R

The Ethics of Aquinas

MORAL TRADITIONS SERIES
A series edited by James F. Keenan, S.J.

The Ethics of Aquinas

Stephen J. Pope, Editor

Georgetown University Press
Washington, D.C.

Georgetown University Press, Washington, D.C.
©2002 by Georgetown University Press. All rights reserved.
Printed in the United States of America

10 9 8 7 6 5 4 3 2 1   2002

This volume is printed on acid-free offset book paper.

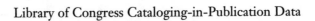

Library of Congress Cataloging-in-Publication Data

The ethics of Aquinas / Stephen J. Pope, editor.
    p. cm.— (Moral traditions series)
    Includes bibliographical references.
    ISBN 0-87840-888-6 (pbk. : alk. paper)
    1. Thomas, Aquinas, Saint, 1225?–1274. Summa theologica. Pars 2. 2. Thomas,
Aquinas, Saint, 1225?–1274—Ethics. 3. Christian ethics—Catholic authors. 4. Ethics,
Medieval. I. Pope, Stephen J., 1955– II. Series.

B765.T53 S8164 2002
241'.042'092—dc21

To the Society of Jesus,
with gratitude and appreciation

Contents

PART II: The Second Part of the Second Part of the *Summa Theologiae*

PART III: The Twentieth-Century Legacy

Preface

Recent years have witnessed a remarkable revival of interest in the ethics of Thomas Aquinas. Scholars have produced books and articles on the life of Aquinas, his spirituality, and his understanding of the relation between faith and reason, nature and grace, reason and faith, and other theological themes. Moralists have written on his accounts of human acts and agency, happiness, the will, the virtues, and various special topics. Some authors provide brief and very general overviews of Thomistic ethics, but none offers a comprehensive treatment of the basic moral arguments and content of Aquinas's major moral work, the Second Part of the *Summa theologiae*. This work intends to fill this lacuna.

This book addresses a fairly wide audience. It intends to attract the attention of experts, but also to assist readers who are interested, but not necessarily specialists, in the moral thought of Aquinas. Its essays complement, but do not substitute for, a careful study of the primary texts.

The chapters in this volume reflect a variety of intellectual perspectives. The contributors come from numerous fields, including intellectual history, medieval studies, moral philosophy, religious ethics, and moral theology. Some authors have spent a lifetime working with specific texts of Aquinas, others draw from Aquinas as one among a number of resources that help address their primary concerns with contemporary moral issues. As a whole, the contributors to this volume represent a spectrum of views

about the meaning and contemporary normative significance of Aquinas's moral thought. They certainly do not comprise a single school of thought. This variety underscores the way in which Thomistic ethics continues to be the scene of lively intellectual development.

The citations in the essays come from a variety of Thomistic texts (including various different texts of the *Summa*). Some scholars use the latest critical editions made available by the Leonine Commission; others draw from alternative standard editions such as those published by Marietti. Each author furnishes an English translation of the words of Aquinas in the body of his or her chapter; readers who wish to consult the Latin texts can find them in the notes.

A word about the structure of the volume is in order. The initial chapters introduce readers to the sources, methods, and major themes of Aquinas's ethics. These orienting essays will be especially helpful for readers who have less familiarity with Aquinas's theology than some others.

The second, more lengthy, part of the book provides an extended discussion of the treatises presented in the Second Part of the *Summa*. Aquinas himself did not divide the text according to "treatises," but, for the sake of clarity and order, we use this conventional system of demarcation. These chapters are not exactly "commentaries" in the sense of a line-by-line explication of texts; our authors do not provide any critical discussion relating to the establishment of reliable texts, or much in the way of philological and grammatical analysis. They seek only to present cogent interpretations of the structure, major arguments, and themes of each of the "treatises."

The third part of this volume examines various aspects of Thomistic ethics in the twentieth century and beyond. Some of the contributors to this section trace various movements within Thomistic moral philosophy and moral theology in the last century, others take a more prospective view of future developments of Thomistic ethics. These chapters make it abundantly clear that far from being a monolithic and static moral theory, Thomism is a tradition of inquiry that continues to experience the same kind of development that marks other such traditions.

The present study was made possible by the labor of many generous people. A number of friends and colleagues offered valuable counsel on important aspects of the project, not the least of which concerned the selection of its authors. I would like to acknowledge the help given to me in this regard by Jean Porter; Stephen F. Brown; Romanus Cessario, O.P.; and James F. Keenan, S.J. I would also like to thank the translators, Frederick Lawrence, Grant Kaplan, and Sister Mary Thomas Noble, O.P. In a more general but very important way, I express special appreciation for my superb ethics colleagues at Boston College: Lisa Sowle Cahill, David Hollenbach, S. J., and John Paris, S. J.

I also owe a debt of gratitude for the manuscript help given to me by Boston College graduate students Thomas Boland, Grant Kaplan, Michael Moreland, and Virgilio Oliveira-y-Costa. Special thanks are due in this regard to Walter Hannam, a most able student of medieval theology, who worked meticulously to check, complete, and, in some cases, correct references found in the chapters of this volume.

The Office of the Academic Vice President and the Office of Research Administration at Boston College supported work on this book through a faculty incentive grant and a research expense grant. Thanks are due to several supportive administrators at Boston College, including the former Academic Vice President, Fr. William B. Neenan, S.J.; the present Academic Vice President, Michael A. Smyer; and the current Associate Academic Vice President for Faculties, Patricia DeLeeuw.

I am most grateful to my wife, Patti, and to my children, Mike, Katie, and Stevie. Their generous love, support, and humor consistently sustain me.

Finally, I dedicate this book to the Society of Jesus, whose members have done much to promote the study of St. Thomas.

Abbreviations

The following abbreviations are used to refer to the works of Aquinas. Unless otherwise noted, all quotations and citations are from the editions listed.

ST *Summa theologiae*. Leonine edition. Vols. 4–11. *Sancti Thomae de Aquino opera omnia*. Rome, 1882–.

SCG *Summa contra gentiles*. Leonine edition. Vols. 13–15. *Sancti Thomae de Aquino opera omnia*. Rome, 1882–.

In Sent. *Scriptum super libros Sententiarum*. Ed. P. Mandonnet and M. Moos. 4 vols. Paris: P. Lethielleux, 1929–1947.

De correctione fraterna *Quaestio disputata de correctione fraterna*. In *Quaestiones disputatae*. Marietti edition. Ed. P. Bazzi, M. Calcaterra, T. S. Centi, E. Odetto, P. M. Pession. Vol. 2. Turin-Rome: Marietti, 1965.

De veritate *Quaestiones disputatae de veritate*. Leonine edition. Vol. 22. *Sancti Thomae de Aquino opera omnia*. Rome, 1882–.

De malo *Quaestiones disputatae de malo*, Leonine edition. Vol. 23. *Sancti Thomae de Aquino opera omnia*. Rome, 1882–.

De perf. vit. spir. *De perfectione vitae spiritualis*. Leonine edition. Vol. 41. Ed. R. Spiazzi. Turin: Marietti, 1954.

De potentia *Quaestiones disputatae de potentia*. In *Quaestiones disputatae*. Marietti edition. Ed. P. Bazzi, M. Calcaterra, T. S. Centi, E. Odetto, P. M. Pession. Vol. 2. Turin-Rome: Marietti, 1965.

De spe *Quaestio disputata de spe*. In *Quaestiones disputatae*. Marietti edition. Ed. P. Bazzi, M. Calcaterra, T. S. Centi, E. Odetto, P. M. Pession. Vol. 2. Turin-Rome: Marietti, 1965.

De virt. card. *Quaestio disputata de virtutibus cardinalibus*. In *Quaestiones disputatae*. Marietti edition. Ed. P. Bazzi, M. Calcaterra, T. S. Centi, E. Odetto, P. M. Pession. Vol. 2. Turin-Rome: Marietti, 1965.

De virt. in comm. *Quaestio disputata de virtutibus in communi*. In *Quaestiones disputatae*. Marietti edition. Ed. P. Bazzi, M. Calcaterra, T. S. Centi, E. Odetto, P. M. Pession. Vol. 2. Turin-Rome: Marietti, 1965.

De anima *Quaestio disputata de anima*. Ed. J. H. Robb. Toronto: Pontifical Institute of Mediaeval Studies, 1968.

De spiritualibus *Quaestio disputata de spiritualibus creaturis*. In *Quaestiones disputatae*. Marietti edition. Ed. P. Bazzi, M. Calcaterra, T. S. Centi, E. Odetto, P. M. Pession. Vol. 2. Turin-Rome: Marietti, 1965.

Quodlibet *Quaestiones Quodlibetales*. Ed. R. Spiazzi. 9th ed. Turin: Marietti, 1956.

In Post. Anal. *Expositio libri Posteriorum*. Leonine edition. 2d ed. Vol. 1–1.

In Periherm. *Expositio libri Peryermenias*. Leonine edition. 2d ed. Vol. 1–2.

In Ethicorum   Sententia libri Ethicorum. Leonine edition. *Sancti Thomae de Aquino opera omnia*. Vol. 47. Rome, 1882–.

In Politicorum Sententia libri Politicorum. Leonine edition. *Sancti Thomae de Aquino opera omnia*. Vol. 48. Rome, 1882–.

In Physicorum In octo libros Physicorum Aristotelis expositio. Ed. P. M. Maggioli. Turin: Marietti, 1954.

In De caelo In libros Aristotelis De caelo et mundo expositio in *In Aristotelis libros De caelo et mundo, De generatione et corruptione, Meteorologicorum expositio*. Ed. R. M. Spiazzi. Turin-Rome: Marietti, 1952.

In De sensu. Sentencia libri De sensu et sensato cuius secundus tractatus est De memoria et reminiscentia. Leonine edition. *Sancti Thomae de Aquino opera omnia*. Vol. 45–2. Rome, 1882–.

In Metaph. In duodecim libros Metaphysicorum Aristotelis expositio. Ed. M.-R. Cathala and R M. Spiazzi. Turin: Marietti, 1950.

In De anima Sentencia libri De anima. Leonine edition. *Sancti Thomae de Aquino opera omnia*. Vol. 45–1. Rome, 1882–.

In De Trinitate Expositio super librum Boethii De Trinitate. Ed. B. Decker. Leiden: E. J. Brill, 1965.

In De causis Super librum De causis expositio. Ed. H. D. Saffrey. Fribourg: Societe Philosophique / Louvain: Editions E. Nauwelaerts, 1954.

In div. nom. In librum Beati Dionysii De divinibus nominibus expositio. Ed. C. Pera. Turin-Rome: Marietti, 1950.

Postilla super Ieremiam In Jeremiam prophetam expositio, in *Expositio in aliquot libros veteris testamenti et in Psalmos L, Opera Omnia*. Vol. 14. Parma: Fiaccadori, 1863.

Postilla super Isaiam Expositio super Isaiam ad litteram. *Sancti Thomae de Aquino opera omnia*. Vol. 28. Rome, 1882–.

Postila super psalmos In Psalmos Davidis expositio. Parma edition. Vol. 14.

In I ad Cor. Super primam epistolam ad Corinthios lectura, in *Super epistolas S. Pauli lecturae*. Ed. P. Raphaelis Cai, O.P. (Turin: Marietti, 1953). Vol. 1.

In II ad Cor. Super secundam epistolam ad Corinthios lectura, in *Super epistolas S. Pauli lecturae*. Vol. 1.

In ad Heb. Super epistolam ad Hebraeos. In *Super epistolas S. Pauli lecturae*. Vol. 2.

In ad Rom. Super epistolam ad Romanos lectura, in *Super epistolas S. Pauli lecturae*. Vol. 1.

In II ad Thess. Super secundam epistolam ad Thessalonicenses lectura. In *Super epistolas S. Pauli lecturae*. Vol. 2.

In Ioan. Super Evangelium S. Ioannis luctura. Ed. P. Raphaelis. Cai, O.P. 5th ed. Turin-Rome: Marietti, 1952.

In Matthaeum Super evangelium S. Matthaei lectura. Ed. P. Raphaelis Cai, O.P. Turin: Marietti, 1951.

Comp. theol. Compendium theologiae seu Brevis compilatio theologiae ad fratrem Raynaldum. Leonine edition. *Sancti Thomae de Aquino opera omnia*. Vol. 42. Rome, 1882–.

De regno De regno ad regem Cypri. Leonine edition. *Sancti Thomae de Aquino opera omnia*. Vol. 43. Rome, 1882–.

De ente De ente et essentia. Leonine edition. *Sancti Thomae de Aquino opera omnia*. Vol. 43. Rome, 1882–.

De unitate De unitate intellectus contra averroistas. Leonine edition. *Sancti Thomae de Aquino opera omnia*. Vol. 43. Rome, 1882–.

The following abbreviations are used to refer to ancient and patristic texts.

Arist.   Aristotle
Pol.   Aristotle, *Politics*
Ph.   Aristotle, *Physics*
Rh.   Aristotle, *Rhetorica*
Cael.   Aristotle, *De caelo*
De an.   Aristotle, *De anima*
Eth. Eud.   Aristotle, *Eudaimonian Ethics*
Eth. Nic.   Aristotle, *Nicomachean Ethics*
Metaph.   Aristotle, *Metaphysics*
August.   Augustine
Conf.   Augustine, *Confessions*
De civ. D.   Augustine, *De civitate Dei*
Div. quaest.   Augustine, *De diversis quaestionibus 83*
Ep.   Augustine, *Epistula*
Retract.   Augustine, *Retractationes*
Cic.   Cicero
Inv. rhet.   Cicero, *De inventione rhetorica*
Macrob.   Macrobius
Sat.   Macrobius, *Saturnalia*

Pl.   Plato
Lach.   Plato, *Laches*
Prt.   Plato, *Protagoras*
Resp.   Plato, *Republic*
Tht.   Plato, *Theaetetus*
Ti.   Plato, *Timaeus*
Xen.   Xenophon
Mem.   Xenophon, *Memorabilia*
Div. nom. Pseudo-Dionysius, De divinis nominibus

The following abbreviations are used to refer to standard editions of the fathers and ecclesiastical documents.

CCEL   *Corpus scriptorum ecclesiasticorum latinorum* (the "Vienna Corpus").
CCSL   *Corpus christianorum series latina.*
DS   Denzinger, *Enchiridion symbolorum.*
PL   *Patrologia latina cursus completus* (Migne)

The Setting of the *Summa Theologiae* of St. Thomas—Revisited

Leonard E. Boyle, O.P.

Some time in the second half of 1261, nearly two years after he had returned from Paris to Naples as a Master in Theology, there to continue work on his *Summa contra gentiles*, Thomas Aquinas was appointed to the Dominican house at Orvieto as *lector conventus*. At the age of thirty-six, he took his place in the normal stream of the Dominican educational system in the order's Roman Province.

By now, the Dominican order was almost fifty years old and fairly set in its ways. It had emerged as a recognized religious order in January 1217 when the Spaniard Dominic obtained from Pope Honorius III a mandate that turned his small band of local preachers in the diocese of Toulouse into an Order of Preachers-in-General. Four years later, shortly before the death of Dominic, it was entrusted as well by Honorius with a general mission of hearing confessions. The Fourth Lateran Council in 1215 had explicitly allied the function of hearing confessions to that of preaching in its constitution *inter caetera*. From 1221 onward the implementation of that constitution in both its facets was, in effect, the mission of the Dominican order.[1]

Perhaps the young Order of Preachers was surprised a bit by this second papal mandate. A general mandate to hear confessions was as new in the life of the church as the earlier commission of the members of Dominic's Order as Preachers-in-General. But it met the challenge at once. Within a few years of the encyclical letter of Honorius III of 1221, and just about the time of Thomas's birth at Roccasecca in 1224 or 1225, at least four useful manuals on the administration of the sacrament of penance had been compiled by members of the Order at Bologna, Paris, Cologne, and Barcelona, and soon were circulating with the Dominicans as they spread in those years between 1221 and 1225 beyond France, Italy, Spain, and the Rhineland—the confines of the order in its first flush—to Britain, Ireland, Scandinavia, Poland, Hungary, and the Near East.

These four manuals, the most celebrated of which is Raymund of Pennafort's *Summa de casibus*, first drafted at Barcelona about 1224, represent the very first literary activity of the Dominican order, something all too readily forgotten, if ever mentioned, by historians of the order. They were the forerunners of a remarkable flow of pastoral manuals of various sizes and shapes from Dominican pens over the three centuries before the Reformation, the better-known of which, to confine ourselves to the thirteenth and fourteenth centuries, are the revised edition of Raymund's *Summa* in 1234–35, Hugh of St. Cher's *Speculum ecclesiae* (ca. 1240), Willelmus Peraldus's *Summa vitiorum* (ca. 1236) and *Summa virtutum* (ca. 1236–49/50), Vincent of Beauvais' *Speculum maius* (1244–59), James of Varazze's *Legenda aurea* (1265–67), Hugh Ripelin of Strasbourg's *Compendium theologicae veritatis* (1265–68), John of Genoa's *Catholicon* (1286), John of Freiburg's *Summa confessorum* (1298), and John Bromyard's *Summa praedicantium* (1326–49).

By and large, these manuals and aids were meant for the generality of the members of the Dominican order, for the *fratres commune* generally engaged in the twin function of the order, preaching and hearing confessions, whose "whole zeal and labor should be directed chiefly toward the advancement of souls," as Vincent of Beauvais apologetically said of himself in his *Speculum maius*.[2] These *fratres communes*, no matter what their age, are the "juniors" (*iuniores*), "beginners" (*incipientes*), and "the simple" (*simplices*) addressed in so many Dominican prefaces. They are, on the whole, those who had not had the chance of a higher education in the manner of Albert, Thomas, Peter of Tarentaise, or other intellectual lights of the "teachable" (*docibiles*) or Lector class. It was for them, principally, that Raymund, William Peraldus, and John of Freiburg wrote. It was for them, explicitly, that Simon of Hinton, probably in the 1250s when Provincial of England, composed his *Summa iuniorum*, and Aag of Denmark, when Provincial of Scandinavia at intervals between 1254 and 1284, his *Rotolus pugillaris* ("for the instruction of young and other Dominicans who have to engage in preaching and hearing confessions").[3]

This wide and varied pastoral output hardly needs explanation. From its very beginnings, the Dominican order was dedicated to education with a distinctly pastoral bent: "All our training," the prologue to the first constitution of 1220 states, "should principally and wholeheartedly be directed toward making us useful to the souls of our neighbors."[4] Any and every aid and possible resource was therefore pressed into the service of the "care of souls" (*cura animarum*). Preachers had to have the Bible at their fingertips, so a great alphabetical concordance, the *Concordantiae S. Iacobi*, was begun by the community of St. Jacques in Paris before 1239, probably under Hugh of St. Cher, and was perfected over the next two generations.[5] The education of youth in faith and morals was a special challenge, so William of Tournai put together his *De instructione puerorum*, a work commended to the whole order by the General Chapter at Paris in 1264.[6] As chess was a popular game, Jacobus de Cessolis of the Dominican house in Genoa composed a mnemonic treatise on virtues and vices in terms of a chess board and chess pieces (ca. 1290), a treatise that had an enormous general circulation and was translated before 1500 into English (by Caxton), Dutch, French, Italian, Catalan, Spanish, Swedish, and Czech.[7]

Every Dominican house, too, was geared to study in the interests of the pastoral care,

and was supposed to have its own Lector to look after the instruction of the community. And even after the younger *fratres communes* had become priests and were engaged in preaching and hearing confessions, only an ad hoc dispensation could excuse them at any point from attendance at the Lector's classes. In this sense, the *fratres communes* were forever *iuniores*.

THOMAS AT ORVIETO

Thomas, as far as we know, had his first taste of this ordinary Dominican world of *fratres communes*, pastoral aids, and practical theology when, after a seemingly studious period of almost two years at Naples, he took on the post of Lector at Orvieto in September or October 1261.[8] He was far removed from the bubbling atmosphere of the *Studia generalia* at Cologne and Paris, between which he had spent some thirteen or fourteen years in all. Although he had the local stimulus and challenge of the papal court, then at Orvieto, his main job was to be at the disposal of his own *fratres communes*, the old with the young.

As we know from Humbert of Romans, who was general of the Dominican order precisely at this time (1254–63) and compiled an invaluable *Liber de instructione officialium Ordinis Praedicatorum*, Lectors were supposed to be totally at the disposition of their brethren. Their vacations were to be taken only at times when the greater part of the community was absent, during the summer, for example, or during the preaching seasons of Advent and Lent. In their lectures, they should always aim at practical and uncluttered instruction. In their periodic disputations, they should confine themselves to "useful and intelligible matters."[9]

In theory at least, Thomas was not unaware of the demands on Lectors and of the limitations of these priory schools. In June 1259, some six months before he left Paris for Naples and, eventually, Orvieto, he had been, with Albert the Great and Peter of Tarentaise, a member of a committee of five that presented a *Ratio studiorum* for the whole order to the general chapter at Valenciennes, north of Paris. In their report, Thomas and his fellow masters had suggested, among other things, that each conventual Lector should have a tutor to assist him, that no one, not even the Prior of the community, was to be absent from lectures, and that priories that found themselves temporarily without Lectors should set up private classes for the brethren on the *Historia scholastica* (of Peter Comestor), the *Summa de casibus* (of Raymund), or some such manual, to offset any danger of idleness.[10]

Thomas himself, as Lector at Orvieto, may have lectured on the Bible as such rather than on the standard medieval work of biblical history, the *Historia scholastica* of Peter Comestor. His literal *Expositio in Job* is probably a reworking of lectures delivered during his four-year term at Orvieto. Possibly the *Postilla super Ieremiam* and *Postilla super Threnos* come from the same stable.[11] But these are works of an exceptional Lector. In all conventual schools, practical theology—"*Collationes de moralibus*," in Humbert's terms—was the order of the day, and this was the principal function of any conventual Lector, St. Thomas not excluded. And although we do not possess any record of "*Collationes*" over which Thomas may have presided, some idea of the type of question with which a Lector might be confronted is afforded by some questions sent to Thomas at Orvieto in 1262–63 by his fellow Lector of Santa Maria Novella in Florence, James of Viterbo, later archbishop of Taranto.

Presumably because he was unable to frame an answer from the *Summa de casibus* of Raymund to some tricky questions on buying and selling on credit in various Tuscan merchant circles, James sent the questions from Florence to the Lector of Orvieto. Thomas, in turn, consulted with Marinus of Eboli, archbishop-elect of Capua, and with the Dominican Cardinal Hugh of St. Cher, both of whom were then at the papal curia in Orvieto. Then, with a passing glance at what Raymund of Pennafort had to say in the *Summa de casibus*, he penned the brief, lucid reply that is now among his *Opera omnia* as *De emptione et venditione ad tempus* and upon which he later based a part of an article in the *Secunda secundae* of his *Summa theologiae* (IIa IIae, q. 78, a. 2, ad 7).[12]

As one may see from a collection of moral problems put together about this time by a Lector in the North of England, solving *casus* was one of the principal methods of teaching practical theology in the Dominican order.[13]

Inevitably, and like any other Lector—this English Dominican, for example, or, notably, John of Freiburg—Thomas would have used Raymund's *Summa de casibus* as his springboard for occasional *casus* and for the regular conventual "*Collationes de moralibus*." By 1261, and indeed long before that date, the *Summa* of the former General of the Dominicans (1238–40) had become an integral part of Dominican training. William of Rennes, Lector of the house at Orléans, had written a valuable *Apparatus* to it about 1241, as well as a series of *Quaestiones adiectae*, and Vincent of Beauvais had incorporated long extracts from both Raymund and William into Books IX and X of his *Speculum doctrinale* between 1244 and 1259. The acts of the General Chapter at Valenciennes in 1259, echoing the commission on which St. Thomas had served, single the *Summa de casibus* out by name, as does Humbert of Romans when speaking of conventual libraries. According to Simon of Hinton a few years earlier, it was "possessed everywhere by the brethren," and there is evidence that abbreviations of it were common within and outside of the Dominican order.[14]

Scholars allow that Thomas, who may have embarked upon his *Summa contra gentiles* (1259–64) at Raymund's request, probably owes many of his civil and canon law references in the *Summa* and in the *Scriptum super Sententiis* to the *Summa de casibus*. But the dependence runs much deeper than this. Thomas had a healthy respect for Raymund as both a fine legist and an able moralist. There is a manifest reliance on Raymund in St. Thomas's treatment of matrimony in his *Scriptum super Sententiis* (1252–56).[15] There are large and unsuspected borrowings from the *Summa de casibus* in the one question I have examined closely in the *Summa theologiae*, that on simony in the *Secunda secundae*, which corresponds to the opening chapter of Raymund's *Summa*. The whole of the *Ad quintum* in IIa IIae, q. 100, a. 1 is word for word from Raymund, as are the *Ad sextum* in IIa IIae, q. 100, a. 2 and the long *Ad quintum* in IIa IIae, q. 100, a. 6.[16]

A professional familiarity as Lector at Orvieto with the *Summa de casibus* and with the system of *casus* and "*collationes morales*" certainly aided Thomas when he began composing his *Summa theologiae*, and particularly the

Secunda secundae; furthermore, it enabled him to field with ease the many questions concerning pastoral care at the six *quodlibets* (I–VI) held during his second Parisian sojourn from 1268 to 1272. All the same, Thomas may have felt that practical theology was too much with the Dominican order and that the *fratres communes*, and the students in particular, both at Orvieto and in the Roman Province, as well as in the order at large, were not being allowed more than a partial view of theology. Perhaps this is why, as I shall now suggest, Thomas began a *Summa theologiae* at Rome soon after his move there from Orvieto in 1265. Perhaps, indeed, this is precisely why he moved.

THOMAS AT SANTA SABINA

On or about 8 September 1265, the annual Chapter of the Roman Province to which Thomas belonged enjoined on him from Anagni, and probably in his presence as Preacher General for the house in Naples, the task of setting up a *studium* at Rome for students from various houses of the Province. The place selected, although not specified in the acts of the Chapter, was Santa Sabina on the Aventine Hill, Dominic's second Roman foundation. Thomas probably took up residence there in late September or early October of that year, remaining for three, full, scholastic years until posted to Paris in, probably, summer 1268 by the general of the order, John of Vercelli.[17]

During his three years at Santa Sabina, Thomas was very active. He preached, made journeys out of Rome, and held *Quaestiones disputatae de potentia*, *De malo* (probably), and "*De attributis divinis*" (the latter of which he then inserted into his *Scriptum super Sententiis* as I d. 2, a. 3).[18] He also supervised and taught the students at Santa Sabina.

Just what he taught them is a little difficult to ascertain. According to Tolomeo of Lucca in 1315–17, who, as a young Dominican, had been his friend and confessor at Naples between 1272 and 1274, Thomas "expounded almost all of the philosophical works of Aristotle, whether natural or moral, while in charge of the *studium* at Rome, and wrote his lectures up in the form of a *scriptum* or commentary on each work, particularly on the *Ethics* and *Metaphysics*."[19]

While this might suggest that Thomas taught these books to his students, Tolomeo does not say so. He confirms only that while Thomas was in charge of the *studium* at Rome, he lectured on certain aspects of Aristotle. In fact, it is highly unlikely that the immediate audience of Thomas at these lectures was his young and presumably untried bunch of students. Some of these may have been bright enough to audit without undue stress Thomas's learned and lengthy expositions of Aristotle, but the majority would likely have needed basic instruction in the fundamentals of Christian teaching.

Santa Sabina, in any case, was not an advanced *studium generale* like the five official *studia* of the order (Paris, Bologna, Cologne, Montpellier, Oxford), to which each Province was allowed to send no more than two promising students (*docibiles*) or, in the case of Paris, the senior *studium*, three. It is doubtful even that Santa Sabina was a *studium provinciale*, or half-way house between a priory school, under the control of a Lector, and a *studium generale* or *solemne*, presided over by a Regent-Master or Principal Lector. Central houses of study, or *studia provincialia* as they were later known, certainly were established in the Roman Province, at Viterbo and Naples, in 1269, but all that we know of the *studium* at Santa Sabina between 1265 and 1268 is that Thomas was ordered to set it up, that "the students there with him for the sake of study" were to have "sufficient clothing from the priories of their origin," and that Thomas was in complete charge of them, having "full authority to send them back to their respective houses" if they did not come up to scratch.[20]

Santa Sabina has the look of what I call a "*studium personale*," a *studium* set up for or by a given master. The Anagni enactment of 1265 speaks of the students as "studying with" Thomas, and makes no mention of any assistants or *Sublectores* (the term used by Humbert). It is not without interest, too, that when Thomas was transferred to Paris in the summer of 1268, the Roman *studium* seems to have died with his departure.

Perhaps the *studium* at Rome was simply an experiment to allow Thomas special scope and to expose select students from all over the Province to his influence. It may well be, indeed, that at the Chapter of Anagni in September 1265, which he as a Preacher General would have attended, a suggestion on his part that something more than mixed priory schools was necessary for the training of students in theology had been taken up by the Chapter, and that he had been given a free hand to open and conduct a personal *studium*.

On the other hand, what we may be witnessing at Anagni is simply the beginnings of a movement inspired by Thomas to improve education in his Province in the wake of the Valenciennes General Chapter of 1259, and which led not long afterwards to the establishment of *studia provincialia* for theology in Italy.

Something of the sort probably was sorely needed in Thomas's large and scattered Roman Province. Before his arrival in late 1259, studies seem not to have had any priority in the province. The first time, indeed, that a Lector as such is mentioned in the extant *Acta* of the Province is in 1259, when a house, with the constitutional "Prior and Lector," was founded at Pistoia. As for references of any kind to study, they are few and far between, apart from a prohibition, for example, of the study of astronomy and "*artes saeculares*" in 1258 at Viterbo.

Thomas was commissioned as Preacher General for Naples in September 1260. As this gave him a voice in the annual Provincial Chapter, he probably began to attend Chapters from the following September. He may not have made his presence felt at once; however, in view of the singular act in his respect of the Chapter at Anagni in 1265, that voice is hardly to be mistaken in the two Chapters that immediately preceded it. At Rome in 1263, the Chapter for the first time ever comes out openly on studies, ruling that all the brethren, the old with the young, should attend classes and "repeat" what they had learned. At Viterbo in 1264, the Chapter stated bluntly that "study in this Province is neglected." It made provision for the financial support of the three students that the Province could send to Paris. It ordered that Lectors should not drop classes at will, that Priors should compel the brethren to study, that they should see to it that weekly "*repetitiones*" were held for all, and that they should direct the Master of Students to examine everyone, and the young especially, in what had been taught during each week.[21]

Perhaps this was not enough for Thomas, and as a result the Chapter at Anagni a year later gave him his head.

At all events, the *studium* at Santa Sabina probably was no more than an attempt by the Roman Province to allow select students to prepare themselves under a single master, Thomas, for the priesthood and the Dominican apostolate. Basically, the course there would have had the same pastoral orientation as that in which I presume Thomas to have been engaged for the previous four years at Orvieto.

But there was at least one great difference between Orvieto and Rome. Where in the former, Thomas would have had to divide his time between students and community, now at Santa Sabina he had the students all to himself. He was on his own, no longer tied to a basic curriculum geared to the pastoral education of the *fratres communes* at large. He was, in a word, free to devise a curriculum of his own—one that would have the *student* body as its focus. More importantly, he was now in a position to expand the students' theological education and to break out of the narrow tradition of practical theology that had hitherto marked the Dominican educational system.

One hint of a change of direction is that, according to Tolomeo, Thomas wrote on the first book of the *Sentences* while teaching at Rome. Although Tolomeo notes that a copy of this commentary existed in his home priory at Lucca, there is no trace of such a text today. But, as I suggest below, modern scholars are lucky to possess a part of a student *reportatio* of that classroom commentary that shows, among other things, that it was not at all, as has been conjectured, a reworking of his *Scriptum super Sententiis* (1252–56) at Paris. Rather, this was an independent work in a simple, direct style not unlike that of the later *Summa*, which drew at times on the *Scriptum* itself, the *De veritate*, and the commentary on Boethius's *De trinitate*.[22] What is important, however, for the present argument, is not the nature of that "Roman" commentary, but the fact that this appears to be the first time that a book of the *Sentences* was taught formally to Dominican students outside of the *studia generalia*. Later on, of course, as *studia provincialia* began to be the fashion, first in the Roman Province in 1269 (possibly a result of the Roman experiment with Thomas), then generally in the order, the *Sentences* of Peter Lombard became a set text in these *studia* in each Dominican province. But there is no evidence that formal lectures on the *Sentences* were among the duties of the ordinary conventual Lectors before or after this time. On this view, it is notable that it was at Rome and not during his Lectorship at Orvieto that Thomas is reputed to have lectured on the *Sentences*.

This is not to say that Peter Lombard's work was unknown in Dominican houses. In his *Instructiones*, Humbert of Romans lists the *Sentences*, with the Bible and Comestor's *Historia*, as a text on which Lectors gave practical instruction.[23] In the summer of 1267, while Thomas was still teaching the students at Santa Sabina, the Chapter at Lucca urged the brethren in general and young priests in particular, to apply themselves "more than usual" to the study of "the Bible, the *Sentences*, the *Historiae*, the writings of the saints, and the *Summa de casibus*."[24]

But Humbert and the Lucca Chapter probably did not have the *Sentences* as a whole in mind but rather the fourth book, and this in order to supplement Raymund's *Summa* in its treatment of the sacraments. For Raymund himself, when dealing with aspects of the administration of some of the sacraments, probably set a headline for the whole Dominican order when he noted there that any of the *simplices* who wished to know more about the sacraments should read certain parts of the *Decretum* and the *Decretales* "and the fourth book of the *Sentences*."[25]

Book IV was, of course, the *locus classicus* for sacramental theology, which is the reason why, for example, John of Freiburg in his *Summa confessorum* of 1298 cites extensively the commentaries of Albert, Thomas, and Peter of Tarentaise on that book of the *Sentences* and, generally, on that book alone. Yet, significantly, it was not Book IV upon which Thomas lectured at Rome. What he taught the Dominican students at Santa Sabina was not, if both Tolomeo of Lucca and the newly identified *reportatio* prove trustworthy, the expected sacramental theology, the subject of the fourth book, upon which he had commented professionally a decade or so earlier at Paris, but rather God, Trinity, and Creation, the burden of the first book. By opting for

Book I (upon which, of course, he had lectured at great length while a Bachelor at Paris), Thomas gives fair warning that he was setting a new course. By concentrating on God, Creation, Trinity, and other *dogmatic* or *systematic* areas of theology, he makes it clear that he was breaking away from the customary "practical" theology of the order to which the Valenciennes Chapter, Humbert, and, needless to say, Raymund's *Summa de casibus*, are eloquent witnesses.

A second hint of the revolutionary character of the *studium* at Santa Sabina is the fact that it was there that Thomas began his great work "for the instruction of beginners," the *Summa theologiae*. Since the *Prima pars* of the *Summa* covers much the same ground as Book I of the *Sentences*, and since Thomas is not reputed to have taught at Rome on any book of the *Sentences* but the first, this suggests that the commentary which Tolomeo saw at Lucca on Book I of the *Sentences* and which now survives at second or third hand in a *reportatio* or copy thereof, may well represent all or most of his teaching during Thomas's first scholastic year (October 1265–July 1266), while the *Prima pars* of the *Summa* (with, probably, a part of the *Prima secundae*) is the outcome of his second and third years of teaching (October 1266–July 1268).

In other words, having availed himself of the freedom of the *studium* in Rome to depart from the practical theology traditional to his order by commenting in his first year there on Book I of the *Sentences*, Thomas in his second and third year dropped the *Sentences* altogether and set out on a road of his own. It was no chance road, but one that he was determined to travel. Even when plucked out of Rome in summer 1268 for university teaching at Paris far removed from the "beginners" at Santa Sabina, he did not abandon his design. By the time he departed Paris four years later, there to embark on, although not to finish, his *Tertia pars*, he had completed the *Prima secundae* and had compiled the massive *Secunda secundae*.

This persistence with the *Summa* over five heavy years at Paris and Naples (1268–73) during which he wrote voluminously on Aristotle's *Perihermeneias*, *Analytica posteriora*, *De caelo*, *De generatione et corruptione*, *Meteora*, *De anima*, *Metaphysics*, *Physics*, *Politics*, and, possibly, *Nicomachean Ethics*, to mention only some of his writings in these years—this persistence at least suggests that, for Thomas, the *Summa* was something out of the ordinary and, indeed, meant much to him. It was, one may suggest, his legacy as a Dominican to his order and to its system of educating the brethren in priories all over Europe. It may have been begun at Santa Sabina in Rome where the *incipientes* were young students of the order, but it was Orvieto and his four years of practical teaching there among the *fratres communes* that had really occasioned it. With the *Summa*, in effect, Thomas made his own personal contribution as a Dominican to the longstanding manualist and summist tradition of the order in which he had been a participant at Orvieto (and at Valenciennes), and at the same time attempted to set the regular training in practical theology in the Dominican Order on a more truly theological course.

BEGINNING THE *SUMMA*

What had been missing in the curriculum before Thomas's tenure at Santa Sabina was what one may term "dogmatic" or "systematic" theology. Writing roughly a decade before Thomas began his *Summa*, General of the Dominicans Humbert of Romans noted in his *Liber de instructione officialium* that the librarian of each Dominican house was responsible for providing a ready-reference area containing good, legible copies of, among other books, Gratian's *Decretum*, Gregory IX's *Decretales*, canonist Geoffrey of Trani's *Summa super titulis*, *Distinctiones morales* (of which there were many in circulation), *Concordantiae* (probably those of the Paris Dominicans noted above), Raymund of Pennafort's *Summa de casibus*, and William Peraldus's *Summa de vitiis et virtutibus*, "so that the community may always have them to hand." Humbert also lists the Bible and the *Historiae* of Peter Comestor, but if there is anything at all obvious about the professional volumes above, it is that they are wholly legal or "moral." There is not a trace, for example, of any specific *summa de sacramentis*, nor any *summa* of "*Sacra doctrina*" as such. "Scientific" theology, in so far as it occurs in the list, is represented by Raymund's *Summa de casibus* and Peraldus's *Summa de vi-*

tiis et virtutibus, the two well-springs, as it happens, of Dominican practical or moral theology.[26]

This doctrinal gap in the system is precisely what Thomas attempted to fill with his *Summa*. All Dominican writers of *summae* previous to Thomas had valiantly covered various aspects of learning for their confrères in pastoral care—Raymund and his fellows for confessional practice, Peraldus for vices and virtues, Aag of Denmark for missionaries, William of Tournai for the instruction of children, James of Varazze for the lives of saints and preaching, Simon of Hinton for the practical theological needs of his English brethren. Thomas, on the other hand, went well beyond anything hitherto attempted. He provided a *summa* of general theology, a manual that dealt with God, Trinity, Creation, and Incarnation, as well as with the strengths and weaknesses of human nature.

Thomas, of course, had nothing against practical theology. After all, he had presumably taught it himself for some years, and is far from neglecting it in his *Summa*; indeed, the largest part, the *Secunda pars*, specifically covers human beings and their acts. But he now gave that practical theology a setting not evident in Dominican circles before him. By prefacing the *Secunda* or "moral" part with a *Prima pars* on God, Trinity, and Creation, and then rounding it off with a *Tertia pars* on the Son of God, Incarnation and the Sacraments, Thomas put practical theology—the study of Christian life, its virtues and vices—in a full theological context. Christian morality, once for all, was shown to be something more than a question of straight ethical teaching of vices and virtues in isolation. Inasmuch as the person was an intelligent being who was master of himself and possessed of freedom of choice, he was in the image of God. To study human action is therefore to study the image of God and to operate on a theological plane. To study human action on a theological plane is to study it in relation to its beginning and end, God, and to the bridge between, Christ and his sacraments.

Thomas, one might add, was not alone in his dissatisfaction with the Dominican curriculum and tradition of theology. Just about the time that Thomas was beginning his *Summa*, Hugh Ripelin, Lector of Strasbourg, wrote a *Compendium theologicae veritatis* in seven books (God, Creation, Sin, Christ, Virtues, Sacraments, Last Things) which, with some 620 manuscripts, numerous printed editions, and translations into Armenian, Flemish, French, German, and Italian, had a huge success and might have inspired Thomas's own *Compendium theologiae* (1269–73).[27]

But if Thomas and Hugh Ripelin were at variance with the practical tradition of vices and virtues, *casus* and "*Collationes de moralibus*" within their Order, all the same both Hugh's *Compendium* and Thomas's *Summa* very much belonged in intent and purpose to the Dominican strain of practical manuals. Like Raymund of Pennafort, Aag of Denmark, Simon of Hinton and other Dominican manualists who had written specifically for the *iuniores* and *simplices*, and for the generality of their Dominican brethren, Thomas in particular probably had young and run-of-the-mill Dominicans primarily in mind and not a more sophisticated, perhaps university audience when in chiselled prose and in easy, logical steps he put his *Summa theologiae* together: "My purpose," he wrote, "is so to propose the things that pertain to faith that the instruction of beginners will better be served."[28]

This, needless to say, is far from evident in the Prologue. As the Prologue stands, Thomas could be referring to any and every beginner. But given the context of the genesis of the *Summa* at Santa Sabina, and the remarkable commission given him at Anagni in 1265, the assumption is hardly out of question that his beginners are Dominican beginners first and foremost, in the manner of other Dominican colleagues of his.

There is certainly nothing in the Prologue to indicate that his sights were set on university students, although, of course, he would later release at Paris for general consumption all that he had then completed of the *Summa*. In any case, there was nothing in 1266–67 to suggest that Thomas would ever again return to Paris or, in fact, teach in any university whatever. All that he says in the Prologue is that he found existing expositions of theology inadequate. They were a hindrance under three heads for beginners. They indulged in a multitude of useless questions, articles, and arguments. They did not give the essentials of Christian teaching in an ordered fashion but

only as these came up in whatever text the writers were commenting on (*secundum quod requirebat librorum expositio*) or whenever the writers seized on a particular point and dilated on it (*vel secundum quod se praebebat occasio disputandi*). Finally, writers treated these fundamentals in so many places that the result on the part of the hearers was aversion and boredom.

It is often assumed that Thomas is here speaking of texts such as the Bible and the *Sentences*, but on the surface his plaint, rather, is against writings or commentaries on texts ("*ea quae scripta sunt a diversis*") and the procedures employed by their authors ("*secundum quod requirebat librorum expositio . . . vel se praebebat occasio disputandi*"). Père Chenu and others, however, understand the Prologue as "a reflection on the current teaching method," where the teacher was bound to the text (*librorum expositio*) and the principal in a *quaestio disputata* to "the contingent circumstances of controversy" (*occasio disputandi*).[29] Yet although the subject of this part of the Prologue is texts by various authors ("*ea quae scripta sunt a diversis*") and not authoritative texts from the tradition ("*ea quae traduntur*"), there is a possible ambiguity in the passage, as though Thomas were speaking on two levels at once. For his complaint against the longueurs and disorder in the writings on theology in question ends with a seeming reference to classrooms and teaching ("*eorumdem frequens repetitio et fastidium et confusionem generabat in animis auditorum*") rather than, as one would have expected, to reading and studying.

If, as well may be, the Prologue has this second edge, criticism on the part of Thomas of his own Dominican educational system is not to be ruled out in favor of the more obvious setting of universities and *studia generalia*—if, that is, "*expositio librorum*" also means "teaching a text" and "*occasio disputandi*" also denotes disputations and disputed questions ("*quaestiones disputatae*"). For as we know from Humbert of Romans in his *Liber* a few years earlier, "expositions" of texts (Thomas's own *Expositio in Job*, for example) and "disputations" (complete with "*opponentes*" and "*respondentes*" and even invited guests) were very much part of the Dominican curriculum.

These criticisms by Thomas may even betray a memory of some remarks of his former General there on the office of Lector. Where, for example, Humbert cautions the Lector, when teaching the Bible, the *Historiae*, and the *Sententiae*, to keep to the text, to avoid "too many divisions of the matter and frivolous expositions," and to strive always for the sake of the hearers ("*auditores*") after "useful and intelligible questions" (*quaestionum utilium intelligentiam*), Thomas notes the hazard of a multitude of "useless questions, articles, and arguments" (*inutilium quaestionum, articulorum et argumentorum*). Again, where Humbert gives advice on the care to be taken to select "useful subjects" for the regular conventual disputations, Thomas underlines the "occasional" role, with respect to the fundamentals of theology, which disputations played. Finally, and more significantly, where Humbert begs the Lector, for the good of his *auditores*, to refrain from the boring prolixity that is bound to result from too excessive repetition ("*a fastidiosa prolixitate quae accidere solet ex nimia repetitione eiusdem*"), Thomas likewise makes the point that frequent repetition of the same things tended to generate confusion in the minds of the readers ("*eorumdem frequens repetitio et fastidium et confusionem generabat in animis auditorum*").[30]

On the view, then, of both commentaries on theological texts (the primary plaint, as it seems, of the Prologue) and teaching methods (a secondary or at least implied plaint), the "beginners" there are just as likely to have been Thomas's students at Santa Sabina and his Dominican brethren in general as beginners at large or in the *studia generalia* and universities. And even the Prologue was simply concerned with current methods of teaching theology, then these are as arguably Dominican as those described by Humbert in his Liber are explicitly, and would have been recognizable as such by any of Thomas's colleagues.

But probably it was the drawbacks to the commentaries and glosses in use at the time in the Dominican order that stirred him more than anything else to write his *Summa*. Remembering his own four years at Orvieto as Lector, and the pronounced summist tradition of practical theology within the order, it is therefore not at all unreasonable to suggest that the texts by various authors ("*quae a diversis scripta sunt*") that principally impeded the *novitii* and *incipientes* of his Prologue are just as

likely to have been the various *summae* of Dominican authorship to which the young students and the body of *fratres communes* had to turn for their theology as the better-known or standard treatises of the universities and schools.

THE *SECUNDA SECUNDAE*

How conscious Thomas was of both that summist tradition and its limitations is, to my mind, clearly to be seen in the *Secunda secundae* of the *Summa theologiae* and its Prologue. I base my certainty here on the fact that the *Secunda secundae* is, in its own right, a straight *summa de virtutibus et vitiis*, a *summa* of moral theology if you wish, although not at all of the *casus* or anecdotal type hitherto in vogue in the Dominican order.

Thomas himself specifies that the first part of the *Secunda pars* covers "moral matter" in general, while the second part or *Secunda secundae* deals with it in particular: "After a general consideration of virtues and vices and other points pertaining to moral matter in general," he writes in the Prologue to the *Secunda secundae*, "it is necessary to consider each of these one by one"[31] (IIa IIae, Prol.). Hence, he goes on, the best procedure will be to devote a tractate in turn to "each virtue, the gift corresponding to it, and the vices opposed to it" (ibid.).[32] In this way, he says, " the whole of moral matter is placed in the context of the virtues," and so "nothing in morals will be overlooked" (ibid.).[33]

His point of departure, and possibly the chief target of his strictures on works in this area, was, I suspect, the great and hallowed *Summa de vitiis et virtutibus* of his senior colleague, William Peraldus or Peyraut, the two parts of which were written over a span of thirteen or fourteen years between 1236 and 1249–50. In Dominican circles, it clearly had the role of "speculative" companion to Raymund's *Summa de casibus*. With Raymund's *Summa*, it is one of the volumes recommended by Humbert of Romans for a ready-reference area in houses of the order, and it is presumably the *Summa de vitiis et virtutibus* that is mentioned with the *Summa de casibus* in Humbert's *Liber* as one of the sources from which Lectors could draw points for discussion at the weekly or biweekly "*Collationes de moralibus.*" A Chapter of the Province of Spain at Toledo in 1250 ordered each house in the Province to inscribe its name on its copies of breviaries, Bibles, and these two *Summae.* In 1267, the two *Summae* are again mentioned in one breath at a Chapter at Carcassonne of the Province of Provence. Some five hundred manuscripts of the *Summa* of Peraldus are extant. It was translated in whole or part into French, Italian, and Flemish in, respectively, the thirteenth, fourteenth, and fifteenth centuries, and was printed repeatedly from 1469 onward.[34]

Needless to say, the *Summa* of Peraldus is looser in structure and far more discursive than the *Secunda secundae* of St. Thomas, but the ground it covers is roughly the same. Peraldus opens with the topic "*De virtute in communi*"; so does Thomas, but unlike Peraldus he devotes a whole volume to it, the *Prima secundae.* Peraldus then goes on, with a vast array of quotations from Scripture, the fathers (Augustine, Gregory, Isidore, John Damascene, in particular), classical "Philosophers" such as Aristotle, Cicero, Seneca, and Ovid, and, finally, more recent authors such as Anselm, Bernard, and Guigo the Carthusian, to define and document the theological and cardinal virtues, the gifts, the beatitudes, and the seven "capital vices" or deadly sins.[35]

This, too, is exactly the range of the *Secunda secundae.* And although there is no cogent evidence that Thomas relied on or borrowed very much from Peraldus, save, perhaps, for a quotation here and there from his battery of authorities, I am sure that Thomas was as aware of the *Summa de vitiis et virtutibus* as he was of Raymund's *Summa de casibus.* His colleague Peraldus had written a thorough, learned, and valued piece of work, and Thomas appears to have made sure that nothing Peraldus had touched upon did not find a place in the *Secunda secundae.* It is hardly by chance, for example, that when Peraldus notes immediately after his brief opening chapter on virtues in general, "We have spoken of the virtues in general. Now we will be speaking of the species of virtue" (*Dictum est de virtute in communi. Nunc dicendum est de speciebus virtutum*), Thomas marks the transition from the first to the second part of the *Secunda* in almost the same words: "After having considered the virtues and vices and other

matters pertaining to morals, it is now necessary to consider specific details in each" (*Post communem considerationem de virtutibus et vitiis et aliis ad materiam moralem pertinentibus, necesse est considerare singula in speciali*); (ibid.). This sort of "bridge" can hardly be a commonplace, particularly when one remembers that the division between "the virtues in general" (*De virtutibus in communi*) and "special virtues" (*De virtutibus in speciali*) has been claimed as original to Thomas.[36]

There is, nevertheless, a world of difference between Thomas's approach to moral matters and that of Peraldus. This is not least the case because Thomas relates the gifts, beatitudes, and vices to each of the seven theological and cardinal virtues where Peraldus simply takes the virtues, vices, gifts, and beatitudes in turn, each in its own right.

Thomas seems to have been very much aware of his departure from the customary treatment of virtues and vices in *summae* and manuals and in particular, one may suggest, in this semi-official *Summa* of his own order. There is probably an oblique apology for abandoning the scheme in Peraldus's *Summa* when in the Prologue to the *Secunda secundae,* and in terms reminiscent of the Prologue to the *Prima pars,* Thomas notes that it is "more expeditious by far to take in turn each virtue with its corresponding gift, the vices opposed to it, and the appropriate precepts, than to take each virtue, gift, vice, and precept in isolation, for the latter course begets much repetition." Besides, he adds, this is a more logical and theological procedure, since it nicely includes all moral matter under the seven great virtues.

It is a commonplace that of all Thomas's writings, the *Summa theologiae* "was the most widely circulated work both in manuscript and in print."[37] Yet if one examines the extant manuscripts, it soon becomes evident that "the *Summa*" as often as not means the *Secunda secundae,* not the tripartite *Summa.* It is, in fact, rarely or relatively so that one finds all the parts of the *Summa* as a unit. Each part—and here I mean the two sections of the *Secunda pars* as well as the *Prima pars* and the *Tertia pars*—seems to have circulated independently, as though each had its own identity, with the *Secunda secundae* the clear winner. By my rough count, and out of a total of almost six hundred manuscripts examined thus far for all parts on their own of the *Summa* as Thomas wrote it, the *Tertia pars* accounts for only 18 percent, the *Prima secundae* for 20 percent, the *Prima pars* for 25 percent, and the *Secunda secundae* for 37 percent.[38]

The popularity of the *Secunda secundae* is hardly to be wondered at. As it stands, and for all its originality and watertight Aristotelianism, the *Secunda secundae* has the trappings of a *Summa de virtutibus et vitiis*, replete with dicta of Aristotle, Cicero, Macrobius, and the rest, and the Prologue quoted above does not dispel that impression. Tolomeo of Lucca, in his note on Thomas's works (ca. 1315), wrote of it that "this part of the *Summa* contains a specific treatment of all the virtues and vices, and is totally based on, and adorned with, the sayings and teachings of Philosophers and the authentic opinions of sacred doctors"—a description that is equally applicable to the *Summa* of Peraldus or any other manual of virtues and vices.[39] This is precisely how some of Thomas's contemporaries saw it, and this is surely why it outdid any other part of the *Summa* in circulation. It is not for nothing that the copy of the *Secunda secundae* that the theologian Geoffrey of Fontaines had made for himself at Paris in the 1290s bears the following explicit, "*Summa de virtutibus et vitiis edita a fratre Thoma de Aquino.*"[40]

As for the axiomatic influence of the *Summa* as a whole within the Dominican order, the dogged effort on the part of Thomas to give a full theological direction to the pastoral preparation of Dominicans seems to have gone over the head of the generality of his brethren. Even after his canonization in 1323 and the withdrawal of the ban of 1277 on Thomas at the University of Paris, the *Summa* never became a part of the curriculum of the priory schools that, as I have suggested, really occasioned it. In these priory schools, practical theology in the old mold continued to dominate the curriculum, with Raymund and Peraldus ruling the roost, although Raymund's *Summa de casibus* gave way in the fourteenth century to John of Freiburg's *Summa confessorum* (1298).

In the various provincial *studia* that have come to light in the last quarter of the thirteenth century, and which may have been a result of Thomas's Roman experiment be-

tween 1265 and 1268, Peter Lombard's *Sentences*, in line with the usage of *studia generalia* and universities, became and remained throughout the Middle Ages the textbook of theology.

Thomas's own Roman Province, which in 1269 began what was to become a network of *studia provincialia*, seems never to have granted the *Summa* a place in its system. There is no sign even that any of the annual Provincial Chapters ever recommended Thomas or any of his works in the way in which, a shade unrealistically, the Chapter of 1284 at Aquila ordered that, "Lectors and others of the brethren in their lectures and disputations" should use the formulary book of papal and other letters compiled by Marinus of Eboli, lately archbishop of Capua.[41] Some bright spirits in the Province seem to have attempted to replace the *Sentences* with the *Summa* at the beginning of the fourteenth century, but they were firmly put in their places by the Chapter at Perugia in 1308: "We wish and order that all Lectors and Bachelors lecture on the *Sentences* and not on the *Summa* of Thomas."[42] However, the General Chapter of the order at Metz in 1313 was a little more accommodating. It allowed that Lectors, when teaching the *Sentences*, "should treat briefly of at least three or four articles of Brother Thomas" (presumably from his commentary on the *Sentences*), and ruled that no one was to be sent to the *studium generale* at Paris "unless he has studied diligently the teaching of Thomas for three years."[43]

The *Summa* had rather more sucess at another level. There were Dominicans who were aware of the "pastoral" possibilities of the work and were not slow to exploit it in that direction. Around 1290, the anonymous Dominican who added the *Speculum morale* to Vincent of Beauvais' great *Speculum maius* of fifty years earlier, borrowed liberally from the *Secunda secundae*.[44] A decade or so later, Albert, Lector of Brescia, who campaigned mightily for Thomas's canonization, and allegedly had a vision of Augustine and Thomas together, wrote a *Summa de instructione sacerdotis* in three books (virtues, vices, sacraments), drawing almost all his material from the *Secunda secundae* and the *Tertia pars*.[45] Between 1310 and 1314, William of Paris, of the priory of St. Jacques, composed a *Dialogus de septem sacramentis*, which is extant in fifty manuscripts and at least fifteen printed editions, and leans heavily on the *Tertia pars* as well as on the commentary of Peter of Tarentaise on Book IV of the *Sentences*.[46]

Almost inevitably, given the bias of the order, it was the *Secunda secundae* that captured the attention of Dominicans at large. Shortly before his death in 1283, General of the Dominicans John of Vercelli (the same who, recently elected, had snatched Thomas away unexpectedly from Rome and his students there in 1268, sending him to the University of Paris with Peter of Tarentaise), commissioned Galienus de Orto, probably while he was Lector at Pisa, to make an abridgement of the *Secunda secundae*. This summary, now extant in at least five manuscripts, had no success.[47] It is schematic and perfunctory, and, in any case, another Dominican Lector of the period, John of Freiburg, took the ground from under Galienus by doing more or less the same thing in a more imaginative fashion a few years later. Where John scored over Galienus was not by engaging in any sort of *précis* of the *Secunda secundae*, but rather by relating Thomas's work to the curriculum of practical theology in the priories and, specifically, to Raymund's *Summa de casibus*, which he was then teaching as Lector in the priory at Freiburg-im-Breisgau.[48]

JOHN OF FREIBURG

"Johannes Lector," as he was known, was a remarkable man whose place in the spread of the teaching of Thomas has largely escaped historians. He had been a pupil of the Lector of Strasbourg, Ulrich Engelbert, prior to 1272; had accompanied Albert the Great to Mecklenberg in 1269; and seems to have studied at Paris for a time, perhaps between 1268 and 1272, when Peter of Tarentaise and Thomas occupied the Dominican chairs there for a second time and when Thomas held his second batch of *quodlibets*, which are so prominent in John's *Summa confessorum*.

Posted about 1280 to the Dominican house at Freiburg-im-Breisgau as Lector, an office he held even as Prior until his death shortly before 1314, John at first occupied himself with an index to Raymund's *Summa* and to William of Rennes' *Apparatus* on it. Then, in

typical Lector fashion, he began to collect "*quaestiones casuales*" for purposes of teaching. In his search for these (meaning, as he states in his preface, "useful questions which bear on the counselling of souls"), he combed councils, canonists, theologians and, naturally, the writings of his teachers and *confrères*, Albert, Peter, Thomas, and Ulrich. On this view, both the second sextet of Thomas's Parisian *quodlibets* and the *Secunda secundae* proved most valuable.

As a result of this intense research while lecturing on the *Summa de casibus*, John of Freiburg was able to produce his own *Summa confessorum* (1298)—the first manual to bear such a title—in which he totally revamped Raymund and deployed as much as possible of the material he had collected in his *Libellus quaestionum casualium*, notably the corpus of some twenty-two *quaestiones* from those Parisian *quodlibets* of St. Thomas, bits and pieces from the *Prima* and *Tertia partes* of the *Summa*, and passage after passage from the *Secunda secundae*. The moral teaching of Thomas, with borrowings as well from Albert, Peter, and Ulrich, is the backbone of John's *Summa*, and sharply differentiates it in tone and content from Raymund's *Summa de casibus*—or, for that matter, any other previous *summa* of the administration of the Sacrament of Penance. Furthermore, the *Summa confessorum* is much broader than Raymund's, and is as much a *summa de sacramentis* as it is of penitential practice.

John's text was a resounding success. Some 160 manuscripts of it are extant, and it enjoyed three printed editions before 1500 and several afterward. In the century after its publication, it inspired in Dominican circles an abridgement (by William of Cayeux, ca. 1300), a simplified version (the *Summa rudium*, ca. 1333), an alphabetical arrangement (which, as the *Pisanella*, after its compiler, Bartholomew of Pisa, is extant in some 600 manuscripts), and a German adaptation by Berthold of Freiburg (ante 1390).[49]

Despite the great number of manuscripts of the *Secunda secundae* itself from 1300 through 1500, it is probably fair to state that it was largely through John of Freiburg's *Summa confessorum*, or such derivatives as the popular *Pisanella*, that St. Thomas's moral teaching in the *Secunda secundae* became known and respected throughout Europe in that period. Furthermore, as the *Summa confessorum* gradually replaced Raymund's *Summa de casibus* in the course of practical theology, Thomas's influence spread within the Dominican order itself.

In that sense at least, Thomas's legacy in the *Summa theologiae* to beginners and to Dominicans at large, had its reward. But, in the whole context of the *Summa*, this was not quite what Thomas had hoped for. Rather, it only compounded the situation that I have suggested he had attempted to correct. Where Thomas toiled to provide an integral theology for his brethren in their dedication to the *cura animarum*, the *Secunda secundae*—a gutted *Secunda secundae* at that—was now, through the *Summa confessorum* of John of Freiburg, irretrievably adrift from the other parts of the *Summa*, especially the first and the third, to which St. Thomas had so carefully moored it.

But one should not place all the blame squarely on the shoulders of John of Freiburg. John had been attracted to the *Secunda secundae* because it was, as he put it, "for the most part on morals and cases" (*pro maiori parte moralis et casualis*).[50] He had a point. The *Secunda secundae* is indeed *casualis*, if by that one means, as John explicitly does, that it contains "useful questions bearing on the counseling of souls." And, if one is to take Thomas himself at his word in the Prologue, it is also very much *moralis*, because it considers "virtues and vices and other things pertaining to moral matter," and claims not to omit "anything related to morals." John, too, may be excused for not paying much attention to the *Prima secundae*, which establishes the principles on which the *Secunda secundae* rests, for Thomas himself seems to diminish the role of the *Prima* when (in the Prologue to the *Secunda*) he says, "after this general consideration [in the *Prima secundae*] of virtues and vices and other things pertaining to moral matter, it is necessary to take these up in detail one by one. For moral teaching in the abstract is not all that useful, since what takes place in practice is with respect to particular things" (ibid.)[51]

It is hardly surprising, then, to find that far from being invariably accompanied by the *Prima secundae*, the *Secunda secundae* had a circulation that was almost twice that of its sup-posed prerequisite. One could argue, indeed, that Thomas was not particularly concerned about the circulation of these parts individually, or about the inviolability of the *Summa theologiae* as a whole. In the list of taxes for copying university exemplars that the University of Paris issued about 1280, the *Prima pars*, the *Prima secundae*, and the *Secunda secundae* (and, I may add, by these precise titles) all occur as separate items, and with separate sets of *peciae* or certified *quires*.[52] As there is no trace in this list of the *Tertia pars*, written at Naples between 1272 and 1273, and we are sure that the *Secunda secundae*, had been finished before St. Thomas departed Paris for Naples, and probably by the spring of 1272—it is quite likely that Thomas released the three sections already completed for general copying before leaving for Naples in late 1272. This at least would explain to some extent the poor showing of the *Tertia pars* in the circulation stakes, for it accounts for only about 18 percent of all the extant manuscripts of all the parts of the *Summa* as written by Thomas. Clearly, it never recovered from a late start.

One could argue, finally, that the relationship between the parts of the *Summa* is not as clear as it might be in the various prefaces, and that Thomas profitably could have been more forthright regarding his intentions when, in the *Summa theologiae*, he wrote what I may now venture to call his one "Dominican" work, and made what I have suggested was his own very personal contribution to a lopsided system of theological education in the order to which he belonged.

Notes

[1]For what follows, see, in general, L. E. Boyle, "Notes on the Education of the *Fratres communes* in the Dominican Order in the Thirteenth Century," in *Xenia medii aevi historiam illustrantia oblata Thomae Kaeppeli O.P.*, ed. R. Creytens and P. Künzle, 2 vols. (Rome: Storia e Letteratura, 1978), 1:249–67 at 249–51; repr. in *Pastoral Care, Clerical Education and Canon Law, 1200–1400* (London: Variorum, 1981). The present chapter is a slight reworking of *The Setting of the Summa theologiae of Saint Thomas* (Toronto: Pontifical Institute, 1982), being the fifth of the Etienne Gilson Series of Lectures at the Pontifical Institute of Mediaeval Studies.

[2]S. Lusignan, *Preface au Speculum maius de Vincent de Beauvais: réfraction et diffraction* (Montréal-Paris: Vrin, 1979), 138.

[3]Boyle, "Notes," 254.

[4]A. H. Thomas, *De oudste Constituties van de Dominicanen* (Louvain: Bibliothèque de la Revue d'histoire ecclésiastique, 1965), 311–12.

[5]R. H. and M. A. Rouse, "The Verbal Concordance to the Scripture," *Archivum Fratrum Praedicatorum* 44 (1974): 5–30.

[6]T. Kaeppeli, *Scriptores Ordinis Praedicatorum Medii Aevi*, XXX vols. (Rome: Ad S. Sabinae, 1975), 2:167; J. A. Corbett, ed., *The De instructione puerorum of William of Tournai O.P.* (Notre Dame, IN: University of Notre Dame Press, 1955).

[7]Kaeppeli, *Scriptores*, 2:311–17; R. D. Di Lorenzo, "The Collection Form and the Art of Memory in the *Libellus super ludo schachorum* of Jacobus de Cessolis," *Mediaeval Studies* 35 (1973): 205–21.

[8]T. Kaeppeli and A. Dondaine, eds., *Acta Capitulorum Provincialium Provinciae Romanae (1243–1344)* (Rome: Institutum historicum fratrum praedicatorum, 1941), 29.

[9]Humbertus de Romanis, *Opera*, ed. J.J. Berthier, 2 vols. (Rome: Befani, 1888–1889), 2:254–61.

[10]*Acta capitulorum generalium ordinis praedicatorum*, vol. 1 (Rome: Typo. Polyglotta Prop. Fide, 1898), 1:99–100.

[11]For these and other works, see J. A. Weisheipl, *Friar Thomas d'Aquino, His Life, Thought and Works*, 2d ed. (Washington, DC: Catholic University of America Press, 1983), 147–95.

[12]H.-F. Dondaine, ed., *De emptione et venditione ad tempus*, in *Sancti Thomae de Aquino Opera omnia iussu Leonis XIII P.M.*, Tomus 42. Opuscula 3 (Rome: Commission Leonina, 1979), 393–94, with intro., 383–90.

[13]Boyle, "Notes," 259–67.

[14]A. Walz, "S. Raymundi de Penyafort auctoritas in re paenitentiali," *Angelicum* 12 (1935): 346–96; K. Pennington, "Summae on Raymond of Pennafort's *Summa de casibus* in the Bayerische Staatsbibliothek, Munich," *Traditio* 27 (1971): 471–80; A. Dondaine, "La Somme de Simon de Hinton," *Recherches de théologie ancienne et médiévale* 9 (1937): 5–22, 205–18.

[15]J. M. Aubert, *Le droit romain dans l'oeuvre de saint Thomas* (Paris: J. Vrin, 1955), 19–23, 32, 43, 45, 60, 62, 109, 129–30.

[16]Compare ST IIa IIae, q. 100, a. 1, ad 5 and *Summa de casibus* 1.1, par. 2 (Rome: Tallini, 1603), 3a; IIa IIae, q. 100, a. 2, ad 6 and *Summa de casibus* 1.1, par. 16 (18a); IIa IIae, q. 100, a. 6, ad 5 and *Summa de casibus* 1.1, par. 14 (14b).

[17]*Acta Capitulorum Provincialium*, 32. The long-accepted idea (on the suggestion in passing, it appears, of P. Mandonnet) that Thomas spent 1267–68 at Viterbo, has been shown to be groundless in R. A. Gauthier, "Quelques questions à propos du commentaire de S. Thomas sur le *De anima*," *Angelicum* 51 (1974): 419–72, 438–43.

[18]See A. Dondaine, "Saint Thomas a-t-il disputé à Rome la question des attributs divins?" *Bulletin Thomiste* 10 (1953): 171–82; "Saint Thomas et la dispute des attributs divins," *Archivum Fratrum Praedicatorum* 8 (1938): 253–62.

[19]A. Dondaine, ed., *Historia ecclesiastica nova*, Book 22, c. 24, in "Les 'Opuscula fratris Thomae' chez Ptolomée de Lucques," *Archivum Fratrum Praedicatorum* 31 (1961):142–203, 151, ll. 21–25.

[20]"Fratri Thome de Aquino iniungimus in remissionem peccatorum quod teneat studium Rome. Et volumus quod fratribus qui stant secum ad studendum provideatur in necessariis vestimentis a conventibus de quorum predicatione traxerunt originem. Si autem illi studentes inventi fuerint negligentes in studio, damus potestatem fratri Thome quod ad conventus suos possit eos remittere." (*Acta Capitulorum Provincialium*, 32).

[21]Ibid., 22 (1258); 24 (1259); 28 (1263); 29–30 (1264).

[22]Dondaine, ed., *Historia ecclesiastica nova*, bk. 23, c. 15, 155, ll. 160–63: "Scripsit etiam eo tempore quo fuit Rome, de quo dictum est supra, iam magister existens, Primum super Sententias, quem ego vidi Luce sed inde subtractus nusquam ulterius vidi." Since Thomas probably was at the Provincial Chapter of 1267 at Lucca, then the copy of his "second" commentary on the first book of the *Sentences*, which Tolomeo saw there later, may have been one that Thomas left behind him after the Chapter. In a recent article ("'*Alia lectura fratris Thome*'? *[Super I Sent.]*,'" *Mediaeval Studies* 42 [1980]: 308–36), H.-F. Dondaine announces the discovery of a copy (probably before 1286) of the Parisian commentary of Thomas on *I Sent.* (Lincoln College, Oxford, ms. lat. 95, fols. 3r–122ra), which carries in its margins another commentary or partial commentary on *I Sent.* with references on three occasions to an "*alia lectura fratris Thome*." In a later article ("Alia lectura fratris Thome," *Mediaeval Studies* 45 [1983]: 418–29), I suggested that the "alia lectura" was not, as Fr. Dondaine was inclined to think, this commentary in margins of the Lincoln College manuscript, but rather the Parisian commentary of Thomas on the *Sentences* (1252–56), and therefore that this marginal commentary could well be a copy of a *reportatio* of the Santa Sabina classroom lectures of Thomas on *I Sent.* in 1265–66. This suggestion has been accepted by many scholars: see J. P. Torrell, *Initiation à Thomas d'Aquin. Sa personne et son oeuvre* (Fribourg-Paris: Cerf, 1993), 66–69, or, in English, Robert Royal, trans., *Saint Thomas Aquinas*, I: *The Person and His Work* (Washington, DC: Catholic University of America Press, 1996), 45–47.

[23]Humbertus, *Opera*, 2:254.

[24]*Acta Capitulorum Provincialium*, 33.

[25]*Summa de casibus*, 3, 24 (Lyons: n.p., 1603), 327b.

[26]Humbertus, *Opera*, 2:265

[27]Kaeppeli, *Scriptores*, 2:260–69. For Hugh's *Compendium*, see the edition (as of Albert) in J. C. A. Borgnet, ed., *Beati Alberti Magni Opera omnia*, vol. 33 (Paris: Vives, 1893), 1–261.

[28]"Quia catholicae veritatis doctor non solum provectos debet instruere sed ad eum pertinet etiam incipientes erudire, . . . propositum nostrae intentionis in hoc opere est ea quae ad christianam religionem pertinent eo modo tradere secundum quod congruit ad eruditionem incipientium."

[29]See M. D. Chenu, *Toward Understanding St. Thomas*, trans. A. M. Landry and D. Hughes (Chicago: Regnery, 1964), 300–301.

[30] For Humbert see *Opera*, 2:254–56, 259–62.

[31]"Post communem considerationem de virtutibus et vitiis et aliis ad materiam moralem pertinentibus, necesse est considerare singula in speciali."

[32]"Erit igitur compendiosior et expeditior considerationis via si simul sub eodem tractatu consideratio procedit de virtute et dono sibi correspondente, et vitiis oppositis. . . ."

[33]"Sic igitur tota materia morali ad considerationem virtutum reducta. . . . Et sic nihil moralium erit praetermissum."

[34]Kaeppeli, *Scriptores*, 2:133–47; A. Dondaine, "Guillaume Peyraut. Vie et oeuvres," *Archivum Fratrum Praedicatorum* 18 (1948): 164–67.

[35]Peraldus, *Summa aurea de virtutibus et vitiis* (Venice: Paganinus de Paganinis, 1497). The proper title and order should be, of course, *Summa de vitiis et virtutibus*.

[36]T. Deman, *Aux origines de la théologie morale* (Montreal-Paris: Vrin, 1951), 105: "Aucun auteur précédant ne nous annonça rien de pareil."

[37]Weisheipl, *Friar Thomas d'Aquino*, 222.

[38]The percentages are based on an analysis of *Codices manuscripti operum Thomae de Aquino*, vol. 1, *Autographae et Bibliothecae A-F*, ed. H.-F. Dondaine and H. V. Shooner (Rome: Commission Leonina, 1967), vol. 2, *Bibliothecae Gdansk-Münster*, ed. H. V. Shooner (Rome: Commission Leonina, 1973). Two subsequent volumes do not modify these figures). Oddly, the presence of these parts of the *Summa* in the extant catalogues of medieval libraries for Austria (*Mittelalterliche Bibliothekskataloge Oesterreichs*, vol. 1, *Niederösterreich: Register*, ed. A. Goldmann, [Vienna: Holzhausen, 1929], 153) works out at much the same percentage for each part: *Secunda secundae*, 38 percent; *Prima pars*, 29 percent, *Prima secundae*, 15 percent; *Tertia*, 13 percent; all parts of the *Summa* occur together only once, as is also the case for the two parts of the *Secunda pars*, amounting to five percent in all. Again, in vol. 3 (the only one I

have examined) of *Mittelalterliche Bibliothekskataloge Deutschlands und der Schweiz: Augsburg-Basel*, ed. P. Ruf (Münster: Beck, 1932), 3:1073 (Index), the percentages are *Secunda secundae*, 43 percent; *Prima pars*, 25 percent; *Tertia pars*, 18 percent; *Prima secundae*, 14 percent.

[39]Dondaine, ed., *Historia ecclesiastica nova*, bk. 22, c. 39, 151, ll. 37–43.

[40]Paris, Bibliothèque nationale, ms. lat. 15795, fol. 268r: "Explicit summa de uirtutibus et uiciis edita a fratre Thoma de Aquino, scripta sumptibus magistri Godefridi canonici Leodiensis, labore Henrici de Bavenchien." See C. Samaran and R. Marichal, eds., *Catalogue des manuscrits en écriture latine portant des indications de dates, de lieu, ou de copiste*, vol. 3 (Paris: Centre national de la recherche scientifique, 1974), 3:439 and plate LIV. Geoffrey († 1306) donated the copy to the Sorbonne, as well as a copy of the *Prima secundae* (BN lat. 15791) written by the same scribe.

[41]*Acta Capitulorum Provincialium*, 69.

[42]Ibid., 169.

[43]*Acta capitulorum generalium*, 2: 64-65.

[44]Lusignan, *Préface au Speculum maius*, 87. The *Prima secundae* is also used there.

[45]Kaeppeli, *Scriptores*, 1:27–28; D. Prümmer and M.-H. Laurent, *Fontes Vitae S. Thomae Aquinatis* (Toulouse: Revue Thomiste, 1912–1937), 356–58; M. Grabmann, "Albert von Brescia und sein Werk *De officio sacerdotis*," *Mittelalterliches Geistesleben*, vol. 2 (Munich: Hueber, 1956), 2:336–38.

[46]See Kaeppeli, *Scriptores*, 2:130–31.

[47]Ibid., 2:6.

[48]For what follows, see L. E. Boyle, "The *Summa confessorum* of John of Freiburg and the Popularization of the Moral Teaching of St. Thomas and of some of his Contemporaries," in *St. Thomas Aquinas 1274–1974 Commemorative Studies*, ed. A. A. Maurer, vol. 2 (Toronto: Pontifical Institute of Medieval Studies, 1974), 2:245–68, and "The Quodlibets of St. Thomas and Pastoral Care," *The Thomist* 38 (1974): 232–56, both repr. in *Pastoral Care*.

[49]Kaeppeli, *Scriptores*, 2:428–33, nn. 2340–45 (John of Freiburg); 94–95 (Cayeux); 1:157–65 (Bartholomew); 238–39 (Berthold); Boyle, "The *Summa confessorum*," 258–61.

[50]*Summa confessorum* (Lugduni: Saccon, 1517), first pref. (from the *Libellus*).

[51]"Post communem considerationem de virtutibus et vitiis et aliis ad materiam moralem pertinentibus, necesse est considerare singula in speciali: sermones enim morales universales sunt minus utiles, eo quod actiones in particularibus sunt."

[52]H. Denifle and E. Chatelain, ed., *Chartularium Universitatis Parisiensis*, vol. 1 (Paris: Delalain, 1889), 1:645–46. The *Prima pars* was in 56 *peciae* at

3 solidi each, the *Prima secundae* in 60 *peciae*, again at 3 solidi, the *Secunda secundae* in 82 *peciae* at 4 solidi.

Selected Further Reading

Bataillon, L. J. "L'activité intellectuelle des Dominicans de la première génération." In *Lector et Complilator. Vincent Beauvais, frére prêcheur. Un intellectuel et son millieu au XIIIe siècle.* Ed. S. Lusignan and M. Paulmier-Foucart Grâne. France: Créaphis, 1997.

Deman, T. *Aux origines de la théologie morale.* Paris: Vrin, 1951.

Jenkins, John I. *Knowledge and Faith in Thomas Aquinas.* Oxford: Oxford University Press, 1998.

O'Meara, Thomas F. *Thomas Aquinas Theologian.* Notre Dame, IN: University of Notre Dame Press, 1997.

Patfoort, A. *Saint Thomas d'Aquin. Les clerfs d'une théologie.* Paris: Cerf, 1983.

Tugwell, S., O.P. *Albert and Thomas. Selected Writings.* New York: Paulist Press, 1988.

The Sources of the Ethics of St. Thomas Aquinas

Servais-Théodore Pinckaers, O.P.

Translated by Mary Thomas Noble, O.P.

A study of the sources of St. Thomas's moral teaching can be very beneficial, for it gives us new insights into his texts and broadens and deepens our understanding of his thought. To a traditional reading that makes use of the commentators who came after Thomas, it adds an interpretation of the master in light of the authors who preceded him, and of the sources that inspired him and provided him with the materials for his theological project. Thus, a speculative examination of his work is rounded out by a historical consideration that reveals the genesis and unfolding of his thought, helping us to perceive better its vitality and richness. Such a study also aids us in discovering the timeliness of a teaching nourished by the great scriptural and patristic traditions and those of Augustine and Aristotle.

Within the limits of this chapter, I shall focus upon the moral section of the *Summa theologiae*, the *Secunda pars*, always with an eye to the possible contributions of other works. It is not difficult to discover the sources of Thomas's teaching, since he himself indicates them. The method is simple enough: it suffices to list the authors he cites, the authorities he appeals to in his articles. Thus, one can easily establish a list of explicit citations, question by question, taking into account the need to pay special attention to works mentioned in the *sed contra* and in the body of the articles, for these are more likely to refer to a substantial source of his teaching.

LIST OF SOURCES OF ST. THOMAS'S ETHICS ACCORDING TO HIS CITATIONS

Using Busa's concordance, I shall begin with a list of citations of authors. Here are the principal authors cited, arranged according to the number of citations in the *Secunda pars* of the *Summa*: Augustine, 1,630; Aristotle, 1,546; Gregory the Great, 439; Pseudo Dionysius, 202; Cicero, 187; Jerome, 178; John Damascene, 168; Ambrose, 151; Isidore of Seville, 120; Roman law, 102; Nemesius of Ephesus (under the name Gregory of Nyssa), 41; Macrobius, 33; Boethius, 30; Prosper of Aquitaine, 19; Benedict, 18; Basil, 13; Plato, 12; Hilary of Poitiers, 12; Bernard, 9; Caesar, 8; Ptolemy, 1. There are also citations from schools of philosophy: Stoics, 25; Peripatetics, 13; Platonists, 7; Epicurians, 2.

Citations of Scripture are found in all the questions and are the most numerous. Confining myself to the *Secunda pars*, I have counted 1,839 from the Old Testament and 2,003 from the New Testament. Most frequently quoted from the Old Testament are the Psalms, the Pentateuch, the Sapiential Books, and the Major Prophets. Here is the picture in detail: Psalms, 246; Deuteronomy, 192; Sirach, 172; Proverbs, 166; Exodus, 136; Isaiah, 132; Wisdom of Solomon, 103; Genesis, 99; Job, 72; Jeremiah, 56; Ezekiel, 38; Daniel, 29; 1 Samuel, 25; 1 Kings, 22; Hosea, 21; 2 Kings, 17; Malachi, 14; 2 Chronicles, 13; Joshua, 11; 2 Maccabees, 10; Judges, 9; 2

Samuel, 9; Amos, 8; Tobit, 8; Zechariah, 7; Song of Solomon, 7; 1 Maccabees, 6; Jonah, 5; Micah, 4; Esdras, 4; Esther, 4; Nahum, 3; Lamentations, 3; Judith, 3; 1 Chronicles, 2; Baruch, 2; Habakkuk, 1; Ruth, 1. The remaining Old Testament authors are not quoted: Obadiah, Sephaniah, Haggai, and Nehemiah. Among citations from the New Testament, Matthew, Paul, and John predominate: Matthew, 335; Romans, 313; 1 Corinthians, 270; John, 126; Luke, 120; Hebrews, 111; 2 Corinthians, 105; Ephesians, 81; 1 Timothy, 81; Galatians, 80; 1 John, 67; James, 63; Acts, 56; Philippians, 29; Colossians, 29; Revelations, 23; 1 Peter, 21; 1 Thessalonians, 15; 2 Peter, 15; Mark, 14; Titus, 12; 2 Thessalonians, 4; Philemon, 2; 2 John, 1; Jude, 1. Only John's Third Letter is not quoted.

In addition to these explicit citations, one also needs to take into account the special category of references indicated by *quidam* and *aliqui*, designating authors not considered as authorities but who may constitute important sources of teaching, beginning with Peter Lombard, the "*Magister*," and the theologians who have commented on him and who belong to a generation close to that of Aquinas.

THE USE OF CITATIONS IN SCHOLASTICISM

Now that I have established a material, one-dimensional list of citations, I need to highlight the contours of the intellectual landscape that they represent. The first important point is the purpose of these citations, which is very different from our modern use of them. In our scientific books, in theology, exegesis, or history, citations give the opinions of authors, particularly contemporary ones. Such references either confirm the position of the writer or advance the discussion. Numerous citations and an abundance of footnotes all serve, it would seem, to bear witness to the author's vast erudition.

With Thomas, the citations of authors are an application of the scholastic method used in the universities. Citations are placed by the scholastics in the text and not in the notes; they form part of the structure of the argument. Moreover, thirteenth-century scholastics cite by name only ancient authors, those who enjoy accepted authority in their field.

They do not name contemporary theologians, with whom they are at times engaged in very direct discussions, except by way of anonymous references that historians today are seeking to elucidate: "*Aliqui dicunt . . . alii dicunt*"; "Certain people say . . . others say."

This difference has its foundation and takes its significance from the scholastic method itself. This method, inspired by St. Augustine who made listening to the teachings of an authority anterior to the work of reason (*De moribus ecclesiae catholicae* 1.2), contains two complementary operations: the reading (*lectio*) and dialectical disputation (*disputatio*). Reading refers to the teaching of the master, which draws upon great works whose authority stems from their recognized quality. The first function of the master is to explain such works and comment on them. There are the books of Scripture, whose explanation is the prerogative of masters of theology; the writings of the fathers of the church, from which the *Sentences of the Fathers* presented by Peter Lombard are derived, upon which all bachelors had to comment; the works of Aristotle, introduced at the University of Paris in the mid-thirteenth century, and so forth. These authors are cited by name. As for recent and contemporary theologians, they are not named, even though their influence might be great. Thus, St. Albert, who was the greatest living authority in the time of St. Thomas, in the modern sense of the word, was reproached for allowing himself to be quoted by name in university disputations.

Grafted onto the reading of great texts and their commentaries is the second operation of the scholastic method: the disputation. It proposes for discussion, in the form of "questions" (*quaestiones*), problems encountered in the sentences of authorities, questions that even reach the point of pitting one authority against another, as Abelard had done in his celebrated *Sic et non*. This connection between reading and disputation gives a dialectical structure to the questions and articles in scholastic works: "*Videtur quod non*," "*Sed contra*," "*Respondeo dicendum*," "*Ad primum . . . dicendum*," which can be translated as: "objections," "contrary reasons," "a main response," and "responses to the objections."

The citations made by St. Thomas in the *Summa* constitute elements of the reading, especially in the *sed contra* and the body of the article or the solution (*determinatio*) of the master. They then furnish arguments in the discussion of the objections. They thus verify their character as sources of knowledge far better than do our modern citations. Their function is to transmit the riches of the theological heritage into the structure of the teaching and to furnish, at the same time, the material for the rational reflection that it helps to insert into the stream of Christian tradition.

If one counts the authors cited by St. Thomas, it is apparent that they are not very numerous in comparison with the bibliographies of our modern publications; however, their significance far outweighs their numbers. First, within each article, the citations are nonetheless abundant and interconnected. Above all, they are rich in content and play a considerable role in the structure of the argument. They have, in fact, a very precise function: their purpose is not erudition but strictly research and the manifestation of the truth of things. The citations of the *sed contra* and of the body of the article usually serve to build up the master's response to the question posed. In the objections, they demonstrate complementary aspects or solve difficulties.

One should note, too, that in citing his sources, Thomas practices a fine economy. One well-chosen citation is enough for him, sometimes two, rarely three, in order to expose the truth he wishes to affirm or defend. His interest bears less on authors and their authority, which might be strengthened by numbers (does he not say that the argument from authority is the weakest in comparison with reason?), than on the truth itself that they interpret. This is why a single citation, if adequate, suffices to support a truth that enlightens research and sustains argument.

THE HIERARCHY OF SOURCES IN ST. THOMAS'S TEACHING

If one wished to construct a table of the sources used in St. Thomas's teaching, one cannot place them all on the same plane, simply listing them alphabetically or chronologically. The Scholastics distinguish different levels among the authors they cite, according to their degree of authority, their capacity to

communicate knowledge, and manifest truth, or, in a word, their luminosity.

At the highest level of authority is the Word of God, expressed in Scripture. This is what furnishes the prime substance of theology (Ia, q. 1) and constitutes its principal source, the highest and surest one. It is rounded out by the teaching of the great councils, which interpret it in an authentic way in the name of the church, and by the confessions of faith which summarize their teaching.

Next, at a second level of authority are the teachings of the church fathers, considered as qualified interpreters and commentators of Scripture. The works of the fathers show Christian thought and experience to be in continuity with apostolic tradition, while confronting it with the philosophical wisdom whose sources they endeavor to utilize while safeguarding the supremacy of revelation. In the transmission of patristic teaching the *Sentences* of Peter Lombard play a determining role as the required manual for theological teaching. St. Thomas for his part will, throughout his life, be concerned to develop his knowledge of the fathers, Augustine (whom he will read and reread personally), and the Greek fathers (whose works he will research). I should mention, also, a certain authority accorded the glosses of Scripture, which are of varied origin.

To the fathers one could add, without attributing to them the same authority, however, representative authors of the height of the twelfth century such as Hugh and Richard of Saint Victor. Finally, it is well to consider as direct but more hidden sources the thirteenth-century theologians with whom St. Thomas holds discussions in all freedom and whom he utilizes quite frequently. These are the *quidam*, among whom one can distinguish the "ancients," of the three preceding centuries, and the "moderns," of the last generation. These authors can be evaluated according to the quality of their opinions. Certain masters, such as Philip the Chancellor with his teaching on the virtues, Albert the Great, in his teaching at Cologne and Paris, and Franciscan colleagues, such as Alexander of Hales and Bonaventure, provide St. Thomas with much information and many ideas.

Turning to the philosophers, one also finds important sources of authoritative teaching.

Philosophers share in reason's authority and can furnish theologians with probable arguments. They bear witness to human reflection and experience. For Thomas, the chief philosophical source is obviously Aristotle, "the Philosopher," whom he uses throughout his work, even when treating specifically Christian questions. St. Thomas considers Aristotle an expert on human nature and borrows from him the basic structure of his morality: the ordering to happiness as our final end, the organization of the moral virtues, and the analysis of friendship that serves him in defining charity. In Thomas's project of constructing a morality of virtues, he also exploits authors such as Cicero and Seneca in dealing with the virtues, Boethius for the treatise on happiness, and Nemesius for the analysis of human acts. Finally, at this level, Thomas is also in contact and in discussion with the *quidam* of his time, consisting notably of the masters in the Faculty of Arts. Furthermore, one must not forget the Arab (Averroes and Avicenna) and Jewish (Maimonides) philosophers. These commentators on Aristotle are for St. Thomas both adversaries and collaborators in researching the truth about God and the human person.

In considering this rapidly constructed table, I can truly say that the work of St. Thomas, particularly the moral section of his *Summa theologiae*, constitutes the convergence of all the great currents of thought known in the thirteenth century, meeting in the cultural center represented by the University of Paris, in their full theological and philosophical flowering. It should be noted, however, that these currents not only exert a historical influence upon Thomas, but, with the contribution of revelation and the different traditions, they provide him with solid materials for a construction at once faithful and original.

THE UTILIZATION OF THE SOURCES AND THEIR ARTICULATION

How does Thomas utilize his sources and establish order among them? To answer this question, there is a capital point that needs to be clarified first: the "authorities" that he cites do not play a deontological role for him, but an epistemological one. In other words, their

sentences do not impose an obligation to hold one or another proposition as true, even if not understood; rather, they are seen as sources of light and truths to be understood, even if they are as yet understood only imperfectly. The "authorities" (the term designated the person who had authority, and equally the propositions taught) address the intellect first, and not merely the will. As for the latter faculty, it is not constrained by the "authorities," but attracted by the love of truth that they inspire. St. Thomas's teaching is thus situated in the context of an intellectual education, a pedagogy exercised by a teacher toward his disciples, whom he forms as theologians, under the aegis of reason and revelation.

SCRIPTURE COMMENTED ON BY THE FATHERS

From this perspective of intellectual research and formation, our doctor does not use his sources in haphazard fashion; rather, he arranges them in careful order. The citations from Scripture, his first source, because it is the divine Word, are explained with the help of the fathers and the contributions of philosophers, for revelation presupposes reason.

I can affirm that the citations from Scripture in the *Summa*, decisive for a question, are often accompanied by references to patristic works. This reveals that St. Thomas does not read Scripture in isolation but interprets it within the church with the help of authoritative representatives of the best tradition, such as Augustine, Gregory the Great, or Dionysius the Areopagite. Let us take the case of the definition of the Evangelical Law as an interior law (Ia IIae, q. 106, a. 1). The *sed contra* cites the Letter to the Hebrews, which takes up the prophet Jeremiah's proclamation of a new covenant, consisting of divine laws inscribed in hearts. The body of the article appeals to precise texts from the Letter to the Romans and interprets them in light of St. Augustine's *De spiritu et littera*, which is precisely a lengthy meditation on all of these scriptural passages. Article two, on justification through the New Law, cites the Letter to the Romans in the *sed contra* and repeats the teaching of *De spiritu et littera* in the body of the article.

The procedure is not mechanical, however. In articles three and four of the same question, the scriptural quotations are placed in the *sed contra* and the principal response, while the references to Augustine and Dionysius are found in the answers to the objections. Nonetheless, the fact remains that the teaching on the nature of the New Law, which underlies the three questions devoted to it, gets its start from Paul, on whom Augustine comments. A similar connection between Scripture and Augustine will appear again as a key issue in the explanation of the Sermon on the Mount, directly inspired by the commentary of the Bishop of Hippo (Ia IIae, q. 108, a. 2). One finds this link between the Gospel and Augustine once again in the question on the Beatitudes (q. 69) and, to a lesser degree, in the discussion of the fruits of the Holy Spirit (q. 70, a. 4).

From this, one can conclude that, on Thomas's view, the fathers are the necessary interpreters of Scripture, authentic representatives of the church's thought. They express the tradition, which it is the task of theologians to transmit, defend, and develop. In this role, the fathers serve as models: First, in listening to and explaining the Word of God, and, then, in their intellectual work, placing the resources of reason at the service of the Gospel in order to form a sacred science, a solid theology corresponding to the needs of Christians and of all men and women called by God. Thomas, as a doctor and master of theology, is aware that he is continuing the work of the fathers by incorporating them into the new scholastic method.

I should add an important remark about scriptural quotations. Inserted into the scholastic text with its strongly rational structure, scripture quotations at first sight may appear artificial, because they introduce a different type of thought and expression that does not have the same rational structure. They also can be taken too easily as secondary illustrations or proof-texts, which is often the case in modern manuals of moral theology. In reality, these words of Scripture usually play a leading role because they possess a status of their own: they are sparks of a higher light coming from the intellect (*intellectus*), which is superior to discursive reason. This is why they are presented as simple words, rays of light that theological reflection should refract in its reasoning. Such is the case, for example, with the phrase from Psalm 4, "The light of your face has shown upon us, O Lord" ("*Signatum est super nos lumen vultus tui, Domine*"), quoted several times in connection with natural law: in Ia IIae, q. 91, a. 2, to show that a natural law exists within us; in Ia IIae, q. 19, a. 4, concerning the relationship of a good will to the eternal law; and in *De veritate*, q. 16, a. 3, on the subject of *synderesis* and its permanence in the human person. This light, which shows us the good and presides over moral judgments, belongs to the very nature of the soul and flows from the domain of intellect. Finally, this verse signifies the interior light, which is the principal cause of knowledge in teaching given by an external master (Ia, q. 117, a. 1, ad 1).

It is thus possible to do some very fruitful research on the enlightening role of the Psalms Thomas quotes. In this connection, one needs to mistrust the rationalistic mentality, which sees as important only what possesses the drawing power of argumentation. For Thomas, the words of Scripture, even when very simple in their formulation, can open up more direct access—far more than even the most elaborate scholastic reasonings—to the reality theology addresses. This is particularly true of those books and authors of the Bible that he himself comments upon and quotes most frequently, such as the Psalms, Isaiah, Job, the Gospels, Paul, and John. According to Thomas, simple and direct understanding is loftier than the reason it guides. It, in fact, enables communication with angelic and divine intelligence (Ia, q. 79, a. 8).

THE UTILIZATION OF PHILOSOPHICAL SOURCES

The second source of light for St. Thomas is human reason, expressed particularly through the philosophers, with Aristotle as their principal representative. The Philosopher plays a basic role in the Angelic Doctor's ethical theory. He furnishes Thomas with the categories and analyses that serve as the foundation of his morality of virtues. Aristotle is quoted in the majority of articles in the *Summa*. However, Thomas does not separate the two principal sources, revelation and reason, theology and philosophy, as would be done later. On the contrary, one can see in him a very close collaboration in the use of authorities between the content of faith and reason, the Gospel and Aristotle. While discerning perfectly the difference between these two kinds of light, Thomas endeavors to show their convergence, which rests on a fundamental harmony. He is thus heir to the fathers, who saw in nature the work of the creator God of Genesis, and in the human person—through reason and free will—the image of God called to fulfillment in the divine vision and union.

This explains why St. Thomas apparently experiences no hesitation in incorporating Aristotle into the solution of specifically Christian questions arising from the order of grace. On his view, grace and nature are in harmony and call out to each other, in such wise that, by basing oneself upon the movements of spiritual nature, one can discern how grace proceeds in conformity with the wisdom of God (Ia IIae, q. 5, a. 7; q. 110, aa. 2, 3). As a witness to humanity, Aristotle becomes in St. Thomas's eyes a servant of the Gospel. Moreover, this daring perspective authorizes him discreetly to correct and transform the teaching of the Stagirite so as to open it to Christian truth.

This unabashed coordination between the Gospel and Aristotle is shown, for example, in the definition of the principal Christian virtue, charity (IIa IIae, q. 23, a. 1). In order to fashion this cornerstone of the treatise on charity, Thomas associates a quotation from John in the discourse after the Last Supper, "No longer do I call you servants, but friends," with a quotation from the *Nicomachean Ethics* that recalls the entire Aristotelian analysis of friendship in Books VIII and IX. In the study of the virtuous character of charity, there follow quotations from Augustine's *De doctrina christiana* (q. 23, a. 2, *sed contra*) and *De moribus ecclesiae catholicae* (q. 23, a. 3, *sed contra*), and, of course, from 1 Corinthians 13, which provides the *sed contra* of articles 4 to 7. Thus, the study and experience of human friendship serve as a substratum for the study of charity, conceived as friendship with God, with Christ, who is called "*Maxime . . . amicus*" (Ia IIae, q. 108, a. 4), with one's brothers and sisters, and with all people. It is obvious that charity surpasses hu-

man friendship, for Aristotle does not think one could enter into friendship with God because of the extreme inequality that separates humanity from Him (q. 23, a. 1, obj. 1), nor with enemies (q. 23, a. 1, obj. 2). Therefore, Thomas makes profound changes in the Aristotelian analysis so as to adapt it to a higher experience. Nonetheless, it is from that analysis that he borrows the structure of friendly relationships, to apply it to charity and to all the movements it engenders. For him, the experience of human friendship provides the best analogy for the description of divine love. Doubtless he is thinking of, among other things, fraternal friendship in the religious life. Aelred of Rielvaux described it a century earlier in his *De spiritali amicitia*, but stopped short of defining charity as friendship, unable to see how the love of enemies, which is characteristic of charity, could be explained in terms of friendship.

There exists, therefore, a close coordination between theological and philosophical sources in Thomas's moral works. It is based upon the fundamental harmony between revelation and reason, each of which, according to its own level and its own method, flows from the divine truth.

St. Thomas's broad and open use of philosophical sources is confirmed in his analysis of the moral virtues, and particularly in his handling of the related virtues. For these questions, Cicero, in his two books, *Rhetorica* and *De inventione*, is Aquinas's guide, along with Aristotle—whom Cicero rounds out—Macrobius, who commented on Cicero's *Dream of Scipio*, and Andronicus of Rhodes. These authors are quoted and analyzed together in q. 48 of IIa IIae, to establish the parts of prudence. In q. 49, on the integral parts of prudence, Cicero furnishes most of the *sed contra* (aa. 1, 2, and 6), with Macrobius (aa. 3, 5–7), Isidore of Seville (a. 4), and finally, Paul's Letter to the Ephesians (a. 8). Aristotle intervenes in the body of the articles. In regard to the parts of justice, in q. 80, one once more finds Cicero, followed by Aristotle, Macrobius, and Andronicus. One again finds the same constellation in q. 128, which establishes the parts of fortitude, and in q. 143 on the parts of temperance.

Philosophical divisions are thus adopted by Thomas to construct the organization of the virtues that underlie morality. This approach is not without its drawbacks, for it does not always allot to the specifically Christian virtues the place they deserve. This is the case, for example, with humility, which is practically nonexistent in the lists used (Andronicus defined it as modest bearing in the matter of clothing: q. 161, obj. 4), and is connected with modesty in Cicero's list, which is itself a part of temperance. Humility thus receives an overly modest position, which is understandable among pagan authors, but St. Thomas knows perfectly well its importance in Christian tradition: the New Testament (q. 161, aa. 1, 3, 5, *sed contra*); among the fathers: Origen (aa. 1, 4, *sed contra*), Augustine (q. 161, a. 2, *sed contra*; q. 161, a. 5, obj. 2 and 4), John Chrysostom (q. 161, a. 5, obj. 1), and Gregory the Great (q. 161, a. 5, obj. 4); and, in the monastic tradition, with the degrees of humility according to St. Benedict, explained in article 6. It is fitting, moreover, to group this question with the two following questions on pride and Adam's sin, in which, by contrast, the fundamental importance of humility appears to better advantage.

The same is true of vigilance or watchfulness, a typically Christian virtue as presented by Paul, a waiting for the coming of Christ, filled with hope (1 Thess 5:5–6; Rom 13:11–12, among others). Thomas identifies vigilance with solicitude, a part of prudence, according to an etymology of Isidore of Seville (q. 47, a. 9), and thus loses the opportunity to expose its Christian dimension.

Such an overt use of Aristotle, Cicero, and other philosophers may explain the reproach often leveled at St. Thomas, that he gives too much space to philosophical sources in his ethics, especially the moral virtues. As a matter of fact, it certainly would be beneficial to compare his total presentation of the virtues with those of Paul and the fathers, notably Augustine, in order to make some clarifications from a Gospel perspective.

THE THEOLOGICAL ORIENTATION OF THE ETHICS OF ST. THOMAS: THE VIRTUES AND BEATITUDES

One can find in Thomas's treatises on the virtues the same theological perspective as is present in the entire *Secunda pars*. One could say that in each instance philosophical analysis rises toward Christian experience and places itself at the service of revelation. It is patently clear in the case of the virtue of fortitude, whose principal act is not so much courage in war as the witness of the martyr (IIa IIae, q. 124). One can see it, also, in the questions on obedience, in which Scripture and Gregory the Great are the principal sources, and in the study of humility, which ends, as I have demonstrated, with an explanation of the twelve degrees of humility as described by St. Benedict.

Finally, one needs to remember that the virtues form an organism whose head is constituted by the theological virtues. These animate and inspire the moral virtues from within, to such an extent that they transform the measure of the moral virtues. This leads St. Thomas to support the existence of infused moral virtues, needed to proportion the action of the Christian to the supernatural and theological end to which he is called. Furthermore, he associates with each of the virtues, including the moral virtues, a gift of the Holy Spirit that disposes us to receive divine inspirations that empower us to act according to a higher measure. This is shown in the exposition on the evangelical beatitudes, which are attained differently according to whether they are attained through the virtues or through the gifts (Ia IIae, q. 69, a. 3).

The problem of the theological orientation of an analysis employing philosophical sources arises particularly with regard to questions about our final end and beatitude, which constitute the backbone of the entire Thomistic moral theology. It is precisely by means of a study of the sources of this treatise that its evangelical dimension can be better demonstrated, appearances to the contrary notwithstanding.

Let me now take the question of the relationship of this treatise to the Gospel beatitudes. The connection is not apparent from a simple reading of the first five questions of the *Prima secundae*, in which one finds only one quotation from the Beatitudes: the beatitude of the pure of heart in the *sed contra* of q. 4, a. 4. This fact seems to confirm the common opinion that the treatise is a purely philosophical, Aristotelian study. But, all one need do is read the explanation of the beatitudes in Thomas's commentary on the Gospel of Matthew to change one's opinion. In the Beatitudes, Thomas sees Christ's answer to the question of happiness, which no philosopher had ever truly been able to resolve, not even Aristotle. Here, already, one finds the categories later to be used in the *Summa*: Christ overturns both the false answers of those who place happiness in a life of pleasure and the incomplete answers of those who place it in the active and contemplative life in this world. Thus, Christ is shown as the philosopher and sage *par excellence*, bringing the complete answer through the promise of the Kingdom of God. This commentary on the Beatitudes already follows that ascending movement, passing from external and bodily goods to interior and spiritual ones and culminating in the vision of God, which one finds again in the argumentation of the *Summa*. On St. Thomas's view, the teaching on the beatitudes underlies the questions concerning happiness and provides their chief answer. The same approach is found in the first two drafts of this treatise, in Book IV of the *Commentary on the Sentences*, distinction 49, and in Book III of the *Summa contra gentiles*, chapters 1 through 63. Moreover, in his outline of the Sermon on the Mount, which contains all moral teaching ("*totam informationem christianae vitae*"), Thomas gives the beatitudes exactly the same position as in the treatise on happiness in the *Summa*: they establish happiness as the end of human life ("*Post declaratum beatitudinis finem. . .*" [Ia IIae, q. 108, a. 3]).

The fact that St. Thomas studies the beatitudes separately results from the question of the relationship among the virtues, gifts, and beatitudes, which had become classic in scholastic tradition after Peter Lombard (III *Sent.*, d. 34). This problem is important for Aquinas, because it conditions the organization of his ethics, whose point of departure is the virtues. It is for this reason that, in the *Summa*, he is led to treat the beatitudes not with the questions on happiness, but after the virtues and gifts (Ia IIae, q. 69), and to associate with each of the seven principal virtues a gift and a beatitude. This plan immediately poses a difficulty: it rarely occurred to readers of the questions on happiness then to read in turn the study of the evangelical beatitudes, which ap-

peared to them to be a spiritual supplement and a slightly artificial refinement of the teaching on the virtues and gifts. Let me add, however, that the list of citations in the first questions of the *Prima secundae* shows that the scriptural and patristic sources are used as frequently as the works of Aristotle or Boethius's *De consolatione*.

THE METHODOLOGICAL USEFULNESS OF THE STUDY OF ST. THOMAS'S SOURCES

One might think that the study of Thomas's sources is, in the end, only of historical interest. This opinion is reinforced by the idea of many Thomists that the master extracted from his sources the essence of their teaching, their rational substance. It, therefore, does not seem necessary to have recourse to the texts employed by the Angelic Doctor, since they are grasped in his own texts and assembled with conciseness and precision. Thus, all the theological material—Scripture, the fathers, and the philosophers—are summarized and gathered together in the work of Thomas. The study of his text, therefore, suffices for theological reflection. But, on the contrary, it seems to me that if St. Thomas were to come back today, he would tell us almost the opposite: "If I made so many, and such well chosen citations from authorities, it was not to dispense you from consulting their authors, but, on the contrary, to invite you to read their works. All the more so because some of them, beginning with the sacred authors, enjoy a higher theological authority than mine."

In order to show the interest of this reading of sources, it would be well first to pick out the principal texts that inspire Thomas, which vary according to the questions. These works usually are indicated by repeated references. In the questions on happiness, for example, one finds as references: Aristotle, especially the *Nicomachean Ethics* and the *De anima*; Boethius's *De consolatione*; Augustine's *De moribus ecclesiae*, *De genesi ad litteram*, and *De civitate dei*, to name a few. Book XIV of *De civitate dei* is the basis for the study of the passions and their morality. In the analysis of love, Dionysius takes his place with Augustine, particularly in regard to the effects of this first passion (q. 27, aa. 1, 3–6, *sed contra*).

Upon close examination, the citations, usually limited to a sentence, often prove to be merely the tip of an iceberg. The study of happiness refers to Books I and X of the *Nicomachean Ethics*, which take in the entire field of morality. Again, an attentive reading shows that the *De consolatione* supplies the Christian philosophical substratum of the treatise. The comparison between the two works brings out both St. Thomas's dependence and his originality, especially in connection with Christian happiness in the next world. All the same, the definition of happiness as "the perfect state of possessing all goods" would seem rather flat had one not read Book III of *De consolatione*, which shows how this is realized in God, the source of every good thing.

Let us take another example. Approaching the question of happiness by discussing the goods of the soul (Ia IIae, q. 2, a. 7), Thomas quotes, from memory apparently, a half sentence from Augustine's *De doctrina christiana* (I, xxii, 20): "That which constitutes the happy life is that which should be loved for its own sake." Behind this brief quotation is hidden a long and profound reflection by Augustine about the goods that one should use and enjoy, and about love of oneself, of others, and of God in connection with the two commandments of love. This gives all its fullness to Thomas's thought, and indicates at the same time the bond that joins the study of happiness to charity.

I could produce similar examples in all the questions of the *Summa* and demonstrate repeatedly the usefulness of reading the principal sources cited in order to throw light on the text and show the richness of the ideas that Thomas has in mind as he writes. Of course, I realize too that he does not write in isolation but is always in living communion with what is truest and best in ecclesial and philosophical tradition, in order to transmit it according to the method taught in the Gospel: he is the wise scribe who draws forth from the treasure he has received things new and old, the latter being the guarantor of the former.

THE NEED TO KNOW
ST. THOMAS'S SOURCES

I have been talking about the usefulness of reading St. Thomas's sources in order to understand him better. I need to go further and speak of its necessity, both because of who Thomas is and because of who his modern readers are.

I could characterize Thomas's thought and style in two words: rational precision. Thomas speaks the language of reason plainly, abstracting from sensible, imaginative, and affective connotations in order to express as precisely as possible the essence of things. This rational purpose leads him to an extreme conciseness; he seeks to formulate the essential and nothing more. One can see this rational process at work in the elaboration of his definitions, such as that of law, which is reduced to its four constitutive elements in the four articles of Question 90 of the *Prima secundae*. At the same time, Thomas has the art of choosing, from among the texts he uses, the sentence or the phrase that expresses the essence of the issue and provides the exact argument he needs. Such conciseness offers incontestable advantages for the precision and strength of his argumentation. But it has a disadvantage. Separated from Thomas by seven centuries of history and placed in an altogether different cultural setting, practically speaking, one can no longer by solely reading his text discern the richness of its content nor of the traditions that it evokes. Each group of questions is a gold mine to be explored anew. In consulting the sources he indicates, one can manage this task without too much difficulty. The modern reader even has the advantage of wider and easier access to ancient texts than was possible in the Middle Ages.

Yet, when one considers the modern reader's condition, the difficulties increase; any modern student is an heir to modern rationalism, whose earliest roots can already be detected close to Thomas's time, from the end of the thirteenth century. No longer can one conceive spontaneously the relationship of reason to the other human faculties, nor to faith, in the same way as did the Angelic Doctor, and, therefore, one risks interpreting him badly or in an impoverished way.

For Thomas, reason is always in direct relation to, and in natural harmony with, the intuitive intelligence (*intellectus*), the source of light through the knowledge of first principles (Ia, q. 79, a. 8); with the will, whence proceeds love of the good and the desire for happiness;

with affectivity, as witnessed by his beautiful study of the passions; and with the senses, and the body itself, naturally united to the soul. For him, reason operates in synergy with sensible and spiritual experience, and in fruitful collaboration with faith and tradition.

However, the predominance of reason has given rise to certain humanly inevitable limitations in the master's work. He speaks little of affectivity. It is enough to read a few pages of Augustine, Gregory, or Chrysostom, so appreciated by St. Thomas, to see the difference. Nor does Thomas have a great deal of imagination, as is shown by the small number of examples he gives and his schematic way of presenting them. Reading his sources eases this difficulty and makes his teaching more expressive. His teaching brings out the essence and structure of things, of human and divine realities, but it is so rigorous and so finely delineated that it sometimes evokes images of a blueprint. The modern reader needs the help of the authors Thomas cites, in order better to gauge the dimensions and feel the life breath that animates his thought.

Between Thomas and the modern reader, a real rupture was created in regard to the concept of the human person with the advent, in the fourteenth century, of nominalism, which separates the human faculties from each other. From that time on, rationalism has opposed voluntarism. In its attempt to dominate then, reason has cut itself off from affectivity, sensitivity, and the natural and acquired inclinations, and has become increasingly conceptual, even mathematical. Theology loses touch with spiritual and human experience. In line with Descartes, the mind, with its ideas, stands in opposition to the body and to matter, and science establishes itself through a break with tradition, by separating itself from faith, as philosophy separates from theology.

It was inevitable that the reading of St. Thomas by his modern interpreters was influenced by the rationalistic context of the day, which to all appearances can claim to have its roots in the heavily rational character of Aquinas's thought. This was even legitimate to the degree that every reader of an ancient work needs to express the teaching from within the context of his own time. But, perhaps, the time has come to become more aware of the influence of rationalism on our minds, its limitations and shortcomings, the error it occasions in our reading of the great theological and philosophical works, and the resulting impoverishment of our reflections on the problems of our day.

The reading of St. Thomas directly and deeply enriched by the concomitant reading of his scriptural, patristic, and philosophical sources, is certainly a good way to overcome the narrowness of a rationalistic theology and to rediscover in ourselves the spiritual sources that have nourished all renewals throughout the course of history, in theology as well as in philosophy.

INTERIOR SOURCES

The question of St. Thomas's sources is actually broader and deeper than one sometimes thinks. To this point, I have been speaking of the textual sources of Thomas's teaching, indicated principally by the authorities cited. This perspective, which could remain in the purely historical order, is actually not enough, for these external sources would have no effectiveness, according to Thomas's own teaching, without the interior and spiritual sources that play a leading role in the formation of theology.

Personal Reason, Source of Light in Teaching

In his lengthy analysis of the act of teaching (Ia, q. 117, a. 1, and parallel places), which undoubtedly testifies to his personal experience even though he establishes it by bringing to the fore Aristotle and Paul, the Teacher of the Gentiles, Thomas distinguishes a twofold action. First, the external action of the master, who helps the mind of the disciple to acquire knowledge by presenting him the pathways of reasoning to be followed, which he himself has traveled; this is *disciplina*. Second, the interior action of the disciple's mind, growing in knowledge thanks to the light of the agent intellect and to the first principles that the intellect possesses naturally as a participation in divine truth. As a physician serves nature in procuring the recovery of health, so the master who teaches is at the service of the disciple's mind. God alone can act directly on the latter and exercise the role of interior master.

This analysis applies directly to my question about sources. The authorities Thomas cites are masters who lend their aid to the acquisition of theological knowledge and to the discovery of truth in every question under discussion. Whatever their importance and their number, nonetheless, one can never forget that these authors address an interior source within each person, the light of truth, which shines at the summit of the mind and in the depths of the heart, presiding over judgments about truth and goodness and particularly over one's receptivity to the teaching and opinions of others.

In this connection, St. Thomas is an exemplary case. In each of his works, in each question of the *Summa*, he places himself alongside his disciples and readers in the school of the masters, to receive all the fragments of truth contained in their teaching. But, at the same time, his interior source, his personal genius, is manifested in the way in which he organizes and disposes the materials he has gathered, to form of them a new synthesis, original and worthy of the great architects of his age. Thanks to this intimate light, Thomas enters into a living and fruitful communion with his sources, so close that, in large measure, it breaks down historical separations. Can one not say that through his dialogue with Aristotle, Thomas has become a contemporary of the Philosopher, or, if you will, that he has introduced him into his own age, and into the University of Paris, as a contemporary master? Can one not likewise think that Aristotle and Thomas may become our contemporaries, masters present to the modern reader as well, if one knows how to read them by the light of the truth, which shines within us as it does in them? They can be even closer to us than many contemporary authors, through their response to our most intimate questions, such as those about happiness and love, truth and goodness. This is, perhaps, still clearer in the case of Augustine, who has been called the most modern of the fathers of the church.

The Word of God as the Principal Interior Source in Theology

When it comes to studying and teaching theology, there is obviously a still higher and more interior source: the Word of God with the grace of the Holy Spirit. The Angelic Doctor recognizes perfectly the predominant action of this source and expresses its interiority, particularly in his teaching on the New Law. Above the natural law, which expresses our spontaneous sense of the true and the good, he recognizes the existence of a source of light and an inclination that are higher and very interior; this he identifies as the grace of the Holy Spirit, penetrating us through faith and operating through charity. As the natural law has been placed in the heart of everyone by the Creator, so the New Law is inscribed by the spirit in the hearts of believers and endowed with a strength of grace for action (Ia IIae, q. 106, a. 1, ad 2). Thus, the spirit becomes our master in a unique way; he is above all interiorly so by the light of his intimate Word, obtaining for us an understanding of the Scriptures and a knowledge of the ways of providence in our own lives and in the history of the church.

Thomas clarifies what the rays of this spiritual light are by associating the gifts with the virtues. To faith are joined the gifts of understanding and knowledge, to charity the gift of wisdom, to prudence the gift of counsel, and so forth. This is the first source of theological knowledge and of Thomistic moral teaching. This is all the more certain, and the Angelic Doctor's originality in this domain is all the more manifest, when one compares him with the theologians of his day: in his definition of the New Law as an interior law identified with the grace of the spirit; in his definition of the gifts as dispositions to receive spiritual inspirations; and, finally, in his construction of morality around the virtues and the gifts that perfect them.

The recognition of this interior source at the origin of theological work transforms historical relationships and creates a kind of spiritual contemporaneity from Pentecost to our own day, among the Christian faithful and among theologians. When Thomas cites the Gospel (for example, the beatitude of the pure of heart who shall see God), he is not merely accepting a text drawn from a venerable passage; through his faith he receives this verse of the Gospel as a word of the Lord bearing within it a present truth, capable of throwing light upon contemporary life. The beatitude of the pure of heart invites every person to seek the vision of God as his or her ultimate end and supreme happiness. For Thomas, this promise of Christ is not only a historical word, a subject for exegetical study; thanks to the light of the spirit, it becomes a present Word, opening up to him and to humanity a future that surpasses anything Aristotle and the pagan philosophers could have imagined. In this light, a new concept of time emerges, centered upon the person of Christ, the teacher *par excellence*. This vision of history is divided into three periods: the preparation for the coming of Christ, the accomplishment of his work of salvation in the Gospel, and the church's journey toward the kingdom. It will be expressed in the reading of Scripture according to the three spiritual senses (Ia, q. 1, a. 10), and through it passes into theology. One finds it again at the foundation of Christian liturgy from the beginning.

Owing to the action of the spirit, Thomas enters into profound communion, in the love and the search for truth, with all the authors whom he consults: with the fathers, as commentators on the Word in the name of the church, and with the philosophers, as witnesses to the humanity and the nature that God has created in his image and likeness and that remain subject to the wisdom of his Providence in spite of sin. In writing the *Summa*, Thomas is aware that he is listening to the Lord teaching on the mountain, in the company of the fathers and the holy Doctors of the church, in the same fellowship with all those, philosophers and others, who, without having been able to hear this voice directly, had nonetheless known how to welcome, even if imperfectly, the light of truth shining at the summit of their souls. For him, it is not merely a beautiful picture or an ideal, but a living communion in the light of the truth poured into hearts by the spirit, who had already hovered over the waters at the beginning of creation.

Those reading St. Thomas today are invited to enter actively into this communion. In order to do so, however, one cannot be content merely to read his works and study them with methods that are considered scientific, however useful these may be in theological work. In doing so, the reader runs the great risk of seeing them only as monuments of the past or as aspects of a powerful and cold rational system. In my opinion, the indispensable condition for penetrating to the heart of St. Thomas's thought is to begin by opening ourselves to the first source of his teaching: the Word of the Lord spoken by the Holy Spirit in the Scriptures and in our hearts. Before opening the *Summa theologiae*, therefore, we should open the Gospel and meditate upon it in prayer as St. Thomas himself did, without forgetting to put it into practice, so that we may acquire by experience a living knowledge of the realities of which he speaks. Then, nourished by the same spiritual source, we can enter into communion of mind and heart with the Angelic Doctor and engage in fruitful dialogue with him, as well as with the authors whom he quotes, as he invites us to listen to them in our search for the truth. Thus, we will better grasp the timeliness of his teaching, discerning its human riches and limitations. We will know, also, how to find the words needed today to transmit the intellectual treasure contained in his works.

Selected Further Reading

Aubert, Jean Marie. *Le droit romain dans l'oeuvre de saint Thomas.* Paris: J. Vrin, 1955.

Bataillon, Louis J., O.P. "Saint Thomas et les Pères: de la *Catena* à la *Tertia Pars*." In *Ordo sapientiae et amoris.* Ed. Carlos-Josaphat Pinto de Oliveira, O.P. Fribourg Suisse: Éditions Universitaires, 1993.

Bellemare, Rosaire, O.M.I. "La Somme de théologie et la lecture de la Bible." *Église et Théologie* 5 (1974): 257–70.

Boyle, John F. "St. Thomas Aquinas and Sacred Scripture." *Pro Ecclesia* 4 (1995): 92–104.

Dondaine, H.-F., O.P. "Note sur la documentation patristique de saint Thomas à Paris en 1270." *Revue des sciences philosophiques et théologiques* 47 (1963): 403–6.

———. "Les scolastiques citent-ils les Pères de première main?" *Revue des sciences philosophiques et théologiques* 36 (1952): 231–43.

Elders, Leo J., S.V.D. "Santo Tomás de Aquino y los Padres de la Iglesia." *Doctor Communis* 48 (1995): 55–80.

Geenen, G., "En marge du Concile de Chalcédoine. Les texts du Quatrième Concile dans les oeuvres de Saint Thomas." *Angelicum* 29 (1952): 43–59.

———. "The Council of Chalcedon in the Theology of St. Thomas." In *From an Abundant Spring.* The Walter Farrell Memorial Volume of the *Thomist.* New York: J. P. Kennedy, 1952.

———. "Les Sentences de Pierre Lombard dans la *Somme* de saint Thomas." In *Miscellanea Lombardiana*. Novara, Spain: Istituto geografico De Agostini, 1957.

———. "Saint Thomas et les Pères." In *Dictionnaire de théologie catholique* 15:1. Paris: Letouzey et Ane, 1946.

Grillmeier, Aloys. "Du 'symbolum' à la *Somme théologique*. Contribution à l'étude des relations théologico-historiques entre la patristique et la scolastique." In *Eglise et Tradition*. Ed. Johannes Betz and Heinrich Fries. Le Puy-Lyon, France: Xavier Mappus, 1963.

Marc, P., Pera, C., and Caramello, P. "De Modo citandi auctoritates a Sancto Thoma usurpato." In *Liber de Veritate Catholicae Fidei contra errores infidelium qui dicitur Summa Contra Gentiles*. Vol. 1, introductio, excursus 3. Turin: Marietti, 1967.

Pera, C. *Le Fonti del pensiero di S. Tommaso d'Aquino nella Somma teologica*. Turin: Marietti, 1967.

Pinckaers, Servais, O.P. "Notes." In *Saint Thomas d'Aquin, Somme Théologique, Les actes humains*, Vol. 2 (*Ia IIae, QQ. 18–21*). Paris: Desclée et Cie, 1966.

———. *Le Renouveau de la morale*, 2d Ed. Tournai, Belgium: Casterman, 1964.

———. *Sources of Christian Ethics*. Trans. Mary Thomas Noble. Washington, DC: Catholic University of America Press, 1995.

Pinto de Oliveira, C.J. "A teologia de S. Tomás e a Biblia." *Theologica* (1958): 201–7.

Prete, B. "Bibbia e teologia nell'opera di S. Tommaso d'Aquino." *Bollettino S. Domenico* 55 (1974): 79–92.

Principe, Walter H., C.S.B. "Thomas Aquinas' Principles for Interpretation of Patristic Texts." *Studies in Medieval Culture* 8–9 (1976): 111–21.

Valkenberg, W. *"Words of the Living God."* The Place and Function of Holy Scripture in the Theology of St. Thomas Aquinas. Wilhelmus G.B.M., Leuven: Peeters, 2000.

Vansteenkiste, C., O.P. "Cicerone nell'opera di S. Tommaso." *Angelicum* 36 (1959): 343–82.

Waldstein, Michael M. "On Scripture in the *Summa Theologiae*." *Aquinas Review* 1 (1994): 73–94.

Overview of the Ethics of Thomas Aquinas

Stephen J. Pope

INTRODUCTION

Thomas Aquinas worked and thought first and foremost as a theologian. Aquinas wrote an extensive commentary on Aristotle's *Nicomachean Ethics*, but he never produced a counterpart. Nor did he conceive of his work as "moral theology," an independent discipline that arose as such only in the modern era.[1] He was a pious scholar seeking to understand more deeply what he affirmed in faith as a member of the believing Christian community. For this reason, his treatment of morality is fundamentally theological. This overview seeks to communicate the structure and content of the ethics provided in his most famous theological work, the *Summa theologiae*.

Structure and Content of the *Summa*

Aquinas wrote the *Summa theologiae* to provide a concise but comprehensive summary of Christian theology.[2] He organized his great text into three major Parts, each of which is devoted to a major theological theme. The First Part or *Prima pars* (Ia) begins with God and with realities as they are created by God. The Second Part or *Secunda pars* (IIa) examines the human acts by which rational creatures return to God. The Third Part or *Tertia pars* (IIIa) presents an analysis of Christ and the sacraments.[3] This overarching structure represents Aquinas's creative adoption of the Neoplatonic emanation and return (*exitus-reditus*) motif within his Christian depiction of the emergence of all creatures from God the Creator and the return of creatures to God the Redeemer.[4]

Thomas matched form to substance: his pedagogy followed from his theology, according to which God is both the source and the destiny of all things. The prologue to the *Prima pars*, Question 2, explains this order. "Sacred doctrine" is God's teaching, the knowledge of God, which includes both knowledge of God as He is in Himself, but also as "the beginning of things and their last end, and especially of rational creatures."[5] The *Summa* thus first discusses God, then the rational creature's advance toward God, and finally Christ, our way to God.

This suggests that the First Part concentrates on God, the Second on humanity, and the Third on Christ. The *Prima pars* devotes forty-two Questions to God, examining first the divine essence and its attributes (qq. 2–26) and then the Trinity (qq. 27–43). Question 44 initiates a lengthy examination of creatures, lasting up to Question 119, precisely as they proceed from God. This section of the *Prima pars* is subdivided into discussions of creation in general (qq. 44–46), the distinction of creatures (qq. 47–102), and the divine governance of creation (qq. 103–19).

The *Secunda pars* focuses on the human being as returning to God. Its analysis depends upon the preceding anthropological section of the *Prima pars* that runs from Question 75, on the soul, through Question 102, on the human abode in paradise. The account of human nature provided earlier in the *Prima pars* thus complements that developed in the *Secunda pars*. The prologue to the *Secunda pars* explains that whereas the prior treatment given in the *Prima pars* had examined God and things precisely as they proceed from *God's* intellect and will, the *Secunda pars* investigates more precisely humanity as created in the image of God and human actions as they proceed from the *human* intellect and will.[6] God and human nature are related analogously as exemplar to image. The exposition of the divine exemplar and of God's relation to creation elaborated in the *Prima pars* prepares for the parallel investigation of human nature as an image of God and its expression in human acts in the *Secunda pars*. To be a person, to be made in the "image of God," is to act freely and intelligently as the principle of one's own acts. "As God creates the world," Gilson explains, "a human being constructs his life."[7]

The *Secunda pars* constitutes the most extensive discussion of ethics in Thomas's *corpus*. It is divided into two sections. The First Part of the Second Part, or the *Prima secundae* (Ia IIae), concerns general topics pertaining to human nature and conduct: the purpose or end of human life (qq. 1–5), human acts (qq. 6–21), the passions (qq. 22–48), habits (qq. 49–89), law (qq. 90–108), and grace (qq. 109–14). The Second Part of the Second Part, or *Secunda secundae* (IIa IIae), provides the "special" or "particular" consideration of morality. This section examines a vast array of virtues and vices, in part reflecting the influence of the earlier *Summa de vitiis et virtutibus* of the Dominican theologian Peraldus. Thomas organized this extensive body of ethical material within an overarching framework provided by the virtues. His treatment of each virtue typically examines the virtue itself, the vices opposed to it, the appropriate gift of the Holy Spirit, and the precepts or norms related to it. The order of presentation always begins with the virtue itself, but the location of the other topics varies from case to case. For example, the gift of Wisdom (IIa IIae, q. 44) follows the treatment of the vices against charity, but the gift of Counsel (q. 52) precedes Aquinas's treatment of the vices opposed to the virtue of prudence.

The *Secunda secundae* opens by revisiting the question of beatitude previously examined at length in the *Prima secundae* (qq. 1–5), but now considers it in light of the doctrine of grace just completed (in Ia IIae, qq. 109–14). Eschmann points out that "there is not a line in the Second Part that is not 'theological.'"[8] The *Secunda secundae* thus begins with an elaborate discussion of the grace-infused theological virtues of faith (qq. 1–16), hope (qq. 17–22), and charity (qq. 23–46). After having established that the Christian moral life is only made possible by grace, it then

reincorporates the classical cardinal virtues of prudence (qq. 47–56), justice (qq. 57–122), courage (qq. 123–40), and temperance (qq. 141–70). The *Secunda pars* then concludes with a discussion of charisms and special states in life (qq. 171–89).

The *Tertia pars* continues to examine the movement of the person to God, but focuses explicitly on the mediation of Christ (the "*reditus per Christum*").[9] The Christian becomes more deeply the image of God in and through Christ. Christ and the sacraments are the way to beatitude (Thomas did not then proceed to elaborate a theology of the church, a topic given systematic development only later in the history of theology).

The first major section of the *Tertia pars* discusses Jesus Christ, the Savior, both in the Incarnation (qq. 1–26) and in terms of what Jesus did in the flesh for our salvation (qq. 27–59). It next examines the sacraments as the means of salvation. As instrumental causes of grace (IIIa, q. 62, a. 1), sacraments are the foundation of the church (IIIa, q. 64, a. 2 ad 3). They are examined first in general (qq. 60–65), and then in particular, beginning with baptism (qq. 66–71), then proceeding to confirmation (q. 72), Eucharist (qq. 73–83), and finally penance (qq. 84–90). (The *Tertia pars* remained incomplete at the time of Aquinas's death.)[10]

Theological Purpose and Character of the *Summa theologiae*

The *Secunda pars*, then, is not, and was never intended to be, a self-contained moral theory of the sort constructed by modern moral philosophers. Aquinas was a theologian who thought about moral questions in light of God, grace, and sacraments; he was not a professional ethicist merely drawing upon theological claims to resolve moral dilemmas.[11]

Standard treatments of ethics in Thomas's day focused primarily on resolving specific practical moral problems.[12] Inheriting a special concern with the morality of specific acts, Aquinas strove to provide a broader and more profound account of the underlying theological context, meaning, and foundation of the Christian moral life. As Leonard Boyle explains, Thomas began writing the *Summa* in part to provide students in the Dominican order with a more coherent and comprehensible theological grounding for the pastoral work that would occupy them in their future work as clerics. The first prologue offers a concise explanation of Aquinas's rationale for writing the *Summa*, a text intended to present more helpful instruction to beginners often hampered in their study by conventional texts flawed by useless questions and arguments, poor organization, and frequent repetition. Thus before arriving at moral questions proper, Aquinas believed, students ought to proceed through a clear exposition of central themes of theology. This is the goal of the *Prima pars*.

The *Prima pars* discusses the unity of the divine essence, the existence and perfections of God (Ia, qq. 1–26), and the nature of God as Trinity (qq. 27–43). Whereas essence and existence in creatures are distinct, God's essence *is* God's existence (q. 3, a. 4). The mystery of God as Triune is the foundation of all the other mysteries of the Christian faith. The Word is eternally generated by the Father, and the Son and the Spirit proceed from the unbegotten Father. The Holy Spirit proceeds from the mutual love of the Father and Son (q. 37).

God is the first cause of everything that exists (q. 44). God creates in order to communicate the divine goodness to creatures. Moreover, because God's goodness could not be adequately represented by one creature alone, God produced many and different kinds of creatures, "that what was wanting to one in the representation of divine goodness might be supplied by another"[13] (q. 47, a. 1). These include both immaterial creatures (angels; qq. 50–64), and material creatures (qq. 65–74), the most noble of which are human beings (qq. 75–102). Human beings are composed of an intellectual soul united to a body (qq. 75–76) and made in the "image of God," and are therefore called to know and love God in a special way (q. 93). The divine goodness is also manifested in the governance of creation (q. 103, a. 1; see also q. 44, a. 4; q. 65, a. 2).

Ethics is a practical form of knowledge. As "science" in the Aristotelian sense, ethics addresses human conduct generally and therefore cannot be expected to render concrete and specific advice for individuals struggling with personal moral decisions. Practical moral choices are guided by the virtue of prudence

(IIa IIae, q. 47, a. 8), not by the discipline of theology. This having been said, as practical, ethics provides an account of the general ordering of daily life and its activities to God. It is not reducible to knowledge of the commands of God the Lawgiver but more importantly offers a wisdom that makes possible a deepening of friendship with God the loving Father.[14] The intrinsic dynamism of practical action thus leads toward contemplative love. Even in its most practical moments, Aquinas's theological ethics, as Torrell explains, "does not lose its contemplative aim. It is still and always directed by the consideration of God, since he is the End in view of which all decisions are made and the Good in connection with which all other goods are situated."[15]

THE *PRIMA SECUNDAE*

The *Secunda pars* develops the ethical implications of the theological and philosophical anthropology introduced in the *Prima pars* (especially in Ia, qq. 75–102). The *Prima secundae* first examines the intrinsic principles of human acts (power and habit [Ia IIae, qq. 1–89]) and then the extrinsic principles of human acts (law and grace [qq. 90–114]). The former include human happiness (qq. 1–5), the will and its acts (qq. 6–17), goodness and malice (qq. 18–21), the emotions (qq. 22–48), habits, virtues, and vices (qq. 49–89). The latter concern law (qq. 90–108) and grace (qq. 109–14).

Happiness

The explicitly moral section of the *Summa* begins not with the question, "What moral laws must I obey?" but rather with the question, "What is true happiness?" This starting point accords with Aristotle's *Nicomachean Ethics*, but also, and more importantly, with Scripture, especially the Psalms, and the fathers of the church.[16]

Aquinas's ethics is founded upon a profoundly teleological view of created reality in general and of human nature in particular: everything that exists acts purposefully for an end. Thomas's universe, as Gilson puts it, was "saturated with finality."[17] To understand anything, humanity included, depends on comprehending its end or purpose. Aquinas's vision of life was thus teleological in the sense of "goal-directed" (as distinct from the ethical "teleology" of consequentialism).

Aquinas regarded human acts, as Chenu observes, as "so many steps by which human nature on its journey back to the source of its being, realizes its end, thereby achieving happiness and perfection."[18] Everyone desires happiness and seeks it in some fashion, and the quality of one's life depends on the content of the happiness sought. It is fundamental to Aquinas's theology that one can only be satisfied by the universal good, that is, by God, who alone gives true and perfect happiness. Those who pursue happiness in possessions and status, for example, obtain true goods but mistake subordinate goods for the ultimate good—thus generating their own dissatisfaction.

The normative significance of the human desire for happiness underscores Thomas's profound difference from philosophers who identify morality with obligation, duty, or command.[19] For Aquinas, the major question for morality concerned "being" rather than "doing."[20] Virtues are more fundamental than either external acts, the moral laws by which they are judged, or particular choices determining behavior in concrete cases. This is why Aquinas did not dwell on moral dilemmas, hard cases, or moral quandaries.

The Will

The *Summa's* analysis of human acts begins with an examination of the nature of the will as voluntary (q. 6) and then focuses more precisely on the constituent elements of its acts (qq. 7–17). Senses orient us to concrete goods that can satisfy specific needs, such as those for food, drink, and others that we share with animals. The will as "rational appetite" differs radically from sense appetite in its orientation to the *universal* good. The will necessarily seeks the universal good. But since it is not determined to choose particular goods in concrete circumstances, it can ignore or violate what is judged to be morally good in this or that concrete case. Alcoholics continue to drink alcohol, for example, despite full awareness of the destructive effects of so doing. This position thus rejects the thesis that "no one deliberately does wrong."[21] Each person

bears the responsibility for directing all of his or her choices to the universal good and to resist being driven by impulse, social pressure, or other influences.

An act can be said to be morally good only when it fulfills three conditions: when the act itself is morally good or indifferent in kind, when it enacts a good intention, and when it is done in a way that is morally appropriate given the circumstances. It is bad if one or more of these aspects of the act are bad. An act can be bad "in itself," such as murder or theft. A kind of act that is good or indifferent in itself can be bad in a specific instance if done with the wrong end in mind or in the wrong way, such as giving money to a needy person out of vainglory. Moral actions take their "species," the kinds of acts they are, from their end. An agent's intention determines the kind of act he or she does; for example, lying in order to attain career advancement is a sin of ambition more than it is a sin of lying (although it is of course both; see q. 43, a. 4).

Emotions

The emotions (*passiones animae*) are natural ways in which one is moved by one's surroundings; they are also termed "passions" because in feeling them agents are moved as a result of having been acted upon by some external agency. Emotions involve bodily responses to situations. They include love (qq. 26–28), hatred (q. 29), concupiscence (q. 30), delight and pleasure (qq. 31–34), sorrow or pain (qq. 35–39), hope and despair (q. 40), fear (qq. 41–44), daring (q. 45), and anger (qq. 46–48). Thomas distinguished between the "concupiscible passions," which are moved by goods of sense as such, from the "irascible passions," which are moved by goods of sense which can only be obtained through the overcoming of some kind of resistance. Love is the most basic of the concupiscible passions and all the other passions can be understood in relation to it.

Because the emotions are part of our creaturely nature and therefore good in themselves, the key moral challenge they present lies in their proper ordering rather than in their repression. Thomas's extensive treatment of the emotions, taking up twenty-six questions, indicates their importance within human life. Thomas discussed the will before he treated the emotions because the latter are shaped and guided by the former. This order of presentation helps to underscore the difference between distinctively human emotions and those displayed in animal behavior. The unity of the body and soul implies that people are emotional as well as rational beings. Yet what they feel is a matter of identity and character, and not derived exclusively from anatomy and physiology. How one functions emotionally, in other words, results in part from what one has freely chosen and guided oneself to have become through the cumulative history of antecedent acts of the will.

Habits and Virtues

After discussing human acts and passions in the first major sections of the *Prima secundae*, the *Summa* turns to the *intrinsic* principles of human acts—power and habit. The *Prima pars* already examined the powers of the soul—vegetative, sensitive, appetitive, locomotive, and intellectual (see Ia, qq. 77–90)—so this section of the *Summa* begins with the topic of habit.

Both acts of the will and the emotions must be given direction, order, and guidance; they do not automatically unfold in morally mature directions. Human capacities can be either developed or corrupted by the acquisition of habits, permanent dispositions to act in characteristic ways. It is important not to confuse Thomas's notion of "habits" with its conventional usage as thoughtless routine.[22] A "habit" in Thomas's sense is a quality in the soul that orders human conduct in a way that contributes to the human development of the person (Ia IIae, q. 49); habits are developed human capacities. A habit can come from repeated action ("habituation"; q. 49, a. 2), but also from nature (q. 51, a. 1) or from God (q. 51, a. 4), as in the case of what the scholastics called "infused virtues."

"Virtues" are simply stable dispositions to act in ways that are good; "vices" are stable dispositions to act in ways that are bad (q. 54, a. 3). Intellect, will, and emotions are all potential subjects of vices and virtues. One can thus grow intellectually by developing a firmer grasp of first principles of a science, a more refined capacity to reason to conclusions from these principles, a deeper understanding of life, a more discerning sensitivity in making practical judgments, and a more adept skill at making things. One grows morally by becoming habituated to treating people justly and to making the right choices about how to respond to one's own desires. The good life is one guided by "right reason," a distinctive accomplishment made possible by employing one's natural capacity as a "rational animal." Reasonableness is displayed in intellectual virtues (qq. 57–58), but also when human beings properly will what is truly good and exercise the moral virtues (qq. 58–61).

Most important, however, are not the classical cardinal virtues of prudence, justice, temperance, and fortitude, but the theological virtues of faith, hope, and charity. The *Secunda secundae* (IIa IIae, qq. 1–46) thus first examines the latter and only then engages in an extended discussion of the former (qq. 47–170). The theological virtues are caused by divine "infusion" rather than by the gradual process of habituation. In fact, the cardinal virtues are also "infused" by divine grace in those who have been blessed with the theological virtues. The Christian moral life is thus rooted in an appropriation of God's gifts and responds appropriately to God with gratitude, trust, and love.

Sin and Vices

Just as virtue disposes the agent to its ordered and proper acts, so vice disposes the agent to engage in disordered acts (Ia IIae, q. 71, a. 1). Sin is found where a person voluntarily engages in a bad human act, that is, in an act that does not conform to its proper measure as determined either by human reason or divine reason (q. 71, a. 6). Although the effects of sin are felt in the body, the seat of sin is the *will*; it exists in the passions or in the intellect insofar as they operate under the influence of the will (q. 74, a. 2). Sin in the formal sense is essentially a corruption or privation of what belongs to a person naturally. It always involves a kind of imbalance, inordinateness, or deviation from what is good for the person. For this reason, Aquinas held that "we do not offend God except by doing something contrary to our own good."[23]

The internal sources of sin include ignorance (q. 76, a, 4), passion (q. 77, a. 8), and, worst of all, because most deeply rooted in the will, malice (q. 78, a. 4). The external cause of sin is the devil, who by "outward suggestion," causes sin indirectly by temptation (q. 80, a. 1). As a consequence of inherited "original sin" (as distinguished from the "actual sin" of the person; q. 81, a. 1), human nature suffers from "concupiscence" whereby the disorder of the will corrupts the other powers of the soul. This flaw is felt most poignantly in disordered appetites (q. 82, a. 3), but its corrupting power lies in the *soul*, not in the body *per se*. So, for example, the moral problem of gluttony lies in a disordered will and not in the need for food (q. 83, a. 1). Sin leaves the natural powers of the soul intact, dulls the natural inclination to virtue, and entirely destroys the gift of "original justice" (q. 85, a. 1). The inclination to evil constitutes a form of "servitude" to sin that hinders the person's ability to obtain his or her own good (IIa IIae, q. 183, a. 4). Therefore, while Aquinas is sometimes criticized for being excessively optimistic, the eighteen questions dedicated to examining the nature of sin indicate a realistic view of the various levels of human disorder.

Law

The *Prima secundae* next discusses the extrinsic principles that move a person to what is good. The extrinsic principle moving us to good is God, who instructs humans through law and supplies the ability to adhere to this instruction through grace. The preceding analysis of sin called attention to the daily need all people have for practical instruction, guidance, and divine aid. Law explicitly teaches one how to act and grace grants the power to do so. The *Prima secundae* draws attention to the innate tendency all people have to their ultimate end, their capacity for acting intelligently, and their attraction to the good. The explicit treatment of natural law in these questions builds on these themes. It examines the essence, kinds, and effects of law (Ia IIae, q. 90–92), eternal law (q. 93), natural law (q. 94), human law (qq. 95–97), the Old Law (qq. 98–105), and the New Law of the Gospel (qq. 106–8).

"Law" as such is defined as "an ordinance of reason for the common good, made by him who has care of the community, and promulgated" (q. 90, a. 4).[24] Eternal law is the providential government of the universe, and all that is in it, by the Divine Reason (q. 91, a. 1). God governs creation through ordering all creatures to their good (q. 94, a. 2). All other creatures move toward their proper good by acting spontaneously on their God-given natural inclinations, but the "rational creature" acts freely on the basis of reason and therefore is, "subject to divine Providence in the most excellent way, in so far as it partakes of a share of providence, by being provident both for itself and for others" (q. 91, a. 2).[25]

Natural law is the "participation" of the intelligent and free human being in the eternal law by living according to "right reason." The first principle of practical reason is that "good is to be done and pursued, and evil is to be avoided" and all other precepts of the natural law are in some way based upon this principle (q. 94, a. 2).[26] The first principle of practical reason is formal—that is, it does not communicate the content of what is good, which can only be determined by intelligently reflecting on the various natural inclinations and the goods by which they are satisfied.

Thus, every person shares with all beings a natural inclination to preserve his or her own existence, and this inclination issues in a precept to preserve his or her own life. Every person also shares inclinations with other animals to reproduce, and this inclination issues in standards governing sexual intercourse, marriage, and family. Finally, every person shares distinctively human inclinations to live with other people and to know the truth about God, and these inclinations generate standards for appropriate conduct in these spheres of action (ibid.). Natural law is "law" in that it orders the person to act in some ways and to refrain from acting in other ways; it is "natural" in that these requirements are derived from innate human inclinations and are integral to human flourishing. Obligation is thus not imposed arbitrarily on human life but rather receives its intelligibility from its promotion of the human good.

Due to the deficiencies of human reason and the impediments placed in its way by sin, natural law is by no means sufficient for the guidance of daily life (q. 99, a. 2, ad 2). Humans need divine law to be properly directed to eternal happiness, clearly instructed on contingent and particular matters about which it is particularly difficult to judge, helped better to understand interior matters that would otherwise not be properly addressed and yet are essential for complete virtue, and, finally, know that all evil deeds, interior as well as exterior, are forbidden and punished (q. 91, a. 4).

Aquinas adopted the standard division of the divine law into the Old Law and the New. The Old Law commands ceremonial precepts governing worship, judicial precepts establishing justice within the community, and moral precepts required by the natural law (q. 99, a. 4). Whereas moral and judicial precepts received their moral authority from natural reason, the ceremonial precepts derived theirs from divine institution alone (q. 100, a. 11). The New Law thus replaced the historically contingent juridical regulations and ceremonial requirements of the Old Law while retaining the moral requirements based on the natural law. Drawing from St. Paul, Thomas held that the New Law is most fundamentally the grace of the Holy Spirit dwelling in the heart of the believer and only secondarily a written law (q. 106, a. 1).

The New Law fulfills the Old in two ways. First, it justifies the believer, thereby enabling him or her to obtain the ultimate end. Without the indwelling of the Holy Spirit, the commands and precepts of the New Testament would be, after all, "only another set of inefficacious regulations."[27] Second, it fulfills the precepts of the Old Law through explaining the deeper sense of the Law, showing the safest way of fulfilling its requirements (that is, through intention and not simply conduct), and by adding to the Law the counsels of perfection (q. 106, a. 2). The New Law establishes sacraments so that believers may be given much more explicit assistance in their growth in grace and love (q. 108, a. 3).

Grace

The *Prima secundae* culminates in questions on grace (qq. 109–114), the second of the two divinely given extrinsic principles of human acts. Grace, an effect of the divine love on the soul, is the means by which God leads us back to God (q. 111, a. 1). A moral philosopher might find it odd or quaint that Thomas's analysis of human acts reaches its climax in a topic that is so theological. Yet for the theologian grace is the "crowning glory of Christian ethics" because Christian life is "life in the spirit."[28] The first question thus establishes that grace is absolutely necessary if one is to know truth (q. 109, a. 1), to do good (q. 109, a. 2), to love God above all things (q. 109, a. 3), to fulfill the Law, in substance as well as in the mode of charity (q. 109, a. 4), to merit everlasting life (q. 109, a. 5), to prepare for grace (q. 109, a. 6), to rise from and avoid sin (q. 109, aa. 7–9), and to persevere (q. 109, a. 10).

Humanity exists now, after the Fall, in a corrupt state (q. 109, a. 2), yet human beings are not completely "depraved" by sin. Humans are still able to exercise their natural powers in many domains of ordinary life, so, for example, use intelligence to make bridges or to recognize how to treat this or that person justly. But "sick humanity" (*homo infirmus*) can only become truly virtuous if cured by the "medicine" of grace (q. 109, a. 2). This is why a person can do a particular act that is generically good on the basis of some good of nature, but cannot be said to exercise perfect virtue without charity (IIa IIae, q. 23, a. 7). Human nature "cannot do all the good natural to it, so as to fall short at nothing; just as a sick man can of himself make some movements, yet he cannot be perfectly moved with the movements of one in health, unless he be cured by the help of medicine" (Ia IIae, q. 109, a. 2).[29] As *homo infirmus*, the person loves himself or herself more than God and neighbor, and prefers his or her own private good to the common good (q. 109, a. 3). Grace, as "medicine," heals this disorder and enables one to love God more than the self and to love both neighbors and the self "in God."

Grace is a habitual gift, infused by God into the soul, that gives one a capacity to obtain the supernatural good. Grace bestows "certain forms or supernatural qualities, whereby they may be moved by Him sweetly and promptly to acquire eternal good" (q. 110, a. 2).[30] These forms or qualities are called "virtues," but "virtue" here connotes not only a perfection of nature that enables one to attain one's natural good, as in the case of the cardinal virtues, but also a disposition that orients a person to God, the supernatural good (q. 110, a. 3). The natural quest thus examined in detail in the questions on happiness (qq. 1–5) finds its true satisfaction discussed in the section on grace (qq. 109–14). These two series of questions, the "bookends" of the *Prima secundae*, form an elegant pattern of question and answer that goes to the very core of human existence.

THE *SECUNDA SECUNDAE*

The *Secunda secundae* turns from general ethical considerations to the practical challenge of living a Christian moral life. In it, Weisheipl explains, Aquinas "completely revised Lombard's discussion of moral questions, synthesizing man's return to God through the virtues (*secunda pars*) in much the same order as Aristotle treats man's search for happiness in the *Nicomachean Ethics*."[31] Everything in the *Summa* to this point builds to the culminating discussion of this journey to God. The *Secunda secundae* can thus be read as essentially a long disquisition on the virtues or, just as aptly, though with a somewhat more explicitly religious emphasis, as an extended discussion of what is now called "spirituality."

Structure of the *Secunda secundae*

The *Secunda secundae* first examines specific virtues relevant to all human beings (IIa IIae, qq. 1–170) and then those virtues pertaining to particular callings (qq. 171–89). Most of this section of the *Summa* is concerned with the former, which consists of the three theological virtues of faith (qq. 1–16), hope (qq. 17–22), and charity (qq. 23–46) and the four cardinal virtues of prudence (qq. 47–56), justice (qq. 57–122), fortitude (qq. 123–40), and temperance (qq. 141–70). The treatment of acts pertaining only to certain individuals examines first the diversity of gratuitous graces of prophecy, rapture, tongues, preaching, and miracles (qq. 171–78), then the diversity of active and contemplative lives (qq. 179–82), and finally the diversity of states of life, especially the acts of those seeking to live a life of charity through serving the church (qq. 184–89). While Aquinas referred to the latter as "the state of perfection," this language should not be confused with moral perfection

(q. 184, a. 4). "States of perfection" include the episcopal state (q. 185) and the "religious state" of those who have been professed in religious orders (qq. 186–89), which Aquinas described as "a school for attaining to the perfection of charity" (q. 186, a. 3).[32]

From beginning to end, the *Secunda secundae* conceives of the Christian life as essentially one of growth in faith, hope, and charity. The cardinal virtues of prudence, justice, temperance, and fortitude are discussed after the theological virtues because they are understood to be retained and perfected within the Christian life. Because nature is perfected by grace (Ia, q. 1, a. 8), the will is perfected by charity, reason by faith, and the cardinal virtues by the theological virtues. One moves toward the ultimate end most *commonly* through growth in the virtues but in the most *excellent* way through the gifts (Ia IIae, q. 69, a. 1)—dispositions through which one is made more readily amenable to the movement of the Holy Spirit (q. 68, a. 1). Although the sequence of treatment varies from virtue to virtue, each virtue is examined in terms of the same standard conceptual categories. These include the virtue itself, its distinctive acts, its subject and its object, its causes and its effects. After examining its basic identity, Aquinas expounded the virtues associated with it, the vices opposed to it, and the precepts to which it gives rise. The late treatment of the precepts in this order of presentation indicates that they exist to serve growth in virtue and not vice versa. Each virtue is complemented with a corresponding gift, or gifts, of the Holy Spirit.

Aquinas coordinated the seven central virtues of the Christian life with the seven gifts of the Holy Spirit, long associated by St. Gregory with the Book of Job and by St. Augustine with the seven virtues of the Holy Spirit mentioned in the Gospel of Matthew (ibid.). Faith is complemented by the gift of *understanding* that perfects the apprehension of truth in speculative reasoning and the gift of *knowledge* that perfects good judgment in speculative reasoning; hope by the gift of the fear of the Lord; charity by the gift of wisdom; prudence by the gift of counsel; justice by the gift of piety; courage by the gift of fortitude; temperance by the gift of fear (the last is discussed in Ia IIae, q. 68, a. 4, but not actually in the treatment of the virtue of temperance).

The Theological Virtues of Faith and Hope

Aquinas examined faith in light of his standard categories: faith itself (IIa IIae, q. 1), the act of faith (qq. 2–3), the virtue (q. 4), those who have faith (q. 5), its cause and effects (qq. 6–7), and the gifts of understanding and knowledge (qq. 8–9). He next turned to what is opposed to the virtue of faith: unbelief in general (q. 10), heresy (q. 11), apostasy (q. 12), blasphemy (qq. 13–14), and the vices opposed to the gifts of knowledge and understanding (q. 15). He concluded with an examination of the precepts relating to faith, knowledge, and understanding (q. 16).

Faith is a gift of grace that allows for an assent of the mind, commanded by the will, to propositions on the basis of divine authority (q. 1; q. 2, a. 2). Such faith generates a firm conviction of the truth of what is believed. This "inner act of faith" is complemented with an "outer act of faith," the public confession of what one believes as a matter of Christian faith (q. 3, aa. 1–2).

Hope, which receives the briefest treatment among the theological virtues, is examined first as the virtue itself (q. 17) and its subject (q. 18), the gift of fear (q. 19), the opposing vices of despair (q. 20) and presumption (q. 21), and finally the precepts related to hope and fear. Through the theological virtue of hope, the Christian believes that he or she will be granted the good of eternal happiness that lies in the vision of God (q. 17, a. 2). Hope strives for the enjoyment of God Himself and ought not be confused with the "mercenary love" (*amor mercenarius*) that uses God as a means to other goods (q. 19, a. 4, ad 3). Hope gives the believer a confident movement toward the future that enables him or her to overcome everything that restricts this movement to God. Hope moves the believer from the desire to avoid punishment that characterizes "servile fear" (*timor servilis*) to the love of God that marks "filial fear" (*timor filialis*; q. 19, a. 5). Grace-inspired confidence leads the Christian away from the twin evils of presumption and despair (q. 21).

The Theological Virtue of Charity

Faith precedes hope and hope precedes charity (q. 17, aa. 7–8)—hence the order of Aquinas's presentation. Yet the *Secunda secundae* gives more attention to the theological virtue of charity (qq. 23–46) than to the other theological virtues (qq. 1–22); indeed, it devotes roughly the same number of questions to charity as to the other two virtues combined. The significance of the length of treatment should not be overemphasized, of course. Thomas devotes only nine questions to prudence (qq. 47–56), which he considers foremost among the cardinal virtues. Yet the virtue of charity clearly plays a central role in the schema of the *Secunda secundae*. In charity, people attain the end for which they exist; in this virtue, the human desire for happiness is satisfied completely; it alone, among the theological virtues, is retained in eternal life. Thus, whereas the *Prima secundae* examines the essential components that play a dynamic role in the human quest for happiness (the will, emotions, habits, law, grace), the *Secunda secundae* explains how grace brings these elements into a dynamic and transformative unity in the infused virtue of charity, the "form of all the virtues" (q. 23, a. 8).

The *Summa* examines, first, charity in itself (q. 23), its subject (q. 24), object (q. 25) and its acts, including love (q. 27), and its effects (qq. 28–33). It treats first its interior effects in joy (q. 28), peace (q. 29), and mercy (q. 30), and then its exterior effects in acts of beneficence (q. 31), almsgiving (q. 32), and fraternal correction (q. 33). This discussion is followed by an inquiry into the four kinds of vice opposed to charity: first, hatred, the vice opposed to charity itself (q. 34); second, the vices opposed to joy: sloth (q. 35) and envy (q. 36); third, the vices opposed to peace: discord (q. 37), contention (q. 38), schism (q. 39), war (q. 40), strife (q. 41), and sedition (q. 42); and last, the vice opposed to beneficence: scandal (q. 43). After the virtue and its opposite vices, this treatise examines the precepts of charity (q. 44) and then completes this analysis with a discussion of the gift of wisdom (q. 45) and the vice opposed to it, folly (q. 46).

Charity is fundamentally the grace-inspired friendship of the human person for God (q. 23, a. 1). It is not to be confused with what modern philosophers came to call "altruism," and even less with philanthropic "charity." The love of friendship includes three marks: benevolence, mutuality, and communication in a shared good (q. 23, a. 1). Aquinas adopted these traits from Book VIII of the *Nicomachean Ethics*, but its unmistakably Christian character is seen in the affirmation that God wills fellowship with humans, and that, through grace, people can become friends with God.

Charity is something created in the soul, and is thus not simply the direct action of the Holy Spirit in the person (q. 23, a. 2); it generates a special kind of love that has as its object divine good (q. 23, a. 4). Charity is the greatest of all the virtues because it enables us to rest in God—the ultimate and principal good (q. 23, a. 7). *God* is the primary object of charity, and through it one loves all that God loves. It therefore embraces the neighbor (q. 25, a. 1), the soul (q. 25, a. 4), and, indirectly, the body (q. 25, a. 5). Charity respects the natural order inclining us to love friends and family, parents and children (q. 26, aa. 6–11), while also inspiring love for wrongdoers (q. 26, a. 6) and enemies (q. 26, a. 8).[33] The primary act of charity is the voluntary act of love, which gives rise to the internal blessings of joy (q. 28), peace (q. 29), and the virtue of mercy (q. 30)—the greatest of the virtues that unites a person with a neighbor (q. 30, a. 4)—and to external acts of charity exemplified in corporal works of mercy (such as feeding the hungry and clothing the naked [see Mt 25:31–45]) and in spiritual works of mercy (like comforting those who sorrow [q. 32, a. 2]).

The vices against charity constitute assaults either on charity itself, as in hatred (q. 34), or on the divine good, in the case of sloth vis-à-vis the spiritual life (q. 35); on the neighbor's good, in the case of envy (q. 36); or on the peace that binds neighbors together, by intentionally sowing discord (q. 37), stirring up trouble by speech (q. 38), breaking the unity of the church by schism (q. 39), instigating an unjust war (q. 40), harming others out of personal animosity or strife (q. 41), or plotting sedition against authorities responsible for the common good (q. 42).

Given these and other forms of opposition to charity, it is abundantly clear why charity would be commanded, a matter of precept (q.

44), and not left up to spontaneous inspiration. Yet the climactic expression of charity is found not simply in firm obedience to moral law but in the gift of wisdom (q. 45). The Holy Spirit inspires acute and penetrating judgment by creating in a person an internal and non-discursive "connaturality" with what is demanded in concrete situations (q. 45, a. 2). The inner promptings of the Spirit enable a person to act in a manner that goes beyond, but not against, the kind of moral excellence found in acquired virtue.

The gift of wisdom does not pertain to all domains of practical knowledge, from baking bread to automobile mechanics, but rather to specific activities of spiritual discernment: "it contemplates divine things in themselves, and it consults them, in so far as it judges of human acts by divine things, and directs human acts according to divine rules" (q. 45, a. 3).[34] The gift of wisdom corresponds to the seventh beatitude, that of the peacemaker, who sets things in due order and in so doing becomes a child of God (q. 45, a. 6). The disordered life of the fool, in contrast, is marked by the dulling of the spiritual sense. Here inordinate attachment to temporal goods corrupts one's own best judgment, even to the point of creating a distaste for God, and rendering one unaware of one's own foolishness (q. 46, a. 3).

Prudence

Immediately after discussing the gift of wisdom, Aquinas turns to its more familiar counterpart, the virtue of *prudence*. Prudence in the Thomistic sense refers to the virtue of practical wisdom, which should not be confused with the "prudential" pursuit of enlightened self-interest found in the modern usage of this term.

Thomas's introduction of this topic begins an extensive discussion of the cardinal virtues that comprises the bulk of what remains of the *Secunda pars*. Were Aquinas building from the natural or acquired to the supernatural, he would have examined first the cardinal and then the theological virtues. The reverse order employed in the *Summa* underscores the fact that the Christian moral life is based first and foremost on grace and the theological virtues; indeed, faith is the first of the virtues to be generated and the last to be lost (IIa IIae,

q. 162, a. 7, ad 3; also Ia IIae, q. 62, a. 4). Yet the gift of wisdom does not render the virtue of prudence unnecessary. A person blessed with faith, hope, and charity still needs the virtue of prudence to address the usual array of practical moral difficulties that are part of the human condition.

Following the standard procedure, the *Summa* examines first the virtue of prudence in itself (IIa IIae, q. 47) and then its "parts," those traits that must exist for the complete act of the virtue. These consist of three categories: first, "integral" parts of prudence, for example, memory and docility, which are necessary for its exercise in the full sense (q. 49); second, its various species or "subjective" parts, such as political prudence and domestic prudence (q. 50); and third, the dispositions connected with it—its "potential" parts—like the ability to identify exceptions in cases of law (q. 51). This "treatise" then discusses the corresponding gift of counsel (q. 52); the vices contrary to prudence: imprudence (q. 53), negligence (q. 54), and the vices resembling it (q. 55), such as craftiness (a. 3) and duplicity (a. 4); and finally the precepts as enumerated in the Old Law (q. 56).

The virtue of prudence is unique among the cardinal virtues precisely as a perfection of the intellect rather than of the will or sense appetite (q. 47, a. 2). Defined as the ability to apply right reason to action (q. 47, a. 4), prudence enables one to know how to act in the midst of the contingencies of particular situations (q. 47, a. 5). Aquinas believed that all normally functioning human beings have a natural habit (Ia, q. 79, a. 12) of *synderesis* (q. 47, a. 6, ad 1), an immediate, non-inferential grasp of principles, the foremost of which is that one ought to do good and avoid evil (q. 79, a. 12; Ia IIae, q. 94, a. 2). This natural moral knowledge directs one formally to the ends of the moral virtues: that is, it tells a person to be just, temperate, courageous, and so forth, and indicts actions that violate these standards. When someone engages in practical moral reasoning, one reflects on how these given ends might pertain to the concrete situation faced here and now. The person exercising the virtue of prudence, for example, does not ask *whether* to be just, but *what it means* to act justly in this specific situation. Prudence, of course, cannot stand alone: it needs the other

moral virtues to exercise its most distinctive act, which is not only to deliberate effectively but even more to command the proper act in light of the preceding process of deliberation (q. 47, a. 8).

Prudence is not defined as simply finding the best means to any end whatsoever, as the false prudence of the "good crook" or the "worldly wise." As a moral virtue, it takes its bearings from the good. It reflects not only on the end of this or that act (as, for example, how to treat justly a needy but dishonest employee) but also about how all of one's acts considered as a whole fit into the end of human life. Because of their disordered ends, sinners can never have the virtue of prudence (q. 47, a. 13). Conversely, those who have grace always have prudence (q. 47, a. 14), in the sense that infused prudence enables them to make wise decisions with regard to matters necessary for their salvation. Perfect prudence commands the proper means to a particular good end and does so with regard to the good end of the person's whole life (q. 47, a. 13). The relation between the infused virtues and particular acts develops over time. Thus, the infused virtue of young children comes slowly into act and increases gradually as they mature and come into the full use of their reasoning ability (q. 47, a. 14, ad 3).

Justice

Justice is examined in sixty-five questions (qq. 57–122), the most extensive coverage of any virtue in the *Summa*. This kind of attention is to be expected, since Thomas wrote for Dominican students of theology, who, in the course of their pastoral work, would be confronted by practical problems of people buying and selling in the marketplace, going to court, and struggling to support their families under difficult economic circumstances. This lengthy discussion is organized into the following categories: first, justice in itself (qq. 57–60); second, the parts of justice (qq. 61–120); third, the gift of piety (q. 121); and last, the precepts of justice (q. 122).

Justice regards rectitude in external relations between people. This rectitude is called *right* (*ius*; q. 57, a. 1), language that should not be confused with modern individual "rights."[35] *Positive right* results from agreement between parties (q. 57, a. 2), as in the case of private contracts. *Natural right* is rooted in the very nature of things as created by God. Creatures have inherent needs and desires whose fulfillment constitutes their flourishing, the reason for their existence in the divine plan. Right exists when one creature's relations to other creatures allow for the satisfaction of their natural needs. This is why, in human communities, taking what belongs to another under extreme stress of need does not constitute theft (IIa IIae, q. 66, a. 7) and also why the rich sin when they fail to give to the poor (q. 66, a. 3, ad 2)—the former fulfills, and the latter violates, what is right.

The strong sense of natural right is seen in the raising of children by their natural parents, (q. 57, a. 3), whereas the weaker sense of natural right is illustrated in legitimacy of the institution of private property, whose social usefulness and common status in the "law of nations" (*ius gentium*) indicate its appropriateness to human nature (q. 57, a. 3, ad 2). What is right constitutes the deepest intelligibility of human laws, and it is the task of human law to render specific formulations of what is right in particular contexts.

Human laws ought to serve the common good (Ia IIae, q. 90, a. 2; q. 96, a. 1), and that is why violations of right always attack the common good, either directly or indirectly. Aquinas had, as Porter explains, "a great awareness of the communal contexts of the moral life, and more specifically, of the ways in which one can injure another through damaging her standing within the community."[36] Yet for all the significance of the common good, the individual cannot be treated unjustly for the benefit of the wider community (IIa IIae, q. 68, a. 3; although we would of course object to some practices that Aquinas considered to be just, e.g., slavery, as in Ia IIae, q. 94, a. 5, ad 4). Inherently wrong legal arrangements cannot be made just simply by the arbitrary declaration of those in power (IIa IIae, q. 57, a. 2, ad 2); hence, the famous axiom that an unjust law is no law at all (Ia IIae, q. 96, a. 4).

There is a sense in which every virtuous act can be said to be just, but Aquinas distinguished, in more precise terms, general justice (*iustitia generalis*), which orders the agent to the common good (also called legal justice

[*iustitia legalis*]; IIa IIae, q. 58, a. 6), from particular justice (*iustitia particularis*), which directs the person to particular goods (q. 58, a. 7). Particular justice, which orders a part to the good of a whole, is composed of two species (subjective parts): commutative justice, concerning part to part, and distributive justice, concerning the relation of whole to part (q. 61, aa. 1–2). Just as the heightened respect given to a wise political leader is proportionately equal to his or her contribution to the common good, so the payment of just wages for honest labor respects the equality between what has been given and received by both employers and employees.

Favoritism (q. 63) is the vice opposed to distributive justice. The *Summa* treats in extensive detail the vices opposed to commutative justice (qq. 64–78) through deeds, including murder (q. 64), theft, and robbery (q. 66); words, both inside the court (qq. 67–71) and outside the court (qq. 72–76); and unjust economic transactions (qq. 77–78), including fraud (q. 77) and usury, the charging of interest on money lent (q. 78).

This analysis of the virtue of justice is completed with a lengthy discussion of the virtues "annexed" to justice (its potential parts): religion (qq. 81–100), piety (q. 101), respectfulness for those in authority (qq. 102–5), gratitude (qq. 106–7), vindication (q. 108), truthfulness (qq. 109–13), friendliness (qq. 114–16), liberality (qq. 117–19), and equity (q. 120).

Thomas condemned as unjust a wide range of acts that range from thinking ill of another person without sufficient reason (q. 60, a. 4) to the taking of innocent life (q. 64). Injustice is found in wrongful imprisonment (q. 65), theft (q. 66), backbiting (and even consenting to backbiting as a listener [q. 73, a. 4]), and perjury (q. 98). As indications of his own cultural context, Aquinas regarded as just the practices of maiming criminals (q. 65, a. 1), whipping children and slaves (q. 65, a. 2), and executing heretics (q. 11, a. 3; but not the forced conversion of unbelievers [q. 10, a. 12]).

Readers may expect to find religion treated under the discussion of charity or faith, but the *Summa* instead treats it as a requirement of justice. Justice renders to another person what is his or her due, so in religion believers give to God what is God's due. Yet though justice requires a kind of equality of return (q. 58, a. 11), there is no equality between the creature and God and we can never return anything equal to the benefits we have received from God (q. 81, a. 5, ad 3). Nor can God ever be a debtor to us (Ia, q. 21, a. 1, ad 3). This radical asymmetry accounts for why religion is not one of the integral parts of justice. Religion, however, shares with justice a willingness to repay a debt, specifically the debt of honor to, or reverence for, the first principle of creation and government of all things (IIa IIae, q. 81, a. 3). Devotion (q. 82), prayer (q. 83), sacrifice (q. 85), religious vows (q. 88), and other acts of service and worship that endeavor to give God what is God's due are also morally virtuous (q. 81, a. 5). Yet because of the utter inequality between the worshiper and God, who "infinitely surpasses all things and exceeds them in every way," religion has nothing like the *quid pro quo* reciprocity that characterizes strict justice and is therefore simply an approximation to it, that is, as a virtue "annexed" to justice (q. 81, a. 4).[37]

In order to understand properly the importance Aquinas attached to religion, it might be helpful to recall his view of the human condition. The state of "original justice" was one of harmony, concordance, balanced proportion, and right relation between humanity and God (Ia IIae, q. 82, a. 3), within the soul and body of each person (Ia, q. 94, a. 1; q. 95, a. 1; q. 97, a. 1) and between the members of the wider human community (Ia IIae, q. 85, a. 3). The prideful attempt of humanity to grasp more than its due (q. 84, a. 2) destroyed "original justice" and "wounded" human nature (q. 85, a. 3). Our original natural inclination to the good of virtue was diminished but not destroyed by the fall.

Grace not only works to repair injustice and to restore justice in human society but, even more, to reestablish the justice (or right relation) between human beings and God. The proper justification of the sinner takes place only through the gift of grace accepted freely in faith and with the love of charity. How this is accomplished through the work of Christ is the topic of the *Tertia pars*. The *Secunda secundae*, however, is concerned with religion as the way in which conduct is directed to God. By showing proper honor to God, religious acts are properly proportioned to God (q. 81, a. 2).

The requirements of religion are given precedence to other laws in the Scriptures because they are of the greatest importance, even more so than those of the other moral virtues (q. 81, a. 6, *sed contra*; on the first three precepts of the decalogue, see q. 122, aa. 1–3). The rationale for this priority resides in the nature of virtue itself. Whatever is directed to an end takes its goodness from its relation to that end. The virtues are ordered to God as their end, and "religion approaches nearer to God than the other moral virtues, in so far as its actions are directly and immediately ordered to the honor of God" (q. 122, a. 6).[38] For this reason, religion is described as the greatest of the moral virtues (ibid.).

While internal acts of worship are more important than external acts, one ought not minimize the importance of the latter as "mere" ritual (q. 81, a. 7). Worship orders humanity to God through external acts, which engage bodies in movement and senses in images in order to draw the entire person into religious reverence (ibid.). Just as his account of our bodily nature led him to acknowledge our need for ritual, so Aquinas's recognition of our social nature encouraged his appreciation for common worship within an ecclesial community. These acts of reverence do not reflect the presumption that they do something for God, who after all is "full of glory to which no creature can add anything,"[39] but rather for our own sakes, because, "by the very fact that we revere and honor God, our mind is subjected to Him, and in this consists its perfection" (ibid.).[40] The desire for happiness, then, can only be adequately pursued on the basis of true worship, and especially in its highest form, the Eucharist (IIIa, qq. 73–83).

The gift of the Holy Spirit associated with the virtue of justice is piety (q. 121). Whereas the virtue of piety annexed to justice renders due honor to parents and country, and symbolically to one's human father (q. 101), the gift of piety is that whereby "we provide worship and duty to God as our Father through the inspiration of the Holy Spirit" (q. 121, a. 1).[41] The virtue of religion pays worship to God as Creator, but the excellence of the gift of piety resides in the fact that it inspires us to revere and worship God as Father, and, by extension, and on account of their relation to the Father, to honor all human beings, especially the saints in heaven, and the truth of Scripture (q. 121, a. 1, ad 3). Given this context, it makes perfect sense that the bulk of the final question here, dedicated to the precepts of justice in the decalogue, concentrates not on interpersonal justice but on the duties of religion (the first three precepts; q. 121, aa. 2–4) and the obligations of piety (the fourth commandment, treated in q. 121, a. 5). The remaining article (q. 121, a. 6) accords brief summary treatment to the remaining six precepts concerning justice between people.

Fortitude

The other two cardinal virtues pertain to the internal ordering of the agent, specifically with regard to ways in which the will might be hindered from following right reason. The virtue of temperance enables one to respond reasonably to what presents itself as attractive and the virtue of courage enables one to respond reasonably to what evokes fear.

The *Summa's* discussion of courage begins with the virtue itself (q. 123), its principal act, martyrdom (q. 124), and its opposing vices, which include disordered fear (q. 125), fearlessness (q. 126), and irrational daring (q. 127). It then examines its parts in general (q. 128) and its parts in particular (qq. 129–38), including confidence or magnanimity (q. 129), magnificence (q. 134), patience (q. 136), and perseverance (q. 137). It concludes with a discussion of the gift of fortitude (q. 139) and its effects (q. 140).

As a general virtue, courage gives the emotional stability required for the exercise of each and every virtue. As a special virtue, it enables the agent to endure or resist challenges to steadfastness of mind, especially in situations involving mortal danger (q. 123, a. 2). The last qualification indicates the special character of courage, its reasonable refusal inappropriately to withdraw from or to be controlled by what generates fear (q. 123, a. 3). Courage is not to be confused with foolish indifference to danger; Aquinas would concur with Mark Twain: courage is "resistance to fear, mastery of fear—not absence of fear."[42] Far from being the same as courage, fearlessness is one of the vices opposed to courage because it lacks proper love of temporal goods (q. 126, a. 1). The courageous person loves life

and other temporal goods in due measure and recognizes threats to personal well-being, yet he or she faces danger for the sake of higher goods. The soldier in battle, for example, risks losing his own life for the sake of defending the common good of his country (q. 123, a. 5).

Courage, however, is displayed not only in martial contexts, but wherever people remain steadfast in the danger of death on account of virtue. Abelard, Cicero, and Macrobius divided courage in two: courage as attacking evils and courage as enduring the onslaught of evils (q. 128, a. 1). Thomas clearly believed the latter to be its more important expression.[43] Aquinas maintained that, as it is more difficult to control fear than it is to act aggressively, courage is more characteristically disclosed in endurance than in attack (q. 123, a. 6). Martyrdom, in which one endures the greatest of physical evils, constitutes the supreme act of courage, an act of the highest perfection, which among all the acts of the virtues exhibits most completely the perfection of charity (q. 124, a. 3).

How could the endurance of evils be a cardinal virtue, since virtues move one toward the good? The phrase "cardinal virtue" applies to habits exhibiting characteristics necessary for the exercise of any virtue whatsoever, and Aquinas maintained that the steadfastness of courage is required for the exercise of *any* of the virtues when they are threatened. The final end of the virtue of courage is thus not evil *per se*, but the good of reason for the sake of which it resists or endures physical evils (q. 123, a. 11, ad 2). And because the fear of death provides the most powerful motive for withdrawing from good, the virtue which properly subordinates this fear to reason is the greatest of the cardinal virtues concerned directly with the emotions (q. 123, a. 12).

Courage faces chiefly the danger of death, but responds in proper measure to other dangers as well. It inspires a balanced, ordered love for temporal goods that overcomes disordered fear concerning their loss (q. 125, a. 1), just as, conversely, it corrects insufficient love of temporal goods and generates a proper appreciation for their place in life (q. 126, a. 2). The activity of other virtues exercised in the face of less extreme kinds of hardships are its "potential" parts. Lesser dangers must still be met with confidence in planning to act and

then in being resolute in action, but in neither
an ambitious (q. 131) nor a vainglorious way
(q. 132). In its more passive mode, courage
endures these dangers with patience (q. 136)
and perseverance (q. 137).

The gift of courage so inspires the mind
with confidence that it refuses to submit irra-
tionally to fear (q. 139, a. 2). Indeed, it generates confidence of escape from every danger
(q. 139, a. 2, ad 1), thus bestowing a special
kind of freedom from evil (q. 139, a. 2, ad 2).
This gift thus has an affinity with the fourth
beatitude—"Blessed are they who hunger and
thirst after righteousness"—in which "hunger" and "thirst" represent the employment of
strenuous effort exerted to overcome obstacles to attaining the good (q. 139, a. 2).

Not everyone is blessed with the gift of
courage, but every Christian is made aware of
the precepts of courage revealed in divine law.
Whereas the Old Law instructed the Israelites
how to fight for the sake of temporal goods,
the New Law teaches spiritual combat for the
sake of obtaining eternal life (q. 140, a. 1, ad
1). Such precepts as Jesus's, "Do not fear those
who kill the body" (Mt 10:28) thus command
endurance of temporal evils for the sake of the
ultimate end.

Temperance

The treatise on the virtue of temperance
begins with a discussion of the virtue in itself
(qq. 141–42), then its parts (qq. 143–70), both
in general (q. 143) and in particular (qq.
144–69), and its precepts (q. 170). It attends to
the parts in particular, which encompass three
major categories: first, the "integral" parts of
temperance, shame (q. 144) and honesty (q.
145); second, the "subjective" parts of temperance, those concerning the pleasures of food
(qq. 146–50) and sex (qq. 151–54); and third,
the "potential" parts of temperance: continence (qq. 155–56), clemency and meekness
(qq. 157–59), and modesty (qq. 160–69).

Temperance is both a general virtue and a
special virtue. As general, of course, it is found
in all actions exhibiting moderation. As special, the virtue of temperance characteristically orders the sense appetites, especially in matters pertaining to pleasures of
touch, such as, food, drink, and sex, desires
that are especially difficult to control (q. 141,

a. 7). Whereas the appetites of animals are
regulated by their intrinsic natural ordering,
human appetites attracted to the same kinds of
goods must be deliberately regulated by reason. Sensible goods offer the greatest pleasures to the sense of touch and often threaten
to disturb the reasonable ordering of human
action. The virtue of temperance, then, em-
powers the agent reasonably to use pleasurable objects as needed in this life (q. 141, a.
6)—"need" including not only the bare necessities of life but also the things that make
possible a decent life according to one's place
in the social order (q. 141, a. 6, ad 2). The
meaning of temperance, of course, cannot be
set in stone since "the practice of temperance
varies according to different times . . . and
according to different human laws and customs" (q. 170, a. 1, ad 3).[44]

Rather than the particularly abstemious
mindset of the emotionally constricted, as that
name sometimes suggests, the virtue of temperance leads to the moderate fulfillment of
natural desires. The *Summa* notes the need to
be alert not only to the vicious nature of un-
checked sexual desires, but also of insensibility—the rejection of pleasures attending
natural operations that are necessary for self-
preservation (q. 142, a. 1).

The integral parts of temperance, those
necessary for any case of its proper exercise,
include shamefacedness, repulsion from the
disgrace of acting contrary to temperance (q.
144), and "honesty," the spiritual beauty manifested in the clarity and due proportion of the
well-ordered life (q. 145). Thus, the virtue of
temperance, more than any other virtue,
manifests a certain beauty, just as the vice of
intemperance exceeds others in disgrace (q.
143, a. 1).

The subjective parts, or "species," of temperance are differentiated according to the
kinds of objects to which they are directed.
The virtue of abstinence concerns the proper
use of food (q. 146). This includes consumption that observes the mean (q. 146, a. 1, esp.
ad 3), as well as acts of fasting for the sake of
moral discipline, spiritual growth, and making
satisfaction for sins (q. 147, a. 1). Abstinence
is contrasted with the vice of gluttony (q. 148).
Pleasures of drink are moderated and re-
strained by the virtue of sobriety just as they
are used sinfully in drunkenness (q. 150).

The pleasures of sexual activity are ordered by the virtues of chastity and purity. These virtues properly fall under the cardinal virtue of temperance; however, they also pertain to the virtue of justice when the conduct in question has impact on others, as, for example, in cases of rape and adultery.

Chastity, which "chastises" concupiscence, is a special virtue concerned with disordered sexual desires (q. 151, a. 2). The virtue of chastity concerns sexual acts themselves, whereas the virtue of purity regards the external signs of sexual interest. Virginity as a moral rather than simply physiological condition is a virtue only when embraced for the right reason, that is, for the good of the soul and its spiritual growth, and so that one may have the leisure to be devoted to divine things (q. 152, aa. 3–5). The virtue of chastity is not to be confused with avoiding all sexual pleasures through what would now be described as neurotic psychological aversion. Nor does Aquinas praise a person who avoids sex simply because he or she is, as he puts it, "insensible as a country bumpkin" (*insensibilis, sicut agricola*; q. 152, a. 2; also q. 153, a. 3, ad 3).

Lust, of course, is the vice opposed to chastity. Given the importance of reason, the somewhat suspect status of sexual desire is signaled in the observation that, "venereal pleasures above all debauch a person's mind" (q. 153, a. 1).[45] Indeed, the *Summa* argues that even within the morally legitimate context of marriage, sexual intercourse still has some degree of shame because the "movement of the organs of generation is not subject to the command of reason, as are the movements of the other external members" (q. 151, a. 4).[46] Yet, it is important to distinguish lust, which by definition violates the order of reason, from sexual desire *per se*, which is a created good. Sexual acts in themselves are not sinful, as long as they are directed in the right manner to their proper end, procreation, rather than to the experience of sexual pleasure for its own sake (q. 151, a. 2). The disordered satisfaction of sexual appetite follows not from anything evil in the body but from a refusal of the *will* to be ordered by right reason.

Finally, the "potential" parts of the virtue of temperance are secondary virtues moderating and restraining desires for less powerful pleasures. One set of these virtues controls the inward movements of the will. In this category, the virtue of continence enables the will to stand firm in the face of vehement desires or immoderate concupiscences (q. 143, a. 1). Whereas the intemperate person feels no qualms over the choice of wrongdoing, the incontinent person feels guilt over the wrongdoing he or she has done out of disordered passion (q. 156, a. 3). Strictly speaking, continence is not a perfect virtue because it only exists in the presence of an underlying internal struggle, thus signifying the presence of vehement disordered desires. Continence does have "something of the nature of a virtue, in so far as reason stands firm in opposing the passions" (q. 155, a. 1).[47] The root cause of incontinence is not sexual desire but the *will* refusing either to think about its acts (the sin of impetuosity) or to abide by its own best judgment (the sin of weakness; q. 156, a. 1).

The other potential parts of temperance include the virtues of clemency and meekness. Clemency mitigates external punishment, whereas meekness moderates the passion for revenge (q. 157, a. 1). Note that anger, defined as the desire to punish or to have revenge (*appetitus vindictae*), is not necessarily evil (q. 158, a. 1). Anger is legitimate when emotionally moderate and in accord with right reason ("zealous anger"), that is, when it promotes justice and the true correction of the offender. Like other emotions, it can be evil by either excess or deficiency (q. 158, a. 2).

A set of secondary virtues, those concerned with less difficult matters, belong to the virtue of modesty, which governs the external actions of the body. Humility is essentially the reverence through which people are properly subject to God (q. 161, a. 1, ad 5; q. 161, a. 2, ad 3). In humility, every person, "in respect of that which is his own, ought to subject himself to every neighbor, in respect of that which the latter has of God" (q. 161, a. 3).[48] Humility should not be confused with humiliating self-abnegation before others. The vice directly opposed to humility is of course pride, the disordered desire for exaltation (q. 162, a. 1, ad 2). Pride consists essentially in the willing refusal to be subject to God and the divine rule (q. 162, a. 6). As aversion that amounts to contempt for God, pride is the most grievous of all sins as well as the queen and mother of all the vices (q. 162, a. 8).

Other parts of modesty include studiousness in the pursuit of knowledge (q. 166), opposed by the vice of curiosity by which one pursues knowledge sinfully (q. 167), and the extension of modesty in our conduct toward other people (q. 168) and in our outward apparel (q. 169).

This treatise concludes with a brief discussion of its precepts as indicated in the decalogue. Among all the vices opposed to temperance, Aquinas held, adultery would seem most opposed to the love of our neighbor, and for this reason the divine law rightly condemns not only adultery itself but even the intention to commit adultery (to covet; q. 170, a. 1). Similarly, not only is the sin of murder condemned, but also the vice of daring that sometimes leads to murder. More positive common requirements of temperance, Aquinas noted, could not have been given, since the practice of temperance varies according to different times, laws, and customs (q. 170, a. 1, ad 3).

Acts Pertaining to Certain People

This final section of the *Secunda pars* addresses an array of topics that pertain especially to certain vocations, especially as concerns the soul's habits and acts (q. 171, Prol.). There is no one correct answer to the Socratic question, "How ought I to live?" Theologically, the diversity of duties and functions within the church results from the plenitude of the grace that flows from Christ to his "body" (q. 183, a. 2, drawing on Rom 12:4–5; see also IIIa, q. 8, a. 3).

Here, the *Summa* examines first the diversities found in various "gratuitous graces" or "gifts" (*gratiae gratis datae*, based on 1 Cor 12:8–10; qq. 171–78), then the diversities among active and contemplative lives (qq. 179–82), and finally the diversities among various duties and states of life within the church (qq. 183–89).[49] Under the first heading, it investigates graces pertaining to knowledge (prophecy [qq. 171–74] and rapture [q. 175]), to speech (the gift of tongues [q. 176] and the gift of "the word of wisdom and knowledge" [q. 177]), and to miracles (q. 178). Under the second heading, it discusses the division of lives into active and contemplative

(qq. 179–82). Finally, under the third, it examines what constitutes diversities among human beings generally (q. 183) and among those seeking spiritual perfection (qq. 183–89), including bishops (q. 185) and members of religious orders such as the Dominicans (qq. 186–89).

Why do these topics belong in the "moral section" of the *Summa*? First, one must recognize that just as the *Prima secundae* opens with the question of human happiness and closes with a culminating discussion of grace, so the *Secunda secundae* begins by exploring the nature of Christian faith and ends by examining the diversity of ways in which grace is active in the lives of faithful Christians. The "moral section" of the *Summa* is concerned with the human movement to God and so fittingly takes up various ways in which people proceed on the journey to God and, through the grace of God, assist others in doing so. Structurally, the examination of grace at the end of the *Prima secundae* finds its counterpart in this discussion of the states in life in which grace is manifested concretely throughout the Christian community at the end of the *Secunda secundae*.

Gratuitous graces are freely given by the Holy Spirit so that one person can aid another to be brought to God (Ia IIae, q. 111, a. 4). The prophet is thus given special knowledge of supernatural things and called to communicate this knowledge through speech (IIa IIae, q. 171, a. 1). Rapture constitutes a special way in which God draws certain people to Himself (q. 175, a. 1), even, as with Moses and St. Paul, in a kind of vision of God's essence that transcends the state of the "wayfarer" (q. 175, a. 3). The gift of tongues allows one to preach throughout the world (q. 176, a. 1). The gift of miracles produces acts that confirm the knowledge received from God, thereby adding to its credibility in the eyes of the faithful (q. 178, a. 1).

This discussion reflects the standard distinction between active and contemplative lives. Some people delight more in contemplation of truth, and so organize their lives around it, whereas others are more intent on external actions and direct their lives to it (q. 179, a. 1). This accords with the distinction between speculative and practical reason, the former concerning itself with knowledge of the truth *per se* and the latter with practical action of one kind or another (q. 179, a. 2). There are also "mixed" ways of life that, like Aquinas's own, incorporate active and contemplative dimensions; these ways of life can be characterized by whichever of the two fundamental traits is predominant. The contemplative life leads to a knowledge and love of God that permeates primarily the intellect in its consideration of truth, but also the will and affections (q. 180, a. 1). The moral virtues dispose the person to embrace contemplation by providing its preconditions, such as self-restraint, internal ordering of the affections, and so forth (q. 180, a. 2). The present experience of imperfect contemplation and its kind of "inchoate beatitude" (q. 180, a. 4; q. 180, a. 7, ad 3) will be surpassed by the ultimate happiness given in the perfect contemplation of the beatific vision in the life to come. Even this imperfect form of contemplation yields the greatest delight possible in this life, for "the love whereby God is loved out of charity surpasses all other love" (q. 180, a. 7).[50] Because contemplation is the end of human life, the contemplative life is in itself superior to the active life.

In producing external works, active occupations draw most directly on the moral virtues. The chief moral virtue of the active life is justice, since it governs our relations with one another (q. 181, a. 1, ad 1), but of course prudence also pertains directly to the active life (q. 181, a. 2). It is important to note, though, that the active life consists primarily but not exclusively in external actions, since no human life can be decent, let alone Christian, without some contemplative activities, such as conversation, prayer, and worship. Although modern ethicists are accustomed to assigning the greatest value to practical action, Aquinas taught that the love of God pursued in the contemplative life is, in principle at least, more excellent than the life dedicated to good works. Because the contemplative life draws on what is highest in human nature (viz., the intellect), it is intrinsically more delightful than the latter and it is loved for its own sake (q. 182, a. 1). In the concrete, however, Aquinas, echoing Augustine's "compulsion of love," recognized that the urgency of human needs can give an existential moral priority to the active life (q. 182, a. 1, ad 3).[51] It is better to give a starving person a loaf of bread than a lecture in philosophy, even though the latter is a more excellent good in itself.

The third major subsection of this treatise examines various duties and states within the church. This variety of duties and states contributes to the church's perfection, makes possible various actions in service of the multiplicity of human needs, and constitutes an order that reflects the church's dignity and beauty (q. 183, a. 2). Differences within the church are thus directed to perfection, action, and beauty, and distinctions among the church's members can be described in terms of "perfection," duties to action, and the order of "ecclesiastical beauty" (q. 183, a. 3).

"Perfection" is the state in which an agent attains his or her proper end (q. 184, a. 1). Human perfection therefore consists most radically in charity that "unites us to God, Who is the last end of the human mind" (ibid.).[52] The perfection of Christian life consists in love. There are significant limits to the perfection of love in this life, but Christians must at the very least strive to eliminate all obstacles to their movement toward God and, as much as possible, to remove from their affections "whatever hinders the mind's affection from being wholly directed to God" (ibid.).[53]

Of course, it is possible to have degrees of charity without its full perfection. Ongoing conversion from cupidity to charity proceeds through beginning and intermediate stages before reaching the proficient stage exemplified in the life of the saint. The perfection of love consists minimally in having nothing in one's affections that contradicts charity. More positively, it is exemplified in the radical extension of love to strangers and enemies, in the intensification of love that leads to the sacrifice of external goods, physical well-being, and even life itself for the sake of the neighbor, and in the productive love that surrenders temporal and even spiritual goods for the neighbor's sake (q. 184, a. 2). Obedience to the commandments helps first of all to remove obstacles to charity and to avoid occasions of sin, such as adultery and greed. The "counsels of perfection"—forms of goodness that are not morally compulsory for every person—call one to renounce limited but real goods, such as marriage, possessions, and worldly concerns, in order to grow in the love of charity.

The "state of perfection" does not refer to a person's internal holiness; rather, it is concerned with his or her external actions as they pertain to the church. Therefore, a person enters into the state of perfection by "binding himself in perpetuity and with a certain solemnity to those things that pertain to perfection" (q. 184, a. 4).[54] Recognizing that wicked bishops can exist alongside holy lay people, Aquinas observed that, "nothing prevents some people who are not in the state of perfection from being perfect, or others from being in the state of perfection who are not perfect" (ibid.).[55] It is in this precise sense that bishops and members of religious orders exist in the "state of perfection." The former give themselves to demanding pastoral duties for the sake of God and the latter take solemn and perpetual vows of voluntary poverty, continence (or chastity), and obedience (q. 186, a. 6). Employing an "antonomastic" use of the term "religion," the virtue in which a person offers what is due to God (recall IIa IIae, q. 81, a. 2), Aquinas argued that those who take up life in religious orders (the "religious") do so in order to "give themselves up entirely to the divine service, as offering a holocaust to God" (q. 186, a. 1).[56] A bishop is called to be of service to the church (q. 185, a. 1) and to the common good (q. 63, a. 2). It is for this reason that the religious state is described as "a school or exercise for the attainment of perfection, which people strive to reach by various practices, just as a physician may use various remedies in order to heal" (q. 186, a. 2).[57]

Religious perfection consists primarily in the vow of obedience, the fulfillment of which imitates the obedience of Christ himself (q. 186, aa. 5, 8). Obedience, though, is not an end in itself, but rather a means of ordering one's will to God. The same general rule applies to other activities associated with religious orders, including teaching, preaching, involvement in necessary secular business, manual labor, begging, and wearing coarse clothing (q. 187). This is true of hermits who live in holy solitude, for as they grow in holiness they benefit us by their prayers and by their example of radical devotion (q. 188, a. 8, ad 4). Fulfillment of the requirements of religious life exceeds the human will; it is only made possible by grace (q. 189, a. 10).

The focus on grace also accords with Aquinas's theology of the church, which he understands primarily as the community of the faithful who participate in the grace of Christ. The church is the effect of grace, the New Law given to those who follow Christ (Ia IIae, q. 106, a. 1). It is not to be identified with the clergy or hierarchy, but rather as encompassing the community of all believers. Aquinas held a vastly comprehensive vision of this community, which includes not only those living now who are united to Christ by faith and love (IIIa, q. 8, a. 3, ad 2), but also believing sinners who have faith but not the theological virtue of charity (ibid.), those who have died and are united with Christ in glory, the souls in purgatory, and angels in heaven (q. 8, a. 4). The body of Christ also potentially includes non-believers, who in the present life have the potentiality to be united to Christ in the future (q. 8, a. 3). Gradations exist within the Christian community, but the most important gradations concern not access to power within her government (ibid.) but degrees of participation within the "mystical body" of Christ. Institutional structures, political and social organization, visible government, and juridical norms are thus necessary and legitimate aspects of the church, but their function is not to serve the institution as an end in itself but to help people grow closer to God and to attain their ultimate end.[58]

CONCLUDING SUMMARY

The fundamental features of the ethics of Aquinas can be summarized in seven interconnected and mutually reinforcing themes. First, Thomas's ethics is grounded in systematic reflection on sacred doctrine, which considers God Himself and all things in relation to God (Ia, q. 1, a. 8). The study of theology views everything as emerging from and returning to God—the focal point of the Christian moral life. Ethics is rooted in the theological virtues, which take this name because through them humans are properly ordered to God, because God is their cause, and because knowledge of them is given explicitly through divine revelation in Scripture (IIa IIae, q. 62, a. 1).

Second, this vision of life is teleological in the sense that it is "goal-directed." It develops an ethic that is eudaimonistic, that is, an ethic intended to provide an answer to the fundamental question asked by every human being about the content and means of attaining human happiness. Life is a journey toward God, the highest good. Every human being, knowingly or not, desires complete and unending happiness that can only be satisfied when he or she attains the true ultimate end, eternal union with God. At the same time, this end is radically inclusive, encompassing the entire range of natural goods pertaining to soul and body. Human motivation is, then, relatively pluralistic, oriented to a variety of goods from the elemental and common to the most noble and transcendent.[59]

Third, this moral vision is theocentrically humanistic. The anthropology of the *Prima pars* reaches a climax in its discussion of the biblical doctrine of human beings as created in the image and (imperfect) likeness of God (Ia, q. 93). God is glorified in a special way through the flourishing and sanctification of human beings. So describing the person as the "image of God" refers to not only the natural human capacity for knowing and loving God (the "image"), but also its imperfect actualization through grace in this life ("re-creation") and its perfect actualization in the glory of the next ("likeness"; Ia, q. 93, a. 4). Humanity is depicted as the "image" manifested in freedom and responsibility, a special status that is further heightened in the discussion of the Incarnation and the redemptive work of Christ in the *Tertia pars*.

Fourth, this ethic is realistic. It accommodates the limitations of human finitude and weakness without being restricted excessively by them. It accommodates the real possibilities and needs of sensible creatures whose understanding requires contact with concrete, visible realities in the material world. Just as in sacramental theology, exterior, tangible objects and physical activities elevate the human spirit to higher, supernatural realities (IIa IIae, q. 81, a. 7), so in ethics the ordering of nature and the concrete ties of blood, community, and friendship form the matrix within which the virtues are acquired, practiced, and promoted (q. 26). Virtue develops, orders, and refines human desire. Moral reflection delib-

erates on the basis of general widely apprehended precepts, like the golden rule, and strives to determine the practical demands of right reason. In so doing, it accords with the essentially rational ordering (*ordinatio rationalis*) of the moral law (Ia IIae, q. 90, a. 4) and the intrinsic intelligibility of the natural law.

Fifth, the *Summa* assigns primacy of place to the virtues and to personal character formation, and a subordinate role to law. Every act and every habit ought to draw one closer to one's ultimate end. Both acts and habits are morally right when they relate a person properly to that end and they are evil when they do not (q. 21, a. 1). Moral law clarifies the parameters within which moral goodness operates, but it intends not just the specific and detailed enumeration of permitted and proscribed actions but the deepening of our humanity. This emphasis on the virtues accords with an attentiveness to human agency, desire, connaturality, intentionality, and interiority. One cannot expect to consult a fixed and comprehensive catalogue of moral rules that eliminates the need for moral deliberation. The moral law expresses the basic regulations of human action, to be sure, but, since the core of the good life consists in exercising the virtues, practical moral decisions are arrived at through the reflective power of the virtue of prudence rather than simply by means of any formal procedure or calculation of the consequences of various courses of action.

Sixth, this is a view of Christian morality as empowered by grace. Life is conceived not only as a journey to God, but also as a process of ongoing conversion and re-creation through grace. The correction and redirection of human nature is made possible only by the indwelling of the Holy Spirit. Human nature is so wounded by sin that its affections are inevitably disordered without grace. Aquinas's Christian awareness of human sinfulness penetrates more deeply into the nature of the psyche than do philosophical theories of moral weakness. Acknowledgment of sin, acceptance of God's offer of forgiveness, and commitment to spiritual discipline provide the deepest religious bases for moral correction. The greatest manifestation of Christian morality is therefore not seen in its moral treatises or ethical theories but in the lives of holy individuals and communities. While agreeing with Aristotle that the virtues comprise the inner core of the moral life, Aquinas went well beyond the Philosopher in claiming that the theological virtues, made possible by the New Law of grace, constitute the inner core of the Christian moral life. The deepening of our humanity proceeds through the graced process of becoming more and more like God, in whose image we have been created.

Finally, Aquinas emphasized the "primacy of charity." His moral vision begins with an attraction to the true and good, leads to friendship, active service, and prayer, and culminates in loving union with God. He recognized, with Augustine, that every person's life is shaped by the objects of his or her love.[60] The virtues that direct love are inculcated through personal formation and training in good habits within various human communities, but they are also, and most importantly, produced by grace-inspired religious transformation. Religious practices, especially prayer and participation in the sacraments, contribute fundamentally to these processes of formation and transformation. Charity is thus a profoundly communal as well as an interpersonal reality. The Christian community is united by the loving activity of the Holy Spirit, who is also the ultimate source of the movement of human beings to God. The inner dynamics of the ethics of Aquinas, then, reaches its highest climax not in good works but more deeply in a penetrating and transforming appreciative love that finds its proper fruition in contemplation, mystical union, and, finally, the beatific vision.

ACKNOWLEDGMENT

I wish to express my thanks to James F. Keenan, S.J., Jean Porter, Gregory Reichberg, Charles Hefling, and the University of Chicago Writers group of the Society of Christian Ethics for reading earlier versions of this essay and offering helpful suggestions for its revision.

Notes

[1]See John Mahoney, *The Making of Moral Theology: A Study of the Roman Catholic Tradition* (Oxford: Clarendon, 1987) and John A. Gallagher, *Time Past, Time Future: An Historical Study of Catholic Moral Theology* (Mahwah, NJ: Paulist, 1990).

[2]See M.-D. Chenu, *Toward Understanding Saint Thomas*, trans. A.-M. Landry, O.P. and D. Hughes, O.P. (Chicago: Henry Regnery Co., 1963), 298–300. The debate over the structure of the *Summa* was initiated by Chenu's "Le Plan de la Somme Théologique de S. Thomas," *Revue Thomiste* 45 (1939): 93–107.

[3]Unfortunately, Thomas ceased working on the *Summa* after he completed IIIa, q. 90, one of the questions on penance. After his death, some disciples attempted to complete his work in the so-called *Supplement* based on his earlier commentary on the *Sentences*. The *Supplement* cannot be considered an authentic reflection of the mature mind of Aquinas. See Jean-Pierre Torrell, O.P., *St. Thomas Aquinas, volume 1: The Person and His Work*, trans. Robert Royal (Washington, DC: Catholic University of America Press, 1996), 147.

[4]See Chenu, *Toward Understanding Saint Thomas*, chap. 11.

[5]"et non solum secundum quod in se est, sed etiam secundum quod est principium rerum et finis earum, et specialiter rationalis creaturae."

[6]See Ignatius Eschmann, O.P., *The Ethics of St. Thomas Aquinas*, ed. Edward A. Synan (Toronto: Pontifical Institute of Medieval Studies, 1997), esp. 8–9 and 159–60.

[7]Cited by Eschmann in *Ethics of St. Thomas*, 160; an English translation from Etienne Gilson, *L'Espirit de la philosophie médiévale* (Paris: Vrin, 1948), 173.

[8]Eschmann, *Ethics of St. Thomas*, 5.

[9]Torrell, *St. Thomas*, 152.

[10]While the *Secunda pars* provides the most concentrated discussion of ethics, it is also important to realize that ethically relevant material is found virtually throughout the entire *Summa*. For example, in order to understand St. Thomas's view of gender and sexual ethics properly, one must consult his view of women in the *Summa*, Ia, q. 92, "On the Production of Woman," as well as the relevant questions on the virtue of temperance (IIa IIae, qq. 141–70). Similarly, someone wishing to understand Thomas's notion of sin needs to examine not only his analysis of "Vice and Sin" in the *Prima secundae* (qq. 71–89) but also, for example, the "Cause of Evil" in the *Prima pars* (q. 49) and perhaps also the analysis of "Penance as a Virtue" and "Of the Recovery of Virtue by Means of Penance" in the *Tertia pars* (qq. 85, 89). This kind of intertextual referencing pertains to all fundamental moral questions.

One should also note that while the *Summa theologiae* is Aquinas's principal work, a comprehensive examination of his ethics would have to be expanded to include his other texts as well.

Thomas developed his moral reflection in a wide variety of forms throughout his scholarly career, from the early commentary on Peter Lombard's *Books of Sentences* (*Scriptum in IV libros sententiarum*), through his more detailed and comprehensive academic disputations such as the *Disputed Questions on Evil* (*Quaestiones disputatae de malo*) and the *Disputed Questions on Charity* (*Quaestiones disputatae de caritate*). While the commentaries on Aristotle's works, especially *On the Nicomachean Ethics of Aristotle* (*Sententia in X libros ethicorum*) are relevant, the biblical commentaries are of particular importance. Torrell suggests that, "If we wish . . . to get a slightly less one-sided idea of the whole theologian and his method, it is imperative to read and use in a much deeper fashion these biblical commentaries in parallel with the great systematic works" (*St. Thomas*, 55).

11See Thomas P. O'Meara, O.P., *Thomas Aquinas Theologian* (Notre Dame, IN: University of Notre Dame Press, 1997), and S. Pinckaers, *The Sources of Christian Ethics*, trans. Sr. Mary Thomas Noble, O.P. (Washington, DC: Catholic University of America Press, 1995).

12See Leonard E. Boyle, O.P., "Notes on the Education of the Fratres Communes in the Dominican Order in the Thirteenth Century," in *Pastoral Care, Clerical Education and Canon Law, 1200–1400* (London: Variorum, 1981), study 6.

13"Produxit enim res in esse propter suam bonitatem communicandam creaturis, et per eas repraesentandam. Et quia per unam creaturam sufficienter repraesentari non potest, produxit multas creaturas et diversas, ut quod deest uni ad repraesentandam divinam bonitatem, suppleatur ex alia."

14See H.-D. Noble, O.P., *L'Amitié avec Dieu: Essai sur la vie spirituelle d'après Saint Thomas d'Aquin* (Paris: Desclée de Brouwer, 1932).

15Torrell, *St. Thomas*, 157.

16See August., *Conf.* 10.20.: "When I seek for you, my God, my quest is for the happy life. I will seek you that 'my soul may live' (Isa. 55:3), for my body derives life from my soul and my soul derives life from you" (*Conf.*, August., trans. Henry Chadwick [New York: Oxford University Press, 1991], 196). Also Servais Pinckaers, O.P., "La Beatitude dans L'Éthique de Saint Thomas," in *The Ethics of St. Thomas Aquinas*, Proceedings of the Third Symposium on St. Thomas Aquinas's Philosophy, Rolduc, 5–6 November 1983, *Studi Tomistici* 25, ed. L. J. Elders and K. Hedwig (Vatican City: Libreria Editroce Vaticana, 1984), 80–94.

17Etienne Gilson, *The Spirit of Medieval Philosophy* (Gifford Lectures 1931–32), trans. A. H. C. Downes (New York: Charles Scribner's Sons, 1936), 104.

18M.-D. Chenu, *The Scope of the Summa* (Washington, DC: Thomist, 1958), 36.

19Charles Taylor observes that, "Much contemporary moral philosophy . . . has tended to focus on what it is right to do rather than on what it is good to be, on defining the content of obligation rather than the nature of the good life; and it has no conceptual place left for a notion of the good as the object of our love or allegiance or, as Iris Murdoch portrayed in her work, as the privileged focus of attention or will" (*Sources of the Self: The Making of the Modern Identity* [New York: Cambridge University Press, 1989], 3). Contemporary Anglo-American authors generally follow Immanuel Kant in this regard; see *The Critique of Pure Reason*, trans. Norman Kemp Smith (London: Macmillan, 1953), A 800–801 and A 805. See, e.g., Alan Gewirth, *Reason and Morality* (Chicago: University of Chicago Press, 1978); R. M. Hare, *The Language of Morals* (New York: Oxford University Press, 1964); and John Rawls, *A Theory of Justice* (Cambridge, MA: Harvard University Press, 1971).

20This issue is developed carefully by James M. Gustafson, *Can Ethics Be Christian?* (Chicago: University of Chicago Press, 1975), chaps. 2–3.

21Pl., *Prt.*358c.

22On the difficulties with the meaning of "*habitus*," see Yves Simon, *The Definition of Moral Virtue*, ed. Vukan Kuic (New York: Fordham University Press, 1986), chap. 3. For a complete analysis of "habit," see G. Klubertanz, *Habits and Virtues* (New York: Appleton-Century-Crofts, 1963).

23SCG III, 122, in St. Thomas Aquinas, *On the Truth of the Catholic Faith, Summa contra Gentiles*, trans. Vernon Bourke (Garden City, NY: Doubleday, 1956), 143.

24"rationis ordinatio ad bonum commune, ab eo qui curam communitatis habet, promulgata."

25"Inter cetera autem rationalis creatura excellentiori quodam modo divinae providentiae subiacet, inquantum et ipsa fit providentiae particeps, sibi ipsi et aliis providens."

26"bonum est faciendum et prosequendum et malum vitandum."

27Ibid., 479.

28Pinckaers, *Sources*, 13.

29"non tamen totum bonum sibi connaturale, ita quod in nullo deficiat. Sicut homo infirmus potest per seipsum aliquem motum habere; non tamen perfecte potest moveri motu hominis sani, nisi sanetur auxilio medicinae."

30"aliquas formas seu qualitates supernaturales, secundum quas suaviter et prompte ab ipso moveantur ad bonum aeternum consequendum."

31James A. Weisheipl, O.P., *Friar Thomas D'Aquino: His Life, Thought and Works*, rev. ed. (1974; Washington, DC: Catholic University of America Press, 1983), 220.

32"disciplina per quam pervenitur ad perfectionem caritatis."

33On the order of charity, see Stephen J. Pope. *The Evolution of Altruism and the Ordering of Love* (Washington, DC: Georgetown University Press, 1994) and idem, "The Order of Love and Recent Catholic Ethics: A Constructive Proposal," *Theological Studies* 52 (1991): 255–88.

34"conspiciendis quidem, secundum quod divina in seipsis contemplatur; consulendis autem, secundum quod per divina iudicat de humanis, per divinas regulas dirigens actus humanos."

35This distinction is the source of considerable debate within the history of philosophy, with some philosophers regarding Thomas as a precursor to modern rights theories and others regarding his notion of *ius* as contrasting with subjective rights.

36Jean Porter, *The Recovery of Virtue: The Relevance of Aquinas for Christian Ethics* (Louisville, KY: Westminster/John Knox, 1990), 134.

37"inquantum omnia in infinitum transcendit secundum omnimodum excessum."

38"Religio autem magis de propinquo accedit ad Deum quam aliae virtutes morales: inquantum operatur ea quae directe et immediate ordinantur in honorem divinum."

39"in seipso est gloria plenus, cui nihil a creatura adiici potest."

40"quia videlicet per hoc quod Deum reveremur et honoramus, mens nostra ei subiicitur, et in hoc eius perfectio consistit."

41"secundum quod cultum et officium exhibemus Deo et Patri per instinctum Spiritus Sancti."

42Mark Twain, *Puddenhead Wilson* in *Mississippi Writings* (New York: The Library of America, 1982), 985.

43See P. G. Walsh, "St. Thomas and his Authorities," in *St. Thomas Aquinas, Summa Theologiae*, vol. 42, *Courage* (2a2ae. 123–40), ed. Anthony Ross, O.P. and P. G. Walsh (London: Blackfriars, Eyre and Spottiswoode, 1963), 241–43.

44"Non potuerunt autem aliqua praecepta communia affirmativa de temperantia dari: quia usus eius variatur secundum diversa tempora . . ."

45"Maxime autem voluptates venereae animum hominis solvunt."

46"motus genitalium membrorum non subditur imperio rationis, sicut motus aliorum membrorum."

47"habet aliquid de ratione vitutis, inquantum scilicet ratio firmata est contra passiones . . ."

48"Et ideo quilibet homo, secundum id quod suum est, debet se cuilibet proximo subiicere quantum ad id quod Dei in ipso."

49On the distinction between gratuitous grace (*gratia gratis data*) and justifying grace (*gratia gratum faciens*), see ST Ia IIae, q. 111.

50"ipse amor quo ex caritate Deus diligitur, omnem amorem excedit."

51See August., *De civ. D.* 19.19.

52"Caritas autem est quae unit nos Deo, qui est ultimus finis humanae mentis . . ."

53"omne illud quod impedit ne affectus mentis totaliter dirigatur ad Deum."

54"ex hoc quod obligat se perpetuo, cum aliqua solemnitate, ad ea quae sunt perfectionis."

55"nihil prohibet aliquos esse perfectos qui non sunt in statu perfectionis: et aliquos esse in statu perfectionis qui non sunt perfecti."

56"se totaliter mancipant divino servitio, quasi holocaustum eo offerentes."

57"status autem religionis est quaedam disciplina vel exercitium ad perfectionem perveniendi. Ad quam quidem aliqui pervenire nituntur exercitiis diversis: sicut etiam medicus ad sanandum uti potest diversis medicamentis." Mark Jordan observes: "Thomas chooses to end the Second Part of the Summa with the comparison of active and contemplative lives and with the description of the states of perfection. He here exhorts the reader to take up a way of life that will lead to beatitude. Thomas is not describing religious life as an education in charity; he is proposing religious life as a response to the reader's desire for beatitude. Do you want to learn how to enact the coherent human life described in the *Summa*'s Second Part? Take up a way of life that is a school for charity" ("The Care of Souls and the Rhetoric of Moral Teaching in Bonaventure and Aquinas," *Spirit and Life: A Journal of Contemporary Franciscanism* 4 [1993]: 42).

58See Yves Congar, "The Idea of the Church in St. Thomas Aquinas," *The Thomist* 1 (1939): 331–59.

59Aquinas regards pleasure as a good, but, unlike the classical utilitarians, he does not think it is the only, let alone the highest, intrinsic good. See John Stuart Mill, *Utilitarianism*, chap. 2. There are of course ambiguities in what Mill means by "pleasure" in this context, e.g., as physiological sensation, mental state, act of free choice, etc.

60See, *inter alia*, August., *De civ. D.* 14.6–7.

Selected Further Reading

Bourke, Vernon. *St. Thomas and the Greek Moralists*. Aquinas Lecture 1974. Milwaukee, WI: Marquette University Press, 1974.

Donagan, Alan. *Human Ends and Human Actions: An Exploration in St. Thomas's Treatment*. Milwaukee: Marquette University Press, 1985.

Eschmann, Ignatius, O.P. *The Ethics of Saint Thomas Aquinas: Two Courses*. Etienne Gilson Series 20. Studies in Medieval Moral Teaching. 1st ed. Edward Synan. Toronto: Pontifical Institute of Medieval Studies, 1997.

Kluxen, Wolfgang. *Philosophische Ethik bei Thomas von Aquin*. 2d ed. Hamburg: Felix Meiner, 1980.

Lottin, Odon. *Le droit naturel chez saint Thomas d'Aquin et ses prédécesseurs*. 2d ed. Bruges; Beyart, 1931.

———. *Psychologie et morale aux XIIe et XIIIe siècles*. 6 vols. Louvain: Abbaye du Mont César, 1942–1960.

O'Meara, Thomas F., O.P. *Thomas Aquinas Theologian*. Notre Dame, IN: University of Notre Dame Press, 1997.

Pieper, Josef. *Faith, Hope, and Love*. San Francisco: Ignatius, 1997.

———. *The Four Cardinal Virtues*. Notre Dame, IN: University of Notre Dame Press, 1966.

Pinckaers, Servais. *The Sources of Christian Ethics*. Washington, DC: Catholic University of America Press, 1995.

Porter, Jean. *The Recovery of Virtue: The Relevance of Aquinas for Christian Ethics*. Louisville, KY: Westminster/John Knox, 1990.

———. *Natural and Divine Law: Reclaiming the Tradition for Christian Ethics*. Saint Paul University Series in Ethics. Grand Rapids, MI: Novalis/William B. Eerdmans, 1999.

Rhonheimer, Martin. *Natur als Grundlage der Moral: Die personale Struktur des Naturgesetzes bei Thomas von Aquin: Eine Auseinandersetzung mit autonomer und teleogischer Ethik*. Innsbruck: Tyrolia-Verlag, 1987.

Simon, Yves. *Freedom of Choice*. Ed. Peter Wolff. New York: Fordham University Press, 1969.

———. *The Definition of Moral Virtue*. Ed. Vukan Kuic. New York: Fordham University Press, 1986.

Wadell, Paul. *Friends of God: Gifts and Virtues in Aquinas*. New York: Peter Lang, 1991.

Westberg, Daniel. *Right Practical Reason: Aristotle, Action, and Prudence in Aquinas*. Oxford: Clarendon Press, 1994.

PART I

The First Part of the
Second Part of the
Summa Theologiae

Happiness (Ia IIae, qq. 1–5)

Georg Wieland

Translated by Grant Kaplan

One can gather from the title that the *Summa theologiae* is a theological work. Such a statement seems trivial, yet it has significant repercussions. The structure and system of the *Summa* result from theological rather than philosophical presuppositions. The goal of theology is the knowledge of God: in the first place knowledge of God in Himself, that is, in the unity of the divine essence, in the Trinity of His persons, and in the departure of creation from Him; next knowledge of God as the end of creation; finally knowledge of God as Redeemer.

By understanding God as the end of creation, Thomas locates the human person at the center of his reflection from the start. As an image of God, "he is himself the principle of his actions, possessing, so to speak, a free will and control over his actions"(Ia IIae, Prol.).[1] Even when the "so to speak" (*quasi*) seems to hint at a limitation of human possibilities, in the *Secunda pars* of the *Summa theologiae*, Thomas understands the person as a fundamentally acting being (q. 6, Prol.). It is not so in the *Summa contra gentiles*, where, in Book III, Thomas treats the person and his deeds as simply a part of a complete process of the return of all creatures, even irrational creatures, to God. Thus it makes perfect sense in this context for Thomas to discuss questions of evil and divine Providence.[2] For how else but through the guidance and direction of God Himself can created beings reach their end? Book III treats "the complete authority or diginity of God, insofar as He is the end and ruler of all things."[3]

By contrast, the *Summa theologiae* interprets the themes of divine Providence and evil in the context of the doctrine of creation. Therefore, the section concerning the return of creation to God takes the form of a practical treatise, a "consideration of morality" (*moralis igitur consideratio*; ibid.). This treatise considers how the person either reaches or falls short of the proper human end through his or her actions. Such a treatise must determine the end at the beginning, since human life and action only maintain order and structure on the basis of an end. "For the end is the rule of whatever is ordered to the end" (q. 1, Prol.).[4]

THE ULTIMATE END

Following his practical intention, Thomas places the determination of the end of human action in the center of his deliberation. There is again a definite difference from the *Summa contra gentiles*. The latter deals above all with the finality of every form of activity: "Every agent acts for the sake of an end."[5] Human action and the corresponding end only appear as a special case of cosmic movement (which is, however, especially important). In contrast, the *Secunda pars* of the *Summa theologiae* focuses on actions that proceed from reason and free will. They are called *human actions* (q. 1, a. 1).[6] Thomas then answers the question: in what does the final end of human life and actions consist? The first five questions of the *Prima secundae* intend to answer this question.

The first question proposes the fundamental axiom that all human beings strive toward a single end (q. 1, a. 7). Thomas must answer certain questions in order to establish this central axiom. The first question asks: do human beings act for the sake of an end (q. 1,

a. 1)? Thomas approaches this question by examining the finality intrinsic to the intentional structure of human action. Human action is a "movement" that proceeds from a potency—in this case from the will—and is directed to an act. This act receives its "nature" (*ratio*) from the corresponding object (Ia, q. 77, a. 3), that is, the "end" (*finis*) of the will (Ia IIae, q. 1, a. 1).[7] Human action thus entails a disposition toward an end.

The analytical connection between action and end leads to the next question: could it be that only certain beings which possess reason and free will act for the sake of an end because only they are able to know an end, and have their actions directed toward that end? Thomas naturally rejects this suggestion because every action presumes an end and the end allows the process of acting to take its course (q. 1, a. 2). The difference between irrational and rational creatures, according to Thomas, is that the former strive for an end because they are led by something outside themselves, whereas the latter move toward the end conceived and desired by themselves (ibid.). Thomas goes one step further in his theory of action by arguing that human (or moral) actions as such can be identified through the intentionality of the agent (q. 1, a. 3). He gives the example of killing a person either for the sake of justice or to appease one's anger (q. 1, a. 3, ad 3). In the first case, the killing is an act of virtue (at least according to the conventional logic of the thirteenth century), while in the second case, it is a reprehensible act.

This answer still falls short of a complete description of human or moral actions; intention is necessary, but does not suffice as a provision for action. If intention alone were enough, then the floodgates would be open for randomness and complete relativity. One must therefore locate individual intention within a more comprehensive moral context. Thomas thus continues by establishing the necessity of a final end. Such a foundation is essential; without it, the movement of action could not be reached. This is because the final end does not merely consist in the end of one's action and the cessation of one's striving, but also in their respective origins. Striving and action would not be initiated, and would not be able to move from potentiality to actuality,

if they were not already in possession of an end, mediated through the intention. This end puts the process of action in motion (Ia IIae, q. 1, a. 4). And in the sequence toward the end there must be a conclusion.

To prove this claim, Thomas invokes the impossibility of the "infinite regression" (*regressus in infinitum*; Ia, q. 2, a. 3; q. 46, a. 2, ad 7).[8] Without a first, which is the origin of a movement, there could not be a second, third, and so on; therefore, no movement at all. This impossibility pertains to the order of intention: there must be a final end that sets the striving and action in motion, and it is effective in the order of execution. There must be a "point" from which an action derives, because the action could not otherwise begin (Ia IIae, q. 1, a. 4). Thomas is primarily concerned with the order of intention, and for this intention, he proposes a final end. This end exists for the particular goals of a person and means an inner, lasting foundation, not simply an external, contingent impulse.

In article six of the first Question, Thomas examines the final end in the particularity of striving and action. He formulates his thesis in the following manner: "The strength of the first intention, which results with regard to the final end, remains preserved in every striving for every possible object even when one does not expressly think about the final end" (q. 1, a. 6, ad 3).[9] This axiom applies as well for the actions lacking extrinsic purpose and end. Certain actions, such as games or quiet, self-contained reflections, have their purpose in themselves. Delight and rest are brought to the performer of such activities, and they contribute to his or her well-being. The anthropological and ethical significance of this line of thinking is obvious: despite the plurality and particularity of one's striving and action, the person develops not only a natural, but also an intentional and practical unity, and due to such a unity, each person is able at all times to answer for his or her entire life.

Thomas does not hold that the presence of the final end in every particular act of striving means that each person is continually aware of this presence. Experience teaches us that such an awareness is not possible. Yet the final end still has consequences for all our actions. In the final analysis, it actually orders each human life. Hence, an individual cannot simultaneously have more than one final end (q. 1, a. 5).

The connection between human striving and fulfillment provides the decisive argument for this thesis. That which completely fulfills human striving is called the "final end" (*ultimus finis*) (ibid.). This is a purely formal determination, not entailing any specification concerning substantive qualities. Yet simply in light of this idea, it is contradictory to accept several final ends. For if the striving of the person were completely fulfilled, and the person still desired something else, such striving would necessarily not have been completely fulfilled.

It is important to note that Thomas here argues in a formal manner. By contrast, in the *Summa contra gentiles*, he draws the conclusion of unity of the highest good—of God—directly from the teleology of all things: "Since everything strives toward its end insofar as that end is good, then the good must be the end insofar as it is good. The highest good is, accordingly, in the greatest measure the end of all things. But the highest good can only be one thing, and that is God."[10] This logic shows that the formal argumentation in the *Summa theologiae* takes this presupposition into account, namely that the person is a dispositional essence. From this presupposition, Thomas cannot immediately reach a conclusion concerning the unity of the final end. He must find instead the nature of the person and of human striving in order to unpack the essential unity of the person and the nature of the final end.

Thomas holds that there can only be one final end, not only for one person, but for all human beings (q. 1, a. 7). The teleology of movement in general and of human action in particular explains the dynamic of striving. This striving aims at and comes to rest in its fulfillment. The assertion of the "unity" of the final end does not only apply in this form to rational creatures, but in fact to all creatures. Moreover, Thomas believes it obvious that all things strive for their fulfillment.

However, the determination of the final end is the point where opinion divides. Different conclusions are derived from different lifestyles (q. 1, a. 7, ad 2). The politician considers power the final end, and the hedonist pleasure. The question concerning the true final

end can best be answered by the one who lives the most moral life (q. 1, a. 7). This axiom can only apply if all agree on what constitutes the most moral life.

Even if one accepts that the thirteenth century had a universal consensus, Thomas does not argue on this basis; rather, he draws on his insight into the essence of human striving and action. This becomes evident when he pursues the question of whether the final end of human beings differs from that of the rest of creation (q. 1, a. 8). In his doctrine of creation, Thomas holds that "the divine goodness is the end of all things" (Ia, q. 44, a. 4).[11] He speaks of God as "the final end of humanity and all other realities" (Ia IIae, q. 1, a. 8).[12] Thomas does not introduce this proposition in an argumentative manner, but simply uses it to emphasize the special manner in which humans (and other rational creatures like angels) achieve this end. They do so through knowledge and love, which separates them from all other creatures that do not possess reason and free will.

THE CONTENT OF HAPPINESS

The purpose of the first Question is fulfilled: all people have a single end—their completion. Therefore, it comes as no surprise that with the beginning of the second Question, Thomas first officially introduces the concept of happiness (*beatitudo*). Yet even if one accepts the results of the first Question, there remain a number of problems, two of which need to be raised here. If all people have only one final end, why do they pursue completely different ends? Furthermore, what exactly is it that wholly fulfills the person? The formal line of argument in the first Question led to a formal conclusion. This formal conclusion must now be complemented with a substantive, material explanation.

The second Question does not openly examine the basis for the difference of ends. Instead this difference is assumed. This means that Thomas proceeds with the presupposition of different lifestyles. One finds this in the formulation of the Question itself. Thomas's question—"in which forms (concepts) does happiness consist?"—assumes more than one understanding of an "end" (q. 2, Prol.).[13] He does not address this plurality by referring to the unity of the end. In fact, he cannot do this, because he recognizes in principle the different ways in which this one end can be reached. Instead, he analyses the different ends under a formal perspective, that is, whether these ends can guarantee human completion. Thomas is concerned here with understanding the essence of humanity. He does not ask what the person should do, but what different ends can or cannot be achieved.[14] One can see as a result of this discussion that the one good that corresponds to the universality of human striving is capable of achieving the completion of the person (q. 2, a. 8). At this point, Thomas concludes that only God can be the end of all humanity.

The analysis of different accounts of the content of the end connects Aristotelian and Stoic ethics with their Christian reception in Thomas's theological context. In the course of the question, Thomas develops a variety of important ideas meriting examination. The idea that the happiness of a person could consist in wealth was always rejected by classical and medieval ethics. This possibility obviously applies to Thomas's position as well (q. 2, a. 1). He takes up two Aristotelian ideas: the instrumental character of wealth and the potential infinity of human acquisitiveness.

One can describe wealth as the possession of natural goods that directly serve such basic needs as food, clothing, shelter, and the like, or as the possession of such artificial goods as money (above all others). These goods in turn assist in the possession of natural goods, and thus indirectly serve basic needs. In any case, wealth remains only a means and can never have the characteristic of an end, let alone of the final end.[15] Even the boundless attempt to acquire money is better understood as the expression of the principle imperfection of worldly goods that can never suffice, than as an indication of any notion that money has an attribute of fulfillment.

The three kinds of fortune that are found in the political life—namely honor, glory, and power—cannot make any claim to be "final ends." Honor is only a "sign and testament to excellence" (*signum et testimonium quoddam illius excellentiae*) (Ia IIae, q. 2, a. 2). Since it is merely a sign, it cannot itself constitute finality and completion. Thomas gives even less value to glory. It depends chiefly on human estimation—in the text it is called "knowledge" (*cognitionem humanam*) (Ia IIae, q. 2, a. 3). One cannot rely on social estimation, which is highly subject to error. Even if one could ground glory objectively, it would still depend on the good quality of the honorable person. So along with honor, glory remains a derivative phenomenon. Finally, power (Thomas does not speak here, as in the *Summa contra gentiles*, of a "worldly" power) cannot be considered a final end because it is indifferent to good and evil (Ia IIae, q. 2, a. 4).[16] The good use of power does not inhere in the term power itself.

The argument against power applies to the rest of the previously discussed possible ends (ibid.). They do not in themselves guarantee unadulterated goods; for this reason, they do not come into consideration as necessary conditions for happiness. This is because the very concept of complete good excludes the possibility of evil. Thomas introduces two new arguments at this point. First, he observes that genuine happiness includes the character of self-sufficiency, that is, the happy person lacks nothing that he or she needs. Therefore, none of the previous understandings of human goods can be identified with the concept of the ultimate end. Second, Thomas argues that since the person is disposed to happiness through reason and will, his or her happiness cannot depend on external causes that lie wholly or partially outside of human possibility.

While the external goods of wealth, honor, glory, and power have often received consideration as final ends in the practical human understanding, they have never played a role in the theoretical argument of philosophy. However, this is not the case with the goods immediately connected to the person (to body and soul). Thus Thomas next treats the goods of the body: health, beauty, and strength (Ia IIae, q. 2, a. 5). He gives two reasons why happiness cannot consist in these goods. The first argument is based on the intentionality of desire and action. The analysis of human action in the first Question demonstrates that action is directed toward an end. Due to the inherent potency of human life, this end cannot lie in the action or in the person. This is because all motion first arises through the transition from potency to act or object. What is in potency cannot achieve the given act by itself, but instead is related to an object. This object actualizes the potency as another, "exterior" object that fulfills human striving.

The apparent intention of the first argument aims at the following proposition: the human being is not his or her own fulfillment and purpose, "for the human being is not the highest good" (ibid.).[17] Yet this statement assumes, at least in the argumentative context of the second Question, the result of the eighth article—the universality of human striving. Therefore, it seems logical that Thomas introduces a second argument, the aim of which is more conclusive. Anyone who accepts that the person consists of body and soul, and that the body is ordered to the soul, must also grant that the final end cannot consist in bodily goods; as such, goods are ordered to the goods of the soul.

Thomas lists pleasure and desire as the final candidates for happiness. He first treats pleasure, which he describes as one of the consequences of happiness. The person does not strive for pleasure, but for the good that fulfills him or her and is appropriate to the person as a final end. When this is attained, pleasure naturally results. Therefore pleasure is considered a "proper accident" (accidens proprium), which does not belong to the essence of happiness, but is indivisibly connected to it (Ia IIae, q. 2, a. 6).

It is not so with desire, which Thomas describes as a bodily condition. Due to its connection with the senses and the body, what applies to bodily goods also applies to desire. Because of the order of the body to the soul, these goods cannot be considered as final ends. Thomas also rejects the close connection between desire and happiness, although he grants pleasure this connection. His reason lies in the limits of sense knowledge. Desire is tied to sense knowledge, and cannot be compared to the universality of spiritual knowledge. Thomas here wants to show that the desire tied to bodily conditions cannot encompass the "immensity" and universality of human fulfillment.

The examination and consideration of traditional, widely disseminated ideas of happiness leads to a negative result. None of these ideas do justice to the formal concept of happiness—to be the total fulfillment of the person—nor do they guarantee human completion. There remains one possibility to consider: whether humanity itself can be its own end and completion. Thomas forms the question—corresponding to his anthropology—whether human happiness consists in a good of the soul (Ia IIae, q. 2, a. 7).

The meaning of this question is perhaps best demonstrated through the modern idea of "development." Let us understand development as the process of unfolding of human possibilities that ends in self-realization. "Self-realization" can never be the final end of the person for Thomas. Due to its potentiality and openness, the human soul is oriented to become actualized and fulfilled by something else. This "something else" cannot consist in something limited and particular because of the universality of human striving. The soul of a person therefore can neither wholly nor partially have the trait of a final end. On these grounds, Thomas criticizes contemporary positions that see a form of human completion in "acquired reason." Such an illusory end has made reason "the suitable object of knowledge and is devoted only to active reason and itself."[18]

Yet even if the object of happiness must be a good external to the person, its possession and enjoyment remain connected to the human soul. Happiness can only be attained through the soul's faculties and subsequent activities (namely, knowledge and love). Happiness is therefore a good of the soul only insofar as it is an acquisition.

At this point, Thomas concludes that not one created good is in a position to fulfill wholly the infinite striving of the human being. In fact, Thomas believes that this applies to the rest of creation as well. None of the created world is the good itself, and the sum of all partial and limited goods does not yield an absolutely complete good. Due to its infinity, human striving cannot come to rest in creation, therefore, "Human happiness consists in God alone" (Ia IIae, q. 2, a. 8).[19]

THE ESSENCE OF HAPPINESS

After demonstrating that the cause of human happiness cannot be finite and limited, Thomas must show how the finite person comes to possess and enjoy the infinite good.

It is here that he first questions the essence of happiness. To begin his discussion, Thomas recalls a well-known distinction. Happiness is an uncreated good lying outside of the person, and its universality alone can quell human striving. However, the essence of happiness is not this good itself, but its acquisition and enjoyment (Ia IIae, q. 3, a. 1). With this distinction, Thomas takes the two-fold nature of happiness into consideration: from the objective side, because the person cannot achieve completion by himself due to his potency and limits; from the subjective side, since it is the particular, individual person whose completion is in question.

The first, and, in this context, most important, inquiry is whether happiness is a condition or an activity. One should not understand "condition" in terms of psychology, that is, as a feeling or a mood. Instead Thomas uses the term to represent the levels of perfection of being. In an essence of the highest and absolute perfection (that is, in God), condition and activity are interchangeable. God is happy through Himself; His activity is His being, and He is Himself end and completion (Ia IIae, q. 3, a. 2, ad 4).

All other essences can only attain their completion through activity, that is, by accomplishing the transition from potency to act. Hence, human happiness must consist in activity. Yet if one compares the corresponding activity of angels with that of humans, a decisive difference is made apparent. Angels are connected with the highest good through a single and everlasting activity. This activity corresponds to the well-established understanding of happiness: the angelic possession of happiness must be permanent, simple, and without interruption, for one cannot speak otherwise of real completion. Humans are connected with God through activity as well, but under the conditions of the present life, this connection is neither permanent nor simple, because the connection is repeatedly interrupted and must always be newly begun. Therefore the term of "incomplete" happiness is befitting. Complete happiness cannot exist in the present life, but God promises this to us in a future life (ibid.).[20]

One can understand the concept of "incomplete" happiness in a twofold manner. One can read it to a certain degree from above, and one

must primarily understand it as such, for incompleteness assumes the standard of perfection. The different levels of happiness are to be measured by God's simplicity, actuality, and absolute completion. And from this perspective the most complete human activity proves to be deficient and inadequate to such a degree that complete happiness only appears as divine promise, but not as human achievement. If one views the "incomplete" happiness from below, however, that is, from the perspective of humanity under the conditions of the present life, happiness appears as "a participation of (true) happiness" (*participatio beatidudinis*) (ibid.). Hence, happiness does not fall under the verdict of human conceit and it is not presented in a negative fashion.

After Thomas demonstrates that happiness must consist in activity, he must now explain in which human activity happiness essentially consists. First, he examines sensible activities. Sense activities operate as preconditions for incomplete happiness, for reason is oriented "in the present life" toward the senses. In the future life, the human spirit, which connects us to God, is of course independent of sense activity. However after the resurrection, the body and therefore the senses share in the complete happiness of the soul. Thomas stresses this point by appealing to Augustine (Ia IIae, q. 3, a. 3).[21] He thus presents a Christian anthropology that takes seriously the embodied state of humanity.

It remains to be seen whether happiness is an activity of reason or the will. As is known, Thomas clearly opts for reason, and thus splits from the Augustinian tradition. He argues that happiness is "the possession of the final end" (*consecutio finis ultimi*) (Ia IIae, q. 3, a. 4). The act of the will cannot consist in this. Either the act of the will is oriented to striving after the end not yet attained—and in this phase the person is not yet completed, and happiness not yet achieved—or the act of will happily possesses the end. Thomas has already shown that delight is only a consequence that results from this possession. The possession itself or the presence of the end must be differentiated from the resultant delight. Delight does not make the end present; rather, the presence of the end precedes delight. Thomas thus concludes that happiness can only consist essentially in an act of reason. The activity of the will, which expresses itself in delight, is an immediate consequence of happiness (Ia IIae, q. 3, a. 4).

Furthermore, Thomas contends that, "Happiness consists more in the activity of the speculative than the practical reason" (Ia IIae, q. 3, a. 5).[22] In light of the preceding discussion this statement should hardly cause wonder. If God is the final end of human action, and happiness consists in the possession of this end, then the "possessing" activity can only consist in contemplation, that is, in an activity of the speculative intellect. God, as eternal reality, cannot be the object of any activity (Ia, q. 14, a. 16). Were a person one's own final end, happiness would then consist in the activity of the practical intellect, that is, in the order and form of our passions and actions—in a virtuous life (Ia IIae, q. 3, a. 5, ad 3). Therefore, Thomas excludes virtue as an adequate answer to the question of happiness. This applies at least to the highest form of happiness, which "consists wholly" (tota consistit) in contemplation (Ia IIae, q. 3, a. 5).[23] It is not so with an incomplete form of happiness. The precedence of contemplation applies here as well. As Thomas states in order to complete his theory, the person is dependent on the virtues for the rule of his or her passions in the present life. The virtues are therefore a condition of incomplete happiness, that is, of the theoretical life.

With this estimation of speculative intellect, Thomas must deal with the meaning of the speculative sciences for happiness (q. 3, a. 6). For could it not be the case that the person achieves this completion through the practice of these sciences? Albert the Great in fact taught something quite similar. His theory of "acquired reason" (intellectus adeptus) connected human happiness with the process of the theoretical disciplines and made completion a matter of philosophy.[24] Thomas rejects such an understanding. Although the theoretical life of the philosopher presents a kind of "participation" (participatio) in true and complete happiness, there is no continual connection to such a life in this world (ibid.). This is because the speculative sciences remain bound to conditions that underlie all human knowledge—the realm of the senses (Ia, q. 83, Prol.).

Another important issue Thomas addresses is the contention that the recognition of "separated substances", namely, pure spirits without matter (angels), offers sufficient grounds for human happiness (Ia IIae, q. 3, a. 7). Thomas rejects this suggestion, because the universality of human striving cannot be fulfilled by the presence of a limited essence—even if this being is in its ontological standing far superior to humanity. All creatures, even angels, merely partake in being and are therefore necessarily limited. They do not come into question as "objects" of human completion. Thomas holds that angels possess a lower level of blessedness (in comparison to divine beatitude). Similarly, and to an even greater measure, such a view applies also to the level of perfection attained through engagement in the theoretical sciences, which do not yield complete knowledge.

According to Thomas, happiness consists in an activity of the theoretical intellect. Yet, because it is always connected to the sense world, the theoretical intellect can neither guarantee nor cause true human perfection (or completion). Nor can the angels, because of the limitations of their existence, affect true human perfection.

There remains one question in the context of achieving happiness: does happiness consist in the vision of the divine essence (Ia IIae, q. 3, a. 8)? Thomas answers in the affirmative. To buttress his argument, he recalls the natural state of the human intellect. Its searching and desiring come to rest only when the intellect has recognized the essence of something. Completion of the person requires not only the knowledge of God as the cause of the world, but also the knowledge of God's essence.

Thomas's thesis in this article is, in short, that the person has a "natural desire" (desiderium naturale) that first comes to rest by gazing on the divine essence. Thomas's problem here lies in how to bring into harmony the "naturalness" of desire with the "gratuity" of the beatific vision.[25] Unfortunately, Aquinas does not directly resolve the question of this relation. The structure of the Question itself and the topic of the five Questions on achieving happiness shows that the Question does not concern how one achieves the final end, but that one must at least in principle be able to achieve it. Thomas demonstrates at this point only the structure of happiness and gives only an outline of how to conceive it coherently. He avoids the more specific matter of how one can actually achieve happiness.

THE EFFECTS OF HAPPINESS

Question 4 deals with the effects of happiness, or the beatific vision, on the person. This Question is also located on a hypothetical level within the structure of the argument. What follows from the connection of the beatific vision with the highest good, and what prerequisites are required? This is a twofold question that determines the direction of the argument. The argument begins with the consequences of the beatific vision for the person (Ia IIae, q. 4, aa. 1–4), and then moves to the necessary prerequisites for happiness, especially in the present life (Ia IIae, q. 4, aa. 5–8).

Thomas understands delight to be a direct result of the beatific vision. As soon as one has achieved the highest good, joy results, and necessarily accompanies happiness. The two are related like cause and effect: "The vision is the cause of delight" (Ia IIae, q. 4, a. 2, *sed contra*).[26] Delight therefore cannot have the same meaning as the vision, in which happiness exists essentially. Thomas describes one aspect of the beatific vision as the "possession" or the "grasp" of the object viewed. He does not hereby mean a complete grasping of God, which, despite the condition of eternal completion, remains impossible due to the finitude of the creature and divine infinity.

Possession is better understood as explicit visualization of the end (Ia IIae, q. 4, a. 3, ad 3). Thomas regards this aspect of the beatific vision in terms of the orientation of the person to the final end. Incomplete knowledge of the end is remedied in the complete knowledge of the beatific vision, just as the disposition of love toward the final end is completed in delight. Similarly hope participates in happiness through the express possession of the end. Note that the anthropological dynamic suggested here is not described in the language of the theological virtues. I must reiterate that Thomas does not understand possession to be an activity different from the beatific vision. Instead, he views it as an aspect, similar to delight, that accompanies the vision.

The proper disposition of the will proves to be a necessary result of this activity from the perspective of the beatific vision (Ia IIae, q. 4, a. 4). One who views the divine essence cannot help but love this "object." Rectitude of the will consists precisely in the love of God. This rectitude is therefore immediately linked to the beatific vision. What seems like a consequence from the perspective of the beatific vision appears as a presupposition to the present life. The rectitude of the will must be taken as a given so that one can reach happiness. For rectitude implies nothing other than the suitable orientation to the end. With the discussion of rectitude of will, we arrive at the matter of the moral meaning of the end.

Thomas explains what is meant by the "will" in the following articles, particularly in light of human fulfillment and the desire for fulfillment in the present life. In the case of the partial happiness of this life, the person is dependent on his body, on external goods, and on communion with friends. Does this apply as well for the complete happiness of the beatific vision? Thomas answers this question by dealing with the relationships of the present life. As the human intellect is oriented to sense understanding for its activities, temporal happiness depends somewhat on the body and its organs. Naturally this does not apply to the beatific vision, which excludes all sense mediation.

The essence of complete human happiness does not require the body. This is not Thomas's final word on the topic. The integral, natural relationship between body and soul is not abolished; rather, it is completed by the beatific vision. The soul's desire thus rests completely only when this essential relationship is reestablished, and in this the body participates in its own way in the fullness of divine wealth (Ia IIae, q. 4, a. 5). The body-soul relationship experienced in this life is reversed in complete happiness. In this case, the soul, or more precisely the intellect, is not oriented toward the body. Rather, the soul lets the body participate in its perfection (Ia IIae, q. 4, a. 6).

The spiritual existence of the body is formed through the soul. Thus it is understandable that this existence does not require any external goods in the state of eternal completion (Ia IIae, q. 4, a. 7). These goods only serve to support the creaturely body. This, however, is not the case with regard to friendship. The person needs this community in the present life, in both action and contemplation. Thomas does not deem the philosophical life lonely. In completed happiness, it is naturally God to whom one owes completion. In this case, one is not oriented to friends, but like the body, friends contribute to the "well being" (*bene esse*) of happiness (Ia IIae, q. 4, a. 8).

In reflecting on the communion of friends and the meaning of the body in the state of completion, Thomas refers in detail to Augustine. It is noteworthy that he does not handle these Questions in the *Summa contra gentiles*. The reason is obvious: the themes of both the resurrection of the dead and the communion of saints belong to the foundation of the Christian tradition, for which Thomas gets one of the greatest authorities to speak. These themes do not belong in the first three books of the *Summa contra gentiles*, a discourse that relies exclusively on the natural intellect. This is also the case in his treatment of the final happiness of humanity.[27]

This outline of human happiness would remain incomplete without a discussion of whether and how one achieves the final end. The treatment of complete human fulfillment does not necessarily include the idea that one actually attains this goal. Thomas expressly treats this question for a theological reason, which he provides in the *Prima pars* (Ia, q. 12, a. 4). According to Thomas, human nature is so limited by its nature that it cannot reach its goal of the beatific vision by itself. The cognitive ability of a knower depends on his or her natural state. The creatureliness of all creatures, even angels and spirits, excludes the possibility of viewing God, the ground of being, on their own accord. Creatures only participate in being, therefore, they cannot eradicate the fundamental distance from their Creator or know the Creator as He is in Himself.

THE ATTAINMENT OF HAPPINESS

Thomas follows this with an investigation of the possibility of achieving complete happiness. For Thomas, the critical factors are the human intellect and will, which are characterized by their ability to strive for and grasp the universal good (Ia IIae, q. 5, a. 1). The consequences for the fundamental openness or receptivity of the person for the infinite

essence of God are obvious. If this were not so, the gift of the beatific vision would change the person in his or her essence in that the infinity of the gazed-upon object would abolish the supposed limitation of the cognitive power. The one who strives for the good in this life would not be identical with the one who views the infinite goodness of God in eternity. This argument touches on the ontological difference between an infinite potency oriented to its fulfillment by external actualization, and the infinite act in which consists fulfillment itself.

The thesis concerning the human openness for the infinite God leads to the question of whether all people participate in complete happiness in the same way. Thomas rejects this idea by pointing out the differences between people (Ia IIae, q. 5, a. 2). Moral and natural differences form the basis for the claim that one person can be happy to a greater degree than another. The happy person needs no further fulfillment.

It is possible on principle to maintain human openness and receptivity to divine infinity. Whoever does so must explain why there cannot be true and complete happiness in this life (Ia IIae, q. 5, a. 3).[28] Thomas gave the systematic explanation for this claim in the *Prima pars*. The essential dependence of human knowledge on bodily capabilities makes the vision of the divine essence impossible under the conditions of this life (Ia, q. 12, a. 11). Thomas only refers to this explanation in the *Prima pars*.

In the *Secunda pars*, Thomas gives a description of human life that cannot meet the requirements of the concept of true happiness. This life entails certain deficiencies that lack on a rudimentary level any remedy and cannot satisfy the fundamental longing of the human person. Thomas lists familiar evils—ignorance, disordered passions, and bodily pain—that continue as long as life itself. "[L]ife itself passes away . . . [and] we naturally desire to have [life] and would wish to abide in it perpetually, for man naturally flees death" (Ia IIae, q. 5, a. 3).[29] Yet since the fleeting nature of life makes it impossible to fulfill the human desire for longevity and reliability, then there cannot exist true happiness here.

Thomas still concedes, in spite of this vivid description, that something short of complete happiness is possible here on earth. He believes that Aristotle was clear on this point, "that the human person does not attain happiness completely, but only in his own way."[30] The Aristotelian ethic with its doctrines of virtue and happiness is a description of the kind of completion possible under human conditions. But this ethic does not give a description of complete happiness from Thomas's theological perspective.

Fully sensitive to the mutability and transience of human life, Thomas feels compelled to defend the proposition that complete happiness cannot be lost. He grounds the argument by referring to the universal concept inherited from Aristotle: "Happiness is a complete and self-sufficient good" (Ia IIae, q. 5, a. 4).[31] The exclusion of every deficiency follows, as does the exclusion of every fear of ever losing this good. The universal concept of happiness also includes a subjective certainty safe from any loss. From the perspective of the beatific vision, Thomas lists three possible dangers: the refusal of the human will itself, deprivation through divine punishment, and threat from external factors. The will of anyone who has ever gazed upon God's essence is attached to this essence with the same necessity as the mind is attached to the first principle of reason. This necessity does not mean coercion, but a fulfillment of that which the will has always wanted. Neither can deprivation through divine punishment be reconciled with the beatific vision. For the beatific vision inevitably means a proper ordering of the will that makes any wrongdoing impossible. Punishment results only from wrongdoing. On account of divine justice, the beatific vision cannot be withdrawn from the person. Even external factors cannot threaten the beatific vision, since it transcends the movement of space and time.

In late Antiquity and the Middle Ages, pure spirits (or theologically speaking, angels) were given a large role in the connection between the cosmic and the terrestrial realms. This leads one to question the role of angels in the reception of happiness. Thomas argues explicitly that everything exceeding nature happens immediately through God alone (Ia IIae, q. 5, a. 6). As previously mentioned, the beatific vision goes beyond the cognitive faculty of all creatures; therefore, it is due to God alone—there is no relevant participation of angels.

Such deliberations do not command the attention of the modern reader, but they demonstrate, regardless of his cosmological presuppositions, how much Thomas emphasizes the transcendence and free activity of God. According to Thomas, God's immediate relation to humanity applies as well to partial happiness and the corresponding virtues. If these are oriented to complete happiness, they are indebted to divine grace alone. Yet Thomas concedes that there are natural virtues that have their origin in the human intellect and will.

The immediate and encompassing effect of God naturally begs the question of whether humanity itself participates in the reception of happiness. Thomas grants that in a single act, God could dispose the human will toward the final end and simultaneously allow the will to attain this end (Ia IIae, q. 5, a. 7). Even if one accepts this understanding, it remains true that the proper disposition of the will is a necessary presupposition of attaining the final end. Although it is theoretically possible, Thomas rejects this possibility for God's omnipotence under the rubric of the "order of divine wisdom" (*ordo divinae sapientiae*) (ibid.).

Only God is immediately happy because of His essence, and not due to a prior movement or activity. This is not the case with creatures. The difference between their natural capability and complete happiness makes "movements" essential. These movements are actions that have the character of "merits" (*merita*). At this point, Thomas does not discuss the question of the degree to which God motivates these movements. The clear reference to the meaning of human action is decisive for the acquisition of complete happiness. For Thomas, it belongs to the "order of things" (*ordo in rebus*) that the person is not just an objective element of the world, but the origin of his or her actions (Ia IIae, q. 5, a. 7, ad 1).[32] Human actions thus have the character of merit whose reward is happiness.

One problem remains to be solved. If everyone strives for the final end, and this end consists in the vision of God's essence, all must strive for the beatific vision. But this is obviously not the case. How can one explain this? Thomas answers by noting the distinction between the universal and particular concepts of happiness. According to the universal view, the one who is happy "has everything that he or she wants," and his or her will is thus completely fulfilled (Ia IIae, q. 5, a. 8, ad 3).[33] Everyone necessarily strives for *this* state by nature. The universal concept, while unmistakable, needs to be differentiated from the particular. According to Thomas, the particular concept is identified with the beatific vision. The manner in which Thomas develops this understanding of happiness clearly demonstrates that his readers are dealing with a rational reconstruction. One can be quite mistaken regarding the specific concept of happiness.

Thomas has shown what the end of human life consists in: namely, the beatific vision. He has shown that the person is by nature able to possess the infinite good. But this fundamental openness does not *eo ipso* include the active ability of the creature to bridge the infinite distance to the Creator through his or her own efforts. The beatific vision remains a gift and a grace. Thomas insists on the proper order of things. The acquisition of happiness depends also on human activity. "Therefore, since it is necessary to arrive at happiness through actions, it is necessary to consider next human actions" (Ia IIae, q. 6. Prol.).[34] As a result, the *Secunda pars* of the *Summa theologiae* assumes the form of a practical treatise or a "consideration of morality."

Notes

[1]"secundum quod et ipse est suorum operum principium, quasi liberum arbitrium habens et suorum operum potestatem."

[2]SCG III, chaps. 4–15 on the problem of evil; SCG III, chaps. 64, 71–77 on the problem of Providence.

[3]SCG III, chap. 1 § Quia ergo: "Restat in hoc Tertio Libro prosequi de perfecta auctoritate sive dignitate ipsius, secundum quod est rerum omnium finis et rector."

[4]"ex fine enim oportet accipere rationes eorum quae ordinantur ad finem."

[5]SCG III, chap. 2: "Quod omne agens agit propter finem."

[6]"actionum quae ab homine aguntur, illae solae proprie dicuntur humanae, quae sunt propriae hominis inquamtum est homo." See Ralph McInerny, *Aquinas on Human Action. A Theory of Practice*

(Washington, DC: Catholic University of America Press, 1992), 3–24.

[7]"Obiectum autem voluntatis est finis et bonum."

[8]See also Patterson Brown, "Infinite Causal Regression," in *Aquinas. A Collection of Critical Essays*, ed. Anthony Kenny (London: Macmillan, 1969), 214–36.

[9]"virtus primae intentionis, quae est respectu ultimi finis, manet in quolibet appetitu, cuiuscumque rei, etiam si de ultimo fine actu non cogitetur."

[10]SCG I, chap. 17: "Si enim nihil tendit in aliquid sicut in finem nisi inquantum ipsum est bonum, ergo oportet quod bonum inquantum bonum sit finis. Quod igitur est summum bonum, est maxime omnium finis. Sed summum bonum est unum tantum, quod est Deus."

[11]"divina bonitas est finis rerum omnium."

[12]"Deus est ultimus finis hominis et omnium aliarum rerum."

[13]"Deinde considerandum est de beatitudine; primo quidem, in quibus sit . . ."

[14]See Wolfgang Kluxen, "Glück und Glücksteilhabe. Zur Rezeption der aristotelischen Glückslehre bei Thomas von Aquin," in *Die Frage nach dem Glück*, ed. Günther Bien (Stuttgart: Frommann-Holzboog, 1978), 82.

[15]Arist. *Pol.* 1.9 (1257a4 and 1258a1).

[16]SCG III, chap. 31: "Quod felicitas non consistit in potentia mundana."

[17]"non enim homo est summum bonum."

[18]Albertus Magnus, *De anima* III, tr. 2, c. 19: "Cum autem iam habeat scientiam, vocatur intellectus adeptus, et tunc non indiget amplius virtutibus sensibilis animae . . . . sic separatus intellectus, qui habet iam intelligibilia et non convertitur nisi ad agentem et ad seipsum." (ed. Colon VII/I, 206, 49–58). See also, Georg Wieland, *Zwischen Natur und Vernunft. Alberts des Grossen Begriff vom Menschen* (Münster: Aschendorff, 1999), 13–15.

[19]"In solo igitur Deo beatitudo hominis consistit."

[20]"Et propter hoc in statu praesentis vitae perfecta beatitudo ab homine haberi non potest. . . . Sed promittitur nobis a Deo beatitudo perfecta." See also Wolfgang Kluxen, *Philosophische Ethik bei Thomas von Aquin*, 2d ed. (Hamburg: Felix Meiner, 1980), 130–36; Denis J. M. Bradley, *Aquinas on the Twofold Human Good: Reason and Human Happiness in Aquinas's Moral Science* (Washington, DC: Catholic University of America Press, 1997), 369–423.

[21]"post resurrectionem, 'ex ipsa beatitudine animae,' ut Augustinus dicit in Epistola 'ad Dioscorum,' 'fiet quaedam refluentia in corpus et in sensus corporeos, ut in suis operationibus perficiantur . . .'"

[22]"Beatitudo magis consistit in operatione speculativi intellectus quam practici."

[23]"ultima et perfecta beatitudo, quae expectatur in futura vita, tota consistit in contemplatione."

[24]Wieland, *Zwischen Natur und Vernunft*, 13–16.

[25]Kluxen, *Philosophische Ethik bei Thomas von Aquin*, 138–42; Bradley, *Aquinas on the Twofold Human Good*, 424–39.

[26]"visio est causa delectationis."

[27]SCG I, chap. 2: § Secundo quia: "Unde necesse est ad naturalem rationem recurrere, cui omnes assentire coguntur"; SCG IV, chap. 1: § Competunt autem verba: "Nam in praecedentibus sermo est habitus secundum quod ad cognitionem divinorum naturalis ratio per creaturas pervenire potest."

[28]See also SCG III, chap. 48.

[29]"cum et ipsa vita transeat, quam naturaliter desideramus, et eam perpetuo permanere vellemus, quia naturaliter homo refugit mortem."

[30]SCG III, chap. 48: § Propter has autem: "Quia vero Aristoteles vidit quod non est alia cognitio hominis in hac vita quam per scientias speculativas, posuit hominem non consequi felicitatem perfectam, sed suo modo."

[31]"Cum enim ipsa beatitudo sit 'perfectum bonum et sufficiens' (*Eth. Nic.* 1.5, 1097b20), oportet quod desiderium hominis quietet, et omne malum excludat."

[32]"operatio hominis non praeexigitur ad consecutionem beatitudinis propter insufficientiam divinae virtutis beatificantis: sed ut servetur ordo in rebus."

[33]"Beatus es qui habet omnia quae vult."

[34]"Quia igitur ad beatitudinem per actus aliquos necesse est pervenire, oportet consequenter de humanis actibus considerare. . . ." This is called a "moral consideration" (*moralis consideratio*) in the prologue.

Selected Further Reading

Bien, Günther, ed. *Die Frage nach dem Glück.* Stuttgart: Frommann-Holzboog, 1978.

Bradley, Denis J. M. *Aquinas on the Twofold Human Good: Reason and Human Happiness in Aquinas's Moral Science.* Washington, DC: Catholic University of America Press, 1997.

Celano, Anthony J. "The Concept of Worldly Beatitude in the Writings of Thomas Aquinas." *Journal of the History of Ideas* 25 (1987): 215–26.

Forschner, Maximilian. *Über das Glück des Menschen. Aristoteles. Epikur. Stoa. Thomas von Aquin. Kant.* Darmstadt: Wissenschaftliche Buchgesellschaft, 1994.

Gallagher, David M. "Desire for Beatitude and Love for Friendship in Thomas Aquinas." *Medieval Studies* 58 (1996): 1–47.

Kleber, Hermann. *Glück als Lebensziel. Untersuchungen zur Philosophie des Glücks bei Thomas von Aquin.* 2d ed. Münster: Aschendorf, 1988.

Kluxen, Wolfgang. *Philosophische Ethik bei Thomas von Aquin.* Hamburg: Felix Meiner, 1980.

McInerny, Ralph. *Aquinas on Human Action: A Theory of Practice.* Washington, DC: Catholic University of America Press, 1992.

Schulze, Markus. *Leibhaft und unsterblich. Zur Schau der Seele in der Anthropologie und Theologie des hl. Thomas von Aquin.* Freiburg/Schweiz: Univ.-Verlag, Studia Friburgensia, N. F. 76, 1992.

The Will and Its Acts (Ia IIae, qq. 6–17)

David M. Gallagher

At the heart of Aquinas's ethics lies the will. Moral acts are willed acts, for as Thomas teaches at the very beginning of his treatise on the moral life, moral acts are identical with human acts—acts which proceed from intellect and will (Ia IIae, q. 1, aa. 1, 3). Where the will does not operate, action has no moral quality whatsoever and falls back into the category of mere natural activity (Ia IIae, q. 6, a. 7, ad 3; Ia IIae, q. 10, a. 3). And even in moral actions, external acts have a moral quality only because they have been commanded by the will (Ia IIae, q. 20, aa. 1–3). Thus moral goodness is located first and foremost in the will. Indeed, for Thomas a person is said to be good or bad simply, i.e., morally, on the basis of his will, for it is through the will that everything else in the person is used well or badly (Ia, q. 48, a. 6). In sum, moral action is willed action and morally good action arises from a good will (Ia IIae, q. 56, a. 3).[1]

This centrality of the will is evident when Thomas presents his description of the subject matter of moral philosophy at the beginning of his commentary on Aristotle's *Nicomachean Ethics*. In this work, he maintains that every branch of philosophy treats a certain order; logic, for example, deals with the order which reason puts into its own acts of thinking. Moral philosophy, he says, treats the order that is found in voluntary actions, and consequently it considers "human operations insofar as they are ordered to one another and to the end." By "human operations," Thomas goes on to say, are understood those actions "which proceed from the will according to the order of reason." He concludes that "the subject of moral philosophy is human operation ordered to the end, or even man taken as voluntarily act-ing for the end." Hence, *willed action*, or the person as the source of willed action, is the subject of study in ethics.[2]

It comes as no surprise, then, that Thomas should devote an extended discussion to the will and willed action (Ia IIae, qq. 6–17). Nor is it surprising to find the will appearing prominently in all the other major aspects of his moral theory. In the treatise on happiness, he maintains that rectitude of the will—the proper ordination to God—is a prerequisite for beatitude; in fact, one might consider his ethics to be nothing more than an account of how one achieves that rectitude (Ia IIae, q. 4, a. 4). The moral significance of the passions lies in their relationship to the will, either as inclining the will to a certain kind of choice or as being themselves incited or repressed by the will (Ia IIae, q. 24, a. 1). In the treatment of the virtues, Thomas explains that the moral virtues are located only in the will or in powers whose acts can be commanded by the will (Ia IIae, q. 56, a. 3). So too, sin occurs primarily in the will itself and only derivatively in the acts of the other powers insofar as they are commanded by the will; there is no sin where there is no will (Ia IIae, q. 74, aa. 1–3). Finally, Thomas begins his treatment of law, claiming that law, by definition, is a principle of human acts, that is, acts that proceed from the will (Ia IIae, q. 90, a. 1; SCG III, chap. 114).

For a clear understanding of Thomas's ethics, then, it is necessary to have an accurate grasp of the will and its functions. In what follows, I will attempt to achieve this by examining Aquinas's understanding of the will in general; in what ways the will is free and in what ways necessitated in its action, a theme Thomas deals with at great length; the various acts of the will as they are described in Ia IIae, qq. 6–17; and finally, how love is the first affection of the will and the implications of this point for understanding the moral life.

THE NATURE OF THE WILL

In one way, the will may be understood simply as that power or faculty of the soul by which a human agent is in control of his actions. For Aquinas, properly human actions are those actions over which a person has control (*dominium*; Ia IIae, q. 1, a. 1). To have control means that when the person acts, it is possible to act otherwise or not to act at all. This mode of acting is contrasted to the mode of nature in which an agent is determined to act in only one way and cannot do otherwise than it does, as occurs in the instinctual behavior of animals. As Thomas says, "the will is distinguished from nature as one cause from another; some things are done naturally and some voluntarily. The mode of causing of the will which is master (*dominus*) of its acts is other than that of nature which is determined to one" (Ia IIae, q. 10, a. 1, ad 1).[3]

The will here is taken, we might say, as the source of the voluntariness of all voluntary action. There are many voluntary actions, actions in the control of the agent, which are acts of powers other than the will. When a person walks or eats these are acts not of the will but of the body; so too, if a person thinks, remembers, or imagines these are respectively acts of the intellect, of the memory, or of the imagination, all powers distinct from the will. Nevertheless, such actions can be voluntary, and these powers do not themselves account for the voluntariness of their own actions; the imagination, for example, does not account for the fact that someone can control whether or not he will use his imagination nor do the bodily powers alone account for the ability he has to decide to walk. One accounts for this control by appealing to another power, a power whose proper act it is to *choose* either to imagine or not to imagine, to walk or not to walk. This power is the will. Thomas often presents the will in this way, taking it as the source of voluntariness. To so understand the will is to take it as *free-will* (*liberum arbitrium*), the term he assigns to the will when it is con-

sidered precisely as the source of free or fully voluntary action (Ia, q. 83, aa. 3–4).[4]

Thomas presents the will, however, not only as *free-will*, but more fundamentally as *rational appetite*. Hence, to understand his theory of the will, we must place it within the larger context of his general theory of appetition. For Aquinas every being has a determinate appetite corresponding to the kind of being that it is. He bases this doctrine on the empirical observation that each kind of thing has typical motions and rests along with the recognition that the source of these motions and rests is internal to the thing. To take the simplest example, stones generally fall toward the middle of the earth, and if they actually arrive at that point they will tend to stay or rest there. Stones or any heavy body have *an internal source of motion* toward some determinate condition in which, when it is achieved, they will rest. Such bodies may move in other directions, but only if they are moved from outside (violent motion); their motion from the internal source is toward some definite place. This internal source of motion, this internal tending or inclining, is exactly what Thomas understands by appetite.[5]

Thomas distinguishes three levels of appetite. The first, of the sort just described, operates without any cognition on the part of the being which has the inclination. Thomas calls this "natural inclination" or "natural appetite." This kind of appetite is found in all beings not endowed with cognition; the direction of the appetite is determined by the thing's natural form. The second level of appetite is found in beings endowed with sense cognition. In such beings—the brute animals—there is a tending or inclination that follows upon cognition; the animals respond appetitively to stimuli received through the senses (including the internal senses). Aquinas calls this kind of appetite "sensitive appetite." It is here at the level of the sense appetite that Thomas first postulates a distinct appetitive power of the soul, for the inclination or tendency experienced by the animal is not simply the result of its natural form but rather arises upon the apprehension of some object (Ia, q. 80, aa. 1–2). Just how the appetite responds to the apprehended object depends, in the case of animals, on their natural instincts, what Aquinas refers to as the "natural judgment" (*iudicium naturale*) of the "estimative power" (Ia, q. 83, a. 1).[6]

The third level of appetite is "rational appetite," that found in beings endowed with reason. As in the previous two levels, there is an internal source of motion, a tending or inclination, but here the good can be apprehended at the level of intellect—grasped under some universal formality of goodness—and so the agent can tend toward the good by means of an appetite distinct from sensitive appetite. Thomas nicely summarizes the three levels while discussing the angelic will:

> Some things incline toward the good with only a natural relationship to it and without cognition, as is the case with plants and inanimate bodies. Such an inclination is called "natural appetite." Some things, however, incline toward the good with a certain cognition, not such that they know the intelligibility (*ratio*) itself of the good, but they know some particular good, like the power of sense which knows the sweet thing and the white thing or something of this sort. The inclination which follows this cognition is called "sensitive appetite." Some things incline toward the good with a cognition by which they know the intelligibility (*ratio*) itself of the good, and this is proper to intellect. And these things tend most perfectly toward the good, not as if merely directed by another toward the good like those things which lack cognition, nor only toward particular goods like those things in which there is only sense cognition, but as if inclined toward the universal good itself. And this inclination is called "will."[7] (Ia, q. 59, a. 1)

The nature of the will as a rational appetite can be clarified through comparison with the sensitive appetite. The two appetites are similar in that, first, both follow upon apprehension and, second, both are distinct powers of the soul as opposed to natural inclination which simply follows upon a natural form. Third, both are appetites of the whole being and not simply of one part. In an objection against positing any distinct appetitive powers, Thomas entertains the argument that every power of the soul already has a natural appetite for its own object: hearing for sounds, sight for colors, the intellect for truth, and so on. Hence it seems superfluous to posit, over and above these powers, another appetitive power whose object is the

desirable taken generally (*appetibile in communi*). To this objection, Thomas responds that while it is indeed the case that each power, being a certain form or nature, has a natural inclination to its own object, there is still the need for an appetite following upon apprehension by which the animal tends toward objects not just as suitable to a particular power, but as suitable *to the animal simply or as a whole* (Ia, q. 80, a. 1, ad 3).[8]

It now becomes evident that both the sensitive appetite and the rational appetite, as distinct appetitive powers, are powers by which the being that possesses them tends toward that which is good for that being as such; these appetites are appetites of the whole and not simply of any one part. In the case of the will, this point implies that whenever a person wills, one wills that which is good (at least apparently) for oneself as a whole. Even if the good willed is the object of another power as, for example, when someone wills to acquire some truth, that object is willed as being good not just for that other power but as good for the whole person. In willing to pursue this truth, the person is implicitly saying that on the whole, he or she will be better off with this truth than without it. The will, then, *by its very nature as an appetite*, is ordained to the perfection of the person in which it is found, just as the sensitive appetite is ordained to the perfection of the animal in which it is found. In fact, it is impossible to will anything at all that is not taken to be a part of or means to the perfection of the willing person.

While similar, the will and the sensitive appetite are nevertheless different in important ways. These differences follow from the basic difference in the types of apprehension. Sense knowledge, for Aquinas, is always of singulars as such. On the other hand it is proper to intellectual knowledge to grasp universals and to grasp any singular thing under the formality of a universal: as "dog," or as "cat," or as "warm," or as "friendly," and so on. Thus, while the sensitive appetites tend toward particular things that are perceived by the senses to be sensibly pleasant or painful, the will tends toward things insofar as they are seen at the rational level to be good; whatever is willed is taken *as good*, as falling under the formality of the good as such and usually under some more specific formality such as the honest good, the pleasant good, or the useful good.[9] As a result of this difference between the apprehensive powers, a person can will a good which cannot be the object of a sense power, as for example, in willing to understand the Pythagorean Theorem. It also is possible that the same object, taken materially, be the object of both the sense appetites and the will. But here the formality under which it is desired is not the same for the two appetites. For example, I may desire to eat an apple at the sense level simply because at the sense level it appears sensibly pleasant. But at the level of rational appetite, I can will to eat the apple because I understand it to be healthy or as a way to please a friend who has offered it to me. In these latter cases, I will to eat the apple, but under some intellectually grasped formality such as "healthy" or "pleasing to my friend" (Ia, q. 80, a. 2, ad 2). For Thomas, as I will demonstrate, it is also this necessarily universal aspect of the willed object that underlies the will's freedom of choice, a freedom not found in the sensitive appetites.

This universal aspect of the will's object, especially the universal good (*bonum universale*; *bonum in commune*), also enables the will to be the appetite of the whole person, what we might call a "personal appetite." Whatever the will wills, it wills as being somehow good, in technical terms, as falling under the formality of good (*sub ratione boni*). Any and all goods of the person, even if they are first objects of other powers, thus become objects of the will. The will, consequently, plays an integrative role with respect to the acts of all the other powers of the soul. All the goods that are objects of the other powers (for example, truth, sensible pleasures, bodily motions) need to be integrated into the overall good of the person. The will carries out this integration by commanding the acts of the other powers. It is by will that a person decides whether or not to engage in those acts at all, and if so, to what extent, when, where, etc. (Ia IIae, q. 9, a. 1). Of course, this control is not absolute; there are some powers (for example, the vegetative powers of growth and nutrition) outside the will's control, and others, like the sensitive appetites, have motions of their own apart from being commanded by the will. Nevertheless, even the latter cannot bring about actions of the person as such except by the per-

mission of the will (Ia, q. 81, a. 3). It is therefore by the will that a given person integrates all the partial human goods into his overall good. It follows, as an immediate consequence, that the person as a whole is said to be good or evil on the basis of the will; one is said to be good simply (*simpliciter*)—morally good—when one's will is properly oriented toward the good (Ia, q. 48, a. 6).[10]

Thomas's doctrine that the will always seeks the good or perfection of the willer and integrates all partial goods into that larger good may lead to a certain misunderstanding. As discussed above, an appetitive power is directed to the good or perfection of the being in which it is found, and so one might infer that all beings, and especially human beings, are naturally egoistic and seek always and in everything exclusively their own individual good. It may even seem that it is impossible to tend toward any good except one's own good, and that every good that is willed is willed as directed to one's own individual good. But this is not, in fact, Thomas's view, for he maintains that one's good is not limited to one's individual good but can include the good of other beings outside oneself. It is indeed true for him that each thing seeks its own individual perfection, but it seeks even more the good of its species, and yet more the good of the whole universe. For example, when the mother exposes herself to danger for the sake of her offspring as is common among the animals, it is clear that the preservation of the species takes precedence over the good of the individual. And since each species is for the sake of the universe as a whole, the individual seeks the common good of the universe above all else. Individual beings are all parts of the larger whole that is the universe and as such they naturally should find their perfection not primarily in their own individual good but rather in the perfection of that whole (Ia, q. 60, a. 5, ad 3; Ia IIae, q. 109, a. 3). Thus, to say that appetite is necessarily directed to a being's perfection does not mean at all that beings, especially human beings, are self-seeking individualists. This point is crucial for Thomas's understanding of appetite in general and the will in particular.

In sum, the will is the power by which a rational being tends toward its proper good or perfection. In this sense, the will is rational appetite. But insofar as rational beings have control over their actions, the rational appetite can also be taken as free choice. And so we can succinctly define the will as the power or capacity by which a rational being—a person—freely directs his actions to his good or perfection.

NATURE AND FREEDOM IN THE WILL'S ACTS

As I have shown, when the will is taken precisely as the source of free choices it is called *free-will*. Whether or not human agents possess the power to choose freely is not a question that Thomas treats at any great length, since he considers it obvious that humans engage in actions they could do otherwise or not do at all. As he says in *De veritate*, it is manifest that man freely chooses one thing and rejects another (Ia, q. 24, a. 1). The closest Thomas comes to proving the existence of free acts is to defend them negatively, that is, to point out the consequences of denying their existence. To deny free action, action in the power of the agent, is tantamount to denying morality itself and all moral philosophy: "If there is nothing free in us but we are moved necessarily to will, then we destroy deliberation, exhortation, precepts and punishments, and praise and blame, the very things with which moral philosophy deals."[11] What is more, we also remove the possibility of merit and demerit, so that from the theological point of view such a position is heretical. Thomas classes the denial of free action among the "extraneous opinions" of philosophy, opinions that deny the possibility of a particular science by denying its very subject matter.[12] Thomas's usual concern, then, when he deals with free actions, is not whether they exist, but rather how they exist. That is, he analyzes the structure of the cognitive and appetitive powers required for such actions. It is this analysis that leads to the distinction between the will's free acts and its natural acts.

Among the free acts of the will, the principle one is choice (*electio*), for it is by choice that a person actually commits himself to one action or another. Before the choice, there is deliberation about what is to be done but not yet the doing of the act; after choice, there is the execution of the chosen act. Only in the

act of choice itself does a person effectively determine himself to the pursuit of some particular good. But choice, for Aquinas, has a determinate structure. Following Aristotle's analysis, Thomas holds that choice is always of means to an end. In the light of an end to be achieved, a person chooses among at least two possible means. Thus reference to an end is essential to the structure of choice, since it is only in light of an end that one can choose between the possible means; the means chosen is that which somehow promises better to achieve the given end. Hence, choice always has these three elements: a given end to be achieved and (at least) two possible means to achieve it. The two possible means may be two different acts (radiation versus chemotherapy to treat a cancer), or may simply be the options of acting versus not acting (treating the cancer versus not treating it at all; Ia IIae, q. 13, a. 3).

In the act of choice, the person who chooses is actually willing both the chosen means and the end for the sake of which it is chosen. As we shall see below, Thomas calls the willing of the end "intention." Every act of choice, consequently, necessarily presupposes an act of intention. How, then, does it happen that a person comes to will the particular end he intends in a given choice? It is this question that leads to the will's natural acts. It may be that the end now intended is being intended because of a previous choice. Someone may now be choosing between the train and the airplane because of a previous choice to go to Chicago. Here again, however, there had to be some end that influenced the choice to go to Chicago. On what basis is that further end intended? It may be a yet earlier choice, but it quickly becomes clear that this process cannot go on infinitely. There must be some end that a person wills, not as the result of any choice but prior to all choices (Ia IIae, q. 1, aa. 4–6; q. 13, a. 3).

The act of the will that precedes and underlies all choices is, according to Thomas, the will's "natural appetite" or "natural inclination." Just as in the demonstrations of science there must be some first principles to which the intellect naturally assents, so too among the acts of the will there must be some act(s) in which the will is moved naturally and not in the mode of *free-will*, that is, acts wherein the will has no power to act otherwise (Ia, q. 82, a. 1, ad 3; Ia IIae, q. 1, a. 5; q. 10, a. 1). Moreover, as the above line of reasoning implies, the first object of the will, as first, must be the end to which the objects of all other acts of the will are directed (Ia, q. 60, a. 2). This object is, according to Thomas, the last end (*finis ultimus*) or beatitude (*beatitudo*). Whatever a person may choose, he or she necessarily chooses it as somehow contributing to his or her goodness or perfection, and beatitude is the name given to that state in which a person possesses her or his good completely or perfectly, the state in which no good due to her or his nature is lacking and no inclination of the will is unsatisfied (Ia IIae, q. 1, a. 6).[13]

That the object of the will's natural appetite or inclination should be the good that constitutes that person's perfection is perfectly consistent with the notion of the will as an appetitive power. It belongs, as I said earlier, to the nature of appetite to be directed to the good or perfection of the being in which it exists. Accordingly, the most basic inclination of the appetite is toward the complete good or perfection of that being. But the fact that the will is *rational* appetite adds another dimension to this natural inclination, viz., that the inclination's object is not any specific form of beatitude, but simply beatitude in general (Ia IIae, q. 1, a. 7; q. 5, a. 8). As I pointed out earlier, the mark of rational cognition is that it can grasp universals, and, as a natural consequence, rational appetite is directed to generalities, especially the good in general and to particular goods as falling under the desired generality. In the case at hand, the will's natural inclination is directed toward the ultimate end or beatitude in general: "there is put into man an appetite for his last end in general (*appetitus ultimi finis sui in communi*), that is, he naturally desires to be complete in goodness."[14] Whether a person seeks his beatitude in some particular good such as bodily pleasure, knowledge, or God is a matter of free choice. By his natural inclination a person wills simply to be fulfilled or happy: all people "wish to have their perfection fulfilled which is the intelligibility (*ratio*) of the last end" (Ia IIae, q. 1, a. 7).[15]

It is important to emphasize here that the object of the will's natural inclination is not some specific good but a general formality, since this fact provides the ultimate basis for the will's freedom. In this vein, Thomas raises an interesting objection in the context of discussing the will's natural inclination. According to the objection, the will cannot have any natural motion since nature—what occurs always or for the most part—is determined to one (*determinata ad unum*), while the will is open to opposites (*se habet ad opposita*). To have a natural motion, then, would seem to be against the very nature of the will. Thomas replies that nature is indeed always ordered to some one thing, but that that one thing is proportionate to the nature in question. Since the will is a rational appetite and reason is open to universals or generalities, it follows that the one to which the will is determined in its natural motion is also something general (*aliquod unum commune*). This something general is nothing other than the good in general. But a universal of this sort can contain within it many particulars; there are many particular goods that fit within the good taken in general. And so, Thomas concludes, the will, while naturally determined to the good in general, is not determined by nature to any of the particular goods. With respect to them it remains free (q. 10, a. 1, ad 3).

This is Thomas's most fundamental explanation for the will's freedom and its basis in the natural inclination. Because the will tends toward beatitude in general or toward the perfect good in general, it remains free with respect to any specific form of beatitude or good. Each person must choose what specific good will be, for him, his ultimate end, and precisely this choice is the most fundamental of all moral choices (q. 89, a. 6). All subsequent choices made in light of the ultimate end have a similar structure; therefore, they too are free. In each case the will (as rational appetite) is directed first to some generality, and then, by deliberation, seeks the instantiation that best fits that generality. In *De malo*, Thomas presents this reasoning in its clearest form:

an understood form is a universal under which many things can be comprehended. And since acts take place among singulars, in which there is nothing that is adequate to a universal power, the inclination of the will remains undetermined with respect to many, just as, when an architect conceives the form of a house universally, under which different shapes of houses are contained, his will can incline toward making a square house or toward making a round house or a house of another shape.[16]

Thomas's example can, it seems, be taken as representative of how choices are made. There is some good that is desired under a general formality; a particular good is then selected which best instantiates or embodies the desired good. So, for example, a woman wishes to travel to Chicago, and consequently looks for a means to do so. At this point, she desires a general good: a-way-to-travel-to-Chicago. After investigating the possible ways, that is, the particulars that fit under this universal, she chooses that one which seems best to instantiate the good she is seeking. This good may be complex, including many elements such as cost, ease, speed, among others, but it remains the case that she wills this complex good first in general and then finds, by deliberation, the particular instance that best embodies that complex good. Thomas gives clear expression to this understanding of willing when he says, in *De veritate*, that the will tends directly toward the reason for the desirability (*ratio appetibilitatis*) such as goodness or utility and only secondarily toward this or that thing insofar as it participates in the reason for the desirability.[17]

The only object, then, that the will necessarily intends is beatitude in general. This is true, however, only in the present life. According to Thomas, the will also moves naturally toward God when, in the next life, under the influence of grace, it is presented with the vision of God's essence. His reasoning is that, in seeing God, the will is presented with the perfect good, the good that contains all possible goodness. Since the universal good is the natural object of the will, the will, when presented with it, moves toward it naturally (Ia, q. 62, a. 8). Under the conditions of the present life, however, one does not grasp God in this fashion. It is possible then to think that one's good is to be found outside of God; therefore, it is also possible not to will (love) God (q. 82, a. 2). Other than these two objects, beatitude in general and God seen in His essence, all objects are willed freely, that is,

they must be chosen. Thomas refers to these "other" objects as particular goods, that is, goods that do not contain in themselves all goodness. He also refers to them as means to the end (*ea quae sunt ad finem*), because a person wills any such good as a way or means to achieve his beatitude. Thus Thomas commonly states that the will necessarily wills the good in general or beatitude and has freedom of choice with respect to particular goods or the means to the end (Ia IIae, q. 13, a. 6).[18]

The analysis of free action does not end with showing how the will's free acts are based on its natural act. Thomas goes a step further and within the free act describes two distinct ways in which necessity or lack of necessity can be present: in the "exercise" of the act and in its "specification."

The distinction between "exercise" and "specification," one that Thomas used increasingly over the course of his career, is not peculiar to the will.[19] It actually applies to almost any power of the soul, especially in rational beings, who possess other powers that can be exercised by the will. Generally speaking, exercise refers to the fact that a power is actually eliciting an act; to take the power of sight, for example, to say the power is exercised is to say there is an act of seeing. Specification, on the other hand, refers to the act's being directed to one object or another. In the act of seeing, the seeing will be directed to this object or that object. "Specification" is used because Thomas believes that actions are the kind of actions they are—are specified—by the objects at which they aim. This distinction between exercise and specification should not be understood as one between two different acts that could occur separately or even two acts that are always together; rather, they are two aspects of a single act. The act of the power is at once exercised and specified (Ia IIae, q. 9, a. 1).

What interests Thomas in this distinction is the difference in the sources or causes of an act's exercise and of its specification. The specification of the act comes from the side of the object. To continue with the example of sight, what a person sees is determined by the object in front of him. Exercise, on the other hand, has its source in the agent. Whether or not someone has an act of seeing depends upon that person. This is especially the case in beings endowed with a will. The object of the will, as we have seen, is the good in general which contains, so to speak, all particular goods. The acts of all powers are particular goods and as such fall within the will's all-embracing object. Consequently, the will has the capacity to exercise or not exercise the acts of the other powers (ibid.). This is the basis for the will's integrative function.

One will also find this distinction between exercise and specification located in the will itself. The will's act is specified by its object. And since the will is a *rational* appetite, its object is supplied to it by reason. Consequently, Thomas says that the will's act is specified by the intellect. In this way, by providing it with its object, the intellect is said to move the will. This "movement" occurs in the order of formal causality (ibid.). On the other hand, in the line of exercise—efficient causality—the will moves itself. Apart from the will's first natural act, which comes from God, the will exercises its own act, just as it exercises the acts of the other powers. Whether or not there will be an act of the will with respect to any particular object lies with the will itself (Ia IIae, q. 9, aa. 3–6). This power of the will to move itself is crucial to Thomas's account of the will's freedom, for it provides the basis for a person's capacity to refuse to will any good.

It is now possible to describe Thomas's understanding of the interrelationship of the intellect and the will, another pivotal point for understanding Thomas's theory of the will. The intellect is said to move the will in that it specifies the will's act by providing the will its object (Ia IIae, q. 9, a. 1).[20] The will, on the other hand, is able to move the intellect by exercising the intellect's act; that a person thinks at all or even thinks about one object or another (this is called consideration) depends upon the will. At any point, the will can move the intellect to think about some object or to stop thinking about it altogether. Still, the specification of the intellect's act comes from the object; therefore, what one concludes as true about a particular object when one considers it might not be dependent on the will. In the case of the intellect's assent to first principles and the conclusions of scientific demonstrations, for example, if there is willed consideration of these propositions, there is natural assent (Ia IIae, q. 17, a. 6).[21] This power of the will to exercise the intellect's act

is important for the question of whether Thomas's "intellectualist" understanding of the will falls into the trap of intellectual determinism. Precisely because the will can control whether or not a possible act will be considered or even from which point of view it will be considered, the presentation of the intellectually understood object to the will becomes itself a voluntary matter (Ia IIae, q. 6, a. 7, ad 3; q. 10, aa. 2–3).

I will return now to the question of freedom and necessity in the will's acts. Thomas discusses this question both in terms of the will exercising its act and in terms of the specification of that act. What sort of necessity is there, then, with respect to the exercise of the will's act? Is there any act that the will must necessarily exercise? To this, Thomas says no. It may seem that for a given object, there must necessarily be some act either toward or away from it, and, in this sense, the will must exercise its act. But since the will's act depends upon the intellect's presentation of the object, and because the will can command the act of the intellect, it is possible, for any given proposed act, simply to will to cease thinking about the object and so to obviate all acts in its regard.[22] This can occur, says Thomas, even if the object is beatitude itself. Since the act of thinking about beatitude is only a particular good, it is possible for the will to choose not to engage in it, that is, not to command the thinking, and then there will simply be no act of the will in regard to beatitude. In this way, then, the will remains free with respect to the exercise of any of its acts (Ia IIae, q. 10, a. 2).

With regard to specification, the issue is more complicated. The sort of necessity in question here is the following: for a given object of the will, can it be either approved (i.e. loved, desired, rejoiced in) or disapproved (hated, rejected, sorrowed over), or must it necessarily be only one of these? For example, with an object such as an act of adultery, it may be desired as being pleasant, yet it may also be rejected as being contrary to the law of God. So too, the good work of a colleague may be cause for rejoicing because it helps the whole firm or may be cause for sorrow because that colleague might receive more honor than I. In such cases, Thomas argues, there is no necessity present in the way in which the will's act is specified. The same object can be willed in various ways depending upon how the object is considered. If there were, however, some object that was good and desirable from all points of view, then it would not be possible to will that object in just any way, but only to love, desire, or rejoice in it.

Thomas points to two such objects. First, there is beatitude considered in general. Because the very concept of beatitude is to possess all the good of which one is capable while lacking no good, such an object cannot be seen in any way other than as good. It is not possible to think of beatitude and not desire or rejoice in it. It is of course, as I have said, possible not to think of it and so exercise no act in its regard, but if one thinks of it one will desire it. Second, there is God seen in the divine essence as occurs in the beatific vision (*visio beatifica*). Here again, it will be evident that all good that is to be found anywhere besides God is found more perfectly in God; and, that all possible goodness is to be found there. The willer thus sees that his or her total good is to be found in God and nowhere else, and so there is no possible reason to reject God. Apart from these two objects, however, all objects can possibly be seen as evil, if only because pursuing them conflicts with the attainment of some other good. Thus, for all other objects, there is no necessity in willing them either from the point of view of exercising the will's act in their regard, or tending toward or away from them if there is such an act (ibid.; *De malo*, q. 6).

Before leaving the topic of the will's free and natural acts, it is necessary to take up another set of acts of the will which Thomas describes as being natural. There are, he says, certain objects of the will besides beatitude or the good in general toward which the will naturally tends, in some cases even with a certain necessity. These are goods which are particular in the sense of not being themselves the good which wholly beatifies, but they are seen to have a necessary connection with beatitude. The clearest description of these goods comes in the *Prima secundae*, in which Thomas delineates the objects which move the will naturally:

This [what is willed naturally] is the good in general toward which the will naturally tends just like any power toward its own object; and

also the final end itself which stands among appetible objects in the same way as the first principles of demonstration among intelligibles; and universally all those things which are suitable to the willer according to his nature. For we desire by our will not only those things that pertain to the power of the will, but even those which pertain to the individual powers and to the man as a whole. Whence man naturally wills not only the object of the will, but also other objects which are suitable to the other powers, such as the knowledge of the truth, and existing and living and other things of this sort that have to do with one's natural well being. All these things are comprehended under the object of the will as so many particular goods.[23] (Ia IIae, q. 10, a. 1)

The general principle here is that a person naturally wills whatever is suitable (*conveniens*) to human nature. Human nature being complex, many distinct goods are included. The first are the objects of all the other powers besides the will. Each power naturally tends toward its object, as for example, the intellect naturally tends toward the truth, and the sense appetites toward what is sensibly pleasant. As objects of these powers and of the powers' natural inclinations, such things are naturally seen as perfective and as contributing to the general good or beatitude of the person. Thus upon their being apprehended, there spontaneously arises in the will an approving stance, either joy if the good is present or desire if it is absent. For example, when someone becomes aware of one's own ignorance of some point of knowledge, he or she spontaneously desires to have that knowledge. This does not necessarily mean that one will actively seek to acquire the knowledge, but only that there is a spontaneous motion of the will toward it that is not an act of *free-will*. Second, any good that is good for the person as a whole and seen as such will be naturally willed. Thomas gives as examples existing and living. Another might be something like health, which is not the object of a particular power but a condition of well-being for the person as a whole. These too are spontaneously approved by the will either by an act of joy if it is present or desire if it is absent.

One way to express the natural quality of this motion is to say that it is not an act of *free-will*, that is, the will does not move in these cases because it has chosen to do so. These things are willed naturally in the sense that the will spontaneously moves toward them upon their being apprehended. So long as a thing is seen to pertain to one's beatitude or one's perfection, there will be a movement of the will toward it (IIIa q. 18, aa. 3–6). The necessity of this movement has to do with the connection a good has with beatitude. If the good is seen to be necessary for beatitude (for example, existing), then it will be willed necessarily. Nonetheless, the kind of necessity with which such goods are willed is not the same as the necessity with which beatitude is willed. Beatitude is necessarily or absolutely willed because it belongs to the very structure of the will; the desire arises immediately from the very nature of the will. These other goods, by contrast, are willed on the basis of the prior willing of the end, beatitude. Their necessity is, in Thomas's language, the "necessity of the end" (*necessitas finis*), the kind of necessity a thing has when it is a means without which an end cannot be achieved. If the end is desired, it is necessary that this means be desired. And so here, since beatitude is necessarily willed, whatever is seen as required for beatitude will be willed with the necessity of the end (Ia, q. 82, a. 1).

Does it then follow that all such objects are necessarily pursued by the willer? This is not the case. In order to see why, I will discuss the various acts of the will. Having clarified these according to Thomas's descriptions, I will be in a position to explain more completely the natural willing of particular goods.

THE ACTS OF THE WILL

For Thomas, a person does not achieve beatitude by a single act; consequently the moral life consists of many acts of the will together with the external acts arising from them. With God and the angels, it is otherwise. For God, beatitude is identical with essence and no further actualization of a potency, that is, no operation is required in order to attain beatitude. For the angels, on the other hand, just one act is required in which the angel's will is suitably disposed toward beatitude. For human beings, however, many acts over a period of time are required (Ia IIae, q. 5, a. 7). Moreover, these acts differ not only numerically but also in kind. In the *Prima secundae*, qq. 8–17, Thomas

presents a very highly developed theory of the various kinds of will-acts, an understanding of which is necessary if one is to grasp his picture of the moral life. All these acts, as acts of the will, are appetitive motions of the person as a whole; they are the strivings, aversions, rests, and so on of the person. It is precisely through these appetitive motions, especially those that are free, that each person determines himself with respect to goods and evils.

There are many distinctions to be drawn among these acts of the will. The most prominent in Thomas's treatment is that between acts ordered to ends (*simple willing, intention,* and *enjoyment*) and those ordered to means (*choice, consent,* and *use*).[24] There is, in addition, a distinction between the acts that are deliberate and free, arising from *free-will,* and those that are natural or spontaneous and not the result of deliberate choice (IIIa, q. 18, aa. 3–6). There is also a distinction between acts of the will directed to goods not yet possessed and acts directed to possessed goods. This distinction should not be overlooked, for it means that "willing" refers not just to acts directed to the acquisition or achievement of goods or bringing about states of affairs that do not yet obtain, but also rejoicing in goods or being sad about evils.[25] Finally, some of the acts occur in what Thomas calls the order of intention, the affective tending toward goods in which ends precede means, while others occur in the order of execution, the willing of the exterior acts by which the desired good is actually achieved or possessed wherein means precede ends (Ia IIae, q. 1, a. 4; q. 16, a. 4).

Aquinas's understanding of the will-acts is not properly seen by taking isolated acts of the will, but rather by seeing each act in its relation to several other acts. In general, Aquinas sees the relationships of these several acts of the will as parallel to the relationship among their objects. Those objects, goods of one kind or another (or evils to be avoided), are related to one another as means and ends. These means and ends are grouped together into what I will call "chains" of ends; lower links of the chain are goods sought as means for the sake of higher links, which in their turn are sought as means to yet higher ends (Ia IIae, q. 12, a. 2). If we start at a given point on the chain we can go "up" the chain toward some end sought for its own sake or "down" the chain toward goods sought only as means to other ends. In neither direction is it possible to proceed to infinity (Ia IIae, q. 1, a. 4).

Suppose, for example, that a woman learns that her elderly mother in Chicago has become ill and needs to be looked after. The woman decides (chooses) to go and help her mother recover. What end is she pursuing? By virtue of the love of friendship she has for her mother, she considers her mother to be another self, and, consequentially, she considers her mother's welfare to be part of her own (Ia IIae, q. 28, a. 2). Thus, her own good or beatitude includes the health and general well-being of her mother. On Aquinas's view, then, she may have a yet further end. She may love her mother with supernatural charity and so love her mother as ordered to God who is then the ultimate end loved by the woman. This is Aquinas's doctrine that all human friendships can be ordered to the love of charity (IIa IIae, q. 26, a. 7). The woman loves God as the ultimate end in which her beatitude is to be found. These situations represent the "higher" links of the chain, all of which concern beatitude, the ultimate end.

If we go downwards from the decision to go to Chicago, the woman must decide what form of transportation to take. Supposing she decides to fly, she must now choose an airline; to do this, she must call her travel agent; for this, she must find the telephone number and then actually make the call. At each step the person deliberates about what is necessary to achieve the good and then chooses the appropriate means until reaching the point at which exterior action is possible. Up to this point all the willing occurs in the order of intention. Once this point is reached, however, the person begins to execute the choices that have been made (Ia IIae, q. 16, a. 4).

We should also note that in fact there are many other chains descending from the choice to go to Chicago. The woman may have to prepare many things for her family (another set of persons she loves with love of friendship) to provide for her absence; she will have to pack her luggage with all the choices that entails; she will have to make her way to the airport, requiring yet another chain of means and ends. Each person is always caught up in any number of such chains, so that at times the same act may serve as a means to more than one end or what serves one end may hinder another (Ia IIae, q. 12, a. 3). It is in this larger context that a person chooses the various means and ends. Aquinas, however, in treating the different acts of the will (and in generally analyzing moral action) tends to simplify matters, and, for the sake of analytic clarity, often looks at choices or other acts of the will without describing the whole context in which they take place. It is always important to keep this fact in mind, for otherwise there is a danger of taking Aquinas's teaching too abstractly.

At the heart of Thomas's scheme lies the act of choice. From the moral point of view, the most significant acts are those in which the will, taken as *free-will*, exercises dominion over its own act. Such acts are proper to the will *as will* (q. 10, a. 1, ad 1). Thomas also says that what one wills in the mode of *free-will* one wills *simpliciter* (IIIa, q. 21, a. 4). Choice, as the act of *free-will*, is the most significant act from the moral point of view, and, as such, it is the first act to consider.

Choice (*Electio*)

Choice, as we have seen, has the following structure. A person must determine himself to one of two (or more) possible actions. He so determines himself in the light of some end for the sake of which one or the other of the prospective actions is chosen (Ia IIae, q. 13, a. 3). Following Aristotle, Thomas maintains that the object of choice is always some possible action. It is possible or at least taken as possible, for no one chooses what one knows to be impossible (Ia IIae, q. 13, a. 5). It is an action (an *agibile*) for whenever one chooses something other than an action, one is in fact choosing to have or to use that thing by means of an action (Ia IIae, q. 13, a. 4). So, for example, if one chooses to eat apples instead of oranges, one is choosing the eating of the former over the eating of the latter; if one chooses a car, one is choosing to drive that car; if one votes for an individual or body to exercise authority, one is choosing to obey that person or body.

The chosen action is, as I have said, a means to an end. That end is, first, the good immediately above it on the chain of means and ends, but it also includes all ends up to and including beatitude. At any given stage on the chain, the means needed to achieve the higher stages are chosen. But if these means themselves require some other means for their achievement, then a further choice at the next lower level is required. This series of choices proceeds until a point is reached at which all the means are decided upon and only execution is required. Therefore, choice occurs anytime the means to achieve an end (ultimate or mediate) are not yet fixed. In order to fix these means, there is, prior to each choice, a deliberation, a process of thinking about the possible means and judging their relative advantages and disadvantages (Ia IIae, q. 14).

At each point on the chain, a person is determining him or herself, and, with each choice, the person becomes affectively committed to some good. This commitment to a good occurs in the order of intention, which is distinct from the order of execution. These two orders work in different directions. In the order of intention, what is first is the last end, and the higher an end is on the chain of ends, the more priority it has. In the order of execution, by contrast, what is lower is what is first accomplished and only at the end of the activity is the ultimate goal achieved. An important consequence of this distinction between the two orders is that, in temporal terms, a choice is very often made quite some time before it is finally executed. The woman makes the choice to go to Chicago several days before she actually goes. This does not mean that the choice is not real; it simply means that a person can determine oneself to an action long before actually carrying it out (for example, scheduling a doctor's appointment). The gap between making a choice and executing the action chosen does allow that a person can retract a choice before (or even while) carrying it out. This occurs whenever a person ceases to will the previously willed action.

Intention (*Intentio*)

Unlike choice, intention is directed to ends and not to means. It is, however, intimately linked to choice, for wherever there is choice there is also intention. The reason for this is that, in any choice, there is a concomitant willing of the end. And in this case, the end is being willed precisely as that which is to be achieved by the chosen means. This is exactly how Thomas defines intention: the act of the will directed to an end taken as the terminus of the means ordered to it (Ia IIae, q. 12, a. 1, ad 3). So, to return to the earlier example, in buying her ticket, the woman is intending to go to Chicago.

If one thinks of the chain of means and ends, it should be clear that at any link in the chain, all the goods above it are intended. When the woman buys her ticket, she is intending not just to go to Chicago, but also to care for her mother, to have her mother once again healthy, and ultimately her happiness. It should also be clear that any given link, while itself a chosen act, becomes an intended end with respect to the further choices made in order to achieve it. If one considers the choice to call the travel agent, buying the ticket now becomes the intended end. So, the notions of end and means and the corresponding notions of intention and choice are fluid; the willing of an action is a choice when seen in relation to what is above it, but is an intention when seen in relation to what is below it. In this case, there are not two distinct acts of willing to buy the ticket; rather, there is only one act, but it is viewed from different angles (q. 12, a. 2).

It should also be clear that acts of intention are the result of a choice. It is because the woman chooses to buy the ticket that buying the ticket becomes the intended end of her choice to call the travel agent. And this is how it normally occurs in one's voluntary actions: one chooses some action and then proceeds to choose means to accomplish it. It is only the ultimate end, beatitude in general, that is intended without having first been chosen. As I have shown, all other goods, including the specific instantiation of beatitude that a person takes as his own, must be chosen. Once again, then, the centrality of the act of choice is clear. Save for beatitude in general, the intending of any goal or end is the consequence of a free choice, and for this reason, intention is usually an exercise of *free-will* and an essential part of the moral action for which a person is held responsible.[26]

As a final point with respect to intention, I should note that intentions can be of various durations—at times, of quite long duration. For example, a student who decides to earn a bachelor's degree intends that end for at least four years, making during that time a multitude of choices toward that end. During that period, however, the person is only occasionally thinking explicitly about the bachelor's degree. Nevertheless, the person is intending that goal throughout the whole time; the intention of that end is animating much if not all that the person does. For this reason, Thomas distinguishes between actually willing an end and intending the end habitually (Ia IIae, q. 1, a. 6, ad 3). This distinction is important, for it allows one to recognize that intentions can persist for long periods of time (for example, fidelity to one's spouse); it also demonstrates how it is possible that a person, while willing only one thing at a time actually, can have many simultaneous willings. All the choices that a person makes and which have not been completely executed exist in the willer in the habitual form. Here again, one encounters a complexity in the life of the will that Thomas usually leaves aside for the sake of analytic simplicity.

Simple Willing (*Simplex voluntas*)

A second act of the will that is directed to the end is what Thomas calls "will" or "willing" (*voluntas* or *velle*). As he points out, the word *voluntas* refers both to the power of the will and to a specific act of the will, the act which he refers to as "simple willing." A power, Thomas says, receives its name from its most proper act, and that act is the one directed to the power's most proper object. Now the object of the will is the good, and, the means being good only by their relation to the end, the end has more the character of good than the means. The act called "will" is therefore that of simply willing the end (Ia IIae, q. 8, a. 2).[27]

How is this act different from the act of intention? The difference lies in the fact that intention is not "simple." Intention is not directed to the end *simply*, but rather to the end *as that which will be achieved by means*. Or, expressed less formally, in intending an end a person is committed to actually carrying out the actions needed to achieve that end. Simple willing, on the other hand, is simply the willing of some good as perfective of me (or those united to me by love) without any necessary reference to whether I intend actually to acquire that good. To take an example, for years I may want—taken as something that would be good for me—to go see Paris. During those years, I never do anything about actually going there. This is simple willing. But suppose that I finally decide actually to go; I am now *ipso facto* committed to employing all the means necessary for this trip. At this point, I *intend* to go to Paris. Clearly, simple willing precedes intention, since one would not intend an end if one did not first have this simple desire to possess it. But at the same time, to will an end by intending it signifies a much greater personal commitment; a person who intends an end is personally committed to its achievement. This is not the case with simple willings (Ia IIae, q. 12, a. 1, ad 4).[28]

The simple willings include the spontaneous, natural willings I described earlier in speaking of the will's natural acts. These willings, as we saw, are directed first to beatitude and second to all the other things which a person spontaneously grasps as suitable (*conveniens*) to his nature and thereby contributing to beatitude.[29] A spontaneous willing arises upon the apprehension of some suitable good; hence, to say that a simple willing is natural does not mean that all persons have it nor that a given person always has it. For example, according to Thomas, parents naturally love their children—have a desire for what is good for them—while children naturally love their parents (IIa IIae, q. 26, a 9). However, before being parents they clearly do *not* experience this natural desire for the well-being of their children; nor is everyone a parent. Similarly, Thomas speaks of a natural love for God, but also recognizes that a person does not have such a love until she or he has some knowledge of God. Thus, an instance of a person who does not know or love God does not invalidate his theory of a natural love for God.[30] It seems also that when Thomas speaks of natural inclinations, as he does in the well-known text on the precepts of the natural law (Ia IIae, q. 94, a. 2), these inclinations fit into the category of natural willings. They are not merely movements of the sense appetite (for example, the desire for truth), nor are they the result of deliberate choice; rather, they arise spontaneously. This seems to be exactly what Thomas understands by simple willings.

In contrast to intention, a person need not act on his simple willings. That is to say, many simple willings remain nothing more than that and are never transformed into intentions. To use one of Thomas's examples, a person has a natural revulsion to having a wound cauterized, yet for the sake of health wills the operation nonetheless. This revulsion is not merely a motion of the sense appetite, but also occurs at the level of will. The person, however, does not act upon his will to flee the pain but rather intends the good of health (IIIa, q. 18, a. 5).[31] An unintended simple willing such as this is called at times by Thomas a "velleity" (*velleitas*) (IIIa, q. 21, a. 4). It is important to note the existence of these velleities, for they help to explain questions that seem difficult for Thomas's understanding of the will. For example, at times it seems difficult to understand how a person can act against a natural act of the will. How, for example, can a person commit suicide if there is a natural willing of life? The answer lies in recognizing that the natural willing is an act of simple willing and that such an act is not the same as intention. In suicide, the person stops intending to live. It does not seem, however, that the person ceases willing to live altogether, as is evidenced in the interior resistance to their action that such people experience. So too, when Thomas claims that rational beings naturally love God more than self, this does not mean that sin is impossible. The notion of velleity also helps to explain how a person can be tempted—experience an attraction at the level of will toward an evil—and yet not follow that temptation.[32]

Finally, note that, according to Thomas, what a person is said to will simply (*simpliciter*) is not what one wills by the act of simple willing, but rather what one wills by an act of *free-will*. Precisely as spontaneous and natural, simple willings do not involve the degree of self-determination that is found in choice and intention. To have a simple willing is not to commit oneself to action, whereas both intention and choice do necessarily involve such a commitment. Thomas distinguishes between will as producing natural acts (*voluntas ut natura*) and will as producing acts

by means of rational deliberation and in the power of the one acting (*voluntas ut ratio*). It is only in this latter mode that a person is said to will simply; what is willed in the mode of nature is willed only in a qualified sense (*secundum quid*). Consequently, while *free-will* depends upon the will in the mode of nature, the acts of the will that are the most significant for the moral life are those of *free-will* (IIIa, q. 21, a. 4).[33]

Consent (Consensus)

The act of consent, on Aquinas's account, is very close to choice, indeed at times they are identical. Consent names the "application of the appetitive motion to something preexisting in the power of the one applying it" (Ia IIae, q. 15, a. 3).[34] To consent to something is, like choice, to be affectively related to that thing as something actually to be done. Hence, like choice, consent has to do with means to the end, is directed to what is possible, and follows upon deliberation. Also, like choice, consent is an act of *free-will*, an act in the control of the agent (ibid.). If, out of several possible means to the intended end, only one appears to be suitable, then, says Thomas, consent and choice are one and the same act. To choose that means over the non-suitable ones and to apply the appetitive motion to it are the same act.

At times, however, the two acts are not wholly identical. This occurs when more than one means is suitable. It may happen that the woman in my example could either fly or take a train to Chicago, and that either possibility is agreeable, and even that each has its own advantages. It would be possible here to consent to both as acceptable possibilities, but then a further act of choice would be required by which she would decide upon one as preferable to the other. In this case, the acts of consent and choice would not be identical, and only with the act of choice would the previous act of consent actually yield the action. Choice, then, always implies consent, but consent need not imply choice.[35] What is important for the moral life is the fact of self-determination with regard to the means to one's beatitude, and Thomas sometimes refers to this self-determination to action as consent and at other times as choice.

Use (*Usus*)

Use is the connection between the act of choice and the execution of the chosen action. Simple willing, intention, consent, and choice all occur in the order of intention. By all of these acts the agent becomes affectively ordered to various goods; these acts occur within the agent and make the agent be appetitively oriented to the various goods. Choice is the last act in this order, for by choice a person is committed to pursuing or rejecting some good. The choice, however, must be executed. For example, having chosen to go to Chicago, to fly, and to use a travel agent, there is no need for further choices; rather, only execution is necessary—the woman must pick up the phone and call the agent. Thus, a further act of the will beyond choice is required, one that is found in the order of execution, the order of realizing the action (Ia IIae, q. 16, a. 4). The choice having been made and the time for action having arrived (these are not always simultaneous), other powers of the soul and the body must move in order to perform the action. These motions are not instinctual, but, rather, they are guided by reason and will. It is precisely the willing involved here that receives the name "use," for the will uses or exercises the other powers in order to carry out the chosen action. As discussed in the context of treating the exercise and specification of the will's own act, the will can command or exercise the acts of other powers; precisely when it does this, its act is use (Ia IIae, q. 16, a. 1).

As an act of the will (rational appetite), use necessarily follows upon an act of reason. Thomas gives this act of reason a special name, "command" (*imperium*) (Ia IIae, q. 17, a. 1). Command and use are a pair, command naming the rational component and use the volitional component of the voluntary act by which a power is exercised. If a person walks in a rational way (for example, not sleepwalking), then Thomas would say that there is both an act of command, since the walking is being commanded by reason, and an act of use, since the will is exercising the motive power. There is, however, only one act here, called command when seen from the side of reason and called use when seen from the side of will (Ia IIae, q. 17, a. 3). So the sequence as Thomas describes it is that a choice is made, there is then a command to exercise the appropriate powers for the carrying out of the chosen action, and this command governs—gives formal determination to—the act of use. Ultimately there is the exterior act, such as walking, the act of the other, commanded powers.[36]

Enjoyment (*Fruitio*)

Enjoyment is the act of the will which a person has upon possessing or acquiring a desired end, for example, the joy of the woman upon her mother's recovery of health or even upon the securing of the airplane ticket. Enjoyment occurs at the end of the execution of the action, when the desired good has been made present (Ia IIae, q. 11, a. 1). As Thomas states, "Enjoyment seems to belong to the love or delight which a person has for the last thing he hoped for, that is, the end" (ibid.).[37] This act of the will should be seen in the light of Thomas's larger understanding of the affections of the will. The first of these affections is love, which is directed to a good simply. If the good is absent and not yet possessed there arises the further affection of desire; if the good is possessed there is delight or joy (Ia IIae, q. 25, a. 2).[38] Enjoyment is the joy which is produced in the will when the will's object, the good, is actually possessed.

Enjoyment in the fullest sense occurs with the real possession of the ultimate end (Ia IIae, q. 11, a. 3). Thomas points to two ways in which enjoyment can be imperfect. First, the good can be imperfectly possessed as occurs when the good is not possessed in reality but only in intention, as desired (Ia IIae, q. 11, a. 4). This would be the kind of enjoyment associated with hope. Second, the good desired may be not the final end, but only some good that is a means to the end. Such a good, when possessed, gives rise to enjoyment, but not enjoyment in the most perfect sense. Perfect enjoyment occurs when the final end is really possessed. Obviously for Thomas enjoyment in the fullest sense will occur only with the possession of the last end, God, in the next life (Ia IIae, q. 11, a. 3).

LOVE AS THE FIRST AFFECTION OF THE WILL

In order to complete the Thomistic account of the will's role in the moral life, it is necessary to touch briefly on Thomas's doctrine concerning love (*amor*), especially the love of friendship (*amor amicitiae*), which is the first of all the will's affections and the basis for all its acts. This teaching provides the wider context for understanding the will's various acts as described in Ia IIae, qq. 6–17 and also allows us to see that for Thomas the moral life is essentially a matter of relationships among persons.

Thomas teaches, first, that the primary affection of the appetitive powers, both sense and rational, is love. Love denotes an appetite's most basic relationship to the good; it denotes the fundamental suitability of a being to that which constitutes its good. Thomas refers to love as the proportion (*proportio*) that exists between a being and its good, speaking, for example, of the suitability or proportion of a heavy object to the middle of the earth as love (Ia IIae, q. 26, a. 2). On the basis of such a proportion or suitability, there arise two other affections in the appetite: desire (*desiderium*), when the loved good is not yet possessed, and delight or joy (*delectatio/gaudium*) if the good is possessed. All further appetitive motions toward goods such as hope or fear arise on the basis of desire; all motions toward evils (fear, anger, etc.) arise from hate (*odium*), which in turn is derived from love.[39] The consequence of this doctrine is immediately evident: all motions of the appetitive powers are based on the first and most basic affection of love. In an article asking whether agents do all that they do from love, Thomas states: "I reply that every agent acts for an end. . . . The end however is the good which is loved and desired by each thing. Hence it is clear that every agent, whatever it may be, carries out every action from some love" (Ia IIae, q. 28, a. 6).[40]

Second, Thomas distinguishes love at the rational level by referring to it as "dilection" (*dilectio*) (Ia IIae, q. 26, a. 3). Moreover, he points to a determinate structure found in all dilection, that is, in every love of every will. This structure is expressed by the distinction between love of concupiscence (*amor concupiscentiae*) and love of friendship (*amor amicitiae*).

At the rational level—the level of will—love always takes the form of wanting a good for someone; as Thomas often states, appealing to Aristotle, "to love is to will the good for someone."[41] Accordingly dilection always has two objects, the person who is loved and the good which is wanted for that person. The will's motion toward the person who is loved is called love of friendship, while the motion directed to the good(s) willed for that person is called love of concupiscence. Formally speaking, by love of friendship a person is loved as that for whom good is sought; by love of concupiscence something is loved as being good for some person (Ia IIae, q. 26, a. 4). The person loved can be oneself or another person, and the thing willed for the person can be bodily goods such as food or drink or spiritual goods such as honor or knowledge or even virtues. For Thomas, these two loves are always found together and indeed constitute a single act: one does not love someone without wanting what is good for that person, nor does one love goods that are not persons without loving them for some person.[42]

Third, within dilection, love of friendship is more basic than love of concupiscence, for one only wants the good for someone if one first loves that person. Hence, Thomas says that love of friendship is love in the most perfect sense—and even speaks of love of friendship as "including" love of concupiscence.[43] Love of friendship, then, is the will's most basic affection; all motion of the will begins with and is based on the love of a person. Even the will's natural inclination toward beatitude is described by Thomas as a self-love. Each person naturally loves himself (a love of friendship), and so he naturally wants what is the greatest for himself, in other words, desires his beatitude (Ia, q. 60, a. 3).

What are the implications of saying that love of friendship is the will's primary affection or motion? It means, first, that the affection of the will which is the most basic of all and is the source of all others is precisely *love for persons*. Everything other than persons is willed for persons and only persons are willed as being good in themselves. Everything in the universe that is not a person, including even the accidental perfections of persons such as health or virtue, is willed for the persons in which it is found. As Thomas succinctly states it, "The principal ends of human acts are God, self, and others, since we do whatever we do for the sake of one of these" (Ia IIae, q. 73, a. 9, c.).[44] This view of love mirrors Thomas's understanding of the universe as a whole according to which only rational beings—persons—exist for their own sake; all other created beings exist for the sake of rational beings and find their fulfillment in their service to those rational beings.[45] Thus Thomas's moral universe is, in a certain sense, much like Kant's kingdom of ends. The moral life consists primarily in loving persons: loving the right persons in the proper order (*ordo amoris*), and loving the proper goods for those persons.[46]

Second, this doctrine means that in all acts of the will, especially in all acts of choice, what is being chosen is some good for some person(s). While one might speak at times of willing something such as food or knowledge or "state of affairs" (in the sense that, by one's choices, one can bring about a condition that did not previously obtain), the basic structure of willing is always that of willing some good(s) for some person(s). This basic structure is to be found in all the will's acts: in the act of enjoyment, one rejoices in the fact that some person has some good; when one intends an end, one is intending some good for some person; and, even in simple willing, some good is being willed for some person. While the object of the will in general is the good, and while one can also make such formal distinctions among objects as that between means and ends, one can also make a more material distinction among the objects. This is the case when one distinguishes between the persons for whom one wills goods and the goods one wills for those persons. Every object of the will fits into one of these categories. Hence, should one ask what a person wills, materially speaking, we must answer that a person wills, first, oneself and other persons (taking them as part of his or her own self by means of the love of friendship) and wills, second, all the goods of those persons along with the means for achieving those goods.

Finally, this understanding of the love of friendship—the affective affirmation of a person—as the most fundamental motion of the will helps in understanding why Thomas's teaching on the will's natural inclination to beatitude is not an egotistical one. According to Thomas's teaching, each person has a natural inclination in his will toward his own good, the possession of which constitutes his beatitude. This natural inclination is, as was said above, a love of friendship for oneself with a love of concupiscence for the perfecting good. Aquinas's doctrine concerning the love of friendship shows how one can take the good of another person as one's own good; thus, it opens up the possibility that one's perfection can be found outside oneself in another person, especially in God.[47] According to Thomas, it belongs essentially to the love of friendship to take as one's own good the good of the beloved. Thus, one's own good can be expanded, so to speak, when one has a love of friendship for another person. One loves one's own good precisely in loving the good of the other person for that person's sake (Ia IIae, q. 28, aa. 2–3). This happens especially in the case of loving God. If a person loves God with the love of friendship (*caritas*) then the good of God becomes his own good and his beatitude consists in possessing (by the *visio beatifica*) this good (IIa IIae, q. 180, a. 1). The will's natural inclination to beatitude does not lock a person inside himself; rather, it draws him out of himself and into the possession of a larger good, which, through the love of friendship, has become his own.

Notes

[1]"et ideo quod homo actu bene agat, contingit ex hoc quod homo habet bonam voluntatem."

[2]*In I Ethicorum*, lect. 1: "Sic igitur moralis philosophiae, circa quam versatur praesens intentio, proprium est considerare operationes humanas secundum quod sunt ordinatae ad invicem et ad finem. Dico autem operationes humanas quae procedunt a voluntate hominis secundum ordinem rationis; nam, si quae operationes in homine inveniuntur quae non subiacent voluntati et rationi, non dicuntur propriae humanae sed naturales, sicut patet de operationibus animae vegetabilis, quae nullo modo cadunt sub consideratione moralis philosophiae. Sicut igitur subiectum philosophiae naturalis est motus vel res mobilis, ita etiam subiectum moralis philosophiae est operatio humana ordinata in finem vel etiam homo prout est voluntarie agens propter finem" (Leonine, 4, 39–49).

3"Ad primum ergo dicendum quod voluntas dividitur contra naturam, sicut una causa contra aliam:
quaedam enim fiunt naturaliter, et quaedam fiunt
voluntarie. Est autem alius modus causandi proprius
voluntati, quae est domina sui actus, praeter modum
qui convenit naturae, quae est determinata ad
unum." Cf. *De veritate*, q. 22, a. 5, ad 7, in contrarium: "hoc enim est proprium voluntati in quantum
est voluntas, quod sit domina suorum actuum"
(Leonine, 626, 372–74); also *De potentia*, q. 2, a. 3,
c.: "Voluntas, inquantum voluntas, cum sit libera, ad
utrumlibet se habet" (Marietti, 30).

4On Thomas's use of the term *liberum arbitrium*,
see also *In II Sent.*, d. 24, q. 1, a. 3 (Mandonnet,
595–98); *De veritate*, q. 24, aa. 4, 6 (Leonine, 689–92;
694–96). The voluntariness in question here is what
Thomas calls the "perfect voluntary" (*voluntarium
secundum rationem perfectam*), the sort of voluntariness proper to free actions. This is contrasted with
imperfect voluntariness, the sort of voluntariness
found in brute animals, the sort of voluntariness, I
might add, that one finds Aristotle describing (*Eth.
Nic.* 3.1–2 [1109b30–1112a17]). For this distinction
in Thomas, see ST Ia IIae, q. 6, aa. 1–2.

5It is important to note that Thomas uses "appetite" (*appetitus*) to designate both the tending or
desiring and the power by which such tending or
desiring arises.

6See *De veritate*, q. 24, a. 2 (Leonine, 684–87);
SCG II, chaps. 47–48.

7"Quaedam enim inclinantur in bonum, per so-
lam naturalem habitudinem, absque cognitione,
sicut plantae et corpora inanimata. Et talis inclinatio
ad bonum vocatur appetitus naturalis.—Quaedam
vero ad bonum inclinantur cum aliqua cognitione;
non quidem sic quod cognoscant ipsam rationem
boni, sed cognoscant aliquod bonum particulare;
sicut sensus, qui cognoscit dulce et album et aliquid
huiusmodi. Inclinatio autem hanc cognitionem sequens, dicitur appetitus sensitivus. Quaedam vero
inclinantur ad bonum cum cognitione qua cognoscunt ipsam boni rationem; quod est proprium intellectus. Et haec perfectissime inclinantur in bonum;
non quidem quasi ab alio solummodo directa in
bonum, sicut ea quae cognitione carent; neque in
bonum particulariter tantum, sicut ea in quibus est
sola sensitiva cognitio; sed quasi inclinata in ipsum
universale bonum. Et haec inclinatio dicitur voluntas. Unde, cum angeli per intellectum cognoscant
ipsam universalem rationem boni, manifestum est
quod in eis sit voluntas."

8See *De veritate*, q. 22, a. 5, ad 3: "intellectus enim
etsi habeat inclinationem in aliquid non tamen
nominat ipsam inclinationem hominis, sed voluntas
ipsam inclinationem hominis nominat" (Leonine,
624, 238–241).

9For this point, see esp. *De veritate*, q. 25, a. 1
(Leonine, 727–30).

10"Et hoc ideo est quia, cum bonum simpliciter
consistat in actu, et non in potentia, ultimum autem
actus est operatio, vel usus quarumcumque rerum
habitarum; bonum hominis simpliciter consideratur in bona operatione, vel bono usu rerum habitarum. Utimur autem rebus omnibus per
voluntatem. Unde ex bona voluntate, qua homo
bene utitur rebus habitis, dicitur homo bonus; et ex
mala, malus." See also *De malo*, q. 1, a. 5 (Leonine,
21–26).

11*De malo*, q. 6, a. un.: "Si enim non sit liberum
aliquid in nobis, sed ex necessitate movemur ad
volendum tollitur deliberatio, exhortatio, praeceptum et punitio, et laus et vituperium circa que moralis Philosophia consistit. Huiusmodi autem
opiniones que destruunt principia alicuius partis
philosophie dicuntur positiones extranee, sicut
nichil moveri quod destruit principia scientie naturalis" (Leonine, 148, 256–63). See *De veritate*, q. 24,
a. 1 (Leonine, 677–84); ST Ia, q. 83, a. 1.

12*De malo*, q. 6, a. un.: "Hec autem opinio est
heretica. Tollit enim rationem meriti et demeriti in
humanis actibus: non enim videtur esse meritorium
vel demeritorium quod aliquis sic ex necessitate agit
quod vitare non possit. Est etiam annumeranda inter
extraneas philosophie opiniones, quia non solum
contrariatur fidei, set subvertit omnia principia philosophie moralis" (Leonine, 148, 248–56). Another
such "extraneous opinion" named by Thomas is the
view that there is no such thing as motion, a view
that denies the possibility of physics by denying its
subject matter, mobile being. These views are not
dealt with by the science in question, since such
sciences presuppose their subject matter and go on
to demonstrate the properties of it. Rather, the
science which deals with extraneous opinions is
metaphysics, for it falls to metaphysics to defend the
first principles of all the sciences (see ST Ia, q. 1, a.
8). Therefore, it is understandable that Thomas
does not defend the existence of free acts within his
moral treatises.

13For this point, see also the following texts: *De
veritate*, q. 22, a. 7 (Leonine, 629–30); ST Ia IIae, q.
1, aa. 5–8; q. 2, aa. 7–8; q. 5, a. 8; q. 10, a. 2; *De malo*,
q. 6, a. un. (Leonine, 145–53). As a representative
text, ST Ia IIae, q. 5, a. 8: "sic necesse est quod omnis
homo beatitudinem velit. Ratio autem beatitudinis
communis est ut sit bonum perfectum. . . . Cum
autem bonum sit obiectum voluntatis, perfectum
bonum est alicuius quod totaliter eius voluntati sat-
isfacit. Unde appetere beatitudinem nihil aliud est
quam appetere ut voluntas satietur."

14*De veritate*, q. 22, a. 7: "Aliis enim rebus inditus
est naturalis appetitus alicuius rei determinatae,
sicut gravi quod sit deorsum, et unicuique etiam
animali id quod est sibi conveniens secundum suam
naturam; sed homini inditus est appetitus ultimi
finis sui in communi, ut scilicet appetat naturaliter

se esse completum in bonitate. Sed in quo ista completio consistat, utrum in virtutibus vel scientiis vel delectationibus vel huiusmodi aliis, non est ei determinatum a natura" (Leonine, 630, 50–60). See also ad 6.

[15]"quia omnes appetunt suam perfectionem adimpleri, quae est ratio ultimi finis . . ."

[16]*De malo*, q. 6, a. un.: "set forma intellecta est universalis, sub qua multa possunt comprehendi. Unde cum actus sint in singularibus, in quibus nullum est quod adequet potentiam universalis, remanet inclinatio voluntatis indeterminate se habens ad multa; sicut si artifex concipiat formam domus in universali, sub qua comprehenduntur diverse figure domus, potest voluntas eius inclinari ad hoc quod faciat domum quadratam vel rotundam vel alterius figure" (Leonine, 148, 287–96).

[17]*De veritate*, q. 25, a. 1 (Leonine, 727–30).

[18]On this point see also *De veritate*, q. 22, aa. 5–6 (Leonine, 621–29); ST Ia, q. 60, a, 2; q. 82, a. 2; Ia IIae, q. 10, aa. 1–2; *De malo*, q. 6, a. un. (Leonine, 145–53).

[19]The treatment of the freedom of the will's acts in terms of exercise and specification is to be found in Thomas's later works, especially in the *Prima secundae* and in q. 6 of *De malo*. Some commentators have seen the introduction of this distinction as a response to the condemnation of certain propositions in Paris in 1270, maintaining that Thomas wished to emphasize the will's freedom and self-motion. For discussion of these problems see O. Lottin, *Psychologie et morale aux XIIe et XIIIe siècles*, 2d ed., vol. 1 (Gembloux: J. Ducolot, 1957), 207–16, 225–43. O.-H. Pesch, "Philosophie und Theologie der Freiheit bei Thomas von Aquin in quaest. disp. 6 De malo," *Münchener theologische Zeitschrift* 13 (1962): 1–25; and H. M. Manteau-Bonamy, "La liberté de l'homme selon Thomas d'Aquin (la datation de la Q. Disp. De Malo)," *Archives d'histoire doctrinale et littéraire du moyen age* 46 (1979): 7–34, have argued that Thomas's response to the condemnations accentuated a movement to be found throughout his career toward a more "voluntaristic" understanding of choice.

[20]This point underlies the principle that the moral goodness of the will depends upon how the will's object is presented to it by the intellect, a principle that is central to Thomas's discussions of the morality of acting on an erroneous conscience (ST Ia IIae, q. 19, aa. 2–6).

[21]I should note that in cases of non-necessary truths—contingent truths—the will plays a role not only in consideration but also in the assent or withholding of assent. This role of the will is highlighted in Thomas's discussion of the act of faith which is not made on the basis of natural evidence, but by an act of the will under the influence of grace (IIa IIae, q. 2, a. 1, ad 2).

[22]This is what happens whenever a person avoids having to make a choice simply by refusing to think about whatever the matter might be.

[23]"Hoc autem est bonum in communi, in quod voluntas naturaliter tendit, sicut etiam quaelibet potentia in suum obiectum: et etiam ipse finis ultimus, qui hoc modo se habet in appetibilibus, sicut prima principia demonstrationum in intelligibilibus: et universaliter omnia illa quae conveniunt volenti secundum suam naturam. Non enim per voluntatem appetimus solum ea quae pertinent ad potentiam voluntatis; sed etiam ea quae pertinent ad singulas potentias, et ad totum hominem. Unde naturaliter homo vult non solum obiectum voluntatis, sed etiam alia quae conveniunt aliis potentiis: ut cognitionem veri, quae convenit intellectui; et esse et vivere et alia huiusmodi, quae respiciunt consistentiam naturalem; quae omnia comprehenduntur sub obiecto voluntatis sicut quaedam particularia bona."

[24]The Latin terms are respectively, *voluntas, intentio*, and *fruitio* (directed to ends) and *electio, consensus*, and *usus* (directed toward means). I shall generally use the English equivalents.

[25]The act of enjoyment is directed to the possessed good; all others are directed to goods or evils not yet possessed. Sins such as *delectatio morosa* (ST Ia IIae, q. 74, aa. 6–8), envy (IIa IIae, q. 36), or jealousy are instances of morally significant enjoyments and sadnesses.

[26]In considering the factors that affect the morality of an action, Thomas lays special weight on the object and the end (ST Ia IIae, q. 18, aa. 5–7) which are the objects respectively of choice and intention. Thus, in evaluating the morality of a given action, the most important acts of the will are the choice and the intention, both being acts of *free-will*. These two acts, says Thomas, constitute a single willing, although one can always distinguish them on the basis of the distinction in their objects (Ia IIae, q. 12, a. 4).

[27]For Thomas's use of the term *simplex voluntas*, see ST IIIa, q. 18, a. 4; q. 21, a. 4. In *De veritate*, Thomas refers to this act under the name of *simplex velle*; see q. 22, aa. 13–14 (Leonine, 643–48).

[28]"Ad quartum dicendum quod intentio est actus voluntatis respectu finis. Sed voluntas respicit finem tripliciter. Uno modo, absolute: sic dicitur voluntas, prout absolute volumus vel sanitatem vel si quid aliud est huiusmodi. Alio modo consideratur finis secundum quod in eo quiescitur: et hoc modo fruitio respicit finem. Tertio modo consideratur finis secundum quod est terminus alicuius quod in ipsum ordinatur: et sic intentio respicit finem. Non enim solum ex hoc intendere dicimur sanitatem, quia volumus eam: sed quia volumus ad eam per aliquid aliud pervenire." See also *De veritate*, q. 22, aa. 13–15 (Leonine, 643–49).

88   David M. Gallagher

29See n. 22 above.

30*In III Sent.*, d. 29, a. 3, ad 3 (Moos, 930). For Thomas's arguments for a natural love of God, see *In III Sent.*, d. 29, a. 3 (Moos, 927–30); ST Ia, q. 60, a. 5; Ia IIae, q.109, a. 3; IIa IIae, q. 26, a. 3. Two examples Thomas gives of spontaneous willings arising are those of a person willing to be warm when cold (Ia IIae, q. 9, a. 5, ad 2) and of a person naturally being repelled when having a wound cauterized (IIIa, q. 18, a. 5). The latter, being a negative willing by which one tends away from an evil, can be called a *noluntas* (Ia IIae, q. 8, a. 1, ad 1).

31"Similiter voluntas ut natura repudiat ea quae naturae sunt contraria, et quae sunt secundum se mala, puta mortem et alia huiusmodi. Haec tamen quandoque voluntas per modum rationis eligere potest ex ordine ad finem: sicut etiam in aliquo puro homine sensualitas eius, et etiam voluntas absolute considerata, refugit ustionem, quam voluntas secundum rationem elegit propter finem sanitatis."

32When one considers Thomas's understanding of *akrasia* (*incontinentia*), in which there are two ends to which a person is attracted (pleasure versus obedience to the divine law, for example), it seems clear that the willing of the end for which the person does not act is a real willing but does not attain the level of *intentio*. In short, the notions of *voluntas* and *velleitas* help to understand all the cases in which there seems to be a conflict within a person's own will. The notion is also important for Thomas's explanation of how a person can legitimately will what God does not will (ST Ia IIae, q. 19, a. 10; IIIa, q. 18, aa. 5–6; q. 21, aa. 2, 4).

33"Voluntas autem simpliciter hominis est voluntas rationis: hoc enim absolute volumus quod secundum deliberatam rationem volumus. Illud autem quod volumus secundum motum sensualitatem, vel etiam secundum motum voluntatis simplicis, quae consideratur ut natura, non simpliciter volumus, sed secundum quid: scilicet, si aliud non obsistat quod per deliberationem rationis invenitur."

34"consensus nominat applicationem appetitivi motus ad aliquid praeexistens in potestate applicantis."

35Aquinas maintains, moreover, that even when the two acts are identical, they still remain distinct in terms of their intelligibilities (*rationes*). When the will's act is taken as consent it is being understood as simply a being-pleased with the action as an acceptable action; when the will's act is taken as choice the action is taken as an action to be done in preference to other actions not to be done (ST Ia IIae, q. 15., a. 3).

36Thomas defines command (*imperium*) as an act of reason presupposing an act of the will (ST Ia IIae, q. 17, a. 1). What he has in mind is an act of the will prior to the command by which that command gets its moving force (reason alone does not move anything), and not the act of the will governed by the command, that is, not the act of use. The act of the will that is presupposed by command, then, would normally be choice, for the command to exercise the other power has moving force only if the person has already chosen to carry out that act. Thomas does mention the possibility that command and use precede choice. What he has in mind is that in the deliberation that precedes choice the intellect is exercised in a voluntary way and hence there must be acts of command and use, acts which obviously precede the choice. In this case the willing that is prior to command would be the willing of the end, for it is the desire for the end that moves a person to deliberate about the means (q. 17, a. 3, ad 1).

37"Unde fruitio pertinere videtur ad amorem vel delectationem quam aliquis habet de ultimo expectato, quod est finis."

38"Ipsa autem aptitudo sive proportio appetitus ad bonum est amor, qui nihil aliud est quam complacentia boni; motus autem ad bonum est desiderium vel concupiscentia; quies autem in bono est gaudium vel delectatio. . . . Delectatio enim est fruitio boni . . ."

39Hope and despair are affections of the irascible appetite with respect to desired goods whose acquisition presents an aspect of difficulty. Therefore, any good that is hoped for or despaired of is already desired and hence loved (ST Ia IIae, q. 25, a. 1). Hate (*odium*) presupposes love because evil is a privation of a good and so one hates a privation only if one first loves the good that the privation diminishes or destroys, as a person would hate sickness because he first loves health (q. 25, a. 2).

40ST Ia IIae, q. 25, a. 2: "Respondeo dicendum quod omne agens agit propter finem aliquem, ut supra dictum est. Finis autem est bonum desideratum et amatum unicuique. Unde manifestum est quod omne agens, quodcumque sit, agit quamcumque actionem ex aliquo amore." Also ad 2: "Unde omnis actio quae procedit ex quacumque passione, procedit etiam ex amore, sicut ex prima causa." Cf. Ia, q. 20, a. 1.

41Arist. *Rh.* 2.4 (1380b35): "Amare est velle alicui bonum."

42For Thomas's doctrine on *amor amicitiae* and *amor concupiscentiae*, see also Ia, q. 60, a. 3; IIa IIae, q. 23, a. 1; q. 25, a. 2; *In div. nom.*, chap. 4, lect. 9, n. 405.

43*In div. nom.*, chap. 4, lect. 10, nn. 404–5.

44This quotation appears within the discussion of how the gravity of a sin depends upon the person whom it offends: "Respondeo dicendum quod persona in quam peccatur, est quodammodo obiectum peccati. Dictum est autem supra quod prima gravitas peccati attenditur ex parte obiecti. Ex quo quidem tanto attenditur maior gravitas in peccato, quanto obiectum eius est principalior finis. Fines autem principales humanorum actuum sunt Deus, ipse homo, et proximus: quidquid enim facimus, propter aliquod horum facimus; quamvis etiam horum trium unum sub altero ordinetur."

[45]For this doctrine in Aquinas, see esp. SCG III, chaps. 22, 112.

[46]The similarity to Kant's kingdom of ends lies primarily in the fact that the moral life is a matter of treating persons properly, which means as ends in themselves and not as ordered to some other (created) being. All other beings enter the moral life by way of their relation to persons (ST IIa IIae, q. 58, a. 3, ad 3). Thomas does not, however, share Kant's view of the autonomy of these ends such that each is the source of moral law. For Thomas, God is the primary source of law and all other persons have rectitude of will—moral rectitude—by obeying that law.

[47]In III Sent., d. 29, a. 3 (Moos, 927–30); also ST Ia, q. 60, a. 5; Ia IIae, q. 109, a. 3.

Selected Further Reading

Bourke, Vernon. J. *Will in Western Thought: An Historico-Critical Survey*. New York: Sheed and Ward, 1964.

Cajetan (Thomas of Vio). Commentary on the *Summa Theologiae*, qq. 6–17. In *Sancti Thomae de Aquino opera omnia iussu impensaque Leonis XIII*. Leonine ed. Vol. 6. Rome: Editori di san tommaso, 1882–.

Donagan, Alan. "Thomas Aquinas on Human Action." In *Cambridge History of Later Medieval Philosophy*. Ed. N. Kretzmann, A. Kenny, and J. Pinborg. Cambridge: Cambridge University Press, 1982.

Gallagher, David M. "Aquinas on Will as Rational Appetite." *Journal of the History of Philosophy* 29 (1991): 559–84.

———. "Free Choice and Free Judgment in Thomas Aquinas." *Archiv für Geschichte der Philosophie*, 76 (1994): 247–77.

———. "Person and Ethics in Thomas Aquinas." *Acta Philosophica* 4 (1995): 51–71.

Garrigou-Lagrange, R. "Intellectualisme et liberté chez Saint Thomas." *Revue des Sciences Philosophiques et Théologiques* 1 (1907): 649–73; 2 (1908): 5–32. Trans. and repr. (with changes) in *God: His Existence and His Nature*. St. Louis: Herder, 1949.

Klubertanz, George P. *The Philosophy of Human Nature*. New York: Appleton-Century-Crofts, 1953.

Lebacqz, Joseph. *Libre arbitre et jugement*. Brussels: Desclée de Brouwer, 1963.

Lottin, Odon. "La preuve de la liberté humaine chez saint Thomas d'Aquin." *Recherches de Théologie ancienne et médiévale* 23 (1956): 323–30.

O'Conner, William R. "The Natural Desire for Happiness." *The Modern Schoolman* 26 (1949): 91–120.

———. "Natural Appetite." *The Thomist* 16 (1953): 361–409.

Pinckaers, Servais. *S. Thomas d'Aquin. Somme theologique. Les actes humains*. Vol. 1 (Ia IIae 6–17). Paris: Éditions du Cerf, 1962.

———. "Der Sinn für die Freundschaftsliebe als Urtatsache der thomistischen Ethik." In *Sein und Ethos: Untersuchungen zur Grundlegung der Ethik*. Ed. P. Engelhardt. Mainz: Matthias–Grünewald, 1963.

Riesenhuber, Klaus. *Die Transzendenz der Freiheit zum Guten. Der Wille in der Anthropologie und Metaphysik des Thomas von Aquin*. Pullacher Philosophische Forschungen 8. Munich: Berchmanskolleg Verlag, 1971.

Simon, Yves R. *Freedom of Choice*. Ed. Peter Wolff. New York: Fordham University Press, 1969.

Sullivan, Robert P. "Natural Necessitation of the Human Will." *The Thomist* 14 (1951):351–99, 490–528.

Westberg, Daniel. *Right Practical Reason: Aristotle, Action and Prudence in Aquinas*. Oxford: Clarendon, 1994.

Zimmermann, Albert. "Der Begriff der Freiheit nach Thomas von Aquin." In *Thomas von Aquin (1274–1974)*. Ed. L. Oeing-Hanhoff. Munich: Kösel-Verlag, 1974.

Good and Evil in Human Acts
(Ia IIae, qq. 18–21)

Daniel Westberg

Thomas Aquinas placed his discussion of how to assess the morality of human action after his analysis of human action, just before the passions, and well before his treatment of sin. This sequence suggests that the criteria for analyzing good and evil are neither the ingredients that make up the process of action (discussed in Ia IIae, qq. 6–17), nor are they just a template for gauging sin.

Some of the current debates within Catholic moral theology center on Thomas's teaching in this section on the morality of actions. It is well known that the handbooks of moral theology, written with a view for training priests in hearing confession, cast the treatment of human action and virtue in a framework for assessing the relative sinfulness of various acts. This has provoked modern scholars to develop a number of counter-strategies: an emphasis on the agent and character over time rather than a narrow focus on actions; and a method of regarding actions as morally neutral in themselves until embedded in an actual set of circumstances with purpose and goal. This has involved the rejection of the concept of "intrinsically evil acts."

Outside of the Catholic tradition, Protestants have often tended to skip lightly over fine distinctions and ethical discussions regarded as "scholastic." The moral analysis of actions usually distills to intention and circumstances. Without the more refined analysis, Protestant thinking has often had little to offer beyond a rather rigid rule-keeping on the one hand, or an accommodating but loose emphasis on recognizing the circumstances and the importance of good intention. Joseph Fletcher's defective *Situation Ethics* helped to expose these shortcomings and to promote the search for a more solid approach to counter the problems of subjectivism and arbitrariness. The Thomist tradition probably offers Christian ethics in general the richest and most subtle method of assessing human actions within a theological framework.

Another reason for a careful reading of this section is the importance of the concept of intention in modern ethical analysis. Especially with the refinement involved in complicated cases in medical ethics, and in the weight that is placed on the analytical device of "double effect," an accurate understanding of Thomistic teaching on intention is vital.

I propose to treat Questions 18 through 21 in four separate sections, but to group the topics and subquestions a little differently and under various thematic categories. Question 18, which relates most to current controversies, deals with the elements of object, end, and circumstances, and the question of intrinsically evil acts; this question is divided into two sections, while Questions 20 and 21 will be merged together.

THE THREE-PART MORAL ANALYSIS OF HUMAN ACTION

The criteria that Thomas developed for analyzing the morality of human actions fall within the theory of good and evil in general. In Ia IIae, q. 18, a. 1, Thomas draws attention to his theory of good, which links the concept of good to being, desire, and completion (Ia, q. 5). When a being is complete, relative to its nature, that being is good. Conversely, the lack of a good in a being which ought to have it is something evil. Applied to human actions, goodness implies the right ordering of relationships—of the will to reason, and of the person both to created reality and to God. When something is lacking in these relations, that is, when something that ought to be there for complete being is missing, then an action can be called evil (Ia IIae, q. 18, a. 1).[1] The specific things that determine whether a human action is complete and good or not are the circumstances, the overall purpose, and the nature of the action itself.

At this point, I feel a point of clarification is in order. The terms "object," "end," and "circumstances" are used here to translate the Latin terms *objectum*, *finis*, and *circumstantia* found in Question 18. Some variations are certainly possible. For example, Thomas Gilby used objective for *objectum* in his translation of this section, and for *finis*, others have preferred "purpose" or "aim."[2] I raise the matter of terminology to explain why I do not use the term "intention." Thomas described *intentio* as a stage in the process of action (Ia IIae, q. 12); it does not exactly conform to the aspects of moral evaluation required here, nor to the modern meaning of intention. Intention for Thomas is the inclination of the agent—the movement of the will—to an object perceived as good, which may be directed to an ultimate end or to a proximate end. Furthermore, in deciding to act, intention covers both the desired goal and the means, the specific action, leading to it (Ia IIae, q. 12, aa. 3–4). Carelessness in observing the description of intention has contributed to many controversies in interpreting Thomas.

Object of Action

The second article of Question 18 is a crucial one. It establishes what Thomas meant by the object of an act, and the notion of actions that are good or bad in kind. The central defining feature of an action (which establishes its "species," that is, what kind of action it is) is the *objectum*, its object or objective— what the person or agent is planning to achieve in the immediate sense. This must be distinguished from the larger purpose or end, which is also relevant to the moral assessment of an act, but does not give the action its specific nature.

Thomas says that the object is what gives an action its specific character and makes this general comparison: "just as in a physical thing [the specific character] is given by its form, so in an action this is given by its object, as also in motion this comes from its terminus" (Ia IIae, q. 19, a. 2).[3] A thing such as a tree or car is defined by its form, while movements and processes are defined by their starting and ending points. Thus human actions are defined by their objectives: what the agent has in mind to accomplish.

There is an outward, physical aspect to action, but this must be combined with the specific object the agent has in mind to form the composite of a discrete act. If my friend walks into the basement where I am sawing a board, and asks, "What are you doing?" the reply "I am sawing some wood" would not really answer the question, because it adds nothing to the already observable physical motions. Describing the action requires some statement such as "I am going to build a dog house" or "I am putting up more shelves in the basement."

Some actions are immediately clear from their context: playing certain games, doing dishes, driving, and so on. But even some of the simplest actions, such as lying on the bed, can serve different purposes, such as either resting one's muscles or meditating. What makes an action intentional is that there is a *reason* for acting (Ia IIae, q. 18, a. 2, ad 2)."[4]

The "object," as described by Thomas, is the immediate reason, the reason which gives definition to the action—that which makes lying down meditating, not resting, or makes walking exercising rather than sightseeing. The object is what makes an action to be an action of a certain kind—in Thomistic terms, the "matter" of the action, around which the action is formed.[5] Often there will be no difference between the object of the action and the purpose of the agent. But sometimes there is a difference (as I will show in Thomas's treatment of "end"); it is this distinction which gave rise to scholastic terminology: the object of the action (*finis operis*), and the end or purpose of the agent (*finis operantis*).[6]

Only what is intended by the agent is an object of the action *per se*, that is, in virtue of the action itself *qua* action, as initiated by the agent. Only what is intended by the agent enters into the "form" or "substance" of his action. According to Thomas, an operation receives its species and name from its *per se* object, not from what is an object *per accidens*. But in things that are for an end, it is something that is intended which is called *per se*; whereas what is outside intention is called *per accidens*.[7] (IIa IIae, q. 59, a. 2)

Note that there may be a series of discrete actions which make up an organized series of acts that can be called an action on a higher level. Driving a car involves a series of smaller acts; while making telephone calls, asking people for funds, making arrangements to rent a theater, and planning advertisements all have their intelligibility as acts in the context of the action "producing a play." While this can be treated as a discrete action—something done—it clearly involves many actions within it.

An action will have a beginning and an end, and be intelligible as an action with an objective to be accomplished and finished. Writing on a piece of paper needs the structure of an objective for action, such as drawing a picture, writing a letter, making a memo. Writing a sentence or drawing the letters "i" and "t" are not ordinarily understood as discrete actions without a larger context; whereas "writing a letter" or "jotting down a memo" can be actions in themselves or parts of a more comprehensive action.

Because the object gives the basic specification of an action, it is possible to speak of certain types of action as good, bad, or indifferent (Ia IIae, q. 18, a. 8). There is a presumption for or against general categories of action. Here in Ia IIae, q. 18, a. 2, Thomas tells us that using what belongs to you (*uti re sua*) is generally good, while taking what does not belong to you (*accipere aliena*) is something generally bad.

Circumstances

In Ia IIae, q. 18, a. 3, Thomas makes a comparison between the elements of an action and the analysis of being in general. If the specific nature of an action comes from its object, then the object is like the substantial form of an individual being, and the circumstances of an action can be compared to accidents such as the qualities of shape or complexion in a human being which provide

individual identity. Just as stunted growth or lack of pigmentation can mar the perfection of the body, so the full moral goodness of an action depends not just on the object but on something added from certain aspects that occur, like certain accidents: these are the due circumstances (Ia IIae, q. 18, a. 3).[8]

In the *De malo* Thomas offers a more systematic description:

> Now that is called a circumstance which surrounds an act, as it were, outside of, not within, the substance of the act being considered. Now this is in one way on the part of the cause, either the final cause when we consider why a person did the act, or the principal agent, when we consider who did the act, or as regards the instrumental cause when we consider with what instrument or what aids he did the act. In another way that which surrounds the act as regards the measure, i.e., when we consider where and when the person acted. In a third way as regards the act itself, whether we consider the manner of acting, for instance, did the person strike lightly, or forcefully, many times or once, or we consider the object or matter of the action, for instance, did he strike his father or a stranger, or even the effect he caused by acting, e.g., by striking did he wound or actually kill? Which are all contained in the following verse: "Who, what, where, by what aids, why, how, when."[9]

In Ia IIae, q.18, a. 10, Thomas points out that sometimes a circumstance that in one case is incidental, in another situation may become the principal condition of the object determining the specific nature of the act.[10] For example, if you are driving to work, then it usually makes no difference who actually owns the vehicle. But driving a car that you have no right to take constitutes theft, and this circumstance now becomes the main condition—you are no longer (primarily) driving to work, but stealing a car.

The place or time of an action is often only a matter of the description of the circumstances, not altering the substance of the act. However, stealing from a church or sacred place adds a degree of moral repugnance to the act (Ia IIae, q. 18, a. 10). As a general principle, "whenever a circumstance relates to a special order of reason, either for or against it, then that circumstance provides the moral definition for that action, either good or bad."[11] Sometimes the circumstance is not ir-relevant, but affects the degree of good or evil. Theft is still theft, whatever the amount of money; but a greater or lesser amount may lessen or aggravate the offence (Ia IIae, q. 18, a. 11).

One point implied by the treatment of Thomas thus far, and which will be clearer in the section on end, is that there is a certain fluidity between object, circumstance, and end. In one sense (as demonstrated in the extract from *De malo*), the purpose the agent has in mind is part of the circumstances; however, it can also change the moral assessment. Other circumstances, although often not affecting the moral evaluation, may also change the way one assesses what kind of action has been performed.

End

In Ia IIae, q. 18, a. 6, Thomas describes the will as directed toward interior and exterior objectives. The exterior objective is the object of the act itself (as treated above), while the end is the interior purpose of the agent, corresponding to the end of the act (*finis operis*) and end of the agent (*finis operantis*), although these terms are not used by Thomas here.

In many—perhaps most—cases, the end and object will be not only harmonious but by nature related. In Thomas's example (in Ia IIae, q. 18, a. 7), fighting well in battle is directly related to the goal of victory. But in some cases, the connection is incidental (*per accidens*), as when one takes something in order to give to the needy. When the object is not *per se* ordered to the will's end, the specifying feature of the object is not determinative of the end, nor does the end shape the object of action. In other words, instead of one species of action, you might well have a moral action coming under two different kinds of act. In Thomas's example (taken from Aristotle), one might steal in order to commit adultery; adultery is therefore the motive for the theft. In this case, one cannot subsume the theft under the adultery—there are two evils committed in one act.

Revisionists who want to modify the scholastic analysis of action would rather work with the concept of "motive" and thus magnify the subjective aspect of intention. This reduces the moral aspect of the object in the action chosen, placing more emphasis on the motivation of the agent.[12] On the other hand, the traditionalist tends to stress the intrinsic moral object of the act, and reduces the relevance of the role of the end or purpose in shaping the nature of the act chosen.[13]

Both approaches deviate from St. Thomas in that they separate object and end. They envision the specific action as the starting point for moral analysis, and then bring in the purpose or motivation of the agent as the moral qualifer (or disqualifier!) of the act. However, in the Thomistic view of action, intention for the end comes first, and the specific action is chosen as a means in the light of, or as a means to, the more general goal. The revisionist strategy tends to subsume the intentionality (and morality) of the object into the general goal, while the traditional scholastic approach reacts against this danger and stresses the centrality of the objective moral character of the act. Both show a tendency of making motivation subjective (in terms of benevolence, compassion, generosity, or love). The mistake on the part of both approaches is to overlook the close relation between object (*objectum*) and end (*finis*) as means and end, and brought together in the act of choice.[14]

ARE THERE ACTIONS THAT ARE ALWAYS EVIL?

The issue is controversial, due in part to its inherent difficulties, and in part to the sparseness and ambiguity of the account in the *Summa theologiae*. Whether or not there are certain actions that are inherently or inevitably wrong, morally, is a central issue in the theories of certain moral theologians associated with the school of proportionalism, and it is an issue that needs to be tested with the moral criteria provided by St. Thomas.

One of the key principles of the proportionalist approach is that actions from the point of view of the object are *pre-moral*, that is, they lack moral determination until chosen by an agent with a certain intention in a given set of circumstances. Killing a human being describes a kind of action that is *prima facie* wrong, but our ultimate moral evaluation depends on the intention in the context of the circumstances. If the killing represents proportionate force in warding off a deadly attack, it may be justifiable self-defense. Thomas, in arguing for capital punishment, says that it is unlawful to kill anyone, when we consider persons in themselves, with the natures God gave them; however, if the common good is seriously threatened, then it is lawful to execute a sinner (IIa IIae q. 64, a. 6).

Challenging the manualist tradition, Peter Knauer insisted that no moral significance should be attached to any physical evil (such as death, falsehood, sickness, loss of property), until it could be determined whether or not there was a commensurate reason for causing it.[15] This is the case even if the physical evil is directly intended psychologically, as in the surgical operation where the doctor removes a patient's limb for some necessary medical reason. In a psychological sense, the doctor intends to amputate the limb. In the moral sense, the act is a healing intervention that can be justified by "commensurate reason." The psychological intention in such a case is pre-moral and beyond intention. What Knauer did in effect was to deny the possibility of intrinsically evil acts, the claim that certain actions could be wrong regardless of circumstances or consequences.

To this point, this analysis seems to be supported by St. Thomas. At the level of object and action, there would seem to be no acts which, independently of circumstances and intention, could be termed intrinsically evil. Thomas leaves the discussion at Ia IIae, q. 18, a. 2, for example, with a group of actions defined as good or evil in kind (*malum in genere* or *bonum in genere*), which then become good or evil depending on circumstances and the end intended. Thomas offers a classic example: it is generally wrong to keep something that belongs to someone else, except in a situation where you might have someone's knife, and the owner wants it back, threatening to use the weapon in anger. Likewise, an action generally good, such as giving alms to the poor, can be rendered a bad action by having faulty ulterior motives, such as contributing to a reputation that serves one's pride.

St. Thomas did not provide a list of specific actions, which by their object, make them intrinsically evil, although such a list may be implied as possible. Some of the recent attempts at such lists which appear in official documents have occasioned criticism, and offer us further opportunity to consider a Thomistic view.[16] By looking at Thomas's analysis of some of the problems and sins in IIa IIae, some light can be shed on this issue. Such an examination will also reveal a subtlety in both language and ethical analysis that prevents Thomas from being enlisted easily to support either side in the dispute.

When one considers Thomas's discourses on fighting in self-defense (IIa IIae, q. 41) and sedition or rebellion (IIa IIae, q. 42), the analysis seems to support the argument that actions that are wrong in general can be justified in particular circumstances, depending on intention. Attacking someone unjustly is a mortal sin, but in self-defense, it may be venial or no sin at all. If the sole intention is to withstand injury, and the defense is made moderately, then there is no sin (IIa IIae, q. 41, a. 1).[17]

Sedition provides a good example of *prima facie* evil. Because it attacks the unity of law and the common good, it is a mortal sin in its genus (IIa IIae, q. 42, a. 2).[18] However, when it is a question of overthrowing a tyrannical government (provided the tyranny is sufficiently worse than the risk posed by the revolution), then the action may be justified. But note that Thomas does not say that sedition is legitimate in these circumstances, only that the action is not one of sedition (IIa IIae, q. 42, a. 2, ad 3).[19]

Thomas helpfully offers further refinements on the relation of object and intention in his analysis of lying. In IIa IIae, q. 110, a. 1, Thomas points out that the proper object of a statement is what is true or false. Thomas distinguishes two actions prompted by a bad will: first, to utter something false; and second, to deceive someone, which is the effect of a falsehood. Falsehood occurs when three things concur: the falsehood itself, the willingness to tell it, and the intent to deceive.

Intention is the crucial factor here. It is possible to tell a falsehood thinking it to be true, in which case it is materially a lie, but not a full lie since the falseness is beyond the speaker's intention (*praeter intentionem*). On the other hand, it is possible that what one says, though thought to be false, is actually true. In that case, the will to deceive determines the morality of the act, and it is essentially a lie (IIa IIae, q. 100, a. 1).[20]

So far, these examples of Thomas's treatment seem to support a more revisionist view that actions in themselves are not always wrong, and that intention and context determine the moral judgment. However, note that if lying is defined as including the intention to deceive (and not simply as uttering a falsehood), then lying is always wrong. Similarly, while an act of revolution may sometimes be justified, the act of sedition is always wrong.

The position that certain actions are always wrong seems clearer in the treatment of other topics. It is not surprising that Thomas comes very close to the position that certain actions are always wrong in cases of sexual immorality. Incest, rape, masturbation, homosexual relations, and bestiality are considered, and ranked, along with fornication and adultery, in terms of their violation of the order of reason, nature, and God's law (IIa IIae, q. 154). In fact, he takes similar positions in a number of other discussions. Thomas is quite categorical about the sin of simony; for example, buying or selling spiritual grace is always a sin (IIa IIae, q. 100).

The attempt to treat all actions as premoral, and not necessarily good or evil until evaluated in the context of a specific set of circumstances, is neither true to Thomas nor feasible to maintain consistently. Consider the example of mutilation. It has been argued that mutilation, the deliberate maiming or destruction of part of the body, may not be always wrong apart from circumstances and intention. It may be necessary, for example, to sacrifice a limb to save a life, as when a foot is caught in the railroad tracks. The argument is misplaced, however, because the correct description of the act to save a life would be amputation, which in some circumstances cannot be performed with surgical neatness. Thus, mutilation is always wrong, because it is not simply descriptive but includes a nefarious motive. Its relation to amputation or surgery parallels the relationship of murder to killing.

Certain terms used for evil actions should be accepted as always wrong. Murder and adultery are morally evil by definition (unjustified killing, illicit sexual relations). Perjury, as well, is a special class of lying, and blasphemy includes a provocative intention

—merely saying the words or reading the identical phrases from a document without meaning them would not be blasphemous. But there is a problem in the conception of action revealed in these official documents that Richard McCormick accurately addresses. In distinguishing (1) falsehood as an ethical act in protecting a secret, and (2) falsehood as an immoral act in cheating someone who has a right to the truth, one needs to see that in both cases the goal of the agent is part of the object. One can say eventually of the second case that it is a lie. In other words, the object, or description of the action, often includes an intention in it—an intention for a proximate end—and it is disingenuous or misleading to put forward the claim that certain actions have, by virtue of their object, and apart from circumstances and intention, a disordered character that makes them intrinsically evil.[21]

The description of an action may change with more complicated circumstances. In the case of a diseased kidney, the action of the surgeons, described as "removing the kidney," is intelligible and accurate. But if the case is part of a kidney transplant, then is "removal of the kidney" the object, when the person is healthy? In this situation, the operation to remove the kidney becomes part of a larger action within the goal of maintaining life. Some would say that what is happening is that more circumstances are being absorbed into the object. Some would describe the removal of the kidney as the object "in the strict sense," while full assessment of the action requires the total or "entire" object (including circumstances and intention).[22] But is this substantially different from Thomas's point (in Ia IIae, q. 18, a. 7) that sometimes the object and the end may not be intrinsically related and need separate evaluation?

The answer to the question whether there are certain actions that are always wrong is not a straightforward one. Note that while something may be conceded to revisionists (the connection between object and intention), the reality of intrinsically evil acts is certainly implied by a Thomist understanding of the moral analysis of actions. The best way to summarize a fully Thomistic position seems to lie in offering a series of principles that qualify each other.

First, intention cannot be separated from object. As Thomas explains intention in Ia IIae, q. 12, a. 2, when there is a series of stages in movement, there are proximate ends before the ultimate end, and intention may pertain to either proximate or ultimate end. Although intention is always for an end, it is not necessarily the final end (Ia IIae, q. 12, a. 2).[23] Intention for the end extends to the means that are seen to be conducive to it. In a common example used by Thomas, the desire to get well extends to an intention to take the medicine (Ia IIae, q. 13, a. 3).[24] Thomas would resist a position (which can be held by both conservatives and revisionists) that separates intention from the object of action.

Second, it is also true that a particular action does not have its moral evaluation until it has been evaluated with the circumstances recognized and the intentions understood. I have made this point above in observing that specific actions are chosen in connection with a more general intention already formed by the agent. Jean Porter comments helpfully: "The object of an action is not simply given perspicuously in the description of an act. It certainly cannot be equated with 'what is done,' described in a simple, nonmoral way."[25] Whatever is understood as "object" by Aquinas or in traditional moral theology, this is surely a *moral* concept. "Thus the object of an act is the generic moral concept in terms of which the act is correctly described from the standpoint of moral evaluation."[26]

Conversely, the object of an action cannot serve independently as a datum for moral evaluation. The determination of the object of an act presupposes that we have described the act correctly, from a moral point of view; hence, "the determination of the object of an act is the *outcome* of a process of moral evaluation, not its presupposition."[27]

Although the correct description (to the outside observer) of an action might be blasphemy or adultery—and we might be able to agree that this is always wrong—the evaluation of the act in terms of the agent is not straightforward. That is because the person who sins usually does not choose under the description of evil, but employs a combination of acceptable intention and faulty act description that enables the rationalizing of evil.[28]

Even in the very simple example used by Thomas, the taking of medicine in order to get well, the "taking of medicine" is not a simple description of the object of action. One could drink the liquid in the bottle not as medicine but as an interesting drug in order to test its effects, or perhaps to harm oneself. To describe the act as "taking medicine" already implies a certain intention or purpose on the part of the agent.

Third, if many of the words that describe a specific type of action and its object have an implied intention, then there are certainly intrinsically evil acts. "Causing pain to another human being" may be a neutral act description, which in some circumstances is justified, but torture, sexual harassment, blasphemy, and the like have an inherent, implied malevolent intention.

Finally, Thomistic doctrine on action should be seen as entirely consistent with the biblical principle that one may not do evil so that good may come. Many theologians suspect that advocates of proportionalism want to maintain the moral openness of the description of the act (until it is embodied in circumstances and intention) in order to allow for the possibility of securing a desired outcome. If lying, stealing, and torture are not intrinsically evil, then it is possible to choose such an object in a grave situation where the right intention would justify it. But it is precisely in those pressured situations—where an official might be tempted to "bend the rules" of evidence in order to secure a conviction, or for a police force to use "mild torture" to maintain the stability of the state—where the reality of intrinsically evil acts is important. The role that Thomas gives to consequences will be discussed below in dealing with Question 21.

WILL AND CONSCIENCE

In Question 19, Thomas provides some refinements of the teaching offered in Question 18, but moves from the analysis of the qualities of exterior action to a discussion of the interior act of the will. Of course, this removes the possibility of using criteria to judge or to establish the correctness of other people's actions. Judgment of the interior qualities of actions belongs only to God; however, awareness of the principles of will and conscience helps us appreciate the complexity of action, and clarifies the foundation of virtue and spiritual life.

Conscience

In Ia IIae, q. 19, a. 3, ad 1, Thomas reminds his readers that the goodness of the will depends on the goodness of the object proposed by reason. The will is not drawn to a good unless it is first apprehended as such by the intellect.[29]

Thomas briefly anticipates here in Ia IIae, q. 19 a. 4 his subsequent teaching on natural law. The light of reason in humanity is derived from the light of God to the extent that it can show a person good things and regulate the will (Ia IIae, q. 91, a. 2). On the matter of erroneous conscience, Thomas cannot accept the teaching of other scholastic theologians on the implications of the relationship of will and intellect, namely, that if conscience tells one to do something which is evil in itself, or not to do what is in itself good, then the conscience is mistaken, and an act of will that differs and resists this is not bad (Ia IIae, q. 19, a. 5).[30] Although presented in this way by both Alexander of Hales and Bonaventure, Thomas must conclude, on the basis of his own description of practical reasoning, that this makes no sense. The will accepts what is presented by the intellect, and the evil or good in the proposed action will have that character as judged by conscience. Therefore, when a person's mind is operating properly, the will *should* be drawn to (or from) that object.

In Thomas's second example, believing in Christ is obviously a good thing in itself. Conversion is a matter of belief which depends on the will (IIa IIae, q. 10, a. 8). However, the features making belief in Christ something attractive or not depend on the characterization held by reason, which may (by unfortunate experience or misinformation) be considered as something bad or unattractive. In this case, the will does not have an independent basis from which to judge a commitment to Christ as the right thing to do apart from its presentation by reason. In this and all other cases, if the will fails to follow the judgment of conscience (even if the consequence

of the resulting action is good), then there is some interrupting factor or unhealthy aspect in the will.

In Ia IIae, q. 19, a. 6, Thomas discusses the case of a misinformed conscience. There is culpable ignorance when the person should have known better or could have taken steps to supplement his or her knowledge, but prefers to remain ignorant. Even if someone has not been instructed in the Ten Commandments, he or she is held responsible for recognizing the immorality of some of the prohibited actions. According to Thomas's teachings on the Old Law, some precepts are accessible to the natural reason of everyone (the commands not to kill and not to steal), while other matters require more instruction (Ia IIae, q. 100, a.1). Thomas's example (in Ia IIae, q. 19, a. 6) of a man making love to a woman next to him under the mistaken impression that she was his wife lacks credibility to the point of absurdity. A more convincing example might have been taking something belonging to another, which can easily be explained as a matter of misperception.

The quality of the intention normally determines the goodness or badness of the will in choosing specific actions. This is because actions are generated when one desires a certain end (intention), which then leads to a determination of the means and the choice of a specific action (Ia IIae, q. 19, a. 7; Ia IIae, q. 12 a. 4). When an action is chosen, prudently, for the sake of a good end, then the relationship to the end is considered the basis for the goodness of the specific action (Ia IIae, q. 19, a. 7, ad 1). Thomas's example of fasting (Ia IIae, q. 19 a. 7) is useful here. When fasting is done for the sake of God, for a spiritual purpose, then it becomes something good. It is easy to imagine other purposes that people might have in abstaining from food at times (and recognized by Thomas in IIa IIae, q. 147, a. 1)—to enhance health, to train for an athletic event, or to look like a supermodel. Such purposes may be good or evil, and limiting one's diet may be good or bad accordingly, depending on the circumstances.

It is also possible to add an element of goodness to an action by referring or offering the action to God. The first act's goodness is established by a different (more limited) intention, which is then strengthened by a subsequent explicit intention. Of course subsequent intention cannot rectify an action already disordered by questionable intention.

The reply to the third objection provides an excellent summary of the relation between intention and action: the will is evil when it tends to what is evil under the aspect of good, or to the good under the aspect of evil. The will is good when it tends to the good under the aspect of good; in other words, it must will the good for the sake of the good (Ia IIae, q. 19, a. 7, ad 3).[31]

There are occasions when the strength of intention is not matched in action, and this might happen in more than one way. A young man might have the intention to become an Olympic athlete, but then realizes that he is unable to make the psychological commitment required for focused training. This is a problem within the agent, whose commitment in practice does not match the requirements of the goal intended. A person may also be thwarted by circumstances, for instance, in not being able to carry out a trip that she had planned. These examples highlight Thomas's point (in Ia IIae, q. 19, a. 8), that there may be a lack of proportion between the end intended and the choice of action, and there may be exterior obstacles outside of one's control.

Generally speaking, in an agent seeing the situation properly, the strength of the intention will shape the will for the actions leading to accomplishment. The desire to finish a project successfully, or to recover health, or to achieve a level of fitness, or to gain the credentials and training for a certain profession, will inform the will to choose the appropriate arduous or time-consuming actions involving practice, exercise, and discipline in order to achieve the goal.

Is it necessary for the chosen action to be considered actually good, from an objective standpoint? From the viewpoint of God, it is the common good of the whole universe that is the standard of good for actions. From this point of view, then, what a Japanese businessman, an American farmer, a Spanish truck driver, or a British academic may intend and base their actions on will differ, of course, according to national and cultural perspectives, union views, economic pressures, and perhaps historic prejudices. The American farmer might be surprised by the European view of genetically altered crops, for example. There would also be different decisions made on other points: the amount of time to be worked each week, family obligations, whether to strike, and the place of alcohol in social life. Is it necessary for the Christian moralist to express reservations about the goodness of these actions seeing that they are made from limited, partial, and perhaps distorted viewpoints?

Thomas allows (in Ia IIae, q. 19, a. 10) a vantage from which to understand the goodness of acts based on partial vision. Individuals may have conflicting desires for different goods for particular reasons, and it is not necessary for the individual to have the larger point of view. For example, in the case of a man convicted of theft, the judge, having the common good in mind, sees the punishment of the offender as a good. The wife of the thief, on the other hand, must consider the good of her family and be opposed to the punishment. Under the aspect of the good of the family, which she is correct to judge the situation from, the wife's petition for her husband's freedom is a good. Allowing the validity of actions based on limited frameworks correlates well with the teaching of Thomas on the order of charity in IIa IIae, q. 26, aa. 7–11. The greater love for family and friends over the community in general means that the greater care and attention shown in actions with them are proportionate and in accordance with reason.

Notice, however, that the will is still in conformity with God's will, even if there is a discordance at the level of a specific material good. The desire for the good of the family is in line with the common good; and following the inclination of preserving the family accords with a natural perception which has its efficient cause in God. In this sense, the will of such a person may be said to conform to the divine will, because one wills that which God wants that person to will (Ia IIae, q. 19, a. 10).[32] This points to the fundamental principle of the harmonization of partial viewpoints and different orders of charity—that each person loves God above all, and desires that everyone will have what is due according to the justice of God (Ia IIae, q. 20, a. 13).[33]

CONSEQUENCES AND RESULTS

In assessing morality, the interior act of the will and the exterior deed compose a single act. However, sometimes an act that takes place exhibits a double good (or evil), and sometimes only one. Thus, sometimes the moral goodness or evil of an act is identical from the interior and exterior points of view, and sometimes it is distinct. For the act to be good, willing a good end is not enough, because the object must also be good (Ia IIae, q. 20, a. 2).

Sometimes the exterior act is good because of the good end. In a medical treatment such as taking injections of insulin, the maintenance of the healthy sugar level is the good that applies to both end and means; but if the doctor has prescribed a vacation for mental health, then the cure has some inherent goodness or attractiveness to it. The two goods are not so separated, of course, that they do not affect each other; in fact, the goodness of intention overflows into the outward act, and the good in the circumstances of the external act melds into the intention (Ia IIae, q. 20, a. 3).

In Ia IIae, q. 20, a. 4, Thomas considers whether an exterior act adds something to the goodness or badness of the interior act. He analyzes this in three ways. He first addresses the act of repetition, which can increase the quality of the will's intention. He follows this with an examination of extent, the tenacity in pursuing the goal to conclusion. This may of course serve either the goodness or the badness of the act. The one who perseveres in a course of action, even when it becomes clear that it is wrong, gets no credit for will-power or perseverance—it merely increases the badness of the action. The one who presses on to accomplish a good, despite obstacles and hindrances, increases the goodness of the action. Thomas concludes with an examination of intensity, because certain actions, as instances of pleasure or pain, make the will more intense or more remiss. These considerations explain why the lives of martyrs or the stories of underdog athletes show an added dimension of goodness, because not only were the results admirable, but their agents labored under difficult and adverse circumstances. In cases where the will is not deficient but circum-

stances totally prevent the execution of the act, there is no diminishment of the goodness of the will.

In Ia IIae, q. 20, a. 5, Thomas discusses whether the consequences of an action increase its goodness or badness. Because modern thinking about ethics, both on the popular and academic levels, has been influenced by consequentialism, the view that the good or bad outcome is the primary factor in its moral evaluation, it is useful to understand Thomas's position in relation to some of the arguments in favor of consequentialism. The third objection will serve here. Thomas puts forward the argument that according to Jewish law, punishment is related to the consequences; for example, in Exodus 21:29, should an ox gore someone to death, the punishment is more severe than when there is no death. Does this not indicate that consequences affect the morality of the action?

In the *sed contra* of this article (Ia IIae, q. 20, a. 5), Thomas states that the consequences do not make an action that was evil to be good, nor one that was good to be evil. For instance, if one gives alms to a poor man, who then misuses the gift of money, the generosity of the giver is not diminished. Similarly, if someone bears up patiently and endures a wrong done to him, the perpetrator is not thereby excused because good was produced out of the wrong (Ia IIae, q. 20, a. 5).[34] Were this not the case, Thomas would have had to modify substantially his whole theoretical position, which posited that the goodness or badness is established by object, intention, and circumstances.

In the body of Ia IIae, q. 20, a. 5, Thomas admits that foreseen consequences are part of the goodness and badness of an act. If someone sees that certain evils flow from an act, and yet persists in it, the will is all the more disordered.[35] If, however, the consequences are not foreseen, then more careful analysis is required. When they are naturally connected to the action itself, where a reasonable person would normally expect such results, the agent should be anticipating them, and these increase the goodness or malice of the action—the consequences determine the object of the action. If, on the other hand, the consequences are rarer or more incidental, and one would not normally anticipate them, then they do not increase the goodness or badness of the act. In his replies to the initial objections, Thomas applies the same distinction: anticipated effects that are inherent to the act are part of the morality, but those that are more accidental are not. This is the principle also recognized by the law, where a person can be held accountable for results that can reasonably be considered foreseeable.

In Ia IIae, q. 20, a. 6, Thomas examines whether an action can be both good and evil. There can be various ways in which an action might be both good and bad, depending on the category of analysis. In the natural order, an action like walking or making a phone call can be considered as a unity, and may be either good or bad. But such an act might also be subdivided morally, that is into distinct phases of differing moral character. A call might include, for example, neutral statements of fact or plans, an expression of gratitude, and a piece of malicious gossip; these elements would have separate moral assessments. Thus, there could be a number of various moral acts, reflecting changes in the person's will during the telephone conversation.

In Ia IIae, q. 21, a. 1, Thomas discusses the difference between sin and evil. Sin is more specific than evil, because evil is the privation of good in any subject, and so it can occur generally in nature. Sin, however, consists in an action done for a certain end, and lacking due order to that end (Ia IIae, q. 21, a. 1).[36] In things that are done by the will, human reason and the eternal law are the two standards. The action is right if it tends toward the end in accordance with both standards, and wrong when it veers away.

This section closes with a discussion of praise and blame, merit, and retribution. To be praised or blamed, according to Thomas (in Ia IIae, q. 21, a. 2), is really nothing other than to be charged with the responsibility for a good or bad act. All voluntary acts are in this category, because human beings have control over their actions through their will. This leads to the conclusion that in the realm of voluntary actions (and there only), good and bad constitute the basis for praise and blame; and with respect to actions, evil, sin, and guilt amount to the same thing (Ia IIae, q. 21, a. 2).[37]

The discussion of merit (Ia IIae, q. 21, a. 3) is a useful corrective to the perspective of contemporary ethical discussions. Most treatments of human action, whether philosophical or theological, stress individual decision and freedom, and leave the link between individual and society vague. Thomas reminds his readers that when good and evil are done to others, there is not only the relationship to the other individuals, there is also a relationship to the whole of society. Because one belongs to the community, a person's actions affect the whole community, and one deserves merit or demerit that corresponds to the goodness or badness of one's actions (Ia IIae, q. 21, a. 3, ad 2).[38]

If one takes the communal perspective to the widest level, namely God's governance of the universe, then a person's actions ought to be directed to God as the proper final end. One who commits an evil deed, which cannot be directed to the service of God, fails to give God the honor due (Ia IIae, q. 21, a. 4). If God did not reward or punish actions, then it would follow that God really had no interest in human actions. Unlike the society or community, where some actions are individual and need not be referred to a social end, every human action takes place within God's universe, and thus deserves merit (or the contrary) from God (Ia IIae, q. 21, a. 4, ad 3).[39] Thomas discusses the doctrine of merit in relation to grace and justification at the end of the treatment of law (Ia IIae, q. 114).

I have noted that this section in the *Summa*, which deals with goodness and badness in human actions, is linked to the discussion of good in general in the *Prima pars*, and to the doctrine of grace as the means of the return to God as final end. The criteria for judging actions as good or bad point to the crucial role of intention, to understanding the nature of what needs to be done, and to the proper recognition of circumstances. This provides the foundation for seeing the role played by the virtues, both moral and theological. Prudence, or practical wisdom, is essential for correct assessment of the situation and coming to sound decisions; justice provides the proper orientation to others as individuals and to the community as a whole; while courage and temperance help to prevent improper desires (greed, anger, lust, and so on) from compromising the intention for the ends one ought to have for good actions. And finally, the theological virtues orient the mind and heart to recognize and rejoice in God's sovereignty, and to be able to decide and carry out all our actions for God's honor and glory.

Notes

[1]ST Ia IIae, q.18, a. 1: "inquantum vero deficit ei aliquid de plenitudine essendi quae debitur actioni humanae, intantum deficit a bonitate, et sic dicitur malum."

[2]Thomas Gilby, *Summa Theologiae* Vol. 18 (1a 2ae 18–21), *Principles of Morality*, Blackfriars ed. (New York: McGraw Hill, 1966).

[3]"Sicut autem res naturalis habet speciem ex sua forma ita actio habet speciem ex obiecto, sicut et motus ex termino."

[4]Elizabeth Anscombe, *Intention*, 2d ed. (Ithaca: Cornell University Press, 1969), § 5–6.

[5]ST Ia IIae, q. 18, a. 2, ad 2: "obiectum non est materia ex qua, sed materia circa quem."

[6]See Stephen Brock, *Action and Conduct: Thomas Aquinas and the Theory of Action* (Edinburgh: T. and T. Clark, 1998), 91.

[7]"[operatio] recipit speciem et nomen a per se obiecto, non autem ab obiecto per accidens. In his autem quae sunt propter finem, per se dicitur aliquid quod est intentum: per accidens autem quod est praeter intentionem." See also *In II Physicorum*, lect. 8, § 214; and Brock, *Action and Conduct*, 89.

[8]ST Ia IIae, q.18, a. 3: "Nam plenitudo bonitatis eius non tota consistit in sua specie, sed aliquid additur ex his quae adveniunt tanquam accidentia quaedam; et huiusmodi sunt circumstantiae debitae."

[9]*De malo* q. 2, a. 6, c.: "Dicitur autem circumstantia quod circumstat actum, quasi extrinsecus extra actus substantiam consideratum. Hoc autem est *uno* quidem *modo* ex parte causae sive finalis, cum consideramus cur fecerit; sive ex parte agentis principalis, cum consideramus quis fecerit; sive ex parte instrumenti, cum consideramus quo instrumento fecerit vel quibus auxiliis. Alio modo circumstat actum ex parte mensurae, puta cum consideramus ubi vel quando fecerit. *Tertio modo* ex parte ipsius actus, sive consideremus modum agendi, puta utrum lente vel fortiter percusserit, frequenter, aut semel; sive consideremus obiectum sive materiam actus, puta utrum percusserit patrem vel extraneum; sive etiam effectum quem agendo induxit, puta utrum percutiendo vulneraverit, vel etiam occiderit; quae omnia continentur hoc versu: quis, quid, ubi, quibus auxiliis, cur, quomodo, quando" (Leonine, 47, 177–94). English translation by Jean Oesterle, *Saint Thomas Aquinas: On Evil* (Notre Dame, IN: University of Notre Dame Press, 1995), 73.

[10]ST Ia IIae, q. 18, a. 10: "potest iterum accipi a ratione ordinante ut principalis conditio obiecti determinantis speciem actus."

[11]"quandocumque aliqua circumstantia respicit specialem ordinem rationis, vel pro vel contra, oportet quod circumstantia det speciem actui morali, vel bono vel malo."

[12]See Timothy O'Connell, *Principles for a Catholic Morality*, rev. ed. (San Francisco: HarperCollins, 1990), 99.

[13]See John A. Oesterle, *Ethics: The Introduction to Moral Science* (Englewood Cliffs, NJ: 1957), pp. 102–4.

[14]For further analysis of the relation of end and object in the process of choice, see Chad Ripperger, "The Species and Unity of the Moral Act," *Thomist* 59 (1995): 69–90.

[15]Peter Knauer, "The Hermeneutic Function of the Principle of Double Effect," *Natural Law Forum* 12 (1967): 132–62.

[16]See, for example, the encyclical of John Paul II, *Splendor of Truth*, § 80: some actions are evil *"always and per se*, in other words, on account of their very object, and quite apart from the ulterior intentions of the one acting and the circumstances." Quoting the Second Vatican Council, the encyclical gives examples of such acts: "Whatever is hostile to life itself, such as any kind of homicide, genocide, abortion, euthanasia and voluntary suicide; whatever violates the integrity of the human person, such as mutilation, physical and mental torture and attempts to coerce the spirit; whatever is offensive to human dignity, such as subhuman living conditions, arbitrary imprisonment, deportation, slavery, prostitution and trafficking in women and children; degrading conditions of work which treat laborers as mere instruments of profit, and not as free responsible persons. . . ."

[17]ST IIa IIae, q. 41, a. 1: "Nam si solo animo repellendi iniuriam illatam, et cum debita moderatione se defendat, non est peccatum."

[18]ST IIa IIae, q. 42, a. 2: "Et ideo ex suo genere est peccatum morale."

[19]ST IIa IIae, q. 42, a. 2, ad 3: "Et ideo perturbatio huius regiminis non habet rationem seditionis."

[20]ST IIa IIae, q. 100, a. 1: "Si vero formaliter aliquis falsum dicat, habens voluntatem falsum dicendi, licet sit verum id quod dicitur, inquantum tamen huiusmodi actus est voluntarius et moralis, habet per se falsitatem, et per accidens veritatem."

[21]Richard McCormick, "Killing the Patient," in *Considering Veritatis Splendor*, ed. John Wilkins (Cleveland, OH: Pilgrim, 1994), 15–16.

[22]Bernard Hoose, "Circumstances, Intentions, and Intrinsically Evil Acts," in *The Splendor of Accuracy*, ed. Joseph A. Selling and Jan Jens (Grand Rapids, MI: Eerdmans, 1995), 138–39.

[23]ST Ia IIae, q. 12, a. 2: "Unde, etsi semper sit finis, non tamen oportet quod semper sit ultimi finis."

[24]ST Ia IIae, q. 13, a. 3.

[25]Jean Porter, "The Moral Act in *Veritatis Splendor* and in Aquinas's *Summa Theologiae*: A Comparative Analysis," in *Veritatis Splendor: American Responses*, ed. M. E. Allsopp and J. J. O'Keefe (Kansas City: Sheed and Ward, 1995), 283.

[26]Ibid., 284.

[27]Ibid.

[28]The *De malo* offers Thomas's detailed treatment of this. In *De malo* q. 3, a. 9 (Leonine, 84–88), Aquinas carefully demonstrates, with the structure of the practical syllogism, that the man who commits adultery is choosing the enjoyment of pleasure; he chooses *not* to see the action as one inconsistent with his marriage or his obedience to God. By comparison, the treatment in the *Summa theologiae* (at Ia IIae, q. 77, a. 2, ad 4) is a very sketchy summary.

[29]ST Ia IIae, q.19, a. 3, ad 1: "quia appetitus voluntatis non potest esse de bono, nisi prius a ratione apprehenditur."

[30]ST Ia IIae, q.19, a. 5: "unde in talibus voluntas discordans a ratione vel conscientia errante non est mala."

[31]ST Ia IIae, q.19, a.7, ad 3: "Unde sive voluntas eius quod est secundum se malum, etiam sub ratione boni; sive sit boni sub ratione mali; semper voluntas erit mala. Sed ad hoc quod sit voluntas bona requiritur quod sit boni sub ratione boni, idest quod velit bonum et propter bonum."

[32]ST Ia IIae, q.19, a.10: "Quia hanc propriam inclinationem consequentem naturam vel apprehensionem particularem huius rei habet res a Deo sicut a causa effectiva. Unde consuevit dici quod conformatur quantum ad hoc voluntas hominis voluntati divinae, quia vult hoc quod Deus vult eum velle."

[33]See ST IIa IIae, q. 20, a. 13, on the status of the order of charity in heaven.

[34]ST Ia IIae, q. 20, a. 5, *sed contra*: "eventus sequens non facit actum malum qui erat bonus, nec bonum qui erat malus: puta si aliquis det eleemosynam pauperi, qua ille abutatur ad peccatum, nihil deperit ei qui eleemosynam facit. Et similiter, si aliquis patienter ferat iniuriam sibi factam, non propter hoc excusatur ille qui fecit."

[35]ST Ia IIae, q. 20, a. 5, c.: "cum enim aliquis cogitans quod ex opere suo multa mala possunt sequi, nec propter hoc dimittit, ex hoc apparet voluntas eius esse magis inordinata."

[36]ST Ia IIae, q. 21, a.1, c.: "Sed peccatum proprie consistit in actu qui agitur propter finem aliquem, cum non habet debitum ordinem ad finem illum."

[37]ST Ia IIae, q. 21, a. 2: "Unde reliquitur quod bonum vel malum in solis actibus voluntariis consti-tuit rationem laudis vel culpae, in quibus idem est malum, peccatum et culpa."

[38]ST Ia IIae, q. 21, a. 3, ad 2: "ipse etiam, inquantum est alterius, scilicet communitatis, cuius est pars, meretur aliquid vel demeretur, inquantum actus suos bene vel male disponit."

[39]ST Ia IIae, q. 21, a. 4, ad 3: "Sed totum quod homo est, et quod potest et habet, ordinandum est ad Deum; et ideo omnis actus hominis bonus vel malus habet rationem meriti vel demeriti apud Deum."

Selected Further Reading

Anscombe, Elizabeth. *Intention*. 2d ed. Ithaca, N.Y.: Cornell University Press, 1969.

Brock, Stephen L. *Action and Conduct: Thomas Aquinas and the Theory of Action*. Edinburgh: T. and T. Clark, 1998.

D'Arcy, Eric. *Human Acts: An Essay in their Moral Evaluation*. Oxford: Clarendon, 1963.

Dedek, John. "Intrinsically Evil Acts: An Historical Study of the Mind of St. Thomas." *Thomist* 43 (1979): 385–413.

Finnis, John. "Object and Intention in Moral Judgments according to Aquinas." *Thomist* 55 (1991): 1–27.

Flannery, Kevin. "What Is Included in a Means to an End?" *Gregorianum* 74 (1992): 499–513.

Gallagher, David M. "Aquinas on Goodness and Moral Goodness," in *Thomas Aquinas and His Legacy*. Ed. David Gallagher. Studies in Philosophy and the History of Philosophy, Vol. 28. Washington, DC: Catholic University of America Press, 1994.

Hoose, Bernard. "Circumstances, Intentions and Intrinsically Evil Acts." in *The Splendor of Accuracy*. Ed. Joseph A. Selling and Jan Jens. Grand Rapids: Eerdmans, 1995.

McInerny, Ralph. *Aquinas on Human Action: A Theory of Practice*. Washington, DC: Catholic University of America Press, 1992.

Pinckaers, Servais. "Le rôle de la fin dans l'action morale selon saint Thomas." *Revue des sciences philosophiques et théologiques* 45 (1961): 393–421.

Porter, Jean. "The Moral Act in *Veritatis Splendor* and in Aquinas's *Summa Theologiae*: A Comparative Analysis," in *Veritatis Splendor: American Responses*. Ed. M. E. Allsopp and J. J. O'Keefe. Kansas City: Sheed and Ward, 1995.

The Passions of the Soul (Ia IIae, qq. 22–48)

Kevin White

The theme of the "passions of the soul" invites reflection both because of its moral and practical urgency and because of its vivid contribution to theoretical consideration of human nature. Analogously, Aquinas's unprecedentedly elaborate "treatise" on the passions is of interest both for its part in the great argument of the *Summa theologiae*, where it is subordinated to the goal of clarifying the action by which the rational creature finds happiness in a return to its Creator and Exemplar, and for its own absorbing argument and detail, which make it a precursor of early modern philosophical treatises on the passions that had other aims.[1] In his youthful *Sentences* commentary and *De veritate*, Aquinas took up a patristic tradition of occasional reflection on the passions in connection with such topics as the suffering of Christ, the theological virtues of hope and charity, fear as a gift of the Holy Spirit, and the rewards and punishments of the afterlife.[2] In the treatise in the *Summa*, he uses his theological and philosophical sources on the passions, his skill at arranging material for maximum intelligibility, and his highly "formal" use of language to produce a comprehensive survey of the passions from the point of view of human nature and human action.[3]

"PASSION" AND ITS SUBJECT

The treatise is characterized by special distinctions between proper and improper senses of words. Meaning is extended on two sides. On one hand, particular passions lend their names to acts of will that resemble them (Ia IIae, q. 23, a. 1, ad 3); in this respect the treatise both transcends its assigned topic and prepares an imagery and a vocabulary for dis-

cussions of more important, spiritual realities in the *Secunda secundae*.[4] On the other hand, because passions are "motions" of sense-appetite that resemble motions of bodies, they and their effects are metaphorically described in terms of the latter (Ia IIae, q. 23, a. 4; q. 37, a. 2); in this respect the treatise seems to support the view that poetry is the appropriate kind of speech about passion. With likeness to both, passions are motions situated "between" spiritual and bodily motions. All three kinds of motion occur in human nature, making up a complex "human motion" that, in its complexity, is morally problematic.

Aquinas's vocabulary gives the actuations of intellect, will, sense-powers, and the locomotive power no distinctive names corresponding to *passiones*, the generic term for actuations or motions of sense-appetite. This term itself has several meanings, which the treatise begins by sorting out. The related verb *pati* in its widest sense refers to any reception, although reception without elimination should rather be called *perfici*, "a being brought to a perfection." More properly, *pati* means reception accompanied by elimination; what is eliminated may be either unsuitable, as when a body gets rid of sickness in being healed, or suitable, as when a body loses health in becoming sick. The latter corresponds to the most proper sense of *passio*, because *pati* connotes a "being pulled" (*trahi*), and it seems to be the violence implied by "pulling" ("yanking" or "jerking" might be better here) that suggests a thing's being taken away from what is suitable to it; *pati* in this most proper sense signifies a worsening, a production (*generatio*) of the worse out of the better that is, more precisely, a destruction (*corruptio*). Passion as mere reception occurs in the soul when it senses or understands; passion as reception with elimination occurs in the composite of soul and body when it is "affected" (*patitur*), and so only incidentally in the soul itself. Since change for the worse more properly has the nature (*ratio*) of passion than does change for the better, pain is more properly called a passion than is joy (Ia IIae, q. 22, a. 1). This point anticipates a striking theme of the treatise, that pain more fully has the nature of passion than does *any* of the other ten passions distinguished (Ia IIae, q. 35, a. 1), being seconded in this respect by fear (Ia IIae, q. 41, a. 1). Pain is analogous to, as well as a direct cause of, bodily distress, and is itself called a sickness (Ia IIae, q. 35, a. 1; Ia IIae, q. 37, a. 4). The treatise's question on the dire effects of pain on soul and body (Ia IIae, q. 37) is followed by one that, in keeping with classical and Arabic presentations of philosophy as a healing art,[5] as well as with Dominican concern for *cura animarum*[6] (cf. "psychiatry"), offers practical advice on alleviating pain. Is this advice emblematic of a quasi-medical intention throughout the treatise? Is passion a sickness of soul?

The opening comparisons of passion to disease and destruction, together with the second article's approving report of Cicero's term for passions, "perturbations" (Ia IIae, q. 22, a. 2, *sed contra*), do form an impression that passion is essentially disorder. Two questions later, however, Aquinas argues that Cicero's Stoic view of passions as intrinsically evil was mistaken, and that they are called perturbations or diseases only when not moderated by reason (Ia IIae, q. 24, a. 2). The initial perspective is clarified by remarks later in the *Prima secundae* concerning the effects of the fall into sin on the human sense-appetite; the second, wider perspective depends on the presentation in the *Prima pars* of human nature as a creature.

Aquinas's view of the integrity of human nature is suggestively sketched by Anton C. Pegis in an interpretation that proceeds by dramatic emphasis. The human soul is "not a substance *and* a form, but a substance *as* a form, a substance whose spiritual nature is essentially suited to informing matter." Explanation of this suitability must answer a question: "How does it happen that the soul, which is an immaterial and intellectual substance, has *lesser* than intellectual powers?" The question implies that understanding of the unity of

human nature must take its bearings from the highest human power, intellect. "The crux of the matter lies in seeing that, though man has powers in addition to the intellect, he is not *more* than intellectual. . . . [T]he human intellect is not fully an intellect *without the sensible powers*. . . . [T]he *intellect and the senses taken together* constitute in their togetherness the adequate intellectual power of the human soul as an intellectual substance." The human being is an intellect; but it is the kind of intellect that includes, because it needs, sense-powers; and sense-powers require the human body as their instrument, a body whose *raison d'être* is thus intellectual.[7]

While Pegis's remarks are based directly on *Quaestiones de anima*, the doctrine they sketch is implicit in qq. 75–76 of the *Prima pars*, and is therefore a premise of the questions on human action in the *Prima secundae*. The thematic difference between Ia, qq. 84–89 and Ia IIae, qq. 6–48 corresponds to Aquinas's contrast between the assimilating cognitive powers Pegis mentions, by which the soul takes things in, and the powers of will, sense-appetite, and locomotion, by which it "goes out" to things (Ia, q. 78, a. 1). One could ask about the part passion has in this complex "outgoing" of the soul (cf. "emotion") by echoing Pegis: how is it that an immaterial, intellectual substance is subject to passion, particularly in view of the fact that passion often vehemently interferes with intellectual operation (Ia IIae, q. 24, a. 3; Ia IIae, q. 33, a. 3; Ia IIae, q. 37, a. 1; Ia IIae, q. 44, a. 2; Ia IIae, q. 45, a. 4; Ia IIae, q. 48, a. 3)?

The *Summa*'s accounting for passion begins with the apparently axiomatic observation that "appetite"—a needy predilection to pursue a good—is a consequence of form (Ia, q. 80, a. 1): each still "shape" or form, it seems, is accompanied by a propelling "weight," that is, a tendency to move toward something good. In things without knowledge, which possess only their own forms, appetite is "natural"; in things capable of knowing, that is, of taking in forms of other things and containing them in a God-like way, the forms so received cause a higher kind of inclination, an appetitive power of soul (ibid.). Such a power is passive, for its nature is to be moved by what is apprehended in cognition; and because intellect and sense are distinct kinds of apprehensive power, intellectual appetite or will is correspondingly distinct from sense-appetite (Ia, q. 80, a. 2). If the human intellect is not fully an intellect without sense-powers, neither is it wholly itself without two further powers: will, the tendency following from its own universal apprehensions, and sense-appetite, the tendency following from the time-and-place-conditioned apprehensions of its sense-powers. The completed intellectual power of the human soul as an intellectual substance is constituted by intellect, senses, will, and sense-appetite together. Sense-appetite and its movements, the passions, are themselves "intellectual"—present on account of intellect—in the human soul.

So described, the four powers suggest a four-sided figure in which sense and will each terminate lines flowing from intellect, and sense-appetite terminates two other lines flowing from sense and will: sense-appetite is more remote from, more "opposed" to, intellect than are either will or sense. The progression from sense-powers to sense-appetite parallels the progression from intellect to will; is there also co-operation between sense-appetite and will that parallels co-operation between sense and intellect in abstractive knowledge? And what relation is suggested by the diagonal from intellect to sense-appetite?

Sense-appetite has a complex role in human action, to which it contributes both its own actuation (passion) and a bodily performance (*executio*) of passion. Its actuation, in keeping with the rule that appetite follows apprehension, is directed by the universal apprehension of reason acting through the intermediary of the "cogitative" power or "particular reason," an inner sense-power that apprehends and compares invisible *intentiones* or "values," such as danger, in objects of the outer senses. This mediation allows universal premises to produce particular conclusions that modify passion, as when anger or fear is aroused or diminished by the application of general considerations. Moreover, human passion, unlike that of brute animals, does not at once or inevitably carry out its bodily performance, but awaits approval or disapproval by the higher appetitive power, the will (Ia, q. 81, a. 3).

PASSION AND ACTION

Although Aquinas is much concerned in the *Summa* with the upsetting by sin of this delicate order of reason, will, passion, and body, his deeper consideration is that human nature allowed for the upset, a point he regularly makes with reference to a comparison in Aristotle's *Politics* according to which soul governs body with "despotic" rule and intellect governs appetite with "politic or kingly" rule.[8] Aquinas's commentary on the *Politics* explains that despotic rule is over slaves, who, because they belong entirely to the ruler, cannot offer any resistance, and so immediately, without contradiction, carry out the ruler's command, whereas politic or kingly rule is over free citizens, who, as free, are able to contradict the ruler.[9] The *Summa* reverses the comparison, making the political point illustrate the psychological one: in contrast to the slavish body, which "belongs entirely" to the soul and immediately obeys its command, sense-appetite, like a free citizen, has "something of its own" by which it can, even if it should not, resist reason's command (Ia, q. 81, a. 3, ad 2; Ia IIae, q. 17, a. 7). Although sense-appetite's resistance to reason is a result of sin, its partial self-possession is an essential, spirited aspect of human nature as it was in the beginning.

At first a mere possibility in the little kingdom of human nature, the uprising of passion against reason has since become the rule, as ordinary observation and the New Testament confirm: "What I would, that I do not; but what I hate, that I do"; and "I see another law in my members, warring against the law of my mind" (Rom 7:15, 23; cf. Ia, q. 81, obj. 2; Ia IIae, q. 17, obj. 1 and ad 1; Ia IIae, q. 77, a. 2, *sed contra*). Rebellion can occur in the body because of a native or momentary disposition to foster and magnify a passion independently of reason's direction (Ia IIae, q. 17, a. 7, ad 2). Human nature in the particular must be considered not only generically as animal and specifically as rational, but also with reference to the bodily makeup that is an individual's own "nature": predisposition to anger, for example, is more "natural," in the sense of being more liable to be physically transmitted from parent to child, than is predisposition to desire for pleasure (Ia IIae, q. 46, a. 5). Such "genetic" considerations argue for mildness in moral judgments of particular cases of disordered passion and, more generally, respect for the material limitations of human freedom.

Sense-appetite itself can get ahead of reason because, together with its subordination to reason through the cogitative power, it has "something of its own" inasmuch as it can be moved by imagination and external senses, and so can resist reason by submitting to a sensing or imagining that dwells on something pleasant vetoed by reason or something unpleasant commanded by it (Ia, q. 81, a. 3, ad 2). Moreover, a movement of sense-appetite can be suddenly aroused by an apprehension of imagination or sense, and such movement, called "antecedent" passion, pre-empts reason's command, although it could have been prevented had reason foreseen it (Ia IIae, q. 17, a. 7).[10]

By conditioning one to take as good what otherwise would not seem so, sense-appetite can move and dominate the will. In fact, it has an edge over will in predisposing action, for action concerns what is individual, and sense-appetite, unlike will, is a power directed to individual things, capable of making them appear in a certain light (Ia IIae, q. 9, a. 2, ad 2; Ia IIae, q. 77, a. 1). Predisposition to action may come wholly from the intellectual part. If, however, intellect is "clouded" by passion, there is still some movement of will, and passion may be driven off, but human nature has become divided, with different "seemings" in different parts of its soul; in the extreme case of madness, passion compels the will to follow it (Ia IIae, q. 10, a. 3).

Of itself, as a movement of sense-appetite, passion is morally neither good nor evil, although there is something like moral goodness in the passion of brute animals inasmuch as it is directed by the knowledge and will of the Creator (Ia IIae, q. 24, a. 1; Ia IIae, q. 24, a. 3, ad 3). But as subject to the command of reason and will in human beings, passion is voluntary, being either commanded or not forbidden by will, and is morally good or evil to an even greater extent than is bodily movement, for sense-appetite is more "inward," "closer" to the will, than are bodily members (Ia IIae, q. 24, a. 1). The apparently severe view of the Stoics that all passion is evil was due to their failure to distinguish between intellectual appetite and sense-appetite, which led them to use the term "will" to describe any rational movement of appetite and the term "passion" for any irrational one; the Peripatet-

ics, by contrast, called every movement of sense-appetite a passion, holding that such movement is good when made orderly by reason and bad when not (Ia IIae, q. 24, a. 2).

The Stoics of course held that all passion lessens the goodness of a human act. But according to the Peripatetic view, the perfection of human goodness requires that passion be not removed, but rather moderated by reason, for the human good, being based on reason, is more perfect when reason's domain is extended in human nature. Passions, no less than bodily movements, should be made orderly, not suppressed, by reason, so that, besides willing good and accomplishing it in bodily action, one may be moved toward it by the sense-appetite (Ia IIae, q. 24, a. 3). Goodness or evil of action may be increased by "consequent" passion, which follows a judgment of reason, either by "overflow" of the will's movement into sense-appetite, or by reason's choice to let sense-appetite be affected in a way that allows reason to act more readily (Ia IIae, q. 24, a. 3, ad 1). Aquinas does argue that some passions, such as compassion and shame, are inherently good, and others, such as envy, inherently evil (Ia IIae, q. 24, a. 4), but the paucity of his examples suggests that most kinds of passion are of themselves morally neutral, allowing the presence or absence of reason's moderating influence.

The treatise's general point concerning the moral need to have passion moderated and made orderly by reason prepares for subsequent discussions of sense-appetite as the subject both of the cardinal virtues courage and temperance (Ia IIae, q. 56, a. 4), and of ravages in human nature caused by man's fall into sin (Ia IIae, q. 85, a. 3).

DISTINCTION OF PASSIONS

> Then, as fire moves upward by its form,
> being born to mount where it most abides
>   in its matter, so the mind thus seized
>   enters into desire, which is a spiritual
> movement, and never rests till the thing
>   loved makes it rejoice.[11]

—Dante, *Purgatory*, Canto XVIII, 28–33

The discussions of specific passions that occupy the bulk of the treatise contribute many observations to the analysis of human action, which is Thomas's goal in the *Secunda pars*. The distinction among kinds of passion depends on the chain of inference by which Aristotelian psychology attempts to penetrate and clarify the obscure inwardness of souls: actuations of soul are distinguished by their objects, powers of soul by their actuations, and kinds of soul by their powers.[12] Accordingly, specific differentiation among the actuations of soul called passions is based on formal distinctions among objects of sense-appetite. The result is an enumeration of eleven passions related to one another in a fixed natural order. Consideration of this order can take its bearings either from the aim and endpoint of appetite, the delightful, or from its starting-point, the lovable (Ia IIae, q. 25, a. 1). The latter perspective reconstructs the order of emergence of the passions, which constitutes a suite or sequence that is like a narrative, of which genres of poetry such as comedy and tragedy represent portions. Knowledge of the whole story might be especially useful to one charged with care of souls, enabling him to quickly "find his place" when dealing with a particular soul caught up in some passion.

Formal differences among objects of passion are differences between effects of their moving powers (Ia IIae, q. 23, a. 4; Ia IIae, q. 30, a. 2), of which three are crucial: that between the attractive "pull" of what is good and the repelling "push" of what is evil; that between the calming effect of a present good and the agitating attraction of an absent one; and that between the simple attraction of good as such and the struggle provoked by a great or momentous (*arduum*) good not easily possessed.[13] A good that is an object of appetite is, more exactly, something "delightful" or "calming," as distinct from a "useful" or a "noble" (*honestum*) good (Ia, q. 5, a. 6). The delightful is the constant goal of appetite, always at least remotely in view—in responding to an evil, to an absent good, or to what calls for struggle, appetite anticipates the calm of something delightful beyond these objects. The three contrasts between objects on the basis of their motive power, then, may be stated as follows: between the calmingly delightful and the disturbingly painful that opposes it; between the present and the absent

delightful; and between the delightful as merely attractive and as something to be struggled toward.

The delightful is a subdivision of the good; good in turn is a transcendental property of beings.[14] The objects of passion (that is, the delightful and its adumbrations) are *beings*, presented and apprehended in such a way as to move the soul. Good is a property of any being as such; in things themselves, an evil is a privation of good, but when apprehended, it becomes a "being of reason," taking on the status of a positive contrary (Ia IIae, q. 36, a. 1). The consequence for the appetite that follows apprehension is that what is evil is something to be fled, just as what is good is to be pursued; although, in knowledge and appetite, as in things themselves, good remains prior to and more forceful than evil. Hence, most passions belong to ordered pairs consisting of a primary response to the delightful and a secondary response to the painful.

The opposition between the delightful's presence and absence is the basis of the sequence of passion (Ia IIae, q. 30, a. 2). The completeness of a sequence, like completeness as such, is determined by the number three, which represents the togetherness of a beginning, middle, and end.[15] In the sequence of passion, the threesome is illustrated by the three moments of natural action, namely inclination, movement, and rest, evident in the weight, fall, and repose of a body dropped to the ground (Ia IIae, q. 23, a. 4; Ia IIae, q. 26, a. 2). The three corresponding moments of passion are distinguished by the three appearances of the delightful, which most basically is agreeable (*conveniens*); but which also, if absent, is attractive; and if present, is wholly itself, that is, delightful or calming. The agreeable, the attractive, and the calming cause, respectively, the passions of love, desire, and delight, the basic moments in the sequence of passion.[16] Each of these moments is matched by a passion caused by the appearance of the delightful's shadow and contrary, the painful, which most basically is disagreeable; but which also, if absent but approaching, is repellent, and if present, disturbing. The disagreeable causes love's contrary, hatred; the repellent desire's contrary, aversion; the disturbing delight's contrary, pain.

The first object of passion, the delightful as agreeable, is a good presented as simply good by apprehension and taken as simply good by appetite. In something like an act of attention, appetite fixes on—or, better, is "taken" by—this good so as to acquire a "kinship" (*connaturalitas*) or "harmony" with it, a "proportion" or "adaptation" to it, a state of being "well-pleased" with it (*complacentia*), these being so many characterizations of the primary passion, love (Ia IIae, q. 26, aa. 1–2; Ia IIae, q. 27, a. 1; Ia IIae, q. 29, a. 1).[17] A loved good is something known to, if only to the extent of having been seen by, one who loves it; and it either actually or potentially resembles the one who loves it (Ia IIae, q. 27, aa. 2–3). Resemblance is oneness between lover and loved that precedes love; oneness of resemblance causes the "affective" oneness that is love itself; and love's first effect is to lead the lover to "real" oneness with the known, loved good (Ia IIae, q. 28, a. 1, ad 2). Union of resemblance anticipates love; the union that is love anticipates the terminus of passion, delight; and "real" union coincides with delight.

The passion of love is a special case in Aquinas's cosmic and metaphysical understanding of love, an understanding whose comprehensiveness rivals that of ancient pagan discussions of *eros*, but is alien to narrower, sentimental modern views. On one hand, he believes, as a Christian, that God *is* love and that the supreme human virtue is the love called charity (Ia, q. 20, a. 1; IIa IIae, q. 23, a. 6). On the other hand, he thinks that all natural things are moved by love. There is, in his view, an inevitable advance from knowledge to appetite, and from appetite to love, appetite's first moment. In unknowing "natural" things (plants, for example), "natural appetite" and "natural love" follow solely from the Creator's knowledge. Higher creatures have their own ability to know, and thus to originate the progression from knowledge to appetite to love. The appetite and love of the higher creatures is divided into two categories: "sensitive" in animals; "rational" in spiritual creatures (Ia IIae, q. 26, a. 1).

Human beings, as rational animals, are subject to both higher kinds of love. Although only sensitive love is a passion in the proper sense, the principal theme of the questions on love is "human" love, which is ambiguously sensitive, rational, or both. Human love is clarified by two important distinctions: one contrasts love in general with the chosen, rational love called "dilection" and the perfect, appreciative love known as "charity"; the other divides all loves into "friendship-love" of someone—oneself or another—for his or her own sake and "concupiscent love" of what is loved *not* for its own sake, but as a good wanted *for* oneself or someone else (Ia IIae, q. 26, aa. 3–4).[18]

If sense-appetite begins by "harmonizing" with a kindred good thing, its second moment is a clash with what is alien and evil, that is, the painful as disagreeable (Ia IIae, q. 29, a. 1). This "discord" of hatred can easily seem more forceful than love, but a hatred is always secondary to and weaker than some love, both because its object is intelligible only as the destruction of or obstacle to an agreeable good that is loved, and because its shrinking from harm is instrumental to love's approach to a good (Ia IIae, q. 29, aa. 2–3). When transferred from sense-appetite to will, the notion of hatred is associated with two moral evils, self-hatred and hatred of truth. Although self-hatred, properly speaking, is impossible, since a thing can want only good for itself, a man, for example, may be said to "hate himself" inasmuch as he takes as good what is bad for him, or takes himself to be what is less than best in him, namely the mind (Ia IIae, q. 29, a. 4). Again, while hatred of truth in general is impossible, a particular truth may be hated if someone wishes that it were not so, or wishes that it was left unknown (Ia IIae, q. 29, a. 5). A peculiarity of hatred, even as a passion in the proper sense, is that its object may be universal, in contrast to the singularity of anger's object (Ia IIae, q. 29, a. 6). This seems to indicate a pre-rational basis for the hatreds that move groups of human beings against one another.

The static harmony and dissonance of love and hatred are followed by two lively movements of appetite: "concupiscence" or "desire," the pursuit of a loved good that promises delight, and "aversion," the flight from a hated evil that threatens pain. The first of these passions, and presumably the second, have analogues in movements of will (Ia IIae, q. 30, aa. 1–2). Desire is the attraction of appetite by and toward an approachable delightful good, aversion the repelling of appetite by and from an approaching painful evil. Both the endless successiveness of natural desire and the unlimited complications of desire by rational calculation imply infinity and dissatisfaction (Ia IIae, q. 30, aa. 3–4).

IRASCIBLE PASSIONS

The generic object of love and hatred, desire and aversion, and delight and pain is sensible good and evil "as such"—the delightful and the painful. But sometimes, Aquinas observes, the soul feels difficulty in acquiring a sensible good or avoiding a sensible evil inasmuch as these actions are above one's ability to perform them easily. Such cases, he argues, reveal a different generic object of passion, namely sensible good or evil *as* momentous in itself and difficult to approach or avoid. Following Aristotle's inference from objects to actuations to powers, Aquinas thinks that these two generic objects indicate not merely a distinction between classes of passion, but a division of sense-appetite into a *concupiscible* power that responds to sensible good or evil as such, and an *irascible* power that responds to them as momentous and difficult (Ia, q. 81, a. 2; Ia IIae, q. 23, a. 1). There are long-standing objections to the distinction between concupiscible and irascible powers;[19] but suggestive parallels may be seen in Plato's distinction between "desiring" and "spirited" parts of the soul, in Freud's distinction between "erotic" and "aggressive" instincts, and, more remotely, in the early modern distinction between "the beautiful" and "the sublime."[20]

The concupiscible appetite seems to operate as continually as perception, the irascible only in special circumstances. Arousal of the latter signals interruption in the smooth concupiscible flow of love toward the delightful and of hatred away from the painful: suddenly simple desire and aversion are no longer enough to ensure this flow; an obstacle has appeared; the soul responds by tensing for struggle. In meeting its new, elevated object, the soul seems to become more alert and potentially stronger. The irascible appetite is a higher perfection of animal nature than is the concupiscible insofar as, by taking on a present difficulty for the sake of a remote good, it

approximates the foresight of reason; but despite its appearance of superior strength and knowingness, it depends on the concupiscible appetite, which it serves as a defender (Ia, q. 81, a. 1).[21]

The objects of the irascible appetite are complex: they are either good *and* hard to get, or evil *and* hard to avoid or defeat. The range of response in appetite is symmetrically complex: whereas the concupiscible appetite inclines simply toward good and away from evil, the irascible may either approach a promising difficult good *as* good, in hope, or fall away from it *as* unreachable, in despair. Furthermore, it may either shrink from a menacing difficult evil *as* evil, in fear, or attack it *as* a conquerable difficulty, in daring (Ia IIae, q. 23, a. 2). What decides whether it will hope for or despair of a momentous good, and whether it will timorously shrink from or daringly face a momentous evil, is a comparison between one's own forces and the object's difficulty (Ia IIae, q. 40, aa. 1–2, 4; Ia IIae, q. 41, a. 2; Ia IIae, q. 42, a. 5; Ia IIae, q. 43, a. 2; Ia IIae, q. 45, a. 2), a comparison that seems further evidence of the irascible appetite's canniness. Since daring follows on hope of victory and despair on fear of difficulty (Ia IIae, q. 45, a. 2), hope and fear are the primary irascible passions. The objects of all these passions share the features "future" and "difficult," and are differentiated by the contrarieties "good-evil," and "possible-impossible": a great future good that seems difficult but possible to obtain is hoped for (Ia IIae, q. 40, a. 1); a great future evil that seems not only difficult but nearly impossible to overcome is feared (fear presumes *some* hope of escape [Ia IIae, q. 42, a. 2]); a great future evil that seems difficult but possible to overcome is daringly opposed (Ia IIae, q. 45, aa. 1–2); a great future good that seems not only difficult but impossible to obtain is despaired of (Ia IIae, q. 40, a. 4).

The treatise's discussion of these passions draws attention to their dependence on and fostering of distinctive, sometimes distorting perspectives on time, particularly on the future. Experience causes hope inasmuch as it allows the time for acquiring skill at doing something easily, or reveals that what seemed impossible is not; but it also causes despair by showing that what seemed possible is impossible (Ia IIae, q. 40, a. 5). On the other hand, hope is prominent in those without foresight, such as the young, the drunken, and the thoughtless (Ia IIae, q. 40, a. 6); despite its element of calculation, hope easily becomes foolish. In fear, the irascible appetite's projection onto the future is confined to a middle ground between unimaginably remote and apparently inevitable evils, both of which exclude fear (Ia IIae, q. 42, a. 2). Fear is especially aroused by the appearance of a sudden or an irremediable evil, which, respectively, focus attention on an imminent and an everlasting future (Ia IIae, q. 42, aa. 5–6). Daring makes one enter into action confidently, but quickly become discomfited by unforeseen danger; this effect is contrary to that of the virtue of courage, which makes one begin to act slowly and deliberately, but then persevere in the midst of expected danger (Ia IIae, q. 45, a. 4).

The irascible passions in general elevate the soul above the level of the comparatively sluggish concupiscible appetite. Anger, the passion with no contrary, is an extreme condition of the irascible appetite itself. Anger presupposes a complex configuration of other passions; it simultaneously looks to both good and evil, and to both past and present; and it implies the workings of reason and justice (Ia IIae, q. 46, aa. 1, 2, 4, 7). The moving cause of anger is something done against one angered (Ia IIae, q. 47, a. 1). Although the objects of all irascible passions imply difficulty, and so some kind of "againstness," only anger essentially presupposes opposition by a person, specifically one who has performed an act manifesting a deliberate, unjust slight of the one made angry. But the remembered evil act is only part of anger's complex object: an angry man looks not only back on the demeaning pain he has suffered, but also forward to a vengeance that he dares as a victory, and desires and hopes for as a pleasant, reasoned act of justice. The reasoning consists in comparing and inferring: "Since you have done this unjust harm to me, I will repay you with another, similar harm that will restore justice between us" (Ia IIae, q. 46, a. 4). The prospect of a justice accomplished both by and for oneself is singularly enticing, and the pleasure of revenge is already present in the thought of and hope for it (Ia IIae, q. 48, a. 1). Anger's object is bittersweet, blending past painful injustice into future pleasant revenge, the latter appearing as an attractive restoration of equilibrium.

Despite its "intelligent" sophistication, anger, more than any other passion, disturbs the body and therefore the power of reason (Ia IIae, q. 48, aa. 2, 4). Anger listens to reason, but imperfectly—the harm suffered provokes it to begin to follow reason, but not to submit to the measure of reason in meting out revenge. Its syllogism thus tends to be specious, inasmuch as the vengeance planned tends *not* to be comparable to the harm suffered, but rather excessive (Ia IIae, q. 46, a. 4, ad 3). In its reasoned beginning, anger, aware of its potential for excess, holds back speech; at an intermediate point, when it begins to eclipse reason but has not yet wholly seized the body, it may give way to loquacity; but eventually it immobilizes the body in general and the tongue in particular, and so again hinders speech (Ia IIae, q. 48, a. 4). It advances from lively, percipient reasoning to blind, mute paralysis. Still, successful anger—as distinct from the lingering resentment of the "embittered" (Ia IIae, q. 46, a. 8)—issues in the pleasure of revenge, and because its intensely imagined end is finite, it is, unlike the more steady state of hatred, transient (Ia IIae, q. 46, a. 6). Its limited temporal arc, its union of past, present, and future, its presumption of reason and justice, and its development of relations between persons make anger an eminently dramatic passion.

DELIGHT AND PAIN

The objects of irascible passions result from complications of the absent good and evil that are objects of desire and aversion. The absence of all these objects is converted into presence when a remote good or evil is united with the subject of appetite to produce delight or pain. These final passions, anticipated by earlier ones, are the two ways in which appetite's movement, toward or from, comes to a stop, delight resembling a "natural" repose, pain a violent arrest (Ia IIae, q. 31, a. 8, ad 2). In love and hatred, appetite seems indifferent to time; in desire, aversion, and the irascible passions, it projects itself onto the future; in delight and pain, it is absorbed into the present. Although delight may be prolonged, it, like eternity, is *simul tota*, complete in the instant (Ia IIae, q. 31, aa. 1–2; cf. Ia, q. 10, a. 1). It is thus, for one delighted, a momentary escape from time's successiveness, and from estimations of time entailed by desire, aversion, and the irascible passions. The ever-renewed sequence of passion causes attention to alternate between an approaching future moment and a consuming present one.

The objects of delight and pain are, respectively, a good embraced and an invading evil. Delight is the perceived achievement of a completion (Ia IIae, q. 31, a. 1). It is the conscious taking possession of a good that was loved and desired—and perhaps hoped for, despaired of, or sought in anger. Its proper cause is operation: delight consists in *doing* something, or rather two things together, namely taking hold of a good and taking cognizance of the taking-hold (Ia IIae, q. 32, a. 1). Pain, delight's formal contrary, is a perceived, forced union with an evil that was hated and avoided—and perhaps feared or met with daring (Ia IIae, q. 35, a. 1). In keeping with the priority of good to evil, pain presupposes removal of an enjoyed or desired good (Ia IIae, q. 36, aa. 1–2). It also presupposes both a disposing and an efficient cause: the former is the subject's longing for what is proper to it as a being, namely unity, a unity that pain seems to sever in the experience of a "falling apart" (Ia IIae, q. 36, a. 3); the latter is an overwhelming force (Ia IIae, q. 36, a. 4).

After establishing the complex operation of "knowing appropriation" as the cause of delight, Aquinas identifies particular ways of knowing and objects of knowledge that cause human delight. An important general point is that change causes human delight for three reasons: because our nature, being itself changeable, finds different things suitable at different times; because an object of our delight may become excessive and so no longer please; and because our desire to know things wholly leads us to enjoy considering their parts one by one (Ia IIae, q. 32, a. 2). Thus, our delight, which is a stasis complete in the moment, nevertheless thrives on change, either because the moment passes in ourselves or our situation, or because the moment *must* pass for the sake of completeness of knowledge and delight.

As ever-looming end-points in the sequence of passion, delight and pain, whether expected or actual, constantly sway human choice. Precisely as end-points, that is, as encounters with anticipated good or evil, they are difficult to explain, for there is nothing beyond them with reference to which they can be analyzed. They are partially clarified by distinctions Aquinas draws between contraries, between what is essential ("of itself") and what is accidental, between prior and posterior, and between greater and less. Pursuit of delight is of itself prior to flight from pain (Ia IIae, q. 35, a. 6). Both delight and pain have intellectual analogues, joy and sorrow, which of themselves are more powerful than their bodily counterparts (Ia IIae, q. 31, aa. 3–5; Ia IIae, q. 49; Ia IIae, q. 35, aa. 2, 7). While delight and pain are formally contrary to one another, they may, with respect to different objects, be simply disparate or even complementary (Ia IIae, q. 35, a. 4). The instrumental delights of touch are most powerful of bodily delights, but the cognitive delights of sight are superior by association with intellectual delight (Ia IIae, q. 31, a. 6). The delight of contemplation is directly opposed by no corresponding pain, although the distraction of bodily pain severely hinders it (Ia IIae, q. 35, a. 5). Delights are applied as remedies for pains (Ia IIae, q. 38, a. 1). Taken together, these distinctions portray intense competition for attention between delights and pains, among delights, and among pains. The moral significance of all passions is due to their capacity to attract, command, or absorb the soul's attention. The principal irascible passions, hope and fear, are particularly attention-getting (Ia IIae, q. 40, a. 8; Ia IIae, q. 44, a. 4), but the theme of attention is most prominent in the discussions of delight and pain.

It is the complexity of human nature, the multiplicity of powers rooted in its soul's single essence, that makes possible a contest for attention among objects of different powers: since one soul can have but one attention, attraction of attention to an object of one power involves withdrawal from that of another, so that consideration of what absorbs much attention is incompatible with consideration of anything else requiring much attention (cf. Ia IIae, q. 77, a. 1). Accordingly, because pain, in particular bodily pain, commands the soul's attention imperiously, to an even greater extent than does delight, it interferes with learning and with consideration of what is already known (Ia IIae, q. 37, a. 1).

Pain's capacity to distract may be countered by love of learning and of contemplation, but pain is a powerful natural enemy of intellect. Pain is felt as a weight on the soul that tends to immobilize the movements of soul and body (Ia IIae, q. 37, a. 2). It also tends to impair action it accompanies, since one who is pained by what he does to that extent does it badly, although pain accompanied by hope of escape is an incentive to the action of getting rid of it (Ia IIae, q. 37, a. 3). Delight is to pain as rest is to weariness: the natural remedy. Aquinas allows that any delight mitigates pain, but particularly recommends weeping, condolence by friends, bathing and sleep, and the greatest of delights, contemplation of truth, which he says can lessen even bodily pain (Ia IIae, q. 38). Thus pain hinders learning and contemplation, and contemplation alleviates pain. The treatise's most far-reaching conclusion concerning the passions seems to be that intellectual knowledge is at odds with pain, but at its highest coincides with the greatest delight.

When it supervenes on another operation, the operation of delight perfects by adding to the good of the other operation the completing good of appetite's natural repose. Delight also perfects operation indirectly inasmuch as one who delights in what is done gives it an attention and care that help in doing it well (Ia IIae, q. 33, a. 4). Hence, delight in an act of reasoning is no impediment; rather, it is a help to the reasoning, although bodily delight may hinder the use of reason by distracting the soul's attention, by opposing the measure of reason through excess, or by incapacitating reason (Ia IIae, q. 33, a. 3).

The doctrine that delight as such is morally evil is doubly wrong: it is based on the erroneous assumption that all delights are bodily; further, it is rhetorically self-defeating, since no one can live without bodily pleasures, and when they who teach the doctrine are discovered taking such pleasure their hearers will be more impressed by what they do than what they say. Delight may be good or evil, depending on whether it is taken in what is in keeping with reason, and whether it accompanies right action (Ia IIae, q. 34, a. 1). In fact, the measure

of moral goodness is the delight one's will takes in right action (Ia IIae, q. 34, a. 4). The Epicurean view that delight as such is good fails to distinguish between what is of itself good and what is good "to" someone: if the latter is merely a qualified good on the assumption of a diseased condition, or an appearance of good based on misjudgment of what is suitable, then the delight is not, simply speaking, good, nor even, simply speaking, delight (Ia IIae, q. 34, a. 2).

Of itself, as the troubling of appetite by a present evil that interferes with its repose in a good, pain is an evil. But on the supposition that something painful is present, pain is good, for its absence would imply failure either to recognize the presence of the painful or to see and resist it as repugnant. In the case of bodily pain, this recognition and resistance are evidence of a healthy nature (Ia IIae, q. 39, a. 1); in the case of interior pain (sadness or sorrow), perception of evil based on right judgment of reason and resistance to it based on a well-disposed will make of sorrow a noble good (Ia IIae, q. 39, a. 2). Sorrow can also be a useful good, not in its mere opposition to a present evil, but in its further impulse to avoid evils that ought to be avoided, notably sin and its occasions: by taking these as not only evil but also painful, sorrow usefully doubles the motive for avoiding them (Ia IIae, q. 39, a. 3). This allusion to a useful sorrow for sin in general anticipates the discussion in the *Tertia pars* of repentance, the sorrow for past sins that is a virtue and a sacrament (IIIa, q. 84, a. 1; IIIa, q. 85).

To the extent that they involve recognition of and reaction to their respective objects, delight and pain operate symmetrically. To the extent that their recognition is accurate and their reaction appropriate, delight and pain are both good. No pain or sorrow, then, can be the greatest human evil. Sorrow for what appears evil but is, in fact, good is a lesser evil than would be loss of that good; sorrow for what is truly evil at least retains the goods of right judgment and right reaction (Ia IIae, q. 39, a. 4). On the other hand, there *is* a delight that is the greatest human good, namely the intellectual enjoyment of God, which is the rational creature's happiness. The immediate relevance of the treatise on the passions to *sacra doctrina* concerns the moral need to have what are properly speaking passions moderated by reason. But the treatise's wider significance lies in its remarks on "passions" of will and their involvement in the Christian divine comedy of sorrowful repentance leading to joyous vision.

Aquinas states that Plato steered a middle course between Stoics and Epicureans, holding that some delights are good and some bad, but also that none is the best good. This last point, Aquinas argues, was based on two errors. Plato thought that delight as such results from the imperfect actualities of coming-to-be and movement, and so cannot be an ultimate perfection. This clearly is true of bodily but not of intellectual delight, which accompanies not only the coming into being of knowledge in wonder and learning, but also contemplation of what is already known. Furthermore, Plato took as best the highest good simply speaking, an abstracted and unparticipated "good itself" comparable to the creator God. But, Aquinas says in an echo of Aristotle's response to this "good itself," we are speaking of what is best in human things. What is best for a thing is its ultimate end. But since "its end" may mean either what it desires to have or the very having (*usus*), the "ultimate end" may refer to God Himself, the highest good simply speaking, or to enjoyment of God, a delight that can be called "the best of human goods" (Ia IIae, q. 34, a. 3). Having already established that enjoyment of God consists in an act of contemplation (Ia IIae, q. 3, a. 8), Aquinas leaves it to the reader to bring together his two arguments against Plato. Although the enjoyment of contemplating the first cause is not a passion in the proper sense, it is the thematic high point of the discussion of delight, as well as of the entire treatise on the passions.

The refutation of Plato has an interesting genealogy. On one hand it introduces into the analysis of passion a topic that *The Book of Sentences*, as well as the tradition of *Sentences* commentaries, including that of Aquinas himself, had reserved for the very end of their survey of Christian doctrine, namely the rewards and punishment following the last judgment.[22] On the other hand, it is a response to doctrines from Plato's *Republic* and *Philebus* mediated and corrected by the *Nicomachean Ethics*.[23] Here, as elsewhere, Aquinas turns to this Aristotelian text to give expression to the Christian teaching that our last end, that is, the intellectual vision of the greatest good, is

also our greatest delight.[24] In analogous ways, then, the delightful, itself an analogous subdivision of the good, is presented by the treatise on the passions as the goal both of passion and of human life as a whole

Notes

[1] Servais Pinckaers, "Les passions et la morale," *Revue des sciences philosophiques et théologiques* 74 (1990): 379.

[2] *In III Sent.*, d. 15, q. 2 (Moos, 481–506); d. 26, q. 1 (Moos, 813–30); d. 27, q. 1 (Moos, 853–71); d. 34; *In IV Sent.*, d. 49, q. 3 (Vivès, 505–24); *De veritate*, q. 26 (Leonine, 745–87).

[3] Mark D. Jordan, "Aquinas's Construction of a Moral Account of the Passions," *Freiburger Zeitschrift für Philosophie und Theologie* 33 (1986): 71–97.

[4] Pinckaers, "Les passions et la morale," 382.

[5] See Thérèse-Anne Druart, "Al-Kindi's Ethics," *Review of Metaphysics* 47 (1993): 329–57, which points out similarities between Al-Kindi's *The Art of Dispelling Sorrows* and Boethius's *Consolation of Philosophy* (348, n. 61).

See also Edward M. Macierowski, "The Thomistic Critique of Avicennian Emanationism from the Viewpoint of the Divine Simplicity, with Special Reference to the 'Summa Contra Gentiles'" (Ph.D. diss., University of Toronto, 1979), 147–53, which, in connection with Avicenna's allusive, possibly esoteric, manner of writing, discusses the names of his philosophical work titled "Book of Healing," and of its abridgement, titled "Rescue." The principal sources of Aquinas's remedies, however, seem to be Aristotelian and patristic rather than Arabic; see Mario E. Sacchi, "La terapéutica del dolor y la tristeza según Santo Tomás," *Psychologica* 2 (1979): 85–104.

[6] See Leonard E. Boyle, O.P., *The Setting of the Summa theologiae of Saint Thomas*, The Etienne Gilson Series 5 (Toronto: Pontifical Institute of Medieval Studies, 1982), 3–4.

[7] Anton C. Pegis, "St. Thomas and the Unity of Man," in *Progress in Philosophy: Philosophical Studies in Honor of Rev. Doctor Charles A. Hart*, ed. James A. McWilliams (Milwaukee, WI: Bruce Publishing Co., 1955), 168–69. Michael Sweeney, in "Allan Bloom and Thomas Aquinas on Eros and Immortality," (*Interpretation* 23 [1996]: 445–56), states the point concisely: "As Anton Pegis puts it, the whole human being is an intellect" (452). In his Thomistic response to a contemporary authority on passion, Sweeney makes effective use of Pegis's important but rarely exploited work.

[8] Arist. *Pol.* 1254b5–7.

[9] *In I politicorum*, chap. 3 (Leonine, A87, 143–66).

[10]Antecedent passion is a consequence of sin and therefore absent from unfallen human nature (ST Ia, q. 95, a. 2; IIIa, q. 15, a. 4).

[11]*The Divine Comedy of Dante Alighieri*, with translation and comment by John D. Sinclair; *II Purgatorio* (New York: Oxford University Press, 1961), 232–35. "Poi, come 'l foco movesi in altura/ per la sua forma ch'è nata a salire/ là dove più in sua matera dura,/così l'animo preso entra in disire,/ ch'è moto spiritale, e mai non posa/ fin che la cosa amata il fa gioire."

[12]*In II De anima*, chap. 6 (Leonine, 93–94, 118–90). See Lawrence Dewan's discussion of early thirteenth-century use of the term *obiectum* in his "'*OBIECTUM*': Notes on the Invention of a Word," *Archives d'histoire doctrinale et littéraire du moyen-âge* 48 (1981): 37–96.

[13]My rendering of *arduum* as "great or momentous" follows R.-A. Gauthier's conclusion, "*L'arduum*, c'est le grand," in *Magnanimité: L'idéal de la grandeur dans la philosophie païenne et dans la théologie chrétienne* (*Bibliothèque Thomiste* 28) (Paris: Librairie Philosophique J. Vrin, 1951), 325; see 321–5 for the argument.

[14]ST Ia, q. 5, aa. 1–3; see "Good as Transcendental," in Jan A. Aertsen, *Medieval Philosophy and the Transcendentals: The Case of Thomas Aquinas* (Leiden: E. J. Brill, 1996), 290–334.

[15]Arist. *Cael.* 1.1 (268a12–19); *In I De caelo*, lect. 2, nn. 4–6 (Leonine, 6–7).

[16]All passions are called *movements of soul* (ST Ia IIae, q. 22, a. 2, *sed contra*). But in the detailed analogy between natural agents and objects of passion, the image of movement is restricted to the intermediate moment, between inclination and repose, of passion (Ia IIae, q. 23, a. 4; q. 25, a. 1); only desire, aversion, and the passions of the irascible appetite are movements in this narrower sense. The apparent inconsistency is partially resolved by the explanation that delight both is and is not movement: in delight the movement of getting hold of a good (*motus executionis*) ceases, but appetite's movement of intending its end continues. This is because, although the presence of the good in one way stills the appetite, the alteration of appetite by its object continues, making delight in another sense a movement (Ia IIae, q. 31, a. 1, ad 2).

[17]On these and other terms Aquinas uses to describe love, see H.-D. Simonin, "Autour de la solution thomiste du problème de l'amour," *Archives de l'histoire doctrinale et littéraire du moyen-âge* 6 (1931): 176–97; Frederick E. Crowe, "Complacency and Concern in the Thought of St. Thomas," *Theological Studies* 20 (1959): 26–9. On love as a "being taken," see the lines from Dante quoted above; and David M. Gallagher's "Person and Ethics in Thomas Aquinas" (*Acta Philosophica* 4 [1995]: 51–71), which construes Aquinas's use of *complacentia* as "emphasizing

. . . the *psychological* experience of being taken, so to speak, by the object" (54).

[18]Some important implications of both distinctions are clarified by Gallagher in "Desire for Beatitude and Love of Friendship in Thomas Aquinas," *Mediaeval Studies* 58 (1996): 1–47.

[19]Descartes, *Les passions de l'âme* (Paris: Librairie Philosophique J. Vrin, 1988), 2d pt., art. 68, 114–15.

[20]Pl. *Resp.* 439d–441c (see also Pl. *Ti.* 69c–72d); Sigmund Freud, *Civilization and Its Discontents*, trans. James Strachey (New York and London: W. W. Norton, 1961), 77.

Inasmuch as it founds the sublime on pain and the beautiful on pleasure, Edmund Burke's *A Philosophical Enquiry into the Origin of Our Ideas of the Sublime and Beautiful* (Notre Dame, IN: University of Notre Dame Press, 1958) does not provide a parallel with the concupiscible-irascible distinction; but Burke does associate the sublime with greatness and difficulty, and regards it as a cause of several passions treated by Aquinas as irascible. Paul Ricouer calls it "the penetrating insight of scholastic psychology, that the irascible is not reducible to the concupiscible, but aims at the arduous as the concupiscible aims at pleasure." *Freedom and Nature: The Voluntary and the Involuntary*, trans. Erazim V. Kohák (Evanston, IL: Northwestern University Press, 1966), 116, n. 14.

[21]*In De sensu, Prohemium* (Leonine, 8, 222–49).

[22]*In IV Sent.*, d. 49, *divisio textus* (Vivès, 456).

[23]Arist. *Eth. Nic.* 10.3 (1173a29–b7); 1.6 (1096b10–350).

[24]See the prologue to Aquinas's *In De causis* (Saffrey, 2, 12–13), which, like ST Ia IIae, q. 3, a. 4, quotes Jn 17:3.

Selected Further Reading

D'Arcy, Eric. "Introduction" to St. Thomas Aquinas, *Summa Theologiae*, Vol. 19: "The Emotions." London/New York: Blackfriars, 1967.

Boganelli, E. "Alcuni aspetti della psicologia e fisiologia delle passioni secondo S. Tommaso." *Bolletino Filosofico* 1 (1935): 56–68.

Brennan, Robert Edward. "The Passions and Actions of Man." In *Thomistic Psychology: A Philosophic Analysis of the Nature of Man*. New York: Macmillan, 1941.

Chenu, Marie-Dominique. "Les passions vertueuses: l'anthropologie de saint Thomas." *Revue Philosophique de Louvain* 72 (1974): 11–18.

Floyd, Shawn D. "Aquinas on Emotion: A Response to Some Recent Interpretations." *History of Philosophy Quarterly* 15 (1998): 161–75.

Gilson, Etienne. "Love and the Passions." In *The Christian Philosophy of St. Thomas Aquinas*. Trans. L. K. Shook. New York: Random House, 1965. Repr.

Notre Dame, IN: University of Notre Dame Press, 1994.

Jacob, Josef. *Passiones: Ihr Wesen und ihre Anteilnahme an der Vernunft nach dem hl. Thomas von Aquin.* (Dissertatio ad Lauream in Facultate Philosophica Pontificiae Universitatis Gregorianae). Mödling bei Wien: Missionsdruckerei St. Gabriel-Verlag, 1958.

James, Susan. "Passion and Action in Aquinas." In *Passion and Action: The Emotions in Seventeenth-Century Philosophy.* Oxford: Clarendon, 1997.

Jordan, Mark D. "Aquinas's Construction of a Moral Account of the Passions." *Freiburger Zeitschrift für Philosophie und Theologie* 33 (1986): 71–97.

Mansfield, Richard K. "Antecedent Passion and the Moral Quality of Human Acts According to St. Thomas." *Virtues and Virtue Theories: Proceedings of the American Catholic Philosophical Association* 71 (1997), ed. Michael Baur, pp. 221–31.

Manzanedo, Marcos F. "La naturaleza de las pasiones o emociones." *Studium* 23 (1983): 47–69.

———. "La clasificación de las pasiones o emociones." *Studium* 23 (1983): 357–78.

———. "Las pasiones en relación a la razón y a la voluntad." *Studium* 24 (1984): 289–315.

———. "El amor y sus causas." *Studium* 25 (1985): 41–69.

———. "Propiedades y efectos del amor." *Studium* 25 (1985): 423–43.

———. "El odio según Santo Tomás." *Studium* 26 (1986): 3–32.

———. "El deseo y la aversión según Santo Tomás." *Studium* 27 (1987): 189–233.

———. "La delectación y sus causas." *Studium* 28 (1988): 265–95.

———. "Efectos y propiedades de la delectación." *Studium* 29 (1989): 107–39.

———. "La moralidad de la delectación." *Studium* 30 (1990): 113–34.

———. "El dolor y sus causas." *Studium* 31 (1991): 63–97.

———. "Efectos y propiedades del dolor." *Studium* 32 (1992): 505–40.

———. "La esperanza y la desesperación." *Studium* 33 (1993): 79–108.

———. "Relaciones y moralidad de la esperanza." *Studium* 33 (1993): 389–410.

———. "El temor según Santo Tomás." *Studium* 34 (1994): 85–130.

———. "La audacia según Santo Tomás." *Studium* 34 (1994): 437–53.

———. "La ira y sus causas." *Studium* 35 (1995): 85–107.

———. "La ira: efectos, propiedades y remedios." *Studium* 35 (1995): 401–30.

Marmo, Constantino. "*Hoc autem etsi potest tollerari . . .*: Egidio Romano e Tommaso d'Aquino sulle passioni dell'anima." *Documenti e studi sulla tradizione filosofica medievale* 2 (1991): 281–315.

Mauro, L. "*Umanità*" della passione in Tommaso d'Aquino. Firenze: Felice Le Monnier, 1974.

———. "Le passioni nell'antropologia di san Tommaso." In *Tommaso d'Aquino nel suo settimo centenario: Atti del congresso internazionale (Roma-Napoli, 17–24 aprile 1974).* Napoli: Edizioni Domenicane Italiane, 1977. Vol. 5: *L'agire morale.*

Meier, Matthias. *Die Lehre des Thomas von Aquino De passionibus animae in quellenanalytischer Darstellung* (Beiträge zur Geschichte der Philosophie des Mittelalters, Band XI, Heft 2). Münster: Aschendorff, 1912.

Morgott, Franciscus (de Paola). *Die Theorie der Gefühle im Systeme des heiligen Thomas.* Eichstätt: Jahres-Bericht über das Bischöfliches Lyceum zu Eichstätt, 1863–1864.

Noble, Henri Dominique. *Les passions dans la vie morale.* 2 vols. Paris: P. Lethielleux, 1931–1932.

Otten, A. "Die Leidenschaften." *Jahrbuch für Philosophie und spekulative Theologie* 1 (1887): 113–36, 196–223, 391–402; 2 (1888): 413–43, 559–87.

Pinckaers, Servais. "Les passions et la morale." *Revue des sciences philosophiques et théologiques* 74 (1990): 379–91.

Quinto, Riccardo. "Per la storia del trattato tomistico *de passionibus animae*: il *timor* nella letteratura teologica tra il 1200 e il 1230 ca." *Thomistica (Recherches de théologie ancienne et médiévale).* Supplementa I (1996), ed. E. Manning, pp. 35–87.

Roberts, Robert C. "Thomas Aquinas on the Morality of Emotions." *History of Philosophy Quarterly* 9 (1992): 287–305.

Sarot, Marcel. "God, Emotion and Corporeality: A Thomist Perspective." *The Thomist* 58 (1994): 61–92.

Schmid, Karl. *Die menschliche Willensfreiheit in ihrem Verhältnis zu den Leidenschaften nach der Lehre des hl. Thomas von Aquin.* Engelberg: Verlag der Stiftsschule, 1925.

Sweeney, Eileen. "Restructuring Desire: Aquinas, Hobbes, and Descartes on the Passions." In *Meeting of the Minds: The Relations between Medieval and Classical Modern European Philosophy. (Rencontres de Philosophie Médiévale, 7).* Acts of the International Colloquium held at Boston College June 14–16, 1996, organized by the Société Internationale pour l'Étude de la Philosophie Médiévale. Ed. Stephen F. Brown. Turnhout: Brepols, 1999.

Wallace, William A. "Appetition and Emotion." In *The Modeling of Nature: Philosophy of Science and Philosophy of Nature in Synthesis.* Washington, DC: Catholic University of America Press, 1996.

Westberg, Daniel. "Intellect, Will, and Emotion." In *Right Practical Reason: Aristotle, Action, and Prudence in Aquinas.* Oxford: Clarendon, 1994.

———. "Emotion and God: A Reply to Michael Sarot." *The Thomist* 60 (1996): 109–21.

Habits and Virtues (Ia IIae, qq. 49–70)

Bonnie Kent

odern readers sometimes see in the scholastic practice of citing "authorities" an excessive concern with tradition, or an aversion to original thinking, or both. In interpreting the *Summa theologiae*, this is a serious, though natural, mistake. In fact, Thomas operates very much like a host laboring to produce congenial, fruitful conversation among guests deeply at odds with each other. Like all good hosts, he conceals how hard he must work to ensure that conflicts are defused and the party goes well. Sometimes Thomas repeats, approvingly, the words of an authority while giving them a meaning rather different from what the author intended. (One would need a knowledge of the history of ethics independent of the "history" offered by the *Summa* to recognize such distortions.) Sometimes he sounds as if he agrees wholeheartedly when he actually agrees only with significant reservations. And sometimes his reservations become clear only later in the *Summa*, so that his earlier statements appear, retrospectively, in an altogether different light.

SECOND NATURE

Thanks to this triumph of diplomacy, the whole project of synthesizing the chaotic array of Greek, Hellenistic, Muslim, and Christian sources into a single, coherent theory of virtue appears far less demanding than it actually was. In explaining the *Summa*'s account of habits and virtues, I shall accordingly try to provide enough historical background to compensate for Thomas's finesse. To appreciate his own innovations, one needs some sense of the serious philosophical problems he actually faced and worked to solve.

When Aristotle places virtue in the metaphysical genus of *habit* (or *hexis*), he runs true to form for classical ethics. Philosophers of antiquity were much impressed by the many years of learning and practice necessary to become a thoroughly admirable human specimen. While they all emphasized the intellectual prerequisite of "practical wisdom" (Greek: *phronesis*; Latin: *prudentia*), they also emphasized the long conditioning, habituation, and sheer practice necessary to produce excellent moral character. Hence Aristotle's definition of moral virtue: "a *hexis* concerned with choice, lying in a mean relative to us, this being determined by a rational principle and in the way in which the man of practical wisdom would determine it."[1]

The Greek *hexis* was translated into Latin as *habitus* and thence into English as "habit." The English word tends to mislead insofar as habit can signify for English speakers any routine performance, however trivial or mechanical—tugging at one's necktie, for example, or wincing at the scream of a police siren. A *hexis* or *habitus*, in contrast, is a durable characteristic of the agent inclining to certain kinds of actions and emotional reactions, not the actions and reactions themselves. Acquired over time, habits grow to be "second nature" for the individual. Aristotle himself appeals to this factor in distinguishing habits from other qualities he labels mere "conditions":

A habit (*hexis*) differs from a condition in being more stable and lasting longer. Such are the branches of knowledge and the virtues. . . . It is what are easily changed and quickly changing that we call conditions, e.g., hotness and chill and sickness and health and the like. For a man is in a certain condition by dint of these, yet he changes quickly from being hot to cold and from being healthy to being sick. Similarly with the rest of the conditions, unless indeed even one of these were eventually to become through length of time part of a man's nature and irremediable or exceedingly hard to change—and then one would perhaps call this a habit.[2]

The idea of virtue as a habit and habit itself as a second nature was a commonplace for the Romans as well as the Greeks. There was, however, some divergence in terminology. When commenting on Aristotle's works, Latin authors tended to use the word *habitus* for the Greek *hexis*—an etymologically sound translation, as Thomas points out, because both words have their root in the verb "to have" (Ia IIae, q. 49, a. 1). On the other hand, when writing without any special reference to Aristotle, Latin authors commonly spoke of "custom" or "usage" (*consuetudo*) rather than habit (*habitus*) as "another nature" or a "second nature."[3] Despite their differences, both words can indeed signify those characteristics which become natural and enduring through long practice, thereby making the individual, in one way or another, the person she is: a brilliant mathematician, a brave soldier, or a faithful wife, and likewise, negatively, a mathematical moron, a contemptible coward, or a despicable cheat.

The arcane topic of translation deserves mention on two grounds. First, Augustine gave serious thought to the process of habituation, spoke of habits in many of his works, but typically used the word "custom" (*consuetudo*), not *habitus*. Second, although he was well aware that classical philosophers described moral virtue as the product of habituation, as a second nature we create through our own activities, Augustine himself insisted that all true virtues are forms of charity: the love of God that God alone can give. What good is the learning and practice so prized by the ancients when genuine virtue requires a radical, divinely produced change in values? According to Augustine, apparent virtues in pagans are actually hidden vices. Even when pagan virtues are sought for their own sake, those attaining them are inflated by pride in their own characters.[4] As Augustine regarded charity as the root of all virtues, so he regarded pride as the root of all sins. He thus

saw habit not as the genus of virtue but closer to the enemy of virtue—so many chains forged by our own wills, making it all the harder for us to love most what most deserves to be loved.[5]

Indeed, Augustine lived to regret having reproduced in one of his works Cicero's famous definition of virtue as "a habit of the soul conforming to the mode of nature and of reason" (*animi habitus naturae modo atque rationi consentaneus*).[6] As Augustine's works were copied and circulated, so, too, was this definition, leading him finally to complain that it was *Cicero's* definition, not his own, and that he included it at the request of others.[7] What, then, should we make of Thomas's decision to define virtue as a habit (Ia IIae, q. 55, a. 4)? Does it represent a rejection, however tactful, of Augustine's teachings? To answer the question, we need to understand exactly what Thomas means by a habit.

RETHINKING HABITS

In the section of the *Summa* known as "the treatise on habits" (Ia IIae, qq. 49–54), Thomas draws so heavily on Aristotle and his commentators that he seems at first glance to be following ancient thought quite closely. Like Aristotle, Aquinas places habits in the category of quality, where they are distinguished from other qualities by both their durability and their tendency to dispose the possessor well or badly (Ia IIae, q. 49, aa. 1–2). As he explains that habits are, by their very nature, principles of action (Ia IIae, q. 49, a. 3), Thomas appears to be continuing in the Aristotelian vein, but already a strangely un-Aristotelian idea has crept in. Citing a commentary by Averroes on Aristotle's *De anima*, Thomas declares that "a habit is that whereby we act when we *will*" (Ia IIae, q. 49, a. 3).[8] He quotes this dictum again and again, not only in the *Summa theologiae* but also in other works, from his youthful commentary on the *Sentences* onward, despite the fact that Aristotle himself claimed no such relationship between habit and will.[9] When Thomas proceeds to argue that certain habits are infused in us by God, it becomes all the more evident that ancient philosophy has been left behind (Ia IIae, q. 51, a. 4). Our second natures need not be generated naturally and gradually, through our own long practice (Ia IIae, q. 52).[10]

At the time, the notion of divinely produced habits would not have raised eyebrows. Theologians as early as the twelfth century had stretched the ancient concept of habit wide enough to include dispositions produced directly by God, not only in adult converts but even in newborn babies, through the sacrament of baptism.[11] In endorsing the view that certain habits are God-given, Thomas explains:

> There are some habits by which man is disposed to an end exceeding the capacity (*facultas*) of human nature, which is the ultimate and perfect happiness of man, as was said above; and since habits should be in proportion to that to which man is disposed by them, for this reason it is necessary that habits disposing one to such an end likewise exceed the capacity of human nature. Hence, such habits can never exist in man except by divine infusion, as is the case for all virtues of grace.[12] (Ia IIae, q. 51, a. 4)

Aristotle linked all virtues to happiness in this life; Augustine linked them all to happiness in the afterlife. Thomas himself argues that humankind has as ends *both* kinds of happiness and so needs *two* kinds of virtue: divinely infused as well as naturally acquired (Ia IIae, q. 51, a. 4).[13] Notice, though, that our need for God-given virtues would be a reason for positing God-given habits only if all virtues should be taken as habits, which will not be argued until later.

Where Aristotle speaks now one way, now another, Thomas consistently teaches that only qualities of the soul, not qualities of the body—such as beauty or health—can be habits *simpliciter* (Ia IIae, q. 50, a. 1). Habits arise from actions of a power capable of exercise in one way or another, not determined by its very nature to operate as it does. When the body digests food, it does so strictly as a matter of nature; hence, it neither needs nor acquires some digestive habit. In contrast, when the body is moved by the soul—in pitching a baseball, for example—it can indeed acquire a habit, albeit merely a habit in the secondary sense.

Imagine a major-league player who has learned to pitch with impressive accuracy, speed, and control. According to Thomas, the pitcher owes his motor skills more to the soul than the body, for the body engages in the long hours of practice necessary to develop such skills only because the soul commands it to do so. The habit of skillful pitching, then, belongs to the soul without qualification (*simpliciter*) and to the body only in an extended sense. The skillful movements of the body, caused by its disposition to function in a skillful way, should be seen mainly as residual effects of the soul's control.

Consider now how well or ill this conception of a habit jibes with our own intuitions. Even if we grant Thomas the point about major-league pitchers, we ourselves might still be inclined to regard animals as much better examples of habituation than human beings. As the star pitcher learns to throw the ball, so the cat learns to run expectantly to its dish when it hears someone open the cupboard where the cat's food is stored. When shown a baseball, the pitcher does not automatically seize and throw it: his behavior in sporting goods stores differs strikingly from his behavior on the mound. In contrast, the mere opening of the cupboard might well send the cat running to its dish even when mealtime is hours away and its food, disappointingly, has never appeared at any other time. Should we not then consider the cat, rather than the major-league pitcher, the true "creature of habit"?

Thomas defends the opposite position: that human beings can acquire habits properly so-called, but animals cannot (Ia IIae, q. 50, a. 3, ad 2). Of course, animals can be trained through a combination of punishment and reward. We can modify their behavior by cashing in on their natural instincts. Yet Thomas believes that even the best-trained animals always act from instinct. Hence he claims that the dispositions they acquire fall short of the essential character (*ratio*) of a habit as regards "the use of the will." Unlike human beings, animals do not have the power to exercise a habit or not, "which seems to belong to the very *ratio* of habit."[14]

For Thomas, then, habits in the strict sense are never the product of bodily constitution, mere "animal" instinct, upbringing, or some combination. Nor can they ever compel us to act or react as we do. On the contrary,

Thomas argues that we can always refuse to act in accordance with our habits and can even choose to act against our habits. Where Aristotle repeatedly suggests that the truly virtuous are beyond danger of degeneration, just as the truly vicious are beyond hope of improvement, Thomas has no such confidence.[15] Habits make it harder, but never impossible, for the virtuous among us to degenerate and the vicious among us to improve (Ia IIae, q. 53, aa. 1–3; Ia IIae, q. 63, a. 2).

Among the powers of the human soul, some are better suited than others to developing habits, just as people are better suited than animals. Insofar as a power acts from natural instinct, it cannot acquire habits in the strict sense. Thomas accordingly sees more room for habits in the sensory *appetite*, the seat of emotions, than in powers of sensory *apprehension* such as memory and imagination (Ia IIae, q. 50, a. 3, ad 3). In downgrading the latter powers he appeals to their connection with the body, the force of sheer repetition in conditioning them to operate in certain ways, how they tend to influence, instead of being influenced by, our intellectual judgment of the particular situation in which we find ourselves, and just how far removed they are from the control of the will (Ia IIae, q. 56, a. 5, ad 1). Here we see the influence of Aristotle's psychology, but perhaps Thomas also recalls Augustine's agony at the inability to control his own memory and the tempting images it produced.[16] Dreams of what we believed we long ago stopped wanting, what we would now never seek in our waking lives, might be taken as evidence of the deeply uncontrollable aspect of imagination and memory.

The *Summa* uses the saying of Averroes—that a habit is that whereby we act when we *will*—to support an even more radical claim: from the essential character (*ratio*) of a habit alone, it is plain that a habit is *principally* related to the will (Ia IIae, q. 50, a. 5).[17] To say the least, this represents a substantial departure from Aristotle's teachings. Aristotle holds people responsible for actions proceeding from passion or non-rational appetite even when the agent acts against her own choice, her own reasoned and settled conception of the good. No single power of the soul is even the indirect source of all moral actions. Thomas, however, regards the will as just such a source.[18] In his view, human beings are blamed for tantrums, fits of gluttony, and other such actions because we never act from passion without the consent of our wills. Animals cannot fairly be blamed for apparently similar behavior because they lack the power of will. They are not, as are human beings, "masters" of their own actions. Although reason might at first appear more important, the will receives increasing attention as the *Prima secundae* unfolds.

THE DEFINITION OF VIRTUE

The *Summa's* discussion of human virtue as a habit, an "operative" habit, and a good habit (Ia IIae, q. 55, aa. 1–3) should be seen not only in relation to the preceding treatise on habits but also in relation to the definition of virtue that immediately follows (Ia IIae, q. 55, aa. 1–3). For the topic is initially *human* virtue, a restriction Thomas stresses (for example, Ia IIae, q. 55, a. 3), and yet the definition is not restricted to human virtue. Why, one wonders, does the adjective "human" drop out?

The aim cannot be to make the definition wide enough to accommodate the virtues of animals, for animals are unable to develop habits in the strict sense, much less virtues. Instead, Thomas wants his definition to cover both the human virtues acquired through our own natural resources and the superhuman virtues Christians have through God's grace. Aristotle, he believes, had some valuable insights in the first area. Thus the division between moral and intellectual virtues provided by the *Nicomachean Ethics* can be considered adequate for human virtues (*virtutes humanas*). But as Aristotle failed to consider faith, hope, and charity, those virtues of human beings (*virtutes hominis*) that surpass our nature and make us participants in God's grace, his definition of virtue proves myopic (Ia IIae, q. 58, a. 3, ad 3).

The definition of virtue chosen for discussion accordingly comes not from the *Nicomachean Ethics* but from Peter Lombard's *Sentences*, the standard theological textbook of the day: "Virtue is a good quality of the mind, by which we live rightly, of which no one makes bad use, which God works in us without us" (Ia IIae, q. 55, a. 4).[19] Recognizing that the textbook definition was pieced together from the words of Augustine, Thomas expresses firm approval: "It should be said that this definition embraces perfectly the whole essential character (*ratio*) of virtue. For the complete essential character of anything is gathered from all of its causes. The preceding definition, however, comprehends all the causes of virtue" (Ia IIae, q. 55, a. 4).[20] The article continues by discussing the formal, material, final, and efficient causes of virtue, along with some apparently modest suggestions for revision.

In discussing virtue's formal component, for example, Thomas proposes to substitute "habit" (*habitus*) for "quality" in order to make the definition "more appropriate." He gives no justification other than a perfunctory allusion to Aristotle's categories. Remember, though, that Thomas has already stretched the ancient concept of habit to cover God-given dispositions and described all habits as principally related to the will. In the next question of the *Summa* he also takes pains to distinguish his own position from Cicero's (Ia IIae, q. 56, a. 5). Granted, there are certain habits acquired in the mode of nature, from mere repetition or frequent usage (*consuetudo*). The natural effects of such brute repetition cannot be denied; we commonly see them in our powers of memory and imagination. Yet Thomas denies that these are habits in the strict sense. Even if they were, he adds, they could not be called "virtues." In a similar vein, he argues that the Latin "moral" can signify either *mos* as custom (*consuetudo*) or *mos* as an inclination that has become quasi-natural for the individual (Ia IIae, q. 58, a. 1). When we speak of "moral virtue," moral has the second meaning, so that one should not imagine some essential connection between moral virtue and custom.

Thomas's distinction between habit and custom seems rather strained—and, from the perspective of ancient philosophy, hopelessly misguided. Augustine, however, would probably have appreciated Thomas's efforts. Why should Augustine object to defining virtue as a habit when the concept of habit itself has undergone such a significant change? At the same time, Augustine might reasonably wonder about the reasons for this conceptual revisionism. What advantages could there be to describing even God-given virtues as "habits"?[21]

To answer this question, it helps to move beyond the *Prima secundae* to Thomas's criticisms of Peter Lombard's teachings on charity (IIa IIae, q. 23, a. 2). Suppose that charity, as Peter had suggested, is not something created in the human soul. Suppose that human acts of charity come not from some divinely infused habit but rather from the soul's being moved directly by the Holy Spirit. No doubt Peter was trying to flag the unique excellence of charity, but to Thomas's mind, his position is still "ridiculous."[22] If charity is not something created in the soul—if it is not a habit inclining the human agent to act from the love of God, not a "second nature," albeit divinely produced, so that acts of charity continue to run counter to the individual's inclinations—how could such acts ever be done easily, promptly, and with pleasure? How could acts of charity even be considered "voluntary"? If the person experiences no internal alteration but instead is moved by God to act contrary to her nature, how is she any more the cause of her own behavior than a rock is the cause of its own "behavior" when God snatches it from its natural descent toward the sewer and sends it shooting toward the heavens? In sum, Thomas does have his reasons for wanting all virtues, including the infused, classified as habits.

Only when he turns to the efficient cause of virtue does Thomas venture a clear criticism of the Augustinian definition: God is the efficient cause of infused virtue, to which the definition applies. Thus it says, "which God works in us without us." If this phrase were omitted, the remaining definition would be common to all virtues, both acquired and infused (Ia IIae, q. 55, a. 4).[23] In other words, the textbook formula suffices for God-given virtues but lacks sufficient generality to cover the full range of virtues—a serious philosophical objection to its adequacy as a definition. Thomas never mentions that the narrowness of the definition was no mere oversight. Because Augustine himself regarded all the "virtues" of pagans as vices in disguise, he had no reason to seek a definition of virtue encompassing them.

Thomas's more generous assessment of non-Christians was common among scholastic theologians. Just the standard distinction between "acquired" and "infused" virtues suggests that genuine virtues can indeed be developed without God's grace. To understand why this departure from Augustine's teachings proves less than revolutionary when seen from the perspective of the *Summa* as a whole, we need to consider the place that naturally acquired virtues actually occupy.

VIRTUES IN A RELATIVE SENSE

Soon after defining virtue, Thomas argues that a virtue without qualification can belong only to the will or some other power of the soul insofar as it is moved by the will (Ia IIae, q. 56, a. 3). Intellectual habits such as science and art must therefore be considered virtues in only a relative sense (*secundum quid*). The aim here is to distinguish virtues that make one a good mathematician, painter, or auto mechanic, or good relative to some other specific role, from virtues that make one an all around good human being. Most habits of intellect fall in the first category, as evidenced by their potential for abuse. Consider, for example, how knowledge and skills acquired in medical school could go to make both an excellent doctor and a talented, undetected murderer. An ambitious toxicologist might use her expertise to develop antidotes for previously untreatable poisons; then again, she might use it to dispatch rivals for research funding by adding to their morning coffee little-known toxins from Amazonian jungles. While her intellectual virtues give her capacities for action not to be found in most people, she needs moral virtues to ensure that her capacities are put to good use.

When he turns to a more specific discussion of intellectual virtues, Thomas again reminds us that such habits make the mind function well, but they do not ensure that the person puts his mind to good use (Ia IIae, q. 57, a. 1). As virtues of the speculative mind, wisdom, science, and understanding enable us to grasp the truth. Art, a virtue of the practical mind, gives us skill in making things. Yet none of these intellectual virtues has any necessary relationship to a good will or well-ordered emotions. The most brilliant theorist might well have a streak of cruelty or a short temper; so, too, might the most expert craftsman (Ia IIae, q. 57, aa. 3–5). Prudence, a habit of the practical intellect, is the sole intellec-

tual virtue inseparable from moral virtue and hence from good moral character. Following Aristotle, Thomas argues that no one can have justice, courage, or any other moral virtue without prudence, nor can one have prudence without the moral virtues (Ia IIae, q. 58, aa. 4–5).

As philosophical readers continue with the *Prima secundae*, they will probably take an interest in the differences between moral and intellectual virtues, differences between the moral virtues themselves, the connection between prudence and moral virtue, and other topics addressed in the *Nicomachean Ethics*. But Aristotle's influence should not be overestimated, for the *Summa* posits a whole species of moral and intellectual virtues with the same names as virtues discussed by Aristotle (prudence, justice, temperance, and so on), but which are infused by God along with the theological virtues of faith, hope, and charity. When Thomas refers to moral and intellectual virtues, he might therefore be referring either to naturally acquired virtues or to virtues that Christians possess due to God's grace. Should one focus on the division between acquired and infused virtues instead of the division between moral and intellectual virtues, the rest of the *Prima secundae* looks rather different.

In discussing the cardinal virtues, for example, Thomas considers the assertion of Macrobius that they belong to four different genera: "political, purifying, purified, and exemplary" (Ia IIae, q. 61, a. 5).[24] Far from dismissing the suggestion that there are very different kinds of prudence, justice, and so on—not only different species but possibly different genera—Thomas supports it. He distinguishes sharply between virtues suited to our natural status as "political animals," disposing us to behave well in the social interactions characteristic of the present life, and the purifying virtues of persons striving for a likeness to God. The purifying virtues lie between the exemplary virtues, which truly belong to God alone, and the political virtues:

Prudence of this kind, by contemplating the divine, scorns all the things of this world and directs all its thoughts to divine truths; temperance sets aside what the body requires, insofar as nature allows; courage prevents the soul from being terrified about losing the body as it approaches heavenly things; and justice lies in the consent of the whole soul to the way thus proposed.[25] (Ia IIae, q. 61, a. 5)

In a related article of his *Disputed Questions on the Cardinal Virtues*, Thomas adds that the political virtues fall short of the true essential character (*ratio*) of virtue. As moral inclinations without prudence fall short, so too, from a wider perspective, do moral virtues acquired together with prudence. Unless directed to God through charity, naturally acquired (alias "political") virtues are deficient in the truly essential character of virtue. The purifying virtues, by contrast, infused by God together with charity, are unqualifiedly perfect and make a person's actions good without qualification.[26]

The *Prima secundae* moves more slowly. Having briefly sketched a distinction between the different species of cardinal virtues (political, purifying, and so on), Thomas turns to the three theological virtues: faith, hope, and charity (Ia IIae, q. 62). These are the sole virtues that have God as their object. Because they enable us to share in the divine nature and direct us to a happiness attainable in the present life, we cannot acquire them through our own resources; we can have them only through the grace of God.

Thomas follows St. Paul in praising charity or love as the greatest of the theological virtues (Ia IIae, q. 62, a. 4; 1 Cor 13:13). Although God infuses all three virtues together, one can still discern a conceptual order. Through faith, we believe what God has revealed of Himself and of the future life; through hope, we come to love Him as the source of our own happiness; but only through charity can we love Him as an end in Himself—as the supreme good, deserving of more love than any other, not merely as good for *us*. The love characteristic of hope is the love of desire; charity alone produces the genuine love of friendship. The crucial difference in motivation explains why Thomas describes charity as the "mother," "root," and "form" of all the virtues, even going so far as to declare that faith and hope are not virtues properly so called in the absence of charity (Ia IIae, q. 62, a. 4; Ia IIae, q. 65, a. 4; Ia IIae, q. 66, a. 6).

Readers must wait until the next question, concerning the causes of virtue, to learn more about the prudence and moral virtues given by God. Thomas argues first that we need these infused virtues to attain the complete happiness of the afterlife, then that they differ not merely in degree of perfection but in kind (*species*) from virtues acquired naturally (Ia IIae, q. 63, aa. 3–4). The difference in kind derives partly from the different goods to which the virtues are ordered. While naturally acquired moral virtues make people well suited to the human affairs and earthly happiness that concern all—because we are all human—infused moral virtues make people well suited to the life Christians must live because they are Christians: persons belonging to the household of God, with love of God as the highest good, faith in God's word, and hope for the happiness of the afterlife. The difference in perceived goods and related motivations dictates different standards of conduct. This is Thomas's second reason for regarding naturally acquired and infused moral virtues as different species. For instance, while human reason alone establishes that people should not eat or drink in ways harmful to body or mind, the higher rule of divine law requires more in the way of abstinence (Ia IIae, q. 63, a. 4).

The next question (Ia IIae, q. 64), about how virtues observe a mean, only appears to shift the focus away from God-given virtues and narrow it to naturally acquired virtues. As Thomas previously transformed Aristotle's concept of virtue as a habit, he now transforms Aristotle's doctrine of the mean, so that it applies not only to naturally acquired virtues but also to infused moral virtues (Ia IIae, q. 64, a. 1, ad 3; a. 4). Thus he lays the groundwork for the next, crucial discussion of how various virtues are connected with each other (Ia IIae, q. 65).

At first, Thomas seems to follow Aristotle in arguing that nobody can have a perfect moral virtue without prudence, nor can somebody have prudence without perfection in all the moral virtues.[27] Of course, one can have what people call "temperance" without what people call "courage" and vice versa. We often praise the "courage" of soldiers who habitually drink to excess, the "temperance" of abstemious but spineless neighbors, and so on. The character traits in question can indeed exist independently of each other; we might even regard them as imperfect virtues. But strictly speaking, they are only inclinations to certain kinds of actions or emotional responses that people have by native temperament, or frequent repetition or usage (*ex naturali complexione vel ex aliqua consuetudine*). Strictly speaking, someone who behaves well in one aspect of human life but not in another acquires a habit. Such a habit, however, will lack the essential character of a *virtue* unless accompanied by prudence (Ia IIae, q. 65, a. 1).

The argument that no proper moral virtue can exist without prudence makes more sense if one recalls that a virtue cannot be put to bad use. The ability to face danger, in its own right, would go just as well to make a daring bank robber as an admirable war hero. A person needs prudence to judge correctly which dangers would be *good* to face. As moral virtue requires prudence, so, too, prudence requires moral virtue. A fearful person, with an excessive desire for safety, will naturally tend to judge too dangerous by half situations that it would actually be good to face. Someone's sense of justice cannot consistently govern her actions if she often lacks the courage to do the right thing.

To this point, Aristotle would have been nodding supportively. However, the very next article of the *Prima secundae* reapplies the distinction between perfect and imperfect virtues along lines undreamed of by Aristotle. Thomas argues that the moral virtues people acquire through their own natural resources can exist without charity, as was the case in many pagans. These virtues, however, are intrinsically imperfect—virtues merely in a relative sense. Only the moral virtues infused by God along with charity "perfectly and truly have the essential character (*ratio*) of virtue," and therefore deserve to be called virtues without qualification (Ia IIae, q. 65, a. 2).[28] As no one can have the naturally acquired moral virtues without naturally acquired prudence, so no one can have the distinctively Christian (infused) moral virtues without the God-given theological virtue of charity.

Note that the naturally acquired moral virtues, which enable one to attain the imperfect happiness possible in human society in this life, are unified by the intellectual virtue of prudence, just as Aristotle claimed. In contrast, what Thomas considers the only perfect, unqualified moral virtues are those unified by charity, a virtue of the will given by God. Again, the connection is reciprocal: we cannot have the infused moral virtues without charity, nor can we have charity without the infused moral virtues (Ia IIae, q. 65, aa. 2–3). At the same time, Thomas sees no essential connection between the infused virtues and the naturally acquired virtues. Christians might accordingly be well directed to the happiness of the afterlife and yet lacking in those virtues that enable a person to be happy in the ordinary human society of the present life. The virtues discussed by Aristotle, however useful to us now, are unnecessary for attaining our ultimate end of happiness in the company of God. Indeed, when Thomas argues in q. 65, a. 3, that "all the moral virtues are infused together with charity,"[29] he seems to have forgotten the kind of moral virtues discussed in the first article. The conversation has turned, by stages, so much away from Aristotle that the ancient conception of virtues as naturally acquired habits now represents an exception to the increasingly Christian "rule."

The series of moves just sketched should help to explain why the *Summa* can be better understood as a conversation continuing over the course of many evenings than as the straightforward textbook discussion modern readers might expect. Naturally acquired habits described as perfect, unqualified virtues by comparison with habits unrelated to a good will and uninformed by prudence gradually emerge as imperfect virtues and virtues only in a relative sense by comparison with God-given habits. Scholastics would have been better able to appreciate the finesse of Thomas's gradual shift of focus and less likely to be confused by it.[30]

The connection of the virtues represents another case where positions apparently endorsed earlier in the *Summa* are modified later. In Question 65, Thomas writes approvingly of Aristotle's claim that one cannot have prudence without having *all* the moral virtues. He seems to make an exception only for the large-scale virtues of magnificence and magnanimity, arguing that someone might have acquired all the other moral virtues and yet have lacked the opportunity to acquire these special ones. On the other hand, a person who already has the virtue of generosity (*liberalitas*) *would* acquire the virtue of magnificence, and with very little effort, if he ever came into a large sum of money; so, generally speaking, all the moral virtues are connected (Ia IIae, q. 65, a. 1, ad 1). In Question 66, however, we find that generosity properly belongs to the same class of virtues as magnificence and magnanimity, so that the connection of the moral virtues must be reconsidered. Here Thomas distinguishes between the four principal or cardinal virtues and various secondary virtues, which merely serve to enhance these four. Generosity belongs to the second group. Thus, Thomas argues, a person cannot have the virtue of generosity without justice. (If I do not have a stable disposition to understand and give people what I owe them, how would I have a stable disposition to give them more than I owe?) In contrast, a person might indeed have the virtue of justice without generosity (Ia IIae, q. 66, a. 4, ad 1). In the *Secunda secundae*, Thomas explains that the virtue of justice might eventually be enhanced by the related virtue of generosity, but generosity is only a "potential" part of justice, not a species of justice or an "integral" part of it (IIa IIae, q. 117, a. 5). By distinguishing between the cardinal virtues and various secondary virtues potentially related to the cardinals, a distinction that figures prominently in the *Secunda secundae*, Thomas respects the common intuition that certain virtues are simply more essential than others to good moral character. Patristic writings often award the cardinal virtues this special status; the *Nicomachean Ethics* does not.

However marginalized the virtues discussed by Aristotle might become as the *Prima secundae* proceeds, Thomas never declares that Christians alone have genuine virtues. He continues to insist that persons of different faiths, even of no faith at all, be given moral credit where credit is due:

True unqualified virtue is that which directs one to mankind's principal good . . . and understood in this way, no true virtue can exist without charity. But if virtue is understood in relation to some particular end, something can be called a virtue without charity, insofar as it is directed to some particular good. However, if that particular good is not a true good, but

merely apparent, the virtue related to this good will not be a true virtue but merely a false likeness of virtue, as the prudence of the greedy is not a true virtue. . . . Yet if that particular good actually is a true good, such as the preservation of the community or the like, it will indeed be a true virtue, although imperfect unless it is referred to the final and perfect good.[31] (IIa IIae, q. 23, a. 7)

Thomas's account of God-given prudence and moral virtues nonetheless raises problems. Why does he posit this separate species of virtue? Other scholastics faulted him for multiplying virtues beyond necessity; only his most loyal followers defended him. Many of today's Thomists likewise regard the positing of infused moral virtues as a mistake by an otherwise brilliant philosopher-theologian.[32] Of course, no moral theorist posits more virtues than he himself deems necessary. The key, then, is understanding the explanatory value that Thomas believes infused prudence and moral virtues offer.

COMPLEXITIES OF CHRISTIAN LIFE

We already know that Thomas endorses two ends of humankind: the limited happiness attainable in human society through our own natural resources, and the perfect happiness of the afterlife attainable by Christians with God's grace. The virtues discussed by Aristotle prove generally adequate with regard to the first kind of happiness. Were there no greater happiness possible, and no higher measure than human reason, the *Nicomachean Ethics* would be a fine guide to the moral life. As it is, Christians must regard the work as seriously flawed, not only in its ignorance of supernatural happiness and the God-given virtues ordered to it, but also as a guide to the moral life here and now. Those motivated by charity, who have faith in God and hope for happiness after death, must respect the rule of divine law governing their conduct. What Christians regard as reasonable—such as laypeople's observance of the Church's fasting regulations, or more poignantly, a life of religious poverty and complete sexual abstinence—could therefore look unreasonably ascetical to a non-Christian.

Note that someone who regards the Christian life as a matter of beliefs, hopes, and motivations, with no observable effect on behavior other than prayer and church attendance, would not be acutely concerned about the influence of faith on people's everyday lives. Christianity would be mostly a private relationship between the individual conscience and God—chiefly a matter of one's heart and mind, so that one's everyday behavior might be hard to distinguish from the behavior of non-Christians. Thomas, however, expects Christianity to have a significant influence on people's day-to-day conduct. In describing (for example) infused temperance as different in kind from acquired temperance, he at once acknowledges and counters likely objections to the way Christians live. A pagan who chose to avoid all sexual activity might appropriately be suspected of finding sex repugnant, or of trying to awe others with his powers of self-control, or otherwise running to an extreme instead of observing the mean; however, for Christians, Thomas argues, with their own distinctive ends and motivations, reason will dictate a mean more exacting than that revealed by natural reason unaided by grace (Ia IIae, q. 63, a. 4; Ia IIae, q. 64, a. 1, ad 3; Ia IIae, q. 65, a. 3). What would be prudent for a Christian might thus appear, and even be, imprudent for a non-Christian.[33]

At the same time, Thomas has a healthy respect for human nature and the happiness attainable through people's natural resources in human society. His steadfast defense of pagan virtues as genuine virtues attests to this. But in insisting on the two ends of humankind, he sees more at stake than the moral credit that Christians should award non-Christians. The earthly happiness of Christians themselves deserves attention. Thomas firmly resists any attempt to reduce life to some dreary waiting room on the train route to heaven—as if its value were purely instrumental to salvation, or as if the loves, friendships, and work Christians enjoy here and now were so many false goods. Purely human goods are still genuine goods, for Christians no less than other people.

How does this bear on the positing of infused prudence and moral virtues? While Thomas believes that only the infused virtues are necessary for happiness in the afterlife, he also believes that people need the acquired virtues to be happy in the ordinary human society of this life.[34] Infused prudence does not enable one to deliberate well about everything under the sun, but only about things related to salvation.[35] People must learn from experience how to succeed in business, deploy troops in combat, and exercise judgment in other worldly affairs. Having as one's ultimate end the complete happiness possible only in the presence of God does not prevent one from regarding the happiness of this life as an intrinsic good. A good can be loved both for its own sake and for the sake of God, as an end in itself and yet as subordinate to a higher end (Ia IIae, q. 70, a. 1, ad 2). Book I of the *Nicomachean Ethics* explains how ends are architectonically ordered, with some as ends in their own right and yet subordinate to further ends. To deny that some good is the *ultimate* end is not necessarily to assert that it has, like a tetanus shot, merely instrumental value. Putting the Aristotelian lesson to theological use, Thomas envisions what might be described as the sanctification of a Christian's everyday life in human society.

In Thomas's view, the virtue of charity, which has God as its object and enables people to act from the love of God, exceeds every other virtue. As Aristotle was correct to praise the intellect as the power of the soul most crucial to attaining earthly happiness, so Augustine was correct to praise the will as the power most crucial to deserving eternal happiness. Because God far surpasses what the human intellect can comprehend, the love of God—a virtue of the will—is more essential to living as a Christian than any virtue of the intellect.[36] While this does not mean that all actions by non-Christians are sinful, it does mean that they cannot be "meritorious," that is, reckoned by God as deserving of reward in the afterlife (Ia IIae, q. 62, a. 4; IIa IIae, q. 10, a. 4). People are capable of merit only if they have, through God's grace, the end and motivations provided by the theological virtues. Those with the virtue of charity might nonetheless develop the natural virtues and exercise them both for their intrinsic worth and for the sake of God. When they do, Thomas says, the acts of these naturally acquired virtues are meritorious.[37] Thus a Christian's daily conduct in selling cars, caring for patients, or teaching philosophy, and likewise, her routine behavior with family and friends, can express both her love for strictly human goods *and* her love for God.

To put it crudely, Thomas does not regard God as some jealous lover who insists that people care for no one but Him and for no happiness other than the happiness they could have in His presence. God Himself gave human beings bodies and emotions; God Himself made human beings social (political) animals, inclined by their very nature to seek happiness in the company of others of their kind. Heaven itself should not be regarded as some eternal tête-à-tête with God. Like Augustine, Thomas describes heaven as a community (or city), where Christians enjoy not only the company of God but also the company of the saints.

Thomas's efforts to legitimate both pagan virtues and Christian concern for worldly happiness are carefully balanced with efforts to avoid giving the erroneous impression that various Christian saints were morally inferior to ancient sages. Recall the words of St. Paul in Romans 7: "I delight in the law of God in my inmost self, but I see in my members another law at war with the law of my mind." Also consider Augustine's description of temperance: "What is the activity of virtue here but a perpetual war with vices?—not external vices but internal, not alien but clearly our very own—a war waged especially by what is called *sôphrosynê* in Greek and *temperantia* in Latin which bridles our fleshly lusts lest they drag our will to consent to crimes of every sort."[38]

In fact, what Aristotle calls temperance (*sôphrosynê*) produces harmony between the possessor's emotions and rational judgment. The temperate person no longer need struggle to resist temptation because he no longer feels tempted to do anything bad. While Aristotle recognizes that some people have emotions that they must perpetually work to control, he labels this state of character "continence" (*enkrateia*) and distinguishes it from virtue.[39] Should we conclude, then, that saints praised as a virtue what ancient philosophers judged second-rate—or worse, that Augustine and Paul were themselves second-rate in moral character?

Thomas's discussion of merit alone should help to answer the question. But he has at least two more answers. First, the saints, with infused virtues, judge themselves by *higher* standards than pagans. Because they measure themselves by the rule of divine law, they inevitably see more shortcomings in themselves.[40] Second, naturally acquired, infused moral virtues have different effects on one's emotions. Like Aristotle, Thomas holds that virtues acquired naturally, through long practice, work to eliminate contrary emotions. In time the agent feels much less troubled by his emotions and comes to find virtuous actions pleasant. Infused moral virtues, Thomas explains, can indeed have such an effect (that they *can* is important), but they might not have it immediately. Christians can continue to feel internal conflict and have difficulty in exercising the virtues given by God (Ia IIae, q. 65, a. 3, ad 2–3).[41] Infused moral virtues nonetheless provide a Christian with the strength to lead a good life (emotionally tumultuous or not) and keep her from feeling distress (*tristitia*). Should anyone object that virtues are supposed to make the possessor find virtuous actions uniformly enjoyable, Thomas reminds us that even Aristotle defended a more qualified position.[42]

Many of Thomas's contemporaries believed it sufficient to posit only naturally acquired virtues and the three theological virtues of faith, hope, and charity.[43] In contrast to Augustine, they acknowledged naturally acquired habits as genuine (albeit limited) virtues in pagans; in support of Augustine, they suggested that Christians do not have such virtues—because any virtues naturally acquired by Christians are redirected to the end of charity (in effect, "supernaturalized") through divine infusion of the theological virtues. I have already presented various reasons why Thomas declined to adopt this view. The one point that remains to be considered is his concern for a fine-grained analysis of moral actions.

According to Thomas, we should distinguish between the love of God produced by charity and actions of other virtues performed for the sake of God. For example, when a Christian abstains from food, drink, or sex, she might well do so for the sake of God; but having God as the final cause of such actions does not prevent them from being acts of temperance. Of course, the same acts "elicited" by the virtue of temperance may be "commanded" by the virtue of charity. Perfection in charity may also be needed extrinsically for perfection in temperance. Nevertheless, Thomas wants us to be precise in describing the moral actions of Christians. Should one blur the distinctions among formal, final, and material causes; between elicited and commanded acts; between intrinsic and extrinsic perfections of virtues, one runs the risk of having distinct virtues collapse into just so many different aspects of charity.[44] A plurality of virtues, related and interdependent, but each with its specific goods, would become essentially one and the same virtue.

More precise descriptions of actions represent a gain in moral analysis. While the general lesson was learned by studying Aristotle, who suggests that illicit sexual intercourse for the sake of money be considered less an act of intemperance than an act of greed, Thomas uses it to distinguish between different virtuous actions by Christians.[45] Lenten fasting for the sake of God remains "materially" an act of temperance, so that Christian acts of abstinence should never be conflated with Christian acts of charity. Confuse declining to eat meat with loving God, or loving one's neighbor for the sake of God, and one still has some way to go toward understanding charity's unique status as the foundation, form, and "mother" of all the virtues.

ACKNOWLEDGMENT

I would like to thank the National Endowment for the Humanities for supporting my research into the disputed role of habit in scholastic ethics. This chapter represents part of this larger project.

Notes

[1]Arist. *Eth. Nic.* 1106b36–1107a2.

[2]Arist. *Cat.* 8b28–9a4. See also *Eth. Nic.* 1100b2, 1105a34–35, 1152a29–33.

[3]A few examples: Cic. *De finibus bonorum et malorum*, 5.25; Macrob. *Sat.* 7.9; August. *De civ. D.* 12.3.

[4]See, for example, August. *De civ. D.* 21.16.

[5]For an excellent study of Augustine's treatment of *consuetudo* see John Prendiville, "The Development of the Idea of Habit in the Thought of Saint Augustine," *Traditio* 28 (1972): 29–99. For present purposes, the reader might simply recall that Augustine's famous *Confessions* bears eloquent testimony to the negative role of habituation, both in delaying his own conversion ("Lord, give me chastity and continence, but not yet") and in tormenting him with what he regarded as sinful yearnings even after his baptism. Consider, for example, *Conf.* 10.30: "Assuredly you command that I contain myself from 'the lust of the flesh, the lust of the eyes, and the pride of life' [1 Jn 2:16]. You commanded me also to abstain from fornication, and in the matter of marriage, you advised me a better course, though you allowed me a lesser good. And since you gave me the power, it was done, even before I became a dispenser of your sacrament. Yet there still live in my memory images of those things of which I have already spoken so much which my long habit (*consuetudo*) has fixed there. When I am awake they beset me, though with no great power, but in sleep they not only seem pleasant but even to the point of consent and the likeness of the act itself."

[6]August. *Div. quaest.* 1. 31; Cic. *Inv. rhet.* 2.53.

[7]August. *Retract.* 1.25.

[8]"Et Commentator dicit in 3. de Anima, quod habitus est, quo quis agit cum voluerit." See below, n. 17.

[9]A few examples: *In III Sent.*, d. 23, q. 1 (Moos, 696–718), and d. 34, q. 3 (Moos, 1157–68); *In III Ethicorum.*, lect. 6 (Leonine, 135–39); *De virt. in comm.*, q. un., a. 1 (Marietti, 707–10).

[10]In ST Ia IIae, q. 52, where he discusses the growth of habits, Thomas returns to speaking chiefly of naturally acquired habits. Although the change of focus might prove rather disorienting for the reader, Thomas does indicate that the special case of virtuous habits will be considered later: "Quomodo autem circa virtutes se habeat, infra dicetur"; "Quomodo autem se habeat circa virtutes, infra dicetur" (q. 52, aa. 1–2).

[11]On important developments during this period see Cary Nederman, "Nature, Ethics, and the Doctrine of 'Habitus': Aristotelian Moral Psychology in the Twelfth Century," *Traditio* 45 (1989–1990): 87–110, and Marcia Colish, "*Habitus* Revisited: A Reply to Cary Nederman," *Traditio* 48 (1993): 77–92.

[12]"Aliqui habitus sunt quibus homo bene disponitur ad finem excedentem facultatem humanae naturae, qui est ultima et perfecta hominis beatitudo, ut supra dictum est [Ia IIae, q. 5, a. 5]. Et quia habitus oportet esse proportionatos ei ad quod homo disponitur secundum ipsos, ideo necesse est quod etiam habitus ad huiusmodi finem disponentes, excedant facultatem humanae naturae. Unde

tales habitus nunquam possunt homini inesse nisi ex infusione divina: sicut est de omnibus gratuitis virtutibus."

13For some examples, see ST Ia IIae, q. 3, a. 6; Ia, IIae, q. 4, aa. 5–6; Ia, IIae, q. 62, a. 1; Ia, IIae, q. 63, a. 3.

14On the face of it, the *Summa* describes animals as so many appetite-driven robots, incapable of calculation, self-assertion, or much of the behavior that people routinely attribute to their cats and dogs. This is a mistake; it might be better to say that Thomas simply believes animals act "on principle." Sadly, limitations of space preclude further discussion of this topic.

15Arist. *Eth. Nic.* 1100b35–1101a8, 1146a9–11, 1150b32–34.

16See above, n. 5.

17It seems no small irony that Thomas should cast Averroes as his authority for the doctrine that habits, by their very nature, are principally related to the will. In the passage Thomas cites repeatedly, Averroes's actual contention is that a habit is that whereby one may *understand* (versus the more general "act") *quando voluerit*, which should perhaps be translated as "when one wants" or "when one wishes" rather than as "when one wills," given that Thomas's own conception of the will is just as alien to Averroes as it is to Aristotle. Commenting on Aristotle's account of the intellect, Averroes is only pointing out that understanding, an intellectual "habit," frees the agent from dependence on external aid or stimulation. See Averroes, *In Aristotelis De Anima, Lib. III*, n. 18 [re 430a15–16]: "Et oportet addere in sermone: secundum quod facit ipsum intelligere omne ex se et quando voluerit. Haec enim est diffinitio habitus, scilicet ut habens habitum intelligat per ipsum illud quod est sibi proprium ex se et quando voluerit, absque quod indigeat in hoc aliquo extrinseco."

18In III *Ethicorum*, lect. 4 (Leonine, 129–30). For further discussion of the difference between Thomas and Aristotle on this topic see Charles Kahn, "Discovering the Will: From Aristotle to Augustine," in *The Question of "Eclecticism": Studies in Later Greek Philosophy*, ed. John Dillon and A. A. Long (Berkeley: University of California Press, 1988), 234–59, esp. 239–45, and my *Virtues of the Will: The Transformation of Ethics in the Late Thirteenth Century* (Washington, DC: Catholic University of America Press, 1995), 156–74, esp. 171–74.

19"Virtus est bona qualitas mentis, qua recte vivitur, qua nullus male utitur, quam Deus in nobis sine nobis operatur." Cf. Peter Lombard, *Sententiae in IV libris distinctae*, d. 27, chap. 1, d. 27, q. 5 (ed. Ignatius Brady [Rome: Editiones Collegii S. Bonaventurae ad Claras Aquas Grottaferrata,

1971], 480): "Virtus est, ut ait Augustinus, bona qualitas mentis, qua recte vivitur et qua nullus male utitur, quam Deus solus in homine operatur."

20"Dicendum quod ista definitio perfecte complectitur totam rationem virtutis. Perfecta enim ratio uniuscuiusque rei colligitur ex omnibus causis eius. Comprehendit autem praedicta definitio omnes causas virtutis." In a disputation on the same topic Thomas was more straightforward, mentioning the chief problem with the definition at the outset. See *De virt. in comm.*, q. un., a. 2: "Dicendum quod ista definitio complectitur definitionem virtutis, etiam si ultima particula omittatur; et convenit omni virtuti humanae" (Marietti, 710–14).

21Note that gifts of the Holy Spirit are likewise classified as habits (Ia IIae, q. 68, a. 3).

22*De caritate*, q. un, a. 1 (Marietti, 753–57); cf. IIa IIae, q. 23, a. 2. The withering term of dismissal, "ridiculous," appears in the disputed questions but not in the *Summa theologiae*. This is only one of many cases where the "host" of the *Summa*, a textbook written for beginning theology students, proves somewhat less diplomatic when debating with peers.

23"Causa autem efficiens virtutis infusae, de qua definitio datur, Deus est. Propter quod dicitur, 'quam Deus in nobis sine nobis operatur.' Quae quidem particula si auferatur, reliquum definitionis erit commune omnibus virtutibus, et acquisitis et infusis."

24*In somnium Scipionis.*, a commentary by Macrobius on Cicero's *Dream of Scipio*, represents a Neoplatonic influence on Aquinas's moral thought now widely ignored. Thomas cites Macrobius repeatedly in the *Secunda secundae*, just as he often cites Cicero himself.

25"Ita scilicet quod prudentia omnia mundana divinorum contemplatione despiciat, omnemque animae cogitationem in divina sola dirigat; temperantia vero relinquat, inquantum natura patitur, quae corporis usus requirit; fortitudinis autem est ut anima non terreatur propter excessum a corpore, et accessum ad superna; iustitia vero est ut tota anima consentiat ad huius propositi viam."

26*De virt. card.*, q. un, a. 2: "Secundus autem gradus virtutum est illarum quae attingunt rationem rectam, non tamen attingunt ad ipsum Deum per caritatem. Hae quidem aliqualiter sunt perfectae per comparationem ad bonum humanum, non tamen sunt simpliciter perfectae, quia non attingunt ad primam regulam, quae est ultimus finis, ut Augustinus dicit *contra Iulianum*. Unde et deficiunt a vera ratione virtutis; sicut et moralis inclinationes absque prudentia deficiunt a vera ratione virtutis. Tertius gradus est virtutum simpliciter perfectarum, quae sunt simul cum caritate; hae enim virtutes faciunt actum hominis simpliciter bonum, quasi attingentem usque ad ultimum finem. . . . Oportet igitur quod similiter cum caritate infundantur habituales formae expedite producentes actus ad quos caritas inclinat. Inclinat autem caritas ad omnes actus virtutum, quia cum sit circa finem ultimum, importat omnes actus virtutum" (Marietti, 818–819).

[27]Arist. *Eth. Nic.* 1144b36.

[28]"perfecte et vere habent rationem virtutis."

[29]"cum caritate simul infunduntur omnes virtutes morales."

[30]For example, while modern readers of the *Summa* might assume that Thomas's discussion of how virtues endure in the afterlife applies to naturally acquired as well as infused moral virtues, he states explicitly in another work that he is referring *only* to infused virtues. See also ST Ia IIae, q. 67, a. 1; *De virt. card.*, q. 1, a. 4 (Marietti, 825–28).

[31]"Virtus vera simpliciter est illa, quae ordinat ad principale bonum hominis. . .; et sic nulla vera virtus potest esse sine caritate: sed si accipiatur virtus, secundum quod est in ordine ad aliquem finem particularem, sic potest aliqua virtus dici sine caritate, inquantum ordinatur ad aliquod particulare bonum: sed si illud particulare bonum non sit verum bonum, sed apparens, virtus etiam quae est in ordine ad hoc bonum, non erit vera virtus, sed falsa similitudo virtutis: sicut non est vera virtus avarorum prudentia. . . . Si vero illud bonum particulare sit verum bonum, puta conservatio civitatis, vel aliquid huiusmodi, erit quidem vera virtus, sed imperfecta, nisi referatur ad finale, et perfectum bonum."

[32]For admirably candid reservations, see Odon Lottin, *Principles de morale*, vol. 2 (Louvain: Éditions de l'Abbaye du Mont César, 1947), 213–25. Twentieth-century authors are usually more prone to reveal their doubts about infused moral virtues by mentioning this aspect of Thomas's ethics only in passing or even altogether ignoring it. The policy of silence is especially pronounced among philosophical authors who seek to abstract Thomas's moral philosophy from his moral theology and treat it independently. I think it safe to say that Thomas would have frowned upon this practice.

[33]See *De virt. in comm.*, q. un., a. 13, ad 6, where Thomas argues that Christian poverty and virginity are means of *reason*, not to be confused with the pagan vice of *insensibility* (Marietti, 750).

[34]*De virt. in comm.*, q. un., a. 1, ad 11: "Dicendum quod ad utrasque operationes habitu indigemus; ad naturales quidem tribus rationibus superius positis [in corp. art.]; ad meritorius autem insuper, ad naturalis potentia elevetur ad id quod est supra naturam ex habitu infuso. Nec hoc removetur ex hoc quod Deus in nobis operatur; quia ita agit in nobis, quod et nobis agimus; unde

habitu indigemus, quo sufficienter agere possimus" (Marietti, 710).

[35]*De virt. card.*, q. un., a. 2, ad. 3 (Marietti, 819).

[36]*De caritate*, q. un., a. 3, ad 13 (Marietti, 762).

[37]*De virt. in comm.*, q. un., a. 10, ad 4 (Marietti, 736).

[38]August. *De civ. D.*, 19.4.

[39]Arist. *Eth. Nic.* 1145a35–36.

[40]For discussion of this point see Norman Kretzmann, "Warring against the Law of My Mind: Aquinas on Romans 7," in *Philosophy and the Christian Faith*, ed. T. Morris (Notre Dame, IN: University of Notre Dame Press, 1988), 172–95.

[41]My explanation of this point draws on Thomas's *De virt. in comm.*, q. un., a. 10, ad 14–15.

[42]Arist. *Eth. Nic.* 1117b9–19.

[43]Both Henry of Ghent and Godfrey of Fontaines, leading secular masters at Paris in the last quarter of the thirteenth century, argued at length against positing infused moral virtues. For helpful selections from their works, as well as from works by other masters critical of Thomas on this issue, see Odon Lottin, "Les vertus morales infuses pendant la seconde moitié du XIIIe siècle," in Lottin, *Psychologie et morale aux XIIe et XIIIe siècles*, vol. 3, pt. 2 (Louvain_Gembloux, 1949), 487–534. See also Duns Scotus, *Ordinatio* III, suppl. dist. 36, in *Duns Scotus on the Will and Morality*, ed. Allan Wolter (Washington, DC: Catholic University of America Press, 1986), 414–17; and especially the strong criticism by Thomas's fellow Dominican, Durand of St. Pourçain, in *Durandi a Sancto Porciano in Setentias theologicas Petri Lombardi commentarium*, III, dist. 33, q. 6 (Lyons, 1587), 613–14.

[44]For discussion of these distinctions see *De caritate*, q. un., aa. 3, 5 (Marietti, 760–62, 765–66).

[45]Arist. *Eth. Nic.* 113024–26.

Selected Further Reading

Gallagher, David M. "Aquinas on Goodness and Moral Goodness." In *Thomas Aquinas and His Legacy*. Ed. D. M. Gallagher. Washington, DC: Catholic University of America Press, 1994.

Gilson, Etienne. *Moral Values and the Moral Life: The Ethical Theory of St. Thomas Aquinas*. Translated by Leo Ward. Haden, CT: Shoe String, 1961.

Inagaki, Bernard. "*Habitus* and *Natura* in Aquinas." In *Studies in Medieval Philosophy*. Ed. John Wippel. Washington, DC: Catholic University of America Press, 1987.

Kent, Bonnie. *Virtues of the Will: The Transformation of Ethics in the Late Thirteenth Century*. Washington, DC: Catholic University of America Press, 1995.

Klubertanz, George. "Une théorie sur les vertus morales 'naturelles' et 'surnaturelles.'" *Révue Thomiste* 59 (1959): 565–75.

————. *Habits and Virtues*. New York: Appleton-Century Crofts, 1965.

Kluxen, Wolfgang. *Philosophische Ethik bei Thomas von Aquin*. Hamburg: F. Meiner, 1980.

McInerny, Ralph. *Ethica Thomista*. Rev. ed. Washington, DC: Catholic University of America Press, 1997.

Porter, Jean. *Moral Action and Christian Ethics*. Cambridge: Cambridge University Press, 1995.

————. "Recent Studies in Aquinas's Virtue Ethics: A Review Essay." *Journal of Religious Ethics* 26 (1998): 191–215.

The Intellectual Virtues (Ia IIae, qq. 57–58)

Gregory M. Reichberg

The link between intellectual proficiency and moral uprightness is tenuous at best. History is replete with individuals whose moral heroism is beyond question but whose intellectual accomplishments are quite meager. Similarly, there are gifted and even brilliant scientists, philosophers, or artists, whose moral bearing seems in inverse proportion to their cognitive attainments. In this respect the testimony of experience militates in favor of the distinction, first explicitly drawn by Aristotle in Book IV of his *Nicomachean Ethics*, between virtues that rectify our emotions, desires, and choices (*moral* virtues) and virtues that ensure expertise in our scientific, artistic, and technical endeavors (*intellectual* virtues).

Thomas Aquinas takes up the Aristotelian distinction between intellectual and moral virtue in a section of the *Secunda pars* that is striking in its conciseness. Intuitive insight (*intellectus*), science (*scientia*), and theoretical wisdom (*sapientia*) are presented together in a single article (Ia IIae, q. 57, a. 2), followed by just one article (Ia IIae, q. 57, a. 3) on the virtue of art (*ars*). This brevity differs sharply from Thomas's rather extended analysis of the particular moral and theological virtues, each of which occupies one or more questions.[1] Furthermore, the intellectual virtues (save *prudentia*) are discussed without the least mention of possible contravening vices. In this respect as well, their treatment varies dramatically from that of the moral and theological virtues, which never appear without the benefit of such a contrast.

Some vital difference clearly separates the intellectual virtues from their moral and theological counterparts. Thomas alerts the reader to this in Ia IIae, q. 56, a. 3, apropos the question whether virtue may be seated within the intellect. There he remarks that the intellectual virtues do not confer or require an uprightness of will; in q. 58, a. 5, he will go so far as to declare that even persons without good moral character may be possessed of these virtues. The name "virtue," he concludes, applies to the intellectual habits only in a qualified sense of the term.[2] By contrast, the moral and theological virtues merit this designation without attenuation; they are, in his terminology, virtues *simpliciter*.

Why does Thomas persevere in bestowing the name "virtue" on wisdom, intuitive insight, science, and art, even in the absence of any intrinsic connection to an upright will—the internal principle which renders people good moral agents?[3] I shall take up this question in the first section of this chapter. I will show how, on Aquinas's system of classification, the intellectual virtues (*virtutes intellectuales*) constitute a subdivision within the category of cognitional habits. Within this category, intuitive insight (*intellectus*), science (*scientia*), wisdom (*sapientia*), art (*ars*), and prudence (*prudentia*) enjoy a special eminence: they are stable dispositions for apprehending truth. For this reason, Thomas sees fit to follow Aristotle in honoring them with the title "virtue."

Then, in the second section of this essay, I will expressly consider how Thomas goes about distinguishing these intellectual habits from the moral and theological virtues. Of decisive importance in this regard is the faculty of will (*voluntas*); as I have already noted, it is because the intellectual habits prescind from the rectitude of this faculty that Thomas deems them virtues only "in a manner of speaking" (*secundum quid*). Yet, so construed, the intellectual virtues seem removed from the guiding theme of the *Secunda pars*: how human beings advance to God (achieve beatitude) by their freely chosen acts. An appraisal of the ethical significance of the intellectual virtues, in the light of Thomas's reasons for including them within the thematic development of the *Secunda pars*, will accordingly provide this essay with a third line of inquiry, "The Intellectual Virtues in Moral Science."

INTELLECTUAL VIRTUE AND ITS VIRTUES

This section is divided into two parts: the first examines Thomas's definition of intellectual virtue; the second considers its diversification into five separate virtues (intuitive insight, science, wisdom, art, and prudence).

The Definition of Intellectual Virtue

The *Prima secundae* treatment of intellectual virtue is set against the background of Thomas's general account of human virtue, the main lineaments of which appear in Ia IIae, q. 55. There he summarizes his teaching that "virtue" denotes activity-directed habits (*habitus operativus*) that facilitate the *good* operation of the soul's powers. A good operation is one that stands in conformity with the natural finality of the powers in question (and, by extension, the finality of the person of whom these powers are functional parts; Ia IIae q. 55, a. 3).[4] Activity-directed habits are of three basic kinds: some give rise to acts that contravene a faculty's natural finality; these are termed "vices." From other habits issue good operations and good operations only: these are termed "virtues." Finally, some habits are sources of both good and bad operations: they have no special name and are known simply by the generic title "habits."[5] Applying this classificatory schema to the intellectual virtues, Thomas first notes that, as the name suggests, these habits are seated in the faculty of thought. Moreover, in view of his endorsement of Aristotle's distinction between the potential and the agent intellects (*intellectus possibilis, intellectus agens*), Thomas designates the former and not the latter as the seat of intellectual virtue, maintaining that because the active intellect is "always in act" it

has no need of the readiness conferred by a habit (Ia IIae, q. 50, a. 5, ad 2).

He describes the potential intellect as a power for receiving intelligible objects into the soul. The universal amplitude of this faculty sets it apart from the senses: each of the latter can apprehend what exists solely within certain parameters (for example, sight can grasp only what is colored). By contrast, the human mind knows whatever it knows under the formality of *being*, a formality that enfolds in its analogical unity all actual and possible existents. Yet, owing to the finitude characteristic of our creaturely condition, the human mind can approach this totality (*ens universale*) in piecemeal fashion only. Hence, the diversification of our knowledge into various disciplines, each of which falls under the purview of a different intellectual virtue (into different *scientiae*).

Understood in the light of this diversification, the notion of an intellectual virtue satisfies Thomas's definition of an activity-directed habit: a quality or form, adhering to a faculty, disposing it to acts of a determinate kind, acts which represent one of several different lines of exercise for that faculty. A habit of this sort is required whenever a faculty is *under-determined* with respect to the possible range of its acts.[6] Thomas elucidates the nature of this exigency by appealing to the notion of disposition:

> The kinds of things that we call "dispositions" or "*habitus*" are qualities . . . which involve a particular proportion between elements which may be variously combined. For this reason the Philosopher says [*Metaph.* 5, chap. 20 (1022b10)] that "a *habitus* is a disposition" and that a disposition is "a relation between the parts of a complex. . . ." Because, therefore, there are many beings whose natures and actions cannot be brought to completion without the presence of many elements that can be combined in various proportions, it follows that there should be such a thing as a *habitus*.[7] (Ia IIae, q. 49, a. 4)

On this rendering, "disposition" signifies a condition in which the parts of a whole are arranged with a view to an effect pertaining to that whole; for, if "a whole is to produce its desired effect, its parts must be disposed accordingly."[8] An activity-directed habit may thus be understood as a *dynamic* whole: a cohesive *arrangement* of several faculties (or functional aspects of a single faculty) in view of accomplishing a specific range of operations.

With respect to an intellectual habit, say that of a biologist, historian, or mathematician, the corresponding activity is first and foremost one of *judgment*. In each instance the mind's capacities (senses, memory, imagination, reason) are so arranged that they conduce to true assertions about a particular zone of intelligibility. Since in each of the three disciplines just mentioned—biology, mathematics, history—the subject matter varies, so too will the mental judgment by which the subject matter of each is known, and *a fortiori* the constellation of acquired mental abilities that make each sort of judgment possible. It has long been recognized that the mind-set of the mathematician—the use of the imagination, for example—is quite different from that, say, of the historian or biologist. Similarly, the extent and manner of a biologist's use of the external senses will contrast significantly with that of the historian or mathematician. Needless to say, in the disciplines just mentioned the very same cognitive faculties come into play (the external senses, memory, imagination, and the like), as well as the various facets of the intellect itself (the ability to conceptualize, remember, compare, infer, judge, and so on). Each discipline will require a distinctive configuration of the said faculties, however.

Early in the *Prima secundae* treatment of this theme, Thomas introduces a quote from Averroes: "a *habitus* is something that a man can exercise in action at will," to elucidate the difference between such activity-directed habits and dispositions as beauty or health (Ia IIae, q. 49, a. 3, *sed contra*).[9] Unlike the former, the latter lie in large measure outside the scope of one's deliberate control. Significantly, however, he does think that voluntariness is intrinsic to the very notion of an activity-directed habit: "from the very nature of a *habitus*, it is clear that it is chiefly ordered to the will; inasmuch as a *habitus* is something 'which a man can exercise at will' . . ." (Ia IIae, q. 50, a. 5).[10]

I will return to this principle later. It is worth noting however that Thomas believes that any faculty of the soul that is not subject to the free exercise of the will must carry out its operation by the necessary determination of some natural impulse. Because faculties of this kind leave open little or no margin of active variability, they cannot be reinforced in their operations by the adjunction of habits. As illustration, Thomas invokes the nutritive faculties in human beings; also mentioned are the sensorial faculties of animals.[11]

The issue of free (voluntary) use leads Thomas to inquire whether any habits may develop in the *human* faculties of inner and outer sensation. With respect to the inner senses, he answers in the affirmative: "these powers can be moved to act at the command of reason (*ex imperio rationis*), thus a man may acquire facility of memory, estimation, or imagination" (Ia IIae, q. 50, a. 3, ad 3).[12] Importantly, however, while conceding that these dispositions may rightly be called "habits" (albeit in a derivative sense), Aquinas nevertheless denies them the honorific title "virtue."[13] This name, he asserts, pertains solely to habits that enable the soul to *consummate* its cognitive operations. No such consummation is possible within the limits set by the inner senses.[14] A nonmaterial mode of presence whereby the thing known exists in the knower, cognition begins in the sense powers but comes to completion solely within the intellect. Hence, it is in this faculty, not the inner senses, that cognitional "virtue" may be found.[15]

Turning to the faculties of *external* sensation, Thomas observes that hearing, sight, and the like are ordained to their respective acts according to a natural necessity. When, for example, the organ of sight comes into contact with certain arrangements of light and color, perceptions eventuate according to the fixed structure of the eyes' physical nature. Possessed of little or no active variability within their respective acts, the external sense powers accordingly leave no room for habits, nor *a fortiori* for virtues.[16]

In sum, then, Aquinas is quite emphatic in denying the existence of any habits within the powers of external sensory apprehension; and, while conceding that habits may accrue to the inner sense powers, he asserts that they merit neither the qualification "intellectual" (except derivatively) nor the denomination "virtue."

Additionally, even if we restrict our consideration to habits that are directly seated in the
possible intellect itself (that is, intellectual
habits), still it remains the case that not each
and every one of them will merit the name
"virtue." To elucidate this point, Thomas underscores the praiseworthiness of virtue: it denotes an intrinsic principle of acts that are
unfailingly good. "Virtue," he writes, "is a perfect habit by which it never happens that anything but good is done" (Ia IIae, q. 56, a. 5).[17]
Since truth—the mind's conformity with a real
state of affairs—is the connatural good of the
theorizing intellect (*verum est bonum intellectus*) and falsehood its evil (*falsum est malum
intellectus*), only those intellectual habits which
promote *unerring* judgments may properly be
called "virtues."[18]

Thomas thereby follows Aristotle's lead in
excluding opinion, beliefs grounded in testi-
monial evidence and other such habits which
alternate between the true and the false, from
membership in the category of virtue. The
imperfection of these habits is advanced as the
reason for this exclusion: the mind cannot be
habitually disposed to render *unfailingly* true
theoretical judgments about matters which are
intrinsically variable (*contingentia*). A theoretical habit for grasping items "that could be
otherwise, either universally or particularly,"
opinion is contrasted by Thomas to the virtues of wisdom, science, and intuitive insight.[19] The latter, "implying a rectitude of
reason about matters which are necessary
(*circa necessaria*)," are "concerned solely with
the true" (*semper se habent ad verum*), while
opinion is directed to both the true and the
false.[20] And even when opinion elicits true
judgments, it does so without apprehending
the item in question in the light of its necessary reasons (or causes); hence these judgments are characterized by a certain instabil-
ity.[21]

In Thomas's eyes, then, only habits that
empower the cognitive agent to make judgments on the strength of *necessary* truths count
as theoretical intellectual virtues. Here necessity obtains both on the part of the objects to
which assent is given and on the part of the
mind which does the assenting. The first sort
of necessity is the cause of the latter: for when
the mind apprehends that some feature necessarily belongs to a given subject, the judg-

ments that follow upon that apprehension are
themselves necessitated in turn (Ia IIae, q. 17,
a. 6). Judgments of this sort do not consist in
a choice between alternative propositions.
The absence of choice does not entail, however, that assent can be given to these necessary truths with little or no preparation on the
part of the knower. On the contrary, only
minds endowed with the relevant intellectual
virtues will consistently have the wherewithal
to pronounce inwardly such fine-tuned judgments about necessary things (*necessaria*), as in
mathematics, for example.

It goes without saying that Thomas does
not deny the existence of contingent properties or events. Nor does he deny that the
human mind may sometimes acquire stable
dispositions for making true speculative judgments about them (as in the *habitus* of a historian, for example).[22] He disallows, however,
that such dispositions may rise to the level of
intellectual virtue. This negation turns chiefly
on the meaning of the term virtue: a virtue is
a habit ordered to *good acts* and good acts *only*.
Since the pronouncement of true judgments
(assent to true propositions) is the *raison d'être*
of the speculative mind—its proper good—
then any habit which alternates between true
and false beliefs (even if it gives rise to beliefs
that are more often true than false) does not
merit the name "virtue."[23]

To this point, I have spoken chiefly of the
theoretical virtues. The reader should not forget that the practical intellect also is directed
to the apprehension of truth; consequently the
habits that accrue to it will be called virtues
only to the extent that they promote unfailingly true judgments about actions to be done
(prudence) and things to be made (art; Ia, q.
79, a. 11, ad 2).[24] Unlike the speculative virtues, however, the virtues of the practical intellect cannot derive their certitude from the
apprehension of necessary truths. On the contrary, the very *raison d'être* of these practical
virtues is to guide agents in tasks that have yet
to be performed, tasks which, with respect to
their futurity, are contingent in kind.

Far, then, from abjuring contingency, the
virtues of the practical intellect absolutely require it; contingency necessarily enters into
the very fabric of their specifying objects. Yet
it enters into this fabric without imperiling the
truth-value of the corresponding judgments.

This is possible, Thomas explains, because, unlike the truth of the speculative intellect, which involves a conformance of the mind to independently existing things, the truth of the practical intellect consists in the converse relation: the conformance of things to the human mind. This practical truth arises only within contingent states of affairs, the effectuation of which depends upon the free determination of the human will. When a state of affairs thus has a human agent for its cause, the agent in question, under the precise aspect of being the author of the said state of affairs, can accordingly apprehend it with the certainty characteristic of an intellectual virtue.

This same reasoning clearly does not hold for theoretical cognition, where truth is defined by reference to states of affairs which lie outside the free initiative of the epistemic agent, a point which Thomas neatly sums up as follows: "The intellect cannot indefectively (*infallibiliter*) achieve conformity with the contingent aspect of things, but only with their necessary aspects. Thus no speculative habit bearing on contingent items (*contingentia*) can be an intellectual virtue; only one concerned with what is necessary (*necessaria*) can achieve this status." Moreover, it is only by reference "to the contingent items (*contingentia*) which may be effected by us (whether they be matters of interior action, or the products of external work) that intellectual virtue can rightly be posited in the practical intellect, *viz.*, art, as regards things to be made, and prudence, as regards things to be done" (Ia IIae, q. 57, a. 5, ad 3).[25]

Despite the asymmetry of their respective objects, the habits of intuitive insight, wisdom, and science, on the one hand, art and prudence on the other, are alike insofar as they are dispositions for rendering true judgments only. Their indefectible ordering to the true is what sets them apart from all the other habits that may arise in the potential intellect (opinion, human faith, dialectical agility, and the like). This unwavering orientation to the true is the decisive reason that merits for them the name virtue. To bring home this point, Thomas reminds us of two principles: the true is a particular kind of good, and virtue an internal principle of good action. In connection with the second principle, Thomas quotes a famous line from *Nicomachean Ethics*

6.6—"virtue is that which makes both its possessor and its acts good"—to show that that goodness is the formal element in virtue. Consequently, "virtue" will apply to habits of intellect, he maintains, insofar as these habits elicit acts that have the character (*ratio*) of goodness. An act of the intellect will possess the character of goodness to the degree that it is desirable as an end (that is, an end that is really, not just in appearance, perfective of the subject). The apprehension of truth is the end to which intellectual acts are ordered.[26] Hence, only those habits which conduce to the apprehension of truth are properly termed intellectual virtues (Ia IIae, q. 57, a. 2, ad 3).[27] These virtues may thus be defined as "right dispositions by which the intellect is inclined toward truth."[28]

Truth is grasped principally in the inward act of judgment, which Thomas names "composition" and "division," since it consists in asserting or denying a connection between the realities signified by the terms of a proposition.[29] Intellectual virtue therefore consists first and foremost in habits of sound judgment. It disposes the agent vis-à-vis other mental acts (of the senses, inner and outer, or of the intellect, as in concept formation and reasoning) to the extent that these acts are preparatory to the act of judgment. Finesse in handling concepts, or acumen in constructing syllogisms, are not of themselves intellectual virtues; they only become such when conjoined with truth-bearing assertions about reality.

The Diversification of Intellectual Virtue into Five Separate Virtues

The *Summa theologiae*'s treatment of intellectual virtue appears to presuppose that the reader is already acquainted with the Aristotelian distinction between the speculative and practical virtues; in any event no attempt is made to justify this division. After some introductory comments on how virtue rightly applies to the speculative habits (Ia IIae, q. 57, a. 1), comments in which Thomas contrasts these habits to the moral virtues (see my discussion of this contrast in "How Moral and Intellectual Virtue Differ"), he quickly advances to Aristotle's classic distinction between three speculative virtues (ibid., a. 2).

In the twelfth article of his *Disputed Question on the Virtues in General*, Thomas does however offer a brief explanation for the division of intellectual virtue into speculative and practical habits, followed by a succinct analysis of the fivefold division inherited from Aristotle. There is no single way (*ratio*) by which human beings can apprehend the truth about things; accordingly, Thomas reasons, our knowledge must be diversified according to a determinable set of formal principles. Of such principles the one most broad in scope divides the objects of our knowledge into necessary truths on the one hand and contingent truths on the other, a division which in turn yields two sets of truth-conductive dispositions: speculative virtues for knowing the former and the practical virtues for knowing the latter.[30]

There are two types of necessary truths. One set is known immediately (through themselves, *per se notum*)—such truths are grasped without the mediation of an inference working through a middle term. The virtue that assures ease in the apprehension of these self-evident truths Thomas names after the mental act by which these same truths are known: "understanding" or "intuitive insight" (*intellectus*, the Latin equivalent of the Greek *nous*). "Intuitive insight" highlights the positive character of this mental act (and the resulting habit), as well as its noninferentiality. Unlike the negative qualifier immediate, "intuitive" has the advantage of characterizing understanding (*intellectus*) in positive terms, as does Thomas himself, who accords it high words of praise: "understanding denotes a certain excellence of a knowledge that penetrates into the heart of things" (IIa IIae, q. 8, a. 1, ad 3).[31]

Conversely, there exist a wide range of necessary truths that come into our awareness only after one has engaged in deductive ratiocination. Conclusions of prior reasoning (*notum ex alio*), these inferred truths are apprehended by a distinctive mental act, which Thomas names "science" (*scientia*, the Latin translation for the Greek *epistēmē*). Two different virtues assure the effective functioning of our scientific judgments. Because some judgments bear on the highest reality, the habit responsible for their elicitation merits a special name: wisdom (*sapientia*, the Latin equivalent for the Greek *sophia*). By contrast, the habit for drawing inferences about necessary

conclusions of lower rank receives no special name and simply goes by the generic title "science" (*scientia*). In this fashion, Thomas enumerates three virtues of the speculative mind: intuitive insight, wisdom, and science.

As noted above, Thomas believes that there can be no speculative *virtue* about contingent matters. Contingent occurrences can be taken up by the human mind with the assurance requisite of intellectual virtue only within the practical order, because here some human agency is causally responsible for their emergence. Contingent happenings that issue from an agent's conscious exertion (*operabilia*) are formally of two different kinds: some, such as deliberations, choices, hopes, fears, loves, and hates, are internal (*in nobis*); others, such as houses, bridges, medical remedies, musical performances, books, and the other things one constructs, are external (*extra nobis*). Governing the first is prudence, the virtue of practical wisdom (*prudentia*, the Latin equivalent for the Greek *phronēsis*), while over the second rules art (*ars*, the Latin expression for the Greek term *technē*), the virtue of correct judgment about things to be made. Thomas, like all medievals, applied the term art to a broad range of practical skills, including medicine, engineering, and logic; in fact, the so-called "fine arts" would not have served as the primary referent of this term—in contrast to our contemporary usage.

Having considered the teaching of Thomas's *De virtutibus* on the five-fold division of intellectual virtue, I will now turn to his treatment of these virtues in Ia IIae, q. 57. First, I will discuss the virtues of the speculative intellect. Grouped together in Ia IIae, q. 57, a. 2, under a single heading, intuitive insight, wisdom, and science are discussed with great concision. To be sure, Aquinas does not take it as the task of moral science to delve very deeply into the nature of these speculative habits. Such an investigation belongs more properly to first philosophy.[32] In this context, he says just enough to situate these habits within the organism of the virtues. Moreover, these brief comments serve as a backdrop to his discussion of the gifts of the Holy Spirit in the *Secunda secundae*, three of which (understanding, wisdom, and science) are understood according to an analogy with the corresponding speculative virtues.

Intuitive insight is the act by which we immediately apprehend (*percipitur statim*) underived (*per se notum*) necessary truths. Truths of this sort earn the title of *principles* because they are a *source* from which other truths may be drawn. The *im-mediacy* of this apprehension must be taken formally: the negation in question bears only on the mediation exercised by the middle term in a syllogistic deduction. Other forms of cognitive mediation are fully compatible with and even necessary to the act of intuitive insight: prior reflection upon sensory data, conceptual analysis, and even dialectical and inductive reasoning. This helps explain why intuitive insight requires the reinforcement of a habit: without such reinforcement the act in question would remain feeble in its penetration and clarity. It would, moreover, be severely restricted in the range of its possible application: for while some principles are knowable by all that have unimpaired faculties, other principles are accessible only to persons with the requisite education ("the wise").[33] Thus, while acknowledging that the "habit of principles" arises naturally in the mind—"bestowed on us by nature" (*nobis naturaliter indita*) (Ia, q. 79, a. 12)—produced by very first exercise of the intellectual powers in a manner so spontaneous that no person can be entirely bereft of it, Thomas nevertheless maintains that mental application of a special sort is needed if this habit is to develop aright.[34]

The mental act of apprehending two or more principles together, such that from their union a new insight is born, is, for Thomas, science. An insight of this kind will emerge only when the mind is able to identify a feature that in some relevant sense is common to each of the said principles. Aristotle called this common feature a "middle term," because, through its mediation, two distinct insights are conjoined in a third. The middle term supplies the reason or explanation that grounds this new insight. Thus, for example, the statement "every man is a substance" derives from the ordered conjunction of the principles "every body is a substance" and "every man is a body," a conjunction effected in the light of the common term "body." Here, the truth of the proposition "every man is a substance" is formally dependent upon the truth of the antecedent propositions; it issues from them as a conclusion from its premises.

The Latin *scientia* is the name for both an act and a habit. The preceding paragraph describes the cognitive *act*. In this sense, "to have *scientia* with respect to some proposition P is to hold P on the basis of a demonstrative syllogism, that is, to hold P where one's epistemic grounds for P are the premises of the syllogism and the fact that P is entailed by those premises."[35] A syllogism of this sort draws out its conclusions by reference to necessary and universal truths.

When science names a habit, it denotes an acquired *ability* for deducing conclusions of the kind just mentioned. Science carries out this function by first serving as an intellectual memory from which a demonstrative inference can be recalled at will; it then enables its possessors to *extend* their knowledge to new conclusions (new absolutely, when these conclusions enlarge the boundaries of the discipline itself; new qualifiedly, when they enlarge the knowledge had by this or that individual). The first of these two functions is plainly more amenable to voluntary choice than the second, since it is easier to remember a conclusion (including the demonstration on which it depends) once learned, than to deduce it in the first place. In either case, however, the habit of science represents a mode of potency between simple intellectual capacity (the state of a mind without training in a particular discipline) on the one hand, and actually thinking through a demonstration, on the other.[36]

Theology, metaphysics, ethics, mathematics, and physics (natural philosophy) are some of the disciplines to which Thomas accords the status of science. This is not however the place to detail his classification of the different scientific habits. The text with which I am now concerned (Ia IIae, q. 57, a. 2) is instead directed to the elucidation of a contrast between science and wisdom. Thomas's reply to the article's first objection sets up the parameters for this contrast. According to Thomas, wisdom should not be divided from science as though it were a *habitus* of an entirely different sort. Rather, "wisdom has what is common to all the sciences; namely, to demonstrate conclusions from principles" (Ia IIae, q. 57, a. 2, ad 1).[37]

Yet, although it is itself a science, wisdom has, on this account, three characteristics that set it apart from every other science. First, wisdom considers not just what is supreme within a particular zone of intelligibility (as, say, physics studies the highest principles of mutable being, or mathematics the highest principles of quantified matter), but what is supreme purely and simply—the first or ultimate causes of being itself. Second, because it knows what is supreme in the universe, wisdom can function as the architectonic science. It reflects upon the principles of all the other sciences, coordinates the sciences in relation to each other, and even defends its own principles against those who would deny them. Finally, while the secondary sciences are many (each having a particular region of being for its proper object), wisdom, the primary science, is universal in scope. In this respect, it is unique: "there is," Thomas writes, "one wisdom only" (*sapientia non sit nisi una*).[38] Supreme among the speculative intellectual virtues, wisdom accordingly merits a place of choice within the moral life.[39] To cultivate the sciences at the expense of wisdom (neglecting the latter for the sake of the former) is a disorder of the spirit that Thomas later denounces as a form of sinful curiosity (*curiositas*) (IIa IIae, q. 167).

In Ia IIae, articles 3 through 6 of Question 57, Thomas takes up a discussion of art and prudence, the two virtues that ensure right reasoning about practical matters. Here again his approach is chiefly comparative. On the one hand, he considers what prudence and art have in common, in opposition to the three speculative virtues. On the other hand, he differentiates prudence from art, thereby spotlighting the fact that, of the five intellectual virtues, prudence alone confers moral rectitude or uprightness of character.

Art and prudence are generically alike, Thomas remarks, with respect both to their seat in the soul (*quantum ad subiectum*) and their subject matter (*materiam*). Habits of the practical intellect, these two virtues are concerned with contingent happenings, not of just any sort whatsoever, but only such as can issue from human initiative (Ia IIae, q. 57, a. 4, ad 2). The role of art and prudence consists not so much in apprehending these contingent happenings as it does in *steering* the very

process by which they come into existence. These are operative, not speculative virtues. By contrast, even if the speculative virtues were able to procure certainty regarding contingent happenings caused by human beings, the knowledge in question would remain contemplative, not causal, and hence would differ essentially from the practical cognition of art and prudence.[40]

Thomas defines art as "right reason about things to be made"; he follows by defining prudence as "right reason about things to be done" (Ia IIae, q. 57, a. 4).[41] "Making" (*facere*), he explains, designates an action that results in the production of things external to the agent, while "doing" (*agere*) names an action that abides in the agent. These definitions are classic Aristotelianism. The distinction between immanent and transitive action is not about spatiality; it points rather to a difference in finality. An operation is deemed "transitive" when it is ordered to (for the sake of) the good of the work (*finis operis*), even if the work in question should exist solely in the mind of its maker. Thus, a composer can merely imagine a sonata, mentally revising it to render the melody more mellifluous, all in perfect conformity with the canons of that art. Immanent activity, by contrast, is directed to the actuality or perfection of the agent (*finis operantis*). Wine can thus be consumed, not just to slake one's thirst (the transitive operation of digestion), but also for the sheer enjoyment of the palate. "Immanent" and "transitive" need not name separate operations; it is possible (in fact usually is the case) that these two coexist as aspects of one operational unit. Thus, a composer can take great pleasure in the exercise of that art, and a gourmet can find nourishment in wine.

Taken alone, without further specification, the distinction between transitive and immanent can hardly suffice to differentiate the sphere of art from that of prudence. For one thing, Thomas employs this same dichotomy to divide art from the contemplative activity of theoretical science, which represents an order of competence quite distinct from prudence. For another, prudence is not solely about the inner states that accompany outward actions, for it is directive of those actions themselves; it takes into account all the factors that conduce to their success or failure.

From his various comments on this topic, one can infer that when Thomas identifies the acting that is the concern of prudence with immanent action, he thereby wishes to specify just one special sort of such action, namely, the action of the will (*voluntas*). More precisely, it is choice (*electio*), the inner act by which the will selects among possible goods, that prudence is especially meant to guide. The various powers of the soul (intellective, sensitive, and locomotive) enter the purview of prudence to the degree that their respective acts may be exercised freely, at the command of the will (Ia IIae, q. 57, a. 4).[42] Consequently, when Thomas asserts that prudence is about actions that abide in the agent (in contrast to art that is directed to an outward matter), the claim bears on the precise formality under which they are known by prudence, namely, insofar as they spring from choice and "use" (*usus*) in the will. On Thomas's view, this volition represents a distinctive mode of immanent action (ibid.).[43]

Once it is understood that prudence is directive of our actions under the aspect of their voluntariness, the other key properties of this virtue become readily apparent. Summarizing these properties below will enable us to perceive more clearly how prudence differs from art.

(1) The will (*voluntas*) is the faculty responsible for safeguarding the overall good of the person; through its mediation, all actions spring from a unitary source and possess a common point of reference. Since the other faculties aim at more limited goods (the concupiscible power is ordered to the experience of sensory pleasure, sight to vision, and the intellect to the apprehension of truth), the will, whose defining referent is goodness as such (*bonum universale*), enfolds each of these particular human goods within its inclination to a total, all-encompassing goodness.

Of itself, however, the will is blind: it can tend only to goods that have been apprehended by reason. Moreover, the will's inclination to particular goods is indeterminate; rational desire becomes effective only as the result of a choice between competing options. Consequently, if voluntary action is to occur at all, a practical judgment must intervene to guide the process in a determinate direction. Such judgments can be made well or poorly.

Practical judgments are good (true) when they command acts in keeping with the person's ordination to integral fulfillment (*beatitudo*). Prudence names the inner disposition for pronouncing judgments of this kind. Art, by contrast, does not concern itself with the well-being of the agent (*finis operantis*). It looks rather to the good of the work (*finis operis*). Thus, to ask whether the thing made will benefit or harm its maker is a question rightly addressed to prudence, not to art. "The craftsman," Thomas concludes, "needs art, not that he may live well, but that he may produce a good work of art, and maintain it in good condition: whereas prudence is necessary to man, in order that he may lead a good life" (Ia IIae, q. 57, a. 5, ad 1).[44]

(2) Deeds are morally good when they are appropriately directed to their due end. A steady orientation to the goods of human life is provided by the moral virtues. These virtues rectify the will (and allied sensory appetites) vis-à-vis the ultimate end—integral human fulfillment. Prudence is concerned with promoting that end. It does so by selecting from the range of available alternatives the sequence of actions most likely to bring it about. In order to carry out this task prudence requires that the agent be rightly disposed toward the end in question. Because moral virtue guarantees this disposition, prudence must ally itself with the full complement of moral virtues if it is to judge rightly of its objects. Rectitude of the will (and lower appetites) is thus a prerequisite to prudence, such that this virtue cannot adequately be defined without it. Art, by contrast, ordered as it is to the good of a particular kind of work (a tunnel to be built, fish to be caught, a patient to be healed), presupposes neither moral virtue nor, consequently, an upright will (Ia IIae, q. 57, a. 4).[45] "It does not depend on the disposition of our appetite whether we judge well or ill of the principles of art," Thomas writes, "as it does when we judge of the end which is the principle in moral matters: in the former case our judgment depends on reason alone. Hence art does not require a virtue perfecting the appetite, as prudence does" (Ia IIae, q. 58, a. 5, ad 2).[46]

(3) The moral virtues are attitudinal dispositions: thus in addition to ensuring the right sort of behavior with respect to the concrete

situation confronting the agent, they also prompt an appropriate emotional response. Prudence, similarly, takes into account how the agent's appetite is affected while performing a particular action. "For in order to do good deeds," Thomas notes, "it matters not only what someone does but also how he does it" (Ia IIae, q. 57, a. 5).[47] Art, by contrast, bears a likeness to the speculative virtues insofar as it prescinds from how the agent feels toward the object: "For as long as the geometrician demonstrates the truth, it matters not how his appetitive faculty may be affected, whether he be joyful or angry: even as it does not matter for the craftsman" (Ia IIae, q. 57, a. 3).[48] This is not to say that such feelings are irrelevant, for, in connection with one's fulfillment as a person, they may matter a great deal. Yet it is prudence, not art or the speculative virtues, that will take them into account.

(4) Prudence takes no holidays. It represents an existential readiness to do what is right, at all times and in all places. Its supervision is demanded of every sort of voluntary act, without exception. Not only does prudence judge of what ought to be done, it also (and especially) ordains the actual accomplishment (*imperium*) of the deed in question.[49] Art, by contrast, is solely a disposition for pronouncing sound judgments; it does not require *per se* the very application of these judgments to a work produced at some determinate time and place. Art, like the speculative virtues, confers only a qualitative (not an existential) readiness to perform actual works: "for if a man possess a habit of speculative science, it does not follow that he is willing to make use of it, but solely that he is able (*fit potens*) to consider the truth in those matters of which he has this knowledge" (Ia IIae, q. 57, a. 1).[50]

(5) Similarly, the artistic habit does not require of its possessor that he produce works conformably with its dictates. A grammarian does not deserve blame for uttering a solecism, provided however that one does so knowingly and deliberately (Ia IIae, q. 56, a. 3). Prudence, by contrast, is wholly incompatible with any conduct that would intentionally contravene what it commands: "thus more praise is given to a craftsman who is at fault willingly, than to one who is unwillingly; whereas it is more contrary to prudence to sin

willingly than unwillingly, since rectitude of the will is essential to prudence, but not to art" (Ia IIae, q. 57, a. 4).[51]

(6) Extending as it does to the very execution of voluntary action—no two instances of which are strictly identical—prudence can follow no fixed and settled rules of conduct. The matters about which it deliberates are open-ended; each constitutes a unique situation in which there is often more than one way to obtain the desired end. Art, by contrast, requires adherence to pre-established rules, rules that must be mastered by the craftsman in order to succeed consistently at work (see Ia IIae, q. 47, a. 2, ad 3).[52]

(7) Finally, although people require the arts in order to serve many needs, no single art is indispensable to moral integrity. Not so, however, with prudence; this virtue is absolutely necessary for a life well lived.

THE INTELLECTUAL AND THE MORAL VIRTUES

This section is divided into two parts: the first considers how Aquinas differentiates the intellectual virtues from the moral virtues; the second examines the ethical relevance of the intellectual virtues.

How Moral and Intellectual Virtue Differ

Unproblematic at first sight, the distinction between moral and intellectual virtue appears to call for little commentary. Seated in different parts of the soul, the moral virtues rectify the will and sense appetites, while the intellectual virtues strengthen the potential intellect and the internal sense powers. Aquinas refrains, however, from drawing the distinction in question solely on this basis, with nothing more said. For if the differentiation of virtue into these two kinds were reducible merely to a diversity of faculties, it would result in a univocal predication of the genus "virtue." Thomas argues however that this division follows the pattern of analogical predication. In other words, these two sets of habits do not merit being called virtues in quite the same way. Virtue pertains chiefly and most properly to good habits of the will; only secondarily, according to a broader and less rigorous connotation of the term, does it apply to the truth-conducive dispositions of the mind.[53] Qualities that ensure uprightness of will, the moral (and theological) virtues accordingly merit the name virtue *simpliciter*. The intellectual virtues, by contrast, acquit their function without any intrinsic relation to the will (*absque omni ordine ad voluntatem*); hence, they are called virtues *secundum quid* (Ia IIae, q. 56, a. 3).

In Ia IIae, q. 56, a. 3, Aquinas presents the rationale behind this division of virtue into two analogical kinds. Following Aristotle, he notes that, in its full-fledged meaning, virtue denotes a habit that "makes its possessor good and his operation good likewise."[54] The intellectual virtues (save prudence) fall short of this definition in each of its aspects. With respect to the second aspect, Thomas notes that although intellectual virtue bestows a *capacity* to perform cognitive tasks well, it does not dictate the actual occurrence of the said acts. Fully possessed of the medical art, an eminent surgeon may nevertheless refuse to operate on a sick individual who clearly stands to benefit from this intervention. The same may be said of a mathematician who chooses not to reflect on a quandary about which one is confident of finding a solution, or of a lawyer who deliberately pushes aside thoughts of a pending lawsuit while on a family vacation. In each instance, the inaction is due not to the agent's lack of ability, but rather to a free choice of the will. The speculative virtues and art confer, in Aquinas's words, "only aptness to act" (*solum facit facultatem agendi*), not the "right use of that aptness" (*[non] facit quod aliquis recte facultate utatur*) (ibid.). As Thomas remarks in *De virtutibus*, it does not follow from the fact that a person has science that "he efficaciously wills the consideration of truth, but only that he is capable of doing so."[55] Efficacious willing is nevertheless integral to virtue in the most proper sense of the term—virtue *simpliciter*. Virtue, Thomas reminds us, bespeaks goodness; goodness (*bonum*) in turn bespeaks actuality. Consequently, virtue applies as such solely to habits that ordain the actual performance of their respective operations. Since the faculty of will is the inner principle responsible for the inception of human actions, only habits rooted in the will merit such an appellation.[56]

Thomas likewise denies that the intellectual virtues can render their possessors unqualifiedly good:

A man is not said to be good absolutely because he may be good in some part, but because he is wholly good; and this he is when his will is good. . . . A man who is good in one of his powers, without having a good will, is said to be good as regards that power, e.g., because he has good vision or hearing. . . . It is clear then that a man is not said to be absolutely good from the fact that he has science, but only to have a good mind or good understanding. The like may be said of art and of other habits of this sort.[57]

Because the moral and theological virtues rectify the will vis-à-vis the overarching good of the whole person, their possession renders a person unqualifiedly good, i.e. of good character. Not so for the intellectual virtues, which rectify the agent's engagement toward particular ends only (such as healing, as in medicine, or the correct apprehension of quantitative relations, as in mathematics).

Directed as they are to limited, particular ends, unity is not required of the intellectual virtues, as it is for the moral virtues. This is especially true of the different arts and sciences, each of which is defined by a sphere of operation that may entail little or no connection with the others. The moral virtues, by contrast, are all ordered to the unique last end—yoked together in prudence and charity, they constitute an organic whole that combines the variegated aspects of an entire life (*de his quae conferunt ad totam vitam*) (q. 57, a. 4, ad 3).[58]

The reference that moral virtues bear to the last end also helps to explain why each stands opposed to the contrary vices of excess and deficiency.[59] The goodness of human acts is taken from their consonance with the ultimate end. Acts that are in discontinuity with that end have the character of sin, and the corresponding habitual dispositions, vice. These bad acts are committed under the attraction to items that are repellent to the order of right reason. Within the realm of human action, evil is not merely a privation; it gives positive specification to deeds.[60] The intellectual virtues, however, are not defined by a reference to the unity of the last end. Nor are they *per se* related to practical (moral) reasonableness or rectitude of the will. Hence, the only opposition possible in their case is simple privation, the ignorance that results from not having cultivated a particular branch of learning. Therefore, Aquinas sees no reason to posit a category of intellectual vice to complement his treatment of the intellectual virtues.

In other contexts, however, Thomas makes it abundantly clear that virtue (*simpliciter*) and vice can indeed accrue to the intellect.[61] This occurs when the intellect operates under the direct influence of the will. On this basis Thomas adduces that theological faith and the cardinal virtue of prudence should be deemed virtues in the full and complete sense of the term (that is, virtues *simpliciter*). And when faith is vivified by charity a new set of intellectual dispositions arise in the mind—infused wisdom, insight, and science—which permit the unhindered contemplation of divine things. In conformity with tradition, Thomas calls these dispositions "gifts of the Holy Spirit" (*dona Spiritus Sancti*). This underscores their special connection with the order of grace. These three gifts confer "purity of mind" (*munditia mentis*) much as theological charity confers "purity of heart" (*munditia cordis*).[62] On the other hand, heresy, unbelief, blindness of mind, dullness of sense, negligence and imprudence, stemming as they do from a disordered will, are listed among the intellect's vices.[63] Significantly, Thomas completes his treatment of the gifts that confer knowledge with an examination of the opposing intellectual vices.[64]

At this juncture, Thomas draws an important conclusion vis-à-vis his topology of the virtues: the infused knowledge of the Holy Spirit—the gifts of wisdom, insight, and science—represents the sole instance when truthful thinking coincides purely and simply with the exigencies of an upright will.[65] This may not be said of the intellectual virtues, which, taken in themselves, can function in separation from the moral virtues (see below). Theological faith, for its part, requires only a beginning of moral goodness, not the full complement of the virtues; it is, Thomas asserts, compatible with the absence of charity (IIa IIae q. 4, a. 7, c., and ad 5). By contrast, the knowledge of God, which issues from faith

formed by charity (the gifts of wisdom, insight, and science), is bestowed *solely* on the upright of heart.

One should not be misled into viewing these gifts as extraordinary and momentary interventions of religious inspiration into the ordinary course of human existence, and thus as somehow akin to prophecy. Rather, by likening them to the intellectual virtues,[66] and by calling them *dispositions* (*habitus*),[67] Thomas intimates that they are the crowning achievement of a virtuous moral and intellectual life.

The Intellectual Virtues in Moral Science

In Ia IIae, q. 58, aa. 4–5, Thomas asks whether the moral and intellectual virtues are interdependent. Can there be intellectual virtue without moral virtue? And inversely, can a person be morally virtuous without also possessing at least some of the intellectual virtues? The doctrine expounded in these two articles downplays the necessity of an interconnection between the two sets of virtues. Of the intellectual virtues, prudence and intuitive insight are absolutely requisite for moral virtue—the former, because it sets the mean for each of the moral virtues and coordinates their respective acts; the latter, because it is a prerequisite to prudence (Ia IIae, q. 58, a. 4). A habit of right reason, prudence depends upon a prior awareness of the primary moral principles (*synderesis*). The apprehension of first principles in the practical order is ultimately traceable, in the dynamics of human knowing, to intuitive insight (*intellectus*). By contrast, from the perspective of moral virtue, the arts, sciences, and theoretical wisdom are dispensable habits: "A man may be virtuous without having full use of reason as to everything, provided that he have it with regard to those things which have to be done virtuously" (Ia IIae, q. 58, a. 4, ad 2).[68]

Similarly, Aquinas maintains that the intellectual virtues—save prudence—can subsist in the soul without the support of moral virtue. "A bad will is not opposed to science or to art," he writes, "as it is to prudence, faith, or temperance."[69] This is a direct corollary of his view that the specification of our theoretical and artistic judgments is intrinsically independent of a motion from the will. To quote again from *De virtutibus*, a. 7: "The consideration itself of truth is not science insofar as it is an object of volition, but according as it tends directly to its object. The like may be said of art with respect to the practical intellect."[70] Thomas is implying that scientific judgments arise naturally once the relevant terms are seen in all their clarity; hence no special act of the will is required to elicit these judgments. The judgments of prudence, on the other hand, are elicited in dependency upon an upright will.[71]

Of course, several questions can be raised against the thesis that the intellectual virtues (save prudence) are morally neutral: Does not the attainment of proficiency in a science or art require at least a modicum of moral virtue? What great thinker is without perseverance, courage, moderation (showing due reserve, say, in the formation of scientific beliefs), impartiality, and other such moral qualities?[72]

Aquinas could respond to the just-mentioned objection by appealing to his distinction between "perfect" and "imperfect" moral virtue (Ia IIae, q. 65, a. 1).[73] A perfect virtue is one that inclines a person to make good use of it in all circumstances, according to the dictates of prudence and charity. Such a virtue accordingly disposes a person to act according to the requirements of the final, overarching end of human life. Because this end is *one* simply, the acts directed toward it by the different perfect virtues are knotted together in unity. In contrast, an imperfect virtue is an inclination to do some deed, the goodness of which is defined by reference to a goal of more limited scope. Since such limited, particular goals (succeeding in one's chosen profession, accumulating wealth, becoming a skilled athlete, and so on) are many, the dispositions that conduce to their respective fulfillment can survive without being interconnected: "If we take the moral virtues in this way," Thomas concedes, "they are not connected" (ibid.).[74] Along similar lines, I would argue that the moral traits of character requisite for the acquisition and maintenance of the intellectual virtues need not rise to the level of perfect virtue. No one will advance very far in learning a new language, acquire expertise in mathematics, or compose a novel without some degree of studious perseverance, for example. Yet this perseverance need not reach into all areas of one's life, and in fact may be

sorely lacking in matters that are of grave moral significance.

In light of the ethical neutrality of the intellectual virtues, what, then, is one to make of Thomas's treatment of them in the *Secunda pars*, a section of the *Summa theologiae* expressly devoted to the consideration of morals? To this question, Thomas offers a twofold reply. First, he remarks that despite the fact that the speculative habits and art do not function as dispositions for choosing well (*habitus electivus*)—such is the office of prudence and the moral virtues—it nevertheless remains true that they are always exercised by *choice*. Recall his endorsement of Averroes's claim that "a *habitus* is something a man can exercise at will." In Ia IIae, q. 57, a. 6, this conception of habit is expressly applied to the intellectual habits. There Thomas argues that the act of reason can always be put to voluntary use (Ia IIae, q. 16, a. 1, ad 3).[75] Considered as a free operation of an individual agent, occurring at a definite time, aiming at an end, and using determinate means, engagement in the work of speculation or the practice of an art is never morally neutral. Making "use of an acquired habit is due to a motion of the will"; therefore "a virtue which perfects the will, as charity or justice, confers the right use of these speculative habits" (Ia IIae, q. 57, a. 1).[76] Inversely, vices such as pride and injustice can vitiate the appetite for knowledge, breeding a "vain curiosity (*curiositas*) about speculative sciences," destructive of human fulfillment (IIa IIae, q. 167, a. 1, *sed contra*).[77] Aquinas explicitly discusses the ethical employment of the mind under the heading of "studiousness" (*studiositas*), a moral virtue whose office consists in rectifying the will to knowledge.[78]

Thus, with respect to their voluntary use, the intellectual virtues fall squarely within the ambit of ethics. They do so not as principles of moral action, but rather as *objects* of moral choice.[79] And although these virtues can indeed be put to a morally bad use, and thereby subsist in the soul apart from any vital connection to the moral virtues, this is plainly not the arrangement Thomas recommends. A unity of the two sets of virtues, whereby the intellectual habits are made conducive to moral integrity, is what Thomas envisages as the optimal situation for these habits.

Finally, Thomas points to a second, complementary, respect in which the intellectual virtues come under the purview of moral science. This time his argument appeals to the special nobility of the speculative virtues. It appears as a reply to an objection which alleges that, since these virtues are occupied neither with giving direction to human acts nor with studying how human beings might best achieve their fulfillment, they consequently remain wholly detached from the concerns of ethics and moral virtue. Thomas counters that the speculative habits are in fact of acute interest to the ethicist, "both because the acts of these virtues can be meritorious [that is, when, as free acts, they are exercised under the influence of charity] . . . and because they are a kind of beginning of perfect felicity, which consists in the contemplation of truth" (Ia IIae, q. 57, a. 1, ad 2).[80] While the first claim is a point I have already covered, the second opens up a new perspective. The intellectual virtues—wisdom in particular—have special affinity with beatitude, the state of ultimate human fulfillment and the very end to which the whole of morality is ordered. Consequently, as "habits," these virtues are more excellent than justice, courage, temperance, prudence, and all the other habits of good moral character.

The moral virtues may very well possess the character of "virtue" more completely than the speculative intellectual habits. They are nevertheless subordinate to the latter in the order of perfection, as what conduces to an end is subordinate to the end itself. Beatitude inchoate, science and wisdom are thus accorded a place of honor in St. Thomas's architecture of the moral life.

ACKNOWLEDGMENT

I wish to thank David Gallagher for his helpful comments on an earlier draft of this paper.

Notes

[1]Of the intellectual virtues, only prudence (*prudentia*) is given ample development in the *Secunda pars* (ST IIa IIae, qq. 47–51). Yet, unlike the others, prudence is also a moral virtue (and a cardinal virtue

at that); therefore, it receives a treatment on a par with its eminence.

[2]Prudence again is the exception, since it is both an intellectual and a moral virtue. As a moral virtue it presupposes rectitude of the will and hence is a virtue *simpliciter* (ST Ia IIae, q. 56, a. 3).

[3]ST Ia IIae, q. 57, a. 1: "[H]abitus intellectuales speculativi non perficiant partem appetitivam, nec aliquo modo ipsam respiciant, sed solum intellectivam."

[4]"[V]irtus importat perfectionem potentiae."

[5]On the distinction between good and bad habits, see esp. ST Ia IIae, q. 54, a. 3. Throughout this chapter, I follow customary usage in rendering the Latin "*habitus*" by the English "habit." The reader should be cautioned, however, that *habit* carries connotations at variance with the proper meaning of *habitus*. See Yves R. Simon, *The Definition of Moral Virtue* (New York: Fordham University Press, 1986), 55–61 for a useful discussion of this terminological difficulty.

[6]Inversely, a power will have no need of a *habitus* if it is by nature fully determined to one operation only; in this case, the faculty's constitutive form is sufficient to direct it aright. Such, for instance, are the operations of the nutritive faculties: growth and reproduction. Such, likewise, are the sentient operations of non-human animals. For what is done by instinct is done in a settled manner with little or no margin for variation (ST Ia IIae, q. 49, a. 4, ad 2).

[7]"[D]icimus autem dispositiones vel habitus sanitatem . . . quae important quandam commensuationem plurium quae diversis modis commensurari possunt. Propter quod Philosophus dicit, in V *Metaphys.*, quod habitus est dispositio, et dispositio est ordo habentis partes . . . . Quia igitur multa sunt entium ad quorum naturas et operationes necesse est plura concurrere quae diversis modis commensurari possunt, ideo necesse est habitus esse."

[8]Simon, *The Definition of Moral Virtue*, 79.

[9]"Habitus est quo quis agit cum voluerit."

[10]"Habitus est quo quis utitur cum voluerit."

[11] Thomas does allow however that some cognitively sophisticated animals can be trained to act at the behest of a human being; in this manner habits may arise in their sensorial faculties; see ST Ia IIae, q. 50, a. 3, ad 2.

[12]"[I]n ipsis interioribus viribus sensitivis apprehensivis possint poni aliqui habitus, secundum quos homo fit bene memorativus vel cogitativus vel imaginativus."

[13]In a derivative sense, meaning that these sensory dispositions function more as auxiliaries to the work of reason than as habits in their own right (ST Ia IIae, q. 50, a. 4, ad 3).

[14]Appetition, by contrast, comes to fruition when the agent is effectively joined to things as they exist

in rerum natura. Accordingly, the appetitive acts that respond to the attraction of *sensible* things will be consummated in the sense-appetite itself; for this reason there may be *virtues* in it and not just in the rational appetite or will (ST Ia IIae, q. 56, a. 5, c., and ad 1).

[15]Against Averroes, who held that intellectual habits have their seat in an inner sense power (the imagination), Thomas argued that habits can develop in the possible intellect itself, because this faculty includes a potentiality for diverse actuations: "Unde relinquitur quod habitus intellectivus sit principaliter ex parte ipsius intellectus: non autem ex parte phantasmatis, quod est commune animae et corpori. Et ideo dicendum est quod intellectus possibilis est subiectum habitus: illi enim competit esse subiectum habitus, quod est in potentia ad multa; et hoc maxime competit intellectui possibili. Unde intellectus possibilis est subiectum habituum intellectualium" (ST Ia IIae, q. 50, a. 4, ad 1). The body of the article provides a fuller discussion of Averroes's position.

[16]He does agree, however, that these powers are not wholly without the enrichment of *habitus*, inasmuch as dispositions may be found *in the higher powers* that *direct* the external senses to their respective operations (see ST Ia IIae, q. 50, a. 3, ad 3). Although each external sense has its own proper object and specific mode of operation, nevertheless, practically speaking, these powers function in close association with the other faculties of the person: the inner senses (especially the common sense and the cogitative sense), the intellect itself, as well as the powers of appetition (sensory and rational), each of which may receive the complement of a *habitus*. Upon acquiring the relevant *habitus*, these faculties become fit to guide the operations of the external senses: either by organizing the sensory data into meaningful wholes or by selectively directing the perceiver's attention within the perceptual field. Hence, a pathologist, gazing into a microscope at a tissue sample, is alert to features (color, texture, lines) that the layman also sees, but hardly notices.

[17]"Virtus enim est habitus perfectus, quo non contingit nisi bonum operari."

[18]However, an unfailing ordination to the true is a necessary but not a sufficient condition for conferring the name *virtus* on an intellectual habit. This becomes clear if one considers Thomas's teaching on synderesis, the habit for apprehending the first principles of moral action. Despite its indefectibility—"there can be no error in it" (*in ea peccatum esse non potest*; De veritate, q. 16, a. 2 [Leonine, 508, 92–93])—*synderesis* nevertheless should not be counted among the intellectual virtues, because the practical consideration to which it gives rise does not terminate with it, but rather with the decisional judgment of prudence: "Ad quintam dicendum

quod actus synderesis non est actus virtutis simpliciter, sed praeambulum ad actum virtutis . . ." (*De veritate*, q. 16, a. 2, ad 5 [509, 138–40]). On this basis, two elements are requisite for predicating virtue of an intellectual habit: the habit must be truth-conducive, and elicit acts that are final in their order.

[19]"Ostendit [Aristoteles] quid pertineat ad opinionem, scilicet quod sit circa contingencia aliter se habere, siue in uniuersali siue in particulari." *In I Post. Anal.*, 44 (Leonine, 167, 36–38). In the same chapter of this commentary, Thomas observes that opinion can take two forms: (1) a disposition to make judgments about matters which are inherently contingent; (2) a disposition to judge of necessary matters as though they were contingent, as when, through lack of learning, a person takes as possible to be otherwise some matter which another person, who has scientific knowledge, correctly perceives as impossible to be otherwise. On the Thomistic theory of opinion, see Simon, *The Definition of Moral Virtue* (61–67), who distinguishes *substitutional* opinions (those that are in principle replaceable by scientific demonstration) from *essential* opinions (those that are concerned with inherently contingent matters).

[20]*In I Post. Anal.*, 44 (Leonine, 170, 291–92, 284–85).

[21]Thomas counts opinion among those mental acts that are "devoid of a firm assent"; someone who opines correctly about some proposition, does so with "fear" that its opposite may be true: "Quidam vero actus intellectus habent quidem cognitionem informem absque firma assensione . . . sive uni parti adhaereant, tamen cum formidine alterius, quod accidit opinanti" (ST IIa IIae, q. 2, a. 1).

[22]For a nuanced discussion of Thomas's teaching on necessity and contingency, and its implications for science, see Jacques Maritain, *Grande logique*, in Jacques and Raïssa Maritain, *Oeuvres complètes*, vol. 2 (Fribourg: Éditions Universitaires, 1987), 706–30.

[23]See *De veritate*, q. 14, a. 8 (Leonine, 458–61).

[24]"Intellectus enim practicus veritatem cognoscit, sicut et speculativus; sed veritatem cognitam ordinat ad opus."

[25]"Et quia intellectus non potest infallibiliter conformari rebus in contingentibus, sed solum in necessariis; ideo nullus habitus speculativus contingentium est intellectualis virtus, sed solum est circa necessaria. . . . [S]olum in contingentibus quae possunt a nobis fieri, sive sint agibilia interiora, sive factibilia exteriora. Et ideo circa sola contingentia ponitur virtus intellectus practici; circa factibilia quidem, ars; circa agibilia vero, prudentia." See *In I Post. Anal.*, 44 (Leonine, 170, 283–313).

[26]In his *Sentences Commentary* Thomas offers a representative statement of this view: "Ad tertium dicendum quod ipsa veritas est materialiter bonum

intellectus, cum sit finis eius: finis enim habit rationem boni, ut dicitur in III *Meta*" (*In III Sent.*, d. 23, q. 1, a. 4, § 84 [Lethielleux, 712]).

27"Ad tertium dicendum quod, sicut supra [q. 55, aa. 3–4] dictum est, habitus virtutis determinate se habet ad bonum, nullo autem modo ad malum. Bonum autem intellectus est verum, malum autem eius est falsum. Unde soli illi habitus virtutes intellectuales dicuntur, quibus semper dicuntur verum, et nunquam falsum. Opinio vero et suspicio possunt esse veri et falsi. Et ideo non sunt intellectuales virtutes, ut dicitur in VI *Ethic.*"

28Y. R. Simon, J. J. Glanville, G. D. Hollenhorst, trans., *The Material Logic of John of St. Thomas* (Chicago: The University of Chicago Press, 1955), 505.

29The act of judgment is hereby termed "inward" in order to distinguish it from acts of outward communication. The intellectual virtues are not directly concerned with the accurate representation of one's thought to others. Truth-telling, on Thomas's account, is the concern of a moral, not an intellectual virtue (ST IIa IIae, q. 109). A person can have an aptitude for knowing the truth (have intellectual virtue) but choose not to communicate this knowledge to others, or deliberately deceive them about what he or she has understood.

30*De virt. in comm.*, q. un., a. 12 (Marietti, 742–47).

31"Sed intellectus nominat quandam excellentiam cognitionis penetrandi ad intima."

32*In I Post. Anal.*, 44 (Leonine, 170, 306–9): "Determinare autem de sapiencia quid sit et quomodo se habeat, et de sciencia et intellectu et arte, pertinet aliqualiter ad philosophiam primam."

33In ST Ia IIae, q. 94, a. 2, for example, Thomas contrasts self-evident propositions that are known to all (*omnibus noti*) to other such propositions that are known only to the wise (*per se notae solis sapientibus*). Similarly, in his *In I Post. Anal.*, 18, Aquinas distinguishes between "common first principles," which are shared by all the sciences (truths like the principle of noncontradiction) from "proper principles," which are specific to each particular science. Perception of the proper principles will, he suggests, require more training than the grasp of common principles, since the latter are, in *actu exercito*, known by all men.

34In ST Ia IIae, q. 51, a. 1, Thomas denies that the "habit of principles" is given with our nature at birth, for two reasons: (1) the habit stands in need of external sense data, from which intelligible forms are abstracted; (2) the apprehension of these forms presupposes some reflection, however minimal. Thus, the judgment "the whole is larger than its part," Thomas's stock example of an underived truth, requires the prior abstraction (and comparison) of the concepts "whole" and "part" from sensory data, an abstraction which can occur with greater or lesser clarity, depending on a number of factors not directly controlled by natural processes (the attentiveness of the knower, the other concepts that may be in his possession, and so on). Thomas does allow, however, that "in the apprehensive powers there may be a natural habit by way of a beginning" (in apprehensivus enim potentiis potest esse habitus naturalis secundum inchoationem), in the sense that certain judgments arise naturally (secundam naturam) once their terms are understood, as in the example just given. Here "naturally" signifies that which flows from the constitutive structure of a being (in this case an intellectual being) with a kind of necessity, hence without effort, deliberation, or contrivance.

35Scott MacDonald, "Theory of Knowledge," in *The Cambridge History of Later Medieval Philosophy* (Cambridge: Cambridge University Press, 1982), 164.

36In *De malo*, q. 16, a. 6, ad 4 (Leonine, 311, 319–34), Saint Thomas contrasts these two forms of cognitive potency, simple and intermediate, in the following terms: "[A]liter dicitur aliquis esse potentia sciens ante addiscere, quando scilicet nondum habet habitum scientae, et aliter ante considerare." In the same reply, he describes the intermediate potency as a kind of incomplete *actuality*: "Ad quartum dicendum quod habere notitiam in actu dicitur dupliciter: uno modo quantum ad actualem considerationem . . . alio modo quantum ad habitualem notitiam."

37"Sapientia est quaedam scientia, inquantum habet id quod est commune omnibus scientiis, ut scilicet ex principiis conclusiones demonstret."

38Less often remarked, however, is the fact that the third trait mentioned (the unity of wisdom) appears to contradict Aquinas's own teaching (see, for instance, ST Ia, q. 1, a. 6) that at least two different sciences properly merit the name wisdom: philosophic or human wisdom (*metaphysica*), and the divine wisdom that issues from faith (*sacra doctrina*). Each of these sciences takes up the study of first causes and principles. Sometimes he refers even to a third way of insight, one specially imparted by the Holy Spirit, as yet another sort of wisdom (Ia, q. 1, a. 6, ad 3). Unfortunately, to my knowledge, Thomas never directly takes up the question whether or not these three modes of wisdom can co-exist (as distinct habits) within one and the same person.

39The supremacy of wisdom vis-à-vis the other intellectual virtues is taken up in ST Ia IIae, q. 66, a. 5.

40Similarly, in his *In I Ethicorum.*, lect. 1 (Leonine 4, 16–39), Thomas distinguishes "the order of things that human reason *considers* but does not *establish*" (ordinem rerum quem considerat sed non facit) from "the order that reason *in planning* estab-

lishes in external things" (*ordo autem quem ratio considerando facit in rebus exterioribus*) and "in voluntary actions" (*ordo actionum voluntariarum*). The first order pertains to the speculative sciences, while the second pertains respectively to art and moral philosophy.

[41]"Recta ratio factabilium" and "recta ratio agibilium."

[42]"Sic igitur hoc modo se habet prudentia ad huiusmodi actus humanos, qui sunt usus potentiarum et habituum, sicut se habet ars ad exteriores factiones."

[43]"Agere autem est actus permanens in ipso agente, sicut videre, velle, et huiusmodi."

[44]"Et ideo ars non est necessaria ad bene vivendum ipsi artifici: sed solum ad faciendum artificiatum bonum, et ad conservandum ipsum. Prudentia autem est necessaria homini ad bene vivendum."

[45]"Et ideo ad prudentiam, quae est recta ratio agibilium, requiritur quod homo sit bene dispositus circa fines: quod quidem est per appetitum rectum. Et ideo ad prudentiam requiritur moralis virtus, per quam fit appetitus rectus. Bonum autem artificialium non est bonum appetitus humani, sed bonum ipsorum operum artificialium: et ideo ars non praesupponit appetitum rectum."

[46]"Ad secundum dicendum quod principia artificialium non diiudicantur a nobis bene vel male secundum dispositionem appetitus nostri, sicut fines, qui sunt moralium principia: sed solum per considerationem rationis. Et ideo ars non requirit virtutem perficientem appetitum, sicut requirit prudentia." Some commentators argue, however, that art does stand in need of an appetitive rectitude within its own, limited sphere, and that in the passage just cited Thomas wishes only to deny that art need include a rectitude of the will vis-à-vis the last end. In ST Ia IIae, q. 57, a. 5, ad 3, for instance, Thomas writes that "verum autem intellectus practici accipitur per conformitatem ad appetitum rectum," without specifying that this principle obtains for prudence only (in fact, later in this passage he refers to both art and prudence); this lends credence to the view that the principle in question applies analogically to both art and prudence: whereas prudential judgment depends upon an upright appetite *simpliciter*, the rectitude presupposed by artistic judgment is relative to the requirements of a particular kind of work. On this, see Cajetan's commentary on ST Ia IIae, q. 57, a. 5, ad 3 (Leonine, vol. 6); and Jacques Maritain, *Art and Scholasticism* (New York: Charles Scribner's Sons, 1962), 46–47.

[47]"Ad hoc autem quod aliquis bene operetur, non solum requiritur quod faciat, sed etiam quomodo faciat."

[48]"Dummodo enim verum geometra demonstret, non refert qualiter se habeat secundum appe-

titivum partem, utrum sit laetus vel iratus: sicut nec in artifice refert . . . "

[49]On the distinction between judgment and command, see ST Ia IIae, q. 57, a. 6, and IIa IIae, q. 47, a. 8. In the second of these texts, Thomas explicitly compares prudence to art—the former commands (that is, applies to action the things counseled and judged), while the latter merely judges.

[50]"Ex hoc enim quod aliquis habet habitum scientiae speculativae, non inclinatur ad utendum, sed fit potens speculari verum in his quorum habet scientiam." The terms *qualitative* and *existential readiness* are borrowed from Simon (*The Definition of Moral Virtue*, 71–79), who uses them to render Thomas's distinction (in ST Ia IIae, q. 56, a. 3, for instance) between habits that confer competence only (*facit facultatem agendi*) and habits that confer competence with moral good use (*facit quod aliquis recte facultate utatur*).

[51]"Et inde est quod magis laudatur artifex qui volens peccat, quam qui peccat nolens; magis autem contra prudentiam est quod aliquis peccet volens, quam nolens: quia rectitudo voluntatis est de ratione prudentiae, non autem de ratione artis."

[52]"Sed ad prudentiam non pertinet nisi applicatio rationis rectae ad ea de quibus est consilium. Et huiusmodi sunt in quibus non sunt viae determinatae perveniendi ad finem, ut dicitur in III *Ethic*." In art, by contrast, reason can proceed with certitude down fixed paths (*secundum certas et determinatas vias*). Thomas does allow, however, that some arts (he mentions warfare and seamanship) involve more indeterminacy than others; in such cases a kind of *consilium* will be necessary, yet not of the same sort as prudence: "Unde in artibus aliquibus est consilium de his quae pertinent ad fines proprios illarum artium. Unde aliqui, inquantum sunt bene consiliativi in rebus bellicis vel nauticis, dicuntur prudentes duces vel gubernatores, non autem prudentes simpliciter; sed illi solum qui bene consiliantur de his quae conferunt ad totam vitam" (ST Ia IIae, q. 57, a. 4, ad 3). On the question of art and fixed rules, see Jacques Maritain, *Art and Scholasticism*, 38–48.

The claim that prudence deals with situations that permit of more than one viable course of action, and hence to which no fixed and settled rules can apply, does not hold in all cases, however. With respect to the negative precepts, for instance, the only proper response to the possible action (e.g., adultery) is inaction.

[53]Aquinas distinguishes the broad from the rigorous usage of *virtus* in III *Sent.*, d. 23, q. 1, a. 4 (Moos, 712): "Sic ergo virtus potest dici dupliciter. Uno modo habitus perficiens ad actum bonum potentiae humanae, sive sit bonus materialiter sive formaliter; et sic habitus intellectuales et speculativi virtutes dici possunt . . . . Alio modo potest dici virtus *magis stricte*, et secundum quod est in usu loquendi,

habitus perficiens ad actum qui est bonus non solum materialiter sed formaliter; et sic solum habitus respicientes appetitivam partem virtutes dici possunt, non autem intellectuales, et specialiter speculativi."

54Arist. *Eth. Nic.* 2. 6 (1106a22–23), quoted by Aquinas in ST Ia IIae, q. 56, a. 3, c.: "Virtus est quae bonum facit habentem, et opus eius bonum reddit," Aquinas uses a slightly modified version of this quote in his *In II Ethicorum.*, lect. 6: "hominis virtus erit utique habitus ex quo bonus homo fit et a quo bene opus suum reddit" (Leonine, 93, 16–17).

55*De virt. in comm.*, q. un., a. 7: "Non enim ex hoc quod homo habet scientiam, efficitur volens considerare verum, sed solummodo potens" (Marietti, 724)

56Thomas denotes virtue *simpliciter* not only habits that are seated in the will itself (such as charity or justice), but also habits seated in other faculties, whose acts are commanded by the will—temperance in the concupiscible appetite, courage in the irascible appetite, faith and prudence in the intellect. On the distinction between elicited and commanded acts, with reference to virtues seated in the intellect, see ST Ia IIae q. 16, a. 1 and q. 17, a. 6.

57*De virt. in comm.*, q. un., a. 7, ad 2: "Ad secundum dicendum, quod homo non dicitur bonus simpliciter ex eo quod est in parte bonus, sed ex eo quod secundum totum est bonus: quod quidem contingit per bonitatem voluntatis. . . . Ille autem qui habet bonitatem secundum aliquam potentiam, non praesupposita bona voluntate, dicitur bonus secundum quod habet bonum visum et auditum . . . . Et sic patet, quod ex eo quod homo habet scientiam, non dicitur bonus simpliter, sed bonus secundum intellectum, vel bene intelligens; et similiter est de arte, et de aliis huiusmodi habitibus" (Marietti, 725).

58See ST Ia IIae q. 65, a. 1, ad 3, where Thomas contrasts the unity of the moral virtues to the separability of the intellectual virtues.

59The mean of intellectual virtue is situated between the extremes of excess and deficiency, yet these extremes do not have the character of opposing vices; on this, see ST Ia IIae, q. 64, a. 3.

60On the specification of moral acts by good and evil, see ST Ia IIae, q. 18, a. 5. See also SCG III, chap. 9: "Ex quo etiam patet quod malum et bonum sunt contraria secundum quod in genere moralium accipiuntur: non autem simpliciter accepta . . . sed malum privatio est boni, inquantum est malum."

61The question whether the intellect may be a seat of virtue *simpliciter* is taken up expressly in ST Ia IIae, q. 56, a. 3: "Contingit autem intellectum a voluntate moveri, sicut et alias potentias: considerat enim aliquis aliquid actu, eo quod vult.

Et ideo intellectus, *secundum quod habet ordinem ad voluntatem*, potest esse subiectum virtutis simpliciter dictae." This same article mentions theological faith as a virtue *simpliciter* of the speculative intellect, and prudence a virtue *simpliciter* of the practical intellect. See *De virt. in comm.*, q. un, a. 7 (Marietti, 723–25).

62On this twofold cleanness (*duplex munditia*), of heart and mind, see ST IIa IIae, q. 8, a. 7.

63The question whether vice may be seated in the intellect is addressed in ST Ia IIae, q. 74, a. 5 and q. 76, a. 2.

64He introduces this consideration of intellectual vice in relation to the gift of insight: "Deinde considerandum est de vitiis oppositis scientiae et intellectui. Et quia de ignorantia, quae opponitur scientiae, dicitur est supra [Ia IIae, q. 76], cum de causis peccatorum ageretur; quaerendum est nunc de caecitate mentis et hebetudine sensus, quae opponuntur dono intellectus" (ST IIa IIae, q. 15, Prol.). After thus presenting blindness of mind and dullness of sense in opposition to the gifts of insight and science, he later treats the vice of folly (*stultitia*) in opposition to the gift of wisdom (IIa IIae, q. 46). Likewise, vices against theological faith are taken up in IIa IIae, qq. 10–14, while IIa IIa, qq. 53–55 discuss the intellectual vices opposed to prudence.

65Thomas notes that those gifts of the Holy Spirit which perfect the activity of the human intellect cannot be exercised in an immoral manner, in contrast to the intellectual virtues, which can be put to a morally bad use: "Et ideo sapientia et intellectu et aliis huiusmodi nullus male utitur, secundum quod sunt dona Spiritus Sancti" (ST Ia IIae, q. 68, a. 8, ad 3).

66See, for instance, ST IIa IIae, Prol.: "[T]res intellectuales virtutes, scilicet sapientia, intellectus, et scientia, communicant in nomine cum donis quibusdam Spiritus Sancti, unde simul etiam de eis considerabitur in consideratione donorum virtutibus correspondentium."

67See ST Ia IIae, q. 68, a. 3, where Thomas refers to the gifts as kinds of *habitus*.

68"Ad secundum dicendum quod in virtuoso non oportet quod vigeat usus rationis quantum ad omnia: sed solum quantum ad ea quae sunt agenda secundum virtutem."

69*De virt. in comm.*, q. un., a. 7, ad 5: "[M]ala voluntas non opponitur scientiae vel arti, sicut prudentiae, vel fidei, aut temperantiae" (Marietti, 725). See also ST IIa IIae, q. 23, a. 7, ad 3: "[S]cientia et ars quaedam virtutes sunt. . . . Sed huiusmodi inveniuntur in hominibus peccatoribus non habentibus caritatem." Aquinas concedes this point in the reply.

70*De virt. in comm.*, q. un., a. 7, c.: "[V]eri consideratio non est scientia in quantum est volita, sed secundum quod directe tendit in obiectum. Et similiter est de arte respectu intellectus practici . . . "

(Marietti, 724). In a similar vein, Yves Simon remarks (in his *Practical Knowledge* [New York: Fordham University Press, 1991]) that theoretical and artistic expertness are characterized by a detachment from the demands of moral virtue: "none would hold that the conclusions of the algebraist are determined by his virtuous inclinations" (18). "The part played by affective dispositions in philosophy remains entirely extrinsic. These dispositions do not concern the philosophic assent." Simon adds significantly, however, that "extrinsic does not mean unimportant" (ibid): "That debased morality should be accompanied by metaphysical excellence is not ruled out by any objective necessity, but it is made, in terms of fact, extremely improbable by the psychological relation between metaphysical truths, or some of them, and the dispositions of the human appetite" (40, n. 23). Moreover, Simon points to another way in which moral dispositions are of significance to the intellectual habits: "a man possessed of a certain science, art, or expertness is normally and inevitably the object of two descriptions. He may be treated as the sheer bearer of a certain habitus, but under many circumstances he is considered a social character, as a complex agent who, by reason of the habitus that he bears, is expected to discharge definite duties in society and to abide by rules of *human* use" (28). Simon's comments nicely complement Aquinas's conception of intellectual virtue.

[71]On the link between practical judgments (concerning action) and dispositions of the will, see Aquinas's discussion in *In III Ethicorum.*, lect. 13.

[72]For a contemporary analysis of intellectual virtues and vices, see Linda Trinkaus Zagzebski, *Virtues of the Mind* (Cambridge: Cambridge University Press, 1996). Zagzebski faults Aristotle (and Aquinas by extension) with among other things driving too sharp a distinction between intellectual and moral virtue, a distinction that, in her opinion, led him to neglect the moral aspects of intellectual virtue. Instead she recommends that we embrace a more unified outlook: "an intellectual virtue does not differ from certain moral virtues any more than one moral virtue differs from another . . . the processes related to the two kinds of virtue do not function independently" (139). In the case of Aquinas, however, Zagzebski overlooks that he too recognized the need for moral qualities in connection with the acquisition and exercise of the intellectual virtues. Yet, unlike Zagzebski, Aquinas does not include moral traits like perseverance *within* his definition of intellectual virtue; rather, he prefers to say that certain moral virtues (*studiositas*, for instance) are necessary as auxiliaries to the intellectual virtues. Aquinas defines the intellectual virtues more narrowly than does Zagzebski (and other contemporary authors). This is because he wishes to uphold the autonomy of the intellect within its own proper sphere of operation (the order of specification). He nevertheless acknowledges that these virtues are not free-floating—in the order of exercise, they require the support of the will and its allied virtues.

[73]"[V]irtus moralis potest accipi vel perfecta, vel imperfecta."

[74]"Et hoc modo accipiendo virtutes morales, non sunt connexae."

[75]This is not to say that volition is itself responsible for the mind's *assent* to propositions. Judgments based on immediate or inferred evidence are necessitated by the object; only when such evidence is lacking does the will intervene to determine the intellect's adhesion to an object (see Ia IIae, q. 17, a. 6). For a treatment of Aquinas's views on the possibility and nature of moral responsibility within the activity of speculative thought, see Gregory Martin Reichberg, "Aquinas on Moral Responsibility in the Pursuit of Knowledge," in *Thomas Aquinas and His Legacy*, ed. David Gallagher (Washington, DC: Catholic University of America Press, 1994), 61–82.

[76]"[S]ed quod utatur scientia habita, hoc est movente voluntate. Et ideo virtus quae perficit voluntatem, ut caritas vel iustitia, facit etiam bene uti huiusmodi speculativis habitibus."

[77] "Ergo circa intellectivas scientias potest esse curiositas vitiosa."

[78]On the virtue of *studiositas* and the opposing vices, see ST IIa IIae, qq. 166–67.

[79]On the distinction between *acts* of choice and *objects* of choice, see ST Ia IIae, q. 58, a. 1, ad 2.

[80]"Tum quia actus harum virtutum possunt esse meritorii . . . . Tum etiam quia sunt quaedam inchoatio perfectae beatitudinis, quae in contemplatione veri consistit. . . ."

Selected Further Reading

Garceau, Benoit. *Judicium: Vocabulaire, sources, doctrine de saint Thomas d'Aquin.* Montréal: Institute d'Études Médiévales; Paris: J. Vrin, 1968.

Gauthier, René Antoine and Jolif, Jean Yves. *L'Ethique à Nicomaque: Introduction, traduction, et commentaire.* Tome II, Commentaire. Louvain: Publications Universitaires, 1959.

Gilson, Etienne. *Wisdom and Love in Saint Thomas Aquinas.* Aquinas Lecture Series. Milwaukee: Marquette University Press, 1951.

Labourdette, Marie-Michel. "La morale de l'intelligence." *Revue thomiste* 100 (2000): 372–83.

Leroy, Marie-Vincent. "Le savoir spéculatif." *Revue thomiste* 48 (1948): 236–339.

MacDonald, Scott. "Theory of Knowledge." In *The Cambridge History of Later Medieval Philosophy.* Cambridge: Cambridge University Press, 1982.

MacLellan, Thomas M. "The Moral Virtues and the Speculative Life." *Laval Théologique et Philosophique* 12 (1956): 175–232.

Maritain, Jacques. *Science and Wisdom*. New York: Charles Scribner's Sons, 1940.

———. *Art and Scholasticism*. New York: Charles Scribner's Sons, 1962.

———. *The Responsibility of the Artist*. New York: Charles Scribner's Sons, 1962.

———. *Grande logique*. In Jacques and Raïssa Maritain, *Oeuvres complètes*. Vol. II. Fribourg, Éditions Universitaires, 1987.

Reeve, C. D. C. *Practices of Reason: Aristotle's Nicomachean Ethics*. Oxford: Clarendon, 1995.

Reichberg, Gregory M. "Aquinas on Moral Responsibility in the Pursuit of Knowledge." In *Thomas Aquinas and His Legacy*. Ed. David Gallagher. Washington, DC: Catholic University of America Press, 1994.

———. "*Studiositas*, the Virtue of Attention." In *The Common Things: Essays on Thomism and Education*. Ed. Daniel McInerny. Mishawaka, IN: American Maritain Association, 1999.

Simon, Yves R. *The Definition of Moral Virtue*. New York: Fordham University Press, 1986.

———. *Practical Knowledge*. New York: Fordham University Press, 1991.

Stump, Eleonare. "Wisdom, Will, Belief, and Moral Goodness." In *Aquinas's Moral Theory*, ed. Scott McDonald and Eleonore Stump. Ithaca, NY, and London: Cornell University Press, 1998.

William, Mary. "The Relationships of the Intellectual Virtue of Science and Moral Virtue." *The New Scholasticism* 36 (1962): 475–505.

Zagzebski, Linda Trinkaus. *Virtues of the Mind*. Cambridge: Cambridge University Press, 1996.

Vice and Sin (Ia IIae, qq. 71–89)

Eileen Sweeney

In *The Symbolism of Evil*, Paul Ricoeur argues that the Hebrew Bible contains two different notions of sin, one *legalistic* and another *prophetic*. The prophetic sense of sin expresses the demand of God speaking to human being and of human being standing before God and found wanting.[1] At the opposite pole, the legal approach to sin breaks down the absolute demand (which has always already been transgressed) into particular commands. Ricoeur relates these views dialectically. When separated from one another, one leads to the view of human evil as transgression of an abstract ethical standard or value set by no one in particular, and the other to a view of it as the unlimited demand of the wholly other before whom one can only fail.[2]

I will examine Aquinas's discussion of vice and sin in terms of an expanded version of this dialectic. The legalistic view is also essentially rationalistic. Reason first articulates specific moral imperatives that can then be acted on. It then interprets, justifies, and prioritizes those imperatives. The examination of the what and the why is crucial to the ethical act, as Socrates makes clear in his discussion with Euthyphro, asking how he knows his act is demanded by piety. The Platonic and Aristotelian versions of the rationalistic view also locate moral obligation in the obligation to one's own happiness and fulfillment.

The prophetic view, on the other hand, expresses the ethical obligation, first, as absolute and unconditional on the individual's happiness. Second, although that obligation is unconditional—as obligation is for Kant—for the prophet, it originates in the demand of the other, a demand which is, in Kant's terms, "heteronomous." Heteronomy is not on this view, as it is for Kant, an abdication of ethical obligation but the realization that one's own standards do not constitute the whole of the world of value, and that one's grasp of the good and the right is limited not only by one's ability to act ethically but even to imagine it. It is to experience oneself in relationships in which one always falls short in a fundamental, unavoidable, and unforeseen way. In the modern era, with the exception of the work of Blaise Pascal, Søren Kierkegaard, and perhaps Emmanuel Levinas, this construction of the moral predicament of human beings has been rejected by philosophers. In Aquinas, this interpretation exists, placed in dialectical tension with the legalistic, rationalistic approach that most philosophers support.

Aquinas's discussion of vice and sin represents an attenuation of this dialectic, in which the voice of ancient religious notions about the offense of God is muted by its displacement into the scholastic form and Aristotelian vocabulary. The form of the disputed question, its strategy of breaking down complex questions into smaller ones and restating large differences in terms of multiple distinctions, gives the stronger voice to reason's requirements of explanation and justification. The Aristotelian account of virtue as self-fulfillment (and vice as its opposite) gives reason the language of autonomous nature, replacing that of the supernatural other. For Aquinas, nature does not quite replace God; however, it is used to explain God in a strategy in which nature, as God's creation, does not contradict God but rather expresses and orients itself toward God's will.

On this view, sin is made analogous to physical illness, and virtue to health. The analogy to bodily health is part of a larger thematic movement in the *Summa*, which is also found in the discussion of the will, passion, and virtue in terms of the Aristotelian pattern of nature and natural motion. Many have noted the sense in which Aquinas transforms Christian theological notions by expressing them in Aristotelian terms, but Aquinas also stretches and reshapes the Aristotelian categories of nature and motion to fit notions like freedom, grace, and union with God connected with his accounts of will, passion, and virtue.[3]

What I intend to consider in this chapter is how these two notions of moral transgression, the "legalist" or "rationalist," revealing the influence of Aristotle, and the "prophetic" or "religious," showing the influence of Scripture, are interwoven in the *Summa theologiae*. I will trace the tension between the legalistic (naturalistic, rational, immanent) and the prophetic (supernatural, transcendent) models of vice and sin that animate Aquinas's discussion of the definition, punishment, and effects of sin, as well as in his attempts to describe the principles of ranking the various sins in terms of gravity and responsibility. All of these themes are, perhaps not coincidentally, sources for distinctions that became part of the scholastic manuals and catechisms of previous generations that now seem hopelessly irrelevant and even irrational: the distinctions between mortal and venial sin, between original and actual sin, and between penal and satisfactory punishment, and the endless and apparently arbitrary ranking of sins by their gravity.

My point is not to defend these elements of Aquinas's account, and it is certainly not to recommend a return to scholastic manuals. It is to understand these notions in the context of his discussion, to see the purposes they serve in his text. They are, I contend, strategies and distinctions called up to retain and explain the complexity of human wrongdoing, to retain the insights of the legalistic/rational and the prophetic/religious accounts of vice and sin. To the degree that I achieve this aim, another will be attained—seeing Aquinas's reflections on sin not as scholastic legalism but as a complex view in dialogue with major ethical thinkers and confronting major ethical questions.

TWO MODELS OF SIN: OFFENDING GOD AND FORSAKING VIRTUE

The opening question considering vice and sin brings out the tension between the two main categories organizing Aquinas's discussion: vice (the Aristotelian category) and sin (the religious category). Aquinas begins by exploring the nature of vice, defining it as contrary to a human nature as defined by reason (Ia IIae, q. 71, a. 2). One objection notes Augustine's definition of sin as "word, deed, or desire *contrary to the Law of God*" (Ia IIae, q. 71, a. 2, obj. 4, emphasis added).[4] The response readers of Aquinas know to expect is not long in coming: that the two definitions amount to the same thing: to be against human nature, i.e., reason, is to be against the law of God (Ia IIae, q. 71, a. 2, ad 4).[5]

This equation of the human and divine as touchstones for judging sin is one that Aquinas restates throughout this discussion. Only three articles later, he reconsiders the definition of sin as contrary to the will of God. In this article, the previous definition of vice reappears as an objection. Human evil, the objection argues, is against reason, not contrary to eternal law (Ia IIae, q. 71, a. 6, obj. 5). Although still promoting the notion of a single order in which both accounts of human evil coexist, in this context Aquinas supports the supremacy of eternal law in evaluating human acts. There are, he argues, two rules of the human will: one "proximate and homogeneous" (human reason) and another which is "first" and, it is implied, distant, and heterogeneous (eternal law, which is God's reason; Ia IIae, q. 71, a. 6).

Responding to the objection containing the naturalistic account of human evil, he distinguishes between the theologian's consideration of sin as offense against God and the moral philosopher's criticism of it as against reason. The theological definition is "more fitting" (whether within the context of a theological work only or in general Aquinas does not say) "the more so," Aquinas continues, "as the eternal law directs us in many things that surpass human reason, e.g., in matters of faith" (Ia IIae, q. 71, a. 6, ad 5).[6] This response orders and subordinates reason to faith and nature to grace, which is Aquinas's hallmark.

In his discussion of the distinction of sins, Aquinas argues that it is the intention of the sinner that defines the sin essentially, not its degree of departure from the law of God (that departure is accidental to the act since no one acts intending evil; Ia IIae, q. 92, a. 1). The ensuing discussions of different ways of distinguishing sin, however, appeal to both divine and human ways of regarding sin. Aquinas considers two other ways of distinguishing sin: first, in Isidore's terms: sin is either against God, against self, or against neighbor and, second, sin is either mortal or venial (Ia IIae, q. 72, aa. 4–5). These formulations seem to create two categories of sin, those against God and those against humanity. One objection argues that *all* sin is against God; the second claims that all sins are simultaneously against God, human being, *and* self. The third points out that these distinctions are based on external factors rather than on the true nature of sin (Ia IIae, q. 71, a. 4, objs. 1–3).

Aquinas's response coolly brings all three of these apparently incompatible ways of describing sin together. First, Aquinas makes of these three kinds of sin three modes of acting against a threefold order existing *in* the human being. Thus, the external is made internal. Second, he makes of the three orders concentric circles, sin against neighbor the smallest, sin against self or reason the second, and sin against God encompassing the others. Thus, all sins *are* in a sense against God but are still distinguished in that one order goes beyond the others (Ia IIae, q. 71, a. 4, ad 2–3).

The division of sin into mortal and venial is also, it is objected, based on something external to the sinful act itself, that is, punishment, for mortal sins are those deserving of eternal punishment, while venial sins earn something less. The determination of whether a sin deserves eternal or temporary punishment, Aquinas responds, is based on an essential feature of the act: the degree of its inordinateness, the character of the good from which the sinner turns. Infinite punishment thus follows from the rejection of the final and infinite good. Like the destruction of the life principle which results in death as opposed to the disorder of disease out of which a return to health is possible, he who rejects God destroys the principle of moral life, and "falls irreparably" (*lapsum irreparabilem*), while he who rejects

only some lesser good can recover based on a principle which is intact (Ia IIae, q. 72, a. 5).

This way of describing the act of mortal sin resonates with the Platonic/Aristotelian account of the life of vice as like one of addiction from which, at a certain point, it is virtually impossible to free oneself, and with the prophetic notion of absolute failure and separation from God as the substance and wages of sin. The category of venial sin, on the other hand, is Aquinas's way of including the notion of incremental failure from which one can recover. The difference between mortal and venial sin parallels from below the distinction between human and supernatural happiness. Thus, venial sin is in a sense an offense against the happiness of virtue achievable by human effort, and mortal sin is an offense against the happiness of the beatific vision.

A more detailed discussion of the distinction between mortal and venial sin again places in question the notion that there are merely human, finite, and reparable ways of going wrong (or right). Here the voice of St. Paul articulates the absolute obligation to God that overtakes the whole of human life: "Whether you eat or drink, or whatever else you do, do all to the glory of God" (1 Cor 10:31). All life's acts are a way of choosing, honoring, and loving God, or not; thus, according to the objection, all sins are mortal, all are the failure to choose God (Ia IIae, q. 88, a. 1, obj. 2). It is a moment where through the voice of the apostle, Aquinas echoes the view expressed by Anselm in *Cur Deus Homo*. No matter how slight an action might be in itself, Anselm brings Boso to admit, if it is contrary to the will of God, it cannot be preferred even to the preservation of all of creation.[7] The point of both St. Paul's exhortation and Anselm's radicalizing of its implications is that the obligation to God is total, absolute, and not in the least moderate or proportional.

In response, Aquinas repeats his account of the distinction between mortal and venial sin based on the distinction between curable and fatal illness. To the Pauline-derived objection he counters with the distinction between the habitual and actual reference of one's actions to God, that is, with a solution based on the model of vice rather than sin. But this is a case where the Aristotelian language belies the radically different concept it is being used to express. On the one hand, Aquinas softens the Apostle's exhortation, arguing that one need only *habitually*—rather than *actually*—refer all human acts to God's glory. On the other, his argument implicitly rejects one view of the distinction between mortal and venial sin—that it divides the activities of human life into those devoted to God and those devoted to oneself: all acts are and need to be as a matter of habit dedicated to God.

Any departure from charity is for Aquinas an instance of mortal sin, and charity takes in all those activities related to the fellowship of those united in love or charity: self, other human beings, and God (IIae IIae, q. 23, aa. 1, 5). Virtually all relationships and all actions are here included; the reference to the goal of union with God for self and others may be only implicitly rather than explicitly recognized in the act. Even cloaked in Aristotelian language, even defined in such a way as to be consistent with the model of vice as the rejection of one's own good, the nature of that good and the way in which all acts are related to that good have been significantly redefined in these passages by being reoriented toward God.

PENAL VS. SATISFACTORY PUNISHMENT

The distinction between mortal and venial sin raises questions not only about how sin is defined by and in relationship to God rather than in terms of one's own nature or good, but also about the nature and source of moral obligation. To define sin in terms of punishment by God seems to define acts in terms of how they are viewed from the outside, in relation to the other, in this case by God as the ultimate judge, rather than in terms of standards that develop from within. Aquinas, as we have seen, does not accept these as alternatives; rather, he sees them as consistent, even identical with one another. His analogy between venial and mortal sin and illness and death recasts punishment as imposed from the outside as the loss of the good desired, God, and hence as self-imposed destruction.

The analogy, however, obscures for a moment the anomaly in the two types of sin and their punishment. They are infinitely different from one another. Mortal sin carries with

it the punishment of damnation. It is a fall from which the individual cannot recuperate, while venial sin is a minor, correctable straying. In an important sense mortal sin is the creation of a category to express the consequences of sin on the prophetic model: absolute failure whose consequence is eternal deprivation and isolation. Venial sin, on the other hand, and its consequence come closer to the legalistic model: there is a debt to be paid but it is defined; it is one the individual can step forward to make, and which rehabilitates the individual and restores justice to the community.

The first objection in Aquinas's text to the distinction of sin in terms of mortal and venial notes the infinite distance between the two kinds of punishment, sounding the prophetic note of falling utterly short and away from God. However, Aquinas supports that distinction with a classically legalistic notion of sin and its punishment from Deuteronomy: "According to the measure of the sin shall the measure also of the stripes be" (Ia IIae, q. 72, a. 5, obj. 1, citing Deut 25:2).[8] The objection thus defends the notion of infinite punishment and separation on the grounds of justice and order. Scripture supports a religious view, but in rationalistic and ethical rather than explicitly religious terms.

A later question entirely devoted to punishment returns to puzzle over the notion of infinite punishment. Aquinas first considers whether punishment can be temporally infinite, lining up objections to such a view. In this context he quotes Isaiah to the same effect as the Deuteronomic passage cited above. No punishment can be eternal because of the very notion of justice as a kind of equality, requiring punishment in time just as the sin is committed in time; hence, Isaiah writes, "In measure against measure, when it shall be cast off, thou shalt judge it" (Ia IIae, q. 87, a. 3, obj. 1, citing Isa 37:8).[9] In this case, a prophetic passage supports a legalistic and Aristotelian view of justice, that the notion of measure or proportion requires the finitude of punishment.

Furthermore, an objection argues, according to Aristotle, punishment is a kind of medicine, administered to the end of health, but nothing directed to an end can be infinite since, of course, it would never reach that end

(Ia IIae, q. 87, a. 3, obj. 2; Arist. *Eth. Nic.* 2.3 [1104b15–18]). The model of punishment as healing makes it a means to an end, but unending punishment must be an end itself. As such, it cannot, then, aim at the recovery of the sinner; rather, its goal is merely vengeance or justice. Even from a religious perspective, another objection notes, infinite punishment seems to attribute to God a kind of enjoyment of the destruction of human beings inconsistent with the divine nature (Ia IIae, q. 87, a. 3, obj. 3).

While the previous discussion concerned a punishment that is infinite in time, the next article asks whether punishment can be infinite *per se*. In this article, Aquinas sets up the objections to argue from the other side: punishment for sin *can* be infinite in quantity. To support this view, he again quotes Deuteronomy on the measure of stripes equaling the measure of sin (Ia IIae, q. 87, a. 4, obj. 2, citing Deut 25:2; see also Ia IIae, q. 72, a. 5). He thus relies on the notion of measure and proportion to support the possibility and appropriateness of infinite punishment. Another objection cites Jeremiah's prayer to have God respond to his sin with judgment but not fury "lest Thou bring me to nothing" (Ia IIae, q. 87, a. 4, obj. 1, citing Jer 10:24).[10]

God's vengeance can be infinite, and it derives from infinite power. Jeremiah pleads for the mercy of less than infinite punishment, an infinite punishment that , it is implied, would be justly applied. The passage also makes concrete the notion of infinite punishment as the absolute destruction of the sinner. Jeremiah surely does so as a way of describing divine power, as well as the necessity of divine favor to save the sinner. In responding, Aquinas focuses on justice to argue against this form of infinite punishment; the destruction of the sinner is inconsistent with the eternal punishment required by divine justice (Ia IIae, q. 87, a. 4, ad 2).

The construction of these sets of objections and responses illustrate how carefully Aquinas balances the two models of punishment and the two views of sin they imply. So, as one might expect, do the bodies of both articles. Aquinas has already laid the groundwork for the justification of punishment in general; sin is the disturbance of the orders of reason, human government, and God, each of which

requires payment of its own debt (Ia IIae, q. 87, a. 1).

Punishment could be understood as the internal result of sin; just as virtue is its own reward, vice is its own punishment. Aquinas roundly rejects such a view, though he adds that there are a number of accidental ways in which sin can be its own punishment. But punishment *per se* is against the will and, hence, from outside the recipient (Ia IIae, q. 87, a. 2). He bases the justification of eternal punishment on the same distinction used to ground the difference between venial and mortal sin: some disturbances of order are complete, destroying the principle, and as long as that disturbance lasts, so does the punishment. Some disturbances are less complete, and so, hence, are their punishments (Ia IIae, q. 87, a. 3).

Moreover, the rejection of the principle of good, of the final end, even though happening in time in a single finite choice or a series of them, is in a sense in eternity: "from the very fact that he fixes his end in sin, he has the will to sin everlastingly" (Ia IIae, q. 87, a. 3, ad 1).[11] God inflicts such punishment not out of the pleasure of destruction but, Aquinas argues, from "delight in the order of his justice" (*delectatur in ordine suae iustitiae*) (Ia IIae, q. 87, a. 3, ad 3). And while, as with human punishment, divine punishment is not always medicinal to the sufferer, it is to others who are deterred by it (Ia IIae, q. 87, a. 3, ad 2). Aquinas supports this rather harsh view with a beautiful passage from the Psalms that transforms his conclusion into a prophetic context, one of relationship, of absolute demand but also absolute love and mercy: "Thou hast given a warning to them that fear Thee, that they may flee from before the bow, that Thy beloved may be delivered" (Ia IIae, q. 87, a. 3, ad 2, citing Ps 59:6).[12] While this passage does not make for a fully convincing argument, it does express a view of deterrence (to use an anachronistic term) that is not a condemnation of others to suffer for our sake—harsh punishment is to protect the just in the community from those who might be tempted to injustice otherwise—but a taking of the punishment of others as a reminder that "there but for the grace of God go I."

The two *sed contras* map the boundaries beyond which Aquinas does not wish to venture.

They support opposite views, and they do so from different perspectives, the first, prophetic; the second, legalistic. Supporting the possibility of eternal punishment in Ia IIae, q. 87, a. 3, Aquinas again turns to Scripture: "he that shall blaspheme against the Holy Ghost shall never have forgiveness, but shall be guilty of an everlasting sin" (Ia IIae, q. 87, a. 3, *sed contra*, citing Matt 25:46/Mark 3:29).[13] The *sed contra* of the following article argues that infinite punishment is contrary to the measure of justice because it would make the punishment for all mortal sins equal (Ia IIae, q. 87, a. 4, *sed contra*). Aquinas's response locates the infinity of the punishment in the sinner's "pain of loss" (*poena damni*), the loss of the good he rejects—God. In this sense, all mortal sins are equal.

On the other hand, different kinds of sins are the choice of different, lesser goods for which God is rejected; hence, the punishments for these different choices are different and finite, inflicted as a "pain of sense" (*poena sensus*) rather than loss (q. 87, a. 4). Thus, instead of choosing between the two models of punishment, Aquinas keeps both, and orders them by the distinction between the good chosen and the good forgone. Further, in an important sense, the argument makes mortal sin, which consists in the rejection of God, its own punishment, a punishment consisting in forgoing forever the enjoyment of that perfect good in order to "fix one's end in sin," thus willing "to sin everlastingly" (Ia IIae, q. 87, a. 3, ad 1).[14] It is a punishment less inflicted by God than a wish on the part of the sinner (mistaken though it is) that is granted by God.

The distinction between the good chosen and the good forgone may seem artificial, but it captures two different perspectives on immoral acts. For, on the one hand, when you fail someone, you fail them utterly, and it is completely irrelevant what or who pulled you away. That is why explanations that include an account of what someone did instead of what they should have done are heard by the injured party as, first, thoroughly irrelevant and, second, as compounding the injury in an attempt to escape responsibility. Hence, from the point of view of the good forsaken, all offenses are equal. On the other hand, the reason for which one was forsaken does mitigate (or deepen) the wrong done, and the punishment is adjusted accordingly.

The question of how one repays the debt owed for forsaking the good again reveals the tension between the more rationalistic, internal model of sin and punishment and one that emphasizes divine judgment and injury to the other. The Aristotelian/Platonic notion of vice and virtue holds that there is no debt once vice is gone. When one "returns to virtue," the sin is gone and the virtuous man deserves no punishment, owes no debt (Ia IIae, q. 87, a. 6, obj. 2). Moreover, Aquinas repeats, punishment is a kind of medicine, which is no longer needed once the illness is cured (Ia IIae, q. 87, a. 6, obj. 3). The *sed contra*, however, tells in brief the disturbing story of King David's forgiveness by God and the remaining debt to God in the wake of his adultery and treachery. God takes away David's sin yet takes the life of his first child from Bathsheba as payment (2 Kings 12:13, 14; Ia IIae, q. 87, a. 6, *sed contra*).

The language of debt places the focus less on the state of the individual soul and more on the interpersonal nature of human action. The wrong done to the other requires repayment, a payment due even after the wrongdoing has ceased. Again Aquinas tries to keep elements of both views of punishment by means of a distinction. There are, he argues, two aspects of the need for repayment. One, an act of retributive justice for "the guilty act" (*actus culpae*), another for "the stain of sin" (*macula sequens*). While the idea of the stain of sin conjures up images from grade school catechism of black spots on the pure white soul, Thomas views it as a metaphor expressing the separation of the soul from God, having lost the brightness it has from the source of its light (Ia IIae, q. 87, a. 6; see also Ia IIae, q. 86, a. 1). He thinks of this light as twofold—the natural light of reason and the divine light. The key notion is the contact with that light which is lost in sin and must be restored: "When the soul cleaves to things by love, there is a kind of contact in the soul, and when man sins, he cleaves to certain things against the light of reason and of the Divine law . . ." (Ia IIae, q. 86, a. 1).[15]

To explain this contact, Aquinas uses the metaphor of physical separation. "Thus if one man be parted from another on account of some kind of movement, he is not reunited to him as soon as the movement ceases, but he needs to draw near to him and to return by a contrary movement" (Ia IIae, q. 86, a. 2).[16] So too, the will to sin must be countered by a contrary movement back toward the one injured.

Grace calls the sinner back and makes possible the return to God. The principle of moral action is charity, which unites the parties in fellowship. Since charity is destroyed by mortal sin, an act of grace from God is necessary to bring the sinner back into the right relation with God and the community (ibid.). Grace makes possible what Aquinas calls "satisfactory punishment" (poena satisfactoria), by which he means a movement of return made willingly rather than under duress (Ia IIae, q. 87, aa. 6–7). While justice strictly speaking is served by punishment, reunion is achieved only by satisfactory punishment. Aquinas notes that the concept is something of an oxymoron: that "when punishment is satisfactory it loses somewhat of the nature of punishment; for the nature of punishment is to be against the will" (Ia IIae, q. 87, a. 6).[17]

Aquinas's responses blend the interpersonal characterization of moral action with the more individualistic model of virtue as self-fulfillment expressed in the objections. He argues that the virtuous person (once returned to virtue) demands punishment as satisfactory, that is, wills that punishment (Ia IIae, q. 87, a. 6, ad 2).[18] The internal standard of virtue, in other words, requires and joins in the restoration of connection to others and to God. The act of repayment, Aquinas argues further, repairs not the will (which in the virtuous has already returned to good order) but the rest of the faculties (presumably the passions and the intellect), and restores justice to the one injured and to the community scandalized by the evil done (Ia IIae, q. 87, a. 6, ad 3). Hence, the same act repairs both the internal order of powers and ends and relationships in the community.

In terms of the distinction between the legal and prophetic notions of sin, "satisfactory punishment" is a hybrid, one part a prophetic view of punishment, punishment imposed from the outside and against one's will, and one part rationalistic and virtue-based, punishment as a healing desired by the wrongdoer. The latter notion of punishment is, of course, best known from Plato's Gorgias. Plato's claim that punishment is the perpetrator's true desire becomes problematic when one realizes that evil individuals do not in fact line up willingly for punishment. Plato solves the problem by distinguishing between what the vicious think they want (continuation in evil) and what they really want (their own good restored by punishment). However, what is enacted in the dialogue is the apparent impossibility of coming to know what one truly wants; no one in the Gorgias or in any other Platonic dialogue, one might argue, is converted to this new perspective. According to the argument of Platonic dialogues of the middle period, education is supposed to solve this problem. However, their dramatic form suggests a more pessimistic outcome.

Confronting the same issue, Aquinas accounts for the possibility of conversion by grace. This is not simply the insertion of God where no other explanation can be found. A version of it is present in secular form in the therapeutic model. On this view, the guilty party cannot take responsibility for his actions and make amends until he feels accepted. Grace is that divine call back to community before the sinner is fit to rejoin it; grace makes it possible to ask for the forgiveness the sinner cannot request until he or she can once again be imagined as part of the community.

ORIGINAL AND ACTUAL SIN

If the account of punishment emphasizes the interpersonal, the offense and the need to repair the fellowship of charity, the account of the effects of sin, including that of original sin, emphasizes its individual, internal effects. The dominant language used to elucidate these effects is, once again, the language of illness, applied first to original sin: "For [original sin] is a disordered disposition, arising from the destruction of the harmony which was essential to original justice, even as bodily sickness is a disordered disposition of the body, by reason of the destruction of that equilibrium which is essential to health" (Ia IIae, q. 82, a. 1).[19]

The same language occurs in all of the subsequent articles of the question and in the following question, i.e., in its discussion of the degree of "infection" of the will and other powers by original sin (Ia IIae, q. 82, aa. 2–4; Ia IIae, q. 83, aa. 3–4). Yet the naturalistic analogy is used to describe conditions both before and after the fall, which for Aquinas are anything but natural. The present condition of humankind is a fall from the integrity of nature, as Aquinas makes clear in his analogy of original sin to illness and his account of concupiscence. The effect of original sin is the inordinate turning to changeable goods (Ia IIae, q. 82, a. 3).[20]

Yet the "harmony" lost in the fall was not a natural state of health but a "supernatural endowment of grace" in which reason was perfectly subjected to God, lower powers to higher, and body to soul (Ia, q. 95, a. 1). If it had been natural, he argues, it could not have been lost by sin (ibid.). Thus, although original justice is lost by the fall, the principles of nature (though not the ability to carry through with them) are intact after the fall (Ia IIae, q. 85, a. 2). What is strange about Aquinas's view is that a purely "natural state" of humankind has strictly speaking never existed; before the fall nature had a kind of supernatural strength, and, after that, nature is somewhat, though not radically, depleted.

The whole notion that the effects of original sin are analogous to the debilitation of illness rests, of course, on the notion that original sin is transmitted from Adam to the rest of humanity. However, Aquinas explicitly rejects the model of illness to express the transmission of original sin. This account fails, he argues, because children cannot be held responsible for something they contract involuntarily from their parents (q. 81, a. 1). His own explanation, couched in the subjunctive, rests on a way of considering all human beings as one person because of their common human nature, as if, he explains further, they were "so many members of one body" (*multa membra unius corporis*) (ibid.). A murder committed by the hand is not attributed to it alone but only as a member of the body. "In this way then, the disorder which is in this human being born of Adam, is voluntary not by his will, but by the will of his first parent, who, by the movement of generation, moves all who originate from him, even as the soul's will moves all the members to their actions"(Ia IIae, q. 81, a. 1).[21] *Qua* individual, then, descendants do not share in guilt, but *qua* sharers in the human

nature originating with Adam descendants do take on the blame, much as children take on a family disgrace (Ia IIae, q. 81, a. 1, ad 1, 5).

Aquinas's position, employing the language of essence and hence Aristotelian metaphysics to explain original sin, attempts to save both the sense in which human beings are, on the one hand, autonomous individuals who carry guilt and responsibility only for their own acts and, on the other hand, members of a single group who share both gifts and defects, and whose fates are linked.[22] Thus, Aquinas grounds the notion that the taint is transmitted to subsequent generations in an analogical way rather than by means of either a linear or literal familial identity with Adam, on the one hand, or a merely mythic or metaphorical link to Adam, on the other. He attempts, in other words, to carve out a position somewhere between a fundamentalist and merely literary reading of Scripture.

When he turns to the effects of actual sin (everything other than original sin), Aquinas asks whether and to what degree nature is destroyed by such sins. First, he divides the "good of human nature" (*bonum naturae*) (Ia IIae, q. 85, a. 1) into three parts: the principles of nature, the inclination toward the natural end of virtue, and the achievement of that end of virtue. He arranges them on a trajectory of motion as starting, middle, and end points.[23]

The starting point, the principles of nature, is never affected by sin. The end point, the complete achievement of virtue under one's own power, is destroyed by sin, but the middle, the inclination to virtue, remains, albeit in diminished form (ibid.). Aquinas argues that this inclination can be diminished indefinitely, just as obstacles can indefinitely impede motion toward the end, but not totally, in the same way that a transparent body remains transparent even though shadowed by intervening clouds (Ia IIae, q. 85, a. 2). Nonetheless, the perfect order of the faculties is lost in original sin and the inclination to virtue is diminished by actual sin. All the faculties of the soul are thus affected: reason's order to the true, the will's order to the good, the irascible power's order to the arduous, and the concupiscible power's order to the delectable. Thus, Aquinas explains Bede's "wounds of nature" (*vulnera inflicta toti humanae naturae*), which follow from sin—ignorance, weakness, malice, and concupiscence—in terms of his own psychology (Ia IIae, q. 85, a. 3).

Aquinas also incorporates Augustine's formulation of the wages of sin as "the privation of mode, species, and order" (*privatio modi, speciei et ordinis*) (Ia IIae, q. 85, a. 4, citing *De natura boni*, 4). He explains its application in terms of the threefold good of human nature: the substance of nature, inclination to good, and the good of virtue or grace. The first retains its mode, species, and order, the second has them only in diminished form; and the third is completely deprived of all three. Augustine's description of the effects of sin becomes an opportunity to reiterate Aquinas's emphasis on the integrity of nature before and after the fall, before and after actual sin. But both Bede's and Augustine's accounts also afford him the opportunity, once his own view of the basic integrity of nature remaining both after original and actual sin is in place, to include also the reality of human weakness, both that brought to the first ethical act as original sin and that exacerbated by the accumulation of sin.

The discussion of the "wounds" of sin and loss of "mode, species, and order" in sin thus provides the transition from a naturalistic to a religious view of the effects of sin, leading up to the last two articles' discussion of death and bodily defects as consequences of sin. In these discussions Aquinas clearly uses the distinction between original and actual sin, which sounds quite arcane to modern ears, to maintain a legal and rationalist account of responsibility, punishment, and justice in the realm of actual sin. Hence, Aquinas rejects arguments which would see death and physical suffering as a result of an individual's actual sin, even as he retains the Genesis account of the consequences of the original sin and the Pauline interpretation of the supreme consequence as death (Ia IIae, q. 85, a. 5, *sed contra*, and ad 3, citing Rom 5:12).

The only way actual sin can cause bodily defect, Aquinas argues, is in the sense that a sin such as overeating can cause sickness; actual sin affects the ability to "regulate the acts of the soul" (*ad rectificandum animae actus*), not those of the body (Ia IIae, q. 85, a. 5, ad 3). Further, death and defect are not the result of a loss of natural but rather supernatural order present before the fall; in this state, the lower rational powers are subject to reason and the body subject to the soul to such a degree as to preclude the corruption of the body at any level. The physical and material consequences of original sin, Aquinas argues, are like the results of displacing a pillar on which a stone rests: when the column is removed, the stone falls, but its nature was to fall with or without the support by the pillar (Ia IIae, q. 85, a. 5).

One might argue that Aquinas is simply saving the appearances of the story of the fall and its consequences while in fact supporting the Greek, philosophical notion of responsibility and the consequences of vice. However, Aquinas's view of original sin is ultimately, I think, not that different from Pascal's: original sin is the most improbable of stories, except that it is the only story which accounts for important but apparently contradictory aspects of human experience.[24] Original sin explains the human propensity to sin in the prophetic sense—sin as inevitable failure before the other, sin as stain or contagion, and human moral limitation as not chosen but given.

It is equally part of human being on the prophetic view to aspire to overcome not only these limits but those of nature itself. But for Aquinas, as opposed to Pascal, part of the truth about the human moral condition is that individuals are autonomous agents capable of virtue as well as vice, free and responsible, not "fated" to fail or afflicted with an inclination toward evil: human nature inclines toward virtue, an inclination it is largely capable of satisfying. Aquinas's account of the definition of sin, its punishment, and its effects all exhibit the tension between these two views of the human moral predicament.

RANKING SINS

The articulation and justification of the requirements of the moral life are the means to fulfilling a rational ethical demand, a justification that must include an account of which of those requirements are the most inviolable. Such an analysis is also required for a system of justice; it is represented in Scripture by the ordinances of Exodus enumerating proper punishments for the restoration of justice. Aquinas's ranking of sins provides the account of the gravity of sins which is a condition for such guidelines. Both his ranking and the

Exodus texts themselves assume that restoration of both communal order and individual virtue is possible. Such projects conflict with the prophetic model as reflected in the notion of mortal sin in two ways. First, the obligations outlined by mortal sin, those describing obligations to God, are all absolute and hence equal. Second, their seriousness is a result of their intention, of the desire to reject God and divine rule. Moreover, the ranking of sins poses difficulties even within a rational or legal framework. One purpose of such a project might be to provide a code in which one may "look up" a transgression and its punishment. This is certainly the *cliché* about Aquinas made real in the confessional manuals which preceded his *Summa* and the catechisms which followed it.

However, the sheer number of distinctions and different orders of gravity and responsibility in Aquinas's analysis yield nothing like the clear charts of a catalogue or rulebook. Instead, the pattern created is a web of overlapping but very different ways in which one's actions and motives have to be scrutinized. The point of Aquinas's exercise cannot be to oversimplify moral analysis, something a rulebook would accomplish; it can only be to complicate and deepen moral thinking—in short, to develop practical wisdom (*phronesis*). He achieves this by an analysis of the various elements of which the Aristotelian wise person (*phronimos*) must be aware: the who, what, when, where, why, and how. Aquinas's goal is, first, pastoral, the reintegration of sinners into the community through an understanding of the degree and type of their alienation, the mitigating circumstances, and the difference between intended and actual outcomes. Any given act has to be ranked on these several scales of gravity. But his goal is not just pastoral care of the other but also of oneself, an invitation to explore and reform one's own motives and intentions.

Aquinas's argument that sins differ in gravity uses the same analogy he employs to distinguish between mortal and venial sin: there are two kinds of privation, one that admits of no degrees, such as death, and another that does, such as sickness or deformity. Vice and sin are in the latter category, Aquinas argues, "because in them the privation of the due proportion of reason is not such as to destroy the

order of reason altogether" (Ia IIae, q. 73, a. 2).[25] Hence, Aquinas argues, sins are graver the more they corrupt principles higher in the order of reason, that is, in terms of the good they reject: "in matters of action the reason directs all things in view of the end, and thus the higher the end which attaches to sins in human acts, the graver the sin" (Ia IIae, q. 73, a. 3).[26] On this scale, sins against God are more grave than those against human beings, and those against human beings are more grave than those against external objects (ibid.). The same principle, Aquinas adds, further differentiates sins within each of these more general categories.

When harm is factored in to the scales of gravity, it is factored in with intention. Thus, Aquinas distinguishes between cases where harm is intended and foreseen, foreseen but not intended, and neither foreseen nor intended. In the first two cases, it is the connection to intention and will which makes the harm aggravate the gravity. In the first case, the harm is directly intended, but in the second, performing the act in spite of knowing the harm it will cause shows a greater will to sin, which increases the gravity of the sin. Even harm one does not foresee makes the sin more grave, as people are responsible for what they should have known would follow from their acts (Ia IIae, q. 73, a. 8).

Aquinas argues that the more "excellent" the person (*magnitudo personae*) sinning, the graver the sin because such persons (a) should more easily resist sin, (b) show more gratitude to God for their gifts, (c) sin against their specific excellence (for example, if a prince sins against justice), and (d) cause greater scandal by their sin (Ia IIae, q. 73, a. 10). Moreover, those against whom one sins also can make the sin more grave. Since there are three ends of one's acts—God, self, and neighbor—sins against persons more united to God (by sanctity or station), to family (or other intimates), and to the community as a whole (public persons) are more grave (Ia IIae, q. 73, a. 9). These additional distinctions affecting gravity do not contradict Aquinas's basic principles for ranking sins, but they do complicate the process considerably. They follow, first, from his view that it is the will and the intent of an act that classifies it and its seriousness, and second, from his view that sins are more grave as they are against God, human beings, and objects, respectively.

Having articulated his own principles, Aquinas then confronts the view that carnal sins are graver than spiritual sins. This view is represented in the objections by biblical, patristic, and Aristotelian sources, all arguing that carnal sins are graver. As with the account of goodness and evil acts in general (and the definitions of the sciences), Aquinas's mode of defining and distinguishing is always formal rather than material. For example, the sciences are distinguished by the principles or *rationes* under which things are considered rather than of the things considered, and moral acts are defined by the end intended rather than the matter of the act. The same is true for sins; they are defined and ranked by the object which is specified by the end, not by the content of the act. The distinction between carnal and spiritual sins is one based on matter rather than form; hence, it cannot be the basic distinction for Aquinas.

Yet Thomas considers this question by seeming to agree with the terms in which the distinction is drawn, but he argues, *contra* the views he cites, that spiritual sins are graver in general. He grounds that answer on aspects of the agent, the sufferer, and the motive rather than the nature of the act itself as spiritual or carnal. First, the spirit of a spiritual sinner turns *away* from God, which occasions more guilt than when the appetite of a sinner turns *toward* physical pleasure in carnal sin. Second, spiritual sin is against God and neighbor and, hence, worse than carnal sin, which is against one's own body. Last, spiritual sin is worse because the impulse to carnal sin is stronger, caused by "the innate concupiscence of the flesh" (*concupiscentiam carnis nobis innatam*), which, he argues, mitigates voluntariness and hence guilt (Ia IIae, q. 73, a. 5). Motive, as this answer implies, can function to make a sin either more or less grave. Finally, he adds, the fact that spiritual sins are graver in general "does not mean that each spiritual sin is of greater guilt than each carnal sin" (Ia IIae, q. 73, a. 5).[27] This treatment as a whole places sin more in the mind than the body. It moves, as Aquinas's account as a whole does, away from a literal or fundamentalist reading of moral action. Aquinas reinforces this view when he argues that a sin of sensuality can never be

mortal. Reason, not sensuous desire, directs a person toward an end; hence, only reason can lead someone fundamentally astray (Ia IIae, q. 74, a. 4). The final caveat, that even though spiritual sins are graver *in general*, they may not be in any given case, simply continues the same line of thought.

Aquinas presents the view he rejects as having broad support in sources as diverse as Leviticus, Augustine, Proverbs, and Aristotle, and, as he responds to those objections, he manages to find the common ground in Gregory the Great, an important ethical authority in medieval moral thought, and, like Aquinas, a thinker who blends Greek and biblical sources. Aquinas's careful use of sources has substantive implications. First, Gregory argues that spiritual sins are greater but also explains the tendency to see matters otherwise: we have less guilt but more shame for carnal sins (Ia IIae, q. 73, a. 5, *sed contra*). According to Aquinas, Aristotle's claim that anger is less shameful than incontinence demonstrates that the latter is less connected to reason and has to do with the pleasures humans share with animals (Ia IIae, q. 73, a. 5, ad 3).[28] For Aristotle, Aquinas implies, the scale of shamefulness is the same as that of gravity. However, for Aquinas (and Gregory), human beings might be ashamed of their animal nature; it may hurt one's sense of dignity, nay vanity, to be (and to be seen to be) in any way vulnerable to desire and pain as animals are; however, what constitutes a true loss of humanity for Aquinas and Gregory is not the humiliation of physical desire but the prideful rejection of the spiritual end in God.

The last reason Aquinas gives for the gravity of spiritual over carnal sins is, as I noted above, the stronger desire which moves one to carnal sin, a strength that mitigates guilt. Aquinas explains in the following article that the will is the cause of sin. Thus, on the one hand, the greater the will to sin, that is, the more evil the end intended, the greater the sin; on the other hand, the more voluntariness is diminished through causes that weaken free choice—ignorance, violence, fear, and even concupiscence as a passion rather than as a movement of the will—the less grave the sin (Ia IIae, q. 73, a. 6, c., and ad 2). An act for Aquinas is only immoral to the degree that it is chosen; those elements which weaken and ultimately destroy choice also lessen and eventually excuse from guilt altogether. Conversely, sins are made worse when motivated by malice because the move to such acts "belongs more to the will, which is then moved to evil of its own accord . . ." (Ia IIae, q. 78, a. 4).[29]

The notion of malice both explains the greater role of intention in determining the nature and degree of evil in human acts and reveals yet another area of tension between philosophical and religious models of human action. Aquinas claims that human beings can truly choose evil and reject good, not just when motivated by passion or ignorance. Nonetheless, in the discussion of weakness of will, he basically repeats Aristotle's view that knowledge is overcome in such acts only in a qualified sense—only knowledge of the universal, not the particular; only habitual, not actual knowledge (Ia IIae, q. 77, a. 2).

Aquinas seems to espouse the view that true knowledge cannot be overcome, that the cause of wrongdoing is ignorance of some kind. As the account of malice makes clear, however, he holds that true and complete knowledge cannot be overcome by passion, but it can by a disordered will. In his discussion of malice, Thomas makes it clear that choice can go wrong in three ways: through a disorder of the passions (as in weakness of will), of the intellect (as in sins of ignorance), and of the will (as in malice or vice). Aquinas thus takes Aristotelian vice and makes it a defect of the will. In malice, one can simply prefer a lesser to a greater good, and although one cannot choose evil as evil for its own sake, evil nevertheless "can be intended for the sake of avoiding another evil or obtaining another good" (Ia IIae, q. 78, a. 1, ad 2).[30]

The fine line Aquinas walks on this issue is well-documented.[31] What is of interest here is how the problem of human beings' apparently knowing choice of evil bears on Aquinas's ideas of vice and sin. It displays, I think, the same tension demonstrated throughout his account. The prophetic model of sin emphasizes the concept of intentional evil, of the desire to reject divine law, to rebel against God, while the philosophers emphasize the role of ignorance in wrongdoing. Aquinas cites authorities from both sides: Aristotle's claim that "every evil man is ignorant" (*omnis malus est*

ignorans) (Ia IIae, q. 78, a. 1, obj. 1), and the Book of Job's description of those who "on purpose have revolted from God" (*de industria recesserunt a Deo*) (Ia IIae, q. 78, a. 1, *sed contra*).[32] Aquinas retains but qualifies both views. Thus, he argues that Aristotelian vice is a disorder of the will and not the intellect (though, to be sure, the will is a faculty of rational choice). Yet, he also argues that though the sinner in one sense rebels against God, no human being could look fully on the face of God and reject that good.

The sin of pride in a way specifies the same tensions as those found in the psychology of sin—the roles of passion, knowledge, and malice in determining gravity. Pride arguably does not even exist in the Platonic or Aristotelian catalogs of vice; however, it has a central place in Aquinas's account.[33] Pride is the first sin, the source of all other sins, and the worst sin. He defines pride as an excessive desire for one's own excellence which rejects subjection to God (Ia IIae, q. 162, aa. 1, 5). It is the worst sin, Aquinas argues, because it is of its very nature an aversion from God and his commandments, something that is indirectly or consequently true of all sins (Ia IIae, q. 162, a. 6). Pride is the source of all other sins, Aquinas argues, in the sense that it is first in intention. First, every sin begins in turning from God and hence all sins begin in pride. Second, he argues, the motive for acquiring all the lesser goods one prefers to God is pride, that through them one "may have some perfection and excellence" (*quandam perfectionem et excellentiam habeat*) (Ia IIae, q. 84, a. 2). Covetousness is the first sin in the order of execution, Aquinas observes, since it desires what become the means for the commission of other sins (ibid.).

In the *Secunda secundae*, Aquinas depicts pride as the original sin. Adam and Eve could not have sinned first in a carnal sin, a desire for physical pleasure against the order of reason, because in the state of nature the physical appetites were perfectly subordinated to reason. Nor was their sin disobedience, unbelief, or the desire for knowledge. Their sin is not essentially disobedience since they could not have desired to rebel for its own sake unless their wills were already disordered (IIa IIae, q. 163, a. 1, ad 1). And Eve's belief of the serpent's claim (and hence disbelief of God) about the results of eating and the desire for knowledge excited by his false promise were, Aquinas argues, results of pride, not themselves the original sin (Ia IIae, q. 163, a. 1, ad 4). Hence, the first sin must have been the coveting of some spiritual good, not ordinately but disordinately, "above one's measure as established by the Divine rule," and, Aquinas concludes, this pertains to pride (Ia IIae, q. 163, a. 1).[34] In terms of Aquinas's threefold schema, the location of the first sin was the will, rather than either the intellect or the sensible appetite.

Pride displays at the level of a particular sin all the elements of the account of sin in general. First, Aquinas's account of pride reinforces his view of the gravity of spiritual over carnal sin. The tendency toward carnal sin is a punishment for original sin, a burden later generations bear for a spiritual sin rather than, as some Christian sources would have it, the first and most grievous sin. Moreover, the desire for money and possessions is, as it is for Rousseau, itself largely a result of pride rather than, as Hobbes would have it, the primary sin to which human beings are prone.[35] For Aquinas, neither the body nor the material world is the source of moral failure; self-aggrandizement is.

Second, Aquinas's view of the place of pride in the motivation further to sin emphasizes the location of the gravity of sin primarily in intention. Pride, the intent to defy God, is what constitutes sin. When it is the motive to other types of sin as the means to this end, it makes those sins worse. Hence, adultery motivated by the desire to lord it over the cuckolded partner is worse than when motivated by mere lust.

However, Aquinas's account of pride also displays the tension between the models of vice and sin for human wrongdoing. He first defines pride as "the appetite for excellence in excess of right reason" (Ia IIae, q. 162, a. 1, ad 2).[36] The language of excess and right reason is, of course, Aristotle's, but Aquinas has to work hard to get this non-Aristotelian vice into the Aristotelian schema. His first problem is to distinguish pride from magnanimity, for both seem to reject subordination and bear a sense of entitlement to great things.[37] He does so by arguing that pride is opposed both to humility and magnanimity by way of excess.

Pride is the *inordinate* desire for great things as opposed to magnanimity's "urging of the mind to great things against despair" opposed as well as to humility, which "withdraws the mind from the inordinate desire of great things against presumption" (Ia IIae, q. 162, a. 1, ad 3).[38]

Aquinas shifts the definitions of humility and magnanimity to make them parallel and compatible instead of opposites. So he adds the inordinateness (*inordinatio*) of the desire humility resists, keeping humility within the model of virtue as mean, and he adds magnanimity's resistance to despair to parallel humility's battle against presumption. It is as if magnanimity's aspiration to great things needs to be justified; in order not to be presumptuous entitlement, the strength of the desire for greatness must be necessary in the face of adversity.

But Aquinas adds more to his definition in a discussion of pride as a mortal sin. It is, he explains, the rejection of subordination to God. Therefore, pride is, as I noted above, the worst sin because it is essentially, like all sins, a rejection of God. Within the account of pride, the same tension as that between the notions of vice and sin is repeated: pride is the defiance of God *and* the rejection of the right order of reason. Once again, Aquinas claims these two views are not opposed or even complementary; indeed, they are essentially the same.

This mode of shifting between the models of vice and sin also appears in the attempt to locate the exact character of the first sin. Aquinas interprets the first sin as the coveting of God's likeness in regard to knowledge and operation (Ia IIae, q. 163, a. 2). Adam and Eve desired to decide for themselves what was good and evil and to foreknow the good and evil that would befall them. Further, they desired to achieve happiness by their own natural power. The sin is to have desired to set one's own standards and limits, to be in control—in other words, not to be confronted by the other in the prophetic model of sin.

The decision to describe these desires as sinful could not be more opposed to Platonic and, to a lesser extent, Aristotelian ethics. For Plato, the prime task is to know the principles of good and evil and to know why they are the principles which should guide one's actions. Moreover, to make oneself happy through knowing one's own good is the task of an ethical life. But Aquinas does not completely part company with the philosophers. Citing the opening line from Aristotle's *Metaphysics*, he makes it clear that the desire for knowledge is natural to us. He not only says it, but, of course, enacts the desire to know in his project. The desire to be like God too is natural, Aquinas notes: "Let us make man to our image and likeness"[39] (IIa IIae, q. 163, a. 2, obj. 2 and c., citing Gen 1:26). Thus, there is a prime place for knowledge and autonomy in human nature.

The depiction of pride as the greatest sin and the source of other sins, like that of weakness of will, reveals the different roles of intellect and will in the psychology of wrongdoing in Aquinas from those of Aristotle and Plato. The oft-acknowledged weak point in Plato and Aristotle's moral psychology is that, given their view that virtue is the good one truly desires for oneself, the fulfillment of one's humanity, it is hard for them to explain exactly how human beings so consistently reject their own good. For Aquinas, just as grace provides the remedy for going awry, pride provides the account of how and why humans go wrong.

Pride taken as the universal motive for sin is derived from Gregory the Great's notion of the seven capital vices. Gregory's schema takes as its main task the explanation of how sin begins and spreads. Capital vices are those which are the principle or director of other vices, vices which in turn have consequences of further vice, which Gregory calls the "daughters" of that particular vice. Gregory's model for organizing the vices at first seems only to have a minor role in Aquinas's account.[40] But as Aquinas discusses the various vices, essentially defining them in Aristotelian terms, he incorporates Gregory's version and his notion of the "daughters" of each of the capital vices. Aquinas also uses Gregory's classification under the subject of the cause of sin, insofar as one sin begets another. It serves, as does Aquinas's analysis of intention, as a psychology of sin, as an instrument for self-examination. The assumption of such an account is, I think, that the individual knows (or should know) the truth about his actions and

effects and can and should be his own worst accuser. On Aquinas's view, the problem is not ignorance but willful turning from self-knowledge and to lesser goods.

CONCLUSION

Perhaps no other topic in Aquinas's writings so concretely displays his total commitment to both rationalism and theism. In this case, it is a double commitment that makes him easy to caricature, as he attempts to subject obligations, failures, and desires, which fall outside the realm of nature, to the rigors of reason, order, and justice. Readers coming from a Catholic background, schooled in the definitions and classificatory schema for sins found in Catholic catechisms, tend to bring to Aquinas's account their childhood memories of lists of sins and punishments, and either support or reject such rigid and dogmatic applications of its conclusions. Philosophically minded readers hope for something on the order of Aristotle, in terms of which the notions of mortal and original sin, and their punishments, eternal damnation and mortality, simply seem atavistic oddities. The most sympathetic politely ignore such talk in deference to great thinkers who, like Homer, sometimes nod; the rest simply write off the entire enterprise.

A wonderful and unexpected example of the former tendency is found in the work of Erich Fromm. In *To Have or To Be?*, Fromm cites Aquinas with great approval as having a humanistic notion of sin; "sin," for Aquinas, Fromm writes, "is not disobedience of irrational authority, but the violation of human well-being."[41] Fromm goes on to note, however, that Aquinas, as "obedient son of the Church," retains a notion of sin as disobedience, and chides him for his "contradictory position." But, impossible as it sounds to modern ears, the whole point of Aquinas's argument is to show that disobedience of God and abandonment of human nature are equivalent rather than contradictory.

In some ways, similarly disconcerting dissonances emerge in the rather legalistic process for evaluating candidates for sainthood. For both sin and sainthood, ironically, the very attempt to rationalize and order them leads to the accusation that the distinctions and structures themselves are irrational and arbitrary.

Yet, not to bring rationality to them is to give up on reason, justice, and order. The alternative, to hold on to reason but to give up on sin and sainthood as categories which fall outside human nature, is the road taken by modernity. The weakness of that strategy, Aquinas would argue, is that it fails to give a complete account of human action and motives.

One way of comprehending Aquinas's project is as an attempt to bring together the two models of human failure and its remedy, one found in Plato, and the other in Greek tragedy. Martha Nussbaum has argued that Plato attempted to provide a solution to the problem of human life in philosophical contemplation and control of life and fortune, while Greek tragedy recognizes the limits of human control in its exploration of human failure and communal disintegration, in the way in which life confronts human beings with complexity and conflicts that philosophical casuistry and formulae cannot resolve. The philosopher's *hubris*, for Nussbaum, is his view that he can "make the goodness of a good human life safe from luck through the controlling power of reason," and successfully construct a single scale of value which will resolve all ethical conflicts.[42] From one point of view, Aquinas appears to be the exemplar of what Nussbaum calls this "aspiration to rational self-sufficiency," since he attempts to "answer" such a wide range of questions in a "*summa*," a text containing everything one needs to know.[43] But this is a misreading of both the form and content of Aquinas's text.

Aquinas's use of the many different vocabularies and traditions, like Aristotle, is grounded in the idea that human acts are irreducibly multiple and particular, and that the intentions and effects of those acts are many and complex. The distance between principles and the variety of human acts and their circumstances is for Aquinas best traversed by enlisting multiple terminologies: the many voices of Scripture, Aristotle, Plato, Gregory, Bede, Augustine, and others supply a plurality of insights on the many aspects of human action. This is similar to Aristotle's (less formal) approach of canvassing the opinions of both the many and the wise to arrive at his view of the ethical life. Aristotle subjects these views to critical evaluation rather than merely accepting them at face value. In a similar way,

Aquinas uses the disputed question to create a context in which such different modes of approach to wrongdoing can speak the same language and speak to the same issues, and uses his own categories to order and distinguish between apparently contradictory views. Thus, his rhetorical form engages other views in a dialectical rather than dogmatic way.

However, what holds the dialectic and the many different vocabularies and traditions together is Aquinas's conviction that the truth about sin and vice is ultimately (though not yet in our understanding) one, not many. Even though, as Aristotle notes and Aquinas confirms, there are many ways to miss (and only one way to hit) the mark ethically, radically different accounts of the nature and cause of wrongdoing, its gravity and punishment, unite in describing the deviation from the one, common human good. Aquinas's commitment to this unity makes it possible for him to introduce these different vocabularies, not just prophetic and legalistic categories, but also the distinctions of Gregory the Great, Bede, and Augustine, Plato, Aristotle, and the Stoics—they are, after all, all attempting to express the same truth. These attempts, however, like Aquinas's own, are partial visions of that single truth. His complex way of consulting and retaining the views of others signifies the incompleteness of any one account and the need to consider and shift from one perspective to another.[44]

Moreover, the substance of Aquinas's view, his attempt to retain the prophetic view of moral life, privileges the same elements of the human condition as does Greek tragedy: human finitude, failure, and dependence. Nussbaum wishes to replace Plato's vision with Aristotle's ethics, which, she argues, "makes human beings self-sufficient in an appropriately human way."[45] If it is supposed to represent a more modest view of the degree to which understanding and doing the good is possible to human beings, Aquinas agrees with and incorporates into his view this qualified affirmation of human autonomy. But Nussbaum's view of the Aristotelian model leaves out the crucial element of moral life found in the prophetic voice of Scripture and, arguably, in Greek tragedy from which Aristotle apparently learned to scale back the aspirations of reason. On the prophetic view,

dependence is dependence on God and finitude is finitude in the face of the infinite
God, and failure is failure to meet the demand of the transcendent other. "Human
self-sufficiency" for the prophets (and in a
different way the Greek tragedians) is not
self-sufficiency at all, because it cannot
achieve its own completion, fails to know itself and its obligations; Aquinas's account of
sin is about how human beings both fall below the possibilities of their own natures in
sin and fail to rise to their aspirations to the
transcendent good.

Notes

[1] Paul Ricoeur, *The Symbolism of Evil*, trans. Emerson Buchanan (New York: Harper and Row, 1967),
55.

[2] Ibid., 62.

[3] See Eileen C. Sweeney, "From Determined Motion to Undetermined Will: Aristotelian Change
and Free Choice in Aquinas," *Philosophical Topics* 2
(1992): 189–214; see also Sweeney, "Restructuring
Desire: Aquinas, Descartes, and Hobbes on the Passions," in *Meeting of the Minds*. in *Rencontres de Philosophie Médiévale* 7, ed. Stephen F. Brown
(Turnhout: Brepols, 1998), 219–37.

[4] "esse dictum vel factum vel concupitum *contra
legem Dei*."

[5] A version of the debate about the relationship of
vice to sin is evident in twentieth-century Protestant
theology, with Karl Barth on one side, claiming that
"only Christians sin," and Reinhold Niebuhr on the
other, arguing that the experience of sin is a universal experience deriving from our inability to deal
with the limits of human existence. At least these are
the terms in which William H. Willimon casts a
debate between the two theologians: "Thus Barth
could assert *only* Christians sin. Only Christians
have a story that makes our actions comprehensible
not as minor slipups, mistakes of judgment, or even
as our inappropriate response to the facts of the
human condition (Niebuhr), but as *sin*, as our determined effort to live our lives as if God were not the
author of our lives" (William H. Willimon, "A Peculiarly Christian Account of Sin," *Theology Today* 50
[1993]: 228). Aquinas's project is to show that these
two views are largely equivalent.

[6] "praecipue cum per legem aeternam regulemur
in multis quae excedunt rationem humanam, sicut
in his quae sunt fidei."

[7] Anselm, *Cur Deus Homo*, in *St. Anselm: Basic
Writings*, trans. S. N. Deane (La Salle, IL: Open
Court, 1972), bk. 1, chap. 21, 239.

[8] "Pro mensura delicit erit et plagarum modus."

[9] "In mensura contra mensuram, cum obiecta
fuerit, iudicabit eam."

[10] "ne forte ad nihilum redigas me."

[11] "ex hoc ipso quod finem in peccato constituit,
voluntatem habet in aeternum peccandi."

[12] "Dedisti metuentibus te significationem, ut
figiant a facie arcus, ut liberentur dilecti tui."

[13] "Qui autem blasphemaverit in Spiritum Sanctum, non habebit remissionem in aeternum, sed erit
reus aeterni delicti."

[14] "quod finem in peccato constituit, voluntatem
habet in aeternum peccandi."

[15] "Est autem quasi quidam animae tactus,
quando inhaeret aliquibus rebus per amorem. Cum
autem peccat, adhaeret rebus aliquibus contra lumen rationis et divinae legis. . . ."

[16] "Sicut si aliquis sit distans alicui per aliquem
motum, non statim cessante motu fit ei propinquus,
sed oportet quod appropinquet rediens per motum
contrarium."

[17] "Poena autem satisfactoria diminuit aliquid de
ratione poenae. Est enim de ratione poenae quod sit
contra voluntatem."

[18] "quia hoc ipsum ad virtutem pertinet, ut satis-
faciat pro his in quibis offendit vel Deum vel hominem."

[19] "Est enim quaedam inordinata dispositio
proveniens ex dissolutione illius harmoniae in qua
consistebat ratio originalis iustitiae: sicut etiam ae-
gritudo corporalis est quaedam inordinata dispositio
corporis, secundum quam silvitur aequalitas in qua
consistit ratio sanitatis."

[20] See Stephen J. Duffy, "Our Hearts of Darkness:
Original Sin Revisited," in *Theological Studies* 49
(1988): 604–5. Duffy argues that, for Aquinas, the
result of original sin is only the loss of the grace, not
a more thoroughgoing perversion of nature. This
interpretation of Aquinas places his view in opposition to Luther and Calvin's darker view of human
nature. While clearly less pessimistic than they,
Aquinas still makes it clear that nature limps rather
than walks full upright after the fall. He writes,
"Accordingly the privation of original justice, by
which the will was made subject to God, is the
formal element in respect of original sin, while every
other disorder of the soul's powers is a kind of
material element in respect of original sin. Now the
lack of order of the other powers of the soul consists
chiefly in their turning inordinately to changeable
good . . ." ("Sic ergo privatio originalis iustitiae, per
quam voluntas subdebatur Deo, est formale in peccato originali: omnis autem alia inordinatio virium
animae praecipue in hoc attenditur, quod inordinate
convertuntur ad bonum commutabile . . . "; ST Ia
IIae, q. 82, a. 3).

[21] "Sic igitur inordinatio quae est in isto homine,
ex Adam generato, non est voluntaria voluntate ipsius sed voluntate primi parentis, qui movet motione

generationis omnes qui ex eius origine derivantur, sicut voluntas animae movet omnia membra ad actum."

22Duffy argues convincingly that a similar tension is present in Augustine's account of original sin as he attempts to avoid both the Pelagian and Manichean view of human evil: "Against the Manicheans he [Augustine] maintained that evil is not identifiable with human finitude. It erupts freely, contingently, and not by ontological necessity. Against the Pelagians, on the other hand, Augustine maintained that sin is not merely accidental or purely contingent. Universal in its range, though not synonymous with or a structure of essential humanity, it nevertheless is a kind of 'second nature,' a positive propensity to evil." Duffy, "Original Sin Revisited," 600.

23The same use of the patterns of Aristotelian motion is used to explain free choice, the development of virtue, and the definitions of the various passions. See Sweeney, "Restructuring Desire" and "From Determined Motion to Free Choice."

24Blaise Pascal, Pensées, trans. A. J. Krailsheimer (New York: Viking Penguin, 1966), sec. 1, VII, 65.

25"Et similiter dicendum est de vitiis et peccatis: sic enim in eis privatur debita commensuratio rationis, ut non totaliter ordo rationis tollatur."

26"Ratio autem ordinat omnia in agibilibus ex fine. Et ideo quanto peccatum contingit in actibus humanis ex altiori fine, tanto peccatum est gravius."

27"Quod non est sic intelligendum quasi quodlibet peccatum spirituale sit maioris culpae quolibet peccato carnali."

28See Arist. Eth. Nic. 7.6 (1149b2); 3.10 (1118b2).

29"Est magis proprius voluntati, quae ex seipsa in malum movetur . . ."

30"potest tamen esse intentum ad vitandum aliud malum, vel ad consequendum aliud bonum . . ."

31The parallel and more discussed question is whether one may reject good in full knowledge of its goodness. Aquinas argues earlier in the Summa theologiae that one may not reject that which is good in all respects, but one may choose either not to act or not to will anything in regard to it (ST Ia IIae, q. 6. a. 3). See also De malo, q. 6 (Leonine, 145–53); and De veritate, q. 22, a. 6 (Leonine, 626–29). For a discussion of this issue in Aquinas and whether his views remained constant throughout his writings, see D. Odon Lottin, Psychologie et morale aux XIIe et XIIIe siècles, vol. 1 (Gembloux: Duculot, 1942), 258; see also Mark D. Jordan, "The Transcendentality of Goodness and the Human Will," in Being and Goodness, ed. Scott McDonald (Ithaca, NY: Cornell University Press, 1991), 141, 146–47.

32Arist. Eth. Nic. 3.1 (1110b28); Job 34:17; see also ST Ia IIae, q. 78, a. 4, sed contra, which cites the same Job passage.

33Alasdair MacIntyre has noted the crucial place of pride in the Augustinian account of justice, and its absence in Aristotle. MacIntyre argues that for Augustine, the sin of the Romans (heirs to Greek conceptions of virtue) was their desire for glory, pride in other words, to which value Augustine strongly contrasts the Christian value of humility. For MacIntyre this is one crucial element in the conflict between the traditions of Aristotle and Augustine which Aquinas attempts to overcome. See Alasdair MacIntyre, Whose Justice? Which Rationality? (Notre Dame, IN: University of Notre Dame Press, 1988), 155, 163.

34"Relinquitur igitur quod prima inordinatio appetitus humani fuit ex hoc quod aliquod bonum spirituale inordinate appetit. Non autem inordinate appetivisset, appetendo illud secundum suam mensuram ex divina regula praestitutam."

35Jean-Jacques Rousseau, Discourse on the Origins of Inequality, in The Basic Political Writings, trans. Donald A. Cress (Indianapolis: Hackett, 1987), pt. 2, 64, 77. For Rousseau, inequality and vice of all kinds (including possessions) is a result of amour-propre, the desire to be regarded as better than others. For Hobbes, the desire for power is the root of all vice, but I think it is clear that though glory is a source of conflict in society, the main reason for needing power is security in one's person and possessions. See Thomas Hobbes, Leviathan (London: Penguin Books, 1987), pt. 1, chaps. 10–11.

36"appetit excellentiam in excessu ad rationem rectam . . ."

37See Pierre Manent's description of Aquinas's "magnanimous" reading of Aristotle on magnanimity in order to make it consistent with the virtue of humility. Manent argues persuasively that the conflict between the self-sufficiency of the magnanimous man and the dependence of the humble on God and other human beings is irreconcilable. Pierre Manent, The City of Man, trans. Marc A. LePain (Princeton, NJ: Princeton University Press, 1998), 200; see also ST IIa IIae, q. 129, a. 6, ad 1. I am grateful to Richard Cobb-Stevens for bringing this reference to my attention.

38"Nam sicut ad magnanimitatem pertinet impellere animum ad magna, contra desperationem; ita ad humilitatem pertinet retrahere animum ab inordinato appetitu magnorum, contra presumptionem."

39"Faciamus hominem ad imaginem et similitudinem nostram."

40By contrast, Aquinas unifies his account of vice around the four cardinal and three theological virtues. This categorization follows from his faculty psychology in terms of which he explains the Stoic concept of the four cardinal virtues. Hence the virtues correspond to the faculties of reason (prudence; faith), the concupiscible appetite (temperance, charity), the irascible appetite (courage, hope); justice is reason's ordering of the goods society has to distribute (ST Ia, q. 61, a. 2; q. 62, a. 2).

[41] Erich Fromm, *To Have or To Be?* (New York: Harper and Row, 1976), 122.

[42] Martha Nussbaum, *The Fragility of Goodness* (New York: Cambridge University Press, 1986), 3.

[43] Ibid.

[44] Alasdair MacIntyre argues that what he calls Aquinas's "singleness of purpose," his subordination of all other goods to the one good, is in sharp opposition to the views of Nussbaum (and her interpretation of Aristotle) and Rawls, both of whom contend that there is not one, final good, but many, heterogeneous goods in human life. For Rawls's and Nussbaum's critique of the pursuit of a single good as the project of human life, see John Rawls, *A Theory of Justice* (Cambridge, MA: Harvard University Press, 1971), 554; and Martha Nussbaum, *Aristotle's De Motu Animalium* (Princeton: Princeton University Press, 1978), essay 4. For MacIntyre, Aquinas integrates different and opposing traditions by "making a claim to truth of a kind which appeals beyond their own particular scheme of concepts and beliefs, to something external to that scheme" (MacIntyre, *Whose Justice*, 173). The difference between my view of Aquinas's method and MacIntyre's is that I take Aquinas's project to be a less thoroughly integrated hierarchy of those different traditions and different goods. Although MacIntyre admits our knowledge of the final end, God, is "inadequate," he argues that "it is an inadequacy in respect of the nature of that which we shall enjoy if we achieve our ultimate end, not at all in respect of its sufficiency in specifying how we ought to act"(ibid.). My contention is that lack of knowledge of the end and the irreducible complexity of particular human acts leaves open-ended both the top and bottom of the hierarchy Aquinas creates.

[45] Nussbaum, *Fragility*, 8.

Selected Further Reading

Bernard, R., O.P. *Le Péché II*. Commentary in *S. Thomas d'Aquin, Somme Théologique*. Paris: Éditions de la Revue des Jeunes, 1931.

Colvert, Gavin. "Aquinas on Raising Cain: Vice, Incontinence and Responsibility." *American Catholic Philosophical Quarterly* 71 (1997, suppl.): 203–20.

Dewan, Lawrence. "Saint Thomas, Lying, and Venial Sin: Thomas Aquinas on the Validity of Moral Taxonomy." *Thomist* 61 (1997): 279–99.

Duffy, Stephen. "Our Hearts of Darkness: Original Sin Revisited." *Theological Studies* 49 (1988): 597–622.

Eschmann, T., O.P. "Thomistic Social Philosophy and the Theology of Original Sin." *Mediaeval Studies* 9 (1947): 19–55.

Festugiére, A. "La Notion du Péché Presentée par S. Thomas." *New Scholasticism* 5 (1931): 332–41.

Fitzpatrick, E. J. *The Sin of Adam in the Writings of Saint Thomas Aquinas*. Mundelein, IL: Saint Mary of the Lake Seminary, 1950.

Huguény, O.P. "Adam et le Péché Originel." *Revue Thomiste* 19 (1911): 68.

Jordan, Mark D. "The Transcendentality of Goodness and the Human Will." In *Being and Goodness*. Ed. Scott McDonald. Ithaca, NY: Cornell University Press, 1991.

Keenan, James F. "The Problem with Thomas Aquinas's Concept of Sin." *Heythrop Journal* 35 (1994): 401–20.

Kors, J.-B., O.P. *La Justice Primitive et le Péché Originel d'après S. Thomas*. Le Saulchoir: Kain, 1922.

Langen, John. "Sins of Malice in the Moral Psychology of Thomas Aquinas." *The Annual of the Society of Christian Ethics* 12 (1987): 179–98.

Lefébure, Marcus. "Evil in Angels and Men: Thomas Aquinas and Melanie Klein." *New Blackfriars* 63 (1982): 460–69.

Lottin, Odon, O.S.B. *Psychologie et morale aux XIIe et XIIIe siècles*. Vol. 4, pt. 3. Gembloux: J. Duculot, 1954.

———. "Le Péché Originel chez Albert le Grand, Bonaventure et Thomas d'Aquin," *Recherches de Théologie Ancienne et Médiévale* 12 (1940): 306–28.

Ricoeur, Paul. *The Symbolism of Evil*. Trans. Emerson Buchanan. New York: Harper and Row, 1967.

Weithman, P. J. "Augustine and Aquinas on Original Sin and the Function of Political Authority." *Journal of the History of Philosophy* 30 (1992): 353–76.

Westberg, Daniel. "Did Aquinas Change His Mind about the Will?" *The Thomist* 58 (1994): 41–60.

Natural Law and Human Law
(Ia IIae, qq. 90–97)

Clifford G. Kossel, S.J.

PREAMBLES

These eight questions have long circulated in English translation as *St. Thomas Aquinas: Treatise on Law*.[1] In fact, they constitute one-third of Aquinas's treatise on law. As a theologian, his aim was a fuller understanding of the Old Law and the New Law, which he treats in Questions 98 through 108. These latter treatises, along with the treatment of justice in the *Secunda secundae*, are very helpful for understanding our treatise. This does not deny the foundational importance or excellence of the architectonic treatment of law in our eight questions; it emphasizes that this treatise does not stand alone.

Moreover, in these questions, Aquinas frequently refers to previous questions in the *Summa* as to matters that the auditor should already know. Aside from things one can know only by divine revelation, the *Prima pars* considers what can be known about God and creatures by applying one's intelligence to an examination of the world of experience. This includes that God exists and is intelligent and loving; that out of love He creates an intelligible universe to share in His being and goodness; and that He cares for, plans (*providentia*), and governs (*gubernatio*) the being and activity of the universe and of every creature, without detracting from the creatures' own causal activity by which they share in this government (Ia, q. 103, a. 6).

In his philosophical anthropology (Ia, qq. 75–88), Thomas studies the structure of the human being and particularly the human capacities for knowing, loving, and choosing by which the human person is especially the "image of God," the "horizon" being, rooted in earth but stretching beyond the heavens (*capax infiniti*) (Ia, q. 77, a. 2; Ia IIae, q. 2, a. 8, ad 3). His Prologue to the Second Part places human beings at the center of theology. "Having spoken of God, the exemplar, and the things that proceed from his power and will, it remains to consider His image, man, insofar as he is also the principle of his own works, having free choice and control of his actions."[2]

The First Part of the Second Part deals generally with all the internal and external sources (*principia*) of human actions. In the first five questions, Aquinas examines the internal dynamism underlying every human activity and, therefore, the activities of practical reason. Such activities have a goal or end, and there is an ultimate end, an end of ends for the whole of human life. This end is intentionally present in the agent as the horizon of personal activity. It is variously described as "the notion of ultimate end" (*ratio ultimi finis*), "self-fulfillment" (*impletio sui*), "perfection of the agent," the "satisfaction of all desires," the whole or "total good," or "happiness" (*beatitudo*).[3]

Aquinas maintains that this final goal as an intentional presence in mind and will is the same for all humans because all desire their perfection, which is the notion of the ultimate end. Yet this is a vague and indistinct idea which requires experience and scientific study for clearer understanding.[4] Thus there is much disagreement among people (and philosophers) about what concretely constitutes such perfection or happiness. Some place it in wealth, pleasure, virtue, or some combination of these (Ia IIae, q. 1, aa. 6–7). But whatever they desire, they desire it *as good*, either the complete good or as somehow contributing to their complete good or happiness.

Thomas holds that only the unmediated vision of God can ultimately fulfill this desire, but to achieve it one needs "a friend," our gracious God, who has promised this reward for a life of genuinely seeking Him (Ia IIae, q. 3, a. 8; Ia IIae, q. 5, aa. 5, 7).[5] This is an instance of Aquinas's frequent statement that grace does not destroy but perfects nature, and it foreshadows the treatise on grace, "which helps us to live rightly" (Ia IIae, q. 109, Prol.) and which closes this part (Ia IIae, qq. 109–14).[6]

But the process of moving from the "ultimate end in intention" to the end achieved ("in execution") is the whole human life of choosing among those things that are "for the end" (*ad finem*).[7] Aquinas analyzes the complex interaction of the spiritual powers of intellect and will that constitutes the essence of the properly human and moral act (Ia IIae, qq. 6–17), and the moral quality of those acts (Ia IIae, qq. 18–21). Because a person is not a pure spirit but has an animal body with its *own* appetites, he thoroughly examines the "passions" (or emotions [*passiones*]) that, for good or ill, can strongly influence our choices (Ia IIae, qq. 22–48). He then treats of the habits and virtues by which one tries to bring these passions under the rule of reason (Ia IIae, qq. 49–70). Finally, he treats vices and sins, which mark the failure of the rule of reason (Ia IIae, qq. 71–89). In following this course, Thomas has established the foundation for an examination of law and grace, the extrinsic principles of action.

DEFINING LAW

In most English dictionaries, the primary usage of "law" is usually presented as a binding rule of conduct established by custom or authority. Aquinas, in his attempt to define law, starts from the common usage, which leads him to something close to the language of modern dictionaries. According to Thomas, law is some binding rule (*regula*) or norm (*mensura*) of human actions; it *commands* or *orders* (*imperat*) by prescribing or prohibiting actions (Ia IIae, q. 90, a. 1).[8] He then moves quickly to a causal definition of law.

The first principle of human action is reason. So law belongs to reason; a sheer act of will by a ruler (*quod principi placuit*), not regulated by right reason, is an iniquity, not a law (Ia IIae, q. 90, a. 1, ad 3). So certain *universal* propositions of practical reason ordered to actions are *formally* law (Ia IIae, q. 90, a. 1, ad 2–3).

As a work of practical reason, a law has a purpose or end, namely that which in practical reason itself is the first principle, the ultimate end of happiness or beatitude (*felicitas vel beatitudo*).[9] But every part is ordered to the whole as the imperfect to the perfect, and since every individual is part of the city, the perfect community, law must have in view primarily the common happiness of the community (Ia IIae, q. 90, a. 2).[10] He refers here to the *Politics*, 1.1, where Aristotle describes the growth of community from family, through village, to the *polis*, which he calls the complete community (*koinonia teleia*). Its mark is "self-sufficiency," that is, through the common endeavor everything necessary for a good human life is at hand. And good human life is that of the activity of the intellectual and moral virtues. It is a moral community, not one of power or economic management—although these may be required as "instruments." Aquinas accepts this, but he extends the idea of "perfect community" (*communitas perfecta*) both politically and for the cosmos.[11]

At this point, Aquinas has to determine the efficient cause of law. The crux of this issue is the question: Whose reason makes law? Law establishes an order for the sake of the common good. Whose good and end is this? It is the good of the whole community. So, as in other matters, ordering to an end is the responsibility of the person(s) whose end it is. Thomas concludes that the establishment of a law is the work of either the whole community or of a public person who represents and has the care of the multitude (Ia IIae, q. 90, a. 3).[12] He notes that the *paterfamilias* may lay down rules for the family, but the latter is also only a part of the political community; as such, those rules are not properly law (Ia IIae, q. 90, a. 3, ad 3).

Finally, he introduces another aspect of the efficient cause of law, the instrumental cause of promulgation. To be a principle of human action, the law must somehow "get into" the subject of the law. Since law is not a matter of force or violence but of directing practical reason, it must "touch" the subject by oral or written communication. Without promulgation, an individual would not know the law; therefore, the law would not have its obligatory force. Promulgation is clearly necessary to effective law, and its force continues into the future, especially when it is written (Ia IIae, q. 90, a. 4, c., and ad 3).[13]

By causal analysis, Thomas arrives at the common nuclear yet comprehensive definition of law: It is nothing other than a dictate of practical reason for the common good promulgated by one who has care of the community. It should be noted, first, that this establishes the criteria for every law; a supposed law that lacks any of these four criteria is not a genuine law. Second, coercion is not of the essence of law, although he grants that the community, as opposed to a parent or personal advisor, does have the power to coerce. Coercion by threat of sanctions is necessary because not all subjects will readily listen to the law (Ia IIae, q. 90, a. 3, ad 2).

THE TYPES OF LAW

Because law is an analogous notion, one needs to reveal and to some extent define its major kinds. Aquinas undertakes this in Question 91. The articles are all headed by the question "Is there" an eternal, a natural, and a human law? Only of divine law is the question: "Is it necessary that there be?" Starting with Question 93, Thomas takes up each of these types in detail. Although I discuss the natural and human laws in detail below, I feel some comments on the eternal and divine laws are necessary at this point.

On the question of eternal law, Aquinas, using some matters already determined in the First Part of the *Summa*, starts from the definition of law outlined in the previous question: "Law is nothing else than a dictate of practical reason in a ruler who governs some perfect community. Now it is clear that, granted the world is governed by Divine providence (Ia, q. 22, aa. 1–2), the whole community of the universe is governed by divine reason. And, therefore, the very idea of the governance of things existing in the Divine mind has the nature of law, and since divine reason transcends time, this conception must

be eternal" (Ia IIae, q. 91, a. 1).[14] And this plan looks principally to the order of the whole to its common good (Ia IIae, q. 93 a. 1, c., and ad 1). [15]

Eternal law is comprehensive; it applies to the movement of all creatures, rational or irrational, but in different ways. All other laws are derived from eternal law, and it is imperfectly known to all humans insofar as they know the natural law (Ia IIae, q. 91, a. 2; q. 94, aa. 2–4). I will discuss these matters at greater length in the examination of natural and human laws.

As both are laws of God, people often confuse or conflate eternal law and divine law. Aquinas, however, is perfectly clear, at least when he is treating the matter directly. Divine law is law divinely revealed (*divinitus revelata*); this refers to the biblical revelation of God's directives for human beings. In fact, there are two divine laws, related not as two species, but as the imperfect to the perfect. It was part of the divine pedagogy to prepare His people through fear of punishment for the new covenant of love poured into our hearts by the Holy Spirit. This law is necessary especially because humans are called to a destiny which transcends the natural order and the human power of achievement; so special directives were needed for the achievement of this end (Ia IIae, q. 91, aa. 4–5).[16]

NATURAL LAW

Natural law remains a controversial issue for both Thomists and their critics. As John Finnis has explained so carefully, there have been many theories of natural law (and he is not reluctant to propose a somewhat new one).[17] Perhaps the most prominent objection to the "traditional natural law theory" (including that of Aquinas) arises from the fact that this theory is embedded in a teleological view of human beings and the universe, which modern science claims is an unnecessary obstacle to progress in a scientific understanding of the world. Legal theorists, on the other hand, often without adequate understanding of natural law (or at least of Aquinas's theory), tend to deny its relevance to human law. First, it is a *moral* law, which clashes with the claims of legal positivists that morals and law must be separated. Second, it appears as a deductive system eventually directing every area of human activity and putting the legislator or judge in a strait-jacket, without genuine discretion or creativity. Finally, there is the natural law claim to "universality," which, they say, cannot fit the liberal pluralistic societies and governments of our age.[18]

I believe that Aquinas's position on natural law is intelligible and forceful in its own right and can respond to these issues. As such, I will simply expose his view, from his texts, as clearly as I can in a short space, with these objections in mind but without directly confronting each one.[19] I will begin with Ia IIae, q. 91, a. 2: whether there is in us some natural law. In locating natural law in the hierarchy of law, it provides the general perspective for understanding law in its ultimate causes.[20] The argument is simple: If there is an eternal law existing in the reason of the ruler of the whole community of the universe, then it is participated in some way by every creature, because God impresses on them the inclinations to their proper acts and ends (Ia IIae, q. 94, a. 1).

Yet the rational creature is under divine providence in a more excellent way insofar as it shares in divine providence by itself exercising providence for itself and others. Thus, it participates actively in the eternal reason from which it receives its natural inclination to its own appropriate acts and end. This participation in the eternal law is called natural law. Since this is an intellectual and rational participation, it is *properly* law, for law, as I have said, belongs to reason (Ia IIae, q. 94, a. 1, ad 3). This does not exclude free choice, but it does insist that underlying free acts (and every operation of intellect and will) there is some natural determination and necessity (Ia IIae, q. 94, a. 1, ad 2).[21]

This exposition may give rise to the usual objections that Aquinas is engaged in a series of deductions from providence to eternal law to natural law and eventually to human law (which is derived from eternal law). This, however, is a misconception. The order Thomas uses here is that of the theologian (and somewhat of the metaphysician) in the synthetic mode, moving from ultimate causes (the existence of which he has already proven) to effects. But as to the *order of dis-covery*, everything is reversed. This should be clear from Ia IIae, q. 93, a. 2: "Is the eternal law known to everyone?" First, the eternal law in itself is known to no one but God and, perhaps, the blessed in heaven. Second, yes, it is known by everyone in its effects, or participations, at least as to the common principles of natural law.[22] So the knowledge of natural law and human law does not depend on the knowledge of God or eternal law, but vice versa. This will be made clear in discussing Question 94, but this does not exclude the requirement of a "reduction" to the ultimate causes for an adequate *understanding* of law.

So I now turn to Ia IIae, q. 94. a. 2, rightly considered the showpiece of Aquinas's natural law theory and the basis of his moral philosophy. This article is comparatively long but also very compact, and he "unpacks" it to some extent in subsequent articles and in Question 100. Thomas begins this article by pointing out that both speculative and practical reason are based on some self-evident (*per se nota*) propositions. What the human intellect first grasps is the notion of being, which is the basis for the first indemonstrable principle: one cannot simultaneously affirm and deny (the same predicate of the same subject). But practical intellect, being ordered to action, first grasps the notion of good, which is the end of action. So the first practical principle is that good is what all things desire. And the first precept of natural law is that good is to be pursued and evil avoided. All other precepts are based on this precept.

Hence, all the things to be done or avoided that practical reason *naturally* apprehends as *human* goods [or evils] belong to the precepts of natural law. But reason *naturally* apprehends as goods and ends all those things to which man has a *natural* inclination. The order of natural law precepts thus follows the order of natural inclinations. He then enumerates the order of these inclinations from lowest to highest in accord with the levels of human reality. That is, man is a being (self-preservation), an animal (preservation of the species), and, specifically, a *rational* animal (to know truth and associate with others). It is quite clear here that the highest of these, and therefore the measure of all, is the latter, reason.[23] I will now examine each of these aspects of natural law.

Indemonstrable, Self-evident Propositions

Thomas often says, as he does here, that a proposition is self-evident when the predicate pertains to the definition of the subject, such as: "Man is rational." But they are self-evident *to humans* only if one knows the nature of the things designated by the subject (and the predicate); in short, they are self-evident only if one knows the *meaning* of the subject and predicate terms. The meaning of some such terms is known only to the experts, the wise, who have devoted long study to the matters involved. But others are known to *all*.

As an example of the latter, Thomas regularly refers to the proposition: Every whole is greater than any part of it. This is not a tautology drawn from dictionary definitions, and, although he sometimes uses the term "innate," this is also misleading. He insists on his Aristotelian position that all human knowledge begins in the senses.[24] One derives notions of such terms from sense-experience. Given the appropriate experience, one can see some necessary relation between these terms (Ia IIae, q. 51, a. 1).[25] In this example, the experience may be as simple as a child seeing its mother cut the cake and giving the child only a piece. Other propositions may require much longer experience, both individual and communal. So the "all" in "known to all" often refers to a (mostly) mature person with adequate experience of social life.

Nor does knowing these propositions require that one has articulated them in clear, distinct formulas. One who has never heard of the principle of contradiction or studied the metaphysics of being or studied logic implicitly knows that human discourse presupposes this principle. Everyone realizes that in discussion one cannot simultaneously maintain contradictory or incompatible positions at the same time. This would lead to incoherence and end all discourse. Likewise with the basic precepts of natural law. One does not have to study ethics or moral science to know them; they are much deeper than our articulated formulas. As Lon Fuller once remarked, one does not have to work out a theory of the ultimate end of human life in order to know that murder is wrong.[26]

Hence, the basic and self-evident principles, speculative or practical, are not ready-made propositions with which one is born. Nor do they refer to some "non-natural properties" grasped by some "intuition," as G. E. Moore might hold. Born of sense knowledge, these principles contain more than the senses grasp, namely, some necessary relations involved in their terms. They require more or less experience and are open to development with experience. And it is possible that one might never adequately formulate them; however, one knows well enough to employ them in rational discourse and in practical life. The issue now is to determine which experiences offer knowledge of the basic precepts of the natural law.

Natural Knowledge of Natural Inclinations

Thomas accepts the fact that there is a human nature, that is, a specific ontological structure that all humans share and that makes them a kind of being distinct from all others. They share much with other sorts of being; they are *living bodies* and *animals* and they share the activities of all these levels of being. The difference is human *rationality* manifested in a different kind of activity. From this, naturally, comes the term *rational animal*. Yet each human being is comprised of many parts, unified by one substantial form, the rational or *intellective* soul, which gives being to the whole and is the ultimate intrinsic source of its activities (Ia, q. 76, aa. 1, 3–4). Such a definition marks the minimum of actuality that a thing must have to be one of this kind, but it leaves open the possibility of growth toward a maximum. A baby is a human being, but, as one might say, "not much of a one yet." However, all good parents have high expectations: will he or she become a great artist, president of the United States, outstanding physicist, computer whiz, or the best shortstop in baseball?

Nature, as specific definition or essence, is, in itself, static. But Aquinas is more interested in this other aspect of nature: the "intrinsic principle of movement and rest," which makes development possible.[27] Growth occurs by reason of a panoply of passive and active capacities (*potentiae*), that is, capacities to be acted on by other agents or to act. These capacities are not identical to the essence or to the substantial form, but they are rooted in it as its necessary and essential properties—lacking them, it would be rendered a closed book, a "monad" (Ia, q. 77, aa. 1–7). By observing the activities of such powers, one recognizes the dynamic structure of human and other beings; it is only through analyzing the activities of these powers that one comes to know the essence of any natural entity whatever.[28]

Corresponding to these levels of being are levels of "appetite," which is simply an "inclination" to something, and every inclination is consequent on some form (Ia IIae, q. 8, a. 1).[29] At this point in the text, Thomas explains that in non-cognitive beings (mineral and plant) the inclination follows directly on the substantial form and nature, and is called "natural appetite" (appetitus naturalis). In cognitive agents, an inclination follows on a form apprehended by the cognitive power. There is, therefore, a "sensitive" or "animal" appetite in things possessing sense cognition. In humans, it follows also on the intellectual grasp of some object, and is called "rational appetite" (also Ia, q. 59, a. 1). In cognitive beings, the appetitive power is a distinct power over and above the natural appetites of the substantial form and the inclination of each power to its own activity. It is the inclination to the well-being of the whole. This also indicates that every power of the soul is itself a form and nature; therefore, it has a natural inclination to its proper act and object (Ia, q. 80, a. 1, ad 3).[30]

Before returning to Ia IIae, q. 94, a. 2, one other matter must be noted. The spiritual powers of the soul (intellect and will) not only reflect on themselves but also interact with one another. I am not only aware of my knowing but can reflectively study my knowing. I am also aware that I see, hear, and so on, and I especially know my own will acts—desire, wish, enjoyment, and such, and their objects (Ia, q. 82, a. 4, c., and ad 1; Ia IIae, q. 87, aa. 3, 4; Ia IIae, q. 10, a. 1, among others).[31] This compenetration of intellect and will underlies the whole question of naturally known natural inclinations.

So Aquinas says that the first thing known without qualification (simpliciter) is "being." Of course this being is found only in the individual things presented by sense experience. But intellect recognizes the universal in the particular. This is not "being as being" disengaged from all its modalities by the metaphysician. It is "common being" (ens commune), being as shared by all the objects of our experience. I also know that I know things, that being is related to intelligence; this constitutes the true (ratio veri) (Ia, q. 16, aa. 1–2).[32]

But practical reason, which is ordered to action, first apprehends good, which is the end of action. This apprehension of the character of the good (the ratio boni) is itself a cognitive act. On what experience can this be based? It can only be in that awareness intellect has of the first act of the will which is its natural and spontaneous reaction to common being as apprehended by intellect. Often Aquinas talks about the two common acts of appetite: desire for the absent good and enjoyment of the good present. But the prior act of love (amor) is the basis and root of all movements of appetite (Ia IIae, q. 25, a. 2).[33] In the same passage, Thomas notes that whatever tends to an end must have "an aptitude and proportion to the end," and "that very aptitude and proportion to the good is love, which is nothing else than being pleased in the good" (complacentia boni) (ibid.).[34]

Thomas uses the latter term—accompanied by such terms as adaptatio, coadaptatio, proportionatum, among others—throughout this treatise (Ia IIae, qq. 25–28).[35] Thomas understands this to mean that, prior to any act of the will, which is a passive power, it must be formed (specified) by some object. This object is provided by intellect, which in all cases gives specification to the will (Ia IIae, q. 9, a. 1). And the first specification is common being and the true, which is the first object of the intellect and arouses the natural love of the will (ibid.).[36] Being cognitively aware that apprehended being forms and attracts, as the object of love, an appetitive power in humans, one "adds" a new relation to being. Not only is being intelligible (perfective of our cognitive power), it is likeable in itself. And this is the nature of good and end. The primary and simple act of the will (velle) is always of the end which is willed absolutely (absolute) for itself as the basic object of the power, that is, the good as such (Ia IIae, q. 8, aa. 2–3).[37] Therefore, the object of the natural love of will, good in general (*bonum in communi*), exactly corresponds to the natural object of the intellect, common being (*ens commune*).

Having understood that "good is that which all things desire," a question of action arises: What shall I do? Practical reason replies: "do good, of course, since it is the only object of love and so the only desirable end, and avoid the contrary (evil)." This is the *natural necessity* that *binds* practical reason and will; it is the first precept of the natural law.[38] All subsequent obligations with regard to particular goods, which are means to the end (*ea quae sunt ad finem*), arise from their relation to this primary precept. This precept simply puts in imperative form the natural necessity of our basic orientation to the ultimate end, which is the complete good or happiness.

Aquinas distinguishes carefully between those *objects* to which one is *naturally* moved and those to which one is *necessarily* moved (Ia IIae, q. 10, aa. 1–2). One is *naturally* moved by good in general, and by the ultimate end, the first principle in matters of appetite as the principles of demonstration are in matters of reasoning. But there are a host of others: in general, whatever is appropriate to the nature of one willing; what pertains to every power and to the whole person (*ad totum hominem*); the knowledge of truth, to be, to live, and other things that have in view the natural integrity of human nature. Each comes within the object of the will as *particular goods* (Ia IIae, q. 10, a. 1; Ia IIae, q. 9, a. 1)

But no object moves the will *necessarily* except that which is totally good, with no deficiencies. The only thing that meets the qualifications is the perfect good (*bonum perfectum*, beatitude), which the will cannot *not* will. The particular goods always have some defect and can be considered under this aspect; thus, they do not move the will necessarily. Thomas adds that an object apprehended as a necessary means to the end can move the will by the "necessity of the end" (Ia IIae, q. 9, a. 2, ad 3; Ia, q. 82, a. 1). In this life, even adherence to God (which is, in fact, human beatitude) might not be seen as having a necessary connection to the ultimate end (Ia, q. 82, a. 2). While the enumeration of natural inclinations in Ia IIae, q. 94, a. 2, is not intended to be exhaustive, it should be noted that these are all *particular* goods that come under deliberation

and choice. Yet here, Thomas says that reason naturally grasps these as *goods*, and *consequently* to be pursued in action (*opere prosequenda*); their contraries are, of course, evils *to be avoided* (*vitanda*). These are imperatives.

But, as he says in Ia IIae, q. 94, a. 2, ad 2–3, as particular goods of the whole person, these goods belong to natural law (as imperatives) according to the rule (ordering) of reason, the governing natural human inclination. They oblige only when reason sees them as necessary or appropriate to the ultimate end. Of course the negative imperative (avoid the contrary evils) obliges in every action. But one is not required to pursue all these goods in every action but only at the right time, place, and so on, according to a reasonable order determined by the judgment of prudence. They constitute the horizon of reasonable goals for practical reason in ordering human living.[39]

Derived Precepts

Thomas holds that other moral precepts can be derived from the first indemonstrable principles by some reasoning (*industria rationis*). This process runs from those known very quickly (*modica consideratione*) to those which require much study and expertise (*multa consideratio*). Thomas seems to identify the first type (sometimes called "secondary principles") with the precepts of the decalogue (except for the Sabbath rest; Ia IIae, q. 100, a. 1; Ia IIae, q. 94, a. 4). He almost always refers to all of these not simply as conclusions from first principles, but as *quasi conclusiones*. He is indicating that these other precepts are not derived simply by deductive reasoning, as are conclusions in theoretical reasoning. I will return to this topic later.

Speculative intellect moves from necessary premises to necessary conclusions, as required for a strictly scientific demonstration. But practical reason deals with human actions, which are individual and contingent; hence, its conclusions do not have absolute necessity (Ia IIae, q. 13, a. 6, ad 2). These universal quasi-conclusions will be true for the most part (*ut in pluribus*), but adjustments might be required owing to "impediments" in particular circumstances. For example, it is invariably true, a first principle, that one should not injure one's neighbor. Taking or retaining their goods is an injury to them. But what if my neighbor is clearly in an angry rage at someone, and asks me to return the gun he left in my care? Would it be reasonable or not to return the gun?

The further one moves from first principles in practical reasoning, the more room for a deficiency in the rule owing to the almost infinite variety of circumstances. Rules and laws, being ordered to the common good and meant to endure over time, are always universal propositions, open to defect and to adjustment for individual cases (Ia IIae, q. 96, aa. 1, 6).[40] Nevertheless, such derived precepts are true for most cases and require attention in making moral decisions. The law is one reason for action (Ia IIae, q. 14, a. 3, ad 2).

They are also subject to another kind of deficiency. Everyone knows the first principles, especially that one must act according to reason. But the more one moves to reasoned precepts about more particular areas, the more likely it becomes that fewer people will know them, especially those that require much study. This ignorance is often the result of something more than error or weakness of reasoning power; in fact, reason can be misdirected by passions, evil customs, or poor natural dispositions (Ia IIae, q. 94, a. 4).[41] Aquinas amplifies this remark when he grants that, although the "common" principles of natural law cannot be abolished from the mind (*a corde hominis*) as universals (*in universali*), they may be eliminated (*deletur*) in a particular action (*in particulari operabili*) because reason may be impeded from applying the universal principle to the particular action by some passion. The "derived precepts" can be deleted by reason of bad beliefs (*malas persuasiones*), evil customs (*pravas consuetudines*), or corrupt habits (*habitus corruptos*; Ia IIae, q. 96, a. 6).[42]

The source of the ignorance that impedes right reasoning in all these cases seems to be a passion.[43] This may also be a clue to Aquinas's reluctance to use the simple term "conclusions" for the conclusions of practical reason. This may also indicate that other factors are involved in such reasoning, namely, experience and the operation of moral virtues. Aristotle argues (seconded by Aquinas) that a proper auditor of courses in "political science" must be neither a "youth" (inexperienced in human affairs) nor a follower of passion (a

youth of any age). Only a mature, well-bred person, who knows some "facts," will be able to understand the "reasoned fact." Such a person already knows that certain acts are wrong and others right. And, although this person may not know "why" an action is right or wrong, he or she is ready to listen and easily grasps the reasons.[44] The vicious and prejudiced, on the other hand, are unlikely to listen to arguments contrary to their "feelings"—they just "don't get it." In light of this, one can easily understand the Aristotelian stress on the importance of training and education both by parents and by the laws of the city.

Natural Law and Virtue

In the trend to construct a "virtue ethic" many seem to think that this ethic not only is only superior to the "legalism" of natural law ethics but replaces it.[45] No doubt an emphasis on moral virtue, especially on prudence, is a gain. There can be no just society unless there are just people. Yet I believe that virtue ethics cannot be separated from a foundation in natural law. Virtue, and every habit, is said to be a "second nature"; however, second nature cannot exist without "first nature." There would be no basic criterion by which to determine virtue and vice.

Aquinas, of course, addresses this problem. In stating that one "must act according to reason," he means, of course, *right* reason. This naturally raises the issue of how one keeps reason straight (*recta*). He agrees with Aristotle that the truth of practical reason is not in conformity to things but in its conformity to right appetite. But an appetite is right when it is in accord with true reason. In his *Commentary on the Ethics*, he directly raises a problem (*dubium*) about this matter (Bk. 6, lect. 2, n. 1131). As this is a problem that Aristotle does not raise, the problem and the response are Aquinas's alone.

For if the truth of practical intellect is determined by relation to right appetite, while the correctness (*rectitudo*) of the appetite is in its consonance with true reason, there is a circle in such judgments. So we must note that appetite is of the end and of those things which are to the end: now *the end is determined for human beings by nature,* as he has said in Book 3. But those things which are to the end are not determined by nature, but must be sought out (*investiganda*) by reason. Thus it is clear, that the correctness of appetite with regard to the end is the measure of truth in the practical intellect. And in this the truth of the practical intellect is determined by its accord with right appetite. But the truth of practical reason itself is the rule of right appetite regarding those things which are to the end. And in this way an appetite is said to be right which follows what true reason says.[46]

So the first rule of the truth of practical intellect is the end set by nature, the object of the natural inclination and love of the will. Aquinas insists that natural love and natural knowledge are always true and right (Ia, q. 60, a. 1, ad 3).[47] Practical reason (understanding will and its objects) seeks the means to achieve these ends by guiding the appetite in subsequent acts. Yet, as I have shown, reason can fail in judgments about the implications of those first principles for more specific situations. And this derives mostly from bad dispositions of the appetites, especially of the sense appetites, which can obscure reason.[48]

One requires the moral virtues precisely to keep the appetites right, readily obeying reason as to the means to secure the ends of human life. And the acquisition of virtue (as of any habit except that of first principles) is itself a work of reason as prudence, which directs good deliberation and choice (IIa IIae, q. 47, a. 8).[49] Habits are developed through exercise in the kind of acts at which the habit aims (Ia IIae, q. 51, aa. 2–3). At first, this exercise, like learning grammar, normally is done under the direction of someone else's reason, that of parent or lawgiver, although some, by individual temperament, may be more inclined to one or another virtue or vice. But virtue is not complete until it is not only "according to right reason, but *with* right reason" (Ia IIae, q. 58, a. 4, ad 3).[50] The learner finally comes to a stage where he or she acts virtuously with ease, regularity, and joy; it becomes "second nature."[51]

But neither moral virtue nor prudence nor their combination are "stand alone" moral guides. They require both the first principles of natural law and often some theoretical knowledge as well as sense knowledge (Ia IIae,

q. 14, a. 6).[52] There are numerous passages that bring out the dependence of prudence and the virtues on the first principles of practical reason, held by the habit of synderesis. A notable one occurs in the treatise on prudence, where Thomas states quite clearly that prudence does not provide the ends of the moral virtues. The ends must preexist in reason "as principles naturally known, and such are the ends of the moral virtues"; other things exist in practical reason as conclusions that concern things that are for the end (*ea quae sunt ad finem*). And the latter are in the realm of prudence; their job is to set in order (*disponere*) the means to the end by applying universal principles to particular action (IIa IIae, q. 47, a. 6).[53]

There is, then, a certain priority of prudence; this is in the deployment of the means, the particulars, to secure the overall human good as set by nature and expressed in the first principles of practical reason. Prudence and virtue are not given by nature; their judgments are acquired by teaching and experience (IIa IIae, q. 47, a. 15). Although reasons can be given for them, the final judgments of prudence cannot be demonstrated. This judgment is always about particular actions: this is the right time and place to eat, to preserve my life, or to risk my life for a friend or for the common good. If I have the virtues of temperance and fortitude, my reason will not be led astray by concupiscence or fear (IIa IIae, q. 47, a. 7). I can trust the inclination of virtue.

Because one is most often preoccupied with this ordering of life, and because hardly anyone explicitly refers to the first principles, one might think those principles are not operative. But this is a mistake. Actions cannot be ordered save in view of some end, and, at least in their actions, people reveal that they do know that those basic ends are good and to be preserved. Such ends have actually been "in the back of their minds." Eventually, people will refer to what makes them happy, although they may be mistaken as to what constitutes happiness.[54] So, people brought up with good moral training in a good tradition can surely live good lives without ever explicitly adverting to first principle or moral science. This certainly attests to the importance of community and tradition.[55]

This, of course, is also the area where reason can be distorted by "bad beliefs and customs." At some point these customs and traditions must themselves come under scrutiny, and at that point people want to know the "reasons" for the "facts." Alasdair MacIntyre has pointed out the disarray in the many post-Enlightenment moral philosophies and the breakdown of traditions.[56] But beyond appealing to an older tradition (Aristotelian-Thomist), one must show that this tradition has a sounder basis and can deal with the issues raised by modern moral philosophy and by life in large and diverse communities. This can be done only by returning in some way to human nature, not necessarily as antecedently known by speculative science, but as revealed in our natural knowledge of our natural inclinations.[57] But this knowledge can, and for better understanding should, be related to the speculative knowledge of human nature and to the universal teleology of the universe and divine providence.[58]

HUMAN LAW

As he did with natural law, Aquinas first locates human law in the continuous flow of law and reason: divine reason and eternal law; human natural reason and natural law; finally, human reasoning to further conclusions and determinations of the generalities of natural law, which yield human law when they fulfill the other requirements for law as stated earlier in Ia IIae, q. 90. This process leads to a fuller, but always imperfect and fallible, participation in eternal law (Ia IIae, q. 93, a. 1, c., and ad 1).

In the treatise on human law itself, he makes a major distinction between two ways in which human law is derived from natural law. The first is by way of conclusions from natural law; for instance, that one must not kill is easily derived from the primary principle that people are social animals and should not injure their neighbors. The second is by way giving determination to matters left indeterminate by natural law; for instance, by natural law a criminal ought to be punished, but what punishment is appropriate natural law does not say; rather this is the determination of the human lawgiver. Today, one might apply this to traffic regulations; there seems to be no

intrinsic reason for driving cars on the right or left of the street, but there is good reason to make a decision about this—to avoid injury to ourselves and others. Both types of determinations are included in human positive law. The first have force from both natural and human law; the second only from human law (Ia IIae, q. 95, a. 2).[59]

The Purposes of Human Law

The end of every law, as Thomas notes in Ia IIae, q. 90, a. 2, is the common good of the community that it governs, in this case, the common good of the political community. However, he notes that the common good is made up of many things (*constat ex multis*; Ia IIae, q. 96, a. 1). In various passages, he refers to the goal of human law as justice, virtue, peace, tranquility, friendship, communication, and communion. Can these be sorted out and ordered? From the *Summa contra gentiles*, III, chap. 80, 14–16, and *In I Ethicorum*, lect. 1, it seems that Aquinas distinguishes three general types of common good. The first is an *extrinsic common good*, which is distinct from the community and its members but is some object to be made or achieved by common effort. While very important, it is not relevant here. There are two types of *intrinsic common goods*. First is the common good of *order*, which inheres in the community as a whole, a set of relations among the parts, such as the organization of an army. This is followed by a *common good of many*, goods that inhere in individual persons but are useful to many through communication and communion, such as faith or virtue.

It seems clear that good order of the community, which results in peace and tranquillity, is the first aim of human law. It is foundational; without it, people cannot live together.[60] This may require many sets of laws to order the various functional groups working for the common good (Ia IIae, q. 95, a. 4). The main requirement for such laws is that they be just; especially they must observe distributive justice by an equitable sharing of the burdens and rewards of social life among the citizens according to function and merit (Ia IIae, q. 96, a. 4; Ia IIae, q. 100, a. 2). So it seems that all of these terms can be placed under the head of the intrinsic *common good of order*.

While a just peace, order, and tranquillity are good in themselves, they also serve a further end, the growth of *virtue* and *friendship* among the citizens. Thomas seemingly repeats himself in noting that the end of law is to make men good (virtuous). But this is not accomplished overnight. First, human law cannot directly command or prohibit interior acts or states. It deals solely with the exterior acts of justice by which people communicate with one another. But there is the hope that through accustoming them to do the right thing, even through fear, people may gradually take this way of life to heart and become virtuous (Ia IIae, q. 95, a. 1; Ia IIae, q. 96, a. 2, c., and ad 2).[61] As to acts of the other virtues, they come under the law only as they may have something of the character of justice and affect the common good (Ia IIae, q. 96, a. 3).[62]

The shift in modern ethical and legal theory from the centrality of natural law to that of natural rights gave rise to elaborate jurisprudential theories about "rights talk" and to disputes over the relation of law to rights and duties.[63] If one holds that the primary purpose of law is to secure "natural," or "human," or even "animal" rights, which every human (or sentient) being possesses just by reason of what this "autonomous" being is, rights precede law. In practice, law becomes a means to settle disputes over these individualistic claims. Thomas provides no thematic discussion of the relation of "law" (*lex*) to "right" (*ius*). But several passages, as well as the general movement of his thought on law and right, clearly give law the priority.

One must first understand that this modern conception of rights has little to do with Thomas's notion of right, which presupposes a social context. Right is the object of the virtue of justice, which governs transactions among people; it is the just thing or action (*iustum*) as owed (*debitum*) to someone. It therefore points to an objective state of affairs, not primarily to a subjective power or claim, although the state of affairs may result in a *justified claim* by one person on others. It always involves at least two persons (but may involve the whole community, as in general or distributive justice) and some thing or action that is owed or belongs to someone (IIa IIae, q. 57, a. 1; IIa IIae, q. 58, aa. 1, 11). Thus it is

always a matter of association or community and presupposes the rules or laws of that community (IIa IIae, q. 57, aa. 2–3).

The most explicit and decisive text in this regard is IIa IIae, q. 57, a. 1, ad 2. The objection quotes Isidore saying that law is a species of right (*iuris*), and therefore the object of prudence, not of justice. Thomas replies that, as with art, the idea or plan (*ratio*) of the artifact must preexist in the mind of the artist as the rule (*regula*) of art, so there must preexist in the mind an idea or plan of the just act as the rule (*regula*) of prudence. If this plan is put in writing (promulgated), it is law. Therefore, law is not the right itself, but some idea (*ratio*) of the right.[64] The language here is almost the same as that used to characterize eternal law and divine providence and their relation to divine governance (*gubernatio*). "The very plan (*ratio*) of the governance of things existing in God as the ruler of the universe is (eternal) law" (Ia IIae, q. 91, a. 1).[65] Applying this to the text on right, it means that law is the blueprint and that rights (*iura*) are the set of relationships actually existing and operative in the human universe, as laid down by law. From natural law, there arise natural rights; from positive law, there arise positive rights (IIa IIae, q. 57, aa. 2 and 3). Law defines these relationships and the actions appropriate to them.

Must law protect rights? Human law must certainly protect natural rights, which is the same as saying that it must not be contrary to natural law.[66] And of course civil authorities must respect rights given by the civil law—or change the law by legitimate procedures. Rights are always embedded in the order set out by the law of some community, and the law of the superior community (federal law) always supersedes that of a lesser community (state law). Natural law sets out the order of the "community of men under God"; this is the highest community, and defines basic human dignity (*dignitas*), the latter being for Aquinas one's rank, status, or function in some community. As he says, God in creating and governing exercises distributive justice by giving to each what is necessary or needed according to its dignity (Ia, q. 21, a. 1). And these are the things or actions owed to him (*debita*) and are his (*suum*) (Ia, q. 21, a. 1, ad 3).[67]

It seems then that the immediate and direct aim of law is to set up an order of just relations in the community and its parts. This constitutes that peace and tranquillity in which the citizens know and understand the rules of their communities. But not any order will do. It must be such that it guides the citizens to the achievement of moral virtue and the cultivation of friendships, and also frees them to pursue the intellectual virtues, art, career, and family life according to their interests within the parameters of law and justice.[68]

Limits of Human Law

Some of these limits have already been mentioned; I will now examine them more thematically. The best place to start is with Ia IIae, q. 91, a. 4, where Aquinas asks why divine law is necessary. The first and obvious reason is that humans have a supernatural destiny, an ultimate end, revealed to them by God; they need divine direction as to the means to achieve this end. Although this may seem outside the concerns of human law, in reality, it is not. Christianity (and some other religions) have used this to put reins on the ambitions of political powers. It is the most serious source for the "injustice" of human law, namely, that it is contrary to divine law (Ia IIae, q. 96, a. 4). This is a constant caution to rulers that humans live in a higher community with a superior common good; they are not totally absorbed in the political community (Ia IIae, q. 21, a. 4, ad 3).[69]

The second limitation arises from the uncertainty of human judgment, especially in particular and contingent matters with which morality and law deal. This can be a cause of confusion and demoralization in the citizenry. Yet for human law, it suffices that one knows that something is true "for the most part" (*verum ut in pluribus*) (Ia IIae, q. 96, a. 1, ad 3). This is one reason why the laws must be general and why it is sometimes permissible to act against the letter of the law, and why a rule by law is better than a rule by judges (Ia IIae, q. 96, a. 6, c., and ad 3).[70]

This is where the "evil beliefs" (*malae persuasiones*) and depraved customs enter the field. Misreasonings and uncontrolled passions can effect a different ethos both in the populace and the legislators to demand laws favoring such an ethos.[71] As a corrective of such possible bad beliefs and customs, and so that people could know without doubt what to do and avoid, it was necessary that they be guided by divinely revealed law. Since people generally get their surest moral guidance from religious faith, it might be well for government and law, even pragmatically, to foster sound religious life among its people, as a help for the development and observance of the law.

Third, humans can make law only about matters they can judge, and these are exterior acts of virtue (*agere virtuosa*). But the perfection of virtue (*agere virtuosa virtuose*) requires the internal acts about which men cannot judge and law cannot command. So that those interior acts be rightly ordered, divine law was necessary. Again and again in this treatise, Aquinas insists that law (and human judgment) can only relate to the exterior act of justice (or of the other virtues as they relate to justice and the common good). By accustoming people to do the right thing, it is the *hope* of law to lead them to virtue; but again, the best hope for this may be in fostering the religious life of people who listen to divine revelation.[72]

Finally, human law cannot prohibit or punish all evils. Law is made for the multitude, and most of them are not perfect in virtue. The attempt to repress all evils can lead to a contempt of law and then to greater evils (Ia IIae, q. 96, a. 2). One might think here of the criminal activity engendered by the Prohibition laws. As this point demonstrates, human law must tolerate (though not approve) some evils (ibid.).[73] Legislators must look to the condition and customs of the many for whom they are making the laws. In this area of factual possibilities, Thomas seems to be a minimalist; while in the area of hope, he seems a maximalist—people can improve under the tutelage of good laws.[74]

Therefore, it is important that God reveal that all evils are forbidden and will receive appropriate retribution.[75] People should not fall into the belief that because human law does not forbid some acts, they are therefore morally permissible, that legality is morality. From this discussion, it is clear that one must now examine the relation of morality to legality.

Moral and Legal Obligation

Practically all utilitarians and positivists, from John Stuart Mill and John Austin to H. L. A. Hart, hold that legal obligation arises from power, fear, or social pressure, and that a law is a law and legally binding if it is procedurally just, that is, that it is posited by a proper authority according to the rules of procedure in a given community. However, the "morality" of the law's content has nothing to do with its "legality." On the other hand, Thomas places (in Ia IIae, q. 90) law clearly in the stream of that practical reasoning which is moral reasoning. On his view, law is a pronouncement of the practical reason of the appropriate authority guiding the community to its common good, which is happiness. To be a genuine law, it must meet *all* the requirements of this definition, not simply that of proper authority.

So in his examination of whether law binds in conscience, Thomas makes no distinction between legal and moral obligation; law is a part of the moral order. If a law does not bind morally, it does not bind legally. Law, or a legal system, is not some entity separate from the moral order with completely independent rules. He therefore affirms that an unjust law is not a law but an act of violence (Ia IIae, q. 96, a. 4; Ia IIae, q. 90, a. 1, ad 3; Ia IIae, q. 93, a. 3, ad 2; Ia IIae, q. 95, a. 3).[76]

Thomas maintains that if a law is just, it has obligatory force from the eternal law from which it is derived. And laws are just by reason of their end, serving the common good and not private gain; by reason of their author not exceeding his or her range of authority; and by reason of its form, when it distributes the burdens of society on its subjects with proportional equality in relation to the common good. Laws can be unjust in two ways. First, if it is contrary to the human good by violating any of the above requirements. Second, when it violates the divine good or divine law, such as laws requiring idolatry (Ia IIae, q. 96, a. 4)

But he distinguishes between these categories. Laws contrary to the divine law should never be obeyed. Laws against the human good may be obeyed, not by reason of the law, but to avoid scandal or turmoil (*turbationem*), situations where one should yield her or his

own right. Such laws do not carry "legal obligation" by themselves; an obligation to obey these laws may arise from charity (avoiding scandal) or from the obligation of general justice to the community (avoiding turmoil; Ia IIae, q. 96, a. 4). There is not even a hint here that unjust laws have any "legal" status at all; once they are out of line with right reason, eternal and natural law, they are out of the legal and moral order and so have no force. In short, they contravene the nature of law.[77]

The relation between law and morality, then, may be summarized thus. First, the lawgiver must set up an order of justice and peace in which people can live in relative security. Second, the details of this order are up to the legislator; natural law requires only that it be just; otherwise much depends on the people for whom the order is set up.[78] Third, human law is not required to enforce all the precepts of the natural law, especially the derived ones, but only those without which people cannot live together. Fourth, morality and the natural law set up primarily negative parameters within which the law must remain, even to be true to its own nature; it may not contravene natural or divine law by commanding or approving what is contrary to them. Fifth, the authority of rulers and their law does derive, indirectly, from eternal and natural law.[79] From these, it receives its power and majesty, a high and indispensable work for human creativity.[80]

SUMMARY

Aquinas's natural law theory is not that of a simply deductive process, as in mathematics. Any "derived precepts" are gathered from the experiences of living and are "reduced to," as he says, and tested against the primary precepts, which look to the good of the *whole person* as well as to the parts. Nor are they rigid rules. They are true "in most cases" (*ut in pluribus*), and need adjustment where the rule does not serve the ends formulated in the basic principles. This is also true of human law (Ia IIae, q. 96, a. 6).[81] The final judgment in such cases, of course, belongs in the sphere of prudence, which supposes the moral virtues lest one too easily judge from fear, greed, lust, and the like. But the latter receive their ends from the basic precepts of natural law.

The basic principles themselves, which formulate the ends of human life, are self-evident and indemonstrable. Most people never "think about" them, but they act according to them; they are the final "reasons" why people act at all. Especially in times of stress and confusion, many people want to know the reasons so as to find surer direction or to uphold what they believe is a good way of life. Many find this assurance in divine revelation, but they still want to relate this to their deepest experiences of life. Of course, there is no guarantee that everyone will see or agree to those basic principles. There are many obstacles such as vicious habits, prejudices, or pride, which blur human vision. One can only break through these obstacles, sometimes, by dialectical argument—sometimes, by disastrous experience.

Human lawmakers have a vast and difficult area for responsible creativity in guiding the political community. They do not have to enforce the whole moral law; however, if they are to contribute to the genuine human well-being of themselves and their subjects, they need the highest kind of prudence, political prudence (IIa IIae, q. 47, a. 10). And for this, they need to be aware of the genuine human goods formulated in the basic precepts of the natural law and of the educative power of laws. After all, the common good is both a *good* and an end.

Aquinas's view of human action is certainly teleological; human actions are surely "goal-oriented"—if there is nothing *to be done*, there is nothing *to do*. In this area it is extremely difficult to deny teleology. Can scientists, for instance, explain their writing books, giving lectures, or doing research (and using vast sums of taxpayers' money) if they are acting without purpose? Aquinas, of course, roots human teleology in the natural teleology of beings universally; although humans are the only natural beings who know their ends as ends, they are not an anomaly in the universe but have a function as all other things do. It is spelled out in their dynamic structure, which one can know.

One says that other things (pine trees, flowers, dogs, and cats) "act as if they knew what they were doing" to promote their own well-being. They even "adapt" to new situations. Aquinas holds that they do not actually know

the relation of means to ends; they act by natural instinct (*ex instinctu naturae*). But Someone does know both their intrinsic structure and order and their relation to the rest of the universe. Order and relations can be known or effected only by intellect. Both macro- and micro-scientists are working hard to discover the relations and order among the parts of individual entities and of the cosmos. To eliminate teleology is to eliminate order and meaning in the universe, to make it a "tale told by an idiot, full of sound and fury, signifying nothing."

Notes

[1] There is now a more helpful edition: R. J. Henle, S.J., ed., *St. Thomas Aquinas: The Treatise on Law* (Notre Dame, IN: University of Notre Dame Press, 1993). This was written primarily for law students, but Henle's "Introduction" provides a good account of the methods, doctrinal background, and sources of the treatise.

[2] "postquam praedictum est de exemplari, scilicet de Deo, et de his quae processerunt ex divina potestate secundum eius voluntatem; restat ut consideremus de eius imagine, idest de homine, secundum quod et ipse est suorum operum principium, quasi liberum arbitrium habens et suorum operum potestatem."

[3] Thomas clearly distinguishes the "objective" aspect, the good to be achieved, which makes us happy (*quod beatum facit*) and the subjective achievement (*adeptio*) of this good. They are not two ends, but two aspects of a single end. See ST Ia IIae, q. 1, a. 8; q. 2, a. 7; q. 11, a. 3, ad 1.

[4] This is in keeping with Aquinas's general principle that we know the more universal, the confused whole, before we acquire a distinct knowledge of the parts and their relationships. See ST Ia, q. 85, a. 3; and Ia, q. 2, a. 1, ad 1: Is the existence of God self-evident? To which, Aquinas says no. But an objection, leaning on the authority of St. John Damascene, claims that the knowledge of the existence of God is naturally placed (*inserta*) in everyone. Thomas replies: "Cognoscere Deum esse in aliquo communi, sub quadam confusione, est nobis naturaliter insertum, inquantum scilicet Deus est hominis beatitudo; homo enim naturaliter desiderat beatitudinem, et quod naturaliter desideratur ab homine, naturaliter cognoscitur ab eodem. Sed hoc non est simpliciter cognoscere Deum esse, sicut cognoscere venientem, non est cognoscere Petrum, quamvis sit Petrus veniens; multi enim perfectum hominis bonum, quod est beatitudo, existimant di-

vitias; quidam vero voluptates, quidam autem aliquid aliud."

[5]ST Ia IIae, q. 5, a. 5, ad 1: "Sicut natura non deficit homini in necessariis, quamvis non dederit sibi arma et tegumenta sicut aliis animalibus, quia dedit ei rationem et manus, quibus possit haec sibi acquirere: ita nec deficit homini in necessariis, quamvis non daret sibi aliquod principium quo posset beatitudinem consequi; hoc enim erat impossibile; sed dedit ei liberum arbitrium, quo possit converti ad Deum, qui eum faceret beatum. 'Quae enim per amicos possumus, per nos aliqualiter possumus, ut dicitur in III *Eth.* (1112b27).'"

He does not demean the "imperfect beatitude," which one can achieve in this life, described by Aristotle as the activity of the moral and intellectual virtues. Rather, he elevates it seeing it as a part or participation in the whole good. The grasp of any truth is a beginning (*inchoatio*) of our sharing in Truth, and so is a genuine value. See ST Ia IIae, q. 2, a. 3: Fame and glory cannot constitute beatitude, rather they presuppose and are caused by "*beatitudo, vel inchoata vel perfecta.*" See also q. 3, aa. 5, 6, 8; q. 4, aa. 5–8.

[6]"per gratiam adiuvamur ad recte agendum."

[7]The phrase "*ea quae sunt ad finem*" is often translated as "means." This obscures the distinction between purely instrumental means and what might be called "constitutive means." The latter means are ends, *bona honesta*, good and desirable in themselves but subordinate to and serving a more complete and higher end. They are beginnings of the ultimate end, as indicated in n. 3. A "good dinner" might be made up of a salad, a slice of succulent prime rib with baked potato, a tasty dessert, and a glass of fine wine. As parts of the whole, these are constitutive means; knives and forks would be instrumental means. All the virtues and their activities in which Aristotle placed human happiness (*beatitudo imperfecta*) Aquinas would consider as constitutive means or beginnings of complete beatitude.

Nevertheless, no end *as* end is the object of deliberation or choice. But as subordinate ends which serve higher ends they may be. In view of his happiness one may choose to be a doctor rather than a lawyer. But *as a doctor* he does not deliberate or choose whether or not to work for the health of his client; that is the end of doctoring. He deliberates about how best to achieve health for this person. See ST Ia IIae, q. 13, a. 3 and q. 14, a. 2.

[8]At ST Ia IIae, q. 17, a. 1, as he describes the psychological process of decision and action, Aquinas explains the act he calls *imperium*: "Imperare autem est quidem essentialiter actus rationis; imperans enim ordinat eum cui imperat, ad aliquid agendum, intimando vel denunciando . . ." This act is preceded by the act of will choosing means for an intended end, and these acts of will give the *impe-*

rium its moving force. He uses etymology rather freely. Here, he derives *lex* from *ligare*, to bind or obligate. In a. 4, ad 3, to emphasize the permanence of written law, he derives it from *legere*, to read.

[9]While Aquinas often uses these terms as synonyms, he seems to prefer *felicitas* to describe the imperfect happiness that can be achieved in this life and *beatitudo* for the perfect beatitude in the next life. Human law, of course, can only directly aim at the first.

[10]He cites Arist. *Eth. Nic.* 5.1 (1129b17): "And so in one way what we call [legally] just is whatever produces and maintains happiness and its parts for a political community." Thomas certainly uses what is most familiar to us, civil law, as a general model. Yet every step of the definition leaves the terms broad enough to apply to other analogous types.

There can be no doubt that he is serious about the reference of law to the ultimate end. See the reply to the second objection in this article: "Sicut nihil constat firmiter secundum rationem speculativam nisi per reductionem ad prima principia indemonstrabilia, ita firmiter nihil constat per rationem practicam nisi per ordinationem ad ultimum finem, qui est bonum commune. Quod autem hoc modo ratione constat, legis rationem habet." ·

[11]See his reference to the "community of men under God" in *De perf. vit. spir.*, chap. 13 (Leonine, B81–B84) and frequent references to the "community of the universe." As to the identification of the political *communitas perfecta*, he is somewhat elusive. He refers variously to *civitas, provincia, regnum, imperium,* and even to *respublica christiana.* Perhaps these are *relatively* complete communities, but in some hierarchical order. The modern national state has *juridical* independence and "sovereignty"; however, it is not genuinely independent economically, politically, or morally.

[12]Political interpretations of this article are considered in the sections on Maritain and Simon in "Thomistic Moral Philosophy in the Twentieth Century," in this volume.

[13]Aquinas knows the need of a legal profession. Not everyone has to know all the laws, but if one is going to start a corporation, he or she needs a corporation lawyer to make clear the legal requirements for this (ST q. 90, a. 4, ad 2).

[14]"nihil est aliud lex quam quoddam dictamen practicae rationis in principe qui gubernat aliquam communitatem perfectam. Manifestum est autem, supposito quod mundus divina providentia regnatur, ut in primo habitum est, quod tota communitas universi gubernatur ratione divina. Et ideo ipsa ratio gubernationis rerum in Deo sicut in principe universitatis existens, legis habet rationem. Et quia divina ratio nihil concipit ex tempore, sed habet aeternum conceptum . . ."

[15]See ST Ia, q. 15, a. 2: (The question is whether there are many ideas or exemplars in the divine mind.) "In quolibet effectu illud quod est ultimus finis proprie est intentum a principali agente. . . . Illud autem quod est optimum in rebus existens est bonum ordinis universi. . . . Sed si ipse ordo universi est per se creatus ab eo [Deo] et intentus ab ipso, necesse est quod habeat ideam ordinis universi. Ratio autem alicuius totius haberi non potest, nisi habeantur propriae rationes eorum ex quibus totum constituitur." God, of course, is the extrinsic common good of the universe; the order of the parts to the whole is the intrinsic common good. He refers to Arist. *Metaph.* 12 (1075a13ff). Thomas discusses this matter in his *In XII Metaph.*, 12.

[16]There are other important reasons for this necessity, but they will be mentioned later in connection with natural and human law. I will skip the *lex fomitis* (ST Ia IIae, q. 91, a. 6); it is "law" improperly and in a passive sense, referring to unbridled passions which lead to sin insofar as they are not ruled by right reason. See also q. 90, a. 1, ad 1.

[17]John Finnis, *Natural Law and Natural Rights* (Oxford: Clarendon, 1980), 24–25. Yves Simon gives an account of the ideological genesis of some of these theories in *The Tradition of Natural Law* (New York: Fordham University Press, 1965), 16–40.

[18]See Robert George, ed., *Natural Law Theory: Contemporary Essays* (Oxford: Clarendon, 1992). Almost every essay in this collection brings out one or more of these issues plus several others—the is/ought problem, relativism of moral and judicial judgments, the claim of "virtue ethics" to replace natural law, and other such topics.

[19]One would do well to consult some of the lively essays in Henry B. Veatch, *Swimming against the Current in Contemporary Philosophy* (Washington, DC: Catholic University of America Press, 1990). Essays 5–9 and 13–15 are particularly relevant to natural law theory. All of these essays were previously published in various journals. And, of course, Simon deals with most of the issues raised here in *Tradition of Natural Law*.

[20]This article seems clearly intended to establish the existence of natural law in humans (against Henle, ed., *Treatise on Law*, 155). The main problem is human freedom, as brought out by objs. 2–3. Thomas's main point is to show that natural law exists in rational creatures in a different way than in irrational creatures and does not cancel free choice.

Oscar J. Brown effectively uses the *Summa contra gentiles* as central to his study, because, for one reason, it sets the study of natural law within the overall legal framework of the divine law, as opposed to the framework of moral theology in the *Summa theologiae*. See Brown, *Natural Rectitude and*

Divine Law: An Approach to an Integral Interpretation of the Thomistic Doctrine of Law (Toronto: Pontifical Institute of Medieval Studies, 1981), ix. I think that the setting for natural law in the *Summa theologiae*, as a principle of action in the human movement toward God, the ultimate end, is most fitting; furthermore, it also places it within the framework of eternal law.

[21]He uses this distinction of two ways of sharing in eternal law in several places, perhaps most succinctly expressed in ST Ia IIae, q. 90, a. 1, ad 1: "Cum lex sit regula quaedam et mensura, dicitur dupliciter esse in aliquo. Uno modo sicut in mensurante et regulante. Et quia hoc est proprium rationis, ideo per hunc modum lex est in ratione sola. Alio modo, sicut in regulato et mensurato. Et sic lex est in omnibus quae inclinantur in aliquid ex aliqua lege, ita quod quaelibet inclinatio proveniens ex aliqua lege, potest dici lex non essentialiter, sed quasi participative." See q. 91, a. 6 for an application of this to the so-called *lex fomitis*. See q. 93, a. 6 and SCG III, chap. 113: "Participat igitur rationalis creatura divinam providentiam non solum secundum gubernari, sed etiam secundum gubernare . . ." This should be a caution to those who too easily identify natural law with natural *appetitive* inclinations alone.

Again, the insistence that all free activity is founded on nature is repeated often. See especially ST Ia IIae, q. 10, aa. 1–2, where he confronts natural necessity with the indetermination of subsequent acts of intellect and will. And this should be a caution to those who would separate reason and nature or would change the terminology to eliminate the "natural" from Aquinas's basic position on ethics or natural law. Vernon Bourke has suggested "ethics of right reason" or "orthological ethics" as a substitute. But this evades the chief problem: How is reason made right? On the relation of reason and nature see q. 71, a. 2.

[22]"Omnis enim cognitio veritatis est quaedam irradiatio et participatio legis aeternae, quae est veritas incommutabilis . . . . Veritatem autem omnes aliqualiter cognoscunt, ad minus quantum ad principia communia legis naturalis. In aliis vero quidam plus et quidam minus participant de cognitione veritatis; et secundum hoc etiam plus vel minus cognoscunt legem aeternam." See ST Ia IIae, q. 93, a. 2, ad 2: Humans cannot know the total order of things, "quo omnia sunt ordinatissima," for the cause cannot be totally revealed in its effects. This, of course, is Aquinas's normal procedure in all matters concerned with God. The proofs for His existence are *quia* proofs (effect to cause), and proofs for all other attributes (except those known only through divine revelation) depend on those proofs along with other observations about the nature of the effects.

[23]See ST Ia IIae, q. 94, a. 2, ad 2: "Omnes huius-modi inclinationes quarumcumque partium naturae humanae, puta concupiscibilis et irascibilis, secundum quod regulantur ratione, pertinent ad legem naturalem, et reducuntur ad unum primum praeceptum, ut dictum est. Et secundum hoc, sunt multa praecepta legis naturae in seipsis, quae tamen communicant in una radice."

[24]See the section on Lottin in "Thomistic Moral Philosophy in the Twentieth Century," in this volume. Also ST Ia, q. 78, a. 4, ad 4: "Licet intellectus operatio oriatur a sensu, tamen in re apprehensa per sensum intellectus multa cognoscit quae sensus percipere non potest."

[25]See De potentia, q. 7, a. 2, ad 11 (Marietti, 190–93). In his earliest major work, Aquinas had already settled this. See In I Sent., d. 3, q. 1, a. 2: "ea quae per se nobis nota sunt, efficiuntur nota statim per sensum; sicut visis toto et parte, statim cognoscimus quod omne totum est maius sua parte sine aliqua inquisitione" (Mandonnet, 94).

He often uses the terms reason (ratio) and intellect (intellectus) without distinction. But in appropriate places he makes it clear that these terms properly refer to two different acts of the same power. They differ, not in their objects, the universal and necessary, but in their way of knowing. See ST Ia, q. 59, a. 1, ad 1: "Sed intellectus et ratio differunt quantum ad modum cognoscendi, quia scilicet intellectus cognoscit simplici intuitu, ratio vero discurrendo de uno in aliud. Sed tamen ratio per discursum pervenit ad cognoscendum illud, quod intellectus sine discursu cognoscit, scilicet universale." Angels are intellectual creatures because they know purely by intellectus. Ratio, reasoning, is the typical human way of knowing, so man is a rational not an intellectual animal. But at his best man shares something angelic, that is, intellectus, for the primary principles, at least, are known in precisely this way. Hence the habitus by which the first speculative principles are retained is called intellectus principiorum. Its counterpart, for first practical principles, is called by that strange, but traditional, name synderesis. See Ia IIae, q. 94, a. 1, c., and ad 2; Ia, q. 79, a. 12.

[26]Cited by Russell Hittinger, "Natural Law and Virtue" in Natural Law Theory, 61 (with reference to Fuller, The Morality of Law, 11). See also in the same essay: "As Lon Fuller remarked, natural law is the method men naturally follow when they are not consciously or unconsciously inhibited by a positivistic philosophy" (67, n. 31).

Hadley Arkes brings out well the implicit character of our most basic moral convictions (in "That 'Nature Herself Has Placed in Our Ears a Power of Judging': Some Reflections on the Naturalism of Cicero," in Natural Law Theory, 245–77). Also, Alasdair MacIntyre (in Three Rival Versions of Moral Enquiry: Encyclopaedia, Genealogy, and Tradition

[Notre Dame, IN: University of Notre Dame Press, 1990], 134–39) discusses this in the larger context of a "holistic" reading of Aquinas.

[27]See ST Ia, q. 29, a. 1, ad 4; q. 115, a. 2; IIIa, q. 2, a. 1. He derives this, and other definitions, from Arist. Ph. 2.1 (192b14 ff).

[28]See ST Ia, q. 87, aa. 1–4. Here, he examines the most delicate cases of all: (1) How does the soul know itself? and (2) What is in the soul? His answer: habitus, intellect itself, and will. He insists that such knowledge begins from awareness of its acts and their objects; potencies are known through their acts. From this immediate knowledge, one can begin the long and subtle study which can terminate in a scientific understanding of the nature of the soul.

[29]"Appetitus nihil aliud est quam quaedam inclinatio appetentis in aliquid . . . omnis inclinatio consequatur aliquam formam." Likewise, every form gives rise to some inclination. ST Ia, q. 80, a. 1: "Quamlibet formam sequitur aliqua inclinatio."

[30]"Unaquaeque potentia animae est quaedam forma seu natura, et habet naturalem inclinationem ad aliquid. Unde unaquaeque appetit obiectum sibi conveniens naturali appetitu. Supra quem est appetitus animalis consequens apprehensionem, quo appetitur aliquid non ea ratione qua est conveniens ad actum huius vel illius potentiae, utpote visio ad videndum et auditio ad audiendum, sed quia est conveniens simpliciter animali." A more expansive development of this, as regards the will, is found at De veritate, q. 22, a. 5 (Leonine, 621–26). While the will is not subject to coercive necessity, it is subject to natural necessity; hence its basic act is not one of free choice; it cannot not will good and the ultimate end which is the complete good; free choice enters only with regard to the particular goods presented by reason. This involves the freedom of exercise (to will or not to will) and the freedom of specification (to will this or that). This distinction runs through the treatise on the two wills in Christ (ST IIIa, q. 18, esp. aa. 1, 3, 5), where he variously describes will as voluntas ut natura or naturalis as opposed to voluntas ut rationalis.

In describing the interaction of intellect and will, Aquinas several times faces the objection that this leads to an infinite series; to close the series he refers to the natural appetites of these powers. See ST Ia IIae, q. 17, a. 5, ad 3: "Cum imperium sit actus rationis, ille actus imperatur, qui ratione subditur. Primus autem voluntatis actus ex rationis ordinatione non est, sed ex instinctu naturae aut superioris causae . . ." (The "superior cause" is God, the creator of "nature" [q. 9, a. 6].) See also q. 9, a. 9, ad 2: "In his quae ad intellectum et voluntatem pertinent, primum invenitur id quod est secundum naturam, ex quo alia derivantur; ut a cognitione principiorum naturaliter notorum, cognitio conclusionum, et a voluntate finis naturaliter desiderati, derivatur electio eorum quae sunt ad finem." And Ia, q. 82, a. 4, ad 2: "Non oportet procedere in infinitum, sed statur in intellectu sicut in primo. Omnis enim voluntatis motum necesse est quod praecedat apprehensio; sed non omnem apprehensionem praecedit motus voluntatis . . ." And *De veritatae*, q. 22, a. 12, ad 2: "Non est procedere in infinitum; statur enim in appetitu naturali, quo inclinatur intellectus in suum actum" (Leonine, 642, 127–30).

[31]Aquinas maintains that actions should properly be attributed to the individual person, although we often use shorthand, such as "the intellect knows, the will desires, the eyes see," etc. See for instance: ST IIa IIae, q. 58, a. 2: "Actiones sunt suppositorum et totorum, non autem, proprie loquendo, partium et formarum, seu potentiarum; non enim proprie dicitur quod manus percutiat sed homo per manum, neque proprie dicitur quod calor califaciat, sed ignis per calorem" (he is explaining that justice is *ad alterum*, and that this requires distinct persons).

[32]See ST Ia, q. 87, a. 3: "Et ideo quod primo cognoscitur ab intellectu humano, est huiusmodi obiectum [extrinsecum]; et secundario cognoscitur ipse actus quo cognoscitur obiectum; et per actum cognoscitur ipse intellectus, cuius est perfectio ipsum intelligere." See q. 87, a. 3, ad 1: "Obiectum intellectus est commune quoddam, scilicet ens et verum, sub quo comprehenditur etiam ipse actus intelligendi. Unde intellectus potest suum actum intelligere. Sed non primo; quia nec primum obiectum intellectus nostri secundum praesentem statum est quodlibet ens et verum; sed ens et verum consideratum in rebus materialibus, ut dictum est (q. 84, a. 7), ex quibus in cognitionem omnium aliorum devenit." In every text where Aquinas discusses the "transcendentals" (properties of being), which do not add to being in itself but to our understanding of being, the sequence is always the same: being, one, true, and good. The primary passage is *De veritatae*, q. 1, a. 1 (Leonine, 3–8); but see also q. 21, aa. 1–3 (Leonine, 591–99) and ST Ia, q. 5, aa. 1–2; q. 11, a. 1; q. 16, aa. 3–4. These passages reveal that the true and the good are based on *being*, ultimately on the existence, *esse* of things. They are relationships of being to cognitive and appetitive powers, so being cannot be eliminated from the true or the good.

[33]See also ST Ia, q. 20, a. 1 (Is there love in God?): "Primus motus voluntatis, et cuiuslibet appetetivae virtutis, est amor. . . . Rursus quod est communius, naturaliter est prius, unde et intellectus per prius habet ordinem ad verum commune quam ad particularia quaedam vera. Sunt autem quidam actus voluntatis et appetitus respicientes bonum sub aliqua speciali conditione, sicut gaudium et delectatio est de bono praesenti et habito; desiderium autem et spes de bono nondum adepto. Amor autem respicit bonum in communi, sive habitum sive non habitum. Unde amor naturaliter est primus actus voluntatis et appetitus."

"Et propter hoc omnes alii motus appetitivi praesupponunt amorem quasi primum radicem. Nullus enim desiderat nisi bonum amatum; neque aliquis gaudet nisi de bono amato." At Ia, q. 20, a. 1, ad 2, and in other passages, Thomas points out that passions (*passiones*) are properly predicated only of the sensitive appetitive power, not of the will. Yet the will is a passive power insofar as it must be moved by some object apprehended. See Ia, q. 80, a. 1: "Potentia enim appetitiva est potentia passiva, quae nata est moveri ab apprehenso . . ." Other passages emphasize the radical nature of love. See *De virt. in comm.*, q. un., a. 12, ad 9 (Marietti, 745); *De caritate*, q. un., a. 2 (Marietti, 757–60). And this paves the way for the primacy over all the virtues of the infused virtue of charity which directly relates us in love to God, the ultimate end and supreme rule and measure of human acts (ST IIIa, q. 23).

[34]"Ipsa autem aptitudo sive proportio appetitus ad bonum est amor, qui nihil aliud est quam complacentia boni; motus autem ad bonum est desiderium vel concupiscentia; quies autem in bono est gaudium vel delectatio."

[35]At ST Ia IIae, q. 27, a. 1, ad 3, Thomas applies this to beauty, *quod visui placet*. In this case the will rests in, enjoys, simply the vision or knowledge of the object without tending to real union with it as it does in the case of good and end. He also points out some indetermination in the use of the word *appetite*. Ia, q. 59, a. 1, ad 2: "Licet nomen appetitivae partis sit sumptum ab appetendo ea quae non habentur, tamen appetitiva pars non solum ad haec se extendit, sed etiam ad multa alia." So he easily puts together the two terms. For example, Ia, q. 60, a. 1: "Et hoc est commune omni naturae, ut habeat aliquam *inclinationem*, quae est *appetitus naturalis vel amor*." See ST Ia IIae, q. 11, a. 1, ad 3: "In delectatione duo sunt: scilicet perceptio convenientis, quae pertinet ad apprehensivam potentiam; et complacentia eius quod offertur ut conveniens, et hoc pertinet ad appetitivam potentiam, in qua ratio delectationis completur." See the fine study by Frederick E. Crowe, S.J., "Complacency and Concern in the Thought of St. Thomas," *Theological Studies* 20 (1959): 1–39, 198–230, 343–82. This *complacentia* might well be translated in verb form: to like. As Thomas says, one does not desire something or delight in its presence unless one likes it.

[36]"Sed obiectum movet determinando actum ad modum principii formalis, a quo in rebus naturalibus actio specificatur, sicut califactio a calore. Primum autem principium formale est ens et verum universale, quod est obiectum intellectus. Et ideo isto modo motionis intellectus movet voluntatem, sicut praesentans ei obiectum suum."

³⁷These two articles leave some ambiguities. They deal with the relations of will to ends and means. The will as a power is related to both because both have the character of good. But he insists that *willing simply* (*velle*) is only of the end, and that this may be separated even temporally from "willing the end *in* the means," as we can will health and only later deliberate about means to attain (or preserve) health (ST Ia IIae, q. 8, a. 3). If this *velle* is the simple and primary movement of will, it must be the same as the *amare* of which he speaks in earlier passages, where the object is simply the good. But since good also has the character of end, and he is engaged here with human actions as tending to the ultimate end (and good), he can refer to it simply as end. Yet end and action as such enter only in the phase that he calls *intention* (*intentio*), by which one effectively wills to achieve (or preserve) some apprehended good (q. 12, a. 1, c., and ad 3–4). See also Ia, q. 83, a. 4, ad 1, where he relates simple will (*velle*) for the end to *intellectus* and the choice of means to *ratiocinari*. This seems to mark the difference between *complacency* (liking) and *concern*.

³⁸Some might say that this is an illicit move from "is" to "ought." Why does Aquinas see no problem here? I think it is because he sees that all moral "oughts," like other value judgments, arise from an intellectually perceived set of relations in a situation, not from some independent source; in this case it is from the perceived relation among being, reason, and appetite, which, in this first instance, arise from perceived natural structures. When someone says, with joy: "He made a home run," this is a value judgment. Home runs are not empirical *things* you can *make* or *see*. What he did was to hit a pitched ball over the left field fence in a game called baseball, which has its own prior structures and relationships. If he had hit a ball over the fence in batting practice, it would not be a home run, although it might still be a *good* hit. See ST Ia IIae, q. 99, q. 1: Obligation arises from the necessity of the end as seen in the means.

³⁹There may be a reason for Grisez and Finnis to fall back on this one negative precept as the only moral absolute: Do not directly destroy or damage any good in any action. But it is odd to call these *human goods* "pre-moral." Of course, like other goods (good horses, good paintings) these could be studied speculatively. But as objects of practical intellect, they are the principles (ends) that enter into and make any subsequent practical reasoning possible. Practical reason directs human acts and human acts are moral acts. "Nam idem sunt actus morales et actus humani" (ST Ia IIae, q. 1, a. 3). True, these principles precede moral science, just as the first principles of speculative intellect precede any demonstrations of speculative science; for science is "of conclusions." Without them there would be noth-

ing to "intend" or "deliberate about." In short, nothing for reason to "put in order."

And there is hierarchy. "Do good" simply refers to the natural inclination to seek the ultimate end, the whole and complete good of the whole person. "Act according to reason" is both a natural inclination and the first precept for ordering and choosing among "those things which are to the end." Among the other inclinations, there is, most notably, the social imperative, which results in the primacy of the common good over any private good of the same order. For the common good, one may risk (not take) even his or her own life. Moreover, one may entirely bypass some of these "natural" goods for the sake of a higher good. See Thomas's defense of consecrated virginity, which leaves one free for contemplating "divine things" and at the same time promotes the common good of society, which needs not only material multiplication and farmers and carpenters, but "contemplators" to enrich society by the fruits of their "study" (IIa IIae, q. 152, aa. 2–3; q. 182, a. 1).

This still leaves a vast area of choice among "life-styles." Whether one is to be doctor, plumber, priest, or singer is not determined by the nature of the species, but by what Aquinas sometimes calls "individual nature" (Ia IIae, q. 51, a. 1). In short, these are left to personal aptitudes, inclinations, and opportunities. See SCG III, chap. 134: (He is discussing the many functions required for human living) "Haec autem distributio diversorum officiorum in diversas personas fit divina providentia secundum quod quidam inclinantur magis ad hoc officium quam ad alia."

⁴⁰Even if a lawgiver such as God knew all possible circumstances, it would be impossible to enumerate them in a law. That is why one needs the virtue called *epieikeia*, which, as the better part of justice, guides the judgment in the matter of departing from the letter of the law. See ST IIa IIae, q. 120.

⁴¹This is the reason Aquinas thinks it appropriate that God reveal not only things which human reason could not know, but matters which people *could* know by using natural intelligence, but which it is unlikely that many will know in fact. See ST Ia IIae, q. 99, a. 2, ad 2. He repeats this in many other places with regard to both speculative and practical issues and treats them thematically in SCG I, chap. 4; ST Ia, q. 1, a. 1; Ia IIae, q. 91, a. 4. One should also consider the passages in which he describes how the will is affected by the sense appetite: Ia IIae, q. 9, a. 2; q. 10, a. 3. On how ignorance affects the voluntariness of acts: q. 6, a. 6; q. 19, a. 5.

⁴²Again, as in ST Ia IIae, q. 96, a. 4, he refers to Julius Caesar's account of the barbarians who considered theft to be good, and adds a reference to St. Paul on homosexuality. It would seem that evil beliefs and customs refer to social or cultural pressures;

the corrupt habits more to individual defects. Here, one should study q. 76, a. 1; q. 77, a. 2; and the parallel passages on the ways in which passion can cause ignorance and so impede reason in applying its universal knowledge to a particular action.

[43]The bad customs, evil habits, and the like must also have their start in such a passion. But this does not necessarily imply that such defects are always culpable. When bad customs or beliefs become embedded in society, the individuals living in such a society can hardly be blamed for their ignorance. But some who see the evil in society might be culpable, that is, if they do not do what they can to make people aware of this evil and try to change it.

[44]Arist. *Eth. Nic.* 1.4 (1095a4–12); and 5 (1095b4–13). Thomas comments on this in *In I Ethicorum.*, lect. 3, nn. 38–40; and lect. 4, nn. 53–4 (Marietti, 10–11, 14) .

[45]Daniel Mark Nelson in *The Priority of Prudence: Virtue and Natural Law in Thomas Aquinas and the Implications of This for Modern Ethics* (University Park: Pennsylvania State University Press, 1992) seems to have persuaded many that Aquinas is basically a "virtue ethicist." He thinks that the followers of Aquinas ("the standard interpretation") have "read into him" a primacy of natural law. "In contrast, according to the interpretation I shall give, prudence and the virtues are primary. One looks to the accumulated moral wisdom and the habitual behavior and judgments of virtuous individuals in one's community as the basic source of information about the rightness and wrongness of human action" (2).

[46]"Nam si veritas intellectus practici determinatur in comparatione ad appetitum rectum, appetitus autem rectitudo determinatur per hoc quod consonat rationi verae, ut prius dictum est, sequitur quaedam circulatio in dictis determinationibus. Et ideo dicendum est, quod appetitum est finis et eorum quae sunt ad finem: finis autem determinatus est homini a natura, ut scilicet in tertio habitum est. Ea autem quae sunt ad finem, non sunt nobis determinata a natura, sed per rationem investiganda. Sic ergo manifestum est, quod rectitudo appetitus per respectum ad finem est mensura veritatis in ratione practica. Et secundum hoc determinatur veritas rationis practicae secundum concordiam ad appetitum rectum. Ipsa autem veritas rationis practicae est regula rectitudinis appetitus, circa ea quae sunt ad finem. Et ideo secundum hoc dicitur appetitus rectus, qui prosequitur quae vera ratio dicit."

[47]"Sicut cognitio naturalis semper est vera, ita dilectio naturalis semper est recta, cum amor naturalis nihil aliud sit quam inclinatio naturae indita ab Auctore naturae." See also *De veritate*, q. 16, a. 2 (Leonine, 507–9).

[48]Of course, justice and its many related virtues are in the will, which has no passions in itself, but does need reason's guidance in applying the principles of justice in the face of such passions as greed and fear. See ST Ia IIae, q. 60, a. 2; q. 100, a. 5, ad 1: "Fuit autem dandum praeceptum homini de dilectione Dei et proximi, quia quantum ad hoc lex naturalis obscurata erat propter peccatum; non autem quantum ad dilectionem sui ipsius, quia quantum ad hoc lex naturalis vigebat."

[49]Choice (*electio*) is an act of the will *accepting* the judgment of reason. See ST Ia, q. 83, a. 3, c., and ad 2. But the will is not necessitated to accept the judgment of reason, except the ultimate end and what is clearly seen as necessary to the ultimate end (ST Ia IIae, q. 10, a. 2, c., and ad 3). Perhaps Aquinas's best exposition of how moral evil occurs is *De malo*, q. 1, a. 3 (Leonine, 13–18). It happens when the will does not use in *act* the rule which it possesses *habitually*.

[50]"Et ideo etsi virtus moralis non sit ratio recta, ut Socrates dicebat, non tamen solum est secudum rationem rectam, inquantum inclinat ad id quod est secundum rationem rectam, ut Platonici posuerunt, sed etiam oportet quod sit cum ratione recta, ut Aristoteles dicit in VI *Eth* (1144b21)."

[51]This is the sequence from *consuetudo* to *habitus*. See ST Ia IIae, q. 58, a. 1: "Dicitur autem virtus moralis a more, secundum quod mos significat quandam inclinationem naturalem, vel quasi naturalem, ad aliquid agendum. Et huic significationi moris propinqua est alia significatio, quae significat consuetudinem; nam consuetudo quodammodo vertitur in naturam, et facit inclinationem similem naturali." As Thomas often states, the appetites are not governed as slaves by a master (like our hands or feet), but by "politics," a rule over free men who have a mind of their own (for example, q. 58, a. 2). Nor must passion be eliminated as the Stoics seem to have held; this would make the sense appetite useless (*otiosum*); rather they must be put in order by the force of reason (q. 59, aa. 3–5). Today, one would perhaps say that this is the "interiorization" of the law, at once a cognitive and appetitive growth—one comes to see that virtuous acts are good and is pleased in doing them.

[52]Prudence guides deliberation (*concilium*), but the latter presupposes an end, which could be some subordinate end but above all the ultimate end; also sense knowledge, as that this is bread or iron; and things known by some other speculative or practical science such as that God has forbidden adultery or that one cannot live without appropriate food.

[53]"Necesse est quod fines moralium virtutum praeexistant in ratione . . . ita in ratione practica praeexistunt quaedam ut principia naturaliter nota; et huiusmodi sunt fines virtutum moralium, quia finis se habet in operabilibus sicut principium in speculativis; et quaedam sunt in ratione practica ut conclusiones, et huiusmodi sunt ea quae sunt ad

finem, in quae pervenimus ex ipsis finibus. Et horum est prudentia, applicans universalia principia ad particulares conclusiones operabilium. Et ideo ad prudentiam non pertinet praestituere finem virtutum moralium, sed solum disponere de his quae sunt ad finem." See ad 3: "Finis non pertinet ad virtutes morales tamquam ipsae praestituant finem, sed quia tendunt in finem a ratione naturali praestitutum. Ad quod iuvantur per prudentiam, quae eis viam parat, disponendo ea quae sunt ad finem. Unde relinquitur quod prudentia sit nobilior virtutibus moralibus, et moveat eas. Sed synderesis movet prudentiam, sicut intellectus principiorum scientiam."

In IIa IIae, q. 47, a. 3, Thomas writes that prudence applies universal principles to singular actions, so the *prudens* must know both. See also Ia IIae, q. 13, a. 2, ad 3: the ends of the virtues are ordered to the ultimate end and so can be subject to choice; Ia IIae, q. 53, a. 1: the habits of first principles, speculative or practical, are not subject to corruption by being forgotten or deceived by contrary judgments; Ia IIae, q. 54, a. 3, c., and ad 2: good and evil habits are distinguished by their disposition to acts in accord with or contrary to human nature, and this is the same as their being or not being in accord with reason; Ia IIae, q. 57, a. 4, c., and ad 3: prudence presupposes the rectitude of appetite with regard to ends which is the rectitude of the moral virtues, but prudence is concerned about matters which relate to the *whole life of man* and to the ultimate end of human life; q. 58, a. 4: moral virtue can exist without some intellectual virtues but not without prudence and *intellectus*, that is, without the principles, speculative or practical, naturally known; *De malo*, q. 2, a. 4 (Leonine, 37–42): in human acts good and evil are determined by relation to that which is proper to man as man, that is, reason, so an act is good when it is conformed to reason *informed by divine law either naturally, or by teaching, or by infusion.*

One of the best passages in an early work is *De veritate*, q. 16, a. 2 (Leonine, 507–9). Here, he emphasizes the need of stability and permanence in moral matters. Every movement must be anchored in something immobile. In the case of human actions this unchangeable center is the knowledge of first principles in which there can be no error and in the light of which all other cognitions are examined and approved or rejected. The act of *synderesis* is a preamble to the act of virtue, as the natural is a preamble to acquired or infused virtues.

[54]John Finnis brings out well the evidence of this for some of the "basic goods" in *Natural Law and Natural Rights*, chaps. 3–4.

[55]Several times Aquinas approvingly refers to Aristotle's saying that we must attend to the undemonstrated positions of the experienced, the elders,

and the prudent because experience has given them an eye to see the right thing to do (*Eth. Nic.* 6.12 [1143b11]). Thomas cites this at ST IIa IIae, q. 49, a. 3, where he is discussing *docility* as an integral part of prudence; and at Ia IIae, q. 95, a. 2, ad 4, where he is explaining why there seems to be no reason for some "determinations" of natural law.

[56]See Alasdair MacIntyre, *After Virtue* (Notre Dame, IN: University of Notre Dame Press, 1981); MacIntyre, *Three Rival Versions of Moral Inquiry: Encyclopedia, Genealogy, and Tradition.*

[57]Religion is still the main source for most peoples' moral education, but religious belief also needs the help of reason and philosophy to relate its claims to human needs and to the universe as a whole. Walker Percy has explored this theme in *Lost in the Cosmos: The Last Self-Help Book* (New York: Pocket Books, 1981).

[58]Nelson, in *Priority of Prudence*, reiterates two main complaints about natural law theory. First, it is too general, without specific moral content to give moral guidance. But, as Aquinas frequently remarks, the first principles contain virtually all conclusions, and the latter are tested by reference to the former. Moreover, direction to act virtuously, or justly, or according to reason also have no specific content. The only completely specific content is in the prudential judgment as to what I am to do *now*, in this set of circumstances, and this is beyond moral science.

Second, without prior preparation, Aquinas introduces natural law as "merely explanatory," not as an integral part of his moral theory, which is centered on the virtues. I believe that the texts I have cited about the natural movements of intellect and will, and the problems with the passions, are very good preparation for a culmination in natural law theory; and Aquinas continues to refer to these principles even in his treatise on prudence. As to being explanatory, Aquinas would probably say: "Of course. I am not engaged in personal counselling or or giving 'how to' advice. I am doing moral science, and the function of science (and wisdom) is exactly to explain things through their causes, especially in their ultimate causes."

[59]This raises the question of just where "natural law" ends and human law begins. Thomas is not always clear on this. In ST Ia IIae, q. 100, a. 1, he says that practical reasoning begins with naturally known principles; however, some derived precepts are so clear that they are known quickly with little thought (*statim, cum modica consideratione*); more particular areas require more thought, mostly by experts, as in the speculative sciences. Those first derivations (and here, he enumerates most of the Decalogue) should be known to everyone and are *absolutely* of the law of nature (*absolute de lege naturae*). The more particular determinations, which

require much more thought, belong to the law of nature but require teaching (*disciplina*) by which the wise instruct the inexpert.

When he deals with the traditional Law of Nations (*lex* or *ius gentium*), so-called, according to Isidore, because "almost all peoples use it," he says this law is derived from the law of nature by way of conclusions "not very remote from the principles." Because of this, men easily agree to it. Purely civil law is that appropriate to each community, as determinations of the general principles of natural law. Yet the law of nations is distinct from natural law, especially that common to all animals (Ia IIae, q. 95, a. 4, c., and ad 1). This article must be read in conjunction with IIa IIae, q. 57, a. 3.

It seems that one can say that natural law unconditionally includes the primary principles and very proximate conclusions; further conclusions belong in a way to natural law as conclusions from it, but they are also, in a way, human law as being worked out by human reason, and both are distinct from purely civil laws, which are peculiar to each city. Nevertheless, all natural law precepts may be taken into and sanctioned by civil law. In fact, almost all civil laws are a confection of both these types. They are usually phrased conditionally: If one is convicted of murder in the first degree . . . he or she shall be liable to such and such penalties. In this treatise, Aquinas is primarily concerned with the force and function of civil positive law.

[60]In ST Ia IIae, q. 95, a. 1, Aquinas remarks that those prone to evil are not easily moved by advice, but the force and fear of the laws can at least inhibit them from doing evil and thus leave the rest of the citizens to a "quiet life" (*et aliis quietam vitam redderent*). In q. 96, a. 2, he says that it is not proper to human law to prohibit all the acts of all the vices, since most men are imperfect in virtue, but only the more serious which are harmful to others, without whose prohibition human society could not be preserved. He mentions homicide, theft, "and other such acts." At q. 98, a. 1, he remarks that the end of human law is "the temporal tranquillity of the city" (*temporalis tranquillitas civitatis*) and it arrives at this by prohibiting exterior evil acts which can disturb the peaceful state of the city. It should be remembered that peace has been defined as the tranquillity of order (IIa IIae, q. 29, a. 1, ad 1).

[61]The best succinct expression of this is ST Ia IIae, q. 92, a. 2, ad 4: "Per hoc quod aliquis incipit assuefieri ad vitandum mala et ad implendum bona propter metum poenae, perducitur quandoque ad hoc quod delectabiliter et ex propria voluntate hoc faciat. Et secundum hoc, lex etiam puniendo perducit ad hoc quod homines sunt boni." In q. 96, a. 3, ad 2, he makes clear the distinction between "doing the virtuous acts" (*agere virtuosa*) and doing such acts "virtuously, the way the virtuous person

would do them" (*agere virtuosa virtuose*). Human law requires payment of debts, but it cannot force someone to enjoy it and thus be an honest person. And he says of the latter: "Et talis actus semper procedit a virtute, nec cadit sub praecepto legis, sed est finis ad quem legislator ducere intendit."

[62]Law may command an act of courage for "the preservation of the city, or preserving the right of one's friend" (*vel propter conservationem civitatis, vel ad conservandum ius amici sui*) (ST Ia IIae, q. 58, a. 3). A more familiar example would be that the law cannot demand that one be a temperate person; however, it can command acts of temperance (with regard to drinking) if one is going to drive a car on the streets. This should be read in conjunction with IIa IIae, q. 58, aa. 5–6. General or legal justice deals with what is owed by all citizens to the community and its common good. It is general by its causality (not by predication), for it can demand the acts of any virtue insofar as they affect the common good. He compares this to charity, the finally supreme virtue, which can command the acts of all the other virtues (see q. 23, a. 8).

In Ia IIae, q. 100, a. 9, ad 2, he clearly distinguishes the content of the law (sometimes called its *object*), which is some act of virtue, from its end, which is virtue. "Intentio legislatoris est de duobus. De uno quidem, ad quod intendit per praecepta legis, et hoc est virtus. Aliud autem est de quo intendit praeceptum ferre, et hoc est quod ducit vel disponit ad virtutem, scilicet actus virtutis. Non enim idem est finis praecepti et id de quo praeceptum datur, sicut neque in aliis rebus idem est finis et quod est ad finem."

[63]Finnis gives a good account of this in *Natural Law*, 198–230. See also MacIntyre's critique of Alan Gewirth's theory in *After Virtue*, 64–69.

[64]He had already noted in response to the first objection that terms are often transferred, by metonymy, from their primary meaning to other related meanings (he refers to various meanings of "medicine"). "Right" primarily meant the "right thing" (*rem iustam*), then was transferred to knowledge of right (law) or to the place (court) where right is declared, and so on. This is why he often uses *ius* and *lex* interchangeably.

[65]"Et ideo ipsa ratio gubernationis rerum in Deo sicut in principe universitatis existens, legis habet rationem." Divine providence (*providentia*) and eternal law are the plan or blueprint of the creation and movement of every creature and the universe as a whole to their ends. Governance (*gubernatio*) is the execution of the plan in the movement of the universe, like building the house. Thus, the activity of creatures, as secondary causes, share in governance but not in providence; but humans also share in providence in the sense that, as intelligent and free beings, they can also plan for themselves and others,

as we have seen (ST Ia IIae, q. 91, a. 2; q. 93, a. 2). On the relation of providence (and eternal law) to governance, see Ia, q. 22, aa. 1, 3; q. 103, aa. 1, 6. This is most succinctly expressed in q. 22, a. 1, ad 2: "Ad curam duo pertinent, scilicet ratio ordinis quae dicitur providentia et dispositio; et executio ordinis, quae dicitur gubernatio. Quorum primum est aeternum, secundum temporale."

66There are many other passages on the priority of law. See, for instance, ST Ia IIae, q. 71, a. 6, ad 4: "Si autem referatur ad ius naturale, quod continetur primo quidem in lege aeterna, secundario vero in naturali iudicatorio rationis humanae, tunc omne peccatum est malum quia prohibitum . . ." See also q. 95, a. 4: (Human laws can be divided according to the various functional groups which serve the common good: priests, rulers, soldiers, etc.) "Et ideo istis hominibus specialia quaedam iura aptantur." IIa IIae, q. 60, a. 5: (Must the judgment of courts always follow the written law?) "Iudicium nihil aliud est quam quaedam definitio vel determinatio eius quod est iustum. Fit autem aliquid iustum dupliciter: uno modo ex ipsa natura rei, quod dicitur ius naturale; alio modo ex quodam condicto inter homines, quod dicitur ius positivum . . . . Leges [humanae] autem scribuntur ad utriusque iuris declarationem, aliter tamen et aliter. Nam legis [humanae] scriptura ius quidem naturale continet, sed non instituit; non enim habet robur ex lege [humana] sed ex natura. Ius autem positivum scriptura legis et continet et instituit, dans ei auctoritatis robur." In q. 60, a. 6, ad 1, he repeats that a written (human) law that is contrary to natural right is unjust and has no power of obligating; it is not a law; rather, it is a "corruption" of law.

Also see Ia, q. 21, a. 2, ad 1: "iustitia, quantum ad legem regulantem, est in ratione vel intellectu; sed quantum ad imperium, quo opera regulantur secundum legem, est in voluntate." In Ia, a. 1, ad 2, he says that since the object of the will is the understood good (bonum intellectum), God can will only what is contained in the plan (ratio) of his wisdom, which is, at it were, the law of justice (lex iustitiae). Hence what He does according to His will, He does justly, just as people act justly when they act according to the law.

67Reflection on ST Ia, q. 21, aa. 1–2, and on Ia IIae, q. 21, aa. 3–4, will provide a good overview of what might be called the social architecture of the universe as Aquinas views it.

68This is much more than "settling disputes" and "keeping law and order" as many legal positivists would have it. Law represses evils and educates toward the good.

69See ST Ia IIae, q. 100, a. 5 (communitas seu respublica hominum sub Deo); q. 21, a. 4 (tota communitas universi); IIa IIae, q. 40, a. 4 (respublica fidelium). On God as the extrinsic common good of man and

the universe, see Ia IIae, q. 109, a. 3; IIa IIae, q. 26, a. 3; SCG III, chap. 117; De perf. vit. spir., chap.13, n. 634 (Marietti, 131). The best outline of the hierarchy of ends and of the relation of parts to wholes in man and in the order of the universe is ST Ia, q. 65, a. 2.

70"Nullius hominis sapientia tanta est ut possit omnes singulares casus excogitare; et ideo non potest sufficienter per verba sua exprimere ea quae conveniunt ad finem intentum. Et si posset legislator omnes casus considerare, non oporteret ut omnes exprimeret propter confusionem vitandam; sed legem ferre deberet secundum ea quae in pluribus accidunt." Why then not leave all cases to the determination of wise judges? First, it is easier to find a few wise men to make good laws than to find the multitude of judges necessary for deciding every single case. Second, those who make laws can consider the matter for some time, while judges determine cases, which arise quickly. And it is easier to rightly make a law after the consideration of many cases than from one. Legislators can consider universally and for the future; judges look to the present case and are more likely to be moved in their judgment by love, hate, greed, or some other passion. Hence as far as possible there should be laws to guide judges, and as little as possible left to human judgment (ST Ia IIae, q. 95, a. 1, ad 2). Yet, there are singular matters which cannot be determined by law and must be left to judges (Ia IIae, q. 95, a. 1, ad 3).

71Aquinas holds that law may be changed for two reasons: (1) the development of understanding, which is characteristic of human reason; and (2) a change in the populace and the conditions of life. But he is cautious about changing the law. Custom itself contributes much to the observance of the law (and, of course, makes it difficult to change even for the better). So law should be changed not just for any improvement but when more can be gained by the change than is lost, or when the old law contains manifest injustice or is harmful to many citizens (Ia IIae, q. 97, aa. 1, 2).

72This is obviously difficult in a pluralist society, but even the law should not let morality go by default to the confusions of atheism and relativism. The proliferation of so-called "anti-hate laws" makes one wonder. In criminal investigation, "looking for the motive" is good procedure; furthermore, the despicable motives of a criminal can also move a jury. But strictly speaking, one cannot be charged or punished for his or her motives, but only for the crimes—murder, theft, and the like, and perhaps for inciting a crime by overt acts of speech or writing. Beyond that, legislators are attempting "thought control." See ST Ia IIae, q. 100, a. 9: "Homo autem, qui est legis lator humanae, non habet iudicare nisi de exterioribus actibus. . . . Lex enim humana non punit eum qui vult occidere et non occidet; punit autem lex divina . . ."

[73]In ST Ia IIae, q. 96, a. 2, ad 2, he refers to a saying from Proverbs: If you blow your nose too hard, you draw blood. In another passage, he refers to the Gospel parable of the "wheat and the tares": Let them grow together and separate them at the harvest. This "non-intervention" itself derives from eternal law: "Quod lex humana dicitur aliqua permittere, non quasi ea approbans, sed quasi ea dirigere non potens . . . plura subduntur causae superiori quam inferiori. Unde hoc ipsum quod lex humana non se intromittat de his quae dirigere non potest, ex ordine legis aeternae provenit. Secus autem esset si approbaret ea quae lex aeterna reprobat. Unde ex hoc non habetur quod lex humana non derivetur a lege aeterna, sed quod non perfecte eam assequi possit" (Ia IIae, q. 93, a. 3, ad 3).

In IIa IIae, q. 77, a. 1, ad 1, he refers to two matters which the law leaves alone: simple fornication and moderate fudging on the price of an item in buying and selling. He also remarks that the "just price" for goods or services in not an exact point but an estimate that leaves some stretch. As such, one can hardly expect perfect justice in this life.

[74]He obviously likes Isidore's description of the *quality* of human laws as adapted to the situation of the people (ST Ia IIae, q. 95, a. 3); he refers back to this several times in his own treatise.

[75]See ST Ia IIae, q. 21, aa. 3–4. These best bring out the human and divine realms of distributive justice in communities. Note that since each person is a *part* of a community, even injury to oneself (private sin?) redounds to the community and merits retribution. But, in q. 21, a. 4, ad 3, Thomas makes a clear distinction as to what is owed to the political community and what is owed to the community of humans under God.

[76]All of these are precisely in passages where Thomas deals with the derivation of human law from eternal and natural law. One must also note that Aquinas holds that, among a free people, custom (*consuetudo*) can make, interpret, or abolish human law (ST Ia IIae, q. 97, a. 3). This is consistent with his position in q. 90, a. 3: making law belongs primarily to the people as a whole. Finnis gives a good account of custom becoming law in the international community (*Natural Law*, 238–45).

[77]In ST Ia IIae, q. 93, a. 3, ad 2, he does grant that such laws have some "similitude" to law, because they come from a legitimate authority which itself derives from eternal law. Yet, "Inquantum vero a ratione recedit, sic dicitur lex iniqua; et sic non habet rationem legis, sed magis violentiae cuiusdam." This does not justify calling such "procedurally just laws" analogously law, and merely a declension from the prime analogate. Not every similitude makes an analogy. Some cavil at the expression: "An unjust law is not a law," as though it were an oxymoron. But they seem to accept: "An unconstitutional law is invalid, that is, is not a law." Has "false gold" become proper gold?

[78]See ST Ia IIae, q. 104, aa. 1–5, where Thomas is dealing with the judicial precepts of the Old Law, which concern the social and political organization of the chosen people. In q. 104, a. 1, ad 2, he describes the scope of the *iudicialia*. It is clear that he considers such precepts binding only *ex institutione*, divine or human. Since the Old Law has been superseded, there is no particular form of government and social organization which is mandatory, although Aquinas clearly prefers the "mixed constitution." The "art" of the legislator must adapt the regime to the people, and the people may change from one type to another and so change the legal *determinationes*.

[79]This is explained in this volume's "Thomistic Moral Philosophy in the Twentieth Century," specifically in the section on Yves Simon.

[80]Aquinas refers to it (*scientia civilis*) as the principal and architectonic work of human practical reason, as concerned with the ultimate and complete good in human affairs. *In I Politicorum*, Proemium, 7 (Marietti, 2).

[81]This is licit even for a private person when there is an emergency, but if there is time and opportunity the private person should consult the prince, who has the power to dispense from the law (ST Ia IIae, q. 97, a. 4). For directions for judges on interpreting the written law, see IIa IIae, q. 60, a. 5, ad 2–3.

Selected Further Reading

Arkes, Hadley. "'Nature Herself Has Placed in Our Ears a Power of Judging': Some Reflections on the Naturalism of Cicero." In *Natural Law Theory*. Ed. Robert P. George. Oxford: Clarendon, 1992.

Armstrong, Ross A. *Primary and Secondary Precepts in Thomistic Natural Law Teaching*. The Hague: Nijhoff, 1966.

Bourke, Vernon J. "Is Aquinas a Natural Law Ethicist." *The Monist* 58 (1974): 52–66.

Brown, Oscar J. *Natural Rectitude and Divine Law: An Approach to an Integral Interpretation of the Thomistic Doctrine of Law*. Toronto: Pontifical Institute of Medieval Studies, 1981.

Budziszewski, J. *Written on the Heart: The Case for Natural Law*. Downers Grove, IL: Intervarsity, 1996.

Chroust, Anton-Hermann. "The Philosophy of Law of St. Thomas Aquinas: His Fundamental Ideas and Some of His Historical Predecessors." *American Journal of Jurisprudence* 19 (1974): 1–38.

Collins, Joseph, O.P. "God's Eternal Law." *The Thomist* 23 (1960): 497–532.

Cromartie, Michael, ed. *A Preserving Grace: Protestants, Catholics, and Natural Law*. Grand Rapids, MI: Eerdmans, 1996.

Crowe, Frederick. "Complacency and Concern in the Thought of St. Thomas." *Theological Studies* 20 (1959): 1–39, 198–230, 343–82.

Crowe, M. B. "St. Thomas and Ulpian's Natural Law." In *Commemorative Studies*. Vol. 1. Ed. Armand Maurer. Toronto: Pontifical Institute of Medieval Studies, 1974.

D'Entrèves, A. P. *Natural Law: An Introduction to Legal Philosophy*. 2d ed. London: Hutchison University Library, 1970.

Eschmann, I. T., O.P. "A Thomistic Glossary on the Principle of the Preeminence of a Common Good." *Medieval Studies* 5 (1943): 125–65.

Finnis, John. *Natural Law and Natural Rights*. Oxford: Clarendon, 1980.

Fortin, Ernest. "Thomas Aquinas." In *History of Political Philosophy*. Ed. Leo Strauss and Joseph Cropsey. 3d ed. Chicago: University of Chicago Press, 1987.

George, Robert P., ed. *Natural Law Theory: Contemporary Essays*. Oxford: Clarendon, 1992.

———. *Natural Law and Moral Inquiry*. Washington, DC: Georgetown University Press, 1997.

Grisez, Germain. "The First Principles of Practical Reason: Commentary on S.T., I–II, Q.94, a. 2." *Natural Law Forum* 10 (1965): 168–201.

Hart, H. L. A. *The Concept of Law*. Oxford: Oxford University Press, 1961.

Hauerwas, Stanley, and Charles Pinches. *Christians among the Virtues: Theological Conversations with Ancient and Modern Ethics*. Notre Dame, IN: University of Notre Dame Press, 1997.

Henle, R. J. *St Thomas Aquinas: The Treatise on Law*. Notre Dame, IN: University of Notre Dame Press, 1993.

Hittinger, Russell. "Natural Law and Virtue." In *Natural Law Theory*. Ed. Robert P. George. Oxford: Clarendon, 1992.

———. *A Critique of the New Natural Law Theory*. Notre Dame, IN: University of Notre Dame Press, 1987.

May, William E. "The Meaning and Nature of Natural Law in Thomas Aquinas." *American Journal of Jurisprudence* 22 (1977): 168–89.

Maritain, Jacques. *Man and the State*. Chicago: University of Chicago Press, 1951.

McInerny, Ralph. *Ethica Thomistica: The Moral Philosophy of Thomas Aquinas*. Washington, DC: Catholic University of America Press, 1982.

Nelson, Daniel Mark. *The Priority of Prudence: Virtue and Natural Law in Thomas Aquinas and the Implications of this for Modern Ethics*. University Park: Pennsylvania State University Press, 1992.

O'Connor, D. J. *Aquinas and Natural Law*. London: Macmillan, 1967.

Phelan, Gerald B. "Law and Morality." In *Progress in Philosophy: Philosophical Studies in Honor of Rev. Doctor Charles A. Hart*. Ed. James A. McWilliams, S.J. Milwaukee: Bruce, 1955.

———. "Justice and Friendship." In *G. B. Phelan: Selected Papers*. Ed. Arthur G. Kirn. Toronto: Pontifical Institute of Medieval Studies, 1967. Also published as "Justice and Friendship," *The Thomist* 5 (1943): 153–70.

Pieper, Josef. *The Four Cardinal Virtues*. Notre Dame, IN: University of Notre Dame Press, 1966.

Schall, James V. *Reason, Revelation, and the Foundations of Political Philosophy*. Baton Rouge: Louisiana State University Press, 1987.

Sigmund, Paul. *Natural Law in Political Thought*. Cambridge, MA: Winthrop, 1971.

Simon, Yves R. *The Tradition of Natural Law: A Philosopher's Reflections*. Ed. Vukan Kuic. New York: Fordham University Press, 1965.

Strauss, Leo. "Natural Law." In *International Encyclopedia of the Social Sciences*. Vol. 2. Ed. David L. Sills. New York: Macmillan, 1968.

Tonneau, J., O.P. "The Teaching of the Thomist Tract on Law." *The Thomist* 34 (1970): 13–83.

Veatch, Henry. *Swimming Against the Current in Contemporary Philosophy*. Washington, DC: Catholic University of America Press, 1990.

Werne, Stanley J. "Natural Law: A Way to Meaning in the World of Law." *Proceedings: American Catholic Philosophical Association* 64 (1991): 231–39.

The Old Law and the New Law
(Ia IIae, qq. 98–108)

Pamela M. Hall

Aquinas's treatment of divine law comes last among his treatment of laws within the *Summa theologiae*, following upon his discussions of eternal, natural, and human law.[1] In turning to the Old and New Laws, he does not leave behind his earlier discussions of law. Rather, Aquinas understands divine law to function in relation to both natural and human law, and, as must all authentic law, to be an expression of eternal law (God's governance of the cosmos). Natural, human, and divine law all pertain to God's means of governance of human beings. Aquinas explains that natural law is the rational creature's "participation" in eternal law (Ia IIae, q. 91, a. 2). Human law works to determine and specify natural law, and it derives its authority from natural law (Ia IIae, q. 95, a. 2).

Divine law is then necessary for human beings for four reasons, according to Aquinas (Ia IIae, q. 91, a. 4). First, natural law is itself inadequate to direct men and women to their ultimate end, union with God. Human beings require help from God to achieve this supernatural end.[2] Likewise, divine law is needed to correct and supplement the uncertainty of human judgment about "what [one] should do and what one should avoid."[3] Aquinas's last two reasons pertain to the scope of human law's regulation: divine law can extend beyond the governing of action to the regulation of interior acts, thus promoting "perfection of virtue"; further, in keeping with this goal, divine law must "forbid or punish" all sins, even those which might go uncorrected by human law.[4]

Aquinas then considers the diversity of the divine law: it is comprised of the old and the new (Ia IIae, q. 91, a. 5). Both are given by God, but are distinct "as perfect and imperfect in the same species, such as a boy and a man."[5] The Old Law is imperfect law for the imperfect: it orders toward an earthly good; it orders external acts alone; it motivates obedience by fear. The New Law, on the other hand, orders men and women toward "an intelligible and celestial good."[6] It directs even interior movements of the soul; lastly, it moves men and women through love to obey it, a love which is given in the grace of Christ. In this initial description of these laws' differences, Aquinas harshly contrasts the work of the Old and New Laws. It is only in this last point, regarding the motivations for obedience to divine law, that Aquinas indicates more clearly a connection between the works of the Old and New Laws: the grace of Christ which confers love for the law is "prefigured" in the Old Law. In his replies to objections, Aquinas also suggests a moral pedagogy at work in the historical transition from the Old to the New Law:

> Just as a father in a household sets forth different mandates for children and adults, also in this way the one king God in his one kingdom gave to men one law when they were yet imperfect and another more perfect law when, through the prior law, they had been led to a greater capacity for divine things.[7] (Ia IIae, q. 91, a. 5, ad 1)

Aquinas's substantive discussions of the Old and New Laws (Ia IIae, qq. 98–108) will expand and transform these specifications of the Old Law's work—of prefiguration and moral preparation for the New Law—in surprising ways.

THE OLD LAW

Thomas begins Ia IIae, q. 98, with a discussion of the Old Law's purposes and limits. The Old Law could not effect the union with God which is the end of divine law; it was thus imperfect. How then did it serve as divine law, ordering the Jewish people to God? First, the Old Law ordered to Christ by "giving testimony to Christ" (Ia IIae, q. 98, a. 2, c.).[8] Second, it ordered to Christ by moral education: "by drawing men away from idolatry, it confined them to the worship of the one God, by whom humankind was to be saved through Christ" (Ia IIae, q. 98, a. 2).[9] Thus far, the Old Law's work seems clear enough: it testifies to Christ by foreshadowing in prophecy. It also prepares morally by educating the Jewish people in worship of the true God. Aquinas then proceeds to complicate this picture.

> God sometimes permits some to fall into sin so that then they may be humbled. Thus did he wish to give a law which men by their own powers were not able to fulfill: so that, while relying on themselves, they would discover they were sinners, and, humbled, turn to the help of grace.[10] (Ia IIae, q. 98, a. 2, ad 3)

God commanded the Jews to obey a law they could not fully obey. The Old Law could not confer the grace necessary for complete fulfillment of its own precepts. Aquinas tells us that the Old Law's impotence in this regard was part of its pedagogy: by commanding what they could not fulfill, the Old Law taught the Jews their own sinfulness and, thereby, their need for grace.[11]

He concludes this section with the questions of who was bound by the Old Law and why it was given at the time of Moses. His answers serve to deepen and clarify the Old Law's pedagogy by connecting it to knowledge of the natural law. Aquinas first argues that all men and women (apart from the Jewish people specifically) were not in fact obligated to obey the Old Law, except insofar as the law "manifested" the natural law. In this way, all were bound to observe the Old Law at least in these precepts, "not because [the precepts] were of the Old Law but because they were of the natural law" (Ia IIae, q. 98, a. 5).[12] The Old Law thus expressed at least in part a moral teaching accessible to even gentiles through the natural law.

Aquinas proceeds to the question of the appropriateness of the time of the Old Law's revelation. In his answer, he deepens his narrative of the Old Law's pedagogy.

> [Law] is imposed on two kinds of men, on the hard and the proud, who through law are curbed and mastered, and the good, who instructed by law are helped to complete what they intend. Therefore it was appropriate that the Old Law was given at such a time for the overcoming of human pride. For man was proud of two things—knowledge and power. [He was proud in his] knowledge, as though natural reason were sufficient for salvation; thus, so that his pride should be overcome in this regard, man was given up to the rule of his reason without the support of a written law. And man was able to learn from experience through this that he suffered from a defect of reason, since around the time of Abraham men lapsed into idolatry and the basest vices. Therefore it was necessary after this time that a written law be given for the remedy of human ignorance. . . . But after man had been instructed by the law, his pride was overcome by weakness, since he was not able to do what he knew. With respect to the good, the Law was given as an aid, which was then most necessary for the people, since the natural law had begun to be obscured through the profusion of sins.[13] (Ia IIae, q. 98, a. 6, c.)

Here, Aquinas sketches a narrative of the moral deterioration of men and women after the fall (and note the forms of their pride: knowledge and power).[14] Left on their own, without even a written law, human beings fell into habitual sin of the "basest" sorts, including idolatry. This Aquinas seems to take as a rebuke to human pride in knowledge, since their reason could not suffice even to show them the error of idolatry. But the education of the Jewish people does not end there. Even with the revelation of the Old Law, human beings "learned from experience" that they could not do even what they now recognized as good. So too is human pride in their power humbled. Even for those "good" who had not lapsed into such sins, Aquinas tells us, the Old Law was given as a kind of clarification of the natural law, knowledge of which was somehow "obscured" by sin.

Note a comprehensive assumption within Aquinas's narrative of moral decline here. Aquinas clearly indicates that ignorance of the natural law *and* recognition of that ignorance were both historical and empirical processes.[15] Both ignorance and rediscovery took place over time and through experience. How could this be so? To understand, one must consider what Aquinas has earlier said concerning the natural law. Aquinas explains in Ia IIae, q. 91, a. 2, that the natural law is, at core, our way of being directed to our connatural end. He tells us that this end is constituted by our "directednesses" to certain sets of natural goods: self-sustenance, family and generation, and specifically rational goods, including communal life and knowledge of God (Ia IIae, q. 94, a. 2, c.).[16] The natural law is primarily this ordered hierarchy of desires to sets of goods. As rational creatures, therefore, we must learn to discover and enact this ordering, thus actualizing our teleology. Discovery can only accompany enactment of the natural law, and enactment occurs progressively, not just within discrete actions: humans appropriate the teleology of our natures, more and more, as we reflect it in our lives as a whole. Thus do we effectively order ourselves (in keeping with our dignity as rational creatures) to the ends that we possess by natural law. Should we fail in so appropriating the natural law, Thomas is very clear that our knowledge of the natural law also fails. We lose the (prudential) understanding of our good as we cease to enact ordination to our good.

Within his narrative of the Jewish people under the Old Law, Aquinas indicates that knowledge of the natural law was so lost after the fall progressively—as it ceased to be enacted within individual lives *and* whole communities. Aquinas argues so too knowledge had to be regained progressively, by the renewal of actions, practices, and habits that expressed the natural law as a hierarchy of ordinations to natural goods. But not just this: expressed in the Jewish way of life must also be acknowledgement of all these goods as given by God, their creator and source.

The Old Law at its core thus prepared the way for the New Law by its moral pedagogy: it helped the Jewish people to relearn the natural law. Part of the Old Law's pedagogy was to teach the Jews that they *were* sinners,

idolatrous and venal; it was to teach them that they were unable even to secure their natural good and thus that they stood in need of help from God. The Old Law, that first stage of the Divine Law, functions as both clarification of the need for help and as the initiation of the remedy needed. Within the whole of his remaining discussion of the Old Law (Ia IIae, qq. 99–105), Aquinas presents this law's purpose as a historical—and lived—process of reorientation toward God.

With Ia IIae, q. 99, Aquinas begins a meticulously detailed discussion of the Old Law's precepts. He tells us that there are many and diverse precepts belonging to the Old Law, all conducing toward the end of friendship between human beings and with God (Ia IIae, q. 99, a. 1, ad 2).[17] Old Law contained "moral precepts," distinct from the moral teaching of the natural law, in two respects at least. The Old Law adds to or clarifies the natural law in part by providing clarification of the "particulars regarding what is to be done" (Ia IIae, q. 99, a. 2, ad 2).[18] Such clarification was needed because of the moral obscurity produced by the "consuetude" of sinning. Also, the Old Law provided an authoritative correction to grosser errors of reason: because "the reason of many judged to be lawful things that are evil in themselves" (ibid.).[19] In both respects, the moral precepts of the Old Law corrected and clarified interpretations of the natural law.

But the Old Law also contained other kinds of precepts, the ceremonial and judicial. These, Aquinas tells us, pertain to the life of the Jewish people in distinct ways. The ceremonial precepts direct those acts and observances pertaining to the worship of God. As such, they are "determinations" of the natural law, precepts that command acknowledgement of the true God as God (Ia IIae, q. 99, a. 3, ad 2). The judicial precepts direct and command the Jewish people with regard to justice among themselves; as such, the judicial precepts also determine and specify the natural law, which in its generality requires determination (Ia IIae, q. 99, a. 4, c.). Note already the root characterization of the three kinds of precepts within the Old Law: the moral precepts themselves restate or clarify the natural law with regard to what is good and evil; the ceremonial precepts determine, in a way specific to the Jews, the part of the natural law pertaining to God and right worship of God; and the judicial precepts direct the relations of the Jewish people with respect to what is just. All the precepts of the Old Law thus belong, diversely, to the natural law by way of clarification or further specification of it. All the precepts likewise are intended for the reconsecration of the Jews to God. I will follow Thomas's own ordering and proceed to his detailed discussion of the moral precepts.

All the moral precepts of the Old Law "pertain to the law of nature, but in diverse ways," depending on the clarity and the simplicity of the natural law reasoning that would support them (Ia IIae, q. 100, a. 1, c.).[20] Certain moral precepts, for example, "honor your father and mother," seem accessible to natural reason with little reflection. Other precepts pertain to the natural law, but as judged so by the wise in the community. (Aquinas cites a command to respect the aged in this regard.) Other precepts even require "divine instruction," although they belong to the natural law: Aquinas cites the decalogue's prohibition against carved images as an example of this kind of moral precept (ibid.).[21]

All the moral precepts of the Old Law, Aquinas goes on to argue, can be reduced to the decalogue. It contains precepts evident to natural reason and "those which were made known at once by faith divinely infused" (ibid.).[22] The decalogue omits two sorts of natural law precepts: those "first and general" principles that are evident to natural reason, and those principles that are known through the counsel and teaching of the wise (q. 100, a. 3, c.).[23] Aquinas clearly indicates that the decalogue did not articulate all natural law precepts; instead, it addressed only those that needed clarifying. Those most general principles, he explained earlier, cannot utterly be effaced from the "human heart" (q. 94, a. 6, c.).[24] Thus, they do not need restatement in the decalogue. The teachings of the wise rely on, and presuppose, the community for their transmission. These too do not require rearticulation, since the decalogue itself is revealed to a community. What then is commanded in the decalogue and why?

In ordering the precepts of the decalogue, Aquinas organizes it in terms of two regions of

attention: God and neighbor (Ia IIae, q. 100, a. 4, *sed contra*). The first three precepts pertain to how God is to be worshipped; the last seven pertain to relations between human beings. All the precepts of the decalogue "order man to a community or republic of men under God" (Ia IIae, q. 100, a. 5, c.).[25] Thus, the first three precepts command and help to determine "fidelity, reverence, and service" in relation to the master of this community, God (ibid.).[26] Idolatry is expressly forbidden (in keeping with fidelity), God is to be honored in speech (in keeping with reverence), and the Sabbath should be observed as service to God "in memory of the creation of all things" (ibid.).[27] The other seven precepts direct the Jewish people in relation to each other both with regard to specific relationships (as in child to parent or between spouses) and more universally (as in the prohibition against murder). Aquinas notes that the decalogue's precepts are intended to direct not only actions, but words and thoughts as well. The decalogue is therefore intended to promote full virtue (Ia IIae, q. 100, a. 9, ad 2).

The decalogue is meant to foster virtue. Yet it seems silent on certain matters, such as a person's duties to himself or herself. In explaining this, Aquinas recurs explicitly to his earlier narrative about the deterioration of knowledge of the natural law after the fall. The decalogue speaks of love of God and neighbor "because in this regard the natural law had become obscured because of sin, but not with respect to love of oneself, because in this regard the natural law flourished" (Ia IIae, q. 100, a. 5, ad 1).[28] The very selection of the decalogue's precepts is determined not just by the natural law itself, but by the ignorance of the natural law created historically through the effects of sin. Idolatry is expressly forbidden, for this is one vice to which the Jewish community is prone. Love of God and neighbor is directed and specified because understanding of what this consists in has been obscured by sin.

The Jews are reeducated in the very law of their natures by the decalogue. Thus, observance of it orders men and women toward God. The decalogue's precepts themselves for this reason hold without exception and do not admit of dispensation (Ia IIae, q. 100, a. 8, c.).

If therefore there are precepts which themselves contain the preservation of the common good or the order of justice and virtue, such precepts contain the intention of the legislator, and for this reason are indispensable . . . . And the precepts of the Decalogue contain the intention itself of the legislator, namely God. For the precepts of the first table, which order to God, contain the order itself to the common and final good, which is God. And the precepts of the second table contain the order to be observed among men, namely that no one do what is undue, and that to each should be returned what is owed: for in this manner the precepts of the Decalogue should be understood. For this reason, the precepts of the Decalogue are altogether indispensable.[29] (ibid.)

The decalogue cannot be dispensed with because it expresses in its laws what it means to be rightly ordered to God and in relation to created goods. This is the very intention of God in giving the divine law. As Aquinas notes in a remarkable reply to an objection, for God to dispense someone from the decalogue would be to "make lawful that a man not order himself toward God, or not to be under his order of justice . . ." (Ia IIae, q. 100, a. 8, ad 2).[30] To fail in the decalogue is to fail to be directed to God as last end and to others in relation to God. To be rightly tutored by the Old Law is to recognize that this is the law's heart. To be rightly tutored by the Old Law is to enact this law pervasively in individual lives and in the life of a community.

In this way, in the enactment of ordination to God and of all things to God, do the ceremonial and judicial precepts work together with the moral precepts. Recall that Aquinas has already characterized the ceremonial and judicial precepts of the Old Law as "determinations" of the natural law with regard to Divine worship and with regard to justice among the Jews. He notes that they are as well "determinative of the precepts of the Decalogue" because they were divinely "instituted" to serve as such for the Jewish people (Ia IIae, q. 100, a. 11, ad 2).[31] That is, the ceremonial and judicial precepts are related to the natural law, to which the decalogue can be reduced, as special determinations (for the Jewish people) of what it means to be ordered rightly to God and neighbor. In this regard, they do not *express* the "intention of the legislator" in the same way that the decalogue's precepts themselves do. They are not intrinsically constitutive of virtue for all people everywhere. Still, for the Jews, they specify precisely and in a multitude of ways how God should be worshipped and how justice is to be enacted among persons. Thus, they conduce toward the acquisition of virtue, which is the decalogue's pedagogical purpose.

Following his analysis of the decalogue, Aquinas addresses first the ceremonial precepts, examining them "in themselves," then their "causes," and their "duration" (Ia IIae, qq. 101–3). He assigns to these precepts a twofold purpose: moral education of the Jews and prefiguration of Christ and the grace of Christ, the New Law (Ia IIae, q. 101, aa. 1–2). Aquinas describes the Old Law's ceremonial precepts as designed in part to suppress the habits of the idolatrous among the Jews—by supplanting these habits with a multitude of alternative pieties in honor of the true God:

Again, [it was necessary] to impose many things on such people, so that as though weighed down by these things, by which they were devoted to the worship of God, they would have no time to serve idols. With regard to those inclined to good, the multiplication of the ceremonial precepts was necessary: because through this their minds were referred to God in diverse ways and more constantly, and because the mystery of Christ, which the ceremonial precepts prefigured, brought many benefits to the world.[32] (q. 101, a. 3, c.)

The ceremonial precepts thus address, just as did the selection of the decalogue's precepts, the exigencies of the Jewish community at this time in history. Old habits of idolatry must be uprooted for new habits of right devotion to the one God. At worst, for the worst, these ceremonial precepts curb idolatrous acts. At best, for those inclined already to the true God, such practices make more comprehensive their ordination to God and to created goods in relation to God. Note thus that the ceremonial precepts reinforce and express specifically what is commanded in the first three precepts of the decalogue.

The ceremonial precepts themselves pertain to four areas: sacrifices, sacred things (objects such as the tabernacle), sacraments (acts of consecration), and observances (religious rites of observance; Ia IIae, q. 101, a. 4). Aquinas addresses each in turn, locating in minutely detailed discussion the literal and figurative "causes" of each of the ceremonial precepts within each of these categories (Ia IIae, q. 102, a. 2). His discussion is a concentrated search to locate in each such prescription or prohibition a purpose and intelligibility—in terms of the moral reformation of the Jewish people *and* in terms of prefiguration of Christ, the Old Law's fulfillment (ibid.). The ceremonial precepts possess a "literal cause" insofar as they serve present ends of moral pedagogy for the Jews; they have a "figurative" or "mystical cause" insofar as they pertain more directly to the New Law in some respect: "In another way reasons can be assigned to them as they are ordered to the prefiguring of Christ. In this way, they have figurative and mystical reasons, whether they are taken from Christ himself and the church, which pertains to allegory, or to the mores of the Christian people, which pertains to morals, or to the state of future glory, as we are brought to it through Christ, which pertains to anagogy" (Ia IIae, q. 102, a. 2, c.).[33]

An illustration of this mode of discussion is in order. Consider Aquinas's discussion of the literal and figurative reasons for the ceremonies pertaining to sacrifices. He begins by mounting a number of objections to there being "appropriate" causes of the precepts, debating what should have been included or excluded for sacrifice (q. 102, a. 3, obj. 1–14). He then responds, affirming again that all the ceremonial precepts had a literal and figurative cause. And what were they for the sacrificial prescriptions? Aquinas assigns two literal causes for sacrifices:

> in one way, according to which the sacrifices represented the ordination of the mind to God, to which the person offering the sacrifice was aroused. For the right ordination of the mind to God, man should recognize that all things he has are from God as first principle and order them to God as ultimate end. And this was represented in oblations and sacrifices. . . . In another way [a literal cause can be found], from the way that men were withdrawn from sacrificing to idols. Whence the precepts about sacrifices were not given to the Jewish people until they had descended into idolatry . . . as

though these sacrifices were instituted so that the people, quick to sacrifice, would offer sacrifices to God rather than idols.[34] (Ia IIae, q. 102, a. 3, c.)

Note some features of this explanation. First, Aquinas establishes the spiritual lesson to be drawn from the sacrificial prescriptions; this lesson pertains precisely to the decalogue's point and purpose. Such sacrifices, as instances of the ceremonial precepts, are intended to refer the minds of the participants to God, to remind them that God is giver of all good things, and that all created goods are subordinated to God as last end. The decalogue itself commands that God be loved with the entire heart and that all things be subordinated to God as last end (Ia IIae, q. 100, a. 10, ad 2). Thus the ceremonial precepts specify and, when observed, help the Jewish people to enact their ordination to God. Second, Aquinas again suggests in the selection of the ceremonial precepts, as with the decalogue's prohibition of graven images, a historical context and concern within the Old Law's formation. The sacrificial prescriptions were commanded in part to target, and then to transform, the practice of sacrificing to idols by some of the Jews. The mystical cause of the sacrificial precepts was, Aquinas goes on to say, of course the sacrifice of Christ himself, God's highest gift to men and women, for the redemption of humankind.[35]

But these ceremonial precepts cease to bind, and become even occasions of mortal sin, with the coming of Christ. The moral precepts of the Old Law, as stated in the decalogue, have enduring authority and will not be superseded (Ia IIae, q. 100, a. 8, ad 3). But these ceremonies (*caeremonialia*) are intended to be prefigurations, and thus they function as false "professions of faith" in the time of the New Law (Ia IIae, q. 103, a. 4).[36] What is honest devotion in the Jews before Christ, to testify to the coming of Christ by the ceremonial precepts, is grievous sin after Christ: for it is to say what is now false about Christ, that he is still to come. Aquinas asserts in his argument here both the connection of the Old Law to Christ and its (ceremonial) obsolescence within the New Law.

Next, I will turn to the third group of precepts of the Old Law, the judicial precepts (Ia

IIae, qq. 104–5). Aquinas, just as in his treatment of the ceremonial precepts, assigns the judicial precepts both literal and figurative causes. He reiterates that the Jews were ordered rightly with regard to others by means of the judicial precepts. As such, they operated as specifications of what justice was within their particular community, and this, he tells his readers, is their chief purpose (Ia IIae, q. 104, a. 1, c.). But they serve also to prefigure Christ "by consequence" rather than in themselves (as with the ceremonial precepts), "insofar as the whole state of that people, who were disposed by these precepts, was figurative" (Ia IIae, q. 104, a. 2).[37]

Aquinas's meaning here is obscure, and he attempts to clarify later: since God chose the Jews so that Christ would be born from them, the "entire state of that people" was "prophetic and figurative," including even their laws and their wars (Ia IIae, q. 104, a. 2, ad 2).[38] It is at least evident from these remarks that Aquinas marks a difference between the kind of prefiguration of the ceremonial precepts and that of the judicial precepts. The latter seem to prefigure Christ only insofar as everything the Jewish people did prefigured Christ in some way.[39] Their literal cause, however, is clearer: to specify for the Jewish community what justice requires in various relationships. Aquinas's ensuing discussion of the judicial precepts in fact centers on the ways they regulated conduct with respect to rulers, other Jews, aliens, and household members, including slaves (Ia IIae, q. 105, aa. 1–4). Aquinas's treatment marks the appropriateness of the precepts in their content and in what they sought to regulate. They do not bind forever because now, Aquinas argues, the coming of Christ has altered "the state of that people," namely the Jews (Ia IIae, q. 104, a. 3).[40] Now, Aquinas tells us, there is "in Christ no distinction between Gentile and Jew, as there was before" (q. 104, a. 3, ad 3).[41] Since the coming of Christ the Jews have no reason to exist within a separate state. They were chosen by God, set apart by God as the people into which Christ would be born; they were prepared for Christ by all the multifarious operations of the Old Law—and now Christ has come. The civil laws of the Jewish state thus cease to bind as the legitimacy of that polity ends.[42]

To summarize Aquinas's account of the Old Law: the moral portion of the Old Law is reducible to the decalogue according to Thomas; and the decalogue, he argues, is itself a restatement of the natural law. Such a restatement was necessary, he notes, because of human fallibility *and* because of the progression of our sinful ignorance. Thus the decalogue clarified what needed clarifying because of increasing failure to enact the natural law: specifically, how to worship God and respect our neighbor. Taken as a whole, the Commandments are, if obeyed in the spirit of the Law, constitutive of virtue. They "contain the very intention of the legislator, namely God" (Ia IIae, q. 100, a. 8). For the Jews, perfect obedience to the Law was a loving enactment of their human orientation to the good and a love expressed through the many ceremonial practices of the Law and through the civil laws of the Jewish community. This enactment was a reactivation of the teleology of their natures and of their desire for God as last end. Full obedience to the natural law, and of the Old Law, simply is the realization of a way of life ordered to God and to created goods in relation to God. The ceremonial precepts in this regard, with the judicial precepts, helped to create and support right ordination to God and to God's creation *as a way of life*.

Aquinas also repeatedly stresses the continuities in faith between the Old Law and the New Law, beyond even that of prefiguration and moral preparation. Both Old and New Laws are divine in origin, and of the same kind. He states, within a denial of the ceremonial precepts' power to justify, that some

> at the time of the law were united to Christ incarnate . . . as they were justified by faith in Christ, of which faith the observance of these ceremonies was a declaration, insofar as they were prefigurations of Christ. For this reason they offered sacrifices for sins in the Old Law, not because such sacrifices themselves purified from sin but because they were declarations of faith, which purified from sin.[43] (Ia IIae, q. 103, a. 2, c.)

This is a remarkable passage in many respects. Aquinas argues flatly that the ceremonial precepts did not justify and could not purify from sin. But the *faith of those who prayed for purification*, within these rites, which prefigured the redemption though Christ, could accomplish union with Christ. Here, the distinction between the moral and the prefigurative functions of the Old Law's ceremonial precepts seems to waver: the prefigurative purpose of the precepts transforms the moral purpose, and what is prayed for in fact is accomplished. Aquinas even seems to suggest that some of the Jews had a faith in Christ that was "explicit," not merely imbedded in the prefigurative aspects of the precepts.[44]

Yet the Old Law as a whole cannot function to justify or to reconcile for Aquinas. The ceremonial and judicial precepts can order toward God, but they cannot confer the grace necessary to accomplish their own purposes. Even in the passage above, it is the faith in Christ, and Christ's (retroactive?) grace that makes possible purification. But now we reach the limits of the natural law and of the Old Law. On Aquinas's view, the Old Law, observed most ardently, can only magnify desire for God; it cannot satisfy it.[45] For the Jewish community as a whole, the Old Law cannot accomplish reconciliation with God. The New Law is the law which completes the Old for Aquinas.

THE NEW LAW

Aquinas's treatment of the New Law is comparatively brief (Ia IIae, qq. 106–8). His discussion of New Law opens into a treatment of grace (Ia IIae, qq. 109–14), which is the New Law's core, and then into the *Secunda secundae's* magisterial examination of the virtues within the life of grace. Aquinas's account of the Old Law is intended to address an epoch, and a community, within salvation history. He thus deals there in careful detail with what is given in the Old Law, which is a written law. But Aquinas's treatment of the New Law is contained not just in his explicit address of the topic but in what follows in the rest of the *Secunda pars* of the *Summa*. How the New Law differs from the Old is the focus of these early questions. What the New Law means as a way of life is a story told for the rest of the *Secunda pars*.

Aquinas wishes to make clear at once two things about the New Law: its superiority to the Old Law and its continuity with it. The first thing Thomas states about the New Law

is that, while it is the Law of the Gospel, it is not a written law (Ia IIae, q. 106, a. 1, c.). The New Law is "principally the grace of the Holy Spirit, which is given to those with faith in Christ" (ibid.).[46] The New Law is distinguished by its entry into the very soul, transforming and strengthening. Aquinas contrasts its work to that of the natural law, arguing that the New Law is "superadded to nature through the gift of grace, not only indicating what should be done but also helping to accomplish it" (ibid.).[47] Written law is only a secondary aspect of it, pertaining to disposition toward, or the right expression of, this grace (ibid.). The New Law simply is the grace of the Spirit which justifies (q. 106, a. 4, c.).

Thus in his initial treatment of the New Law, Aquinas immediately and unequivocally draws a stark contrast between the Old Law and the New Law. The Old Law constitutes the Jews as a community through a multitude of precepts; the New Law is only derivatively a written law at all. The Old Law orders the Jews toward reconciliation with a distant God, but it can never bring this reconciliation about; the New Law is the very indwelling of God in the soul of the justified. Aquinas deepens the contrast with the Old Law by affirming the New Law's historical placement (Ia IIae, q. 106, aa. 3–4). In arguing against the claim that the New Law should have been given from the beginning of the world, he gives three familiar reasons for its historical location: the need for the redemptive work of Christ, the need for the pedagogy of the Old Law, and (part of this pedagogy) the need for human beings to discover under the Old Law their sinfulness and their need for grace (Ia IIae, q. 106, a. 3, c.). Thus the Old has prepared the way for the New. But the New Law itself will know no obsolescence until the end of the world: "for nothing [in the present life] can be closer to the ultimate end than that which immediately leads to the ultimate end" (Ia IIae, q. 106, a. 4).[48]

Aquinas uses this language of perfection and completion both to connect and then to distinguish the New Law from the Old. Both the Old Law and the New Law, he tells us, have a common end: "namely that men be subjected to God" (Ia IIae, q. 107, a. 1, c.).[49] And those under the New Law and the Old share a oneness of faith, a faith which differs in state because "what they believed as future, we believe has been accomplished" (ibid.).[50] The New Law's distinctive perfection is not in a distinct end; rather, it is in the *achievement* of the end and, thereby, in the expression of an animating love, which is charity. Thus, alluding to an Augustinian play on words, Aquinas calls the Old Law the law of fear (*timor*), and the New Law the law of love (*amor*) (Ia IIae, q. 107, a. 1, ad 2). People of the New Law cleave to God for God's own sake, and not out of fear of punishment or from hope of temporal reward. Such adherence expresses a kinship with God and is, Aquinas indicates, a sign of the indwelling of grace. This emboldens Aquinas to argue that even some in the time of the Old Law, manifestly moved by love of spiritual things, should be considered as being of the New Law. "For there were some in the state of the Old Testament who, having charity and the grace of the Holy Spirit, hoped principally for spiritual and eternal promises. And accordingly they belonged to the New Law. Just so, there are some carnal ones in the New Testament who have not yet attained to the perfection of the New Law . . ." (Ia IIae, q. 107, a. 1, ad 2).[51]

Aquinas carries forward this characterization of the New Law as the law of love for the rest of his discussion of love. (Note then that the treatment of laws in the *Prima secundae* begins with eternal law, God's ordering of the cosmos, and concludes with God's merciful reordering of human beings to union with God.) It is by the New Law's animating charity, which effects a transformation of the very soul of the believer, that he distinguishes the content of the Old and New Laws.

Christ fulfills the Old Law in three ways, Aquinas argues (Ia IIae, q. 107, a. 2). First, Christ fulfills the Old Law by more completely expressing the Old Law's true meaning: he forbids not only external sinful acts, but internal acts as well. Further, he sets forth the safest way to keep the law of God. Third, Christ adds to Old Law certain "counsels of perfection." Note that all of these aspects of fulfillment do not alter the moral content of the Old Law. Indeed, Aquinas explicitly affirms that this remains unchanged (Ia IIae, q. 107, a. 2, ad 2). Rather, the New Law commands, yet also effects, a greater perfection of

spirit, a perfection that (finally) makes possible perfect obedience to the Old Law. This last point is crucial—Aquinas understands the regulation of internal acts as ultimately required for perfect obedience of the moral precepts of the Old Law (the ceremonial and legal precepts no longer bind, for reasons already discussed). He states, "The precepts of the New Law are said to be greater than the precepts of the Old Law with respect to [their] explicit expression. But with respect to the very substance of the New Testament, all is contained in the Old Testament" (Ia IIae, q. 107, a. 3, ad 2).[52]

This regulation of internal acts of the soul would seem to make the New Law more burdensome than even the burdensome Old Law (Ia IIae, q. 107, a. 4). But, in this case, the charity that is the New Law makes possible, and even pleasant, perfection of obedience. Indeed joy in obedience itself expresses the right and comprehensive ordering of the soul to God which the New Law requires. And from this internal ordering springs all the external acts commanded within the New Law.

The kingdom of God consists principally in internal acts, but by consequence all things without which internal acts cannot exist also belong to the kingdom of God. Thus if the kingdom of God is internal justice and peace and spiritual joy, it is necessary that all external acts which oppose justice and peace and spiritual joy be opposed also to the kingdom of God, and for this reason are forbidden by the Gospel of the kingdom.[53] (Ia IIae, q. 108, a. 1, ad 1)

The strategy of this reasoning gives us another point of contrast between the Old and New Laws according to Aquinas. The Old Law commanded external acts in order to habituate the Jewish people into (internal) virtue. The New Law commands external acts only insofar as they are opposed to, or expressive of, the internal perfection of the law of love. In the New Law, the internal virtue of the believer is the standard by which external acts are permitted or forbidden.

Aquinas concludes his treatment of the New Law with an exploration of the way in which internal acts are regulated within the New Law; he answers this question through discussion of Christ's "Sermon on the Mount"

(Ia IIae, q. 108, a. 3). He carefully argues that the Sermon contains a "complete representation of the Christian life" (ibid.).[54] It orders internal acts of the believer with regard to God, self, and neighbor; in doing so, the Sermon presents the completion and fulfillment of the Law given on Mount Sinai. Each of the first three of the objections that Aquinas raises against the New Law's adequate regulation of internal acts refers to one set of the Old Law's precepts. How can the New Law order internal acts adequately, in comparison with the moral, ceremonial, and legal precepts of the Old Law? Aquinas answers by affirming again the New Law's regulation of internal acts as revealing the way to perfect obedience of the commandments, the moral core of the Old Law (Ia IIae, q. 108, a. 3, ad 1). The New Law is superior even to the judicial precepts by showing, and by achieving, a more perfect justice of internal and external act (Ia IIae, q. 108, a. 3, ad 2). The New Law does nothing explicitly to replace or amend the ceremonial precepts, which are abolished with the redemptive work of Christ. The New Law now requires a change to a "spiritual worship" of God (Ia IIae, q. 108, a. 3, ad 3).[55] In his defense of the New Law's adequacy in regulating internal acts, Aquinas repeatedly affirms that the New Law accomplishes, in the soul of the believer, that which the Old Law intended.

In Ia IIae, q. 108, a. 4, Thomas takes up the *counsels of perfection* (poverty, chastity, and obedience). Aquinas interprets these counsels as designed to enhance adherence to the spiritual goods which those within the New Law seek always to love more completely. These counsels are not, however, commandments. The New Law is a "law of liberty," and these counsels, freely adopted, can intensify union by drawing men and women away from earthly goods (Ia IIae, q. 108, a. 4).[56] Note that in both his treatment of the Sermon on the Mount and in discussion of the counsels of perfection, Aquinas stresses the way in which obedience of the New Law permits, even requires, the exercise of mature judgment by the believer. This requirement is warranted by the transformation of the soul worked by grace. Now truly ordered toward God, and moved by the indwelling love of God, the believer knows and does reliably what expresses that love (Ia IIae, q. 108, a. 2). Here, too, one can see how far Aquinas places the New Law from the pedagogy of the Old Law.

In other ways, however, the Old and New Laws are very close indeed. As connected stages of the Divine Law, they both work to bring men and women to God. The New Law never alters or subverts the moral precepts of the Old Law (themselves articulations of the natural law). And both the Old and the New Laws attend to virtue as a way of life within community, ultimately within the same community of the faithful. For Aquinas, however, the New Law is distinct from the Old because it fulfills the Old. What the Old Law foreshadows is made plain in the Incarnation and redemptive work of Christ. What the Old Law intends, the healing of sin and union with God, is accomplished in the grace won by Christ. In this way, the impotence which he attributes to the Old Law is itself a ground for the expression of God's mercy. This being repeatedly asserted, Aquinas still acknowledges that some during the time of the Old Law were manifestly possessed of charity. The oneness of faith shared by the Jews of old and Christians thus was, at least for certain individuals, also a oneness in the very life of God. Thomas never comes closer to allowing for holiness among those living by the Old Law. But he is clear that such holiness is the point of Divine Law, Old and New.

Notes

[1]This chapter is a partial retreatment of the texts I discuss in my *Narrative and the Natural Law: An Interpretation of Thomistic Ethics* (Notre Dame, IN: University of Notre Dame Press, 1994). See esp. chaps. 2–4 for an account of the connections between natural law and the Old and New Laws.

[2]Two authors who address the issue of whether there is a "natural" end for human beings on Aquinas's view are Kevin Staley and Jean Porter. See Staley, "Happiness: the Natural End for Man?," *Thomist* 53 (1989): 215–34. Porter builds on Staley's arguments in her *The Recovery of Virtue: The Relevance of Aquinas for Christian Ethics* (Louisville, KY: Westminster/ John Knox, 1990), 63–68.

[3]"quid ei sit agendum et quid vitandum."

[4]"punire vel prohibere."

[5]"sicut perfectum et imperfectum in eadem species, sicut puer et vir."

[6]"bonum intelligibile et caeleste."

7"sicut paterfamilias in domo alia mandata proponit pueris et adultis, ita etiam unus rex Deus in uno suo regno aliam legem dedit hominibus adhuc imperfectis existentibus, et aliam perfectiorem iam manuductis per priorem legem ad maiorem capacitatem divinorum."

8"testimonium Christo perhibendo."

9"dum retrahens homines a cultu idolatriae, concludebat eos sub-cultu unius Dei, a quo salvandum erat humanum genus per Christum."

10"Deus aliquando permittit aliquos cadere in peccatum, ut exinde humilientur. Ita etiam voluit talem legem dare quam suis viribus homines implere non possent, ut sic dum homines praesumentes de se peccatores se invenirent, humiliati recurrerent ad auxilium gratiae."

11Note that this characterization in no way countermines Aquinas's claim of the Old Law's inferiority. Aquinas is emphatic and unyielding on this issue. Rather, it gives the Old Law's inferiority a further meaning in the moral development of the Jews. For an excellent discussion of Aquinas and his treatment of the Old Law and of the Jewish people, see John Y. B. Hood, *Aquinas and the Jews* (Philadelphia: University of Pennsylvania Press, 1995). The clarity of Hood's reading of Aquinas on the Old Law and its precepts has been very helpful to me in my own research on the Old Law. Hood addresses the important issue of the cultural context and negative cultural consequences of Aquinas's (and others') beliefs for the Jewish people of that time. While treatment of this issue is beyond the scope of this exegetical essay, I want to go on record as rejecting the "assimilation" of the Old Law to a Christian understanding of revelation and history.

See also the very fine discussion of Aquinas on the Old Law by Thomas S. Hibbs, "Divine Irony and the Natural Law: Speculation and Edification in Aquinas," *International Philosophical Quarterly* 30 (1990): 419–29. I am indebted to Professor Hibbs's essay for his insights into divine "pedagogy."

12"non quia erant de veteri lege, sed quia erant de lege naturae."

13"lex duobus generibus hominum imponitur. Imponitur enim quibusdam duris et superbis, qui per legem compescuntur et domantur; imponitur etiam bonis, qui per legem instructi adiuvantur ad implendum quod intendunt. Conveniens igitur fuit tali tempore legem veterem dari ad superbiam hominum convincendam. De duobus enim homo superbiebat: scilicet de scientia et de potentia. De scientia quidem, quasi ratio naturalis ei posset sufficere ad salutem. Et ideo ut de hoc eius superbia convinceretur, permissus est homo regimini suae rationis absque adminiculo legis scriptae; et experimento homo discere potuit quod patiebatur rationis defectum, per hoc quod homines usque ad idolatriam et turpissima vitia circa tempora Abrahae sunt

prolapsi. Et ideo post haec tempora fuit necessarium legem scriptam dari in remedium humanae ignorantiae. . . . Sed postquam homo est instructus per legem . . . dum implere non poterat quod cognoscebat. . . . Ex parte vero bonorum, lex data est in auxilium. Quod quidem tunc maxime populo necessarium fuit, quando lex naturalis obscurari incipiebat propter exuberantiam peccatorum."

14See ST Ia IIae, q. 84, a. 2, for a discussion of pride.

15I argue at greater length, and no doubt with greater clarity, for what follows in *Narrative and the Natural Law*. See esp. 31–36 , 49–52.

16Aquinas uses the word *inclinationes* for what I am calling directednesses.

17In this emphasis on the Old Law's connection to friendship with God, Aquinas of course establishes a connection with the New Law, which accomplishes friendship with God, and his characterization of the virtue of charity as friendship. See ST Ia IIae, qq. 106–8; q. 65, a. 5; and IIa IIae, q. 23.

18"in particularibus agendis."

19"quaedam quae sunt secundum se mala, ratio multorum licita iudacaret."

20"omnia praecepta moralia pertineant ad legem naturae, sed diversimode."

21"divina instructione." Aquinas indicates in his comment that this (counter-intuitive?) connection to the natural law may be needed within the Old Law because the precept specifically addresses what is divine (*de divinis*).

22"illa quae statim ex fide divinitus infusa innotescunt."

23"illa scilicet quae sunt prima et communia."

24"Quantum ergo ad illa principia communia, lex naturalis nullo modo potest a cordibus hominum deleri in universali."

25"[ita praecepta legis divinae] ordinant hominem ad quandam communitatem seu rempublicam hominum sub Deo."

26"primo, fidelitatem; secundo, reverentiam; tertio, famulatum."

27"in memoriam creationis rerum."

28"quia quantum ad hoc lex naturalis obscurata erat propter peccatum; non autem quantum ad dilectionem sui ipsius, quia quantum ad hoc lex naturalis vigebat."

29"Si qua ergo praecepta dentur quae contineant ipsam conservationem boni communis, vel ipsum ordinem iustitiae et virtutis, huiusmodi praecepta continent intentionem legislatoris; et ideo indispensabilia sunt . . . . Praecepta autem decalogi continent ipsam intentionem legislatoris, scilicet Dei. Nam praecepta primae tabulae, quae ordinant ad Deum, continent ipsum ordinem ad bonum commune et finale, quod Deus est; praecepta autem secundae tabulae continent ordinem iustitiae inter homines observandae, ut scilicet nulli fiat indebitum, et cuilibet reddatur debitum; secundum hanc enim rationem sunt intelligenda praecepta decalogi. Et ideo praecepta decalogi sunt omnino indispensabilia."

30"[ut homini] liceat non ordinate se habere ad Deum, vel non subdi ordini iustitiae eius."

31"praecepta caeremonialia et iudicialia sunt determinativa praeceptorum decalogi ex vi institutionis." See also a restatement of this point at ST Ia IIae, q. 104, a. 1.

32"[oportebat] et iterum multa talibus imponi, ut quasi oneratis ex his quae ad cultum Dei impenderent, non vacaret idolatriae deservire.—Ex parte vero eorum qui erant proni ad bonum, etiam necessaria fuit multiplicatio caeremonialium praeceptorum. Tum quia per hoc diversimode mens eorum referabatur in deum, et magis assidue. Tum etiam quia mysterium Christi, quod per huiusmodi caeremonialia figurabatur, multiplices utilitates attulit mundo."

33"Alio modo possunt eorum rationes assignari secundum quod ordinatur ad figurandum Christum. Et sic habent rationes figurales et mysticas, sive accipiantur ex ipso Christo et Ecclesia, quod pertinent ad allegoriam; sive ad mores populi Christiani, quod pertinent ad moralitatem; sive ad statum futurae gloriae, prout in eam introducimur per Christum, quod pertinent ad anagogiam."

Note that Aquinas's use of the terms of *allegory*, *morality*, and *anagogy* corresponds to and refer to his earlier discussion of the senses of Scripture in Ia, q. 1, a. 10. In his remarks there, he makes explicit the application of these interpretive senses to the Old and New Laws.

34"Uno modo, secundum quod per sacrificia repraesentabatur ordinatio mentis in deum, ad quam excitabatur sacrificium offerens. Ad rectam autem ordinationem mentis in deum pertinent quod omnia quae homo habet, recognoscat a Deo tanquam a primo principio et ordinet in Deum tanquam in ultimum finem. Et hoc repraesentabatur in oblationibus et sacrificiis. . . . Alio modo, ex hoc quod per huiusmodi homines retrahebantur a sacrificiis idolorum. Unde etiam praecepta de sacrificiis non fuerunt data populo Iudaeorum nisi postquam declinavit ad idolatrium . . . quasi huiusmodi sacrificia sint instituta ut populus ad sacrificandum promptus, huiusmodi sacrificia magis Deo quam idolis offerret."

35John Hood offers an excellent critique of Aquinas's "methodology" of reading for the prefigurative aspects of the Old Law's ceremonial precepts, noting the arbitrariness and ahistoricism of many of his symbolic associations. See *Aquinas and the Jews*, 54–57. He links this to Aquinas's Christocentric (and thereby religiously hegemonic) interpretation of human history.

36"protestationes fidei."

37"inquantum scilicet totus status illius populi, qui per huiusmodi praecepta disponebatur, figuralis erat."

38"Et ideo oportuit totum illius populi statum esse propheticum et figuralem."

39The meaning of Aquinas's claim here still escapes me to a great degree. Hood discusses Aquinas's marked "vagueness" about the judicial precepts in *Aquinas and the Jews*, 57–60.

40"statum illius populi."

41"iam in Christo non esset discretio gentilis et Judaei, sicut antea erat."

42Aquinas is never clearer about his triumphalist Christianity. As part of this, the Old Law has only derivative legitimacy for him: it exists only for the sake of preparation and prefiguration of Christ. Thus, on his view, a Jewish state after Christ is illegitimate and (presumably) a political consolidation of religious error. He never entertains alternative grounds for such a state or justification for the persistence of the Jewish faith after Christ. A critique of this position is morally important, but beyond the scope of this exegetical piece.

43"coniungi Christo incarnato . . . ; et ita ex fide Christi iustificabantur. Cuius fidei quaedam protestatio erat huiusmodi caeremoniarum observatio, inquantum erant figura Christi. Et ideo pro peccatis offerebantur sacrificia quaedam in veteri lege, non quia ipsa sacrificia a peccato emundarent, sed quia erant quaedam protestationes fidei, quae a peccato mundabant."

44John Hood discusses this passage and the implication of an "explicit" faith in Christ by the Jews in *Aquinas and the Jews*, 54–56. I am indebted to his remarks.

45Aquinas also seeks to prove this belief with the claim that, in fact, a person cannot fulfill all of the Old Law's precepts without charity. For charity, a theological virtue, accomplishes the ordination to God which is the Old Law's goal. See ST Ia IIae, q. 100, a. 10, ad 2; q. 65, a. 5; and q. 66, a. 6.

46"principaliter lex nova est ipsa gratia Spiritus Sancti, quae datur Christi fidelibus."

47"superadditum per gratiae donum. Et hoc modo lex nova est indita homini, non solum indicans quid sit faciendum, sed etiam adiuvans ad implendum."

48"Nihil enim potest esse propinquius fini ultimo quam quod immediate in finem ultimum introducit."

49"scilicet ut homines subdantur Deo."

50"Nam quod illi credebant futurum, nos credimus factum."

51"Fuerunt tamen aliqui in statu veteris testamenti habentes caritatem et gratiam Spiritus Sancti, qui principaliter expectabant promissiones spirituales et aeternas. Et secundum hoc pertinebant ad legem novam. —Similiter etiam in novo testamento sunt aliqui carnales nondum pertingentes ad perfectionem novae legis." See also Aquinas's remarks about the "implicit faith" of some of the Jews in ST Ia IIae, q. 106, a. 1, ad 3, and a. 3, ad 2.

[52]"praecepta novae legis dicuntur esse maiora quam praecepta veteris legis, quantum ad explicitam manifestationem. Sed quantum ad ipsam substantiam praceptorum Novi Testamenti, omnia continentur in Veteri Testamento." See also ST Ia IIae, q. 108, a. 3, ad 3, for the same point.

[53]"regnum Dei in interioribus actibus consistit principaliter: sed ex consequenti etiam ad regnum Dei pertinent omnia illa sine quibus interiores actus esse non possunt. Sicut si regnum Dei est interior iustitia et pax et gaudium spirituale, necesse est quod omnes exteriores actus qui repugnant institiae aut paci aut gaudio spirituali, repugnent etiam regno Dei; et ideo sunt in Evangelio regni prohibendi."

[54]"totam informationem Christianae vitae."

[55]"erat in spiritualem commutandus."

[56]"lex libertatis."

Selected Further Reading

Brown, Oscar J. *Natural Rectitude and Divine Law in Aquinas.* Toronto: Pontifical Institute of Medieval Studies, 1981.

Hall, Pamela M. *Narrative and the Natural Law.* Notre Dame, IN: University of Notre Dame Press, 1994.

Hauerwas, Stanley. *Character and the Christian Life: A Study in Theological Ethics.* San Antonio, TX: Trinity University Press, 1975.

Hibbs, Thomas S. "Divine Irony and the Natural Law: Speculation and Edification in Aquinas." *International Philosophical Quarterly* 30 (1990): 419–29.

Hittinger, Russell F. "After MacIntyre: Natural Law Theory, Virtue Ethics, and Eudaimonia." *International Philosophical Quarterly* 29 (1989): 449–61.

Hood, John Y. B. *Aquinas and the Jews.* Philadelphia: University of Pennsylvania Press, 1995.

Jordan, Mark D. *Ordering Wisdom: The Hierarchy of Philosophical Discourses in Aquinas.* Notre Dame, IN: University of Notre Dame Press, 1986.

Porter, Jean. *The Recovery of Virtue: The Relevance of Aquinas for Christian Ethics.* Louisville, KY: Westminster/John Knox, 1990.

———. "Desire for God: Ground of the Moral Life in Aquinas." *Theological Studies* 47 (1986): 48–68.

Staley, Kevin. "Happiness: The Natural End of Man?" *Thomist* 53 (1989): 215–34.

Grace (Ia IIae, qq. 109–114)

Theo Kobusch

Translated by Grant Kaplan and Frederick G. Lawrence

THE LOCATION OF THE TREATISE ON GRACE IN THE *SUMMA THEOLOGIAE*

The structure of Thomas Aquinas's *Summa theologiae*—that wondrous work whose life elixir is metaphysics—is in itself very clear: the *Prima pars* deals with God and creation under the title, "On the procession of creatures from God" (*De processione creaturarum a Deo*); the *Secunda pars*, with the movement of nature endowed with reason toward God; and the *Tertia pars*, with Christ insofar as he, as a human being, is the way to God. Since Chenu's fundamental work, people have wanted to recognize in this ordering the Neoplatonic *egress-regress* or *emanation-return* (*exitus-reditus*) schema.[1] In fact, Thomas used these Neoplatonic terms in the *Commentary on the Sentences* to indicate the total scope of theology's objects.

However, that these concepts are supposed to indicate a schema in accord with which Thomas also structured the *Summa theologiae* should rightly be questioned. Doubts immediately arise because the Neoplatonic schema originally consisted of a triad. In addition to "procession" (*prohodos*) and "return" (*epistrophe*), Neoplatonism also regarded "subsistence" (*mone*) as a properly significant element (in the sense of subsisting-in-itself) pertaining to the One. Because the *Commentary on the Sentences* emphasizes that the processions of the persons already fall under the concept of "egress" (*exitus*), there would remain for subsistence (*mone*) to some degree only the subsection, "On the one God" (*De deo uno*), which treats God in His self-subsistent essence with-

out being separated from the sections on egress. Thus, one cannot completely avoid the impression that the original Neoplatonic schema was reduced to a twofold pattern, in order to be suitable as an aid to interpretation.

Moreover, R. Heinzmann has shown that the plan of *Summa theologiae* betrays the influence of the earlier *Commentary on the Sentences* and *Summas*, which are themselves based on a conception of salvation history.[2] To understand the *Prima secundae* in particular, which treats the human act, this is especially pertinent, since it has irritated so many theologians that Thomas deals with the virtues and the problem of grace without bringing their interpretation in relation to grace in Christ, and in general, that the theme of the human act is handled before Christology.[3] Taking into account the tradition pointed out by R. Heinzmann, in which the work of creation (*opus creationis*), the work of recreation (*opus recreationis*), and the work of final retribution (*opus ultimae retributionis*) are distinguished, then it is evident that Thomas aligns himself with that interpretation according to which, within the work of recreation, the treatise on the virtues and on justification (and therefore of grace) precedes the treatise on the Incarnation.[4]

Yet it is not only due to these rather extrinsic reasons that the treatise on grace cannot be regarded as an anticipation of the doctrine of the Incarnation, but as an integral component of the *Prima secundae*, and so must be seen as the teaching on human acts. Above all, it is most important to examine the true scientific character of this part of the *Summa theologiae*.

There can be no doubt that it is not a matter of a purely philosophical ethics; the movement that runs through the entire work starts from God and leads back to Him, so that the total theological character is unmistakable. However, whether on this account the moral teaching contained in the *Secunda pars* of the *Summa* is a moral theology depends on one's notion of moral theology.

In his fundamental study on Aquinas and philosophical ethics, W. Kluxen has pointed out that a unique form of metaphysics is immanent in Thomas's moral teaching, and this is to be highlighted especially in relation to the *Prima secundae*. Like the physicist, who contemplates natural things as mobile, and does not pose the question about their being as such, so also the "moralist" (that is, ethically engaged reason as such) does not ask about what good and evil are in general. "Only the metaphysician asks about that."[5] It is similar with the question about the nature of the rule of reason in action, the natural law.[6] If one looks more closely, it even becomes clear that the entire *Prima secundae* does not have a practical character at all; instead, its nature is a speculative one.[7] It does not say what should be *done*, but what is the *end*, the essential and the accidental, and what the human act's principles are. In other words, the *Prima secundae* deals with the human act (*actus humanus*) as a being of a specific kind, which Thomas had already distinguished from the natural, intellectual, and artificial kinds of being at the beginning of the *Commentary on the Ethics*.

Already in Ia IIae, qq. 18–21, on the moral act, Thomas sets the "moral being"—be it in the form of the "moral act" (*actus moralis*) or also as the category of "morality" (*genus moris*)—as a thematic object in opposition to natural things (Ia IIae, q. 21, a. 2, ad 2).[8] In this sense, the entire *Prima secundae* is a "universal," that is, speculative moral teaching, the proper object of which is moral being, also known as the human act. But since the end of the act as well as its circumstances, its essence, and the affective element (as the act common to other animals) are all implied in the notion of act, these themes all belong to the objective field of universal morality, that is, they are of a speculative nature (Ia IIae, q. 6).

According to Thomas, however, the internal and external principles of the human act are also the object of this universal treatise (Ia IIae, q. 49; also Ia, q. 87, a. 2, *sed contra*; Ia, q. 93, a. 7). Habits, virtues, and the like are to be regarded as internal principles; however, the external principles of the act are the law as the guiding element given us by God, and the grace that supports us (Ia IIae, q. 90). Here Thomas differentiates internal from external principles, just as in his formulation of the subject matter of metaphysics where, for example, in the case of natural things form and matter or being and essence are understood as internal principles whereas God and the intelligences are external principles. Already on the basis of this analogy, one has a certain right to talk about a metaphysics of the moral sphere, or of the act. Just as in Aristotelian metaphysics, God finally appears as the unmoved mover of the world of nature, so in the metaphysics of act God at last appears as the one who moves the will—that is, He appears as grace.

On the whole, therefore, a philosophical order seems to lie at the basis of the *Prima secundae*, which, according to the famous specification in the *Summa contra gentiles* II, chap. 4, begins with the contemplation of creaturely being and leads to the knowledge of God. The *Prima secundae* also begins with the creaturely being of human beings insofar as they are acting natures. Its first questions present God as the final end inasmuch as every act is goal-oriented and, in the words of the first article, insofar as the end, "even when it is last in execution, is first in the intention of the agent" (q. 1, a. 1, ad 1).[9] In the moral sphere, the final end occupies in this manner the rank of a first, indemonstrable, self-evident principle (a theoretical-scientific principle that is taken for granted and cannot itself be called into question; Ia IIae, q. 72, a. 5).[10]

If one also remains aware that it is precisely the human act, which in a later period in Christian Wolff, Samuel Pufendorf, and others constitutes the main object of "universal ethics" (*ethica universalis*), or "universal practical philosophy" (*philosophia practica universalis*), and which ultimately is termed a "metaphysics of morality" (*metaphysica moralis*) in the school of Wolff, or, as in Kant, the "metaphysics of morals," then one cannot deny that in his treatise on the human act in the *Prima secundae*, Thomas invented a new genre in theological form. While omitting the qualification of theological, this genre was taken up by philosophy and bore significant fruit.[11]

If it is correct that the universal morality of the *Prima secundae* is a metaphysics of morals, then this is also decisive for understanding the character of the treatise on grace. Just as universal metaphysics contemplates "common being" (*ens commune*) as its proper object, and yet also asks about the final principles and causes of beings, by which it becomes philosophical theology, so the metaphysics of act thematically contemplates the human act and asks at the same time about its condition of possibility as the first external principle of all action. Just as in the earlier perspective of philosophical theology, God is shown to be the first principle insofar as He is the unmoved mover of all natural things; for the metaphysician, who seeks the external principle of human action, God is presented as self-giving freedom or grace, the condition that makes free action possible.

In this sense, the doctrine of grace (as well as the doctrine of law) is the philosophical theology that belongs to the metaphysics of act. Symptomatically, even in the treatise on grace, God is designated as the "first mover" in relation to human will, thereby making a central concept of traditional philosophical theology relevant to the teaching on grace. The doctrine of grace is thus not an accidental addition to the doctrine of act, but substantially necessary for the metaphysician of morals or anyone wishing to trace human action to its root. This connection between grace and action is also underlined by the terminology already given to Thomas: according to Alexander of Hales and others, the "graced being" (*esse gratiae*) is the supernatural super formation of "moral being" (*esse morale*).[12] Thus, it can be understood why grace is treated as the final topic of a treatise devoted to the subject of human acts or, more generally, the category of morality (*genus moris*).

THE LIGHT OF GRACE

The treatise on grace at the end of the *Prima secundae* belongs to the doctrine about the human act or, more generally, about being moral. Typically, the whole treatise ends with the statement: "And let these things said on moral matters in general suffice" (Ia IIae, q. 114, a 10).[13] In scholasticism, the concept of moral matters is the most universal name for everything connected in any way with our freedom. Therefore, the treatise on grace is the conclusion of the teaching on freedom, insofar as the *Prima secundae* is the treatise on the free act, that is, on the human act. Hence, grace for Thomas must have an intrinsic relation to human freedom. However, this is only possible if the character and status of this principle given immediately by God can be clarified, which is to be considered as the ground of all supernatural knowledge and so of all mediated willing: the "light of grace" (*lumen gratiae*). Thereby, one is led to what is, for Thomas, the most important meaning of "grace," namely, that divine motion by which the human will is directed toward the final end, perfect beatitude (Ia IIae, q. 109, a. 5).[14] When this goal seems often to be obscured in individual moral acts, it is still never actually forgotten, but is present instead as what is always willed already in all acts of will, just as the principle of noncontradiction is present in all speaking and thinking in the mode of validity, without indeed being handled thematically itself in individual acts of thinking. For this reason, Thomas even says explicitly that, just as the intellect necessarily depends on first principles, so also does the will depend necessarily on the last end, which consists in beatitude (Ia, q. 82, a. 1).

But the parallel structure between intellect and will—between theoretical and practical knowledge—goes still further. As the reflexive cognitional analysis performed by Thomas shows, knowledge of the life-world always contains an *a priori* element, which Thomas calls "intellectual light" (*lumen intellectuale*) or "light of reason" (*lumen rationis*). By it, a person is enabled to see the first principles in which all human knowledge is contained in a specific way, and to obtain insight into its truth. In this sense, Thomas speaks of a formation of first notions preceding concrete knowledge, "which is immediately known by the light of the agent intellect through the species abstracted from sense data, whether as complex concepts, such as axioms, or simple ones, such as the concept of being, of the one, etc.,"; that is, the so-called transcendental concepts, "which the intellect immediately grasps."[15]

As Thomas teaches throughout, this light of reason, which enables people to apprehend the so-called self-evident principles (*principia per se nota*), is given or "innate" in us as "a similitude of the uncreated truth in us."[16] But since these self-evident principles are to be regarded as the "seeds of knowledge," it can also be said of the light of intellect that all knowledge is somehow already in it. And conversely, for Thomas it must be the case that "everything known as such (contains) the intellectual light in itself," which is co-known whenever something intelligible is grasped; this light will also be understood without necessarily implying the knowledge of God (who is the source of this light) according to His essence.[17] However, in everything known, being is co-known as the universal being of things, and because this being is not independent (that is, is not subsistent), it is understood as "a participation and image of the subsistent, divine Being." For this reason, Thomas can say that all knowers know God implicitly in each thing.[18] This holds true analogously for the realm of practice as well. For God, insofar as He is the final end and beatitude, is implicitly striven for in everything sought.[19] That which is first in the order of intention—not of execution—must be considered the first moving principle of human action, and this is nothing else than the final end (Ia IIae, q. 1, a. 4).

For Thomas, there is a peculiarity for the realm of the will (of practicality or morality) that is of fundamental importance for the problem of grace. It has already been noted that in the realm of moral being, the final end assumes the scientific-theoretical status proper to first principles in speculative philosophy (Ia IIae, q. 72, a. 5).[20] To be sure, the will is such that it assumes with natural necessity the first, indemonstrable, self-evident principles as starting points of its activity (just as does the theoretical intellect), without this kind of necessity's implying compulsion.[21] Nevertheless, in accord with the famous closing of the commentary on Boethius's *De trinitate*, it cannot do this in a purely natural mode, but only with the help of divine grace.[22] In a natural mode the intellect can only attain whatever can be reduced to the first, self-evident principles perceived by it in the light of reason. Thomas refers to whatever transcends the limits of rea-

son as the *supernatural*. On the theoretical side, this knowledge includes, for example, knowledge of "future contingents" given only through a supernatural light, the light of prophecy; but also the mystery of the Trinity, which can be seen only in the light of faith. The principle of such supernatural knowledge, however, is God Himself.[23] On the practical side, there is knowledge of the external principles of human acts, which transcend human reason. Hence, for Thomas, a supernatural light is needed for the knowledge of human action insofar as it is guided by God as the eternal law (Ia IIae, q. 8, a. 3, ad 3). Similarly, according to the basic thesis of the treatise on grace, even that practical knowledge in accord with which the human will turns toward the final end on account of the motion of the first mover alone is due to the light of faith, which Thomas also refers to as the light of grace.

It is of enormous significance for understanding the treatise on grace to penetrate the parallel structure of supernatural knowledge and natural knowledge. For just as in natural knowledge there is the "natural light" (*lumen naturale*), by which the principles arising from sense knowledge are seen, yet which precedes all sense experience, and in this sense provides an *a priori* element, so must the light of faith, the graciously infused habit of faith, be regarded as an *a priori* element of the knowledge proper to faith, which makes possible the assent to both the articles of faith received by hearing, and knowledge of the final end.[24] If, however, the final end is the principle of the "processes of rational action," as Thomas says, and thus of the will, and if this final end can only be grasped in light of faith or grace, so that it acts upon the will as a supernatural principle, which is God himself, then faith must be understood as an element intrinsic to the will. Insofar as the final end is present as a principle of every intention in every act and questing, faith must be thought of as a supernatural element immanent in natural reason. But faith is also the initial anticipation of eternal life.[25] Therefore, faith is the only element of the supernatural through which the final goal can be *known* with certainty. However, the treatise on grace makes it clear that the remaining theological virtues, hope and charity, orient the human being as an entity striving toward the final goal. This entails—and hope fulfills—that the final goal is held to be possible, and that beyond this, as charity mediates it, the final goal is also regarded as good (Ia IIae, q. 111, a. 4, ad 2).[26]

From exactly this perspective philosophy is to be criticized for having failed in reflection on how the human being can attain the final end (because this depends on supernatural virtues immanent in the will), or as the treatise on grace formulates it, how a person can enter into "immediate union with the final end" (*immediate ad coniunctionem ultimi finis*; Ia IIae, q. 111, a. 5).[27] The purpose of grace is to unite human beings with the highest good, God (Ia IIae, q. 112, a. 4).

In the treatise on grace, faith appears in this way as an inner moment of human action. This corresponds completely to the intention documented elsewhere in Aquinas that the habit of faith "is moved not by the intellect, but by the will, so that it effects the free assent to what is believed."[28]

GRACE AND FREEDOM

In the measure that the treatise on grace handles divine grace as an exterior principle of the moral act, that is, of free action, it is related from the start to human freedom in a special manner. For Thomas, it is in virtue of the "freedom of choice" or "decision" (*liberum arbitrium*) that the human turns toward or away from God. Whatever may be the case with the possibility of doing evil and of turning away from God, for Thomas all movements that lead from a possibility to a reality are conditioned originally by a divine motion. This also holds true for the motions of the human will. The first mover does not cause this motion in the same way as it causes the motion of a physical being. From a theological point of view, it must therefore be said that without the divine motion, human freedom would not be possible. The motion of grace is to this extent the condition of the possibility of human freedom (Ia IIae, q. 109, a. 6, ad 1–2). Because the prime mover moves all secondary causes each in a different way, the movement of the human will by divine grace is different from the movement of natural things. As the condition of the possibility of finite freedom, divine grace can move the hu-

man will only inasmuch as the essence of this will—freedom itself—is preserved. In contrast, the movement of natural things signifies natural compulsion.[29]

If, in the context of the teaching on grace, Thomas speaks of freedom in the sense of freedom of decision, he means something like the moment of subjectivity that must be conceived as the indispensable principle of a free act. In this sense, through His grace, God cannot justify the sinner without him, that is, the person cannot be justified without a movement of his or her subjective freedom. This movement of the will consists in consent to the justice of God (Ia IIae, q. 111, a. 2, ad 2).

Thomas has recourse here to the old motif, stressed especially by the Stoics and Augustine, of subjective freedom as consisting in consent to something (Ia IIae, q. 113, a. 7, ad 1).[30] Divine grace is precisely that divine motion of the first mover by which the subjective freedom of the person first becomes valid. Thomas calls "love" that which strives for the good under the presupposition of freedom. Therefore, divine grace must also be understood in the sense of the eternal love of God, who as such wills to give to creatures endowed with reason the eternal good, which He Himself is, thereby allowing them to participate in the divine good. Grace, then, has the character of a gift insofar as the divine goodness itself is communicated to the human will, and so mediates to it "the community of divine nature" (*communicatio consortium divinae naturae*; Ia IIae, q. 112, a. 1).

Correspondingly, the virtue of love poured out on the human being has the property of producing a "spiritual communion with God" (*societatem spiritualem cum Deo*; Ia IIae, q. 190, a. 3, ad 1). What stands in the background of the treatise on grace is Thomas's teaching on charity as a "supernatural communication" (*communicatione supernaturali*) of the highest good, or of divine grace, by which a share in the divine life is granted to the human being.[31] But when grace is thought of as the self-communication of God, the opposition between created and uncreated grace is shown to be logically bridgeable and compatible.[32] Considered from a purely philosophical point of view, grace is to be specified as the "free gift of the Other" that simply escapes all grasp and every power to dispose of it by human beings. Therefore, it is the "self-gift of the non-manipulable" that is spoken of here.[33] Only thus can one assess what Thomas actually intends to say: The absolutely nonmanipulable is present only in the mode of gift (*donum*).

If I say that a person has the grace of God, then according to Thomas, I mean that there is something supernatural bestowed by God on her or him, that to some extent offers the effect of divine love. In this manner divine love makes the person pleasing (*gratum*) to God (Ia IIae, q. 110, a. 1, ad 1).[34] In another passage Thomas says that this expression means also that God "accepts" the human being. Being in the presence of God by grace means being accepted by him into a common eternal life.[35] Considering that, according to Thomas, the gift of divine grace so understood is designated as a "presupposition" of "human acts," that is, of free acts, then there can be no doubt that this engages the essence of finite freedom most profoundly. Finite (that is, human) freedom can only be and achieve validity (this is the treatise on grace's theological goal) inasmuch as it mediates finite freedom in the mode of gifted being, and it is made possible through the acceptance of the human person by divine goodness.

In this context, it must be pointed out that any opposition such as that between the personal and the ontological, or the like, is a construct of modern theologians and does not match the intentions of Thomas. To be sure, there is a certain thoroughgoing justification for speaking about the character of the "personal" in the treatise on grace, precisely insofar as this treatise supplies the conclusion of the *Prima secundae*, which deals with the moral act, or, more generally, with moral being. In the scholastic portrayal, this is in fact the being of the person. There is a great, albeit for a long time unnoticed, tradition of the ontology of the personal or of the moral entity.[36] Even Thomas himself speaks throughout the treatise on grace of a "new being" in which the human being is constituted through the bestowal of grace, and this, in a certain way, means created out of nothing (Ia IIae, q. 110, a. 2, ad 3). This is nothing else than the being of grace that Thomas in several passages contrasts with the being of nature, and to which he attributes its own proper mode of coming-to-be-present.[37]

MERIT

To the human work there is added the character of justice in the sense of equality when it experiences a corresponding compensation or wage in comparison with another: "for instance the recompense of pay due for a great service" (IIa IIae, q. 57, a. 1).[38] The reflections on merit in Ia IIae, q. 114, are linked to the fundamental ideas of the Aristotelian theory of justice. At the same time they also lead further in terms of theology beyond what had already been suggested in Ia IIae, q. 21, aa. 3–4, on retribution or recompense in the sense of justice.[39] To do something meritorious, so that there is a claim to a reward, can in general only be done by a free being who freely fulfills the demands of the moral law. The activity of animals or of a natural thing that acts out of natural necessity can never possess this character of merit. In his *Commentary*, G. Vazquez explains that natural objects can surely attain a specifically appraisable worth, but never the specificity proper to merit, for this is not based on a value that can be appraised at a price, but on a moral value that deserves praise or some other reward.[40] To this extent, the theme of merit in fact pertains to the above-mentioned theme of human (free) action. For this reason, Thomas can say that the meritorious acts of human beings are the product of their freedom (Ia IIae, q. 114, a. 3).[41]

The treatise on grace deals with human freedom inasmuch as it is made possible by divine grace and willed as such. Therefore, in this treatise, it is a matter of the possibility of the meritoriousness of human acts before God. In the strict sense of a "condign merit" (*meritum condigni*), the character of merit cannot be attributed to the human act. The Aristotelian specification depends on the equality of human beings to each other, but an infinite difference exists between God and humanity. Thus, human action can be meritorious before God only in a certain sense, namely, insofar as it corresponds to a divine ordering (Ia IIae, q. 114, a. 1).[42]

Scholars disagree as to what this ordering really is. For example, O.-H. Pesch shifted Thomas's "ordering" (*ordinatio*) completely into proximity with the Scotist "divine acceptance" (*acceptatio divina*).[43] B. Hamm and

J. P. Wawrykow have justly criticized this shift, and interpreted the concept in the sense of a teleology proper to an ontology of creation, or of predestination in the broad sense that selects certain people to life with God, which they then attain through their good works, achieved with the help of grace.[44] Without going into this theological discussion in detail, it can be established in like manner for the understanding of the nature of merit for Thomas (and since we are dealing with the possibility of meritoriousness before God), that there has to be a norm fixed by God that affords the condition of the possibility of merit.[45] Such a norm can also be expressed, for example, as in the early work of Thomas, by a divine promise.[46] The specificity of meritoriousness can for this reason be meted out to human action not only on the basis of this divine orientation toward the good but also on the basis of freedom. But both elements are united in love, for through it alone does the human being attain the enjoyment of divine good, namely, of eternal life; and in it at the same time the human being reaches the highest degree of freedom (Ia IIae, q. 114, a. 4). According to Thomas the nature of this orientation to the final goal is such that human nature can reach it not by means of its own power, but through the help of divine grace (Ia IIae, q. 114, a. 2, ad 1). For this reason no human act can be the sufficient ground of the merit unto eternal life.

Human beings can then merit something from God and before God *only* when they have already received the always prevenient gift of grace, the initial grace. In this respect, Thomas says that every merit has divine grace as a presupposition and foundation, wherefore it is also called the "principle of meritorious work" or "cooperative grace" (Ia IIae, q. 112, a. 2, ad 1).[47] The concept of merit necessarily implies—Wawrykow has often pointed this out correctly—the right to expect a corresponding reward from God.[48] That to which one has a right cannot at the same time also be as such a gift of grace. In this respect, merit and grace are opposed to one another (Ia IIae, q. 114, a. 3).[49] God does not become a debtor to human beings in this respect, but rather a debtor to Himself, insofar as He must act in accord with His own ordering.

Undoubtedly, Thomas expressed the substantial part of his doctrine of merit in a juridical language. This is also made clear in the description of merit in the sense of correspondence (*meritum congrui*), where he has recourse to the concept of "recompense" (*recompensare*), a concept that indeed was already resonant with Aristotelian reciprocal justice, the starting point of his exposition.[50] When modern theologians believe they can recognize in Thomas's doctrine of merit an "emptying out of all juridical images" in favor of a personalist viewpoint, they do not notice that at the beginning of the tradition of the metaphysics of the moral sphere, there is no opposition whatsoever between the personal and the juridical.[51] Instead, rights and person are intrinsically linked with each other because both belong to the sphere of moral being (*esse morale*). Thus, as long as the character of being meritorious is supposed to be ascribed to an act, one can never prescind from that right to a reward, even in the case of a "transmundane" reward, which is only made possible by divine grace. In the degree that it is regarded as meritorious, there belongs, so to speak, to the moral act, which is the act performed from freedom, an essential right's claim, which appeals to the divine promise or to some other ordinance. This right's claim is as such also an element of hope. To be sure, Thomas did not make this idea explicit in the treatise on grace itself, but he certainly did so in his earlier works: besides divine grace, hope as a sure expectation of future beatitude is supported also on merits—not on actual ones, but proleptically; otherwise it could be confused with presumption (*presumptio*).[52] As Josef Pieper has expressed it, hope says: "It will turn out well for ourselves and for myself," and the element of merit contained in it adds the further claim that from me there arises no obstacle to allowing divine grace to be effective.[53]

THE LIMITS OF THE THOMIST DOCTRINE OF GRACE

Everything I have said to this point was to demonstrate that the *Prima secundae* provides the beginning of the development of a novel philosophical genre: the metaphysics of the moral being at the center of which stand humans and the ethical acts they perform.

The doctrine of grace appeared as the apex and culmination of the teaching on the human person as an essence characterized by freedom, as presenting the condition (which is itself unconditioned) of the possibility of finite (human) freedom. Divine grace is the theological expression for the divine freedom that wills and makes possible another, finite, freedom.

Thomas conceived of the being of divine grace (as distinct from the being of nature) as indeed the more perfect being, but also as always analogous to natural being.[54] For this reason, precisely even in the treatise on grace, reference is frequently made in comparison to the realm of nature (Ia IIae, q. 109, a. 5).[55] But the world of nature serves not only as a comparison. In reality, the Aristotelian ontology of natural things also lies at the basis of the doctrine of grace in the *Prima secundae*. This is expressed most clearly in that grace itself is understood as an accident inherent in the soul, or an accidental form of the soul. Thomas, noticing the inadequacy of the Aristotelian ontological terminology, remarks that grace itself, which supplies the participation in divine goodness as an accident, has a more imperfect manner of being than the human soul subsisting in itself, in which grace inheres (Ia IIae, q. 110, a. 2, ad 2).[56] Therefore, Thomas saw that the world of freedom and grace constitutes a realm of being (distinct as a completely different mode from the world of nature) that stands as the condition for the possibility of finite freedom for this world, which is proper to moral being (*ens morale*). Nevertheless, he tried to express it in categories valid for natural things, such as that of "quality" (Ia IIae, q. 111, a. 2, ad 1). Thus, the impression could arise that something like grace can be regarded as an extramental natural thing.[57]

The limits of the Thomist doctrine of grace are obvious by reason of another, though related, element. It is a characteristic of the treatise on grace in the *Prima secundae* that here, in contrast to the earlier work, the causing of divine grace is understood as a divine motion. The frequent use of the terminology of motion indicates that Thomas is making the concept of grace dynamic. Bouillard thinks that this move is connected to a more intensive preoccupation with the Pauline doctrine of grace, while Wawrykow assumes that it can be traced to a growing familiarity with Augustine's late theology of grace.[58] Whatever the influence of Christian thinkers, there can be no doubt that the concept of motion, which in actuality plays a determinative role in the treatise on grace, stems from Aristotelian philosophy, or more exactly, the physics, and is transferred to the world of the will and of freedom. The unmoved mover is in Aristotle a mover of natural things; in Thomas, it is also a mover of the will and of the heart. The divine motion of grace is precisely that motion that both precedes and first enables the self-movement of the free will. What at first sight seems to be an enlargement of the ancient concept of motion soon stands out as just what it has to be seen as historically: a transfer of a category from the world of nature—along with others, for example, the "influx of grace" (*influx gratiae*) or the "intention" (*intentio*) and "remission" (*remissio*)—to the world of freedom (Ia IIae, q. 112, a. 4, ad 2).[59] The question, however, is whether the essence of grace and freedom can ever be adequately expressed in such natural categories as motion, although Thomas himself, even in the treatise on grace, employs other categories such as those of self-communication and gift (which transcend the Aristotelian imaginative world), and these seem to be more appropriate to freedom and grace.[60] But it was reserved for a later time to think out fully the categories which are proper and adequate to the world of freedom.[61]

Notes

[1]See M.-D. Chenu, *Introduction à l'étude de St. Thomas d'Aquin* (Paris: Vrin, 1950), 255–76. On this discussion, see Max Seckler, *Das Heil in der Geschichte* (München: Kösel, 1964), 36, who states that the egress-regress schema mirrors "the most fundamental law of all being." Similarly, Otto Hermann Pesch speaks out as well in "Um den Plan der Summa Theologicae des hl. Thomas von Aquin," in *Thomas von Aquin*, ed. K. Bernath, Bd. I (Darmstadt: Wissenschaftliche Buchgesellschaft, 1978), 411–37.
The most convincing critique of the schema comes from A.-M. Patfoort, "L'unité de la Ia Pars et le mouvement interne de la Somme théologique

de St. Thomas d'Aquin," *Revue de Sciences Philoso-phiques et Théologiques* 47(1963): 513–44, who shows that the *reditus* already begins in the *Prima pars* and extends into the *Tertia pars*, so that the entire schema does not suffice to make intelligible the division of the work into three parts. Considerations of a similar type are expressed also by Thomas F. O'Meara, "Grace as a Theological Structure in the *Summa Theologiae* of Thomas Aquinas," *Récherhes de Théologie ancienne et médiévale* 55 (1988): 130–53, 150. Indeed whoever wishes to hold the view *partout* may read O.-H. Pesch (cited above) at 426 f.; or M. V. Leroy, "Review of *Saint Thomas d'Aquin, Les clefs d'une théologie*," *Révue Thomiste* 84 (1984): 298–303; and J.-P. Torrell, *Magister Thomas. Leben und Werk des Thomas von Aquin*, trans. Katharina Weibel (Freiburg: Herder, 1995), 170.

[2] R. Heinzmann, "Die Theologie auf dem Weg zur Wissenschaft," in *Thomas von Aquin*, 453–69. See also Heinzmann's "Der Plan der 'Summa Theologiae' des Thomas von Aquin in der Tradition der frühscholastischen Systembildung," in *Thomas von Aquin. Interpretation und Rezeption. Studien und Texte*, ed. W. P. Eckert (Mainz: Grünewald, 1974), 455–69; and "Die Entwicklung der Theologie zur Wissenschaft," in *Aufbruch-Wandel-Erneuerung. Beiträge zur "Renaissance" des 12. Jahrhundert*, ed. G. Wieland (Stuttgart: Frommann-Holzboog, 1995), 123–38.

[3] On this, see M. Seckler, *Das Heil in der Geschichte*, 39.

[4] R. Heinzmann, "Die Theologie," 462–63.

[5] W. Kluxen, *Philosophische Ethik bei Thomas von Aquin* (Mainz: Matthias Grünewald, 1964), 61. See also ibid., 170: "The question about good and evil is necessarily a question not of practical science, but belongs to the metaphysics of action."

[6] Ibid., 113.

[7] Ibid., 109: "It is less a matter of practical than of speculative knowledge of the human act."

[8] See also Domingo Báñez, "*Comentarios ineditos a la Prima Secundae de Santo Tómas*," ed. V. B. de Heredia. T. I (Salamanca: San Esteban, 1942), 23: "because in this part the consideration on moral matters is more universal" ("quia in hac parte universalior est consideratio de rebus moralibus").

[9] "etsi sit postremus in executione, est tamen primus in intentione agentis." On the difference between the order of intention and of execution, see ST Ia IIae, q. 1 a. 1, ad 1; q. 18, a. 7, ad 2; q. 20, a. 1, ad 2; q. 25, a. 2; and q. 84, a. 2.

[10] "But the principle of the whole order in things moral is the ultimate end, because it functions in matters of operations just as the indemonstrable principle does in speculative matters . . ." ("Principium autem totius ordinis in moralibus est finis ultimus, qui ita se habet in operativis, sicut principium indemonstrabile in speculativis . . . ").

[11] See Theo Kobusch, *Die Entdeckung der Person. Metaphysik der Freiheit und modernes Menschenbild*, 2. Aufl. (Darmstadt: Wissenschaftliche Buchgesellschaft, 1997).

[12] See Kobusch, *Die Entdeckung der Person*, 51–53.

[13] "Et haec de moralibus in communi dicta sufficiant."

[14] "However eternal life is an end exceeding the proportion of human nature . . . but this requires a higher virtue, which is the virtue of grace." ("Vita autem aeterna est finis excedens proportionem naturae humanae . . . at hoc exigitur altior virtus, quae est virtus gratiae.") See also ibid., a. 6.

[15] See *De veritate*, q. 11, a. 1 (Leonine, 348–54).

[16] *De veritate*, q. 10, a. 6: "it must be said that first principles whose knowledge for us is innate, are certain similitudes of the uncreated truth" ("dicendum quod prima principia quorum cognitio est nobis innata, sunt quaedam similitudines increatate veritatis"; Leonine, 313, 265–67). Also q. 11, a. 1: "The light of reason of this kind by which principles of this kind are known to us is bestowed on us by God, as it were, a certain similitude of uncreated truth resulting in us" ("Huiusmodi autem rationis lumen, quo principia huiusmodi sunt nobis nota, est nobis a Deo inditum, quasi quaedam similitudo increatae veritatis in nobis resultantis"; Leonine, 351, 353–56). See also *In De Trinitate*, q. 3, a. 1, ad 4 (Decker, 114, 4–117, 10).

[17] *De veritate*, q. 18, a. 1, ad 10.

[18] *De veritate*, q. 22, a. 2, ad 1.

[19] Ibid.

[20] "In matters of morality the principle of the whole order is the final end, because it functions in matters of action the way indemonstrable principle does in speculative matters . . ." ("Principium autem totius ordinis in moralibus est finis ultimus, quia ita se habet in operativis, sicut principium indemonstrabile in speculativis . . .").

[21] See *De veritate*, q. 22, a. 5: "It is manifest therefore that the will does not necessarily will by the necessity of coercion, yet wills something necessarily by the necessity of natural inclination" ("Patet igitur quod voluntas non necessario aliquid vult necessitate coactionis, vult tamen aliquid necessario necessitate naturalis inclinationis"; Leonine, 624, 219–22).

[22] *In De Trinitate*, q. 6, a. 4: "For although the human being may be naturally inclined to the last end, it nevertheless cannot naturally attain it, but only through grace, and this is on account of the eminence of that end" ("Quamvis enim homo naturaliter inclinetur in finem ultimum, non tamen potest naturaliter illum consequi, sed solum per gratiam, et hoc est propter eminentiam illius finis"; Decker, 229, 9–12).

[23] See *De veritate*, q. 12, a. 1 (Leonine, 365–70); q. 12, a. 3 (Leonine, 373–80); q. 18, a. 4 (Leonine,

538–44). Already, similarly, *In II Sent.*, d. 28, q. 1. a. 5 (Mandonnet, 706–8).

24On the parallel structure of the two kinds of knowledge of God, see esp. L. Oeing-Hanhoff, "Gotteserkenntnis im Licht der Vernunft und des Glaubens nach Thomas von Aquin," *Thomas von Aquin 1274/1974*, ed. L. Oeing-Hanhoff (München: Kösel, 1974), 97–124.

25*De veritate*, q. 14, a. 2 (Leonine, 439–44).

26See also *In III Sent.*, d. 23, q. 1 a. 5: "therefore faith is required, which makes the end known, and hope, according to which trust in the attainment of the last end is present, as if concerning something possible for it, and charity, through which the end is considered good to the one intending it" ("ideo requiritur fides, quae facit finem cognitum, et spes, secundum quam inest fiducia de consecutione finis ultimi, quasi de re possibili sibi, et caritas, per quam finis reputatur bonum ipsi intendenti") (Moos, 717). Also *In III Sent.*, d. 26, q. 2 a. 2, ad 2: "therefore theological virtues which have the last end for their object . . ." (ideo virtutes theologicae quae habent finem ultimum pro obiecto . . . ; Moos, 836).

27See *In III Sent.*, d. 27, q. 2, a. 3, ad 5 (Moos, 881); q. 2, a. 4, ad 3 (Moos, 888).

28*In De Trinitate*, q. 3, a. 2, ad 4: "Hic tamen habitus non movet per viam intellectus, sed magis per viam voluntatis; unde . . . facit voluntarie assentire." (Decker, 114, 28–115, 2).

29On the movement of the will by the infusion of grace, see ST Ia IIae, q. 113, a. 3, ad 3; q. 113, a. 7; and esp. SCG III, chap. 148.

30See also ST Ia IIae, q. 113, a. 7, ad 1. On the historical background of the medieval doctrine of assent, see G. Verbeke, "Éthique et connaissance de soi chez Abélard," *Philosophie im Mittelalter*, ed. J. P. Beckmann, L. Honnefelder, G. Schimpf, and G. Wieland (Hamburg: Meiner, 1987), 81–101. It plays a significant role in Augustine, as, for example, *Enarratio in Ps. 75*; *Contra Iulianum 3*; *Expositio quorundam propositionum ex epistula ad Romanos* § 27; *Ep. 6*; *De gratia Christi et de peccato originali* 2.39.

31See *In III Sent.*, d. 24, q. 1, a. 3, ad 2: "(the highest good) . . . according as he pours out himself by a supernatural communication; and in accord with this ground, the highest good is the end of our life . . ." ("[summum bonum] . . . secundum quod diffundit se communicatione supernaturali; et secundum hanc rationem summum bonum est finis nostrae vitae . . .") (Moos, 775). See also ST IIa IIae, q. 24, a. 2, ad 1: "but charity is founded upon a certain supernatural communication" ("sed caritas fundatur super quadam communicatione supernaturali").

32See K. Rahner, "Zur scholastischen Begrifflichkeit der ungeschaffenen Gnade," *Zeitschrift für Katholische Theologie* 63 (1939): 137–56.

33J. Splett, "Gnade. Zu einem Grundbegriff—philosophisch," *Zeitschrift für Katholische Theologie* 117 (1995): 152–66, 161.

34ST Ia IIae, q. 110, a. 1, ad 1; q. 110, a. 3; q. 111, a. 1, ad 3; see also SCG III, chap. 150: "for it is said that someone is grateful to someone because he is beloved to that one" ("dicitur enim aliquis alicui esse gratus, quia est ei dilectus").

35*De veritate*, q. 27, a. 1: "For God to accept someone or to love, which is the same, is nothing other than to will something good for him" ("Deum enim acceptare aliquem vel diligere quod idem est nihil est aliud quam velle ei aliquod bonum"; Leonine, 790–91, 123–25).

36See on this Kobusch, *Die Entdeckung der Person*, 23–25. The evaluation of the moral over against the physical sphere (mostly following Cajetan) is still clearly discernible in R. Garrigou-Lagrange, *Grace: Commentary on the Summa Theologica of St. Thomas Ia IIae*, q. 109, a. 114, trans. The Dominican Nuns, Corpus Christi Monastery, CA (St. Louis: B. Herder, 1952), 128: "Sanctifying grace is a participation in the divine nature, not only moral but physical, not only virtual but formal, analogical however . . ."

37See *In I Sent.* d. 17, q. 1, a. 1, ad 3 (Mandonnet, 395–96); *In II Sent.* d. 26, q. 1, a. 1, ad 4 (Mandonnet, 670); d. 5, q. 1, a. 3 (Mandonnet, 148–50); *Super II Ad Cor.* 5:4 (Marietti, 476–77, nn. 158–59).

38"puta recompentio mercedis debitae pro servitio impenso."

39On the connection between the concepts of recompensatio and of commutative justice, see also ST IIa IIae, q. 61, a. 4; q. 61, a. 4, ad 1; q. 77, a. 2; q. 78, a. 2, ad 2.

40See Gabriel Vazquez, *Commentarium ac Disputationum in Primam Secundae Sancti Thomae*, Tomus Secundus (Antwerpiae, 1620), 763b: "For although in things, which are not deeds, there may be a value, and in the case of a horse, wine, oil, and money: nevertheless in them there is no ground of merit whatsoever" ("Nam quamvis in rebus, non sunt operationes, sit valor, ut in equo, vino, oleo et pecunia: tamen in eis nulla est ratio meriti"). 737a: "For as the ground of merit is not in value, which ought to be estimated in terms of price, but only in the value of moral goodness, which is repayed either by praise or something similar" ("Etenim sicut ratio meriti non est in valore, qui pretio aestimari debeat, sed solum in valore bonitatis moralis, quae laude aut aliquo huiusmodi remuneretur").

41"a human being's work can be considered meritorious in two ways: in one way, inasmuch as it proceeds from free decision . . ." ("opus meritorium hominis dupliciter considerari potest: uno modo, secundum quod procedit ex libero arbitrio . . .").

42"And therefore human merit before God cannot exist unless in accord with the presupposition of a divine ordination" ("Et ideo meritum hominis apud Deum esse non potest nisi secundum praesuppositionem divinae ordinationis"); see also ad 3, and q. 114, a. 2.

[43]O.-H. Pesch, "Die Lehre vom 'Verdienst' als Problem für Theologie und Verkündigung," *Festschrift für Michael Schmaus*, ed. L. Scheffczyk, et al. (Paderborn: Schöningh, 1967), 1865–1907, 1904.

[44]Berndt Hamm, *Promissio, Pactum, Ordinatio. Freiheit und Selbstbindung Gottes in der scholastischen Gnadenlehre* (Tübingen: J.C.B. Mohr, 1977), 334; see also Joseph P. Wawrykow, *God's Grace and Human Action. Merit in the Theology of Thomas Aquinas* (Notre Dame, IN: University of Notre Dame Press, 1995), 189, 33.

[45]See also Wawrykow, *God's Grace*, 181: "For Aquinas, it is the divine ordination which makes merit before God possible."

[46]Ibid., 78.

[47]"there can be no merit except from grace" (nullum meritum potest esse nisi ex gratia); see also q. 114, a. 2. Also, q. 111, a. 2: "but inasmuch as it is a principle of a meritorious work, which also proceeds from a free choice, it is called cooperative" (inquantum vero est principium operis meritorii, quod etiam ex libero arbitrio procedit, dicitur cooperans).

[48]See Wawrykow, *God's Grace*, 181, 221. See also Domingo Báñez, *Comentarios inéditos a la prima secundae de Santo Tomás*, T. III (Salamanca: San Esteban, 1948), 317: "Properly, merit consists in a good and free operation, wherefore it acquires a right to a reward" (Proprie meritum consistit in operatione bona et libera unde quod adquiritur ius ad mercedem).

[49]"and thus it is clear that all merit is opposed to grace" ("et sic manifestum est quod omne meritum repugnat gratiae").

[50]Ibid.: "for it seems fitting that to the human being operating in accord with his virtue, God gives a reward in accord with the excellence of his virtue" ("videtur enim congruum ut homini operanti secundum suam virtutem, Deus recompenset secundum excellentiam suae virtutis").

[51]O.-H. Pesch, *Die Theologie der Rechtfertigung bei Martin Luther und Thomas von Aquin* (Mainz: Matthias Grünewald Verlag, 1967), 775, 780. See also B. Catâo, *Salut et rédemption chez St. Thomas d'Aquin L'acte sauveur du Christ* (Paris: Aubier, 1965). Wawrykow, *God's Grace*, 27, rightly criticizes the fact that Pesch underplays the role of justice in the ideas of merit and reward. For the critique of Catâo, see esp. 31. On the metaphysics of the moral sphere, see Kobusch, *Die Entdeckung der Person* s.v. "Recht."

[52]See especially *In II Sent.*, d. 24, q. 2, a. 4 (Mandonnet, 611–614); *In II Sent.*, d. 43, q. 1, a. 5, ad 4 (Mandonnet, 1109); *In III Sent.*, d. 24, q. 1, a. 1, ad 3 (Moos, 762–63); *In III Sent.*, d. 26, q. 2, a. 3, ad 1 (Moos, 839); later on also *De spe*, q. un., a. 1, ad 2–3 (Marietti, 805); ST Ia IIae, q. 62, a. 4, ad 2; and IIa IIae, q. 17, a. 1, ad 2.

[53]See J. Pieper, *Über die Hoffnung* (München: Kösel, 1949), 52.

[54]See *In I Sent.*, d. 17, q. 1, a. 3, Marg. 2: "just as substantial form is related to the existence of nature, so charity is related to the existence of grace" ("sicut se habet forma substantialis ad esse naturae, ita caritas ad esse gratiae"). *In IV Sent.*, d. 17, q. 1, a. 35: "for the existence of grace is above the natural existence . . . " ("est enim esse gratiae supra esse naturale . . . "; Moos, 207). *In IV Sent.* d. 17, q. 1, a. 35: "because in creation the thing occurs according to the existence of nature, which is less than the existence of grace, which is given in justification" ("quia in creatione fit res secundum esse naturae, quod est minus quam esse gratiae, quod datur in justificatione") (Moos, 851). *In IV Sent.* d. 31, q. 1, a. 3: "just as the existence of nature is more essential to the human being than the existence of grace, although the existence of grace is more worthy" ("sicut etiam homini est essentialius esse naturae quam esse gratiae quamvis esse gratiae sit dignius") (Parma, 956). *De caritate*, q. un., a. 1, obj. 13: "the human being in accord with the existence of grace is nearer to God than it is in accord with the existence of nature . . . " ("homo secundum esse gratiae est propinquior Deo quam secundum esse naturae . . . "; Marietti, 754).

[55]See also ST Ia IIae, q. 109, a. 7; q. 111, a. 5, ad 2; q. 112, a. 3, ad 3; q. 113, a. 6, ad 2.

[56]Similarly in ST Ia IIae, q. 110, a. 2, ad 1; see also q. 111, a. 2, ad 1; already in *De veritate*, q. 24, a. 8, ad 6 it says: "so also grace according to its existence is in the free choice through its mode as an accident in a subject" ("ita etiam gratia secundum esse suum est in libero arbitrio per modum eius sicut accidens in subjecto"; Leonine, 701, 181–83).

[57]See Theo Kobusch, "Ens inquantum ens und ens rationis. Ein aristotelisches Problem in der Philosophie des Duns Scotus und Wilhelms von Ockham," *Aristotle in Britain During the Middle Ages*, Société Internationale pour l'Étude de la Philosophie Médiévale: Proceedings of the International Conference at Cambridge, 8–11 Apr. 1994, ed. J. Marenbon (Turnhout: Brepols, 1996), 157–75.

[58]See Henri Bouillard, *Conversion et Grace chez St Thomas d'Aquin* (Paris: Aubier, 1944), 135–37; and Wawrykow, *God's Grace*, 15.

[59]On this see B. J. F. Lonergan, *Grace and Freedom*, ed. J. P. Burns (London: Darton, Longman, and Todd, 1971), 61. The work of Bouillard, *Conversion et Grace*, which goes most thoroughly into the concept of motion, has been the subject of a prolific critique by Thomas Deman, review of *Conversion et grâce chez S. Thomas d'Aquin*, by H. Bouillard, S.J., *Bulletin Thomiste* 7 (1943–1946): 46–58. Deman

points out that just after the treatise on grace, grace as motion is to be distinguished from grace as *habitus*. This criticism is also the position of M. G. Lawler ("Grace and Free Will in Justification," *The Thomist* 35 [1971]: 601–30, esp. 623–25), which takes up that of Bouillard. Deman speaks of the synthetic genius of St. Thomas that develops the distinction between the motion of grace and the universal motion of the first mover, between the supernatural and the natural motion (I attempted to make this distinction familiar above). Yet it must also be critically questioned whether the concept of motion in general is suitable for expressing personal relationships.

60On *donum* as distinct from *datum*, see for example *In I Sent.* d. 18, q. 1, a. 2: "Wherefore gift can be eternal, but not a datum. . . . For a gift, as the Philosopher says, is the giving of what cannot be bought back, not what is not worth being recompensed, but that which does not seek any recompense. Wherefore the gift means liberality in the one giving" ("Unde donum potest esse aeternum, sed non datum . . . . Donum enim, ut dicit Philosophus, IV Top., cap II, est datio irredibilis, non quae recompensari non valeat, sed illa quae recompensationem non quaerit. Unde donum importat liberlitatem in dante"; Mandonnet, 439).

61See Theo Kobusch, "Die Kategorien der Freiheit. Stationen einer historischen Entwicklung: Pufendorf, Kant, Chalybäus," *Allgemeine Zeitschrift für Philosophie* 15 (1990): 13–37.

Selected Further Reading

Auer, Johannes. *Die Entwicklung der Gnadenlehre in der Hochscholastik*, 2 Vols. Freiburg: Herder, 1942–1951.

Deman, T. *Der Neue Bund und die Gnade*. Heidelberg: F. H. Kerle, 1955.

———. "Review of *Conservation et grace chez S. Thomas d'Aquin.*" *Bulletin Thomiste* 7 (1943–1944): 46–58.

Fitzgerald, L. P. "The Divisions of Merit in the Early Scholastics." Ph.D. diss., Pontifical University of St. Thomas, Rome, 1972.

Ladrille, G. "Grace et motion divine chez saint Thomas d'Aquin." *Salesianum* 12 (1950): 37–84.

Lais, H. *Die Gnadenlehre des Hl. Thomas v. Aquin in der Summa contra Gentiles und der Kommentar des Franziskus Silvestris von Ferrara*. Munich: K. Zink, 1951.

Laporte, J.-M. *Les structures dynamiques de la grâce: grâce médicinale et grace élevante selon Thomas d'Aquin*. Tournai: Desclée, 1973.

Lawler, M. G. "Grace and Free Will in Justification: A Textual Study in Aquinas." *The Thomist* 35 (1971): 601–30.

Pesch, Otto Hermann. "Die Lehre vom "Verdienst "als Problem für Theologie und Verkündigung." In *Wahrheit und Verkündigung: Festgabe M. Schmaus*, Vol. 2. Ed. L. Scheffczyk. Paderborn: Schöningh, 1967.

Schenk, Richard. *Die Gnade vollendeter Endlichkeit. Zur transzendentaltheologischen Auslegung der thomanischen Anthropologie*. Freiburg: Herder, 1989.

Schockenhoff, Eberhard. *Bonum Hominis. Die anthropologischen und theologischen Grundlagen der Tugendethik des Thomas v. Aquin*. Mainz: Matthias-Grünewald, 1987.

Schröer, Christian. *Praktische Vernunft bei Thomas von Aquin*. Stuttgart: W. Kohlhammer, 1995.

Stoeckle, B. *Gratia supponit naturam. Geschichte und Analyse eines theologischen Axioms*. Rome: Herder, 1962.

PART II

The Second Part of the Second Part of the *Summa Theologiae*

The Theological Virtue of Faith:
An Invitation to an Ecclesial Life of Truth
(IIa IIae, qq. 1–16)

Stephen F. Brown

The Scriptures speak in different ways of faith. The Letter of James (2:19), with its declaration "Demons believe," describes the loveless, and indeed ironic, faith that demons possess. Habakkuk (2:24), on the other hand, underscores the effect of a love-filled faith, as it declares: "The just man lives by faith" (see also Rom 1:17; Gal 3:11; Heb 10:38). In his Letter to the Hebrews (11:13), Paul (according to the Vulgate's attribution) manifests the achievements of strong faith: "The holy ones by faith have conquered kingdoms." The various Scriptural descriptions of faith well provide the principal source of the questions that filled the *summae* of medieval theologians in their treatises *De fide*.[1] The next most important source for these medieval questions were the commentaries of the fathers, especially those of St. Augustine and St. Gregory the Great.[2] Augustine speaks of explicit beliefs, as when he affirms that "our faith is sound if we believe that no man, old or young, is delivered from the contagion of death and the bonds of sin, except by the one Mediator of God and men, Jesus Christ."[3] Gregory set up the contrast between evident knowledge and inevident faith: Thomas the Apostle "saw one thing and believed something else. He saw a man; he believed him to be God and bore witness to this, saying 'My Lord and my God'."[4] Medieval theological questions, spawned by their Biblical and Patristic sources, were formed and formulated to spur a deeper understanding of the scriptural message. The biblical words "Demons believe" aroused in Aquinas's *Summa theologiae* the *aporia*: "Do demons have faith?" ("*Utrum in daemonibus sit*

fides?"; IIa IIae, q. 5, a. 2); and his answer described the nature and ground of their equivocal faith and how it differed from that of those who enjoyed the virtue of faith. Paul's words in 1 Cor 1:10—"That you all speak the same thing, and there be no schisms among you"—came to establish the ecclesial nature of faith (IIa IIae, q. 1, a. 10, c.).[5] Gregory the Great's declaration that "faith to which human reasoning gives proof is a faith without merit"[6] led to the justification of the science of theology by Aquinas and many of his predecessors (IIa IIae, q. 2, a. 10).

FAITH AS A SEARCH FOR TRUTH

When, however, medieval theologians focused on the virtue of faith, they most frequently centered their attention on Paul's Letter to the Hebrews (11:1), which describes faith as "the substance of things hoped for, the argument for things not seen." Faith is the argument for the realities of Christian belief, especially for the Triune God, the Incarnate Son of God, and the beatific vision as the fulfillment of human life. This centering on truth is not a purely medieval construction. The fathers of the church often focused on this intellectual aspect of the faith; Augustine even presented the Hebrews text of Paul (11:1) as the definition of faith.[7]

The stimulus for the medieval focus on the truth aspect of the virtue of faith most likely was set by a debate between Bernard of Clairvaux and Peter Abelard. Abelard defined faith somewhat ambiguously as "a judgment (*existi-*

matio) of things not seen."[8] Bernard caught the ambiguity of Abelard's restatement of Paul's definition ("judgment" instead of "argument" or "conviction"), and he interpreted Abelard as saying either that Christian faith only has the character of opinion or that each believer can choose which truths of the faith he or she wishes to affirm.[9] This was not exactly what Abelard was attempting to say by "judgment (*existimatio*) of things not seen." A more careful look at his language would indicate that on the whole Abelard used three terms to speak about the realities of the Christian faith: comprehension (*comprehendere, comprehensio*), cognition (*cognoscere, cognitio*), and understanding (*intelligere, intellectio*). "Comprehension," for him, is the type of knowledge that God alone enjoys in knowing himself, while "cognition" is the kind of knowledge that the angels and the blessed have of the divine realities. Human beings ordinarily do not have this kind of knowledge, although there are exceptions, such as the transported experiences of the prophets and of Paul who was rapt to the third heaven.[10] "Understanding" is the kind of knowledge that follows upon faith. It was understanding that was pointed to by the Vulgate text of Isaiah 7:9: "Unless you believe, you shall not understand." In sum, the kind of knowledge that Abelard meant when he spoke of an *existimatio* or "judgment of things not seen" does not signify probable knowledge, but rather indicates a knowledge that really excludes error. It is not the kind of human faith that is pure opinion, but rather a type of faith that is not grounded on evidence that brings *cognition*. Faith as Abelard meant it only excludes experimental knowledge based on the compelling presence of the thing known; it does not exclude certitude. Faith, for Peter Abelard, baits humans into search. It excites an inquiry that one hopes will beget in this life a deeper *understanding*, but it in no way excludes firm assent to Christian truths.

The principal attempt at settling the debate between Abelard and Bernard by underscoring the sure or certain character of the nature of faith is found in Hugh of Saint-Victor's *De sacramentis fidei Christianae*. He gave a more precise definition of faith, contrasting it more distinctly with opinion and evident knowledge:

Faith is a kind of certainty of the mind in things absent, established beyond opinion and short of knowledge. For there are some who straightway repel with the mind what is heard and contradict those things which are said, and these are deniers. Others in those things which they hear select any one side whatever for consideration but they do not approve for affirmation. For although they believe one of the two as more probable, yet they do not presume to assert whether it itself is still true. These are the conjecturers. Others thus approve the other side, so that they assume its approbation even unto assertion. These are the believers. After these kinds of cognition that more perfect kind follows when the thing is made known not from hearing alone but through its presence. For more perfectly do they know who comprehended the thing itself as it is in their presence. These are the knowers. First, therefore, are the deniers, second the doubters, third the conjecturers, fourth the believers, fifth the knowers. From this, therefore, it can be conjectured why we have called faith certainty, since when there is still doubt, there is not faith. It is clear also why we say that certainty itself which we call faith was established beyond opinion or conjecture and short of knowledge.[11]

One of the most detailed expressions among medieval authors before Aquinas of the sure confidence that informs Christian faith is found in the Prologue question of the *Summa aurea* of William of Auxerre. Commenting on Paul's claim that "faith is the argument for things not seen," William asks whether the fathers of the church and the Masters of Sacred Scripture before him did not appear to act perversely when they attempted to prove the articles of the faith by providing human reasons. After all, "faith is the argument for things not seen," not a conclusion justified by rationally grounded arguments. In his response, William offers three reasons why Christian teachers are justified in presenting rational arguments for the faith: first of all, natural reasons increase and strengthen the faith of believers, even though they are not the principal reason causing the faithful to assent to their truth. Second, rational arguments allow the learned to defend the faith against heretics. Third, arguments supporting Christian teaching lead the unlearned to accept the faith: they realize that learned believers have responses for the flood of objections that may come from nonbelievers. William's three reasons, in fact, summarize the position that St. Augustine supported when he said that not all knowledge is worth pursuing, but only "that knowledge by which that most wholesome faith that leads to eternal happiness is begotten, nourished, defended and strengthened."[12] William of Auxerre concludes:

> It is for these three reasons that blessed Peter commanded prelates in particular that "they be ready to render an account to anyone who asks an explanation of those things that are in them by faith and hope" (1 Peter 3:16).[13] Nonetheless, when someone has true faith and also has reasons by which this faith can be manifested, he does not rest upon the First Truth because of these reasons but rather he accepts these reasons because they agree with the First Truth and bear witness to it.[14]

While other facets of the virtue of faith are not neglected in Aquinas's *Summa theologiae*, the focus on the truth aspect of faith is central to his treatise *De fide*. The very first article of the first question asks: "whether the object of faith is the First Truth" (IIa IIae, q. 1, a. 1). Thomas continues with such questions as: "whether an object of faith can be seen," that is, can it be evident (IIa IIae, q. 1, a. 4)? "Can an object of faith also be an object of science" (IIa IIae, q. 1, a. 5)? As he moves on to the act of faith, he wonders whether Augustine is correct in his claim that "to believe is to think with assent" (IIa IIae, q. 2, a. 1). Thomas also questions Augustine over whether it is necessary to believe those things which can be proved by natural reason (IIa IIae, q. 2, a. 4), and whether reasons in support of what one believes lessen the merit of faith (IIa IIae, q. 2, a. 10). When he turns to the virtue itself of faith, he examines the fittingness of Paul's definition of faith—"the substance of things to be hoped for, the evidence of things not seen" (IIa IIae, q. 4, a. 1)—and whether faith resides in the intellect (IIa IIae, q. 4, a. 2). He also attempts to determine if it is more certain than science and the other intellectual virtues (IIa IIae, q. 4, a. 8). There is thus a strong accent on the truth aspects of faith in Aquinas. Yet, he did not create this accent—it was already there in his biblical, patristic, and medieval predecessors.

AQUINAS ON PAUL'S DEFINITION OF FAITH

When Aquinas deals with the virtue of faith (IIa IIae, q. 4, a. 1), he examines whether Paul's description of faith as "the substance of things to be hoped for, the evidence of things not seen" is a fitting or suitable definition. Aquinas's response to those who declare that it is technically not a definition contrasts, in brief, the methods of Plato and Aristotle: Aristotle provides arguments that are explicitly syllogistic in form; Plato employs implicit syllogisms that he hides behind his more rhetorical questions and declarations. Both philosophers, however, treat, either explicitly or implicitly, the substance of the issue. Similarly, Aquinas judges that although Paul's description of faith is not an explicit definition, it does contain all the essential elements of a suitable, albeit implicit, definition.

Hugh of Saint-Victor, whose treatise on faith is so well-respected by Aquinas, declares that Paul's statement tells us less of what faith is than what it does.[15] Aquinas, however, is more subtle in his judgment: "If we consider the matter more rightly, this definition overlooks none of the points in reference to which faith can be defined, although the words themselves are not arranged in the form of a definition . . ." (Ia IIae, q. 4, a. 1).[16]

At this point, as Aquinas examines the suitability of Paul's description of faith, he gets to the heart of the matter concerning the nature of Christian faith:

> In order to make this clear, we must observe that since habits are known by their acts, and acts by their objects, faith, being a habit, should be defined by its proper act in relation to its proper object. . . . Now it has been already stated that the object of faith is the First Truth, as unseen, and whatever we hold because of it, so that it must needs be under the aspect of something unseen that the First Truth is the end of the act of faith.[17] (Ibid.)

In short, the First Truth is not only the ground of faith. The First Truth is also the end or goal of faith. In his *Exposition on the 'De Trinitate' of Boethius*, Thomas argues: "Consequently, since the goal of human life is perfect happiness, which consists in the full knowledge of divine realities, the direction of human life toward perfect happiness from the very beginning requires faith in the divine, the complete knowledge of which we look forward to in our final state of perfection."[18]

THE NECESSITY OF FAITH

I will begin this attempt at understanding Aquinas's treatise on faith by dealing with this end or goal of faith. All humans seek fulfillment as their end. Philosophers have explained that fulfillment cannot be found in sense pleasures, since, as pleasant as such pleasures might be, they sell people short by making them focus on the same kind of fulfillment that is pursued by lesser, non-rational, animals. Neither is wealth humanly satisfying, since the gathering of wealth aims at a material goal, and, of course, humans are more than material beings. A human should strive for higher things. Is one's goal in life to be honored and recognized by other spiritual beings? Certainly, honor is a more noble goal than wealth; yet acclaim seems more to depend on others and their judgments, which are often fickle and based on appearances. For fulfillment, one needs something more suitable to his or her nature: one wants to base life on more than appearances and external judgments that often have little to do with true judgments of the individual as a human being. One might suggest, then, artistic or scientific goals. Yet, whatever goals are set and met, a person seems to have a capacity for yet more. The human estimate of fulfillment always seems to fall short.

With a taller yardstick, God tells us, through his prophets, that we are made to expect even more: "Eye has not seen, nor ear heard what God has prepared for those who love Him" (1 Cor 2:9). Basically, Aquinas's text concerning faith points to a goal or an end for human life that even the most intelligent humans, the philosophers, had not thought or imagined. Aquinas indicates this by distinguishing between the philosophers' imperfect happiness and the perfect happiness that God has prepared for the faithful.

The goal of faith is thus beyond humanity. Never in the highest human thoughts would one have discovered it. It is in this sense, from the perspective of its origin, beyond human nature. One only could know of it if the unlimited First Truth, who is not only the end or goal of one's life but also the ground, reached down and told about it in a way that limited minds could grasp to some degree. This He did in His immediate revelation to the prophets or sacred writers, whose words comprise the Scriptures. They paint a new picture of human fulfillment and aim. In other words, a human being's goal is actually beyond his or her nature; it is "supernatural."

When Aquinas asks in IIa IIae, q. 6, a. 1, whether faith is infused into man by God, he answers by stressing two distinct points. First, in order to have faith, it is necessary that something be presented to human beings for their belief. Since what is proposed for their belief surpasses human reason, human beings would not know about the divine plan for them unless God chose to reveal it to them. To the apostles and prophets this revelation was given immediately; to others it has been and is given through preaching. Aquinas's second point concerns the acceptance of and assent to what is preached. Revealed truth is not a self-evident message that forces assent. Faith is an assent to what is not self-evident. It is an assent to what is beyond human invention and grasp. Why then do believers assent?

Aquinas rejects certain explanations. At times, divine revelation has also been accompanied by miraculous events. At other times, preaching seems effective because of the persuasive power of the speaker. Such external inducements, as helpful as they might be, cannot be sufficient causes of assent. If they were, then all those who experienced them would assent. Yet, the Scriptures often speak of the rejection of Christ despite his many miracles and the refusal to accept Paul's message despite his powerful preaching. So, assent to revealed truth can only be explained by an appeal to a grace from God. In response to the Pelagians who claimed that the assent came from human free choice, Aquinas answers: "But this is false, for since, by assenting to what belongs to faith, man is raised above his nature, this must needs come to him from some supernatural principle moving him inwardly; and this is God. Therefore, faith, as regards the assent which is the chief act of faith, is from God moving man inwardly by grace" (IIa IIae, q. 6, a. 1).[19]

Faith is the virtue that first leads Christians to accept the elevated beatitude that God has prepared as our fulfillment. To establish the elevated or grace-given status of perfect happiness, Aquinas has to point out the limits of the natural seekers for wisdom, even those whom he respects highly. He notes the limits of a person's natural abilities frequently in his writings. At the very beginning of the *Summa theologiae*, when he asks whether human beings need more knowledge than their natural abilities can provide to attain salvation, he indicates that few people aim at the highest levels of knowledge, and then only late in life; sadly, even these few end up with a mixture of error in regard to whatever ultimate truth they attain. This is the case in regard to what one can naturally know about divine realities; in the case of supernatural truths human limits are even more obvious.[20] In the *Summa contra gentiles*, the *Quaestiones disputatae De veritate*, and the *Expositio in librum Boethii De Trinitate*, Thomas offers very similar reflections.[21] In the latter two works, he indicates the source of his reflections: the five causes that limit human attainment of a knowledge of God presented by Moses Maimonides in *The Guide of the Perplexed*.[22] In his treatise on faith in the *Summa theologiae*, Thomas states that there are three reasons why human beings need biblical faith to compensate for their best natural efforts to know what divine things are about: (1) Without faith a person would come to a knowledge about God only late in life. (2) Many people, due to dullness of mind, the conflicting cares and needs of daily life, or their own apathy towards study, would be deprived of a knowledge of God if divine things were not proposed to them by way of faith. (3) Even the philosophers in their search into questions about God and humanity have erred on many points. To the end, therefore, that a more secure knowledge of God might be present among people, even the few who seek a knowledge of God, it is necessary that divine things be taught by way of faith.[23]

However, Thomas casts Maimonides' observations within the context of Christian faith. Christian faith provides a perspective beyond that offered by Maimonides: "There are, however, some aspects of the divinity that human reason is utterly incapable of knowing fully: we await their clear knowledge in the life to come, where our happiness will be complete."[24] Moses Maimonides showed how the biblical faith of the Jewish people supplied for the weaknesses of human beings left on their own. This makes Torah absolutely necessary for the non-philosophers. But even the few philosophical-minded must be close to the Torah's presentation of God and his laws until they mature philosophically late in life. Maimonides did not, obviously, take into consideration the triune God or our union with God in the beatific vision that is proper to Christian faith. Aquinas thus is in a different context when he concludes: "We shall be advanced to this knowledge not by anything due to our nature but only by divine grace."[25] Faith does not merely compensate for reason's weakness and for general human distractions, or help the philosopher in the more mature search for God, as Maimonides argues; it elevates the believer to a perspective beyond that of reason limited to its own general or philosophical endeavors. This alternative vision is the Christian-faith contribution: it reveals the triune God, the importance of Christ, the divine Mediator between God and humanity, and the blessed vision of God that is the completion of the search of the Christian believer for the goal that God has set for our fulfillment. Without Christian revelation and its grace-supported acceptance, one would not know of his or her supernatural dignity nor pursue the supernatural end.

THE ASSISTANCE OF REASON: PREACHERS AND TEACHERS

If Aquinas at one level underscores the weakness of the human intellect in knowing divine things—those that are naturally knowable and those that are the supernatural objects of faith—he also stresses the importance of human effort in regard to faith and the search for truth. Following St. Paul's declaration that "faith comes from hearing," he acknowledges the importance of preaching in bringing the divine message to human beings. He likewise continues the tradition of St. Augustine, who urged Christians to pursue the kind of knowledge that "begets, nourishes, defends and strengthens" the faith.

One might wonder how it is compatible to say that faith is a divine gift that can only be explained as an infused grace from God, and yet claim at the same time, as Augustine does, that Christians should pursue the kind of human knowledge that "begets" faith. Aquinas answers objections of this kind by saying that "science begets and nourishes faith by way of external persuasion afforded by some science; but the chief and proper cause of faith is that which moves man inwardly to assent" (IIa IIae, q. 6, a. 1).[26] God uses human instruments, such as preachers and teachers, to beget, nourish, defend, and strengthen faith, but such instruments are not sufficient on their own to produce faith. If they were, then every competent preacher would be effective in leading his or her listeners to affirm the faith preached, and every teacher would be successful in his or her faith endeavors.

Aquinas, while insisting that faith is a divine gift and not solely the product of preaching or teaching, still stresses the importance of preaching and teaching concerning divine things. He even claims that theology or the study of the Scriptures can not only provide inspirational or moral lessons, but that it can be a science or very solid form of knowledge. Looking at the model that Aristotle gave for science, Thomas in his Commentary on the *Sentences* of Peter Lombard and in his Exposition on Boethius's *De trinitate* uses the expressions "*quasi 'principia'*" and "*quasi 'conclusiones'*" to indicate that the theological premises or principles are, strictly speaking, not evident, but that they act in a parallel fashion to the way philosophical principles or premises act in relation to philosophical conclusions.[27]

The main purpose of the *Summa theologiae* is to set up a more scientific organization of the scriptural message. Peter Lombard's *Sentences*, which became the basic textbook in theology in the Middle Ages, had flaws, as Thomas explains in the Prologue to his *Summa*: too many useless questions, illogical organization, and boring repetitiveness.[28]

Aquinas wanted theology to be a more scientifically organized discipline. One of his Parisian predecessors, Peter Comestor, had attempted to organize the forest of the Scriptures into a unified story and crafted the *Historia scholastica*, a history of salvation. Others, like Peter Lombard and those who commented on his work, tried a logical ordering of

the scriptural message instead of an historical one. Aquinas wanted to improve on their earlier *Summae quaestionum* by bringing forth a more scientifically satisfying work that, like them, followed a logical instead of an historical approach. Peter Lombard and many of the twelfth- and early thirteenth-century teachers of Scripture had taken this logical approach, and Aquinas, as I noted earlier, found them wanting.

Some twenty years before Aquinas, William of Auxerre, in his *Summa*, attempted to organize Christian teaching in a scientific way. He started with principles or premises and then developed conclusions along the Aristotelian model of science. Yet, his principles or premises were chosen according to the capability of believers, not according to an intrinsic importance belonging to the truths themselves. William started with principles or premises that were true and knowable to any believer—that Christ was a man, that he was humble, meek, and patient. For Aquinas, the premises or principles that controlled his view of a scientific version of the Scriptures were the articles of the faith expressed in the creed. In his more scientific study of theology, he focused more on the essential elements of the faith. He does not concentrate on premises that are first known by any reader, but on principles or articles that are in themselves more essential to the faith.

Recognizing that the articles of the Christian faith cannot be proved, but that they are the premises whose truth guarantees all the truths that are deduced from them, Thomas sees these premises of faith as parallel to Aristotle's first principles or premises. You cannot prove everything, according to Aristotle; you must start with some self-evident premises. In a similar way, you cannot prove the articles of the creed that serve as the first principles of theology. You accept them on faith. Yet, even here, Aquinas does not desert his attempt at understanding. When Aristotle acknowledged the necessity to admit first principles that are not demonstrable, he still did not lapse into blind assertion of them. What did he do in their regard? Aquinas, in his exposition of Boethius's *De trinitate*, tells of the first principles of theology or articles of the creed and what can be done in their regard: "They are also defended against those who attack them, as the Philosopher argues against those who deny principles. Moreover, they are clarified by certain analogies, just as principles that are naturally known are made evident by induction but not proved by demonstrative reasoning."[29]

In dealing with the first principles of theology, then, Aquinas, is not a fideist. He insists on the human efforts of theologians to defend in suitable ways the principles accepted on faith. He argues that at the very least theologians must be able to explain the terminology and meaning of the principles or basic truths of the faith in a way that shows that they are not contrary to reason. Furthermore, they must search for suitable analogies that will help searchers to arrive at some understanding of these fundamental truths.

The other aspect of the scientific nature of theology is its deductive character. Throughout the history of the Christian understanding of revelation, a certain type of deduction, in the sense of making explicit what was already implied in the Scriptures, has been admitted as necessary. One finds such "deductions" in the later declarations of the councils that opposed heretical interpretations regarding the Trinity or Christ and in the explicit articles of the various formulations of the creeds. Aquinas, in his view of theology, sees such procedures as an important aspect of its study. Theological conclusions, drawn from revealed premises, follow as explicit declarations of basic theological principles or premises. Theology is not just carrying out in a mechanical way the rules of logic. It is a deepening through its deduction of the understanding of the rich message of the scriptural revelation and of the divine mysteries contained therein.

Another side of this process of making things more explicit also shows the scientific organization that Aquinas desires. When he deals with the object of faith in IIa IIae, q. 1, a. 7, he indicates that some of the articles of the creed, which serve as principles or premises for deducing other truths, have a certain hierarchy among them:

In like manner, all the articles are contained implicitly in certain primary truths of the faith, such as God's existence, and His providence over the salvation of man, according to Heb 9: "He that cometh to God, must believe that He

is, and is a rewarder to them that seek Him." For the being of God includes all that we believe to exist in God eternally, and in these our happiness consists, while belief in His providence includes all those things which God dispenses in time for man's salvation, and which are the way to that happiness; and in this way, again, some of those articles which follow from these are contained in others. Thus faith in the Redemption of mankind includes implicitly the Incarnation of Christ, His passion and so forth.[30] (IIa IIae, q. 1, a. 7, c.)

If the mark of a wise person is to order things properly, then Aquinas's efforts to discover the wise order of reality according to God's plan would qualify his well-ordered form of Christian teaching as a wisdom participating in the Divine Wisdom. It is a serious attempt at understanding God's order of reality. Not only, then, is theology a science; it is the highest and noblest science, providing the divine order within which all the other sciences, and thus all other realities, have their place. Theology is our human way of seeing the divine order of things. Its teachers have this office and challenge: to present to the degree that is humanly possible the divine order of reality, an order that is beyond purely human imagination and purely human attainment (IIa IIae, q. 2, a. 6, ad 1).[31]

THE ECCLESIAL CHARACTER OF FAITH

Universities themselves were created under church auspices in the Middle Ages, and a university theologian held an office that required him to perform various duties. These duties were responsibilities associated with his office. He had the duty to be a person who "begot, nourished, defended, and strengthened" the moral and doctrinal truth of Christian revelation. One of Thomas Aquinas's contemporaries at Oxford University, the Franciscan Richard Rufus, describes well the duties or responsibilities that were expected of these more learned believers:

At this point the overall work of the theologian is divided into four parts, or, as it were, into four quadrants, namely, into celebration, reading, preaching and dealing with questions. In regard to the first quadrant (in celebration), we praise God in the liturgy. In the second place (in our formal reading), we set forth the original meaning of the holy Scriptures by employing our natural talents to expound, or, as it were, bring forth, its message. Thirdly (by preaching), we form by moral training those who are unlettered and who are, as it were, unformed. Fourthly (through questions), we untie knotty issues, explain difficult points, clear up ambiguous elements, and bring clarity to obscure things to the degree possible.[32]

Not every Christian had the talent and calling, and thus the office, to be a theologian, so theologians in their office of preaching had to guide the unlearned believers, according to ecclesial understanding, to the goal of Christian life and to indicate the necessary means to attain it. Believers are baptized into the church and thereby enter the Christian community of faith and understanding. The ordinary believer affirms explicitly the articles or essential beliefs of the Christian faith found in the declarations of the Apostles' Creed and of the Nicene Creed; they also accept implicitly all that God has revealed in the Scriptures. Theologians by their offices as theologians have to have a more explicit knowledge in order to "beget, nourish, defend, and strengthen the faith" in themselves and the Christian community. Yet, their faith is not different from the faith of the simple believers. It is the church's faith—all of them believe what God has revealed through the prophets and apostles as taught by the church.

The explicit beliefs of the church are found in the creeds, which are a digest of God's essential revelation. It might be of some significance to know that David was the son of Jesse (IIa IIae, q. 2, a. 5, c.), but it is much more important to know that Christ is the Son of God, that He became man, that He suffered, died and was buried, and rose again (IIa IIae, q. 1, a. 8, c.). The creeds of the church differ only in their explicitness, rather than in substance, from one another. Later creeds, such as the Nicene Creed, bring out more explicitly what is really, but only implicitly, contained in the Apostles' Creed and the Scriptures (IIa IIae, q. 1, a. 9, ad 2). These more explicit declarations of later creeds manifest the church's effort to ward off errors and distortions regarding divine revelation. They are the result of the church's mission to

"defend the faith," a mission in which theologians, such as Athanasius, shared at the Council of Nicea (IIa IIae, q. 1, a. 10, ad 3).

The creed or symbol is "a collection of the truths of the faith" expressed in set words (IIa IIae, q. 1, a. 9, c.).[33] The truths are expressed in statements or propositions. The true believer, however, does not stop at the words; he believes in the realities expressed in the words. Believers live their lives in accord with these realities. They enter a different world than the one revealed by human discovery. They receive from God an invitation to a new way of seeing and a new way of living. Aquinas captures this well in the opening words of his *Compendium theologiae*:

Faith is a certain foretaste of that knowledge which is to make us happy in the life to come. The Apostle says, in Hebrews 11:1, that faith is "the substance of things to be hoped for, " as though implying that faith is already, in some preliminary way, inaugurating in us the things that are to be hoped for, that is, future beatitude.[34]

Notes

[1]On the various biblical sources for the questions concerning faith, see William of Auxerre, *Summa aurea*, lib. III, tract. XII, cap. 1, ed. J. Ribaillier (*Spicilegium Bonaventurianum*, XVIII A: Paris-Rome, 1986), 197–99.

[2]Peter Abelard in his *Introductio ad theologiam*, lib. 1, II, provides numerous references to Gregory the Great and St. Augustine concerning the nature of faith (PL 178, 984–85).

[3]August. *Ep.* 190, "Ad Optatum Episcopum": "Illa fides sana est qua credimus nullum hominem, sive maioris sive parvae aetatis, liberari a contagio mortis et obligatione peccati nisi per unum mediatorem Dei et hominum, Iesum Christum" (cited in IIa IIae, q. 2, a. 7, *sed contra*; cf. PL 33, 858).

[4]Gregory the Great, *XL Homiliarum in Evangelia Libri duo*, II, 26: "Sed aliud vidit, aliud credidit. . . . Hominem ergo vidit, et Deum confessus est, dicens: 'Dominus meus, et Deus meus'" (PL 76, 1202).

[5]"Idipsum dicatis omnes, et non sint in vobis schismata."

[6]Gregory the Great, *In Evangelia*, II, hom. 26: "nec fides habet meritum, cui humana ratio praebet experimentum" (PL 76, 1197).

[7]August. *De trin.* 13.1.3: "Numquid enim adhuc fides dicenda est cum definita sit in epistula ad

hebraeos fides dictumque sit eam esse convictionem rerum quae non videntur" (PL 42, 1015).

[8]Peter Abelard, *Introductio ad theologiam*, lib. I, I: "Est quippe fides existimatio rerum non apparentium" (PL 178, 981).

[9]Bernard of Clairvaux, *Disputatio adversus Abaelardum*, cap. l: "Fidem definivit aestimationem rerum non apparentium, nec sensibus corporis subiacentium, aestimans fortasse vel communem fidem nostram aestimationem esse, vel licitum esse in eo quodlibet cuilibet ad libitum aestimare" (PL 182, 1051).

[10]2 Cor 12:1–4.

[11]Hugh of St.-Victor, *De sacramentis fidei Christianae*, I, 10, c. 2: "Fidem esse certitudinem quamdam animi de rebus absentibus, supra opinionem et infra scientiam constitutam. Sunt enim quidam qui audita statim animo repellunt et contradicunt his quae dicuntur: et hi sunt negantes. Alii in iis quae audiunt alteram quamcumque partem eligunt ad existimationem, sed non approbant ad affirmationem. Quamvis enim unum ex duobus magis probabile intelligunt, utrum tamen adhuc idipsum verum sit asserere non praesumunt: hi sunt opinantes. Alii sic alteram partem approbant, ut eius approbationem etiam in assertionem assumant: hi sunt credentes. Post ista genera cognitionis illud perfectius sequitur cum res non ex auditu solo, sed per suam praesentiam notificatur. Perfectius enim agnoscunt qui ipsam rem ut est in sua praesentia comprehendunt: hi sunt scientes. Primi ergo sunt negantes, secundi dubitantes, tertii opinantes, quarti credentes, quinti scientes. Ex his ergo conici potest quare fidem certitudinem appellamus, quoniam ubi adhuc dubitatio est fides non est. Patet etiam quare ipsam certitudinem quam fidem appellamus supra opinionem vel aestimationem, et infra scientiam dicimus esse constitutam" (PL 176, 330). Hugh of St.-Victor: *On the Sacraments of the Christian Faith*, I, 10, c. 2, trans. Roy J. Deferrari (Cambridge, MA: Medieval Academy of America, 1951), 168.

[12]August. *De trin.* 14.1: "Non utique quidquid sciri ab homine potest in rebus humanis, ubi plurimum supervacuae vanitatis et noxiae curiositatis est, huic scientiae tribuo, sed illud tantummodo quo fides saluberrima, quae ad veram beatitudinem ducit, gignitur, nutritur, defenditur et roboratur" (PL 42, 1037).

[13]On the wording and use of this text, see J. de Ghellinck, *Le mouvement théologique du XIIe siècle* (Bruges: Éditions 'de Tempel', 1948), 279–84.

[14]William of Auxerre, *Summa aurea*, I, prol. : Propter has tres rationes precipit beatus Petrus maxime prelatis ut parati sint omni poscenti reddere rationem de ea quae inest eis fide et spe, 1a Petri iii. Cum autem habet quis veram fidem et rationes quibus ostendi possit fides, ipse non innititur primae

veritati propter illas rationes, sed potius acquiescit illis rationibus quia consentiunt primae veritati et ei attestantur" (Ribaillier, 16).

[15]Hugh of St.-Victor, *De sacramentis fidei Christianae*, I, 10, c. 2: "Sic itaque fides est substantia rerum sperandarum, quia per eam iam quodammodo quae futura sunt subsistunt in nobis, et argumentum non apparentium, quoniam per ea quae occulta sunt approbantur a nobis. Sed quia in hac descriptione non quid sit fides, sed quid faciat fides ostenditur, nec ea quae de praeteritis vel de praesentibus habetur fides diffinitur, si quis plenam ac generalem diffinitionem fidei signare voluerit dicere potest: fidem esse certitudinem quamdam animi de rebus absentibus, supra opinionem et infra scientiam constitutam" (PL 176, 330). Deferrari trans.: "And so faith is the substance of things to be hoped for, because through it indeed in some manner the things which are to come and the proof of things which are not apparent subsist in us, since through these the things that are hidden are proven by us. But since in this description not what faith is but what faith does is shown, and since that faith is not defined which is held regarding past or present matters, if any one wishes to note a full and general definition of faith, he can say that faith is a kind of certainty of the mind in things absent, established beyond opinion and short of knowledge."

[16]"Tamen, si quis recte consideret, omnia ex quibus fides potest definiri in praedicta descriptione tanguntur, licet verba non ordinentur sub forma definitionis . . . "

[17]"Ad cuius evidentiam considerandum est quod, cum habitus cognoscantur per actus et actus per obiecta, fides, cum sit habitus quidam, debet definiri per proprium actum in comparatione ad proprium obiectum. . . . Dictum est autem supra quod veritas prima est obiectum fidei secundum quod ipsa est non visa, et ea quibus propter ipsam inhaeretur. Et secundum hoc oportet quod ipsa veritas prima se habeat ad actum fidei per modum finis secundum rationem rei non visae."

[18]*In De Trinitate*, q. 3, a. 1: "Cum ergo finis humanae uitae sit beatitudo, quae consistit in plena cognitione diuinorum, necessarium est ad humanam uitam in beatitudinem dirigendam statim a principio habere fidem diuinorum, quae plene cognoscenda exspectantur in ultima perfectione humana" (Leonine, 107–8, 123–28).

[19]"Sed hoc est falsum. Quia cum homo assentiendo his quae sunt fidei elevetur supra naturam suam, oportet quod hoc insit ei ex supernaturali principio interius movente, quod est Deus. Et ideo fides quantum ad assensum qui est principalis actus fidei, est a Deo interius movente per gratiam."

[20]"Ad ea etiam quae de Deo ratione humana investigari possunt, necessarium fuit hominem in-

strui revelatione divina. Quia veritas de Deo per rationem investigata, a paucis, et per longum tempus, et cum admixtione multorum errorum homini proveniret; a cuius tamen veritatis cognitione dependet tota hominis salus, quae in Deo est. Ut igitur salus hominibus et convenientius et certius proveniat, necessarium fuit quod de divinis per divinam revelationem instruantur."

[21]SCG q. 1, a. 4 (Leonine, 11); *De veritate*, q. 14, a. 10 (ed. Leonina, XXII/2), 466–67; *In De Trinitate*, q. 3, a. 1 (Leonine, 108).

[22]Moses Maimonides, *The Guide of the Perplexed*, I, 34, vol. 1, trans. S. Pines (Chicago: University of Chicago Press, 1963), 72–79.

[23]See ST IIa IIae, q. 2, a. 4: "Dicendum quod necessarium est homini accipere per modum fidei non solum ea quae sunt supra rationem, sed etiam ea quae per rationem cognosci possunt. Et hoc propter tria: Primo, quidem ut citius homo ad veritatis divinae cognitionem perveniat. Scientia enim ad quam pertinet probare Deum esse et alia huiusmodi de Deo, ultimo hominibus addiscenda proponitur, praesuppositis multis aliis scientiis. Et sic non nisi post multum tempus vitae suae homo ad Dei cognitionem perveniret. Secundo, ut cognitio Dei sit communior. Multi enim in studio scientiae proficere non possunt, vel propter habetudinem ingenii, vel propter alias occupationes et necessitates temporalis vitae, vel etiam propter torporem addiscendi. Qui omnino a Dei cognitione fraudarentur nisi proponerentur eis divina per modum fidei. Tertio modo propter certitudinem. Ratio enim humana in rebus divinis est multum deficiens, cuius signum est quia philosophi de rebus humanis naturali investigatione perscrutantes in multis erraverunt et sibi ipsis contraria senserunt. Ut ergo indubitata et certa cognitio apud homines de Deo, oportuit quod divina eis per modum fidei traderentur, quasi a Deo dicta, qui mentiri non potest." See also Ia, q. 1, a. 1, supra, n. 23; and SCG q. l, a. 4 (Leonine, 11).

[24]*In De Trinitate*, q. 3, a. 1: "Quedam uero diuinorum sunt ad que plene cognoscenda nullatenus ratio humana sufficit, set eorum plena cognitio expectatur in futura uita, ubi erit plena beatitudo . . . " (Leonine, 108, 164–67).

[25]Ibid.: "Et ad hanc cognitionem homo perducetur non ex debito sue nature, set ex sola diuina gratia . . . " (Leonine, 108, 168–70).

[26]"Dicendum quod per scientiam gignitur fides et nutritur per modum exterioris persuasionis, quae fit ab aliqua scientia. Sed principalis et propria causa fidei est id quod interius movet ad assentiendum."

[27]*In De Trinitate*, q. 2, a. 2, ad 4: "Articuli autem fidei in hac scientia non sunt quasi conclusiones, sed quasi principia . . . " (Leonine, 96, 134–35).

[28]ST Ia, Prol.: "Consideravimus namque huius doctrinae novitios in his quae a diversis conscripta sunt plurimum impediri; partim quidem propter

multiplicationem inutilium quaestionum, articulorum et argumentorum; partim etiam quia ea quae sunt necessaria talibus ad sciendum non traduntur secundum ordinem disciplinae, sed secundum quod requirebat librorum expositio, vel secundum quod se praebebat occasio disputandi; partim quidem quia eorundem frequens repetitio et fastidium et confusionem generabat in animis auditorum."

[29]*In De Trinitate*, q. 2, a. 2, ad 4: "Articuli autem fidei . . . etiam defenduntur ab impugnantibus, sicut Philosophus in IV *Metaphysicae* disputat contra negantes principia, et manifestantur per aliquas similitudines, sicut principia naturaliter nota per inductionem, non ratione demonstrativa, probantur" (Leonine, 96, 134–40).

[30]"Et similiter omnes articuli implicite continentur in aliquibus primis credibilibus, scilicet ut credatur Deus esse et providentiam habere circa hominum salutem, secundum illud ad Hebr., 'Accedentem ad Deum oportet credere quia est, et quod inquirentibus se remunerator sit.' In esse enim divino includuntur omnia quae credimus in Deo aeternaliter existere, in quibus nostra beatitudo consistit. In fide autem providentiae includuntur omnia quae temporaliter a Deo dispensantur ad hominum salutem, quae sunt via in beatiudinem. Et per hunc etiam modum aliorum subsequentium articulorum quidam in aliis continentur, sicut in fide redemptionis humanae implicite continentur et Incarnatio Christi et eius Passio et omnia huiusmodi."

[31]Thomas here speaks of theologians whose duty or office it is to teach others. At about the same time at Oxford, Franciscan theologian Richard Rufus writes that a theologian has four officies or duties: (1) the duty of celebrating the Eucharist; (2) the duty of preaching ; (3) the duty of disputing theological questions; and (4) the duty of reading, in the technical sense of explaining the very text itself.

[32]Richard Rufus, *In I Sententiarum*, Prol. (Oxford, Balliol College, cod. 62, f. 6rb): "Dividitur autem hic universus labor in quattuor partes, quasi in quattuor quadrantes, scilicet, in iubilationem, lectionem, praedicationem, quaestionem. Primo quadrante in ecclesiasticó officio Deum laudamus. Secundo, originalem litteram sacrae Scripturae nomine ingenii exponendo, quasi exarando, reseramus. Tertio, rudes et quasi informes moribus informamus. Quarto, nodosa enodamus, difficilia explanamus, ambigua certificamus, obscura, prout possibile est, elucidamus." For a discussion of these various offices of the theologian, see Jean-Pierre Torrell, *Saint Thomas Aquinas: The Person and His Work*, vol. 1, trans. R. Royal (Washington, DC: Catholic University of America Press, 1996), 54–74. For an earlier discussion of the offices of the theologian, see Peter Cantor, *Verbum abbreviatum*, cap. l: In tribus igitur consistit exercitium sacrae scripturae, circa lectionem, disputationem et praedica-

tionem" (PL 205, 25). It should be noted that Torrell stresses that, in the formula of Peter Cantor, and in the fulfillment of these duties by Thomas, preaching comes after reading and disputation, since preaching must have a solid theological basis.

[33]"Et ab huiusmodi sententiarum fidei collectione nomen symboli est acceptum."

[34]*Comp. theol.* , chap. 2: "Fides autem praelibatio quaedam est illius cognitionis quae nos in futura beatos faciet. Unde et Apostolus dicit quod est 'substantia sperandarum rerum,' quasi iam in nobis res sperandas, id est futuram beatitudinem, per modum cuiusdam inchoationis subsistere faciens" (Leonine, 83, 1–6).

Selected Further Reading

Alfaro, Juan. "Supernaturalitas fidei iuxta S. Thomam." *Gregorianum* 44 (1963): 501–42; 731–87.

Aubert, Roger. "Le caractère raisonnable de l'acte de foi." *Revue d'histoire ecclésiastique* 39 (1943): 22–99.

———. *Le problème de l'acte de foi. Données traditionneles et résultats des controverses récentes.* 4th ed. Louvain: E. Nauwelaerts, 1969.

———. "Le role de la volonté dans l'acte de foi d'après les théologiens de la fin du XIIIe siècle."In *Miscellanea moralia A. Janssen.* Vol. I. Louvain: E. Nauwelaerts, 1948.

———. "Le traité de la foi à la fin du XIIIe siècle." In *Theologie in Geschichte und Gegenwart. Michael Schmaus zum 60. Geburtstag.* Ed. J. Auer and H. Volk. Munich: K. Zink, 1957.

Bourgeois, Daniel. "'Inchoatio vitae eternae.' La dimension eschatologique de la vertu théologale de foi chez saint Thomas d'Aquin." *Sapienza* 27 (1974): 272–314.

Cessario, Romanus. *Christian Faith and the Theological Life.* Washington, DC: Catholic University of America Press, 1996.

Dulles, Avery. *The Assurance of Things Hoped For: A Theology of Christian Faith.* New York: Oxford University Press, 1994.

Duroux, B. *La psychologie de la foi chez S. Thomas d'Aquin.* Tournai: Desclée de Brouwer, 1963.

Guzie, Tad W. "The Act of Faith according to St. Thomas: A Study in Theological Methodology." *The Thomist* 19 (1965): 239–80.

Jenkins, John I. *Knowledge and Faith in Thomas Aquinas.* Cambridge: Cambridge University Press, 1997.

Labourdette, M.-M. "La vie théologale selon saint Thomas: L'affection dans la foi." *Revue thomiste* 60 (1960): 364–80.

Leclercq, Jean. "L'idéal du théologien au moyen âge. Textes inédits." *Revue des sciences religieuses* 21 (1947): 121–48.

Ross, James. "Aquinas on Belief and Knowledge." In *Essays Honoring Allan B. Wolter.* Ed. W. A. Frank and G. J. Etzkorn. St. Bonaventure, NY: The Franciscan Institute Press, 1985.

Sokolowski, Robert. *The God of Faith and Reason: Foundations of Christian Theology.* Notre Dame, IN: University of Notre Dame Press, 1982.

Torrell, Jean-Pierre. "Théologie et sainteté." *Revue thomiste* 71 (1971): 205–21.

The Theological Virtue of Hope
(IIa IIae, qq. 17–22)

Romanus Cessario, O.P.

THE VIRTUOUSNESS OF THEOLOGICAL HOPE

Aquinas holds that the theological virtues observe an order. Specifically, the virtues of love follow in their inception the virtue of knowledge. The progression implies more than a logical sequence. Rather the order of faith, hope, and charity represents the actual development of the theological life in the Christian believer.

As a specific virtue of the Christian life, theological faith perfects human intelligence.[1] At the same time, though faith properly speaking remains a virtue of the intellect, the act of faith requires more than the exercise of human intelligence. Christian belief relies on the energies of human appetite. Because the mysteries of faith surpass the inbred capacities of human intelligence, the human will must supply the required momentum for engendering the act of fiduciary assent. Furthermore, because belief demands that one rely on the word of another, the theological virtue of faith necessarily involves commitment to a person, to the loving God who reveals his truth in the world. Faith commitment of this sort occurs only under the influence of some kind of divine grace, drawing a person to embrace the ultimate goodness that the church announces through the preaching of the gospel.

Aquinas understood that intellect and will operate differently. Whereas the intellect finds its perfection in knowing the truth, the human will, because of its particular psychological structure, achieves its own proper perfection through embracing the good. For Aquinas, "good" always denotes a real, predicamental quality of being that exists in the world as a result of the divine causality. "God's love," Aquinas insists, "pours out and creates the goodness in things" (Ia, q. 20, a. 2).[2] For the Christian believer, theological hope represents a reaching out for the ultimate goodness that is God himself, and so initially perfects the passive capacity in the human person to find complete fulfillment only in God, a capacity that God has made part of being human.[3]

To grasp the virtuousness of the second theological virtue, it is useful to recall some of the anthropological presuppositions that undergird a Thomist treatment of the theological virtue of hope. The German philosopher Josef Pieper summarizes the main features of hoping as an exercise of the appetitive in a human being: "Hope, like love, is one of the very simple, primordial dispositions of the living person. In hope, man reaches 'with restless heart,' with confidence and patient expectation toward . . . the arduous 'not yet' of fulfillment, whether natural or supernatural. As a characteristically human endeavor, then, hoping incarnates a reaching out for anything that is perceived as good, and for the anticipated fulfillment that the possession of something good brings."[4]

In Aquinas's writings, one finds four characteristics common to every kind of hoping. First, hope concerns only the movement toward what perfects the human person, toward good objects or ends that enhance the personal dignity of one endowed with spiritual powers. On the other hand, when a person encounters something destructive, the reaction takes on a different shape, such as the repugnance or fear we experience in the face of evil. Second, hope looks toward the future, for a person never hopes for what he or she already possesses. Hope seeks a good object that still lies in the future; the person who presently and actually realizes the attainment of something desired reacts with joy. Third, one speaks of hoping only when the attainment of the good, future object involves some difficulty or an element of arduousness. Otherwise, when it is a case of someone seeking a good that is easily achieved, the person experiences the simple emotion of desire, which properly pertains to the concupiscible appetite. In fact, the precise note of being difficult to attain establishes the formal object of hope and explains why we find hope among the irascible or contending emotions, instead of the primary concupiscible or impulse emotions. For if there were nothing difficult to surmount in achieving a particular good, the concupiscible or impulse emotions themselves would suffice to ensure that the person aspired to such goods. Finally, only something that is attainable elicits hope; a person must judge that the hoped-for reality lies within the realm of possible options. When this is not the case, the individual definitively impeded from obtaining some good that is required for human perfection experiences instead the emotion of despair.

The emotion of hope shares in the general dynamics of human longing and expectation. As part of the psychological makeup of the human person, hope expresses itself in two ways. First of all, hope exists at the level of the basic sense appetites, specifically as one of the five irascible or contending emotions that serve to strengthen one against the difficult situations that life presents. As a human emotion, sense hope arises spontaneously whenever a person encounters a good that, though its achievement might entail sizable difficulties, still emerges as a realizable good. This expectation comprises the simple, primordial movement of the person toward an expected good. However, the natural emotion of hope, like the simple disposition of love, lacks the distinctive quality of virtue. For by definition, virtue establishes a person in the stable pursuit of the good. The virtuous person remains so ordered toward embracing the good that he or she can commit serious evil only with fully conscious and deliberate effort.[5] The spontaneity associated with a pure emotional response excludes the sort of stability that the definition of virtuousness requires.

On another level, hope designates a moral or human virtue. As is true of all human virtue, the moral virtues that resemble hope, such as magnanimity and munificence, involve a reasoned choice toward the achievement of a good course of action. But in the form of a *moral* virtue, hope specifically affects the human appetite, strengthening the irascible or contending appetites to withstand whatever threatens its well-being in the world. In other words, moral hope begets courage. Since natural hope involves excelling in formidable activities or undertaking lavish projects, these virtues, as I have said, include qualities of soul such as magnanimity and munificence. "Magnanimity," says Aquinas, "coincides with courage inasmuch as it strengthens the mind for a strenuous task" (IIa IIae, q. 129, a. 5).[6] And from this connection, the Thomist recognizes the excellence that hoping achieves in other virtues related to cardinal fortitude, such as long-suffering and constancy.

Aquinas makes a great deal of the fact that the theological virtues relate the believer directly to God. Faith, hope, and charity together place the human person in full communion with the Persons of the blessed Trinity, a relationship made possible for us only by the saving work of Jesus Christ. As a theological virtue, hope specifically unites the believer with God as his or her supreme and ultimate good. At the same time, even as Aquinas accentuates the God-centeredness of hope, he also explains that the theological life subsists in the Trinitarian communion to which hope tends.

By definition, virtue makes its possessor good here and now. It might seem, then, that any as yet future good, even the divine goodness itself, could not serve as a suitable object for virtue. Some theologians in fact have argued that hope should not be numbered among the theological virtues, for by hoping, one does not attain God; rather, one establishes a certain state of affairs confined to the human condition. These theologians see hope as the self's movement toward the possession of God, not the attainment of a perfecting end. Aquinas, on the other hand, insists on the virtuous character of hope. He explains that "in all things subject to regulation and measure, their being good is reckoned on the basis of their reaching the rule (or measure) proper to them" (IIa IIae, q. 17, a. 1).[7] Virtue puts right reason into emotion, and like all virtue, hope looks to establish the proper measure for a specific human activity. Put otherwise, the virtues of hope shape the proper emotional response that a person should demonstrate when faced with some future, difficult, but attainable good. Thus, while hope by definition never attains its object, the act of hoping possesses a suitable perfection in itself, qualifying it as a truly virtuous activity. Hoping remains centered in the tendential, and can best be interpreted under the sign of what the French refer to as *"une herméneutique du temps."*

Aristotle distinguishes magnanimity from hope precisely on the basis of whether someone is able to attain a difficult good by his or her own efforts, as happens in the case of magnanimous men and women, or alternatively whether they are able to reach a goal only with help from others. For Aquinas, this distinction opens up a way to clarify further the distinctively virtuous quality of theological hope. He says: "When it is a case, then, of hoping for something as possible to us precisely through God's help, such hope, *by reason of its very reliance upon God*, reaches God himself. Evidently, then, it is a virtue, since it makes one sphere of human activity to be good and to reach one of the rules it is supposed to reach" (ibid., emphasis added).[8] In other words, the perfection involved in hoping emerges from the virtuous way in which the believer actually relies on God. This reliance, moreover, constitutes the basis for establishing the proper measure or rule that the definition of virtue requires in order that both doer and action manifest a certain perfection.

In this reliance on the divine help, we can again distinguish theological hope from the simple emotion of desire. While desire implies a sure movement toward a future good, it does not form the basis for a theological virtue. Why not? Aquinas replies: "No virtue is called desire, because desire does not imply any present clinging or spiritual contact with God himself."[9] In another text, Aquinas expands on this topic: "To be sure one who hopes is imperfect with respect to what he or she hopes to obtain and does not yet possess. But such a one is perfected as to this that he or she already reaches the rule proper to his actions, namely God on whose help he relies" (IIa IIae, q. 17, a. 1, ad 3).[10] Hoping belongs to the wayfarer, but it also perfects the Christian on life's journey. By assuring one's reliance on God, hope, says Aquinas, braces the believer to confront the difficulties and spiritual trials that frequently emerge in Christian living.

HOPE AND THE PROMISE OF HAPPINESS

In order to clarify the formal object of theological hope, Aquinas emphasizes a central claim of the *Secunda pars*, namely, that God alone constitutes the supreme good for the human person. When Aquinas inquires whether human happiness ultimately consists in the vision of God's very essence, he concludes that the personal relationship with God (beatitude) is indeed the supreme happiness for each member of the human species (Ia IIae, q. 3, a. 8.).[11] To speak about humankind's ultimate beatitude as consisting in a "direct vision of the divine essence" implies that the rational soul is capable of an immediate intuition of God's very being, upon which follows a spontaneously elicited joy, the thorough beatification of the whole person.[12] The scholastics traditionally designate the human creature's share in God's blessedness as "formal" *beatitude*, and so distinguish it from "objective" *beatitude*, the incomparably blessed life that God alone both constitutes and enjoys.[13]

The theological virtue of hope relates the believer to objective beatitude, that is, the very blessedness of God as it connotes formal beatitude, or the blessed vision of God which the company of the saints actually enjoys and which fulfills all their desires. The Christian who hopes seeks God *for himself or herself*. In the technical language of the commentatorial tradition, God-as-possessed expresses the formal object of theological hope.

During the excesses of seventeenth-century French spiritual idealism, some authors actually spoke about *l'amour pur*, a love so disengaged from the self that it could conceivably continue even in the damned.[14] Their postulate obviously has nothing in common with

Aquinas's view of Christian hope. At the same time, when Aquinas affirms that theological hope seeks God for the hoper, he does not thereby subordinate God either to the human creature or to the whole of creation. The believer does not hope for God as one might instrumentally use something created in order to achieve a specific personal perfection. Rather, the Christian desires God for himself or herself because God alone stands as the true ultimate end or goal of each human being's personal existence. As is clear from the general norms that govern Christian loving, we can never subordinate another person to serve as a means of self-fulfillment. Since this is true of our love for human persons, it is all the more true of our love for God. With precision, Dominican commentator Cardinal Cajetan observes of theological hope: "we hope for God for ourselves, but not indeed on account of ourselves" (*Speramus Deum nobis, non vero propter nos*).[15]

What motivates Christians to hope that they will eternally possess God? What grounds the confident expectation that they will receive such great benefits from him? How does one maintain this hope throughout a lifetime of falling many times and in the face of numerous other signs of our unworthiness? In his *Disputed Question on Hope*, Aquinas takes up these questions, and provides the answers to them.

First, Aquinas recapitulates the basic teaching that hope's virtuousness lies precisely in its proper reliance on the divine help. "Faith is not considered a virtue except in so far as it assents to the testimony of the First Truth . . . likewise hope obtains the status of virtue from the fact that one clings to the help of the divine power while moving toward eternal life. However, were one to seek out human assistance, either one's own or from another, in order to look for this perfect good without the divine help, this would be a serious sin."[16] Theological usage distinguishes a virtue's formal terminative object—in the case of theological hope, objective beatitude as connoting formal beatitude—from the formal mediating object. The scholastic theologians describe the formal mediating object as the medium whereby the virtuous person reaches the formal object of the virtue. This amounts to explaining what exactly motivates a person to cling to God in theological hope.

Therefore, as the formal [mediating] object of faith is First Truth [Speaking], whereby as through a certain medium the believer assents to those things which he or she believes—the material object of faith—so also the formal [mediating] object of hope is the help of the divine power and mercy (*auxilium divinae potestatis et pietatis*), on account of which the movement of hope reaches out for the goods hoped for, *viz.*, the material object of hope.[17]

It is clear that this text places the experience of God's all-powerful mercy at the very heart of the theological life. When, moreover, Aquinas underscores reliance on the divine mercy and compassion as an indispensable part of the Christian life, he reflects authoritative Christian teaching on salvation.

The broad and sometimes eclectic commentatorial tradition that followed Aquinas questioned the reason for a Christian's expectation to attain the full possession of God. Some commentators agreed that God's merciful omnipotence explains the efficient cause of one's actually attaining the vision of God, but rejected the view that the divine power can serve as a formal cause of our hoping for it. In other words, they argued that there is nothing in the divine omnipotence that gives a specific reason for theological hope as such, and so denied that God's omnipotence serves as hope's formal mediating object. For example, one early seventeenth-century Jesuit commentator, Francisco Suárez, who departed from Aquinas on many key points in philosophy and theology, alleged that the very goodness of God himself suffices to explain why the believer would be motivated to hope in God.[18]

Suárez's position fails to acknowledge that the divine power must not only account for the actual achievement of eternal happiness, but also support one's tending toward it, that is, the spiritual clinging to God amidst the difficulties and obstacles of the present life. Thomists recognize that only God's all-powerful mercy adequately explains how a Christian believer in the present sin-marked economy of salvation can still hope to attain beatitude. Hope enables the Christian believer to pursue the vision of God precisely as it represents a possible good. For the sinner, such a reaching out demands God's merciful aid, the effective expression of his disposition to save the human race. Thus, both the divine omnipotence and mercy specify hoping in a motivational way.[19] Aquinas's position supports the view that the pilgrim church constantly requires succor in its journey to the heavenly homeland or *patria*. Alone, the human creature remains impotent to reach the goal of beatific fellowship with the saints and, moreover, experiences frustration in this effort as a result of personal and communal sin. The formal mediating object of theological hope reminds us that God's omnipotent mercy both can and will overcome these obstacles to the believer's eternal well-being.

Since God communicates His redeeming mercy through the sacrifice of Christ, the mystery of the Incarnation grounds every exercise of theological hope. Aquinas recognized that the New Testament explicitly points to Christ as the one who guarantees hope's efficacy: "But I am not ashamed, for I know whom I have believed, and I am sure that he is able to guard until that Day what has been entrusted to me" (2 Tim 1:12). At the same time, the virtue of hope enables each believer to participate already in the promised eschatological salvation. Aquinas likewise heeds St. Paul's words to the Romans: "and hope does not disappoint us, because God's love has been poured into our hearts through the Holy Spirit which has been given to us" (Rom 5:5). Aquinas stresses God's merciful omnipotence, reminding his readers that, because of personal sin, the believer never outgrows the need to develop a loving confidence in God's mercy. Later, the church incorporated the Thomist view into an official statement: "And because 'we all make many mistakes' (Jas 3:2)," the Council of Trent states, "each of us ought to keep before his eyes the severity of judgment as much as the mercy and goodness . . . for our whole life must be examined and judged not by our judgment but by that of God."[20]

Theological hope relates the Christian directly to God, so it includes among its material objects all of the good things that the Christian believer lovingly looks forward to receiving: the vision of God, the accompanying bliss, the resurrection of the body and its glorification, and fellowship with the blessed.[21] Theological hope also entitles the Christian to expect the secondary material objects, that is, created instruments of hope that

form part of the Christian dispensation for salvation. This means above all the instrumental causality of Christ's humanity; however, it also includes spiritual goods such as grace, the infused virtues, the gifts of the Holy Spirit, the maternal mediation of the Blessed Virgin Mary, the intercession of the saints, and the forgiveness of sins (especially mediated through the sacraments of Penance and Holy Anointing). Furthermore, one can rely on theological hope for temporal goods, such as holy friends, good health, psychological equilibrium, at least to the extent that these things conduce toward beatitude.

Aquinas compares the material objects of hope with the material objects of theological faith, namely, the articles of the Creed:

> Just as those things that are believed as faith's material objects are all referred to God even though some of them are created, e.g., the dogma that God created all creatures and that the person of the Word takes up the body of Christ in a hypostatic unity, so also all those things which are hoped for as material objects of hope are ordained to the one hoped-for end which remains the enjoyment of God. Toward this kind of formal beatitude we hope to be helped by God not only spiritually, but also with physical benefits.[22]

This text illumines Aquinas's strategy for overcoming the apparent tensions between future and realized eschatology, and for avoiding the modern propensity to dichotomize the material and spiritual worlds. Earlier, Augustine made the same point: "Those blessings alone are the object of the theological virtue of hope that are contained in the Lord's Prayer."[23]

HOPE AND THE LOVE OF DESIRE

In its root meaning, to love means to will a good to someone.[24] On this basis, the Thomist tradition distinguishes between two kinds of love, namely, the "love of benevolence" (*amor benevolentiae*) and the "love of desire" or "concupiscence" (*amor concupiscentiae*). Benevolence signifies willing well to another, or the disinterested affection that properly characterizes the love of friendship (*amor amicitiae*). Furthermore, because the person to whom one benevolently wills a good becomes thereby united with the willing individual in a true bond of friendship, only other persons ought to comprise the authentic recipients of true benevolence. The Christian believer can embrace in this kind of loving not only the self and other persons—neighbors on earth and angels in heaven—but, according to a gracious design, even God.

Concupiscence signifies willing a good to oneself, or a desire for what is good for the subject. Since it is implanted in us by the author of nature and continues to function even under the reign of grace, this sort of wanting forms part of a well-ordered life. By loving this way, humans seek authentic goods, particularly those things that are predominately useful or delightful goods. Theological hope remains rooted in this kind of love. Again, Aquinas holds that a person can hope for God as formal beatitude without subordinating God to the interests of self. This properly Christian consideration prompts Aquinas to develop an extended philosophical analysis of the interrelationship between the two kinds of love.

> Love is twofold: one kind is perfect; the other kind is imperfect. Love of something is imperfect when someone loves a thing not that he might wish the good in itself to the "thing," but in order that he might wish its good to himself. This is called by some "concupiscence," as when we love wine, wishing to enjoy its sweetness, or when we love some person for our own purposes or pleasure. The other kind of love is perfect; in this the good of anything is loved in itself, as when loving someone, I wish that he himself have the good, even if out of that fact nothing falls to me. This is said to be the love of friendship, whereby anyone is loved for himself (*secundum seipsum*). This is perfect friendship, as is said in *VIII Ethicorum*.[25]

The love of desire (*amor concupiscentiae*), though an imperfect expression of love, constitutes a perfection in its own order, just as motion truly perfects a mobile being, even though the mobile thing in order to remain in motion has always yet to reach its terminus.

When the object of the love of desire includes reference to some non-personal thing, the ultimate referent (the end "to which" or *finis cui*) must always be the one who loves. For example, I love money because I can put food on the table for my family or sexual pleasure because it involves joyful union with my spouse. Otherwise such love would be disordered, as when a miser loves money only for the sake of money or the profligate sexual gratification only for the sake of sexual gratification. But when God is loved with desire, as happens in theological hope, one can still wish the goodness of God for the self without entailing a disordered subordination of God to one's own personal purposes. In this regard, God and even created persons differ from such things as wine, money, or sexual gratification. Although one can seek within the proper circumstances and under the right conditions created goods solely on account of the self, the Christian can never approach God in that way. Indeed, to seek to use any person only as a means for one's own fulfillment forms the core of vicious selfishness, not the heart of virtuous hope.

Virtuous hoping does not leave the one who hopes isolated from others. As Aquinas notes, there exists a mutual relation between the hope of desire and the love of friendship. Moreover, this interconnectedness of loves reflects a more basic integration that transpires within the human person. Aristotle describes "a sort of circle formed by the acts of the soul: for a thing outside the soul moves the intellect, and the thing known moves the appetite, which tends to reach the things from which the motion originally starts."[26] Insofar as hope looks for and moves toward the hoped-for good, it springs from a love of desire for that good. But insofar as the one hoping looks out for the help needed to attain this good, the hoping disposes him or her toward a love of benevolence or friendship. For the person who hopes comes to love the one who provides the means for attaining the sought-after good.[27] Hope leads to charity, writes Aquinas, "for when a person hopes to receive something good from God, he or she is led to see that God should be loved for His very self."[28]

Because the theological virtues always point to God as their proper and immediate object, they remain radically different from any ordinary kind of human believing, hoping, or loving. Still, one can discern a model for the way that faith leads to hope and hope to charity in the experience of human friendship. Aquinas offers a good illustration of this analogy in the *Summa contra gentiles*:

> The love that a man has for others arises in man from the love that he has for himself, for a man stands in relation to a friend as he does to himself. But a person loves himself inasmuch as he wishes the good for himself, just as he loves another person by wishing him good. So, by the fact that one is interested in his own good he is led to develop an interest in another person's good. Hence, because a person hopes for good from some other person, a way develops for him to love that other person in himself, from whom he hopes to attain the good. Indeed, a person is loved in himself when the lover wishes the good for him, even if the lover may receive nothing from him. Now, since by sanctifying grace there is produced in us an act of loving God for Himself, the result was that we obtained hope from God by means of grace. However, though it is not for one's own benefit, friendship, whereby one loves another for himself, has of course many resulting benefits, in the sense that one friend helps another as he helps himself. Hence, when one person loves another, and knows that he is loved by that other, he must get hope from him. Now by grace one is so established as a lover of God, through the love of charity, that he is also instructed by faith that he is first loved by God, according to the passage found in 1 John 4:10: "In this is charity: not as though we had loved God, but because he hath first loved us." It follows, then, from the gift of grace that we get hope from God. It is also clear from this that just as hope is a preparation of man for the true love of God, so also man is conversely strengthened in hope by charity.[29]

This text explains the organic connection that binds together theological faith, hope, and charity. As virtues of the Christian life, each of these infused qualities of soul unites the human person to God in ways that radically modify the principal human powers. It is easy to recognize that there exists a connection between the truth that the believer comes to accept from hearing (*ex auditu*) and the hope that this saving message kindles in his or her heart. Dominican friar Thomas Aquinas never lost sight of the fact that Jesus began his ministry "proclaiming the good news of God, and saying, 'The time is fulfilled, and the kingdom of God has come near, repent, and believe in the good news'" (Mk 1:14–15).

THE PROVISIONAL CHARACTER OF HOPE

While every virtue affects the whole person, Aquinas always specifies the human capacities that a particular virtue shapes. Faith constitutes a perfection of the intellect; it makes people knowers of the truth. The virtues of theological love perfect the powers of human appetite, that is, the rational appetite or will of the believer. As the rational appetite forms the subject of theological hope, this virtue deals with the desires of the heart, for, as Aquinas explains, "corresponding to the movement of the inferior appetite where there is emotion, there is a movement of the superior appetite without emotion" (IIa IIae, q. 18, a. 1).[30] By describing hope as a virtue of the rational appetite, Aquinas departs from the Augustinian tradition that classified hope as a virtue of the memory. Hope of course can purify the human memory of the recollection of past sins, but it only accomplishes this by helping one confront the future with a renewed confidence in God's merciful omnipotence.

Aquinas defines hope as a confident movement toward the future, and therefore catalogs it as a virtue that belongs to the provisional order, to the "state of the wayfarer" (*status viatoris*). Hope will always be the province of the traveler because neither the blessed nor the damned can possess hope. The blessed already possess the beatitude that hope longs after; in them, hope gives way to the joy that accompanies the beatific vision. But in hell, no hope of reform remains. In fact, the very realization that one can never reach beatitude intensifies the anguish that a damned person would suffer. And so Aquinas argues that "it is no more possible for the damned to consider blessedness as still open to them than for the blessed to conceive of it as not already possessed" (IIa IIae, q. 18, a. 3).[31] But wayfarers whose future destiny remains open find themselves in neither condition, and so theological hope urges them on. In the 1930s, Father Paul de Jaegher titled a volume of meditations on hope, simply, *Confiance!*[32]

Aquinas's treatment of theological hope excludes forms of hoping based exclusively on expectations from here below. Most of the mistaken views arise from an inadequate appraisal of the wayfaring condition—a wrong-headed conception of temporality. Because time marks the movement of change, forms of philosophical idealism, which largely assume a split between mind and body, find it difficult to embrace, except in oblique ways, the concreteness of time. On the other hand, optimistic existentialist philosophies, which refuse to place limits on human temporality, deny the provisional status of the wayfarer by fabricating a myth that gives ultimate significance to this passing world. Because the heavenly city is sought on earth, humanists turn hope into a form of expectation for a better life, a sort of imagining of the real. Today, this view still affects some corners of theological investigation. But the theological character of hope as Aquinas argues for it challenges philosophical positions that aim to confine the virtue of trust to human hope, while at the same time it confronts authors such as Nietzsche, Schopenhauer, Kafka, and Camus, who have each called into question the reasonableness of all expectation for a future good.

Being a wayfarer marks human creatureliness. For Aquinas, hope aims at overcoming everything that keeps the human spirit from reaching perfection.[33] Indeed the various replacements for Christian hope proposed by different ideologies (and sometimes uncritically adopted by theologians) inevitably presuppose that sin and its effects remain permanent features of the human situation. Some refuse to accept that the sinful status of the creature can be overcome; others are willing to concede that the penalties of sin form part of authentic human existence. Views such as these, however, leave no place for the Christian to welcome the merciful omnipotence of God made available in Christ. At this point, it is significant to recall that Aquinas discusses the gift of Fear of the Lord in connection with the virtue of hope (IIa IIae, q. 19). Since theological hope serves the state of the wayfarer, this virtue together with its gift provide everything that the pilgrim church requires in order to reach its goal.

The Catholic Reform of the sixteenth century steadfastly withstood the remonstrance made by Protestant theologians that knowledge of one's own salvation ought to be included among the material objects of faith, that is, as something positively revealed by God. Here the attempt to ensure a personal experience of fiduciary faith engendered a confusion between what the mind can know in faith and what the will can achieve through hoping. Aquinas respects the limitations that belong to both kinds of human activity. "Let the one who stands," St. Paul exhorts us, "take care not to fall" (*Qui stat, caveat ne cadat*) (1 Cor 10:12). Again, the Council of Trent espouses a Thomist theme by reaffirming that every believer should maintain an unshaken hope that God will provide what is required for salvation: "Even though all should place a most firm hope (*firmissimam spem*) in God's help and rest in it, let no one promise himself with absolute certainty any definite outcome."[34]

Renaissance Thomists helped clarify further some of the sixteenth-century theological debates by distinguishing between certitude in its cognitive form, when the intellect is fixed on a truth, and a noncognitive or affective certitude.[35] Affective certitude is a form of practical knowledge that directs any operation to its proper end, that is, either as realized or as tending toward an end. According to Aquinas's explanation, this special kind of certitude compares with the sureness that moral virtues exhibit with respect to their objects, a tendency that can be described as conative. "The tendency of hope toward its end is marked by such certitude as this," says Aquinas, "in actual fact a derivation from faith's certitude found in the cognitive power" (IIa IIae, q. 18, a. 4).[36] But because hope's certitude resides in the will, the character of the rational appetite predominates in its operations. In this sense, it differs both in kind and degree from the certitude that only the intellect can achieve.

As a virtue of the wayfarer, hope develops a connatural clinging to God, a sure expectation that God will provide whatever is needed to reach happiness, even though the thought of one's own resources and the feebleness of one's own efforts might otherwise lead to different conclusions. The infallibility of the moral virtues serves as model for hope's certitude. The moral virtues supply the person with "second natures," which serve as real principles for human action, so that human appetites will follow infallibly the order of right reason. In a similar way, theological hope offers a "new nature," one that places human desire for God firmly within the ambience of His merciful omnipotence. In summary, the graced Christian believer possesses the cognitive certitude of faith that a mercifully omnipotent God offers the gift of salvation to all men and women and, as long as one personally appropriates this truth held by faith, the affective certitude of hope enables the believer to live a life of mature confidence in God's power. Among the blessed, the certitude of hope gives way to joyful realization of the divine goodness, whereas in the wayfarers, the members of the pilgrim church, this certitude still exists in a tendential state.

Because it embodies a true theological virtue, hope conditions the Christian to trust in God's merciful omnipotence as the formal means whereby he or she anticipates a full share in the divine goodness. But within the present economy of salvation, Christians must appeal as well to the personal agents that the divine goodness has established in the world. So the Christian hoper confidently relies on the merits of Christ, on the maternal mediation of the Blessed Virgin Mary, on the intercessory prayer and help of the communion of saints, and on any other means that aid Christian hoping.

DESPAIR AND PRESUMPTION, THE SINS AGAINST HOPE

Aquinas holds that despair is neither a sentiment nor a mood, but an error in faith-judgment that supposes that God will not provide what is required for the wayfarer to reach salvation. Its sinful character stems from what the tradition calls an "offensive turning" (*conversio offensiva*), the special character of the vices associated with the theological virtues. Rather than turn toward another creature in a disordered way (*conversio ad creaturam/aversio a Deo*), as happens in the case of vices that corrupt the moral virtues, the creature by sinning against the theological virtues turns or relates toward God in a disordered, offensive way.

Spiritual sloth—what Kierkegaard calls the "despair of weakness"—and unchastity are the two vices that Aquinas, following an ancient spiritual tradition, assigns as the most likely causes of despair. Despair enacts a special sin against the redemption. Elsewhere St.

Thomas writes, "If sin could truly not be forgiven, then it would not be a sin to doubt forgiveness of sin."[37] But the fact is that sin has been forgiven and the formal object *quo* of theological hope is meant to bring the sinner into contact with a merciful God.

Presumption denotes an affective movement of the creature which is motivated by a false judgment about how God's mercy conforms to his justice and wisdom. In the final analysis, the one who presumes does not understand that God's plan for our salvation includes our transformation. Because despair acts directly against the formal motivating object (*quo*) of theological hope, this vice readily appears as a sinful disorder. Presumption, however, mimics theological hope, even though this anti-theological vice also constitutes an "offensive turning" toward God. Those who presume on God's merciful omnipotence want the benefits of the divine attributes which hope assures, but presumptuous persons want this goodness and mercy outside of the order which is established by the divine wisdom and justice. Thomas gives the example of one who "hopes to obtain pardon without repentance or glory without merits" (IIa IIae, q. 21, a. 2).[38] In other words, presumption establishes an "unwarranted reliance upon God" (IIa IIae, q. 21, a. 2, ad 2).[39]

According to ancient tradition, presumption is born of pride, the most serious of the deadly sins. For it implies "that one thinks so much of himself that he imagines God will not punish him nor exclude him from eternal life in spite of his continuing in sin" (IIa IIae, q. 21, a. 4).[40] Against this false seduction, Aquinas proposes the spiritual attitude of a child, one inflamed by the gift of filial fear, which so fixes the believer's gaze onto the Heavenly Father that nothing can deter him or her from hastening toward the love that never ends.

Notes

[1]On this topic, see my *Christian Faith and the Theological Life* (Washington, DC: Catholic University of America Press, 1996). For a general treatment of the virtuous life, see my *Virtues, or the Examined Life* (New York: Continuum, 2002).

[2]"Sed amor Dei est infundens et creans bonitatem in rebus." For the Christian moral theologian, this notion implies that extramental good shapes the

development of human freedom and choice. In this sense, real moral good is to be distinguished from what some British moral philosophers consider moral realism, namely, a form of moral argument that supposes that the grounds for moral truth lie only in some part outside of the moral agent. British philosopher Roger Scuton, for instance, distinguishes between a strong and a weak naturalism on the basis of how strongly one makes the logical inference between the "good" and whatever is judged to be good. See Scutton, "Attitudes, Beliefs and Reasons" in *Morality and Moral Reasoning: Five Essays in Ethics*, ed. John Casey (London: Methuen, 1971), 57.

[3] See Servais Pinckaers, O.P., "Le désir naturel de voir Dieu," *Nova et Vetera* 51 (1976): 255–73.

[4] Josef Pieper, *Hope*, trans. Mary Frances McCarthy, S.N.D. (San Francisco: Ignatius Press, 1986), 27. For a current survey of hope in contemporary moral philosophy, see Bernard Schumacher, "Esperance," in *Dictionnaire d'Éthique et de Philosophie Morale* (Paris: Presses Universitaires de France, 1996), 524–28.

[5] See *De virt. in comm.*, q. un, a. 2 (Marietti, 710–14).

[6] "Sic ergo patet quod magnanimitas convenit cum fortitudine, inquantum confirmat animum circa aliquid arduum . . ."

[7] "In omnibus autem regulatis et mensuratis bonum consideratur per hoc quod aliquid propriam regulam attingit . . ."

[8] "Inquantum ergo speramus aliquid ut possibile nobis per divinum auxilium, spes nostra attingit ad ipsum Deum, cuius auxilio innititur. Et ideo patet quod spes est virtus, cum faciat actum hominis bonum, et debitam regulam attingentem."

[9] *De spe*, q. un., a. 1, ad 6: "desiderium autem importat quidem motum in futurum, sed sine aliqua praesenti inhaesione vel spirituali contactu ipsius Dei; unde nec desiderium nominat virtutem aliquam" (Marietti, 805).

[10] "dicendum quod ille qui sperat est quidem imperfectus secundum considerationem ad id quod sperat obtinere quod nondum habet, sed est perfectus quantum ad hoc quod iam attingit propriam regulam, scilicet Deum, cuius auxilio innititur."

[11] Aquinas also considers whether a creature can find fulfillment in "seeing" the divine essence in ST Ia, q. 12, aa. 1–11. He further contrasts this kind of vision-knowledge of the divine essence with the knowledge of God which the human person has in this life both through natural reason and through the gift of divine grace. In his commentary on IIa IIae, q. 4, a. 8, Cajetan observes that in this life the knowledge of God through grace is not necessarily a higher mode of knowledge than that through reason, which provides its own sort of evidence. Rather faith's excellence derives from its formal object, namely, First Truth-Speaking. For a discussion of God's own knowledge, which he shares with the blessed in heaven, as source of faith and the *sacra doctrina*, see ST Ia, q. 1, a. 2; and IIa IIae, q. 2, a. 3.

[12] Thomists traditionally distinguish the mind's grasp of the divine essence from the will's joyful elation that results from beholding it. Moreover, they insist that this beatific joy relates to the vision of God in the same way that a specific property belongs to an essence. On this question, Scotus held the view that joy itself is the formal constitutive of beatitude. For Aquinas, however, "the ultimate happiness of humankind consists in its highest activity, which is the exercise of one's mind" (Cum enim ultima hominis beatitudo in altissima eius operatione consistat, quae est operatio intellectus) (ST Ia, q. 12, a. 1).

[13] Although grounded in Aquinas's own treatment of beatitude, the distinction becomes formalized in the sixteenth-century commentatorial tradition. For further discussion, see William J. Hill, O.P., *Hope*, IIa IIae. 17–22 (New York: McGraw-Hill, 1966), 146–47.

[14] Pope Innocent XII's *Cum alias ad apostolatus* (12 Mar. 1699) censured certain propositions taken from the writings of Bishop François de Fénelon (1651–1715), who was unsuccessful in his attempt to defend certain views on "pure" or "disinterested" love as set forth by the French spiritualist Madame Guyon. Ronald A. Knox recounts the story of Madame Guyon (1648–1717) and her circle in his volume, *Enthusiasm* (Westminister, MD: Christian Classics, 1983), 319–55.

[15] *In secundam secundae*, q. 17, a. 5, no. 8.

[16] *De spe*, q. un., a. 1: "Fides autem non habet rationem virtutis, nisi in quantum inhaeret testimonio veritatis primae . . . unde et spes habet rationem virtutis ex hoc ipso quod homo inhaeret auxilio divinae potestatis ad consequendum vitam aeternam. Si enim aliquis inniteretur humano auxilio, vel suo vel alterius, ad consequendum perfectum bonum absque auxilio divino, esset hoc vitiosum . . ." (Marietti, 804–5).

[17] Ibid.: "Sic igitur, sicut formale objectum fidei est veritas prima, per quam sicut per quoddam medium assentit his quae creduntur, quae sunt materiale objectum fidei; ita etiam formale objectum spei est auxilium divinae potestatis et pietatis, propter quod tendit motus spei in bona sperata, quae sunt materiale objectum spei" (Marietti, 805).

[18] Francisco Suárez (1548–1617), an eclectic Thomist, is best known for his discussion on the relationship between divine grace and human freedom. For Suárez on the formal cause of hope, see his posthumously published *De Triplici Virtute Theologica, Fide, Spe, et Charitate* (1621).

[19] This paragraph follows Hill, *Hope*, 148, n. 11, for this summary of the position that the Iberian

commentator John of St.-Thomas defends in his *Cursus Theologicus* XVII, Disp. IV, art. 1, no. 17. English translations of qq. 17–22 come from Hill's vol. 33 of the Blackfriars ed. of the *Summa*.

[20]Council of Trent, "Decree on Justification," chap. 16 (*DS* 1545–50).

[21]Christian hoping ceases at death, when the believer hears Christ say, "Come, you that are blessed by my Father, inherit the kingdom prepared for you from the foundation of the world" (Mt 25:34). The church, moreover, has officially taught that beatific vision does not await the general resurrection of the dead, and so holds that the separated souls of the just experience the beatitude of heaven (*DS* 1304–6). Furthermore, one confesses in faith that these blessed ones together comprise the company of the saints with which the church on earth enjoys a special form of communion. At the same time, the resurrection of the body also belongs to the body of Christian truths to which believers give their profession of faith in the Creed. Although theological reflection on matters which pertain to eschatology necessarily involves a certain degree of speculation, the common teaching of the church maintains that the resurrected body also participates in the effects of beatitude. Aquinas expresses this belief beautifully when he says that "participation in the glory of Christ's body renders our bodies glorious" (Sed participando gloriam corporis Christi, effcientur corpora nostra gloriosa) (ST IIIa, q. 56, a. 2, ad 1).

[22]*De spe*, q. un., a. 1: "Sicut ergo ea quae creduntur materialiter, omnia referuntur ad Deum, quamvis aliqua eorum sint creata; sicut quod credimus omnes creaturas esse a Deo, et corpus Christi esse a Filio Dei assumptum in unitate personae, ita etiam omnia quae materialiter sperantur, ordinantur in unum finale speratum, quod est fruitio Dei; in ordine enim ad hanc fruitionem speramus adiuvari a Deo non solum spiritualibus, sed etiam corporalibus beneficiis" (Marietti, 805). See also, ST IIa IIae, q. 17, a. 2, ad 2.

[23]*Enchiridion de fide, spe et caritate*, chap. 114; see August. "Faith, Hope and Charity,"in *Writings of St. Augustine*, "The Fathers of the Church," vol. 2, trans. Bernard M. Peebles (New York: Cima, 1947), 369–472.

[24]See ST Ia, q. 20, a. 2: "God therefore wills some good to each existing thing, and since loving is no other than willing good to someone, it is clear that God loves everything" (Cuilibet igitur existenti Deus vult aliquod bonum. Unde, cum amare nil aliud sit quam velle bonum alicui, manifestum est quod Deus omnia quae sunt, amat).

[25]*De spe*, q. un., a. 3, "Utrum spes sit prior caritate": "Est autem duplex amor: unus quidem imperfectus, alius autem perfectus. Imperfectus quidem amor alicujus rei est, quando aliquis rem aliquam

amat non ut ei bonum in seipsa velit, sed ut bonum illius sibi velit; et hic nominatur a quibusdam concupiscentia, sicut cum amamus vinum, volentes ejus dulcedine uti; vel cum amamus aliquem hominem propter nostram utilitatem vel delectationem. Alius autem est amor perfectus, quo bonum alicujus in seipso diligitur, sicut cum amando aliquem, volo quod ipse bonum habeat, etiam si nihil inde mihi accedat; et hic dicitur esse amor amicitiae . . . unde ista est perfecta amicitia, ut dicitur in VIII Ethic." (Marietti, 808). The reference to Arist. *Eth. Nic.* 8.3 (1156b7–9) runs as follows: "Perfect friendship is the friendship of men who are good, and alike in virtue; for these wish well alike to each other *qua* good, and they are good in themselves."

[26]See *De veritate*, q. 1, a. 2 (Leonine, 8–10) where Aquinas gives this account of Aristotle's teaching in *De an.* 3.9 (433a14ff).

[27]Hill, *Hope*, 137, offers this helpful illustration: "In willing food to the hungry, it is apparent that my love goes out to both bread and man, but hardly in comparable ways. There are actually two goods here, one (loved with an *amor concupiscentiae*) enriches my hungry fellow man, the other (loved with an *amor amicitiae*) enriches me. The enriching act is in the former case an 'appropriation;' in the latter it is only a 'communion.' The good which derives to me is precisely the full realization of my humanity, the most perfect deployment of my liberty under the direction of intelligence, the fulfillment of myself in the construction of the human community. In short, one cannot truly love a friend—and in supernatural charity it is God who is now the friend—without becoming thereby ennobled."

[28]*De spe*, q. un., a. 3: "dum aliquis per hoc quod sperat se aliquod bonum a Deo consequi, ad hoc deducitur ut Deum propter se amet" (Marietti, 809). In its most proper and formal sense, hope concerns only the one who makes the act of hope; and so formally speaking, Thomists argue that a person cannot hope for another person's eternal beatitude. The Christian tradition, however, does allow that someone can draw other persons into his or her hoping on the condition that there exists a true bond of charity so that such persons are regarded as "other selves."

[29]SCG III, chap. 153: "Dilectio enim quae est ad alios, provenit in homine ex dilectione hominis ad seipsum, inquantum ad amicum aliquis se habet sicut ad se. Diligit autem aliquis seipsum inquantum vult sibi bonum: sicut alium diligit inquantum vult ei bonum. Oportet igitur quod homo, per hoc quod circa proprium bonum afficitur, perducatur ad hoc quod afficiatur circa bonum alterius. Per hoc igitur quod aliquis ab alio sperat bonum, fit homini via ut illum diligat a quo bonum sperat, secundum seipsum: diligitur enim aliquis secundum seipsum quando diligens bonum eius vult, etiam si nihil ei

inde proveniat. Cum igitur per gratiam gratum fa-cientem causetur in homine quod Deum propter se diligat, consequens fuit ut etiam per gratiam homo spem de Deo adipisceretur. Amicitia vero, qua quis alium secundum se diligit, etsi non sit propter pro-priam utilitatem, habet tamen multas utilitates con-sequentes, secundum quod unus amicorum alteri subvenit ut sibi ipsi. Unde oportet quod, cum aliquis alium diligit, et cognoscit se ab eo diligi, quod de eo spem habeat. Per gratiam autem ita constituitur homo Dei dilector, secundum caritatis affectum, quod etiam instruitur per fidem quod a Deo prae-diligatur: secundum illud quod habetur 1 Ioan. 4–10: in hoc est dilectio, non quasi nos dilexerimus Deum, sed quoniam ipse prior dilexit nos. Conse-quitur igitur ex dono gratiae quod homo de Deo spem habeat. Ex quo etiam patet quod, sicut spes est praeparatio hominis ad veram Dei dilectionem, ita et e converso ex caritate homo in spe confirmatur" (Leonine, 447).

[30]"similes motus qui sunt in appetitu inferiori cum passione, in superiori sunt sine passione . . ."

[31]"ad conditionem miseriae damnatorum pertinet ut ipsi sciant quod nullo modo possunt damnationem evadere, et ad beatitudinem perve-nire." The translation is somewhat free.

[32]See Paul de Jaegher, S.J., *The Virtue of Trust, Meditations* (London: Burns, Oates, and Wash-bourne, 1935).

[33]See especially *De spe*, aa. 1–4 (Marietti, 803–12).

[34]Council of Trent, "Decree on justification," chap. 13 (*DS* 1540–41): "nemo sibi certi aliquid absoluta certitudine polliceatur, tametsi in Dei aux-ilio firmissimam spem collocare et reponere omnes debet."

[35]For a general survey of the history of Thomism, see my *Le thomisme et les thomistes* (Paris: Éditons du Cerf, 1999).

[36]"Et sic etiam spes certitudinaliter tendit in suum finem, quasi participans certitudinem a fide, quae est in vi cognoscitiva."

[37]*De malo*, q. 3, a. 15, *sed contra*: "Si igitur impos-sibile esset aliquod peccatum remitti, desperans de remissione illius peccati non peccaret" (Leonine, 100, 40–42).

[38]"ita falsum est quod in peccato perseverantibus veniam concedat, et a bono opere cessantibus gloriam largiatur . . ."

[39]"sperat de Deo aliquid quod Deo non con-venit."

[40]"ac si ipse tanti se aestimet, quod etiam eum peccantem Deus non puniat vel a gloria excludat."

Selected Further Reading

Bernard, Charles A. *Théologie de l'espérance selon s. Thomas d'Aquin*. Paris: Vrin, 1961.

Cessario, Romanus. *Le Virtu*. Manuali di Teologia Cattolica (AMATECA) Vol. 19. Sezione sesta: *La persona umana* (Milan: Editoriale Jaca Book, 1994). Spanish trans.: *Las virtudes* (Valencia: Edicep, 1998). English edition: *Virtues, or the Examined Life* (New York: Continuum, 2002).

Conlon, W. M. "The Certitude of Hope." *The Thomist* 10 (1947): 75–119; 226–52.

De Letter, P. "Hope and Charity in St. Thomas." *The Thomist* 13 (1950): 204–48; 325–52.

Gillon, Louis B. *Christ and Moral Theology*. Trans. Cornelius Williams, O.P. Staten Island: Alba House, 1967.

Glenn, Sr. Mary Michael, "A Comparison of the Thomistic and Scotistic Concepts of Hope." *The Thomist* 20 (1957): 27–74.

Hill, William J. *Hope. Summa Theologiae* IIa IIae. 17–22. Vol. 33. Blackfriars ed. Eds. Thomas Gilby et al. New York: McGraw-Hill, 1966.

Knox, Ronald A. *Enthusiasm*. Westminister, MD: Christian Classics, 1983.

Pieper, Josef. *Hope*. San Francisco: Ignatius Press, 1986.

Ratzinger, Josef. *To Look on Christ: Exercises in Faith, Hope, and Love*. Translated by Robert Nowell. New York: Crossroad Publishing Co., 1991.

Wadell, Paul J. *The Primacy of Love: An Introduc-tion to the Ethics of Thomas Aquinas*. New York: Paulist, 1992.

The Theological Virtue of Charity
(IIa IIae, qq. 23–46)

Eberhard Schockenhoff

Translated by Grant Kaplan and Frederick G. Lawrence

In the architectonic plan of the *Secunda secundae*, the treatise on charity holds a prominent place. This doctrinal piece with twenty-four sections forms not only a culmination in the treatment of the theological virtues but also a highpoint. In it are packed the basic lines of the theological and ethical conception that Thomas brings to sight in discussing the single material themes in the area of special ethics. Because the analysis of the treatise on charity cannot be understood without constantly referring back and cross-checking throughout the entire work, an interpretation of Thomas's teaching on charity must at least briefly mention the first presuppositions: (1) the thesis of the unity of human practice on the basis of the final end, and (2) the theory of perfect and imperfect happiness linked to it.

THE PRESUPPOSITIONS: GOD AS THE FINAL END AND HIGHEST GOOD

In order to investigate the movement of charity as the highest of the theological virtues in its anthropological structures, Thomas has recourse to the results of his theory of acts already developed in the *Prima secundae*. Particularly important are Thomas's differentiation of proximate, intermediate, and superordinate ends, as well as their orientation to a final end. Based on the intentional structure of the human act, human beings, insofar as they are occupied with particular things and individual acts, are already always on the way to the goal of their proper perfection. Human acts always have first of all to do with an immediate object, by which they are distinguished specifically from others. The specification of human acts by the object to which they are intentionally directed is already clear in such descriptions in speech as, "to take a walk," "to read a book," "to visit a friend," "to take a stand for justice," or "to accomplish an act of love." But by constantly orienting their acts toward "something," human beings strive for a final end, which Thomas understands as their utmost potentiality and as their comprehensive life-achievement. This final end is the basis of all individual acts; hence, it cannot be objectively imagined and realized as the last member in a chain of acts like the usual goals of action. The idea of a final end does not mean a categorical but a transcendental determination; it names the necessary presupposition for rendering individual acts intelligible as aspects of a unified process. Just as the Thomist analysis of acts is determined by the primacy of intention over execution of the end over the particular object, and of the "final end" (*finis ultimus*) over the "proximate end" (*finis proximus*), so the orientation in terms of the idea of a comprehensive achievement dominates the entire ethics of virtue: Because the final end is present in everything one does, one's actions gain their unity and inner coherence only in the measure that they succeed in uncovering this final end, to affirm it consciously, and to accept it in free decisiveness.

In addition to the most important structural components of the theory of the human act,

Thomas takes over from Aristotle a philosophical conception of happiness that sees the fulfillment of human longing not primarily in the condition of sense happiness but as a quality of the whole person attained in the perfection of the highest capacity for activity—or, more exactly, of the supreme faculty of the human soul. This philosophical image of happiness is based essentially on the assumption of a strict relationship between one's actions and one's being. Because human persons are in agreement with their acts and express themselves in them, the question of happiness coincides with the issue of the morally good act. Thomas, along with Aristotle, sees in this an elementary truth of our humanity: lasting happiness, that maintains what it promises until the end, cannot consist solely in the possession of single particular goods such as power, wealth, and physical appearance, nor in the experience of sense pleasure. Nor, in general, can it be enacted through objective acts directed immediately toward reward or gain. Reliable happiness instead comes indirectly, as a concomitant of good moral acts. It is only acquired and maintained in such a manner that whatever one does, one remains open for a greater perfection to which each good moral act is related as an integral part of a whole, or as individual tones within the larger melody of one's life.[1]

According to the delineation of this insight into the human condition, happiness enlarges people not by adding up various experiences of prosperity and emotional satisfaction but by the orientation to the good that transforms their acts. Whereas in Aristotelian ethics the idea of happiness or *eudaimonia* is understood in a formal sense, meaning simply the final encompassing end within which one's single acts can be interpreted as more or less fortunate moments of a whole life-plan, for Thomas the concept of happiness or *beatitudo* is strictly theological. Human practice does not find its point of unity in itself, but is completed in communion with God as the unique fulfilling good. Man's path to God is thus thought of not simply as a preparation for the reception of future happiness after death but rather as a growth process of a happiness already realized initially in moral acts, which will lead from its now imperfect shape to eschatological perfection. Thus, the fundamental ideal of the Thomist theology of charity is a variation within the realm of ethics of the one grand theme of the entire *Summa*: that God out of unbounded love for his Triune nature, and in a movement in response to this original event of love, draws all creatures in accord with their own dignity back to Himself as end.

The fundamental conception of the procession-return scheme recurs throughout the total plan of the *Summa theologiae* on different levels. On the level of the human being as the image and likeness of God, God's general providence for all creation is promoted to the inner instinct of grace, by which God exerts pressure on the human will to freely bind itself with the good and toward the goal of community with him. The inward movement by grace, which does not want to attain its goal without the consent of the human will, is enacted as the infusion of the three theological virtues and the gifts of the Holy Spirit, which Thomas analyzes in their mutual effectiveness. In accord with the biblical sequence of 1 Cor 13:13, the primacy within the triadic reciprocal interplay of the three theological virtues is once again attributed to charity: Charity brings about the arrival at the final goal meant for all human beings and the highest fulfillment of their longing for definitive community with God. So the circular movement that originated in the Creator's decision is closed and, since this is characterized by understanding and free will, was aimed from the start at the free "Yes" of His loving counterpart.[2]

The infinite God, in whose image the human being is made, is at once the goal of every act. People become conscious of their orientation to God through faith. By acknowledging God as their final end, they now bear within themselves inchoately the eternal life to which they are called (IIa IIae, q. 4, a. 1). In hope, they aim at God's helpful omnipotence, and in this striving for fulfillment, attain the strength to resist all barriers along their earthly paths (IIa IIae, q. 17, aa. 2–6).

In his theological and ethical theory of charity, Thomas goes a further step by conceiving the union between the human being and the God of his faith and hope as "friendship." Just as God gives Himself to be known to everyone in the two previous theological virtues, each under a determinate aspect (as first truth, or as powerful aid, respectively), so too is charity aimed at God unrestrictedly: "Charity reaches God as He is in Himself" (IIa IIae, q. 23, a. 6).[3] In charity, God becomes the person's friend, and the person, separated by an infinite distance from God, becomes God's friend. The relationship of the person to his or her origin and end is conceived through a transformation of the cosmological procession-return motif, in accord with the model of personal relationships, as a mutual friendship. To the degree and manner that Thomas unfolds this one thought step-by-step, and even makes the Aristotelian analysis of friendship as instrumental as his elaboration of intra-theological sources, the methodical procedure and systematic character of his theological and ethical thought can be observed in an exemplary way.

THE THEOLOGICAL DEFINITION: CHARITY AS FRIENDSHIP WITH GOD

Thomas is the first medieval theologian to bring the Aristotelian idea of friendship to bear on the speculative analysis of God's charity.[4] The short outline that precedes the treatise on charity as a prelude still lets us suspect very little about the intellectual course of thought that Thomas had to relinquish. In the *Commentary on the Sentences* Thomas develops the concept of friendship from a wide-ranging articulation of all the forms of love.[5] In this phenomenological perspective, "friendship" (*amicitia*) appears to him as the most complete realization of "love" (*amor*), which embraces both the desire for a friend as well as the corresponding benevolence and the readiness for doing good to one. Such friendship is expressed in mutual exchange and the companionship of friends that is accompanied by reflective knowledge of the particular quality of their relationship. Following Aristotle, therefore, Thomas names as the specific element of friendship that most distinguishes it from passionate love the mutual character of relationships of friendship, common knowledge about it, and finally the two-sided, free choice of the other.

For Thomas, divine charity falls under the concept of friendship defined in this way, so that God and human beings mutually love each other, and, according to the First Letter of John: "we have an abiding union" (*societam habemus ad invicem*) (1 Jn 1:7)—that is, people live in "community" or "fellowship" (*koinonia*) with one another. In the *Commentary on the Sentences*, Thomas does not offer a deeper reflection on the basis for such an exchange of life between God and human beings, or on how friendship between both, attested to by Aristotle only in a mythical mode of speech, can be conceived of at all. God's charity is simply a friendship of human beings with God, in the same way that any friendship appears as an outstanding variation of love. What makes it a particular friendship distinct from all other kinds of friendship is the uniqueness of the divine friend, who is precious and dear to the human being—Thomas here plays on the Latin terms *carus* and *caritas*—and hence is loved with a special friendship.

In the corresponding article of the *Summa* (IIa IIae, q. 23, a. 1), Thomas takes a decisive step beyond the enumeration of the phenomenological characteristics of friendship. Among the presuppositions required for the complete concept, he counts only good will (*benevolentia*) and a certain mutuality of love (*mutua amatio*) as the concepts meeting the necessary requirements. Only the personal love of friendship that loves the other for his or her own sake becomes an issue as an insertion point for the theological interpretation of charity. It simply makes no sense and is already excluded by the word's meaning to denote as friendship the desire-filled love for objects by which persons "love" their horse or wine. More important, however, than this terminological delimitation to the forms of "love of desire" (*amor concupiscentiae*) related to objects is a third condition Thomas already mentioned in a *Quodlibetum* and that he now numbers among the determinations that pertain to the essence of charity.[6] The reciprocal good will between God and the person in whom it is manifested, itself requires a sustaining ground upon which alone the exchange of life in common can be actuated.

Thomas uncovers the basis of divine charity, which he carefully calls "a certain communication of the person with God" (*aliqua communicatio hominis ad Deum*). The Latin expression *communicatio* is only rendered in modern languages with some difficulty. It encompasses both an active, dynamic aspect as well as an intransitive one, which, on account of its substantive character, is gladly understood as a possession of a common essential form.[7]

As applied to God's love for human beings, *communicatio* means a sharing and commonality that consists in the fact that the Triune God gives everyone His own beatitude and calls people to participate in His divine life. Thomas arrives at this content, packed with theological significance, by joining its biblical meaning with a central element of the Aristotelian analysis of friendship. In the text cited in IIa IIae, q. 23, a. 1 (1 Cor 1:9), fellowship (*koinonia*), together with a subjective genitive, indicates the participation of the faithful in Christ and the vital union of all Christians with the Son.[8] Aristotle, too, regards the nature of different friendships as grounded in a vital union each of its own kind, but always pertaining to people with one another. The common execution of a voyage on a ship or the craft of war, or being together in a family or in a city creates different kinds of friendship (*philia*) among people, which is built up in accord with the mode of their fellowship.[9] Thomas combines the Pauline idea of the calling of all the faithful to a vital union with Christ with the Aristotelian key for making relevant distinctions that reduces the friendship of sailors, soldiers, artisans, and tent-dwellers to their respective forms of being together. In so doing, he can clarify why the human love of God based on a sharing and a commonality of divine life can be called a friendship that is at the same time radically distinct from all other friendships. Human love for God proceeds from a communication that cannot be compared with any human compact. In this communication, the infinite God in the fullness of His Triune life is opened up to human beings and so calls them to friendship with Himself. It is thus friendship in the full sense of the word, and with the rigorous precision of the Aristotelian notion. And yet it is at once such a wholly unique type that it realizes its destiny on a foundation created by God Himself.

One can only measure the range of Thomas's thought when one asks in what sense the communication of life that proceeds from God assumes the function of the "fellowship" (*koinonia*) that according to Aristotle is indispensable to any friendship. It surely does not speak of friendship between human beings and God in the same sense that the Philosopher describes the commonality required between friends. Aristotle's "lasting friendship" exists only between equals, who are similar in dignity, virtue, and social status.[10] To be sure, he also recognizes friendships based on the superiority of one of the two partners as is the case with parents and children, rulers and subjects, or between older and younger people. But even in these asymmetrical relationships, the postulate is fulfilled at least in the mode of an adequate proportion between friends, so that the better partner is loved more, corresponding to her or his higher rank.[11] However, when the distance becomes too large, the willingness for friendly companionship dies away on both sides. This is already noticeable conduct in relation to sovereigns; and the relationship to the gods is properly characterized by Aristotle in terms of distance. For them, only honor and gratitude, but not friendship, is appropriate. Their superiority removes them to a remoteness where neither can they approach human beings, nor can human beings turn to them.[12] Indeed, for their part, the gods take pleasure in human beings, especially in the wise and virtuous, but what they love in them is solely their reenactment of the divine spirit in human thought. The self-thinking thought of the godhead is shown in the human spirit as in a mirror, and finds joy in this self-image. But this is not the friendship that breaks out of the circle of self-reference and reaches the others for their own sake to wish them well. If human friends are already helpful to one another above all in remaining constant in their mutual exercise of virtue—how can the Godhead, unqualified perfection in its self-sufficiency, be a friend of human beings?[13] The Aristotelian ideal of friendship acknowledges no overcoming of distance and differences in rank; it is neither desire (*eros*) nor *agape*, but "friendship" (*philia*): love of like for like and exchange among equal partners.[14]

Thomas's intellectual achievement consists in his interpretation of the concept of *communicatio* against the background of the Christian understanding of God. According to Aristotle, lack of equality excludes friendship between gods and human beings. Thomas's God is neither the unmoved mover nor the highest thought who sees only his own essence in the finite spirit. He is the God of love, who yearns for intimate community with human beings and seeks companionship and exchange with them. Thomas does not shy away from using the vocabulary of "society" (*societas*), "to live together" (*convivere*), and "conversation" (*conversatio*), which are all taken from the realm of intimate human communication.[15] The Triune God establishes the foundation upon which the friendship of human beings for God can emerge by bending down to him in God's becoming human, and becoming equal to human beings in the descent of love. Conversely, human life is given new dignity in the mystery of the Incarnation that renders it worthy of the love and friendship of God. Thomas gains the possibility of considering divine love for human beings as friendship not by any discounting of the equality between friends demanded by Aristotle, but in the measure that he conceives of God's effective dealing with human beings in creation, Incarnation, and election. He interprets the concept of *communicatio* in light of his Christian understanding of God, which makes possible the equality required. God's love draws human beings up into the community of his blessed life, and gives them that character and dignity that altogether and alone enable a friendship with him.

The theological virtue of charity, the divine friendship of graced human beings, is thus realized on a level of equality, as Aristotle requires of any friendship. The interrelatedness of the conceptual coordinates of his analysis has remained, but it has taken on a new theological nuance of meaning in the idea of the self-communication of divine love to human beings. Fellowship (*koinonia*) no longer means merely the external affinity of friends, as becomes visible in their frequent companionship and in their social equality. Instead, with the dynamic and creative communication of the new being proper to grace and the share in beatitude is named the foundation on which human love is elevated as friendship with the Triune God.[16] However, because God's grace transforms the person inwardly and impinges

on him in his created reality, there emerges from the active self-communication to the human being a new "quality" (*quaedam qualitas*) or a "permanently given form" (*habituale donum*). Both strata of meaning pass over immediately into IIa IIae, q. 23, a. 1, when Thomas, speaking on the application of one and the same notion, states, "Since therefore there is some communication of human beings to God, inasmuch as God shares his beatitude with us, it is moreover necessary that some friendship be founded by this communication."[17]

In light of the earlier controversies among Thomas's interpreters, it can therefore be stated that, only when the term *communicatio* is interpreted to embrace both strata of meaning (the active-dynamic and the intransitive-ontological), can it fulfill the function intended by Thomas in the speculative analysis of divine charity. The use of a central concept of Aristotelian ethics exemplifies how in the appropriation of his philosophical vocabulary, Thomas, following his philosophical model, unites exactness in applying his concepts and intellectual freedom in newly determining its theological content.[18]

THE ANTHROPOLOGICAL STRUCTURE: CHARITY AS A NEW CREATION OF HUMANITY

While recourse to the Aristotelian theory of friendship pursues a clearly recognizable intellectual intuition that frees its interpretive elements out of the horizontal ordering and transfers them to the creative relationship of God to humanity, its relationship to the presuppositions of the Augustinian theology of grace is more complicated. Material references to Augustine, which are far more frequent than citations from the *Nicomachean Ethics*, oscillate between agreeable reception and critical revision. This is a byproduct of a carefully demarcated and multilayered model that conceals rather than reveals significant departures from Augustine. It is clear that, for Thomas, the theological authority of the Bishop of Hippo is paramount. He never directly contradicts Augustine, even though he opposes Augustine's contemporary proponents, even Peter Lombard, with great candor.

This failure on the part of authority may be noted especially on two issues in the treatise on charity that document the resolute resumption of Augustine's positions as well as the covert critique. The disagreement with one of Peter Lombard's particularly infamous theses can serve as a first example of an openly conducted debate over an issue on which Augustine does not appear as a direct proponent of the opposed opinion. Thomas addresses it in his question on the nature of caritas in the article, "Whether charity is a created reality in human beings" (IIa IIae, q. 23, a. 2). On the speculative level, the second article can be regarded as a necessary expansion of the first article. That is, it contains a counterbalance to the strong emphasis of the previous article's perspective on the theology of grace, in which charity appears as friendship with the Triune God. In connection with the passage in Paul often cited in the medieval period, Romans 5:5b ("God's love has been poured out into our hearts through the Holy Spirit that has been given to us"), Lombard had construed love in his *Sentences* as an immediate effect of the Holy Spirit and of His indwelling in the soul. Initially, Thomas takes this remarkable opinion under his protection in the face of an obvious misunderstanding, and stresses that the act of divine love on the part of the human being cannot simply be identified with the third divine person. Thomas does not credit his theological opponent with such theological nonsense. He instead meets the challenge of the high academic culture of disputation, which lies at the basis of the medieval *disputatio*, by seeking as benevolent an interpretation as possible.

According to Thomas's *interpretatio benignior*, by which he repeats Lombard's counterthesis, Lombard had only wanted to underline the primacy of charity over the other virtues, inasmuch as he interprets it as an immediate effect of the Holy Spirit. While this makes all other actions of the graced human being effective through the prior faculties of the soul and the virtues, it should necessitate no creaturely mediation whatsoever in the case of charity. On this interpretation, the power of the Holy Spirit fills the soul directly and immediately, so that individual acts of charity overflow as from a constantly bubbling spring. In terms of an image developed in twentieth-

century Protestant theology, which closely approximates the historical position of Lombard, it may also be said that the individual believers serve the movement of divine love as a passive instrument or as a "channel" through which, in the ideal case, the circle of Trinitarian love courses without any refraction by the creaturely personal will of the human being.[19]

For Thomas, such an interpretation can, if it is understood as a scientific conceptual clarification of the issue, only lead in its logical consequences to error. It achieves the opposite of its intent; instead of ensuring the priority of charity over the other virtues, it allows charity to be eclipsed by the specific capacities of the other virtues to perform. Thomas avers a double intellectual failure of Lombard's position, which, in each case, leads to the destruction of charity. If, in the act of charity, the freedom of the human will is completely excluded, and the soul does not actuate its own effectiveness, but is moved from the outside, then such an act can no longer be understood as charity. What is considered as a hymnic eulogy to the highest of the three divine virtues actually leads to an intellectual self-contradiction, since in terms of its very concept, "love means an act of the will" (IIa IIae, q. 23, a. 2).[20] If the voluntary moment is excluded from it, then one not only abstracts from an imperfection of the finite human being, but essentially destroys its creative structure. When human love for God does not arise from an inner principle infused into the created structure of its soul, then it can no longer remain the human being's free act in response to the antecedent love of God. A love as an effect of grace that gets around the human will, and replaces its antecedently habitual activity, can only be conceived on the side of God, but not also on the side of the human being. Since love in its proper sense demands the free response of the human being, the Aristotelian understanding of reciprocal friendship maintains its unconditional validity for Thomas.

Besides its inner contradictoriness, Thomas raises yet a second objection to the Lombardian thesis. In so doing, he combines a principle from his analysis of the human act with a simple phenomenological observation. He assumes that a human act only results spontaneously and easily from the respective spiritual faculty when the faculty is disposed through a previously added predisposition to the relevant act. The empirical assumption Thomas presupposes as an indisputable experiential fact is furnished by remarking that acts of divine charity are accompanied, in a stronger measure than is the case with acts of the rest of the virtues, by a spontaneous joy in the good. From these two premises, Thomas raises an interesting question: if even simple things are guided to their corresponding goals by a disposition of a form, how is one supposed to deny the human being the possession of an analogously enabling form in his or her orientation to God as the uniquely fulfilling goal? He concludes that, because the act of divine charity transcends the scope of the natural will's capacity, the spontaneity of charity is only explainable by the imprinting of a form as dispositive to its acts, or of a created principle of action. "When therefore some form is not superadded to the natural faculty of the will, which inclines it to the act of charity, then this act would be less perfect than the natural acts and the acts of the other virtues. Above all, such an act would not be done with ease, and would provide no joy" (ibid.).[21] Since, experientially, the acts of divine love have a special spontaneity and ease, these acts must be considered as a created reality in human beings, that is, as a habitual capacity or a principle of action prior to its own acts.

Thomas's discussion in IIa IIae, q. 23, a. 2, obj. 1, gives a historical explanation of how the misunderstanding of the Lombardian thesis could come about. This indication is informative above all because Augustine is made indirectly responsible for the later misunderstanding. The reflection is as follows: if one correctly states that people are good solely by virtue of God's goodness, and wise only by virtue of his wisdom, this does not mean that God's goodness and wisdom are in each person immediately, but that one has a share in them in a created manner. In the same way, charity with which one loves God and neighbor is understood in a certain sense as a created participation in divine love—if only one interprets the idea of participation correctly. On this, Thomas states in a lapidary way: "Such a manner of speech is usual among the Platonists, with whose doctrines Augustine was imbued; and because they did not notice this background, his word could later lead to error" (IIa

IIae, q. 23, a. 2, ad 1).[22] With these few remarks, Thomas also profiles his relationship to Augustine inasmuch as he distinguishes literary levels of relationships from the actual theological subject matter at stake in his train of thought. Augustine is spared on the former level, although the proper distance toward his Platonic style of thought is unmistakable. On the second level, Thomas indirectly criticizes Augustine for laying, by his imprecise *modus loquendi*, the basis for the misunderstandings by his disciples.[23]

THE ROLE OF THE ETHICAL LIFE: CHARITY AS THE FORM OF ALL THE VIRTUES

The way in which Thomas unites respect for the Bishop of Hippo with objective criticism is documented in IIa IIae, q. 23, a. 7. In his answer to this question ("Whether any true virtue is possible without charity"), Thomas distinguishes between a twofold human good and a twofold goal of actions.[24] Just as the particular goods of human existence are truly good because they may be ordered to God as the uniquely fulfilling good for human beings, so among the ends of actions there are particular proximate goals that similarly do not contradict the orientation to the ultimate end (*finis ultimus*). Such particular proximate ends are not absorbed by the dynamic of their orientation toward the final end. They also remain limited by the specifically theological perspective of the human being's return home to God, but they are still true and so valid partial ends. Wherever the human being is oriented by the virtues of justice, prudence, courage, bravery, and generosity, or by human civility to the realization of such ends, he or she brings about a provisional and imperfect happiness that can achieve a certain stability even when it is not directed by charity to the complete happiness of community with God. Not so much by the lack of charity, but only if the relevant partial goal proves to be only an apparent good, the pursuit of which destroys the orientation to the last end, do such prior inclinations to action lose their virtuous character. Only when they keep him from pursuing his final end do the imperfect virtues of the natural human being become "false appearances of virtue" (*falsa similitudo virtutis*)

(IIa IIae, q. 23, a. 7), which are, in truth, vices, as Thomas illustrates with a strikingly long quotation from Augustine.

Given that Thomas cites Augustine at special length in this passage, one could easily overlook the gulf between Augustine's opinion on reality and his own. While for Augustine, the lack of charity from any human action makes it an act of sinful self-love, because a created good keeps one from love of God, for Thomas, the particular structure proper to human acts wins greater relevance even in its own respective sphere. Where Augustine acknowledges only a contradictory opposition between charity and cupidity, or between love of God (*amor Dei usque ad contemptum sui*) and self-love (*amor sui usque ad contemptum Dei*), Thomas reckons on a third alternative. For him, the virtues of the natural human being in their orientation to the particular ends of human practice preserve their own human significance, which is not destroyed by the absence of charity. Therefore, Thomas could not make his own either the hyperbole that the virtues of the Romans were merely splendid vices, or the oft-quoted dictum of Augustine: "love and do what you want" (*ama et quod vis fac*).[25] For Thomas, the success of human practice does not depend only on its orientation to the final end, but also on *what* love does in the sphere of proximate ends of action. Neither do the virtues ordered to such proximate goals lose their proper meaning without charity, nor is this erased by the orientation toward the ultimate end when charity intervenes and transforms these virtues. Instead, charity gathers the effective power for the good present already in the moral virtues to guide them to the ultimate end that transcends the natural tendency of the will. This is the point of the concluding thesis of this article, according to which charity does not suppress the individual virtues but rather orders them as their inner form to their utmost perfection to which, in friendship with the Triune God, the human being is called.

In this interpretation of the axiom "charity is the form of the virtues" (*caritas forma virtutum*) is manifest the new departure of a form of theological thought to which the Augustinian dialectic between grace and freedom, revelation and reason has become alien (IIa IIae, q. 23, a. 8). Just as revelation does not extinguish

natural reason, and grace does not destroy human freedom, so charity is effective *in* justice and *through* justice, *in* courage and *through* courage, and *in* the tactful conduct of prudence and *through* the tactful conduct of prudence. Where charity is effective as an inner form of the moral virtues, their acts to some extent shape the concrete form in which they accomplish their proper work. The human being upon whom divine friendship is bestowed does not persist in pure receptivity so that infused charity can be effective in him without hindrance; instead, charity permeates the moral virtues as its "strategies."[26] Attuned by charity, the moral virtues serve friendship with God. The more strongly these virtues are activated, the more God can work in a human being and vice versa. In this instance, one can see the same relationship of reciprocal causality between charity and the moral virtues that Thomas, in his doctrine of justification, pits against the Augustinian antagonism between grace and freedom (IIa IIae, q. 113, a. 6).[27] If through the effect of charity people become friends of God, two things must happen: (1) God acts in them and (2) they make themselves available to the affairs of God in the world by means of their natural capacities.

THREE POLES OF CHARITY: LOVE OF GOD, LOVE OF SELF, AND LOVE OF NEIGHBOR

The *Denkform* of analogy, in which nature and grace, virtue and charity, and provisional and perfect happiness remain constantly related to each other, also marks the discussions Thomas sets forth in IIa IIae, qq. 25–26, on the inner unity between love of God, self, and neighbor as well as on the order of charity (*ordo caritatis*). Even when he allows qualifications to the radical nature of biblical demand in many concrete observations, Thomas follows the interpretation he gives to the fundamental tendency of charity, indeed, precisely the triangular structure of charity as presented in the New Testament (IIa IIae, q. 25, a. 8).[28] In the synoptic Gospels, as well as the Pauline and Johannine letters, the term *agape* has the constant meaning of the creative love of God for human beings, the responsive love of human beings for God, and included in that love, the love of human beings for one another.[29] In line with this biblical understanding, Thomas emphasizes above all the inner unity of charity that only afterward and secondarily is differentiated into different acts of love of God, of one's own self, of fellows near and far, or of personal enemies. Because there is only *one* foundation and *one* motive for charity—namely, the calling to the blessed community with God and love for Him as the origin of all good things—charity always formally remains one and the same virtue (IIa IIae, q. 23, a. 5; IIa IIae, q. 23, a. 5, ad 2). In the enumeration of all forty-four separate virtues (which are brought together in the *Secunda secundae* in the outline-plan for the treatment of themes in material ethics), love of God and love of neighbor count as one specifically identical virtue, in spite of their distinct acts and objects. When, in contrast, the synoptic formulation always refers to two commands, this occurs above all for the sake of simpler people who conceive only with difficulty that the acts of love of God and love of neighbor mutually entail each other (IIa IIae, q. 44, a. 2, ad 4).

The decisive reason for the inner unity between love of God and neighbor is once again taken from a formal principle of the Thomist analysis of the human act. Since specification of human acts by the respective objects to which they are related follows the formal aspect under which they attain their object, an act that is related to this formal horizon within which it is apprehended has to be specifically identical with any act that is directed to an individual object under the same aspect (IIa IIae, q. 25, a. 1). As one example makes clear, this principle states that there is one and the same eyesight by which one perceives the light and the colors of objects. Colors in things shine forth only with the radiation of light; in darkness, the colors disappear. For Thomas, the unity of love of God and neighbor is to be understood according to this same principle. Charity is aimed at the Triune God, who destines human beings to friendship with Himself, and, along with this aspect directed to its inmost center, encompasses as its concrete object the neighbor, who is called to the very same end. The human being's responsive love of God necessarily includes the love for all those put on the path alongside us to the same final goal, who are called to share in the same

beatitude (IIa IIae, q. 25, a. 12). In *caritas*, the neighbors are loved for God's sake, or—if one may be permitted to combine the formulation of the *Summa theologiae* with the more precise elaborations of the parallel *Quaestio disputata*—*because* God is in the neighbors, and *so that* they can be in God and God can be in them.[30] In this way, love does not just mean the love for one's own good, or for the good of another, but a common movement toward God; because humans are united with God as their highest good, they also become worthy of each other's love. "In this way we love all our neighbors with the same love of charity, because they are related to God as our common good" (IIa IIae, q. 25, a. 1, ad 2).[31]

The principle in accord with which one loves the neighbor on account of the common call to share in one divine life holds good for Thomas as the key for understanding all other forms of charity. It explains why one can love the irrational creatures, not for their own sake, but in honor of their divine Creator and for personal use (IIa IIae, q. 25, a. 3). It explains why and in what manner one could love one's body (IIa IIae, q. 25, a. 5), and how one may already love the angels, who wait in the heavenly kingdom (IIa IIae, q. 25, a. 10). With the help of the same principle, Thomas finally explains why and in what manner one should love both sinners and enemies. One obviously cannot love them because they are evil and oppose us with hostility. That would be both too demanding for the one loving and an utter perversion of love itself. To be required to love enemies *as* enemies, and to treat them with benevolence *because* they have malicious attitudes, cannot be the sense of Jesus' command in the Sermon on the Mount (Mt 5:44), cited by Thomas in the *sed contra* for the article on love of enemy as the central text from the Bible. He sharply repudiates such an interpretation as "perverse and contradictory to love" (*perversum et caritati repugnans*; IIa IIae, q. 25, a. 8). He reasons that this would lead to loving the sin together with the sinner, and the hostility in the enemy, which is bad for both the sinner and the one who loves.

One cannot love sinners and enemies insofar as they are separated from the believer, but only insofar as they coincide with one's humanity and in the common calling to live as children of God. One must hate in sinners that they are sinners, and love them as human beings who are called to beatitude (IIa IIae, q. 25, a. 8, ad 2).[32] Similarly, one should detest enmity as such, but show oneself constantly ready to help one's enemies in case of emergency. "That is to say, they are not opposed to us insofar as they are human beings capable of beatitude" (ibid.).[33] Following the same logic, Thomas reduces the sinners' love of themselves not to an excess of self-love, but to the fact that they love themselves in a perverse way. In connection with the characteristics differentiated by Aristotle, in accord with which true friendship can exist only among the virtuous, Thomas sees the proper nature of sin in people's self-deception about their true good. Because sinners pursue an illusory good out of false self-knowledge, by which they destroy the orientation of their inner persons toward the knowledge of the true and the good, they also remain caught in a false self-love. They love themselves not in what constitutes their true good, but in what leads at length to the corruption of a reasonable existence and of their inner persons. Thus they sin not on grounds of self-love as such, but because they do not love themselves in the right manner (IIa IIae, q. 25, a. 7).

On the contrary, Thomas evaluates the self-love of virtuous persons as a basic creative energy, which can serve all the forms in which love appears. Natural self-love is by no means understood by Thomas on the model of longing love, as in the different variations on "pure love" (*amor purus*) or of disinterested love from the medieval mystics down to Fénelon. Like love of neighbor, it has instead a basically personal status and must therefore be set alongside love of neighbor in the order of "love of friendship" (*amor amicitiae*). Already in his derivation of the two basic forms of love, aimed either at a good wished for another or at the person for whose sake one desires this good, Thomas speaks in a parallel ordering of love of self and love of neighbor. "The friend is loved as one for whom one desires good; and the human being also loves himself in this way" (Ia IIae, q. 2, a. 7, ad 2).[34] In another passage, there is also talk about an ontological priority of self-love that appears as the primordial form and root of the love of neighbor (*forma et radix amicitiae*). If it is occasionally stated that each one loves oneself more than

the other, Thomas intends neither a diminishing of the biblical commandment of love nor any concession to egoism (IIa IIae, q. 27, a. 4). By his ontological analysis of the natural movement of love, Thomas wants instead to provide an explanation of how the "as yourself" (*sicut teipsum*) of the biblical demand of love is to be understood. Because self-love is "the inwardly most familiar form of love," it can serve as a model of how immediately and unreservedly we ought to love our neighbor.[35] "Friendship consists in this, that we conduct ourselves toward [our neighbors] just as we do toward ourselves" (IIa IIae, q. 25, a. 4).[36]

For Thomas, the primacy of self-love over love of neighbor on this level is not a statement of normative ethics. He simply describes the natural weight of the human will, which is inscribed in it as an ontologically fundamental direction. In a specific way, the human will also stands under the fundamental law of all creaturely being according to which *being*-one is prior to *becoming*-one (*unitas est potior unione*). The natural assertion of one's own good precedes the free love that is supposed to reach the neighbor, just as it already includes the self of the one loving. At any rate, Thomas does not always clearly distinguish between the natural assertion of one's own good and the free self-love of virtuous human beings who follow the ethical order of love. Hence, he has lent plausibility to the misunderstandings of many modern interpreters who acknowledge in human love only the "physical" tendency to one's own good and overlook the analogical levels in which the natural weight of being is realized on the level of human beings by their free will.[37]

The greater priority with which self-love precedes love for the other is not to be confused with the psychological suspicion that casts the highest forms of love of God and neighbor as little more than an epiphenomenon of egoism or a sublimated variant of libido. While egocentrics subordinate the whole world to the standpoint of their own "Is," the one who loves truly follows the objective order of love, according to which spontaneous self-love is supposed to be the origin and measure of neighborly love. The principle according to which being-one-with-oneself is more primal than becoming-one-with-the-other requires indeed precisely that the more fundamental element (on the level of the will's natural tendency) will be a standard for later elements (on the level of conscious love in its ethical order). Yet this implies that the relationship by which a person *is* one with himelf or herself is considered as the exemplar in accord with which even love finds its standard by which one is supposed to *become* one with the other. In the measure that the form of love, which is most familiar to each in his or her own self-experience, is thought of as the form of our love in relation to others, the standpoint of "I" is enlarged into the community of love.

The Thomist understanding of the biblical demand to love your neighbor "as yourself" does not aim at a moral compromise or at a balance between egoism and altruism, but at the overcoming of this opposition. The "as yourself" (*sicut teipsum*) of the biblical love command requires, in agreement with the basic structure of personal love, that "one loves the neighbor, neither for one's own profit, nor for one's own pleasure, but wishes the neighbor good for the same reason for which one wills the good for oneself" (IIa IIae, q. 44, a. 7).[38] The dynamic of the natural tendency toward one's own good is so transformed into the ethical order of love as to encompass in equal measure both free and conscious self-love (as a voluntary assertion of this tendency, in order to underpin the objective order of love), and personal love of neighbor (as a voluntary assertion of what is good for him or her).

THE REALIZATION OF CHARITY: THE ORDER OF CHARITY (*ORDO CARITATIS*)

With this insight into the triangular structure of love and into the intrinsic relationship between love of God, self, and neighbor, Thomas has arrived at an important outcome of his speculative analysis of charity. Yet, he does not rest satisfied with this level of analysis. The brief article on the order of charity can be understood as an initial bridge to concrete ethics. A further step toward the multiplicity of everyday life, which in material terms requires the greatest scope within the whole treatise, is provided in Thomas's discussion of all the partial virtues connected with

charity—joy, peace, mercy, beneficence, almsgiving, and fraternal correction (IIa IIae, qq. 28–33)—and of their opposed vices—hatred, boredom, envy, discord, contentiousness, schism, war, quarrel, and riotousness, as well as bothersomeness (IIa IIae, qq. 34–43).

The importance of the hierarchical ordering of the Thomist presentation of the order of charity within the history of theology lies in its specific mode of systematic grounding. Thomas does not confine himself merely to listing the individual parts, as occurs in Augustine and Lombard (God above me; the inner person in me; the neighbor next to me; my body below me). He wants once again to demonstrate that such a list is adequate to the underlying nature of reality by appealing to the basic principle of the doctrine of charity. The order of charity, accordingly, follows through into its ultimate subdivisions of the ordering of its objects toward God. The differentiated levels of nearness to and distance from God as the origin and end of charity at the same time supply people with a rule of preference for their practical acts.

Within the bounds of this chapter, I cannot trace all the ramifications of the order of charity. Instead, I will again illustrate Thomas's methodical mode of procedure in relation to love of self and neighbor. The order of charity also recognizes and restrains the precedence of self-love over the acts of neighborly love rooted in the natural tendency toward one's own good. Only love for one's spiritual self, but not just any good for oneself, should be preferred to the love for the neighbor. The good of one's own body, physical health, and people's physical existence in general must be subordinated to the duties of proper love of neighbor as the reason for caring (*ratio diligendi*), for one's own bodily integrity weighs less than the motive of love of neighbor. I am bound to my neighbor by the full participation in beatitude, while the ordering of my physical existence to beatitude is only realized in a reduced fashion (IIa IIae, q. 26, a. 5). The harming of the body and even the sacrifice of my own life can even be demanded by rightful self-love, as when martyrdom leads to perfect virtue and love is displaced to our inner person (IIa IIae, q. 26, a. 5, ad 2).[39] Yet individuals may never place the ethical integrity of their spiritual selves at risk. The hypothetical possibility of preserving another from sin could not justify ruining one's own salvation and excluding oneself from the immediate orientation toward beatitude (*beatitudo*).

By strictly pursuing the threads proper to ontological participation in the good, Thomas garners further preferential rules: those among my neighbors who stand closer to me by being related to me are to be loved more due to the shared stronger natural bond, while as regards the intimacy of friendship they should be more intensive. One should love one's father in relation to his dignity more than one's own children, whereas one's children deserve the priority due to their dependence but also on account of their more intensive love in return (IIa IIae, q. 26, aa. 8–9). Corresponding to the Aristotelian understanding of the process of biological procreation, the father is the principle of one's being in a more outstanding way than is the mother, and so is to be loved more (IIa IIae, q. 26, a. 10). A wife is owed greater and more passionate love, but parents more lofty respect (IIa IIae, q. 26, a. 11).

Thomas reckons realistically with the fact that the order of charity must remain capable of being fulfilled, and so each can be assigned only a limited number of neighbors to be loved immediately. Thomas does not share the opinion of an anonymous member of the early school of Anselm of Laon, who held that the duty of emotional benevolence ought to be extended to all people, and who believed that love of neighbor is only limited in its external demonstration.[40] Thomas denies any such division of love into internal affect and external deed. The biblical command of love cannot be fulfilled by attributing universal breadth to the inner desire and its confinement to the external doing of love.[41] Instead, the insight that not all human beings are equally worthy of everyone's love lies at the basis of Thomas's necessary differentiation between one far away, nearby, and the neighbor. This is not just on account of the natural limitedness of individual ability to love, but an acknowledgment that in the stratified order of being some stand closer to us than others. Only insofar as one wishes for every human being the same highest good without curtailment can one's love be considered valid for all without distinction. The intensity and

the form of expression of our orientation to others must on the other hand be directed to accord with the relationships in which human beings stand in relation to one another (IIa IIae, q. 26, a. 6, ad 1).

Since the order of charity (*ordo caritatis*) is not primarily grounded by the natural limits of the human ability to love but by the many-leveled orientation to God as the principle and foundation of love, its validity remains unconfined to one's "state in life" (*status vitae*). If indeed in the state of perfection, the necessary delimitation of love unfolds in relation to only a few close human beings, the order of charity is still maintained, even in this universal limitation. If, that is to say, the happy life consists in the fact that the human being is brought home to God forever, and all being is definitively ordered to God in the right way, then the order of charity, whose work this is on earth, far from being eliminated in eternal life, is actually perfected in it. Here, Thomas's speculative cognitive certainty reaches its limit, since he must take into account that all the day-to-day reasons that make people worthy of each other's love will be eclipsed in an incomparable way by the presence of God (IIa IIae, q. 26, a. 13).

THE FRUITS OF CHARITY: JOY, PEACE, AND THE GIFT OF WISDOM

The organization of material in the *Secunda secundae* follows the structural scheme of the ordering used in the analysis of fundamental ethics in the *Prima secundae*. The sequence between the virtues, the gifts of the Holy Spirit, and the beatitudes is repeated within the smaller units of the *Secunda secundae* as well. The entire material ethic is treated here under the heading of a theological virtue or the cardinal virtues following upon them. Thomas concludes this treatise with a discussion of whether charity is related specially to one of the gifts of the Holy Spirit or to a certain beatitude.

A saying from Augustine's *Commentary on the Sermon on the Mount*, which Thomas cites in the *sed contra* of this article before his own discussion, refers to the close correspondence between the promise to those who are peacemakers and the gift of wisdom, which produces the same effect on the passions of the soul.[42] The connection of both with charity results effortlessly for Thomas from the idea of the order of charity. The point of comparison resides in the ordering function that can be affirmed under the diverse aspects of charity, of the peacemaking activity, and of the gift of wisdom, respectively. Even if these correlations are not logically rigorous, the uncovering of such background correspondences within the total architecture of the *Summa* represents an important partial advance that has more than an ornamental function for Thomas's theological method. The systematic recourse to biblical groups of texts, such as the table of charisms in Isa 11:2, or the beatitudes from the Sermon on the Mount, allows for an interpretation of the meaning of charity that is richer in content than the analysis of the essential structure of human acts could be on its own.

By no means should the reader understand that, in the disclosure of hidden correspondences, Thomas follows a free-floating theological construction. The linking of single quotations from the Bible leads instead to material statements that are solidified through the correlations accessible to philosophical reason, as is manifest in the use of texts from Aristotle's *Metaphysics* and *Ethics*. This is especially the case when Thomas is directed by the discussion of the charisms, the fruits of the Holy Spirit, and the beatitudes to the close connection between charity and its fruits, between joy and peace, and the gift of wisdom. This is the relation between charity and its fruits, which consists in the gift of wisdom.

The last article of his treatise on charity expresses *in nuce* the most important cornerstone of his theological conception of peace. Let me quote it more fully as a conclusion:

> Those persons are called peacemakers who bring about peace to a certain extent in themselves and in others. Both occur because those in whom peace is established can be reduced to right order. Peace consists, as Augustine says in Book XIX of the *City of God*, precisely in a "state of orderly rest" (*tranquilitas ordinis*). But this order, as the Philosopher indicated in the beginning of his *Metaphysics*, is the task of wisdom. In this manner, readiness for peace is adequately correlated with wisdom.[43] (IIa IIae, q. 45, a. 6)

Because human beings love themselves by charity in its orientation to God as their uniquely fulfilling good, joy and peace are its most noble effects (*nobilissimus effectus*), which are immediately united with the possession of the highest good. The "most noble effect" is directly interwoven with the possession of the highest good. Thomas comments in his interpretation of Paul's phrase, "May the Lord of peace give you peace" (2 Thess 3:16), true peace consists in peace with both oneself *and* others. External harmony is a necessary presupposition for peace, but this can only last if one lives with oneself in peace and finds the right order of one's own strivings, passions, and wishes. Yet both—the peace in the self and peace among the community—are only possible in God. For God is for each person the highest, unique fulfilling good, and at the same time, what is most in common for all.[44] The longing of the human heart is so great and so deep that God alone is great enough to fulfill it. Only those finding rest in God, in whom there remains nothing of unsatisfied yearning that can become anew a cause of unrest, envy, and hate, can find peace. "A human being will not have a peaceful heart, even if he should possess what he wants, so long as there is still something for which to strive that he cannot possess all at once" (IIa IIae, q. 29, a. 1).[45] This longing comes to fulfillment in God; in Him, universal peace and universal communication among human beings become real. God is the peace that all strive for and the last goal of every person. This is Thomas's intent when he writes in the beginning of the *Prima secundae*, in his treatise on happiness, that "The final end must therefore so fulfill the total seeking of human beings that nothing remains to be sought outside it" (Ia IIae, q. 1, a. 5).[46]

In his treatise on charity, Thomas provides an answer to the fundamental question of morality. It promises that any persons who have entrusted themselves to the path of love and who pursue God's invitation to friendship with Him will be given a definitive coming-to-rest and attaining-the-goal of human life. The last word spoken about human life does not speak of battle, struggle, and exertion, but instead of peace over all grasping, rest without boredom, and joy beyond measure: "Since, however, no creature is capable of the joy worthy of God, so that this joy cannot be apprehended by human beings without remainder, according to Matt 25:21, the human being enters into it: 'Come, share in the joy of the Lord'" (IIa IIae, q. 28, a. 3).[47]

Notes

[1]See Wolfgang Kluxen, *Philosophische Ethik bei Thomas von Aquin* (Mainz: Matthias Grünewald, 1964), 157–63; and Herman Kleber, *Glück als Lebensziel. Untersuchungen zur Philosophie des Glücks bei Thomas von Aquin* (Münster: Aschendorff, 1988), 185.

[2]Paul J. Wadell, *The Primacy of Love: An Introduction to the Ethics of Thomas Aquinas* (New York: Paulist, 1992), 57–61.

[3]"caritas attingit ipsum Deum ut in ipso sistit."

[4]See A. Stévaux, "La doctrine de la Charité dans les Commentaires des Sentences de Saint Albert, de Saint Bonaventure et de Saint Thomas," *Ephemerides Theologiae Louvaniensis* 24 (1948): 59–97, 83–87.

[5]See *In III Sent.*, d. 27, q. 2, a. 1 (Moos, 872–79).

[6]*Quodlibet* I, q. 4, a. 3, ad 1 (Marietti, 9).

[7]See Luigi Cacciabue, *La carità soprannaturale come amicizia con Dio. Studio storico sui commentatori di S. Tommaso dal Gaetano ai Salmanticesi* (Brescia: Quiriniana, 1972), 26–29.

[8]See Charles K. Barrett, *A Commentary on the First Epistle to the Corinthians* (London: Black, 1968), 39.

[9]Arist. *Eth. Nic.* 8.9 (1159b24–1160a30).

[10]Ibid., 8.7 (1157b37–1158b1).

[11]Ibid., 8.8 (1158b23–26). For more on this, see William F. R. Hardie, *Aristotle's Ethical Theory* (Oxford: Clarendon, 1980), 320.

[12]See Arist. *Eth. Nic.* 8.9 (1158b35–1159a6).

[13]On this see Innocenzo Francini, "Vivere insieme? Un aspetto della 'koinonia' aristotelica nella teologia della carità secondo s. Tommaso," *Ephemerides Carmeliticae* 25 (1974): 301–3; and Avital Wohlmann, "L'élaboration des éléments aristoteliciens dans la doctrine thomiste de l'amour," *Revue thomiste* 82 (1982): 251.

[14]See also René Antoine Gauthier and Jean-Yves Jolif, *L'Éthique à Nicomaque, Tome II: Commentaire, IIième Partie* (Paris: Éditions Béatrice-Nauwelaerts, 1970), 689.

[15]See *In III Sent.*, d. 32, a. 2 (Moos, 1004–5).

[16]See Wohlmann, "L'élaboration des éléments aristoteliciens," 256–61; and Louis M. Hughes, "Charity as Friendship in the Theology of Saint Thomas," *Angelicum* 52 (1975): 169.

[17]"Cum igitur sit aliqua communicatio hominis ad Deum secundum quod nobis suam beatitudinem communicat (1), super hac communicatione (2) oportet aliquam amicitiam fundari."

[18]For a more detailed grounding, see Eberhard Schockenhoff, *Bonum hominis. Die anthropologischen und theologischen Grundlagen der Tugendethik des Thomas von Aquin* (Mainz: Matthias Grünewald, 1987), 508–10, 516–18.

[19]See Anders Nygren, *Eros und Agape. Gestaltwandlungen der christlichen Liebe. Zweiter Band* (Gütersloh: Bertelsmann, 1937), 557. English trans.: *Agape and Eros*, trans. Philip S. Watson (Chicago: University of Chicago Press, 1982).

[20]"amor de sui ratione importet quod sit actus voluntatis."

[21]"Nisi ergo aliqua forma superadderetur naturali potentiae per quam inclinaretur ad dilectionis actum, secundum hoc esset actus iste imperfectior actibus naturalibus et actibus aliarum virtutum: nec esset facilis et delectabilis. Quod patet esse falsum: quia nulla virtus habet tantam inclinationem ad suum actum sicut caritas, nec aliqua ita delectabiliter operatur."

[22]"Hic enim modus loquendi consuetus est apud Platonicos, quorum doctrinis Augustinus fuit imbutus. Quod quidam non advertentes ex verbis eius sumpserunt occasionem errandi."

[23]On this, see Giles Hibbert, "Created and Uncreated Charity," *Recherches de théologie ancienne et médiévale* 31 (1964): 63–84, which likewise comes to the conclusion that Thomas has understood the Augustinian position better than did Peter Lombard.

[24]"Utrum sine caritate possit esse aliqua vera virtus?"

[25]August. *Tractatus in epistolam Joannis*, 7.8 (PL 35, 2033).

[26]See Wadell, *The Primacy of Love*, 90.

[27]See Henri Bouillard, *Conversion et grâce chez S. Thomas d'Aquin. Étude historique* (Paris: Aubier, 1944), 40–54.

[28]In this passage, Thomas makes a differentiation within the command to love one's enemies, which is alien to the biblical passage. He distinguishes between the necessary requirements (*de necessitate caritatis*) and a required intervention of love for the enemy in special emergencies (*in articulo necessitatis*), and confines the first stage to the inner readiness (*secundum praeparationem animi*) for actually demonstrating it, whereas the actually performed love of enemy outside an extreme emergency pertains to the perfect fulfillment of the command.

[29]See Helmut Kuhn, *Liebe. Geschichte eines Begriffs* (München: Kösel, 1975), 73.

[30]*De Caritate*, q. un., a. 4: "Thus it must be said that charity loves God by its very nature; and by its nature loves all other things insofar as they are ordered to God: so in a sense it in every neighbor; for thus the neighbor is loved by charity, because

God is in him, or so that God may be in him." ("Sic igitur dicendum, quod caritas diligit Deum ratione sui ipsius; and ratione eius diligit omnes alios in quantum ordinantur ad Deum: unde quodammodo Deum diligit in omnibus proximis; sic enim proximus caritate diligitur, quia in eo est Deus, vel ut in eo sit Deus") (Marietti, 764).

[31]"Unde eodem amore caritatis diligimus omnes proximos, inquantum referuntur ad unum bonum commune, quod est Deus."

[32]"Unde hoc debemus in eis odio habere: debet enim nobis displicere quod nobis inimici sunt. Non autem sunt nobis contrarii inquantum homines sunt et beatitudinis capaces. Et secundum hoc debemus eos diligere."

[33]"Non autem sunt nobis contrarii inquantum homines sunt et beatitudinis capaces."

[34]"amicus autem amatur tanquam id cui concupiscitur bonum; et sic etiam homo amat seipsum."

[35]Josef Pieper, *Über die Liebe* (München: Kösel, 1972), 126.

[36]"in hoc enim amicitiam habemus ad alios, quod ad eos nos habemus sicut ad nosipsos."

[37]On the controversies about the "physical" interpretation of Thomas's doctrine of *caritas* by French Jesuit Pierre Rousselot (1878–1915), see esp. Louis B. Geiger, *Le Problème de l'Amour chez s. Thomas d'Aquin* (Montreal: Vrin, 1952), 28, 93–94; Jordan Aumann, "Thomistic Evaluation of Love and Charity," *Angelicum* 55 (1978): 536–56; and Avital Wohlmann, "Amour du bien et amour de soi dans la doctrine thomiste de l'amour," *Revue thomiste* 81 (1981): 231–33.

[38]"ut scilicet non diligat aliquis proximum propter propriam utilitatem vel delectationem, sed ea ratione quod velit proximo bonum, sicut vult bonum sibi ipsi." See Pieper, *Über die Liebe*, 126.

[39]This text makes clear how strongly the Aristotelian influence on Thomas can overlay the basic biblical layer of his thought. See Wohlmann, "L'élaboration des éléments aristoteliciens," 258.

[40]See Odon Lottin, "Aux origines de l'école théologique d'Anselme Laon," *Recherches de théologie ancienne et médiévale* 10 (1938): 101–22, 114.

[41]See *In III Sent.*, d. 29, a. 2 (Moos, 925–27); and *De caritate.*, q. un., a. 9 (Marietti, 776–78).

[42]August. *De sermone Domini in monte*, 1.4.11 (PL 34, 1235).

[43]"Pacifi autem dicuntur quasi pacem facientes vel in seipsis vel etiam in aliis. Quorum utrumque contingit per hoc quod ea in quibus pax constituitur ad debitum ordinem rediguntur: nam pax est 'tranquillitas ordinis,' ut Augustinus dicit, XIX *de Civ. Dei*. Ordinare autem pertinet ad sapientiam; ut patet

per Philosophum, in principio *Metaphys*. Et ideo esse pacificum convenienter attribuitur sapientiae."

[44]*In II ad Thess.*, chap. 3, lect. 2, n.89: "God is said to pertain to peace in two respects. For peace consists in two things: that a person be in harmony with himself and with others. And neither can be had sufficiently except in God; for one does not sufficiently achieve harmony with oneself except in God, and still less as regards others, since human desire achieves harmony in itself only when what is desired in accordance with one [appetite] suffices for all; and this can be nothing except God. . . . For nothing else whatsoever besides God can suffice for all [desires], but God suffices. . . . Likewise, human beings do not achieve unity among themselves, except in that which is common among them, which is chiefly God. ("Deus dicitur esse pacis quantum ad duo. Pax enim consistit in duobus, ut scilicet homo concordet ad seipsum, et ad alios. Et neutrum potest haberi sufficienter nisi in Deo: quia sibi non concordat sufficienter nisi in Deo et minus aliis quia tunc affectus hominis concordat in seipso quando quod appetitur secundum unum, sufficit quantum ad omnes, quod nihil potest esse praeter Deum. . . . Quaecumque enim alia, praeter Deum, non sufficiunt ad omnes, sed Deus sufficit. . . . Item homines non uniuntur inter se, nisi in eo quod est commune inter eos, et hoc est maxime Deus") (Marietti, 209).

[45]"Non enim homo habet pacatum cor quandiu, etsi habeat aliquid quod vult, tamen adhuc restat ei aliquid volendum quod simul habere non potest."

[46]"Oportet igitur quod ultimus finis ita impleat totum hominis appetitum, quod nihil extra ipsum appetendum relinquatur."

[47]"Quia tamen nulla creatura est capax gaudii de Deo ei condigni, inde est quod illud gaudium omnino plenum non capitur in homine, sed potius homo intrat in ipsum: secundum illud Matth. 25 [v. 21, 23]: 'Intra in gaudium Domini tui'."

Selected Further Reading

Kleber, Herman. *Glück als Lebensziel. Untersuchungen zur Philosophie des Glücks bei Thomas von Aquin*. Münster: Aschendorff, 1988.

Kluxen, Wolfgang. *Philosophische Ethik bei Thomas von Aquin*. 3d Aufl. Hamburg: Felix Meiner, 1998.

Porter, Jean. *The Recovery of Virtue: The Relevance of Aquinas for Christian Ethics*. Louisville: Westminster/John Knox, 1990.

Wadell, Paul J. *The Primacy of Love: An Introduction to the Ethics of Thomas Aquinas*. New York: Paulist, 1992.

The Virtue of Prudence (IIa IIae, qq. 47–56)

James F. Keenan, S.J.

The virtue of prudence places the entire discussion of moral reasoning into an anthropological context. While some ethical systems reflect on moral reasoning without reflexive anthropological considerations, Thomas's ethical method maintains that the ability to reason well depends in part upon the extent to which the agent's personality is rightly ordered. Conversely, the ability to develop a well-ordered personality depends not only upon the intended exercise of well-ordered actions, but also on the prudential determination of those intended exercises. In fact, the function of prudence or right moral reasoning is to determine, intend, and choose actions that will lead to the right realization of those appetites. The mutual dependency of prudence and the moral virtues (this is an evolving spiral, not a vicious circle) incorporates and integrates moral reasoning into an evolving vision of the human person.[1]

Prudence functions to perfect a person's natural inclinations through integrating them into a coordinated way of acting and living in a right manner. From the outset, prudence is not simply the virtue that makes particular choices. Rather, prudence has a privileged place among the cardinal virtues: it recognizes the ends to which a person is naturally inclined, it establishes the agenda by which one can pursue those ends, it directs the agent's own performance of the pursued activity, and, finally, it measures the rightness of the actions taken. Prudence, in short, guides the agent to living a self-directed life that seeks integration.

This overarching dimension of prudence emerges from Thomas's comments about how prudence pertains to the whole of life. Thomas reiterates these in order to bring his reader to an appreciation of the scope of prudence. For instance, at the end of the *Secunda pars* where Thomas discusses the active life, he invokes Aristotle's claim (*Metaph.* 9.8 [1050a30–b2]) that prudence is "right reason about things to be done " (*recta ratio agibilium*) (Ia IIae, q. 57, a. 4). He notes that the works of the moral virtues are the end of prudence: the function of prudence is to determine rightly the works of the moral virtues. He concludes, "the ends of the moral virtues are the principles of prudence, as the Philosopher says in the same book" (IIa IIae, q. 181, a. 2).[2] As the end of prudence is the right realization of works of virtue, the principles of prudence are the ends of the moral virtues themselves. The entirety of the person's moral life is governed by prudence, which is that virtue able both to recognize the ends of our natural inclinations and to bring them to realization through virtuous activity: "Prudence is of good counsel about matters regarding man's entire life and the end of human life" (Ia IIae, q. 57, a. 4, ad 3).[3]

PRUDENCE AND ENDS

Thomas distinguishes the intention of the end, which belongs to the moral virtues, from the specific choice, which belongs to prudence (Ia IIae, q. 56, a. 4, ad 4), and concludes that prudence is "about things ordained to the end" (*ad ea quae sunt ad finem*) (Ia IIae, q. 57, a. 5). Then, when discussing the priority of an intellectual virtue over a moral virtue, he adds that prudence directs the moral virtues not only in the choice of the means, "but also in appointing the end" (Ia IIae, q. 66, a. 3, ad 3).[4] He stipulates here the end that he has in mind: "Now the end of each virtue is to attain the mean in the matter proper to that virtue; which meaning is appointed according to the right ruling of prudence, as stated in *Ethic* ii. 6, vi.13" (ibid.).[5] Prudence's central function is to direct the moral virtues to their end, which is their respective mean (Ia IIae, q. 64, a. 3). Prudence also pursues the end of all the virtues, which is the common end of all life (IIa IIae, q. 47, a. 2).

Later in the *Secunda secundae*, Thomas seems to shift slightly his position regarding prudence and the end. Here, Thomas writes a specific article asking whether it belongs to prudence to appoint the end and concludes, "it does not belong to prudence to appoint the end, but only to regulate the means" (IIa IIae, q. 47, a. 6).[6] Then, Thomas introduces *synderesis* as that which appoints the end: "natural reason, known by the name *synderesis* appoints the end to moral virtues" (IIa IIae, q. 47, a. 6, ad 1).[7] In setting the priority of *synderesis* over prudence, Thomas does not jeopardize the priority of prudence over the moral virtues; rather, he specifically excludes the moral virtues as themselves appointing the end: "the end concerns the moral virtues, not as though they appoint the end, but because they tend to the end which is appointed by human reason" (IIa IIae, q. 47, a. 6, ad 3).[8]

What Thomas identified earlier, he now distinguishes. The end was the mean that prudence appointed; the end is now something different than the mean. In making this distinction, he also introduces another slight change. In the *Prima pars*, Thomas describes the *synderesis* as little more than inciting to the good and murmuring at evil (Ia, q. 79). In the *Secunda secundae*, Thomas writes:

> The proper end of each moral virtue consists precisely in conformity with right reason. For temperance intends that a man should not stray from the right judgment for the sake of his concupiscences; fortitude, that he should not stray from the right judgment of reason through fear or daring. Moreover, this end is appointed to man according to natural reason, since natural reason dictates to each one that he should act according to reason. But it belongs to the ruling of prudence to decide in what manner and by what means man shall obtain the mean of reason in his deeds.[9] (IIa IIae, q. 47, a. 7)

In this later comment, *synderesis* appoints the end of each moral virtue, which ends are still the same: to act according to reason.

Thomas identifies these ends as the naturally known principles that pre-exist in the practical reason. *Synderesis* appoints, therefore, the ends of the moral virtues, which are the naturally known principles in the practical reason: "in the practical reason, certain things pre-exist, as naturally known principles, and such are the ends of the moral virtues, since the end is in practical matters what principles are in speculative matters" (IIa IIae, q. 47, a. 6).[10]

In making this identity, Thomas still reasserts the importance of prudence over the moral virtues. In addressing the appointment of ends he concludes that though *synderesis* moves prudence, prudence is more excellent than the moral virtues (IIa IIae, q. 47, a. 6, ad 3). An implicit hierarchy—*synderesis*, prudence, and the moral virtues—is clearly evident (IIa IIae, q. 47, a. 6).

Thomas demonstrates the superiority of prudence in a multitude of ways. Because prudence directs the moral virtues in the choice of means and, more importantly, because it appoints the mean that all virtues are to attain, prudence is the most excellent of the acquired virtues (Ia IIae, q. 66, a. 3, ad 3). Elsewhere, he argues that prudence is superior because it puts order into acts of reason (Ia IIae, q. 61, aa. 2–4). Moreover, since the cause of *human* "good" or "perfection" is reason (Ia IIae, q. 18, a. 5; q. 61, a. 2; q. 66, a. 1), the virtue nearest the cause is more excellent (Ia IIae, q. 66, a. 1). Furthermore, in the subjects that they perfect, prudence in perfecting reason is more excellent than those perfecting the appetites (Ia IIae, q. 61, a. 2; Ia IIae, q. 66, a. 1). Finally, he states that prudence alone is goodness essentially (inasmuch as the "good" is what reason appoints as the mean), whereas the other virtues are good by their participation in prudence (IIa IIae, q. 123, a. 12). Prudence supersedes the other virtues simply (*simpliciter*; Ia IIae, q. 66, a. 3), and is the principal of all the human virtues (Ia IIae, q. 61, a. 2, ad 1).

This hierarchy is needed because the end that *synderesis* appoints cannot be attained by the moral virtues without prudence: "Moral virtue after the manner of nature intends to attain the mean. Since, however, the mean as such is not found in all matters after the same manner, it follows that the inclination of nature, which ever works in the same manner, does not suffice for this purpose, and so the ruling of prudence is required" (IIa IIae, q. 47, a. 7, ad 3; also IIa IIae, q. 47, a. 15).[11] The ends of the moral virtues appointed naturally by *synderesis* are thus the principles that prudence heuristically pursues.

Still, prudence relies on the moral virtues to dispose themselves to those ends that *synderesis* has appointed (Ia IIae, q. 58, aa. 2, 5; q. 59, a. 4; Ia IIae, q. 68, a. 8). This requirement makes Thomas's interplay between prudence and the moral virtues dynamic. For although the moral virtues need prudence to set the mean to realize the ends of the moral virtues, prudence needs those moral virtues disposed to their ends in order for prudence and those virtues to advance. This interdependency means that to the extent that the moral virtues develop, there is the concurrent possibility of further development in prudence, and vice versa.

Although rarely mentioned in the questions dealing with natural law, prudence is very much in the background of the relationship between natural law and virtue. As the principles of prudence are the ends of the moral virtue, so the principles of natural law are the ends of our natural inclinations. Thomas writes that the first precept of the natural law is that good is to be done and pursued, and evil is to be avoided. This, as shown in the *Prima pars*, is that to which *synderesis* incites a person. Thomas invokes *synderesis* or natural reason when he adds, "all other precepts are based upon this: so that what the practical reason naturally apprehends as man's good (or evil) belongs to the precepts of the natural law as something to be done or avoided" (Ia IIae, q. 94, a. 2).[12] He adds, "the order of natural law is according to the order of natural inclinations"(ibid.).[13] He addresses the inclinations that prudence specifically perfects, referring to the natural ends of those inclinations as related to the one end of being ruled by reason. "All the inclinations of human nature, e.g., of the concupiscible and irascible parts, insofar as they are ruled by reason, belong to the natural law, and are reduced to one first

precept, as stated above: so that the precepts of the natural law are many in themselves, but are based on one common foundation" (Ia IIae, q. 94, a. 2, ad 2).[14] He therefore connects natural law to virtue via "the natural inclination to act according to reason: and this is to act according to virtue. . . . Considered as virtuous . . . all virtuous acts belong to the natural law" (Ia IIae, q. 94, a. 3).[15]

Dennis Billy, in an essay dedicated to the relationship between prudence and natural law, argues that "[they] refer to one another by virtue of their intrinsic relationship to right reason."[16] That intrinsic relationship is through the natural reason whose principle appoints the ends of natural inclinations. Maria Carl takes this one point of agreement, right reason, and adds to it another one, the natural inclinations themselves: Thomas's "conceptions of natural law and virtue are based on the theory of natural inclinations and, more precisely, on the specifically and properly human inclination to reason."[17]

> Billy explicates the relationship between prudence and the natural law: Without the moral virtues, natural law and prudence would not be properly synchronized: primary and secondary goods of human life must be *given* as general ends (i.e., by synderesis and natural law) and proximate goals *appointed* and *personalized* (i.e., by prudence) before they can be *focused upon* (i.e., by the moral virtues), and then *implemented* by appropriate rational means (i.e., by prudence).[18]

Prudence then recognizes the ends of the virtues, appoints the means so that the inclinations can attain their ends, proposes the means to the disposed moral virtues, and directs the right realization of those means.

Carl similarly attempts a summary of the relationship between natural law and the virtues:

> The fundamental relationship between the natural law and the virtues, then, is twofold: The subject matter or content of the precepts—what they are about—is virtuous actions, and the end or final cause of the precepts is virtuous dispositions. Thus, while the natural law is ontologically prior to virtue in the order of generation as cause to effect, virtue is teleologically prior to law as final cause to that which is for the sake of the final cause.[19]

On this, Jean Porter helpfully notes, however, that *synderesis* is not the natural law itself; rather, it is "the habitual knowledge of the fundamental principles of the natural law" (see Ia IIae, q. 90, a. 1, ad 2).[20]

In summary, prudence depends on *synderesis*.[21] Without *synderesis* appointing the end, prudence would not have the pre-existent principles to be applied to the inclinations. As Thomas writes, "to prudence belongs not only the consideration of reason, but also the application to action, which is the end of practical reason" (IIa IIae, q. 47, a. 3).[22]

PRUDENCE PERFECTS

I will now examine Thomas's ideas on prudence and perfection. In the *Prima secundae* Thomas states that virtue perfects the person in view of doing good deeds (Ia IIae, q. 58, a. 3; q. 68, a. 1). These deeds are *good* because they are perfect: the good is that which is perfect. The good perfects, but the good perfects because it is perfect.[23] In his *Commentary on the Sentences*, Thomas writes "goodness pertains to the communication of perfection."[24] In *De veritate*, he explains similarly that "good is the status of that which perfects."[25] The *Compendium of Theology* states, "The perfection of anything is its goodnesss."[26] In *De malo* 1, a work contemporary with the *Prima pars*, Thomas proposes three uses of the word good, and each use is a perfection: "The perfection of a thing is called good."[27]

In the *Summa theologiae*, the question of God's goodness (Ia, q. 6) follows the question of God's perfection (Ia, q. 4). In the question between these two, Thomas states "something is good insofar as it is perfect" (Ia, q. 5, a. 5).[28] When he asks whether God is good, he repeats his earlier remark that "something is good insofar as it is perfect" and offers three ways in which something is perfect. He concludes that no created thing but only God fulfills this threefold perfection within one's essence (Ia, q. 6, a. 3). God is, therefore, good in that God is at once the perfection or fulfillment of God's self. God *is*. Nothing about God waits for completion.[29]

The virtues are good inasmuch as they are perfect and inasmuch as they help one attain perfection. As Thomas writes at the end of the *Summa*, nothing is perfect unless it attains its end (IIIa, q. 44, a. 3, ad 3). In the human, however, the end or the perfection is twofold (Ia, q. 62, a. 1; Ia IIae, q. 3, a. 2, ad 4; Ia IIae, q. 3, a. 6). The first is what we on our own natural powers attain; the second is beyond our powers. The difference in the two perfections, therefore, is the difference of the ends attainable: only by grace does one attain the second perfection (Ia IIae, q. 62, a. 1). In either case, the good or the perfect is so called insofar as it *attains* its end (IIa IIae, q. 184, a. 1). Inasmuch as the virtues are about perfection, therefore, the virtues are about making us right or complete. What then makes perfect the acquired moral virtues?

Prudence perfects us with regards to things to be done (IIa IIae, q. 47, a. 5). Thomas underlines first that prudence perfects practical reason (Ia IIae, q. 61, a. 2; Ia IIae, q. 66, a. 1; Ia IIae, q. 61, a. 3; Ia IIae, q. 61, a. 4; Ia IIae, q. 63, a. 2, ad 3). Thus, prudence is an intellectual virtue. But unlike the other intellectual virtues, it engages a different material object (IIa IIae, q. 47, a. 5); it engages instead the same object as the moral virtues. Although the moral virtues perfect the rational, irascible, or concupiscible appetites, they do so inasmuch as they engage objects that will perfect these appetites. The objects engaged are right if they are prudential. If the object of justice, temperance, or fortitude is not prudential, the act will not be just, temperate, or fortitudinous, nor will it perfect the agent.

In sum, the fundamental inclinations of each person in particular and of the human species in general are innate;[30] they are realized into moral virtues by prudence. Thomas makes this point in an interesting article on vengeance: "It is evident that virtues perfect us so that we follow in due manner our natural inclinations. Wherefore to every definite natural inclination there corresponds a special virtue" (IIa IIae, q. 108, a. 2).[31] But, to attain its proper perfection, moral virtues must attain, as we saw, the rule of reason (Ia IIae, q. 63, a. 2; Ia IIae, q. 63, a. 4; Ia IIae, q. 71, a. 6; Ia IIae, q. 74, a. 7; IIa IIae, q. 8, a. 3, ad 3; IIa IIae, q. 17, a. 1; IIa IIae, q. 27, a. 6, ad 3). Natural inclinations become virtues, then, to the extent that they become "good," which is to attain that rule (Ia IIae, q. 64, a. 1, ad 1). They attain this rule to the extent that they attain their mean, because for moral virtues, the mean has the character of rule and measure (Ia IIae, q. 64, a. 3). Therefore prudence, in establishing that rule or mean of reason, makes the virtues good, since the good in the acquired virtues is the good as defined by reason (Ia IIae, q. 61, a. 2; Ia IIae, q. 62, a. 3; Ia IIae, q. 63, a. 2).[32]

PRUDENCE DIRECTS

If "prudence perfects" describes prudence realizing the inclinations into virtues, then "prudence directs" explains how that realization occurs. In order to appreciate this *directive* function, I return, for a moment, to the natural law. Since the specific precepts of the natural law cannot be simply deduced from its first principles, prudence must direct the inclinations into the means to achieve the ends.[33] These means are not simple deductions from those ends; on the contrary, as we have seen, the means are means *to* the end. As Stephen Pope notes, these principles are really ends, that is, "what nature teaches is to be determined teleologically."[34] Although the natural law is "a set of fundamental, innately known principles by means of which more specific moral judgments are formed," one must understand how those specific moral judgments are formed.[35] That understanding is key for grasping Thomas's conceptions of the natural law and prudence.

As I have shown, Thomas establishes the priority of prudence over the moral virtues because they cannot appoint the means to attain the end appointed by *synderesis*. The virtues depend on prudence to realize those ends. Josef Pieper describes prudence as providing the inclinations, "a passage to reality"; the principle of *synderesis* requires prudence so that a specific good or end can be known, pursued, and realized.[36] As Jean Porter writes, "This principle does not take on substantive content apart from an account of what the concrete specific good of the human creature is."[37] That concrete specific good is attained under the direction of prudence.

Prudence directs in two ways: it perfects the practical reason as it determines and pursues the means for attaining the natural inclination's perfection. This twofold perfection is, as we have seen, approached through the same object, since "prudence in applying right reason to action is not done without right appetite" (IIa IIae q. 47, a. 4).[38] The perfection of those natural inclinations is "the good as fixed by reason, with regard to which Dionysius says (*Div. nom.* iv) that the good of the soul is to be in accord with reason" (Ia IIae, q. 55, a. 4, ad 2).[39] Prudence directs the inclinations to their realizations as virtues, which is their good according to the rule of reason (Ia IIae, q. 63, a. 2).

Prudence does not only direct those inclinations. It "is needed in the reason to perfect the reason and to make it suitably affected toward things ordained to the end" (Ia IIae, q. 57, a. 5).[40] Its twin functions of perfecting practical reason and leading the inclinations to their virtuous realization is what gives prudence that overarching role of directing the entire person in the way of life: "prudence is necessary to man, that he may lead a good life, and not merely that he may be a good man" (Ia IIae, q. 57, a. 5, ad 1).[41]

The directive function of prudence is the guide in our passage to reality, because contingency marks the practical order. Facing that contingency, prudence directs the agent toward the end of life: "Future contingents, insofar as they can be directed by man to the end of life, are the matter of prudence" (IIa IIae, q. 49, a. 6).[42] Thomas appeals to *direction* as prudence's specific function to describe its ability to negotiate this contingency: "It is only about contingent matters that an intellectual virtue is assigned to the practical intellect" (Ia IIae, q. 57, a. 5, ad 3).[43]

Thomas derives this directive function of prudence from his sources. Commenting on Augustine's definition of virtue as the art of right conduct, Thomas writes that "this applies to prudence essentially; but to other virtues, by participation, for as much as they are directed by prudence" (Ia IIae, q. 58, a. 2, ad 1).[44] From Aristotle (*Eth. Nic.* 2.6), the essential meaning of virtue revolves around prudence as directive; it is a habit of choosing the mean appointed by reason as the prudent man would appoint it"(Ia IIae, q. 59, a. 1).[45] Likewise, reflecting on Gregory's insistence on the necessity of the unity of the virtues, Thomas writes: "the qualities of prudence overflow onto the other virtues insofar as they are directed by prudence" (Ia IIae, q. 61, a. 4, ad 1).[46]

Thomas summarizes: "there is but one virtue to direct all such (moral) matters, viz. prudence" (Ia IIae, q. 60, a. 1, ad 1).[47] Elsewhere, he repeats this central insight: "the whole matter of the moral virtues falls under the one rule of prudence" (Ia IIae, q. 65, a. 1, ad 3).[48]

Under the concept of direction, one can understand the relationship of the moral virtues to prudence. The moral virtues dispose the powers in which they inhere so as to be directed by prudence (Ia IIae, q. 68, a. 8), since reason is to direct all inclinations (Ia IIae, q. 94, a. 4, ad 3). These inclinations dispose the powers by providing prudence the subject matter that prudence is to direct (Ia IIae, q. 65, a. 2), since prudence has the same matter as the moral virtues (IIa IIae, q. 47, a. 5, ad 1). If these inclinations are not directed to their mean, then they do not become virtues (IIa IIae, q. 47, a. 7, ad 3). Thus, "natural inclinations fail to have the complete character of virtue, if prudence be lacking"(Ia IIae, q. 65, a. 1, ad 1).[49]

Specific moral judgments can only be determined in the concrete order by prudence, which determines the means and thus directs the practical reason and the inclinations toward the end to be attained. Prudence directs because it "belongs to the ruling of prudence to decide in what manner and by what means man shall obtain the mean of reason in his deeds"(IIa IIae, q. 47, a. 7).[50] That "mean of reason" in one's deeds is the stuff of right specific moral judgments. As Porter writes: "prudence determines what amounts to a substantive theory of the human good, at least as it applies to this individual in this particular setting, although of course the individual may not be able to formulate that theory in any systematic way."[51]

Thomas uses prudence as directive as a segue into political prudence, which is prudence directed to the common good (IIa IIae, q. 47, a. 11, ad 1).[52] Because "it belongs to prudence rightly to counsel, judge, and command concerning the means of obtaining a due end, it is evident that prudence regards not only the private good of the individual, but also the good of the multitude" (IIa IIae, q. 47, a. 10).[53] With this insight, he approaches good governance and the prudence of an individual king: "Now it is evident that there is a special and perfect kind of governance in one who has to govern not only himself but also the perfect community of a city or kingdom; because a government is the more perfect according as it is more universal, extends to more matters, and attains a higher end. Hence prudence in its special and most perfect sense, belongs to a king who is charged with the government of a city or kingdom" (IIa IIae, q. 50, a. 1).[54]

Thomas calls this prudence "reignative," and when he contemplates its relationship with justice, he provides us with a proper summary for this section:

All matters connected with moral virtue belong to prudence as their guide. . . . For this reason also the execution of justice, insofar as it is directed to the common good, which is part of the kingly office, needs the guidance of prudence. Hence these two virtues—prudence and justice—belong most properly to a king. . . . Since, however, direction belongs rather to the king and execution to his subjects, reignative prudence is reckoned a species of prudence which is directive, rather than to justice which is executive.[55] (IIa IIae, q. 50, a. 1, ad 1)

Prudence as directive expresses the overarching way through which it perceives the end, provides the heuristic means to the self-disposed moral virtues, and directs them in their operations as they express those means to that end.

Fifty years ago, French Dominicans turned to the directive function of prudence to resituate prudence as the virtue of moral reasoning.[56] In the last three centuries, during which time the moral manuals dominated moral theology, moral reasoning looked more like obedience to particular deductive casuistic judgments made by moral theologians and their surrogates, the confessors.[57] Replacing this type of paternalistic casuistry with the virtue that directs the moral agent to rightly realize her or his inclinations into moral virtues has been the work of many contemporary Catholic revisionists.[58] In doing so, they restored to Christians their rightful duty to be accountable for their own consciences.[59]

This turn to prudence was a turn not only away from blind obedience to bishops, moral theologians, and confessors, but also away from the domination of speculative reasoning and its universal principles on the horizon of moral reasoning. In the three hundred years between the end of high casuistry in 1660 and the Second Vatican Council, consistently, univocally applied universal principles replaced any particular prudential judgments. This reliance on speculative knowledge and their universal principles obscured, however, the purpose of practical reasoning. As Daniel Westberg notes: "The primary difference between theoretic reason and practical reason is not between abstract and concrete, but in the purpose: theoretic reasoning is done in order to know something, practical reasoning in order to do something."[60] The return to prudence prompted theologians and philosophers to reexamine the suitability of those absolute universals put in place during the deductivist, manualist period.[61] This turn to practical reasoning furthermore reawakened a new examination of casuistry not as a deductive method of moral reasoning but as an analogical, inductive method.[62] The retrieval of this particular form of casuistry furthered in turn the distinctive claims of practical reasoning.[63]

PRUDENCE INTEGRATES

Art and prudence are the virtues that perfect practical reason, though prudence is different from art, a point that Thomas appears to enjoy making (Ia IIae, q. 57, a. 4; Ia IIae, q. 58, a. 2, ad 1; Ia IIae, q. 58, a. 3, ad 1; Ia IIae, q. 58, a. 4; Ia IIae, q. 65, a. 1; IIa IIae, q. 47, a. 4; IIa IIae, q. 47, a. 4, ad 2). Art concerns transient operations, while prudence concerns immanent ones (Ia IIae, q. 57, a. 5, ad 1; q. 68, a. 4, ad 1). Likewise, art is right reason about things to be made (Ia IIae, q. 57, a. 3), while prudence is right reason about things to be done (Ia IIae, q. 57, a. 4). The difference between something being made or done simply revolves around the question of whether the activity engages not only the practical intellect of the agent, but also the appetites of the agent as well. If an action is transient, then the work that the agent is performing passes from the agent to the object and transforms the object being made. By art, an object is perfected as well as the agent's practical reason. For instance, by art, a cabinetmaker learns more about cabinetmaking and makes better cabinets, but the personal moral virtues of the cabinetmaker are not affected. If an action is immanent, the work that the agent is performing so engages the agent that his or her performance redounds to one's whole person through the activity. In prudence, the agent's operation, his or her practical reason and personality are perfected simultaneously. For instance, by prudence a governor reigns well; therefore, the society ruled benefits, the sovereign's reasoning improves, and his or her appetites ("concupiscible," "irascible," and "intellectual") become more virtuous. The operation and the agent become identified in prudential activity. Thus, Thomas asserts that "actions and passions, which are within us, are more the concern of prudence and virtue than of art" (Ia IIae, q. 34, a. 1, ad 3), because prudence puts reason into the operations and passions (Ia IIae, q. 61, a. 2).[64]

By prudence, an agent becomes what she or he intentionally does.[65] The agent's engagement of particular activities occasions the further development of particular dispositions that the agent has. Thomas's appropriation of Avicenna's formula for the acquisition of virtue through "reflection and exercise" (*studium et exercitium*) is evident here: to be virtuous requires right exercises of immanent activity (Ia IIae, q. 65, a. 1, ad 1; IIa IIae, q. 47, a. 14, ad 3; IIa IIae, q. 47, a. 16, ad 2).[66]

Prudence directing immanent activity means, therefore, that prudence integrates the appetites and practical reason. Thomas states six times that *among themselves* the four virtues are interconnected (Ia IIae, q. 65, a. 1, ad 1, 3–4; Ia IIae, q. 66, a. 1; Ia IIae, q. 66, a. 2). Because prudence constitutes the inclinations as virtues, Thomas argues, not surprisingly, that the virtues are interconnected through prudence. Interestingly, he underlines this interconnection by paralleling prudence to charity. In one section, Thomas writes that the moral virtues are united together through prudence, just as the gifts of the Holy Spirit are connected through charity (Ia IIae, q. 68, a. 5). In another, he states, "the connection among moral virtues results from prudence, and as to the infused virtues, from charity" (Ia IIae, q. 66, a. 2).[67]

If the virtues require prudence, do they equally require charity? Thomas defines virtue by prudence and parallels the functions of prudence and charity in uniting the virtues.

But what does he say about the person who is without charity but has acquired prudence? On several occasions Thomas raises the matter. First, in his definition of virtue, Thomas considers Augustine's definition of virtue: "Virtue is a good quality of the mind, by which we live righteously, of which no one can make bad use, which God works within us, without us" (Ia IIae, q. 55, a. 4, obj. 1).[68] He accepts the definition insofar as he can eliminate the coda, "that God works within us, without us. . . . If we omit this phrase, the remainder of the definition will apply to all virtues in general, whether acquired or infused" (Ia IIae, q. 55, a. 4; also Ia IIae, q. 55, a. 4, ad 6).[69] Thomas makes clear that virtue is not necessarily derived from infused grace. Rather, from the beginning of his treatise on the acquired virtues, Thomas entertains the possibility of virtue in a purely secular ambit.[70] Moreover, he considers explicitly the interconnection of the acquired moral virtues without charity.

Thomas asks whether the acquired moral virtues are virtues without having charity and responds that even though they are not perfect in attaining the last end, they are still virtues (IIa IIae, q. 23, a. 7, ad 1, 3). He concludes that, although the virtuous acts do not attain of themselves the final perfection, they remain virtuous. The final perfection is the second happiness which humanity can only attain out of charity.[71] On another occasion, he affirms that acquired virtues were in the Gentiles and similarly can be considered *per se* as a perfection of the human natural powers (Ia IIae, q. 65, a. 2). The absence of charity here is not on account of a lack of personal goodness, but rather a lack of faith.

On two other occasions, however, Thomas considers the absence of charity in the virtuous person specifically in terms of one's goodness or badness (our terms). First he considers that a virtuous person without charity can sin (Ia IIae, q. 63, a. 2, obj. 2) and adds that the acquired virtues are compatible with sin, even mortal sin (Ia IIae, q. 63, a. 2, ad 2). Second, he considers that virtues without charity can be in the good and bad alike (Ia IIae, q. 65, a. 2, obj. 1), and adds that this is the imperfect meaning of virtue (Ia IIae, q. 65, a. 2, ad 2). That a person is a believer or unbeliever, in mortal sin or not, even good or bad, does not change whether a person has the four acquired cardinal virtues.

The absence of charity may actually be found not only in the good Gentile, but also in the bad Christian who enjoys a virtuous life. The possibility makes sense in a system wherein the acquired virtues are measured by the attainment of the rule of reason (IIa IIae, q. 17, a. 1). This measure is different from the measure of charity.

This internal and external coherence of human action is achieved by prudence, which connects the virtues. In the question on the connection of the virtues, Thomas begins his integrated anthropology by passing through several tiers. Rather than starting with charity as Augustine did in his letter to Jerome, Thomas starts with prudence.[72] He argues that, without prudence, an individual virtue is no more than an inclination (Ia IIae, q. 65, a. 1). He adds: "natural inclinations fail to have the complete character of virtue if prudence be lacking" (Ia IIae, q. 65, a. 1, ad 1).[73] In the same article, he later notes: "the whole matter of moral virtues falls under the one rule of prudence" (Ia IIae, q. 65, a. 1, ad 3).[74] In the closing words of the long article, he writes, "Consequently the lack of prudence in one department of things to be done, would result in a deficiency affecting other things to be done" (Ia IIae, q. 65, a. 1, ad 4).[75]

Clearly, through prudence, one can attain our natural ends, but prudence needs charity to be disposed to the supernatural end. Just as the natural inclinations are the ends or principles for prudence in the active life, so charity becomes the end or principle for the prudent person in the pursuit of supernatural happiness (Ia IIae, q. 65, a. 2).

Nonetheless, the moral virtues and the virtue of charity make the person well disposed to the ends that one should pursue. For this reason, charity alone makes the agent disposed to his or her end: "Now for prudence to proceed aright, it is much more necessary that man be well disposed toward his ultimate end, which is the effect of charity, than that he be well disposed in respect of other ends, which is the effect of moral virtue" (ibid.).[76] To attain the supernatural end, charity is absolutely necessary. It is clear that, just as prudence sets the mean and is the measure of the moral virtues, so, too, charity has its own measure.

Thus, when Thomas asks whether charity observes the mean, he responds that the love of God is not subject to a measure because there is no mean to be observed (IIa IIae, q. 184, a. 3): the measure of charity is to love God above all (IIa IIae, q. 26, aa. 2–3; IIa IIae, q. 27, aa. 3, 5–6; IIa IIae, q. 44, aa. 4–5). This measure is, therefore, a measure without mean. The greater one's love for God, the better one's love actually is (IIa IIae, q. 27, a. 6).

In this light, charity and prudence have different measures. Prudence measures whether an action has attained the mean. Charity measures whether one loves God to the greatest possible extent. In fact, Thomas acknowledges these distinct measures and states that external acts must be measured by two rules, by charity and by reason (IIa IIae, q. 27, a. 6, ad 3). On one hand, one must ask whether one is acting out of a striving for greater union with God; on the other hand, one must examine whether the reasonable mean has been attained.[77]

Therefore, the lack of prudence not only means that an inclination does not become a virtue, but also that, left without this directive and integrating virtue, the agent moves toward disintegration. Vice is itself the lack of integration: "Acts of virtue are suitable to human nature since they are according to reason; whereas acts of vice are discordant from human nature since they are against reason" (Ia IIae, q. 54, a. 3).[78] Later, Thomas writes, "sin does not consist in passing from the many to the one, as is the case with virtues, which are connected, but rather in forsaking the one for the many" (Ia IIae, q. 73, a. 1).[79]

Thomas has accorded to prudence this integrating and directive function through which an agent moves toward right realization through immanent action. In so doing, Thomas has partially attributed to prudence that which Augustine dedicated exclusively to charity. This move allows Thomas to speak across confessional lines so as to engage all human beings to see that the quest we each have for the right realization of our own selves is accessible to each one of us. The thirteenth-century Dominican offers through prudence not only a way that one can determine oneself according to one's own inclinations, but also a way to recognize that each person is called to exercise this same competency.

Notes

[1] I take the metaphor from Thomas Kopfensteiner, "Science, Metaphor, and Moral Casuistry," in *The Context of Casuistry*, ed. James Keenan and Thomas Shannon (Washington, DC: Georgetown University Press, 1995), 207–20, at 209.

[2] "fines virtutum moralium sunt principia prudentiae sicut Philosophus dicit."

[3] "prudentia est bene consiliativa de his quae pertinent ad totam vitam hominis, et ad ultimum finem vitae humanae."

[4] "sed etiam in praestituendo finem."

[5] "prudentia non solum dirigit virtutes morales in eligendo ea quae sunt ad finem, sed etiam in praestituendo finem. Est autem finis uniuscuiusque virtutis moralis attingere medium in propria materia; quod quidem medium determinatur secundum rectam rationem prudentiae, ut dicitur Eth. Lib ii, cap. 6 et Lib vi, cap. 13."

[6] "ad prudentiam non pertinet praestituere finem virtutibus moralibus, sed solum disponere de his quae sunt ad finem."

[7] "virtutibus moralibus praestituit finem ratio naturalis, quae dicitur synderesis."

[8] "finis non pertinet ad virtutes morales, tanquam ipsae praestituant finem, sed quia tendunt in finem a ratione naturali praestitutum."

[9] "hoc ipsum quod est conformari rationi rectae, est finis proprius cuiuslibet virtutis moralis. Temperantia enim hoc intendit, ne propter concupiscentias homo divertat a ratione; et similter fortitudo, ne a recto iudicio rationis divertat propter timorem vel audaciam; et hic finis praestitutus est homini secundum naturalem rationem: naturalis enim ratio dictat unicuique ut secundum rationem operetur. Sed qualiter et per quae homo in operando attingat medium rationis pertinet ad rationem prudentiae."

[10] "ita in ratione practica praeexistunt quaedam ut principia naturaliter nota; et huiusmodi sunt fines virtutum moralium, quia finis se habet in operabilibus, sicut principium in speculativis."

[11] "virtus moralis per modum naturae intendit pervenire ad medium. Sed quia medium, secundum quod medium, non eodem modo invenitur in omnibus; ideo inclinatio naturae, quae semper eodem modo operatur, ad hoc non sufficit, sed requiritur ratio prudentiae."

[12] "super hoc fundantur omnia alia praecepta legis naturae, ut scilicet omnia illa facienda vel vitanda pertineant ad praecepta legis naturae, quae ratio practica naturaliter apprehendit esse bona humana."

[13] "Secundum igitur ordinem inclinationum naturalium est ordo praeceptorum legis naturae."

[14] "Omnes huiusmodi inclinationes quarumcumque partium naturae humanae, puta concupiscibilis et irascibilis, secundum quod regulantur

ratione, pertinent ad legem naturalem, et reducuntur ad unum primum praeceptum, ut dictum est; et secundum hoc sunt multa praecepta legis naturae in seipsis, quae tamen communicant in una radice."

15"Si igitur loquamur de actibus virtutum, inquantum sunt virtuosi, sic omnes actus virtuosi pertinent ad legem naturae."

16Dennis Billy, "Aquinas on the Relations of Prudence," *Studia Moralia* 33 (1995): 250.

17Maria Carl, "Law, Virtue, and Happiness in Aquinas's Moral Theory," *Thomist* 61 (1997): 427.

18Billy, "Aquinas on the Relations of Prudence," 153.

19Carl, "Law, Virtue, and Happiness in Aquinas's Moral Theory," 442.

20Jean Porter, "Contested Categories: Reason, Nature, and the Natural Order in Medieval Accounts of the Natural Law," *Journal of Religious Ethics* 24 (1996): 218. Porter's important essay demonstrates that, for the high scholastics, the natural law was not a fixed set of precepts (217).

21Maria Carl writes "Aquinas is explicit and consistent about the interdependence of prudence and *synderesis*." ("Law, Virtue, and Happiness in Aquinas's Moral Theory," 446). Carl's claim of consistency should not lead us to think that Thomas's thoughts on *synderesis* did not develop. See Giuseppe Abbà, *Lex et virtues: Studi sull'evoluzione della dottrina morale di san Tommaso d'Aquino* (Rome: Libreria Ateneo Salesiano, 1983). For further discussion on the relationship between *synderesis* and the natural law, see Oscar Brown, *Natural Rectitude and Divine Law in Aquinas* (Toronto: Pontifical Institute of Medieval Studies, 1981).

22"ad prudentiam pertinet non solum consideratio rationis, sed etiam applicatio ad opus, quae est finis practicae rationis."

23See Joseph de Finance, *Essai sur l'agir humain* (Rome: Gregorian University Press, 1962), 86.

24*In IV Sent.*, d. 46, q. 2, a. 1, sol. 2.: "bonitas ergo respicit commuicationem perfectionis" (Index thomisticus, 663)

25*De veritate*, q. 21, a. 6: "respectus autem qui importatur nomine boni, est habitudo perfectivi" (Marietti, 387).

26*Comp. Theol.*, I, chap. 103 : "perfectio enim cuiuslibet rei est bonitas eius." (Index thomisticus, 611).

27*De malo*, q. 1, a. 2: "ipsa perfectio rei bonum... dicitur" (Leonine, 11, 87–88).

28"Unumquodque dicitur bonum inquantum est perfectum."

29Dalmazio Mongillo, "Le componenti della bontà morale," *Studia Moralia* 15 (1977): 483–502.

30There is considerable debate over the amount of information those inclinations provide and how much of a fixed agenda those ends establish. For

instance, Daniel Mark Nelson remarks that "Nature provides only the most general sort of guidance in the sense that natural inclinations provide the very wide boundaries within which prudential reason operates" (*The Priority of Prudence: Virtue and Natural Law in Thomas Aquinas and the Implications for Modern Ethics* [University Park: Pennsylvania State University Press, 1992], 121). However, all participants in that debate insist that the principles of prudence are derived from the innate ends of the particular moral virtues. See the discussion in Pamela Hall, *Narrative and the Natural Law: An Interpretation of Thomistic Ethics* (Notre Dame, IN: University of Notre Dame Press, 1994).

31"Unde patet quod virtutes perficiunt nos ad prosequendum debito modo inclinationes naturales quae pertinent ad ius naturale. Et ideo ad quamlibet inclinationem naturalem determinatam ordinatur aliqua virtus specialis."

32On the importance of prudence as measurement, see Karl Merks, *Theologische Grundlegung der sittlichen Autonomie* (Düsseldorf: Patmos, 1978), 125ff. See also Klaus Riesenhuber, *Die Transzendenz der Freiheit zum Guten. Der Wille in der Anthropologie und Metaphysik des Thomas von Aquin* (Munich: Berchmanskolleg, 1971).

33Porter writes, "Aquinas appears to be one of the few authors in this period who even considered the possibility that the specific precepts of the natural law might be deduced from first principles, and he decisively rejected this on logical grounds (ST Ia IIae, q. 94, a. 4; see also IIa IIae, q. 47, a. 2, ad 3)" ("Contested Categories," 212).

34Stephen J. Pope, "Scientific and Natural Law Assessments of Homosexuality," *Journal of Religious Ethics* 25 (1997): 101.

35Porter, "Contested Categories," 217.

36Joseph Pieper, *The Four Cardinal Virtues* (Notre Dame, IN: Notre Dame University Press, 1966), 125. See also Stanley Hauerwas and Charles Pinches, *Christians among the Virtues: Theological Conversations with Ancient and Modern Ethics* (Notre Dame, IN: Notre Dame University Press, 1997), esp. 100–104.

37Jean Porter, *The Recovery of Virtue: The Relevance of Aquinas for Christian Ethics* (Louisville: Westminster/ John Knox, 1990), 161. She adds, "Natural reason, functioning as *synderesis*, generates the principle that the good of the human person is to be in accordance with reason. Prudence, which takes account of the specifics of an individual's own character and circumstances, determines what, concretely, it means for this individual to be in accordance with reason; prudence does this in and through determining the mean of the virtues relative to the individual and to the demands of equality and the common good" (162).

38"Ad prudentiam autem pertinet, sicut dictum est, applicatio rectae rationis ad opus quod non fit sine appetitu recto."

39 "sed est bonum rationis, secundum quod Dionysius dicit quod 'bonum animae est secundum rationem esse."

40"Et ideo necesse est in ratione esse aliquam virtutem intellectualem, per quam perficiatur ratio ad hoc quod convenienter se habeat ad ea quae sunt ad finem, et haec virtus est prudentia."

41"prudentia autem est necessaria homini ad bene vivendum, non solum ad hoc quod fiat bonus."

42"Unde consequens est quod contingentia futura, secundum quod sunt per hominem in finem humanae vitae ordinabilia, pertineant ad prudentiam."

43"Et ideo circa sola contingentia ponitur virtus intellectus practici."

44"secundum hoc quod dicit quod virtus est ars recte vivendi, essentialiter convenit prudentiae, participative autem aliis virtutibus, prout secundum prudentiam diriguntur."

45"est habitus electivus in medietate consistens determinata ratione, prout sapiens determinabit."

46"Id enim quod est prudentiae, redundat in alias virtutes, inquantum a prudentia diriguntur."

47"unde est una sola virtus in eis dirigens, scilicet prudentia."

48"et ideo tota materia moralium virtutum sub una ratione prudentiae cadit."

49"naturales inclinationes non habent perfectam rationem virtutis, si prudentia desit."

50"qualiter et per quae homo in operando attingat medium rationis, pertinet ad rationem prudentiae."

51Porter, *The Recovery of Virtue*, 162.

52See Giuseppe Gullo, *Prudenza e Politica* (Naples: Edizioni Domenicane Italianae, n.d.).

53"Quia ergo ad prudentiam pertinet recte consiliari, iudicare et praecipere de his per quae pervenitur ad debitum finem, manifestum est quod prudentia non solum se habet ad bonum privatum unius hominis, sed etaim ad bonum commune multitudinis."

54"Manifestum est autem quod in eo qui non solum seipsum habet regere, sed etiam communitatem perfectam civitatis vel regni, invenitur specialis et perfecta ratio regiminis; tanto enim regimen perfectius est, quanto universalius est, ad plura se extendens, et ulteriorem finem attingens. Et ideo regi, ad quem pertinet regere civitatem vel regnum, prudentia competit secundum specialem et perfectissimam sui rationem."

55"omnia quae sunt virtutum moralium, pertinent ad prudentiam sicut ad dirigentem. . . . Et ideo etiam executio iustitiae, prout ordinatur ad bonum commune, quod pertinet ad officium regis, indiget directione prudentiae. Unde istae duae virtutes sunt maxime propriae regi, scilicet prudentia

et iustitia . . . . Quia tamen dirigere magis pertinet ad regem, exequi autem ad subditos; ideo regnativa magis ponitur species prudentiae quae est directiva, quam iustitiae quae est executiva."

Thomas also treats the specific virtues of political prudence by which a person "directs himself in relation to the common good" (regit homo seipsum . . . per politicam [prudentiam] . . . in ordine ad bonum commune) (IIa IIae, q. 50, a. 2, ad 3); domestic prudence (a. 3); and military prudence (a. 4).

56See the discussion in Daniel Westberg, *Right Practical Reason: Aristotle, Action, and Prudence in Aquinas* (Oxford: Oxford University Press, 1994), 3–14. A classic expression of the directive function is found in A.-M. Henry, ed., *Prudence chrétienne* (Paris: Cahiers de la vie spirituelle, 1948).

57On this obedience, see John Mahoney, *The Making of Moral Theology: A Study of the Roman Catholic Tradition* (Oxford: Clarendon, 1987). On the attempts to replace obedience to deductive casuistic judgments with a personalist inductive form of moral reasoning guided by the directive function of prudence, see Herbert McCabe, "Manuals and Rule Books," in *Understanding Veritatis Splendor*, ed. John Wilkins (London: SPCK, 1994), 61–68. See also my comments in "Casuistry," in *For that I Came: Virtues and Ideals of Jesuit Education*, ed. William O'Brien (Washington, DC: Georgetown University Press, 1997), 93–116; "Learning to Reason Well: Moral Theology since Vatican II," in *Vatican II: Continuing the Agenda*, ed. Anthony Cernera (Fairfield, CT: Sacred Heart University Press, 1997), 199–222.

58The forebear of this French Dominican turn to prudence was certainly the Belgian Benedictine, Dom Odon Lottin. See Mary Jo Iozzio, *Self-Determination and the Moral Act: A Study of the Contributions of Odon Lottin (OSB)* (Leuven: Peeters, 1995).

59See Klaus Demmer, "La competenza normativa del magistero ecclesiastico in morale," in *Fede cristiana e agire morale*, ed. Klaus Demmer and Bruno Schüller (Assisi: Cittadella editrice, 1980), 144–71.

60Westberg, *Right Practical Reasoning*, 4.

61Here the essay by Josef Fuchs stands out, "The Absoluteness of Moral Terms," in *Readings in Moral Theology No.1: Moral Norms and Catholic Tradition*, ed. Charles Curran and Richard McCormick (New York: Paulist, 1979), 94–137.

62Albert Jonsen and Stephen Toulmin, *The Abuse of Casuistry: A History of Moral Reasoning* (Berkeley: University of California Press, 1988); Keenan and Shannon, *The Context of Casuistry*.

63Kathryn Hunter, "A Science of Individuals: Medicine and Casuistry," *Journal of Medicine and Philosophy* 14 (1989): 193–212; Albert Jonsen, "Of Balloons and Bicycles or The Relationship between Ethical Theory and Practical Judgment," *Hastings Center Report* 21 (1991): 14–16; Jonsen, "The Con-

fessor as Experienced Physician: Casuistry and
Clinical Ethics," in *Religious Methods and Resources in
Bioethics*, ed. P. F. Camenisch (Netherlands: Kluwer
Academics, 1993), 165–80; Jonsen, "Casuistry: An
Alternative or Complement to Principles?," *Kennedy Institute of Ethics* 5 (1995): 237–52; Stephen
Toulmin, "The Tyranny of Principles," *The Hastings
Center Report* 11 (1981): 31–39; Toulmin, "The Recovery of Practical Philosophy," *The American
Scholar* 57 (1988): 337–52.

[64]"Circa operationes autem et passiones quae
sunt in nobis, magis est prudentia et virtus quam
ars."

[65]Servais Pinckaers reminds us that humans are
not creatures of habit and that they are not simple
products of their actions; rather, virtues are acquired
by intended, desired, prudential activity ("Virtue Is
Not a Habit," *Cross Currents* 12 [1962]: 65–82).

[66]Thomas invoked the phrase early in his writings; see *In III Sent.* d. 33, q. 1, a. 2, sol. 2 (Index
thomisticus, 380).

[67]"et secundum hoc, ratio connexionis virtutum
moralium accipitur ex parte prudentiae et ex parte
caritatis quantum ad virtutes infusas."

[68]August. *De libero arbitrio*, 2.19: "Virtus est bona
qualitas mentis, qua recte vivitur, qua nullus male
utitur, quam Deus in nobis sine nobis operatur."

[69]"quae quidem particula si auferatur, reliquum
definitionis erit commune omnibus virtutibus, et
acquisitis et infusis."

[70]Rightly, Renée Mirkes writes, "perfect moral
virtue is materially an acquired moral virtue and
formally a virtue of prudence" ("Aquinas's Doctrine
of Moral Virtue and Its Significance for Theories of
Facility," *The Thomist* 61 [1997]: 195). See also John
Peterson, "The Interdependence of Intellectual and
Moral Virtue in Thomas Aquinas," *The Thomist* 61
(1997): 449–54.

[71]On charity, see Gerard Gilleman, *The Primacy
of Charity in Moral Theology* (Westminster: Newman,
1959); on the attainment of the last end, see Jean
Porter, "Desire for God: Ground of the Moral Life
in Aquinas," *Theological Studies* 47 (1986): 48–68.

[72]See the discussion on Augustine's interconnection of the virtues in John Langan, "The Unity of
the Virtues," *Harvard Theological Review* 72–73
(1979): 81–95. August. *Ep.* 167 in *Letters*, vol. 30
(New York: Fathers of the Church, 1955). See also
Enchiridion 31.117.

[73]"naturales inclinationes non habent perfectam
rationem virtutis, si prudentia desit."

[74]"et ideo tota materia moralium virtutum sub
una ratione prudentiae cadit."

[75]"Et ideo defectus prudentiae circa unam partem agibilium induceret defectum etiam circa alia
agibilia."

[76]"Ad rectam autem rationem prudentiae multo
magis requiritur quod homo bene se habeat circa
ultimum finem, quod fit per caritatem, quam circa
alios fines, quod fit per virtutes morales."

[77]Conrad van Ouwerkerk, *Caritas et Ratio: Étude
sur le double principe de la vie morale chrétienne d'après
S. Thomas d'Aquin* (Nijmegen: Drukkerij Gebr.
Janssen, 1956). See also my *Goodness and Rightness in
Thomas Aquinas' Summa theologiae* (Washington,
DC: Georgetown University Press, 1992); and my
"Distinguishing Charity as Goodness and Prudence
as Rightness: A Key to Thomas' *Pars Secunda*," *The
Thomist* 56 (1992): 407–26.

[78]"Sicut actus virtutum naturae humanae conveniunt, eo quod sunt secundum rationem; actus
vero vitiorum, cum sint contra rationem, a natura
humana discordant."

[79]"Non enim peccatum committitur in accedendo a multitudine ad unitatem, sicut accidit in
virtutibus, quae sunt connexae; sed potius in recedendo ab unitate ad multitudinem." On whether sin
is measured against charity or prudence, see my
"The Problem with Thomas Aquinas's Concept of
Sin," *Heythrop Journal* 35 (1994): 401–20.

Selected Further Reading

Endres, Josef. "Anteil der Klugheit am Erkennen
des konkreten Wahren und an dem Wollen des
Wahrhaft Guten." *Studia Moralia* 1 (1963): 221–53.

Gullo, Giuseppe. *Prudenza e Politica*. Naples:
Edizioni Domenicane Italianae, n.d.

Henry, A.-M., ed. *Prudence chrétienne*. Paris: Cahiers de la vie spirituelle, 1948.

Hibbs, Thomas S. "Principles and Prudence."
New Scholasticism 61 (1987): 271–84.

Keenan, James. *Goodness and Rightness in Thomas
Aquinas' Summa Theologiae*. Washington, DC:
Georgetown University Press, 1992.

———. "Distinguishing Charity as Goodness
and Prudence as Rightness: A Key to Thomas' Pars
Secunda." *The Thomist* 56 (1992): 407–26.

Kluxen, Wolfgang. *Philosophische Ethik bei Thomas
von Aquin*. 2d ed. Hamburg: Felix Meiner, 1980.

Merks, Karl. *Theologische Grundlegung der sittlichen Autonomie*. Düsseldorf: Patmos, 1978.

Nelson, Daniel Mark. *The Priority of Prudence:
Virtue and Natural Law in Thomas Aquinas and the
Implications for Modern Ethics*. University Park:
Pennsylvania State University Press, 1992.

Pieper, Josef. *Prudence*. New York: Pantheon
Books, 1959.

Pinches, Charles. "Pagan Virtue and Christian
Prudence." *Journal of Religious Ethics* 23 (1995):
93–115.

Porter, Jean. *The Recovery of Virtue: The Relevance
of Aquinas for Christian Ethics*. Louisville, KY: Westminster/John Knox, 1990.

Riesenhuber, Klaus. *Die Transzendenz der Freiheit zum Guten. Der Wille in der Anthropologie und Metaphysik des Thomas von Aquin*. Munich: Berchmanskolleg, 1971.

Simon, Yves. *Practical Knowledge*. New York: Fordham University Press, 1991.

van Ouwerkerk, Conrad. *Caritas et Ratio: Étude sur le double principe de la vie morale chrétienne d'après S. Thomas d'Aquin*. Nijmegen: Drukkerij Gebr. Janssen, 1956.

Westberg, Daniel. *Right Practical Reason: Aristotle, Action, and Prudence in Aquinas*. Oxford: Oxford University Press, 1994.

The Virtue of Justice (IIa IIae, qq. 58–122)

Jean Porter

According to Aquinas, justice is a virtue, which he defines, following Justinian's *Digest*, as "the constant and perpetual will to render to each one that which is his right" (IIa IIae, q. 58, a. 1).[1] Together with prudence, fortitude, and temperance, it is a primary or cardinal virtue (Ia IIae, q. 61, a. 2). Its subject is the will (Ia IIae, q. 56, a. 6; IIa IIae, q. 58, a. 4), and its proper object is *ius*, or right, the proper order of interrelationships established by divine or human reason (IIa IIae, q. 57, a. 1). As such, it is paradigmatically expressed in exterior actions directed toward other persons (Ia IIae, q. 60, aa. 2–3; IIa IIae, q. 58, a. 8).

The discussion of justice (IIa IIae, qq. 58–122) is the longest, the most complex, and arguably the most difficult treatment of a particular virtue in the *Summa theologiae*. Even a cursory examination of Aquinas's remarks on justice reveals why he attended to this virtue in such detail. As a virtue of the will, justice is the only cardinal virtue which directly concerns the distinctively human capacity for rational desire. Moreover, it is the cardinal virtue directly concerned with external actions, and as such, it includes most of the norms of nonmaleficence and respect for others which are central to his moral theology.

On further examination, one finds that the length and complexity of Aquinas's treatment of justice is not only a reflection of its importance for him. It also reflects the complexity of the traditions which informed his own discussion. Among Christian patristic authors, both Augustine and Gregory the Great are extensively cited; among classical authors, Aristotle plays a central role, but Cicero is also much in evidence, as are other classical authors.

The conceptions of justice mediated through these authors were complex. There was general agreement among Aquinas's sources that justice is a virtue; at the same time, however, there was considerable diversity of views about what this means. For some of the church fathers, justice is equivalent to rectitude in any of the affairs of life, and thus it is to be understood as a general virtue, or even as equivalent to virtue *tout court*. Justice can also be understood as a general virtue in a second sense, following Aristotle, according to which justice is preeminently the virtue of a lawgiver, and its proper object is the common good of the community. Finally, justice can be understood as a particular virtue, and more specifically as one of the four traditional cardinal virtues. In addition, it was generally agreed that there is a connection between justice and the natural law, whether that connection is understood in terms of Aristotle's "natural justice," as the equity that played a central role in civic jurisprudence, or the "natural law," or "right" (*ius*), which was central to both civil and canonical jurisprudence in Aquinas's time.

Aquinas's own theory of justice as developed in the *Summa theologiae* draws on all of these conceptions. What is distinctive about his theory is the way in which he integrates them into a systematic account. In the course of developing this account, he analyzes and coordinates the different perspectives on justice, as a general virtue, as one particular virtue among others, as the virtue preeminently concerned with right relations among people, and as an integral component of the Christian life. In this chapter, I will attempt to outline Aquinas's complex conception of justice while still conveying its analytic coherence. I will focus on the account presented in the *Summa*, generally following the order of Aquinas's presentation in the *Secunda secundae*, while taking account of his remarks on justice in the *Prima secundae*.

JUSTICE AS A VIRTUE

In the course of setting out his overall theory of virtue, Aquinas appropriates the traditional schema of four "primary" or "cardinal virtues," which provides him with an organizing framework for his subsequent analysis of the moral virtues (Ia IIae, q. 61; he offers his argument for the traditional list, including justice, at Ia IIae, q. 61, a. 2). In the course of developing his interpretation of this schema, he lays the groundwork for organizing the different conceptions of justice which have been bequeathed to him.

The key text is Ia IIae, q. 61, a. 4, in which he asks, "Whether the four cardinal virtues are different from one another?" He replies that the answer depends on one's interpretation of the cardinal virtues. In one sense, these virtues can be considered as "general conditions of the human soul, which are found in all virtues"; understood in this way, prudence is distinct from the other three virtues, but the latter are not distinct from one another.[2] In another sense, the cardinal virtues can be considered as particular virtues, with their own distinctive spheres of operation, and, in this sense, all four are specifically distinct from one another. The latter sense Aquinas adds is the preferred way of understanding the cardinal virtues.

The distinction between general and particular can be applied straightforwardly to fortitude and temperance. For example, fortitude may be said to be a "general virtue," in the sense that every act of virtue displays a certain firmness of soul, thanks to which it can be described as an act of fortitude. But fortitude may also be considered as a "particular virtue," which characteristically has situations of danger or hardship as its characteristic field of operation, and which is paradigmatically expressed by reacting appropriately, without excessive fear or daring, to those difficult or dangerous situations.

The application of this schema to justice is more complex, however, because justice is said to be a general virtue in at least two senses.

First, justice may be equated with rectitude or moral goodness, and in this sense it can be called a general virtue in the same fashion as fortitude and temperance, that is, as a general condition for any act of virtue (Ia IIae, q. 61, a. 4). However, Aquinas also takes the view, which he draws from Aristotle, that there is a kind of general justice that has the common good of the community as its object.[3] Understood in this sense, justice is said to be a general virtue because it directs the acts of the other virtues to its own object, the common good, which transcends the good of the individual toward which the other particular virtues are directed (IIa IIae, q. 58, aa. 5–6). In other words, justice, understood in this sense, is architectonic with respect to the other virtues. At the same time, this form of justice is not essentially equivalent to the other virtues and is thus a particular virtue (IIa IIae, q. 58, a. 6). However, note that when Aquinas speaks of particular justice, he normally means that form of justice that rectifies relationships to individual persons.

Aquinas also describes general justice as legal justice. This terminology can be misleading, unless one is mindful that for Aquinas, "it pertains to the law to govern in accordance with the common good" (IIa IIae, q. 58, a. 5).[4] Aquinas does not value observance of positive law *per se*; in fact, justice may require someone to disregard the letter of the positive law in some cases (IIa IIae, q. 120, a. 2, ad 1). The moral value of legal justice lies rather in respect for the common good, which will normally be mediated through respect for the valid laws of the community, which by definition will themselves be ordered to the common good (Ia IIae, q. 90, a. 2).

In addition to legal justice, Thomas identifies yet another kind of justice, namely "particular justice" (IIa IIae, q. 58, a. 7). Through this form, the individual is disposed to act rightly in all matters having to do with other persons, neither withholding from another that which is due, nor injuring another person (IIa IIae, q. 58, a. 11). Since particular justice concerns the person's relationships to other individuals, its actions are directed toward the common good by legal justice, in the same way as are the actions of the other particular moral virtues (IIa IIae, q. 58, a. 5). Moreover, because one's relationships with others are mediated through exterior actions, particular justice finds its proper sphere of action in external actions, rather than in the proper disposition of the passions (Ia IIae, q. 60, aa. 2–3; IIa IIae, q. 58, a. 2).

These two points, that particular justice is oriented toward others rather than oneself, and concerns actions rather than passions, jointly serve to distinguish particular justice from the other moral virtues, that is, fortitude and temperance.[5] Fortitude and temperance are oriented toward the good of the individual, and they are virtues of the sensual appetites, that is to say, the passions (Ia IIae, q. 60, a. 2). For this reason, their norm consists of the rational mean, which is to say, the appropriate affective reaction to whatever situations fall within their proper spheres of operation (Ia IIae, q. 64, a. 2). Since individuals differ with respect to their emotional makeup, this mean can only be determined by reference to the individual's own temperament and situation; moreover, these virtues are essentially directed toward the individual's own overall good, and so the mean that they observe is set with reference to the agent in a second sense. Justice, on the other hand, is expressed in actions that observe interpersonally valid criteria for fairness and equity. Hence, justice observes a real, and not only a rational mean (ibid.; IIa IIae, q. 58, a. 10).

The analysis of the virtues in terms of a doctrine of the mean is of course taken from Aristotle.[6] At the same time, the application of the Aristotelian doctrine of the mean to the virtue of justice raises a problem, as Aristotle himself seems to have recognized.[7] The difficulty is this: when one speaks of a mean, a criterion located between extremes of deficiency and excess is implied. Neither Aristotle nor Aquinas holds the silly doctrine that the mean of virtue is characterized by feeling a moderate quantity of emotion in every circumstance, no matter how trivial or extreme (Ia IIae, q. 64, a. 1, and, still more explicitly, IIa IIae, q. 92, a. 1).[8] However, for Aristotle, the doctrine of the mean does seem to imply that for every virtue, there are corresponding states of character that cannot be equated straightforwardly with degrees of emotion, but that are characterized nonetheless by tendencies toward excess or deficiency in the passions. Hence, fortitude is a mean between

cowardice (exhibiting more fear than a situation warrants) and recklessness (expressing insufficient fear in given situations); temperance is a mean between a self-indulgent love of sensual pleasures and inappropriate insensibility to them; and so on.

The difficulty now becomes clear. If justice observes the mean between vices, understood in this sense as vicious tendencies of the passions, what should one identify as its correlative vices? Aristotle answers, somewhat lamely, that the corresponding vice is greed. But the problem here is obvious: it is possible to be motivated by something other than greed when acting unjustly. More generally, it is possible to act unjustly without any motive that would ordinarily be described as vicious at all, as, for example, when a teacher grades a student too leniently out of a misplaced compassion.

How does Aquinas deal with this difficulty? In order to answer this question, it is first necessary to recall that he understands virtues as qualities that perfect the intellectual and affective capacities of the human person, in such a way as to enable the individual to act in certain characteristic ways (Ia IIae, q. 55, a. 1). "Perfect" should here be understood in two senses; the virtues are perfections of the person who has them, insofar as they are the full development of the individual's capacities for knowledge and action, and at the same time they lead to actions that are perfect, that is to say, good in every relevant respect (Ia IIae, q. 55, aa. 2–4). Hence, for Aquinas, a particular virtue is defined by reference to the characteristic kind of good action it produces, and not in terms of the vice which it serves to check (as he observes in passing, in the context of defending a definition of virtue in general; Ia IIae, q. 55, a. 4). Correlatively, he argues, following Aristotle, that the truly virtuous person is characterized by the ease and readiness with which he performs the acts of virtue, although this observation must be qualified with respect to someone whose moral virtues have been infused directly by God (Ia IIae, q. 65, a. 3, ad 2).

This overall theory, which is Aristotelian in its main lines, enables Aquinas to define justice in terms of the form of goodness toward which it is oriented, rather than having to identify a particular vicious motive which it

serves to correct (IIa IIae, q. 58, a. 1). Moreover, Aquinas follows through on this Aristotelian analysis in a way that improves on Aristotle's own treatment by making a further
claim that Aristotle does not explicitly state.
That is, he identifies justice as a virtue of the
will, seen in contrast to the other moral virtues, which perfect the passions (as I have
noted above).

In order to appreciate the significance of
this claim, it is necessary to understand what
Aquinas means by the "will." For him, the will
is a rational appetite; that is, it is the distinctively human capacity to desire whatever the
intellect judges to be good, in contrast to the
passions, which respond to good and bad as
perceived through the senses (Ia IIae, q. 8, a.
1). As such, the will always presupposes an
intellectual judgment that a given object of
choice is in some way good (Ia IIae, q. 9, a. 1;
q. 19, a. 3). At the same time, the will is free
with respect to the objects presented to it by
the intellect, because no finite object is good
in every respect (Ia IIae, q. 10, a. 2). The
passions may be said to move the will, but only
indirectly, by means of influencing one's intellectual judgments; and so, for example, I am
more inclined to judge that prime rib, medium rare, would be a healthy meal, than
marinated tofu (Ia IIae, q. 9, a. 2; Ia IIae, q. 10,
a. 3; Ia IIae, q. 77, a. 1).

Aquinas argues that justice is necessarily a
virtue of the will and not the passions, because just action presupposes an evaluative
judgment about the relationship between persons, and this judgment can only be made by
the intellect (IIa IIae, q. 58, a. 4; see also IIa
IIae, q. 58, a. 9). For this reason, it should be
understood as a settled policy or a standing
commitment to act in certain ways, rather
than as a tendency to feel in certain ways and
then to act accordingly. At the same time,
justice, like every virtue, is more than a tendency to perform good acts of a certain kind.
It also implies that the just individual is motivated by a desire to preserve and promote
justice, in such a way that she does what is
just precisely *because* it is just, and not out of
some other motive, for example fear of punishment (IIa IIae, q. 32, a. 1, ad 1; IIa IIae,
q. 82, a. 2). Moreover, this rational love of
justice is not a passion, although normally it
both presupposes and gives rise to a whole

range of passions (Ia IIae, q. 60, a. 2; IIa IIae,
q. 58, a. 9).[9]

By identifying justice as a virtue of the will,
Aquinas is able to allow for the greater complexity of injustice, seen in relation to the vices
which correspond to the other moral virtues.
At IIa IIae, q. 59, a. 2, he asks whether someone is said to be unjust, simply because he
performs an unjust act. After disposing of the
case of someone who performs an unjust act
unknowingly, hence involuntarily (*qua* unjust
act) and without culpability, he observes that
there is a difference between someone who
does something unjust out of a vicious desire,
and someone who acts out of the habitual vice
of injustice. The former would be the paradigmatic case of sinful behavior for many of
Aquinas's contemporaries, but, for Aquinas,
this is only one form that sinful behavior can
take, and not necessarily the most corrupt
form (Ia IIae, q. 77, a. 3; however, these sins
can certainly be mortal sins, [Ia IIae, q. 77, a.
8]). On the other hand, someone who acts out
of the vice of injustice is motivated to act by
the injustice of the act *per se*. In such a case, the
individual may act without any disordered
passion at all, simply out of a desire to do harm
to another (IIa IIae, q. 58, a. 9, ad 2).

This claim would seem to run counter to
Aquinas's well-known view that every act is
oriented toward some good. However, in returning to his discussion of sins of deliberate
malice, the reader is reminded that there is a
form of sin that involves the deliberate choice
of evil, not for its own sake, but out of an
inordinate love for some other good (Ia IIae,
q. 78, a. 1). Hence, sins of deliberate malice
reflect an orientation of the will that is contrary to the orientation conferred by justice;
someone who sins out of deliberate malice
prefers some temporal good to the order of
reason or to charity, whereas the just individual paradigmatically prefers the common
good to her or his own private good. (However, this does not mean that every sin of deliberate malice is an expression of the vice of
injustice, or indeed of any other settled vice
[Ia IIae, q. 78, a. 3.])

What is the relationship between justice
and the other virtues? I have already noted
that, for Aquinas, justice is characterized by an
orientation toward exterior actions, in contrast to the other moral virtues, which are

defined in reference to the passions they rectify. This might be taken to imply that for Aquinas, the acts of the other moral virtues are subsumed under justice in such a way that only justice may be said to be expressed in our exterior actions. Correlatively, on this view, fortitude and temperance would not have their own distinctive exterior actions. However, this line of interpretation oversimplifies Aquinas's understanding of the relationship of justice to the other moral virtues.

It is true that for Aquinas, justice is characteristically oriented toward the rectification of one's exterior actions, as the other moral virtues are not (Ia IIae, q. 60, a. 2; IIa IIae, q. 58, a. 9). It is also true that for him, there is a sense in which every exterior act of every moral virtue may be said to be an act of justice. Yet he also explicitly states that every moral virtue expresses itself through exterior actions (Ia IIae, q. 60, a. 2). Moreover, since justice is also characterized by its orientation toward other persons, acts of temperance or fortitude that involve only one's own good are not acts of justice, except, again, in a qualified sense (IIa IIae, q. 58, aa. 7–8). How are we to sort these claims out?

Recall, first, that Aquinas allows for more than one sense in which justice may be said to be a virtue. If we are speaking of justice in the most general sense, that is, justice considered as a condition for every virtuous act, then every act of every virtue is an act of justice in just the same way as it is an act of temperance or fortitude. If what is in question is legal justice, by which the individual is directed toward the common good, then every act of moral virtue may be said to be an act of justice in this sense, because the good of the individual is a part of the common good (Ia IIae, q. 60, a. 3, ad 2; however, this should be read in conjunction with IIa IIae, q. 58, a. 6).[10] Hence, if an individual acts out of temperance or fortitude in pursuit of her or his own private good, or if she or he aims at the good of some other individual through particular justice, that action is *ipso facto* directed to the common good, precisely because the latter includes the good of every individual in the community (IIa IIae, q. 58, a. 5). However, this does not mean that the act in question is not also an act of temperance, fortitude, or particular justice. Rather, the act retains its character as an expression of the particular virtue that elicits it, while, at the same time, it is referred to the common good through the more comprehensive virtue of legal justice (IIa IIae, q. 58, a. 6; also IIa IIae, q. 32, a. 1, ad 2).

Note that the exterior acts of the moral virtues are attributed to legal justice, and not to the particular justice that concerns relationships to other persons.[11] Particular justice is also said to be paradigmatically a virtue of exterior operations, but that does not imply that every exterior operation is an act of particular justice; to the contrary, Aquinas notes that the other moral virtues are sufficient to rectify those exterior actions that concern the individual alone (IIa IIae, q. 58, a. 2, ad 4). One who temperately declines a third piece of pie for the sake of personal health and equanimity is not acting out of particular justice at all, and this act is an act of legal justice only insofar as one is promoting the common good by preserving one's own well-being. How can we square this with Aquinas's claim that justice is paradigmatically the virtue of exterior actions?

His argument is as follows: Each particular moral virtue is to be understood in terms of the distinctive form of moral goodness at which it aims, and correlatively in terms of the paradigmatic kinds of actions that express that form of goodness. Fortitude and temperance are essentially directed toward morally praiseworthy orientations of the passions, expressed in modalities of responsiveness and feeling. This does not mean that these virtues are not expressed through exterior actions, but only that the moral value of such actions is derived from the praiseworthy states of passion which they express (ibid.; also Ia IIae, q. 60, a. 2). Justice, on the other hand, is essentially directed toward securing right relations with others, with the community as a whole in the case of legal justice, or with other individuals, in the case of particular justice. One's relationships with others, in turn, can only be mediated through exterior actions, and *that* is why justice is paradigmatically the virtue of exterior operations (IIa IIae, q. 58, aa. 2, 9). For the same reason, the norm of justice is set by transpersonal standards of equity and not by reference to the agent's own overall good; to put the same point in another way, justice respects a real and not merely a rational mean (IIa IIae, q. 58, a. 10).[12]

ACTS OF JUSTICE

Because particular virtues are dispositions to act in certain ways with respect to some distinctive sphere of action, they are defined in terms of the kinds of action which they characteristically produce (Ia q. 87, a. 2; Ia IIae, q. 55, a. 4). The kinds of actions which are paradigmatic for a particular virtue are in turn defined with reference to the formal character of the good at which they aim, formulated in the context of the sphere of action of the virtue in question (Ia IIae, q. 54, a. 2). Hence, in the analysis of the particular virtues in the *Secunda secundae*, Aquinas consistently begins his analysis by asking what is the object of the virtue, and what are the paradigmatic actions by which it aims at that object; he ends by considering the precepts of the divine law (that is to say, the scriptural precepts) that correspond to that virtue.

In order to give some account of the norms and precepts of justice as Aquinas understands them, it is therefore necessary to begin, as Aquinas does, by asking what the object of justice is. We will then turn to a consideration of the paradigmatic acts of justice.

At the beginning of his analysis of justice in the *Secunda secundae*, Aquinas asserts that the object of justice is *ius*, that is to say, the right (IIa IIae, q. 57, a. 1).[13] This, in turn, is understood in terms of whatever is due to the community or to another individual, as established by natural or positive law (IIa IIae, q. 57, a. 2). This connection between justice and the right is consistent with Aquinas's claim that justice is the moral virtue proper to the will. Since the will is a rational appetite, it is not surprising to find that the proper object of its characteristic moral virtue is not only discerned through rational judgment (this is true for every virtue), but is determined by reference to laws, whether natural or positive, which are by definition ordinances of reason (Ia IIae, q. 90, a. 1). At the same time, in IIa IIae, q. 57, Aquinas explicitly draws out the implication of the traditional view, which he has already affirmed, that the natural law is expressed through the precepts of the decalogue (Ia IIae, q. 100, a. 1), which, as we later read, are also the precepts of

the divine law associated with the virtue of justice (IIa IIae, q. 122, a. 1).

In the next questions (IIa IIae, qq. 58–59), Aquinas sets out the main lines of his conception of justice as a virtue and of injustice as a vice. Near the end of IIa IIae, q. 58, he reminds his readers that the proper act of justice is to render to each one that which is his or her due, a definition that he will expand and clarify through the next sixty questions.

After examining the meaning of injustice (IIa IIae, q. 59), he turns to an examination of judgment, which is the paradigmatic act of a judge, and is as such an act of justice (IIa IIae, q. 60, a. 1). He then sets forth the conditions under which judgment may legitimately be rendered: it must proceed from the inclination of justice; it must be rendered by one who is authorized by the leader of the community to act as a judge; and it must be in accord with right reason, as determined through prudential judgment (IIa IIae, q. 60, a. 2). The following articles expand upon these conditions (IIa IIae, q. 60, aa. 3–6).

This question provides a striking illustration of the difference between Aquinas's idea of what a theory of justice should be and our own views on the matter. Near the beginning of *A Theory of Justice*, John Rawls asserts that justice is "the first virtue of social institutions," and in this respect, he would seem to speak for nearly all contemporary philosophers.[14] For Aquinas, on the other hand, justice is always considered as a personal virtue to be analyzed in terms of those actions of individuals which either express justice or are contrary to it. Moreover, in this respect he would seem to be typical of his own contemporaries, just as Rawls typifies the contemporary scholar. Throughout his analysis of justice, Aquinas addresses what we would describe as social issues, and he is also thoroughly convinced of the importance of legality and political authority. However, neither he nor his contemporaries (so far as I have been able to determine) provides an analysis of social structures, seen in abstraction from the individuals who move within those structures.[15]

Aquinas's distinctive orientation is still more evident when we turn to the next question, which sets out the parts of justice (IIa IIae, q. 61). These he identifies as the species or kinds of justice, that is, "distributive" and "commutative"; the integral parts of justice that must be present in every act of the virtue (IIa IIae, q. 79); and the potential parts of justice, that is, the virtues annexed to justice (IIa IIae, q. 80). The latter resemble justice in some key respect, and yet fall short of the ideal definition of justice in some way (ibid.). I will return to a closer examination of the integral and potential parts of justice later.

At this point, what should be noted is the brevity of Aquinas's account of distributive justice, particularly seen in contrast to his discussion of commutative justice. Distributive justice is analyzed in tandem with commutative justice in the four articles of IIa IIae, q. 61; additionally, he devotes another question to the vice opposed to distributive justice, that is, consideration of persons (IIa IIae, q. 63). He only devotes one further question to the primary act of commutative justice, restitution (IIa IIae, q. 62), but he then takes fifteen more questions (IIa IIae, qq. 64–78) to examine the sins opposed to commutative justice.

Moreover, his analysis of distributive justice in IIa IIae, q. 61 and q. 63, focuses on the questions which arise for the individual who is charged with distributing social goods. He says that the norm of distributive justice in specific situations is set by reference to whatever is the organizing principle of the community in question (IIa IIae, q. 61, a. 1). Further on, he adds that this norm varies with respect to what is being distributed; honors are distributed with reference to personal worth, public offices are to be distributed with reference to individual qualifications, and so forth (IIa IIae, q. 63, a. 1). Beyond this, however, he has little to say about the norms of distributive justice *per se*, which he assumes to be straightforward.[16]

In the course of his analysis of distributive and commutative justice, Aquinas explains how each of these forms of justice attains the mean of the virtue, but in a different way. As we have already noted, distributive justice renders what is due to each person, as determined by a criterion of proportionality between individual worthiness and the goods being distributed; hence, Aquinas notes that distributive justice preserves equality among persons, not absolutely, but in accordance with a geometric proportionality (IIa IIae, q. 61, a. 2). Commu-

tative justice, on the other hand, preserves equality in accordance with an arithmetical mean, that is to say, with respect to the quantity of the things exchanged between persons or the benefits and burdens that accrue to each one (ibid.). He adds that commutative but not distributive justice may thus be said to be equivalent to *contrapassum*, that is, to a state of affairs in which the suffering or loss of one is balanced by the suffering or loss of another (IIa IIae, q. 61, a. 4).

What precisely does all this mean? Aquinas's mathematical images for the different senses of equality proper to justice, which he takes from Aristotle, are notoriously unclear, as is the idea of *contrapassum*.[17] However, his general idea is clear enough; justice between persons is preserved so long as neither party to a transaction suffers unduly, nor benefits at the expense of another. He goes on to further develop the meaning of commutative justice through his analysis of restitution (the primary act of commutative justice; IIa IIae, q. 62) and of the sins opposed to commutative justice. From IIa IIae, q. 64, through IIa IIae, q. 76, he takes up an analysis of sins against commutative justice which involve involuntary transactions, resulting in bodily harm, damage to one's connections or goods, injustice in a legal proceeding, or loss of social standing due to slander or other forms of "extra-judicial speech." This represents Aquinas's most detailed treatment of the norms of nonmaleficence, including his analysis of murder, theft and robbery, and detraction. (Those sins against the neighbor involving sexual acts, such as adultery, are taken up in his analysis of sins against temperance, since these are sins of lust as well as sins against justice [IIa IIae, q. 65, a. 4, ad 3].) Next, he turns to those offenses that occur in the course of voluntary transactions. Here one finds his treatment of the various forms of economic injustice, including fraud and usury (IIa IIae, qq. 77–78).

In IIa IIae, q. 79, Aquinas turns to the integral parts of justice, which he gives as "to avoid evil and to do good" (IIa IIae, q. 79, a. 1).[18] In this context, as he goes on to explain, good and evil should be understood specifically with reference to the good of the neighbor and the common good, in such a way that one does good by promoting the common good of the community and respecting the legitimate claims of other persons, and one avoids evil by avoiding harm to the community or to other individuals. So understood, these are said to be integral parts of justice, since each of them is required for a perfect, that is to say a complete, act of justice. It should be noted that this question establishes a further link between justice and the natural law as it was understood in Aquinas's time, since, in this period, the natural law itself is frequently said to be the avoidance of evil and the performance of good.[19]

Over half of the sixty-one questions that Aquinas devotes to justice in the *Secunda secundae* address the virtues annexed to justice and the sins opposed to those virtues (IIa IIae, qq. 80–120). These are virtues which resemble justice in some respect, while falling short of the complete ideal of justice in another respect; either they concern obligations to those to whom full recompense can never be made, such as God or one's parents, or they concern qualities which are morally desirable but not strictly obligatory, for example liberality and friendliness (IIa IIae, q. 80, a. 1). This does not imply that these are lesser virtues, considered as moral qualities. To the contrary, one of the annexed virtues, religion, is preeminent among all the moral virtues, including justice (IIa IIae, q. 81, a. 6; see esp. ad 1).

Religion is understood by Aquinas as the moral virtue through which one offers due homage to God through cultic acts of worship (IIa IIae, q. 81, aa. 1, 5, 7). As such, it is distinct from and subordinate to the theological virtues, even though it is preeminent among the other moral virtues, as just noted (IIa IIae, q. 81, aa. 5–6). Since we are embodied creatures whose thought processes are grounded in sense data, it is necessary for us to express our devotion and love for God by means of exterior signs. These signs provide the sphere of operation proper to the virtue of religion (IIa IIae, q. 87, a. 7). The inclination to show honor to a divine creator through cultic acts is grounded in human nature, and in this sense, religion is a part of the natural law, even though the specifics of particular cults are established by human or divine decree (IIa IIae, q. 81, a. 2, esp. ad 3; see also IIa IIae, q. 85, a. 1). At the same time, throughout his discussion of religion, Aquinas treats it as an infused moral virtue; that is to say, he assumes that true

religion will be grounded in grace and guided in its expressions by the theological virtues, above all by charity (in particular, IIa IIae, q. 81, a. 5, ad 1; IIa IIae, q. 82, a. 2). Aquinas has very little to say about the possibility of a natural religion that avoids the sinful perversities of idolatry, although he seems to leave open the possibility that such might exist (IIa IIae, q. 94, a. 4, esp. ad 2).

After discussing the acts of religion and the sins opposed to it (IIa IIae, qq. 82–100), Aquinas turns to the other annexed virtues and their correlative sins or vices (IIa IIae, qq. 101–20). Space does not permit a detailed examination of these, which include piety toward parents, gratitude toward benefactors, and obedience toward superiors, as well as friendliness, affability, and liberality in one's social relations.

Aquinas ends his analysis of justice with discussions of the gift of the Holy Spirit and the precepts of the divine law corresponding to the virtue. The gift of the Holy Spirit that he associates with justice is "piety," through which an individual is disposed to pay due reverence to God as Father (IIa IIae, q. 121, a. 1). The precepts of the decalogue are given as the precepts of the divine law corresponding to justice (IIa IIae, q. 122).

PROPERTY: THEFT AND ROBBERY

In order to understand fully Aquinas's analysis of justice, it may be helpful to consider his treatment of one particular moral issue in more detail. Therefore, in this section, I will examine Aquinas's analysis of theft and robbery, which consist in taking the material goods of another, either secretly (*furtum*, theft) or by force (*rapina*, robbery [IIa IIae, q. 66]; for an explanation of the distinction, see IIa IIae, q. 3).

In his introduction to the question dealing with the parts of justice, Aquinas indicates that he will consider the two species of justice, namely "distributive" and "commutative" justice, first with reference to the distinction between them, and second, through an examination of restitution, which is the paradigmatic act of commutative justice (IIa IIae, q. 61, intro.). He then proceeds to an examination of the vices opposed to these parts of justice. He identifies only one sin directly opposed to distributive justice: respect for persons, that is, the distribution of goods by criteria other than those relevant to the principle of distribution in question (IIa IIae, q. 63). In contrast, he identifies a number of sins directly opposed to commutative justice, which, as noted above, would be considered today under the rubric of violations of norms of nonmaleficence. Theft and robbery are included among the sins that take place through involuntary transactions (in contrast to those committed in the course of voluntary transactions such as buying and selling), and that are directed against the material goods of another, in contrast to the body or near personal connections of another (in contrast to, for example, murder or adultery; these divisions are set forth in the introductions to IIa IIae, qq. 63–64).

It might seem that theft and robbery offer clear cases of sins against justice, since they evidently involve a failure to render to another that which is her or his own. In fact, at IIa IIae, q. 66, a. 3, Aquinas does make this point; however, he must first establish that material goods fall within the category of those things that can belong to someone. This is not as obvious as it might appear; there was a long-standing tradition that private property was contrary to the natural law. But by the same token this was a standard problem for scholastic jurists and theologians, and, by Aquinas's time, the main lines of a solution were well established.[20]

Aquinas's analysis of property follows these general lines. However, seen in comparison to his immediate predecessors and contemporaries, Aquinas is noteworthy for his insistence that ownership of material goods is natural to human beings considered as a species, since they are meant to serve our bodily needs (IIa IIae, q. 66, a. 1). Nonetheless, this does not mean that the ownership (as opposed to the simple use) of material goods on the part of individuals stems directly from the natural law. At this point, Aquinas's analysis becomes very similar to that of other thirteenth-century theologians.[21] The institution of private property, he explains, is an addition to the natural law, devised by human reason to serve the well-being of the human community (IIa IIae, q. 66, a. 2). The natural law injunction that material goods should be held in common still has force, in that those who own such goods are obliged to share them with others in time of need (ibid.). Hence, the individual's right to private property is a positive rather than a natural right, and as such it presupposes the existence of social conventions (IIa IIae, q. 66, a. 1, ad 1).

In this context, it is worth noting once again the differences between Aquinas's approach to questions of justice and our own view. Certainly, he considers the institution of private property to be important, but that does not mean that it merits its own discussion. Rather, he discusses this topic in the context of an examination of the claims of justice between individuals with respect to material goods, as a necessary preliminary to establishing what those claims are. Furthermore, he says only enough to indicate that private property is a legitimate addition to the natural law; he does not consider the relative merits of different forms of property, nor does he address such questions as the legitimacy of title or the possible injustice of inequalities of wealth. His focus throughout this question is on individual relationships within the framework of an institution of property, not on the institutional framework itself.

Having established the legitimacy of private property, Aquinas then goes on to place theft within his overall framework of sins against commutative justice, along the lines indicated above (IIa IIae, q. 66, a. 3). This is yet another point that appears incongruous. What is distinctive to theft is not only the appropriation of the material goods of another, but the fact that this is carried out in secret, in distinction from robbery, which is carried out through violent force (ibid). There is a tangible difference, so to speak, between having one's purse stolen from an empty room and having it taken at gunpoint; but why should this difference translate into two specifically distinct kinds of sins, as Aquinas explicitly claims (IIa IIae, q. 66, a. 4)? As he goes on to explain, theft and robbery take their specific character from the fact that they involve the appropriation of another's property against the owner's will, and correlatively, they are distinguished in accordance with the two ways in which something is involuntary, namely, through ignorance (and one is ignorant of what is done to him or her in secret), and through violence (ibid; see also Ia IIae, q.

6, aa. 5, 8). Of the two, robbery is the greater sin, since what is done through violence is more directly contrary to the will than an offense of which one is ignorant, and thus involves a greater harm (IIa IIae, q. 66, a. 9; see esp. IIa IIae, q. 66, a. 9, ad 3).

Of course, theft is also a sin. It involves a direct violation of justice, since it consists of taking from another that which is due to him or her; furthermore, it involves the practice of a kind of deceit or fraud on its victim (IIa IIae, q. 66, a. 5). Moreover, it is specifically a mortal sin, first, because it involves harming the neighbor contrary to the demands of charity, and, second, because were it to become a general practice, human society would be destroyed (IIa IIae, q. 66, a. 6).

Having made these points, however, Aquinas goes on to qualify them in a number of respects. Aquinas explains at IIa IIae, q. 66, a. 6, ad 3, that taking something small from another is not a mortal sin, perhaps not even a sin at all, since presumably the owner would not consider such an act to be seriously harmful. In other words, it would be reasonable to presume in such a case that one is not acting against the owner's will, and therefore, that one's act is not a violation of justice, or at any rate not a serious violation. Hence, the occasional appropriation of a paper clip or a cookie is not a mortal sin, unless perhaps the agent acts as he or she does with the explicit intention of harming another through theft.

At IIa IIae, q. 66, a. 5, ad 3, Aquinas considers the rarer but perhaps more interesting case of someone who retrieves his or her own property from another who holds it. This kind of action can hardly be said to be theft in the strict sense, because it does not involve taking what belongs to another. Yet such an act involves other kinds of injustice. If the property in question is being held legitimately, for example, as a deposit, the one who takes it back secretly places the holder in an awkward position, since she or he will be obliged either to restore it or to prove that she or he is not responsible for its loss. Hence, individuals who take back their own property secretly sin by injuring the one holding the item in question, and are obliged to relieve the holder of implicit accusation of negligence or theft, which she or he would otherwise have to refute. In contrast, if the one holding the prop-

erty of another is doing so unjustly, the latter does not sin *against the holder* if the owner secretly takes back his or her own property, nor is that person bound to make restitution in such a case. Nonetheless, the owner does sin against common justice, insofar as the owner usurps the right of judgment to him or herself, instead of going through established channels for the redress of rights. Hence, he or she is obliged to make satisfaction, not to the one from whom the property was taken, but to God.

This is a particularly interesting passage, because it reflects a more general tendency in Aquinas to restrict the infliction of certain kinds of harms to those who have responsibility for the community as a whole. Only those having a legally sanctioned responsibility for the common good may kill wrongdoers (IIa IIae, q. 64, a. 3; the case of self-defense presents a difficult and much debated exception to this rule, see IIa IIae, q. 64, a. 7), or subject them to lesser but serious injuries such as mutilation (IIa IIae, q. 65, a. 1). In the case at hand, Aquinas argues that only those in public authority may take the goods of another through force (IIa IIae, q. 66, a. 8). Furthermore, in all these situations, coercive force can only be used against someone who has forfeited life or security through sinful acts or aggression against the community. And so, just as it is not permissible to kill the innocent, even for the well-being of the community (IIa IIae, q. 64, a. 6), so it is not licit to take from another what is one's own unless one has in some way forfeited it through one's own fault, through aggression against the community or through some wrongdoing that merits punishment (IIa IIae, q. 66, a. 8). Otherwise, as with a private person, a public official who takes what is another's is bound to make restitution (ibid.).

Finally, Aquinas holds that someone in immediate and serious need may take what is another's, either secretly or by force, in order to sustain one's life (IIa IIae, q. 66, a. 7). Aquinas argues as follows. The right to private property depends on human laws, which cannot derogate from natural or divine law. More specifically, this right is limited by the fact that material things are intended by their Creator to serve the physical needs of human beings. Ordinarily, the institution of private property serves this intention by providing a structure for distributing material resources. But when it fails to do so, the claims to which this institution gives rise are superseded by the more fundamental claim to make use of material goods to sustain one's life. For this reason, someone who takes from another what is necessary to sustain life is not only justified, but, strictly speaking, the "thief" cannot be said to be guilty of theft or robbery at all.

As Brian Tierney has recently shown, some thirteenth-century scholastics went further in this direction than did Aquinas, treating the claim of the poor person in such a case as a subjective right which can be vindicated through a quasi-judicial procedure.[22] In contrast, Aquinas does not speak of the claim of a poor person in this situation as a subjective right.[23] Yet neither is this claim just a pious ideal. By asserting that the poor person who takes from another in such a situation is not guilty of theft or robbery at all, Aquinas implies that this person should be free from punishment for this action. Significantly, in the first objection, Aquinas refers to a church law that imposes a penalty on someone who takes under the pressure of need. He then responds to this objection by remarking that this canon applies only to someone who takes from another out of a lesser need, with the clear implication that someone who takes what is another's out of urgent and serious need should not be penalized at all (IIa IIae, q. 66, a. 7, ad 1). While this is not tantamount to asserting a subjective right on the part of the poor person, it does at least provide for subjective immunity.

The limitation on property rights implied in IIa IIae, q. 66, a. 7, is particularly important, because it mitigates (without removing) the problematic character of private property. As Anabell Brett has observed, the concept of ownership (*dominium*) is a social as well as an economic concept; it implies power over persons as well as objects. Correlatively, the poor person, the pauper, is normally also in a state of "servitude" or "subordination" (a *servus* or *subditus*).[24] Hence, the institution of property is in tension, at least, with the ideal of equality implied by the virtue of justice. Aquinas's delineation of the limitations of property rights does not do away with this tension, but it does at least give practical force to the view that natural equality is more fundamental than the inequalities introduced by human society.

JUSTICE AND CHARITY

To this point, I have bracketed the question of the relationship of justice to charity. This relationship must be understood first as a relationship of one virtue to another if one is to respect the logic of Aquinas's moral theology. At the same time, this question introduces wider issues concerning the place of justice in the Christian life, which have figured prominently in recent literature. Now that I have the outlines of Aquinas's overall account of justice in place, it is possible to address these issues.

The main lines of Aquinas's treatment of charity and the infused moral virtues will be familiar to many readers. In his initial examination of virtue, Aquinas distinguishes between the acquired moral virtues, which, as the name suggests, can be attained through human effort, and the infused virtues, which are brought about in humans directly by God (Ia IIae, q. 63, a. 3). The former are sufficient to bring humans to the most complete happiness possible to us as creatures, although given the vitiating effects of sin, only a very few will be able truly to acquire the virtues. However, since men and women also have been called to the supreme happiness of direct union with God, an end that completely exceeds the capacities of any created nature, the human person stands in need of principles that enable one to act in such a way as to attain that end. These can only come through God's immediate action, transforming the soul and bestowing on it principles of action that it could not have attained by itself (Ia IIae, q. 62, a. 1). This transformation is brought about by grace, and the operative dispositions through which grace is rendered active are the infused virtues and the gifts of the Holy Spirit (Ia IIae, q. 110, a. 3).

The infused virtues, in turn, include not only the three traditional virtues of faith, hope, and charity, but also infused analogues of the acquired virtues, which have the same spheres of operation as their counterparts but aim at a different end, and therefore are specifically different from them (Ia IIae, q. 63, aa. 3–4). To be more exact, the infused cardinal virtues are infused together with charity, which presupposes all the other virtues even as it directs them toward its end, direct union with God (Ia IIae, q. 65, aa. 3–4).

In the first place, then, one can say that charity stands in the same relationship to justice as it does to the other virtues. That is, charity is architectonic with respect to justice and the other virtues, bringing them in proper relationship with one another and directing their acts to the final end of union with God, which is the proper end of charity itself (IIa IIae, q. 23, a. 4, ad 2). At the same time, charity cannot function without justice and the other infused moral virtues, because these latter are necessary to bring a proper orientation to the different capacities of the person and the spheres of action proper to human life.

There is more to be said on this subject, however. Justice is more similar to charity than any of the moral virtues, and for this very reason, one must carefully distinguish them in order to gain a more precise sense of their relationship. Both charity and justice are virtues of the will (as is hope), through which the individual is directed toward goods that transcend one's private good (IIa IIae, q. 18, a. 1). Both are expressed in exterior actions through which the individual sustains relationships with other persons and with God (with respect to charity, see IIa IIae, q. 31, a. 1; IIa IIae, q. 32, a. 1; IIa IIae, q. 33, a. 1). As noted above, the cultic acts through which charity is expressed in public worship are the proper acts of religion, a moral virtue annexed to justice. Finally, the precepts of the divine law corresponding to charity, namely the commands to love God and neighbor, correspond to the fundamental principles of the natural law from which the basic precepts of justice are derived (Ia IIae, q. 100, a. 3, ad 1; IIa IIae, q. 44, a. 2).

Both legal justice and charity function as architectonic virtues, in the sense that both function in such a way as to direct the acts of the other virtues to an end transcending the good of the individual. For this reason, both may be said to be general virtues, even though each of them is essentially different from other virtues, in such a way that neither can be said to be a general condition for the exercise of any virtue (IIa IIae, q. 58, a. 6). At the same time, however, Aquinas also considers charity

to be a particular virtue, with its own characteristic interior and exterior acts (IIa IIae, q. 23, a. 4; IIa IIae, q. 27, a. 1). These acts cannot be subsumed under legal justice, because the end toward which charity is directed, namely God considered as the object of personal love, is a higher and more perfect good than the common good toward which legal justice is oriented. At the same time, the acts of justice are not immediately acts of charity, although like all other virtuous acts, they are commanded by charity and directed by it to the final end of human life. Indeed, Aquinas is careful to distinguish the exterior acts proper to charity from those which are proper to justice; the latter, in contrast to the former, are done on account of some strict obligation, as would be the case, for example, with an act of restitution (IIa IIae, q. 31, a. 3, ad 3; IIa IIae, q. 32, a. 1, ad 2; IIa IIae, q. 33, a. 1).

The virtues of charity and justice, and the actions through which they are expressed, are thus interlinked in the life of the Christian for Aquinas, without losing their character as two distinctive virtues. The charitable person, understood in accordance with Aquinas's conception of charity, typically undertakes a great many things that she or he is not obliged to do by any general or particular obligation but out of sheer gratuitous love for her or his neighbor, offering money to the poor, bringing assistance and consolation to her or his neighbors in time of loss, befriending the lonely, helping to guide the young, and in general, going beyond the bounds of strict duty for the sake of the neighbor, whom she or he loves in God. These are most properly understood as acts of charity. At the same time, however, charitable love of others also prompts this person to respect the legitimate claims of others, to avoid harming them, and to carry out special obligations to particular people, which are all expressions of justice. These are properly acts of infused justice, but as with all the infused virtues, they are ultimately motivated by and directed toward the final aim of charity, that is, the love of God and of the neighbor for God's sake (IIa IIae, q. 58, a. 1, ad 6).

Aquinas makes the same point in a negative way in the course of asking whether sins against justice are mortal sins, which is equivalent to asking whether they are offenses against charity. He answers that they are, because they involve harming the neighbor, and since charity includes love of the neighbor, an act of deliberate harm to the neighbor is directly contrary to charity (IIa IIae, q. 59, a. 4). In other words, justice matters to the Christian because the norms of justice safeguard the well-being of the neighbor.

This should be underscored. Aquinas does not say that injustice is to be deplored and avoided because unjust acts always express a vicious depravity of the passions (to the contrary, he denies this; see IIa IIae, q. 59, a. 9, ad 2). Nor does he say that justice matters because the norms of justice are the means by which a community of virtue can be sustained. He does say that one of the functions of law, including natural and divine as well as positive law, is to render persons good, but he qualifies this claim by restricting the goodness in question to observance of the laws themselves (which by definition are directed to the common good [Ia IIae, q. 92, a. 1]). For Aquinas, justice is not an instrumental virtue, which derives its value from its role in fostering good character or virtuous communities. Justice matters to the Christian because the well-being of other people matters to the Christian.

It appears, therefore, that the Christian is motivated to respect the demands of justice out of that love of neighbor which is fundamental to charity. However, a further question arises at this point. That is, what is the basis for justice, as the Christian understands and practices it? Does charity place justice on a new foundation, so to speak, with the result that for the Christian the meaning of harm and obligation is radically transformed? Aquinas does not address this question in these general terms; rather, he asks more than once whether the obligations of charity or religion supersede the claims of natural justice. Consistently, he answers such questions in the negative (most explicitly, at IIa IIae, q. 104, a. 6). The demands of natural justice are grounded in reason, and grace is not less reasonable than nature; nor can one say that the fundamental needs and exigencies of human nature are abolished or rendered irrelevant to charity (IIa IIae, q. 26, a. 6; see also Ia IIae, q. 108, a. 2). For this reason, Christians can live in community with non-Christians, and they are constrained by natural justice in their dealings with them (IIa IIae, q. 10, aa. 10, 12). It

should also be noted that for Aquinas, men and women can attain true virtues, including presumably justice, without grace, even though these virtues are imperfect seen in comparison to the infused virtues (Ia IIae, q. 65, a. 2; IIa IIae q. 23, a. 7). This would seem to imply that a non-Christian society can nonetheless be a just society, which the Christian can recognize as such.

Here, one can see the significance of the fact that Aquinas considers charity and justice to be two distinct, particular virtues. Charity is a greater virtue than justice, and is architectonic with respect to it; however, justice retains its own independent content by virtue of which it places constraints on charity. At the same time, justice provides a framework for human life that does not owe its validity to Christian revelation, and therefore places limits on what may be done in the name of that revelation. We may wish that Aquinas's contemporaries had taken this lesson more seriously; we, ourselves, can profit from it as well.

ACKNOWLEDGMENT

I would like to express my appreciation for a grant from the Institute for Scholarship in the Liberal Arts in the College of Arts and Letters, the University of Notre Dame, which supported my research for this article.

Notes

[1]"Iustitia est constans et perpetua voluntas ius suum unicuique tribuens." The quotation is taken from Justinian's *Digest* I.1, tit.1, leg. 10.

[2]"generales conditiones humani animi, quae inveniuntur in omnibus virtutibus."

[3]Note, however, that Aquinas goes beyond what Aristotle explicitly says; see Arist. *Eth. Nic.* 5.1–2 (esp. 1129b10–1130a15 and 1130b15–30).

[4]"ad legem pertinet ordinare in bonum commune."

[5]Strictly speaking, prudence is an intellectual virtue; however, Aquinas adds, it is considered to be a moral virtue in a wider sense, since the moral virtues properly so called cannot exist without it, nor can it exist without them (ST Ia IIae, q.58, a.3, ad 1).

[6]See Arist. *Eth. Nic.* 2.6 (1106a15–1107a26) for Aristotle's own explanation of the mean of virtue.

[7]Bernard Williams sets forth the problem in Aristotle's treatment in "Justice as a Virtue," in *Essays on Aristotle's Ethics*, ed. Amelie Oksenberg Rorty (Berkeley: University of California Press, 1980), 189–200.

[8]For an analysis of Aristotle's position, see J. O. Urmson, "Aristotle's Doctrine of the Mean," in *Essays on Aristotle's Ethics*, 157–70.

[9]Because the modern reader is accustomed to think of the virtues as intrinsically connected to modalities of feeling and responsiveness, Aquinas's analysis of justice as a virtue of the will might seem implausible at first. However, if one thinks of the virtue of justice as a settled commitment, on a par with a commitment to a marriage, for example, it is easier to see the point of his analysis. One normally expects two people to marry out of love for each other. Yet the commitment that an individual makes to his or her marriage, even though it may be motivated by feelings of love for one's spouse, is not equivalent to that love. It involves a settled policy to act in such a way as to promote the marriage relationship and to avoid actions that would tend to undermine that relationship. Included in this policy is a commitment to nurturing and fostering the love that originally motivated the marriage. Yet a commitment to a marriage is compatible with a whole range of other feelings toward one's spouse, and it may persist after the original feelings of love have faded away.

[10]Note that Aquinas says only that exterior acts of the moral virtues can be attributed to justice in this sense (ST Ia IIae, q. 60, a. 3). Yet among the theological virtues, both faith and charity also have characteristic exterior acts (IIa IIae, q. 3; IIa IIae, q. 31, a. 1; IIa IIae, q. 32, a. 1; IIa IIae, q. 33, a. 1). Aquinas does not say that these are attributed to legal justice, and by the logic of his analysis, it is difficult to see how they could be, since the theological virtues are oriented toward a good, namely God considered as the direct object of human beatitude, which transcends the common good that is the object of legal justice.

[11]Hence, particular justice is attributed to legal justice in the same way as are the other particular moral virtues; ST IIa IIae, q. 58, a. 7.

[12]It would be easy to be misled on this point by the assumption that a given act can only express one virtue. But Aquinas explicitly rejects this assumption. In the first place, if the particular cardinal virtues are connected, as Aquinas holds, one would expect any good action to reflect more than one particular virtue. At a minimum, any truly virtuous act will at least be an act of prudence as well as one of the moral virtues, since prudential judgment is always necessary to determine what it means to act in accordance with the moral virtues in concrete instances of choice (ST IIa IIae, q. 33, a. 1, ad 2; see

also q. 47, a. 7). Moreover, there is no reason why one action might not be morally praiseworthy in more than one respect (just as a bad action may be sinful in more than one respect). Aquinas gives the example of a soldier fighting for his country; his brave actions are acts of fortitude, because they express his courage, and at the same time they are acts of justice because they express his commitment to the common good of his community (q. 104, a. 2, ad 1).

[13]*Ius* may also be translated as "law," but since Aquinas consistently uses *lex* rather than *ius* in his analysis of different kinds of laws (see ST Ia IIae, qq. 90–108), I have translated *ius* as "right."

[14]John Rawls, *A Theory of Justice* (Cambridge, MA: Harvard University Press, 1971), 3.

[15]Why should this be the case? Part of the reason, I believe, lies in a general tendency among medieval authors to think of social structures in terms of the juridical relationships among individuals. It is also the case that Aquinas is writing near the end of a two hundred year period of social and economic expansion and institutional reform throughout western Europe, a process in which the organization and reform of civil and ecclesiastical court systems played a central role. The courts were centrally important to Aquinas and his contemporaries because throughout the medieval period there was very little legislative activity; civil society was largely governed by customary law, and the church was governed by canons which only began to be organized in a coherent system in the eleventh century. In this context, it is not surprising that Aquinas and his contemporaries would give considerable attention to the juridical procedures by which law is interpreted and made effective in a community and relatively less to those processes, still largely obscure to them, by which laws are made and institutional structures are formed.

These processes have been the subject of extensive discussion since Marc Bloch's classic *Feudal Society* (trans. L. A. Manyon, 2 vols. [Chicago: University of Chicago Press, 1961], esp. 2:359–440). For more recent work on this subject, with extensive bibliographies, consult the essays collected in *The Cambridge History of Medieval Political Thought c.350– c.1450*, ed. J. H. Burns (Cambridge: Cambridge University Press, 1988).

[16]Contrast this to contemporary discussions of justice, which are overwhelmingly focused on debating the norms which should govern the distributions of social benefits and burdens. The moral problems of individuals responsible for making these allocations receive less attention, although Rawls does discuss the natural duties of individuals in *A Theory of Justice*, 333–94. For other examples of studies which focus on distributive justice, see Robert Nozick, *Anarchy, State, and Utopia* (New

York: Basic Books, 1974); Michael J. Sandel, *Liberalism and the Limits of Justice* (Cambridge: Cambridge University Press, 1982); and Michael Walzer, *Spheres of Justice: A Defense of Pluralism and Equality* (New York: Basic Books, 1983). One can see here a further indication of Aquinas's focus on individual relationships, and his relative unawareness of issues pertaining to institutional structures.

[17]Arist. *Eth. Nic.* 5.3–4 (1131b25–1132b20).

[18]"declinare a malo et facere bonum."

[19]Numerous examples may be found in the texts on natural law by twelfth- and thirteenth-century authors collected by Odon Lottin, *Le droit naturel chez saint Thomas d'Aquin et ses predecesseurs*, 2d ed. (Bruges: Charles Beyaert, 1931), 106–25, and Rudolf Weigand, *Die Naturrechtslehre der Legisten und Dekretisten von Irnerius bis Accursius und von Gratian bis Johannes Teutonicus* (Munich: Max Hueber, 1967), 121–258.

[20]For a helpful discussion of the scholastic analysis of property, together with a collection of relevant texts from canon lawyers in the twelfth and thirteenth centuries, see Weigand, *Die Naturrechtslehre*, 259–82, 307–60.

[21]See for example the *Summa aurea* of William of Auxerre, III, q. 17, a. 1, and *De bono* of Albert the Great, V, q. 1, a. 3, ad 6.

[22]Brian Tierney, *The Idea of Natural Rights: Studies on Natural Rights, Natural Law and Church Law, 1150–1625* (Atlanta, GA: Scholars, 1997), 59–76.

[23]I agree with Tierney (among others) that Aquinas does not have a doctrine of subjective rights, although (I would add) he comes close at some points; see Tierney, *The Idea of Natural Rights*, 45.

[24]Anabell Brett, *Liberty, Right and Nature: Individual Rights in Later Scholastic Thought* (Cambridge: Cambridge University Press, 1997), 24; for a more extended discussion of these issues, see 10–48.

Selected Further Reading

Burns, J. H. *The Cambridge History of Medieval Political Thought c.350–c.1450.* Cambridge: Cambridge University Press, 1988.

Crowe, Michael Bertram. *The Changing Profile of the Natural Law.* The Hague: Nijhoff, 1977.

Gilby, Thomas. *Principality and Polity: Aquinas and the Rise of State Theory in the West.* London: Longmans, 1958.

Lottin, Odon. *Le droit naturel chez saint Thomas d'Aquin et ses predecesseurs.* 2d ed. Bruges: Charles Beyaert, 1931.

———. "Notes sur la justice et deux questions connexes." In *Psychologie et Morale Aux XIIe et XIIIe Siècles, Tome III: Problemes de Morale.* 2d ed. Louvain: Abbaye du Mont César, 1949.

MacIntyre, Alasdair. *Whose Justice? Which Rationality?* Notre Dame, IN: University of Notre Dame Press, 1988.

Maritain, Jacques. *The Person and the Common Good.* Notre Dame, IN: University of Notre Dame Press, 1947.

Pieper, Josef. "Justice." In *The Four Cardinal Virtues.* Notre Dame, IN: University of Notre Dame Press, 1954.

Porter, Jean. *The Recovery of Virtue: The Relevance of Aquinas for Christian Ethics.* Louisville, KY: Westminster/John Knox Press, 1990.

Tierney, Brian, *The Idea of Natural Rights: Studies on Natural Rights, Natural Law and Church Law, 1150–1625.* Atlanta, GA: Scholars, 1997.

Weigand, Rudolf. *Die Naturrechtslehre der Legisten und Dekretistren von Irnerius bis Accursius und von Gratian bis Johannes Teutonicus.* Munich: Max Hueber, 1967.

Sins Against Justice (IIa IIae, qq. 59–78)

Martin Rhonheimer

Translated by Frederick G. Lawrence

JUSTICE AND INJUSTICE

The knowledge of moral failure or sin depends on the knowledge of the relevant opposed virtue (IIa IIae, Prol.). Sins and vices are a defect in relation to the good. They are, like all evil, properly nothing when taken in themselves and hence as such are also not knowable. What sin is becomes clear only in view of the good with respect to which a sinful act is defective. This holds true for injustice as well. Any talk about it depends upon and is oriented toward the knowledge of what is just.

> Injustice is, therefore, the shadow of which justice is the substance, the negative of which justice is the positive, the privation of which justice is the realization. In the experience of injustice, therefore, we do not, strictly, apprehend injustice so much as glimpse the justice implicit in it: the commission of injustice exposes the justice to be realized. Injustice is, as it were, a negative which we have only to develop in order to find out what justice is.[1]

Yet justice has to do with the relationship to one's fellow human beings: to them as persons, to their lives, their physical integrity, and the material and spiritual goods to which they are entitled. Justice aims at "a certain balance" (*aequalitas*; IIa IIae, q. 57, a. 1), which possesses the character of anything due respectively to another. This is any fellow human being's *right* (*ius* or *iustum*); for the agent, it is something given, based on objectively existing circumstances, laws, and other relevant conditions.[2] This is precisely the object of the virtue of justice. For justice is nothing else but "a habit in virtue of which the human being bestows on each one his due with a constant and lasting will" (IIa IIae, q. 58, a. 1).[3]

Injustices are thus the sum of rights violations. They deprive one's fellows of recognition by denying them that to which they are entitled. They destroy the balance between rights and duties. Thus, Thomas distinguishes general justice from special justice. The former regards whatever one owes others in their universality, that is to say, the common good. This priority of the relationship to the common good may be startling. However, it is an expression of the fact that, for Thomas, the relationship to one's fellow is also necessarily and always mediated by the community-structure of life together in society.[4] "Accordingly, the acts of all the virtues can pertain to justice, insofar as they direct human beings to the common good" (IIa IIae, q. 58, a. 5).[5] Since it is proper to law to order the actions of human beings to the common good, this is called *general justice* or *legal justice* (ibid.). In this most general of senses, as well, "all vices, insofar as they are opposed to the common good," can "have the make-up of injustice" (IIa IIae, q. 59, a. 1).[6] Whenever one does something evil, one thus transgresses against justice—in this most general and unspecified sense.

However, the interesting points here are the ideas of *special justice* and the transgressions against it. It is related in a direct and immediate way to the relationship to one's fellow human being, whether in the sharing of goods (*iustitia distributiva*), or in relations of exchange (*iustitia commutativa*). Here injustice is an "imbalance in relationship to others, insofar as the person wants to have too many goods, for example, wealth or honors, and fewer evils, for example, work and harm" (IIa IIae, q. 59, a. 1).[7] Therefore, for each objective realm of justice, there is an opposite respective injustice.

According to Thomas, special justice is a matter of a "proper ordering" (*coordinatio*) with fellow humans, based on external actions and in view of the subjects of those actions (IIa IIae, q. 58, a. 8). Justice is inseparable from social coordination and cooperation. At its core, justice always already possesses a social character. As such, it is the virtue by which the person, independently of the laws, is oriented to the welfare of the society, and thereby to his or her fellow humans as a body. For this reason, it is also inseparable from love—*caritas*—even though it remains essentially distinct from it. Fundamentally, on the level of what is due, justice is shown nevertheless to be a basic form of any benevolence, of which "charity" (*caritas*) is the ultimate perfection brought about by grace. That is exactly why every act injurious to justice also transgresses love for one's fellows, since whatever corresponds to justice is what love also demands in the first place (the reverse does not hold true: love demands much that mere justice does not require).

In this way Thomas also shows why injustice is specified as a mortal sin (q. 59, a. 4). Mortal sins are those moral failures by which the soul loses (supernatural) life. The soul possesses this life through love, and therefore mortal sin is constituted by whatever is opposed to love. Every injustice, however, means harm to another in some manner, and each harming intrinsically stands in opposition to the love that moves one to strive for the welfare of the other (IIa IIae, q. 59, a. 4).[8] Not only love but also justice find their common root in *benevolence* toward one's fellows; love is indeed a higher form of this benevolence—the "love of friendship" (*amor amicitiae*)—which complements and transcends justice (as Aristotle held in relation to friendship). But precisely the common structure of benevolence reveals the nature and scope of injustice: it implies an unsocial relationship lacking solidarity to one's fellows under the most diverse aspects. Thomas expressed this relationship between justice and social relations even more emphatically than Aristotle.[9]

The specification of injustice nevertheless embraces a still further essential element: the perspective of *intentionality* (I will return to this in more detail). Injustice, to be sure, is always some form of injuring a right, and the "right" of the other, "that which is owed" to him or her, is something objectively given in the concrete situation of action, but without intention and conscious choice there is actually no real injustice (IIa IIae, q. 59, a. 2).[10] This does not mean that a guiltless bad action is only "materially," but not "formally," a sin; this would trivialize the issue. Rather, it ought to be said that it is altogether possible knowingly to violate the just good of one's fellow without the corresponding action's being an act of injustice, since the injury to the right involved was neither an object of choice nor a more far-reaching intention of the one acting. This is so in certain cases of killing: there are actions in which the death of a person is consciously taken into account and even physically caused, wherein (a) the one killed has a complete right to life, yet (b) the injury to this right is neither envisaged immediately as a means nor in any other manner, and the *action* can consequently not be designated as "unjust" (as in the cases of self-defense and waging a just war). Injustice is a property of intentional actions and not of a certain constellation of events.

THE MANIFOLD OF JUST ACTS AND THE UNITY OF PRINCIPLES

The manifold of just acts and of corresponding sins against justice is correlated to the variety of interhuman relationships, human activities, and concrete situations. Yet, throughout this manifold a common structural principle is at work: the principle of justice. As I already mentioned, Thomas reduces justice to the structure of benevolence, whereby justice first comes to sight as the seed of what, with the aid of grace, is capable of expanding to the point of supernatural love.

This structural principle is a principle of practical reason, and Thomas calls the ensemble of such practical principles the "natural law" (*lex naturalis*).[11] This is based on the nature of good as the essential correlative of any desire (the *ratio boni*), and is manifest in its most general, still utterly unspecified form as the imperative, "The good is to be pursued and done, evil is to be avoided" (Ia IIae, q. 94, a. 2).[12] This is the first principle of practical reason and, as such, the first precept of the natural law (ibid.). In the truest sense, it is the *principle of practice*.[13] Of course, nothing can be inferred from this principle alone. But, according to Thomas, reason grasps in the natural inclinations immediately and, as it were, spontaneously (which is why Thomas speaks of natural reason) the basic human goods, which, literally governed under the imperative power of the first principle and by reason, become goods to be pursued (*bona prosequenda*). They are still universal practical principles not explicated in terms of specific actions. Among them is found also "the natural inclination to live in community with other people" (ibid.).[14] Precisely this inclination delimits the realm in which the principle of justice has its place.[15]

Thomas stresses repeatedly that the first and fundamental principles of justice are also found among the first and most general principles of the natural law. According to his commentary on Aristotle's treatise on natural justice in the *Nicomachean Ethics*, among the "naturally known and the as it were indemonstrable principles nearest to these" is chiefly named the "first principle" ("evil is to be avoided"), and immediately thereafter the principle that "no one should be unjustly harmed," and lastly, "one should not steal."[16] These three examples adduced by Thomas correspond to the three levels (1) of first principles in general, (2) of "common principles" (*principia communia* or *communissima*), and (3) of "secondary principles."[17] In contradistinction to the prohibition of stealing, the principle to harm no one unjustly is not yet specific; it expresses the content of the violation of justice on the level of the universal, for any injustice is in some manner doing unjust harm. It still does not specify any special type of unjust action (such as, say, murder or robbery).

The principle of justice is thus among the first principles of practical reason. Accordingly, injustice affects human beings most profoundly in their identity as subjects of action.[18] This is expressed by Thomas in various manners in different places. The most famous is the passage from *De veritate* in which the first practical principles contained in the so-called habit of *synderesis* are equated with the "natural principles of natural law."[19] Among the most universal and evident principles not

disclosed by reflection, Thomas counts the principle that "a person should do no harm to anyone" (Ia IIae, q. 100, a. 3).[20] In general, "love for one's fellow human being" is in like manner reckoned by Thomas among the evident principles that arise from natural reason (Ia IIae, q. 100, a. 11). Thus there pertains to that which is "right by nature" (*ius naturale*), to what is naturally due to the other, all "that nature tends toward: as for instance, one should do the other no injustice" (Ia IIae, q. 94, a. 5, ad 3).[21]

This initial, still inspecific principle of justice is unfolded subsequently into the already mentioned partial virtues, corresponding to the multiplicity of human relationships and modes of action. In every activity of justice or in all violations against it, the social nature of the human being comes to the forefront for Thomas. Precisely *because* the person, by nature, by need, and by inclination, is geared toward a communal life, natural reason dictates to people the fundamental principle of justice "to maintain for each his own, and to refrain from unjustice."[22] This is the most general expression of that which pertains naturally to the person; otherwise, life together in society would not be possible.[23]

For Thomas, therefore, every act of injustice brings into play a relation not only to the concrete fellow human being to whom the injustice is done, but also the relationship to society as a whole, and, hence, to a certain degree, the relationship to every other person as a member of this community. The formulations of the principle of justice mentioned above might seem to be trivial and empty formulae. Such an appraisal, however, would fall prey to the mistake of confusing the basic for the trivial. In fact, one is dealing here with *principles*, with the starting points for any further discourse about justice. Without these principles, there can be no such discourse. Even more, in these principles, which themselves are contents of judgments on the part of the practical reason of the acting subject, the person is constituted in his or her identity as social by nature and as a subject of justice. The question that emerges at this moment is a rather different one: Where does the concept of right (*ius, iustum*) as well as that of what is owed (*debitum*) come from? Must they not be reduced to still more basic givens?

INJUSTICE AS A FUNDAMENTAL VIOLATION AGAINST EQUALITY

As a matter of fact, such a reduction of the concept of "what is owed or due" to something more basic has to be possible, so that the principle of justice is capable of falling under the efficacy of the first principle of practical reason, "Good is to be done . . ."; the just, the division of right, the concept of "what is due" must fall under the concept of the *good* to be pursued (the *bonum prosequendum*). This is the decisive point. In fact, one again finds Thomas expressing a seemingly trivial, but nevertheless pregnant, statement: "To render what is due to anyone possesses the rationale of the good" (IIa IIae, q. 81, a. 2).[24] It follows that what is due comes under the first principle of practical reason. Can concept of right (*ius*) or of the due be reconstrued? If so, can one precisely reconstrue the genesis of the principle of justice, as well, in terms of the concept of the good?

Thomas offers few explicit points to support this approach. Such a reconstruction would still be possible, by way of the concept of recognition that leads to the Golden Rule.[25] Indeed, the basic rise of the concept of right is that of "my right" in self-assertion over against the claims of others. Altruism is not the starting point. The concept of justice, which extends to the right of the other, only arises from the recognition of the other as a fellow human being, as "equal to me." This act of recognition is, as it were, the fundamental act of justice; and so injustice is always a form of inequality. From this acknowledgment of the other as "equal-to-me," there immediately follows, for practical reason, the Golden Rule: "Do not do to anyone else what you do not want anyone to do to you" (this can also be expressed positively: "Do to others what you want others to do to you"). Following the Golden Rule (hardly a theme in Thomas) consists in transforming "what is good" and adequate "for us," even our right, into a good due respectively to another, and so into the fundamental structure of benevolence.[26] One knows exactly—one grasps in an immediate way—what one wants others to do or not to do to oneself. By means of the fundamental recognition of the other as an equal, one apprehends that the other is owed this good.[27] In other words, the denial of the Golden Rule implies, in a way that is as trivial as it is fundamental, the nonacknowledgment of others as equals in respect to their *being human*.

In these contexts of recognition of the other as equal to oneself, and of the Golden Rule that accompanies it, the fundamental structure of justice is, therefore, demonstrable. The good is, in principle, graspable as something due to the other, and, hence, what is due, or right, is subsumable under the good. All of these matters pertain undoubtedly to the basic principles of the natural law. Every injustice is a concrete and specific violation against this fundamental recognition of the other as an equal.

Justice as a habit of benevolence is nevertheless not natural, but an acquired virtue. With Aristotle, to be sure, Thomas explains that a person is a friend to another person by nature; one can see this especially in situations when one is abroad or in an emergency.[28] Yet Thomas is still aware that the human being, by nature, is only capable of striving for his own good with the affective consistency and connaturality of a habit; to seek the good of one's fellow in this manner—just as to seek one's own good—transcends the natural potentiality of human willingness (Ia IIae, q. 56, a. 6). With respect to seeking the good of the other, this habit is, therefore, not natural, but an acquired, moral virtue. Justice is not only an act, but a habit (*habitus*) of benevolence. Consequently, acts of injustice not only injure the right of the other, but also harm the benevolent orientation of the agents (as a fundamental attitude) to their fellows. They thereby destroy the bond that holds people together.[29]

THE DIVISION OF THE PRINCIPLES INTO PARTIAL SPHERES AND THE CORRESPONDING VIOLATIONS AGAINST JUSTICE

In IIa IIae, qq. 63–78, Thomas treats the different specific sins against justice. Later on, there follows, in the treatment of the so-called "potential" parts of justice (qq. 80–121), the explication of the sins opposed to these (different forms of irreligiosity, disobedience, ingratitude, and the like), among which the violations against the truth (lies) are of greater importance, since they are connected in a special way with justice as it relates to fellow human beings.

The treatise on the virtue of "truth" or "truthfulness" (*veritas*) and its transgression—what I will name "justice in communication"—might have deserved a more prominent place in the organization of the *Summa theologiae*. But Thomas believes that truthfulness indeed overlaps with justice in that they are similarly "related to the other," and that they bring about a certain equality, that nonetheless the character of what is due does not accrue to it in the sense of "right" properly speaking, and that it possesses this character only in a moral sense (IIa IIae, q. 109, a. 3). Even so, shortly thereafter there follows the pregnant proposition: "Because the human being has a social nature, by nature one owes the other that without which human society could not be maintained. Human beings could not lead a common life if they did not believe each other as the kind of people who communicate the truth. Hence, the virtue of truthfulness pertains in a certain sense to something owed or due" (IIa IIae, q 109, a. 3, ad 1).[30]

It almost seems as if what is due in the case of the virtue of truthfulness, even when it does not properly possess the character of a right, is owed in an even more fundamental sense than that of the debt (*debitum*) that arises in other partial virtues of justice. Justice in communication is constitutive for social life, and so is, as it were, a transcendental condition for justice in all frameworks of human relations. Everywhere that people interact with each other and relationships of justice inhere, they do so through communicative acts. Hence, in spite of the understandably didactic arrangement of the treatise on truthfulness and lying, it would surely not be amiss to allot a special status for this, which also appears justified by the fact that lying traditionally assumes a prominent place among the so-called actions that are intrinsically evil.[31]

I will now return to the specific parts of justice properly speaking, and to their opposed failures. How does Thomas organize their treatment? First, Thomas distinguishes sins against distributive justice from those against commutative justice. Among the violations against distributive justice there is ac-

tually only one kind: showing favoritism, unjust preference, or discrimination of persons (*acceptio personarum*; IIa IIae, q. 63). Obviously, this is possible in every situation and relationship. Thomas concentrates especially on positive and negative acts of discrimination in the administration of spiritual goods, on the occasion of bestowing honors, and in trial procedures.

All of the remaining sins treated by Thomas are directed against commutative justice and thus are related to actions having to do with exchange (actions in which something is given or taken). These can, for any given action, be involuntary or voluntary. An involuntary exchange means harming the neighbor by actions performed against his will. These can occur by words or by deeds; by deeds, inasmuch as one does harm to the other by murder (IIa IIae, q. 64); or by mutilation, beating, and incarceration; or inasmuch as another person belonging to him is harmed (IIa IIae, q. 65). Finally, others can be harmed in their property, by theft or robbery (IIa IIae, q. 66). In contrast, by words harm occurs to one's fellow human being either within a trial, and so in the context of a judgment or verdict through the unjustness of the judge (IIa IIae, q. 67) or by unjust accusation (IIa IIae, q. 68). But there are also injustices on the side of the accused (IIa IIae, q. 69), of witnesses (IIa IIae, q. 70), and of attorneys (IIa IIae, q. 71). Outside of trials, there are injustices by invective (IIa IIae, q. 72), the cutting off of honor (IIa IIae, q. 73), a whispering campaign for the purpose of dividing friends from each other (IIa IIae, q. 74), derision (IIa IIae, q. 75), and cursing (IIa IIae, q. 76). Voluntary exchanges include buying, as well as lending and borrowing, money. Thomas speaks here about the sins of deception (IIa IIae, q. 77) and of usury (IIa IIae, q. 78). These are activities that in themselves arise in business with others on a voluntary basis but in which one holds back from the other what is owed.

It is, obviously, impossible to go into all the details here with respect to the particular kinds of unjust actions and their corresponding vices. The question of lending at interest in particular would demand its own treatment, but is now merely of historical interest.[32] Likewise, the theme of "private property" would warrant a deeper analysis (IIa IIae, q.

66, aa. 1–2).[33] Thomas's elucidations of the possible failures against justice in the context of judicial verdicts are still of astonishing relevance and precision—Thomas is obviously quite informed about the relevant problems—but they would need to be nuanced and refined in more than a few ways.

One of the *Summa*'s most controversial and oft-discussed questions is certainly that about killing (IIa IIae, q. 64). In this section, Thomas addresses homicide, capital punishment, self-defense, and suicide. In this treatise, he develops various relevant issues: besides the question of the justification of the death penalty, there is especially the problem of the tenability of such a thing as "actions that are intrinsically evil," which relates to Thomas's affirmation of the "permissibility" of killing in certain cases. This issue is posed also in connection with lying, and arises in another way in relation to the question of theft, as regards respecting someone else's property. In what follows, I will confine myself, by way of example, to the question of the prohibition of killing.[34]

INJUSTICE IN CONCRETE MODES OF ACTION AND "INTRINSICALLY EVIL ACTIONS" AGAINST JUSTICE (IN THE INSTANCE OF KILLING)

Intentional Actions and the Absoluteness of the Prohibition of Killing

Concrete actions contradict individual virtues, and, therefore, human goods, by reason of certain *formal* properties that characterize them as actions opposed to those virtues. This means that one does not violate justice because one, in a material and physical sense, does this or that, but because this deed, as a consciously chosen act, possesses the property of violating what is due to the other—his or her rights. Not because John takes the amount X from the pocket of Paul does he violate justice, but because the sum X was Paul's property, he has a right to it, and John appropriates this amount against Paul's will. The material elements are, of course, necessary to bring about an unjust act, but they do not suffice for describing some mode of behavior as an *injustice*.

As I have already demonstrated, any *unjust* action, according to Thomas, is unjust pre-

cisely because it is a violation of a right, and because this *violation* is consciously chosen as a means, or sought as a goal (not, of course, because, say, the goal of the action as such would have been the violation of the right, but because one consciously chooses or seeks as a goal something one knows is a violation of a right). Thomas solves questions of possession in relation to theft without any strain from this perspective. According to the *Secunda secundae*, the existence of private property does not eliminate the ordination of external goods toward the totality of human beings, and so property rights can become irrelevant in extreme situations (think, for instance, of taking away another's property in situations of extreme and acute emergency [see IIa IIae, q. 66, a. 7]). Does he also apply this consideration to the issue of killing? Is killing *as such* (a series of corporeal movements by A, which leads in a causally direct connection to the death of B) already a rights violation, an unjust action, or does it require other elements in order to describe it as such and to formulate a relevant norm?

In fact, nowhere does Thomas say that the killing of humans as such is not permitted.[35] He questions whether one ought to kill sinners, whether this is also permitted for private persons, whether clerics should do this, whether one ought to kill oneself, whether it is permitted to kill the innocent, and whether killing in self-defense is permissible. A general prohibition of killing human beings is nowhere to be found.

The Norm, "One Ought not Kill the Innocent"

Along with the entire preceding Christian tradition, Thomas nevertheless supports the categorical claim that it "is in no way allowed to kill an innocent person" (IIa IIae, q. 64, a. 6).[36] The decisive aspect of the rights violation, and thus, of the injustice, is integrated into the formulation of the norm by means of the notion of the innocent person. At first, the formulation once again sounds trivial, but it is not. It is important to examine more closely the reasoning behind this point. In general, one ought to kill no person "taken as such," for one ought to love the nature created by God, which is destroyed by killing even a sinner. At any rate, the common welfare is also assailed by the sin; for the sake of protecting the common good, the killing of the sinner is, therefore, permitted. The life of a just person on the other hand would precisely promote the common weal; and so, in no way is it permissible to kill the innocent.

The foundation for the absolute prohibition of killing has, then, two levels: first, an, as it were, merely provisional barrier, the dignity of the human nature created by God (a necessary but not sufficient condition for the prohibition of killing); and, second, the promotion of, or noninjury to, the common welfare by those in question (that is, their *innocentia* or lack of guilt). The innocent person, to whom the killing prohibition is related absolutely, is, therefore, the person who stands in a relationship of justice toward the community and its welfare. Accordingly, the "absoluteness" of the prohibition of killing seems to be limited to, and, indeed, to just that extent, only a "conditioned absoluteness." But, then, it seems, the prohibition of killing actually would not be called absolute at all. The absoluteness of the prohibition against killing would reside only in the formulation. To be sure, one can *formulate* the precept or prohibition absolutely, if one includes certain conditions or circumstances in the formulation (as is done here, for example, in the case of "being innocent"). From this, many have concluded that such a thing as "intrinsically evil actions" simply do not exist; every action, considered in itself, could be good or evil, which would depend on the intentions of the agents and on the circumstances, and on a corresponding formulation of the moral norm. An occasional appeal has been made to Thomas's treatment of the question of killing in behalf of this perspective.[37]

In addition, Thomas's argumentation sounds a bit utilitarian. This is still clearer in IIa IIae, q. 64, a. 2, where he handles the death penalty explicitly: "Each individual however stands to the whole community in the relationship of a part to the whole. When, therefore, a person becomes dangerous and destructive to the community on account of a crime, it is reasonable and salutary to kill him, so that the good as a whole will be saved."[38] Somewhat later, Thomas adds, it is indeed "intrinsically evil [*secundum se malum*] to kill a

person as long as he perdures in his dignity"; furthermore, it can "be good to kill a person who lives in sin, like a beast; for the evil person is worse than an animal and brings about greater harm (*plus nocet*), as the Philosopher says" (IIa IIae, q. 64, a. 2, ad 3).[39]

The categories of "innocent" (*innocens*) and "guilty" (*nocens*; IIa IIae, q. 64, a. 6, ad 3) possess a certain ambiguity. They can mean both "not harmful" or "harmful" and "innocent" or "guilty." In fact, however, guilty is also a juridical term for "guiltiness." It is clear that according to whether we understand innocent (*innocentia*) as "unharmfulness" or "guiltlessness," the reasoning then becomes either utilitarian or nonutilitarian. That Thomas uses the terms somewhat ambiguously cannot be denied. His explanations awaken the impression of a certain ambivalence.

Killing as Punishment

In order to clarify Thomas's exact position, one must have recourse to the superordinate concept of *punishment*—and the death penalty is surely a form of punishment. According to the utilitarian perspective, punishments are meted out only in order to fend off future harm to society. At the center stands not the "guilt" of the one to be punished, but the risk-potential for society of his action. It is clear that Thomas does not support such an opinion, since he always speaks about the sinner. Sin, of course, implies guilt. The risk to the common welfare does not consist in a sheer "harming" of public order. For this reason, Thomas would not agree with the opinion that under some circumstances it might be permitted to condemn an innocent person, such as cases in which provisionally a greater evil might be avoidable. For the utilitarian, on the contrary, the innocent person becomes a pest by virtue of such a possibility, and, consequently, his condemnation under justice is at least *discussible*.[40]

For Thomas, there is no punishment without guilt. Indeed, only the *guilty* "harming" of fellow persons and of the common good can be treated as a violation of justice. According to Thomas, punishments have the sense of making good a violation of justice. The actual "harming" of the common good that calls for punishment is the violation of the justice upon which the people's living together rests. A society in which violations of justice are not punished in a consistent way cannot exist.

Because it refers punishment strictly back to guilt, this theory is no longer utilitarian, since injustice is only present when justice is knowingly and freely injured. Thomas amplifies this point when he states, "One should however bring harm to bear on anyone only in the mode of punishment for the sake of justice" (IIa IIae, q. 65, a. 2).[41] In IIa IIae, q. 65, a. 3, he distinguishes between two kinds of taking away one's freedom: for punishment, or, privately, to avoid some evil. Nevertheless, both kinds have to take place "in accord with the order of justice."[42] Justice is, therefore, not identical with "avoiding harm." In any case, one can describe the violation of justice as a quite special, basic kind of harm to the human community. And, this is, then, intended as well whenever harmfulness and guiltiness are thought of together in the concept of the guilty. Finally, Thomas explicitly establishes that "a penalty can only be meted out for a sin: for the balance of justice is only restored by the punishment" (IIa IIae, q. 108, a. 4).[43] Only a *voluntarily* committed injustice, therefore, can be punished.[44]

Thus, penalties are awarded basically for the restoration of justice; the advantage, gained by the lawbreaker in an unfair manner at the cost of the other, must be compensated by the fact that he or she is harmed against his or her will, and, indeed, only by the public official competent in this matter, based on a judicial verdict. A peaceful life together in society would not be possible in any other way. It is clear that the preservation of justice and the protection of society are thought of together on a fundamental level. Here, one might almost speak of a "utilitarianism of justice" on Thomas's part. It is also important to notice that Thomas in no way supports a one-sided theory of retribution. Instead, he is of the opinion that, no matter what, the present world is not the place for the definitive restoration of justice. This is why punishments are also not *intrinsically* required in this life, "except as a means of salvation, and so they serve either for the improvement of the sinner or for the benefit of the community, whose re-

pose is assured by the punishment of evildoers" (IIa IIae, q. 68, a. 1).[45]

Thomas proposes a multileveled and differentiated theory of punishment, which unfortunately manifests a lack of conceptual clarity because it was not constructed systematically. First and foremost, punishment has a retributive sense ("guilt" is, therefore, a necessary but not sufficient condition for the requirement of punishment). Furthermore, it is nevertheless true that retribution can only be demanded when it also possesses a certain usefulness beyond simply this, whether it be on the level of the protection of life together in the society and of peace among human beings themselves, or whether it be the improvement of the evildoer.[46]

In death penalty cases, capital punishment would be justified only to the extent that it is really a *punishment*; however, were it merely a socially useful measure or a form of revenge, killing the offender would be unjust. The executioner should, according to Thomas, in no way aspire to the death of the criminal as such. In principle, to desire the evil inflicted on the evildoer by the penalty, and even to enjoy it, would be a sign of hatred, and, so, is directly opposed to love, and, therefore, sinful (IIa IIae, q. 108, a. 1). The one inflicting the penalty must, instead, through the punishment strive to keep justice and peace in the society, and to render the criminal harmless, and so forth. Only in this context can the death penalty be an act of justice for Thomas.

Precisely for this reason, killing as an enactment of the death penalty is a totally different action *intentionally* than one specified as murder. In the case of murder, a private person *wills* the death of another, whether as a means or as an end. This, considered from the side of the act's object, is essentially a rights violation, whereas the death penalty is essentially an act of justice (insofar as one is not acting out of revenge). Thomas confirms this in another well-known passage, in which he explains the distinction between the natural species and the moral species of an act. The object of the action could differ completely in accord with the end of the will (*finis voluntatis*) for the sake of which this action is chosen: "Just as this is the case in relation to the killing of a person, which is (always) one and the same in terms of the natural species; it can be directed both toward the end of preserving justice, as well as toward the satisfaction of rage. Correspondingly, in terms of the moral species, we are dealing with two distinct acts: in one case, with an act of virtue; in the other, with an act of depravity" (Ia IIae, q. 1, a. 3, ad 3).[47]

Problems with the Death Penalty

On the basis of this argument, it becomes clear that the legitimacy of the death penalty implies no exception to the prohibition of killing. "Killing" as an action on the level of nature (*genus naturae*) cannot be defined as a human, chosen action. From the side of the object, killing as an act of punishment is a specifically different moral action than murder. Murder is *always* an action in which killing occurs because one *wills* the *death* of the victim, whether as a means or as an end. However, the meting out and exercise of the death penalty is exactly like a murder and hence a sin, if one wills the death of the evildoer *above all*, instead of simply trying to preserve justice by administering a penalty.

Yet, to be sure, not all problems are solved in this way. At this point, one must ask why, then, inasmuch as Thomas is really dealing with a transgression seriously harmful to the society, does he insist so categorically upon death for the punishment of the sinner? Thomas's logic includes yet a further premise (thereby depending again on the fact that the killing of the innocent is absolutely not allowed, but, on the other hand, killing one who is guilty is permitted). This premise could, perhaps, be reconstructed as follows: The killing of one innocent by public penal justice is legitimate, because the criminal has only already *lost the right to life* by acting in a manner that was seriously harmful to the common welfare (and, as already cited above, sunk back to the level of a brute). In the end, however, this premise seems fundamentally more problematic. One might be more inclined to say that someone's right to life is not restricted on the basis of self-imposed guilt (and thereby the already effective harm), but by the risk to society his or her survival would present (whereby one might also conceive of a calculus of deterrence). Is sheer retribution for the sake of retribution justifiable as an act of terrestrial justice?

It is not entirely clear whether Thomas believes that one must punish serious transgressions with death simply because they are serious. That would contradict his opinion that earthly penalties have above all a salutary and not a vengeful character, and thereby also contradict his utilitarianism of justice. As a matter of fact, in IIa IIae, q. 108, a. 3, ad 2, Thomas argues exactly in this way: "But penalties in this present life have more of a healing character. Consequently, the death penalty is only given as regards those transgressions which present enormous perniciousness to others."[48] Here, therefore, Thomas presents a utilitarian, that is, prospective, element in his theory of the death penalty. In spite of the fundamental defect in the utilitarian penal theory (at the level of the concept of punishment), on another level it has the advantage of assessing the seriousness of a transgression not retrospectively, but prospectively, as Thomas seems to do here. At any rate, then, the premise according to which the criminal would have already lost the right to life by his or her guilt is weak. This right could only be legitimately restricted in cases in which the continued existence of the society—the peaceful living together of people—could not be assured in any other way. Nevertheless, in other passages, Thomas seems to propose instead a retrospective view aimed at retribution.[49] The question remains whether Thomas pleads for pure retribution, or whether here, too, a calculus of deterrence is tacitly implied.

Perhaps not every vague point in Thomas's theory of punishment is cleared up in this manner. It also remains problematic, for instance, that Thomas, in the prior context, does not distinguish between sinner and criminal.[50] In fact, it sometimes seems that Thomas holds that the serious sinners would have already lost the right to human dignity only by reason of a seriously harmful fault to the common good. Today, one would no longer argue in this manner. On the other hand, it is also significant that Thomas holds it is immoral and sinful for there to be any administration of the death penalty, even in cases of one unequivocally guilty, out of motives of revenge.[51]

Given today's possibilities for enacting punishment and protecting society from serious criminals, and in view of the primarily healing task of human punishment always stressed by Thomas, there remains very little room for the appropriateness of the death penalty. But, such an insight is only a subsidiary point of this analysis. The key concern is to clarify how the absolute norm of the prohibition of killing is to be understood. Favoring the death penalty, whether it is appropriate or not, would be no exception to such an absolute prohibition.

The norm that one ought never kill an innocent, however, covers not only actual murder by a private person, but also murders in the name of justice—the misuse of the instruments of penal justice by a public official. That is the advantage of this formulation of the norm. But, it does not yet cover two cases in which killing seems to be allowed: killing in a just war and killing in self-defense. Unfortunately, I can only go into these cases briefly here.[52]

Killing in Self-defense and Killing in War

Killing in self-defense is not directly intentional; it is "besides the intention" of the agent (*praeter intentionem*). Thomas affirms categorically, "it is not permitted that someone intentionally kill anyone in order to defend himself" (IIa IIae, q. 64, a. 7).[53] This is only permitted by a public authority (ibid.). Thereby Thomas reaches the intermediate result that a *private person* is never allowed to kill. "Thou shalt not kill" holds true for the actions of private persons absolutely. Here, the mention of *an innocent person* is not even necessary, since private persons are not competent to exercise penal justice.

Legitimate self-defense with lethal consequences means that the attacker's death is not intended along with the goal of saving one's own life but, rather, that an action is chosen by which one seeks to stop the aggression of the attacker. The force used in this case must be proportionate to the force of the aggressor. The death of the attacker, should it occur, is, then, intentionally only a byproduct of the defensive activity. As for its moral species, the action itself would not be a killing action, but only one of self-defense, "since moral actions get their species on the basis of what is intended, and not of what lies outside the intention" (IIa IIae, q. 64, a. 7).[54]

Therefore, simply to choose the death of the attacker and to act accordingly would be impermissible.

This argument for the nonintentional character of killing in legitimate self-defense appears cogent, although it is understood falsely or misused by not a few interpreters of Thomas.[55] Nevertheless, the formulation that intending death for the sake of self-defense is allowed for public authority as distinct from the private person remains somewhat open to misunderstanding, insofar as it "relates [this] to the public welfare" (ibid.).[56] That is, such killing is only possible in the context of punishment (the preservation of justice) or of a just war. It is not dealing with mere actions in self-defense, as Thomas's formulation somewhat misleadingly suggests.

The case of killing in just war, however, has certain things in common with self-defense; it is similarly akin to killing as a punishment. What killing in just war has in common with self-defense is that in the former case it is not a matter of a mode of action directed against the life of determinate persons, but one of defending against aggression and so protecting one's own goods. One, therefore, does not will the death of the attacker, but only to render him harmless, in order to fend off the assault (one ought not kill the wounded soldier no longer capable of battle; one even, if possible, has to give him medical care). In the death penalty, naturally the death of the condemned person has to intervene so that the purpose of the punishment be fulfilled. (Thomas nevertheless asserts one ought not to desire simply the death as such; rather, one must always seek only the preservation of justice).

In the case of the just war, this is even more the case (IIa IIae, q. 40, a. 1). The fighting soldier is acting here in the commission of public power. A just war, accordingly, is always an act of public authority and, in this sense, of the society as a whole. In their very notion, private wars are unjust. However, Thomas also affirms that a just war presupposes some guilt. And so, in some way an injustice has to be redeemed. Nevertheless, even such an apparently useful or "just" end does not justify any warlike action. Beyond this, the war has to have good effects; it is not supposed to increase the evil.

The Formulation of the Absolute Prohibition against Killing

Thus, one attains an absolute norm, valid under all circumstances, that a private person is never allowed to kill another person (one need say nothing here about innocence). In terms of a theory of action, this formulation is univocal, and distinguishes murder as an objectively distinct action from the death penalty and killing in war (however, killing in self-defense is not another species of killing, nor even a species of killing at all; the species here is self-defense, and the killing, considered in terms of its intention, is a secondary result, occurring beside the intention [*praeter intentionem*]).

On the other hand, Thomas's statement that one ought never kill an innocent person has the advantage of covering both the case of murder by a private person (in which it is always a matter of "an innocent," since no trial verdict is present) and the case of a misuse of military or police means (for instance, secret and illegal commando actions for the sake of assassinating political opponents). Killing in war or handing down a death penalty with any guilty spirit (*animus nocendi*) or hatred has the character of "private" killing, because in such a case one is no longer acting in one's character as a public person.

The treatment of the issue of killing by Thomas still allows one to conceive the prohibition against killing in a more concise way—in terms of the theory of action—that one never ought to want the death of a person, either as an intended end or as a means chosen for an end. That this holds for private persons is readily illuminating. However, neither in the case of the death penalty is killing chosen to attain the goal of justice, since the killing here is already chosen as an *act of punishment*, that is, an act preserving justice (and, then, perhaps, as an act also directed toward yet other goals, such as deterrence). Here, what one actually wills is not the death of evildoers, but their just punishment.[57] This nuance is manifest precisely in contrast to one calling for the death of criminals out of revenge and hatred toward them. In war, something analogous can be said, and the above-mentioned duty to provide help for wounded enemy troops shows that killing as such, either as a

means or as an end, is actually not intended. In terms of action theory, these particular killing activities have the character of protection against aggression (for Thomas, of making good an injustice as well). From the basis of a reasonable standpoint, all this is consistent with the formulation of an absolute prohibition of killing in the sense given above.

As already mentioned, human actions and their moral identity can never be defined on the level of a purely "physical" occurrence of an act. It always requires an initial, basic, intentional content, a basic intentionality.[58] In these actions against justice, this intentional content always has something to do precisely with the rights of the other. In and of itself, any individual's right to life is unassailable, but there are cases in which it conflicts with general justice—the common good—and does so in a *guilty* manner according to the criteria of justice. In this way, one can justify the death penalty as well as killing in a just war. That one *can* justify the death penalty as an act of justice, without entering into contradiction with the absolute prohibition against killing, is far from meaning that one has to support the introduction or maintenance of the death penalty. There are indeed always enough other reasons that speak against the death penalty and can demonstrate it to be unjust.

JUSTICE, PRUDENCE, AND LOVE

It was mentioned earlier that Thomas apprehends any act of injustice not only as a transgression against basic benevolence toward the neighbor, but also as a transgression against the theological virtue of love. Because sins against justice are also sins against love, in terms of its species any injustice is connected with the loss of the supernatural life of the soul, and thus a mortal sin (q. 59, a. 4). Like any moral virtue, only more emphatically, justice can only exist when joined to prudence. In many cases, prudence *already in itself* commands one to refrain from certain actions (namely, those forbidden by an absolutely prohibitive norm, such as killing or lying). To reach a judgment about action in other cases, prudence has to establish concretely what concerns the rights of others. As already stated above—and here it is essential—love is always involved in all of this. Love, justice, and prudence—to name only these three—form an indissoluble unity. Love presupposes the moral virtues, depending on them in a certain manner, while also simultaneously transforming them, and so it transcends mere justice.

On the other hand, in Catholic moral theology of the last thirty years, theories have been developed (proportionalism or consequentialism, among others) according to which the moral goodness of an action (in contrast to mere rightness) is constituted only on the level of benevolence, of love, and the like, but not on the level of practical judgment proper. Let me only say here that Thomas's teaching about the norm regarding killing can teach precisely how the rightness of action and the goodness of the person are mutually intertwined precisely on the level of concrete practical judgment. A right action in the realm of justice is precisely always also a *just* action and, thus, the action of a just person—it entails a fundamental benevolence in relation to the neighbor and is suited to be informed by infused love. In the domain of justice, *right* always means rightness in *willing* (on the level of choice of action and of the further intention of an end); rightness of the will, however, is always already moral goodness of the person. This is why a right action is also already a morally good action. Conversely, the morally false action is, for the same reason, also an *unjust* and, hence, a morally evil action. Therefore, it also automatically transgresses against love.

In a particularly clear manner, James F. Keenan has recently advanced the view criticized here, and appealed to Thomas Aquinas in doing so.[59] He coherently supports the opinion that the rightness of striving and, consequently, the acquired moral virtue has nothing at all to do with the goodness of the person. The goodness of the person is only brought about by the grace of infused love.[60] As an interpretation of Thomas, this ultimately could not be tenable. Thomas's explicit teaching, that *according to their species*, sins against justice are mortal sins because they altogether violate love, shows this.

Then, too, in terms of ethical theory generally, Keenan's conception does not seem equipped for coming to grips with the properly ethical problem that asks what do we have to do to be good human beings, even as regards its starting point. According to Keenan,

all one needs is love; it is a matter of indifference what one does, or whether one does, or even wants, the right thing, which is to say, whether one acts justly. In this case, there would be no more sins against justice, not even when a person willingly violates the rights of another. Only sins against love would still be conceivable. This idea has to be characterized as defective.

Thomas's teaching on the relationship between justice and concrete actions thus remains relevant, precisely even as a *propaedeutic* to and integral component of a Christian morality of love. "To love means to want the good for someone;" this Aristotelian basic formula for the love of friendship taken up by Thomas is already valid for the kind of benevolence I am calling *justice*.[61] Since, in every human and freely chosen action, a will aimed at the truly or only apparently good is involved, every unjust act essentially contradicts benevolence in relation to one's fellow human being, and not only on the basis of an additional intention directed against love. For Thomas, sins against justice—in both deeds and words—are sins against love precisely *because* they violate justice. On a level prior to the supernatural love of charity (*caritas*), but not totally independent of it, sins against justice constitute a turn of the will away from the good. Consequently, in Thomas's sense, one cannot relativize the importance of doing justice and the prudence connected with it in favor of a falsely understood morality of love, whose two feet would no longer be firmly planted on the earth. This world, as Thomas teaches, can only become a better world through a kind of love that becomes effective by means of justice.

Notes

[1]Marcus Lefébure, O.P., "Introduction," in St. Thomas Aquinas, *Summa Theologiae*, Vol. 38 (London: Blackfriars, Eyre and Spottiswoode, 1975), xvi.

[2]The concept *ius* or *iustum* can only be rendered into English with difficulty. "Right" is not the suitable expression, since "right" and "rights" mean *subjective* claims. On the contrary, with *ius* is meant whatever is owed or "accrues to." The English expression for this would be "the due." So, too, Thomas Gilby, O.P., (in the Blackfriars edition of the *Summa theologiae*, 37:21) in the subsequent defi-

nition of the virtue of justice translates the term *ius suum* with "his due."

³"habitus secundum quem aliquis constanti et perpetua voluntate ius suum unicuique tribuit."

⁴Compare also the subchapter, "Individual and Social Justice," in Thomas Gilby, O.P., *Principality and Polity: Aquinas and the Rise of State Theory in the West* (London: Longmans, Green and Co., 1958), 219–27.

⁵"Et secundum hoc actus omnium virtutum possunt ad iustitiam pertinere, secundum quod ordinat hominem ad bonum commune."

⁶"Sicut etiam omnia vitia, inquantum repugnant bono communi, iniustitiae rationem habent."

⁷"iniustitia secundum inaequalitatem quandam ad alterum: prout scilicet homo vult habere plus de bonis, puta divitiis et honoribus; et minus de malis, puta laboribus et damnis."

⁸"Omne autem nocumentum alteri illatum ex se caritati repugnat, quae movet ad volendum bonum alterius" ("However, every harm inflicted on another is repugnant to charity, which moves us to will the good of the other") (ST *IIa IIae*, q. 59, a. 4).

⁹Therefore, of particular importance is the virtue of truthfulness or honesty, which, at any rate, is only spoken of later along with the vices of lying that are opposed to it (ST IIa IIae, qq. 109–10, under the *partes potentiales* of the virtue of justice). One can understand truthfulness as "justice in communication": precisely the medium of language is the precondition and most fundamental externalization of the social relation; misuse and destruction of this medium is treated by Thomas as unjust in a fundamental sense. I will come back to this.

¹⁰"Facere ergo iniustum ex intentione et ex electione est proprium iniusti" ("Therefore it pertains to the unjust to do something unjust from intention and choice") (ST IIa IIae, q. 59, a. 2).

¹¹For details, see my more extensive studies of the concept of *lex naturalis* in Thomas: *Natur als Grundlage der Moral: Die personale Struktur des Naturgesetzes bei Thomas von Aquin: Eine Auseinandersetzung mit autonomer und teleologischer Ethik* (Innsbruck-Wien: Tyrolia, 1987) (English trans.: *Natural Law and Practical Reason: A Thomist View of Moral Autonomy* [New York: Fordham University Press, 2000]).

¹²"bonum est faciendum et prosequendum, et malum vitandum."

¹³That the first principle of practical reason, as well as all the subsequent principles, is a principle of practice and not of ethics means more proximately that it is the principle of action for concrete acting subjects, and not a principle of discourse *about* practice, for example, of a discourse about norms carried on by ethicists. It is that principle that always already underpins reasonable human action, and shapes its inner, intelligible drive. Practical principles are not principles of thought or

reflection but, rather, principles of action. Practical reason and its principles, first of all, are not "ethics" or normative discourse, but the rational insight of the moral subjects themselves motivating them to action. Precisely for this reason, it appears to be shortsighted to regard the first principle as the expression of the "structure of practical rationality in general," which "establishes the formal absence of contradiction of whatever is known as good" (Ludger Honnefelder, "Wahrheit und Sittlichkeit. Zur Bedeutung der Wahrheit in der Ethik," in *Wahrheit in Einheit und Vielheit*, Beiträge zur Theologie und Religionswissenschaft, ed. Emerich Coreth [Düsseldorf: Patmos, 1987], 147–69, esp. 156, 167). See also Honnefelder, "Absolute Forderungen in der Ethik. In welchem Sinn ist eine sittliche Verpflichtung 'absolut'?" in *Das Absolute in der Ethik*, ed. Walter Kerber (München: Kindt, 1991), 13–33, esp. 25f. Honnefelder designates the first principle of practical reason as the "principle of practical *non-contrariety*." The purely logical characterization predominates over the dynamic-practical aspect or the psychology of action, which, in my opinion, is decisive here.

¹⁴"ad hoc quod in societate vivat."

¹⁵With the delimitation of a realm the content of the principle of justice is also decided—on the most universal level. Hence, it seems less meaningful—and unfounded from Thomas's perspective—to view in the first principle of practical reason as it were the quintessence of the natural law, in the sense of the admonition to "act in accord with reason," so that the natural inclinations in their natural "non-disposability" are only regarded as the field (determinate and not surrendered to arbitrariness) of the ordering acts of reason, without considering them simultaneously also, in the sense of the matter/form scheme, as the material ground of determination for any ruling by reason. To have reconnected reason too much with "nature" and thus to have threatened it in its autonomy was reproached to me especially by Georg Wieland, "Secundum naturam vivere. Über das Verhältnis von Natur und Sittlichkeit," in *Natur im ethischen Argument*, ed. Bernhard Fraling (Freiburg-Schweiz: Universitätsverlag, 1990), 13–31, esp. 21–26; and Ludger Honnefelder, "Natur als Handlungsprinzip. Die Relevanz der Natur für die Ethik," in *Natur als Gegenstand der Wissenschaften*, ed. Ludger Honnefelder (Freiburg: Verlag Karl Alber, 1992), 151–83, esp. 179. An explicit answer to this critique is found in my postscript to *Natural Law and Practical Reason*; and in my article, "Praktische Vernunft und 'das von Natur aus Vernünftige'. Zur Lehre von der Lex naturalis als Prinzip der Praxis bei Thomas von Aquin," *Theologie und Philosophie* 75 (2000): 493–522. For a critique of Honnefelder's interpretation of Thomas, see also Christian Schröer, *Prak-*

tische Vernunft bei Thomas von Aquin (Stuttgart: Verlag W. Kohlhammer, 1995), 205ff.

[16]*In V Ethicorum.*, lect. 12: "etiam in operativis sunt quaedam principia naturaliter cognita, quasi indemonstrabilia principia et propinqua his, ut malum esse vitandum, nulli esse iniuste nocendum, non esse furandum, et similia" (also in matters of operation there are certain naturally known principles, almost indemonstrable principles, and those closest to these, such as evil is to be avoided, no one is to be unjustly harmed, do not steal, and similar things; Leonine, 305, 52–56).

[17]Secondary principles are divided by Thomas into those more proximate, those knowable for all, and those remote and not always knowable by all. On the distinction of the different levels of practical principles or precepts of the natural law, see the classic work by R. A. Armstrong, *Primary and Secondary Precepts in Thomistic Natural Law Teaching* (The Hague: Martinus Nijhoff, 1966).

[18]In the same measure that the above-named interpretations by Honnefelder and Wieland confine the materially pregiven content of the natural law to the precept that one must live in a manner coherent with reason, they fail to conceive practical reason as a reason that grounds the *material identity of the person.* The identity established by practical reason is reduced by these authors to formal characteristics, such as *rationality, autonomy,* and *ethical nature.* The principle of justice, and the relation to the other it entails, is nevertheless a (rationally determined, of course) *material* principle, founded on the effectual presence of an *inclinatio naturalis.* One should not reduce the latter, as Honnefelder and Wieland appear to do in the preceding context, to the natural drives that spring forth from the corporeal nature of the human being; instead, it also encompasses the tendencies arising from the *appetitus rationalis,* the will. Justice is counted among these. Both Honnefelder and Wieland present a dualistic structural specification of the relationship between nature and (practical) reason (Wieland, "Secundum naturam vivere," 25). This is indeed connected with the fact that, in these two authors, under the influence of Wolfgang Kluxen (*Ethik des Ethos* [Freiburg: Karl Alber, 1974], 27 ff.), nature (here, *naturalis inclinatio*) is generally designated as *meta-norm* (or a purely negatively effective "*norma normarum*"), whereas reason is designated as the moral norm. That reason is the standard of morality is incontestable. Yet it can only be this inasmuch as in each one of its acts it is embedded in a *naturalis inclinatio*; a "free ranging" practical reason, which stands as it were over against "nature," relating itself to it (which is Wieland's way of expressing the matter), is unthinkable. As I have tried to show in my more complete analyses of Thomas's teaching on natural law, only in the mode of reflection upon its

own acts does reason acquire a distantiated relationship to nature and only approaches it insofar as it is a good, known and ordered *by reason.* In its normatively fundamental acts, practical reason is bound much more to nature than Wieland and Honnefelder—standing under the influence of Kant—want to admit. See my "Praktische Vernunft und 'das von Natur aus Vernünftige'."

[19]*De Veritate*, q. 16, a. 1: "in ipsa est quidam habitus naturalis primorum principiorum operabilium, quae sunt naturalia principia iuris naturalis; qui quidem habitus ad synderesim pertinet" (in it there is a certain natural habit of first principles concerning operables, which are the natural principles of the natural law; which habit indeed pertains to synderesis; Marietti, 322). On Thomas's equation of the Aristotelian intellectual grasp of first principles with synderesis, see Michael Bertram Crowe, *The Changing Profile of the Natural Law* (The Hague: Martinus Nijhoff, 1977), 136–41. See also my *Praktische Vernunft und Vernünftigkeit der Praxis. Handlungstheorie bei Thomas von Aquin in ihrer Entstehung aus dem Problemkontext der aristotelischen Ethik* (Berlin: Akademie Verlag, 1994), Teil V; and *Natur als Grundlage der Moral*, 229ff; *Natural Law and Practical Reason*, 278ff.

[20]"nulli debet homo malefacere . . ." ("the human being should do evil to no one").

[21]"quia ad hoc natura inclinat, sicut non esse iniuriam alteri faciendam" ("for nature inclines toward this: as no injury is to be done to another").

[22]SCG III, chap. 129: "unicuique quod suum est conservare, et ab iniuriis abstinere" ("to save for each what is his own, and to abstain from injuries").

[23]Ibid. This same consideration is also found in the specification of the content of the so-called *ius gentium* in ST Ia IIae, q. 95, a. 1.

[24]"reddere debitum alicui habet rationem boni" ("to render what is due has the intelligibility of the good").

[25]See Martin Rhonheimer, *La prospettiva della morale. Fondamenti dell'etica filosofica* (Rome: Armando, 1994), 242–46; Rhonheimer, *Die Perspektive der Moral. Philosophische Grundlagen der Tugendethik*, enlarged German ed. (Berlin: Akademie Verlag, 2001), 247–51.

[26]Thomas's commentary on the relevant passage from the Gospel of Matthew (Mt 7:27) is not very helpful.

[27]By this, of course, is not meant that this recognition and justice implies an effective equality of claims and rights. What is meant is that, based on this recognition, all are equal in the fulfillment of their respective rights claims; it implies, so to speak, the equality of the rights of all to attain their respective right. The Golden Rule does not, then, mean that what is due to me is *eo ipso* due also to the other; but, rather, that we owe the other what *in the other's*

place we would figure is good for and due to us. It is, thus, a principle of impartiality.

[28]See SCG III, chap 117; and Arist. *Eth. Nic.* 8.1 (1155a21–22).

[29]The virtue of justice thus stands in immediate continuity with friendship, since according to Aristotle this consists in loving the other as "another self" (Arist. *Eth. Nic.* 9.4 [1166a32]), which Thomas understands in such a way that for one's friend the friend "wants the good as if for himself" (vult ei bonum sicut et sibi ipsi [ST Ia IIae, q. 28, a. 1]); this is, as it were, the surpassing of the Golden Rule by affective identification with the other.

[30]"quia homo est animal sociale, naturaliter unus homo debet alteri id sine quo societas humana conservari non posset. Non autem possent homines ad invicem convivere nisi sibi invicem crederent, tanquam sibi invicem veritatem manifestantibus. Et ideo virtus veritatis aliquo modo attendit rationem debiti."

[31]On the question of lying, see my explications in *Natur als Grundlage der Moral*, 346f (which corresponds to *Natural Law and Practical Reason*, pt. 2, 9.1); *La prospettiva della morale*, 288f; and *Die Perspektive der Moral*, 313ff.

[32]Classic studies of the theme are those of Benjamin N. Nelson, *The Idea of Usury* (Princeton: Princeton University Press, 1949); and John T. Noonan, Jr., *The Scholastic Analysis of Usury* (Cambridge, MA: Harvard University Press, 1957). See also the commentary by Arthur F. Utz in the German edition of Thomas's *Summa theologiae*, vol. 18 (Heidelberg-Munich/Graz-Vienna-Salzburg: F. H. Kerle/Anton Pustet, 1953), 545–59.

[33]On this, see Appendix 2 by Lefébure in the Blackfriars edition of the *Summa theologiae*, 38:275–83; by way of summary, see also J. H. Burns, ed., *The Cambridge History of Medieval Political Thought c. 350–c. 1450* (Cambridge: Cambridge University Press, 1988), 621–25.

[34]See also my two articles, "'Intrinsically Evil Acts' and the Moral Viewpoint: Clarifying a Central Teaching of *Veritatis Splendor*," *The Thomist* 58 (1994): 1–39; and "Intentional Actions and the Meaning of Object: A Reply to Richard McCormick," *The Thomist* 59 (1995): 279–311. On some questions having to do with action theory, see also William E. May, *Moral Absolutes: Catholic Tradition, Current Trends, and the Truth* (Milwaukee, WI: Marquette University Press, 1989); and John Finnis, *Moral Absolutes: Tradition, Revision, and Truth* (Washington, DC: Catholic University of America Press, 1991).

[35]We can prescind here from the question of killing animals (ST IIa IIae, q. 64, a. 1).

[36]"nullo modo licet occidere innocentem."

[37]On this, see the well-known articles by moral theologians such as Louis Janssens, Josef Fuchs, and Richard A. McCormick in Charles E. Curran and Richard A. McCormick, S.J., eds. *Moral Norms and Catholic Tradition: Readings in Moral Theology No. 1* (New York: Paulist, 1979).

[38]"Quaelibet autem persona singularis comparatur ad totam communitatem sicut pars ad totum. Et ideo si aliquis homo sit periculosus communitati et corruptivus ipsius propter aliquod peccatum, laudabiliter et salubriter occiditur, ut bonum commune conservetur."

[39]"Et ideo quamvis hominem in sua dignitate manentem occidere sit secundum se malum, tamen hominem peccatorem occidere potest esse bonum, sicut occidere bestiam: peior enim est malus homo bestia, et plus nocet, ut Philosophus dicit."

[40]So, for instance, in Bruno Schüller, *Die Begründung sittlicher Urteile. Typen ethischer Argumentation in der Moraltheologie*, 2d ed. (Düsseldorf: Patmos, 1980), 291. See also H. J. McCloskey, "A Note on Utilitarian Punishment," *Mind* 72 (1963): 599.

[41]"Nocumentum autem inferre alicui non licet nisi per modum poenae propter iustitiam."

[42]"secundum ordinem iustitiae."

[43]"poena non debetur nisi peccato, quia per poenam reparatur aequalitas iustitiae."

[44]However, Thomas admits that one can also treat punishment activities, not insofar as they are penalties (restoration of justice), but as it were as preventive measures for the avoidance of future sins, or the promotion of a good. Then there is no guilt present, but a cause. Examples are lacking in his account. In any case, we find ourselves outside the context of politics and law, where it is always a matter of restoring justice.

[45]"sed inquantum sunt medicinales, conferentes vel ad emendationem personae peccantis, vel ad bonum reipublicae, cuius quies procuratur per punitionem peccantium."

[46]ST IIa IIae, q. 109, a. 1 enumerates a whole series of legitimate motives for punishment (betterment of the sinner, rendering him harmless, security of others, preserving justice, and God's honor), whereby there is no further distinction between the motive of preserving justice, which pertains to the concept of punishment itself, and the others.

[47]Here, it is a matter of the end of the *electio*, of choice, of the first and fundamental act of will, which constitutes the object of the action: "sicut hoc ipsum quod est occidere hominem, quod est idem secundum speciem naturae, potest ordinari sicut in finem ad conservationem iustitiae, et ad satisfaciendum irae. Et ex hoc erunt diversi actus secundum speciem moris: quia uno modo erit actus virtutis, alio modo erit actus vitii." We can say that the mere infliction of an evil against the will of the victim is the *genus naturae* of the act of punishment, a *genus* that is also common to other, perhaps unjust, actions

as well. The moral species of "punishing" maintains the "inflicting of an evil" by the intentional direction of this event, in itself only physical, toward the goal of the preservation of justice.

[48]"Sed poenae praesentis vitae sunt magis medicinales. Et ideo illis solis peccatis poena mortis infligitur *quae in gravem perniciem aliorum cedunt.*" Emphasis mine.

[49]See ST IIa IIae, q. 66, a. 6, ad 2. The death penalty is demanded here for all transgressions "quae inferunt irreparabile nocumentum, vel etiam pro illis quae habent aliquam horribilem deformitatem" ("which inflict irreparable harm, or also for those that involve some horrible deformity"). For Thomas, this also covers sacrilege or the embezzlement of public money (in contrast to mere theft, which is reparable [*reparabile*]).

[50]Although, of course, Thomas is perfectly aware of the difference between sin strictly understood and that which has to be punished by civil law ("crime") (see ST Ia IIae, q. 96, a. 2; IIa IIae, q. 69, a. 2, ad 1). On this topic, see also Gilby, *Principality and Polity*, 176ff.

[51]The motive of revenge and hence the desire for the death of the evildoer out of hatred and contempt for him in many cases seem to be the dominant motive for the demand for the death penalty. The public pressure upon juries in such cases, through the influence of the mass media, can be so great that cases of unbiased verdicts are becoming ever more difficult.

[52]For a more systematic treatment of this question, see also Rhonheimer, "Intentional Actions and the Meaning of Object," as well as Rhonheimer, *La prospettiva della morale*, 280ff; and *Die Perspektive der Moral*, 303ff.

[53]"illicitum est quod homo intendat occidere hominem ut seipsum defendat."

[54]"Morales autem actus recipiunt speciem secundum id quod intenditur, non autem ab eo quod est praeter intentionem."

[55]See esp. Peter Knauer, S.J., "The Hermeneutic Function of the Principle of Double Effect," in *Moral Norms and Catholic Tradition: Readings in Moral Theology No. 1*, 1–39.

[56]"refert hoc ad publicum bonum."

[57]The same holds for *any* punishment: monetary punishments are not given to do harm to the one being punished, to make him poorer, etc., nor because one has an interest in his money (as in the case of theft), but precisely in order to *punish*, in the sense of allowing justice to prevail.

[58]On the concept of a "basic intentionality" and of the "intentional basic action," see Rhonheimer, *La prospettiva della morale*, 85ff; and *Die Perspektive der Moral*, 96ff.

[59]See James F. Keenan, S.J., *Goodness and Rightness in Thomas Aquinas's Summa Theologiae* (Washington, DC: Georgetown University Press, 1992); see also his article, "Die erworbenen Tugenden als richtige (nicht gute) Lebensführung: Ein genauerer Ausdruck ethischer Beschreibung," in *Ethische Theorie praktisch. Der fundamental-moraltheologische Ansatz in sozialethischer Entfaltung*, ed. Franz Furger (Münster: Aschendorff, 1991), 19–35.

[60]One could understand this in the trivial sense of *rightness* as *natural moral perfection* and *goodness* as *supernatural moral perfection*. But, surely, this is not Keenan's meaning. He would like to establish that, "under the threshold of love," that is to say, on the level of right and wrong and its corresponding desire, one cannot yet judge the goodness of a person at all.

[61]"cum amare nil aliud sit quam velle bonum alicui" ("since to love is nothing but willing the other good") (ST Ia, q. 20, a. 2). The formula comes from Arist. *Rh.* 2.4 (1380b 36). On this, see Eberhard Schockenhoff, *Bonum hominis. Die anthropologischen und theologischen Grundlagen der Tugendethik des Thomas von Aquin* (Mainz: Matthias-Grünewald, 1987), 493ff.

Selected Further Reading

Armstrong, R. A. *Primary and Secondary Precepts in Thomistic Natural Law Teaching*. The Hague: Martinus Nijhoff, 1966.

Burns, J. H., ed. *The Cambridge History of Medieval Political Thought*. Cambridge: Cambridge University Press, 1988.

Cessario, Romanus. *Le Virtù*. AMATECA Manuali di Teologia Cattolica Vol. 19. Milano: Jaca Book, 1994.

Crowe, Michael B. *The Changing Profile of the Natural Law*. The Hague: Martinus Nijhoff, 1977.

Curran, Charles E. and McCormick, Richard A., eds. *Readings in Moral Theology No. 1: Moral Norms and Catholic Truth*. New York: Paulist, 1979.

Finnis, John. *Moral Absolutes: Tradition, Revision, and Truth*. Washington, DC: Catholic University of America Press, 1991.

———. *Aquinas. Moral, Political, and Legal Theory*. Oxford: Oxford University Press, 1998.

Geach, P. T. *The Virtues. The Stanton Lectures 1973–4*. Cambridge: Cambridge University Press, 1977.

George, Robert P. *Making Men Moral: Civil Liberties and Public Morality*. Oxford: Clarendon, 1993.

Gilby, Thomas. *Principality and Polity: Aquinas and the Rise of State Theory in the West*. London: Longmans, Green and Co., 1958.

González, Ana Marta. "*Depositum gladius non debet restitui furioso*: Precepts, Synderesis, and Virtues in Saint Thomas Aquinas." *The Thomist* 63 (1999): 217–40.

Honnefelder, Ludger. "Absolute Forderungen in der Ethik. In welchem Sinne ist eine sittliche Verpflichtung, 'absolut'?," In *Das Absolute in der Ethik*. Ed. Walter Kerber. München: Kindt, 1991.

———. "Wahrheit und Sittlichkeit. Zur Bedeutung der Wahrheit in der Ethik." In *Wahrheit und Vielheit*. Ed. Emerich Coreth, Düsseldorf: Patmos, 1987.

———. "Natur als Handlungsprinzip. Die Relevanz der Natur für die Ethik." In *Natur als Gegenstand der Wissenschaften*. Ed. Ludger Honnefelder. Freiburg: Karl Alber, 1992.

Keenan, J. F., S.J. *Goodness and Rightness in Thomas Aquinas's "Summa Theologiae."* Washington, DC: Georgetown University Press, 1992.

———. "Die erworbenen Tugenden als richtige (nicht gute) Lebensführung: Ein genauerer Ausdruck ethischer Beschreibung." In *Ethische Theorie praktisch*. Ed. Franz Furger. Münster: Aschendorff, 1991.

Kluxen, Wolfgang. *Ethik des Ethos*. Freiburg/München: Karl Alber, 1974.

Lefébure, Marcus. "Introduction," in St. Thomas Aquinas, *Summa theologiae*, Vol. 38. London: Blackfriars, Eyre and Spottiswoode, 1975.

May, William, E. *Moral Absolutes: Catholic Tradition, Current Trends, and the Truth*. Milwaukee, WI: Marquette University Press, 1989.

McCloskey, H. J. "A Note on Utilitarian Punishment." *Mind* 72 (1963): 599.

Nelson, B. N. *The Idea of Usury*. Princeton: Princeton University Press, 1949.

Noonan, J. T., Jr. *The Scholastic Analysis of Usury*. Cambridge: Cambridge University Press, 1958.

Rhonheimer, Martin. *Natural Law and Practical Reason: A Thomist View of Moral Autonomy*. English trans. New York: Fordham University Press, 2000. *Natur als Grundlage der Moral: Die personale Struktur des Naturgesetzes bei Thomas von Aquin: Eine Auseinandersetzung mit autonomer und teleologischer Ethik*. Innsbruck-Wien: Tyrolia, 1987.

———. *Praktische Vernunft und Vernünftigkeit der Praxis. Handlungstheorie bei Thomas von Aquin in ihrer Entstehung aus dem Problemkontext der aristotelischen Ethik*. Berlin: Akademie Verlag, 1994.

———. *La prospettiva della morale. Fondamenti dell'etica filosofica*. Roma: Armando, 1994.

———. "'Intrinsically Evil Acts' and the Moral Viewpoint: Clarifying a Central Teaching of *Veritatis Splendor*." *The Thomist* 58 (1994): 1–39.

———. "Intentional Actions and the Meaning of Object: A Reply to Richard McCormick." *The Thomist* 59 (1995): 279–311.

———. "Fundamental Rights, Moral Law, and the Legal Defense of Life in a Constitutional Democracy." *The American Journal of Jurisprudence* 43 (1998): 1–49.

———. "Praktische Vernunft und 'das von Natur aus Vernünftige'. Zur Lehre von der Lex naturalis als Prinzip der Praxis bei Thomas von Aquin," *Theologie und Philosophie* 75 (2000): 493–522.

———. *Die Perspektive der Moral. Philosophische Grundlagen der Tugendethik*. Berlin: Akademie Verlag, 2001.

Rodríguez Luño, Angel. *Etica*. Firenze: Le Monnier, 1992.

Schockenhoff, Eberhard. *Bonum hominis. Die anthropologischen und theologischen Grundlagen der Tugendethik des Thomas von Aquin*. Mainz: Matthias Grünewald, 1987.

Schüller, Bruno. *Die Begründung sittlicher Urteile. Typen ethischer Argumentation in der Moraltheologie*. Düsseldorf: Patmos, 1980.

Utz, A. F. *Kommentar zu: Thomas von Aquin, Summa Theologica. Die Deutsche Thomas-Ausgabe: Band 18, Recht und Gerechtigkeit (II–II 57–79)*. Heidelberg-München: F. H. Kerle, 1953.

Wieland, Georg. *Secundum naturam vivere*. Über den Wandel des Verhältnisses von Natur und Sittlichkeit." In *Natur im ethischen Argument*. Ed. Bernhard Fraling. Fribourg: Universitätsverlag Fribourg, 1990.

The Virtue of Courage (IIa IIae, qq. 123–140)

R. E. Houser

ANTIQUE COURAGE

To understand courage, the ancients began with Achilles, the greatest of the Greek warriors, sulking in his tent before the lofty walls of Troy. He combined physical prowess with mental boldness in a "manly" manner, the literal meaning of the Greek words for courage: *arete* (sometimes linked to Ares, the god of war) and *andreia* (formed from *aner* or "male"). The anger which drove Achilles, however, also made him refuse to fight, which was unjust, and lend his armor to Patroklos, which was surely imprudent. By so combining virtue and vice, Achilles was a tragic and literarily effective figure, if one hard to understand.

The sophists made short work of such difficulties, by using their techniques of rhetorical analysis to deconstruct traditional morality. Protagoras's dictum "man is the measure of all things" meant that morality is based on culturally relative custom (*nomos*) rather than unvarying nature (*physis*), and that correct action is guided by right opinion rather than certain wisdom.[1] Socrates then defended traditional norms by turning sophistic techniques on their creators. He thought goodness based on nature, good action coming from virtue (*arete*) understood as a craft (*techne*) and virtue coming from knowledge: "Whoever knows the fine and good will never choose anything else, and whoever is ignorant of them cannot do them and, even if he tries, will fail. Therefore, the wise do what is fine and good, the unwise cannot and fail if they try."[2] This *logical* identity between wisdom and virtue seems to have led Socrates to assert an *ontological* identity between them: "justice and every other form of virtue *is* wisdom."[3] It follows that courage is "knowledge of the grounds of fear and hope," so an imprudent Achilles could not be a courageous Achilles.[4]

Plato did not go so far, reducing the multitude of virtues not to one but to four: courage, temperance, justice, and wisdom. His argument was based on the geography of the soul, which can be understood indirectly through the classes of the *polis*. To the three classes in the city—guardians, auxiliaries, and craftsmen—correspond three parts of the soul—"reason" (*logistikon*), "emotion" (*thymos*), and "desire" (*epithumia*). The virtues for these parts are wisdom, courage, and temperance; justice, a harmony produced when the three parts of the soul function well, is the virtue of the whole soul. Wisdom, courage, and temperance, taken together, are the necessary and sufficient conditions for justice: "That which preserves and fosters this inner harmony is called a just and fine action"; and "an action which destroys this harmony is unjust."[5] Each of the four cardinal virtues is distinct from the others, but functionally unified with them. Consequently, "there is but one form of virtue [in the aristocratic philosopher-king], while there are unlimited forms of vice, four of which are worthy of examination"—the timocrat, oligarch, democrat, and tyrant.[6] It follows that for Plato, like Socrates, if Achilles were unjust or imprudent, he could not be courageous.

Aristotle thought Plato's conclusions only as secure as his questionable claims about the structure of the soul. Modeling the whole of virtue theory on Plato's account of justice, which took its bearings from its end, not its "subject," produced Aristotle's teleological approach to ethics, where the moral virtues are means for attaining the ultimate end of happiness, and virtue is a good moral habit, defined as the *mean* between two extremes. The mean is determined concretely; to find it, Aristotle used as a model his account of the sense powers, such as sight and hearing, each of which is severely limited to perceiving a small range of "objects," such as color or sound. By analogy, Aristotle limited each specific moral virtue to a circumscribed area of moral life.

His treatment of courage is a case study in how Aristotle turned general Platonic virtues into specific ones. Courage helps one deal with the passions of fear and confidence brought on by facing evil, and one certainly fears many evils: "disgrace, poverty, disease, and friendlessness," among others. While Plato thought courage governs all these cases and more, Aristotle insisted that real courage is limited to facing the greatest evil—death—and even then only facing a "noble death" on the battlefield, fighting for the city. He dismissed courage apart from war as only "metaphorical" or "due to a similarity," not true courage at all.[7] Even in war, there are many cases which lack some feature of true courage and are courageous only by extension. The "courageous" deeds of the "citizen-soldier" who "seems to face dangers because of the penalties imposed by the laws and the reproaches they would otherwise incur,"[8] or of the mercenary soldier who fights for money, are performed in battle, but not out of the moral habit of courage. Aristotle thought even as fine a figure as Hektor had only the second-level courage of the "citizen-soldier."[9]

One is tempted to ask: if the strength to face disgrace and disease, or lesser problems like a relentless foreman or rigorous teacher, are not truly courage, then what are they? Aristotle, however, seems majestically unconcerned with such a question. True courage, or any other real virtue, is the outstanding excellence exhibited by the elite "few." True virtue is simply not found among the "many," and Aristotle seemed little concerned with describing their moral character.

On the issue of the unity of the virtues, Aristotle abandoned the doctrine of unity, claiming that each specific moral virtue is connected with prudence (*phronesis*), construed narrowly as practical decision-making, and which is a necessary and sufficient condition for courage and every specific moral virtue: "It is clear, then, from what has been said, it is not possible to be good in the principal way without prudence; nor prudent without ethical virtue."[10] Although there is a logical identity between prudence and each moral virtue, there is no ontological identity between them, for they are not the same virtue. Imprudence is merely a kind of blindness that makes it impossible to exercise a moral virtue such as courage; while lack of courage makes it impossible to put prudence into practice, at least in that realm of moral life courage concerns.

Aristotle's innovations finally provided a way of explaining how Achilles could be truly courageous but not just. This achievement, however, did have a cost: Aristotle left behind Plato's central idea of four cardinal virtues, and moved courage far away from those everyday fears where it seems most often needed.

Stoicism was the last ancient school to influence Aquinas's thought about courage. Following the Stoics, Cicero defined virtue as "a habit of mind consonant with the order of nature and with reason,"[11] and he held that virtue has four "parts"—the four Platonic virtues—each subdivided in turn. He said that courage is the conscious undertaking of dangers and the endurance of hardship and that it has four parts: (1) magnificence, the planning and execution of great and expensive projects by putting forth ample and splendid effort of mind; (2) confidence, that through which, on great and honorable projects, the mind self-confidently collects itself with sure hope; (3) patience, the voluntary and lengthy endurance of arduous and difficult things, whether the case be honorable or useful; and (4) perseverance, ongoing persistence in a well-considered plan.[12] Cicero failed to elaborate the relation between courage and its parts successfully, and resolution of this difficult point had to wait over a millennium.

THE CHRISTIAN DOCTRINE OF CARDINAL VIRTUES

In the interval, the advent of Christianity saw Ambrose of Milan, an inveterately allegorical thinker, coin the term "cardinal virtue." In his day, the Latin term *cardo* was a cosmological term and referred to the earth's poles, points on the ecliptic, days when the seasons change, the four principal winds. When Ambrose structured his funeral oration for his brother Satyrus around the four Platonic virtues, it seemed right to call them cardinal virtues, because they invested his brother's life with cosmic significance by leading him to its author.[13] Ambrose explored the nature of such cardinal virtues in an attempt to reconcile Matthew's account of eight beatitudes with Luke's four. He concluded that each beatitude entails *all* the others and that the same conclusion holds for the virtues: "Therefore, the virtues are so connected and chained together, that whoever has *one* seems to have them all. And there accrues to the saints [though not to pagans, he implies] *one* virtue; since the reward of what is more fruitful is itself more fruitful."[14]

Other fathers—Jerome, Gregory, and Augustine—followed Ambrose's reductionism. Augustine reduced all the virtues to love, just as Socrates had reduced them all to knowledge: "But if virtue leads us to the happy life, I would say that virtue altogether is nothing other than the highest love of God. For what is called fourfold virtue is named, so far as I can tell, from certain varied affections of love itself."[15] Since there are no longer four virtues but one "fourfold virtue," there is no space between virtuous Christians and vicious pagans, the terrain experience says is inhabited by virtuous pagans and vicious Christians. Augustine struggled mightily—and, ultimately, unsuccessfully—with this difficulty.

When Albert wrote his commentaries on the *Sentences* and the *Nicomachean Ethics* (1245–52), two points especially influenced his young student, Thomas of Aquino. First, Albert's approach to virtue was based on a fundamental analogy between the natural world and the moral world. Just as nature is composed of individuals whose essences one can understand universally, so in the moral realm there are individual human actions that one can describe in terms of moral classes. As well as being individual habits of mind, then, the virtues and vices are moral universals because every action has a certain universal, moral essence.

Second, Albert tried to integrate the many Aristotelian virtues with Plato's four cardinal virtues, by focusing on a central distinction: As the essence of a natural object can be described at the level of species or of genera, so also moral universals fall into species and gen-

era. Albert thought the Aristotelian virtues are like species, while the cardinal virtues are like genera, and attributed this doctrine to Cicero: The cardinal virtues are "properly in *every* virtuous act," for "Cicero says the four attributes which are present in virtuous actions argue for the four virtues. For the knowledge required argues for prudence; the strength to act resolutely argues for courage; moderation argues for temperance; and correctness argues for justice." These four "general acts of virtue," however, do not ensure that an action is *morally* right. Even "if one has these general traits, one does not necessarily possess all the specific types of virtues." Courage is an example: "It is not the same strength which is proper to courage and which is found in all virtuous actions, for what is proper in courage is to act against difficult passions, while what is common in courage is the strength to act according to virtue." When Albert viewed the cardinal virtues, then, he saw four general, Platonic attributes of every good action, but he also recognized that each cardinal virtue has a specific sense, and becomes specific by a process of *appropriation* to a limited area.[16]

Aquinas developed Albert's insights in exhaustive detail in the *Secunda secundae*, producing a theory of virtue more elaborate than anything found in earlier authors—in great measure because of the care he took to distinguish different senses of each virtue.[17] Understanding the analogous senses of the virtues, however, has proven notoriously difficult for Aquinas's commentators over the centuries. Josef Pieper, for example, tried to connect the different kinds of courage by claiming they all involve "facing death," which is what makes an action courageous in the first place: the ultimate injury is, of course, death. And even nonlethal injuries are prefigurations of death; this extreme violation, this final negation, is reflected and effective in *every* lesser injury. Thus, all fortitude has reference to death. All fortitude stands in the presence of death.[18] Pieper tellingly makes no mention of the distinction between general and special virtues, and for good reason. By using what Aristotle said limits courage to connect all the various kinds of courage together, Pieper obliterates any distinction between general and special courage. On his account, all courage is at least implicitly the courage to face death, which is special courage.

Thomas himself, however, approached the matter quite differently, using the four Aristotelian causes to define virtue. On this view, virtue is "an operative habit" (*habitus operativus*), with a *proximate end* of "operation itself" (*ipsa operatio*), and a *remote end* in happiness (Ia IIae, q. 55, a. 2). Humans are the intrinsic *efficient* causes of "acquired" virtue, while God is the extrinsic *efficient* cause of "infused" virtues, a distinction unknown to Plato and Aristotle (Ia IIae, q. 55, a. 4). Neither end nor agent, however, helped Aquinas distinguish general from specific virtues; to address this, he turned to "matter" and "form."

Aquinas recognized two meanings of form. Considered ontologically, a form is part of a composite and different from its matter. In definitions, however, by form, he means the essence of the thing defined, including matter. Thus, for humans, "the form of the part, which is signified by the term 'soul'," is different from "the form of the whole, which is signified by the term 'humanity'."[19] For the purpose of *defining* virtue, "form" means "the form of the whole," that is, the universal essence of virtue. "Now the formal cause of a virtue, like the formal cause of anything, is taken from its genus and difference" (ibid.).[20] Since the species of a natural genus are distinguished from each other by differentiating notes, distinguishing general from specific virtues involves a similar search. Aquinas first searches for the attribute common to all the special virtues lying under a cardinal virtue. This is the cardinal virtue conceived as a general virtue. He then searches for differentiae that distinguish the cardinal virtue, conceived as a special or specific virtue, and other special virtues, from the general virtue. In this way, Aquinas uses the "genus and difference" model of definition for each specific virtue. Pieper's mistake is to take what for Aquinas is the differentia distinguishing the *special* virtue of courage from other virtues, and treat that difference as though it were a genus common to all types of courage.

Aquinas also used "matter" to distinguish general from special courage. He recognized three senses of matter. Matter "out of which" (*ex qua*) refers to the material components of a physical substance, which are irrelevant to the virtues. But the other two are helpful. The matter "in which" (*in qua*) is the "subject" or seat of a virtue, a power of the soul. This sense of matter helps identify the general cardinal virtues. By contrast, "matter about which (*circa quam*) is the object of a virtue," a limited area of human action which "determines a virtue as to its *species*" by providing the differentia that distinguishes one specific virtue from another (Ia IIae, q. 55, a. 4).[21]

These different senses of matter and form helped Aquinas distinguish *general* from *special* courage, by opening up three ways to argue for the cardinal virtues (Ia IIae, q. 55, a. 4). Arguments based on generic "form" and on the "matter in which" display courage as a *cardinal and general virtue*; its "matter about which" or object shows how courage is a *special virtue*.

COURAGE AS A CARDINAL AND GENERAL VIRTUE

The simpler argument for the general cardinal virtues is based on their "matter in which." To the Platonic tripartite structure of the soul, Aquinas added a fourth power, free will, which is different from intellect, emotions, and desire. Appetite follows on the heels of cognition. Therefore, appetites resulting from "sensation" (*appetitus sensibilis*), which includes both "emotion" (*appetitus irascibilis*) and "desire" (*appetitus concupiscibilis*), are different from "intellectual appetite" (*appetitus intellectualis*) or "will" (*voluntas*), which arises from mental thought. Since human emotions and desires can be shaped by reason, Aquinas, unlike some other scholastics, did not hesitate to place some virtues there.[22] All four powers must be engaged properly for an act to be good, making each of them the seat of one cardinal virtue: intellect for prudence, the will for justice, the emotions (*appetitus irascibilis*) for courage, and desire (*appetitus concupiscibilis*) for temperance. Because each cardinal virtue governs *all* the good acts of its respective power, courage is conceived here as a *general* virtue (Ia IIae, q. 61, a. 2).

The other argument for the general cardinal virtues is based on the "formal principle of the virtues now under consideration," which "is the good discerned by reason" (ibid.).[23] Since "good" signifies the intended end, while "reason" shows how this end is grasped, "the good discerned by reason" (*rationis bonum*) is a convenient formula for the teleology of human action. It involves four necessary conditions: Awareness of a goal and the means to achieve it require "rational direction"; to proceed to one's ends requires "correct" choice; to keep one's attention on the goal chosen, one must moderate any inclinations that might lead away from it; and one must be "resolute" in overcoming obstacles on the way to the goal. These four cardinal features of good human action *flow from its goal-oriented character*. Both the end and the means to it must be cognized, desired, willed, and clung to, attributes formally similar to, but not identical with, the special cardinal virtues of prudence, temperance, justice, and courage respectively. Aquinas understood the four *general* cardinal virtues in a purely teleological way and realized that an action successfully attaining its end might be immoral. Consequently, he highlighted the difference between the cardinal virtues, understood as general "formal aspects" (*rationes formales*) of actions that are good in a minimal sense of attaining their intended ends, and the *specific* cardinal virtues, which make an action *morally* good, by choosing four different terms to describe the "general" cardinal virtues: "Now these four things—*rational direction, correctness, resoluteness, and moderation*—are required for *any* virtuous action."[24]

General courage helps with one kind of impediment to reasonable action—being repelled from the good by "something difficult" (*aliquod difficile*) (IIa IIae, q. 123, a. 1), and it "signifies universally a kind of resoluteness of mind" (*absolute importat quamdam animi firmitatem*) (IIa IIae, q. 123, a. 2). *Absolute*, meaning "essentially" or "universally," indicates that general courage has the widest possible application, while "resoluteness" (*firmitas*), that is, the determination to overcome obstacles on the way to an end, is the generic formality common to all subdivisions of courage.

To understand courage more precisely, Aquinas searched his sources for Cicero's "part": "confidence" (*fiducia*), "magnificence" (*magnificencia*), "patience" (*patientia*), and "perseverance" (*perseverantia*). But of these four, Aristotle had included only magnificence on his list of moral virtues. To reconcile these

two authorities, Aquinas interpreted patience and perseverance as specific, Aristotelian virtues, such as magnificence is. He then searched through Aristotle's list for a fourth special virtue, one akin to confidence, and found magnanimity. Thus arose the four parts of courage listed in the *Summa*: magnanimity, magnificence, patience, and perseverance. Ciceronian confidence, however, is not just another name for magnanimity, but is a different virtue. Aquinas understood it to be general in scope, a kind of genus for magnanimity and the first of the four parts of "general" courage, the other three parts being "accomplishing the deed" (*executio operis*), "enduring evils" (*sustinentia quorumcumque malorum*), and "constancy" (*constantia*).[25] Without some level of confidence in preparing to act, some ability to accomplish the task at hand, some ability to endure obstacles, and some constancy in pursuing the end, no act could ever be accomplished. These traits are not full-blown virtues, but are universally present in all deeds which achieve their ends.

In order to reconcile these two lists of analogous virtues, Aquinas clarified Cicero's notion of the parts of a virtue by dividing them into three kinds: "*integral*, as wall, roof, and foundation are parts of a house; *subjective*, as ox and lion are parts of animal; and *potential*, as nutritive and sensitive are parts of the soul" (IIa IIae, q. 48, a. un.).[26] The two lists of the parts of courage are consistent with each other, because they refer to different kinds of parts. The general traits make up the "integral" parts of courage, while the others, the specific virtues, constitute its "potential" parts:

> When they [the parts of courage] are limited to the proper matter of courage, that is, to danger involving death, they [i.e. confidence, accomplishment, endurance, and constancy] will be its integral parts, without which there can be no courage. But when they are referred to other matters in which there is less difficulty, they will be virtues different in species from courage [i.e. magnanimity, magnificence, patience, and perseverance], but connected with it as the secondary is connected with the primary.[27] (IIa IIae, q. 128, a. un.)

Thus, just as every good action requires rational direction, correct choice, moderation, and resoluteness (the four general cardinal virtues), so, in turn, every act of resoluteness (*firmitas*) or general courage, and every act of special courage (*fortitudo*), requires confidence, accomplishment, endurance, and constancy (the four integral parts of courage). Parallel to the general cardinal virtues are the four special cardinal virtues (prudence, justice, temperance, and courage), and parallel to the four integral parts of courage are four specific virtues, the "potential parts" of special courage (magnanimity, magnificence, patience, and perseverance).

A clear sign of the difference between general and special virtues is the way in which they are connected. Because general virtues are conditions necessary for any good act, they are *unified* in a Platonic way: "Without all the conditions dovetailing together, one of the conditions by itself is insufficient to produce what is truly a virtue."[28] By contrast, each specific virtue functions independently of other specific moral virtues, depending only upon prudence: "No moral virtue can exist without prudence, nor can one who lacks moral virtue possess prudence. On the other hand, if we consider the four cardinal virtues as signifying the general conditions for virtue, in this respect they are connected in this way, that the presence of just one of these conditions, without fulfilling all four, is not sufficient to produce a virtuous act."[29]

Aquinas's doctrine of the general cardinal virtues allows one to account for Achilles even better than had Aristotle. To exercise the *special* virtue of courage, as in defeating Hektor, an Achilles must have all four *general* cardinal virtues, though by no means must he be just or temperate in any specific way. These four general traits may help in doing what is morally good, but Aquinas realized they may also help us do what is morally wrong. Thus, Aquinas would distinguish the good bank robber, who has the admirable skills necessary for success, from the bad bank robber, who is incompetent beyond description. The successful robber does not possess all four *specific* cardinal virtues and, conceivably, does not possess even one of them, but he does have all four *general* cardinal virtues, for without them, the robbery would end in utter failure.[30] Distinguishing general from special cardinal virtues, then, allowed Aquinas to account for the vast range of human behavior, especially the moral middle, more accurately than anyone before him.

COURAGE AS A SPECIFIC VIRTUE: THE MORAL COURAGE OF HERO AND MARTYR

Neither the soul's powers nor the teleology of action shows courage to be a "specific moral virtue" (*virtus specialis*), a habit fostering actions that follow the moral law within a definable area of human life. To prove that courage is a virtue of this kind, Aquinas offers a third argument for the four cardinal virtues, one focusing on the object of each virtue. While depending heavily on Aristotle, Thomas presents two significant alterations on the Philosopher's arguments.

First, the object of the special virtue of courage is wider than Aristotle had thought. Aristotle had limited true courage to the battlefield and had gone out of his way to show that being fearless in "emergencies that involve death," such as shipwrecks and disease, is *not* the same as courage. Sailors and physicians do not face death directly because they hope their respective skills will save them.[31] For his part, Aquinas turned Aristotle around and refused to narrow courage to the battlefield. There are two sorts of *true* courage: "Now a man is not reputed brave absolutely (*simpliciter*) owing to his enduring just any kind of adversities, but only because he endures the greatest evils [those of death]. Owing to his enduring other evils someone is called brave in a certain respect (*secundum quid*)" (IIa IIae, q. 123, a. 4, ad 1).[32] Being brave "in a certain respect" is the kind of *true* courage found in its potential parts. And within special courage, which faces "the greatest dangers, namely the dangers of death," Aquinas made a second distinction. "Danger of death from illness, or a storm at sea, or robbers, or similar things, do *not* seem to threaten anyone directly (*directe*) insofar as he pursues some good. By contrast, the dangers of death in war *do* threaten a man directly (*directe*) because of some good, insofar as he defends the common good through just warfare" (IIa IIae, q. 123, a. 5).[33] Both cases of facing death—direct and indirect—include the *formal nature* of courage—fearlessly and resolutely and morally facing obstacles—as well as its proper *matter*—the danger of death. Consequently, where Aristotle had placed facing death at sea *outside* the bounds of true courage, Aquinas brought it *within* the special virtue of courage.

Second, Aquinas added a special, Christian form of courage, one that is found in the first Christian ideal: the courage of the martyrs, who "undergo personal battles for the sake of the highest good, who is God. Therefore, their courage is especially praised and is not outside the type of courage which concerns warfare" (IIa IIae, q. 123, a. 5, ad 1).[34] The martyr's courage includes both the form and matter of secular courage, which, because exhibited for a Christian end, is thoroughly unique. Thomas explains that, "Martyrdom is related to faith as the end for which one becomes resolute, while it is related to courage as the habit which elicits the act of martyrdom" (IIa IIae, q. 124, a. 2, ad 1).[35] Martyrdom, then, is not merely the oldest Christian ideal, "of all human acts martyrdom is the most perfect in its kind, as it were a sign of the greatest charity, as it says in John 15:13: 'Greater love has no man than this, that a man lay down his life for his friends'" (IIa IIae, q. 124, a. 3).[36] Although he expanded Aristotle's civil courage to include more than battlefield courage, Thomas revives the parallel between classical and Christian virtue in the exemplar of Christian courage. The "perfect nature of martyrdom" requires "suffering death for the sake of Christ," much as Aristotle had said that only the man willing to face noble death in battle was truly courageous (IIa IIae, q. 124, a. 4).[37] If the virtue of civil courage does not require the last full measure of devotion, the virtue of religious courage does, which is why martyrdom is the primary exemplar of courage.

COURAGE AS CARDINAL AND SPECIAL VIRTUE

To label only four of the many virtues with the term "cardinal" indicated their primary status in relation to other virtues. As I have shown, the secular courage of the knight and the Christian courage of the martyr are species exhibiting the formal nature of the general cardinal virtue of courage. The relation here is that between genus and species. The special virtue of courage—whether secular or Christian—is in turn a principal virtue, in relation to other, lesser virtues, its "potential parts," though in a different way. Logically this relation is one of "special virtues over against other special virtues" (Ia IIae, q. 61, a. 3).[38] These subordinate virtues possess the formality of general courage (overcoming obstacles) and that of special courage (doing so in a rational and moral way), but they apply these formal traits to other matter, areas of life less harmful than death. I will now turn to a discussion of these subordinate virtues—magnanimity, magnificence, patience, and perseverance.

SPECIAL VIRTUES SUBORDINATE TO COURAGE

Magnanimity

Magnanimity is arguably the most difficult virtue for Aquinas to explain. Ciceronian confidence (*fiducia*) is not to be confused with Aristotelian magnanimity. Cicero had not defended the connection between confidence and courage; and Aristotle had not connected magnanimity and courage at all. Above all, however, because none of Aristotle's virtues is more closely connected to pagan Hellenic culture than his "great-souled" man (*megalopsychos*), what he had called the "ornament of the virtues" (*ornatus omnium virtutum*) seems inconsistent with Christianity.

In reply, Aquinas offered an account of the relations among courage, confidence, and magnanimity, which the ancients had neglected. Confidence "pertains to preparing the mind, so that one will have a mind ready for the aggression" that courage broadly construed demands (IIa IIae, q. 128, a. un.).[39] This definition makes confidence an integral part of *general* courage. Such confidence becomes the special virtue of magnanimity only when applied to the "matter about which" the special virtue is concerned—public "honor" and recognition for great deeds done (IIa IIae, q. 129, aa. 1, 2, 4). In accord with the model of defining special virtues through genus and differentia, then, Aquinas defined magnanimity by using general courage or "resoluteness in the face of difficulties" as remote genus, "confidence" as proximate genus, and "honor" as differentia. On the other hand, he distinguished magnanimity from special courage by noting that "magnanimity agrees with courage, in making the mind resolute about difficult tasks, but it falls short of courage because it makes the mind resolute about matters where it is easier to be resolute," for death, the matter of special courage, is a greater obstacle than any other (IIa IIae, q. 129, a. 5).[40] Approaching these virtues by way of logical definition allowed Aquinas to sort out courage (both general and special), confidence, and magnanimity more precisely than his predecessors.

As sophisticated as they were, however, these distinctions did not form the focal point of his treatise on magnanimity. Thomas needed to address the serious problem posed by Aristotle's own words, which seemed to argue that it *cannot* be a Christian virtue. "Magnanimity is the opposite of humility, for the magnanimous man 'considers himself worthy of great rewards, and is dismissive of others'" (IIa IIae, q. 129, a. 3, obj. 4).[41] And at least five traits of magnanimity Aristotle had lauded seem unworthy of a Christian: ignoring benefactors, overplaying *gravitas*, irony, unwillingness to associate with others, and preferring useless to productive possessions (IIa IIae, q. 129, a. 3, obj. 5).[42] Following this line of argument, Dante used magnanimity to describe the virtuous pagans in limbo, at the top of hell:

> There were people with eyes *grave and slowly moving*,
> With *looks of great authority*;
> They *spoke seldom, with muted voices*.
> Right before me, on the enameled green,
> Were shown to me the great spirits (*li spiriti magni*).
> In seeing them I am myself exalted.
> I saw Electra, and a great company,
> Of whom I knew Hector, and Aeneas, and Caesar.[43]

Aquinas offered two answers to the problem of how magnanimity might be made Christian. He first offered a structural argument: Magnanimity and humility are not really opposed, since they fit within two different areas on the scheme of the virtues. Magnanimity is a kind of courage, while humility falls under temperance. Humility gives one self-control about wanting goods hard to obtain (*boni ardui*), but when they are appropriate for us to pursue, magnanimity gives us the courage to go after them (IIa IIae, q. 161, a. 1). Consequently, humility is not the opposite of magnanimity, and even Aristotle had said its opposite was being "small-souled" (*pusillanimus*), that is, lacking the courage to pursue goods "commensurate" with one's "own potential" (IIa IIae, q. 133, a. 1).

Aquinas seems to have recognized, however, that such an answer is not fully satisfying, and his second reply was to baptize magnanimity, rather than cede it to the pagans:

> In a human is found something great, which comes as *a gift of God*, and something defective, which comes from *the infirmity of nature*. Therefore, magnanimity makes a man "esteem himself worthy of great rewards" *in view of the gifts he possesses from God*.[44] For example, if he has great mental ability, magnanimity makes him try to perfect the operations of that ability. And the same can be said about using any other good, such as knowledge or wealth. Humility, on the other hand, makes a human esteem himself low *in view of his own natural defects*. . . . *Thus it is clear that magnanimity and humility are not contrary to each other, though they seem to tend in contrary directions, because they concern diverse features of the human.*[45] (IIa IIae, q. 129, a. 3, ad 4)

In this way, Aquinas made magnanimity a Christian virtue, whose essence is to recognize that gifts natural and acquired, for which one is due some measure of honor, are ultimately owed to God. Quite different from Aristotle's idea of virtue, this is a type of magnanimity Augustine, Jerome, or Innocent III would have certainly understood.

Aquinas listed four vices opposed to magnanimity. In addition to being pusillanimous, one shoots beyond the mean in desiring honor through "presumption" (*praesumptio*), "ambition" (*ambitio*), or "vainglory" (*inanis gloria*). Although Aquinas structured his presentation of all four as opposites of the "special" virtue of magnanimity, these vices all have more than one sense, and Aquinas explained each one by beginning with its broader sense and then narrowing it.

Presumption is taking on what is above one's own powers (IIa IIae, q. 130, a. 1), a broad definition Aquinas narrowed by adding that we overestimate our abilities to perform "something great" (IIa IIae, q. 130, a. 2, ad 2). Its opposite is pusillanimity. Aquinas illustrated this vice (one with an Aristotelian name) through a Gospel tale, the story of "the servant who buried in the ground the money received from his master, and did nothing with it, due to the kind of fear connected with pusillanimity" (IIa IIae, q. 133, a. 1).[46] Because a servant is presumably not capable of great deeds, pusillanimity is here meant in a broad sense. After beginning this way, Aquinas then limited the vice to persons who *are* capable of great deeds, but unwilling to do them (IIa IIae, q. 133, a. 2). Pusillanimity is a kind of fear, taken broadly and not limited to fear of death. Just as the formal nature of courage flows through the virtues allied to it, though their areas are different, so fear flows through its allied vices.

Aquinas's treatment of ambition and vainglory follows the same pattern. Defined generally, ambition "signifies an inordinate desire for honor," one that can become disordered either because one wants to be honored for some non-existent excellence, or one neglects God or neighbor in distributing earned honors (IIa IIae, q. 131, a. 1).[47] Broadly construed, Aquinas understood ambition in Christian terms. He then narrowed it to become a vice opposing magnanimity by noting that the magnanimous person strives for both great deeds and honor for them. If presumption leads one to something beyond one's abilities, ambition leads one to look for more honor than is rightfully due (IIa IIae, q. 131, a. 2, ad 1). Desire for glory in itself is not bad, but such desire becomes vain when the basis for glory is insufficient, or one seeks glory from the wrong people, or when one seeks glory for an end other than "the honor of God or the salvation of our neighbor" (IIa IIae, q. 132, a. 1).[48] This gives even the broad sense of vainglory a Christian meaning.

In dealing with magnanimity and its opposed vices, Christian magnanimity makes possible the kind of heroic deeds performed by such knights as Richard the Lion Heart or St. Louis IX, whose feats both Aristotle and Dante would clearly recognize as worthy of honor. But greatness of soul also can be exhibited in small deeds made great by their eternal consequences. It is not unfaithful to the thought of Aquinas to find in his treatise on magnanimity the seeds of St. Therese's Little Way, a mode of life Aristotle would doubtless find wrongheaded and deplorable. For the vices opposed to magnanimity, the narrow senses of the terms—their opposition to striving for great honor and great deeds—seem less important to Aquinas than their broader meaning. There are doubtless some who need to learn not to presume to accomplish great deeds of valor, but all must learn that, without God, nothing can be done.

Aquinas had a keen feel for when the narrow and when the broad sense of each virtue is relevant to practical decision making. Above all, he was never inclined to confuse the two. We see here at the level of detail, advantages which flow from distinguishing general from special cardinal virtues, at the level of principles. This fundamental distinction allowed Aquinas to make subtle use of multiple, analogous senses of the various virtues and vices.

Magnificence

Aquinas's splendid little treatise on magnificence illustrates to perfection his relation to Aristotle. The Philosopher's doctrine by no means determined the scope or structure of Aquinas's concept of this virtue, even though he integrated into his own view the essentials of Aristotle's thought on the subject. Aristotle had connected magnificence (*magnificentia*) with "liberality" (*liberalitas*), virtues concerned with various sums of money. They represent antidotes to the vicious love of money found in Plato's oligarchic and democratic men, because Aristotle had wanted to show that there can be virtue "with regard to the giving and taking of wealth, and especially in respect of giving."[49] They do not concern equity in normal business transactions (which falls under commutative justice), but expenditure of money for the public good.

Free citizens should give freely of their substance, liberality is simply a form of the word for "freedom." Aristotle had his eye on citizens whose inherited wealth freed them from caring too much about money, and allowed them to develop good taste, so that they pursue what is noble. The vice of deficiency is "unfreedom" (*illiberalitas*), which one might render "mean" or "tightfisted," as found in pimps and usurers, gamblers and robbers. The vice of excess is prodigality, not so much spending too much as aiming at results less than noble.

When Aristotle turned from liberality to magnificence, examples flowed from his pen because a city like Athens depended upon the largesse of her wealthy patrons. Magnificence covers subsidizing votive offerings and sacrifices to the gods, supporting temples like those on the Acropolis, mounting a chorus in a play, equipping a trireme in war, building fine houses for all to see, and putting on lavish weddings. All of these contribute in some measure to public culture. Its opposites are the deficiency of "pettiness" and excesses of "vulgarity" and "lack of taste."

Aquinas approached liberality and magnificence quite differently. He disconnected them, making liberality a part of justice and magnificence a part of courage. The questions he raised about magnificence follow perfectly the model of defining a species through genus and differentia. He began with the genus, which constitutes a general kind of magnificence, much broader than Aristotle's specific virtue, then turned to the differentia which distinguishes the special virtue of magnificence (q. 134, a. 1). This is its "matter about which." The result is a precise definition of the *special* virtue of magnificence. Aquinas then returned to the formal side of the virtue, asking "whether magnificence is a part of courage" (IIa IIae, q. 134, a. 4).

Etymology uncovers a broad sense of magnificence, which is "making something great" (*facere aliquid magnum*). "Great" takes the work of magnificence beyond "what pertains to the person," which "is small in comparison with what concerns God or the community" (IIa IIae, q. 134, a. 1, ad 3).[50] Placing magnificence beyond the individual realm sets it apart from most of the virtues falling under courage and temperance, which focus on personal morality. Aquinas then distinguished general from special magnificence, based on two senses of the term "make." Construed broadly, making is performing "*any* sort of action," whether transitive or immanent. This

sense of making delineates a kind of magnificence which "is not a special virtue," but is a general virtue producing "great" deeds done for God or community, not just ourselves (IIa IIae, q. 134, a. 2).

Understanding "making" narrowly (*proprie*) limits the virtue to "producing something in external material, like a house," and narrows magnificence to a "special virtue" by isolating its object: "the product made by art," which "is great, either in size, in how precious it is, or in dignity." Aquinas focused first on the quality of the product (ibid.), then turned to the large outlay of money necessary to produce it (IIa IIae, q. 134, a. 3). Consequently, even "the matter of magnificence" is an analogous term, referring in the first instance to the work produced, but by extension also to "the spending the magnificent man uses to produce a great work, and the money he uses on such a great building job, and the love of money the magnificent man moderates, in order not to hamper such a costly project" (ibid.).[51]

From this, Thomas develops a precise definition of the special virtue of magnificence. Its genus, according to Thomas, is "great works done for God and community," while its differentia narrows the "works" down to "expensive public projects" underwritten by magnificent patrons. Aquinas developed this sort of a formal definition, not to demonstrate his dialectical skill, but to uncover multiple, analogous senses of magnificence. Only in seeing its full range can one come to appreciate the essence of the virtue. In particular, this definition allowed Aquinas to fill out his account of magnificence in ways unknown to Aristotle, by comparing the specific sense of magnificence with two other virtues.

First, moving from magnificence conceived as a species to its genera reveals a highest genus, which is the broadest sense of the virtue. Accomplishing or executing (*executio*) the work is the second component of general courage. It must be added to confidence to produce the aggressive acts courage requires: "Now the second pertains to execution of the task; so that one will not be deficient in executing what was begun in confidence" (IIa IIae, q. 128, a. 1).[52] As confidence is the general analogue of the specific virtue of magnanimity, so accomplishment is the general analogue of the specific virtue of magnificence. In addition to the magnificence required to lavish vast sums on great works, then, Aquinas recognized its proximate genus, a broader sense of magnificence that issues in other sorts of "great" works. Beyond both of these, an even wider analogue becomes apparent—its highest genus: the ability to *accomplish* works or deeds set in the face of difficult obstacles. While this kind of magnificence is so thin that Aristotle would never have called it magnificence at all, Aquinas recognized the *formal* similarity between the general attribute of "accomplishing the deed" and the magnificence of the rich.

Focusing on the formal rather than the material aspect of magnificence reveals how magnificence is a part of courage, a relation never envisioned by Aristotle. The special virtue of magnificence is not a subjective part of courage because they do not deal with the same "matter." It is, however, a potential part *related* to courage "as a secondary virtue is related to its primary virtue" (IIa IIae, q. 135, a. 4).[53] The two virtues "agree" in "striving for what is arduous and difficult" in the face of obstacles to be overcome, an agreement that situates both virtues "in the emotional" part of the soul. They differ in the kind and amount of difficulty to be overcome. The difficulties magnificence faces—having the courage to spend money on expensive projects, for example—is "far less than danger to person."[54] Courage and magnificence, then, are formally similar while materially different, which places magnificence under the cardinal virtue of courage, as one of its potential parts (ibid.).

On the vices opposed to magnificence, Aquinas quoted Aristotle that the deficiency of the petty person is to "'lose the good' of a magnificent work 'for a trifle' he is unwilling to spend" (IIa IIae, q. 135, a. 1).[55] Aquinas's limited Greek did not allow him to understand Aristotle's terms for excess, nor their focus on the vulgar display of the rich. But Aquinas was not limited to textbooks for examples of the difference between magnificence and its opposites. In the case of King Louis IX of France, saint, patron of the Dominicans, and personal acquaintance of Aquinas, he had an exemplar of the kind of Christian magnificence sketched in the *Summa*. No finer example of the exercise of this virtue

could be found than the Sainte Chapelle, which Louis built around 1245 to hold the Crown of Thorns, just the time Aquinas arrived in Paris. In this regent, then, Aquinas had a Christian exemplar of magnificence, courage, *and* magnanimity.

Patience

If the treatise on magnificence is a finely sculpted arcade in Aquinas's intellectual cathedral, his study of patience is a corridor not entirely finished. No opposing vices are mentioned, even though impatience is familiar to all. Nor did Aquinas move from general to a more specialized sense of the virtue, but went directly to patience as a Christian virtue, even though he recognized a general sense of patience termed "enduring all kinds of evils" (*sustinentia quorumcumque malorum*) (IIa IIae, q. 136, a. 4, ad 1).

The reason for his focus may well be the scriptural answer to the question about patience uppermost in the mind of Aquinas: What is its matter? St. Paul addressed this issue when he said, "As it is, I rejoice, not because you were grieved, but because you were grieved into repenting; for you felt a godly grief, so that you suffered (*patiamini*) no loss through us. For godly grief (*tristitia*) produces a repentance that leads to salvation and brings no regret, but worldly grief (*saeculi tristitia*) produces death."[56]

Aquinas was as fascinated by etymologies as Aristotle and Heidegger. Patience (*patientia*) has the same root as *pati* (to suffer) and *passio*, the Aristotelian category that describes receiving the results of action. Understood etymologically, patience is the virtue of "suffering" well. St. Paul pointed out that the Corinthians had "suffered" grief (*tristitia*) at his hands. Grief or sorrow, then, is the proper "matter" of patience. Grief is a normal but not a necessary consequence of suffering evils, which distinguishes general from special patience. In the narrow sense, patience keeps the grief produced by an evil suffered from becoming overwhelming; while, speaking in a broader sense, patience helps one withstand evil, even when it does not produce feelings of grief.

St. Paul also led Aquinas to the belief that there are two diametrically opposed ways to deal with grief, which are bound to two fundamentally different ways of life (*vitae*). The *worldly* way had been well distilled in the high art of Hellenic culture, where the end of human life is death, the absolute dissolution of the human person. To react to the sorrow of death in a *godly* way, by contrast, opens up the true end of human life, salvation beyond the grave, achieved by means of repentance. What opens the second way is a specific virtue for "suffering well." If patience is the virtue that makes grief godly by turning one toward heavenly beatitude, the *special* virtue of patience, on Aquinas's conception of it, must be an infused, Christian virtue. In light of this, he immediately concluded that, "Patience, in so far as it is a virtue, is caused by charity. . . . From which it is clear that patience cannot be obtained without the help of grace" (IIa IIae, q. 136, a. 3).[57] Aquinas did not mean to deny the existence of a kind of secular patience—the kind Cicero knew; but in the end, such patience, like the grief it endures, is worldly and inadequate.

However, following St. Paul complicates matters for Thomas. Courage is situated in the emotions (the "irascible power" of the soul), while the "subject" power of grief is the desiring element (the "concupiscible power"), whose major virtue is temperance. Based on the part of the soul where it exists, it seems more reasonable to ally patience with temperance than with courage (IIa IIae, q. 136, a. 4, obj. 2). Aquinas responded that "the connection of one virtue with another is not due to their *subject*, but is due to their *matter* and form" (IIa IIae, q. 136, a. 4, ad 2).[58] While grief does exist in the desiring element, rather than the emotions, its matter and form show that patience is subordinate to courage. The *matter* of patience is not just any grief, but sorrows which lead us to "turn away from the good of virtue" (*recedat a bono virtutis*). It follows that, *formally* speaking, patience consists "in enduring what presently harms us" (*in patiendo quae praesentialiter nocent*) and therefore is an obstacle standing in the way of realizing our goals. This formal feature—overcoming obstacles—is what allies patience with courage. Because the fear of death is a greater obstacle than grief, courage is the superior virtue. Patience is attached as a subordinate virtue, even though patience

actually exists as a habit in a different region of the soul (ibid.).

One can see in the resolution of this objection a willingness to embrace both Plato and Aristotle that allowed Aquinas to develop an account of the virtues related to courage more subtle than anything found in his predecessors. The special virtues of Christian and secular patience have the same matter (grief) and form (endurance), though exercised for different ends. Special patience is different from special courage, as grief is different from death. The formality of enduring grief is clearly like enduring death, but only "like," contrary to Pieper. The two special virtues of patience and courage are similar in that "enduring evils" is a general sense of patience, which is a component part of resoluteness or the general virtue of courage. Seeing multiple virtues where Cicero had only seen one, and Aristotle had seen none at all, gives Aquinas a finely woven net with which to capture the subtleties of human moral life.

Perseverance

The last of the potential parts of courage is perseverance, and here Aquinas's sources seemed in complete disagreement. Aristotle omitted it from his list of virtues, and, in fact, even provided an argument that perseverance is not a virtue: "Continence is better than perseverance," and since "continence is not a virtue," it seems to follow *a fortiori* that perseverance cannot be a virtue (IIa IIae, q. 137, a. 1, obj. 1).[59] Ranged against the Philosopher were Cicero and Augustine, who had called perseverance "a gift of God" (*donum Dei*) (IIa IIae, q. 137, a. 4, *sed contra*).

Cicero had done a better job on perseverance than on patience. His definition of perseverance as "ongoing persistence (*perpetua permansio*) in a well-considered plan" points out its matter: "For persisting *for a long time* at something difficult contains its own special kind of difficulty; and therefore persisting for a long time at some good, until we accomplish it, pertains to a special virtue" (IIa IIae, q. 137, a. 1).[60] Exercising a specific virtue over a long period of time actually requires a second "specific virtue, whose job in the performance of these two or other virtuous deeds is to endure for as long a time as is necessary" (ibid.).[61]

To answer the Aristotelian objection that perseverance is not a virtue requires movement beyond a narrow sense of perseverance, because the objection envisions a kind of perseverance co-ordinate with continence, which is not a virtue. Continence and incontinence, sometimes called strength and weakness of will, are states between temperance and intemperance. The temperate person finds it easy to make the right choices about food, drink, and sex, because virtue has moderated desire for "necessities of life." On the other hand, the intemperate person consistently makes bad choices, because desire has not at all been moderated. Between the temperate and intemperate are people who struggle with strong desires. Those who do what is right are continent (*continens, egkrates*); those who do not are incontinent (*incontinens, akrates*). These intermediate states are neither virtuous nor vicious. If continent acts are extended over a long period of time, as virtuous acts can be, then continence should be accompanied by perseverance, as virtue is. But it would be incongruous to combine the virtue of perseverance with continence, which is not a virtue. Aquinas concluded that "if perseverance is understood in this way it is *not* a perfect virtue, but is *something imperfect in the genus of virtue*" (IIa IIae, q. 137, a. 1, ad 1).[62] This kind of perseverance is imperfect because it is neither a fully formed virtuous habit nor is it joined to another virtue. On the other hand, imperfect perseverance does help one achieve a good end by overcoming the difficulty of time. Clearly, the two senses of perseverance are analogous.

To these two senses of perseverance Aquinas then added two more. There are two types of ends: "one which is the end of an action, the other which is the end of human life."[63] The two kinds of perseverance thus far identified allow one to persevere to the *end of an action* (*finis operis*). The *end of human life* requires a special kind of perseverance, accompanying "virtues whose acts have to last for a whole life long," the theological virtues of "faith, hope, and charity" (IIa IIae, q. 137, a. 1, ad 1).[64] Because these virtues are infused, the perseverance which accompanies them must also derive from grace (IIa IIae, q. 137, a. 4). This third kind of perseverance, then, is a special and Christian virtue.

The last kind of perseverance involves the widest sense of the term. Perseverance is conceived here as a general virtue, a component part of the *general* virtue of courage. Aquinas thought this general virtue so important that he devoted a distinct article to it, and gave it a special name: constancy (*constantia*). It is similar to perseverance in that they both "agree in being about the end, since both concern resolutely persisting in some good" (IIa IIae, q. 137, a. 3).[65] The key difference is that the special virtue of perseverance is limited to its particular matter—actions that take a long time. "Constancy, however, makes one resolutely persist in the good, against difficulties which come from *all* other external impediments" (ibid.).[66] This makes constancy a general, formal aspect of good action. This widest sense of perseverance is important because, like the other attributes of the general cardinal virtue of courage, it must be present in *any* successful act.

Aquinas thus distinguished four analogous senses of perseverance: (1) The special and Christian virtue of perseverance is an infused habit whose matter concerns a whole life geared to beatitude, while its form is "preserving resoluteness against the difficulty of length of time" (IIa IIae, q. 137, a. 2, ad 1).[67] (2) Special and secular perseverance energizes other specific virtues to continue over long periods of time, until they reach their particular ends, like winning at Agincourt. (3) Imperfect perseverance allows one over time to develop virtuous habits in the first place, as the apprentice does. (4) Finally, constancy is part of any act that achieves its end. Chaucer's Wife of Bath and Clerk of Oxford can both be said to persevere in this broad sense, even if they were quite different in other respects.

After negotiating the details of Aquinas's treatise on courage, one might ask why he went to so much trouble to identify multiple senses of what is essentially the same virtue, especially in light of the fact that he himself professed to have little tolerance for "useless multiplication of questions, articles, and arguments" (Ia, Prol.).[68] Homer and Socrates, Plato and Aristotle, each focused only on the most outstanding human excellence. But between Aquinas and the ancients came Christianity, and as a Christian, Aquinas sought an all-inclusive moral continuum, one on which to place not just each and every human, but each and every human act. Only God can know every person so intimately, but the divine exemplar of moral knowledge led Aquinas to try to develop an all-encompassing vision of the hierarchy of the virtues and vices.[69] To establish this hierarchy, Aquinas employed Platonic division and collection to develop genus-species trees as a means of understanding the virtues in detail. His guiding principle for generating definitions was to distinguish the two senses of the cardinal virtues, and in this way what was peripheral for Albert became central to Thomas's ethics. An important result is that Aquinas was more successful than many of his disciples or predecessors at avoiding the extremes of an ethics of mere intention, as could be found in Abelard, or an ethics of pure consequentialism, a view he did not find in books, but which was certainly familiar to him from growing up in a family willing to use whatever means necessary—including the celebrated courtesan—to try to keep him away from the Dominicans. The general cardinal virtues show that a truly moral act must succeed in achieving its end, while the special cardinal virtues show that a truly moral act must follow the standards of the moral law, in intention as well as execution and results.

Just as it is better that a human both will the good and do it with an exterior action, so it pertains to the perfection of the moral good that a human be moved to the good not only by the will but also by the sense appetite, as is said in Psalm 84:2: "My heart and my flesh exalt in the living God," where we take "heart" as intellectual appetite and "flesh" as sensitive appetite (Ia IIae, q. 24, a. 3).[70]

Notes

[1]Cited, *inter alia*, in Pl. *Tht.* 152a, in F. M. Cornford, trans., *The Collected Dialogues of Plato*, ed. Edith Hamilton and Huntington Cairns (Princeton: Princeton University Press, 1973), 859.
[2]Xen. *Mem.* 3.9.5.
[3]Xen. *Mem.* 3.9.4.
[4]Pl. *Lach.* 196d.
[5]Pl. *Resp.* 4 (443e5–444a1).

[6]Pl. *Resp.* 4 (445c5–7).
[7]Arist. *Eth. Nic.* 3.6 (111a15, 19).
[8]Arist. *Eth. Nic.* 3.8 (1116a16–17).
[9]Arist. *Eth. Nic.* 3.8 (1116a14–b2).
[10]Arist. *Eth. Nic.* 6.13 (1144b30–2).
[11]Cic. *Inv. rhet.* 2.53.159: "Nam virtus est animi habitus naturae modo atque rationi consentaneus."
[12]Cic. *Inv. rhet.*, 2.54.163: "Fortitudo est considerata periculorum susceptio et laborum perpessio. Eius partes magnificentia, fidentia, patientia, perseverantia. Magnificentia est rerum magnarum et excelsarum cum animi ampla quadam et splendida propositione cogitatio atque administratio; fidentia est per quam magnis et honestis in rebus multum ipse animus in se fiduciae certa cum spe collocavit; patientia est honestatis aut utilitatis causa rerum arduum ac difficilium voluntaria ac diuturna perpessio; perseverantia est in ratione bene considerata stabilis et perpetua permansio."
[13]Ambrose, *De excesu fratris Satyri* 1.57: "Superest, ut ad conclusionem cardinalium virtutum etiam iustitiae partes in eo debeamus adverter" (CSEL 73, 239). See P. G. W. Glare, *Oxford Latin Dictionary* (Oxford: Clarendon, 1982), 276; Lewis and Short, *A Latin Dictionary* (Oxford: Clarendon, 1879), 291; P. Courcelle, *Recherches sur les Confessions de S. Augustin* (Paris: E. de Boccard, 1968), 323.
[14]Ambrose, *Expositio evangelii secundum Lucam* 5. 63: "Conexae igitur sibi sunt concatenataeque uirtutes, ut qui *unam* habet plures habere uideatur, et sanctis *una* conpetit uirtus, sed eius quae fuerit uberior uberius est praemium" (CCSL 14, 157, 677–80; emphasis added).
[15]August. *De moribus ecclesiae* 15.25: "Quod si virtus ad beatam vitam nos ducit, nihil omnino esse virtutem affirmaverim nisi summum amorem Dei. Namque illud quod quadripartita dicitur virtus, ex ipsius amoris vario quodam affectu, quantum intelligo, dicitur" (PL 32, 1322).
[16]Albert, *In Nic. Eth.* 2.6 (Kübel, 120): "(3) Praeterea, Tullius dicit, quod quattuor, quae sunt in operibus virtutum, vindicant sibi quattuor virtutes, quia scire, quod requiritur, vindicat sibi prudentia; strenuitatem, ut firmiter operetur, vindicat sibi fortitudo; medium temperantia; rectitudinem iustitia; et sic medium non est aequaliter in omnibus. . . . Ad tertium dicendum, quod illa quattuor proprie sunt in omnibus, sed appropriantur uni vel alteri secundum convenientiam ad materiam cuiuslibet virtutis, nec est eadem strenuitas, quae est propria fortitudinis et quae convenit omnibus, quia propria fortitudinis est in aggressione difficilium passionum et communis est in strenuitate operandi secundum virtutem." See also *In III Sent.* d. 36, a. 1 (Borgnet, 28:666–67). See O. Lottin, "Les vertus cardinales et leur ramifications chez les théologiens de 1230 à 1250" in *Psychologie et morale aux XIIe et XIIIe siècles*,

vol. 3 (Louvain: Abbaye du Mont César, 1949), 154–94.

[17]See Servais Pinckaers, *The Sources of Christian Ethics*, trans. Sr. Mary Noble (Washington, DC: Catholic University of America Press, 1995), 230–32, on how Catholic theologians later lost sight of the cardinal virtues. On analogous senses of the virtues, see Lee Yearly, *Mencius and Aquinas* (Albany: State University of New York Press, 1990), 32–36.

[18]Josef Pieper, *The Four Cardinal Virtues* (Notre Dame, IN: University of Notre Dame Press, 1965), 117.

[19]*In VII Met.*, lect. 9, n. 1467: "forma totius quae significatur nomine humanitatis, et forma partis, quae significatur nomine animae…" (Marietti, 358) See A. A. Maurer, *Thomas Aquinas. On Being and Essence*, 2d ed. (Toronto: Pontifical Institute of Medieval Studies, 1968), 31, n. 7.

[20]"Causa namque formalis virtutis, sicut et cuiuslibet rei, accipitur ex eius genere et differentia."

[21]ST Ia IIae, q. 55, a. 4: "Materia autem circa quam est obiectum virtutis."

[22]For example, Bonaventure, Henry of Ghent, and Scotus. See B. Kent, *Virtues of the Will* (Washington, DC: Catholic University of America Press, 1995), 200.

[23]"Principium enim formale virtutis, de qua nunc loquimur, est rationis bonum."

[24]*De virt. card.*, a. 1: "Haec igitur quatuor scilicet cognitio dirigens, rectitudo, firmitas et moderatio, etsi in omnibus virtuosis actibus requirantur" (Marietti, 815).

[25]On executing the deed, see ST IIa IIae, q. 128, a. 1. For enduring evils, see IIa IIae, q. 136, a. 4, ad 1. For constancy, see IIa IIae, q. 137, a. 3.

[26]"triplex est pars: scilicet integralis, ut paries, tectum, et fundamentum sunt partes domus; subiectiva, sicut bos et leo sunt partes animalis; et potentialis, sicut nutritivum et sensitivum sunt partes animae."

[27]Speaking of confidence and magnificence in particular, Aquinas says: "Haec ergo duo si coarctentur ad propriam materiam fortitudinis, scilicet ad pericula mortis, erunt quasi partes integrales ipsius, sine quibus fortitudo esse non potest; si autem referantur ad aliquas alias materias, in quibus est minus difficultatis, erunt virtutes distinctae a fortitudine secundum speciem suam, tamen adiungentur ei sicut secundarium principali." He then repeats the same conclusion about patience and perseverance: "Haec etiam duo si coarctentur ad propriam materiam fortitudinis, erunt partes quasi integrales ipsius: si autem ad quascumque materias difficiles referantur, erunt virtutes a fortitudine distinctae; et tamen ei adiungentur sicut secundariae principali."

[28]*De virt. card.*, a. 1, ad 1: "una harum conditionum ad veram virtutis rationem non sufficit nisi

omnes praedictae conditiones concurrant." (Marietti, 815).

[29]*De virt. card.*, a. 2: "Si autem accipiamus virtutes perfectas in secundo respectu boni humani, sic connectuntur per prudentiam; quia sine prudentia nulla virtus moralis esse potest, nec prudentia haberi potest, si cui deficiat moralis virtus. Si tamen accipiamus quatuor cardinales virtutes, secundum quod important generales conditiones virtutum, secundum hoc habent connexionem, ex hoc quod non sufficit ad aliquem actum virtutis quod adsit una harum conditionum, nisi omnes adsint" (Marietti, 819).

[30]The bank robber example comes from J. Porter, *Moral Action and Christian Ethics* (Cambridge: Cambridge University Press, 1995), 160. Her erroneous conclusion that "the cardinal virtues, considered as *specific* and discrete virtues, are *all* necessarily present in the character of the truly virtuous person," comes from insufficiently distinguishing general from special cardinal virtues.

[31]See Arist. *Eth. Nic.* 3.6 (1115a34–b7).

[32]"fortitudo bene se habet in omnibus adversis tolerandis; non tamen ex toleratione quorumlibet adversorum reputatur homo *simpliciter* fortis, sed solum ex hoc quod bene tolerat etiam maxima mala; ex aliis autem dicitur homo fortis *secundum quid*."

[33]"Pericula autem mortis quae sunt ex aegritudine, vel ex tempestate maris, vel ex incursu latronum, vel si qua alia sunt huiusmodi, *non* videntur alicui *directe* imminere ex hoc quod prosequatur aliquod bonum. Sed pericula mortis, quae sunt in bellicis, *directe* imminent homini propter aliquod bonum, in quantum videlicet defendit bonum commune per iustum bellum."

[34]"martyres sustinent personales impugnationes propter summum bonum, quod est Deus; ideo eorum fortitudo praecipue commendatur. Nec est extra genus fortitudinis quae est circa bellica, unde dicuntur fortes facti in bello."

[35]"Et sic martyrium comparatur ad fidem sicut ad finem in quo aliquis confirmatur; ad fortitudinem autem sicut ad habitum elicientem."

[36]"Et secundum hoc patet quod martyrium inter caeteros actus humanos est perfectius secundum suum genus, quasi maxime charitatis signum, secundum illud Joan. 15,13: Maiorem charitatem nemo habet quam ut animam suam ponat quis pro amicis suis."

[37]ST IIa IIae, q. 124, a. 4: "Et ideo ad perfectam rationem martyrii requiritur quod aliquis mortem sustineat propter Christum." See also Arist. *Eth. Nic.* 3.6 (1115a23–34).

[38]"et sic sunt speciales virtutes contra alias divisae."

[39]"Ad actum autem aggrediendi duo requiruntur, quorum primum pertinet ad animi praeparationem,

ut scilicet aliquis promptum animum habeat ad aggrediendum, et quantum ad hoc ponit Tullius fiduciam."

[40]"Sic ergo patet quod magnanimitas convenit cum fortitudine, inquantum confirmat animum circa aliquid arduum; deficit autem ab ea in hoc quod confirmat animum in eo circa quod facilius est firmitatem servare."

[41]"Sed magnanimitas opponitur humilitati: nam 'magnanimus se dignum reputat magnis, et alios contemnit'."

[42]See also Arist. *Eth. Nic.* 3.4 (1124b13–30).

[43]Dante, *Inferno* 4.112–23, emphasis mine. "Genti v'eran con occhi tardi e gravi, /di grande autorità ne' lor sembianti: /parlavan rado, con voci soavi. . . . Colà diritto, sopra 'l verde smalto, /mi fur mostrati li spiriti magni, che del vedere in me stesso n'essalto. I' vidi Elettra con molti compagni, /tra' quai conobbi Ettòr ed Enea, /Cesare armato con li occhi grifagni."

[44]See Arist. *Eth. Nic.* 4.2 (1123b16).

[45]"in homine invenitur aliquid magnum, quod ex dono Dei possidet; et aliquis defectus, qui competit ei ex infirmitate naturae. Magnanimitas ergo facit quod homo se magnis dignificet secundum considerationem donorum quae possidet ex Deo; sicut si habet magnam virtutem animi, magnanimitas facit quod ad perfecta opera virtutis tendat: et similiter est dicendum de usu cuiuslibet alterius boni, puta scientiae, vel exterioris fortunae. Humilitas autem facit quod homo seipsum parvipendat, secundum considerationem proprii defectus. . . . Et sic patet quod magnanimitas et humilitas non sunt contraria, quamvis in contraria tendere videantur, quia procedunt secundum diversas considerationes." See also *In III Sent.*, d. 33, q. 2, a. 1, sol. 4, ad 2 et 3, (Moos, 1050, 167–1051, 170).

[46]"servus qui acceptam pecuniam domini sui fodit in terram, nec est operatus ex ea propter quemdam pusillanimitatis timorem, punitur a domino."

[47]"Ambitio autem importat inordinatum appetitum honoris."

[48]"qui videlicet appetitum gloriae suae non refert in debitum finem, puta ad honorem Dei, vel proximi salutem."

[49]Arist. *Eth. Nic.* 4.1 (1119b26–27).

[50]"Quod autem pertinet ad personam uniuscuiusque, est aliquid parvum in comparatione ad id quod convenit rebus divinis, vel rebus communibus."

[51]"Et ideo materia magnificentiae possunt dici et ipsi sumptus, quibus utitur magnificus ad opus magnum faciendum, et ipsa pecunia qua utitur ad sumptus magnos faciendos, et amor pecuniae, quem moderatur magnificus, ne sumptus magni impediatur."

[52]"Secundum autem pertinet ad operis executionem, ne scilicet aliquis deficiat in executione illorum quae fiducialiter inchoavit."

[53]"magnificentia, secundum quod est specialis virtus, non potest poni pars subiectiva fortitudinis, quia non convenit cum ea in materia; sed ponitur pars eius, inquantum adiungitur ei sicut virtus secundaria principali."

[54]"arduum autem in quod tendit magnificentia, habet difficultatem propter dispendium rerum, quod est multo minus quam periculum personae."

[55]"Unde Philosophus dicit quod 'parvificus maxima consumens, in parvo' scilicet quod non vult expendere, 'bonum perdit' scilicet magnifici operis."

[56]2 Cor 7:9–10 (RSV).

[57]"Unde manifestum est quod patientia, secundum quod est virtus, a charitate causatur, secundum illud 1 Cor. 13,4 'Charitas patiens est.' Manifestum est autem quod charitas non potest haberi nisi per gratiam."

[58]"adiunctio virtutis ad virtutem non attenditur secundum subiectum, sed secundum materiam vel formam."

[59]"ut Philosophus dicit, continentia est potior quam perserverantia. Sed continentia non est virtus, ut dicitur. Ergo perseverantia non est virtus."

[60]"nam hoc ipsum quod est diu insistere alicui difficili, specialem difficultatem habet."

[61]"ita etiam perseverantia est quaedam specialis virtus, ad quam pertinet in his vel in aliis virtuosis operibus diuturnitatem sustinere, prout necesse est."

[62]"Et ideo si accipiatur hoc modo perseverantia, non est virtus perfecta, sed est quoddam imperfectum in genere virtutis."

[63]"Est autem duplex finis: unus quidem qui est finis operis; alius autem qui est finis humanae vitae."

[64]"Sunt autem quaedam virtutes quarum actus per totam vitam debent durare; sicut fidei, spei, et charitatis, quia respiciunt ultimum finem totius vitae humanae."

[65]"Perseverantia et constantia conveniunt quidem in finem, quia ad utrumque pertinet firmiter persistere in aliquo bono."

[66]"Constantia autem facit firmiter persistere in bono contra difficultatem, quae provenit ex quibuscumque aliis exterioribus impedimentis."

[67]"Licet perseverantia magis videatur convenire in materia cum temperantia quam cum fortitudine; tamen in modo magis convenit cum fortitudine, inquantum firmitatem servat contra difficultatem diuturnitatis."

[68]"Propter multiplicationem inutilium queastionum, articulorum et argumentorum."

[69]We should not forget the practical purpose this part of the *Summa* had for Dominican confessors and preachers. See Leonard E. Boyle, *The Setting of*

the Summa (Toronto: Pontifical Institute of Medieval Studies, 1982); Leonard E. Boyle, this volume, pp. 1–16.

[70]"Sicut igitur melius est quod homo et velit bonum, et faciat exteriori actu; ita etiam ad perfectionem boni moralis pertinet quod homo ad bonum moveatur non solum secundum voluntatem, sed etiam secundum appetitum sensitivum, secundum illud quod Psal. 83,3 dicitur: 'Cor meum et caro mea exultaverunt in Deum vivum,' ut cor accipiamus pro appetitu intellectivo, carnem autem pro appetitu sensitivo."

Selected Further Reading

Bañez, Dominic, O.P. *Scholastica commentaria in secundam secundae*, qq. 47–189. Salamanca, 1586.

Bullet, G. *Vertus morales infuses et vertus morales acquises selon saint Thomas d'Aquin*. Fribourg: Éditions Universitaires, 1958.

Cajetan, Thomas de Vio, O.P. In *Secunda secundae summae theologiae Sancti Thomae Aquinatis cum commentariis cardinalis Caietani*. Vol. 10. Rome: Leonina, 1899.

Casey, John. *Pagan Virtue*. Oxford: Clarendon, 1990.

Cessario, Romanus. *The Moral Virtues and Theological Ethics*. Notre Dame, IN: University of Notre Dame Press, 1991.

Eschmann, I. T., O.P. *The Ethics of Saint Thomas Aquinas: Two Courses*. Ed. E. A. Synan. Toronto: Pontifical Institute of Medieval Studies, 1997.

Farrell, Walter, O.P. *A Companion to the Summa*. Vol. 3: *The Fullness of Life* (Corresponding to *Summa theologiae*, IIa IIae). New York: Sheed and Ward, 1940.

Fathers of the English Dominican Province, trans. *St. Thomas Aquinas: Summa Theologica*. New York: Benziger, 1948.

Folghera, J.-D., O.P., trans. *Somme theologique. La force. 2a–2ae, qq. 123–140*. Paris: Desclée, 1926.

Gauthier, R.-A. *Magnanimité*. Paris: Vrin, 1951.

Geach, Peter T. *The Virtues*. Cambridge: Cambridge University Press, 1977.

Gilson, E. *The Christian Philosophy of St. Thomas Aquinas*. Trans. L. K. Shook. New York: Random House, 1956.

Kent, Bonnie. *Virtues of the Will: The Transformation of Ethics in the Late Thirteenth Century*. Washington, DC: Catholic University of America Press, 1995.

Lottin, Odon, OSB. *Psychologie et morale aux XIIe and XIIIe siècles*. Vol. 3. Gembloux: J. Duculot and Louvain: Abbaye du Mont César, 1949.

Pieper, Josef. *The Four Cardinal Virtues*. Notre Dame, IN: University of Notre Dame Press, 1965.

Pinckaers, Servais. *The Sources of Christian Ethics*. Trans. Sr. Mary Thomas Noble. Washington, DC: Catholic University of America Press, 1995.

Ross, Anthony, O.P., and P. G. Walsh, trans. *Summa theologiae*. Vol. 42. New York: McGraw-Hill and London: Eyre and Spottiswoode, 1966.

Yearly, Lee H. *Mencius and Aquinas: Theories of Virtue and Conceptions of Courage*. Albany: State University of New York Press, 1990.

The Virtue of Temperance
(IIa IIae, qq. 141–170)

Diana Fritz Cates

Human bodies and minds need nourishment. Wholesome foods are necessary goods; without them, people suffer, sicken, and die. Yet for many who have access to these goods, eating poses problems. Ingesting food is so abhorrent to some that they become unwilling and unable to eat anything—in the midst of bounty, they starve to death. For others, ingesting food provides such intense pleasure (or relief from pain) that they will not and cannot stop eating; as they become increasingly obese, they succumb to life-threatening diseases. It is ironic that something so good for humans can become a source of so much debilitation.

Since ancient times, physicians of the soul have taught that functioning well as a human being requires learning to desire, use, and enjoy sensible goods "in the right way." But what is it to have rightly ordered appetites? Thomas Aquinas pursues this question in his treatise on "temperance" in the *Summa theologiae*, IIa IIae, qq. 141–70. This chapter provides a descriptive analysis of the treatise, focusing on three matters: the nature of "temperance" as a virtue, the standard relative to which appetitive excellence is determined, and the main species of temperance, which order desires for food, drink (especially alcohol), and sexual relations. Given the alarming number of people in the modern age suffering from anorexia, bulimia, obesity, alcoholism, drug addiction, sexual addictions, and so many other ills that reflect disordered appetites, it is worth considering whether Thomas's view discloses a path to serenity.

In brief, Thomas defines temperance as a virtue that moderates the affections of the soul (IIa IIae, q. 141, a. 3). Temperance moderates movements of the sense appetite, in particular, by keeping them consonant with the order of reason and divine law (IIa IIae, q. 141, a. 2, ad 1; IIa IIae, q. 141, a. 4). Temperance orders the strongest sense desires and pleasures known to humans, namely, those associated with eating, drinking, and sexual activity (IIa IIae, q. 141, a. 4). The aim of temperance is to ensure that one's desires for, and one's use and enjoyment of, food, drink, and sexual relations are consistent with the preservation of the individual and the species (q. 141, a. 5). The aim is also to ensure that one's engagement with these sensible goods exhibits moral and spiritual beauty or honor (IIa IIae, q. 141, a. 2, ad 3). Temperance is a virtue that restrains powerful impulses that threaten the appetitive integrity of the soul, but more than this, temperance is a virtue whose exercise partly constitutes tranquility and joy (IIa IIae, q. 141, a. 2, ad 2; Ia IIae, q. 31, a. 3).

THE VIRTUE OF TEMPERANCE

In naming temperance a virtue, Thomas identifies it as a habit concerned with choosing both to act and to feel in accordance with the mean, located between the extremes of excess and deficiency, where the mean is defined with reference to the rule of practical wisdom (Ia IIae, q. 59, a. 1). In its infused form, temperance is a gratuitously granted habit concerned with choosing in accordance with the rule of divine wisdom (Ia IIae, q. 63, a. 4).[1] Whether acquired or infused, temperance is a deliberately cultivated, stable disposition to respond well to certain objects of experience. It is partly a disposition to respond well in action, but Thomas's main concern is with the affective dimension of our responsiveness.

Temperance is a disposition to be well-moved. Thomas says that temperance is "about desires and pleasures" (*circa concupiscentiam et delectationem*) (IIa IIae, q. 141, a. 3). It is about the way in which one is drawn toward certain objects that one apprehends as good (IIa IIae, q. 141, a. 3, ad 2), and it is about the pleasure that attends this movement. Temperance is about the pleasure of anticipation as well as the pleasure of attaining the object of desire.[2] According to Thomas, pleasure can be experienced "becomingly" or "unbecomingly," depending on whether it supervenes on the desire for or the attainment of a genuine good or on a merely apparent good, and depending on whether, all things considered, its vehemence, duration, and the like are appropriate to the situation (IIa IIae, q. 142, a. 2; Ia IIae, q. 34, a. 2).

Temperance is about the desires and pleasures that are elicited by objects of sense experience. In Thomas's scheme, the human appetite is divided into the intellective and sense appetites. The "intellective appetite" is the power by which one tends toward (or away from) and enjoys (or experiences pain over) an object that one apprehends, via a judgment of reason, to be good (or bad) (Ia, q. 80, a. 2, ad 2). The "sense appetite" is the power by which a person tends toward (or away from) and takes delight in (or is pained by) an object that one apprehends with the senses to be delectable (or detestable) in its particularity (Ia, q. 81, a. 2). The sense appetite includes the concupiscible and irascible appetites (ibid.). The "concupiscible appetite" is the power "through which the soul is simply inclined to seek what is suitable, according to the senses, and to fly from what is hurtful."[3] Temperance is the cardinal ordering principle of this power. The "irascible appetite" is the power that inclines one to resist obstacles that keep one from seeking what one takes to be suitable or avoiding what one takes to be harmful. "Fortitude," "the virtue that strengthens against dangers of death," is the cardinal ordering principle of this power (Ia IIae, q. 61, a. 3).[4]

Food, drink, and sexual contact are objects of the concupiscible sense appetite. With Aristotle, Thomas holds that the pleasures associated with these goods are best construed as pleasures of touch. Food, drink, and sexual contact are all "attained by the touch" (*in tangendo*) (IIa IIae, q. 141, a. 5). To be sure, humans ordinarily attain sensible goods via the concurrent engagement of several different senses; however, for Thomas, the sense of touch is basic. "The principal thing," he says, is the tactile use "of the necessary means [of preservation], of the woman who is necessary for the preservation of the species, or of food and drink which are necessary for the preservation of the individual."[5] Perception of sensible features like "beauty and adornment in woman, and a pleasing savor and likewise odor in food" can increase an experience of pleasure, but the pleasure remains essentially one of touch (ibid.).[6] Thomas seems to take for granted the folk wisdom to which Aristotle appeals in his reflections on this matter. Aristotle remarks that "gluttons pray for long throats, not for long tongues."[7]

Temperance is the disposition that orders desires and pleasures connected to the use of food, drink, and sexual relations. Following Aristotle, Thomas holds that pleasure is a feeling that accompanies the proper functioning of the human organism (Ia IIae, q. 32, a. 1; IIa IIae, q. 142, a. 1). Because it is proper for humans to use food, drink, and sexual relations for the preservation of self and species, it is proper to feel pleasure in eating, drinking, and sexual activity. It is proper, however, only if this pleasure is felt in a distinctively human way. Thomas notes that, all too commonly, humans experience pleasure in the manner of simple brutes (IIa IIae, q. 142, a. 4); they are easily induced to forsake "the rule of reason and Divine law" (*regula rationis et legis divinae*; IIa IIae, q. 141, a. 2, ad 1). To avoid debasement, humans must not be led by their noses in the use and enjoyment of sensibles; rather, they must be led by reason—ideally, reason formed by faith, hope, and charity. Humans must use the power of reason to bridle their impulses and the feelings of pleasure that attend them (IIa IIae, q. 141, a. 3, ad 2).

Much of what Thomas says about temperance suggests that, for him, temperance is a habit of responding to enticing sense impressions, less with rightly ordered desires and pleasures of touch, and more with a second-order desire defensively to restrict and repress appetitive movements that threaten reason's rule. It sometimes seems that, for Thomas, temperance is a habit of undergoing tightly reined movements of the appetite while feeling the accompanying pleasure of being "in control." There are good reasons, however, for questioning the adequacy of this reading (and for distinguishing Thomas's account from Puritan accounts of temperance). First, Thomas follows Aristotle in distinguishing the temperate and the merely continent person. According to Aristotle, "the continent and the temperate person are both the sort to do nothing in conflict with reason because of bodily pleasures; but the continent person has base appetites, and the temperate person lacks them. The temperate person is the sort to find nothing pleasant that conflicts with reason; the continent is the sort to find such things pleasant but not to be led by them."[8]

Thomas echoes Aristotle: "continence has something of the nature of a virtue, insofar . . . as the reason stands firm in opposition to the passions, lest it be led astray by them: yet it does not attain to the perfect nature of a moral virtue, by which even the sensitive appetite is subject to reason so that vehement passions contrary to reason do not arise in the sensitive appetite" (IIa IIae, q. 155, a. 1).[9] In other words, the temperate person's desires and pleasures are so well-ordered that he or she does not have to struggle to keep them in line. In contrast, the continent person must fight unruly impulses. The continent person is successful in his or her struggles, but the very fact that he or she struggles indicates the lack of rational order in the soul. To characterize temperance as a habit of struggling against temptations to excessive pleasure, then, reduces it to continence.

Beyond this, and in a more positive vein, Thomas indicates that temperance is a habit of responding to sense impressions of food, drink, and sexual relations with desires and pleasures that are beautiful. The desires and pleasures of the temperate person exhibit "a certain moderate and fitting proportion" (IIa IIae, q. 141, a. 2, ad 3).[10] They are internally well-balanced and coordinated relative to the end of excellent human functioning. The desires and pleasures of the temperate person also reflect the dignity of rational animality. One displays the honor peculiar to a

human being when that person experiences desire and pleasure, not in a brutish or slavish way, but in the mode of reflective awareness and rational governance (IIa IIae, q. 141, a. 1, ad 1; Ia IIae, q. 31, a. 5).

G. Simon Harak provides an example of the beauty that is evident in the pleasure of the person of Thomistic temperance: "I had a friend who described once the delight of biting into a freshly picked, vine-grown tomato. When, from within that delight, she reflects on the generosity of God, on God's giving her the ability to delight in this tomato, on God's nurturance of the whole world, she experiences joy. She has found the meaning of her delight. And that, for Thomas, would be rational, human, moral passion."[11] This is not an intellectualization that distracts from the fullness of bodily pleasure; rather, it is a reflection that enhances the pleasure by extending it to several levels of human operation and awareness at once, by allowing it to resonate throughout the various dimensions of the self.

Finally, Thomas indicates that temperance is a habit of responding with tranquility or serenity of soul to sense impressions of food, drink, and sexual relations (IIa IIae, q. 141, a. 2, ad 2). Serenity describes a state that is, negatively, free of distress. It also describes a state that is, positively, characterized by pleasure, especially the pleasure of feeling and knowing that one's appetites are in good working order.

Thomistic temperance is best construed as a habit of being consistently moved and pleased in a beautiful and honorable manner by attractive objects of sense experience. Again, it is not primarily a defensive habit of controlling one's appetites. Nevertheless, Thomas repeatedly sounds an alarm when describing temperance relative to its absence. He urges vigilance, for he is convinced that human habits of desire influence all human encounters with reality. They influence perceptions of particulars, reflections concerning the moral significance of these particulars, and deliberations about how to respond to items of perceived significance (Ia IIae, q. 9, a. 2; Ia IIae, q. 13, a. 1; Ia IIae, q. 77, a. 1).[12] If one's appetites become disordered—if one repeatedly succumbs to powerful impulses to touch sensibles in pleasing but detrimental ways—then one becomes disposed

324 Diana Fritz Cates

to seek what is bad under the impression that it is good. When this happens, one loses the ability to discern this distortion in one's vision and love of the good. One thus sinks ever deeper into confusion and compulsion. Thomas says that disordered pleasures "dim the light of reason from which all the clarity and beauty of virtue arises: wherefore these pleasures are described as being most slavish" (IIa IIae, q. 142, a. 4).[13]

Some fear of going to the bad is fitting in those whose moral and spiritual excellence is insecure. Thomas says that "shamefacedness" (*verecundia*) is an "integral part" (*pars integralis*) of temperance: "wherefore Ambrose says (*De Offic.* i.43) that 'shamefacedness lays the first foundation of temperance,' by inspiring [persons] with the horror of whatever is disgraceful" (IIa IIae, q. 144, a. 4, ad 4).[14] To be more specific, Thomistic shamefacedness takes two related objects. It is first a fear of being base. It is second a fear of being perceived by others to be base and thus deserving of scorn (IIa IIae, q. 144, a. 1, ad 2; IIa IIae, q. 144, a. 2). Shamefacedness does not move anyone to pursue beautifully ordered desires for their own sake, but it moves persons to avoid manifestations of unruly desire in order to avoid reproach from members of the community whose opinion matters to them.[15] For Thomas, this is a step in the right direction.

Thomas complements shamefacedness with another integral part of temperance, namely, "honesty" (*honestas*). Honesty refers to an honorable state, that is, a state of being worthy of honor principally on account of one's excellence. It refers to a state that is fittingly perceived as beautiful: "beauty or comeliness results from the concurrence of clarity and due proportion. For . . . God is said to be beautiful, as being the cause of the harmony and clarity of the universe" (IIa IIae, q. 145, a. 2).[16] Accordingly, "spiritual beauty consists in a [person's] conduct or actions being well proportioned in respect of the spiritual clarity of reason" (ibid.).[17] Thomas seems to have in mind a more specific notion of honesty as well (IIa IIae, q. 145, a. 4, ad 1). Honesty is partly a state of having beautifully configured habits of desire. Thomas's coupling of honesty with shamefacedness suggests that honesty is a state of regarding the moral and spiritual beauty of appetitive recti-

tude, particularly within oneself, as intrinsically delightful (IIa IIae, q. 145, a. 1, ad 3; IIa IIae, q. 145, a. 2, ad 1). An honest person is one who takes joy in expressing with "open-facedness" what is good or fine.[18] Such a person is disposed to be temperate, not out of a fear of disgrace, but out of a love for the beauty of temperance (IIa IIae, q. 143, a. 1).

THE RULE OF TEMPERANCE

Temperance is thus a habit of being rightly pleased as one is drawn toward the use and enjoyment of food, drink, and sexual relations. Understanding further the nature of temperance *qua* virtue requires specifying what it is to be rightly pleased. According to Thomas, appetitive rectitude is determined with reference to the rule of reason and divine law. Reason and divine law concur that human appetites are well-ordered when they direct a person toward the end proper to human beings. In general, this end consists in happiness (IIa IIae, q. 141, a. 6, ad 1).[19] Humans are oriented toward a twofold happiness, namely, a natural, imperfect form of happiness and perfect, supernatural happiness (Ia IIae, q. 5, a. 5).[20] Natural happiness consists in Aristotelian *eudaimonia*, which is "a sort of living well and doing well in action."[21] It is the enjoyment of natural perfection in the operations of thinking, feeling, willing, and acting, aided by the use of certain external goods (Ia IIae, q. 3, a. 2, ad 3; Ia IIae, q. 4, a. 7).[22] Supernatural happiness consists in the beatific vision, which is the enjoyment of supernatural perfection in the divinely assisted operations of knowing and loving God. Such happiness can be experienced proleptically in this life, in friendship with God, but it can be experienced fully only in the life to come (Ia IIae, q. 3, a. 2, ad 4). To say that appetitive rightness is determined with reference to reason and divine law is thus to say that appetites are well-ordered inasmuch as their movements contribute to natural and supernatural human perfection (IIa IIae, q. 141, a. 6, ad 1).

Appetitive rectitude with respect to food, drink, and sexual relations is a consistent desiring and enjoying of these goods in a way that conduces to the good functioning of the human organism and the human community as a whole. For Thomas, proper functioning requires minimally the preservation of self and species (IIa IIae, q. 141, aa. 4–5). "Wherefore temperance takes the need of this life, as the rule of the pleasurable objects of which it makes use" (IIa IIae, q. 141, a. 6).[23] Thomas says, however, that the need of this life may be taken in two ways (IIa IIae, q. 141, a. 6, ad 2). It may be taken for biological necessity, so that reason and divine law require desiring, using, and enjoying objects without which individuals and communities literally could not survive. It may also be taken for "something without which a thing cannot be becomingly," so that reason and divine law permit desiring, using, and enjoying more than what is necessary for individual and collective survival, as long as certain guidelines are followed (ibid.).[24]

First, nonnecessary items of sense must be desired, used, and enjoyed in a way that does not undermine "health or a sound condition of body" (ibid.).[25] According to Thomas, human knowledge, including moral knowledge, is caused partly by sensory perception, which takes place in and through changes in bodily organs (Ia q. 78, a. 4; Ia, q. 84, aa. 6–8). Human passion, which is partly a responsiveness to perceived value, also occurs via corporeal transmutation (Ia IIae, q. 22, a. 2, ad 3). Furthermore, the body as a whole is the organ with which one enacts the moral insight that one attains. Keeping the body in the best condition possible is thus basic to the pursuit of human excellence. For Thomas, "it is clear that [one] can be hindered, by indisposition of the body, from every operation of virtue" (Ia IIae, q. 4, a. 6).[26]

Keeping the body in good operating condition is necessary for attaining supernatural, as well as natural, perfection. To underscore the importance of this, Thomas quotes Augustine: "if the body be such, that the governance thereof is difficult and burdensome, like unto flesh which is corruptible and weighs upon the soul, the mind is turned away from that vision of the highest heaven" (De genesi ad litteram, 12.35).[27] Thomas conceives of the human being as a soul-body composite, and whenever the higher—for Thomas, the more intellectual—powers of the composite are functioning well, feelings of pleasure are generated that resonate throughout the whole of the

person, including the body. The body must be in sound condition if it is to resound well with this pleasure (Ia IIae, q. 24, a. 3, ad 1; IIa IIae, q. 25, a. 5, ad 2).[28]

Second, nonnecessary sensibles must be desired, used, and enjoyed "according to the demands of place and time, and in keeping with those among whom one dwells" (IIa IIae, q. 141, a. 6, ad 2).[29] A becoming engagement with sensible goods is one that accords with the dictates of practical wisdom or prudence (prudentia). A prudent person discerns that a given end ought to be promoted in a given situation. Such a person determines how desirable it is to promote this, rather than some other end, and he or she determines the most desirable way to promote the most desirable end (IIa IIae, q. 47, a. 7). Prudence is a habit that assists persons in choosing how to act. It determines, for example, whether, when, what, where, how much, with whom, and in what manner one ought to eat. Prudence is also a habit that assists persons in choosing how to feel (IIa IIae, q. 47, a. 7, ad 2–3; Ia IIae, q. 15, a. 3; Ia IIae, q. 57, a. 5). It determines such things as whether, when, for how long, and with what intensity one ought to desire particular dining options and enjoy the options that one selects.[30]

A prudent person arrives at different practical conclusions in different situations; one's determinations of the mean with regard to action and appetite are relative to the shifting particulars of the situation at hand, including one's own shifting condition (Ia IIae, q. 64, a. 1, ad 2; a. 2). There are, in Thomas's view, some universal laws of nature that inform the decision making of the prudent person. There are laws inherent in the nature of human being and sociality that set limits to the possibilities of right action and passion. That is to say, there are laws that determine the sorts of responses that can and cannot contribute to human flourishing (Ia IIae, q. 94, a. 2). There are other general rules that inform a prudent person's deliberations and choices (IIa IIae, q. 47, a. 3, ad 2). But the prudent person must perceive when a law or a rule is appropriate to a situation, and he or she must apply all guidelines in a context-sensitive manner, attending with special care to the irreducibly particular features of the situation: "to prudence belongs . . . the application of right reason in matters of counsel which are those wherein there is no fixed way of obtaining the end, as stated in *Ethic*. iii.3" (IIa IIae, q. 47, a. 2, ad 3).[31]

Thomas is explicitly in conversation with Aristotle as he urges the application of prudence to the question of behavioral and appetitive rightness. Keep in mind, however, that, for Thomas, those who do best at discerning what is right are those who are informed, not only by practical wisdom, but also by divine law as revealed in Scripture and grasped in the exercise of the theological and other infused virtues (Ia IIae, q. 93, a. 6). One who has been formed by charity exercises a supernaturally elevated, infused prudence in the pursuit of supernatural, as well as natural, happiness (Ia IIae, q. 65, aa. 2–3).[32] She or he also exercises an infused temperance, which orients a person passionally in light of the final beatitude of the life to come. This orientation sometimes leads one to think, feel, and act differently in regard to sensible objects than one would if oriented toward natural human happiness alone. Evidently referring to the person who exercises infused temperance, Thomas says that

> "virginity abstains from all sexual matters, and poverty from all wealth, for a right end, and in a right manner, that is, according to God's word, and for the sake of eternal life. But if this be done in an undue manner, i.e., out of unlawful superstition, or again for vainglory, it will be in excess. And if it be not done when it ought to be done, or as it ought to be done, it is a vice by deficiency: for instance, in those who break their vows of virginity or poverty" (Ia IIae, q. 64, a. 1, ad 3).[33]

This passage manifests a significant departure from the perspective of Aristotle, even as it reflects Aristotle's doctrine of the mean.[34]

There is a third, related guideline that must be followed in desiring, using, and enjoying non-necessary sensible goods. Thomas says that fitting engagement

> depends not only on the requirements of the body, but also on the requirements of external things, such as riches and station, and more still on the requirements of good conduct. Hence the Philosopher adds . . . that "the temperate [person] makes use of pleasant things provided [not only that] they be not prejudicial to health

and a sound bodily condition, but also that they be not inconsistent with good, i.e. good conduct, nor beyond his substance, i.e. his means." And Augustine says (*De Morib. Eccl.* xxi) that the "*temperate [person] considers the need* not only *of this life* but also *of his station*."[35] (IIa IIae, q. 141, a. 6, ad 3)

Thomas does not elaborate, but I take it that, in his view, a prudent person of small means does not squander material resources on sumptuous food and drink, nor does such a person squander the resources of passion on refined tactile stimulations. Rather, she or he uses these resources wisely to contribute in the best way possible to the overall well-being of those for whom she or he is responsible. A prudent person of more considerable means does not ordinarily spend resources on the pursuit and enjoyment of refined pleasures, either. Although one can afford to do so, such indulgence is inconsistent with a commitment to the common good: "right reason . . . judges the common good to be better than the good of the individual" (IIa IIae, q. 47, a. 10).[36] This commitment impels a person to use wealth and social standing to promote the good of those less fortunate (IIa IIae, q. 32, a. 1; IIa IIae, q. 117, a. 1, ad 1; IIa IIae, q. 145, a. 1, ad 2; IIa IIae, q. 145, a. 3, ad 2).

A person who is not only prudent but is also a friend of God is oriented and drawn toward particular sensibles in a way that reflects his or her spiritual, as well as social, station.

> Thus, for the sake of the body's health, certain persons refrain from pleasures of meat, drink, and sex; as also for the fulfillment of certain engagements: thus athletes and soldiers have to deny themselves many pleasures, in order to fulfil their respective duties. In like manner penitents, in order to recover health of soul, have recourse to abstinence from pleasures, as a kind of diet, and those who are desirous of giving themselves up to contemplation and Divine things need much to refrain from carnal things.[37] (IIa IIae, q. 142, a. 1)

Prudent persons of relatively low spiritual standing refrain from carnal things because this is the best way to bridle and break bad habits of desire. Quoting Augustine (*De musica*, 6.11), Thomas says that, "if the mind be lifted up to spiritual things, and remain fixed 'thereon, the impulse of custom,' i.e. carnal concupiscence, 'is broken, and being suppressed is gradually weakened: for it was stronger when we followed it, and though not wholly destroyed, it is certainly less strong when we curb it'" (IIa IIae, q. 142, a. 2; see also IIa IIae, q. 146, a. 1, ad 3).[38] Persons of relatively high spiritual standing also refrain from carnal things, but they do so because they already recognize, and want others to recognize, that carnal things cannot possibly satisfy the deepest of human longings. Clinging to carnal things, particularly as they are in themselves, without reference to the ultimate ground of their being and goodness, is thus a waste of time and energy. This energy is better spent fostering in oneself and in others a beautiful and resounding joy. Under the formative influence of charity, persons of spiritual excellence acquire "a mind that rejoices in adhering to spiritual things" (IIa IIae, q. 147, a. 4, ad 5).[39]

To summarize briefly, Thomas articulates some guidelines for attaining and exercising habits of appetitive rightness. The desire for, and the use and enjoyment of, food, drink, and sexual relations ought not to harm one's body, which is the necessary vehicle for the pursuit of goodness and happiness. The desire for, and the use and enjoyment of, sensibles ought generally to be appropriate to the circumstance, where it is understood that no two circumstances are ever exactly the same. In each circumstance, one is to compose the intentional content of one's desires and pleasures relative to a well-formed vision and love of excellent human functioning. Insofar as one is temperate, one's desires and pleasures arise rightly, as a matter of habit, in response to objects that are more or less worthy of attention and affection. The temperate person's desires, the actions that they motivate, and the accompanying feelings of pleasure exhibit a beauty and honor proper to a human being. And the reflective awareness of this beauty appropriately enriches the person's pleasure.

THE SPECIES OF TEMPERANCE

Extending his analysis of the nature of temperance in general, Thomas attends to the species of temperance (its "subjective parts" or

partes subiectivae). He also analyzes some related virtues whose exercise contributes indirectly to the cultivation of temperance (its *potential parts* or *partes potentiales*). The following discussion is limited to an examination of the species. As Thomas explains,

the species of a virtue have to be differentiated according to the difference of matter or object. Now temperance is about pleasures of touch, which are of two kinds. For some are directed to nourishment: and in these as regards meat, there is "abstinence," and as regards drink properly there is "sobriety." Other pleasures are directed to the power of procreation, and in these as regards the principal pleasure of the act itself of procreation, there is "chastity," and as to the pleasures incidental to the act, resulting, for instance, from kissing, touching, or fondling, we have "purity."[40] (IIa IIae, q. 143, a. 1)

I will investigate each of these virtues in turn, focusing on their defining characteristics and opposing vices.

The species of temperance that concerns the desire for, and the use and enjoyment of, food is abstinence. Abstinence is a habit of responding to sense impressions of food with well-ordered desires and pleasures (IIa IIae, q. 146, a. 1, ad 2). It is partly a disposition "to bridle the lusts of the flesh" (*ad concupiscentias carnis comprimendas*)—to keep sense desires and feelings of pleasure from getting so spirited that they break free of the reins of reason (IIa IIae, q. 147, a. 1). Thomas does characterize abstinence as a disposition that builds "strength for overcoming the onslaughts of gluttony, which increase in force the more [one] yields to them" (IIa IIae, q. 146, a. 2, ad 2).[41] Beyond this, however, Thomas characterizes abstinence as a habit of undergoing movements of the sense appetite in a fitting way, so that feelings of pleasure associated with desiring and ingesting food correspond consistently to the actual goodness of the food for a given person. Abstinence is a state of having one's gustatory appetite in excellent shape, such that all thoughts, feelings, and actions concerned with consumption are governed by a rational power exercised "through faith and love of God" (*ex fide et dilectione Dei*; IIa IIae, q. 146, a. 1, ad 1) and "with gladness of heart" (*cum hilaritate mentis*; IIa IIae, q.

146, a. 1, ad 4). Abstinence is chiefly a habit of the internal affections (*interiores affectiones*; IIa IIae, q. 146, a. 1, ad 2), but it is expressed and cultivated through the practice of fasting (IIa IIae, q. 147, a. 2). Virtuous fasting is an act of "[abstaining] in some measure from food for a reasonable purpose" (IIa IIae, q. 147, a. 1, ad 3).[42]

The rule of reason and divine law with respect to abstinence and fasting is determined with reference to the end or goal of abstinence, which is determined with reference to the end of human life generally. The end of abstinence is threefold (IIa IIae, q. 147, a. 1). First, an abstinent person abstains and fasts in order to cool down familiar cravings that repeatedly threaten to propel him or her into heated soul-body states; one abstains and fasts in order to restrain desires that are rooted in vices that have yet to be extirpated from the soul. Second, an abstinent person abstains and fasts in order to loosen attachments to sensible goods in general, "in order that the mind may arise more freely to the contemplation of heavenly things" (ibid.).[43] Third, an abstinent person abstains and fasts in order to satisfy for sins. Abstinence and fasting promote the re-establishment of justice (within the self and between the self and God) when efforts at cooling down or detaching fall short.

An abstinent person acts appropriately for one or more of these ends, guided by reason, by well-formed habits of perceptiveness and emotional attunement, by the exercise of infused virtue, and by the wisdom of Scripture.[44] If the person is a member of the church, he or she will be guided also by church precepts, which define with considerable specificity "the time and manner of fasting as becoming and profitable to the Christian people" (IIa IIae, q. 147, a. 3).[45] Informed by these sources, an abstinent person will seek the best course of action in each situation. Thomas says that, "in abstaining from food a [person] should act with due regard for those among whom he lives, for his own person, and for the requirements of health" (IIa IIae, q. 146, a. 1).[46] Exercising due regard requires discerning and weighing all communal and personal goods at stake and responding in a way that preserves the most important of these.

In opposition to abstinence, Thomas posits two vices. One is a vice of "deficiency," a habit of desiring, using, and enjoying too little the goods of the palate. Speaking generally about intemperance Thomas says that

> Whatever is contrary to the natural order is vicious. Now nature has introduced pleasure into the operations that are necessary for [one's] life. Wherefore the natural order requires that [one] should make use of these pleasures, insofar as they are necessary for [one's] well-being, as regards the preservation either of the individual or of the species. Accordingly, if anyone were to reject pleasure to the extent of omitting things that are necessary for nature's preservation, he would sin, as acting counter to the order of nature. And this pertains to the vice of insensibility.[47] (IIa IIae, q. 142, a. 1)

Speaking specifically about the habit of failing to desire, use, and enjoy food as reason and divine law recommend, Thomas quotes Jerome: "It matters not whether thou art a long or a short time in destroying thyself, since to afflict the body immoderately, whether by excessive lack of nourishment, or by eating or sleeping too little, is to offer a sacrifice of stolen goods" (IIa IIae, q. 147, a. 1, ad 2).[48] Afflicted bodies are not well-suited to support the work of moral and spiritual progress.

The vice of deficiency relative to the virtue of abstinence is not given a special name, but the vice of excess is, perhaps because eating too much, too extravagantly, and too compulsively is by far the most common form of missing the mark with respect to food.[49] Gluttony is frequently manifest in the outward act of overeating, but gluttony like abstinence has especially to do with the "internal affections":

> the vice of gluttony does not regard the substance of food, but [consists] in the desire thereof not being regulated by reason. Wherefore if [one exceeds] in quantity of food, not from desire of food, but through deeming it necessary to him, this pertains, not to gluttony, but to some kind of inexperience. It is a case of gluttony only when [one] knowingly exceeds the measure in eating, from a desire for the pleasures of the palate.[50] (IIa IIae, q. 148, a. 1, ad 2)

Thomas regards gluttony as a serious sin because it disposes a person to eat in a way that is "incommensurate and consequently improportionate to the end" of eating, which is the preservation of bodily well-being (IIa IIae, q. 148, a. 2).[51] Gluttony dulls the mind and compels a person to eat in a manner that actually injures one's well-being. Gluttony can also dispose a person to turn away from the enjoyment of God as the highest end, making the glutton "[adhere] to the pleasure of gluttony as his end, for the sake of which he contemns God, being ready to disobey God's commandments, in order to obtain those pleasures" (ibid.).[52] Pleasures of the table are not intrinsically bad, but one makes a pitiful and painful mistake, in Thomas's judgment, when one uses these pleasures to satisfy one's most significant human needs.

The species of temperance that pertains to the desire for, and the use and enjoyment of, liquid nourishment is sobriety (IIa IIae, q. 149, a. 2, ad 1). Sobriety is a habit of responding with measured desires and pleasures to sense impressions of drink. It is a habit that concerns principally one's bearing toward intoxicating beverages. Thomas takes intoxicants like wine to be "most profitable" (*eius usus mensuratus multum confert*) (IIa IIae, q. 149, a. 1) and "necessary to the present life" (*necessaria sunt praesenti vitae*) (IIa IIae, q. 149, a. 1, ad 2). He appears to agree with the authors of Ecclesiastes and 1 Timothy that the moderate use of alcoholic beverages promotes digestive health, eases physical pain, and causes "joy of the soul and the heart" (*exultatio animae et cordis*) (IIa IIae, q. 149, a. 3, *sed contra*). For Thomas, sobriety is partly a disposition to desire and enjoy consuming alcohol in a manner that safeguards its benefits and minimizes its dangers. He notes with concern that even a slight excess of alcohol "disturbs the brain by its fumes" (*perturbat cerebrum sua fumositate*) (IIa IIae, q. 149, a. 2), causing people to do things that they would never do if they were not under its influence (IIa IIae, q. 150, a. 2). The sober person is aware of these dangers, and sobriety disposes him or her to be cautious. Sobriety is also, more fundamentally, a disposition to desire and enjoy alcohol in a manner that reflects serenity of soul. The virtuous person has a beautiful soul, and it

brings that person pleasure to be in his or her own company (IIa IIae, q. 25, a. 7). Insofar as a sober person is broadly virtuous, then, he or she desires to consume alcohol in a manner that enhances, rather than diminishes, self-awareness.

The rule of reason and divine law with respect to desiring, using, and enjoying alcohol is that these activities be consistent with the maintenance of health. Desire, use, and enjoyment must also be consistent with the maintenance of rational self-awareness and self-command. Within the bounds set by these general rules, there is considerable flexibility regarding the mean. As always, determining what is right requires the exercise of prudence. Persons who are "easily the worse for taking wine" (*qui a vino de facili laeditur*) (IIa IIae, q. 149, a. 3), who get sick or drunk every time that they attempt the moderate use of alcohol, ought to avoid alcohol altogether.[53] Others who ought to refrain include those who have taken vows not to drink alcohol and those whose drinking, in a given circumstance, would likely cause offense to others (ibid.). While it is not necessary to avoid alcoholic beverages in order to attain wisdom sufficient for salvation, "a [person] may have wisdom in some degree of perfection: and in this way, in order to receive wisdom perfectly, it is requisite for certain persons that they abstain altogether from wine, and this depends on circumstances of certain persons and places" (q. 149, a. 3, ad 1).[54] Finally, Thomas mentions that the mean must be determined with reference to a person's state of health. What is right for a healthy person may be excessive for someone who is sick, or vice versa (q. 150, a. 2, ad 3).

There are two vices opposed to sobriety. The vice of deficiency is a disposition to desire, use, and enjoy alcohol too little: As the Philosopher says (*Ethic.* iii. 11), "insensibility which is opposed to temperance is not very common, so that like its species which are opposed to the species of intemperance it has no name. Hence the vice opposed to drunkenness is unnamed; and yet if a [person] were knowingly to abstain from wine to the extent of molesting nature grievously, he would not be free from sin" (IIa IIae, q. 150, a. 1, ad 1).[55] Thomas may have in mind someone who is so repulsed by the taste of alcohol or the sensation that she experiences in drinking it that she refuses to take a prescribed dosage of medicinal wine or some other medicine containing alcohol.

The far more common vice opposed to sobriety is the vice of excess, which is drunkenness. Drunkenness sometimes refers to a state that a person falls into accidentally, "through the wine being too strong, without the drinker being cognizant of this" (IIa IIae, q. 150, a. 1).[56] Strictly speaking, however, drunkenness is the state of being a drunkard. For Thomas, a drunkard is someone who "is well aware that the drink is immoderate and intoxicating, and yet he would rather be drunk than abstain from drink" (IIa IIae, q. 150, a. 2).[57] Drunkenness is a disposition to desire and use alcohol in order to experience the pleasure of becoming intoxicated. Thomas regards drunkenness as a habit that has even more devastating effects than gluttony has on the formation and exercise of moral agency (IIa IIae, q. 149, a. 2, ad 1). Drunkenness, as expressed in act, "is a mortal sin, because then a [person] willingly and knowingly deprives himself of the use of reason, whereby he performs virtuous deeds and avoids sin, and thus he sins mortally by running the risk of falling into sin. For Ambrose says (De Patriarch.): "We learn that we should shun drunkenness, which prevents us from avoiding grievous sins. For the things we avoid when sober, we unknowingly commit through drunkenness" (IIa IIae, q. 150, a. 2).[58] Human happiness is found by pursuing rational and moral excellence in the loving company of God and good friends. Excessive drinking confuses and dulls the mind and the affections. It weakens a person's power to reflect upon and order his or her ruling loves. Tragically, the more a drunkard drinks, the less she or he understands and cares about the failing state of her or his soul (IIa IIae, q. 148, a. 6).

CHASTITY

Temperance is a virtue that orders one's appetites rightly with respect to food, drink, and sexual relations. The species of temperance that concerns sexual relations is chastity, which is a disposition to experience sexual desire and pleasure in a becoming manner. Insofar as chastity is distinguished from purity, chastity regards desires and pleasures related to sexual intercourse proper, whereas purity regards desires and pleasures related to external signs (exteriora signa) of intercourse, such as looking, kissing, and touching (IIa IIae, q. 151, a. 4). Because Thomas regards purity not as a virtue distinct from chastity, but as "expressing a circumstance of chastity" (exprimens castitatis circumstantiam), and also because he says so little about purity, this analysis will focus on chastity (IIa IIae, q. 151, a. 4).

Chastity is partly a disposition to respond to impetuous sexual desires with a second order desire to chastise and restrain them (IIa IIae, q. 151, a. 3, ad 2). A chaste person knows that the desires and pleasures of sex "more than anything else work the greatest havoc in a [person's] mind," clouding judgment regarding the kinds of sexual contact that are genuinely good (IIa IIae, q. 153, a. 1, ad 1).[59] Insofar as he or she is still bothered by desires and pleasures that threaten the rational governance of the soul, the chaste person remains ready for battle (IIa IIae, q. 154, a. 3, ad 1). Unless the chaste person has taken a vow of virginity, he or she need not defend against all sexual desire and pleasure; he or she needs only to defend against excess. Chastity is more, however, than a disposition to chasten and restrain. It is also a disposition to experience sexual desire and pleasure in a beautiful way—in a way that reflects the body's status as a temple of the Holy Spirit (IIa IIae, q. 153, a. 3, ad 2). It is a disposition to be moved by sexually attractive objects "in due manner and order" (debito modo et ordine) (IIa IIae, q. 153, a. 2). Chastity is partly a disposition that orders action, and "it belongs to chastity that a [person] make moderate use of bodily members in accordance with the judgment of his reason and the choice of his will," but it belongs to chastity first and foremost that a person have well-ordered desires and pleasures (IIa IIae, q. 151, a. 1, ad 1).[60]

On the face of it, it seems that the deliberate ordering of sexual desire and pleasure is impossible for human beings. Thomas says that "the movement of the organs of generation is not subject to the command of reason" (IIa IIae, q. 151, a. 4, c.; IIa IIae, q. 151, a. 4, ad 3).[61] He says further that the intensity of bodily pleasure experienced during intercourse is not a matter for reason's command; instead, it is simply a function of bodily disposition (IIa IIae, q. 153, a. 2, ad 2). Thomas indicates that during sexual relations, a person's mind can be so captivated by feelings of bodily pleasure that for a time, "the free act of reason in considering spiritual things" can become impossible (ibid.).[62] Yet Thomas also says that humans can consent or not to bodily desires and pleasures: "the lower appetite is not sufficient to cause movement, unless the higher appetite consents" (Ia, q. 81, a. 3; see also IIa IIae, q. 151, a. 2, ad 2; IIa IIae, q. 151, a. 3, ad 2).[63] He says that the virtue of chastity concerns "how much the interior appetite is affected" by the "pleasure experienced by the external sense" (IIa IIae, q. 153, a. 2, ad 2).[64] In addition, Thomas commends (for some persons) the virtue of virginity, which is a disposition, based in a decision and confirmed by a vow, never to experience the pleasure of sexual orgasm, "in order more freely to have leisure for divine contemplation" (IIa IIae, q. 152, a. 2).[65]

I take it that, in Thomas's view, it is not possible to command certain changes in sexual organs, like erections, not to occur; nor is it possible to command oneself to experience merely moderate rather than intense physical pleasure once one makes the choice to use these organs. But sexual desire is more than a pleasing change in a sexual organ. It is a human passion, and like other passions it has intentional (as well as material) content, which means that it can be formed to some extent via the deliberate formation of this content.[66] It can be shaped in and through reflection on the meaning and value of human sexuality.[67] As a sexual urge begins to arise—and as this urge becomes more and more explicitly focused on an object that is conceived in a particular, contingent way—one can reflect critically on this urge and its object. One can reflect on what the urge really amounts to and what the value might be of indulging it in one way or another. One ought to reflect before the desire becomes so intense that it undermines the ability to exercise good judgment.

According to Thomas, reason and divine law require that persons conceive of sexual relations correctly, as having procreation and thus the preservation of the human species as their purpose (IIa IIae, q. 153, a. 2). Reason and divine law also require that persons form

their sexual desires in light of their correct conceptions, so that when such desires arise they are experienced "as directed to" (venereorum) or "in keeping with" (conveniens) the generation of new life and the preservation of the human race (IIa IIae, q. 153, a. 2).[68] Thomas's view on this matter is partly a reflection of his convictions concerning the natural order of things; hence, it is helpful to recall his view of natural law (Ia IIae, q. 94, a. 2).[69] Thomas holds that each created being has within it certain ordering principles (or metaphysical causes). These principles determine the kind of being that the creature is, and these principles determine, accordingly, what it is for the creature to be a good specimen of its kind, to excel at being the particular creature that it is. Humans have their own ordering principles that determine the possibilities of their perfection. Humans can know these principles through the exercise of reason. Thomas thinks it evident to reason that humans have been constituted in such a way that those who engage in sexual relations can do humanly well in their relations only if they engage in them for the purpose of procreation. Intercourse for any reason other than the preservation of the human race reflects an impairment of natural human operations and a diminishment in the quality of a life.

One could argue that Thomas accepted Augustine's teaching concerning the three goods of marriage, which are procreation, the faithful management of each other's unruly sexual desires, and the sacramental signification of Christ's union with the church.[70] Accordingly, Thomas must have thought it fitting to engage in sexual acts with the intention of saving a spouse from sexual vice or enjoying sacramental unity, as long as the spouses remain open to procreation. It is important to know that Thomas does not explicitly state this in his treatise on temperance. It is important also to discern that there is a difference between the goods of marriage, which are things that excuse and compensate for (what Augustine regarded as) the negative features of marriage, and the goods that are properly intended in sexual intercourse per se. The goods of marriage are discussed in the Supplement to the Summa, which was constructed by someone other than Thomas, drawing from Thomas's commentary on the Sentences of

Peter Lombard. The *Supplement* argues that the faithful alleviation of a spouse's temptations to fornication is, along with procreation, an appropriate end to intend in intercourse. There is no indication, however, that the good of sacramental unity is an end that is fittingly intended in intercourse. To the contrary,

> Just as the marriage goods, insofar as they consist in a habit, make a marriage honest and holy, so too, insofar as they are in the actual intention, they make the marriage act honest, as regards those two marriage goods which relate to the marriage act. Hence when married persons come together for the purpose of begetting children, or of paying the debt to one another (which pertains to faith), they are wholly excused from sin. But the third good does not relate to the use of marriage, but to its excuse . . . . [W]herefore it makes marriage itself honest, but not its act, as though its act were wholly excused from sin, through being done on account of some signification. Consequently there are only two ways in which married persons can come together without any sin at all, namely, in order to have offspring, and in order to pay the debt; otherwise it is always at least a venial sin.[71] (*Supplementum*, q. 49, a. 5)

There is one reference to the marriage debt (*uxori debitum*) in the treatise on temperance, but there is no mention of engaging in sexual relations with the intention to pay the marriage debt (IIa IIae, q. 153, a. 3, ad 3).[72] This much is clear in the treatise: the natural law dictates that humans do best as sexual beings when those who engage in sexual acts do so with the intention to procreate.[73] Humans have the freedom to argue with and to contravene the law of their sexual nature; however, they cannot, in Thomas's judgment, flourish while violating this law.

Although he clearly values marital unity and the intimacy of marital friendship, Thomas does not indicate that sexual relations may fittingly be pursued with the intention of promoting this intimacy.[74] Nor does he consider the possibility that the planet could someday become so overpopulated and ecologically overtaxed that conceiving new life would injure, rather than enhance, existing life and future generations. (Lack of consideration along these lines is understandable in someone who lived and wrote during the Middle Ages.) Thomas does acknowledge that some persons indulge in sexual relations simply for pleasure. He states that persons who engage in sex for this purpose are lustful, and that lust is a vice (IIa IIae, q. 153, aa. 3–4). Keep in mind that, in Thomas's view, humans are ordered to attain a supernatural, as well as a natural, happiness, and that they do best at being supernaturally human when they pursue natural goods in light of their contribution to supernatural perfection and beatitude (*sub specie aeternitatis*) (IIa IIae, q. 152, a. 2). Sexual pleasure sought for its own sake does not seem to Thomas to make a significant contribution to knowing and loving God.[75]

Within Thomas's treatise on temperance the general rule with respect to sexual relations, the desires that motivate them, and the pleasure that accompanies them is thus that they be directed to the goal of procreation. Thomas specifies further that, in order to be constitutive of human well-being, sexual relations must take place within the context of a fine, stable, monogamous, heterosexual marriage that is open to providing offspring with the internal and external goods that compose a flourishing human life directed toward God (q. 154, a. 2). Thomas goes on, accordingly, to identify several forms of sexual expression that he takes to be wrong. Exploring a few of these is worthwhile.

Thomas maintains that using contraception during sex, homosexual relations, masturbation, and bestiality are all wrong, and they are wrong for the same reason.[76] They constitute "vices against nature" (*vitia contra naturam*) (IIa IIae, q. 154, a. 12), and sins against the Creator of the natural order because they are nonprocreative (IIa IIae, q. 154, a. 1). In Thomas's view, human nature itself dictates that humans can only excel at being human—and at contributing to the good of the human community—when those who engage in sexual acts do so in order to perpetuate the species. Thomas suggests that the only reason why persons would deliberately engage in nonprocreative sexual activities is because they desire sexual pleasure for its own sake (IIa IIae, q. 154, a. 11, ad 3). But such desire is an expression of lust.

Thomas also regards premarital sexual relations, whether they be consensual (as in seduction) or nonconsensual (as in rape), to be wrongful acts—and especially vile when the girl involved is a virgin. Premarital sex injures a girl by making her less marriageable, thus more likely to live a wanton life (IIa IIae, q. 154, a. 6). Premarital sex also injures possible offspring by bringing them into an undefined relational context in which their most important needs could not possibly be met (IIa IIae, q. 154, a. 2). In both of these ways, premarital sex violates the principle of charity. To understand additional reasons that Thomas gives for holding that premarital sex is wrong, readers must allow themselves to be drawn further into a deeply patriarchal world in which sexual morality reflects the point of view of men—a world in which the nature, the interests, and the value of girls and women are defined by men.[77] For Thomas, premarital sex is wrong partly because it violates the legal rights, the power, or the authority of a father or an intended husband. Thomas says, for example, that a virgin who has been promised in marriage to one man and has been raped by another "must be restored to her betrothed, who has a right to her in virtue of their betrothal: whereas one that is not promised to another must first of all be restored to her father's care, and then the abductor may lawfully marry her with her parent's consent. Otherwise the marriage is unlawful, since whosoever steals a thing . . . is bound to restore it" (IIa IIae, q. 154, a. 7, ad 3; see also IIa IIae, q. 170, a. 1, c.; IIa IIae, q. 170, a. 1, ad 2).[78] There is, of course, nothing peculiarly medieval about this view. Thomas quotes Hebrew scripture: "For it is written (Deut. xxii. 28, 29): 'If a man find a damsel that is a virgin, who is not espoused, and taking her, lie with her, and the matter come to judgment: he that lay with her shall give to the father of the maid fifty sicles of silver, and shall have her to wife, and because he hath humbled her, he may not put her away all the days of his life . . .'" (IIa IIae, q. 154, a. 6, ad 3).[79] Premarital sex is wrong, in Thomas's view, because it violates the principle of justice, as well as the principle of charity.

Extramarital sex or adultery is wrong for some of the same reasons that premarital sex is wrong, according to Thomas. It causes injury to possible offspring that may be conceived (IIa IIae, q. 154, a. 2). It subverts the adulteress's husband's just authority over his wife (IIa IIae, q. 154, a. 8, ad 3). It also causes injury to existing children in both families (in ways that Thomas does not specify [IIa IIae, q. 154, a. 8]). In addition, it injures the husband of the adulteress by making it uncertain whether the children that she conceives are his (IIa IIae, q. 154, a. 8). It injures the spouses of both parties—it undermines both marriages—by breaking the marital trust (fidem) that ought to bind husband and wife to each other (IIa IIae, q. 154, a. 8, ad 2). Finally, adultery violates the sixth commandment (IIa IIae, q. 154, a. 8).

Thomas thus argues in his discussion of various wrongful sexual acts that reason and divine law require persons to adhere in all of their sexual relations to the law of nature and to the principles of love and justice. If they abide by the law, and their moral character is formed according to the law, then they will choose to engage in sexual relations only for the sake of procreation and only within a particular sort of relationship. It is noteworthy that Thomas does not say in his discussion of chastity, as he does in his discussions of abstinence and sobriety, that within the bounds set by general moral principles, there is room for varied, context-specific determinations of appetitive and behavioral rightness. This is because he does not allow the use of nonnecessary sexual relations in the way that he allows the use of nonnecessary foods and beverages. That is to say, he does not approve of sexual relations that are unnecessary for procreation. Hence, he does not explore the complex particulars of personal and social circumstance that many people in the present age think they need to consider in order to exercise practical wisdom in the expression of their sexuality.

To proceed, there are two vices opposed to the virtue of chastity. One is a vice of deficiency, which is rare: "The opposite of lust is not found in many, since [humans] are more inclined to pleasure. Yet the contrary vice is comprised under insensibility, and occurs in one who has such a dislike for sexual intercourse as not to pay the marriage debt" (IIa IIae, q. 153, a. 3, ad 3).[80] Thomas takes issue with those who regard sexual desire and pleasure as intrinsically evil, for the desire for sexual pleasure was created by a good God, for an exceedingly good purpose (IIa IIae, q. 153, a. 2). "The person who, beside the dictate of right reason, abstains from all pleasures through aversion, as it were, for pleasure as such, is insensible as a country lout" (IIa IIae, q. 152, a. 2, ad 2).[81]

The more common vice opposed to chastity is the vice of excess, which is lust. Lust is a habit of "exceeding the order and mode of reason in the matter of venereal acts" (IIa IIae, q. 153, a. 3).[82] It is, more fundamentally, a habit of undergoing movements of the sexual appetite in a humanly unbecoming manner (IIa IIae, q. 153, a. 1). It is a disposition to desire and enjoy sex with the wrong person or for the wrong reason (ibid.).

In brief summary, abstinence, sobriety, and chastity are the main species of temperance. They enable us consistently to resist any impulses that we may have to respond in destructive or demeaning ways to the sensible goods of food, drink, and sexual relations. Much more than this, they enable us deliberately to form our engagements with these sensibles so that, over time and with the gracious help of God, it becomes second nature for us to desire, use, and enjoy them in a way that befits our rational human nature and our status as children of God.

CONCLUSION

Most persons are confronted regularly with strong desires for food, drink, and sexual relations. The moral and spiritual tenor of a human life rests, to a significant degree, on how one is drawn toward (or away from) what one perceives to be good (or bad). One function of Thomas's treatise on temperance is to encourage readers to form better habits of being moved so that one can consistently experience the pull of desire in ways that contribute to, rather than diminish, the enjoyment of a decent human life. Thomas acknowledges that it is not easy to form the habit of temperance or the more specific habits of abstinence, sobriety, and chastity. Commonly, one must first overcome some bad habits or vices that are currently deforming one's desires and skewing one's perceptions of these desires. Even apart from vicious formation, desires for food, drink, and sexual relations can be difficult to manage. They can be impetuous, for they concern matters of life and death. Finally, food, drink, and sexual stimuli are not goods that most people can simply avoid in an effort to

avoid temptation. They are goods that one must confront frequently, even daily, and sometimes all day long. This constant confrontation does have a positive dimension to it, however, in that it provides plenty of opportunity for practice. Thomas comments that

> it is easier to find a remedy for intemperance than for cowardice, since pleasures of food and sex, which are the matter of intemperance, are of everyday occurrence, and it is possible for [a person] without danger by frequent practice in their regard to become temperate; whereas dangers of death are of rare occurrence, and it is more dangerous for [a person] to encounter them frequently in order to cease being a coward.[83] (IIa IIae, q. 142, a. 3)

As persons practice being moved by sensible goods in a manner that exhibits appetitive rectitude, they are urged to follow the measure of reason and divine law. According to Thomas, reason and divine law require that persons desire, use, and enjoy these goods in ways that protect and enhance the quality of human life and community under the reign of God. Some will disagree with Thomas concerning what makes a life distinctively human, and what makes a distinctively human life worth living. Some will disagree, accordingly, with a number of his recommendations for approximating a good and deeply satisfying life. But one must admit that his basic question about the rational and faithful ordering of human appetites is, in one form or another, as much a question for the modern reader as it was for people in Thomas's day. Innumerable human beings suffer directly and indirectly from painful, crippling, and even deadly addictions to food, alcohol, and dehumanizing sexual activities. Humans also suffer from other forms of desperate grasping that are based in distorted perceptions of what is genuinely good for them. How, indeed, is serenity to be found? Thomas's treatise is an excellent resource for reflection on this matter.

ACKNOWLEDGMENT

I wish to express my gratitude to G. Simon Harak, S.J., who commented extensively on an earlier draft of this chapter. Thanks also to

Joan Henriksen Hellyer, Stephen J. Pope, and Ralph Keen.

Notes

[1]For an analysis of Aristotelian and Thomistic accounts of moral virtue, and a discussion of the relationship between acquired and infused virtue, see my *Choosing to Feel: Virtue, Friendship, and Compassion for Friends* (Notre Dame, IN: University of Notre Dame Press, 1997), chaps. 1–3.

[2]"Pleasure is caused by the presence of suitable good, insofar as it is felt, or perceived in any way" ("delectatio causatur ex praesentia boni convenientis, secundum quod sentitur, vel qualitercumque percipitur"). A suitable good is "present" to some extent in hope or anticipation. Hence, pleasure accompanies our tending toward, as well as our uniting with, an appetible object (ST Ia IIae, q. 32, a. 3).

[3]"Una, per quam anima simpliciter inclinatur ad prosequendum ea quae sunt convenientia secundum sensum, et ad refugiendum nociva . . ."

[4]"fortitudo, quae firmat contra pericula mortis."

[5]"Principaliter quidem ipse usus rei necessariae: puta vel feminae, quae est necessaria ad conservationem speciei; vel cibi vel potus, quae sunt necessaria ad conservationem individui."

[6]"sicut pulchritudo et ornatus feminae, et sapor delectabilis in cibo, et etiam odor."

[7]Charles M. Young, "Aristotle on Temperance," *The Philosophical Review* 97 (1988): 537. Young cites Arist. *Eth. Eud.* 1231a12–17. Young argues that for Aristotle, pleasures associated with the sense of touch are the most basic in that they are the least "cerebral"; they involve the least amount of rational discrimination.

[8]Arist. *Eth. Nic.*, 1151b35–1152a4.

[9]"continentia habet aliquid de ratione virtutis, inquantum scilicet ratio firmata est contra passiones, ne ab eis deducatur: non tamen attingit ad perfectam rationem virtutis moralis, secundum quam etiam appetitus sensitivus subditur rationi sic ut in eo non insurgant vehementes passiones rationi contrariae."

[10]"quaedam moderata et conveniens proportio . . ."

[11]G. Simon Harak, S.J., *Virtuous Passions: The Formation of Christian Character* (New York: Paulist, 1993), 94.

[12]See Cates, *Choosing to Feel*, 18–24.

[13]"minus apparet de lumine rationis, ex qua est tota claritas et pulchritudo virtutis. Unde et huiusmodi delectationes dicuntur maxime serviles."

[14]"Unde Ambrosius dicit, in *de Offic.*, quod verecundia iacit prima temperantiae fundamenta, inquantum scilicet incutit horrorem turpitudinis." Material

quoted by Thomas is italicized, rather than enclosed within quotation marks.

[15]For a critical analysis of Thomas's views regarding excellence and the honor due persons on account of their excellence, see my "Taking Women's Experience Seriously: Thomas Aquinas and Audre Lorde on Anger," in *Aquinas and Empowerment: Classical Ethics for Ordinary Lives*, ed. G. Simon Harak, S.J. (Washington, DC: Georgetown University Press, 1996), 47–88.

[16]"ad rationem pulchri, sive decori, concurrit et claritas et debita proportio: dicit enim quod Deus dicitur pulcher *sicut universorum consonantiae et claritatis causa.*"

[17]"Et similiter pulchritudo spiritualis in hoc consistit quod conversatio hominis, sive actio eius, sit bene proportionata secundum spiritualem rationis claritatem."

[18]The English term *openfacedness* is intended as a contrast to the English term *shamefacedness*. I owe the image to G. Simon Harak, S.J.

[19]Keep in mind that, in Thomas's view, the happiness of the individual is considered with reference to the common good.

[20]For a more extensive analysis of the twofold end of human being and its relation to the twofold rule of human action and passion, see Cates, *Choosing to Feel*, chaps. 2–3.

[21]Arist. *Eth. Nic.* 1098b21–23.

[22]Arist. *Eth. Nic.* 1099a24–1099b8.

[23]"Et ideo temperantia accipit necessitatem huius vitae sicut regulam delectabilium quibus utitur . . ."

[24]"id sine quo res non potest convenienter esse . . ."

[25]"Quaedam enim sunt impedimenta sanitatis vel bonae habitudinis."

[26]"Manifestum est autem quod per invaletudinem corporis, in omni operatione virtutis homo impediri potest." See also ST IIa IIae, q. 25, a. 5; IIa IIae, q. 142, a. 1. See Joseph Pieper, *The Four Cardinal Virtues: Prudence, Justice, Fortitude, Temperance* (New York: Harcourt, Brace, and World, 1965), 186–87.

[27]"si tale sit corpus, cuius sit difficilis et gravis administratio, sicut caro quae corrumpitur et aggravat animam, avertitur mens ab illa visione summi caeli."

[28]See Harak, *Virtuous Passions*, 78–80. Soundness of soul and soundness of body are intimately connected for Thomas, as they were for the ancients. Just as an unsound soul can literally deform a body and inhibit its feelings of full-bodied pleasure, so can a poorly tended body inhibit the pursuit and enjoyment of moral and spiritual goods (ST Ia IIae, q. 31, a. 7).

[29]"pro loco et tempore et congruentia eorum quibus convivit."

[30]For further discussion of the relationship between desire and choice in Thomas, see Cates, *Choosing to Feel*, esp. chaps. 2–3. One who is perfectly

prudent would also be perfectly temperate, and such a one would not need to choose to feel otherwise than she spontaneously does. But most of us are not perfectly virtuous. On the intricate, mutually dependent relationship of prudence and temperance, see ST Ia IIae, q. 58, aa. 4–5.

[31]"Sed ad prudentiam non pertinet nisi applicatio rationis rectae ad ea de quibus est consilium. Et huiusmodi sunt in quibus non sunt viae determinatae perveniendi ad finem; ut dicitur in III *Ethic*."

[32]For a discussion of the relationship between acquired, theological, and infused virtue in Thomas, see Cates, *Choosing to Feel*, chaps. 2–3.

[33]"Abstinet enim virginitas ab omnibus venereis, et paupertas ab omnibus divitiis, propter quod oportet, et secundum quod oportet; idest secundum mandatum Dei, et propter vitam aeternam. Si autem hoc fiat secundum quod non oportet, idest secundum aliquam superstitionem illicitam, vel etiam propter inanem gloriam; erit superfluum. Si autem non fiat quando oportet, est vitium per defectum: ut patet in transgredientibus votum virginitatis vel paupertatis."

[34]For more on the difference between the mean of acquired virtue and the mean of theological and infused virtue, according to Thomas, see ST Ia IIae, q. 64, a. 4.

[35]"Quae quidem attenditur non solum secundum convenientiam corporis: sed etiam secundum convenientiam exteriorum rerum, puta divitiarum et officiorum; et multo magis secundum convenientiam honestatis. Et ideo Philosophus ibidem subdit quod in delectabilus quibus temperatus utitur, non solum considerat ut non sint impeditiva sanitatis et bonae habitudinis corporalis, sed etiam ut non sint *praeter bonum*, idest contra honestatem; et quid non sint *supra substantiam*, idest supra facultatem divitiarum. Et Augustinus dicit, in libro *de Moribus Eccle.*, quod temperatus respicit non solum *necessitatem huius vitae*, sed etiam *officiorum*."

[36]"Repugnat etiam rationi rectae, quae hoc iudicat, quod bonum commune sit melius quam bonum unius."

[37]"Sicut propter sanitatem corporalem, aliqui abstinet a quibusdam delectationibus, cibis et potibus et venereis. Et etiam propter alicuius officii executionem: sicut athletas et milites necesse est a multis delectationibus abstinere, ut officium proprium exequantur. Et similiter poenitentes, ad recuperandam animae sanitatem, abstinentia delectabilium quasi quadam diaeta utuntur. Et homines volentes contemplationi et rebus divinis vacare, oportet quod se magis a carnalibus abstrahant."

[38]"mente in spiritualia suspensa atque ibi fixa et manente, consuetudinis, scilicet carnalis concupiscentiae, impetus frangitur, et paulatim repressus extinguitur. Maior enim erat cum sequeremur: non omnino nullus, sed certe minor, cum refrenamus."

[39]"Aliud autem est quod pertinet ad *gaudium mentis in spiritualia suspensae*."

[40]"Oportet autem diversificare species virtutum secundum diversitatem materiae vel obiecti. Est autem temperantia circa delectationes tactus, quae dividuntur in duo genera. Nam quaedum ordinantur ad nutrimentum. Et in his, quantum ad cibum, est abstinentia; quantum autem ad potum, proprie sobrietas. Quaedam vero ordinantur ad vim generativam. Et in his, quantum ad delectationem principalem ipsius coitus, est castitas; quantum autem ad delectationes circumstantes, puta quae sunt in osculis, tactibus et amplexibus, attenditur pudicitia."

[41]"quia dum homo abstinet, magis redditur fortis ad impugnationes gulae vincendas, quae tanto fortiores sunt quanto homo eis magis cedit."

[42]"ex rationabili proposito, a cibis aliqualiter abstinet."

[43]"ad hoc quod mens liberius elevetur ad sublimia contemplanda."

[44]Perception, especially the perception of moral salience and significance, is a key element in the exercise of moral agency, as is the emotional attunement that qualifies perception. Thomas agrees with Aristotle that "if each person is in some way responsible for his own state [of character], then he is also himself in some way responsible for how [the end] appears" (*Eth. Nic.* 1114a32, referred to at ST Ia IIae, q. 9, a. 2). For further discussion of Thomas on the role of perception and emotion in deliberation and decision making, see Cates, *Choosing to Feel*, chap. 3. See also Etienne Gilson, *The Christian Philosophy of St. Thomas Aquinas* (Notre Dame, IN: University of Notre Dame Press, 1956), pt. 3, chap. 2.

[45]"determinatio temporis et modi ieiunandi secundum convenientiam et utilitatem populi Christiani . . ."

[46]"ut scilicet homo a cibis abstineat prout oportet, *pro congruentia hominum cum quibus vivit et personae suae, et pro valetudinis suae necessitate*."

[47]"Respondeo dicendum quod omne illud quod contrariatur ordini naturali, est vitiosum. Natura autem delectationem apposuit operationibus necessariis ad vitam hominis. Et ideo naturalis ordo requirit ut homo intantum huiusmodi delectationibus utatur, quantum necessarium est saluti humanae, vel quantum ad conservationem individui vel quantum ad conservationem speciei. Si quis ergo in tantum delectationem refugeret quod praetermitteret ea quae sunt necessaria ad conservationem naturae, peccaret, quasi ordini naturali repugnans. Et hoc pertinet ad vitium insensibilitatis."

[48]"non differt utrum magno vel parvo tempore te interimas; et quod de rapina holocaustum offert qui vel ciborum nimia egestate, vel manducandi vel somni penuria, immoderate corpus affligit." According to the translator's note (*The Summa*

Theologica of St. Thomas Aquinas, trans. The Fathers of the English Dominican Province, vol. 3 [Allen, TX: Christian Classics, 1981], 1780), this passage is not found in Jerome's work, although it is assigned to him by Gratian in the Corpus of Canon Law (Cap. *Non mediocriter*, *De Consecrationibus*, dist. 5).

[49]The idea that a moral agent aims at the mean of virtue like an archer aims at a target (hoping to hit the bull's eye) goes back at least to Aristotle: "surely knowledge of [the highest] good is also of great importance for the conduct of our lives, and if, like archers, we have a target to aim at, we are more likely to hit the right mark" (*Eth. Nic.* 1094a23).

[50]"vitium gulae non consistit in substantia cibi, sed in concupiscentia non regulata ratione. Et ideo si aliquis excedat in quantitate cibi non propter cibi concupiscentiam, sed aestimans id sibi necessarium esse, non pertinet hoc ad gulam, sed aliquam imperitiam. Sed hoc solum pertinet ad gulam, quod aliquis, propter concupiscentiam cibi delectabilis, scienter excedat mensuram in edendo."

[51]"non sunt ita commensurata ut sint proportionata fini."

[52]"Quod quidem contingit quando delectationi gulae inhaeret homo tanquam fini propter quem Deum contemnit, paratus scilicet contra praeceptia Dei agere ut delectationes huiusmodi assequatur."

[53]Thomas says that "sobriety is most requisite in the young and in women, because concupiscence of pleasure thrives in the young on account of the heat of youth, while in women there is not sufficient strength of mind to resist concupiscence. Hence, according to [V]alerius Maximus among the ancient Romans women drank no wine" (sobrietas maxime requiritur in iuvenibus et mulieribus: quia in iuvenibus viget concupiscentia delectabilis, propter fervorem aetatis; in mulieribus autem non est sufficiens robur mentis ad hoc quod concupiscentiis resistant. Unde, secundum Maximum Valerium, mulieres apud Romanos antiquitos nonbibebant vinum; ST IIa IIae, q. 149, a. 4). For further reflection on Thomas's problematic attitude toward women's rational capacities, see Cates, "Taking Women's Experience Seriously," 64–67, especially nn. 92, 101.

[54]"Alio modo, secundum quendam perfectionis gradum. Et sic requiritur in aliquibus, ad perfecte sapientiam percipiendam, quod omnino a vino abstineant: secundum conditiones quarundam personarum et locorum."

[55]"sicut Philosophus dicit, in III Ethic., insensibilitas, quae opponitur temperantiae, *non multum contingit*. Et ideo tam ipsa quam omnes eius species, quae opponuntur diversis speciebus intemperantiae, nomine carent. Unde et vitium quod opponitur

ebrietati innominatum est. Et tamen si quis scienter in tantum a vino abstineret ut naturem multum gravaret, a culpa immunis non esset."

[56]"ex nimia vini fortitudine, praeter opinionem bibentis."

[57]"aliquis potest contingere quod aliquis bene advertat potum esse immoderatum et inebriantem, et tamen magis vult ebrietatem incurrere quam a potu abstinere."

[58]"Quia secundum hoc, homo volens et sciens privat se usu rationis, quo secundum virtutem operatur et peccata declinat: et sic peccat mortaliter, periculo peccandi se committens. Dicit enim Ambrosius, in libro *de Patriarchis*: 'Vitandam dicimus ebrietatem, per quam crimina cavere non possumus: nam quae sobrii cavemus, per ebrietatem ignorantes committimus.'"

[59]"voluptatibus venereis, quae maxime et praecipue animum hominis resolvunt."

[60]"Pertinet enim ad castitatem ut secundum iudicium rationis et electionem voluntatis, aliquis moderate utatur corporalibus membris."

[61]"motus genitalium membrorum non subditur imperio rationis . . ."

[62]"liberum actum rationis ad spiritualia consideranda . . ."

[63]"appetitus inferior non sufficit movere, nisi appetitus superior consentiat."

[64]"Et praeterea ad virtutem non pertinet quantum sensus exterior delectetur, quod consequitur corporis dispositionem: sed quantum appetitus interior ad huiusmodi delectationes afficiatur."

[65]"ut liberius divinae contemplationi vacet . . ."

[66]Thomas also indicates that sexual desire can be affected by a change in diet (ST IIa IIae, q. 146, a. 2, ad 2; IIa IIae, q. 147, a. 1; IIa IIae, q. 153, a. 1, ad 2).

[67]Recall Harak's example of the person biting into the ripe tomato and reflecting upon the goodness of God. As Harak would say, fitting sexual pleasure is not squelched when a person reflects upon this pleasure in light of the goodness of God's created order; rather, it is intensified by being extended throughout the various dimensions of the self.

[68]Thomas implies that it is not necessary, during moments of sexual ecstasy, to retain one's explicit intention to procreate, as long as the habit of intending sex for procreation be present. As he puts it, "Nor does it follow that the act in question is contrary to virtue, from the fact that the free act of reason in considering spiritual things is incompatible with the aforesaid pleasure. For it is not contrary to virtue, if the act of reason be sometimes interrupted for something that is done in accordance with reason, else it would be against virtue for a person to set himself to sleep" (Nec hoc etiam quod ratio non potest liberum actum

rationis ad spiritualia consideranda simul cum illa delectatione habere, ostendit quod actus ille sit contrarius virtuti. Non enim est contrarium virtuti si rationis actus aliquando intermittatur aliquo quod secundum rationem fit: alioquin, quod aliquis se somno tradit, esset contra virtutem) (ST IIa IIae, q. 153, a. 2, ad 2).

[69]In interpreting Thomas on natural law, I am particularly influenced by Aristotle's *Metaphysics*.

[70]See Augustine, *The Good of Marriage*, trans. Rev. C. L. Cornish, in *Nicene and Post-Nicene Fathers, Vol. 3, Augustine: On the Holy Trinity, Doctrinal Treatises, Moral Treatises*, ed. Philip Schaff, D.D., LL.D. (Peabody, MA: Hendrickson, 1994), 399–413. For an insightful analysis of Augustine on marriage and sexuality, see Paul Ramsey, "Human Sexuality in the History of Redemption," in *The Ethics of Augustine*, ed. William S. Babcock (Atlanta: Scholars, 1991), 115–45.

[71]"sicut bona matrimonii, secundum quod sunt in habitu, faciunt matrimonium honestum et sanctum; ita etiam, secundum quod sunt in actuali intentione, faciunt actum matrimonii honestum, quantum ad illa duo bona matrimonii quae ipsius actum respiciunt. Unde quando coniuges conveniunt causa prolis procreandae, vel ut sibi invicem debitum reddant, quod ad *fidem* pertinet, totaliter excusantur a peccato. Sed tertium bonum non pertinet ad usum matrimonii, sed ad essentiam ipsius, ut dictum est. Unde facit ipsum matrimonium honestum: non autem actum eius, ut per hoc actus eius absque peccato reddatur, quia causa alicuius significationis conveniunt. Et ideo duobus solis modis coniuges absque omni peccato conveniunt: scilicet causa procreandae prolis, et debiti reddendi. Alias autem semper est ibi peccatum, ad minus veniale."

[72]Furthermore, it is not immediately obvious what the marital debt amounts to in this passage, for Thomas could be referring to the obligation to provide a spouse with offspring. Compare Augustine: "Therefore married persons owe one another not only the faith of their sexual intercourse itself, for the begetting of children, which is the first fellowship of the human kind in this mortal state: but also, in a way a mutual service of sustaining one another's weakness, in order to shun unlawful intercourse . . ." (*The Good of Marriage*, 6).

[73]Thomas believes that some people (a limited number) do best at being human and at being friends of God by remaining celibate (ST IIa IIae, q. 152, a. 2, ad 1).

[74]See, for example, ST IIa IIae, q. 26, a. 11; and SCG II, chap. 123. For a brief discussion of the development of church teachings concerning the end(s) of human sexuality, including the promotion of marital unity, see James P. Hanigan, *Homosexuality: The Test Case for Christian Sexual Ethics* (New York: Paulist, 1988).

[75]John Giles Milhaven explores the question of why, given that Thomas does not take sexual pleasure to be intrinsically evil, he nevertheless holds that it is a venial sin to pursue it simply for its own sake. He argues that, for Thomas, "sexual pleasure is the lowest of human pleasures and lacks all intrinsic value for the person. . . . The cause is not that sexual pleasure interferes most with the exercise of human reason. It does so interfere in a person's purely natural state, but the cause lies deeper. . . . The crucial reason for sexual pleasure's lack of intrinsic value is that it has in it nothing resembling rational knowledge. Unlike higher sense pleasure, it is grounded in pure sense knowledge that has no share in reason" ("Appendix: Thomas Aquinas on the Pleasure of Sex and the Pleasure of Touch," in *Hadewijch and Her Sisters: Other Ways of Loving and Knowing* [Albany: State University of New York Press, 1993], 140).

[76]Thomas includes in this group of sexual acts "other monstrous and bestial manners of copulation" (alios monstruosos et bestiales concumbendi modos), which may refer to forms of nonvaginal intercourse like oral or anal sex.

[77]For a clear, concise, and critical discussion of Thomas's view of women and their sexuality, see Lisa Sowle Cahill, *Between the Sexes: Foundations for a Christian Ethics of Sexuality* (Philadelphia: Fortress, 1985), chap. 6.

[78]"Illae enim quae sunt aliis desponsatae, restituendae sunt sponsis, qui in eis ex ipsa desponsatione ius habent. Illae autem quae non sunt aliis desponsatae, restituendae sunt primo patriae potestati: et tunc, de voluntate parentum, licite possunt eas in uxores accipere. Si tamen aliter fiat, illicite matrimonium contrahitur: tenetur enim quicumque rem rapit, ad eius restitutionem."

[79]"Dicur enim *Deut.* 22, [28–29]: 'Si invenerit vir puellam virginem, quae non habet sponsum, et apprehendens concubuerit cum illa, et res ad iudicium venerit, dabit qui dormivit cum ea patri puellae quinquaginta siclos argenti, et habebit eam uxorem: et quia humiliavit illam, non poterit dimittere eam cunctis diebus vitae suae.'"

[80]"oppositum luxuriae non contingit in multis: eo quod homines magis sint proni ad delectationes. Et tamen oppositum vitium continentur sub *insensibilitate*. Et accidit hoc vitium in eo qui in tantum detestatur mulierum usum quod etiam uxori debitum non reddit."

[81]"ille qui abstinet ab omnibus delectationibus praeter rationem rectam, quasi delectationes secundum se abhorrens, est insensibilis, sicut agricola."

[82]"Hoc autem pertinet ad rationem luxuriae, ut ordinem et modum rationis excedat circa venerea."

[83]"Tertio, quia contra intemperantiam potest magis de facili remedium adhiberi quam contra

timiditatem: eo quod delectationes ciborum et venereorum, circa quas est intemperantia, per totam vitam occurrunt, et sine periculo potest homo circa ea exercitari ad hoc quod sit temperatus; sed pericula mortis et rarius occurrunt, et periculosius in his homo exercitatur ad timiditatem fugiendam."

Selected Further Reading

Augustine. *The Good of Marriage*. Trans. Rev. C. L. Cornish. In *Nicene and Post-Nicene Fathers*. Vol. 3: *Augustine: On the Holy Trinity, Doctrinal Treatises, Moral Treatises*. Ed. Phillip Schaff, D.D., LL.D. Peabody, MA: Hendrickson, 1994.

Cahill, Lisa Sowle. *Between the Sexes: Foundations for a Christian Ethics of Sexuality*. Philadelphia: Fortress, 1985.

Cates, Diana Fritz. *Choosing to Feel: Virtue, Friendship, and Compassion for Friends*. Notre Dame, IN: University of Notre Dame Press, 1997.

———. "Taking Women's Experience Seriously: Thomas Aquinas and Audre Lorde on Anger." In *Aquinas and Empowerment: Classical Ethics for Ordinary Lives*. Ed. G. Simon Harak, S.J. Washington, DC: Georgetown University Press, 1996.

Gilson, Etienne. *The Christian Philosophy of St. Thomas Aquinas*. Notre Dame, IN: University of Notre Dame Press, 1956.

Hanigan, James P. *Homosexuality: The Test Case for Christian Sexual Ethics*. New York: Paulist, 1988.

Harak, G. Simon, S.J. *Virtuous Passions: The Formation of Christian Character*. New York: Paulist, 1993.

Milhaven, John Giles. "Appendix: Thomas Aquinas on the Pleasure of Sex and the Pleasure of Touch." In *Hadewijch and Her Sisters: Other Ways of Loving and Knowing*. Albany: State University of New York Press, 1993.

Pieper, Joseph. *The Four Cardinal Virtues: Prudence, Justice, Fortitude, Temperance*. New York: Harcourt, Brace and World, 1965.

Porter, Jean. *The Recovery of Virtue: The Relevance of Aquinas for Christian Ethics*. Louisville, KY: Westminster/John Knox, 1990.

———. "The Unity of the Virtues and the Ambiguity of Goodness: A Reappraisal of Aquinas's Theory of the Virtues." *Journal of Religious Ethics* 21 (1993): 136–63.

———. *Natural and Divine Law: Reclaiming the Tradition for Christian Ethics*. Grand Rapids, MI: William B. Eerdmans, 1999.

Ramsey, Paul. "Human Sexuality in the History of Redemption." In *The Ethics of St. Augustine*. Ed. William Babcock. Atlanta: Scholars, 1991.

Young, Charles M. "Aristotle on Temperance." *The Philosophical Review* 97 (1988): 521–42.

Charisms, Forms, and States of Life
(IIa IIae, qq. 171–189)

Serge-Thomas Bonino, O.P.

Translated by Mary Thomas Noble, O.P.

If it is true that our supernatural vocation neither destroys nor overlays our nature but on the contrary evolves within its structures so as to heal them and bring them to perfection, it is logical that humans—as social and political animals—should develop a supernatural life within a society or community of grace—the church of Jesus Christ. The Christian life, the subject of the *Secunda pars*, is therefore by definition an ecclesial life. Now the church, much like every society, forms an intrinsically diversified yet organic whole. *Sanctifying grace*, a created supernatural participation in the divine nature, establishes among all those who possess it a profound communion that insures the specific unity of the mystical Body of Jesus Christ. But this communion of grace is incarnated in juridical-social structures in which each of the faithful, or each group of the faithful, has a clearly determined place and plays a particular ecclesial role in the service of the spiritual common good.

It was fitting that, after having discussed in the first 170 questions of the *Secunda secundae* "the virtues and vices which pertain to all men, whatever their condition and state," Thomas should complete his exposition of particular Christian morality by the study of "what pertains to certain men in a special way"[1] (IIa IIae, q. 171, Prol.). For the study of these organic diversifications within ecclesial life, Thomas takes his inspiration from St. Paul's teaching in 1 Cor 12–13.[2] From this text, Thomas draws the threefold structure presented in IIa IIae, qq. 171–89: "There are varieties of gifts (*charismatôn, gratiarum*), but

the same Spirit; and there are varieties of service (*diakoniôn, ministrationum*), but the same Lord; and there are varieties of working (*energematôn, operationum*), but it is the same God who inspires them all in everyone" (1 Cor 12:4–6).

Gifts, service, and *working* constitute the three fields of ecclesial activity in relation to which social differences within the Christian community are defined. The first distinction, therefore, flows from differences with regard to the various gratuitously given graces (*gratis datae*) or *charisms* (IIa IIae, qq. 171–78). The second distinction is that of *forms of life*; it flows from working, by which Thomas means types of occupation (active or contemplative) that give a Christian life its shape and general orientation (IIa IIae, qq. 179–82). Finally, the third distinction is based on ministries and states of life (IIa IIae, qq. 183–89). Each of these distinctions finds its origin in that which specifies a human being insofar as he or she is a person, namely, a properly rational activity. In fact, all other differences—difference in race, for example—remain infra-human and can in no way determine a principle of differentiation adequate for the structure of a truly human society.

Because of the continuity implied by the analogy between the natural and supernatural orders, these distinctions within the church are often rooted in distinctions in the natural order. For example, the difference between a form of active life and a form of contemplative life already exists within political societies in the natural order, and it is significant that the two great sources of Thomist reflection on this diversification should be, on the one hand, Aristotle's *Nicomachean Ethics* and, on the other, the spiritual teaching of Gregory the Great. Moreover, because of the many distinctions based on the hierarchical plurality of conditions, states, and functions within both secular societies and the church, the issues I will address here implicitly contain elements of reflection important for a social and political philosophy.

THE CHARISMS

The Charisms in General

It was an idea dear to Aquinas that God, for His own greater glory and not out of any need or indigence, uses intermediaries to govern the universe (Ia, q. 103, a. 6.). If creative action is, by definition, strictly incommunicable to the creature (Ia, q. 45, a. 5), God makes generous use of intermediaries, who thus enjoy the role of instruments of the divine government. This great law is valid also in the supernatural order, and it allows one to understand the meaning of the particular distinction between sanctifying grace and the charisms. Sanctifying grace (or grace *gratum faciens*) is a created participation in the divine nature, as much at the level of being as of acting. It brings about one's union with the last end, which is God. Graces gratuitously given (*gratis datae*)—or charisms—are given to some so that they may dispose others to receive sanctifying grace. In this way, the former cooperate instrumentally in the return of souls to God (Ia IIae, q. 111, a. 1). Charisms are thus wholly ordered to sanctifying grace (ibid.).[3]

Graces gratuitously given, therefore, are defined essentially in relation to their end, which is their instrumental use for "others," i.e., the ecclesial community or, more broadly, anyone connected with the church. As their primary object is not the good of the one who is gifted, charisms can (this is obviously *not* the ideal) be exercised by someone with evil moral dispositions, and who does not necessarily live in grace and charity.[4]

In this segment of the *Summa*, the typology of the charisms depends strictly on the list given by Paul in 1 Cor 12:8–10. From this list, Thomas takes three general categories, which he presents for examination: (1) *charisms of knowledge*, all of which are connected in some way with prophecy (IIa IIae, qq. 171–74); (2) *charisms of communication* or *eloquence* (*locutio*), such as the gift of tongues and the grace of sapiential or learned speech (IIa IIae, qq. 176–77); and (3) *charisms of action* (*operatio*), especially the gift of working miracles (IIa IIae, q. 178).[5]

Thomas does not simply juxtapose these categories. In fact, the charisms of speech and action are ordered to the charisms of knowledge. The object of the charisms of speech is the transmission of supernatural teaching as revealed in prophecies, and miracles (charisms of action) are intended to confirm that teaching (IIa IIae, q. 171, a. 1; IIa IIae, q. 174, a. 4). This primacy accorded to prophecy among the charisms corresponds well to the primacy Thomas attributes to faith as supernatural knowledge in the constitution of the church, which he often defines as the *gathering of believers* (*congregatio fidelium*). This idea becomes clear when one understands that faith depends heavily on prophetic revelation, which then provides faith with its object (IIa IIae, q. 174, a. 6).[6]

Prophecy[7]

Thomas's theological reflection on prophecy can be situated at the intersection of two doctrinal traditions with distinctive motifs.[8] The first is the Latin theological tradition, which is the vehicle for themes developed from assiduous meditation on the Scriptures. In this tradition, for example, Thomas finds the distinction between the various forms of prophecy (*predestination, foreknowledge,* and *denunciation*; IIa IIae, q. 174, a. 1). Book XII of Augustine's *De genesi ad litteram* is a major source of this tradition. Aquinas draws on the Bishop of Hippo's work to incorporate the three kinds of prophetic vision: *corporeal vision, spiritual (imaginative) vision,* and *intellectual vision.*[9] Furthermore, Thomas also inherits from this tradition certain problematics, more recent and already stamped with the scholastic style, such as that of the *medium* of the prophetic vision.[10] However, while Aquinas is certainly indebted to this tradition, which provides him with numerous elements that enter into his own theological synthesis, he often needs to reshape or develop earlier thought, for with the invasion of Aristotelian philosophy, Christian theology was faced with altogether new epistemological and psychological exigencies.

Nevertheless, the immediate (though implicit) horizon of Thomistic reflection is the confrontation with the prophetology of the *falasifa*.[11] The generally rationalistic orientation of *falasifa* sometimes reduces religion to a philosophy full of imagery aimed at common people. From this perspective, religious revelation, transmitted by the prophets, is merely another way of conveying what strictly philosophical rationality reaches through scientific reflection. Prophecy is never a gift granted by a free initiative on the part of God, which opens onto supernatural truths; rather, it appears as the highest expression of the natural knowledge of man. Prophetic knowledge results necessarily from the perfection of the natural virtues of intellect and imagination, which allows the prophet to be united to separate intelligences. Thus grafted on these intelligences, the prophet receives at the lower level a communication of the intelligible flux that travels from the top to the bottom of the spiritual world. Prophetic vision, therefore, does not imply any special supernatural intervention.

Another basic characteristic of the prophetology of *falasifa* is its political dimension.[12] The prophet (in this case, Moses or Mohammed) is not a pure contemplative; he is primarily a religious legislator. He gives the Law and thus founds policy. But, in order to be able to act upon the crowds in this way, the prophet must possess, in addition to knowledge, certain pedagogical gifts that are dependent on imagination. Most particularly, he must be able to translate the intelligible into symbols accessible to the ignorant. In this he is superior to the simple philosopher.

Thomas devotes four questions, therefore, to prophecy. In the first (IIa IIae, q. 171), he is at pains to define the very essence of prophecy. Prophecy, he explains, is formally knowledge, even though, in the broadest sense, the prophetic charism also includes all that concerns communicating the revealed message to humanity (IIa IIae, q. 171, a. 1). The object of this knowledge is not limited to future happenings. In fact, prophetic knowledge is a cre-

ated participation in the one divine light that embraces all intelligible reality—past, present, or future. This confers on it both a strong formal unity and a universal material extension (IIa IIae, q. 171, a. 3, ad 3). Prophetic knowledge includes, first, truths that are natural to, but not necessarily accessible by, all people, so that God has judged it good to reveal them.[13] Second, one finds truths that absolutely surpass the power of human reason left to itself, such as the mystery of the Trinity. Finally, there are truths bearing on objects that are totally *sui generis*, such as future contingents. The last type of truth has the particular note of being absolutely unknowable in themselves, because they are purely non-existent and their truth is not actually determined. If God knows those truths, it is by reason of the transcendence of His knowledge, which, in its eternity, embraces all time (IIa IIae, q. 171, a. 3).[14]

The ontological state of prophecy in the prophet is not that of a *habit* (*habitus*), that is, a stable principle of action. Rather, prophecy is a passing illumination, a "kind of passion or transitory impression" (*quaedam passio sive impressio transiens*), a category that Thomas often uses in regard to the diverse effects of instrumental causality. He means, in fact, to bring out the purely instrumental role of the prophet: the divine light falls across the prophet to illuminate others, but does not inhere in him in a habitual way. By way of comparison, the prophetic light is in the prophet as physical light is in the air, but *not* as it is in the sun. Light is in the sun as a stable and permanent form, whereas in the air, it has no profound ontological root. That is, if a light source ceased to radiate light, the air would immediately return to darkness. A clear sign of this needy ontological state is that the prophet does not initiate the prophetic illumination—he or she cannot dispose of the prophetic light at will, as would be the case if it were an internal stable principle in the manner of a habit.

But the profound reason for this is that a habitual intellectual light—for example, the habit of metaphysics—renders the mind capable of knowing the fundamental principles of the order of truths that this light illumines, in such a way that the metaphysician knows not only the truth of a particular metaphysical conclusion, but also knows *why* it is true by reducing it to the first principles of metaphysics. By way of contrast, the light the prophet receives does indeed give knowledge of a supernatural truth; however, it does this without revealing its cause, which would render it fully enlightened. This cause is nothing less than the divine essence itself (IIa IIae, q. 171, a. 2). It follows, moreover, that the prophet does not know all that can be known in virtue of the prophetic light, but only certain truths it illumines selectively for the prophet (IIa IIae, q. 171, a. 4).

Despite this weak ontological condition, prophetic knowledge, insofar as it is a participation in the divine foreknowledge, is infallible. In every case, it is important to discern whether the supernatural revelation bears directly on the future event as such, or merely on the fact that this future event is programmed or "set in motion" within its causes. In the latter case, which corresponds to the prophecy that is called a *denunciation* (*prophetia comminationis*), the event prophesied may not take place if a change is produced at the level of its causes. For example, if people are converted, the chastisement that was prophesied for them will not be carried out (IIa IIae, q. 171, a. 6). The fact remains that infallibility has to do with prophetic revelation as such. Now, although in the higher forms of prophecy the prophet enjoys clear evidence of the supernatural character of this knowledge, it can happen, in the lower forms, that the prophet does not always discern clearly whether this has been received by means of prophetic instinct or simply is the result of the prophet's own reflection (IIa IIae, q. 171, a. 5).

In his reflection on the causes of prophecy (IIa IIae, q. 172), Thomas remains aloof in regard to the rationalistic naturalism of the *falasifa*'s prophetology. Prophecy, says the common Doctor, is a gift; in the last analysis, it comes from God alone, who communicates it to whom and when He wills. It is true that a person, solely by virtue of natural resources, can have a certain anticipated knowledge of the future. In fact, a number of future events are already present in a sense in their causes. Because of this, an astute mind, aided by acquired experience, can deduce the future from the present. But, short of foundering in a strict determinism that would suppress all contin-

gency, this purely human knowledge of the future is generally conjectural and fallible. In any case, it is only valid for events which are in some manner programmed in their causes. Note, however, that certain things—free actions, for example, which make up the warp and woof of all human history—are absolutely not preprogrammed. Because of this, such actions can be known *only* to God. That being the case, a prophet's knowledge of them is necessarily the result of supernatural revelation (IIa IIae, q. 172, a. 1).

If God is effectively the first cause of prophetic knowledge, in the absolute sense of the word, then the prophet needs neither natural dispositions (IIa IIae, q. 172, a. 3) nor even moral predispositions (IIa IIae, q. 172, a. 4). Just as the creative action of God presupposes absolutely nothing on the part of the creature, so God, in the sovereign divine freedom, can communicate prophetic revelation to whomever He wishes, even to the person most lacking in natural aptitudes. Moreover, this seems to be a law of the divine action—many examples can be found in the Bible. Instead, God gives the prophet both the knowledge *and* dispositions needed to receive it.

This, however, does not exclude the fact that, in conforming to the general law of hierarchical mediation as explained by Dionysius, God uses angels to illuminate human beings and communicate revelation to prophets (IIa IIae, q. 172, a. 2). Conversely, Thomas also addresses the possibilities of "prophecies" inspired by demons. Thomas, in fact, notes the possibility of "prophets of demons" sometimes being authentically inspired by the Holy Spirit, as was the case with the prophet Balaam (IIa IIae, q. 172, a. 6). However, in most cases, such "prophets" are actually inspired by the natural knowledge of demons. Although it is superior to that of human beings, one cannot speak of supernatural prophecy in the strictest sense (IIa IIae, q. 172, a. 5). Only God can inspire true prophecy.

To continue his examination of prophecy, Thomas turns, in IIa IIae, q. 173, to the *manner* of prophetic knowledge, that is, the psychological processes by which the prophet comes to know supernatural truths.[15] Aquinas, careful to distinguish prophecy from every anticipated beatific vision, begins by rejecting the Latin theory of vision in the mirror of eternity (*in speculo aeternitatis*), held at the beginning of the thirteenth century by such theologians as Philip the Chancellor and William of Auxerre. According to this theory, the prophet would see in God the transcendent models of creatures (*rationes creaturarum*), yet he or she would not see the divine essence under the aspect by which it beatifies the blessed. For Thomas, this explanation is purely and simply contradictory. It is, in fact, absolutely impossible to separate the vision of Ideas of creatures in God from the beatifying vision of the divine essence (IIa IIae, q. 173, a. 1).

Aquinas then proposes another theory of prophetic knowledge, one which does greater justice to the scientific demands of Aristotelian psychology (IIa IIae, q. 173, a. 2). Like all human intellectual knowledge, prophecy includes two movements: the *acceptance* or *representation* of things (*receptio*) and the *judgment* about the thing presented. This judgment, which is always the fruit of a supernatural illumination, formally defines prophecy: it is its principal and determining element. By this judgment, the prophet perceives both the truth and the supernatural origin of what is known. The representational material on which the judgment is exercised may come from extremely varied sources. It may be purely natural in origin, such as when, for example, the hagiograph assesses under a prophetic light truths grasped in the normal course of human knowledge (IIa IIae, q. 174, a. 2, ad 3). But this is a very inferior form of prophecy. In prophecy properly so-called, the origin is always supernatural. In this case, however, there are two models, both of which, on Thomas's view, have their own validity. There can be a miraculous granting of data, either by the direct infusion of intelligible representational forms (*species*) in the passive intellect, or by the impression of sensible *species* in the imagination. One may also think that the prophetic light suffices to confer on the mind of the prophet the ability to organize in a supernaturally significant manner preexisting cognitive data which has been acquired according to the natural mode of knowledge, that is by abstraction from what is sensible.[16]

Reflection on the different types of prophecy (IIa IIae, q. 174) again shows a combination of thematic issues taken from Judaeo-Arabic prophetology and the Latin theological

tradition. From the latter, Thomas pulls the distinction between prophecies of predestination, of foreknowledge, and of denunciation (IIa IIae, q. 174, a. 1). On the other hand, the articles devoted to the degrees of prophecy (q. 174, aa. 3–6), if they are somewhat linked to the Latin tradition, are understood chiefly in the setting of a discussion with the *falasifa*. In particular, the recognized objective superiority of a purely intellectual vision over an intellectual vision combined with an imaginative vision is perhaps, for Aquinas, a way of opposing the prophetology of the *falasifa*.[17] For these, in fact, the imaginative vision is unquestionably a part of prophecy, in which the prophet is essentially the founder of a political order. But, without underrating this dimension of prophecy, Thomas seems to want to relativize it (for example, IIa IIae, q. 172, a. 1, ad 4).

As in the *Quaestiones de veritate*, the reflection on the charism of prophecy is immediately extended to a question on *ecstasy* (*raptus*).[18] Ecstasy, in the strict sense, is the experience wherein certain people, when their sensible activity is totally suspended, are raised by the Spirit to a supernatural vision (IIa IIae, q. 175). The main body of Thomas's treatise is devoted to the theological interpretation of St. Paul's mysterious experience as alluded to in 2 Cor 12:2–3. Oddly enough, the borderline case of ecstasy seems to run counter to Aquinas's strong empiricism.

There is considerable philosophical *and* theological interest in these five questions on prophecy and ecstasy. In fact, the formally theological study of prophecy as a supernatural form of knowledge leads Aquinas to verify the pertinence of his intellectual and philosophical models, and even to fine-tune them. The theological stakes are not slight. With prophecy come the foundations of a theology of revelation, which Aquinas poses in close harmony with his theology of Scripture or again with his conception of the virtue of faith. Actually, this treatise on prophecy has been the subject of assiduous rereading on the part of Thomist theologians of the twentieth century, since the need has arisen, in the face of questions posed by biblical criticism, to better define the exact nature of scriptural inspiration.[19] Today, in a theological context marked by a certain reassessment of extrabiblical religious traditions, Thomas's reflections on prophetic activity outside the institutional frontiers of the church offer new, potentially valuable perspectives.

ACTIVE LIFE AND CONTEMPLATIVE LIFE[20]

Within the church—as already in the wordly city—believers are divided into two categories, in which they are privileged to direct their lives toward the pure knowledge of truth (a form of contemplative life), or toward external activity (a form of active life). The distinction between these two forms of life is profoundly human because it hinges on the human intellect, which defines the person as such. It, in fact, exercises both speculative and practical functions.[21]

The distinction between the contemplative and active life clearly does not mean that some persons would be exclusively occupied with contemplating, while others would be completely immersed in practical activities. Nor does it point to a purely quantitative estimate, according to which anyone who spent more than one-half of his or her time in contemplation would be considered a contemplative. The meaning of the distinction, rather, is that of a difference in the choice, deliberate and cultivated, of a general orientation of one's life. Here, Thomas has recourse to the notion of *intent* (*intentio*), or again of *study* (*studium*). Study here refers to a persevering and even vehement application of the mind toward obtaining a particular end (IIa IIae, q. 166, a.1). A contemplative, then, is one who applies the totality of his or her strength and orders his or her entire life to contemplation. Conversely, the active person is one who orders life directly to action. Thus, "the active and contemplative lives differ on the basis of the different activities of people intent on different goals. One of these is the consideration of truth, which is the end of the contemplative life, and the other is external activity, to which the active life is directed"(IIa IIae, q. 181, a. 1).[22]

Thomas's distinction between a life ordered to the pure contemplation of God and a life directed to action—briefly, between the contemplative and the active life—is actually a very common theme in Christian spiritual tradition. For vivid examples, one need only look to the two wives of Jacob, Rachel and Leah, or, again, to the two sisters, Mary and Martha, of Bethany.[23] In the four questions devoted to this issue, Thomas makes particular reference to Gregory the Great (*Commentary on Ezekiel, Moralia*), yet he does so without excluding either Pseudo-Dionysius or the more recent Latin tradition (such as Bernard or the Victorines).

However, in the thirteenth century, this classic theme returned to relevance through its connection with the distinction between the theoretical and practical life that Aristotle established in Book X of the *Nicomachean Ethics*. In fact, Aristotle's exaltation of the theoretical life, which is, concretely, the philosophical life, became one of the major themes developed through a doctrinal trend traditionally called "Latin Averroism," which was in reality radical Aristotelianism. In developing this approach, radical Aristotelians, such as Boethius of Dacia in his *De summo bono*, took up this glorification of a theoretical life in the natural order, not without opposing it tacitly to the Christian concept of a life whose primacy was charity.

Thomas uses his usual tactic of cutting short the pretensions of Aristotelian ethics by exploiting the existence of a natural desire in every spiritual creature to see the very essence of God. Purely philosophical contemplation cannot attain the vision of God, which alone can satisfy the innate ontological desire of the human intellect to know the ultimate source of intelligibility. Consequently, the philosophical life procures only an *imperfect* form of happiness. The supernatural vision of the divine essence—the reward promised for a life of charity—alone can constitute true happiness. Also, even if not stated explicitly in these questions devoted to the forms of life, Thomas probably intended not only to show the reasonableness of a venerable position of tradition, but also to illustrate the truth that the Christian realization of the ideal of the contemplative life fulfills and, at the same time, transcends the Aristotelian ideal.

The contemplative life (IIa IIae, q. 180) is defined according to its ultimate act: the simple gaze of the intellect upon a truth (*simplex intuitus veritatis*) (IIa IIae, q. 180, a. 3, ad 1). Of course, Thomas does not mean simply *any* truth. Rather, this life is centered around divine truth, the contemplation of which is the end of all human life (IIa IIae, q. 180, a. 4). All other forms of knowledge are definitively ordered to this one (IIa IIae, q. 180, a. 4, ad 4). This contemplation of God is still imperfect, but it offers a foretaste of beatitude (IIa IIae, q. 180, a. 3, ad 1).[24] Does the contemplative never rise, then, to the pure vision of the divine essence? Thomas admits it in the case of rapture, that of St. Paul especially (IIa IIae, q. 180, a. 5).

Although contemplation as such is formally an act of the intellect, it goes without saying that the pursuit of a contemplative life presupposes the affective engagement of the whole person, who mobilizes all his or her powers in view of this end (IIa IIae, q. 180, a. 1). It is love, the love of contemplation and, above all, the love for the object contemplated ("aflame to gaze on the beauty of God"), that moves the intellect to contemplation (ibid.).[25] Thus, contemplation, once attained, is a source of utter joy (IIa IIae, q. 180, a. 7).

However, this simple gaze, sustained by love, which the contemplative directs to God and which defines contemplation, is not given outright to the human being. For reasons linked to the conditioning of the intellectual life as it actually exists in human beings, it presupposes a whole assemblage of preliminary dispositions that enter indirectly into the contemplative life. First, contemplation requires a certain quality of moral life that assures the purification of the passions (IIa IIae, q. 180, a. 7, a. 2). In this sense, the contemplative life presupposes the active life, not so much in terms of external activity itself, as in the interior calm that it produces in return (IIa IIae, q. 182, aa. 3–4). Second, the act of contemplation for the discursive and rational intellect of humanity can only take place at the end of a complex intellectual process. This process sets in motion several types of activity through which the spirit makes its way progressively toward this simple grasp of the truth, which is its rest (IIa IIae, q. 180, a. 3). Thomas tries to illuminate the progressive stages that spiritual authors distinguish along the path to contemplation, as, for example, the triple distinction, so dear to the Victorines, between reading, meditation, and contemplation (IIa IIae, q. 180, a. 3, ad 1).

As for the active life (IIa IIae, q. 181), it consists in putting the moral virtues to work under the direction of the practical wisdom that is the virtue of prudence (q. 181, a. 2). The active life is ordered to external activity. All the same, this "exteriority" does not refer only to the order of doing, and of transitive action (the rational, that is, the human organization of the world and society), but, also, to the order of moral action and self-management. It is under this second aspect that action is exceedingly important for the contemplative life itself, as we have noted.

The objective comparison between the contemplative and active lives (IIa IIae, q. 182) can never fail to turn to the advantage of the first. Does not the contemplative life realize the vocation proper to the person as person? In an amazing text, which joins inextricably Aristotelian themes and Christian traditions, Thomas easily establishes that the contemplative life is superior to the active (IIa IIae, q, 182, a. 1). Furthermore, it is objectively more meritorious than the active life, because, in itself—contrary to current thought—the contemplative life manifests greater charity than the active life (IIa IIae, q. 182, a. 2). If the pain one suffers in order to serve Christ through external works is a beautiful sign of charity, to leave all things in order to devote oneself solely to contemplation is a still greater one (IIa IIae, q. 182, a. 2, ad 1). Clearly, Thomas has led his readers to the pole opposite from a theology in which merit is measured by the disagreeable nature of the action accomplished!

However, while denying nothing of the bold intellectualism presiding over this view of things, Thomas quickly notes that, in certain circumstances, the active life can actually prove superior to the contemplative life. Not only when the material necessities of human existence demand it—first of all to live—but also when it is the urgency of charity that moves the contemplative to perform works of the active life. In this case, the passage from the contemplative to the active life is actually a matter of addition (IIa IIae, q. 182, a. 1, ad 3).[26] Moreover, there are, in fact, works of the active life, such as the preaching and teaching of Christian truth, that require, by very reason of their object, contemplation. Certainly, one devoted to the liberation of captives would gain much, personally, by developing the contemplative orientation of life through prayer and study, but this work does not intrinsically require contemplation. On the other hand, teaching Christian truth requires a certain amount of contemplation. This is not a sort of mystical contemplation; rather, it is the particularly human thought of theological contemplation, the only sort that can be communicated in teaching.[27] An active life devoted to teaching is, therefore, objectively better than a purely contemplative life. In fact, this is the kind of life Christ chose: "[T]he active life according to which a person, by preaching and teaching, gives to others the fruits of contemplation is more perfect than the life by which a person contemplates alone, because such a life presupposes an abundance of contemplation. And therefore, Christ chose such a life" (IIIa, q. 40, a. 1, ad 2).[28]

THE STATES OF LIFE

The third great organic diversification within the ecclesial community flows from ministers. It includes, according to Thomas, a diversity of *states* (*status*), of *functions* (*officia*; IIa IIae, q. 168, a. 3, ad 3), and of degrees of *dignity* (*gradus*; IIa IIae, q. 183).[29] These three categories reproduce, in an analogical way, certain divisions already present in civil society.

The diversity of functions (*officia*) is explained by the necessity of publically identifying and deputizing certain persons in order to perform the many public activities necessary for the life of the church (IIa IIae, q. 183, a. 3). The diversity of degrees of dignity (*gradus*)—often linked with functions or states—contributes, by the resulting harmonious order, to the beauty of the church (IIa IIae, q. 183, a. 2). However, Aquinas focuses his reflection here on the concept of a state of life. In fact, thirteenth-century law gave Thomas a certain civil "analog" in the established difference between the *state of servitude* and the *state of freedom* (IIa IIae, q. 183, a. 1). A *state of life* is defined here as a stable social situation, recognized by society, and, therefore, juridically determined.[30] This notion of a state of life (or of a condition) supports a direct relationship with the tandem of freedom and servitude.[31] It achieves this through

the mediation of the idea of *permanent obligation*, which enters into its definition.[32] To be in a given state of life is always to be either obliged or free in relation to something else.

In spite of the vast overview planned in IIa IIae, q. 183, Thomas in no way becomes involved in a systematic study of the proliferating diversity of ministries and states of life. Moreover, certain aspects concern canon law rather than theology, while others are better placed with the study of the social sacraments, which structure the ecclesial community (Holy Orders and Matrimony; IIa IIae, q. 184, Prol.).[33] Thomas, therefore, confines himself here to the question of the state of perfection.

The State of Perfection

The Christian life, Thomas never ceases to repeat, "consists principally in charity, by which the soul is united to God" (IIa IIae, q. 184, a. 1, ad 2).[34] Thomas is signifying here that the perfection of the Christian life is nothing else than the perfection of charity.[35] Although, in the life of heaven, it is the intellectual act of the beatific vision that establishes the most perfect possible union with God, on earth, in the human condition as wayfarer, it is the supernatural love of charity that unites a person most closely to God. Understand, however, that there are degrees of charity. It can increase, or inversely, diminish (IIa IIae, q. 24, aa. 4–10). This growth is not, however, linear. It passes through qualitative thresholds, which allow the identification of stages or degrees of the spiritual life. A venerable spiritual tradition marks three of these: the state of *beginners*, of the *advanced*, and of the *perfect* (IIa IIae, q. 183, a. 4; IIa IIae, q. 24, a. 9).[36] The state of the perfect is, thus, the term of growth in charity in this world.

According to Thomas, the perfection—not the one which in heaven consists in the complete love of God and of neighbor—is found in a state in which every aspect of a Christian's life, at least in a habitual way, refers to God, who is loved beyond all else (IIa IIae, q. 184, a. 2). This implies that all that might oppose the dynamism of the love for God be resolutely discarded. Such a perfection of charity is mandatory—all Christians without exception should tend toward it. "You shall love the

Lord your God with all your heart . . ." (Deut 6:5). This commandment is addressed to everyone and allows of no half-measures. All Christians, therefore, are bound to observe the *precepts* (*praecepta*), beginning with the twofold commandment of charity and the precepts that forbid conduct directly opposed to the life of charity.

This perfection of charity, to which every Christian is called, is tied directly to inner spiritual freedom. The more charity attaches a person to God, the freer and more detached that person is from all that is not God. "He is perfect in charity," writes Thomas, inverting the celebrated Augustinian definition of sin, "who loves God to the point of despising himself and all that belongs to him."[37] But this spiritual freedom, the effect and sign of perfect charity, can be obtained in many ways. One privileged way consists in practicing the counsels recommended by the Lord Jesus in the Gospels. These evangelical counsels—voluntary poverty, chastity, and obedience—are not the perfection itself of the Christian life, nor are they the absolutely necessary means for attaining it, as are the precepts. Nonetheless, they are "a certain type of instrument for attaining perfection" (IIa IIae, q. 184, a. 3, ad 1).[38] They are relative means, but particularly appropriate for reaching the state of perfect charity. In fact, they free the Christian in relation to certain things, such as marriage or secular business, which are not contrary to charity in themselves, but which often hinder the complete spiritual freedom of belonging only to God.

The liberating practice of the evangelical counsels may be left to personal initiative, but ordinarily it is sanctioned in a public and stable way. Thus, those who make profession to follow the counsels and commit themselves to this by vow enter into a very clearly defined state of ecclesial life which is called "the state of perfection." It is a state of servitude—since Thomas defines the state in relation to freedom or to obligation—but a servitude that is paradoxically liberating. Those who embrace this state of life become, at the heart of the Christian community, the social symbol, the image, of that holiness that defines the church of Jesus Christ in its totality.

But Thomas is quite aware that all those who are perfect are not living in the state of perfection (IIa IIae, q. 184, a. 4). Not only can the evangelical counsels be lived in a non-institutional manner, but the full Christian freedom they favor can also be found actualized in Christians engaged in states of life incompatible with the effective practice of the counsels. The example of Abraham, who was wealthy, married, and free to dispose of himself and his affairs, is offered to show that holiness can be achieved independently of the practice of the counsels. Abraham's situation resulted from perfect charity, which gave him true spiritual freedom by detaching his human heart from all purely earthly affections.[39]

The Religious Life

The ecclesial state of perfection admits of a twofold fulfillment, which Aquinas does not hesitate to say is equivocal: the *episcopal state* (IIa IIae, q. 185) and the *religious life* (IIa IIae, qq. 186–89).[40] The state of perfection is comprised of persons who solemnly commit themselves to something that is connected to perfection.[41] The "something" in question might either dispose a person to perfect charity or manifest this charity. Thus, the evangelical counsels, publicly vowed, prepare believers for perfect charity by freeing them from the cares of earthly business, so as to leave them more open to the things of God. As for the "care of souls" (*cura animarum*), it is in itself an effect of perfect charity. As the bishop is irrevocably committed to this by virtue of his consecration, and as he is obliged to exercise the most perfect charity in fulfilling his pastoral duties, especially in accepting the possibility of "laying down his life for his sheep" (Jn 10:11), which is the highest expression of charity, the episcopate truly constitutes a state of perfection.[42]

The state of perfection, therefore, does not have the same meaning for the episcopate and the religious life. One might say that the bishop is in a state of acquired perfection that is to be exercised, in the sense that he assumes a ministry that in some way presupposes and develops charity. As for the religious person, she or he is in a state of perfection to be acquired (IIa IIae, q. 186, a. 1, ad 4).[43] Such a person takes certain means leading to perfect charity, so that the religious life might be defined as a school of perfection.

Thomas's examination of the religious state is among the most committed in the *Summa theologiae* (IIa IIae, qq. 186–89). Indeed, the evangelical reawakening of the thirteenth century found expression in the appearance of new forms of religious life, the mendicant orders, particularly the Order of Friars Minor of St. Francis of Assisi and the Friars Preachers of St. Dominic, whose ideal of doctrinal preaching in evangelical poverty attracted the young Thomas Aquinas. But soon enough, in certain places, such as the University of Paris, these new religious orders had to face the hostility of the secular clergy.[44] The conflict between the mendicants and the secular clergy had many facets, and, quite rightly, the ecclesiological stakes were especially high, but the theology of the religious life was also directly involved; it was the very legitimacy of these new forms of religious life, irreducible to classical monasticism or even to the canonical life, which was under attack.[45] Thomas undertook the defense of the Dominican ideal, and the collection of texts where he treats this question, whether in his works of synthesis or his occasional works, forms an important *corpus* on the theology of the religious life.[46]

In IIa IIae, q. 186, Thomas defines the very essence of the religious life. The expression "religious" life indicates a particular affinity between this state of life and the moral virtue of religion, by which one is devoted to the service of God through worship, and, thus, "reconnects" (*re-ligare*) to God. Now, this union with God, which charity actualizes fully, defines Christian perfection. Thus, the religious person, who is devoted completely and, therefore, in a stable and definitive way, to divine worship, going so far as to make of his or her own life a holocaust, is in a state of perfection. This is the purpose of public vows to observe the evangelical counsels of poverty,[47] chastity, and, above all, obedience.

Thomas next turns to "the activities of religious," an argument that clearly bears the marks of contemporary controversies (IIa IIae, q. 187). Thus, Thomas defends the compatibility of, and even the special appropriate-

ness existing between, religious life and the apostolic works of preaching and teaching (IIa IIae, q. 187, a. 1). He also challenges the idea that manual work is an essential part of religious life (IIa IIae, q. 187, a. 3), and justifies the practice of begging (IIa IIae, q. 187, aa. 4–5).

The diversity of religious institutes, or types of religious life, is the object of the following question (IIa IIae, q. 188). According to Thomas, this distinction is based on the diversity of the works of charity to which a religious order may be dedicated, and, only secondarily, on the diversity of the exercises or practices that characterize a given religious institute (IIa IIae, q. 188, a. 1). Thus, religious orders dedicated to contemplation may be fundamentally distinguished from those devoted to some work of the active life, ranging from the armed defense of Christianity (IIa IIae, q. 188, a. 3) to preaching (IIa IIae, q. 188, a. 4), a work which presupposes study ordered to knowledge (IIa IIae, q. 188, a. 5). The plurality of religious congregations calls for some ordering. There must be a hierarchy among them. It flows from the hierarchy of ends these congregations pursue (IIa IIae, q. 188, a. 6). Here, Thomas uses the principles already employed when comparing the active and contemplative lives (IIa IIae, q. 182). Of themselves, religious orders devoted to contemplation are superior to those that give themselves to works of the active life, unless the work of the active life in question intrinsically implies contemplation, which is the case with apostolic orders devoted to preaching and teaching. These apostolic orders are, therefore, objectively superior to purely contemplative orders and are at the summit of the hierarchy of religious orders.[48]

Charity, Thomas often explains, is the form or soul of all Christian virtues (for example, IIa IIae, q. 23, a. 8). "The bond of perfection" (Col 3:14), charity effects the unity of the personal life of the Christian, as well as that of the ecclesial community. How apt, then, for the *Secunda pars* of the *Summa theologiae* to close, in connection with the state of perfection, by recalling the primacy of charity in the Christian life. Henceforth, the gaze of the theologian could turn in the *Tertia pars* toward the One who, in the concrete economy of salvation, is for everyone

the superabundant source of this charity: Jesus Christ.

Notes

[1]"Postquam dictum est de singulis virtutibus et
vitiis quae pertinent ad omnium hominum conditiones et status, nunc considerandum est de his quae
specialiter ad aliquos homines pertinent." See also
the General Prologue of IIa IIae.

[2]It would be helpful to refer to the commentary
that Thomas gives on these chapters in his *Lectura
prior in epistulas Pauli* (1263–65).

[3]Some charisms, such as prophecy or the gift of
tongues, played a role of primary importance in the
foundation of the church. In fact, they will not
disappear for as long as the church perdures. In this
segment of the *Summa*, many indices attest that the
charisms Aquinas addresses are *always* active in the
church. On the different ages of prophecy, see ST
IIa IIae, q. 174, a. 6.

[4]For example, the gift of prophecy could be bestowed on someone who does not have charity.
ST IIa IIae, q. 172, a. 4: "[D]atur enim prophetia
ad utilitatem Ecclesiae, sicut et aliae gratiae gratis
datae . . . ; non autem ordinatur directe ad hoc
quod affectus ipsius prophetae coniungatur Deo,
ad quod ordinatur caritas. Et ideo prophetia potest
esse sine bonitate morum . . ."

[5]See ST IIa IIae, q. 171, Prol.: "Omnia vero quae
ad cognitionem pertinent, sub prophetia comprehendi possunt. Nam prophetica revelatio se extendit
non solum ad futuros hominum eventus, sed etiam
ad res divinas . . ."

[6]On the Thomist teaching on revelation, see
Leon Elders, ed., *La doctrine de la révélation divine de
saint Thomas d'Aquin*. [*Actes du symposium sur la pensée
de saint Thomas d'Aquin, tenu á Rolduc, les 4 et 5
novembre 1989*] (Rome: Libreria Editrice Vaticana,
1990).

[7] Thomas returned to the theme of prophecy on
several occasions, notably in his scriptural commentaries: *De veritate*, q. 12 (Leonine, 365–414); SCG
III, chap. 154; *Postilla super psalmos, Proemium*, and
L, 8 (Parma, 148–50, 349–50); *Postilla super Isaiam*,
c. 1, 6 (Leonine, 8–19, 47–53); *Postilla super Ieremiam*, c. 18 (Parma, 622–24); *In Mattheum*, c. 1, lect.
5 (no. 145–46) (Marietti, 21); *In Ioan.*, c. 11, lect. 7
(no. 1577–79) (Marietti, 294–95); *In ad Rom.*, c. 12,
lect. 2 (Marietti, 181–84), and c. 14, lect. 3 (Marietti,
211–13); *In I ad Cor.*, c. 12, lect. 1–2 (Marietti,
367–72); c. 13, lect. 3–4 (Marietti, 384–88); and c.
14, lect. 1, 6 (Marietti, 389–91, 400–401); *In ad Heb.*,
c. 11, lect. 7 (Marietti, 474–76).

[8]The reference work on this question remains
that of Bruno Decker, *Die Entwicklung der Lehre von
der prophetischen Offenbarung von Wilhelm von Aux-*

erre bis zu Thomas von Aquin, (Breslau: Kallmünz
über Regensburg: Lassleben, 1940). On the histo-
rico-doctrinal context in which Thomistic reflection took place, see Jean-Pierre Torrell, O.P.,
*Recherches sur la théorie de la prophétie au Moyen Âge,
XIIe–XIVe siècles. Études et textes* (Fribourg: Éditions
universitaires, 1992). Marianne Schlosser, *Lucerna
in caliginoso loco Aspekte des Prophetic-Begrilles in der
scholastischen Theologie* (Paderborn: Ferdinand
Schöningh, 2000).

[9]Serafino M. Zarb, O.P., "Le fonti agostiniane del
trattato sulla profezia di S. Tommaso d'Aquino," in
Angelicum 15 (1938): 169–200.

[10]On the theory of prophecy in Latin theology of
the first half of the thirteenth century, see *Théorie de
la prophétie et philosophie de la connaissance aux environs
de 1230. la contribution d'Hugues de Saint-Cher (Ms.
Douai 434, Question 481)*, ed. Jean-Pierre Torrell,
O.P., Spicilegium sacrum lovaniense 40 (Louvain:
Peeters, 1977).

[11]Thomas seems to take up this position especially in regard to Avicenna and Maimonides. On
Avicenna, see Louis Gardet, *La pensée religieuse
d'Avicenne (Ibn Sina)* (Paris: Librairie Philosophique
J. Vrin, 1951), 107–41. On Maimonides, who treats
of prophecy in *The Guide of the Perplexed*, II, chaps.
32–48, see Avital Wohlman, *Thomas d'Aquin et
Maïmonide: un dialogue exemplaire* (Paris: Cerf,
1988), 267–317.

[12]See Leo Strauss, *Maïmonide* (Paris: Presses universitaires de France, 1988), 101–42.

[13]On the status of these natural revealed truths,
see P. Synave, O.P., "La révélation des vérités divines
naturelles d'après saint Thomas d'Aquin," in
*Mélanges Mandonnet. Études d'histoire littéraire et doc-
trinale du Moyen Âge*, vol. 1 (Paris: Librairie Philosophique J. Vrin, 1930), 327–70.

[14]On the question of the knowledge of future
contingents in Thomas, see, among recent works,
Harm J. M. J. Goris, *Free Creatures of an Eternal God:
Thomas Aquinas on God's Foreknowledge and Irresistible
Will* (Leuven: Peeters, 1996).

[15]See Jean Richard, "Le processus psychologique
de la révélation prophétique selon saint Thomas
d'Aquin. Commentaire historique et doctrinal de
IIa IIae, q. 173, a. 2," *Laval théologique et philosophique*
23 (1967): 42–75.

[16]In my "Le rôle de l'image dans la connaissance
prophetique d'après saint Thomas d'Aquin"(*Revue
Thomiste* 89 [1989]: 533–68), I tried to show that the
"miraculous" origin of the underlying imagery of
prophecy was not essential to the Thomist theory,
and that one might bypass it in favor of a theory of
the supernatural organization of *species* by the intellect, activated by the *lumen propheticum*, which allows one to promote a theory of prophecy that
insists on a certain immanence of supernatural
knowledge.

[17]It is necessary to emphasize that the purely intellectual vision is not cut off from all relationships to images. Even the direct knowledge of intelligible truths presupposes some imaginative support in this world. See ST IIa IIae, q. 174, a. 2, ad 4. The difference between an intellectual and an imaginative vision does not lie in the presence or absence of a reference to images, but in the fact that in the imaginative vision the intelligible truth must be deduced from a symbol while it is given directly as such in the intellectual vision.

[18]*De veritate*, q. 12 addresses prophecy, and q. 13 treats of rapture. Note also that q. 14 begins the theme of faith, which shows the structural bond, in Thomist theology, between reflection on faith and reflection on prophecy (Leonine, 365ff.).

[19]See, for example, Pierre Benoit, O.P., "Révélation et inspiration. Selon la Bible, chez saint Thomas et dans les discussions modernes," *Revue biblique* 70 (1963): 321–70.

[20]See Jean Leclercq, "La vie contemplative dans saint Thomas et dans la tradition," *Recherches de théologie ancienne et médiévale* 28 (1961): 251–68; Jean-Hervé Nicolas, *Contemplation et vie contemplative en christianisme* (Paris: Beauchesne, 1980); Inos Biffi, *Teologia, storia e contemplazione in Tommaso d'Aquino* (Milano: Jaca Book, 1995), chap. 1.

[21]Speculative and practical knowledge are distinguished by their ends. But it is important to understand clearly that practical knowledge is not, as is often imagined, an initially speculative knowledge that has become practical because a person wants to apply it, of his free choice, to action. People imagine that there is some kind of undifferentiated knowledge which, at the person's choice, remains speculative or becomes practical. In this case, when it is affirmed that practical and speculative knowledge are distinguished according to their ends, it is a question of a finality extrinsic to knowledge: the *finis operantis*, that is, the end sought by the person in his or her knowing. But this is not the case. Speculative and practical knowledge are in reality distinguished by the *finis operis*, that is, the finality intrinsic to the knowledge. It is as the knowledge stands in itself, and not in virtue of some superadded intention, that practical knowledge differs from speculative knowledge. The speculative knowledge of a house (which consists in knowing the quiddity of the house, its essence) is, therefore, not the same thing as the practical knowledge of the house (which consists in knowing the house as something that is to be built). The principle of this practical knowledge is not the essence of the house, but the end of the house, and a person reasons in order to know by what means and through what steps this end may be attained concretely. On this question, see Marie-Michel Labourdette, "Note sur les diversifications du savoir:

connaissance spéculative et connaissance pratique," *Revue Thomiste* 44 (1938): 564–68.

[22]"Vita activa et contemplativa distinguuntur secundum diversa studia hominum intendentium ad diversos fines, quorum unum est consideratio veritatis, quae est finis vitae contemplativae, aliud autem est exterior operatio ad quam ordinatur vita activa."

[23]Thomas often refers to these types. See, among many others, ST IIa IIae, q. 179, a. 2, *sed contra*; q. 182, a. 1.

[24]"Per eam fit nobis quaedam inchoatio beatitudinis."

[25]"Aliquis ex dilectione Dei, inardescit ad eius pulchritudinem conspiciendam."

[26]"Et sic patet quod, cum aliquis a contemplativa vita ad activam vocatur, non fit per modum subtractionis, sed per modum additionis."

[27]On this mixed work of teaching Christian truth and its relation to contemplation, see Marie-Michel Labourdette, "L'idéal dominicain," *Revue Thomiste* 92 (1992): 344–54.

[28]"Sed vita activa secundum quam aliquis praedicando et docendo contemplata aliis tradit, est perfectior quam vita quae solum contemplatur, quia talis vita praesupponit abundantiam contemplationis. Et ideo Christus talem vita elegit."

[29]In ST IIa IIae, q. 168, a. 3, ad 3, the term *officium* is applied to the profession of a comedian! It designates any profession, any social function.

[30]See *Quodlibet* I, q. 7, a. 2, ad 2: "aliquid enim sollemne et perpetuum dicitur habere statum, sicut patet de statu libertatis vel matrimonii, et similium" (Leonine, 197)

[31]See *Quodlibet* III, q. 6, a. 3: "Cum dicimus aliquos esse in statu perfectionis, accipitur status pro conditione" (Leonine, 269–70).

[32]See J.A. Robilliard, "Sur la notion de condition (*status*) en saint Thomas," *Revue des sciences philosophiques et théologiques* (1936): 104–7.

[33]"Nam consideratio officiorum, quantum quidem ad alios actus, pertinet ad legis positores."

[34]"Vita autem Christiana specialiter in caritate consistit, per quam anima Deo coniungitur."

[35]"Et ideo secundum caritatem simpliciter attenditur perfectio Christianae vitae." See *De perf. vit. spir.*, chap. 1: "Simpliciter ergo in spirituali vita perfectus est qui est in caritate perfectus" (Leonine, B69, 39–40).

[36]One can refer, for this distinction, as in a more general way for the theme of Christian perfection, to Reginald Garrigou-Lagrange, *The Three Ages of the Interior Life, Prelude of Eternal Life*, trans. Sr. M. Timothea Doyle (St. Louis: Herder, 1948).

[37]*In Mattheum*, 19, n. 1593: "Ille ergo est perfectus in caritate, qui diligit Deum usque ad contemptum sui et suorum" (Marietti, 244).

[38]"Consilia sunt quaedam instrumenta perveniendi ad perfectionem."

[39]Abraham was a model of perfection and yet he was rich, see ST IIa IIae, q. 185, a. 6, ad 1: "Potest esse summa perfectio cum magna opulentia: nam Abraham, cui dictum est, Gen 17, 'Ambula coram me,' legitur dives fuisse." Likewise, he was married and this in no way deflected him from the love of divine things. See SCG III, chap. 137.

[40]*In Matthaeum*, 19, no. 1594: "Status perfectionis duplex est, praelatorum et religiosorum; sed aequivoce . . ." (Marietti, 244).

[41]See *Quodlibet* I, q. 7, a. 2, ad 2 (Leonine, 196–97).

[42]Secular priests, even if they have the care of souls, cannot be said to be in a state of perfection, basically because their *cura animarum* is in itself revokable, see ST IIa IIae, q. 184, a. 6, and parallel places.

[43]"Religionis status principaliter est institutus *ad perfectionem adipiscendam* per quaedam exercitia quibus tolluntur impedimenta perfectae caritatis."

[44]On the history of the first phase of the Parisian controversy, see Michel-Marie Dufeil, *Guillaume de Saint-Amour et la polémique universitaire parisienne, 1250–1259* (Paris: A. et J. Picard, 1972).

[45]See Yves Congar, "Les enjeux ecclésiologiques de la querelle entre mendiants et séculiers dans la seconde moitié du xiiie siècle et le début du xive," *Archives d'histoire doctrinale et littéraire du Moyen Âge* 28 (1961): 34–151.

[46]See Jean-Pierre Torrell, *Initiation à saint Thomas. Sa personne et son oeuvre* (Paris: Cerf-Editions universitaires, 1993), chap. 5.

[47]Thomas firmly opposed certain Franciscan theologians who sometimes tended to identify poverty and perfection. For him, poverty is and should remain a means to perfection. See ST IIa IIae, q. 185, a. 6, ad 1: "Perfectio Christianae vitae non consistit essentialiter in voluntaria paupertate, sed voluntaria paupertas instrumentaliter operatur ad perfectionem vitae. Unde non oportet quod ubi est maior paupertas, ibi sit maior perfectio." See also q. 188, a. 7. These texts in which Thomas relativizes evangelical poverty are at the heart of the controversies aroused at the end of the thirteenth century and the beginning of the fourteenth century by the Franciscan partisans of radical poverty. See Ulrich

Horst, *Evangelische Armut und Kirche: Thomas von Aquin und die Armutskontroversen des 13. und beginnenden 14. Jahrhunderts* (Berlin: Akademie Verlag, 1992).

[48]In ST IIa IIae, q. 189 (on entrance into religious life), Thomas offers the main elements of his response to the grievance held against mendicants by the secular clergy, that the candidates they received into religion were too young. Thomas amply developed this question in his brief work *Contra doctrinam retrahentium a religione* (around 1271) as well as in his *Quodlibet* IV, q. 23.

Selected Further Reading

Biffi, Inos. *Teologia, storia e contemplazione in Tommaso d'Aquino*. Milano: Jaca Book, 1995.

Bonino, Serge-Thomas. "L'image dans la connaissance prophétique." *Revue thomiste* 89 (1989): 533–68.

Decker, Bruno. *Die Entwicklung der Lehre von der prophetischen Offenbarung von Wilhem von Auxerre bis zu Thomas von Aquin*. Kallmünz über Regensburg: Lassleben, 1940.

Leclercq, Jean. "La vie contemplative dans saint Thomas et dans la tradition." *Recherches de théologie ancienne et medievale* 28 (1961): 251–68.

Nicolas, Jean-Hervé. *Contemplation et vie contemplative en christianisme*. Paris: Beauchesne, 1980.

Pocquet du Hank-Jussé, Laurent-Marie. *La Vie religiuse d'aprés saint Thomas d'Aquin*. Paris: Téqui, 2000.

Richard, Jean. "Le processus psychologique de la révélation prophétique selon saint Thomas d' Aquin. Commentaire historique et doctrinal de IIa–IIae, q. 173, a. 2." *Laval théologique et philosophique* 23 (1967): 42–75.

Torrell, Jean-Pierre. *Recherches sur la théorie de la prophétie au Moyen Âge, XIIe-XIVe siècle, Etudes et textes*. Fribourg: Editions universitaires, 1992.

———. *Initiation à saint Thomas. Sa personne et son oeuvre*. Paris-Fribourg: Cerf-Editions universitaires, 1993.

Wohlman, A. *Thomas d'Aquin et Maïmonide. Un dialogue exemplaire*. Paris: Cerf, 1988.

PART III

The Twentieth-Century Legacy

Interpreting Thomas Aquinas: Aspects of the Dominican School of Moral Theology in the Twentieth Century

Thomas F. O'Meara, O.P.

This essay, a contribution to a volume whose purpose is to present in a vital way Thomas Aquinas's theology of the Christian life, sketches some figures in recent moral theology. The following pages do not examine an ethical issue; rather, this is a study of the approaches of moral theologians who themselves claim the same teacher. This chapter is a study of that work's commentators and disciples—an exercise in the hermeneutics of a thinker's teaching as it perdures in a tradition or school.

Each century is heir to the centuries gone before: one understands better the directions for theology chosen in the 1920s or 1950s when some attention is given to theologies from earlier ages such as Trent, the Baroque, and the Enlightenment—although here I can only intimate earlier times. How did Dominican theologians in the twentieth century interpret Aquinas's moral theology, the Second Part of the *Summa theologiae*? We are interested not so much in what they said about the virtue of fortitude or about certain sins against chastity but in their use of the *Summa theologiae* and its foundational themes—the missions of the Trinity, the structure of the human person, the presence called grace, and the interaction between grace and the human personality in virtues and gifts.

I would not want to imply that six centuries of Dominican Thomism is the only approach to understanding the *Summa theologiae*; however, it is clearly one important cluster of traditions. How did twentieth-century Dominican interpreters retain a certain fidelity to Aquinas? Were they similar to each other? Were they faithful to the letter of the *Summa theologiae?* First, I will examine the basic structure of the *Prima secundae*, the central role of grace, and its modalities like virtues; I will then turn to four Dominican theologies from different periods and different countries that work within that framework. My goal is to outline the modern interpretations of the graced life as it is presented in Aquinas's great work.[1]

THE GRACED LIFE IN THE *SUMMA THEOLOGIAE*

Leonard Boyle has argued that the *Summa theologiae* was originally conceived as a work on moral theology (hence its lengthy Second Part), a handbook for the theological students in Rome preparing for the Dominican ministry of preaching and hearing confessions.[2] "By prefacing the Secunda or moral part with a Prima pars on God, Trinity, and Creation, and then rounding it off with a Tertia pars on the Son of God, Incarnation, and the Sacraments, Thomas put practical theology, the study of Christian man, his virtues and vices, in a full theological context."[3] Thomas's *Summa* was to be a manual on virtues and vices aimed at preachers and confessors. Perhaps an earlier Dominican work served as a model: William Peyraut (1200–71) was a contemporary of Albert the Great and Vincent of Beauvais. Living in the Lyons priory with Stephen of Bourbon, author of *De septem donis Spiritus Sancti*, and with Peter of Tarentaise, theologian and later pope, he worked on his *Summa de vitiis et virtutibus* in the 1230s and 1240s. The first part treats forty-one vices in the framework of the seven capital sins; the second part has five tracts dealing with the virtues in general, with faith, hope, and charity, with the gifts of the Holy Spirit, and with forty subsidiary virtues. In both parts, the author develops sermon topics and gives biblical documentation and examples. As William Hinnebusch noted, "hundreds of manuscripts and many printed editions testify to its popularity."[4]

One should approach Thomas's *Summa* first, not as a warehouse of theological conclusions, but as a structure of interrelated themes and thought-forms. Benedictine Guy Lafont compares the *Summa* to a cathedral: "The Christian reality is too complex. . . . In this sense the *Summa theologiae* resembles the great churches of the Middle Ages. Its architectural perfection appears at first glance and which nevertheless manifests to close observation a richness of invention and adaptation in its totality and in its detail, but for which it is not easy to express in a formula the idea of the builder."[5] Certain characteristics of Aquinas's mindset are well-known: a confidence in human ideas and thought-forms explaining revelation; an attention to the real and an appreciation of the activity of secondary causes; grace not condemning or replacing human nature but really mediated through person and sacramentality.[6] All of the Second Part is a treatise on grace. Grace, like justification and sanctification, salvation and redemption, is simply one traditional word for what underlies most of religion. There are many theologies of grace in Christianity, East and West, and Aquinas represents but one. Grace bespeaks a deeper relationship to God than does nature; it is what Jesus called the reign of God, or what John and Paul called the Spirit indwelling. Having established human and divine principles of supernatural life (Ia IIae), Aquinas turned to its realization in active persons (IIa IIae). Personality and grace combine to enact a Christian life; they delineate the subjects and agents, the virtues and beatitudes, and finally the states and offices where grace is concretized in social life.

The first article of the *Summa theologiae* announces the vast work's subject: a special *ordo*, a realm above human nature. Every question and each article is engaged by a teleology of the supernatural, which is the result of a divine plan (predestination) and a presence (Trinitarian mission) unfolding in a new life-principle, grace. The Word and Spirit come to people to enable that special life.

> It is not suitable that God provides more for creatures being led by divine love to a natural good than for those creatures to whom that love offers a supernatural good. For natural creatures God provides generously . . . kinds of forms and powers which are principles of acts so that they are inclined to activity through their own beings . . . . Even more for those moved to reach an eternal supernatural good he infuses certain forms or qualities of the supernatural order according to which easily and enthusiastically they are moved by God to attain that good which is eternal. And so the gift of grace is a kind of quality.[7] (Ia IIae, q. 110, a. 2)

Preacher at the cathedral of Notre Dame and member of the French Academy, A. M. Carré described the panorama of the *Summa theologiae* in this way: "So I take my place in a universe on the move. And God himself proposes my destiny to me. But this destiny I must make my own. St. Thomas sees in this personal appropriation the religious act par excellence."[8] The *Summa* is a kind of physics of salvation, a psychology of the presence of the Spirit described in the eighth chapter of Paul's Letter to the Romans.

The Second Part of the *Summa theologiae* studies the human journey amid sin and grace. This is no geographical trip; rather, this is life itself, a journey built of actions described by Aristotle's psychology. Aquinas's moral theology describes active potentialities in both nature and grace. Grace is not the multiple actual graces of the Baroque (not mentioned) but a new life-principle ("a kind of quality" or "a created form"; Ia IIae, q. 110, aa. 1–4);[9] its array of powers living within an organic life assist human beings in reaching a destiny which is both human and divine.[10] In the *Prima secundae*, Aquinas moves from psychological powers through realms of realities ("laws" of nature, religion, the Jewish people) to a climax: a law that is *presence*, a divine power, a gift to humans, which is the Holy Spirit. "That, however, which is most powerful in the law of the New Testament and in which its entire power consists is the grace of the Holy Spirit given by Christ to believers" (Ia IIae, q. 106, a. 1).[11] God instructs not through epiphany but through presence. If the New Law is the Spirit of the Risen Jesus, that life is described by Jesus's teaching and life, particularly by the Sermon on the Mount.

Why does grace come after infused virtues and spiritual gifts have been considered? That is a puzzling structural question, and its answer lies in the nature of Aristotelianism, which begins as a science of natural and living bodies. Actions disclose natures, and so the actions of the human person and even those actions of self-sacrifice for others in love or courage lead us to the stable principles of the person. The active graced person leads the conclusion of the need for and reality of a principle, grace. Thomas then considers activities in light of *that* source.

The relationship of virtues to grace is similar to that of the faculties of the personality to the vivifying soul or of actions to their specifying nature. "Just as from the essence of the soul powers flow to be the principles of activities, so also from grace itself powers flow forth in the potencies of the soul by which these are moved to their activities" (Ia IIae, q. 110, a. 4, ad 1).[12] Just as faith, hope, and charity are infused with grace, so, too, do the cardinal virtues and their subvirtues emerge, not as philosophical or biblical ideas or exercised practices, but from the Spirit.[13] Virtues, on Thomas's view, are not simply duties attached to biblical words or grooves for actions, both sparked by some faint divine influence. "Theological virtues conferred on us by God direct us to a supernatural destiny. So it is right that also there correspond to these theological virtues other habits divinely caused in us which are related to theological virtues just as moral and intellectual virtues are related to the natural principles of the virtues" (Ia IIae, q. 63, a. 3).[14]

For Aquinas, unlike some of his predecessors, charity was not synonymous with the Holy Spirit or grace. "The grace of God is called the form of the virtues inasmuch as it gives spiritual existence to the soul, so that it is able to receive the virtues. But charity is the form of the virtues since it forms their operation."[15] Charity is one virtue, "the most excellent virtue," but it is not the motor or source of virtues (IIa IIae, q. 23, a. 6). Remaining on

the same level as all the other virtues, it confers a dynamic orientation because love in this life reaches to the loved object, to the Trinity itself. In this sense, a "form" gives a special causal and teleological direction while not replacing the virtues' own work.[16] Justice has its own form, object, and goal; prudence, moreover, the virtue of the practical intellect, is a second directing force with similarities to charity.[17] Grace cannot be the same as the theological virtues, because habits and actions like the virtues necessarily imply a subject; there are virtues beyond the acquired natural virtues, for these latter cannot reach a supernatural destiny.[18]

Grace and virtues have further, climactic modes: gifts, beatitudes, fruits of the Spirit (Ia IIae, q. 69, a. 70). Here, virtue has reached a connatural contact with the reign of God—and yet this occurs not in extraordinary or transient charisms but in ordinary Christian life (Ia IIae, q. 68, a. 2). The Dominican school emphasizes the gifts of the Spirit; for them, moral theology does not end with an ascetically developed set of virtues nor with will power or rational discussion; instead, its object is an intuitive familiarity with the divine.[19]

Aquinas's theology of grace and virtues must be understood within the entire sweep of the missions of the Trinity, the incarnate Word in Jesus's life, and the ongoing incarnation of Christian sacraments and life leading to an eschatological flowering of the life-principle of grace in the style of Dante's *Paradiso*. Albert Patfoort sees in the Second Part of the *Summa theologiae* "three zones of great pneumatological concentration: gifts, the new law, and a treatise on grace."[20] There is in the *Summa* a distinct harmony of creation and grace. Furthermore (among other patterns), Thomas's argument takes the form of crescendo. That process moves from philosophical analysis to the explicitly revealed, while in other moments it builds toward a greater intensification of supernatural being. For instance, the First Part leads to a climax of being or goodness which is particularly God's own (Ia, q. 6, a. 4); Trinitarian processions flow out on missions to earth; creation leads to that creature where matter and spirit intersect. In the Second Part grace appears slowly in a series of intensifications, "Zones of pneumatic concentration": supernatural destiny, graced habits, evangelical law, grace. The *Summa* thus reaches the divine presence manifest in some intensity—in the quasi-form of sanctifying grace, in Christ's uncreated and created grace, in the instrumentality of the sacraments.

THOMISMS, PAST AND PRESENT

To the outsider, the Catholic Church can appear to be a large group upon which authority has bestowed monoformity. In fact, it includes considerable diversity, a diversity derived from the variety of religious orders, spiritualities, movements, educational and caritative institutions, and theological schools. This last organization, the theological school, is perhaps one of the most important contributors to the internal diversity of the church. A theological school crafts a perspective on Christianity, that is, a theological theory developed within a university or a religious order. Citing Scotism and Suarezianism, the Baroque École Française, and the Tübingen school, Karl Rahner described theological schools as "structures which within the church and its creeds form a more or less deep and unified perspective on theology or spirituality. . . . The church has (one could say with some shock, in a generous and naive way) recognized, indulged, and protected the simultaneous existence (even in points where they were mutually contradictory) of diverse moral theologies."[21] These schools have their births, their demises, their contributions, and their disputes. An article in the *Dictionnaire de spiritualité* observes how "the fact of a diversity of schools of spirituality in the church is inevitable" and sees schools as the intersection of individuals and movements and cultural periods. "It would be accurate to say that the life of the church *requires* this multitude of particular spiritualities."[22] Still, the more a particular school realizes that it is but one ministry and one perspective, the more it will help the entire church; its limitations serve its insight and fidelity.

Thomism is a theological school—perhaps it is best seen as a family of theological schools—committed in different ways to the principles and insights of Thomas Aquinas's thought. The history of Thomism up to the present has had four periods: the age of defenses (the thirteenth to fifteenth centuries); the age of commentaries (the mid-1400s to the early 1600s); the age of controversies, encyclopedias, and compendia (the mid-1500s to the mid-1700s); and the modern neo-Thomist revival (1840 to 1960).[23] The long history of Thomism is marked by two major neo-Thomist revivals, one in the sixteenth century and one lasting from 1860 to 1960.[24]

As Vatican II began in 1962, Roman Catholic moral theology was found in seminaries, houses of studies for religious orders, and the orders themselves. The ethics for clergy and laity came from textbooks whose Aristotelian language and theological conceptuality were neoscholastic (but not necessarily neo-Thomist). For the Dominicans, the text of Aquinas's *Summa theologiae* has served as the text for moral theology in one way or another from the fourteenth century, and, in 1571, the Dominicans divided theological education into speculative theology and moral theology (both studied in that *Summa*), and "practical moral" treating concrete problems in morality, canon law, and liturgy.[25] Dominicans saw negative consequences resulting from the Baroque: a separation of moral theology from the rest of theology, a loosening of the moral virtues from the habit of grace treated apart in dogmatic theology, a view of the Christian life as natural virtuous habits sparked by actual grace, and a separation of spirituality from theology involving an emphasis on the extraordinary. But, that which was criticized eventually entered into the Dominican books.

The Dominican school, in contrast to later theologies of actual graces or philosophies of human virtues, placed a constant emphasis on grace as the supernatural source and character of the virtuous life. Naturally, there were criticisms of the Dominican school, which existed amid several other neo-Thomist ones and many neoscholastic directions; its emphasis on grace might obscure psychological effort in cultivating virtue, or its insistence on infused virtues beyond the three theological ones might end in a dualism. On the other hand, the Dominicans protested that some neoscholastic theologies, while never fully setting aside Aquinas's principles, focused on verbal categories and psychological faculties and did not emphasize the Trinitarian milieu and telos of the virtuous life. The graced personality, the mature climax of the image of God in the Spirit's new law and gifts were set in the shadows of the more luminous Baroque heroics and failings.

NEO-THOMIST INTERPRETATIONS OF VIRTUES AND GRACE

To explicate the tradition of the Dominican school through the twentieth century, I will briefly examine four theologies. Of these four (from five writers), the first comes from a Fribourg moral theologian, who pursues a historical and thematic Thomism beyond earlier neo-Thomisms; the second and third come from American textbook authors; while the last is presented by a Roman teacher and commentator on the *Summa*. The critical questions one must address are as follows: How did they retain and alter the theological principles of the *Summa theologiae*?[26] How did they apply Thomism to ethical systems and issues?

Dominic Prümmer: From *Summa* to Manual

Dominic Prümmer (1866–1931) taught moral theology applied to practical areas at Fribourg in Switzerland from 1908 to 1930. He wrote a three-volume handbook for seminarians and priests.[27] The large volumes of that "manual of moral theology" (a condensed version eventually appeared in English translation) follow the pattern of the *Summa theologiae*; however, Prümmer's approach was marked by several significant differences. (It should be recalled that the Dominican seminarians were studying the Second Part of *Summa theologiae* as, or before, complementing it with Prümmer's "practical moral" text.) A discussion of the ultimate human destiny (clearly a "supernatural destiny") begins his moral theology. According to Prümmer, "God is the principle [and goal] of human actions because his revelation is the first rule of morality; moreover this end which is the ultimate destiny of all moral actions is union with God in eternal happiness."[28] Prümmer then treats the nature of human actions, kinds of laws, conscience, sins, and virtues in general; he closes with the seven key virtues followed by

the sacraments. Prümmer's approach, however, was not entirely unique. In fact, this alteration of the *Summa theologiae*'s order is actually rooted in systems dating from the sixteenth to the nineteenth centuries, while its proximate model can be found in manuals from the turn of the twentieth century.

This particular manual subsumed the law of the Gospel (in Aquinas it is not primarily a positive law but the graced presence of the Holy Spirit) under "positive divine law." Prümmer alludes to the evangelical law but proceeds to focus on different kinds of laws in the New Testament, and then on charity. The bridge from personality and history to grace is thus obscured in this system; because of this, it loses something of the Spirit's original force. At the point where the *Summa* treats the evangelical law ending in grace, Prümmer omits grace and instead considers at some length issues of conscience and numerous moral systems from recent centuries. Prümmer knows that grace is a necessary means for the Christian life, "a proximate means to attain a supernatural end."[29] Nevertheless, because theology has been divided into two large segments (dogmatic and moral), with grace usually located in the former, modern theology has for some time treated grace elsewhere. Grace figures in moral theology only because "sanctifying and actual grace is conferred upon us, and increased, mainly in the sacraments" (grace is occasionally mentioned as a proximate means of human actions).[30] But then grace is discussed in the context of merit, for merit of a supernatural eschaton implies supernatural actions. Prümmer's analysis soon becomes absorbed in divisions of actual graces which are the inner dynamics of merit. Such a treatment overlooks Thomas's belief that merit flows from grace as the life of the Spirit, as a permanent disposition of the person and not from the nature of an actual grace.[31] In the section on virtues in general, moral infused virtues and gifts of the Holy Spirit are touched upon, but the manualist's interest lies with virtues' growth, interplay, and diminution.[32]

He had undertaken, Servais Pinckaers observed, "a renewal in the presentation of this classic moral by focusing on the virtues rather than the commandments in an effort to return to St. Thomas." But according to Pinckaers, "the virtues furnish little more than an alternative framework so that the matter remains formed by obligations and sins."[33] Prümmer treats selected themes from the *Summa theologiae*, retaining the motifs of supernatural life in a lengthy exposition of the virtues; grace is a topic both speculative and practical, but its removal into dogmatic theology leads to viewing moral theology as an ethics of habits and cases apart from life in the reign of God. The prominence after the sixteenth century of actual grace—in Aquinas, it is grace as a perduring life-principle is central, and actual grace is rarely treated—both furthers and is sustained by this removal of grace from ethics.

American Thomists: Callan and McHugh

Two Dominicans, Charles Callan and John McHugh, who taught in the Dominican *studium* in Washington, DC, and at Maryknoll, produced two volumes in the late 1920s for use in American seminaries. Mentioning that of the "many modern works published abroad, not a few are in the vernacular,"[34] they wrote in English. The team worked hard to give a practical bent to the consideration of moral issues in American life at that time, and they mentioned how they sought advice from lawyers and doctors.

The two-volume work is divided into general and special moral theology. The first part treats the ultimate end of the human person and subsequently human acts and habits; it also contains several sections on law. Discussions of law in general and natural law in particular yield to a "positive divine law," part of which is the law of the New Testament. There are, however, only a few references to Aquinas's evangelical law (*lex evangelica*); human law and civil law yield instead to a substantial section on ecclesiastical law. Where grace follows the Spirit's law in the *Summa*, here conscience and the various moral schools are treated (as in Prümmer). Special moral theology appears under the curious heading, "the duties of all classes of men," the theological and moral virtues, which is followed by individual sections on clusters of issues that the authors saw as prominent in society at that time—the commandments of faith (joining forbidden societies, taking part in Protestant worship, professing the Catholic faith publicly), sins against love and joy, and sins against

"beneficence" (scandal, cooperation in sins and crimes). Callan and McHugh conclude their effort with a look at the commandments of charity and the gift of wisdom.

Callan and McHugh make quite clear their beliefs that the end toward which people move is supernatural and that the special help of grace is needed to achieve that end. According to the volumes' index, the term grace is mentioned only once (it is, in fact, mentioned in a few other places). The introduction mentions that divine grace "is discussed fully in dogmatic theology and hence may be omitted here."[35] Virtues are divided into theological and cardinal or moral. The two topics of grace as the source of the infused virtues and or the interplay between infused and acquired moral virtues are not discussed. And the phrase, "infusion from on high" denominating those virtues might imply a constant gift of actual grace rather than a habitual emergence from a new life-principle.[36] No mention is made of why the goal of the moral life requires moral virtues to be graced; nor is the relation of virtues and gifts to grace addressed anywhere. Instead, the specificity of the Christian life fades, leaving mostly a philosophy without specifically religious acts and ends. The gifts of the Holy Spirit are presented as special impetuses from the Holy Spirit but without the psychological interpretation of gifts as similar to connatural instincts, a theme central to Aquinas and his commentators.

Aquinas's position—the evangelical law is the very grace of the Spirit—is not treated; instead, pages are devoted to comparisons between Old and New Laws and to a division of mandates and works. "Since the New Law is the law of grace, it commands only those things by which we are brought to grace, or by means of which we make use of grace already received. We receive grace only through Christ, and hence there are commandments regarding the Sacraments; we make right use of grace by faith that worketh through charity, and hence there are the precepts of the Decalogue to be kept."[37] In comparisons with Hebrew law, the authors choose a slightly skewed emphasis: "In both Testaments grace and the Holy Spirit are given through faith in Christ, and doctrines, commandments, and ceremonies are prescribed.

But, whereas the Old Testament is principally a law of works, the New Testament is principally a law of faith."[38] Charity is "the informing principle of the other virtues." Form does not mean that it is the model or specific content of the others but, as the authors explain in metaphors and unclear pieties, charity brings "the quality of *perfect* virtue." The role of being the end and mother, foundation and root of the others, is found in love's commanding good.[39]

Interestingly, what the Callan and McHugh volumes lack are not practical applications; rather, Thomas's theology is all but invisible. They have accepted the position that dogmatic areas are treated elsewhere, and that moral theology does not relate much to them as it treats actions, principles, and cases. In examining the table of contents, a skeleton of ultimate end, human actions, virtues, vices, and gifts becomes readily apparent; unfortunately, the theological foundation for all this, like Trinitarian mission and the headship of Christ, has been seriously diminished.

These two volumes bear a strong resemblance to Prümmer's work. In light of this, it is safe to assume that these Dominicans drew from a Latin manual (probably) written by another member of the Order. The Americans are less theological, more focused on practical issues, and more likely to contain some non-Dominican facets of the manual genre. They produced a handy textbook of information about a moral life, but morality is left without much explanation of its cause or ground, or about its relationship to the often mentioned beatitude. In some areas, the object of discussion is a natural life adorned with religious terms and actions.

Reginald Garrigou-Lagrange: From Manual to Timeless Commentary

In his series of commentaries on the *Summa theologiae*, Reginald Garrigou-Lagrange included a book on the questions on grace and another on virtues in general. While meant to be perennial, his commentaries relied heavily on sixteenth- and seventeenth-century masters, including Thomas de Vio (Cardinal Cajetan), Domingo Bañez (one of "the greatest Thomists"), and John of St. Thomas.[40] These philosophers and theologians provided the

sources for a work constructed in a later form of the Baroque collections; that is, they combined scholastic commentary, recent issues, and devotional meditations.[41] With the twentieth-century Roman theologian, excurses on particular issues interrupt the order and exposition of the *Summa*. For instance, four chapters on *grace*, almost one-third of the book, comprise an inserted unity on sufficient and efficacious grace. Garrigou-Lagrange's perspective articulates a conservative French and Roman neo-Thomism of the first half of this century joined to French and Carmelite spiritualities. Garrigou-Lagrange's many pages move rapidly between centuries to muster an argument or a bad example; for instance, within two pages, Thomas Aquinas and Romans are followed by Augustine and the fifth-century Gallic theologians; after references to John Chrysostom, the line of thought moves directly to Luther, Calvin, Jansenists, and Trent.[42]

Garrigou-Lagrange's work was a compendium of Aquinas's thought, that is, of texts and commentaries, and of critical rejections of other theological and philosophical opinions, medieval and modern. He was a relentless advocate of a Thomism where grace is seen basically as uncreated grace and as a gratuitous, created gift of the supernatural order in us, sharers in the divine nature.[43] This stands in contrast to some, even most nineteenth- and twentieth-century Baroque theologians and manualists, for whom grace is a motive force igniting and directing natural virtues. In fact, the Baroque emphasis on actual grace makes grace too "natural," too suggestive of cooperation by mind or will. "Grace is in us a supernatural gift of God, inhering in the soul, by which we are truly children of God, born of God, and participators in the divine nature."[44]

He saw Aquinas's thought as quite different from that of Tanquerey and other manualists, whose respective approaches generally place actual grace before habitual grace. Transitory actual graces are something decidedly secondary, and in the long run presuppose habitual grace.[45] "Sanctifying grace, the seed of glory, introduces us into this higher order of truth and life and is an essentially supernatural life, a participation in the intimate life of God, in the divine nature . . . immensely superior to a perceived miracle and above the natural life of our intellectual and immortal soul."[46] At times his theological anthropology of divine presence in human life is reminiscent of some schools of monastic and patristic spirituality, where grace is first and foremost the divine presence in humans. Nevertheless, Garrigou-Lagrange does not explain in new or concrete ways what participation in the divine might mean in the twentieth century. Analyses of the graced habit and quality abound in qualifications; however, individual journeys through ministry and prayer throwing light on the theologian's own century are absent.

For Garrigou-Lagrange, Duns Scotus began the tradition that veered away from an all-encompassing supernatural order. Scotus "says that if God so willed, he could give us grace and the light of glory as natural properties; and that the supernatural differs from the natural only on the part of the efficient cause as sight supernaturally given to a man born blind differs from natural sight. Hence grace would not be something intrinsically and essentially supernatural."[47] The Dominican called "nominalists" those who could not get beyond religious words to the reality of grace, and he scolded those neoscholastic schools who posited the motive force (actual grace) and the goal (heaven) as supernatural but who viewed the virtues and actions to be on a natural plane and acquired through good endeavors. "Some who read the *Summa theologiae* in an entirely material manner reach the conclusion that our act of faith is a substantially natural act clothed with a supernatural modality. . . . [But] Virtues are supernatural in their very essence raising infinitely the vitality of our intelligence and of our will. They are specified by a formal object, or a formal motive, which infinitely surpasses the natural powers of the human soul and those of the highest angels."[48]

In looking at the volume commenting on the theological virtues, one finds the expected emphasis upon supernatural action and life, with *supernatural* representing the realm of Incarnation and Trinitarian presence. Moreover, a habit of loving God as Savior and not just as Creator cannot be engendered by good human acts. "It is compulsory to deny that there are any such things as acquired theological virtues. Theological virtues have

to be infused and their existence cannot be known without revelation."[49] In this view, the interplay of faith, hope, and charity, rather than charity alone, directs the Christian journey.[50] Similarly, if acquired moral virtues constitute the natural perfection of humanity, they cannot make someone a citizen in the kingdom of God. Acquired moral virtues, even directed by charity, are inadequate for moving directly to the eschaton because the life of grace transcends human psychological habits. The life of the Spirit is a life, not simply a mechanism inspired by the Bible or switched on by transitory actual graces. Garrigou-Lagrange did not write a commentary on other virtues, and these two books hold very little on concrete moral problems and very much on the Thomist organization of the Christian life. He clearly emphasized the activity of human actions on two quite distinct lines of human nature and Trinitarian grace. Grace and its emergences in theological virtues and gifts of the Holy Spirit, perhaps because they are central to the supernatural order, are always highlighted. Aquinas's theology of the law of the Gospel, as was often the case until the 1970s, was little considered, and Garrigou-Lagrange's theology of moral acts was not based upon a consideration of the natural law.

Garrigou-Lagrange did not only apply scholastic words and forms from a particular philosophy to central Christian beliefs but concluded that the Aristotelian expression did not ultimately need biblical or other philosophical modes of expression. Garrigou-Lagrange's elements were *notiones* proving and explaining; their mechanism is an exposition of an area with its multiple divisions and charts. Topics like potency, analogy, the supernatural order, mystery, and terms like "habit," "virtue," or "love" are arranged more to establish the coherence of a long established, perduring system than the truth or power of Christian faith. In Garrigou-Lagrange's eyes, the employment of Aristotelian terms by both Aquinas and Trent had given those works an unchangeable truth, which is similar to an axiom or a fixed point in geometry. He had read in Henri Bouillard, a Jesuit advocate of a new theology, that not only philosophers and physicists but ordinary people think differently about what form as grace might mean, and that after 1945 Catholicism should develop other terms and theologies to present what Trent intended, the inner, lasting supernatural presence. Garrigou-Lagrange could not imagine yet another new "notion"; instead, he insisted that Trent had approved not only the theological reality and idea but the notion, too, because things and their ideas constitute each other. For him, when one has changed not just the words but also the notion, one has changed the meaning, and that leads to being unfaithful to the intention of the council and the teaching of the church.[51] The Dominican thus defended a conceptual-linguistic identity between Aristotelian concepts, Latin language, and Christian teaching. The idea of Aquinas that concepts and judgments reach realities (even those of faith) but do not exhaust them is overlooked. (See IIa IIae, q. 1, a. 2, ad 2.)[52]

A pluralism in understanding the Incarnation and gospel seems impossible. M.-R. Gagnebet wrote of Garrigou-Lagrange's thinking: "The objective concept is an aspect of reality itself, present to the human spirit in an intelligible analogical representation chosen by God himself. . . . When a notion (of philosophy) is assumed by the light of faith, it does not enter into the expression of the dogma with a special meaning but only as a stable notion of human spirit accessible to common sense."[53] Entire books are devoted to analogy, even if that religious epistemology undercuts any identity of the mental and the real. Ultimately, there can be only one theology—and the differences between Origen and Bérulle are overlooked. It is illusory to think that theological expression can be found outside Aristotelianism. For instance, one cannot observe that it is the real presence that is a dogma and not the Latin term, "transsubstantio."[54] Here lies the climax, the embarrassment, and the source of the collapse of rigid neoscholasticisms.

Audiences determine thinking, and audiences of Kantians and Molinists were quite real in the Roman theologian's mind; Molinists lived down the hill from the Angelicum at the Gregoriana, and some Kantians were suspected of having crept into the Society of Jesus north of the Alps. As often happens with apologetics, the clearer the author's position the fewer the people who find it attractive. Paradoxically (and this is true of much of Ro-

man Catholicism at this time), this neo-Thomism reached its high level of productivity in the years after 1945, and yet it was largely of past centuries: it opposed a Baroque theology to modern German philosophies. Gagnebet wrote: "Garrigou-Lagrange never ceased to ponder these documentary actions of the magisterium (*Lamentabili* and *Pascendi*). His entire work is their explication and defense against modernist theology."[55] But that Catholic modernism in France was long gone and in Germany it had never existed.[56] Garrigou-Lagrange may have been correct to note that some of Henri de Lubac's criticisms of the results of neo-Thomism were not necessarily true of Aquinas's texts, but the Dominican completely missed the effect of neoscholastic rigidity and separateness in the practical theology of clergy and laity. After World War II, Garrigou-Lagrange's writings, in terms of their apologetic and philosophical framework, had no real extra-ecclesial audience and were read for their theological exposition of a neo-Thomism. Garrigou-Lagrange is not a moral theologian; rather, he serves as a commentator on the moral sections of the *Summa theologiae*. In reading his works, one does not find a manual aimed at life and issues; instead, his reader is presented with an exposition of grace, virtues, and gifts in the *Summa* in terms of the Baroque Dominican school as resurrected in the twentieth century.

A Biblical Thomist: Servais Pinckaers

Longtime professor of moral theology at Fribourg, Servais Pinckaers is an altogether different kind of theologian from those discussed above. In contrast to the previous authors, he is neither a manualist nor a commentator, nor is he a neo-Thomist schooled before 1925. Even prior to Vatican II, Pinckaers had published essays on aspects of a renewal in moral theology. There needs to be a search, he wrote, for new perspectives even as one comes to appreciate the singular role of Thomas Aquinas:

> The teaching of St. Thomas reunited in a remarkable way rational power and penetrating contemplative experience in order to understand the faith. This work [the *Summa theologiae*] has rightly become a classic both as a basis of reference and as a model in theology

(and even in philosophy) up to our own time. Nevertheless, from the fourteenth century, this moral construction so carefully elaborated was confusingly altered and supplanted by a profoundly different conception upon which we are still somewhat dependent.[57]

Rather than working from an ontological isolation (imposed by a past philosophy), Pinckaers held that moral theology should be based on a critical appreciation of the new studies of Aquinas in historical and philosophical contexts. In Pinckaers's program—beyond its critique of neoscholastic language, it included a deeper view of the moral act, happiness, habit, and virtue—charity and hope guided the entire moral life in light of a "supernatural finality coloring it from one end to the other."[58] Pinckaers repeated the century-old Dominican call not to further a distinction between systematic theology, spirituality, and practical issues of morality.[59] However, Pinckaers offered many essays in which he argued that the theology of Aquinas offers a model precisely in giving an important place to the gospel in the formation of Christian morality. "His example does not oblige us to construct something neogothic but encourages and helps us to return to the Gospel to find there light, inspiration, and materials for fashioning a Christian morality in the style required for today."[60]

Two collections offer a quasisystematic presentation. *The Sources of Christian Ethics* (1985) was written in light of the renewal of moral theology after Vatican II and in terms of widespread awareness of today's moral issues. Pinckaers defines moral theology as "the branch of theology that studies human acts so as to direct them to a loving vision of God seen as our true, complete happiness and our final end. This vision is attained by grace, the virtues and the gifts in light of revelation and reason."[61] After examining that definition and delineating basic moral questions, the first section addresses human acts and morality, the specificity of Christian morality and Christian morality according to St. Paul and the Sermon on the Mount. Serving as a bridge to a historical section is an inquiry as to how the moral teaching of Aquinas is Christian and not purely one of Aristotelian virtue. The historical section reaches from

the first centuries to the Middle Ages (again treating Aquinas) and then further through the late Middle Ages and Protestant theologians to the age of manuals; it concludes with post-Tridentine texts, neo-Thomism, and the period leading up to Vatican II. The third section treats "Liberty and Natural Law," which allows a number of specific questions on social life and sexuality to be treated in light of the contemporary and creative tension between individual freedom and natural law. The volume represents a moral theology where theological sources, both Thomist and biblical, are stressed, and where the approach and orientation of Christian anthropology (what the manuals had deposited with dogmatic theology) are not a foundational *propadeutic*, but the living source of moral thinking and life. While virtues are prominent, this is not a simple virtue-ethic; rather, Pinckaers presents a moral theology of Pneumatic dynamics empowering various aspects of the human personality.

A second book, *L'Évangile et la morale*,[62] arranges published essays into sections covering moral theology and aspects of the gospel; happiness and love; and finally, church and conscience, where a number of concrete topics such as marriage, chastity, and erroneous conscience are treated. Working from the perspective of moral theology, Pinckaers has been an important, creative force in understanding how themes and structures link elements like virtues to Christ, Trinity, and grace; and second, in drawing out New Testament themes at work in the moral theology of the *Summa theologiae*. A focus on the place of God's supernatural presence within the plan of Thomas's *Summa* is sustained by locating virtuous moral behavior in the central panel of a triptych: preceded by the evangelical law, which is itself grace, and followed by the gifts of the Spirit. Noting the absence for a long time of the Holy Spirit in the formation of moral theology, he returns to the spotlight the brief but important questions in the *Summa* on the evangelical law. "Beyond the treatise on the natural law there is the theology of the new law or the evangelical law, a small masterpiece composed by St. Thomas, serving as the key in the construction [of the totality] and containing a definition where all the lines of the *Summa* meet: the new law understood as an interior law, as the grace of the Holy Spirit received by faith in Christ and operating by love of which the Sermon on the Mount provides the text . . . which the sacraments bear and offer."[63] There the Holy Spirit enters ("the law of the New Testament . . . consists in the grace of the Holy Spirit" [Ia IIae, q. 106, a. 1]) to empower moral life divinely but intimately. The treatise on law flowing into an evangelical law serves as an anticipation of, and a bridge to, the subsequent questions on grace. In other words, with the gospel, the realms of human discourse and activity called "laws" have become human, interiorized but also active. In short, law has become grace, and this divine presence is the source of all (and all is secondary) whether texts or sacraments. "If moral theology has for its object responding to the question of happiness, it gives immediate importance to the knowledge of the Father, Son, and Holy Spirit who are inviting us to enter into intimacy with them and partake of their happiness. When the law of the Gospel is principally constituted by the grace of the Holy Spirit received by faith in Christ, the moral theology it inspires will be intimately linked to the person of Christ and will not turn grace into an abstraction. . . . How one sees this issue of the key and gate of entry into the house of moral theology plays a determining role."[64]

Pinckaers distinguishes between spiritual and material elements in the gospel law. It is an interior law and not one written in a codification; it is rooted in faith in Christ as the center of salvation-history, it works through love. Materially the new law is found in the person and teaching of Jesus, and it is his Sermon on the Mount which is the "text" of the new law.[65]

In Catholic theologians' new search for a biblical ethics, the Sermon on the Mount must regain the pivotal place it had with Aquinas. Before comparing the Sermon to natural law and then to Paul's Letter to the Romans (a complementary biblical source for morality), Pinckaers locates it (and the gospel law) in the world of the thirteenth century, an age of quests for evangelical life and discipleship.[66] The "proper texts of the new law" are not a series of rules but an invitation to a new regime, to a deeper way of life in familiarity with the Spirit; an inclination born of the attrac-

tions of the Spirit does not bring duty or fear.[67] That teaching, finding a climax in the beatitudes, is permeated by the eschatology of supernatural beatitude. Whatever the obvious differences in genre, Thomas wanted the moral section of his *Summa* to be a commentary on the Lord's sermon and to include the virtues and gifts: "So the treatise on the new law is not an isolated segment but a coordinating center of the *Summa theologiae*; it manifests the Christological and biblical nature of Aquinas's moral theology, and it should serve as a model for stimulating our theological reflection today."[68]

Observing the absence of any separation between dogma and moral in Aquinas and noting how many moralists ignored Jesus's great sermon after Luther's alignment of it with the law and good works, he concludes: "[Going] beyond the divorce in the post-Tridentine morality and in Kantian morality between the desire of happiness and morality . . . , the doctrine on the virtues and the gifts, on the evangelical law and on grace is necessary to give to Catholic moral theology its richness and spiritual vitality, to give to the moral law a dynamic interiority, to give the action of the Holy Spirit its primacy, all within a vigorous systematic framework."[69]

In the *Secunda secundae*, the two dynamic principles, personality and the grace of the Spirit, meet in families of virtues. As the moralist does not spend time with actual graces so acquired, moral virtues are not the center of Christian life. "[Aquinas's] sense of the Incarnation, of the penetration of grace into human nature, like the union of soul and body, inspired in him an original idea which many theologians have later hesitated to take up. Considering that grace calls all our faculties to collaborate in its work, he thought it was understandable that a special elevation of our moral virtues would occur—these he named infused moral virtues."[70]

Pinckaers speaks of an organism of virtues with their special links to prudence, faith, and love. Since the virtuous life is modeled on and destined toward the life of the incarnate Word (unfolded in the Third Part of the *Summa*), they have a Christological orientation. Pinckaers cautions his readers not to have a myopic or divisive viewpoint that "sees the *Summa* like a cathedral with three large naves."[71] The three parts relate to each other intrinsically through vital networks and motifs drawn from the Bible, and the fathers have a preponderance over Aristotelian analyses of virtues. Charity touches and organizes the virtues grounded in the Spirit and in communion with Christ, but it does not replace the proper action of each and every virtue nor does it diminish the work of the Spirit and grace.[72] Ultimately, grace draws virtues to higher levels in the Spirit's gifts, forces in the Christian life mentioned in Isaiah, Matthew, and Paul. The neglect of the gifts of the Spirit lies in the fears of rationalism concerning the instinctive and the mystical in religion, but these further modes of the Spirit are allied to the virtues and their intensity remains within ordinary life according to the new law of the kingdom.[73]

Pinckaers is clearly not the writer of a seminary textbook in the style of the early twentieth century; rather, he is a scholar who is acutely aware of past genres and their limitations and who employs the world of historical and biblical studies to discover the depth of Aquinas's thought. Rarely, however, does he reach concrete issues—and even they are kept at some distance. This may be a consequence of his deep involvement with Aquinas, a speculative thinker, and it is in the Dominican theological style to cultivate a theology of principles rather than of current applications.

CONCLUSION: A THEOLOGICAL SCHOOL CHANGING DURING A CENTURY

I have just touched on something of a school and a century. Different theologians wrote about the Christian life out of a communal hermeneutics generated by common education and religious ethos. I have looked at how each of the writers treated the *Summa theologiae*, and how they retained approaches of the Dominican school. Each offers something about the history of moral theology in the twentieth century, about manuals and commentaries, about the move at Vatican II from textbooks to texts, from frameworks to realities. One learns not to overlook the variety within a tradition, nor to fuse the interpretations with the theologian (as when a

neo-Thomism identified itself with the thought of Thomas Aquinas). These theologians certainly illustrate differences between neo-Thomisms and Aquinas. If Prümmer did not overlook Aquinas, still he diminished some of his ideas and principles, while a comparison of Garrigou-Lagrange and Pinckaers illustrates how a knowledge of history—whether of the thirteenth or the nineteenth century—does not relativize but liberates Aquinas.[74]

Aquinas's moral theology is not a philosophy of virtues nor a psychology of means to contact a Supreme Being or Goodness. It is not a foundation for offering general principles to casuistry in the sacrament of penance or to a canon law of censures. It is neither an applied moral theology of cases nor a logic or metaphysics of ethical principles. As a part of the entire *Summa theologiae*, the Second Part narrates the journeying Christian life touched by the processions of the Trinity and the emerging of a psychology of the human being existing in salvation-history through a life-principle, which is the gift and presence of the Holy Spirit. Precisely by drawing the new currents of his time into a theology, Aquinas became an Aristotelian, a thinker of nature's forms, and in light of the *De anima*, a moral theologian of faculties, habits, and activities flowing from nature and grace (the Dominicans inevitably mentioned the organic nature of the Christian personality). But Aquinas's moral theology begins with the selection of the eschaton as the goal of men and women, and for this, it spotlights a second life-principle, grace. Within the pattern of crescendo acquired and infused virtues, realms of realities (laws), and charismatic gifts enter and remain. A moral theology is not Christian because an Aristotelian philosophy is adorned with passages from the Bible, but because it sees reality in light of the kingdom of God and explains how incarnation continues in so many lives. Incarnation is an underlying pattern of the *Summa theologiae* and it reaches from the mission of the Word to the sacrament of the sick and dying.

The first three theologians examined here did not expend much energy exploring the difference between the text of the *Summa* and their chosen mentors of neo-Thomism (perhaps it did not occur to them to see much difference), nor did they know how dominant in their writings were the formative approaches of the Baroque and nineteenth century. While they retained the centrality of supernatural grace and its necessary role in human activities and virtues (there are no neutral actions for men and women), did Prümmer and the Americans grasp how the separation of dogmatic and moral theology impoverished their ethics, how it left them victims of the fragmentation occurring after the Baroque which they bemoaned? Despite their best efforts to escape modernity, were not Garrigou-Lagrange and the two Americans children of their time? Their theologies mentioned grace as a form prior to actual graces, but their interest like much of Catholicism after the sixteenth century lay with actual grace, with kinds of graces, and with controversies over freedom and grace. There was an interest in syllogisms and proofs to the detriment of the dialectical synthesis of ideas and sources. A less flexible Aristotelianism had forced theology to be static, propositional, and eternal—an enterprise ending in divisions and definitions. Dominican neo-Thomism preserved the supernatural order and the centrality of habitual grace, but grace also became imprisoned in a middle level of mechanical analysis, separated from its biblical roots and rarely applied to any concrete issues or societies.

The first three texts did have their own identities. Garrigou-Lagrange was not the same as John of St. Thomas or Cajetan; the Americans were less theological than their European counterparts. Thus, in neo-Thomisms there was some pluralism in theological schools and approaches, although they all stayed within a general Latin, scholastic, and neo-Aristotelian terminology and frame of reference. The neoscholasticism that reached its peak in the 1950s insisted exclusively on a method which in its neo-Aristotelian clarity responded with difficulty to new issues in modern peoples' lives. It is paradoxical that a moral theology that was revolutionary in the thirteenth century because of its psychology had ended up as one based on an antiquated ontology. Far from imitating Aquinas's search for new texts and ideas and his life-long enterprise of engaging creatively a new culture, some neo-Thomists used medieval or Baroque theologies to reject anything touching modern philosophy, politics and science.

Dominican theology affirmed and distinguished the virtues of nature and of grace, but theories with an ethic drawn from Aristotle or from the humanism of the Enlightenment focused on acquired virtue. Independent human virtues were only extrinsically supernatural—they receive that denomination because human habits had received a transient actual grace or a supernatural elevation (in the eyes of God) achieved by means of willed charity or religious obedience. Intentionality elevated moral action; the specificity of an act as well as its supposed impact upon others came too much from the intention of the doer. Through this approach, liturgy and spirituality lost their moorings in healthy social and psychological life. The emphasis upon actual grace reduced the stability and the depth of an individual's graced life. The rediscovery of Aquinas's mention of grace in terms of formal as well as efficient causality is a gift of the conciliar period.

There is a considerable difference, not only in perception but in education and information, between the earlier Thomists and Pinckaers. Why? What happened in the decades after 1930? The answer is found in the new methodological and theoretical approaches of a new generation of scholars. There was the expansive historical research of scholars such Martin Grabmann, Étienne Gilson, J. A. Weisheipl, and M.–D. Chenu; and a few years later came the insightful reflections of such theologians as Yves Congar, Edward Schillebeeckx, and Karl Rahner. Chenu based his own theology upon the vitality and sublimity of revelation, the personal but supernatural quality of faith, and the social conditions of a period. The science and culture of an age offer the forms for expressing faith; science, architecture, politics, philosophy, and theology often have a certain cultural unity that is disclosed by historical study:

> To analyze the historical and social conditions of Aquinas's work is the best way of observing the truth of his teaching in relationship to its place in civilization and in the course of theological development. We find this realism again today as we understand better how the

Word of God is incarnate in the history of humanity, in the worlds of space and time. Theology should not be a closed chapel set apart from people but a faithful experience and elaboration of the Word of God in a mature faith. To accomplish this was the genius of Thomas Aquinas.[75]

Historical study also disclosed the world, problems, and limitations of different periods of Thomism. There was a dual, beneficial paradox: history's limits lead to a deeper knowledge, and the confrontation of Aquinas's thought with modern issues and pastoral renewal discovered lost insights. Chenu emphasized the theological dimension of knowing and acting morally:

> Without doubt there is a certain kind of moralist who finds [in Aquinas] only considerations which are in fact preliminary, a metaphysical extrapolation or a mysticism at a distance from practical human conduct and from the special characteristic of human liberty. For St. Thomas, on the other hand, moral science is precisely *theological*: interior to this high knowing, both theoretical and practical at the same time. Its purpose is to see and to locate all beings and every being in and by their order to God from whom they flow forth in a delineated participation which leads back to God.[76]

Building upon the foundation of those first and second generations of historians and theologians, a newer group of scholars, such as Walter Principe, Ulrich Horst, Otto Pesch, and J.–P. Torrell, have expanded our realm of understanding.

Without an awareness of the presence of the Spirit in individual Christians considerations of ethical issues can easily lose what is distinctively Christian: not in the sense that they reject the words of Jesus, but in that they overlook the framework of the biblical world where each individual lives between grace and sin. They do not accept a continuing incarnation or sanctification following upon justification. The thin but sturdy framework of a past mechanics of actual graces moving a neutral personality in a secularized world was surpassed in the documents of Vatican II; it is not adequate to the complexity of human life or the power of the Spirit. The Dominican emphasis upon the supernatural goal and in-

ner life-principle has implications for a moral theology which intends to be more biblical, for an ethics of virtues, and perhaps too for specific biomedical issues and for the relationship of church and world. The graced person and the contemporary complexity of discerning grace in society and human religion are the point of intersection for theology, ethics, and spirituality, which is ethics personalized.

Finally, one can see the importance of knowing the long, diverse history of moral theology. Of all fields, ethics should not be antiquarian; nor should it reenact controversies from the past. History dispels the constrictions of the sect and the provincialism of the isolated text.[77] Contemporary awareness and history go together—they are two facets of healthy inquiry. In understanding the past, one must neither fear the present nor despair of the future. In fact, one can only accept the inevitable flow of time, that primal creature of God.

Notes

[1] See my "Grace as a Structure in the *Summa Theologiae* of Thomas Aquinas," *Revue de Théologie Ancienne et Médiévale* 55 (1988): 130–53; and "Virtues in the Theology of Thomas Aquinas," *Theological Studies* 58 (1997): 254–85.

[2] Leonard E. Boyle, *The Setting of the "Summa Theologiae" of Thomas Aquinas* (Toronto: Pontifical Institute of Medieval Studies, 1982), 17ff.

[3] Ibid, 16.

[4] Hinnebusch, *The History of the Dominican Order*, vol. 2 (Staten Island, NY: Alba House, 1966), 243.

[5] Lafont, *Structures et méthode dans la Somme théologique de s. Thomas d'Aquin* (Paris: Desclée de Brouwer, 1961), 469.

[6] See my *Thomas Aquinas Theologian* (Notre Dame, IN: University of Notre Dame Press, 1997), chap. 2.

[7] "quia non est conveniens quod Deus minus provideat his quos diligit ad supernaturale bonum habendum, quam creaturis quas diligit ad bonum naturale habendum. Creaturis autem naturalibus sic providet. . . . eis formas et virtutes quasdam, quae sunt principia actuum, ut secundum seipsas inclinentur ad huiusmodi motus . . . . Multo igitur magis illis quos movet ad consequendum bonum supernaturale aeternum, infundit aliquas formas seu qualitates supernaturales, secundum quas suaviter et prompte ab ipso moveantur ad bonum aeternum

consequendum. Et sic donum gratiae qualitas quaedam est."

[8]*Ces Maîtres que Dieu m'a donné* (Paris: Cerf, 1982), 72. E. Schillebeeckx writes: "God reveals himself as God, because he gives himself to us precisely as the content of our salvation. . . . Aquinas therefore placed the God of salvation, *Deus salutaris*, at the very beginning of the *Summa*, in the first article." "Scholasticism and Theology," in *Revelation and Theology*, vol. 1 (New York: Sheed and Ward, 1967), 247

[9]*De veritate*, q. 27, a. 1 (Leonine, 789–92).

[10]*De veritate*, q. 27, a. 2: "There is a goal prepared by God for human beings exceeding any proportion to human nature, namely eternal life . . . , and it is fitting that humans be given something not only to enable activity toward that goal . . . but that the very nature of the human being be elevated to a dignity and competence toward that goal, and to this grace is given. . . . And just as in natural things the nature is one thing and the inclination of nature is another, and the movement or operation a third, so in the realm of grace—grace is different from charity and the other virtues." (Sed est aliquis finis ad quem homo a Deo praeparatur, naturae humanae proportionem excedens, scilicet vita aeterna. . . . Unde oportet quod homini detur aliquid non solum per quod operetur ad finem . . . sed etiam per quod ipsa natura hominis elevetur ad quandam dignitatem, secundum quam talis finis sit ei competens; et ad hoc datur gratia. . . . Et ideo sicut in rebus naturalibus est aliud natura ipsa quam inclinatio naturae et eius motus vel operatio, ita in gratuitis est aliud gratia a caritate et ceteris virtutibus; Leonine, 794, 130–48). The neo-Thomists carried Aquinas's insight that there might be a supernatural modification of the soul, like grace, into other analyses and coined the term "entitative" or "substantive" habit; A. Michel, "Vertu," *Dictionnaire de Théologie Catholique* 15:2 (Paris: Letouzey et Ané, 1950), col. 2765; R. Garrigou-Lagrange, *Grace* (St. Louis: Herder, 1952), 124.

[11]"Id autem quod est potissimum in lege novi testamenti, et in quo tota virtus eius consistit, est gratia Spiritus Sancti, quae datur per fidem Christi."

[12]"Sicut ab essentia animae effluunt eius potentiae, quae sunt operum principia; ita etiam ab ipsa gratia effluunt virtutes in potentias animae, per quas potentiae moventur ad actus."

[13]ST Ia IIae, q. 110, a. 3, ad 3: "[Grace] is not the same as virtue but is a kind of habitude which is presupposed by infused virtues as their principle and root" ("Nec tamen est [gratia] idem quod virtus: sed habitudo quaedam quae praesupponitur virtutibus infusis, sicut earum principium et radix"). For an extensive treatment of Aquinas's view of the necessity of infused virtues and of other theologies in the

Middle Ages, see E. Shockenhoff, *Bonum hominis. Die anthropologischen und theologischen Grundlagen der Tugendethik des Thomas von Aquin* (Mainz: Matthias-Grünewald, 1987), 295ff.; and Odon Lottin, *Psychologie et Morale aux XIIe et XIIIe siècles* (Löwen: Gembloux, 1942–1960). On possible interplays between acquired and infused virtues, see the lengthy discussion in Jean-Marie Aubert, "Vertus," in *Dictionnaire de Spiritualité* (Paris: Beauchesne, 1992), 485–97; on the topic of infused virtues, the role of prudence, and recent Scotist and Franciscan moralists rejecting infused moral virtues, see R. F. Coerver, *The Quality of Facility in the Moral Virtues* (Washington, DC: Catholic University of America Press, 1946).

[14]"conferuntur nobis a Deo virtutes theologicae, quibus ordinamur ad finem supernaturalem, sicut supra dictum est. Unde oportet quod his etiam virtutibus theologicis proportionaliter respondeant alii habitus divinitus causati in nobis, qui sic se habeant ad virtutes theologicas sicut se habent virtutes morales et intellectuales ad principia naturalia virtutum."

[15]*De Caritate*, q. un., a. 3, ad 19: "gratia Dei dicitur esse forma virtutum, in quantum dat esse spirituale animae, ut sit susceptiva virtutum; sed caritas est forma virtutum in quantum format operationes earum . . ." (Marietti, 762).

[16]Aubert, "Vertus", col. 493 with a bibliography of recent literature on an ethics of virtues, particularly in Europe (cols. 496f.). Schillebeeckx writes: "[Aquinas] did not simply call love the final form of faith as a result of his general teaching that 'love is the form of all the virtues.' He meant much more than this. Mature faith was for him not simply faith-plus-love. The relationship between the two was much more intimate—faith itself was inwardly completed precisely as faith, that is, as intellectual consent, and thus as a direct extension of believing" ("Scholasticism and Theology," 254).

[17]See H. D. Noble, "Prudence," *Dictionnaire de théologie catholique*, vol. 13:1 (Paris: Letouzey et Ané, 1936), cols. 1033–39; Josef Piper, *Prudence* (New York: Pantheon, 1959). On the direction which prudence gives to other virtues, see ST IIa IIae, q. 47, aa. 5–6, and the commentary of Thomas de Vio, Cardinal Cajetan.

[18]Michel writes: "This distinction emerges from the pen of a theologian of the age Philippe de Grève (1236), the helpful distinction between sanctifying grace which perfects the essence of the soul and communicates to it the principle of supernatural life; and the virtues which perfect the powers of the soul in ordaining them to virtuous act. . . . At the time of Albert the Great and St. Thomas one did not argue about this" ("Vertu," *Dictionnaire de théologie catholique*, col. 2762).

[19]Illustrating the importance of the gifts in the Dominican tradition is the influential treatise of John of St. Thomas from the seventeenth century which inspired recent books from figures as different as Ambroise Gardeil, Garrigou-Lagrange, and Walter Farrell. They more or less present a theology summarized by Gardeil: "The gifts of the Holy Spirit are not actual interventions of the Spirit in our life, but habitual dispositions placed in our soul which lead it easily to consent to his inspirations. . . . Through these God shines freely across the Christian's whole moral and supernatural life, initially illumined by the calm light of the virtues." See John of St. Thomas, *The Gifts of the Holy Ghost* [1645] (New York: Sheed and Ward, 1951); A. Massoulié, *Méditations de Saint Thomas sur les trois vies* [1678] (Paris: Lethielleux, 1934); A. Gardeil, *The Gifts of the Holy Ghost in Dominican Saints* (Milwaukee, WI: Bruce, 1937), 31, 20; W. Farrell and D. Hughes, *Swift Victory* (New York: Sheed and Ward, 1955); R. Garrigou-Lagrange, "The Gifts of the Holy Ghost," in *The Three Ages of the Interior Life*, vol. 1 (St. Louis: Herder, 1947), 66ff; J. M. Ramirez, *De Donis Spiritus Sancti de quae vita mystica . . . Thomae expositio* (Madrid: Aldecoa, 1974); J. Arintero, *The Mystical Evolution* (St. Louis: Herder, 1949); M.-M. Labourdette, "Dons du Saint-Esprit, IV, Saint Thomas et la théologie thomiste," *Dictionnaire de spritualité* 3 (Paris: Beauchesne, 1957), 1610ff. (the Jesuit Billot treats the gifts as related to infused virtues stressing more their role in life and perseverance than in mystical instinct; Billot, *De Virtutibus infusis* [Rome: Gregoriana, 1928], 172–92).

[20]Patfoort, *Saint Thomas d'Aquin* (Paris: FAC, 1983), 87.

[21]"Schulen, theologische Schulen," *Lexikon für Theologie und Kirche* 9 (Freiburg: Herder, 1964), 509f.; see A. Landgraf, *Einführung in die Geschichte der theologischen Literatur der Frühscholastik unter dem Geschichtspunkte der Schulenbildung* (Regensburg: Pustet, 1948); Pierre Mandonnet, "Frères Prêcheurs (La théologie dans l'ordre des)," *Dictionnaire de théologie catholique*, vol. 6:1 (Paris: Letouzey et Ané, 1924), cols. 863–924; *Le Scuole degli ordini mendicanti (secoli XIII–XIV)* (Todi: Academia Tudertina, 1978); G. M. Löhr, *Die Kölner Dominikanerschule vom 14. bis 16. Jahrhundert.* (Cologne: Pick, 1948). One sees the historical nature and import of schools in moral theology in the lengthy article on "Probablisme," by T. Deman, in *Dictionnaire de théologie catholique*, vol. 13:1 (Paris: Letouzey et Ané, 1936), cols. 418–619.

[22]Lucien-Marie de Saint-Joseph, "École de spiritualité," in *Dictionnaire de spiritualité*, vol. 4 (Paris: Beauchesne, 1960), cols. 116, 127.

[23]J. A. Weisheipl, "Thomism," in *New Catholic Encyclopedia* 14 (New York: McGraw Hill, 1967), 126ff.; Otto Pesch, "Thomismus," in *Lexikon für Theologie und Kirche* 10 (Freiburg: Herder, 1965), 157; see L. Kennedy, *A Catalogue of Thomists, 1270–1900* (Houston: Center for Thomistic Studies, 1987); O'Meara, *Thomas Aquinas Theologian*, chap. 4.

[24]In the 1950s, Dominican *studia* such as Fribourg, Salamanca, Toulouse, and the Roman Angelicum produced a series of moral theologies of grace and infused virtues that staked out the middle ground between the medieval *summae* with their Baroque expositors, and the practical moral textbooks; see, for instance, books by Michel Labourdette, L. G. Fanfani, Pedro Lumbreras, Reginald Garrigou-Lagrange, and Santiago Ramirez.

[25]Johann Theiner, "Die Dominikaner," *Die Entwicklung der Moraltheologie zur eigenständigen Disziplin* (Regensburg: Pustet, 1971), 335.

[26]Martin Grabmann wrote at the turn of the last century: "Today . . . outstanding Thomists like Garrigou-Lagrange and Gardeil discuss a speculative deepening of moral theology which ordinarily finds its form in an interior and warm affinity with dogmatics and so gains a deeper influence upon Christian life through a deep grasp of grace, the Christian virtues and the gifts of salvation" (*Die Idee des Lebens in der Theologie des hl. Thomas von Aquin* [Paderborn: Schöningh, 1922], 5).

[27]Another Dominican, Benoit Henri Merkelbach, could serve as an example at this point: "Modern authors of manuals are not accustomed to have much on virtues because all of them are involved in distinguishing, enumerating, and measuring sins, so that one would rightly say that their moral theology is only an elenchus or *codex peccatorum*." He then lists Alphonsus Ligouri, Vermeersch, and others who have "nothing" on the topic, while A. Tanquerey and H. H. Noldin have "some" treatment, but the offerings of his confrere Prümmer is "more complete." B. H. Merkelbach, *Summa Theologiae moralis ad mentem d. Thomae . . .* I [1930] (Brugges: Desclée de Brouwer, 1956), 449.

[28]Prümmer, *Manuale Theologiae Moralis secundum Principia S. Thomae Aquinatis* 1 (Freiburg: Herder, 1931), 2; Prümmer's opening volume contains a valuable list of writers in moral theology in recent centuries. The abbreviated version in English is *Handbook of Moral Theology* (New York: Kenedy, 1957).

[29]Prümmer, *Manuale Theologia*, 16.

[30]Ibid., 16.

[31]Ibid., 92ff.

[32]Ibid., 326f.

[33]Servais Pinckaers, "L'enseignement de la théologie morale à Fribourg. Passé et avenir," in *Saint Thomas au XXe siècle*, ed. S. Bonino (Toulouse: Saint Paul, 1994), 432. Pinckaers has analyzed the structure of the moral manualists: "The moral teaching of the manuals can be compared to a build-

ing resting on four foundation stones: human or free action, law, conscience, and sins. The columns are the commandments of God and of the church, and these indicate the obligations, which mark off boundaries and provide the furnishings of moral theology, so to speak. The overarching roof is justice, the legal virtue, or honesty, which, as Suarez declared, crowns the whole edifice and maintains it with the force of obligation" ("Moral Theology in the Modern Era of the Manuals," *The Sources of Christian Ethics* (Washington, DC: Catholic University of America Press, 1995), 267).

[34]Charles J. Callan and John A. McHugh, *Moral Theology: A Complete Course Based on St. Thomas Aquinas and the Best Modern Authorities* (New York: Wagner, 1929) 1, 7; a revision of the work was undertaken in 1958 by Edward P. Farrell.

[35]Ibid., 1, 8, 38 (on grace and merit) .

[36]Ibid., 51.

[37]Ibid., 119.

[38]Ibid., 117.

[39]Ibid., 447.

[40]See Domingo Bañez, "De Comoedia banneziana et recenti syncretesimo," *Angelicum* 23 (1946): 4ff.; Garrigou-Lagrange, *Grace*, 46.

[41]Among the Dominicans the Baroque mixture of theology and spirituality finds a climax in Vincent De Contenson (1641–1674) and his *Theologia mentis et cordis* of Lyons, 1668–69 (Paris: Vivès, 1875).

[42]*Grace*, 71f. John of St. Thomas wrote: "From this it must be inferred that all other virtues are to appear as infused. . . . The supernatural destiny must be appropriated through means, through supernatural choices; and, if this is to occur in a supernatural manner, it happens through infused virtues which order the person well toward the goal" (*Cursus theologicus* 6 [Paris: Vivès, 1885], 514f.).

[43]Garrigou-Lagrange, *Grace*, 114, 399ff.

[44]Ibid., 114.

[45]Ibid., 73f.

[46]Garrigou-Lagrange, "The Spiritual Organism," in *The Three Ages of the Interior Life*, vol. 1 (St. Louis: Herder, 1949), 50f. Similarly, the virtues flow from grace like faculties from the soul as sketched in *Grace*, 139: "The infused virtues . . . which flow from habitual grace are qualities, that is, *permanent principles* of supernatural and meritorious operations; it is then necessary that habitual or sanctifying grace (a *state* of grace), from which these virtues proceed as from their root, is itself an infused and permanent quality and not a motion like actual grace" ("La nouvelle théologie ou va-t-elle?," *Angelicum* 23 [1946], 129). In Garrigou's opinion, this position was defined by Trent. Garrigou noted some Jesuits who supported his Thomist position, but he found the contemporary expressions of Henri de Lubac and Henri Bouillard unacceptable. "It is obvious that Father de Lubac has never explained the

Summa theologica article by article" (*Grace*, 410ff., 445ff.). On the politics of Garrigou-Lagrange and its influence on his theological opposition to the new theologies of French scholars during the time of European fascisms, see Joseph A. Komonchak, "Theology and Culture at Mid-Century: The Example of Henri de Lubac," *Theological Studies* 51 (1990): 601.

[47]Garrigou-Lagrange, *Grace*, 124. "St. Thomas' conclusion is that sanctifying grace is something beyond the infused virtues which are derived from it, just as the natural light of reason is something beyond the acquired virtues derived from that light" (ibid., 143).

[48]Garrigou-Lagrange, *Christian Perfection and Contemplation* (St. Louis: Herder, 1951), 63, 78.

[49]Garrigou-Lagrange, *The Theological Virtues* (St. Louis: Herder, 1965), 11.

[50]Ibid., 11, 22ff.

[51]Ideas of altering the Aristotelian psychology and physics (even his terms!) for contemporary insights and expressions are "an illusion" (Garrigou-Lagrange, *Grace*, 412).

[52]ST IIa IIae, q. 1, a. 2, ad 2.

[53]M.-R. Gagnebet, "L'oeuvre du P. Garrigou-Lagrange," *Nova et Vetera* 39 (1964): 284. There are not many writings on Garrigou: see R. Krieg, "A Fortieth-Anniversary Reappraisal of 'Chalcedon: End or Beginning?'," *Philosophy and Theology* 9 (1995): 77ff.; F. J. Couto, *Hoffnung im Unglauben. Zur Diskussion über den allgemeinen Heilswillen Gottes* (Paderborn: Schöningh, 1973), chap. 2.

[54]Garrigou-Lagrange, *Grace*, 412.

[55]Gagnebet, "L'oeuvre du P. Garrigou-Lagrange," 280.

[56]See my "Through and Beyond Modernism," *Church and Culture* (Notre Dame, IN: University of Notre Dame Press, 1991), 165ff.

[57]Servais Pinckaers, *La moral catholique* (Paris: Cerf, 1991), 37; the following pages of this book give with history and charts an overview of the period of the modern epoque with its collections and manuals.

[58]Servais Pinckaers, *Le Renouveau de la morale* (Tournai: Casterman, 1964), 23: "Between St. Thomas and St. Alphonsus along with the authors of the manuals, even when they espouse a 'Thomistic discipleship' and even when there are some partial agreements, there is always a basic disagreement on the systematic plan. . . . We find in St. Thomas a morality of happiness and of the virtues centered in charity and prudence, and we find in modern moralists a morality of commandments and legal obligations centered on conscience and sins" (Pinckaers, "L'enseignement de la théologie morale à Fribourg," 433).

[59]Pinckaers, "L'enseignement de la théologie morale à Fribourg," 433.

[60]Pinckaers, *L'Évangile et la morale* (Fribourg: Presses Universitaires, 1990), 10.

[61]Pinckaers, *The Sources of Christian Ethics*, 8.

[62]Pinckaers, *L'Évangile et la morale*.

[63]Pinckaers, "L'enseignement de la théologie morale à Fribourg," 437.

[64]Pinckaers, *L'Évangile et la morale*, 11.

[65]Pinckaers, *La moral catholique*, 92–94, 97–100; Pinckaers also relates the sacraments and the church to the new law.

[66]Pinckaers, *L'Évangile et la morale*, 45ff.

[67]Ibid., 52.

[68]Ibid., 55.

[69]Pinckaers, "L'enseignement de la théologie morale à Fribourg," 439f.; see also Pinckaers, "La Loi évangelique, vie selon l'Esprit, et le Sermon sur la montagne," in *L'Évangile et la morale*, 52.

[70]Pinckaers, *L'Évangile et la morale*, 68f.

[71]Ibid., 50.

[72]Pinckaers, *La moral catholique*, 95. On the relationship of the virtues to Christ, through the Spirit and grace, see Pinckaers, "La Loi évangelique, vie selon l'Esprit, et le Sermon sur la montagne," 50.

[73]Pinckaers, *L'Évangile et la morale*, 50; Pinckaers, "L'instinct et l'Esprit au coeur de l'éthique chrétienne," in *Novitas et Veritas Vitae* (Paris: Cerf, 1991), 213ff.

[74]Otto Pesch saw the period around the council as a reversal "from Thomism to Thomas." (*Thomas von Aquin. Grenze und Grösse mittelalterlicher Theologie* [Mainz: Matthias-Grünewald, 1989], 33ff).

[75]M.–D Chenu, preface to H. Petitot, *Life and Spirit of Thomas Aquinas* (Chicago: The Priory Press, 1966), 6.

[76]M.–D Chenu, *St. Thomas d'Aquin et la théologie* (Paris: du Seuil, 1959), 126; in the 1960s, he had called attention to the role of the new law in the renewal of moral theology, a key factor in newer Thomist perspectives ("The Renewal of Moral Theology: The New Law," *The Thomist* 34 [1970]: 1–30).

[77]"I believe that the novelty of Vatican II," Yves Congar wrote, "consisted largely in its acceptance of the historicity of the church, of scripture. . . . The vision of the Council has been resolutely that of the history of salvation completed by eschatology . . ." ("Situation écclésiologique au moment de 'Ecclesiam suam' et passage à une église dans l'itinéraire des hommes," in *Le Concile de Vatican II* [Paris: Beauchesne, 1984], 27). For the measures of the Vatican after 1950 against historical study, see R. Guelluy, "Les Antécédents de l'encyclique 'Humani Generis' dans les sanctions romaines de 1942: Chenu, Charlier, Draguet," *Revue d'histoire ecclésiastique* 81 (1986): 485ff.

Selected Further Reading

Aubert, Jean-Marie. "Vertus." In *Dictionnaire de spiritualité*. Paris: Beauchesne, 1992.

Curran, Charles E. *History and Contemporary Issues*. New York: Continuum, 1996.

———. *The Origins of Moral Theology in the United States*. Washington, DC: Georgetown University Press, 1997.

Deman, Thomas. "Probabilisme." In *Dictionnaire de théologie catholique*. Vol. 13:1. Paris: Letouzey et Ané, 1936.

De Saint-Joseph, Lucien-Marie. "École de spiritualité." In *Dictionnaire de spiritualité*. Vol. 4. Paris: Beauchesne, 1960.

Dublanchy, Edmund. "Morale (Théologie), Histoire Sommaire." In *Dictionnaire de théologie Catholique*. Vol. 10:2. Paris: Letouzey et Ané, 1929.

Gründel, Johannes. "Moraltheologie im Spannungsfeld von Fortschrift und Tradition." In *Zäsur. Generationswechsel in der katholischen Theologie*. Stuttgart: Akademie der Diozese Rottenburg-Stuttgart, 1997.

Hilpert, Konrad. "Moraltheologie." In *Lexikon für Theologie und Kirche*. Vol. 7. Freiburg: Herder, 1998.

Hinnebusch, William A. *The History of the Dominican Order*. Vol. 2. Staten Island, NY: Alba House, 1966.

Kennedy, Leonard A. *A Catalogue of Thomists, 1270–1900*. Houston, TX: Center for Thomistic Studies, 1987.

Lottin, Odon. *Psychologie et Morale aux XIIe et XIIIe siécles*. Löwen: Gembloux, 1942–1960.

Mahoney, John. *The Making of Moral Theology. A Study of the Roman Catholic Tradition*. Oxford: Oxford University Press, 1987.

Mandonnet, P. "Frères Prêcheurs (La Théologie dans l'ordre des)." In *Dictionnaire de théologie catholique*. Paris: Letouzey et Ané, 1924.

Noble, Henri Dominique. "Prudence." In *Dictionnaire de théologie catholique*. Vol. 13:1. Paris: Letouzey et Ané, 1936.

O'Meara, Thomas F. "Bibliography IV. Surveys of the History of Thomism." In *Thomas Aquinas Theologian*. Notre Dame, IN: University of Notre Dame Press, 1997.

Pesch, Otto Herman. "Thomismus." In *Lexikon für Theologie und Kirche*. Vol. 10. Freiburg: Herder, 1965.

Pinckaers, Servais. *Le renouveau de la morale*. Tournai: Casterman, 1964.

———. *The Sources of Christian Ethics*. Trans. Sr. Mary Thomas Noble, O.P. Washington, DC: Catholic University of America Press, 1995.

Shockenhoff, Eberhard. *Bonum hominis. Die anthropologischen und theologischen Grundlagen der*

Tugendethik des Thomas von Aquin. Mainz: Matthias Grünewald, 1987.

Theiner, Johann. "Die Dominikaner." In *Die Entwicklung der Moraltheologie zur eigenständigen Disziplin*. Regensburg: Pustet, 1971.

Weisheipl, James Athanasius. "Thomism." In *New Catholic Encyclopedia*. Vol. 14. New York: McGraw Hill, 1967.

Ziegler, J. G. "Moraltheologie." In *Lexikon für Theologie und Kirche*. Vol. 7. Freiburg: Herder, 1962.

Interpreting Thomas Aquinas: Aspects of the Redemptorist and Jesuit Schools in the Twentieth Century

Raphael Gallagher, C.SS.R.

In order to use the term "school" with regard to Redemptorists and Jesuits, the word needs to be taken in a large sense: it is incorrect to imply that either Redemptorists or Jesuits have a uniform method that could be immediately identified as a univocal school of thought.[1] This is clearer now than at the beginning of the twentieth century, when the residue of a sterile debate over moral systems in the wake of the proclamation of St. Alphonsus as a doctor of the church seemed to classify Jesuits into the apparently self-defining school of probabilism and the Redemptorists into that of the equiprobabilists.[2] The moral theology associated with both is the result of a developing and multiform tradition rather than confined to a univocal school of thought.

It is also important to bear in mind that the similarities between the Jesuit and Redemptorist traditions of moral theology outweigh some obvious differences. The fundamental reason for this is that both developed their moral theology in view of the agenda that was imposed on the discipline as a result of the Council of Trent.[3] Broadly speaking, the decrees of that council dealing with the sacrament of confession obliged Catholic theologians to analyze moral questions through the enumeration of sins according to their number, species, and circumstances. This development entailed, in practice, that moral theology became the theological science that prepared future priest-confessors in the art of the administration of the sacrament of confession from a juridical and practical viewpoint. The agenda of moral theology was dictated by the Roman Catholic conception of the sacra-ment of confession in the Counter-Reformation period. There were some differences of emphasis within this agenda, but there was no substantial disagreement that, from the Council of Trent (1545–63) to the eve of the Second Vatican Council (1962–65), the epistemological structure and methodological aims of moral theology were shaped by the questions arising from the canonical and sacramental need to confess sins in a particular form.

This, in turn, helps to clarify the sense in which I can talk about interpreting Thomas Aquinas in either of the schools: in the specific area of moral theology, neither modern Redemptorists nor modern Jesuits saw it as their primary task to preserve a Thomistic system as such. Both would have been aware of the debates about what this system might mean in the wake of *Aeterni Patris* (4 August 1879), just as both would have been careful to claim that they were working within acceptable interpretations of Aquinas. Although both would have been concerned to be seen to be within the parameters of an acceptable neoscholasticism, it would be more precise to identify the moral theology they produced as preserving the tradition of St. Alphonsus and, implicitly for the Jesuits, that of H. Busenbaum.[4] If it was clear that these had used Aquinas in an acceptable way, then the primary task was to preserve their interpretations rather than, in a direct textual sense, enter the twentieth century debates within neoscholasticism.

In light of these clarifications, it is not strictly necessary for the purposes of this chapter to continue to distinguish between the Redemptorist and Jesuit schools (or traditions, as I prefer). There was a perceived difference between both at the turn of the century linked, as already indicated, to the debate on moral systems in the late nineteenth century. The reality was that both accepted the casuistic purposes of the moral manual, destined for the correct administration of the sacrament of confession, as dictating everything else in moral theology—the broadly similar views of Marc and Slater on the purpose of moral theology confirm this.[5] The Redemptorist and Jesuit schools of moral theology can, consequently, be generically classified as belonging to the casuistic manual tradition.

The casuistic purpose of the manuals was clearly dictated by providing a method for resolving practical doubts in the confessional (Is this act a sin? Which species of sin is it? What are the indicated remedies?). The differences in the systems for resolving these doubts are of minor importance compared to the agreement on the general purpose. It is not that the manuals were unaware of the need for a coherent internal theological rationality. How this was established provides a clue to understanding the influence of Thomas Aquinas on the casuist manual tradition of this century. The casuist manuals sought to provide such a coherence by referring to only those elements of the *Prima secundae* of the *Summa theologiae* that were going to be of practical use to the confessor. At the beginning of the twentieth century, the casuist manuals, probably stung by the growing criticisms of casuistry,[6] continued to react in precisely this way: where the classic manuals (for instance, that of St. Alphonsus) begin with the tracts on conscience and law, the modern casuistic manuals began to increasingly use the tract *On Human Acts* (*De actibus humanis*) as the first part of moral theology.[7] A close reading of this work usually reveals that human acts are discussed, with much reference to Aquinas, but always in view of ultimately clarifying the classification of acts that might or might not be sinful. An external scaffolding of an apparently Thomistic provenance was added to the casuistic manuals, but the inside of the house contained the well-worn furniture of old.

It is important to note, however, that casuist manuals were not, in their origin, a development *outside* the system of Aquinas. The oppo-

site is more true. Alphonsus used Aquinas as his primary theological source.[8] The interpretation made of Aquinas is, admittedly, with a view to the kind of ministerial purposes not envisaged in the structure of the *Prima secundae*. What Alphonsus did—in this way, the later manuals are similar—was to start with the pastoral preoccupation of how to present the solution of moral cases with a view to restoring people to the state of grace (as then understood) or of helping people to remain in that state of grace.

The preoccupation of the casuist manuals with sin is, in fact, based on the positive premise that what matters is the presence of the grace of Christ. Aquinas is used, in an admittedly selective way, in order to give a solid theological foundation to a problem that Thomas never addressed directly. While a Thomist of a purist strain might find this approach problematical, the casuist manualists were driven by the belief that their overall purpose was legitimate. On their view, however great the theological authority of Aquinas (and none doubted this), the authority of a general council (in this case, Trent) was far greater. To consider the theology of grace as the key to understanding the whole theological system of Aquinas is a defensible Thomistic view: the casuist manuals dealt with moral theology from the perspective of sin, but simply because the Decrees of the Council of Trent so dictated.[9] These two facts do not easily sit together, but it is possible to read the underlying theological rationale of the casuist manuals at the turn of the century as preserving the sin-grace dialectic in the following way. The classification of sins was Tridentine: the theological categories of grace were neoscholastic.

The origins of the crisis of the casuist manual begin at this juncture. When the preoccupation with the classification of sins becomes the *dominant* hermeneutical principle of moral theology, the dialectical tension with a theology of grace is quickly lost. This is, in fact, what happened. Aquinas's influence on the manuals became purely formal. The distinctions between the systems of probabilism and equiprobabilism became so intricate as to have, in the end, nothing to do with the sacramental passion out of which the manuals had been born. The purpose of the manuals became the manuals themselves, not the pastoral need for which they had been created. Any changes in the early part of the twentieth century were due to the consequences of the decrees of the various Roman Congregations and, when it appeared in 1917, of the *Code of Canon Law*. The intricacies of the neoscholastic debates were considered more appropriate for the dogmatic theologians.

The more discerning manualists were aware that this was an unpleasant state of affairs. While dogmatic theology was going through some sort of reformulation as a result of the growing influence of neoscholastic thought, the casuist manuals seemed to be caught in a time-warp. The reaction to a significant article by the Dominican Thomas Deman in 1936 can be taken as a useful indicator of how the casuist manuals were eventually to be influenced by Aquinas.[10] Deman's article, at least by implication, suggested that the casuist manuals were not an authentic development of Thomas's thought. This was a serious implication as, by the 1930s, neoscholasticism was positioned as the accepted Catholic view of Aquinas, a situation that would never be challenged by the manualists. It is hardly surprising, therefore, that they were stung by Deman's implication that the only intellectually honest way out of the dilemma was a return to the structure of Aquinas.

One of the more sober responses to Deman was authored by Redemptorist C. Damen, who was among the most renowned manualists of his day.[11] Damen presents two notable arguments. First, he demonstrates that Alphonsus developed his system of moral theology around the Thomistic notion of prudence. Although Damen does not try to place Alphonsus in the virtue-schema of the moral theology preferred by the Dominican school, the linking of Alphonsus to a prudence-based moral system was clearly intended to counter any suggestion that he was a "mere" casuist. More notable, for the purposes of my argument, is Damen's definition of Alphonsus as the master of *pastoral* prudence.[12] Damen is acknowledging that there is a dialectical relationship between Alphonsus and Aquinas: the prudence that gives a practical rationality to the system of Alphonsus is not a commentary on the Thomistic text, *tout court*. Alphonsus, it is claimed, had a legitimate pastoral purpose

in writing his moral theology. But, equally, this pastoral approach has a demonstrably intellectual Thomistic base.

This exchange of views is an aspect of a wider debate that was beginning to affect the manual system, which, though not Thomistic in origin, was to have a decisive influence in shaping the contemporary dialogue between the inheritors of the casuistic manuals and the theological system of Aquinas. The organizing principle of the whole of moral theology (not just the manuals) was radically questioned by Fritz Tillmann and, later, by Theodor Steinbüchel and Johannes Stelzenberger, among others.[13] Their criticisms were based on biblical grounds and personalist philosophy rather than a rereading of Aquinas. It was only with the publication of Bernhard Häring's seminal *The Law of Christ (Das Gesetz Christi)* that the full crisis of the casuistic manuals reached a wide theological audience.[14] It is interesting to note that Häring's work is not a totally consistent rejection of the manuals; furthermore, Häring, especially in the first volume, continues to invoke Thomas Aquinas as the major authority on certain questions.[15] Häring's critics were legion, and they included certain theologians who saw his work as inherently flawed precisely because it was not based on a Thomistic vision of moral theology.[16]

The event of Vatican II overtook this developing debate around the casuist manuals and the efforts at a new formulation, which included not just the Redemptorist Häring but the Jesuit Josef Fuchs.[17] The casuist manual, already being undermined, finally crumbled, blasted under by the reforms of the council. Just as the Council of Trent had the decisive influence in shaping the dialectical relationship between those manuals and Aquinas, so Vatican II is proving to be the catalyst in the contemporary influence of Aquinas on the inheritors of the manual system. The idea of inheritors is important; while no serious theologian now regrets the demise of the casuist manuals, there is a vigorous division of opinion between those who see the reformulation of moral theology as a strictly Thomist enterprise and those who believe that the tradition represented by the casuist manuals can be reformulated in a theologically consistent way. The crucial epistemological question is whether one believes there is, in the Thomistic texts, the key to solving all possible experiential moral conflicts or whether one believes that some of the practical-pastoral questions forced on people by experience need to be supplemented by some other system of knowledge. The inheritors of the casuist manual tradition would, in the main, believe that the tragedies of life and the inevitable conflict of goods and goals need a theological epistemology that is not catered for, in all its aspects, by a material reading of Aquinas.

Although the most quoted text of Vatican II with regard to the renewal of moral theology is the *Decree on Priestly Formation* (*Optatam totius*) 16, one should look elsewhere for clues as to how Aquinas might influence the inheritors of the manual system. It is the redefinition of the church-world relationship in the *Pastoral Constitution on the Church in the Modern World* (*Gaudium et spes*) that is more likely to shape the inheritors of the manual system. This is because this work is redimensioning the precise sense in which moral issues are affecting the historical consciousness of a generation. As a result, a new range of theoretic and practical issues, which one must address, is being created.

The task facing the inheritors of the casuistic manuals is gargantuan. Already in 1969, Joseph Ratzinger saw the potential problems with regard to a slippery-slope interpretation of *Gaudium et Spes* 16, which is a central text with regard to the understanding of conscience (and in the formulation of which, incidentally, some Redemptorists had a key role).[18] Ratzinger fears that the precise relationship between the will and reason could be broken in a way that would lead to what would come to be called the "creative conscience."[19] Should this happen, one is, indeed, faced with the possibility of truth having a double status: truth would contradict truth, which is a clearly silly position. The root of this problem is directly related to my argument here. Aquinas held one view of conscience, and in particular of the erroneous conscience. But not all theologians followed this teaching in detail including, it would seem, Alphonsus.

The heart of the problem is the theological definition of moral truth in the particular circumstances in which one is faced with the practical decision of following the truth as a matter that has consequences for one's salvation. Unless this problem is satisfactorily resolved, the inheritors of the casuist tradition will be unclear as to whether the *formulation* of truth is one question and the *experience* of truth quite another. Interpreting Aquinas adequately is a necessary component of the resolution, and this explains the way in which the inheritors of the casuist manuals are reengaging in dialogue with him.

The first substantial fruit of this reinterpretation of Aquinas has been the acceptance of the essentially theological status of moral theology. Other streams of thought facilitated this, but it was certainly due to the more direct contact with Aquinas that this position has gained ground. There was considerable early resistance to this position because the casuist manuals saw their scientific status as being defined by the (largely legal) requirements of the administration of the sacraments. The question of truth, to take one example, was reduced to technical definitions of a lie (telling an untruth? with a view to deceive? someone who had the right to know?), and whether such a lie was a serious violation of the eighth commandment and merited being mentioned during the sacramental confession of one's sins. The wider significance of truth, as a coherent expression of a life-project, would not have been treated in any manual. There is an interesting subtext in the development of this way of looking at moral questions. Not all interpreters of Aquinas look to him primarily as a theologian; some, for instance, see his contribution as more in the philosophical sphere. For the inheritors of the manuals to accept that Aquinas is, supremely, a theologian places them at odds with some Thomistic schools of thought, but this is not generally regarded as a disadvantage.

Difficulties, however, in this reintegration of a unified vision of theology as one science rather than a discretely connected series of disciplines have resulted from a variety of other developments since the demise of the manuals. The question of moral norms and the specifically Christian nature of morality absorbed much of the energy of moral theologians since Vatican II. While understandable, given the inclination of moral theology to deal with practical matters and the justification of particular positions that were expounded, the absorption with such concerns led to a preoccupation with autonomy in moral decision and authority in moral argument. Interesting and important as these questions are, they are hardly as fundamental as the theological nature of the science in the first place. Because of the preoccupation with second-order concerns, the development from moral theology as a separate discipline (the view of the casuist manuals) through the scriptural basis of all theology (the desire of the council) to theological ethics (which now seems the most acceptable term) has been uneven, and the dialogue with Aquinas consequently intermittent. The renewed appreciation of Aquinas is, however, helping the inheritors of the casuist manuals to be theological in a foundational sense, and thus eliminate any lingering doubts about the theologically scientific status of moral theology. In this crucial sense, the inheritors of both the Jesuit and Redemptorist traditions of moral theology are in the debt of serious Thomistic scholars.

An obvious difficulty remains. The term "theological" could itself be purely formal and the link with Aquinas thus quite tenuous. One should not forget that, in their origin, the casuist manuals represent *one* tradition within the many claiming a Thomistic provenance. Logically, if the originators of the casuist manuals thought that the *theological system* of Aquinas was sufficient, in itself, to solve the tragic conflicts of the moral life then there was no need for *another theological system*. The lesson of history is that they did not think so, and acceptance of the authority of St. Alphonsus by the church can only be interpreted as an agreement with this. Not only, therefore, are there various schools within Thomism itself, but there remains the possibility of other theological systems as valid possibilities within the church—a point recently restated by the ordinary magisterium.[20] The difficult issue must be faced: if moral theology is only properly described as "theology," then in what precise sense can there be different systems of moral theology so that what is covered by that term does not degenerate as the casuistic manuals eventually did?

On precisely this question, the role of Thomas Aquinas is proving crucial. If my hypothesis is correct (that is, the casuist manuals represent a tradition within a tradition), then the inheritors of the casuist manuals face two interpretative tasks, both of which involve dialogue with Thomas. In order to best address these tasks, a contemporary reexamination of the Thomistic categories central to the formation of this tradition is in order.[21] Care should be taken, however, not to use such a discussion to resurrect useless debates about moral systems or as an underhand way of trying to prove that someone is more "Thomistic" than another. The scope of this scientific inquiry should be quite precise in its examination of the tradition of the casuist manuals (tradition as distinct from their final arid and fossilized form) and whether it represents a legitimate expression of Thomas's general theological system. I grant the fact that these manuals are not an exact replica of Aquinas's themes; however, I believe that current research shows that they do not contradict Thomas on the precise question of a theological status. The crucial reason for this has already been implied: if the category of grace (and not, for instance, charity or virtue) is the key to understanding the theology of the *Summa theologiae*, then the casuist tradition is a valid *theological* one insofar as it can be demonstrated that it is the question of grace that also preoccupies them, albeit from a particular aspect. The interest in the theological origins of the manual tradition (as distinct from the system of reflex principles, which, until recently, was the main area of research) is leading, in some cases, to a renewed appreciation of the Thomistic heritage that, in part, the casuist manuals share.

It must be acknowledged that some scholars argue that the whole enterprise of the casuist manuals is so flawed that it would be disingenuous of me to suggest such a heritage. To this charge, I would respond that the effort to relocate the tradition of the casuist manuals within a Thomist tradition is *not* an effort to resurrect the casuist manual form for the twenty-first century. That form died with the demise of the Tridentine theology to which they were inextricably linked—any effort to use the casuist manual form today would be akin to saying the theological position of Vatican II (and, in particular, that of *Gaudium et spes*) should be replaced by the schemata of the Council of Trent.

Trying to resurrect the relationship of the origins of the casuist manual tradition with Thomist theology has logically led to a second interpretative question: How can this tradition be grounded, theologically, in the light of the tasks this tradition has inherited? These tasks can, broadly, be defined as *pastoral* in the sense of *Gaudium et spes*—pastoral, in this instance, indicates those questions raised by the relationship of the church with the world—which, as indicated, is the conciliar context most relevant to that tradition.[22] This relationship has changed so profoundly that the scope of the questions with which the inheritors of the casuist manual have to deal bears practically no relationship with the subject matter of the casuist manuals: the nature of society, the mission of the church, the meaning of a christological anthropology, and the living of the Christian life in the light of the new historical consciousness of our age. These are the pastoral questions, and they clearly involve a fundamental restatement of the tradition represented by the casuist manuals. In these, pastoral broadly referred to the way in which one applied the law to practical cases: manuals were classified as pastorally rigid or benign precisely in the light of how this was done. It is now clear that the concept of the pastoral involves more fundamental questions.

An example of the dialogue with Aquinas among the inheritors of the casuist tradition in this sense is Terrence Kennedy.[23] His work, interestingly, takes its general program from *Gaudium et spes*: his preoccupation is with the meaning of morality, how this is shaped by modern culture and science, and how both of these factors are affecting the practical living of the moral life. This clearly places him in the contemporary tradition once represented by the casuist manuals. The structure of his work is, in part, Thomistic, and, as such, Aquinas is the most quoted author. My interpretation of the living tradition that Kennedy represents is that modern culture is giving rise to new moral experiences and novel questions to be answered. Faced with this, the theologian must address the implications of these questions for the exposition of relevant, current Christian moral teaching. In some of these questions (though not in all), it is Aquinas's own exposition that is judged to be most adequate, both in itself and as offering the possibility of incorporating new interdisciplinary insights into a coherent system.

The clear danger in this approach is that Aquinas could be used as a sort of theological quarry to give apparent substance to an inherently weak theological position. However, if appropriate hermeneutical rules are applied, one can avoid this pitfall. The precomprehension that one brings to the interpretation of the text (in this case, the pastoral concern in the sense used by *Gaudium et spes*) is legitimate, but it should never be forced on the text itself. This dictates that the inheritors of the casuist manual must be more attentive to the exegetical range of interpretations within the Thomist schools to understand the original text and context.[24] I am returning here to my hypothesis of the casuist manuals being a tradition within a tradition: traditions provide unexpected resources when it comes to the foundational theological questions.

It is true that the casuist manuals ceased to be a tradition, in the true sense of a living organism, and became more akin to the dusty, dead bones found in museums (or mausoleums). The renewed contact with Aquinas is helping to revive that tradition in what I believe is a valid sense. The casuist manual tradition is again turning to Aquinas as a major dialogue partner on the critical questions. There is, however, one proviso: if the pastoral questions have changed (that is, the conception of religion, the meaning of morality, and the relationship between the church and the world) then the moral response to these questions must, in the final analysis, be related to *these* questions and not to others, however interesting.

The renewed interest in Aquinas is not being proposed here as a line of inquiry that is being accepted by all in the tradition to which I refer. In his exhaustive study, Vincente Gómez Mier offers an altogether different interpretation.[25] He, too, is concerned with what has happened to the casuist manual tradition; among the authors thoroughly examined are major representatives of the two schools covered in this chapter.[26] Gómez Mier hypothesizes that a paradigm shift, in the sense used by Thomas Kuhn and Larry Laudan, has occurred within moral theology and that the refoundation of moral theology can only be achieved in the light of the result of a paradigmatic revolution.[27] There is, in my view, a flaw in Gómez Mier's study; he analyzes the casuist manuals more as *texts* than as part of a *living tradition*. Judged on a textual basis, there is, as he amply demonstrates, significant substance to his argument. But what if the manuals, in their origins, were not as legalistically inflexible as their representatives in this century undoubtedly became? The shift of paradigm then turns out to be of a different kind than that implied by Gómez Mier. Instead of the "before" and "after" categories used by him with reference to Vatican II, the dynamic becomes more the analysis of the origin, development, and fossilization of a tradition. Those who would accept Gómez Mier's conclusions would see little point in my arguments here on Aquinas and the recovery of a tradition within a tradition.

The influence of Aquinas on the inheritors of the casuist manuals may be discernible in the reformulation of the theological origins of that tradition; less obvious is how Aquinas might be a dialogue partner in the redefinition of casuistry itself. Although casuistry predates the Catholic form of the art, it has to be acknowledged that the disrepute of the term is so total that it may be better avoid it. There is, indeed, merit in the view that the problem is the *abuse* of casuistry, not the theological art to which the term over time referred.[28] Nonetheless, I do not wish to be a propagandist for a word that, dealt a devastating blow by Pascal's critique, is now used even by Catholic theologians as a term of disparagement. But, if the term itself is rejected, what can replace it? It is here that the hypothesis of this chapter may offer a clue. If the contemporary task is to define the ethicotheological purpose of the inheritors of a (casuist) tradition, it could be useful to identify and investigate the historical progenitors of that tradition.

The perennial dream of ethicists, both philosophical and theological, has been to create a theoretic science with universal demonstrability and logical applicability to every possible problem that might arise. Behind this dream lies the legitimate desire to avoid an ethical position devoid of all intellectual credibility where, instead of the demonstrable truth of first and derived principles, one is left to the whims of personal desires or the unverifiable opinions of others. Indeed, I share that fear. But what if it is not possible to construct a system of ethics that is at best a universally

abstract truth or, at worst, a form of a dogmatized imposition that presumes a practical identification between *synderesis*, conscience, and personal freedom? It was the acceptance of the impossibility of the latter that lies at the origin of the casuist manual tradition—whatever about the demonstrability of theological argument in the *aulae* of the university setting of the mediaeval *summae*, it was quite another matter when faced with practical judgments in the tribunal of the confessional, as the dominant sacramentology of the sixteenth and seventeenth centuries saw that sacrament.

To avoid the use of a discredited term (casuistry) and to learn from the lessons of an indefensible methodology (the systems of reflex principles), it may be useful to refer to the fundamental question posed by the practical problem just exposed. Is the road to truth of one form, or can it be diverse without being self-contradictory? The Redemptorist and Jesuit inheritors of the manual tradition would, I believe, wish to explore the latter view. The paradigmatic nature of truth is not simply that derived from the theory of *episteme*—truth is also related to *techne*. For the purposes of my argument, it is not necessary to go into the history of these terms (or the related concept of *phronesis*); rather, it is sufficient to allude to the historical debate on the theory of knowledge.[29] Note, however, that this allusion is not a way of reviving any semblance of a relativist double-status for truth, which is, correctly, a preoccupation. But the *aspect* of truth that is discovered by the one or the other is different. This is the substantial point at the foundation of the theological art that became known as casuistry. Analogically, the truth discovered in the controlled laboratory of medical research should neither contradict nor necessarily coincide *in all the details* with the truth discovered in the course of a clinical encounter. Applying this analogy, it is impossible to overemphasize the context out of which the tradition of the casuist manuals was born, that of the sacramental needs deemed necessary by the Council of Trent. Consequently, the aspect of truth that was sought (particularly that affecting conscience in the sacrament of confession) was not the aspect of truth propounded on the same topic (conscience) but in a different context by St. Thomas.

The external form of what the inheritors of the casuist tradition possessed at the beginning of the twentieth century (the moral manual) is not therefore necessarily the only form, particularly when one considers the Tridentine context of its base. Behind that particular form is an entirely legitimate theological preoccupation. The judgment of Fergus Kerr seems, in my opinion, substantially correct: "Conflicts of values or principles which depend on some human error at some stage for their existence are one thing. There is of course no simple rule in Thomistic moral theory to resolve such conflicts, in the way that Kantian universaliability, the utilitarian calculus or what just 'feels' right is supposed to be able to do. . . . This is where any moral theory requires to be balanced by the practice of casuistry. . . ."[30] (I add the note "substantially" to my approval of Kerr's position, simply because of my preoccupation with the revival of the term "casuistry.")

The correct insight of Kerr is that there are possible issues of the moral life that are not explicitly covered by Aquinas. This is in line with Servais Pinckaers's more general argument: "A virtue-based morality requires a richer and more varied vocabulary than does one based on acts and norms, precisely because of its link with experience. . . . If it is to be fruitful the reading of St. Thomas's works on moral theology therefore calls for contact with experience. . . . [I]t cannot be totally fruitful unless complemented by the reading of authors who use a language more directly associated with experience . . ."[31] Although he does not mention any exemplars of the moral manual in his list of authors (Pinckaers's view of the manual tradition is generally negative), I would suggest that it is his precise point that justifies my hypothesis. It was the contact with experience that forced theologians to develop the manual as a tradition within a tradition; it is the contact with a new experience that can revive that tradition in a theologically credible way.

Aquinas's contribution to this task will be, almost by definition, limited. However, a hitherto rarely explored possibility is the very concept of experience itself in Thomas's writing. Experience has, of course, a particular meaning for him, and it is often linked to the experience of faith rather than to the human dimension of experience, which was the subject of frequent explorations throughout the twentieth century. With these precautions it is, nonetheless, plausible to advance the view that, for Aquinas, experience is a source of certainty, in that it increases hope and gives a greater security and expertise in the context of action.[32] This opens up an intriguing possibility for dialogue between the Redemptorist and Jesuit schools and Aquinas's theology, which has not yet been much pursued.

Introducing this concept of experience, especially as the experience of faith, could help the inheritors of the manual tradition redefine that tradition without falling into the faults of casuistry. The major advantage would be a recovery of a broader understanding of morality precisely as morality. Upon further examination, the foundation of twentieth-century casuist manuals is clearly found in the legal realm rather than the moral one. More to the point, it is based on a process of investigation whether a particular law had been promulgated or not. This is the logical consequence of the connection between moral theology and the administration of the sacrament of confession. It is obvious how, in some cases, the question of sin depended on whether a particular law had been promulgated or not. In the final analysis, it can be said that the minor differences between the schools were based on the interpretation of the axiom: "a doubtful law does not obligate" (lex dubia non obligat). Not only is this a legal formula, but it is a negative one. No wonder there was such difficulty in portraying moral theology as a science geared toward the positive growth of the person—positive visions are hardly the likely fruit of a negative premise.

Returning to my conjecture that it is Gaudium et spes that can provide the matrix for the inheritors of the casuist manuals, there is an intriguing possibility offered by paragraph 46 as a way of envisaging a creative dialogue with Aquinas on the above point. "Having outlined the dignity of the human person and the individual and social task to which he or she is called to fulfill in the world as a whole, the council now draws attention in the light of the Gospel and human experience to certain contemporary needs which particularly affect the human race."[33] The relevance of the perspective offered by this to the inheritors of the casuist manual is twofold. It explains how the problem of the identification of the will of God with a material representation of the law can be overcome and with it any tendency to reduce the human person to being an object who is a mere executor of that law. Second, through the concept of experience taken in its totalizing faith-sense, morality is once more placed in the person-as-subject. The human person in society and community is clearly a theme in Aquinas, and this is of obvious interest to the inheritors of the manual tradition.

How Redemptorist and Jesuit schools interpret Aquinas in the immediate future will depend on their judgment of how the tradition they inherited has fared in the last thirty years. The external form of that tradition represented by the casuist manual is dead. The first efforts to rewrite the tradition were largely inspired by the orientation of *Optatam totius* 16 to give a more scriptural basis to moral theology; this period was followed by a decade of concern with the question of norms and autonomy and an interesting contact with the metaethical discourses of some English and German philosophers as a way of solving practical issues to which the Scriptures did not yield an immediate response.

These two roads of inquiry (a scriptural basis, a philosophically inspired method for dealing with practical normative questions) did not sit easily together. In the 1990s, the Jesuit and Redemptorist schools have both moved more in the direction of a hermeneutical approach that allows for a differentiated interpretation of the human person in particular historical and cultural circumstances. The overriding preoccupation has been to give a full (that is, objective and Christian) account of the human as a subject-in-community; furthermore, there is an openness to new developments (that is, to avoid any fundamentalist use of texts, scriptural or otherwise).

In this personal assessment of the schools across the last three decades, I would highlight the gradual recovering of two elements that are central to the historical origins of those schools in the first place: a theological structure and a preoccupation with the questions which the practical living of the faith presents to theology.[34] In the first of these tasks, the intrinsic theological nature of the discipline,

the ongoing dialogue with Aquinas has already been fruitful. In the second of the concerns, the dialogue with Aquinas is more fitful; yet one can see areas where there has been undoubted benefit to the inheritors of the casuist tradition.

Being a tradition within a tradition, the immediate task of the Jesuit and Redemptorist schools is to consolidate the essentially theological nature of their broadly pastorally oriented concerns. This demands a critical self-awareness that has not been easy to regain after the shock of the disappearance of a method that had served both well for over two centuries. The regaining of this critical self-awareness is being helped by the wider debate on Aquinas in the Thomistic schools generally. It is now clear, for instance, that the discussion on virtue is not unidimensional within Thomist schools: if it can be proven (as I have indicated that it can) that the Redemptorist and Jesuit schools are themselves originally formed in the same broad tradition, then it is possible for these schools to learn from, and perhaps even contribute to, the understanding of Aquinas on some particular questions.[35]

The genius of the Redemptorist and Jesuit schools is a particular one, connected with a spiritual-theological insight into the conscience-dilemmas that ministry among struggling people provokes. The expression of this genius certainly needs a new theological and pastoral foundation in view of the profundity of these dilemmas today.[36] The casuist manuals could reduce questions of truth and truthfulness to a discourse about lying, mental reservations, and the like. The inadequacy of such responses is obvious both theologically and pastorally. The widespread abandonment of the sacrament of reconciliation, once the very purpose of the casuist manual, is directly linked to the unsatisfactory answers for the pastoral questions of the changed relationship between the church, the world, and the endless human quest for meaning. It is likely that the inheritors of the casuist manuals will look to Aquinas for the resolution of some of these fundamental questions, although it is also likely that for other aspects they will continue to explore and develop elements from their own expressions of a particular inheritance of one form within a wider tradition.

Notes

[1] The early years of the Jesuits were marked by vigorous internal differences about moral theology, see Th. Deman, *Aux origines de la théologie morale*, (Paris: Vrin, 1951). These differences have persisted to the present day. The early Redemptorists were more uniform, though contemporary authors such as Bernhard Häring, Marciano Vidal, Brian V. Johnstone, and Sabatino Majorano are by no means of one mind in their methodology.

[2] The debate itself centered on the Redemptorist reaction to the opinions of the Jesuit Antonio Ballerini regarding the interpretation of St. Alphonsus expressed in Ballerini's *Compendium Theologiae Moralis* (Rome, 1866). A fuller account of this curious controversy is given in my "The Moral Method of St. Alphonsus in the Light of the *Vindiciae* Controversy," *Spicilegium Historicum Congregationis Ssmi Redemptoris* 45 (1997): 331–49.

[3] See Louis Vereecke, "L'Enseignement de la théologie morale du Concile de Trente au Concile Vatican II," *Seminarium* 34 (1994): 22–30.

[4] Hermann Busenbaum (1600–1668) was the author of *Medulla Theologiae Moralis facili ac perspicua methodo resolvens casus conscientiae ex variis probatisque authoribus concinnata* (Münster, 1650). The early editions of St. Alphonsus's moral theology are in part a commentary on Busenbaum (usually spelt as Busembaum by Alphonsus): see *Studia et Susidia de Vita et Operibus S. Alfonsi Mariae de Ligorio*, Biblioteca Historica CSSR, Vol. XIII (Rome: Collegium S. Alfonsi de Urbe, 1990), 505–508. Busenbaum continued to be referred to as a "primary" source by Jesuit moralists such as A. Ballerini, mentioned in n. 2.

[5] The Jesuit Thomas Slater, speaking of the moral manuals, says that "They deal with what is of obligation under pain of sin: they are books of moral pathology" (*A Manual of Moral Theology for English-speaking Countries*, vol. 1 [New York: Benziger Brothers, 1909], 6). The Redemptorist Clement Marc, whose manual was still in use in the 1930s, writes that "Theologiae enim moralis est omnia homini implenda officia metire ac definire, ipsisque terminum indicare, quem sine peccato praeterire nequit" (*Institutiones Morales Alphonsianae* [Rome: Philippi Cuggiani, 1885], xviii).

[6] Josef Georg Ziegler, "La Teologia Morale" in *Bilancio della teologia del XX secolo*, ed. Robert Vander Gucht and Herbert Vorgrimler (Roma: Città Nuova, 1972), esp. 341–48.

[7] For representative samples from the two schools, see Arthur Vermeersch, S.J., *Theologiae moralis principia-responsa-consilia*, 3d ed. (Rome: Università Gregoriana, 1933); and the Redemptorist manual, J. Aertnys-C. Damen, *Theologia Moralis*, 16th ed. (Turin: Marietti, 1950).

[8] This view would be contested by respected scholars like Servais Pinckaers (*The Sources of Christian Ethics* [Washington DC: Catholic University of America Press, 1995], 286ff.). It is my judgment that the schools in question in this chapter believed that St. Alphonsus achieved what he announces in the "Praefatio ad Lectorem" of his *Theologia Moralis*, ed. Leonard Gaudé (Rome: Vatican Press, 1905), lvi: "Praesertim autem sedulam operam navavi in adnotandis doctrinis D. Thomae. . . ." That the interpretation of St. Thomas was a primary concern for followers of the manual tradition in this century is amply demonstrated in a doctoral thesis examining one of the foremost representatives of that tradition, William McDonough, "The Nature of Moral Truth According to Domenico Capone" (Ph.D. diss., Accademia Alfonsiana [Rome], 1990).

[9] Thomas F. O'Meara, "Virtues in the Theology of Thomas Aquinas," *Theological Studies* 58 (1997): 255–85.

[10] Thomas Deman, "Probabilisme," in *Dictionnaire de Théologie Catholique*, vol. 13 (Paris: Librairie Letouzey et Ané, 1936), cols. 417–619.

[11] C. Damen, "S. Alfonsus Doctor Prudentiae," *Rassegna di Morale e Diritto*, 5–6 (1939–1940): 1–27.

[12] Damen uses the term "prudentiae pastoralis Magister" (ibid., 19) precisely to show the scope of the manual in the hearing of confessions.

[13] Raphael Gallagher, *The Theological Status of Moral Theology* (Rome: Tipografia Olimpica, 1981), 13–22.

[14] Bernard Häring, *Das Gesetz Christi. Moraltheologie, dargestellt für Priester und Laien* (Freiburg: E. Wewel, 1954). English trans.: Bernard Häring, *The Law of Christ: Moral Theology for Priests and Laity*, trans. Edwin G. Kaiser, C.PP.S. (Westminster: Newman, 1963).

[15] This is more true of the first volume than the succeeding two where the most quoted authorities are recent popes.

[16] Marinko Perovic's recently published doctoral thesis ("*Il Cammino a Dio*" e "*La Direzione alla Vita*" Tesi Gregoriana, Serie Teologia 23 [Rome: Gregorian University Press, 1997]) is a study based on the Dominican moral theologian Jordan Kunicic (1908–74) and provides evidence in this direction.

[17] Josef Fuchs, *Lex Naturae: zur Theologie des Naturrechts^* (Düsseldorf: Patmos, 1955).

[18] On Ratzinger's comment, see Herbert Vorgrimler, ed., *Commentary on the Documents of Vatican II*, vol. 5 (New York: Herder and Herder, 1969), 134–36. William McDonough has chronicled part of this in " 'New Terrain' and a 'Stumbling Block' in Redemptorist Contributions to *Gaudium et Spes*," *Studia Moralia* 35 (1997): 9–48.

[19] Many commentators on *Veritatis Splendor* (August 6, 1993) use this term, for instance that of Ramon Lucas, ed., *Veritatis Splendor: testo integrale e*

commento filosofico-teologico (Milan: San Paolo, 1994), 305–6.

[20]*Veritatis Splendor*, 29.

[21]The relationship between Aquinas, Alphonsus, and Thomistic interpretations on the problems of prudence and conscience was Domenico Capone's very last academic concern, in his eighty-eighth year: see Domenico Capone, *La proposta morale di Sant'Alfonso—sviluppo e attualità*, ed. S. Majorano and S. Botero (Rome: Edacalf, 1997), 335–52.

[22]This is explicitly stated in fn. 1 of the text of *Gaudium et spes*.

[23]Terence Kennedy, *Doers of the Word—Moral Theology for Humanity in the Third Millenium* (Slough: St. Paul's Publications, 1996), which is the first volume of a proposed trilogy.

[24]Géry Prouvost, *Thomas d'Aquin et les Thomistes* (Paris: Éditions du Cerf, 1996) is the type of recent study that could be useful to moral theologians.

[25]Vincente Gómez Mier, *La refundación de la moral catolica* (Pamplona: Editorial Verbo Divino, 1995).

[26]Jesuit manuals studied include those by Sabetti, Génicot, and Noldin; Redemptorist ones include Marc and Damen.

[27]Referring to a paradigm shift has become widespread due to the work of Thomas Kuhn, *The Structure of Scientific Revolution* (Chicago: University of Chicago Press, 1962) and, to a lesser extent, that of Larry Laudan, *Progress and Its Problems* (Berkeley: University of California Press, 1986). The term refers to the epistemological problem involved in understanding and charting change. Working with scientific categories, Kuhn tries to establish how an original matrix can be rendered obsolete by a revolution within a scientific discipline. This revolution results in a paradigm shift in the understanding of the discipline. Laudan's perspective is different, although complementary. He is concerned with understanding how the traditions of investigation can change when their presuppositions alter; the result is akin to a paradigm shift.

[28]This plausible thesis is found in Albert Jonsen and Stephen Toulmin, *The Abuse of Casuistry* (Berkeley: University of California Press, 1988).

[29]A fuller account can be found in ibid., chap. 1.

[30]Fergus Kerr, "Moral Theology after MacIntyre: Modern Ethics, Tragedy and Thomism," in *Studies in Christian Ethics* 8 (1995): 43.

[31]Servais Pinckaers, "Rediscovering Virtue," in *The Thomist* 60 (1996): 377.

[32]Francesco Ventorino, in "Fede cristiana ed esperienza umana in S. Tommaso D'Aquino," *Synaxis* 15 (1997): 89–116, does a textual analysis of this question, though admittedly not from the particular perspective of the moral theologian.

[33]Trans. from Norman Tanner, ed., *Decrees of the Ecumenical Councils*, vol. 2 (Washington, DC: Georgetown University Press, 1990), 1099–1100.

[34]This is a personal assessment. A fuller account of the present state of moral theology, from a different perspective, is the extensive "Literaturbericht" of Franz Furger in three successive issues of *Theologie der Gegenwart* 39 (1996): 54–77, 209–34, 291–307.

[35]James F. Keenan, *Goodness and Rightness in Thomas Aquinas' Summa Theologiae* (Washington, DC: Georgetown University Press, 1992) is one such example from the Jesuit tradition.

[36]Brian V. Johnstone, "From Physicalism to Personalism," *Studia Moralia* 30 (1992): 71–96, is a fine example of how the inheritors of the Redemptorist tradition are also grappling with the basic questions.

Selected Further Reading

Curran, Charles E. *The Origins of Moral Theology in the United States: Three Different Approaches.* Washington, DC: Georgetown University Press, 1997.

Diebolt, J. *La théologie morale catholique en Allemagne au temps du philosophisme et de la restauration 1750–1850.* Strassbourg: F. X. Le Roux, 1926.

Gallagher, John A. *Time Past, Time Future: An Historical Study of Catholic Moral Theology.* New York: Paulist, 1990.

Gucht, Robert Vander, and Herbert Vorgrimler, eds. *Bilan de la théologie au XXe siècle.* 2 vols. Paris: Casterman, 1970–1971.

Hocedez, Edgar. *Histoire de la théologie au XIXe siècle.* 3 vols. Paris: Desclée de Bouwer; Brussels: L'Edition Universelle, 1947–1952.

Mahoney, John. *The Making of Moral Theology: A Study of the Roman Catholic Tradition.* Oxford: Clarendon, 1987.

McCool, Gerald A. *Nineteenth-Century Scholasticism. The Search for a Unitary Method.* New York: Fordham University Press, 1989.

Theiner, Johann. *Die Entwicklung der Moraltheologie zür Eigenständigen Diziplin.* Regensburg: F. Pustet, 1970.

Vereecke, Louis. *De Guillaume D'Ockham à Saint Alphonse de Liguori.* Vol. 12: *Bibliotheca Historica C. Ss. R.* Rome: Collegium S. Alfonsi de Urbe, 1986.

Woods, Walter. *Walking with Faith. New Perspectives on the Sources and Shaping of the Catholic Moral Life.* A Michael Glazier Publication. Collegeville, MN: Liturgical, 1997.

Thomistic Moral Philosophy in the Twentieth Century

Clifford G. Kossel, S.J.

eo XIII's strong endorsement of Thomas Aquinas's philosophy (*Aeterni patris*, 1879) added impetus to a renewal of research on the Dominican's works and thought under way well before the twentieth century.[1] But until about 1935, most philosophical teaching and writing in American Catholic circles was "neoscholastic," a movement that honored Aquinas but was aware of little difference between him and a host of thinkers in the "scholastic tradition." In American Catholic seminaries and colleges, moral philosophy was studied mostly through manuals, and supplemented with a heavy dose of canon law and moral theology.

These textbooks were not without value, but they provided little understanding of the coherent view of the moral life that Aquinas had woven from his biblical, patristic, and Aristotelian sources. Nor did it provide adequate resources for serious discussion and confrontation in the public academic forum with the positions of contemporary philosophy.[2] A genuine revival of Aquinas's moral philosophy required a better understanding of his thought with its proper context and sources. This is the work of the "retrievers," researchers who investigate the text, language, sources, and development of Aquinas's writings to discover as clearly as possible his genuine thought, ever an ongoing task.

Creative thinkers, aware of the retrievers' work and faithful to the principles and themes of Aquinas, are then prepared to explore and develop older themes in new ways. This requires long and careful reflection on the whole of Aquinas's thought. One cannot be *only* a Thomist ethicist; he or she must be aware of the setting of moral philosophy within the whole scheme, for instance, of the *Summa*, the Second Part of which flows from the First Part.[3] In this chapter, I will focus on three significant contributors to the revival of Thomistic moral philosophy in America as it was gradually assimilated from its European sources: Odon Lottin, Jacques Maritain, and Yves Simon.

In the area of moral and political philosophy, the growing influence of Aquinas in America was owing especially to these three men, not only among Catholic thinkers but also in the secular academy. Their writings are particularly valuable today, as they anticipated many current issues. "Virtue ethics," the priority of prudence, psychological determinism, new views of natural law, the nature of civil society and its relations to the church, the status of a Christian philosopher—all are studied deeply and trenchantly by these extraordinary thinkers. Frankly, they deserve to be read or reread. In this limited space, however, I can offer only a sampling of their respective catalogs.

DOM ODON LOTTIN, O.S.B. (1880–1965)

From the many eminent researchers on Aquinas and his background, I chose Lottin because his research dealt chiefly with the moral philosophy and psychology of Aquinas. Between 1922 and 1960, he published about sixty articles in various European philosophical and theological journals. Most of these were painstaking investigations of the language and thought of Aquinas and his predecessors.[4] In these studies, he aims at a fuller understanding of Aquinas's moral theory culminating in the Second Part of the *Summa theologiae*. The issues cluster around three central problems: the definition and scope of natural law and right, freedom of will and free choice, and the nature and connection of the virtues. Some related issues support or complement these three.

Historian and Exegete

His rules of method as historian and exegete of Aquinas are straightforward and simple. First, prescinding from his successors and commentators, let Thomas speak for himself. Study patiently in chronological order the texts relevant to some problem; do not be surprised that Thomas, like any mortal, may change his opinion or at least refine his formulations. Second, since Aquinas was not "a meteor fallen from the heavens," study his intellectual *milieu*. His immediate predecessors provide a state of the question and a language that St. Thomas respects even as he "interprets" them. In his use of old formulas, Thomas often quietly introduces new meanings or emphases; watching these reveals the originality of his thought.[5]

I will briefly look at Lottin's typical procedure and some results as he studies the growth of "natural law" theory.[6] He looks first at the revered texts of Roman Law (Gaius and Ulpian) and of Isidore of Seville. From these texts, it becomes clear that civil laws are those which each nation or people lays down for itself; beyond these is *natural law* (or *right*), common to all people and in some way a norm for civil law.[7] Sadly, at this point, clarity ends. Is natural law the *law of nations* (*ius gentium*) of Gaius, dictated by natural reason (*ratio naturalis*), contemporary with the origins of humanity? Or is Ulpian right: natural right is what is common to all animals—sexual union, procreation, and education of offspring whereas the *law of nations* (*ius gentium*) is peculiar to human beings (slavery, private property, honoring of contracts, free access to the sea, and the like)? Isidore of Seville, the great and "authoritative" encyclopedist, accepts the latter with some modifications.[8]

Now Lottin turns to Gratian's *Decretum* (ca. 1140) and its commentators (Decretists).[9] Gratian himself repeats the division and definitions of Isidore. While he maintains that

natural law, the immutable norm of every human law, began with the origin of rational creatures, it was not codified until the Mosaic Law. Its content is basically what is taught in the Law and the Gospel: Do to others what you would have them do to you, and do not do to others what you would not have them do to you. Here, one cannot help but ask: What is the relation between natural law and divinely revealed law?

After setting this problematic background, Lottin studies a series of commentaries on the *Decretum* from Rufinus (1157) to the *Glossa Ordinaria* of Joannes Teutonicus (ca. 1215). Most of the problems concerning the definition, properties, and scope of natural law are raised in the course of this discussion. The *Glossa*, he thinks, crystallizes the views of the Decretists in its hierarchized synthesis of the definitions. Natural law can be: (1) the tendency of every being to produce its like; (2) the tendency common to animals and humans to procreate and educate; (3) the tendency proper to human beings that is derived from reason, such as the rule that all things are common property; (4) finally, it may be the sum of all the precepts of the decalogue.[10]

He next examines the texts of the theologians from Anselm of Laon (ca. 1100) to Aquinas's contemporaries, Albert and Bonaventure. Twelfth-century theologians seem disinterested in the nature and properties of natural law. But their biblical reading raised difficulties which were to plague later writers, including Aquinas, in regard to its immutability. The polygamy of the Patriarchs, Abraham's readiness to kill his innocent son, Osee's taking a "wife of fornications," and the theft of the Egyptians' goods by the Israelites—all seem contrary to the natural law, yet authorized by God. How can one explain such obvious "changes" in natural law, at least if the decalogue is the expression of that law?[11]

Lottin credits William of Auxerre (ca. 1220) with first integrating natural law into a treatise on theology, considering it the basis and norm of the moral virtues. For William, natural law is specifically human; it is what natural reason (*ratio naturalis*) dictates; it is innate and identified with *synderesis*, which is the higher reason contemplating God and the divine attributes. With Augustine, he maintains that the soul in knowing itself, the image of God, knows God as the supreme good and truth; sense experience is not the source but merely a necessary condition for human thought. He draws the parallel between speculative and practical reason that Aquinas often uses; both begin from innate principles and move discursively to further conclusions.[12]

The latter consideration opens the way for the development of positions, under varying terminology, concerning primary and secondary precepts (or ends). This leads to further refinements on the relation of reason to nature, clearer formulations of the immutability and variability in natural law judgments, and to possible solutions of the many problems raised above. As I cannot trace here all the threads of this intricate discussion, I will turn to Lottin's discussion of Aquinas.[13]

Again, he notes Thomas's great respect for traditional "authorities," not merely a rigid adherence to the past but a deep belief that his predecessors saw some truth. His problem was the need to prune, order, and integrate these truths. For instance, while giving first place to Ulpian's definition, which his teacher, Albert, had simply dismissed and which seems on its face contrary to Thomas's own position, he integrates it with the definitions of Isidore and Gratian. Likewise, he keeps much of the terminology of the Decretists and theologians while reinterpreting them.[14]

Lottin insists that from the *Sentences* to the *Summa*, Thomas stresses the intrinsic nature of natural law—it is not a law imposed by an external authority; instead, it arises from the dynamic structure of the human being.[15] While Thomas frequently applies the term "innate" to natural law, he does not use the term in the Platonic sense. For him, there are no innate ideas, judgments, or *habits* (*habitus*). Rather, the *cognitive* and *appetitive powers* of the human soul, both sensitive and rational, are *natural* to it and have a *natural* inclination to their proper activities. These innate powers and tendencies are, given the appropriate experience, sufficient to perform their human function of forming ideas, judgments, and habits. The primary judgments of practical reason are primary natural law, and they are held by the habit of *synderesis*, which is the counterpart of the "first principles" (*intellectus principiorum*) of speculative reason.[16]

The centerpiece of Aquinas's explanatory synthesis is the article on the unity and plurality of natural law precepts (Ia IIae, q. 94, a. 2).[17] Thomas here goes to basics. Intellect first grasps *being*, which is included in whatever anyone apprehends; on this are based the self-evident (*per se nota*) propositions that speculative reason forms and employs in all its reasonings. Practical reason, concerned with action, first grasps good which as object of the will is the beginning of all practical reasoning.[18] So the first principle of practical reason is: good is to be pursued, evil to be avoided.

This is not the only self-evident principle. "All the other precepts of the natural law are based on this, so that whatever practical reason *naturally* apprehends as a *human* good [or evil] belongs to the precepts of natural law as something to be done or avoided . . . so it is that all those things to which man has a *natural* inclination, reason *naturally* apprehends as good and to be pursued in action and their contraries as evil and to be avoided" (Ia IIae, q. 94, a. 2).[19] To what is the person *naturally* inclined? Here, Thomas sets up an order from the more general to the more specific: (1) to what all substances are inclined, their preservation in being *according to their nature*; (2) to what is common to all animals (he cites the definition of Ulpian), sexual union and training of offspring; (3) to what is proper to human beings, to know the truth about God and to live in society, so that a person should shun ignorance and avoid offense to those with whom he or she must live.[20]

Human beings thus share some basic inclinations with all beings, but each follows from the form which constitutes its specific nature. Since reason is the form that constitutes human nature, reason must give form to all *human* actions. Human natural inclinations, by themselves, are *not* law, natural or otherwise, except as sharing passively in some law which *rules* them (Ia IIae, q. 90, a. 1, ad 1; Ia IIae, q. 91, a. 6). So "all these inclinations in any part of human nature . . . belong to natural law and are reduced to one first precept insofar as they are ruled by reason."[21] Law remains a directive of reason (*ordinatio rationis*), and natural law is the formal principle of order governing the activities springing from all human appetites and giving form to all the virtues.[22]

From these primary, immutable, and indemonstrable principles, other precepts follow,
which he calls "secondary" or "quasi-conclusions" (*quasi conclusiones*). The latter require
some work of reason, which may be very little
or very much.[23] This gives rise to the possibility of deficiency in knowledge—not everyone
knows such conclusions. Also, the variation of
circumstances sometimes changes the objective relationships so that some conclusions,
which remain true "*for the most part*," are not
true *in this particular* situation.[24]

Lottin exhibits Aquinas integrating a long
tradition of natural law thinking and providing a coherent account of its nature, scope,
and variability anchored in immutable principles. His other historical studies complement this one, especially those on freedom
and on the virtues.[25] In these, he reveals
Thomas's originality and freedom in spite of
his adherence to and respect for the traditional formulas.

Moral Theologian

Lottin's interest and work were ultimately
aimed at a reform of moral theology, and later
in his career he produced two systematic
works in this area.[26] The earlier work deals
chiefly with moral philosophy and is substantially integrated into the moral theology of the
second work. He stresses the relevance of philosophy for theology and criticizes many contemporary treatises because they separate
moral theology from both moral philosophy
and dogmatic theology.[27]

While this work is of Thomist inspiration,
he considers Thomas a light for the spirit,
not a confining limit. Thus, he feels free to
omit outdated questions and formulas, fill in
the lacunae, and modify the order of treatment.[28] In fact, he does this quite freely as
one can see by looking at the table of contents.[29] After rejecting, for moral philosophy,
the deductive method (starting with God and
the eternal law), and the sociological method
(Durkheim, Levy-Bruhl, and others) he proposes his own view. For moral philosophy he
suggests the method of "psychological (or
metaphysical) induction," that is, reflection
on the original data of spontaneous moral
judgments that everyone possesses as an objective and immediate norm of morality. This

supplies the *form* of morality. The matter is
also immediate: the rational, social, and contingent nature of humanity.[30]

After a thorough psychological analysis of
the free human act, he takes up the morality
of actions and the formation of conscience. In
his last chapters, he considers the nature and
organization of the virtues, natural and supernatural, and the conditions for living the virtuous and the meritorious life. He emphasizes
the intrinsicism of morality throughout, an
idea he had also stressed in his historical studies of Aquinas. In spite of his freedom with
regard to Aquinas's order and terminology, he
remains a Thomist who supplied invaluable
historical material for future students of
Aquinas.[31]

JACQUES MARITAIN (1882–1973)

The lives of Lottin and Maritain were almost contemporaneous; they shared admiration for Aquinas, but each had a different focus. Lottin was immersed in the history and
exegesis of Aquinas; Maritain's aim was to
bring Thomistic philosophy to bear on contemporary issues. Lottin's work was chiefly
with students and scholars; Maritain was a
friend and collaborator with poets, painters,
statesmen, students, clerics, and popes, as well
as with scholars. One might say that Maritain
brought Aquinas out of the monastery into the
academic public square, where Thomas himself had been at the University of Paris.[32]

In 1901, Jacques met a fellow student at the
Sorbonne, Raïssa Oumansoff, whose family
had left Russia in 1893 to escape a pogrom.
Together, they attended the lectures of Henri
Bergson at the Collège de France and were
heartened by his attack on positivism, opening
the way to spirit and truth. They married in
1904, and were baptized in the Roman Catholic faith in 1906, with Léon Bloy as their godfather. For the next two years, Jacques studied
biology under Hans Driesch at the University
of Heidelberg. In 1909, at the suggestion of
their spiritual director, Fr. Humbert Clérissac,
O.P., they began their study of Aquinas's writings. This inaugurated a new intellectual and
spiritual life for them.[33]

Fired by the combination of his new faith
and Aquinas's thought, he published his first
book, a rather severe criticism of Bergson

(which he later modified).[34] This brought him to prominence—and brought him new friends and a host of enemies. More importantly, though, it gave new impetus to the revival of Thomism in France, and soon in Europe and the Americas.[35] Although he was Professor of Philosophy for several years at the Institut Catholique, most of his writings grew out of lectures at universities in Europe and the Americas, for which he was much in demand. In 1926, he turned his attention to political philosophy, occasioned by Pius XI's condemnation of *Action Française*.[36] He became engaged (but not exclusively) in social and political thought for the rest of his life.[37] Since this is one of two areas (aesthetics being the other) in which he made his most original and influential applications of Thomist philosophy, I will focus on this to show something of his method and important views on social ethics.[38]

Style and Method

Maritain's style is indeed striking. The first aspect of his style, which catches his readers almost immediately, is the eloquence of his expression. Maritain's writing was effective not only because he was an original thinker with fine rhetorical skills, but because he possessed a transparent zeal to find and communicate the truth to the best of his ability, which was motivated by a genuine concern for the well-being of his fellow human beings.[39] Aware of the complexity of language and the diversity of cultures and social situations, he often repeats important ideas in different terms and with a variety of striking images and examples, contemporary or historical. He speaks at times like a prophet, and his writings are never dull.

Then there is *distinguishing and defining*. In the first chapter of *Man and the State* he carefully defines a number of central terms that he will use: community, society, body politic, nation, state. Do not think, however, that Maritain will gloss these seemingly common terms; these are not "one liner" definitions. In fact, each is well described and distinguished from the others in several ways and with many examples, never losing sight of the complex whole.[40] One might prefer other terms, but it is difficult to ignore the distinct aspects of human social engagement to which they refer.

Finally, there is the *careful logic*. While rarely expressing his argument in a simple syllogism, the movement from premises to conclusions is clear. In the first chapter of *Man and the State*, he arrives at a definition of state as the topmost *part* of the *whole* body politic; the state specializes, as it were, in looking to the affairs of the whole and governing for the common good. In the second chapter, he does a careful analysis of the notion of *sovereignty* as it made its way into modern political philosophy through Bodin, Hobbes, and Rousseau. These authors define a sovereign (a person or body of persons) as one who is *above* and *separate* from the body politic, who governs with *absolute and inalienable authority*, and who is *unaccountable* to anyone (save, if they are believers, to God).

The conclusion is clear. No purely human authority can have these attributes. The state is a *part* of, not *above* and *separate* from, the civil community and is *accountable* to the body politic, which can also remove (*alienate*) or modify that authority. Not even the "sovereign people" (of Rousseau) can govern itself from above itself. He appends a corollary to this definition: these attributes of sovereignty still linger in common use and obscure a genuine understanding of a hierarchy of limited authorities and autonomies. Because of the obfuscatory nature of the term as commonly used, he proposes to eliminate the word from the vocabulary of political thought. Should it remain in the language, it poses a danger both to the internal pluralism of civil society and to its dealing with the international community.[41]

Christian Personalism

Several of Thomas's critical texts are gathered to form a center for Maritain's view of the person in society. "Person signifies what is most perfect in all nature, that is, a subsistent individual of a rational nature" (Ia, q. 29, a. 3).[42] "Each individual person is related to the entire community as the part to the whole" (IIa IIae, q. 64, a. 2).[43] "Man is not ordained to the body politic according to all that he is and has. . . . But all that man is, and can, and has, must be referred to God" (Ia IIae, q. 21, a. 4, ad 3).[44] Armed with these texts, he develops his view that, in spite of being genuinely a part of society, every human person transcends all human communities and their common goods by reason of the goals to which human nature is ordained. The human being, even if there were only one, is directly ordered to the Absolute, thus to the contemplative act of the beatific vision.[45]

How can he reconcile this transcendence with being a part, and, so, necessarily serving the whole and its common good? First, Maritain makes his well known distinction between *individual* and *person*. As Aquinas shows, it is by reason of his materiality that each human being is an individual and a member of a species. As such the individual is a *part* and serves the good of the whole. But the human being is a person by reason of his or her spiritual soul and its highest faculties, intellect and will with their drive to truth, good, beauty, and the like, which expand his or her being toward the infinite. These are objects of the speculative intellect, not of the practical intellect, which is engaged in the community and its good.[46]

Secondly, what is the common good of the political community? It is not some special good separate from the members of the community; it is a good or goods that, deriving from the community, must somehow be redistributed to and shared by all the members. Nor is it primarily wealth, power, or good order; these are instrumental goods. It is communion in the *good life*, the goods of the spirit, the opening of mind and heart to values which transcend the political community—science, art, moral virtue—and by which the person achieves genuine freedom. The common good of the political community, a genuine ultimate end in the temporal order, serves personal growth toward freedom and the ultimate end of human life.[47]

Democratic Faith; Christian Inspiration

Maritain grants that there are inevitable tensions between this service of society to the person and the tendency of society to diminish the person, to treat it merely as a part.[48] But he thinks this conflict gives rise to a dynamic in history tending toward democracy, self-government by the people.[49] He maintains that the right of the people to govern itself derives from natural law, and they may share the exercise of their authority with persons they choose to represent them.[50] With Aristotle and Aquinas, he insists on a "moral rationalization" of politics as opposed to a "technical" or "artistic" one (Machiavellianism). The former sees politics as a prudential ordering of society to achieve the common good of persons, which includes justice and morality; the latter sees it as the maintenance of good order by acquiring and maintaining *power*, with disregard for justice and morality. He believes that democracy is the only way to bring about a moral rationalization of society.[51]

This poses a problem. "A genuine democracy implies a fundamental agreement between minds and wills on the bases of life in common."[52] In the "sacral" era of the Middle Ages, this was found in the unity of religious faith. But this is no longer possible.[53] The modern attempt to base civil society on mere scientific reason, segregated from religion, has failed, and it is now clear that "the fact that religion and metaphysics are an essential part of human culture, primary and indispensable incentives in the very life of society." Thus, he proposes a renewed democracy that will be *personalist* and *pluralist*.[54]

Agreement of minds and wills can be achieved by consensus on a set of *practical* judgments that then constitute a secular or democratic faith. The *theoretical* justifications for these practical tenets of a society of free citizens may differ greatly, but they can converge in an analogical similarity in the practical order. This convergence is sufficient for citizens to cooperate in the common task for the common welfare, if they revere "truth and intelligence, human dignity, freedom, brotherly love, and the absolute value of the moral good." Each group may teach and promote its own mode of justification; this is part of the freedom of minds and consciences.[55]

Maritain does not ignore the difficulties of this project; he thinks it requires heroic efforts. But as he believes that it was the inspiration of the gospel that awakened the progress of moral conscience to awareness of the basic tenets of freedom and democracy, so he believes a truly human and moral society "cannot conceivably succeed without the impact of Christianity on the political life of mankind and the penetration of the Gospel inspiration on the substance of the body politic."[56] This raises the difficult issue of the relation of church and state.

Church and State

At least since the Middle Ages and through the Reformation, there has been a more or less close union of church and state, in varying forms. In the predominant Catholic theology and philosophy, this has persisted at least as an ideal (*thesis*) until Vatican II. However, it was granted that accommodations must be made where circumstances made the realization of this ideal impossible (*hypothesis*). The circumstances, of course, were the growing religious pluralism in most Western states, the drive to freedom and equality, and the fact that Catholics were no longer a great majority of the populace—and were, in fact, often a minority. Therefore, a legally established church was difficult to maintain, and even became obnoxious to many citizens.

In the middle of the twentieth century, Maritain and John Courtney Murray were the leading voices in America to question this position.[57] Both argued that "union of Church and State" was never a dogma of the church. It was itself an adaptation to the times when an immature state needed the help of the church in the task of organizing society as it developed a new culture and civilization. Human beings slowly became aware of the properly secular, worldly purpose of the state (or body politic) as distinct from the spiritual, supra-temporal task of the church. The American and French Revolutions paved the way for "disestablishment." But the influence of Enlightenment philosophy tended not only to legal separation of church (any church) and *state*, but to deprive religion of influence on *society* and public affairs, to privatize religion.

Maritain centers his argument for a different view around the person, both a part of the body politic and superior to it, even in the natural realm. But a Christian knows that there is also a supernatural society which guides the person to the ultimate end, God. And this is the "rock of the dignity of the human person." The "law that we are faced with here is the law of the *primacy of the spiritual.*" The churches are associations promoting spiritual values and their moral standards. For the unbeliever, freedom of the church rests on the right to freedom of association and of conscience, "the most basic and inalienable of all human rights." For the believer, the freedom of the church is grounded on God's commission to teach people the way of salvation. Hence the first general principle in this matter is the *freedom of the church to teach, preach, and worship.*

Through its members, the church is *in* the body politic, but by reason of its spiritual and eternal goals, it is also *above* every body politic. The things that are God's are superior to the things that are Caesar's. From this, one finds the second general principle: *the superiority of the church over every body politic or state*. This superiority is one of dignity, rank, or value, not of domination; the body politic remains autonomous in its own temporal realm. But because the same *persons* are members of both societies, and we cannot split the person, a third general principle follows: *the necessary cooperation between church and state*. For Maritain, these are the immutable principles governing this whole issue.[58]

Although these three *principles* are unchanging, their *application* will differ according to different historical situations.[59] Thus, in the Middle Ages, the superiority of the church was realized in that the political powers served the spiritual goals of the church. However, that "sacral" order disintegrated as the state became conscious of its own proper function. The climate now is one bent on "the conquest of freedom and the realization of human dignity." The church does its part in this quest, not by managing the body politic, but by inspiring persons and societies through its Christian message.[60]

The state indirectly cooperates with the church by fulfilling its own function well—creating and protecting legal order and the social, economic, and cultural conditions that favor the ends of persons. More directly, it should guarantee the full freedom of the church to carry out its own mission.[61] Beyond this, without granting the church (or churches) a favored juridical status, there should be mutual assistance between the body politic and the church. "It is rather *by asking the assistance* of the Church for its own temporal common good that the body politic would assist her in her spiritual mission." The various "free agencies and institutions of the body politic" would ask the church's help in the educational and social works by which the church also aids the common welfare. Both church and body politic thus help each other in aiding the person, believer and citizen.[62]

Finally, Maritain looks beyond the national states to the community of the world—in modern parlance, the "global village." The interdependence of nations in almost every sphere calls for a world order of law and of some worldwide political organization. A merely governmental view ("world government") will simply not do. Such organizations must rise, neither from empire nor pacifism, but from the people who have come to recognize the political common good that embraces all nations. Again, it must be pluralist in allowing the present national states to retain their own identity and culture, but subordinate to the requirements of the world body politic.[63]

Maritain's Influence

It is difficult to catch the richness of Maritain's lectures and writings in a few pages; and even more difficult to gauge his influence. I will point out one critical point in Maritain's thought. Political pluralism (vertical and horizontal) and the relations of church and state are inextricably intertwined. He and John Courtney Murray created a new climate for American Catholics (and many others) to ponder these issues. In fact, Maritain's extensive writings on these topics prepared the faithful for the *aggiornamento* wrought by Vatican Council II (especially for the *Declaration on Religious Freedom*), the opening of the church to the world and vice versa, and the personalism and "new evangelization" preached by John Paul II.[64] One may not agree with all of Maritain's positions, but one should not ignore the zeal and cogency of his argument; and we should be grateful for the untiring effort he exerted to bring these issues to the forefront.[65]

YVES R. SIMON (1903–61)

In 1922, a young student at the Sorbonne, Yves Simon, became a disciple of Maritain and attended the Thomist Circles at Maritain's home in Paris. Unlike Maritain he seemed called to be a professor. With a diploma from the Sorbonne (1923) and a doctorate in philosophy from the Institut Catholique (1934), he began teaching at the Catholic University of Lille in 1930 and also gave courses at the Institut Catholique. In 1938, he moved to America and became professor of philosophy at the University of Notre Dame until 1948, when he joined the Committee on Social Thought at the University of Chicago. Owing to illness he retired from teaching (but not from writing) in 1959.[66]

Although Maritain regarded him highly and promoted his work, he remained in Maritain's shadow and was not as widely known as his mentor and colleague. His late recognition is owed partly to the long delay in translations of several of his works and to the fact that many of his wide-ranging courses were not edited for publication until sometime after his death. Simon acknowledged his debt to Maritain, but he was an independent philosopher and the equal of his teacher.

He was devoted to long and careful study of philosophical and social issues and trends. His first two books were remarkable studies of Aristotle and Aquinas on speculative and practical knowledge. Even his studies of the events of World War II are not merely political tracts for the time but thoughtful analyses of social causalities that transcend their immediate subject.[67] His teaching and writing were the fruit of long meditation on his subject matter, enriched with the history of philosophy and social thought.[68]

Freedom and Order: Free Choice

Much of Simon's thought centered around the problems of freedom and order. Like Plato, he saw this as a concern for both the individual and society; each in its own way is a one-and-many that needs order to function well. Order within or among free persons is suggested by nature but is achieved only through human reason and freedom. Simon in one of his finest works takes up the issue of free choice or free will itself: Between scientific determinism and romantic chaos is there room for genuine and intelligible free choice?[69] "The dialectic of the whole issue is often biased from the beginning by the postulate of a conflict between order and freedom."[70]

Facing sensationalist positions, he first asks: *Is there a will*, that is, a rational appetitive power in the person distinct from all the instinctive drives, inclinations, affections, and the like, which he sums up as the "emotional sphere?"[71] By careful causal analysis of the phenomena of human actions, normal and abnormal, with striking examples and lucid argument, he explains the existence of just such a power in the person. He also demonstrates that it penetrates the whole emotional sphere, just as intellect penetrates our sense perceptions. The "common sense" (and legal) distinction between "voluntary" and "involuntary" actions is fully justified by philosophical analysis.[72]

Following the lead of Aquinas, he points out that the object of will is the comprehensive good (*bonum in communi*), the nonparticular good to which all particular goods must conform to be good at all. This good is also called *happiness* and *ultimate end*, from which all other ends and means take their goodness. Adherence to this good is entirely spontaneous and free from constraint. It is not drawn from the necessity of nature; however, it is to the will as light to the eye. Yet, it is not an act of free choice; there are no alternatives to the ultimate end.[73]

This "superdetermination" of the will toward the full actuality of good is the basis of free choice. By it the will enjoys a "dominating indifference" toward all particular and deficient goods presented by reason as possible objects of choice. The will, as efficient cause of all human acts, initiates rational deliberation and closes deliberation when it *chooses*. Choice requires specification (determination) by some judgment of reason, but will makes *this* the final judgment about what to do (or not do) by accepting and acting on it. Will thus actively brings about its own specification and commands that the action *be* and take its *form* from this judgment.[74] Free choice, then, is no exception to the principle of causality. From its natural plenitude in the comprehensive good and with rational deliberation about particular goods, the will determines itself. For this reason, the total act earns the label, "free judgment" (*liberum arbitrium*).[75]

The good chosen in a particular action is not necessarily the moral good; it may be pleasure, wealth, power, or any number of other things. The moral good enters into deliberation as one aspect of a proposed action. Why is choice not always for the moral good? Here lies the problem of order arising from the multiplicity of human tendencies and the likelihood of interference between them. Establishing order in one's personal life is the problem of the nature and development of moral virtue.[76]

Moral Virtue

Although he uses homely examples drawn from common experience, Simon's works are not easy reading and may be somewhat irksome to an impatient reader. But the attentive student will be richly rewarded. Typical of those works derived from his courses is *The Definition of Moral Virtue*, a book of about 130 pages in six chapters. One might think one would simply state the definition and move on to an examination of its applications. But Simon was well acquainted with the history of virtue from Plato to William James; he recognized the vagaries and traps in its usage. It should be no surprise, then, that the definition is not spelled out until the middle of the fifth chapter. What is Simon doing in the meantime?

He is clearing the ground of accumulated confusions about moral virtue, which is generally supposed to provide some stability and reliability in personal and social life.[77] There are what he calls the "modern substitutes" for virtue: the "natural spontaneity" of Rousseau and Emerson, which would rid one of the encrustation of social inhibitions and norms by calling on one's primitive goodness and innocence; the "social engineers" (Fourier, Marxists) who would make traditional virtue unnecessary by structuring society so that everyone's wants would be met; the "psychotechnologists" (under the general aegis of Freud) who use psychology or medicine to eliminate or alleviate undesirable tendencies.[78] As usual, Simon does not deny some value in such views, but they are not adequate substitutes for genuine virtue.[79]

Because his aim is the rehabilitation of the Aristotelian definition, Simon attends to the translation of the word designating the genus of which moral virtue is a species. The term, a persistent source of confusion throughout the ages, in Aristotle is *hexis*; in Aquinas, *habitus*. Unfortunately, there are no English equivalents that could properly express this idea. Out of this have come myriad translations; perhaps the most common one being, of course, the Latin derivative "habit." But this term, both in common use and in philosophical discourse, now has connotations other than, and often conflicting with, its ancestor.[80] The inherent (and inherited) problems are surely obvious.

Habit and *habitus* both signify some disposition in an agent, normally acquired by repetitive actions, to act in certain ways. Like *habitus*, habits may be acquired voluntarily—I want to learn how to ride a bicycle. But the acquired habit, as such, operates "automatically," "mechanically," without freedom and choice—the experienced bicyclist need not "think" or "choose" what to do at every move. But the operation of *habitus*, for Aristotle and Aquinas, is most voluntary and free; the just person wants to do the just action and chooses it against alternatives of gain, pleasure, fear, and so on. She or he knows what she or he is doing, does it because it is the right thing to do, and she or he is happy doing it.[81]

Human virtue is thus not a gift of nature but a personal achievement which opens the way for spontaneity and creativity.[82] Nor is it purely a result of a well-ordered society, important as this is, but a condition which a society of free persons presupposes for willing and achieving the common good.[83] Finally, it is not merely a product of physical, emotional, or mental well-being, although these are very helpful; rather, it is the fruit of personal ordering and using well of all of one's capacities.[84]

Order in Society

Simon's best known work is his application of Thomistic principles to the theory of authority and democratic government.[85] The first chapter of *Democratic Government* lays out a general theory of the need for and proper functions of social authority. This is perhaps the most solid and permanent legacy of Simon in this area. Against views that hold that authority arises only from some evil or deficiency, he argues that it arises from the nature of the person and society. To clarify this position he distinguishes three functions of authority.

The "paternal" (or "substitutional") function does arise from deficiency and takes its name from its most conspicuous example: the authority of parent over child. The child lacks the knowledge and emotional control to care for itself; so parents "substitute" their abilities to guide the child to maturity. When that stage is reached (at whatever age), the authority, which was aimed at the good of the child, is finished; it intends to do away with itself. Some communities also, to achieve their own good, might need temporary management by another community owing to some notable deficiency, abnormal or normal.[86] The identification of all authority with parental authority is one of the chief causes for the "bad name" of authority.[87]

Assuming that community is natural to humanity, and that the aim of community is a *common* good as distinct from a mere sum of private goods (as it is in contractarian theories), he shows that authority provides two essential functions in any community.[88] Even in the hypothesis of a society composed of fully intelligent and virtuous people, *unity of action* with regard to means for achieving the common good requires authority, unless the means is unique and secures unanimity. This need for authority arises from plenitude, not from deficiency. Virtuous people will the common good, and intelligent people can see various ways to achieve it, and none of them is demonstrably the best. How to decide among preferences? Authority is the only way.[89]

Finally, there is the "most essential" function of authority: *direct attention to the matter (content) of the common good*. Every good member of a community must *formally* will the common good and accept the chosen means to achieve it. But most citizens, most of the time, must take care materially of the particular goods for which they are responsible. If they do not, the diversity and plenitude required for the common good would soon diminish and perhaps disappear. "That particular goods be properly defended by particular persons matters greatly for the common good itself."[90]

Two kinds of "particularity" are involved. The first, called "private," he compares to the "homestead," the direct concern of private persons as such. This requires authority to assure that private goods remain in harmony with the common good. The other, termed "special," is concerned with some *aspect* of the common good; the secretary of state and the secretary of health are both concerned materially with particular aspects of the common good, but this requires some authority who looks to the totality, say the president or Congress.[91]

Authority thus complements the autonomy of the private and special particularities. To develop moral virtue and good judgment, as well as to resist abuse of authority, people must be free and responsible for their own lives, families, and enterprises. This is the source of the initiatives that bring about the plenitude of goods, material and spiritual, in which citizens have genuine communion. Favor as much autonomy as possible consistent with the common good. Yet, without authority to assure the harmony of private initiatives with the common good, there would be chaos, and, in chaos, nobody is free.[92] However, if a higher authority, the state for instance, takes over the decision-making for individuals and lesser communities, there may be good order "but liberty is gone and death is coming." This is the way to totalitarian government.[93]

Democratic Freedom

In the second chapter, he begins a discussion of the nature and perils of modern democracy as specified by universal suffrage. Without claiming that it is the only legitimate form of government, he defends it as the most viable form for the modern age.[94] He starts with Aquinas's distinction between "political" rule (over free citizens) and "despotic" rule (over slaves).[95] In the former "the resistance of the people to bad government is institutionally organized"; in the latter it is not. All good civil government must be "political," but not necessarily democratic.

Political systems look to the personal and common good of the governed, and free citizens still act as autonomous agents in their relation to authority. The slave is governed for the good of another; he is alienated, exploited, passive, and instrumental in relation to authority.[96] The revolutions of the last three centuries aimed to increase the autonomy of citizens. In spite of aberrations, this has resulted in better means of resistance to bad

government and more active participation by citizens in the "deliberative" phase of government, mainly through periodic election of their representatives. While this is indeed progress, it is not an infallible guarantee of good government.[97]

But these revolutions have also raised problems about the moral foundations of civil authority. Good people think they have a moral obligation to obey rulers and their laws. But only God can bind one's conscience. How does this power come to reside in some distinct governing personnel? Simon does maintain that God is the ultimate and indirect source of political authority—by creating this naturally social being from whom political society evolves and for which government is a moral necessity. But immediately and primarily it is located in the social body, which must direct itself to its common good.[98] As Simon explains, "Natural law gives political power to the community but does not demand that this power should always remain in the community or be directly exercised by it. It remains in the community so long as the community has not decided otherwise or until a change is lawfully brought about by one having power."[99]

Simply put, if the community retains its authority, it establishes a direct democracy. Although this is rare, it remains the archetype of all democratic institutions.[100] If the community so chooses, it may transmit all or some of its authority to be exercised by someone to whom it gives consent and whom the members must obey by reason of their obligation to the common good. But the community always retains its superior authority.[101] What is special to democracy is that it never transmits all transmissible power to the governing personnel. This is manifest not only in the periodic election and accountability of its officials, but in the requirement that some laws (such as amendments to the Constitution) be submitted to a referendum of the people, and in the persuasive power of public opinion.[102] These means of control characterize the modern ideal of "representative democracy."

After his explanatory defense of democracy, Simon looks deeply into two problems of democracy. First, the demand for *equality* rightly calls for absolute equality in matters of justice, but can be only a hopeful tendency in others (education). And to preserve the vital autonomy of lesser communities, especially the family, he holds that equality must be limited in some areas.[103] Second, he thoroughly examines the effects of technological and industrial society on the development of free, self-governing citizens and compares this to the Jeffersonian ideal of an agrarian society. Simon finds pros and cons to both forms of society. One cannot escape the fact that technology is permanently entrenched in modern society—for good or evil. Again, the issue is one of *right use*; this requires the virtue of prudence in both citizens and leaders. The latter should not be "experts" (though experts are needed in an *instrumental* capacity) but good men and women who have some grasp of the finalities of human nature and its precarious state. Finally, he thinks that a healthy democracy will always require input from the "family farm" to keep in touch with nature and human personality.[104]

With extraordinary insight, Simon integrates the issues of freedom and order from that of the self to that of the world. Both his arguments and his suggestions remain relevant, although new issues have emerged, especially the growing demand (fed by the "information highway") for equality of all views and all "life-styles," a kind of pervasive relativism endangering both democracy and freedom.

Lottin and his fellow researchers prepared the ground for a better understanding of Aquinas's moral and political philosophy, and we owe them a great debt. But Maritain and Simon led the way in deploying this philosophy to current conditions.[105] Their defense and moral grounding of democracy, their insistence on the autonomy of lesser communities within civil society, and their highlighting the requirements of social justice prepared the way, in America at least, for new perspectives on these matters and for a truly Christian humanism, which came to the foreground in Vatican II and in the documents of recent popes. There are still problems to resolve in both church and state, but without the hard intellectual work and persevering teaching of these men the issues themselves would be several steps back in the understanding of American Catholics and of many others.[106]

Notes

[1]For a brief account of the Encyclical's origins and Leo's collaborators, cf. Leonard E. Boyle, O.P., "A Remembrance of Pope Leo XIII: The Encyclical Aeterni Patris," and the following "Commentary" by James A. Weisheipl, O.P. in *One Hundred Years of Thomism: Aeterni Patris and Afterwards*, ed. Victor B. Brezik, C.S.B. (Houston, TX: Center for Thomistic Studies, University of St. Thomas, 1981), 7–27. This work includes an English translation of the *Aeterni patris* (173–97).

[2]The founding of the American Catholic Philosophical Association and its journal, *The New Scholasticism*, in 1926 was a hopeful beginning in the United States. But there was still confusion. For this and for the program and hopes, see the "Inaugural Address" by Msgr. Edward A. Pace in *Proceedings: American Catholic Philosophical Association* (ACPA) 1 (1926): 12–18. Then read Joseph Owens' "Presidential Address" forty years later, "Scholasticism— Then and Now," *Proceedings: ACPA* 40 (1966): 1–12. Another important event was the founding of the Institute of Medieval Studies in Toronto under the direction of Etienne Gilson in 1929. It became a major center for the study and diffusion of Thomistic philosophy. For an appreciation of Gilson, see Armand A. Maurer, "The Legacy of Etienne Gilson," in *One Hundred Years*, 28–44.

[3]The division between retrievers and developers is not exclusive; most retrievers were also developers. Gilson is a prime example. Best known as a historian of medieval philosophy, he contributed much to developing Aquinas's thought, particularly in metaphysics. His sections on the moral life in every edition of *Le Thomisme* are fine and helpful expositions of Aquinas's moral thought, and *Moral Values and the Moral Life*, trans. Leo Ward (St. Louis: Herder, 1931), was widely read, but his main contributions were not in moral philosophy.

[4]There were also several books, including two important systematic works in moral theology. His publications until 1940 are listed in Vernon J. Bourke, *Thomistic Bibliography: 1920–1940* (St. Louis: The Modern Schoolman, Supplement to Vol. 21, 1945). A chronologically ordered bibliography of most of his books and articles is supplied by Mary Jo Iozzio, "Self-Determination and the Moral Act: A Study of the Contributions of Odon Lottin, O.S.B." *Recherches de Théologie Ancienne et Médiévale*, Supplementa vol. 4 (Leuven: Peeters, 1995), 179–84. She also gives a brief account of his life and person, 2–8. Most of the earlier articles were gathered (with some corrective notes and supplementary essays) into a single six-volume work: *Psychologie et morale aux XIIe et XIIIe siècle* (Louvain: Abbaye du Mont César and Gembloux: Duclot, 1942–1957). His works were not translated into

English but were widely studied; look at the list of references in modern editions of Aquinas's works and in serious studies of Aquinas, especially on moral theory.

[5]These directives are spelled out in *Le Droit Naturel chez Saint Thomas d'Aquin et ses Prédécesseurs*, 2d ed. (Bruges: Beyaert, 1931), 3–4. The first edition was a series of articles in *Ephemérides Theologicae Lovaniensis* (1924–1926); these were somewhat revised and some new material added for the second edition. A helpful exposition of medieval uses of authoritative formulas (*auctoritates*) can be found in Chenu's still indispensable *Introduction à l'Étude de s. Thomas d'Aquin* (Montreal: University of Montreal, 1950), 106–31; or *Toward Understanding St. Thomas*, trans. A.-M Landry and D. Hughes (Chicago: Regnery, 1964), 126–55.

[6]It is easy to forget that many "results" now taken for granted were first proposed by Lottin and other early researchers. They did not close all the issues; they located and clarified them.

[7]Lottin recognizes that *lex* and *ius* are not identical in all respects. He remarks that Aquinas, conforming to the usage of his time, often uses them interchangeably (*Droit Naturel*, 69). He also notes that Aquinas and his contemporaries always use the term *ius* in the objective sense, the object of justice, the just thing, never in the modern sense of a subjective power to deploy some object to one's advantage (97). In a later discussion of the relation between *lex* and *ius*, he grants that one may find an occasional text using the subjective sense; but this is not its technical meaning, especially with regard to *ius naturale*. See *Morale Fondamentale* (Tournai: Desclée, 1954), 173–76. A key text of Aquinas on this is ST IIa IIae, q. 57, a. 1, ad 2: "[S]icut eorum quae per artem exterius fiunt quaedam ratio in mente artificis praeexistit, quae dicitur regula artis; ita etiam illius operis iusti quod ratio determinat quaedam ratio praeexistit in mente, quasi quaedam prudentiae regula. . . . Et ideo lex non est ipsum ius, proprie loquendo, sed aliqua ratio iuris."

[8]Lottin, *Droit Naturel*, 7–11.

[9]He does not follow the commentaries on Roman Law except for incidental notes, but suggests that it should be done. On 4 he refers to the work (in progress at the time) of R. W. and A. J. Carlyle as a rich source of texts: *A History of Political Theory in the West*, 6 vols. (Edinburgh: Blackwood, 1903–36).

[10]Lottin, *Droit Naturel*, 23. Since he holds that it was mainly through the *Glossa* that the theologians after 1215 made contact with the Decretists, it is interesting to look at this text (and compare it with ST Ia IIae, q. 94, a. 2), which he cites from the Gloss on Decret. V, 1: "*Ius naturale est commune omnium nationum. Ad intelligentiam istorum nota quod natura multis modis dicitur. Quandoque dicitur natura uis insita rebus similia de similibus procreans.*

Secundo modo dicitur natura quidam stimulus seu instinctus nature ex sensualitate poueniens ad appetendum uel ad procreandum uel ad educandum. Tertio modo dicitur instinctus nature ex ratione proueniens; et jus ex tali natura proueniens dicitur naturalis aequitas; et secundum hoc jus nature dicuntur omnia communia, id est communicanda tempore necessitatis. Quarto modo dicitur jus naturale precepta naturalia, hoc est: non furtum facies, non mechabaris."

[11]Also the problems of the shift from community of goods to private property and from the liberty of all to the institution of slavery, questions already raised by Isidore and the Decretists, become more acute. Almost all attribute this shift to circumstantial changes, the main circumstance being original sin and its consequences. Thomas will give a more positive explanation.

John Mahoney in *The Making of Moral Theology* (Oxford: Oxford University Press, 1987), 111, n. 143, says that "it is well known that he [Aquinas] viewed the institution of private property as necessary for man only after the Fall, due, no doubt, to sin's affecting man's natural predisposition to live in social harmony." He refers to ST Ia, q. 98, a. 1 (surely to ad 3), and to IIa IIae, q. 66, a. 2. Neither of these texts supports Mahoney's statement. The first text (Ia, q. 98, a. 1) does not attribute the division of properties to the fall but to the multiplication of men (the article concerns procreation in the original state). What is attributed to the fall (in ad 3) is the lack of readiness in the will to share the use of private properties with others in need.

The second text (IIa IIae, q. 66, a. 2), Thomas's thematic text on private property, argues that the private possession (*potestas procurandi et dispensandi*) is licit and *necessary* for human social life. By natural right (*ius naturale*) all things are common only in the sense that nature has not divided things and designated them for particular people; the actual divisions of property come about by human agreement and in this sense belong to *ius positivum* (ad 1). (See IIa IIae, q. 57, a. 2 on the ways in which things become related [*adaequatum*] to particular people and IIa IIae, q. 57, a. 3, on the way in which both private property and "slavery" come about as natural to humanity only *secundum rationem naturalem*.) In the body of the article, Thomas emphasizes that the *use* of such properties must remain common to the extent that one readily shares with those in need. The only sin mentioned is the sin of those who prevent others from procuring things or do not share with those in need (IIa IIae, q. 57, a. 2, ad 2).

[12]Lottin, *Droit Naturel*, 33–35.

[13]Ibid., 39–57. He gives special attention to Philip the Chancellor, Alexander of Hales, Bonaventure, and Albert. In all of them there remains some of the Augustinian platonism found in

William of Auxerre. This comes out especially in the explanation of the "innateness" of natural law.

[14]Ibid., 61–67. In this question of the definitions of natural law he looks at each relevant work of Aquinas in chronological order. He follows a similar procedure on the other issues.

[15]Ibid., 70–71, 100–103. His closing paragraph (103): "Il faut le redire, le mérite de saint Thomas ne consiste pas d'avoir créé la formule de préceptes primaires et de précepts seconds, ni d'avoir réduit la loi naturelle aux premiers principes, ni d'avoir souligné l'innéité du droit naturel; son vrai mérite, qui assure la pérennité à sa doctrine, est d'avoir mis en sa plein lumière le caractère intrinséciste du droit naturel. Le loi naturelle n'est autre que la nature humaine s'exprimant rationnellment. C'est le dynamisme aristotélicien appliqué à l'ordre moral: l'homme se perfectionne en réalisant dans sa conduite sa condition d'homme, mais au préalable en l'exprimant par les dictées de sa raison naturelle."

In opening his treatise on law (ST Ia IIae, q. 90, a. 1), Thomas says he is turning to the *extrinsic* principles leading us to good, namely, law and grace. This can be misleading as implying law is wholly heteronomous. He is referring primarily to God "who instructs us by law and aids us by grace." The "law" here is primarily the divinely revealed Law which is the principal aim of this treatise (Ia IIae, q. 90, a. 4; Ia IIae, qq. 98–108). Thomas has expressed eloquently why one needs this divine "instruction" (Ia IIae, q. 91, a. 4; Ia, q. 1, a. 1; SCG I, chaps. 4–5). Also, all law, including civil law, must be *promulgated*, that is, be made known to the subject to become an intrinsic and efficacious principle of action (ST Ia IIae, q. 90, a. 4). Natural law is promulgated by the fact that God gave us the power to know it *naturally* (Ia IIae, q. 90, a. 4, ad 1). Of course, all law is ultimately from God and the eternal law but in different ways.

[16]This effectively excludes any Platonist notion of "innate" as reflected in William of Auxerre and others. It also means that the basic judgments, speculative or practical, precede the *habitus*. See Lottin, *Droit Naturel*, 71–73, where he also suggests that Thomas might well have rid himself of the language of innateness, but he held to the traditional formula while changing its meaning.

[17]John Finnis in an admirable work separates nature from reason; only the latter, he says, is the norm of the morality of acts in Aquinas's view. The "natural" and its inclusion in a universal teleology is "a speculative appendage added by way of metaphysical reflection, not a counter with which to advance either to or from practical *prima principia per se nota*." (*Natural Law and Natural Rights* [New York: Oxford University Press, 1980], 36, and the note, 52–53). This seems to miss the point that reason (or rational soul) is the specifying form of

human nature, and that reason's natural grasp of the natural human inclinations is precisely the grasp of human nature and its essential ends. Of course, one does not need a course in metaphysical anthropology to be aware of one's own nature; one knows it "by experiencing one's nature, so to speak, from the inside, in the form of one's inclinations" as Finnis says so well (34).

In *Morale Fondamentale*, Lottin studies the norm of morality as it developed in Aquinas's works (*Notes Complémentaires*, III, 165–73). He cites many texts to support the position that the ultimate end ("human flourishing" in Finnis), human nature, specific form, and reason all function as norms of human acts, although Aquinas usually shortens it to "right reason." Lottin explains his own view of this in 114–28. A significant text is: ST Ia IIae, q. 71, a. 2: "[V]itium virtuti contrariatur. Virtus autem uniuscuiusque rei consistit in hoc quod sit bene disposita secundum convenientiam suae naturae . . . in qualibet re vitium dicatur ex hoc quod est disposita contra id quod convenit suae naturae. . . . Sed considerandum est quod natura uniuscuiusque rei potissime est forma secundum quam rei speciem sortitur. Homo autem in specie constituitur per animam rationalem. Et ideo id quod est contra ordinem rationis, proprie est contra naturam hominis inquantum est homo; quod autem est secundum rationem, est secundum naturam hominis inquantum est homo."

Of course, sin is also contrary to the eternal law (ST Ia IIae, q. 71, a. 6 and a host of others). The relation to the ultimate end is embedded in the very definition of law: reason is the first principle of human acts and so it is their rule and measure; its function is to order acts to their end, which is the first principle of action. But in (practical) reason itself there is something which has primacy, the ultimate end. See Ia IIae, q. 90, aa. 1–2.

[18]For Lottin's view of this, see *Morale Fondamentale*, 79–81; for a summary of his historical data, see 96–100. Intellect and will, of course, are not two closed boxes. Lottin studied their relation in *La Théorie du Libre Arbitre depuis S. Anselme jusqu'a S. Thomas d'Aquin* (Louvain: Abbaye du Mont-César, 1929). In the section on Aquinas (129–59), he repeatedly emphasizes the compenetration of reason and will and, as spiritual powers, their capacity to reflect on their own acts; in this he sees the basis of human liberty. Important texts of Aquinas on this are: ST Ia, q. 82, a. 4; Ia, q. 87, aa. 3–4; Ia IIae, q. 9, aa. 1–3.

[19]"Et super hoc fundantur omnia alia praecepta legis naturae: ut scilicet omnia illa facienda vel vitanda pertineant ad praecepta legis naturae, quae ratio practica *naturaliter* apprehendit esse bona *humana* . . . inde est quod omnia illa ad quae homo habet *naturalem* inclinationem, ratio *naturaliter* ap-

prehendit ut bona, et per consequens ut opere prosequenda, et contraria eorum ut mala et vitanda" (Emphasis mine). *Natural(ly)* here refers to acts which spring spontaneously from the *nature* of these powers without discursive or inferential thought (*ratio ut natura*), and without prior deliberation (*voluntas ut natura*). But this does not exclude the necessity of sense experience.

[20]See Lottin, *Droit Naturel*, 78–81. Thomas expresses this same position in different ways. A good example is ST Ia IIae, q. 10, a. 1. The question is whether the will is moved to anything naturally. Taking "nature" in the sense of what constitutes the substance of a thing (*quod per se inest rei*), the "natural" must be the primary source of every additional perfection. "Et hoc manifeste apparet in intellectu, nam principia intellectualis cognitionis sunt naturaliter nota. Similiter etiam principium motuum voluntariorum oportet esse aliquid naturaliter volitum. Hoc autem est bonum in communi, in quod voluntas naturaliter tendit, sicut etiam quaelibet potentia in suum obiectum; et etiam ipse finis ultimus, qui hoc modo se habet in appetibilibus sicut prima principia demonstrationum in intelligibilibus; et universaliter omnia illa quae conveniunt volenti secundum suam naturam. Non enim per voluntatem appetimus solum ea quae pertinent ad potentiam voluntatis, sed etiam ea quae pertinent ad singulas potentias et ad totum hominem. Unde naturaliter homo vult non solum obiectum voluntatis, sed etiam alia quae conveniunt aliis potentiis, ut cognitionem veri, quae convenit intellectui; et esse et vivere et alia huiusmodi, quae respiciunt consistentiam naturalem . . ."

[21]"Dicendum quod omnes huiusmodi inclinationes quarumcumque partium humanae naturae, puta concupiscibilis et irascibilis, secundum quod regulantur ratione pertinent ad legem naturalem, et reducuntur ad unum primum praeceptum. Et secundum hoc, sunt multa praecepta legis naturae in seipsis, quae tamen communicant in una radice" (Ia IIae, q. 94, a. 2, ad 2; see also Ia IIae, q. 94, a. 4, ad 3). There can hardly be clearer affirmations that natural law is not a kind of "biological determinism" as some have said. Inclinations are the *material*; reason gives them *form* and thus human determination. Natural law in its basic precepts points to the ultimate ends to be pursued, and deliberative reason must adjust the means (human acts) to these ends. See Lottin, *Droit Naturel*, 77–81.

[22]See Lottin, *Libre Arbitre*, 148–50, passim. This study on liberty complements *Droit Naturel*.

[23]These "secondary" precepts, at least in their generality, Aquinas locates within the *ius gentium* of Isidore; they can be called "human law" because they are derived by way of some reasoning, which is specific to man, not "common to men and animals." But they belong to natural law because they follow

from it as conclusions; hence their universality among all peoples. They are not what Aquinas usually designates as human, positive, or civil laws; these are a different kind of "determination" of natural law flowing from legislative reason. See ST Ia IIae, q. 95, aa. 3, 5; IIa IIae, q. 57, a. 3. The latter article (with Ia IIae, q. 94, a. 5, ad 3) also reveals Aquinas's handling of private property and slavery.

Lottin discusses Aquinas's view of the content and immutability of natural law in *Droit Naturel*, 74–89. The main texts on this are Ia IIae, q. 94, aa. 3–6 and Ia IIae, q. 100, a. 1.

[24]In the well-known example of returning deposits (which Aquinas borrowed from earlier writers), he maintains that *justice must always be done*; but *what is just* in these circumstances is not always the same. One major "circumstance" is the "mutability of human nature." This is not a mutability of essence or specific nature as in "evolution." Rather nature as a principle of operation sometimes fails in its aim, both in the subhuman and in the human. In human nature there may be a change from a "right" (*recta*) to a "perverse" will; this changes the relationships so that what is normally the right action ceases to be so. See ST IIa IIae, q. 57, a. 2, ad 1; *De malo*, q. 2, a. 4, ad 13.

Thomas deals with the biblical problems raised by his predecessors in several places. These do not involve changes or dispensations in natural law. Basically he reverts to God's absolute dominion over all things, including human life; hence He can determine what belongs to whom and thus change the relationships. See Ia IIae, q. 94, a. 5, ad 2; Ia IIae, q. 100, a. 8, ad 3; IIa IIae, q. 64, a. 6, ad 1; IIa IIae, q. 104, a. 4, ad 2.

[25]Sixteen articles on the virtues, natural and supernatural, were published in various journals between 1929 and 1959. In *Morale Fondamentale*, after an exposition of his own view on the virtues (341–434), he again summarizes his historical research in the Notes Complémentaires (434–70). In the same work he presents his own view on liberty (73–83) and a summary of the historical data (96–100). On the question of free choice, one of his most important contributions was his study of the dating of the *Quaestiones disputatae de malo*: "La date de la question disputée 'De Malo' de saint Thomas d'Aquin," *Revue d'Histoire Ecclésiastique* 24 (1928), 373–88. He considered this work a turning point on the issue of free choice, if not in doctrine, at least in emphasis. Prior to this Aquinas had treated reason as supplying the final cause; after this he emphasizes the formal causality of reason, distinguishing the liberty of specification (formal causality) from the liberty of exercise (efficient causality). While his dating has been disputed, the latest biography of Aquinas supports it. See Jean-Pierre Torrell, *Saint Thomas Aquinas*, Vol. 1: *The Person and His Work*,

trans. Robert Royal (Washington, DC: Catholic University of America Press, 1996), 201–5.

Iozzio seems correct in pointing out that Lottin's studies of freedom and the virtues are the beginning of "virtue ethics" and of the centrality of prudence (*Self-Determination*, 38). Alasdair MacIntyre does not mention Lottin in his writings, but these studies would have supplied him with data on two of his main themes, virtue and tradition. Aquinas's tradition, of course, goes back much further than the two centuries on which Lottin concentrates. Lottin points out that Aristotle, especially *Eth. Nic.*, was important in Thomas's reflections in all three areas. But MacIntyre still seems disconcerted with natural law.

[26]Lottin, *Principes de Morale*, 2 vols. (Louvain: Abbaye du Mont César, 1946), and *Morale Fondamentale*, 1954.

[27]Lottin, *Morale Fondamentale*, 23–24; see 19, n. 4, for a brief critique of those who would avoid "speculation." Just as reading his historical studies is somewhat like reading a good detective story, so reading this work, with its ample footnotes and *Notes Complémentaires*, is like following a descriptive bibliography of the theologians of his time and their controversies. Along with a detailed table of contents, it provides good indexes of authors and subjects.

[28]Ibid., vi–vii. (This reminds one of Aquinas's own introduction to his *Summa*.) In concluding this introduction he leaves no doubt about his admiration for Aquinas: "Faut-il ajouter qu'on trouve chez saint Thomas d'Aquin cette conception saine de la nature humaine, de sa dignité, des ses capacités, qui fera un jour l'honneur de l'humanisme chrétien? Aujourd'hui encore, à sept siècles de distance, l'oeuvre du saint docteur se présente comme la synthèse le plus harmonieuse qui, dans l'unité de la personne humaine maîtresse de ses destinées, associe intimement l'humble effort humain, source de l'honnêteté morale naturelle, aux richesses de la vitalité divine que nous prodiguent la grâce sanctifiante et les vertus théologales."

[29]A good example is the way he gives first place among the moral virtues to the virtue of religion, because in the natural order it relates one directly to the ultimate end and is a fundamental disposition necessary for a rational creature to guide his life properly (ibid., 350–63).

[30]Ibid., 38–44. Although he grants that Thomas's description of theology as beginning in God (and eternal law) and moving down to creatures is synthetically correct, it is not an appropriate pedagogical method for moral theology. We move, in the *via inventionis*, from the known to the unknown; so begin with natural morality. The deductive method could obscure the intrinsicism of morality to which those raised on catechetical religious instruction are not accustomed.

[31]Many would not agree with his organization of moral theology. As for moral philosophy, most would still prefer to begin with the issue of the ultimate end, in the manner of *Eth. Nic.* and ST Ia IIae. Nevertheless, in regard to college textbooks in ethics, there was a definite turn, owing to Lottin and others, with greater emphasis on the moral virtues and prudence. For instance, see Henri Renard, *The Philosophy of Morality*, pref. J. Maritain (Milwaukee, WI: Bruce, 1953); Vernon J. Bourke, *Ethics: A Textbook in Moral Philosophy* (New York: Macmillan, 1957); John A. Oesterle, *Ethics: The Introduction to Moral Science* (Edgewood Cliffs, NJ: Prentice-Hall, 1957). And one could do well to consult two works of George Klubertanz, "The Empiricism of Thomistic Ethics," *Proceedings: ACPA*, 31 (1957), 1–24; and *Habits and Virtues* (New York: Appleton-Century-Crofts, 1965).

[32]There are many good introductions to Maritain. A fine start is Donald and Idella Gallagher, *The Achievement of Jacques and Raïssa Maritain: A Bibliography 1906–1961* (Garden City, NY: Doubleday, 1962). The Introduction (7–36) is a brief account of the Maritains' lives and milieu, followed by a descriptive chronology (37–42). The bibliography is complete (to 1961) and chronological for each section, giving the various editions, most translations, a table of contents for the books, and finally a list of books and articles about the Maritains. They estimate that "there are approximately 400 different published writings" by Jacques Maritain (35, n. 38).

See also Joseph W. Evans, ed. and intro., *Jacques Maritain: The Man and his Achievement* (New York: Sheed and Ward, 1963); especially the sensitive article by Maritain's student and colleague Yves R. Simon, "Jacques Maritain: The Growth of a Christian Philosopher," 3–24; and a fine assessment by James Collins, "Maritain's Impact on Thomism in America," 25–45; Donald A. Gallagher, "The Legacy of Jacques Maritain, Christian Philosopher," in *One Hundred Years*, 45–59.

[33]Raïssa collaborated in many of Jacques' works and was a constant inspiration for him. She also published several works of her own, including some volumes of poetry and a study of Aquinas. Best known are her memoirs, which give much information about Jacques, their friends, and the *Cercles Thomiste*, which they hosted for many years in their Paris home: *We Have Been Friends Together*, trans. Julie Kernan (New York: Longmans, Green, 1942). They also had a deep religious life and wrote some works on prayer and Christian spirituality. They were acquainted with the mystics, especially John of the Cross. Perhaps they followed the alleged saying of their godfather that the only thing worthwhile is to become a saint.

They had visited America in 1933, 1936, and 1938 for lectures at universities in the United States,

Canada, and Mexico. They came to stay in 1939; in 1948, Jacques accepted a position as professor of philosophy at Princeton. After Raïssa's death in 1960, Jacques returned to France, where he lived and died with the Little Brothers of Jesus in Toulouse. He continued to write, most notably *The Peasant of the Garonne: An Old Layman Questions Himself about the Present Time*, trans. Michael Cuddihy and Elizabeth Hughes (New York: Holt, Reinhart and Winston, 1968), reflections on persons and events before, during, and after Vatican II. While he praises much about the Council, he is rather harsh regarding some subsequent "interpretations." I am inclined to agree with the view of Donald Gallagher: "Once again I think we have to see him here not speaking in the measured tones of the philosopher, making some kind of critical evaluation, but speaking from the mountain top, lamenting human shortcomings, including his own" (*Legacy of Maritain*, 56–57).

[34]*La Philosophie Bergsonienne: Études Critiques* (Paris: Marcel Riviére, 1914); this publication grew out of lectures at the Institut Catholique in Paris in 1913. The third edition (1948), revised and expanded, was translated into English: *Bergsonian Philosophy and Thomism*, trans. Mabelle Andison and J. Gordon Andison (New York: Philosophical Library, 1955).

[35]To illustrate the dissemination of his ideas, consider that his second book, *Art et Scholastique* (Paris: Louis Rouart et Fils, 1920), was translated into English (1923, 1930), Dutch (1924), Polish (1936), Slovak (1941), and Spanish (Buenos Aires, 1945, 1958). The American English translation is still used as a text in many college classes: *Art and Scholasticism*, trans. J. F. Scanlon (New York: Charles Scribner's Sons, 1930). This is typical of many of his later publications, which were even more widely translated.

The South American translation is notable. Maritain was popular there, especially for his political writings (and subjected to severe criticism); a Maritain Center was opened in Rio de Janeiro in 1925, many years before the opening of the Jacques Maritain Center at the University of Notre Dame in 1958. His first visit to South America was to Buenos Aires, where he gave a series of lectures in 1936.

[36]This was a conservative royalist movement to which many Catholics were attached. (See a judicious account of this movement by one who observed it, Yves Simon, in "Jacques Maritain," 14–18.) Maritain had written a few non-political articles for their review. He accepted the condemnation and the next year published his first work on the relation of church and state: *Primauté du Spirituel* (Paris: Libraire Plon, 1927); in English: *The Things that Are Not Caesar's*, trans. J. F. Scanlon

(London: Sheed and Ward, 1930). As intimated by the French title, the "primacy of the spiritual" will be a central theme in his later political works.

[37]Not only "thought," however. After coming to America more or less permanently in 1939, he provided a meeting place in New York for French intellectuals and artists living in exile. Between 1941 and 1945 he sent about fifty messages to France by radio and the Voice of America. Most of these were published: *Messages, 1941–1945* (New York: Éditions de la Maison Française, 1945). From 1945 to 1948, he served as French ambassador to the Holy See, and in 1947, as head of the French delegation and president of the conference, he gave the opening address and guided the General Conference of UNESCO in Mexico City. Many of his lectures before and during the war were on current subjects such as totalitarianism, Marxism, anti-Semitism, and political freedom.

[38]Two books express Maritain's views most succinctly: *The Person and the Common Good*, trans. John J. Fitzgerald (New York: Charles Scribners, 1947); *Man and the State* (Chicago: University of Chicago Press, 1956), an outgrowth of the 1949 Walgren lectures at the University. Earlier lectures were published as *Scholasticism and Politics*, ed. and trans. Mortimer J. Adler (New York: Macmillan, 1940). He had already expressed his vision of a true humanistic and Christian world, especially in *Humanisme Intégrale: Problèmes Temporels et Spirituels d'une nouvelle Chrétienté* (Paris: Fernand Aubier, 1936); in English: *True Humanism*, trans. Margot Adamson (New York: Scribners, 1938).

[39]Ralph McInerny calls attention to this: "For well over half a century, Jacques Maritain's voice was one to which others attended, giving ear to what was said at least at the outset *because* of the person saying it" (*Art and Prudence: Studies in the Thought of Jacques Maritain* [Notre Dame, IN: University of Notre Dame Press, 1988], 1).

[40]This is practically a trademark of Maritain, signalized by the title of one of his greatest works: *Distinguish to Unite: the Degrees of Knowledge*, trans. Gerald B. Phelan et al. (New York: Scribners, 1959), a translation of the fourth, revised and expanded, French edition of this work.

[41]Maritain, *Man and State*, 28–53. He maintains that this concept can be applied only to God or to the pope in relation to the church. Nor can we arbitrarily change this embedded meaning; we cannot say "sovereignty" and mean "limited government" (49). One might argue, of course, that the term can be used in a purely juridical sense as designating the highest authority in a civic community. Simon, for instance, does not hesitate to use it in his writings on political philosophy. But Maritain is right in pointing out that this causes trouble in dealing with the international community and with

international law. And internally, what can it mean that the United States is a union of "sovereign states," as they still call themselves (especially at party nominating conventions), although they obviously are not? Is Chicago a "sovereign city?"

[42]"persona significat id quod est perfectissimum in tota natura, scilicet subsistens in rationali natura."

[43]"Quaelibet autem persona singularis comparatur ad totam communitatem sicut pars ad totum."

[44]"homo non ordinatur ad communitatem politicam secundum se totum, et secundum omnia sua. . . . Sed totum quod homo est, et quod potest et habet, ordinandum est ad Deum."

[45]Maritain, *The Person*, 5: "The human person is ordained directly to God as to its absolute ultimate end. Its direct ordination to God transcends every created common good—both the common good of the political society and the intrinsic common good of the universe. Here is the fundamental truth governing the whole discussion . . ."

[46]Ibid., 21–36. He had already pointed out the Thomistic position of the superiority of speculative intellect and the contemplative life over practical intellect and the active life (14–18). In Aristotelian and Thomistic philosophy, an individual member of a species exists for the good (perpetuation) of the species. Every species, and every other *part* of the universe serves the *intrinsic* common good of the universe, namely, its *order*. The person, for Aquinas at least, is the only *part* that is also a *whole* and an end in itself (not a mere instrument), which transcends that order to be directly related to the *extrinsic* common good, God. These ordered finalities are succinctly expressed by Aquinas in ST Ia, q. 65, a. 2. Maritain is saying that the person is not merely another *part* of the cosmic order as some current environmentalists seem to hold. As he has said that the person is not for the state, but the state for the person, he might say that the person is not for the environment (cosmic order) but the environment is for the person.

[47]Maritain, *The Person*, 39–44. See 50–51 for a summation: "it is essential to the good of the social whole to flow back in some fashion upon the person of each member. It is the human person who enters into society; as an individual, it enters into society as a part whose proper good is inferior to the good of the whole. . . . But the good of the whole is what it is, and so superior to the private good, only if it benefits the individual persons, is redistributed to them and respects their dignity. . . . On the other hand, because it is ordained to the absolute and is summoned to a destiny beyond time, or, in other words, because of the highest requirements of personality as such, the human person, as a spiritual totality referred to the transcendent whole, *surpasses* and is superior to all temporal societies . . . in respect to things *which are not*

Caesar's both society itself and its common good are indirectly subordinated to the perfect accomplishment of the person and its supra-temporal aspirations as to an end of another order—an end which transcends them." He sees this as transcending the opposition between liberal individualism and totalitarianism: "Anarchical individualism denies that man, by reason of certain things which are in him, is engaged in his entirety as a part of political society. Totalitarianism asserts that man is part of political society by reason of himself as a whole and by reason of all that is in him" (62).

In *Man and State*, Maritain gives several descriptions of the content of the common good, see 11–12, 54–55. In both books he points out that it is not only our *supernatural* goal which transcends political society but also the *supra-temporal* goods of this life—truth, beauty, virtue, etc. While being the chief elements of the common good of a civic community, they also transcend it and constitute the common good of the "community of minds," of culture and civilization. See, *The Person*, 52–54, n. 33; *Man and State*, 148–49. There seems to be a coincidence here of the personal and the common good.

[48]*The Person* was, partly at least, Maritain's response to a noted controversy of the 1940s. In 1943, Charles DeKoninck published a work, *De la Primauté du Bien Commun* (Quebec: Editions de l'Université de Laval: Fides) whose subtitle was "Contre les Personalistes." This led some readers to assume that it was aimed at Maritain, although Maritain himself was not mentioned. Jules Basinée published an article in *The Modern Schoolman* in January 1945 (vol. 22, 59–75) which was an attack on Maritain using some materials from DeKoninck. I. T. Eschmann, a German Dominican teaching at Toronto, published an article "In Defense of Jacques Maritain" in *The Modern Schoolman* in May 1945 (vol. 22, 183–208) in which, practically by-passing Basinée, he attacked DeKoninck; the latter replied with his "In Defense of St. Thomas: A Reply to Fr. Eschmann's Attack on the Primacy of the Common Good" in *Laval Théologique et Philosophique* 1 (1945): 8–109.

There were certainly some misunderstandings among these Thomists, which is understandable in view of the fact that St. Thomas provides no thematic treatment of common good or its relation to the private or personal good. One must gather his views from widely scattered references throughout his writings on other subjects. From later lectures and writings, it seems that Eschmann's thought was closer to DeKoninck's than to Maritain's. He thought that Maritain's was good *political* philosophy, and this was important when the West was encountering totalitarian states; but it was inadequate as a cosmic social philosophy or, as he once put it, the "sociology of beatitude."

A brief critical account of the dispute is given by Ralph McInerny, "The Primacy of the Common Good," in *Art and Prudence: Studies in the Thought of Jacques Maritain* (Notre Dame, IN: University of Notre Dame Press, 1988), 77–91 (but he omits Basinée's article, which was the catalyst for Eschmann). This dispute on the interpretation of Aquinas is not yet adequately resolved. A more recent discussion is provided in Gregory Froelich, "The Equivocal Status of the Bonum Commune," *New Scholasticism* 63 (1989): 38–57. But some points are sure. First, Aquinas never hedges on the priority of the common good to any private good of the same order. Second, there is a hierarchy of communities, family, city, and *communitas universi sub Deo*, and therefore the common goods are subordinate to one another, the lower to the higher. This is the line of final causality which terminates in God, the common good of all creatures. Finally, there does seem to be a coincidence of personal and common good in that the highest common goods are also the highest personal goods.

[49]Maritain, *The Person*, 67–68: "Social life is naturally ordained . . . to the good and freedom of the person. And yet there is in this very same social life a natural tendency to enslave and diminish the person in the measure that society considers the person as a part and as a mere material individual. . . . This movement tends to realize gradually, in social life itself, man's aspiration to be treated as a person in the whole, or, if you will, as a whole and not as a part. To us this is a very abstract but exact expression of the ideal to which, from their very inception, modern democracies have been aspiring, but which their philosophy of life has vitiated."

[50]See Maritain, *Man and State*, 24–26, 48, 35–36, 136–39. Maritain's view of the derivation of political authority is basically the same as that of Simon, which we will discuss later. He seems to use "democratic" in two senses: first, that the primary locus of full authority remains always in the people, whatever the regime; second, the particular regime we call "representative government" or simply "democracy." The latter is the main issue here.

[51]Ibid., 59: "Something particularly significant must be stressed at this point: democracy is the only way of bringing about *a moral rationalization* of politics. Because democracy is a rational organization of freedoms founded upon law." Politics, he says, must be ethical, but there is a distinction between political and individual ethics. For instance, for the sake of the common good, the statesman must tolerate some evils; hence he rejects "hypermoralism" in politics (61–64).

[52]Ibid., 109.

[53]Ibid., 108: "In proportion as the civil society . . . has become more perfectly distinguished from the spiritual realm of the church—a process which was in itself but a development of the gospel distinction between the things that are Caesar's and the things that are God's—the civil society has become grounded on a common good and a common task which are of an earthly, 'temporal,' or 'secular' order, and in which citizens belonging to diverse spiritual groups or lineages share equally. Religious division among men is in itself a misfortune. But it is a fact that we must willy-nilly recognize."

[54]Ibid., 109. Maritain does not explicitly make the distinction, but there are two "pluralisms" in his writings: One might be called "vertical," the ordered set of authorities and autonomies in the civic community; the other "horizontal," referring to the diversities of religions, traditions, ethnic backgrounds, etc., of the citizenry. Here he is talking about the horizontal type. Vertical pluralism is inherent in his whole political philosophy and is identical with the principle of subsidiarity which he calls "organic edification." See, for instance, ibid., 11, 67–68. Joseph W. Evans gives a good account of this in "Jacques Maritain and the Problem of Pluralism in Political Life," in *Jacques Maritain*, 215–36.

[55]Maritain, *Man and State*, 110–12. He says that men "belonging to *most* philosophical or religious" lineages could agree to cooperate for the common good on this practical basis. He deals with "political heretics," who threaten the very basis of civil life, and how a democracy may handle them on 114–19.

The basis for such practical agreement, for Maritain, seems to lie partly in his view of "knowledge by inclination." On 111, he says that these *practical* tenets "depend basically on simple 'natural' apperceptions, of which the human heart becomes capable with the progress of moral conscience." But he also refers to Christian inspiration for such practical convergence; in the same sentence, he adds that these apperceptions: "as a matter of fact, have been awakened by the Gospel leaven fermenting in the obscure depths of human history."

This section is a parallel to chap. 4, "The Rights of Man." There, he says that rights depend on natural law for their validity, and basic natural law is known, not by conceptual or reasoned judgments, but by natural inclinations. Our knowledge of the requirements of natural law and human rights develops with experience in social life, and then is also open to conceptual and reasoned formulation. He refers to his experience with UNESCO, and to the United Nations' *Declaration of Human Rights*, to show the possibility of such agreement on a list of human rights, even among those who do not accept the *theory* of natural law. He held to this to the end; see *The Peasant*, 64–70.

Whether a pluralist society can be held together on the basis of such *practical tenets* is an open question. Maritain himself says that while people of different types of society may lay down a similar or identical list of rights on paper: "They will not, however, play that instrument in the same way. Everything depends upon the supreme value in accordance with which all these rights will be ordered and will mutually limit each other. It is by reason of the hierarchy of values to which we thus subscribe that we determine the way in which the rights of man, economic and social as well as individual . . . pass into the realm of existence" (106–7). Francis J. Canavan brings out some of the difficulties (and some suggestions) in American society today: "Our Pluralistic Society," *Communio* 9 (1982): 355–67.

⁵⁶Maritain, *Man and State*, 55. See also 113–14: "First . . . the more the body politic . . . were imbued with Christian convictions and aware of the *religious* faith which inspires it, the more deeply it would adhere to the *secular* faith in the democratic charter; for, as a matter of fact, the latter has taken shape in human history as a result of the gospel inspiration awakening the 'naturally Christian' potentialities of common secular consciousness. . . . Second: to the extent that the body politic—that is, the people—were imbued with Christian convictions, to the same extent, as a matter of fact, the justification of the democratic charter offered by Christian philosophy would be recognized as the truest one. . . ." By reason of the diverse justifications, he also suggests a pluralistic system of education to transmit this "democratic faith" (119–26).

⁵⁷There was mutual influence; they often cite one another. They worked against formidable opposition, and Murray, a Jesuit priest, was for a time silenced by Rome on this issue but was invited to Vatican Council II as an expert. Gilson in a letter (1 Apr. 1964) to his friend Fr. Henri de Lubac remarks: "My great strength, alas! is that I am not a priest. Had Maritain and I been monks or priests, neither of us would have been able to write the hundredth part of what we've written. . . . But I've nothing to teach you on that score, have I?" (*Letters of Étienne Gilson to Henri de Lubac*, trans. Mary Emily Hamilton [San Francisco: Ignatius, 1986], 69.) These letters are annotated by de Lubac.

⁵⁸Maritain, *Man and State*, 148–54.

⁵⁹Ibid., 156–57: "the *application* of the principle is analogical . . . and that this application takes various typical forms in reference to the *historical climates* or *historical constellations* through which the development of mankind is passing; in such a manner that the same immutable principles are to be applied or realized in the course of time according to typically different patterns. . . . And it is according to these historical climates . . . that we have to conceive the *concrete historical ideals* . . . ideals which are neither absolute nor bound to an unrealizable past, but which are *relative*—relative to a given time—and

which moreover can be claimed and asserted as *realizable.*"

The "analogy" of which he speaks is not a figure of speech; it is an important principle in Aquinas's metaphysics to deal with the similarity and diversity of beings. A "good horse" and a "good speech" are not much alike even in their goodness; but "good" is neither equivocal nor univocal but analogical; both embody goodness but in different patterns.

⁶⁰Ibid., 157–64.

⁶¹Ibid., 171–73. In this passage, he agrees with and quotes Murray extensively. He also believes that a vitally Christian society, aware of the faith that inspires it, would give some public expression to its common belief in the existence of God; other religious confessions would join in this and in the councils of the nation.

⁶²Ibid., 178–79. On 20, he had remarked that "the primary duty of the modern State is the enforcement of social justice." And in his enumeration of human rights (103–7), the emphasis is on social rights. This enumeration seems like a program for the future and certainly has been a major concern of the church, especially since Vatican II.

⁶³Ibid., 188–216. On this topic, he is influenced by Mortimer Adler and Robert M. Hutchins, whom he cites frequently. He is aware that such a hope is far from realization but believes that great efforts of education plus encouragement for existing international agencies may prepare for the eventual realization of this ideal.

⁶⁴Murray, of course, was directly instrumental in the preparation of that decree at the council. He and Maritain certainly were not alone; many European Catholic thinkers (and some American bishops) were moving in this direction.

⁶⁵Michael Novak, *Free Persons and the Common Good* (Lanham, MD: Madison Books, 1989), argues for an updating and merging of two notions of the common good: one implicit in the liberal tradition and the other the view upheld in the Catholic tradition. Throughout the book he leans much on Maritain and Simon. He offers his reflections on this matter "in homage to a thinker [Maritain] whose contributions to the Universal Declaration of Human Rights, to the Christian Democratic parties of the world, and to the vision of a practical, realistic humanism, will long deserve the gratitude of those who thirst for ordered liberty" (xi–xii).

⁶⁶There is no full biography of Simon. Helpful outlines of his life and work may be found in some introductions to his (mostly posthumous) works: Marie-Vincent Leroy, O.P., "Yves R. Simon: A Bio-Bibliography" in Yves R. Simon, *The Definition of Moral Virtue*, ed. Vukan Kuic (New York: Fordham University Press, 1986), ix–xiv; an "Editor's Preface" in Yves R. Simon, *Work, Society, and Culture*, ed. Vukan Kuic (New York: Fordham University Press,

1971), ix-xvi. The latter includes a bibliography of works published to that time (several were published later) and of many articles on Simon, compiled by his son, Anthony O. Simon, 189–226. A recent book of essays includes a more complete bibliography: *Acquaintance with the Absolute: The Philosophy of Yves R. Simon*, ed. Anthony O. Simon (New York: Fordham University Press, 1997).

Early in his studies, Simon was interested in philosophy and social thought. But between 1923 and 1934, besides studying Aristotle, Aquinas, and others, he devoted much time to the natural sciences and to medicine. Also it should be noted that during his time in America he lectured at several other universities in the United States, Canada, Mexico, and, of course, France.

[67]Kuic points out "his grasp of political events and of forces at work in the world" and cites a letter of Simon to his friend Edmond Michelet of 12 June 1940. Michelet at the time was Minister for Cultural Affairs in the French government and kept in touch with Simon after he went to America. Simon wrote: "The Nazis will not win this war; it will be won by the Americans, but God only knows at what price in suffering for our country." As Kuic says "the statement was made six days before the famous appeal by Charles De Gaulle to the French to continue fighting and eighteen months before the attack on Pearl Harbor and the consequent American entry into the war" (editor's preface to *Work*, xiii).

[68]One of his students and editors, Vukan Kuic, remarks on "Simon's practice of writing and speaking strictly on what he knew something about— which means that he always knew exactly what he was speaking or writing about. . . . Teaching, he used to say, is an overflow of contemplation" (ibid., xi).

[69]Yves R. Simon, *Freedom of Choice*, ed. Peter Wolff (New York: Fordham University Press, 1969). This is a translation and revision by Simon and Wolff of *Traité du libre arbitre* (Paris: Vrin, 1952). Mortimer Adler and Wolff discovered the *Traité* during their research at the Institute for Philosophical Research in San Francisco and used it extensively in the two-volume work *The Idea of Freedom* (Garden City, NJ: Doubleday, 1958–1961). See Wolff's Preface, xiii–xvii.

Adler, in his "Foreword," x, is extraordinary in his praise: "[T]his treatise . . . provides the only remedy that could possibly be effective in lifting the controversy [on free choice] to a more fruitful plane, for it not only expounds the doctrine of Aquinas in terms that are accessible to contemporary thinking, but it also employs an imagery that is consonant with contemporary discussion and elaborates the Thomistic doctrine in the light of contemporary psychology."

[70]Simon, *Freedom of Choice*, 3. He continues: "Thus on either side, freedom is interpreted as something disorderly, exuberant, lavish, inventive, creative, and insane, which gives all things color and warmth but carries a threat of universal chaos." Hence many scientists claim that "a free act is an event without a cause, an exception to the law of causality and to the principle of uniformity in natural occurrences. . . . Such a thing cannot exist."

[71]Ibid., 29: "According to all sensationist doctrines, the emotional system constitutes the entirety of human desire, and the word 'will', if still used at all, designates a thing that can be reduced to some component of emotional life."

[72]Ibid., 29–44. He argues that unbridled human passions (but not that of beasts) reveal a search for infinity; and this reveals the presence of another power seeking the total good or happiness (under whatever name) for which the passions are merely instruments. Among other things, he examines "exasperation" (of artists), "sublimation" (psychology), and attempts to limit scientific inquiry (positivism). Of course, he knows that the emotions and imagination can influence reason and will; but reason and will also affect these powers and use them as instruments in their own quest. On 83–93, he has subtle discussion of the relation of "common sense" to science and philosophy.

[73]Ibid., 23–28. The comprehensive good is neither determinately finite nor infinite, but it *admits* coincidence with the infinite good. He compares it to Plato's notion of absolute beauty as described in the *Symposium*. Philosophers may not be able to assert that a finite intellect can have an intuitive vision of this absolute good, but a hypothetical proposition can be philosophically established: "'If there is an intuition of the comprehensive good there is also determinate adherence to it' in spontaneity, in voluntariness and without choice" (27).

[74]Ibid., 142: After giving an example of deliberating whether I should go to Paris or to Montpellier and choosing Paris: "According to all the evidence it is not in acting according to the judgment 'I should go to Montpellier' that the will has conferred to the judgment 'I should go to Paris' the dignity of last practical judgment. It is in acting according to the judgment 'I should go to Paris' that it has determined itself alone according to that judgment. From a slightly different point of view, let us record the division of the will into a dynamic moved part and a dynamic moving part: the dynamic moved part receives, as its form, the practical judgment 'I should go to Paris,' and it is in acting according to this same judgment that the dynamic moving part causes the informing of the dynamic moved part." See also 147–51.

For a discussion of the full range of practical knowledge see: Yves Simon, *Practical Knowledge*, ed. Robert J. Mulvaney (New York: Fordham University Press, 1991). Although this is not a translation of his earlier work, *Critique de la Connaissance Morale* (Paris: Vrin, 1934), it does carry forward that long-term interest. For its immediate sources, see the "Editor's Note," vii–xii. On 128–31, he treats the matter of "superdetermination" and freedom in a discussion of social science.

[75]Simon, *Freedom of Choice*, 97–103: "The force which holds in check the determining power of the practical object . . . is the spontaneous, natural, necessary, and nonvoluntary adherence of the will to its comprehensive good; it is the natural desire for happiness; it is the necessary volition of the last end. By reason of its being a living relation to the comprehensive good, the will invalidates the claim of any particular good to bring about a determinate judgment of desirability. At the instant when the attraction of a thing good in some respect inclines the mind to utter the proposition 'this is good for me,' the infinite ambition of the will reverses the perspective. The thing which is good only in a certain respect discloses uncongenial aspects, and the proposition 'this is not good for me' fights with its contradictory for the assent of the mind."

[76]Ibid., 50–52: "The problem [of separation of achievement and pleasure] would not arise, the normal concomitance of real achievement and pleasure would be realized with perfect regularity, if the human dynamism were not made of a multiplicity of tendencies. Such multiplicity involves the possibility of interference and entails a demand for order. . . . Any dynamic whole demands that order should obtain in the satisfaction of the tendencies which make it up. . . ."

This also relates to natural law and the order of its precepts, which I discussed in the section on Lottin. Simon discusses natural law in *The Tradition of Natural Law*, ed. Vukan Kuic (New York: Fordham University Press, 1965). One might note in this work a procedure similar to that employed in *Moral Virtue*. In the earlier chapters, he discusses the historical adventures of natural law theory, the confusions and misunderstandings, and an analysis of terms and contexts needed to grasp the Thomistic theory.

[77]Simon, *Moral Virtue*, 1: "There is nothing worse from a pedagogical point of view than to begin a discourse with a ready definition unrelated to the reader's personal experience and thoughts. The place to begin a discussion of a subject is always its common understanding. . . . What matters is that everyone recognizes the difference between people who are really dependable and those who are not. . . . And that is also what virtue means in the common understanding. . . ."

[78]Ibid., 4: "Their idea of how to achieve moral excellence is not to work for it but rather to tap in the individual a natural spontaneity toward goodness, which they take to be antecedent to both

rationality and social order." "They" here refers to Rousseau and Descartes; the latter advises one beginning scientific study to rid the mind of all prior judgments.

[79]Ibid., 15: "[I] have not tried to conceal my opinion that none of them, nor all of them together, would solve our problems. But that does not mean that I do not recognize how these ideas contribute to our understanding of the human condition." He returns to these "substitutes" in other contexts and describes what he considers helpful in each.

[80]Ibid., 56: He claims that, "by the time philosophical vernaculars were being established in the seventeenth century, the notion which Aristotle expressed by the term *hexis*, and for which his Latin followers used *habitus*, was already out of the philosophical scene. . . ." He thinks Ross's translation of Aristotle ("a state of character") is better. But this has a weakness: Sciences are also *habitus* and one would hardly call mathematics, for instance, a state of *character*. Unfortunately, a careful translation with abundant notes and glossary was published twenty-five years after his death: Arist. *Eth. Nic.*, trans. Terrence Irwin (Indianapolis: Hackett, 1985). Simon would have liked and learned from this work.

[81]Ibid., 55–61. Anyone who has tried to teach a course on the moral philosophy of Aristotle or Aquinas, and the text being used translates *habitus* by "habit" or "good habit," knows how difficult it is to move students from the habit of thinking "habit" to grasping *habitus*. Simon simply decided to use "habitus" as vernacular English.

This is not merely a "linguistic nicety"; the confusion makes it difficult to grasp the differences. The actions of habitus are free, voluntary, and intend objectively necessary relations; the actions of habit as such are involuntary, not free, and hold only a subjective necessity (as in Hume's account of the habits of the mind). However, Simon holds that habits are very important *instruments* of both scientific and moral habitus; they free the agent from thinking about routine procedures and for creative thinking. See also 76–77.

[82]Ibid., 60: "For while . . . even as they serve specific ends, habits operate automatically or mechanically, the operation of habitus is characterized by unmistakable vitality. Habit relieves us of the need to think; but habitus makes us think creatively." And 85: "For Aristotle, virtue born of rationality and freedom represents a far more distinguished form of spontaneity than what is found, say, in basic human instincts. . . . Compared to 'native goodness,' the cost of achieving a truly virtuous disposition is incomparably higher."

[83]Ibid., 86–87: "in evaluating again the effectiveness of 'social engineering' in assuring human dependability we may well call briefly on Plato. . . . Thus in contrast to, say, Marx or Fourier, among

others, Plato holds firmly that in order to establish a properly working political system, there has to be disposition not only among the many but also within each of them. The personal whole needs to be set in order no less than the social whole. This is what analogies between the individual and the city in *The Republic* are all about: one cannot be properly disposed without the other, but it is vain to expect that taking care of one will automatically take care also of the other. . . . 'Social engineering' looks for an easier way out. But I am convinced that as long as we keep reading Plato, we shall not fall into complete barbarism." And 33: "Instinct and custom may make us both behave and be happy; but it is only if we know what we are doing and why that we become fully human."

[84]Ibid., 86: "Whether one is or is not dependable hinges not so much on the goodness in nature as on the goodness in the use of natures, including especially one's own qualities and abilities." In *Philosophy of Democratic Government* ([Chicago: University of Chicago Press, 1951], 267–74; based on the Walgren Lectures of 1950, reprinted several times, and translated into at least five languages), he applies this to the question of societal control of technology: How can we better assure *good use* of the increasing quantity and improving *perfection* of our technology? He does not overlook the great value of family and community tradition in preparing the ground for acquiring the moral virtues by bringing about effective knowledge of the right thing to do. But at all times, and especially when traditions are breaking down, there is a human desire to *understand* the rules, not merely to *fulfill* them. See also *Moral Virtue*, 32–33; *Practical Knowledge*, 71–74, 96–99.

[85]An earlier work, *Nature and Functions of Authority* (Milwaukee, WI: Marquette University Press, 1940), was the Aquinas Lecture of 1940. A later work, *General Theory of Authority* (Notre Dame, IN: University of Notre Dame Press, 1962), repeats some of *Democratic Government* but expands to include illuminating reflections on authority in science and in moral guidance.

[86]Ibid., 10–13. He refers to a city fallen into disorder which it cannot handle; this would be abnormal. But rule by the federal government over a "territory" until it reaches a stage of sufficient organization to take care of itself as a "state" would be normal. He also discusses rule over "colonies," which might be justified in some instances; but he is suspicious of most such endeavors.

[87]Ibid., 69–71. Other sources of this "bad name" are: frequent and sometimes grave abuse of civil authority, but this should not render the essence of authority suspicious; the most obvious and most widely known function of civil society is the repression of evildoers, which to many means that uncon-

ditional power of coercion defines the state, but coercion is only one instrument of society and does not answer the question of the essence of the institution which has such power; the illusion that good and enlightened people will insure the intention of the common good, but this overlooks the need for particular persons to take care of particular goods. Also *General Theory*, chap. 1, 13–22, gives a good description of the "bad name" arising from the deficiency view of authority. He sums it up on 21: "What thinkers opposed to authority generally mean is that authority can never be vindicated except by such deficiencies as are found in children, in the feeble-minded, the emotionally unstable, the criminally inclined, the illiterate, the historically primitive."

[88]Ibid., 48–50. He discusses the difference between a contractual "society" and a true community. The former may have a "common interest" in a transaction, but this is merely a sum of private interests: "It lacks one of the defining features of the common good, viz., the intelligible aspect by which the common good calls for communion in desire and common action" (49). See also, *General Theory*, 29–31. Joseph Pappin III makes an interesting comparison in "Freedom and Solidarity in Sartre and Simon," *American Catholic Philosophical Quarterly* 70 (1996): 569–84.

[89]He points out that societies of virtuous and intelligent people do exist, a married couple or other small groups (19). He often refers to Aquinas (ST Ia, q. 96, a. 2) on the necessity of governance even in the state of original innocence. This text says nothing about the form of authority in society—one person, a small group, or the whole group acting as an assembly and voting on the issue. Simon considers the locus of authority later. But it does raise an interesting issue. Where is final decision-making authority in the family?

He discusses the nature of the prudential judgment, private or societal, and its indemonstrability and incommunicability in many places. See *Democratic Government*, 19–28, 219–22; *Practical Knowledge*, 71–76; *General Theory*, 33–47. He maintains that this judgment is determined not by demonstration but by "affective knowledge" (inclination, connaturality). In his early work, the *Critique*, 39–50, he examines this under the title: *L'Intelligence: Disciple de L'Amour*. This supposes that the love is made right by the possession of the moral virtues—and more fully by the divine gifts of charity and the gifts of the Holy Spirit. Perhaps his best exposition of this matter is in *Tradition of Natural Law*, 125–36. On 128, he responds to the usual objection to this type of judgment: "Is that arbitrary, a kind of wishful thinking? It certainly is if it is applied in domains where judgment by cognition is available and in all cases where wishes are not what they are supposed to be. But if the inclinations are sound, the judgment which is assented to because of agreement with an inclination is perfectly certain in its own way."

This is based on Aristotle's analysis of *practical truth* in *Eth. Nic.* 6.2, and Aquinas's concurrence with this analysis in several texts which Simon cites. That is, practical truth is not in conformity of the judgment with *things* but in its agreement with *right appetite*. In this he agrees with Maritain, and both cite the text of Aquinas in ST Ia, q. 1, a. 6, ad 3 (and Ia IIae, q. 65, aa. 1–2; Ia IIae, q. 57, a. 5, ad 3; Ia IIae, q. 95, a. 2, ad 4; IIa IIae, q. 45, a. 2). Not only is the prudential judgment of this sort, but natural law itself is first known in this way. *Practical Knowledge*, 33: "The system of natural law, before it is apprehended rationally, is known through affective connaturality." And see *Moral Virtue*, 107–8, on how we know right from wrong. Although Lottin does not use the same terms, he says the same thing, at least with regard to natural law, as we have seen.

It is strange that Finnis, while accepting much of Simon's analysis of authority and government, discounts his view of affective knowledge: "Discount, however, his theory (taken from Maritain) of 'affective knowledge'" (*Natural Law*, 255). He gives no reasons and in fact he seems to appeal to inclinations throughout his treatment of basic values in chaps. 3–4.

⁹⁰Simon, *Democratic Government*, 41. On 37, he cites one of his favorite texts of Aquinas, ST Ia IIae, q. 19, a. 10, where Aquinas asks whether one must conform his will to the will of God *as to the thing willed* by Him, and compares this to the case of a judge condemning a criminal to death and the wife of the condemned wishing that the criminal live. The judge, like God, is looking to the common good; the wife to the good of her family, and *that is what God wants her to do*. On 51–57, he studies Aristotle's defense of pluralism against Plato's call for excessive unity (*Pol.* 2.2–5). He treats this point more fully in *General Theory*, 50–79.

⁹¹Ibid., 59: "Thus the proposition that authority is necessary to the intention of the common good has a double meaning. It means, first, that authority is necessary in order for private persons to be directed to the common good; it means, second, that authority is necessary in order for functional processes, each of which regards some aspect of the common good, to be directed toward the whole of the common good."

⁹²Ibid., 71: "Thus autonomy renders authority necessary and authority renders autonomy possible—this is what we find at the core of the most essential function of government." The principle of autonomy, or subsidiarity, results in a structural hierarchy (another "bad word") of communities and authorities. See 207–8: "If . . . the principle of

autonomy obtains, the larger unit runs only the affairs that cannot be run by any smaller unit, and society is organically divided into several communities characterized by decreasing amplitude of scope . . . . Contrary to a common opinion, hierarchical order is not a proper effect of authority; it is properly effected by the joint operation of the principles of authority and autonomy."

⁹³Ibid., 136–39. This applies to "democratic totalitarianism" as well as to better known types. On 137–38, he lists some protections a democracy may provide against becoming totalitarian: freedom of the church, of the press, and of some other institutions such as the private school, independent labor unions, autonomous cooperatives, private ownership and free enterprise. See Simon, *General Theory*, 138: "Hierarchy disappears, or is at a minimum, in a state that has gotten rid of subordinate organizations and lords it over a sheer multitude of individuals. Such a state is clearly outlined in Rousseau and Jacobinism." In this matter he often refers to Aquinas: ST Ia, q. 103, a. 6, on how God shares the execution of His governance of the universe with secondary causes so that they participate in the good of genuine agency.

⁹⁴Simon, *Democratic Government*, 78: "It seems that the principle of universal suffrage must be numbered among those propositions which, at a given moment of history, have got hold of the human conscience and, from then on, never can be rejected, though they may call for reinterpretation." See 97: "The common man . . . will be crushed unless the constitution of society attaches some power to the only distinction that he certainly possesses, viz., that of having number on his side."

⁹⁵See ST Ia, q. 81, a. 3, ad 2; Ia, q. 96, a. 4. Simon notes that "a despotic system is not necessarily iniquitous. The idea of an enlightened despotism is not absurd, it is only disquieting and suspicious" (*Democratic Government*, 72–73).

⁹⁶Simon, *Democratic Government*, 74–75. He returns to the notion of exploitation in relation to inequality in exchange within the free market economy, a problem for democracy (230–53).

⁹⁷Ibid., 87–89 on some conditions which can vitiate the election process; 125–27 on the power of propaganda, which he likens to psychic coercion. Note that Simon grants that some nondemocratic features can be helpful to a democratic regime, and he refers to the "mixed" regime, combining monarchy, aristocracy, and democracy, proposed by Aquinas, ST Ia IIae, q. 105, a. 1. This seems to be Aquinas's most mature thought, in which he also mixes Moses and Aristotle. On this see, Douglas Kries, "Thomas Aquinas and the Politics of Moses," *Review of Politics* 52 (1990): 84–104.

⁹⁸*Democratic Government*, 154: "there is something paradoxical about one man's having the power

to bind the conscience of another man. Of course a man cannot do such a thing. God alone can. And God can bind a man to obey another man. This he did by the creation of the human species, which is naturally social and political; for the necessity of government and obedience follows from the nature of community life."

99Ibid., 173. After rejecting the "divine right" and "coach-driver" theories, he is explaining the "transmission" theory of Suarez. And this reaches back to Aquinas's argument in ST Ia IIae, q. 90, a. 3. Aquinas, having shown that law is a work of practical reason directing the actions of citizens to the common good, asks: Whose reason makes law? He answers: That of the whole people (since the common good is *their* good) or of someone who is their "vicar" (*vicem gerens*). Supporting this is ST Ia IIae, q. 97, a. 3, c. and ad 3 (Does custom have force of law?). Simon grants that Aquinas's text expresses a "political," not necessarily a "democratic" view. The point is that the *first* locus of political authority is in the *multitudo* whose business it is to take care of *their* common good. Simon holds that a direct democracy (nontransmission of authority to a distinct governing personnel) may be feasible for a small community but would be nearly impossible for a large community; hence the need normally to "transmit" authority to someone or group to represent them in caring for the common good; this could occur through various forms of "consent," not necessarily by elections. See 173–76, and 190–94 on the various modes of "consent" and an analysis of the meanings of the phrase "government by the consent of the people."

See John P. Hittinger, "Jacques Maritain and Yves Simon's Use of Thomas Aquinas in their Defense of Liberal Democracy," in Gallagher, *Legacy of Aquinas*, 149–72, a laudatory but critical article. At 163, he remarks that "it is strange that there is a properly democratic body prior to the establishment of a regime, which is the fundamental political phenomenon according to the Aristotelian political science followed by Aquinas." He may be right about Aquinas's use of *multitudo* to signify an already politically formed body, not a mere mass of individuals. But this may be like asking: When does a child become an adult (aside from strictly legal determinations)? There are stages here from the incomplete to the complete. A number of pioneer ranchers may become aware that they need some concerted action to defend themselves against predators, to provide a school, and hire a teacher for their children, etc., and get together to discuss and decide such issues. This amounts to a growing consciousness of a common good and the beginning of a *regime* called *direct democracy*. Later, with growing common concerns and exhaustion from too many meetings which lead to neglect of their *particular* ranches and families,

they may decide to *transmit* authority to some trusted person or persons (mayor, council) to deal with some or all such matters. They "transmit" authority and establish a new regime. Aristotle proposes this "genetic" approach in *Pol.* 1.2.

100Simon, *Democratic Government*, 181: "Although a regime implying no transmission of power and no distinct governing personnel is a rare occurrence, it is plain that direct rule of the whole community through majority vote is the archetype of all democratic institutions and the fundamental pattern which must be referred to whenever there is a problem of understanding the democratic element in a mixed society."

101Ibid., 179: "Thus, whether the regime is democratic or not, the transmission theory holds that the people, after having transmitted power and having placed itself in a position of mandatory obedience, retains a power greater than the power transmitted; this power is to be exercised when, and only when, the governing personnel are gravely unfaithful to their task." This is well summed up in *General Theory*, "Appendix: On the Meaning of Civil Obedience," 163–67.

102Ibid., 183–85. He devotes 185–90 to the problem of "public opinion." When does one cross the line from moderate campaigns to make our views known to officials (and thus act as a *consultative* body) to over-intensive campaigns to "force" the hand of officials, mainly through fear? The latter may turn into the "coach-driver" view; as the coach-driver *seems* in control but is really only following the direction of the passengers, so officials *seem* to be governing, but are really merely agents of the people who govern them. In the fashion of Rousseau, this means that one obeys only himself through that monster "General Will"; this is a pseudo-transmission of authority that makes rebels of us all and becomes a source of tyranny. On the "coach driver" view, see 146–54.

103In ibid., 228, he gives a criterion for these limits in his discussion of "equality of opportunity": "The excess to be avoided admits of precise definition: as far as opportunity is concerned, equality is carried too far when it impairs the goods to which opportunity is relative; more specifically, a policy of equal opportunity begins to be harmful when it threatens to dissolve the small communities from which men derive their best energies in the hard accomplishments of daily life."

In the preceding pages (222–28) he describes the extreme to which an insistence on absolute equality of opportunity can lead. If all children are to have a completely level start, they must be taken from their parents at birth and raised in nurseries run by a large organization, such as the state. By frequent testing of abilities, emotional stability, etc., they will find their appropriate slot in the world. Nothing but their natural qualities and merits will count; no external factors (wealth, class, and the like) will interfere in the process. This abolishes the family and all the goods that come from family life—*for which everyone should have an opportunity*.

[104]Ibid., 260–322. Humanistic education can be very helpful in subordinating technology to genuine human goals. "The essence of humanism is the use of a reference to man as principle of integration" (300). See also his chapter on "Christian Humanism: A Way to World Order," in *Practical Knowledge*, 137–55.

[105]They constantly insist that moral and political philosophy cannot deal merely with "essences" but with essences existing in a given "state" or situation. Water may be essentially H_2O, but the "water" in the river, ocean, or fountain is never pure H_2O. So "government," "authority," "church," etc., exist in various physical, psychological, and historical climates which must be taken into account in the study of such "essences" in their real existence.

[106]An important influence of Maritain and Simon, along with Gilson, was the encouragement and inspiration they gave to Catholic lay scholars to engage in the philosophical dialogue. One has only to review the roster of the ACPA and its journal from 1926 to the present to see the growth in the number of lay scholars. In their lives of scholarship and devotion these three provided an image of Christian philosophers at work.

Selected Further Reading

Adler, Mortimer, ed. *The Idea of Freedom.* New York: Doubleday, 1958–1961.

Bourke, Vernon J. *Thomistic Bibliography: 1920–1940.* St. Louis: The Modern Schoolman, Supplement to Vol. 21, 1945.

———. *Ethics: A Textbook in Moral Philosophy.* New York: Macmillan, 1961.

Boyle, Leonard E. "A Remembrance of Pope Leo XIII: The Encyclical *Aeterni Patris.*" In *One Hundred Years of Thomism: Aeterni Patris and Afterwards.* Ed. Victor A. Brezik. Houston: Center for Thomistic Studies, University of St. Thomas, 1981.

Brezik, Victor A., ed. *One Hundred Years of Thomism: Aeterni Patris and Afterwards.* Houston: Center for Thomistic Studies, University of St. Thomas, 1981.

Canavan, Francis J. "Our Pluralistic Society." *Communio* 9 (1982): 355–67.

Carlyle, R. W. and A. J. *A History of Political Theory in the West.* 6 vols. Edinburgh: Blackwood, 1903–1936.

Chenu, M.-D. *Toward Understanding St. Thomas.* Trans. A.-M. Landry and D. Hughes. Chicago: Regnery, 1964.

Collins, James. "Maritain's Impact on Thomism in America." In *Jacques Maritain: The Man and His Achievement.* Ed. Joseph W. Evans. New York: Sheed and Ward, 1963.

Evans, Joseph W. "Jacques Maritain and the Problem of Pluralism in Political Life." *Jacques Maritain: The Man and His Achievement.* Ed. Joseph W. Evans. New York: Sheed and Ward, 1963.

———, ed., *Jacques Maritain: The Man and his Achievement.* New York: Sheed and Ward, 1963.

Finnis, John. *Natural Law and Natural Rights.* New York: Oxford University Press, 1980.

Gallagher, Donald, and Idella Gallagher. *The Achievement of Jacques and Raïssa Maritain: A Bibliography 1906–1961.* Garden City, NY: Doubleday, 1962.

Gallagher, Donald. "The Legacy of Jacques Maritain, Christian Philosopher." In *One Hundred Years of Thomism: Aeterni Patris and Afterwards.* Ed. Victor A. Brezik. Houston: Center for Thomistic Studies, University of St. Thomas, 1981.

Gilson, Etienne. *Moral Values and the Moral Life.* Trans. Leo Ward. St. Louis: Herder, 1931.

———. *Letters of Étienne Gilson to Henri de Lubac.* Trans. Mary Emily Hamilton. San Francisco: Ignatius, 1986.

Hittinger, John P. "Jacques Maritain and Yves Simon's use of Thomas Aquinas in their Defense of Liberal Democracy." In Gallagher, ed., *Legacy of Aquinas,* pp. 149–72.

Iozzio, Mary Jo. "Self-Determination and the Moral Act: a Study of the Contribution of Odon Lottin, O.S.B." In *Recherches de Théologie Ancienne et Médiévale, Supplementa.* Vol. 4. Leuven: Peeters, 1995.

Klubertanz, George. "The Empiricism of Thomistic Ethics." *Proceedings: American Catholic Philosophical Association* (ACPA) 31 (1957): 1–24.

———. *Habits and Virtues.* New York: Appleton-Century-Crofts, 1965.

Kries, Douglas. "Thomas Aquinas and the Politics of Moses." *Review of Politics* 52 (1990): 84–104.

Kuic, Vukan. Editor's preface to *Work, Society, and Culture.* Ed. Vukan Kuic. New York: Fordham University Press, 1971.

Leroy, Marie-Vincent, O.P. "Yves R. Simon: A Bio-Bibliography." In *The Definition of Moral Virtue.* Ed. Vukan Kuic. New York: Fordham University Press, 1986.

Lottin, Odon. "La Date de la Question Disputée 'De Malo' de Saint Thomas d'Aquin," *Revue d'Histoire Ecclésiastique* 24 (1928): 373–88.

———. *La Théorie du Libre Arbitre depuis S. Anselme jusqu'a S. Thomas d'Aquin.* Louvain: Abbaye du Mont César, 1929.

———. *Le Droit Naturel chez Saint Thomas d'Aquin et ses Prédécessors,* 2d ed. Bruges: Bayaert, 1931.

———. *Principes de Morale*. 2 vols. Louvain: Abbaye du Mont César, 1946.

———. *Morale Fondamentale*. Tournai: Desclée, 1954.

———. *Psychologie et Morale aux XIIe et XIIIe siècle*. Louvain: Abbaye du Mont César, 1942–1957.

Mahoney, John. *The Making of Moral Theology*. Oxford: Oxford University Press, 1987.

Maritain, Jacques. *La Philosophie Bergsonienne: Études Critiques*. Paris: Marcel Riviére, 1914.

———. *Art et Scholastique*. Paris: Louis Rouart et Fils, 1920.

———. *Primauté du Spirituel*. Paris: Libraire Plon, 1927.

———. *The Things that Are Not Caesar's*. Trans. J. F. Scanlon. London: Sheed and Ward, 1930.

———. *Humanisme Intégrale: Problèmes Temporels et Spirituels d'une Nouvelle Chrétienté*. Paris: Fernand Aubier, 1936.

———. *True Humanism*. Trans. Margot Adamson. New York: Scribners, 1938.

———. *Scholasticism and Politics*. Ed. and trans. Mortimer J. Adler. New York: Macmillan, 1940.

———. *Messages, 1941–1945*. New York: Éditions de la Maison Française, 1945.

———. *The Person and the Common Good*. Trans. John J. Fitzgerald. New York: Charles Scribners, 1947.

———. *Man and the State*. Chicago: University of Chicago Press, 1956.

———. *Distinguish to Unite: the Degrees of Knowledge*. Trans. Gerald B. Phelan et al. New York: Scribners, 1959.

———. *The Peasant of the Garonne: an Old Layman Questions Himself about the Present Time*. Trans. Michael Cuddihy and Elizabeth Hughes. New York: Holt, Reinhart and Winston, 1968.

Maritain, Räissa. *We Have Been Friends Together*. Trans. Julie Kernan. New York: Longmans, Green, 1942.

Maurer, Armand A. "The Legacy of Gilson." In *One Hundred Years of Thomism: Aeterni Patris and Afterwards*. Ed. Victor A. Brezik. Houston, TX: Center for Thomistic Studies, University of St. Thomas, 1981.

McInerny, Ralph. *Art and Prudence: Studies in the Thought of Jacques Maritain*. Notre Dame, IN: University of Notre Dame Press, 1988.

Novak, Michael. *Free Persons and the Common Good*. Lanham, MD: Madison Books, 1989.

Oesterle, John A. *Ethics: The Introduction to Moral Science*. Edgewood Cliffs, NJ: Prentice-Hall, 1957.

Owens, Joseph. "Scholasticism—Then and Now." *Proceedings: ACPA* 40 (1966): 1–12.

Pace, Msgr. Edward A. "Inaugural Address." *Proceedings: ACPA* 1 (1926): 12–18.

Pappin, Joseph III. "Freedom and Solidarity in Sartre and Simon." *American Catholic Philosophical Quarterly* 70 (1996): 569–84.

Renard, Henri. *The Philosophy of Morality*. Milwaukee, WI: Bruce, 1953.

Simon, Anthony, ed. *Acquaintance with the Absolute: The Philosophy of Yves R. Simon*. New York: Fordham University Press, 1997.

Simon, Yves R. *Critique de la Connaissance Morale*. Paris: Vrin, 1934.

———. *Nature and Functions of Authority*. Milwaukee, WI: Marquette University Press, 1940.

———. *Philosophy of Democratic Government*. Chicago: University of Chicago Press, 1951.

———. *Traité du Libre Arbitre*. Paris: Vrin, 1952.

———. "Jacques Maritain: The Growth of a Christian Philosopher." *Jacques Maritain: The Man and his Achievement*. Ed. Joseph W. Evans. New York: Sheed and Ward, 1963.

———. *The Tradition of Natural Law*. Ed. Vukan Kuic. New York: Fordham University Press, 1965.

———. *Freedom of Choice*. Ed. Peter Wolff. New York: Fordham University Press, 1969.

———. *Work, Society, and Culture*. Ed. Vukan Kuic. New York: Fordham University Press, 1971.

———. *General Theory of Authority*. Notre Dame, IN: University of Notre Dame Press, 1982.

———. *The Definition of Moral Virtue*. Ed. Vukan Kuic. New York: Fordham University Press, 1986.

———. *Practical Knowledge*. Ed. Robert J. Mulvaney. New York: Fordham University Press, 1991.

Torrell, Jean-Pierre. *St. Thomas Aquinas*, Vol.1: *The Person and His Work*. Trans. Robert Royal. Washington, DC: Catholic University of America Press, 1996.

Weisheipl, James A. "Commentary." In *One Hundred Years of Thomism: Aeterni Patris and Afterwards*. Ed. Victor A. Brezik. Houston: Center for Thomistic Studies, University of St. Thomas, 1981.

Interpretations of Aquinas's Ethics Since Vatican II

Thomas S. Hibbs

By prefacing the *Secunda* or moral part with a *Prima Pars* on God, Trinity and Creation, and then rounding it off with a *Tertia Pars* on the Son of God, Incarnation and the Sacraments, Thomas put practical theology, the study of Christian man, his virtues and vices, in a full theological context. . . . Christian morality, once for all, was shown to be something more than a question of straight ethical teaching of virtues and vices in isolation. Inasmuch as man was an intelligent being who was master of himself . . . , he was in the image of God. To study human action is therefore to study the image of God and to operate on a theological plane. To study human action on a theological plane is to study it in relation to its beginning and end, God, and to the bridge between, Christ and his sacraments.

—Boyle, *The Setting of the "Summa Theologiae" of Saint Thomas*

The passage states the striking thesis of Leonard E. Boyle's *The Setting of the "Summa Theologiae" of Thomas Aquinas*. Boyle situates the *Summa theologiae* in its historical context and demonstrates its careful restructuring of the popular Dominican ethical manuals for the care of souls. He argues that Thomas's intention was to correct tendencies toward casuistry and to resituate the exposition of the virtues within a Christian anthropology, indeed within the whole of speculative theology. Boyle goes on to note that in the centuries after Thomas's death, his intention was systematically ignored, as the *Secunda pars*, especially the portion that considers moral matters in detail, regularly circulated autonomously.[1]

As one assesses the main currents of interpretation of Aquinas's ethics over the past thirty years, it is both sobering and instructive to take note of the gap between Thomas's ambitious intention and the use to which his moral teaching has been put. Although there was a certain waning of interest in Aquinas in the years immediately after Vatican II, interest has increased steadily since then. This is especially true of ethics studies, as the past twenty years have witnessed a remarkable resurgence of interest in the moral thought of Aquinas. In many ways, post–Vatican II scholars are in a better position now than at any time in modernity to recover the complexity and integrity of Aquinas's moral thought. In part, this is because of careful historical studies like those of Leonard Boyle. But it is also because of fortuitous developments in contemporary ethical discourse, developments often only tangentially related to Aquinas.

In an essay of this length, I cannot hope to address most, let alone all, of the lines of inquiry, interpretation, and dispute that have been pursued in recent years. Forced to make an unhappy choice between composing a lengthy bibliographic essay and presenting the most intriguing debates and schools of interpretation, I have chosen the latter. Even that option is guided less by neutral historical criteria, whatever those might be, than by the controversial thesis that I can detect in the diffuse lines of investigation the possibility of reading Thomas's moral teaching in the way he originally intended it to be read. What, then, are the main lines of interpretation?

There is, first, the ongoing debate that arose in the mid-1960s over Thomas's understanding of the status of the moral precepts and over how one should determine the morality of action in concrete cases, a debate that pits proportionalists against absolutists. Second, there is the debate initiated by the ground-breaking work of Germain Grisez and John Finnis on Thomas's view of the natural law, a debate that includes questions about the knowability of the precepts of the natural law, about the grounds of the precepts in nature and creation, and about the nature of practical reasoning itself. On one hand, this is an extension of the debate between proportionalists and absolutists, with Grisez and Finnis on the latter side. On the other, it is a dispute that pits Grisez and Finnis against nonproportionalist Thomists, who detect in the Grisez-Finnis approach to natural law an unworkable attempt to accommodate modern, especially Kantian, conceptions of morality. The third area of development concerns the retrieval of Aquinas's account of the virtues. The impetus for this comes both from the general revival of interest in the virtues and from questions being raised from within Thomism about the adequacy of approach centered exclusively on natural law. When one realizes that the topic of law occupies a very small, though conceptually significant, part of the *Secunda pars*, and that the structure of the voluminous *Secunda secundae* is built around the virtues, then one begins to see possibilities for a much broader retrieval of Aquinas's ethics. That broader retrieval would involve attention not only to the virtues, but also to the theological structure of Aquinas's moral teaching and to the place of his moral teaching within the context of his comprehensive theological pedagogy. The fourth area, then, concerns the theological intention, structure, and content of Aquinas's ethics.

PROPORTIONALISM AND ABSOLUTISM

The history of proportionalism is complex.[2] To some extent, the roots of proportionalism can be traced to a reaction against the dominant twentieth-century tradition of moral pedagogy in the manuals, an approach to morality that is often denigrated as having been rigid, void of empirical reflection, distant from the original texts and classical sources of Catholic moral thought, and excessively focused on prohibitions. In place of an abstract, impersonal, timeless morality of rules, which possesses a universality more appropriate to theoretical than practical knowledge, proportionalism promises a model of practical deliberation open to historical development and sensitive to concrete situations and to the personal dimensions of moral choice.[3] It also suggests ways of restoring intentionality to its central place in Christian ethics. But it is more ambitious than even this description reveals. For all its differences from utilitarianism, it shares with that ethical system an aspiration for clarity and the great hope that moral philosophy might provide aids, rules, or strategies to discern what a person ought to do in the concrete.

In his study of the history of proportionalism, Bernard Hoose traces the entire movement begun by Peter Knauer's essay, "The Hermeneutic Function of the Principle of Double Effect." Here, Knauer claims to have discovered in Thomas's account of doing harm out of the motive of self-defense (IIa IIae, q. 64, a. 7) a criterion of proportionate reason.[4] Debate still rages over the meaning and appropriate application of the principle of double effect—and even over whether Thomas ever articulated such an idea.[5] Few would now concur with Knauer's claim that this passage contains Thomas's statement of the "fundamental principle of all morality."[6] Indeed, many—and not just those of the moral absolutist school—are skeptical about the purported Thomistic roots of proportionalism, since the language of maximizing and weighing does not figure prominently in Aquinas. What, then, is the Thomistic basis of proportionalism?

One of the most important proportionalists to have written on Aquinas is Louis Janssens, who points to the distinction in St. Thomas between an action's formal component (the interior act of the will) and its material element (the exterior act). An apparently good exterior act such as almsgiving can be rendered evil by a disordered act of the will, as when one gives alms out of vanity. In an essay titled "Saint Thomas Aquinas and the Question of Proportionality," Janssens contrasts a juridical with a moral approach to the appraisal of action. In the former, which is the approach of an outsider with no access to the interior movements of another's will, one considers "all the observable circumstances and other perceptible elements in the situation."[7] In the latter, one begins from the interior act and its object and then judges on the basis of the following principle: "what we do has to be proportioned to the end in the sense that it must be able to be really *id quod est ad finem*, an effective means to the end." If the end is good and the means proportioned to it, an action is licit. The chief alternative to this view holds that certain external acts are, according to Thomas, "of themselves (*secundum se*) morally wicked and can never be justified by relating them to any end, however noble, that the agent may intend."[8] Hoose counters on behalf of Janssens that, while Thomas's texts may contain a "few exceptions to the teleological approach, . . . his approach is overwhelmingly teleological."[9] Later, I will return to this subject and consider the merits of Hoose's claim about Thomas's approach.

In his comments on this early period in the debate, Richard McCormick considers a general shift toward a "morality of consequences."[10] But he goes on to argue that the identification of influential Catholic moralists as utilitarians or consequentialists is simplistic.[11] All proportionalists insist that values other than consequences are to be taken into account. He suggests that other terms such as "mixed consequentialism" or "moderate teleology" would be more apt.

Indeed, the claim that consequences *and* certain basic values and disvalues must inform practical deliberation has become a shibboleth of the proportionalist response to critics. The claim seems sound enough, yet insufficient attention has been given to the grounds on which one determines pre-moral goods and evils.[12] Even if it is not a straightforward utilitarianism or consequentialism, it has nonetheless held out the hope of providing rules or procedures for the resolution of conflicts and dilemmas. Indeed, the proportionalist recurrence to the same tough cases that have bedeviled utilitarians is significant for two reasons: it underscores both how important it is to resolve such cases and how elusive the resolution is.[13]

DEBATE OVER THE NATURAL LAW

The most systematically developed alternative to the proportionalist vision of ethics has been the result of the fruitful collaboration of John Finnis and Germain Grisez.[14] They attempt to reconstruct Thomas's account of natural law in such a way as to avoid the most pressing modern objections to it. They repudiate the notion that Thomas derives the precepts of the natural law from a theoretical account of human nature. On their view, Aquinas does not ground evaluative claims in factual claims and thus does not erroneously derive an "ought" from an "is." Accordingly, Finnis and Grisez abandon the traditional grounding of natural law in the *telos* or goal of human nature, in a hierarchy of goods appropriate to the human species.

In place of a hierarchy of goods, Grisez and Finnis provide a list of goods, each of which "is equally self-evidently a form of good," and "none can be analytically reduced to being merely an aspect of any of the others, or to being merely instrumental in the pursuit of any of the others." Finally, "each . . . can be reasonably regarded as the most important. Hence there is no objective hierarchy among them."[15] The denial of hierarchy is crucial to the attack upon the proportionalist measuring of goods against one another. On the basis of their value egalitarianism, Finnis and Grisez counter that, although one need not pursue each good equally or in the same way, a person must not act against a basic good. To see that there is at least a *prima facie* reason for concern about hierarchy, one need only consult the following claim from Richard McCormick about situations of moral conflict: "Now in situations of this kind, the rule of Christian reason, if we are governed by the *ordo bonorum*, is to choose the lesser evil . . . the only alternative is that we should choose the greater evil, which is patently absurd. This means that all concrete rules and distinctions are subsidiary to this and hence valid to the extent that they actually convey to us what is factually the lesser evil."[16] Clearly, one powerful strategy to undercut the weighing of goods is to deny altogether that there is any natural hierarchy of goods. Yet the alternative, egalitarian approach is not invulnerable. Among the critical, substantive responses to Finnis and Grisez, the most substantial focus upon the elusiveness of demonstrations for the equality of such a diverse set of values; indeed, that task has proven at least as difficult as that of establishing a clear-cut hierarchy.

In spite of the difficulties with basic value equality, many thinkers have been drawn to this position. What makes this view attractive? First, it frees Thomas's account from the impression that it involves a crude and mechanical derivation of rules from an abstract conception of nature. It also corrects the impression that there is only one way of life conducive to the good life. It also allows one to see the rich and endless variety of ways in which excellence and happiness might be pursued. By prescinding entirely from the question of natural teleology, Finnis and Grisez circumvent the objections raised by modern science against the very notion of teleology. Indeed, they bracket theoretical considerations, focus on the peculiar order of practical reason, and offer a novel interpretation of the human inclination toward goods.

Their approach renders natural law theory more congenial to liberal democracy and its language of personal fulfillment. In Finnis's words, any ranking of goods is "made" so by individual choice in accord with a personal life-plan or conception of human fulfillment. Another strength of the Grisez and Finnis recasting of natural law is that it can provide both a justification for limited government and criteria for determining when government has overstepped the bounds of its legitimate authority. Its list of inviolable goods provides the latter, while its liberal account of the good secures the former. As Ernest Fortin and Russell Hittinger have pointed out, much of the language of Finnis's *Natural Law and Natural Rights* is indistinguishable from that deployed in John Rawls's magisterial defense of the liberal political order in *A Theory of Justice*.[17]

But Fortin and Hittinger are not happy about this convergence. They object to what they see as a capitulation to distinctively modern teachings. Furthermore, they question the viability of developing an autonomous natural law ethic.[18] At this point, three problems become evident: (1) the demotion of the virtues that attends the elevation of law, (2) the inadequate attention to Thomas's conception of the

common good, and (3) the neglect of the twofold subordination of natural law to eternal and divine law. Indeed, these criticisms, which are equally applicable to the proportionalists, provide the point of departure for a more comprehensive appropriation of Aquinas's ethical thought.

As part of his denial that there are no basic goods beyond those on his list of seven, Finnis considers a set of virtues and states, "courage, generosity, moderation, gentleness, and so on, are not themselves basic values; rather they are ways (not means, but modes) of pursuing basic values and fit . . . a man for their pursuit."[19] Finnis is careful to distinguish the virtues from mere "means" but he hardly comes close to acknowledging Thomas's emphatic and repeated assertion that the virtues are constitutive of human excellence and happiness. Indeed, prudence itself, whose Aristotelian description Finnis finds unhelpfully hazy, is reinterpreted as simply pursuing the basic goods in accord with a set of rules of practical reasonableness.[20] But this presents a severely truncated view of the virtues, to which Thomas devotes much more attention than he does to the topic of law.

RETRIEVING THE VIRTUES

In philosophical circles, one might trace the explosion of philosophical interest in the virtues to the publication of Alasdair MacIntyre's *After Virtue* in 1981.[21] Although Aquinas was a "surprisingly marginal figure" in *After Virtue*, the argument of the book had a tremendous influence on those writing on Aquinas's views on virtue. Some of the salient theses of *After Virtue* should be noted. First, by reviving the functionalist language of the virtues, MacIntyre repudiated the modern "is/ought" distinction. In the inherently teleological language of the virtues, description cannot be severed from explanation and evaluation. To describe a person as possessing a habit, say, of courage or cowardice is to evaluate simultaneously that person's character as good or bad, at least in a certain respect. Second, MacIntyre locates the virtues within practices, cooperative forms of activity wherein participants come to pursue and to value those goods internal to the activity itself.[22] He thus underscores the communal and political setting of the virtues and the disparity between an ethics of virtue and utilitarianism, which knows no such distinction between internal and external goods. Third, although, at least in *After Virtue*, if not in subsequent works, MacIntyre was suspicious about natural teleology, rejecting as outmoded what he labeled Aristotle's "metaphysical biology," he did speak both of a social teleology and of the need for an ethics of the virtues to retain the metaphysical language of potency and act.[23] Finally, in an oft-neglected passage of *After Virtue*, MacIntyre suggested a way to conceive of the place of rules in an ethics of the virtues. While the virtues describe the goods to be pursued in the practice, rules are typically a set of prohibitions that identify the performance of certain acts as inherently frustrating of the ends constitutive of the practice itself.[24]

The accentuation of goods and virtues over rules, of the communal over the individual of liberalism, and of character over the episodic and atomistic analysis of isolated acts—these themes have informed much recent work on Aquinas's ethics. Among theologians, Stanley Hauerwas was an early and dogged critic of the tendency toward a fragmentary, abstract, and procedural analysis of action in the Kantian and utilitarian systems.[25] Against these ethical systems, the standard strategy in virtue and character ethics has been to argue that rules cannot apply or interpret themselves. An exclusively rules-based ethics seems to generate an unwieldy multiplication of metarules governing the application of subordinate rules and to invite an infinite regress in the process of moral deliberation. Of course, some Thomists might respond that since Thomas supplies a hierarchy of precepts founded on the basic precept to do good and avoid evil, no such regress will occur. But, even if this is so, Thomas provides neither a calculating device nor a list of precepts that would mediate between the primary and more proximate precepts, as both his critics and defenders are fond of pointing out.[26] Even were there such a list, a significant gap would still remain between the proximate precepts and human perception, discernment, and appraisal of the concrete case. At this level, the operation of the virtues, especially that of prudence, is indispensable. Because prudence is the capacity for determining what ought to be done in the

concrete case, it judges whether an action is performed when and where it should be, for the right end and so forth (IIa IIae, q. 47, a. 7). A further advantage of this approach is that it counteracts the tendency in legalistic ethics to discount the role of passion or emotion in deliberation and action. Moral virtue consists in rightly ordered passion.

By way of response to those who hold that morality consists solely or primarily in conformity to rules, one might recur to Thomas's assertion that the "whole structure of good works originates from the four cardinal virtues" (Ia IIae, q. 61, a. 2).[27] Thomas's view differs from the modern tendency to collapse the virtues into one virtue, something like self-control, that enables a person to do his or her duty. Nor does Thomas treat justice as a kind of equal regard for all others. Although all the virtues about operations concur in the "general notion of justice" (*generali ratione iustitiae*), which concerns what is due to another, they differ in that "the thing due is not identical in all the virtues; for something is due to an equal in one way, to a superior, in another way, to an inferior, in yet another, and a debt varies as it arises from a contract, a promise, or a benefit received" (Ia IIae, q. 60, a. 3).[28] The virtues thus differ in accord with their proper objects; for example, religion concerns one's debt to God; piety, one's debt to country or parents; and gratitude, one's debt to benefactors. Thomas's insistence on the plurality of the virtues and on the way they subtly support one another allows him to offer a capacious and remarkably detailed account of moral phenomena.

The emphasis on the indispensable need for experience and training in the moral life has led some recent commentators to shift entirely the balance from natural law to virtue. In his *Priority of Prudence*, Daniel Mark Nelson claims that "Thomas's general point" in his discussion of natural law "is that we have a created, natural ability to act for the good appropriate to our nature and to develop the habits that perfect that capacity."[29] Nelson notes that, in concrete circumstances, natural law cannot "provide a formula" for correct choice.[30]

The problem with turning Thomas's ethics into an ethics solely of the virtues is brought out rather nicely by Pamela Hall in her response to Nelson. She counters that this leaves prudence unguided and neglects the close link in Aquinas between the precepts of the natural law and the articulation of a hierarchy of natural goods to which our species is inescapably ordered. For Thomas, prudence is inoperative without input from the "universal principles of reason." Hall cites Thomas's statement that *synderesis* determines the ends of the moral virtues and informs the deliberations of prudence in the way first principles guide the activity of theoretical reason.[31]

According to Hall, the natural law is an internal disposition toward what is good for, and perfective of, the agent. The force, which has been misunderstood by many, of the first principle "do good, avoid evil" is crucial. Nelson, for example, understands it as a factual comment about a person's always choosing *apparent* goods, not necessarily *actual* goods. But what sense does it make to say that one desires anything under the formality of its being an apparent good? One always desire things as real goods, as perfective of his or her desires and capacities, even when one errs in judgment. As Ralph McInerny puts it, a "merely factual desire . . . does not exist."[32] McInerny nicely develops the relationships between natural inclinations and precepts in the following way: The precept urges a person to pursue what is truly good, to fulfill the formality under which one desires whatever one desires; thus, there is no illicit move from fact to value. Because every agent is already pursuing her or his own good, the natural law can engage dialectically various individuals and cultures. According to McInerny, the negative, exceptionless precepts of the natural law prohibit actions that "always and everywhere thwart the human ideal."[33]

To the casual observer, it might seem that any insistence upon the inviolable role of natural law precepts would, at least from the perspective of the dominant classical and contemporary virtue theories, inordinately constrict the scope of prudence.[34] Indeed, Thomas relegates prudence's role to that of deliberating about the means appropriate to ends provided by *synderesis*. Yet, as many have pointed out, there are various levels, with degrees of generality and specificity, to the articulation of the precepts of the natural law. As Thomas does not adopt a mechanical and

purely proceduralist conception of practical reason, there is ample room for the operation of prudence at all these levels. One might recall with profit in this context Aristotle's division of goods into ends, means, and those which operate in one order as ends and in another as means. There is no obstacle to pursuing some goods as desirable in themselves and also as contributing to other goods. This expands considerably the scope of prudence.

From the perspective of the virtues, what might one make of the seemingly interminable debate between proportionalists and absolutists? The most severe judgment would be this—neither camp can exploit Thomas's rich account of the virtues; in the latter, prudence becomes a matter of successfully following rules, while in the former, prudence surfaces consistently as a virtue of weighing the various features of an action. Both sides exhibit an uncritical reliance upon the now-standard divisions between aretaic, teleological, and deontological moral theories. Indeed, this could be said of many pure virtue theorists as well. The difficulty is not just that Aquinas's ethics fits neatly into none of these categories because it appears to contain a healthy dose of all three. The deeper problem is that, even where there appears to be an overlap with contemporary categories, the terms have strikingly different meanings. How distant, for example, is Thomas's conception of teleology, whose sources are Aristotle and Augustine, from that of Mill or Bentham? If the natural law theories of Finnis and Grisez produce an unstable mixture of Thomistic and Kantian elements, the proportionalist camp risks conflating Thomas with the founders of utilitarianism. It seems rather that the integrity of Thomas's ethics can be preserved only by understanding goods, rules, and virtues in their interconnection.[35]

In her discussion of the principles and virtues of justice, Jean Porter concedes that one can adduce passages supporting both sides of the proportionalist-absolutist divide.[36] She suggests that there is "no satisfactory way out of these quandaries so long as we limit ourselves to the understanding of good and moral evaluation . . . to be found in contemporary Catholic moral theology."[37] A proper understanding of Thomas's account of moral pre-

cepts presupposes a grasp of his view of the
common good, which underscores the reciprocal relationships between individual and
common good. Thomas frequently links the
basic precepts of the natural law—for example, those forbidding murder, theft, and adultery—to prohibitions protective of the basic
goods of civil society. Such acts violate the
"fundamental institutional structures of the
community."[38] Avoiding the approaches of
both the proportionalists and absolutists, she
holds (a) that at the basis of the natural law
there is a hierarchy of goods, grounded in an
order of natural inclinations, (b) that in seeking one's perfection it is appropriate to subordinate lower to higher goods, and (c) that in
the consideration of harm done to individuals,
the "ordering cuts in the opposite direction."[39] Goods located lower on the hierarchy,
such as life, place a greater demand on others
than do higher goods, such as the pursuit of
knowledge. A just community provides for all
its members a certain "immunity from fundamental sorts of harm and coercion."[40] How is
Thomas's account different from that of the
proportionalists?

One of the chief hermeneutic strategies in
the proportionalist interpretation of Aquinas
is to allege that where he provides an apparently nonteleological justification of an "exception" to a precept, the underlying and un-
stated justification is proportionalist in nature.
From this perspective, Janssens and Hoose
accuse Thomas of engaging in "verbal gym-
nastics."[41] Similarly, in response to Finnis's
assertion that to kill the innocent is to act
contrary to the basic value of life, Richard
McCormick argues thus: The only basis for
concluding that such an act is wrong is that the
lives of noninnocent individuals have been
weighed against other competing values and
found wanting. He goes so far as to suggest
that in the history of moral theology exceptions for the killing of the noninnocent have
been made on the basis of a "consequentialist
calculus."[42] As Porter shows, both sides have
ignored Thomas's grounding of precepts in
institutional structures and in natural and social roles. So, for example, when justifying
what appears to be theft in cases of grave need,
he is not engaging in suppressed proportionalist weighing of the good of private property
against the good of the individual. Instead, he

recurs to the subordinate status of the institution of private property with respect to the
common good. Built into the practice of private property is an inherent limitation on its
exercise.[43]

The common good, according to Russell
Hittinger, is one of the "natural law doctrines
which bear upon the transcendent aspect of
practical reason," since it entails a "value
which transcends the individual goods im-
manently enjoyed by individuals."[44] Another
such doctrine concerns our natural ordination
to an "end that transcends participation in
finite goods." Even on the natural level,
Thomas treats the virtue of religion as a "superordinate good—the summit of justice itself."[45] When one examines the teaching on
natural law, its peculiar status among the various kinds of law becomes immediately apparent. Some think that these peculiarities raise
insuperable problems for any attempt to develop an autonomous natural law ethic. Why?

The other kinds of law, say, human or divine, are promulgated in a set of explicitly
stated propositions, violations of which are
attended by sanctions. The natural law by
contrast is promulgated in God's act of creation, by his fashioning beings with inclinations
toward ends appropriate to their nature.
Thomas clearly thinks that one can discern
what one ought and ought not to do by rational reflection upon the goods to which
one's nature is ordered. The question is
whether this knowledge constitutes law in the
full sense. One response is to see the term
"law" as analogical, the focal meaning of
which would be civil law. Thomas does indeed
state that natural law is properly called law,
but this need not conflict with the claim that
natural law involves an analogical usage of law,
since analogical is not opposed to proper in
the way metaphorical is.

An analogical usage of terms pervades the
comparison of natural and supernatural ethics. Aquinas distinguishes between the knowledge of sin had by the philosopher, who considers sins as acts contrary to reason, and by
the theologian, who understands such acts as
"offenses against God" (*offensa contra Deum*)
(Ia IIae, q. 71, a. 6, ad 5). Furthermore, Aquinas holds that there is a certain convergence
or overlap between the precepts of the natural law and the commands of the decalogue.

Yet the precepts of the decalogue that belong to the first table, that is, the precepts concerning love and worship of God, require "divine instruction" (q. 110, a. 1; Ia IIae, q. 104, a. 1, ad 3). Divine law is a much more sure and comprehensive guide to action than is the natural law, which, even in its limited sphere, is obscured by sin.

Another way to underscore the subordinate status of the natural law runs thus: Conformity to the precepts of the natural law is conducive to our achievement of the end of human life, but that end is complex, involving not only the organization of various pursuits to a single end, but also the subordination of all natural activities to our supernatural end. The primacy of that latter end is evident in the structure of the treatise on law itself, which is devoted primarily to an analysis of the revealed laws of the Old and New Testaments. From this vantage point, the natural law is but one moment within a more comprehensive theological pedagogy.[46]

Of course, here, I am touching upon the old question of the distinctiveness of Christian ethics, a question central to the neo-scholastic debates over the existence and nature of Christian philosophy and to moral theories as diverse as those of Josef Fuchs and Stanley Hauerwas. Fuchs traces the specificity of Christian ethics, not to a set of concrete norms, but to a fundamental orientation toward Christ. He contrasts the categorical order of norms for actions with the transcendental order of intentionality. "If we abstract from" the latter, then Christian morality is "basically and substantially a 'Humanum,' that is, a morality of genuine being human. . . . [W]e have reservations about lying and adultery, not because we are Christians, but simply because we are human.[47]

Others, like Stanley Hauerwas, see the Christian life as thoroughly particularist. There is a certain disparity in their approaches, since Fuchs focuses on norms and generic virtues, whereas Hauerwas thinks the specificity of Christian morality arises from the peculiar way of life pursued by members of the Christian church, from the distinctive stories that inform the moral imagination of believers. Like MacIntyre and Porter, Hauerwas puts the formation of character through virtue at the heart of the moral life and thus

makes it possible for us to see the importance of the comprehensive theological structure of Aquinas's moral teaching. Indeed, some recent commentators have underscored the centrality of the Sermon on the Mount for Thomas's ethics. The teachings of that sermon "contain a total representation (*informationem*) of the Christian life" (Ia IIae, q. 108, a. 3).[48] The implication is that Thomas does not limit Christian morality to a list of precepts and prohibitions.

One of the most suggestive ways in which the distinctiveness of Aquinas's Christian ethics has been explored is in terms of narrative. The most compelling and influential interpretations, say those of Stanley Hauerwas or Pamela Hall, of Aquinas in the language of narrative are heavily indebted to the work of Alasdair MacIntyre. Recall that for MacIntyre, the unity of a human life is understood in terms of a specific narrative, which comprehends the goods to which human life is ordered, the virtues conducive to, and constitutive of, the end, and the vices disruptive of the pursuit of those goods. What has made this schema helpful to many is its focus on the teleology of the virtues, undeniably a central feature of Aquinas's ethics. If MacIntyre is right in his historical argument that the lists of virtues and their ranking in relationship to one another differ from community to community, then it would be impossible that there not be a distinctively Christian ethics. Indeed, I should be surprised to find that there were not a variety of Christian narratives of the good life.

Narrative ethics has opened up the possibility of reading the treatise on law as Thomas's speculative consideration of the moral pedagogy of salvation history. It has also, often simultaneously, pointed to the central role of charity, which Thomas calls the form of the virtues.[49] Nowhere is a recovery of the complexity of Thomas's moral pedagogy more valuable than in the treatment of charity. In the contemporary tendency to equate charity with equal regard or altruism, we can detect the influence of Kant's conception of duty as treating everyone with the respect due to rational, autonomous agents. The likely result is a cognitive reductionism that is incapable of discerning the different sorts of things owed to different persons in different circumstances. By contrast to the dominant model of charity as equal regard, Thomas's account is inherently prudential and grounded in an order of love that elevates and reorders rather than obliterates natural associations and duties.[50] In his depiction of charity as friendship with God, Thomas retains and develops Aristotle's doctrine of friendship as a shared participation in the life of intellectual and moral virtue.

In his reading of charity, James Keenan claims to discover the basis for a distinction between "rightness," which is the conformity of one's actions to reason, and "goodness," which consists in striving to live rightly.[51] According to Keenan, charity is itself a kind of striving toward the ultimate good, a matter of motivation and goodness, seeking though not necessarily attaining right reason. The latter is the sphere of acquired virtue. Keenan criticizes the proportionalist identification of goodness with intention and rightness with the external act. The problem is that the proportionalists erroneously separate the end from the object in the determination of the moral species; they suppose that the former, which is a matter of intention, is the determinant of the moral species, whereas the latter is equated with the external act. According to Keenan, a similar segregation of what Thomas holds together can be found in the work of absolutists such as William May. Instead, both intention, end, or internal object and choice, external object, or external act are related in the order of the specification of the act.[52] The proper distinction is between the specification of the act, which is to be in accord with right reason, and the exercise of the act, which falls to the will in its striving. In this distinction, Keenan claims to have discovered a doctrine of the autonomy of the will and the basis for appraising the motivational or formal component of the moral life as good or bad. This is where his novel interpretation of the doctrine of charity is pertinent, since it describes the fundamental motivational structure of a good human life.[53] By contrast, the account of natural virtue describes what it would mean for a life to be rightly ordered.[54]

Keenan's interpretation shares much with the recent revival of virtue ethics. He notes that both absolutists, who are concerned with whether acts instantiate absolute values, and proportionalists, who are concerned with whether acts contribute to welfare, overlook Thomas's accent on the immanent perfection of agents through virtuous acts.[55] Yet his distinction between rightness and goodness is not characteristic of virtue ethics. In fact, James Doig counters Keenan's interpretation by arguing that Aquinas depicts the "virtuous agent as one who effectively and in the correct way wills to pursue the ultimate goal of human living. The morally right person is the morally good person."[56]

Keenan's position rests on the controversial thesis that Thomas develops in the *Summa theologiae* a doctrine of the autonomy of the will, based on the distinction between the orders of specification and exercise.[57] The voluntarist interpretation of Aquinas, at least with respect to goodness, is an alternative to the intellectualist interpretation that has dominated the Thomistic tradition. In another recent book, Daniel Westberg also takes issue with the intellectualist reading of Thomas on human action. Yet he finds the voluntarist reading equally flawed. Both sides err in that they "conceive the will and intellect to function independently, if not in opposition to each other." The confusion arises from the false picture of the two as operating "sequentially." The result is predictable: "the locus of decision is resolved either by positing a judgment of the intellect followed by an acquiescent will . . . , or by an intellectual description of options presented with 'indifference', leaving the will free to make the decision."[58] In place of this sequential approach to the roles of intellect and will in the stages of action, Westberg holds that the two are "complementary" at each stage.[59] Whereas for Westberg the interpenetration of intellect and will in every stage of action is but an exfoliation of Aristotle's notion of choice as reasoning desire or desiring reason, on Keenan's view Thomas's doctrine of charity seems to mark a decisive break from Aristotle's account of virtue as action in accord with right reason.

THE THEOLOGICAL CHARACTER OF THOMAS'S ETHICS

More than any other contemporary approach, that of virtue and narrative has helped to recapture the complex theological pedagogy of Thomas's ethics.[60] Yet it is not without defect. There are the obvious dangers of reducing ethics to stories and of conflating an appreciation of history with historicism. In a recent article, Thomas O'Meara objects that too often contemporary virtue ethicists ignore the precise theological structure of Thomas's ethical teaching. For all their talk about "Christian life, character, and virtues," proponents of virtue fail to investigate the "real ground" of the virtues.[61] None of the virtues, not even charity, is the ground but rather grace, which Thomas distinguishes from virtue as "a kind of habitude . . . presupposed by infused virtues as their principle and root" (Ia IIae, q. 110, a. 3, ad 3).[62] O'Meara proceeds to outline the central teaching of Aquinas's moral theology: an "anthropology of grace."[63] He quotes approvingly from authors such as Otto Hermann Pesch, who links the *Summa's* treatment of habits not primarily to the virtues, but to the doctrine of grace which Aquinas describes as a *"qualitas."*[64]

To recover that teaching would require attending not only to the virtues, the vices, the gifts, and their source in grace, but also to the interconnection between the explicit moral teaching of the *Secunda pars* and the germane theological doctrines of the *Prima* and *Tertia partes*. In short, it would involve recovering what Boyle describes as the integral intention of the *Summa theologiae*. No current author has succeeded at this task better than Servais Pinckaers. As he notes, "How one sees the issue of the key and gate of entry into the house of moral theology plays a determining role."[65] In his magisterial work, *The Sources of Christian Ethics*, Pinckaers attempts to rescue Thomas's ethics from a series of distortions, among which are neglect of the foundational teaching on human happiness, inordinate attention to cases of conscience, the reduction of the passions to obstacles to compliance with duty, and the supplanting of the sections on virtue and grace by those on law.[66] On the basis of a comprehensive and inclusive presentation of Thomas's moral teaching, Pinckaers demonstrates that Thomas's ethics is Christian, that the "evangelical law" is the "cornerstone" of his theology, and that he followed Augustine's view of the Sermon on the Mount as the complete teaching on the Christian way of life.[67]

Pinckaers argues that the fundamental category in Thomas's ethics is happiness or beatitude, which is partially realized in the practice of the virtues and to which the moral precepts direct us. He focuses on the link in both Augustine and Aquinas between the Beatitudes, which constitute Christ's answer to human happiness, and the gifts of the Holy Spirit.[68] Since the gifts combine cognitive and affective elements, a restored appreciation of them would attend to their mystical and contemplative elements. The gifts culminate in wisdom, which involves both a beholding and a loving of what is true, good, and beautiful. It is in fact a communion with the interpersonal life of the divine Trinity.[69] The link between virtue and the divine life is aptly expressed by Romanus Cessario, O.P.: "In the final analysis, Aquinas understands the practice of virtue as nothing less than the full realization of evangelical glory in this life."[70]

FURTHER QUESTIONS

Pinckaers's integrated account of the relationships among happiness, virtue, and law, between knowledge and love, and between contemplation and action points us in the direction of a recovery of Aquinas's peculiar contribution to the ancient debate over the good life, the central claimants to which are the contemplative and the active lives. It is striking that Thomas both begins the *Secunda pars* with an argument that the ultimate end of human life is contemplative and concludes with a consideration of the ways of life. Given Thomas's emphasis on the crucial role of contemplation in the good life, it is surprising how little attention has been devoted to the topic or to the role of the intellectual virtues.[71] I might list the topic of contemplation and intellectual virtue among those features of Aquinas's moral thought that remain neglected in the literature. What are the others?

There are at least three other areas. First, there is the relationship between the natural and the supernatural in Aquinas's ethical teaching. The relationship was hotly debated earlier in the century and to many the relevant issues seem intractable.[72] Thus, many commentators on Aquinas's ethics, even theologians, simply bypass the question. But it is hard to see how an adequate account of the primacy of the theological virtues and the gifts over the natural virtues will ever be created until the relationship between the natural and the supernatural has been explored more thoroughly. It might be useful to approach the large and seemingly interminable debates over nature and grace through a study of the concrete connections between Thomas's ethical teachings, on the one hand, and his explicitly theological doctrines on God, the Trinity, the Incarnation, and sacraments, on the other. Second, there are questions concerning the appropriate political setting for the pursuit of the good life. Thomas follows Aristotle and the ancients generally in depicting ethics and politics as ultimately inseparable. Once again, this is an issue over which there was virulent disagreement earlier in the century, as Thomists differed over the understanding of the common good and whether natural law is compatible with natural rights.[73] Third, there is the question of the sources of Aquinas's moral teachings. While the renewal of virtue has brought about a welcome reconsideration of the status of Aristotle in Aquinas's thought, much remains to be done on other important sources, such as Augustine, Gregory, Damascene, Paul, and others.[74] The past thirty years have highlighted the complex structure of Thomas's moral pedagogy, of its many layers of discourse. Before one can speak confidently of recovering his teaching, one must attend more carefully and comprehensively to his subtle and nuanced orchestration of philosophical and theological sources.

ACKNOWLEDGMENT

Work on this chapter was funded by a grant from the Lynde and Harry Bradley Foundation through the Institute of Medieval Philosophy and Theology at Boston College, directed by Stephen Brown. I am grateful to James Keenan, Michael Moreland, and Stephen Pope for criticisms of early drafts of this chapter.

Notes

[1]Leonard E. Boyle, O.P., *The Setting of the "Summa Theologiae" of Saint Thomas* (Toronto: Pontifical Institute of Medieval Studies, 1982), 23ff.

[2]A succinct introduction to the history can be found in Bernard Hoose, *Proportionalism: The American Debate and Its European Roots* (Washington, DC: Georgetown University Press, 1987). The topical division of Hoose's chapters makes his work useful for those interested in the development of particular issues. The work also contains a helpful bibliography. Also see Todd Salzman, *Deontology and Teleology: An Investigation of the Normative Debate in Roman Catholic Moral Theology* (Leuven: University Press, 1995).

[3]See the comments by Josef Fuchs in "The Absoluteness of Moral Terms," 130–32, and by Louis Janssens in "Ontic Evil and Moral Evil," 84–87. Both essays can be found in Charles Curran and Richard McCormick, eds, *Readings in Moral Theology No. 1: Moral Norms and Catholic Tradition* (New York: Paulist, 1979).

[4]See Hoose, *Proportionalism*, 1.

[5]See Joseph Mangan, "An Historical Analysis of the Principle of Double Effect," *Theological Studies* 10 (1949): 49–61; Donald Motaldi, "A Defense of St. Thomas and the Principle of Double Effect," *Journal of Religious Ethics* 14 (1986): 296–332; James Keenan, "The Function of the Principle of Double Effect," *Theological Studies* 54 (1993): 294–315; and Thomas Cavanaugh, "Aquinas's Account of Double Effect," *The Thomist* 61 (1997): 107–21.

[6]Peter Knauer, "The Hermeneutic Function," in *Readings in Moral Theology No. 1*, 1.

[7]Louis Janssens, "Saint Thomas Aquinas and the Question of Proportionality," *Louvain Studies* 9 (1982), 45.

[8]William May, "Aquinas and Janssens on the Moral Meaning of Human Acts," *The Thomist* 48 (1984): 605. Thomas's action theory has been the subject of numerous interesting studies. In addition to the articles already cited by Knauer, Fuchs, and Janssens, the reader should consult the critique of their lines of reasoning in Brian Mullady, *The Meaning of the Term "Moral" in St. Thomas Aquinas* (Vatican City: Libreria Editrice Vaticana, 1986). Also of interest are Alan Donagan's *Human Ends and Human Actions: An Exploration in St. Thomas's Treatment* (Milwaukee, WI: Marquette University Press, 1985), and his "Thomas Aquinas on Human Action," in *The Cambridge History of Later Medieval Philosophy*, ed. N. Kretzmann, A. Kenny, and J. Pinborg (Cambridge: Cambridge University Press, 1982); Ralph McInerny, *Aquinas on Human Action: A Theory of Practice* (Washington, DC: Catholic University of America Press, 1992); and Daniel Westberg, *Right Practical Reason: Aristotle, Action, and Prudence in Aquinas* (Oxford: Clarendon, 1994).

[9]Hoose, *Proportionalism*, 94.

[10]Richard McCormick, "Reflections on the Literature," in *Readings in Moral Theology No. 1*. His

initial focus is on Josef Fuchs's "The Absoluteness of Moral Terms," in the same volume, 94–137.

[11]McCormick, "Reflections," 301ff.

[12]See Ronald McKinney, "The Quest for an Adequate Proportionalist Theory of Value," *The Thomist* 53 (1989): 56–73.

[13]See Hoose, *Proportionalism*, 82–93, 123–28.

[14]The debates over the position have generated an enormous body of literature. The basic position is articulated in John Finnis, *Natural Law and Natural Rights* (Oxford: Clarendon, 1980); and Germain Grisez, "The First Principle of Practical Reason," in *Aquinas: A Collection of Critical Essays*, ed. A. Kenny (Garden City, NY: Doubleday, 1969), 340–82. A somewhat more recent statement that claims independence from Aquinas is Finnis, Grisez, and Joseph Boyle, "Practical Principles, Moral Truth, and Ultimate Ends," *American Journal of Jurisprudence* 32 (1987): 99–151.

[15]Grisez, "The First Principle of Practical Reason," 92.

[16]Richard McCormick, *Ambiguity in Moral Choice*, (Milwaukee, WI: Marquette University Press, 1973), 38.

[17]See Fortin, "The New Rights Theory and the Natural Law," *The Review of Politics* 44 (1982): 590–612; and Hittinger, *A Critique of the New Natural Law Theory* (Notre Dame, IN: University of Notre Dame Press, 1987). Grisez responded to Hittinger in "A Critique of Russell Hittinger's Book, *A Critique of the New Natural Law Theory*," *The New Scholasticism* 62 (1988): 438–65. See the exchange between Ralph McInerny, Finnis, Grisez in *Readings in Moral Theology No. 7*, ed. Curran and McCormick (New York: Paulist, 1991), 139–170.

[18]The latter criticism would apply not just to Finnis and Grisez but to an array of neo-Thomist construals of Aquinas's ethics.

[19]Finnis, *Natural Law and Natural Rights*, 90–91.

[20]Ibid., 102.

[21]Alasdair MacIntyre, *After Virtue* (Notre Dame, IN: University of Notre Dame Press, 1981). It would be misleading, however, to suggest that little or no work had been done on Aquinas on the virtues prior to the publication of *After Virtue*. Indeed, even the philosophical recovery of the virtues might be said to have Catholic and in some cases explicitly Thomistic roots. The most important and influential attack on rule-based ethics, an attack that argued on behalf of the superiority of an Aristotelian account of the virtues, was an essay titled, "Modern Moral Philosophy," *Philosophy* 33 (1958): 1–19, published by the Catholic philosopher Elizabeth Anscombe. Philosopher Philippa Foot published a collection of essays titled *Virtues and Vices*, which relies heavily on Aquinas, developing his teaching in rich and suggestive ways. In theology, Stanley Hauerwas was already developing in the 1970s his

own character and virtue-based alternative to both the Kantian and utilitarian schools. In the 1950s, long before virtue became popular in moral discourse, Josef Pieper was writing his eloquent essays on the cardinal virtues. See *The Four Cardinal Virtues* (New York: Pantheon Books, 1954). Pieper was preceded by Reginald Garrigou-Lagrange, *De Virtutibus Theologicis commentarius in Summam Theologicam S. Thomae* . . . (Turin: Benufi, 1949); and by Odon Lottin, *Études de Morale histoire et doctrine* (Gembloux: Duclot, 1961)

[22]MacIntyre. *After Virtue*, 177–79.

[23]Ibid., 183.

[24]Ibid., 142–43. He develops the link between virtues and rules in his "Plain Persons and Moral Philosophy: Virtues, Rules, and Goods," *The American Catholic Philosophical Quarterly* 66 (1992): 3–19.

[25]Stanley Hauerwas, *Character and the Christian Life* (San Antonio: Trinity University Press, 1975); more recently, see Stanley Hauerwas and Charles Pinches, *Christians Among the Virtues* (Notre Dame, IN: University of Notre Dame Press, 1997).

[26]Daniel J. O'Connor's trenchant critique of Aquinas focuses on this *lacuna*, as does Finnis's reconstruction. See O'Connor, *Aquinas and the Natural Law* (London: MacMillan, 1967).

[27]"In quatuor virtutibus tota boni operis structura consurgit."

[28]"debitum non est unius rationis in omnibus: aliter enim debetur aliquid aequali, aliter superiori, aliter minori; et aliter ex pacto, vel ex promisso, vel ex beneficio suscepto."

[29]Daniel Mark Nelson, *The Priority of Prudence: Virtue and Natural Law in Thomas Aquinas and the Implications for Modern Ethics* (University Park: Pennsylvania State University Press, 1992), 103. In *Right Practical Reason*, Daniel Westberg adopts a similar strategy but with more careful attention to Thomas's texts.

[30]Nelson, *The Priority of Prudence*, 114, 119.

[31]Pamela Hall, *Narrative and the Natural Law* (Notre Dame, IN: University of Notre Dame Press, 1994), 39–40; also see 19–21.

[32]Ralph McInerny, *Ethica Thomistica* (Washington, DC: Catholic University of America Press, 1982), 37–38, 43–44.

[33]Ibid., 48.

[34]On the link between law and virtue, see Giuseppe Abba, *Lex et Virtues: studi sull'evoluzione della dottrina morale di san Tommaso d'Aquino* (Rome: LAS, 1983).

[35]See MacIntyre, "Plain Persons and Moral Philosophy."

[36]Jean Porter, *The Recovery of Virtue: The Relevance of Aquinas for Christian Ethics* (Louisville: Westminster/John Knox Press, 1990), 124–54.

[37]Ibid., 128.

[38] Ibid., 131.

[39]Ibid., 144.

[40]Ibid., 139.

[41] See Hoose, *Proportionalism*, 99, n. 97.

[42] Ibid., 119.

[43]Also see McInerny on relative moral precepts, *Ethica Thomistica*, 59–62.

[44]*A Critique of the New Natural Law Theory*, 89.

[45]Ibid., 170–71.

[46]See Oscar Brown, *Natural Rectitude and Divine Law in Aquinas: An Approach to an Integral Interpretation of the Thomistic Doctrine of Law* (Toronto: Pontifical Institute of Mediaeval Studies, 1981).

[47]Josef Fuchs, "Is There a Specifically Christian Morality?" in *Readings in Moral Theology, No. 2*, ed. Curran and McCormick (New York: Paulist, 1980). There is something of an echo in these debates of the old neo-scholastic debate over whether there is such a thing as an adequate moral philosophy. Jacques Maritain argued that a "true science of the use of freedom determines how the acting subject can live a life of consistent goodness" (*Science and Wisdom*, trans. Bernard Wall [New York: Scribner's, 1940], 162). A purely philosophical ethics is "essentially insufficient" because it is ignorant of "the real and actual last end of human life" (165). In a recent response to the position of Maritain, Ralph McInerny argues that Maritain is demanding too much of moral science and that Maritain's objections to philosophical morality apply to the science of moral theology as well (*The Question of Christian Ethics* [Washington, DC: Catholic University of America Press, 1993], 51). McInerny goes on to defend the adequacy in its own sphere of the philosophical ethics of Aquinas, in the forms of natural law and natural virtue. He makes the creative suggestion that the precepts of the natural law function in the moral order much the way the naturally attainable truths about God's existence and unity do in the order of speculative reason. They are *preambulae fidei*, that is, truths that God has revealed but that are nonetheless discoverable by natural reason (39–48). Although they move in quite different directions, McInerny and Fuchs see the availability of natural moral knowledge apart from grace as a crucial source of dialogue between believer and nonbeliever.

[48]"totam informationem Christianae vitae continet."

[49]See Paul Waddell, *The Primacy of Love: An Introduction to the Ethics of Thomas Aquinas* (New York: Paulist, 1992); and his *Friendship and the Moral Life* (Notre Dame, IN: University of Notre Dame Press, 1989).

[50]For a treatment of Aquinas on the order of love and its relationship to contemporary sociobiology, see Stephen J. Pope, *The Evolution of Altruism and the Ordering of Love* (Washington, DC: Georgetown University Press, 1994). Also germane is Edward

Vacek, *Love, Human and Divine: The Heart of Christian Ethics* (Washington, DC: Georgetown University Press, 1994).

[51]James F. Keenan, S.J., *Goodness and Rightness in Thomas Aquinas's Summa Theologiae* (Washington, DC: Georgetown University Press, 1992).

[52]Ibid., 83–85.

[53]Keenan cites German authors such as Klaus Riesenhuber (*Die Tranzendenz der Freiheit sum Guten* [Munich: Berchmanskolleg, 1971]) and Wolfgang Kluxen (*Philosophische Ethik Bei Thomas von Aquin* [Hamburg: Meiner, 1980]) as anticipating the line of reasoning he develops.

[54]Keenan, *Goodness and Rightness*, 108–10.

[55]Ibid., 84–85.

[56]James Doig, "The Interpretation of Aquinas's Prima Secundae," *American Catholic Philosophical Quarterly* 71 (1997): 171–95.

[57]Keenan, *Goodness and Rightness*, 23–91.

[58]Daniel Westberg, *Right Practical Reason: Aristotle, Action, and Prudence in Aquinas* (Oxford: Clarendon Press, 1994), 82.

[59]Ibid., 122.

[60]I would be remiss not to refer the reader to the influential work of Lee H. Yearley, *Mencius and Aquinas: Theories of Virtue and Conceptions of Courage* (Albany: State University of New York Press, 1990).

[61]Thomas O'Meara, O.P., "Virtues in the Theology of Thomas Aquinas," in *Theological Studies* 58 (1997): 256–57.

[62]"habitudo quaedam quae praesupponitur virtutibus infusis, sicut earum principium et radix."

[63]O'Meara, "Virtues in the Theology of Thomas Aquinas," 269.

[64]See Pesch's essay, "The Theology of Virtue and the Theological Virtues," in *Concilium 191: Changing Values and Virtues*, ed. D. Mieth and J. Pohier (Edinburgh: T. and T. Clark, 1987).

[65]Servais Pinckaers, O.P., *L'Évangile et la morale*, (Paris: Cerf, 1990), 11.

[66]Servais Pinckaers, O.P., *The Sources of Christian Ethics*, trans. Sr. Mary Thomas Noble (Washington, DC: Catholic University of America Press, 1995), 230–33.

[67]Ibid., 134–90.

[68]Ibid., 151–55.

[69]Ibid., 27–35.

[70]Romanus Cessario, O.P., *The Moral Virtues and Theological Ethics* (Notre Dame, IN: University of Notre Dame Press, 1991), 6.

[71]A conspicuous and instructive exception is Josef Pieper, *Happiness and Contemplation*, trans. Richard and Clara Winston (New York: Pantheon Books, 1958). For an examination of the relationship between the intellectual and the moral virtues, see Greg Reichberg, "Aquinas on Moral Responsibility in the Pursuit of Knowledge," in *Thomas Aquinas and His Legacy*, ed. David Gallagher

(Washington, DC: Catholic University of America Press, 1994), 61–82.

⁷²For a summary of the earlier debate, see Phillip Donnelly, "Discussion on the Supernatural Order," *Theological Studies* 9 (1948): 213–49. For a recent reconsideration of some of these issues that usefully develops the analogical relationship between the natural and the supernatural, see Kevin Staley, "Happiness: The Natural End of Man?" *The Thomist* 53 (1989): 215–34. In "What is the End of the Human Person? The Vision of God and Integral Human Fulfilment," Benedict Ashley provides an account of Thomas's vision of the good life as containing exceptionless moral precepts, contemplation, and an integration of the natural within the supernatural. See his essay in *Moral Truth and Moral Tradition*, ed. L. Gormally (Dublin: Four Courts, 1994), 68–96.

⁷³For a recent summary of that debate and its relevance to contemporary political theory, see Mary Keys, "Personal Dignity and the Common Good: A Twentieth-Century Thomistic Dialogue," in *Catholicism, Liberalism, and Communitarianism*, ed. K. Grasso, G. Bradley, and R. Hunt (Lanham, MD: Rowman and Littlefield, 1995), 173–96. For an argument that Thomas's political theory avoids the "shallow individualism of liberal theory and the social determinism of communitarian theory," see E. A. Goerner and W. J. Thompson, "Politics and Coercion," *Political Theory* 24 (1996): 1–28.

⁷⁴For a conspicuous exception, see Mark Jordan, "Aquinas's Construction of a Moral Account of the Passions," *Freiburger Zeitschrift fur Philosophie unde Theologie* 33 (1986): 71–97.

Selected Further Reading

Abba, Giuseppe. *Lex et Virtues: studi sull' evoluzione della dottrina morale di san Tomasso d'Aquino*. Rome: LAS, 1983.

Alvira, Tomas. *Naturaleza y Libertad*. Pampolona: Eunsa, 1985.

Boyle, Leonard E. *The Setting of the Summa Theologiae of Saint Thomas*. Toronto: Pontifical Insitute of Medieval Studies, 1982.

Brock, Stephen. *Action and Conduct: Thomas Aquinas and the Theory of Action*. Edinburgh: T. and T. Clark, 1998.

Davies, Brian. *The Thought of Thomas Aquinas*. Oxford: Clarendon, 1992.

Eschmann, Ignatius. *The Ethics of St. Thomas Aquinas: Two Courses*. Toronto: Pontifical Institute of Medieval Studies, 1997.

Finnis, John. *Aquinas: Moral, Political, and Legal Theory*. Oxford: Oxford University Press, 1998.

Kent, Bonnie. *Virtues of the Will: The Transformation of Ethics in the Late Thirteenth Century*. Washington, DC: Catholic University of America Press, 1995.

MacIntyre, Alasdair. *Dependent Rational Animals*. Chicago: Open Court, 1999.

Natali, Carlo. *La sagezza di Aristotele*. Venezia: Bibliopolis, 1989.

Pesch, Otto. "Die bleibende bedeutung der thomanischen Tugendlehre." *Freiburger Zeitshcrift für Philosophie und Theologie* 21 (1974): 359–91.

Pinckaers, Servais. *L'Évangile et la morale*. Paris: Cerf, 1990.

———. *Les Actes Humains/Saint Thomas d'Aquin*. Paris: Cerf, 1997.

Spaemann, Robert. *Glueck und Wohlwollen*. Stuttgart: Klett-Cotta, 1989.

Yearley, Lee. *Mencius and Aquinas*. Albany: State University of New York Press, 1990.

The Evaluation of Goods and the Estimation of Consequences: Aquinas on the Determination of the Morally Good

Ludger Honnefelder

A significant increase in options for action and the subsequent increase in the potentially beneficial consequences of action, both the result of the tremendous advances in science and technology in the last decades of the twentieth century, have presented a series of hitherto unknown needs: to choose between alternative practices; to evaluate the goals of action and their associated values and goods; and to estimate whether the consequences and side effects of actions are defensible. This raises the question about which procedure is most appropriate to conduct such choosing and estimating. What criteria can be applied if decisions are to be justified ethically and not just economically, politically or legally?

Speaking from the perspective of moral philosophy, the number of answers to these questions advanced through history is probably as great as the number of moral theories itself. No moral theory can escape these questions completely; on the other hand, each must in its answer refer to the very concepts that it employs in its beginnings. However, this does not mean that any of the traditional moral theories will serve equally well as a reference point for a contemporary answer to the questions on procedure and criteria of moral evaluation. In the more recent discussion, especially among so called "teleological theories," one finds mostly utilitarian procedures and criteria, which relate the moral quality of an action or action-guiding rule to an evaluation of its consequences in terms of a larger or smaller benefit.[1] The rich possibilities which Aristotelian moral philosophy presents

for the problem of moral evaluation receive less consideration.[2] In view of the overall importance of the Aristotelian approach in the current debate about a suitable foundation for moral philosophy, it is therefore opportune to investigate what roles choice, evaluation, and estimation of consequences play in the systematic reception of that approach in scholastic philosophy, especially in the thought of Thomas Aquinas.

This approach is grounded by an expectation that the investigation will reveal insights relevant for a contemporary theory of moral evaluation. In the following pages, I will sketch out which role (1) the principle of practical reason plays as the foundation and basic criterion of every choice and deliberation. Following this, I will briefly investigate (2) how the natural inclinations and (3) the *ethos*, as expressed in a canon of virtues, and the life plan pursued by each individual influence the choice of the good. Finally, I will discuss (4) how an evaluation of side effects can be incorporated. As far as possible, I will point out the ensuing preference rules and their importance for a contemporary theory of moral evaluation.

PRACTICAL REASON

According to Aquinas, the role and function of a preferential choice—an evaluation of goods and an estimation of consequences—emerge from the essence of the morally good itself. Like Aristotle, Thomas assumes that an action is morally good if in it, a human being realizes himself or herself as a human being. As for all living beings, so for humans, nature is a dynamic faculty; it is a potential *to be*, which is expressed in manifold ways of desiring and which is ordered toward realization as its goal. However, Aquinas explicates more clearly than Aristotle what distinguishes human action from animal behavior. Unlike animals, which spontaneously grasp and then follow the goals of their desires, human beings know of a goal as a goal and act by adopting a stance on it. In the *will*, they possess a capacity to grasp previously understood goals and to order themselves toward them through an *intention* (*intentio*; Ia IIae, q. 12, aa. 1–5).[3] In *reason*, they possess the capacity to understand goals, to present them to the will, and to match them to the appropriate means once an intention has been formed (Ia IIae, qq. 8–17).

Since, according to Aquinas, the will is not necessarily concerned with a particular good but only with the good in general, it can opt for what is only apparently good rather than what is the truly good and for the fulfillment of a particular desire instead of the more general and higher one. The will not only has the freedom to will or not to will, it also has the freedom to want this or that depending on which goal reason presents to it.[4] With its freedom to follow or not to follow reason, the will becomes subject to the difference between good and bad; at the same time, reason, as the faculty of a desiring and willing being, becomes *practical*. The individual action appears as the result of a complex sequence of steps that Aquinas analyzes in detail. The first part of this sequence: apprehension (*apprehensio*), volition (*volitio*), cognition (*cognitio*), intention (*intentio*) concerns the action's *goal*; the second part: consideration (*consilium*), consent (*consensus*), judgment (*iudicium*), choice (*electio*), instruction (*praecipere*), and application concerns the appropriate *means* to the end. The sequence culminates in *realization* (*fruitio*).

Practical deliberation (*phronesis*; *prudentia*) features mainly in the second part as the direct action guiding the work of reason, which also determines the moral quality of the concrete action. It has to mediate between the general and necessary principles and the particular and contingent conditions; relate the particular and contingent means to the conceived goal; design and evaluate the individual steps

of the action sequence; and finally prescribe the resulting action as good, that is, as to be carried out (IIa IIae, q. 47, aa. 1–16).[5]

According to Aquinas, a more detailed analysis of the work of practical reason and its structure reveals that the concrete action guiding judgment—the conclusion (*conclusio*) of the practical deliberation—must be clearly distinguished from the general principles, that is, its premises. His explication runs as follows: If human beings, unlike animals, do not simply pursue the goals of their desires, but know of a goal as a goal, and act (1) by taking a position on the goal and (2) by recognizing and acknowledging what is good relative to a given desire and rejecting what is opposed to the good as something to be avoided, then the supreme rule, which defines the form of every concrete rule and which is inherent in every action-guiding statement, is that the good is to be done and the bad is to be avoided (see esp. Ia IIae, q. 94, a. 2).[6] Practical reason can regulate action only because it possesses that supreme rule like a "natural habit" prior to all further regulations.

In addition to the distinction between the goal of desire and the intention of the will, there is another difference, which was not made explicit by Aristotle, but that is characteristic for human action. Stripped of its application, the supreme rule shows its constitutive role as the principle of practical *noncontrariety*. Equivalent to the theoretical law of noncontradiction, it grounds the possibility of acting at all. For to prescribe and prohibit an action at the same time is not to provide any action guidance at all. As a first and supreme *principle*, it not only determines the individual rule but also the consistency of all rules, and hence the consistency of all actions. As an *imperative*, it gives the morally binding force to every action or action rule that has been recognized as good. This is because it expresses the basic tendency of reason toward the good, or, in other words, the fundamental acknowledgment that is the basis for the acknowledgment of any concrete imperatives.

Only if one follows Aquinas in presupposing a compound formation of moral judgments will one apprehend—at least by two steps—the twofold task of practical reason: the planning of future actions in concrete practical judgments and the critical appraisal of past actions in a judgment of conscience. Action guidance by practical reason does not consist in the mere application of the goals of desire, understood as resulting from an essential nature; rather, it is an "order which reason, through understanding, creates in the actions of the will," the recognition of the good "through a comparison with reason" (*per comparationem ad rationem*; Ia IIae, q. 18, a. 5).[7] The supreme principle "grounds" (Ia IIae, q. 94, a. 2) practical reason in desire and ties it to the recognized good, but in itself "it is not sufficient in order to make the right judgment with regards to the concrete action" (Ia IIae, q. 58, a. 5).[8]

As far as the goal of an action is concerned, it is first only with respect to an intention; with respect to the execution, it comes last and has to be discovered. Therefore, merely applying the supreme principle to the concrete action through a synthetic process (*modo compositivo*) proves insufficient.[9] An action can ensue only when the means are sought according to the intended goal by an analytic procedure (*modo resolutorio*; Ia IIae, q. 14, a. 5).[10] If, however, moral judgment and action are an ordering of a complex whole through reason, then human beings are responsible not only for their morally relevant actions but also for the rules that determine such actions.

Alongside the multi-step character of practical reason appears another characteristic: the self-reference of morally relevant actions. If reason and free will are what characterizes human beings as human beings, then morally relevant actions can only be good if they occur "according to reason" (*secundum rationem*).[11] Thomas explains this self-determination of the will through reason with the relatively simple statement, "Natural reason commands to act according to reason" (IIa IIae, q. 47, a. 7).[12] This deliberation follows the principle that, for every thing, good is only what agrees with its form. To contravene the command of reason therefore means not only to act badly in a moral sense, but also to contradict oneself as a moral subject; as Thomas notes, "whatever is against reason is against human nature."[13] According to Aquinas, the action guiding judgment (*prudentia*) is therefore accompanied by the judgment of conscience (*conscientia*), through which practical reason

preserves the moral identity of the agent by testing its own application against its principle, that is, the supreme practical principle which is habitually retained by original conscience (*synderesis*; Ia, q. 79, aa. 12–13).[14] According to Aquinas, to act morally is not merely to grasp a material good in order to become morally good. To grasp the good in the first place is also to grasp oneself as a being that determines itself freely through reason in order to become such a being.

This approach has serious implications for the evaluation of goods. Evaluation of the good is necessary because what is the morally demanded good under the circumstances is not obvious; instead, it must be determined through practical deliberation. That determination does not constitute the morally good; rather, it chooses from among the actions that present themselves, the one that has to be done. Evaluation of goods is an ordering by way of a preferential choice. It is possible only due to the principles that reason possesses prior to any choice; the first of these is the general principle of practical reason: to act according to reason. This yields the first preferential rule: those actions and rules enjoy unconditional preference which directly secure the moral subject itself, in other words, the capacity for self-determination of the agent through reason.[15] Aquinas's doctrine that even the erroneous conscience is morally binding shows that the modern assurance with regard to the inviolability of the freedom of conscience and faith, contained in fundamental human rights, can be interpreted as a consequence of this account (IIa IIae, q. 19, a. 5).[16] According to Aquinas, the foundation of any evaluation of goods is the moral subject itself; the basic criterion is the unconditionally valid rule that what practical reason recognizes and acknowledges as to be done, is to be done; the first preferential rule is to choose those rules over all others that make it possible to adhere to the rules that one acknowledges as binding.

NATURAL INCLINATIONS

The complexity of moral actions is mirrored by the complexity of the criteria by which their moral quality is measured. According to Aquinas and from a formal point of view, these criteria result from the *circumstances* (*circumstantiae*) of an action. For if I know who (*quis*) acts, what (*quid*) he or she does, where (*ubi*) and how (*quibus auxiliis*), and why (*cur*) he or she acts the way (*quomodo*) he or she does, only then (*quando*), can I evaluate the moral character of his or her action (Ia IIae, q. 7). Among the circumstances that Aquinas draws from Aristotle and the Stoics, the "what" and the "why" of an action are the most "important" for him (Ia IIae, q. 7, a. 4). When he analyzes an action in Ia IIae, q. 18, he names as critical for the moral quality of an action the *object* (*obiectum*), i.e., the goal toward which the action is oriented and from which it receives its substantial definition as, say, a theft or lie; the circumstances (*circumstantiae*) in the narrow sense, which complement the substantial definition like accidents; and the *intent* (*finis*), in which the agent grasps the intended object of the action (Ia IIae, q. 18, aa. 1–5, 10).[17] There can be no doubt that according to Aquinas the intent of the agent (*finis operantis*) and its relationship to the goal of the action (*finis operis*) are the crucial elements; however, he concedes that sometimes the circumstances can be so determining that they become almost like an element of the object itself and thus alter the moral quality of the action even in its essence (Ia IIae, q. 18, a. 5, ad 4).[18] According to Aquinas, the circumstances of an action in the narrow sense are more variable determinants rather than mere accidents.[19]

As my analysis shows, an action is morally good only if, besides the good intent of the agent, the object and the circumstances are morally right. Which action ought to be chosen under which circumstances is principally a *contingent* matter. For only the supreme good is good *without limitations*, and only its pursuit is *necessarily* commanded. Which *finite* goal I have to choose under which conditions will be the result of a practical deliberation. Three aspects influence the incumbent material definition of the good which is to be chosen: the relationship of the goal to the basic inclinations in which the human desire for a happy life realizes itself; the status which the goal has in the context of a given *ethos*, that is, a collective definition of the happy life; and the importance the goal has in relation to the ultimate goal that I explicitly or implicitly

pursue (a "life plan"). A preferential choice can determine what is morally correct, and therefore command a particular action, only by integrating those three aspects.

According to Aquinas, the importance of the *first* aspect results from the simple fact of human nature that the one human desire for the good, which reason seeks to realize, can be pursued only through a multitude of different inclinations. Mirroring the triad of being-living-understanding (*esse-vivere-intelligere*), Aquinas lists as examples of such natural inclinations (*inclinationes naturales*) as the human desire to preserve oneself and the species; and the human inclination to communicate with others, to understand the truth, and to transcend oneself in an absolute being (Ia IIae, q. 94, a. 2).

These examples sketch an anthropology according to which a human person, which determines itself freely through reason, is grounded in a biophysical, animal, and sensitive nature; even more, it *is* a person only inasmuch as it is grounded in such a nature, as Aquinas explains when he discusses the separation of the soul from the body in death (Ia, q. 29, a. 1).[20] Because nature and person form such an original unity, membership in the species is sufficient to guarantee a human being's recognition as a person. The rights that result from the biophysical nature of a human being are therefore those of the person. As the examples show, these do not only include the right to the continuation of one's individual existence but also the right to social interaction. Through its grounding in a natural base, the right to the recognition of one's own needs by others is linked to my recognition of others' needs; everyone has the same right to life. Because the natural inclinations are *basic* appetites, which can even conflict with each other, they, like the supreme principle of reason, do not immediately yield action guiding norms. To use modern parlance: they have a *metanormative* character. They do not yield concrete norms but raise demands that become norms only through the ordering intervention of reason. They set limits for action even though they do not determine it directly.[21]

According to the doctrinal tradition that follows Aquinas, the first aspect yields two main preference rules for a practical deliberation leading to concrete action and the evaluation of goods that are part of it. If human nature consists in a unity of body and soul and if "acting according to reason" (*esse secundum rationem*) is based on the conditions set by bodily activities, then, while the activities of the mind must be accorded the higher rank, in any given case, the more urgent action must be carried out before the higher ranking one, and the securing of life must be preferred over the maximization of chances for a happy life.[22] It is therefore appropriate to count among the fundamental human rights that secure the dignity of a human being not only those which guarantee freedom of action, conscience, or creed, but also those which guarantee their necessary conditions such as life, physical integrity, property, work, and others. Wanton manipulations of human nature are a violation of the right to self-determination and the dignity of the person.

Because the dependency on social interaction is part of the natural condition of human beings, the second preference rule which follows from the web of natural conditions underpinning human action is that, under equal circumstances, the rights of the majority or of all take precedence over the rights of an individual or a few.[23] It goes without saying that the precedence of the urgent and of the general welfare applies only as much as the dignity of the person can be maintained; thus both are subordinate to the preference rule which secures the existence of the moral subject itself.

There can be no doubt that the metanormative role of nature as described by Aquinas relates not only to the individual fundamental inclinations but also to their structure and the way they are embedded within the environment which sustains the human being. In modern parlance, it relates to the organic as well as to the ecological system. Thus, Wilhelm Korff is correct when he describes Aquinas's natural inclinations as a nonarbitrary, yet adaptable system of rules. From the perspective of modern human science and with respect to human social interaction, this system manifests itself in the web of conditions that make a human being at once an aggressor, a caregiver, and a being with needs. This triad is modeled on the old tribal urges of intraspecific aggression, caring for the offspring, and joint retreat. However, if all three are already

integral parts of the organic system, it follows that any rule that does not acknowledge this interdependence and isolates one component in favor of the other two will not lead to morally good action.[24] A similar metarule can be formulated with respect to the complete organic system, to the environment, and to their functional requirements.

Aquinas, following the Aristotelian approach, relates all goals back to the natural inclinations; and this is what allows him, in his doctrine of the virtues in the *Secunda secundae*, to interpret the Christian notion of love as that (theological) virtue which shapes all other virtues (IIa IIae, q. 23, a. 8).[25] Thus, Aquinas and the scholastic manuals in his wake discuss the problem of which goals are to be preferred over other goals, and according to which rules, under the heading "order of love" (*ordo caritatis*), and after they have introduced the virtue of love (*caritas*; IIa IIae, qq. 25–26).[26] Because the love of the supreme good, God, is unconditionally obligatory and thus beyond all comparison, the evaluation concerns especially the question of which order the love of other people must follow; in modern parlance: How are the rights of others, which result from morally legitimate fundamental inclinations, to be included in the practical deliberation which determines one's own goals and actions? Like Aristotle, Aquinas answers with an emphasis on *institutions* such as marriage, family, state, law, creed, and the like, which are linked to the success of society and the individual (IIa IIae, q. 26).[27] The ranking order of immediate relationships for the purpose of an evaluation is as follows: spouse, children, parents, siblings, relatives, friends, benefactors. In the area of societal relationships, the rule is that legal obligations take precedence over obligations of charity (IIa IIae, q. 26, aa. 6–13).[28]

ETHOS AND LIFE PLAN

The *second* determining factor that practical reason encounters in its quest for the morally good is the dispositions that human inclinations acquire and that combine in the form of virtues to make a pattern or overall shape of the good life, which can be called the *ethos*. Unlike the talents that a human being has by nature, the virtues arise from the actions of the human being; they can only be passed on and preserved through actions, notably education and practice (Ia IIae, q. 63). As Aristotle's link between the concepts of *ethos* and *polis* shows, the *ethos* is provided *to the individual*, yet *as such* it is something that is made and preserved through society and culture. In Aquinas, the parallel idea is that "in order to make the right judgment with respect to a concrete action it is not sufficient" for practical reason to draw on the general principles that are the result of the supreme principle of reason and on the fundamental inclinations of human nature (Ia IIae, q. 58, a. 5).[29] For if there is not just *one* way that will lead to a given goal, but if there are many and contingent ways, then the truth of a practical conclusion cannot be proven with the same degree of necessity as the truth of a theoretical conclusion, which allows for exactly one middle term (Ia, q. 47, a. 1, ad 3).[30] Thus, before choosing an action, there must be an *inquiry* (*inquisitio*), which, as has been said before, does not proceed in a synthetic fashion but which identifies the appropriate means to an end by way of analysis (Ia IIae, q. 14, a. 1).[31] The concrete action-guiding rules, which take the form of positive, self-imposed laws (*leges humanae positivae*), cannot be derived from the general rules—natural law (*lex naturalis*) in Aquinas's parlance—"by way of deduction" (*per modum conclusionum*) but only "by way of (further) determination" (*per modum determinationis*; Ia IIae, q. 95, a. 2). Such a determination, however, is not possible without some level of design through "creative addition" and "augmentation" (ibid.).[32] Once that further determination has led to action-guiding rules—in the language of virtues: once the individual moral action has led to the formation of moral virtues—there is moral judgment and action which results directly from the context of the virtues and their quintessence—the *ethos*. Such judgment and action result in a quasi-natural way "from an inclination which has been shaped by the relevant virtue" (Ia, q. 1, a. 6, ad 3).[33]

From the above the following will be evident. Not every dispositional form of human existence can claim to be an *ethos*; yet there is also not just one such form that can lay that claim once and for all. There are three decisive criteria. The *ethos* gains its unity, consis-

tency, and formal obligatory force from its genesis in practical reason and its supreme principle. It can claim to be the concrete shape of the ultimate goal, a good life, and its material obligatory force from its origin in the fundamental human inclinations. Together with these metanormative framework conditions, it is its inner cogency, its plausibility and meaning, that gives a concrete *ethos* its moral obligatory force. It follows necessarily that every *ethos* can claim obligatory force inasmuch as it can prove itself in that way. There is thus a legitimate diachronous and synchronous multitude of *ethos* forms, yet a comparison among them will show differences in their moral dignity. According to Aristotle, the *ethos* of the *polis* surpassed all others, because it was shaped under the institutional conditions of freedom and reason. Aquinas holds, on the other hand, that the *ethos*, which is shaped by the demands of the theological virtues of faith, hope, and charity, has obligatory force, because in it, the human being can find its fulfillment as a being with reason and freedom, which is God's image and "itself the origin of its actions" (*ipse est suorum operum principium*; Ia IIae, Prol.).[34]

A consideration of the *ethos* yields a third group of preferential rules. Among the different forms of *ethos* the one with the greater cogency takes precedence. Following Aristotle and Aquinas, an *ethos* is the more cogent the more it acknowledges not only personal dignity and the individual moral subject but also takes in self-determination through reason as one of its constituent components.[35]

This brings into the picture the *third* determining factor underlying the concrete moral judgment, namely, the *life plan* that every individual must pursue in one's actions. If the good life, the ultimate human goal, can be achieved only by choosing appropriate partial goals in the form of actions, the result for the agent is thus an intentional structure with normative binding force. Aquinas is, on this point, even clearer than Aristotle.[36] By carrying out action A in order to want partial goal B, and wanting B because I implicitly or explicitly intend C as the ultimate goal, I intend B and C together as well as separately (Ia IIae, q. 12, a. 2).[37] However, because the choice of B is not necessary on the basis of either the supreme rule of reason or the non-

arbitrary, yet adaptable fundamental inclinations, the moral quality of the contingent
choice of A *and* B appears only in the context
of the ultimate goal; it depends on the position of A within my life plan. Furthermore,
it does not matter whether I have explicitly
devised that plan or am pursuing it only implicitly. It appears that the question: "who do
I want to be?" can only be posed through
the question: "what is the best for me?" But
if the question about the good cannot be di-
vorced from the question about the ultimate
good, and if this question cannot be answered
other than as a question about what is best
for me personally, the connection between
the general moral obligation, the particular
ethos and the individual life plan becomes obvious. *Ethos* and life plan gain their relative
binding force and truth from the general obligation, which becomes real in turn through
the experience of an *ethos* and a life plan.

This means that both the *ethos* (which is
provided to the individual) and the individual
life plan demand consistency and continuity.[38]
Since the *ethos* provides to the individual a
definition of the good life through which it
gains human status in the first place, and guarantees the continuation of the relevant social
order and thus the conditions that make action possible in the first place, it must be
linked to a dual obligation—that its validity is
accepted and preserved, and that the individual follows its rules. If the individual gains its
personal moral identity within the context of
an individual life plan, it must in every action
observe the resulting obligation to preserve
the personal biographical consistency and
continuity.

The two preferential rules—that an action
must fit into an accepted *ethos*, and that it
must fit into an individual life plan—may coincide or may conflict with one another. If the
demand for conformity with the overall *ethos*
is in conflict with the demand for consistency
of the individual's biography, one must rely on
the preferential rules cited above with respect
to the relationship between the individual
moral subject on the one hand and the common good and the social institutions on the
other. For the so-called "conscience case,"
that is, the elimination of the individual moral
identity, however, the preference rule that
safeguards the person always takes precedence. Any absolute claims of one particular
life plan must be regarded as turning a particular, individually meaningful totality into a
totalitarian one.[39] Plurality is the condition of
the possibility of a person's individuality.

CONSEQUENCES AND SIDE EFFECTS

In contrast to utilitarianism and modern
teleological ethics, neither Aquinas nor Aristotle evaluates the morally good primarily
from the consequences of an action; yet *consequences and side effects* are a relevant part of the
evaluation. Consider that if an action's morality is determined by its object, and if that
object is nothing other than the goal which is
intended with that action (Ia IIae, q. 10, a.
1),[40] then the object—from the perspective of
the action—can be regarded as that "toward
which the action is heading naturally,"[41] as the
natural goal (*finis naturalis*; Ia IIae, q. 1, a. 3, ad
3) or the *natural effect* (*effectus per se*) of the
faculty to act (Ia IIae, q. 20, a. 5, ad 1).[42] To
judge actions from their natural goals, is, in
reality, to judge them as consequences, which
are the effects that an agent naturally achieves
through its actions. From this perspective,
Aquinas can confidently state that "an action
is thus called good, because it can achieve a
good effect" (Ia IIae, q. 18, a. 2, ad 3).[43] In this,
all relevant *circumstances* must be taken into
consideration, since they, as has been said already, morally qualify the object of the action
not only accidentally but at times even substantially.[44] If the intention of the agent is not
exhausted by the goal of the action (*finis operis*)
but if the agent chooses the action in question
as a way to a further goal, then its moral quality will be determined by this further goal (Ia
IIae, q. 1, a. 3, ad 3).[45] But because the means
are also intended (Ia IIae, q. 12, a. 4),[46] no
action which employs morally bad means for
a morally good end can be morally good.[47] As
regards the regular or accidental side effects
(*eventus*) of an action, the intentions of the
agent (*finis operantis*) are only morally good if
not only the actually foreseen side effects of its
actions are good, but also those which can be
foreseen, inasmuch as they result as natural
effects "as a rule" (*ut in pluribus*). The case is
different only for accidental and thus unfore-
seeable side effects (Ia IIae, q. 20, a. 5).

Three doctrinal pieces contained in the late- and neoscholastic handbooks are directed toward the evaluation of consequences and side effects. None of them can be found in Aquinas, yet all three can claim to be based on foundations he built. They are the doctrines of the lesser of two evils, of double effect, and of the legitimate breaking of the law. If an action is going to have foreseeable but unavoidable harmful side effects, then the more damaging the side effects, the more weighty must be the ethical justification. This rule is based on the Aristotelian maxim, which appears also in the *Decretum Gratiani*, that "the lesser of two evils is the one to be chosen" (*minus malum de duobus eligendum est*).[48] In the case of otherwise equal circumstances and unavoidable harmful side effects, one must choose the lesser of two evils over the larger, or the one of shorter duration over the long-term one, or the likely one over the certain, or the reversible over the irreversible, or that which affects few over that which affects all. This does *not* apply to morally bad actions, which must never be intended as such. As Aquinas remarks with respect to the obligation to admonish one's neighbor, at most it is permissible to tolerate a moral evil to prevent a larger one.[49] Otherwise, the toleration can be justified either if it generates a good or is necessary to preserve one, so that the lesser evil (*minus malum*) turns into a lesser good (*minus bonum*), as Thomas Sanchez remarks (IIa IIae, q. 10, a. 11).[50]

The "doctrine of double effect" is about actions that at once cause a good and a bad effect and where the bad effect can be foreseen. According to the scholastic handbooks the rule is as follows: the foreseeable bad effect can be tolerated if (1) the action itself is morally good or at least indifferent; (2) the agent intends only the good effect and foresees, but does not intend, the bad one, that is, it only allows the bad one to occur; (3) the bad effect is at once the result of the action, that is, it does not serve as a means to achieve the good effect; (4) through the good or indifferent action an important good is intended, which cannot be achieved without the occurrence of the bad effect and which has an acceptable standing in comparison to the bad effect.[51] Aquinas himself only discusses cases where someone's action causes a bad side effect, such as annoyance "without the inten-

tion of the agent" (*praeter intentionem agentis*) (IIa IIae, q. 43, a. 3). Since in such cases the bad side effect is not intended by the will as either a goal or a means but is only tolerated, it is morally unimportant. A second case concerns an action such as self-defense, which has two effects. Of these two effects, one, the preservation of one's own life, is internal to the intention of the agent; the other, the killing of the aggressor, is external to it. That Aquinas calls the second effect "besides the intention" (*praeter intentionem*) does not mean that he thinks of it as an indirect, merely tolerated one, as would be demanded by the later doctrine of the double effect; instead, he thinks of it as an unavoidable means to a legitimate end that can be morally tolerated if the means is appropriate to the goal in question (IIa IIae, q. 64, a. 7).[52] This case can therefore not be cited as confirmation of the late- and neoscholastic doctrine that bases itself on it; rather, it may support that doctrine's modern interpretation, which employs a more general notion of the evaluation of goods.[53]

The doctrine of the legitimate breaking of the law in Aquinas, who follows the authors of antiquity, notably Aristotle, deals with the right notion of legal justice. Since the actions for which laws are made "consist in individual acts which may differ in infinitely many ways," a law can be just only "as a rule" (*ut in pluribus*) (IIa IIae, q. 120, a. 1).[54] At times, law is damaging; in those cases, it would be against the original just intention of the lawmaker to follow it. Such situations demand an attitude of fairness (*aequitas*). In this scenario, this means a legitimate breaking of the law in order to understand that what is good does not consist in following the letter of the law but in following "that which is demanded by justice and ordinary utility" (IIa IIae, q. 120, a. 1).[55] Thus, the legitimate breaking of the law is not arbitrary but the "subjective part of justice and . . . the quasi higher rule of human action" (IIa IIae, q. 120, a. 2).[56] This rule demands that if reason finds that the consequences of an action carried out according to the law are not appropriate or reasonable, then one must follow justice and act *against* the law. Only later in the development of moral philosophy does the doctrine of the legitimate breaking of the law become a casuistic rule of interpretation which, according to Francisco Suárez, lifts the obligation to follow the law if following the law (1) must in a concrete case be judged to be morally bad; (2) would burden or even harm the individual; and (3) the lawmaker did not intend to bind in the case in question.[57]

In Aristotelian ethics, the evaluation of goods and the estimation of consequences are necessary elements with regard to "the particular contingent human actions, which can differ from each other in infinitely many ways," and thus need to be guided by reason (Ia IIae, q. 120, a. 1). While, on Aquinas's view, the supreme principle—to act according to reason, or, justly—applies necessarily and always, the principle that something held in trust must be returned binds "only as a general rule" (*ut in pluribus*; Ia IIae, q. 94, a. 4). "Because human actions must be distinguished according to the different factors of the agents, the time and other circumstances; the conclusions do not follow from the first regulations of the natural law so that they are always valid but only that they are mostly valid. 'For such is the matter of morality,' as Aristotle states."[58]

The *criteria* for the evaluation of goods and the estimation of consequences follow from the principle that the moral quality of an action results from the totality of its causes (*ex integra causa*), that is, the complex determining causes of the action (goal, intention, and circumstances) as well as the framework that determines their evaluation: the principle of reason, natural inclinations, *ethos*, and life plan (q. 18, a. 4, ad 3).[59] The *process* by which goods and consequences are evaluated is that of a practical deliberation, in which synthetic and analytic method, deduction and determination, consideration of means and ends, and practical syllogism combine to form a specific unity in which the complex web of formal and material causes, of invariant and *ethos*-relative rules, of nonarbitrary and adaptable character finds the concrete expression that binds human action.

Notes

[1] For this term see Charlie D. Broad, *Five Types of Ethical Theory*, 18th ed. (London: Routledge and Kegan Paul, 1971), 278.

[2] Recent Catholic moral theology has referred to the tradition of late-scholastic and neoscholastic handbooks, but instead of investigating their Aristotelian origin, has linked them to modern teleological theories. See, for example, Bernhard Schüller, *Die Begründung sittlicher Urteile. Typen ethischer Argumentation*, 2d ed. (Düsseldorf: Patmos, 1980); Franz Böckle, *Fundamentalmoral* (Munich: Kösel, GmbH and Co., 1977), 302–19, as well as the survey in Franz Furger, "Zur Begründung eines christlichen Ethos–Forschungstendenzen in der katholischen Moraltheologie," in *Theol. Berichte IV*, ed. Josef Pfammatter and Franz Furger (Zürich: Benziger, 1974), 11–87.

[3] See also *De veritate*, q. 22, a. 13 (Leonine, 643–46). See also Antony Kenny, "Thomas von Aquin über den Willen," in *Thomas von Aquin im philosophischen Gespräch*, ed. Wolfgang Kluxen (Freiburg: Alber, 1975), 101–31; Wolfgang Kluxen, "Thomas von Aquin: Zum Gutsein des Handelns," *Philosophisches Jahrbuch*, 87(1980): 327–39.

[4] See *De malo*, q. 6 (Leonine, 145–53). See also Klaus Riesenhuber, *Die Transzendenz der Freiheit zum Guten. Der Wille in der Anthropologie und Metaphysik des Thomas von Aquin* (Munich: Berchmanskolleg, 1971).

[5] See Klaus Hedwig, "Circa particularia. Kontigenz, Klugheit und Notwendigkeit im Aufbau des ethischen Aktes bei Thomas von Aquin," in *The Ethics of St. Thomas Aquinas*, ed. Leo J. Elders and Klaus Hedwig (Rome: Libreria Editrice Vaticana, 1984), 161–87.

[6] For more detail, see my "Praktische Vernunft und Gewissen," *Handbuch der christlichen Ethik 3*, ed. Anselm Hertz, Wilhelm Korff, Trutz Rendtorff, and Hermann Ringeling. 2d ed. (Freiburg: Herder, 1983), 19–43. Also "Wahrheit und Sittlichkeit. Zur Bedeutung der Wahrheit in der Ethik," in *Wahrheit in Einheit und Vielheit*, ed. Emerich Coreth (Düsseldorf: Patmos, 1987), 147–69, 154ff.

[7] *In I Ethicorum*, lect. 1, n. 1: "ordo quem ratio considerando facit in operationibus voluntatis" (Marietti, 3); see also ST Ia, q. 79, a. 11.

[8] "hoc non sufficit ad recte ratiocinandum circa particularia."

[9] *In I Ethicorum*, lect. 3, n. 35 (Marietti, 10).

[10] See Klaus Hedwig, "Circa particularia," 170–74; also, Hedwig, "Praecepta negativa. Die Axiomatik der praktischen Vernunft und das Verbot," in *Lex et Libertas. Freedom and Law according to St. Thomas Aquinas*, ed. Leo J. Elders and Klaus Hedwig (Rome: Libreria Editrice Vaticana, 1987), 200–218, 202ff.

[11] *In II Ethicorum*, lect. 2, n. 257 (Marietti, 74).

[12] "naturalis enim ratio dictat unicuique ut secundum rationem operetur."

[13] *De malo*, q. 14, a. 2, ad 8: "quicquid est contra rationem est contra hominis naturam" (Leonine, 263–64, 218–19); see also ST Ia IIae, q. 71, a. 2.

[14] See also ST Ia IIae, q. 94, a. 2; *De veritate*, qq. 16–17 (Leonine, 501–28); for more detail, see my "Practical Reason and Conscience."

[15] Bernhard Schüller rightly talks about "reflexive" normative propositions, because these propositions refer to the moral judgement itself; Wilhelm Korff speaks of "personal" preferential rules, because these rules are intended to secure human freedom and dignity. See Bernhard Schüller, *Begründung sittlicher Urteile*, 76; Korff, *Kernenergie und Moraltheologie. Der Beitrag der theologischen Ethik zur Frage allgemeiner Kriterien ethischer Entscheidungsprozesse* (Frankfurt: Suhrkamp, 1979), 89.

[16] On Aquinas's doctrine, see also *De veritate*, q. 17, aa. 3–4 (Leonine, 521–27); *In II Sent.*, d. 39, q. 3, a. 1 (Mandonnet, 995–98); *Quodlibet* III q. 12, a. 2 (Marietti, 65–66). On the modern consequences, see my "Menschenwürde und Menschenrechte. Christlicher Glaube und die sittliche Substanz des Staates," in *Grundlagen der politischen Kultur des Westens*, ed. Klaus Wilhelm Hempfer and Alexander Schwan (Berlin: de Gruyter, 1987), 239–64.

[17] See in detail, Wolfgang Kluxen, *Philosophische Ethik bei Thomas von Aquin* 2d ed. (Hamburg: Meiner, 1980), 166–205.

[18] See also ST Ia IIae, q. 18, a. 10; *De malo*, q. 2, aa. 6–7 (Leonine, 45–51).

[19] Franz Scholz, "Objekt und Umstände, Wesenswirkungen und Nebeneffekte. Zur Möglichkeit und Unmöglichkeit indirekten Handelns," in *Christlich Glauben und Handeln*, ed. Klaus Demmer and Bernhard Schüller (Düsseldorf: Patmos, 1977), 243–60, 246–51.

[20] See also ST Ia, q. 75 a. 4, ad 2; *De potentia*, q. 9, a. 2, ad 14 (Marietti, 229).

[21] As regards the role of nature as a "demand" and "limit," see Wolfgang Kluxen, *Ethik des Ethos* (Freiburg: Alber, 1974), 27–49.

[22] See Schüller, *Begründung sittlicher Urteile*, 124–32; Korff, *Kernenergie und Moraltheologie*, 68–71.

[23] See Schüller, *Begründung sittlicher Urteile*, 116–23; Korff, *Kernenergie und Moraltheologie*, 71–77.

[24] See Wilhelm Korff, *Norm und Sittlichkeit*, 2d ed. (Freiburg: Alber, 1985), 76–101.

[25] See also *De virt. in comm.*, q. un., a. 2, ad 3 (Marietti, 712).

[26] Modern moral theologians such as Böckle and Schüller follow the same procedure when they interpret the evaluation of goods as an evaluation of pre-moral goods and moral values which takes place under the demands of love.

[27] On the importance of marriage in this context, see Paul Mikat, *Ethische Strukturen der Ehe in unserer Zeit. Zur Normierungsfrage im Kontext des abendländischen Eheverständnisses* (Paderborn: Schöningh, 1987), 10–27.

[28] As regards the tradition of the scholastic manuals of moral theology, see Augustin Lehmkuhl, *Compendium Theologiae Moralis*, 4th ed. (Freiburg: Herder, 1899), 130–54.

[29] See n. 8 above.

[30] See also ST Ia IIae, q. 57, a. 6, ad 3; Ia, q. 82, a. 2.

[31] See nn. 9, 11 above.

[32] See also ST Ia IIae, q. 91, a. 3; q. 94, a. 5.

[33] "Contingit enim aliquem iudicare, uno modo per modum inclinationis: sicut qui habet habitum virtutis, recte iudicat de his quae sunt secundum virtutem agenda, inquantum ad illa inclinatur . . ." See also ST IIa IIae, q. 45, a. 2. See also Hedwig, "Circa particularia," 175f.

[34] See also ST Ia IIae, q. 93, a. 5.

[35] See Kluxen, *Ethik des Ethos*, 51–72.

[36] See n. 3 above.

[37] See my "Wahrheit und Sittlichkeit," 157, 161ff., 168f.

[38] See Kluxen, *Ethik des Ethos*, 51–61.

[39] See my "Zur Philosophie der Schuld," *Theologische Quartalschrift* 155 (1975): 31–48, 43f., 46ff.

[40] See also ST Ia IIae, q. 19, a. 2, ad 1; qq. 1, 3.

[41] *In II Sent.*, d. 1, a. 2, ad 3.

[42] See also ST Ia IIae, q. 18, a. 2, ad 3.

[43] "ex hoc dicitur actio bona, quod bonum effectum inducere potest."

[44] *In IV Sent.*, d. 16, q. 3, a. 2 (Moos, 798–807).

[45] See also ST Ia IIae, q. 12, a. 4; *De malo*, q. 2, a. 4, ad 9 (Leonine, 41, 335–39); q. 2, a. 7, ad 8 (Leonine, 51, 125–42).

[46] See ST Ia IIae, q. 19, a. 7; q. 18, a. 6.

[47] See also ST Ia IIae, q. 88, a. 6, ad 3; IIa IIae, q. 64, a. 5, ad 3.

[48] See Arist. *Eth. Nic.* 2.9 (1109a35); *Decretum Gratiani* 13 in *Corpus iuris canonici*, ed. Emil A. Friedberg (1879; Graz: Akademische Druckund Verlagsamstalt, 1959). For a contemporary interpretation of the maxim, see Schüller, *Begründung sittlicher Urteile*, 121f.; Korff, *Kernenergie und Moraltheologie*, 78–90.

[49] *De correctione fraterna*, q. un., a. 1, ad 5 (Marietti, 796). See also ST Ia IIae, q. 101, a. 3, ad 2.

[50] See Thomas Sanchez, *De sancto matrimonii sacramento* VII 11 nn. 14–28 (Nuremberg: n.p., 1706), II:39–42.

[51] See John T. Mangan, "An Historical Analysis of the Principle of Double Effect," *Theological Studies* 10 (1949): 41–61.

[52] See also Franz Scholz, *Wege, Umwege und Auswege der Moraltheologie. Ein Plädoyer für begrün-*

dete Ausnahmen (Munich: Don Bosco, 1976), 112, 123.

[53]See Peter Knauer, "Das rechtverstandene Prinzip von der Doppelwirkung als Grundnorm jeder Gewissensentscheidung," *Theologie und Glaube* 57 (1967): 107–33.

[54]"in singularibus contingentibus consistunt, quae infinitis modis variari possunt . . ."

[55]"sequi id quod poscit iustitiae ratio et communis utilitas."

[56]"pars subiectiva iustitiae . . . est quasi superior regula humanorum actuum."

[57]See Francisco Suárez, *De legibus* 1.6 c. 7 n. 11.

[58]*In IV Sent.*, d. 33, q. 1, a. 2: "sed quia actus humanos variari oportet secundum diversas conditiones personarum et temporum, et aliarum circumstantiarum; ideo conclusiones praedictae a primis legis naturae praeceptis non procedunt ut semper efficaciam habentes, sed in majori parte. talis enim est tota materia moralis, ut patet per philosophum . . . " (Index thomisticus, 598). Scholz also talks of the "structural law of the gradually diminishing applicability of the concrete norms" (*Wege*, 128–31).

[59]See also ST Ia IIae, q. 19, a. 6, ad 1; Ia IIae, q. 19, a. 7, ad 3.

Selected Further Reading

Bradley, Dennis J. M. *Aquinas on the Twofold Human Good: Reason and Human Happiness in Aquinas's Moral Science*. Washington, DC: Georgetown University Press, 1997.

Finnis, John M. *Natural Law and Natural Rights*. Oxford: Oxford University Press, 1980.

Honnefelder, Ludger, "Naturrecht und Normwandel bei Thomas von Aquin und Johannes Duns Scotus." In *Sozialer Wandel im Mittelalter. Wahrnehmungsformen, Erklärungsmuster, Regelungsmechanismen*. Eds. J. Miethke and K. Schreiner. Sigmaringen: Thorbecke, 1994.

———. "Praktische Vernunft und Gewissen." In *Handbuch der christlichen Ethik 3*. Ed. Anselm Hertz, Wilhelm Korff, Trutz Rendtorff, and Hermann Ringeling. 2d ed. Freiburg: Herder, 1983.

Kluxen, Wolfgang. *Philosophische Ethik bei Thomas von Aquin*. 2d ed. Hamburg: Meiner, 1980.

Korff, Wilhelm. "Der naturale und theologische Gründungszusammenhang des Normativen nach Thomas von Aquin." In *Norm und Sittlichkeit. Untersuchungen zur Logik der normativen Vernunft*. 2d ed. Freiburg: Alber, 1985.

McInerny, Ralph. *Ethica Thomistica: The Moral Philosophy of Thomas Aquinas*. Washington, DC: Georgetown University Press, 1982.

Merks, Karl-William. *Theologische Grundlegung der sittlichen Autonomie. Strukturmomente eines 'autonomen' Normbegründungsverständnisses im Lex-Traktat der Summa theologiae des Thomas von Aquin*. Düsseldorf: Patmos, 1978.

Pesch, Otto-Hermann. *Commentary to S. Th. I-II, 90–105*. Heidelberg: F. H. Kerle, 1977.

Lonergan and Aquinas: The Postmodern Problematic of Theology and Ethics

Frederick G. Lawrence

INTRODUCTION

The term "postmodern" is controversial. At the 1997 "Religion and Postmodernism" symposium at Villanova University, Jacques Derrida, often identified with the term, claimed that he has never understood himself to be postmodern, while deriding the term's vagueness. Even so, the word has entered contemporary parlance, and like all such mode-words, it expresses a set of concerns commonly felt today.

Those concerns are rooted in the crisis of modernity and cluster around questioning and reflecting upon modernity. "Modernity" here refers to what Hans Blumenberg in *Die Legitimität der Neuzeit* called the "humane self-affirmation" in reaction to the late medieval period's "theological absolutism" from Duns Scotus through William of Ockham to the Reformation theologies of Luther and Calvin and of counter-Reformation Baroque scholasticism.[1] This so-called humane self-affirmation is in turn based on the Machiavellian interpretation of specifically modern science in the mode of Galileo, Newton, and Harvey. It is a project aimed at making human beings "masters and possessors of nature," as Descartes phrased it in the *Discourse on Method*. This project gave rise—through Hobbes, Spinoza, and Locke—to liberal democracy and, in figures such as Adam Smith and Montesquieu, to liberal capitalism. Ironically, it also spawned massive reactions to liberal capitalism in the emancipatory movement from Rousseau through Kant and Hegel to Marx, which seeks to overcome the limits of commerce by various cultural and political limits on the inequities of market capitalism.

Postmodernity's radical questioning of modernity (or of the Enlightenment) centers upon the critique of reason as a sheer instrument of the will-to-power. Its presiding spirit is Friedrich Nietzsche, who sought a more integral form of humanity. It is highly suspicious of the supposedly scientific and universalist justifications for what turn out to be forms of individual or group (that is, class, gender, or race/ethnicity) bias. Hence, Derrida and the late Michel Foucault, thinkers we typically associate with postmodernism, articulate their intent as radically ethical: Derrida debunks artificial discriminations in the name of radical hospitality; Foucault uncovers strategies of control in the name of radical liberty.

A central postmodern preoccupation has been the displacement of the subject. This entails a critique (1) of the liberal utilitarian-individualist subject; and (2) of either the romantic-expressivist subject (favored by certain species of socialism), or (3) the autonomous subject that seeks to completely internalize and generalize all norms. The postmodern critique of the subject as primary object, and so as truncated or immanentized, was needed to make problematic the prevalent modern assumption of the subject as the primary object in the universe and its implicit (and often explicit) image of a moral agent whose motivation is transparent, unbothered by self-deception or the need to engage in socially conditioned role-playing. At the same time, the critique of modernity—as in Etienne Gilson, Jacques Maritain, Hans-Georg Gadamer, Leo Strauss, Eric Voegelin, Paul Ricoeur, Alasdair MacIntyre, Charles Taylor, and Emmanuel

Lévinas—has often gone hand-in-hand with a renewed appreciation of premodern philosophy and theology, precisely because it does not share modernity's possessive individualism and subjectivism. You may be surprised to learn that this is also true of Bernard Lonergan, S.J.

LONERGAN AND THE CONTEMPORARY CRISIS OF FAITH

For Bernard Lonergan, the Christian faith is now undergoing a crisis rooted in Christianity's inability to make a balanced transition to modern society and culture. Christian philosophy and theology should not just be uncritically accommodated to modernity. Lonergan was acutely aware that in the wake of *Aeterni patris* Catholic philosophy and theology had failed to relinquish the fixist norms espoused by a mentality he called "classicist" and to achieve a transcultural normativity compatible with historical consciousness. Yet he was scathingly critical of the historicist or positivist drift toward relativism that more or less renounced any normativity whatsoever along with decadent aspects of the scholastic heritage. Lonergan's life was dedicated to helping Christian theology make the transition to what is now being called "postmodernity" without losing its integrity. His key critique of "classicism" and nuanced acceptance of "historical mindedness" is a balanced yet radically postmodern critique of modernity.

Pivotal to Lonergan's execution of this task is his unique relationship to the paradigm-figure of the Middle Ages, Thomas Aquinas. Writing about the decisive task of dialectic, he stressed "meeting persons, appreciating the values they represent, criticising their deeds."[2] Lonergan's entire appoach to the crisis of modernity was marked deeply by his encounter with Aquinas.

In reading and rereading Aquinas, Lonergan followed Einstein's advice not to listen to what scientists say they do but to watch what they do. Many years of intensive and painstaking research taught him that "*in the practice of Aquinas [theology] was . . . the principle for the moulding and the transformation of a culture.*"[3] Besides "reflecting on revelation," theology "has somehow to mediate God's meaning into the whole of human affairs."

The twenty-first century requires a postmodern transposition of the sweep of Aquinas's theological enterprise.

"Theology mediates between a cultural matrix and the significance and role of a religion in that matrix."[4] Aquinas's wholehearted and unflinching engagement with Greek and Arabic thought in the twelfth century taught Lonergan that the effectiveness of theology's mediating task "depends . . . on the clarity and accuracy of its grasp of the external cultural factors that undermine its achievements and challenge it to new endeavors."[5] As Thomas had done in relation to Aristotle's influence on intellectual culture in his day, Lonergan, too, gave immense time and energy to the "postmodern" problem of coming to terms with modernity.

In his retrieval of Aquinas's thought on "operative grace" (*gratia operans*) and on the "inner word" (*verbum*) Lonergan applied the scholarly canons of critical historical research and interpretation to the saint's *Opera omnia*. He was dismissive of anyone who would "substitute rhetoric for history, fancy for fact, abstract argument for textual evidence."[6] He realized the crucial issue in interpreting Aquinas was more than history, even in the important and indispensable sense of responsible historical scholarship; it was also profoundly existential: "to effect an advance in depth that is proportionate to the broadening influence of historical research." This he named "reaching up to the mind of Aquinas."[7] This project changed him in two ways. First, it made him capable of stating accurately and suggestively in the indirect discourse of responsible scholarship what Thomas Aquinas meant. This goal was of course not unique to Lonergan, having been undertaken by numerous scholars from Marie-Dominique Chenu and Etienne Gilson to Yves Simon and Charles de Konninck. Second, and perhaps uniquely, his study of Aquinas made Lonergan capable of conceiving his own lifework as bringing Aquinas's "compelling genius" to bear on the crisis of our own day—a crisis never directly envisaged by St. Thomas.

In magnificent proportions, Thomas Aquinas came to know, assimilate, and transform Greek and Arabic culture by "think[ing] out the Catholic position in philosophy . . . and put[ting] new order into the sprawling theology dominated by the Lombard's *Sentences*."[8] Lonergan therefore eschewed the common neoscholastic strategy of taking the errors of later thinkers out of the context in which they made sense, and then supplying Thomas's putative refutations of their mistakes. Aquinas inspired Lonergan "to give concrete expression to the sincerity of Catholic thought"[9] by doing all he could to know, assimilate, and transform "the basic developments out of which come the modern world."[10] This is Lonergan's way of fulfilling Leo XIII's challenge: "to increase and perfect the old things by the new" (*vetera novis augere et perficere*).[11] In his project of method in theology, Lonergan transposed Aquinas's massive effort to know, assimilate, and transform culture by addressing the issues of our own day in his own lifework.

METHOD AS WISDOM

What makes the meaning of "method" for Lonergan so profound and unprecedented, therefore, is the manner in which his project of method flows integrally from his encounter with the practice of Aquinas as a theologian. He insisted in *Method*, such "encounter is the one way in which self-understanding and horizon can be put to the test."[12] Ordinary ideas about method tend to be *technical* in the Enlightenment vein of Descartes or Bacon, and so they focus on "a set of verbal propositions enouncing rules to be followed in a scientific investigation."[13] Lonergan places method instead in the context of Aquinas's dictum that "it is characteristic of the wise person to order all things" (Ia IIae, q. 66, a. 5, c., and ad 4).[14] By reconceiving the Thomist highest viewpoint of wisdom in terms of the phenomenological notion of horizon and of Jean Piaget's use of group theory to specify psychological development,[15] Lonergan makes method a matter of utmost radicality and complete concreteness. Method for Lonergan basically means appropriating and articulating the grounds of theological (and *any*) practice in one's own total and basic horizon. His engagement with the thought of Thomas Aquinas led Lonergan to realize that method in its plainer but quite important sense of "distinguishing different tasks, and thereby eliminating totalitarian ambitions" has to be anchored in the human sub-

ject's appropriation of method as "transcendental"—that is, Aquinas's twofold operation (*duplex operatio*) of human intelligence in rational self-consciousness.[16] Making the structure of one's mind and heart one's own reveals the ultimate and so transcultural set of human operations of experiencing, understanding, reflecting, deliberating, deciding, and loving. At root, "method" for Lonergan means (1) appropriating the structures of human conscious intentionality that specify one's horizon as total and basic; and (2) consciously living in accord with one's total and basic horizon by following the "transcendental" precepts to be attentive, intelligent, reasonable, responsible, and loving. This is an enormous order, because, as Lonergan himself was well aware, method in this sense is not, to use Newman's expression, a matter of merely "notional" apprehension and assent; it has to be an achievement of "real" apprehension and assent, or it is just empty words.[17]

CRITIQUE OF THE MODERN MODEL OF CONSCIOUSNESS

Lonergan was able to explicate human consciousness in a manner that was not possible for Aquinas. Because of his study of Thomas, however, he could correct the pervasive modern notion of consciousness as perception. In his work on Aquinas, he realized that consciousness is not so much a matter of inner or outer perception, but of experience.[18] What Lonergan said in a review of Emerich Coreth's *Metaphysik* might help begin to convey what he means by consciousness as experience: "We should learn that questioning not only is about being but is being, being in its *Gelichtetheit* (luminousness), being in its openness to being, being that is realizing itself through inquiry to knowing that, through knowing, it may come to loving."[19] Lonergan describes "being oneself as being in its *Gelichtetheit*" because for him being is not abstract but concrete. As he often insisted, "It is not the universal concept 'not nothing' of Scotus and Hegel, but the concrete goal intended in all inquiry and reflection. It is substance and subject: our opaque being that rises to consciousness and our conscious being. . . ."[20] Lonergan explained that "being oneself as conscious being" "is not an object, not part of the spectacle we contemplate, but the presence to himself of the spectator, the contemplator. It is not an object of introspection, but the prior presence that makes introspection possible."[21] So he disagrees with the Cartesian notion of the subject or *res cogitans* as the primary object, because consciousness as the primordial experience of presence to oneself is not reducible to awareness of an object.

The reader might recall that for Descartes consciousness as a power of inner, reflexive perception is known by a doubling back of inward, reflexive perception upon itself; and that Kant links the objectivity of knowledge indissolubly to external perception that cannot reach an internal power. Instead for Lonergan, "[conscious being] is conscious, but that does not mean that properly it is known; it will be known only if we introspect, understand, reflect, and judge."[22] At a stroke, Lonergan thereby rejects the Cartesian notion of consciousness either as identical with or as knowable only by an inner, reflexive perception; furthermore, he disagrees with Kant's position that consciousness cannot be objectively known.

Lonergan discovered that conscious being can be known by a heightening of consciousness comparable to that which occurs in "high" psychotherapies, in which people come to experience, identify, and name their emotions and feelings. As Lonergan points out: "It is one thing to feel blue and another to advert to the fact that you are feeling blue. It is one thing to be in love and another to discover that what has happened to you is that you have fallen in love. Being oneself is prior to knowing oneself. St. Ignatius said that love shows itself more in deeds than in words; but being in love is neither deeds nor words; it is the prior conscious reality that words and, more securely, deeds reveal."[23]

First, note that feeling, the "prior conscious reality" Lonergan speaks about here, is pure experience in the sense that as an internal experience, it is a mode of consciousness as distinct from self-knowledge. In other words, consciousness itself is prior to and distinct from any later process in which one heightens his or her awareness through inquiring about and understanding, through checking and judging what one undergoes in experiencing feelings.

The following passage about passing from feelings as conscious experience to feelings as integrated into self-knowledge brings out the significance of this distinction:

Feelings simply as felt pertain to an infrastructure. But as merely felt, so far from being integrated into an equable flow of consciousness, they may become a source of disturbance, upset, inner turmoil. Then a cure or part of a cure would seem to be had from the client-centered therapist who provides the patient with an ambiance in which he is at ease, can permit feelings to emerge without being engulfed by them, come to distinguish them from other inner events, differentiate among them, add recognition, bestow names, gradually manage to encapsulate within a superstructure of knowledge and language, of assurance and confidence, what had been an occasion for disorientation, dismay, disorganization.[24]

Second, however, the "feelings as felt" are knowledge in an improper sense precisely because they are conscious before being focused upon, explicated, and thematized. It is important to specify this as performative knowledge or, as I have said, knowledge in an improper sense of the word. Nevertheless, it is knowledge of the subject as subject, not as object—a kind of knowledge to which neither Descartes nor Kant could do justice, because in one way or another, they each identified consciousness with perception. This performative or improper sort of knowing is knowledge under the formal aspect of "the experienced" (*sub ratione experti*), as Lonergan phrased it, and not under the formal aspect either of being, or of intelligible form, or of the true. For both Lonergan and Aquinas, the last of these—knowledge in the proper sense of the term (that is, under the aspect of both the intelligible and of the true)—requires that one add a superstructure to his or her awareness through introspection, inquiry, understanding, and articulation, as well as through reflection and judgment.[25]

The postmoderns following Heidegger have tried to dismantle the predominant model of consciousness as exclusively perception, because it renders one unable to come to terms adequately either with consciousness as external experience in sensation (as distinct from perception), or with consciousness as internal experience in consciousness's own modes and operations. From the postmodern as opposed to the modern perspective, then, consciousness means "an internal experience in the strict sense of the self and its acts."[26]

Let me stress two more points about this postmodern understanding of consciousness. First, consciousness defined as internal experience is more primitive and more originative than standard modern conceptions of consciousness rooted in Cartesian or Kantian epistemologies of the subject, neither of which are empirically accessible or phenomenologically ostensible. And yet, because it is so primitive, one's original access to it is not, as Habermas has said, "the objectifying attitude in which the knowing subject regards itself as it would entities in the external world."[27] As Lonergan insists, "one must begin from the performance if one is to have the experience necessary for understanding what the performance is."[28] Thus, one has to begin from "a performative attitude," in Habermas's phrase—"*in actu exercito*" for the later scholastics.

The second point is that properly to know consciousness as internal experience is to know something that is contingently constitutive of the being of the human subject. Inasmuch as it involves using ordinary language to inquire, grasp, and formulate, and then to assess and judge whether articulations of possibly relevant relationships are contingently verifiable in the experiences themselves, such self-knowledge has the quality Habermas, borrowing from Piaget, calls "reconstruction"—what the later scholastics called "*in actu signato*." In the correct postmodern understanding of consciousness as experience, "reconstructive and empirical assumptions can be brought together in one and the same theory."[29]

The cognitive dimension of consciousness became most clear to Lonergan while writing the *Verbum* articles.[30] Not until the post–1964–65 period did the implications of the dependency of the cognitive dimension of consciousness upon the practical and existential levels gradually become clearer to him. Not only do deliberation, decision, and loving action presuppose and complement knowing, but even more crucially, knowing also presupposes and complements those operations.

During *Method in Theology*'s years of gestation, Lonergan was increasingly able to express Aquinas's metaphysical explanation of human freedom and divine grace (already retrieved in the 1930s and 1940s) in terms of an analysis of conscious intentionality that can verify its basic terms and relations within consciousness as experience. The difficulty with a metaphysical articulation of the relationship between divine grace and human freedom in terms of faculty psychology is not that it is incorrect, but that it relies on a deduction from things directly experienced, and so is not immediately accessible and so empirically verifiable.[31]

In his 1957 book *Insight* (and especially in chapter 11), Lonergan tended to equate the breakthrough to the total and basic horizon with the appropriation of rational consciousness in one's affirmation of oneself as truly a knower. Rational *self*-consciousness takes center-stage only in chapter 18. This ordering places the focus almost exclusively on the clear recognition that knowing is a compound, dynamic structure of experiencing, understanding, and judging, and especially on one's ability "to discriminate with ease and from personal conviction between . . . purely intellectual activities and the manifold of other 'existential' concerns that invade and mix and blend with the operations of intellect to render it ambivalent and its pronouncements ambiguous."[32] Already in lectures on "Intelligence and Reality" delivered in 1950–51 at the Thomas More Institute for Adult Education (Montreal), he had sensed that the key to *Insight*'s breakthrough was a more sweeping affair of "radical intellectual conversion."[33] It involved a revolution in oneself and a purification of oneself from what he then called "inhibiting and reinforcing (that is, reductively utilitarian) desires."[34] The point is to liberate the pure, disinterested, and unrestricted desire to know being from other desires, and to make this specific desire normative in one's actual living. By the time he wrote *Method in Theology*, however, what was earlier implicit became fully explicit. Because of the primacy of the practical and existential levels of conscious intentionality, intellectual conversion (the effective disclosure of our horizons as total and basic by real apprehension and assent) presupposes both moral conversion (from spontaneous likes and dislikes to the truly good or right) and religious conversion (from self-centeredness to being-in-love with God).[35]

As was already clear in *Grace and Freedom*, religious conversion is the result of the gift of God's self-communication, beyond the horizon of finite human knowing and choosing. The missions of God's Spirit and Word make moral and intellectual conversion concretely possible, even though these conversions can be conceived abstractly independently of God's grace. Those conversions in turn demand the exercise of liberty by which one reorients oneself and brings the horizon of day-to-day living into ever closer attunement with the infinite potentiality of one's total and basic horizon. Openness as gift heals by transforming the human's sinful closedness and it elevates a person to the factual, healing, and creative openness of divine adoption.[36]

I will turn now to the salient dimensions of Lonergan's method-project as a radically hermeneutic undertaking indelibly marked by Lonergan's encounter with St. Thomas Aquinas.

HERMENEUTICS OF THEORY

In *Grace and Freedom*, Lonergan exposed the key ideas of Thomas's teaching on grace in terms of a higher theoretical synthesis in relation both to the gradual evolution of theology before him and to the lower viewpoints represented later by the Reformation debates and the Baroque scholastic *De auxiliis* disputes. Lonergan presented an historical reconstruction (which depended on Artur Michael Landgraf and Odon Lottin) of the development of the theory of grace from the *symbola* of the Patristic era to the medieval *summae*. This reconstruction revealed how Aquinas's theology, as instanced in the emergence of the fully rounded theory of operative or actual grace formulated in *Summa theologiae* Ia IIae, q. 111, a. 2, is much more a matter of growing understanding of relevant data than of the stock-in-trade of scholastic manuals: the highlighting of universal and necessary terms and the drawing of certain conclusions via syllogisms. Lonergan, later on quoting Georg Simmel, called the aspect of developing understanding he found at the heart of Aquinas's theologizing *die Wendung zur Idee*[37]—the dis-

placement toward system by which the historically unfolding course of individual and collective questions and answers ascends from the "first-for-us" of commonsense or descriptive understanding to the "first-in-itself" standpoint of scientific theory or explanation. Aquinas represented a high-water mark for this ascent in Catholic theology.

The emerging technique of the *quaestio* made it possible for Thomas Aquinas to distinguish clearly between *lectio* (exegetical commentary on the authoritative sources of revealed truth) and the precise kind of *disputatio* aimed at "the reasons that bring to light the ground of the truth and enable one to know how what is said is true."[38] Thus, in Lonergan's retrieval, Aquinas's theology represented a grand chapter in the process by which Christian meanings and values were translated from the world of community (common sense), which unfolds in the dramatic, artistic, symbolic, and mystical patterns of experience, to the purely intellectual pattern of experience. As long as difficult questions about the intelligibility and meaning of Christian truths and values arise, what the medievals called "speculative" and what is now known as "systematic" theology has a lasting significance for Christian life and practice. Indeed, moral and ethical questions in theology require this dimension as well. Lonergan's initial scholarly encounter with Thomas Aquinas uncovered a hermeneutics of the rigorously theoretic moment in human and Christian life.

HERMENEUTICS OF COGNITIVE INTERIORITY

Thomas Aquinas dedicated himself mainly to bringing Christian thought into the world of theory. Lonergan's *Verbum* studies showed that the basic terms and relations of Aquinas's theology of the Trinity were derived from his grasp of rational process (*emanationes intelligibiles*) in the human mind and heart as the created image of the Triune God. On Lonergan's bold interpretation, Aquinas's statements about human psychology within a metaphysical framework were expressions of his own prior introspectively and experientially grounded analysis of human knowing and willing. Pursuing a line of inquiry initiated by Augustine's *De trinitate*, "The Thomist concept of inner word is rich and nuanced: it is no mere metaphysical condition of a type of cognition; it aims at being a statement of psychological fact and the precise nature of these facts can be ascertained only by ascertaining what was meant."[39] This means that a "turn to the subject" was required in order both to understand and affirm the facts about *intelligere* and *dicere* in the first place; and to reconstruct Aquinas's thought on the procession of the *verbum*. As Lonergan stated at the close of *Insight*: "it is only through a personal appropriation of one's own rational self-consciousness that one can hope to reach the mind of Aquinas."[40]

In contrast to Lonergan's hermeneutics of cognitive interiority,[41] the recovery of Thomist gnoseology by Joseph Maréchal and Karl Rahner were exercises in the metaphysics of knowledge (*Erkenntnismetaphysik*). Only Lonergan made Aquinas's explicit statement that "the human soul understands itself by its understanding, which is its proper act, perfectly demonstrating its power and its nature" (Ia, q. 88, a. 2, ad 3) the starting point of his investigation.[42] The hermeneutics of cognitive interiority concentrates on the act of understanding rather than on truth, certitude, necessity, universality, conception, inquiry, intuition, experience, *a priori* synthesis, apperceptive unity, description, phenomenology, induction, or any combination of these.[43] This approach—which makes explicit the act of conceiving *because* one understands and the act of judging *because* one's intelligence grasps the sufficiency of the evidence—seems to be unparalleled in the literature on Thomist gnoseology. It alone highlights what most crucially distinguishes human and spiritual causality from the causality operative in all subhuman phenomena. As Lonergan shows, Thomas realized that because human intellect is a created participation in uncreated light, *one knows by what one is instead of by what one produces* (universal concepts and propositions, for example). That is why Lonergan's scrutiny of human acts of direct and reflective understanding yields the immense promise expressed in the slogan of *Insight*: "Thoroughly understand what it is to understand, and not only will you understand the broad lines of all there is to be understood, but also you will possess a fixed base, an invariant pattern,

opening upon all further developments of understanding."[44]

The absolute centrality for human existence of the preconceptual act of understanding on the intelligent (What? Why? How? What for?), rational (Is it so? actually? probably? or only possibly?), and practical/existential (What should I/we do? Should I/we do it? Is it worthwhile?) levels of consciousness becomes the key to Lonergan's method-project of knowing, assimilating, and transforming the contemporary external cultural factors that condition Christian faith and theology, about which Aquinas was completely unaware. I will focus on four sets of issues surrounding today's external cultural factors.

First, the technical terms and relations drawn from Aristotelian physics and metaphysics in which Aquinas stated the psychological analogy for the Trinitarian processions have never functioned as deductive premises for the modern empirical sciences of nature. Hence, Lonergan concentrated on the cultural influences on faith and theology arising from the emergence of the new notion of empirical natural science, which is in crucial ways incompatible with Aristotle's notion of *episteme* with which Thomas was at home. He had to take seriously the normative achievements of modern science, while carrying out a postmodern critique of the Enlightenment ideology of scientism, with its mythology of rigor and proof.

Second, even though Aquinas developed and transformed Aristotelian positions to the point where he was able to integrate Augustine's psychological insights into a coherent theology of the Trinity, "he had to leave to a later age the task of acknowledging the discontinuity of natural and of human science and of working out its implications."[45] Thus, a second external cultural factor Lonergan needed to face was the emergence of the empirical *human* sciences that study human beings as they are concretely, and not only abstractly in terms of normative ideals and perfections. Once again, this means discerning the normative achievements in human sciences and scholarship, while rejecting ideological self-misconceptions, such as Weber's famous separation between facts and values.

Third, Aquinas *performed* the "turn to the subject," that is, the introspective exercise of reflecting upon his experiences of understanding and judging, and of distinguishing each from the other (especially, discriminating *sentire* from the *primae et secundae mentis operatio*). He did not *thematize* the turn to intending subjects and the study of their conscious acts and intentional terms. Prompted by the rise of modern empirical sciences, modern philosophies have turned expressly to the subject; they have given the epistemological question (How does one know one knows?) priority over the question of being (metaphysics or ontology). And so a third external cultural factor confronted by Lonergan is the rise of a panoply of modern philosophies, perhaps coherent in themselves, but assuming the mistaken modern notion of consciousness as perception, while also lacking one or another crucial structural element in their analysis of human knowing.

Fourth, as the human sciences, existentialism, phenomenology, deconstructionism, and the genealogical approach all make unmistakable, human horizons emerge through acts or operations (the psychological aspect) with others (the social aspect) within a tradition (the historical aspect). That is why the Thomist-Aristotelian analysis of human development in terms of potencies or faculties and habits (virtues, vices) needs to be transposed methodically in order to do justice to historical consciousness's focus on elicited *acts* of meaning and value. There is a need to take seriously the existential and practical domain in a more concrete way than Thomas, who did so in a more remote and abstract fashion, could manage in his day.

Insight and *Method* represent Lonergan's attempt to know, assimilate, and transform the external cultural factors that play such a massive role in the mediation of the Divine Word and Spirit in history. There follows a sketch of Lonergan's contribution to these four problematics.

Modern Philosophies

Although the best premodern philosophers made the *performative* transition both from the world of commonsense's myths, rituals, and customs, and from the world of theory into the world of interiority (the "turn to the subject"), they did not make either the performance or its correlative realm of interiority into a proper *theme*. Indeed, the classical scholastics—especially those engaged in debates over such questions as whether "first philosophy" consisted in material logic or ontology—simply neglected the subject altogether in order to concentrate on the question of being and its subdivisions (natural theology, rational psychology, and cosmology) from a strictly logical point of view. At their best such philosophies tended to devolve into sets of disputed questions with no grounds (other than logical ones) offered for resolving the disputes. In reaction to and in competition with scholastic decadence and verbalisms, the modern empirical sciences arose independently of the explicit terms and relations of any "adjectival" metaphysics (such as Platonic, Aristotelian, Lucretian, Thomist, Scotist, Ockhamist, Suarezian, and so on). This impelled leading modern philosophers to turn to the subject by starting with the issue of the objective validity of human knowing: the epistemological question.

Lonergan is sympathetic with postmodern concerns about such a strategy. For him it is not so much putting the question about knowing before the question about being that is problematic—in the context of the ongoing scholastic inability to settle disputed questions, this was not unreasonable. However, the typically modern perceptualist (Locke, Hume), idealist (Kant, the neo-Kantians, Husserl), or naive realist (Gilson, Maritain, Gredt) construals of the "problem of the bridge" between subject and object are already based on a false and ungrounded model of knowing. If one negotiates the "turn to the subject" by neglecting the subject, as naive realism does; or by truncating it, as perceptualism does; or by immanentizing it, as idealism does; or by alienating it, as Nietzsche and many deconstructionists and genealogists do, then "putting the cart before the horse" inevitably results: you cannot justify knowledge on the basis of a false account of knowing.

In *Insight*, Lonergan starts *not* with the question of epistemology but with the factual question he names "cognitional theory."[46] What acts are performed when one thinks one is knowing? "Insight as Activity" (chapters 1–10) helps readers identify, distinguish, and appropriate the sets of related acts they perform whenever they understand and know in mathematics, in natural and human sciences, and in everyday human living. Intelligent answers to questions about data received by sensation and sense perception, and represented by imagination, are reached through an interplay of our imaginations and our ability to reach *possibly* relevant descriptions and explanations of these data by operations of direct understanding; and *actually* relevant facts are attained through reflective acts of understanding that reasonably grasp the sufficiency of the evidence in every pertinent field and mode of knowing. The self-assembling structure of knowing is irreducible to what at first blush seems most obvious about knowing, namely, the sensible experience of what is "already out there now." When one knows, one asks questions for intelligence (What is it?) and questions for reflection (Is it so?) about data sensed and/or imagined; and one does not attain knowledge proper until one answers these questions intelligently and reasonably.

Only after one obtains answers about what knowing is that are factual or verified in the data of human consciousness can one pose the question about the objectivity of knowing in a way that makes sense: Why is performing these acts knowing? This is the *critical* way of putting the hoary objection to beginning with epistemology, which says quite sensibly that if one begins by doubting the veracity of one's knowledge of being, one will never succeed in justifying the capacity to know that common sense assumes one has in all his or her living. Rightly understood, the epistemological question only comes after one's factually ascertaining what one does when one knows. Only then can one establish the properties of knowing operations that explain why doing them yields knowledge of reality, namely, experiential, normative, and absolute objectivity. These kinds of objectivity are brought to light in relation to some such set of true judgments as: I know some object. I exist. The object exists. I am not the object.

Whenever one moves from experiencing through direct insight to judgment as an affirmation in which "*is*" expresses the absolute positing of an intelligible synthesis, one knows what is the case objectively. Why? Because this is what the questions for inquiry and reflection natively and spontaneously want to attain. In short, "the possibility of human knowing . . . is an unrestricted intention that intends the transcendent, and a process of self-transcendence that reaches it."[47]

Once the turn to the subject has been made in this fashion, one can see that subjectivity is the opposite to, or exclusive of, objectivity, *only if the latter is misconstrued* in an empiricist, positivist, idealist, or relativist manner. Lonergan can explain plausibly that such misconceptions (with their consequent horizonal distortions) arise when the mistaken (and typically modern) notion of consciousness as perception is compounded by the omission of one or another part of the integral structure of knowledge. Human cognitional structure presents norms or exigences that recur in everyone whenever they know; but they also can be violated as a matter of fact by anyone who, under the pressure of other desires and fears, acts in an inattentive, stupid, silly, and irresponsible way. For Lonergan, anyone who truly wishes to understand the truth about reality will also submit spontaneously to the normativity built *by nature* into their own cognitional structure. He characterizes this normativity as "natural and inevitable" because it is independent of the peculiarities of the relative (psychological, social, or historical) horizon of any particular person.

The answer to the metaphysical question—What does one know whenever one actually knows?—is reality or being. As intelligent and reasonable, human questioning intends being in an unqualified and unrestricted way; and outside of being there is nothing. It follows that being is what is to be known by understanding and judging correctly. But since human questioning and judging regard data either of the senses or of consciousness itself, the being "proportionate" to knowing is what one experiences with his or her senses or as one's finite consciousnesses. Such being has a structure that is isomorphic to a person's knowing: central and conjugate potency (→ experience), form (→ understanding), and act (→ judgment).

Nevertheless, the objective of one's intelligent and rational questioning goes beyond the range of external and internal experience. Lonergan clarifies that although the questions *what* God is and *whether* God exists go beyond being as intrinsically conditioned by space and time (= proportionate being), they do not extend beyond the range of one's inquiring and the reflective intending of being. Philosophically speaking, and in principle (the *quaestio juris*), the answers to these questions depend on exactly the same criteria as does our knowledge of any contingent beings whatsoever, namely, the reasonable apprehension of sufficient evidence.

From the higher viewpoint of theology, and as a matter of fact (the *quaestio facti*), Lonergan is also clear that convinced adherence to the criteria for the rational judgment of being across the board is tantamount to biblical "purity of heart." In other words, actually, true answers to the God-questions depend not just on affirmation of ourselves as knowers but on intellectual conversion; and for Lonergan this rare occurrence, as I have mentioned, entails prior religious and moral conversions—in brief, God's grace. For Lonergan, the God-question is never simply a theoretical one; it always is practical and existential as well.

Modern Science

Aquinas labored under the auspices of Aristotle's logical ideal of science as true and certain knowledge of things by their necessary causes. Lonergan argues that the modern empirical sciences have abandoned this ideal in order to try to explain all phenomena or data. While the ancients tended to regard Euclid's *Elements* as the closest approximation to the logical ideal, modern mathematics as instanced by Gödel's theorem and the "axioms of decision" have relinquished such pretenses altogether. Neither the Greeks nor Aquinas had at their disposal the systematic procedures by which to proceed beyond the application of logic to commonsense descriptions; and so their successors were susceptible of giving too much weight to merely nominal definitions. But modern science employs delicate techniques of measurement, curve-fitting, and implicit definition; and as experimental it uses careful procedures of verification that go far beyond the classical *reductio in principia* to check imagined constructions and perhaps biased perceptions against data.

Lonergan's move from *Verbum*'s hermeneutics of cognitive interiority to *Insight* benefitted from seven centuries of development in mathematics, physics, chemistry, biology, depth psychology, and the social and human sciences. This enormously enhanced his account of explanatory understanding in scientific theory. So, too, his account of judgment recognizes that the term of verification and so of judgment is the virtually unconditioned in contrast to the kind of absolute necessity only instantiated by God as formally unconditioned. Consequently, not only does Lonergan show that the exorbitant requirements of Aristotelian science (*episteme*) might be dropped in favor of the more modest quest for verified possibilities without sacrificing truth or intellectual honesty, but also he sets forth a full clarification of the basic heuristic structure of explanatory understanding in his account of classical, statistical, genetic, and dialectical methods.

Human Sciences and Human Studies or Scholarship

Empirical science investigates data experimentally. Still, within the totality of sense data and of the data of consciousness are data that also are imbued with or constituted by humanly generated meanings and values. As a result Lonergan differentiates the empirical sciences as human from the sciences of subhuman nature because the former have as their objective only the data constituted by meaning. Moreover, he distinguishes human *sciences* as seeking principles or laws either verified universally or else revised (as may occur for example in psychology, sociology, or economics) from *human studies* or *scholarship*.[48] Human studies and scholarship treat the human world constituted by meaning in terms of an extension of common sense's competence regarding persons, places, and things in their historical particularity about which one possesses data (as in literary studies, exegesis, and history, as well as aspects of theology).

It is no novelty to either Aristotle or Aquinas that meaning is constitutive of human knowing as responding to questions, since the *prima et secunda operationes* of the intellect are acts of meaning. Lonergan also reflects philosophically on the way human acts of knowledge and choice are constitutive of human living. Thus, too, according to Lonergan, the human sciences and scholarship go beyond the classicist preoccupation with laws, norms, exemplars, and ideals to grasp the concrete actualities and possibilities of human living making up the human good, which is the historical product of human acts of knowing and choosing.

I must devote an entire section to the fourth set of issues surrounding *Existenz* and *praxis*, which Lonergan had to face only by transposing and developing Aquinas's positions.

Hermeneutics of
Practical-Existential Interiority

To say that meaning is constitutive of human reality is to say that if one changes the meaning of any human thing like a constitution or a law or a promise, one changes that thing; and if one removes its meaning, one eliminates its reality. Since meaning arises from human acts of knowing and choosing in society and within a tradition, human being is intrinsically historical. For Lonergan, historical consciousness is chiefly an explicit awareness that human beings individually are responsible for the life they lead and collectively are responsible for the world in which they lead it. Meaning as constitutive of human potentiality, of human cultural achievements, and of human social institutions may be true or false, good or evil, authentic or unauthentic. As a result, there is a critical need for reflection on meaning and for a certain control of meaning. "For if social and cultural changes are, at root, changes in the meanings that are grasped and accepted, changes in the control of meaning mark off the great epochs in human history."[49]

Lonergan's postmodern analysis of the crisis of modernity reveals that it is rooted in the breakdown of the classical, logically oriented control of meaning still championed by the Enlightenment: classical and modern control of meaning is conceived in terms of a universal fixed for all time; postmodern control of meaning considers controls *as themselves involved in an ongoing process*.[50]

Contemporary anti-foundationalists, deconstructionists, genealogists, relativists, and nihilists deny that whatever controls may be involved in historical process can still possess any normativity; in this denial, they perhaps

unwittingly share the classicist mindset's assumptions about the control of meaning: if it is not a universal, fixed, atemporal, and absolutely necessary, then it cannot be normative. For Lonergan, in contrast, the ultimate set of operations revealed by method disclose exigencies that are immanent, operative, and normative *within* the process of human historical becoming; they are transhistorical and transcultural.

In a similar fashion, Lonergan underlines how theology emerged within the cultural superstructure of the West to perform the sapiential role of the control of meaning: *sapientis est ordinare*. An Aquinas, operating theoretically within the framework of the classical control of meaning, was able to differentiate the theological task into *lectio*, *disputatio*, and *praedicatio*. Lonergan's historically minded conception of theology discriminates eight functional specialties in accord with the basic levels of human conscious operation:

empirical:	*experience*
intelligent:	*understanding*
rational:	*judgment*
responsible:	*deliberation*

1. research	8. communications
2. interpretation	7. systematics
3. history	6. doctrines
4. dialectic	5. foundations

The disciplines of positive theology complicate Thomas's *lectio* into the three tasks implied by historical interpretation and judgment: *research*, *interpretation*, and history. The two kinds of *disputatio* distinguished by Aquinas—the *via inventionis* establishing the teaching of the authoritative sources, and the speculative *via disciplinae* or *doctrinae*—become transformed into *doctrines* and *systematics*. *Praedicatio* becomes the grand collaborative task of *communications*, that is, communicating God's meanings and values to all societies and cultures.

However, there is nothing in Thomas's division that corresponds to Lonergan's *dialectic* and *foundations*. This is due in part to Lonergan's postmodern context. In his critique of modernity and transposition of the vast theological project of Thomas Aquinas, Lonergan had to move (in a way that Aquinas did not) beyond the hermeneutics of interiority as *cog-*

nitive to the hermeneutics of interiority as *practical* and *existential*.

When Lonergan wrote in the Introduction to *Insight* that "more than all else, the aim of the book is to issue an invitation to the personal, decisive act,"[51] he was implying that the "cognitional theoretic" question about what we do when we think we are knowing cannot be asked and answered in a sufficiently thoroughgoing way without eventually negotiating the practical and existential question about how we should live our lives. Self-appropriation requires practical re-orientation, and Lonergan eventually made explicit that radical changes in orientation are conversions. Doing justice to the conversions and the "vertical exercises of liberty"[52] required that Lonergan move expressly beyond the intelligent and rational levels of cognitive self-transcendence called forth by the notion of being to acknowledge the responsible level of real self-transcendence called forth by the transcendental notion of the good or of true values to which we respond with the whole of our being:

> On the topmost level of human consciousness the subject deliberates, evaluates, decides, controls, acts. At once he is practical and existential: practical inasmuch as he is concerned with concrete courses of action; existential inasmuch as control includes self-control, and the possibility of self-control involves responsibility for the effects of his actions on others and, more basically, on himself. The topmost level of human consciousness is conscience.[53]

Furthermore, Lonergan held that, because of the moral impotence caused by personal and social or "structural" sin, intellectual and moral conversion require a prior religious conversion that results from falling in love with God through the sending of the gift of the Spirit. The gift of God's love occurs at the topmost level of consciousness, "but it is this type of consciousness at its root, as brought to fulfillment, as having undergone conversion, as possessing a basis that may be . . . ever more ready to deliberate and evaluate and decide and act with the easy freedom of those that do all good because they are in love."[54] So Lonergan's hermeneutics of practical and existential interiority pinpoints the foundations of authentic versus unauthentic human living, and of philosophical and theological reflection on living, in the converted or unconverted horizons of concrete human subjects living together in traditions. Correlatively, the functional specialty of *dialectic* traces fundamental differences in the *de facto* outcomes of research, interpretation, and history to the presence or absence of religious, moral, or intellectual conversion in the people doing the work. And the functional specialty of *foundations* articulates the horizons of these persons as more or less converted in these diverse ways. People's horizons condition their selection of the truths by which they live (in *doctrines*) and the openness of their minds and hearts to the divine meanings and values in all their theoretical and practical implications (in *systematics* and *communications*). For Lonergan, therefore, the Christian community is enabled to exercise an integral control of meaning and value by means of a functionally specialized theology cooperating with the mission of the Spirit and the mission of the Incarnate Word in history in a healing and creative manner.

THE HUMAN GOOD AND HUMAN MORALITY

Lonergan's breakthrough to a hermeneutics of interiority as practical and existential grounds his move from the descriptive notion of the common good (appealed to by Aristotle and Aquinas) to his quite Thomist development of an explanatory notion of *the human good*.[55]

Both Aristotle and Thomas acknowledged the good as the object of indiscriminate desire—the totality of humankind's needs and wants (*id quod omnia appetunt*). All the things a person does to satisfy one's needs and to obtain what one wants—from the most simple hunger for food to the most sublime aspiration to see God—yield what Lonergan calls "particular goods."

Aquinas also conceived of the totality of the concrete relationships in the universe as an intelligible order grounded in the infinite wisdom of the Creator.[56] Similarly, correlative to one's potentiality to develop his or her human intelligence over time is the set of institutional frameworks, and of habits and skills, that at once integrate and make possible all of the society's particular goods as related to each other by what Lonergan calls the "good of order."

Just as the concrete order of the created universe is related to the freely creative God who is infinitely good, so there is such a thing as human liberty because no finite good can fully satisfy human yearning; so human freedom disposes of itself through reflection and judgment, deliberation and choice. For Lonergan the good of order as a product of human intelligence "lies outside the field of sensitive appetition" and "is in itself an object of human devotion." For example, individualism and socialism are "neither food nor drink . . . [but] constructions of human intelligence, possible systems for ordering the satisfaction of human desires."[57] Correlative to the *originative value* of human liberty, the third level of the human good in *Insight* emerges as *terminal value*, which is in the realm of deliberation and choice only when one becomes conscious of the good of order as a possible object of rational choice and asks: Is it worthwhile? In this context value is an instance of the intelligent and the reasonable. But Lonergan went on later to articulate a richer, more nuanced notion of value:

> In *Method* . . . [the distinct notion of the good] is intended in questions for deliberation. . . . It is aspired to in the intentional response of feeling to values. It is known in judgments of value made by a virtuous or authentic person with a good conscience. It is brought about by deciding and living up to one's decisions. Just as intelligence sublates sense, just as reasonableness sublates intelligence, so deliberation sublates and thereby unifies knowing and feeling.[58]

Note that for Lonergan deliberation's judgments of value sublate and so unify knowing and feeling, and so they are not, as John Finnis alleges, simply a matter of arbitrary feeling.[59] Lonergan explains that the

> prior opaque and luminous being is not static, fixed, determinate, once-for-all; it is precarious; and its being precarious is the possibility not only of a fall but also of fuller development. That development is open; the dynamism constitutive of our consciousness may be expressed in the imperatives: be intelligent, be reason-

able, be responsible; and the imperatives are unrestricted—they regard every inquiry, every judgment, every decision and choice.[60]

If the dynamism constitutive of consciousness is realized in fulfilling those imperatives, then we become ourselves in self-transcendence. For Lonergan, self-transcendence means just what it says, so that Lonergan can fully agree with Walter Davis when he says, "The self is not a substance one unearths by peeling away layers until one gets to the core, but an integrity one struggles to bring into existence."[61] Moreover, the framework of self-transcendence in this universe has an even more radically decentering or eccentric twist, because the concrete evolution of one's "prior opaque and luminous being" is swept up, in Lonergan's account, into a vertical finality that is at once possible, multivalent, obscure, and indeed, mysterious:

> Such vertical finality is another name for self-transcendence. By experience we attend to the other; by understanding we gradually construct our world; by judgment we discern its independence of ourselves; by deliberate and responsible freedom we move beyond merely self-regarding norms and make ourselves moral beings.[62]

Finnis forgets that, in Lonergan's words, "The disinterestedness of morality is fully compatible with the passionateness of being. For that passionateness has a dimension of its own: it underpins and accompanies and reaches beyond the subject as experientially, intelligently, rationally, morally conscious."[63] This passionateness of being, on the one hand, is the vertical finality that characterizes the emergent probability of the created universe:

> Its underpinning is the quasi-operator that presides over the transition from the neural to the psychic. It ushers into consciousness not only the demands of unconscious vitality but also the exigences of vertical finality. It obtrudes deficiency needs. In the self-actualizing subject it shapes the images that release insight; it recalls evidence that is being overlooked; it may embarrass wakefulness, as it disturbs sleep, with the spectre, the shock, the shame of misdeeds. As it channels into consciousness the feed-back of our aberrations and

our unfulfilled strivings, so for the Jungians it manifests its archetypes through symbols to preside over the genesis of the ego and to guide the individuation process from the ego to the self.[64]

On the other hand, in human development from below upward, the passionateness of being refers to consciousness as an immanent source of transcendence (Thomas's *lumen intellectus agentis*). More precisely, in the context of morality, it refers to the extension of our inexorable desire to know into the field of deliberate choices and human action, which is identical with the "fuller flowering of the same dynamic principle that now keeps us moving toward ever fuller realization of the good, of what is worthwhile."[65]

According to Lonergan, value as a transcendental notion "is what is intended in questions for deliberation just as the intelligible is intended in questions for intelligence."[66] This means that just as our spontaneous intention of intelligibility provides an inner norm for human acts of direct understanding, and one's spontaneous intention of truth provides an immanent norm for acts of reflective understanding and judgment, so also does the transcendental notion of value provide the intrinsic norm for judgments of value, decisions, and actions.

Because the transcendental notion of value is at work any time one asks whether a possible course of action is worthwhile, it functions as a criterion for the decisions and choices through which terminal values are realized. One has an inbuilt capacity to distinguish between true and false values, between the truly good and mere satisfactions. As objects of possible choice, the truly good regards particular goods that are in harmony with the good of order, and ultimately with the intelligible order of the created universe. Consequently, values apprehended by feelings as intentional responses are ordered objectively and hierarchically into the *vital values* of health and welfare; the *social values* of a community well-ordered technologically, economically, and politically; the *cultural values* embodied in education, science, scholarship, the humanities, the arts, philosophy, and theology; and the *religious values* integral to living in the presence of an ultimate mystery of love and awe.[67] By freely choosing terminal values, one not only acts to meet common needs, but one also constitutes oneself as an originating value, since "implicitly or explicitly, they modify our habitual willingness, or effective orientation in the universe and so our contribution to the dialectical process of progress or decline."[68]

THE DIALECTIC OF HISTORY AND THE PROCESS OF REDEMPTION

History for Lonergan is part of the unfolding of the emergent probability of the created universe.[69] By the fact of evil that unfolding is a dialectic of progress and decline. Basic sin for Lonergan is the failure of human beings to act in a way that is consistently intelligent, reasonable, and responsible.[70] Moral evil is ultimately a matter not just of moral renunciation but of moral impotence—Lonergan's restatement of Thomas's teaching (Ia IIae, q. 109) that human beings cannot consistently avoid mortal sin without divine grace.[71] The concrete outcome of moral impotence and moral evil is the negation of the human good: the statistical phenomenon of sin and crime on the level of particular goods; structural evils in technology, economy, polity, the educational system, the arts, in organized religions, and the like, on the level of the good of order. The pervasive individual rationalizations and collective cover stories and ideologies that furnish alibis for the ongoing human refusal of rational self-consciousness result from moral impotence on the level of originating and terminal values. Concretely, then, doing good is usually a matter of overcoming inauthenticity and evil within ourselves and in our world.

According to Christian teaching as explained by Thomas Aquinas, however, because of moral impotence the solution for the "reign of sin" is absolutely supernatural,[72] utterly beyond the horizon of human knowledge and choice. The high point of vertical finality in history, therefore, is the pure instance of grace that concretely enables the contingent assumption by the Divine Word of the particular human nature in the Jew, Jesus of Nazareth.[73] The Word Incarnate's dying to rise again reveals the law of the cross by which the historical solidarity "in Christ Jesus" moves from sin through death to eternal life. Human beings are redeemed and enabled to live lives of self-sacrificial love, hope, and faith by the twofold historical mission of the external Word in Jesus and of the internal gift of God's love "poured out into our hearts by the Holy Spirit that is given to us" (Rom 5:5).[74] Such redemption happens in time in order to reverse the dialectical decline brought about by human evil or sin. Lonergan expressed the usual way this redemption is mediated to most people in history as follows:

> There [vertical finality] is the topmost quasi-operator that by intersubjectivity prepares, by solidarity entices, by falling in love establishes us as members of community. Within each individual vertical finality heads for self-transcendence. In an aggregate of self-transcending individuals there is the significant coincidental manifold in which can emerge a new creation. Possibility yields to fact and fact bears witness to its originality and power in the fidelity that makes families, in the loyalty that makes peoples, in the faith that makes religions.[75]

This quotation makes clear that human fulfillment comes not in our capacity to exercise dominative control in a context of disoriented freedom but in conversational care, and indeed, appreciative love for God and the universe as God's cosmic Word. The implications of this postmodern view of experience for the Christian doctrines of creation, redemption, Trinity, and the transformed ethical life that these doctrines imply have not been spelled out, but might be rather evident.

THE WAY OF GIFT AND THE WAY OF ACHIEVEMENT

About the interplay of the two ways in human development Lonergan wrote:

> The structure of human development is twofold. The chronologically prior phase is from above downwards. Children are born into a cradling environment of love. By a long and slow process of socialization, acculturation, education they are transferred from their initial world of immediacy into the local variety of the world mediated by meaning and motivated by values. Basically, the process rests

on trust and belief. But as it proceeds more and more there develops the capacity to raise questions and to be satisfied or dissatisfied with answers. Such is the spontaneous and fundamental process of teaching and learning common to all. It is at once intelligent and reasonable and responsible.[76]

A crucial upshot of a correct analysis of the postmodern notion of consciousness as experience is that there is nothing in our consciousnesses that has not been, in a precise sense, given to people, including consciousness itself.

As for handing on the tradition ourselves, Lonergan wrote:

> [T]he handing on of development . . . works from above downwards; it begins in the affectivity of the infant, the child, the son, the pupil, the follower. On affectivity rests the apprehension of values; on the apprehension of values rests belief; on belief follows the growth in understanding of one who has found a genuine teacher and has been initiated into the study of the masters of the past. Then, to confirm one's growth in understanding comes experience made mature and perceptive by one's developed understanding and with experiential confirmation the inverse process may set in.[77]

This description unintentionally portrays the enactment of the hermeneutic circle in Lonergan's life, with Thomas Aquinas as the crucial "master of the past."

In his final years all Lonergan had learned from Thomas about operative grace—especially the grace of conversion—finally meshed with all he had learned from him about the structured dynamism of human knowledge. Then he was able to thematize fully the two complementary and mutually mediating rhythms of human development.[78] The healing vector moves from above downward, beginning with the God-given dynamic state of being-in-love with God. That state flowers into faith as the eyes of being-in-love with God, which motivates people to believe the truths by which they live, to evaluate in light of love's transvaluation of feelings as intentional responses, to discern and judge, understand and attend with contemplative, prayerful serenity. The creative vector moves from below upward by attending and imagining, understanding and formulating, reflecting and judging, deliberating, deciding, believing, and loving. Thus, the rhythm of human development is marked by an interplay of a way of heritage (or gift or tradition) and a way of achievement. This is the concrete meaning of the hermeneutic circle.

CONCLUSION

Lonergan's ideas on theology and method are the rich outcome of a complex hermeneutical exchange with Thomas Aquinas that involved a hermeneutics of theory, of interiority as cognitive, and of interiority as practical and existential. If Christian ethics today is a part of theology as mediating between a cultural matrix and the significance and role of a religion in that matrix, its relation to Thomas Aquinas cannot simply be that of an authoritative quarry. If it is to integrate into itself the radical postmodern critique of modernity required to operate "on the level of our times," it would be well to negotiate the dimensions of theory, cognitive interiority, and practical and existential interiority that perhaps only a person who had been profoundly changed by encountering Thomas Aquinas could have thematized adequately. For Lonergan, method relieves average persons from the need to be geniuses in their creative work; but it only deepens the demand for personal and communal authenticity.

Notes

[1]*Die Legitimität der Neuzeit* (Frankfurt am Main: Suhrkamp, 1966). English trans.: *The Legitimacy of the Modern Age*, trans. Robert M. Wallace (Cambridge, MA: MIT Press, 1985).

[2]Bernard J. F. Lonergan, S.J., *Method in Theology* (New York: Herder and Herder, 1972), 247.

[3]Bernard J. F. Lonergan, S.J., "Theology in its New Context," in *A Second Collection*, ed. William F. J. Ryan, S.J., and Bernard J. Tyrrell, S.J. (Philadelphia: Westminster, 1974), 55–67 at 62.

[4]Lonergan, *Method*, xi.

[5]Lonergan, "Theology in its New Context," 58.

[6]Bernard J. F. Lonergan, S.J., *Insight: A Study of Human Understanding* (New York: Philosophical Library, 1957), 747.

[7]Lonergan, *Insight*, 748.

[8]Bernard J. F. Lonergan, S.J., *Grace and Freedom: Operative Grace in the Thought of St. Thomas Aquinas*,

ed. J. Patout Burns (London: Darton, Longman, and Todd, 1971).

[9]Lonergan, *Insight*, 744.

[10]Bernard Lonergan, "The Response of the Jesuit as Priest and Apostle in the Modern World,"in *A Second Collection*, 165–87 at 183.

[11]Bernard Lonergan, *Collection: Papers by Bernard Lonergan*, ed. F. E. Crowe, S.J. (New York: Herder and Herder, 1967), 151. Leo's program was laid out in Pope Leo XIII, *On Christian Philosophy (Aeterni Patris*, 4 Aug. 1879) in Etienne Gilson, ed., *The Church Speaks to the Modern World: The Social Teachings of Leo XIII* (Garden City, NY: Doubleday, 1954), 31–54.

[12]Lonergan, *Method*, 247.

[13]Bernard Lonergan, "Theology in its New Context," 64.

[14]"[sapientiae] est ordinare omnes [virtutes]."

[15]For a sample of Lonergan's appropriation of Piaget's developmental psychology, see; "Topics in Education: The Cincinnati Lectures in 1959 on Philosophy of Education," in *Collected Works of Bernard Lonergan*, vol. 10, ed. Robert M. Doran and Frederick E. Crowe (Toronto: University of Toronto Press, 1993), 193–207.

[16]Bernard Lonergan, "An Interview with Fr. Bernard Lonergan, S.J.," ed. Philip McShane, *A Second Collection*, 209–30, 212.

[17]On "notional" and "real" assent, see John Henry Cardinal Newman, *Grammar of Assent* (Garden City, NY: Doubleday, 1955), chap. 4.

[18]See Bernard Lonergan, *De constitutione Christi ontologica et psychologica* (Rome: Gregorian University Press, 1956), 83–99.

[19]Bernard Lonergan, "Metaphysics as Horizon," *Collection*, 202–20, 206.

[20]Bernard Lonergan, "*Existenz* and *Aggiornamento*," *Collection*, 240–51, 248.

[21]Ibid., 248.

[22]Ibid.

[23]Ibid., 248–49.

[24]Lonergan, "Prologomena to the Study of Religious Consciousness of Our Time," in *A Third Collection: Papers by Bernard J. F. Lonergan*, ed. Frederick E. Crowe (New York: Paulist, 1985), 55–73, 58.

[25]Lonergan, "Christ as Subject: A Reply," *Collection*, 164–97, 178–80.

[26]Ibid., 184.

[27]Jürgen Habermas, *The Philosophical Discourse of Modernity*, trans. Frederick G. Lawrence (Cambridge, MA: MIT Press, 1987), 296.

[28]Lonergan, *Collection*, 186.

[29]Habermas, *Philosophical Discourse of Modernity*, 298.

[30]This refers to a series of articles by Bernard Lonergan that appeared in *Theological Studies*, vols. 7–10 (1946–1949) titled, "The Concept of *Verbum*

in the Writings of St. Thomas"; now republished as *Verbum: Word and Idea in Aquinas*, ed. Frederick E. Crowe, S.J., and Robert M. Doran, *Collected Works of Bernard Lonergan* 2 (Toronto: University of Toronto Press, 1997).

[31]This refers to Bernard Lonergan's reworked doctoral thesis published in installments in 1941–1942 in *Theological Studies*, vols. 2–3, under the title, "St. Thomas's Thought on *Gratia Operans*," reedited and published as *Grace and Freedom* (see n. 7 above).

[32]Lonergan, *Insight*, xix.

[33]Ibid., 27.

[34]Ibid., 19.

[35]Lonergan, *Method*, 40–243.

[36]Lonergan, "Openness and Religious Experience," in *Collection*, 198–201.

[37]Bernard Lonergan, *De deo trino: pars dogmatica* (Rome: Gregorian University Press, 1964), n. 10; 10–11.

[38]See Lonergan, *Method in Theology*, 337, where he paraphrases the famous passage from Thomas Aquinas at *Quodlibet* IV, q. 9, a. 3, [18] (Marietti, 83).

[39]Lonergan, *Verbum*, 46.

[40]Lonergan, *Insight*, 748.

[41]"Interiority" refers to internal experience, or the data of consciousness as distinct from the data of sense. See below on the postmodern notion of consciousness as experience as opposed to consciousness as perception.

[42]"anima humana intelligit seipsam per suum intelligere, quod est actus proprius eius, perfecte demonstrans virtutem eius et naturam."

[43]See Lonergan, "Isomorphism of Thomist and Scientific Thought," in *Collection*, 142–51, 149.

[44]Lonergan, *Insight*, xxviii, 748.

[45]Lonergan, *Verbum*, xiii.

[46]Lonergan is unique in this nomenclature: where he distinguishes between cognitional theory as a *quaestio facti* prior to epistemology as a *quaestio juris*, most others use the terms cognitional theory and epistemology interchangeably and only in the sense of the latter. This may be related to the fact that the German term for epistemology is *Erkenntnistheorie*.

[47]Lonergan, "Cognitional Structure," in *Collection*, 221–39, 231.

[48]Lonergan, *Method*, 233.

[49]Lonergan, "Dimensions of Meaning," in *Collection*, 252–67, 255–26.

[50]Lonergan, *Method*, 29.

[51]Lonergan, *Insight*, xix.

[52]On the distinction between horizontal and vertical exercises of liberty, see Lonergan, *Method*, 40, 122, 237–38, 240, 269.

[53]Lonergan, "The Response of the Jesuit," in *A Second Collection*, 168.

[54]Ibid., 173.

[55]Lonergan returned (with modifications) to the notion of the human good repeatedly. The main references are: *Insight*, 212–14, 596–98, 605–7; "The Role of a Catholic University in the Modern World," 114–20, 115–16; for the fullest development, *Topics in Education*, in *Collected Works of Bernard Lonergan*, vol. 10, ed. R. M. Doran and Frederick E. Crowe, S.J. (Toronto: University of Toronto, 1993), 26–157; see also, *Method in Theology*, 47–52, 359.

[56]See John H. Wright, S.J., *The Order of the Universe in the Theology of St. Thomas Aquinas*. Analecta Gregoriana LXXXIX, Series Facultatis Theologicae (Rome: Gregorian University, 1957); see also Bernard Lonergan, "The Natural Desire to See God," *Collection*, 84–95, 93,

[57]Lonergan, *Insight*, 597.

[58]Bernard Lonergan, "*Insight* Revisited," in *A Second Collection*, 263–78, 277.

[59]John Finnis, *Fundamentals of Ethics* (Washington, DC: Georgetown University, 1983), 32, 42–45, 49, 54.

[60]Lonergan, "*Existenz* and *Aggiornamento*," 249.

[61]Walter A. Davis, *Inwardness and Existence: Subjectivity in/and Hegel, Heidegger, Marx, and Freud* (Madison: University of Wisconsin Press, 1989), 105.

[62]Bernard Lonergan, "Mission and Spirit," in *A Third Collection*, 23–34 at 28.

[63]Lonergan, "Mission and Spirit," 29.

[64]Ibid., 29-30.

[65]Lonergan, "The Subject," in *A Second Collection*, 24.

[66]Ibid., 34.

[67]On values see, Lonergan, *Method in Theology*, chap. 2

[68]See Walter E. Conn, "Bernard Lonergan on Value," *The Thomist* 40 (1975): 251.

[69]On "emergent probability," see Lonergan, *Insight*, 123–28, 132–34, 209–11, 259–62, 264–66, 462, 698.

[70]Ibid., 666–68.

[71]Ibid., 627–30; on "psychological continuity," see also *Grace and Freedom* on "psychological continuity," 48–53, 51n., 55, 57, 99.

[72]On the "theorem of the supernatural," see *Grace and Freedom*, 11n., 13–19, 21, 47, 52; on the "absolutely supernatural," see *Insight*, 725-729, 697. On Lonergan's overall retrieval of Thomas Aquinas on grace, see J. Michael Stebbins, *The Divine Initiative: Grace, World Order, and Human Freedom in the Early Writings of Bernard Lonergan* (Toronto: University of Toronto Press, 1995).

[73]Bernard Lonergan, *De verbo incarnato*, 3d ed. (Rome: Gregorian University Press, 1964).

[74]On the divine missions, see the last theses of Bernard Lonergan's *De deo trino*, Vol. 1 (2d ed.)

and Vol. 2 (3d ed.) (Rome: Gregorian University, 1964).

[75]Lonergan, "Mission and Spirit," in *A Second Collection*, 30.

[76]Lonergan, "Theology and Praxis," in *A Third Collection*, 184–201, 196–97.

[77]Lonergan, "Natural Right and Historical Mindedness," in *A Third Collection*, 169–83, 181.

[78]See, for instance, the essay, "Healing and Creating in History," in *A Third Collection*, 100–109.

Selected Further Reading

Barden, Garrett. *After Principles*. Notre Dame, IN: University of Notre Dame Press, 1980.

Byrne, Patrick H. "The Thomist Sources of Lonergan's Dynamic World-View," *The Thomist* 46 (1982): 108–45.

———. "The Fabric of Lonergan's Thought," in *Lonergan Workshop* (Missoula, MT: Scholars Press, 1986), 6:1–84.

———. *Analysis and Science in Aristotle*. Albany: State University Press of New York, 1997.

Conn, Walter. *Conscience: Development and Self-Transcendence*. Birmingham, AL: Religious Education, 1981.

———. *Christian Conversion: A Developmental Interpretation of Autonomy and Surrender*. New York: Paulist, 1986.

———. *The Desiring Self: Rooting Pastoral Counseling and Spiritual Direction in Self-Transcendence*. New York: Paulist, 1998.

Crowe, Frederick E., S.J. *The Lonergan Enterprise*. Cambridge, MA: Cowley, 1980.

———. *Appropriating the Lonergan Idea*. Ed. Michael Vertin. Washington, DC: Catholic University of America Press, 1989.

———. *Lonergan*. Outstanding Christian Thinkers Series. Ed. Brian Davies, O.P. Collegeville, MN: Liturgical, 1992.

Doran, Robert M. *Theology and the Dialectics of History*. Toronto: University of Toronto Press, 1990.

Dunne, Tad. *Lonergan and Spirituality: Towards a Spiritual Integration*. Chicago: Loyola University Press, 1985.

Fallon, Timothy P., and Philip Boo Riley. *Religion and Culture: Essays in Honor of Bernard Lonergan, S.J.* Albany: State University of New York Press, 1987.

———. *Religion in Context: Recent Studies in Lonergan*. Lanham, MD: University of America Press, 1988.

Flanagan, Joseph, S.J. *Quest for Self-Knowledge: An Essay in Lonergan's Philosophy*. Toronto: University of Toronto Press, 1997.

Lamb, Matthew L. *Creativity and Method: Essays in Honor of Bernard Lonergan*. Milwaukee: Marquette University Press, 1981.

Lawrence, Frederick G. "The Fragility of Consciousness: Lonergan and the Postmodern Concern for the Other," *Theological Studies* 54 (1993): 55–94.

———. "Athens and Jerusalem: The Contemporary Problematic of Faith and Reason," *Gregorianum* 90 (1999): 223–44.

Liddy, Richard. *Transforming Light: Intellectual Conversion in the Early Lonergan*. Collegeville, MN: Liturgical, 1993.

Lonergan, Bernard, S.J. *De constitutione Christi ontologica et psychologica supplementum confecit Bernardus Lonergan, S.J.* Rome: Gregorian University Press, 1956.

———. *Insight: A Study of Human Understanding*. London: Longmans, Green, and Co.: New York: Philosophical Library, 1957. Also in *Collected Works of Bernard Lonergan*, Vol 5. Ed. Frederick E. Crowe, S.J., and Robert M. Doran. Toronto: University of Toronto Press, 1992.

———. *Divinarum personarum conceptionem analogicam evolvit Bernardus Lonergan, S.J.* Rome: Gregorian University Press, 1957.

———. *De deo trino. Pars analytica*. Rome: Gregorian University Press, 1961.

———. *De deo trino*. Vols. 1 (2d ed.), 2 (3rd ed.). Rome: Gregorian University Press, 1964.

———. *De verbo incarnato* (3d ed.) Rome: Gregorian University Press, 1964.

———. *Collection: Papers by Bernard Lonergan, S.J.* Ed. Frederick E. Crowe, S.J. New York: Herder and Herder, 1967; also in *Collected Works of Bernard Lonergan*, Vol. 4. Ed. Frederick E. Crowe, S.J., and Robert M. Doran. Toronto: University of Toronto Press, 1988.

———. *Verbum: Word and Idea in Aquinas*. Ed. David B. Burrell. Notre Dame, IN: University of Notre Dame, 1967. Also in *Collected Works of Bernard Lonergan*, Vol. 2. Ed. Frederick E. Crowe, S.J., and Robert M. Doran. Toronto: University of Toronto Press, 1997.

———. *Grace and Freedom: Operative Grace in the Thought of St. Thomas Aquinas*. Ed. J. Patout Burns. London: Darton, Longman and Todd; New York: Herder and Herder, 1971.

———. *Method in Theology*. London: Darton, Longman and Todd; New York: Herder and Herder, 1972.

———. *Philosophy of God, and Theology: The Relationship between Philosophy of God and the Functional Specialty, Systematics*. London: Darton, Longman and Todd; New York: Herder and Herder, 1973.

———. *A Second Collection: Papers by Bernard J. F. Lonergan, S.J.* Ed. William F. J. Ryan, S.J., and Bernard J. Tyrrell, S.J. London: Darton, Longman and Todd; Philadelphia: Westminster Press, 1974; Toronto: University of Toronto Press, 1996.

———. *Understanding and Being. Halifax Lectures on Insight*. Ed. Elizabeth A. Morelli and Mark D. Morelli. New York and Toronto: Edwin Mellen, 1980. Also in *Collected Works of Bernard Lonergan*, Vol. 5. Revised and augmented by Frederick E. Crowe, S.J., with E. A. Morelli, M. D. Morelli, R. M. Doran, and T. V. Daly. Toronto: University of Toronto, 1990.

———. *A Third Collection: Papers by Bernard J. F. Lonergan, S.J.* Ed. Frederick E. Crowe, S.J. New York: Paulist, 1985.

———. *Topics in Education. Cincinnati Lectures of 1959 on the Philosophy of Education* in *Collected Works*, Vol. 10. Ed. Robert M. Doran and Frederick E. Crowe, S.J. Toronto: University of Toronto Press, 1993.

———. *Philosophical and Theological Papers 1958–1964*. Ed. Robert C. Croken, Frederick E. Crowe, S.J., and Robert M. Doran. Toronto: University of Toronto, 1996.

McShane, Philip. *Lonergan's Challenge to the University and the Economy*. Washington, DC: University Press of America, 1980.

Melchin, Kenneth R. *History, Ethics and Emergent Probability*. Lanham, MD: University Press of America, 1987.

———. *Living with Other People: An Introduction to Christian Ethics Based on Bernard Lonergan*. Saint Paul University Series in Ethics. Collegeville, MN: Liturgical, 1998.

Meynell, Hugo A. *An Introduction to the Philosophy of Bernard Lonergan*, 2d ed. Toronto: University of Toronto Press, 1991.

———. *Redirecting Philosophy: Reflections on the Nature of Knowledge from Plato to Lonergan*. Toronto: University of Toronto Press, 1998.

Morelli, Mark D. and Elizabeth A. *The Lonergan Reader*. Toronto: University of Toronto Press, 1997.

Rota, Giovanni. *"Persona" e "Natura" nell'Itinerario Speculativo di Bernard J.F. Lonergan, S.J.* Rome: Pontificio Seminario Lombardo, 1998.

Stebbins, J. Michael. *The Divine Initiative: Grace, World Order, and Human Freedom in the Early Writings of Bernard Lonergan*. Toronto: University of Toronto Press, 1995.

Contributors

Serge-Thomas Bonino, O.P. has been director of *Revue thomiste* and the Institut Saint-Thomas d'Aquin since 1991. After completing doctorates in philosophy (Poitiers) and theology (Fribourg), he taught the history of medieval doctrines in the Faculty of Philosophy at the Université catholique de Toulouse (where he is dean), and dogmatic theology at the Centre d'études des dominicains de Toulouse (where he is director). His publications include his dissertation on St. Thomas's De veritate and numerous articles on St. Thomas and the history of Thomism.

Leonard E. Boyle, O.P. (1923–99) entered the Dominican order in 1943 and was ordained priest in 1949. His studies at Oxford (1947– 56) culminated with a doctoral thesis on a fourteenth-century English parish priest, William of Pagula. He then traveled to Rome, where he did research in the Secret Vatican Archives and taught at the Angelicum. He taught at the Pontifical Institute of Medieval Studies in Toronto and he was the Prefect of the Biblioteca Apostolica Vaticana and President of the Leonine Commission for the editions of the works of St. Thomas Aquinas. At the end of his career, he was honored by his former students and colleagues with the publication of numerous volumes.

Stephen F. Brown is professor of theology and director of the Institute of Medieval Philosophy and Theology at Boston College. He received his doctorate at the University of Louvain in 1964. He has taught at Siena College, Saint Bonaventure University, the University of the South, and came to Boston College in 1979. He is editor of five volumes of the *Opera omnia* of William of Ockham and of numerous articles on Ockham's sources and critics. He is now studying the origins and development of theology as a scientific discipline in the Middle Ages. He has written numerous publications on St. Thomas.

Diana Fritz Cates is associate professor of ethics in the School of Religion at The University of Iowa. She received her doctorate from Brown University in 1990. Her publications include *Choosing to Feel: Virtue, Friendship, and Compassion for Friends* (University of Notre Dame Press, 1997), numerous journal articles and chapters in edited volumes, and she has co-edited with Paul Lauritzen *Medicine and the Ethics of Care*, a collection of original essays in medical ethics (Georgetown University Press, 2001).

Romanus Cessario, O.P., is currently professor of systematic theology at St. John's Seminary, Brighton, Massachusetts. He was ordained for the Eastern Province of the Dominicans in 1971. In 1972, he received a licentiate in sacred theology at the Pontifical Faculty of the Immaculate Conception in Washington. He completed doctoral studies in theology at the University of Fribourg (Switzerland), and published *The Godly Image* (St. Bede's Publications, 1990). He has many publications, and among them is a collection of essays on the fifteenth-century Dominican theologian John Capreolus co-edited with Guy Bedouelle and Kevin White. His most recent publications are an edition of Capreolus's *On the Virtues* and the *Introduction to Moral Theology*.

David M. Gallagher received his doctorate at The Catholic University of America in 1989. He was a member of the faculty of the School of Philosophy at The Catholic University of America from 1988 to 1999. He has been a research fellow at the Thomas Institut at the University of Cologne (1993–94) and at the Center for the Philosophy of Religion at the University of Notre Dame (1998). His research and publications have focused on the ethics of Thomas Aquinas, especially the role of the will and of love. He is presently working on a book on the role of love in the ethics of Thomas Aquinas.

Raphael Gallagher, C.SS.R., is a Redemptorist from Ireland. He is currently an Invited Professor at the Alphonsian Academy in Rome. After graduating with a B.A. (Arts) from the National University of Ireland at Galway, he continued with his seminary training in Galway and Dublin. His postgraduate studies were at the University of Bonn (Germany) and the Alphonsian Academy (Rome), where he was awarded a doctor of sacred theology degree in 1977. Among his recent publications is his contribution to the moral theology section in *Alphonsus de Liguori: Selected Writings* (Paulist Press, 1999).

Pamela M. Hall is currently an associate professor of philosophy and women's studies and the Massee-Martin/NEH Distinguished Teaching Professor at Emory University. She received her doctorate in philosophy from Vanderbilt University. She has authored *Narrative and the Natural Law: An Interpretation of Thomistic Ethics* (University of Notre Dame Press, 1994), and has written numerous journal articles.

Thomas S. Hibbs is an associate professor of philosophy at Boston College. He received his doctorate from the University of Notre Dame in 1987. He is the author of *Dialectic and Narrative in Aquinas: An Interpretation of the Summa Contra Gentiles* (University of Notre Dame Press, 1995), and editor of *Aquinas on Human Nature* (Hackett Press, 1999). He is also the author of numerous articles on Aquinas and contemporary ethics.

Ludger Honnefelder is a professor of philosophy at the University of Bonn. He is the Director of the Albertus-Magnus-Institute (Bonn) and member of the board of the Institute of Science and Ethics at Bonn. In 1992,

he was appointed member of the North Rhine-Westphalian Academy of Sciences. He has written a number of books and articles on metaphysics, ethics, and the history of medieval philosophy, and is coeditor of *John Duns Scotus: Metaphysics and Ethics* (Leiden: E. J. Brill, 1996).

R. E. Houser is an associate professor of philosophy in the Center for Thomistic Studies at the University of St. Thomas, Houston, Texas. He was educated at the University of Texas at Austin, the Pontifical Institute of Medieval Studies, and the University of Toronto. The author of numerous articles on ancient and medieval philosophy, he has edited *Medieval Masters: Essays in Memory of Msgr. E. A. Synan* (Center for Thomistic Studies/University of Notre Dame Press, 1999) and *Laudemus viros gloriosos: Essays in Honor of Armand Augustine Maurer C.S.B.* (University of Notre Dame Press, forthcoming). He is the author and translator of *The Cardinal Virtues: Aquinas, Albert, and Philip the Chancellor* (Pontifical Institute of Medieval Studies, forthcoming).

James F. Keenan, S.J., is a professor of moral theology at Weston Jesuit School of Theology in Cambridge, Massachusetts. He received his licentiate in sacred theology and doctor of sacred theology degrees from the Gregorian University in Rome. He has numerous published articles and among the books he has written are *Goodness and Rightness in Thomas Aquinas's Summa Theologiae* (Georgetown University Press, 1992) and *Virtues for Ordinary Christians* (Sheed and Ward, 1996).

Bonnie Kent is an associate professor of philosophy at the University of California, Irvine. She received her doctorate from Columbia University in 1984, and she has held visiting scholarships at Harvard and the University of St. Andrews, as well as visiting teaching appointments at The Massachusetts Institute of Technology, New York University, and the University of Oslo. Her publications include *Virtues of the Will: The Transformation of Ethics in the Late Thirteenth Century* (Catholic University of America Press, 1995) as well as many contributions to edited volumes.

Theo Kobusch is professor of philosophy (Philosophisch-Theologische Grenzfragen) at Ruhr-Universität Bochum. He received his doctorate from the University of Giessen in 1976 and, in 1982, his Habilitation in philosophy in Tübingen. He is coeditor of the *Historische Wörterbuch der Philosophie*. He has published a wide range of studies on the history of philosophy, focusing on antiquity and the Middle Ages.

Clifford G. Kossel, S.J., is a professor emeritus of philosophy at Gonzaga University, Spokane, Washington, where he has taught courses in philosophy for over forty years. He received his doctorate from the University of Toronto. A past president of the Jesuit Philosophical Association, he was cofounder of the American edition of *Communio, International Catholic Review* and served on its editorial board for many years. He has published articles on the metaphysics and ethics of Aquinas in various journals.

Frederick G. Lawrence teaches in the Theology Department at Boston College. In 1963, he was sent to study theology with Bernard Lonergan at the Gregorian University in Rome. He studied for his doctorate at the University of Basel (1966–71). He has written on Gadamer, Lonergan, Heidegger, Voegelin, Strauss, Metz, and currents of continental thought labeled "postmodern." His recent publications include "The Fragility of Consciousness: Lonergan and the Postmodern Concern for the Other," *Theological Studies*; "The Seriousness of Play: Gadamer's Hermenuetics as a Resource for Christian Mission," in *From One Medium to Another* (Sheed and Ward, 1997); and "Athens and Jerusalem: The Contemporary Problematic of Faith and Reason," *Gregorianum*.

Thomas F. O'Meara, O.P., is the William K. Warren Professor of Theology at the University of Notre Dame. Prior to his twenty years at Notre Dame, he taught at Aquinas Institute of Theology, Weston College of Theology, and the Seminary of Sts. Peter and Paul in Ibadan, Nigeria. His doctoral studies were with Heinrich Fries and Karl Rahner. A past president of the Catholic Theological Society of America, his books include two vol-

umes on the history of German Catholic theology in the nineteenth century, *Theology of Ministry*, rev. ed. (Paulist Press, 1999), and *Thomas Aquinas Theologian* (University of Notre Dame Press, 1997).

Servais-Théodore Pinckaers, O.P., received his license in theology at the Dominican Studium at La Sarte, Huy (Belgium) in 1950 and his doctorate in theology at the Angelicum in Rome in 1952. He taught moral theology at La Sarte from 1952 to 1965; then, after eight years of pastoral work in Liege, he returned to academic theology. He has been teaching at the University of Fribourg (Switzerland) since 1973, and, as a professor emeritus, he continues to research and write. His translated works include *The Sources of Christian Ethics* (Catholic University of America Press, 1995), and *The Pursuit of Happiness: Living the Beatitudes* (Alba House, 1998). He is currently preparing a study of St. Thomas's theology of happiness.

Stephen J. Pope is an associate professor of social ethics in the Theology Department of Boston College. He received his Ph.D. in theological ethics from the University of Chicago. He taught at the Saint Paul Seminary School of Divinity of the University of St. Thomas in St. Paul, Minnesota (1985–1988) before joining the Department of Theology at Boston College (1988–present), where he currently holds the position of associate professor. He published The *Evolution of Altruism and the Ordering of Love* (Georgetown University Press, 1994), and coedited, with Michael Himes, *Finding God in All Things: Essays in Honor of Michael J. Buckley, S.J.* (New York: Crossroad, 1996). He has published articles on love, justice, natural law, and evolutionary ethics in *Theological Studies, The Journal of Religion, Horizons, Zygon: The Journal of Religion and Science*, and elsewhere. He is currently working on a project concerned with the implications of human evolution for Christian ethics.

Jean Porter is John A. O'Brien Professor of Theology (Christian Ethics) at the University of Notre Dame. She received her doctorate from Yale University in 1984, and taught at Vanderbilt Divinity School from 1984 until she joined the faculty of Notre Dame in 1990.

She is the author of *The Recovery of Virtue: The Significance of Aquinas for Christian Ethics* (Westminster/JohnKnox Press, 1990), *Moral Action and Christian Ethics* (Cambridge University Press, 1995), and *Natural and Divine Law: Reclaiming the Tradition for Theological Ethics* (Novalis/Eerdmans Press, 1999).

Gregory M. Reichberg, senior researcher in ethics at the International Peace Research Institute, Oslo, received his doctorate from Emory University. He has been a member of the philosophy departments at Fordham University and The Catholic University of America. His work has concentrated on Thomas Aquinas, contemporary Thomism, and the ethics of war and peace. He has a long list of essays and journal articles. He is coeditor of *The Classics of Western Philosophy* (Blackwell, forthcoming), and the *Ethics of War and Peace at the Dawn of the New Millennium*, a special issue of the *Journal of Peace Research* (forthcoming).

Martin Rhonheimer is currently a professor of ethics and political philosophy at the School of Philosophy of the Pontifical University of the Holy Cross in Rome. He received his doctorate in 1997 and received ordination as a Catholic priest in 1983. In addition to many articles on ethics, action theory, and political philosophy, he is the author of a number of books, including *Natur als Grundlage der Moral* (Tyrolia, 1987), published in English as *Natural Law and Practical Reason: A Thomist View of Moral Autonomy* (Fordham University Press, 2000).

Eberhard Schockenhoff is professor of moral theology at the Albert-Ludwig University of Fribourg, to which he was called in 1994. He attained his doctorate in Tübingen with a work on Thomas Aquinas's ethics (*Matthias-Grünewald-Verlag*, 1987). From 1990 until 1994, he taught in the Faculty of Theology of the University of Regensburg. Other areas of focus for his research are in bioethics and his historical preoccupation with Thomas Aquinas into systematic studies on the problematic of ethical relativism and the grounding of norms.

Eileen Sweeney is currently an associate professor of philosophy at Boston College. She received her doctorate in philosophy from the University of Texas in 1986. She has written many published works on Aquinas's notions of science, reason, and methodology, as well as on his use of supposition theory, and views on theological language and analogy. She is currently completing a book on language use and theory in Augustine, Boethius, Anselm, Abelard, and Alan of Lille titled *The Exile of Language: Logic, Theology, and Poetry in Early Medieval Philosophy*.

Daniel Westberg was ordained in the Anglican Church of Canada, where he served in parish ministry for ten years. In 1988, he earned a doctorate at Oxford University in moral theology. Westberg has taught in the Department of Religious Studies at the University of Virginia, as well as in seminaries in Canada and the United States. He has published a number of articles in the area of natural law and moral psychology.

Kevin White is an assistant professor in the School of Philosophy at The Catholic University of America. He received his doctorate in philosophy from the University of Ottawa in 1986. As the recipient of a postdoctoral fellowship from the Social Sciences and Humanities Research Council of Canada, he traveled to Rome, where he spent three years working with the Leonine Commission and teaching at the Pontifical Beda College. He has published articles on metaphysical, psychological, and moral issues, and has edited a previously unpublished portion of Aquinas's commentary on Aristotle's *Meteora*. He is editor of *Hispanic Philosophy in the Age of Discovery* (Catholic University of America Press, 1997), and coeditor, with Guy Bedouelle and Romanus Cessario, O.P., of *Jean Capreolus en son temps [1380–1444]* (Editions du Cerf, 1997).

Georg Wieland is a professor for Philosophische Grundfragen der Theologie at the University of Tübingen. He received his doctorate from the University of Bochum in 1969, and his Habilitation in 1979 from the University of Bonn. He has written many contributions to the field of medieval philosophy, ethics, and anthropology.

Index

habitus. *See also* habits
 translation of, 116–17, 393–94, 406n80
Hall, Pamela M., 194–206, 416–17, 458
Hamm, B., 211–13
happiness, 32–33, 57–68
 achievement of, 63–64, 65–67
 actions and, 33, 62–63, 66, 67, 245
 in the afterlife, 118, 124–26
 angels and, 62, 66
 Aristotle on, 24–25, 32, 66, 118, 124, 245
 Augustine on, 118
 beatitude and, 63–64, 421
 Boethius on, 20
 Christ on, 24
 common good and, 324, 335n19
 complete, 65, 66, 406n75
 effects of, 64–65
 ends and, 59–61
 grace and, 421
 hope and, 64, 234–36
 intellect and, 65
 law and, 421
 morality of, 364, 371n58
 natural, 324
 perfect, 224, 225
 Pinckaers on, 364
 sources on, 24–25
 supernatural, 324
 temperance and, 326
 theoretical life and, 345
 ultimate end and, 393
 virtues and, 421
 will and, 62–63, 65
 worldly, 118, 124–26
Harak, G. Simon, 323, 337n67
Häring, Bernhard, 376
harm
 avoiding, 294
 bodily, 327, 335n28
 consequential, 432–34
 injustice and, 288, 291
 intention and, 160
 from self-defense, 413
hatred, 107, 108, 294
Hauerwas, Stanley, 416, 419
To Have or To Be? (Fromm), 164
health. *See also* illness
 alcoholic beverages and, 329
 sins and, 158
 the soul and, 335n28
 temperance and, 325, 326
 virtues and, 151–52
heaven, 126

Hebrews, Letter to the, 20, 221
Hegel, Georg, 439
Heinzmann, R., 207
Hektor, 309
hell, 238
heroism, 309–10, 312
heteronomy, 151
hexis. *See also* habits
 translation of, 116–17, 393–94, 406n80
Hibbs, Thomas S., 412–25, 458
Hinnebusch, William, 356
Hippo, Bishop of. *See* Augustine, Saint
Historia scholastica (Comestor), 3, 6, 226
history, 447, 448, 450–51
Hittinger, Russell, 415, 418
Hobbes, Thomas, 163, 167n35
Holy Spirit, 248–50, 256, 357, 370n19
homicide, 292
homo infirmus, 36
homosexuality, 332
honesty, 324
Honnefelder, Ludger, 299n15, 300n18, 426–36, 458
honor, 60, 224, 312
Honorius III, Pope, 1
honors, 291
Hoose, Bernard, 413, 414, 418
hope, 37–38, 232–43
 appetite and, 88n39, 233, 238
 Aristotle on, 234
 attention and, 111
 Augustine on, 236
 beatitude and, 234–35, 238, 242n28
 certitude of, 239, 240
 characteristics of, 232–33, 238–40
 charity and, 122, 237
 death of, 242n21
 vs. desire, 234
 experience and, 109–10
 vs. faith, 236, 237–38
 fear of, 239
 future good and, 233, 238, 240–41n2
 happiness and, 64, 234–36
 in hell, 238
 love and, 236–38
 vs. magnanimity, 234
 memory and, 238
 merit and, 213
 omnipotence and, 235, 236, 240
 perfection of, 234
 sins against, 239, 240
 theological, 234, 236, 242n21
 time and, 238–39

ceremonial precepts of, 36, 196–97,
198–99, 200–201, 203
charity and, 203
on Christ, 195, 199, 200
divine law and, 195, 203
end of, 201–2
fulfillment of, 202
God and, 201
grace and, 201
Jewish people and, 204n11
judicial precepts of, 196–97, 198, 199–201
limits of, 195
on morality, 199, 200, 205n33
natural law and, 195, 196, 197, 198, 201–3
New Law and, 194, 200, 201
revelation of, 195
on sins, 195
on virtues, 198
on worship, 198
O'Meara, Thomas F., 355–73, 421, 459
omnipotence, 235, 236, 240
Opera omnia (Thomas Aquinas), 438
opinion, 134, 145n19
opportunity, equality of, 396, 409–10n103
Optatam totius, 382
order. *See also* supernatural order
of actions, 78, 177, 211–13, 215n16
of charity, 254–55
common good of, 178
of faith, 232
freedom and, 392–93, 396, 405n70
good of, 449
of law, 49, 392
of life, 420
of reality, 227
Simon on, 392–93
in society, 394–95
teleology and, 182
ultimate end and, 211, 215n16
virtues and, 232, 400n29
Order of Friars Minor of St. Francis of Assisi, 349
Order of Preachers-in-General, 1
ordinatio rationalis, 49
ordination, 198
Origen, 363
original sin, 23, 157–58, 159, 164
Augustine on, 167n22
pride as, 162–63
result of, 158, 166n20
sources on, 35
Orvieto, 2–4
Osee, 386

oughts, 187n38
Oumansoff, Raïssa, 388, 400–401n33
overpopulation, 332
owed. *See* debt
ownership, 280, 282

P

pain, 107, 110–13
paradigm shifts, 379–80, 384n27
Pascal, Blaise, 151, 159
passions, 103–15. *See also* emotions
actions and, 105–6
antecedent, 106, 114n10
being and, 449–50
Cicero on, 104
concupiscible vs. irascible, 33
definition of, 103–4
evil of, 106
good and, 106, 113
human nature and, 105
intellect and, 106
movement of, 107, 114n16
natural law and, 176
object of, 108–9
reason and, 105, 106, 112–13
sense appetites and, 103, 108, 174, 186n32, 186n33
sources on, 24
types of, 106–9
virtues and, 416
will and, 69, 105, 106, 113, 119
Pastoral Constitution on the Church in the Modern World, 377, 379, 381–82
pastoral manuals, 1–2, 7, 375, 379, 382
paternal authority, 394
Patfoort, Albert, 357
pati, 103
patience, 308, 314–15
Patriarchs, 386
Paul, Saint
on charisms, 341
on charity, 122
ecstasy of, 344
on faith, 221–22, 223–24
on grace, 356
on grief, 314–15
Letter to the Ephesians, 22
Letter to the Romans, 356, 365
on love, 248–50
on obligation to God, 153–54
on patience, 314–15
on peace, 256

satisfactory, 157
  for sins, 154–57
  theory of, 294
purification, 200–201
purity, 330
pusillanimity, 311–12

Q

Quaestio disputata de virtutibus cardinalibus (Thomas Aquinas), 122
Quaestio disputata de virtutibus in communi (Thomas Aquinas), 136
Quaestiones de anima (Thomas Aquinas), 104
Quaestiones disputatae de malo (Thomas Aquinas), 74–75, 92, 262
Quaestiones disputatae de veritate (Thomas Aquinas)
  on choice, 73
  on human limits, 225
  on passions, 103
  on perfection, 262
  on science, 141
  Scriptum super Sententiis and, 5
  on *synderesis*, 289
  on truth, 142–43
  on will, 75
Quaestiones Quodlibetales (Thomas Aquinas), 246
quality, habits as, 117
questions
  on God, 445, 446
  Lonergan on, 439, 442, 445–46
  role of, 12, 13
quidam, 18, 19, 20
Quodlibet. See Quaestiones Quodlibetales

R

Rachel, wife of Jacob, 345
Rahner, Karl, 358, 443
rape, 332–33
rapture, 346
Ratio studiorum, 2–3
rational appetite, 174
  will and, 70–71, 72–73, 74, 76
rational beings. *See* persons
rationalism, 25, 26
Ratzinger, Joseph, 377
Rawls, John, *A Theory of Justice*, 277, 415
Raymund of Pennafort. *See also Summa de casibus*
  John of Freiburg and, 12, 13
  on *Sentences*, 6
  as a source, 2, 3, 6, 7, 11

readiness, qualitative, 140, 147n50
reality, 227, 445, 447
realization, 427
reason. *See also* practical reason; *synderesis*
  acquired, 63
  actions and, 91, 170, 176–77, 387, 427, 434
  anger and, 110
  appetite and, 177, 188n51
  Aristotle on, 151, 163
  authority of, 20
  in autonomy, 151
  choice and, 393
  definition of, 185n25
  delight and, 112
  ends and, 58, 308
  faith and, 225–27
  good and, 307–8
  human law and, 399n23
  ignorance and, 176
  intellect and, 25–26, 185n25
  justice and, 284
  law and, 35–36, 170
  light of, 209–10, 215n16
  natural inclination and, 175, 289, 387–88
  natural law and, 300n18, 387, 398n17
  passions and, 105, 106, 112–13
  personal, 26–27
  philosophers and, 21
  prudence and, 262–63, 417
  vs. revelation, 21–22
  self-determination and, 428
  in sexual behavior, 45, 331
  sins and, 152, 161
  sources and, 25–26
  speculative, 264–65
  theoretical vs. practical, 265
  ultimate end and, 59
  will and, 256, 377
recklessness, 274
recompense, 213
reconciliation, 382
rectitude, 40–41, 64, 324–27, 334
redemption, 450–51
Redemptorist school, 374–84
Reichberg, Gregory M., 131–50, 460
religion
  culture and, 438–39, 444
  freedom of, 391
  justice and, 41–42, 279, 418
  politics and, 391–92
  religious life and, 349
  values of, 450
religious life, 48, 348–50. *See also* Christian life